✓ **W9-BMC-042**

PAGE 50 ON THE ROAD

YOUR COMPLETE DESTINATION GUIDE
In-depth reviews, detailed listings
and insider tips

Northern Lowlands p453

Northwestern Costa Rica p130

Península de Nicoya p209

Central Valley & Highlands p94

Caribbean Coast p397

San José p52

Central Pacific Coast p274

Southern Costa Rica p334

Península de Osa & Golfo Dulce p358

PAGE 517 SURVIVAL GUIDE

VITAL PRACTICAL INFORMATION TO
HELP YOU HAVE A SMOOTH TRIP

THIS EDITION WRITTEN AND RESEARCHED BY

Nate Cavalieri,
Adam Skolnick, Wendy Yanagihara

welcome to
Costa Rica

The Tropics in Technicolor

Whether you're following the metallic shimmer of a blue butterfly from palm to palm, staring into the yawning mouth of a deep purple orchid or watching wisps of fog roll in to soften the jagged edge of mountains, Costa Rica's vivid colors last a lifetime. The canopies rustle with riotous troupes of white-faced monkeys, hillsides echo with the squawks of scarlet macaws and you can reach up to the trees and pick your day's lunch: a ripe starfruit. It might seem at times like some kind of wondrous tropical fantasy land, but this is Costa Rica.

Outdoor Adventures

Rainforest hikes and brisk high-altitude trails, rushing white-water rapids and world-class surfing: there is a dizzying suite of outdoor adventures. They come in every shape and size – from the squeal-inducing rush of a canopy zip line, to a sun-dazed afternoon at the beach. The country's national parks allow visitors to glimpse the seething life of the tropical rainforest, its simmering volcanoes and cloud forests offer otherworldly vistas and its reliable surf breaks are suited to beginners and experts alike. Can't decide? Don't worry, you won't have to. Given its diminutive size, it's possible to plan a relatively short trip that includes all of the above.

21 TOP EXPERIENCES

Monteverde Cloud Forest

1 A pristine expanse of virginal forest totaling 105 sq km, Monteverde Cloud Forest (p158) owes much of its impressive natural beauty to Quaker expats, who left the US in the 1950s to protest the Korean War and helped foster conservationist principles with Ticos of the region. But as fascinating as the history is, the real romance of Monteverde is in nature itself: a mysterious Neverland dripping with mist, dangling with mossy vines, sprouting with ferns and bromeliads, gushing with creeks, blooming with life and nurturing rivulets of evolution.

Volcán Arenal

2 While the molten night views are gone and the volcano lies dormant, this mighty, perfectly conical giant is still worthy of a pilgrimage. There are several beautiful trails to explore, especially the magnificent climb to Cerro Chato (p136). And although Volcán Arenal (p145) is considered by scientists to be active, you'd never know it from the serene, mist-covered vistas. Even when clouds gather, and there is a chill in the air, you are just a short drive away from its many hot springs.

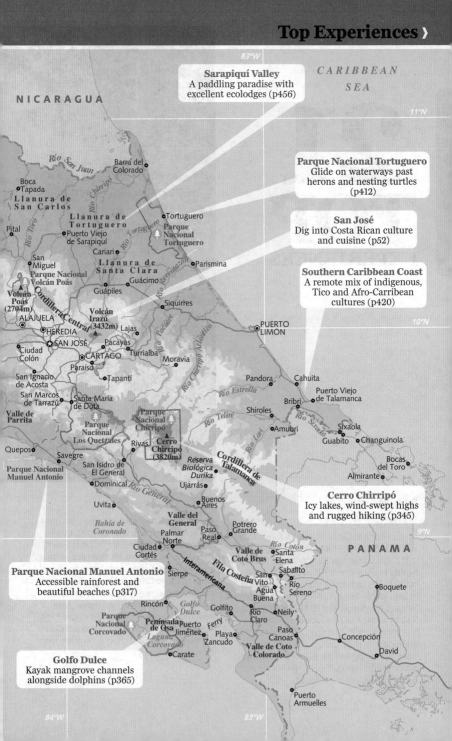

CARIBBEAN
SEA

NICARAGUA

Sarapiquí Valley
A paddling paradise with
excellent ecolodges (p456)

Parque Nacional Tortuguero
Glide on waterways past
herons and nesting turtles
(p412)

San José
Dig into Costa Rican culture
and cuisine (p52)

Southern Caribbean Coast
A remote mix of indigenous,
Tico and Afro-Carribean
cultures (p420)

Barra del
Colorado

Boca
Tapada

Llanura de
San Carlos

Río San Juan

Pital

Llanura de
Tortuguero

Tortuguero

Puerto Viejo
de Sarapiquí

Parque
Nacional
Tortuguero

San
Miguel

Cariari

Parque Nacional
Volcán Poás

Llanura de
Santa Clara

Parismina

Guácimo

Volcán
Poás
(2704m)

Guápiles

ALAJUELA

Volcán
Irazú
(3432m)

Lajas

HEREDIA

Siquirres

Ciudad
Colón

SAN JOSÉ

Pácayas

CARTAGO

Turrialba

PUERTO
LIMÓN

Paraíso

Moravia

San Ignacio
de Acosta

Tapantí

Pandora

Cahuita

San Marcos
de Tarrazú

Santa María
de Dota

Río Estrella

Puerto Viejo
de Talamanca

Valle de
Parrita

Parque
Nacional
Chirripó

Shiroles

Bribrí

Parque
Nacional
Los Quetzales

Rivas

Cerro
Chirripó
(3820m)

Amubri

Sixaola

Quepos

Savegre

San Isidro de
El General

Reserva
Biológica
Durika

Cordillera de
Talamanca

Guabito

Changuinola

Parque Nacional
Manuel Antonio

Dominical

Ujarrás

Bocas
del Toro

Río General

Uvita

Buenos
Aires

Almirante

Bahía de
Coronado

Valle del
General

Paso
Real

Potrero
Grande

Palmar
Norte

Río Cotón

Cerro Chirripó
Icy lakes, wind-swept highs
and rugged hiking (p345)

PANAMA

Ciudad
Cortés

Valle de
Coto Brus

Santa
Elena

Parque Nacional Manuel Antonio
Accessible rainforest and
beautiful beaches (p317)

Sierpe

Sabalito

San
Vito

Río
Sereno

Boquete

Rincón

Golfo
Dulce

Golfito

Río
Agua
Buena

Parque
Nacional
Corcovado

Península
de Osa

Puerto
Jiménez

Ferry

Río
Claro

Neily

Laguna
Corcovado

Playa
Zancudo

Paso
Canoas

Concepción

Carate

Valle de Coto
Colorado

David

Golfo Dulce
Kayak mangrove channels
alongside dolphins (p365)

Puerto
Armuelles

Interamericana

Fila Costeña

Cordillera Central

Río Toro

Río Chirripó

Río Tortuguero

Río Reventazón

Río Pacuare

Río Chirripó Atlántico

Río Telire

Río Sixaola

Río Lari

83°W

84°W

83°W

11°N

10°N

9°N

Costa Rica

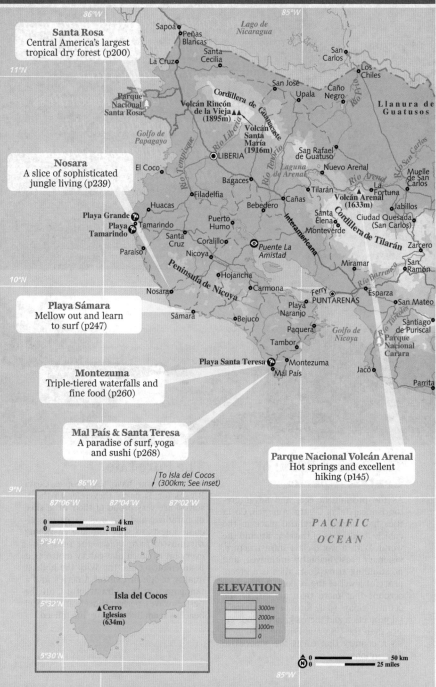

Santa Rosa
Central America's largest
tropical dry forest (p200)

Nosara
A slice of sophisticated
jungle living (p239)

Playa Sámara
Mellow out and learn
to surf (p247)

Montezuma
Triple-tiered waterfalls and
fine food (p260)

Mal País & Santa Teresa
A paradise of surf, yoga
and sushi (p268)

Parque Nacional Volcán Arenal
Hot springs and excellent
hiking (p145)

Lago de
Nicaragua

Sapoá
Peñas
Blancas
Santa
Cecilia
La Cruz
San José
San
Carlos
Los
Chiles
Caño
Negro
Upala

Cordillera de Guanacaste

Parque
Nacional
Santa Rosa

Golfo de
Papagayo

Volcán Rincón
de la Vieja
(1895m)
Volcán
Santa
María
(1916m)

San Rafael
de Guatuso
Nuevo Arenal

Llanura de
Guatusos

LIBERIA

El Coco

Bagaces

Laguna
de Arenal

Tilarán

Muelle
de San
Carlos

La
Fortuna

Volcán Arenal
(1633m)

Jabillos

Huacas

Filadelfia

Bebedero

Cañas

Santa
Elena
Monteverde

Ciudad Quesada
(San Carlos)

Playa Grande
Playa
Tamarindo
Tamarindo

Puerto
Humo

Zarcero

Santa
Cruz

Coralillo

Puente La
Amistad

San
Ramón

Paraíso

Nicoya

Miramar

Peninsula de Nicoya

Hojancha

Carmona

Esparza

San Mateo

Nosara

Ferry
PUNTARENAS

Playa Sámara

Sámara

Bejuco

Playa
Naranjo

Santiago
de Puriscal

Paquera

Golfo de
Nicoya

Parque
Nacional
Carara

Tambor

Playa Santa Teresa
Mal País

Montezuma

Jacó

Parrita

To Isla del Cocos
(300km; See inset)

PACIFIC
OCEAN

Isla del Cocos

Cerro
Iglesias
(634m)

4 km
2 miles

ELEVATION

3000m
2000m
1000m
0

0 — 50 km
0 — 25 miles

In Costa Rica trails lead to rushing waterfalls, mist-covered volcanoes and deserted beaches. Regardless of which you choose, this tropical playland is a feast for the senses.

(left) Costa Rica's iconic blue morpho butterfly (p516)
(below) An empty beach in Parque Nacional Corcovado (p382)

The Peaceful Soul of Central America

As the preeminent eco- and adventure-tourism capital of Central America, Costa Rica has earned a rightful place in the cubicle daydreams of travelers around the world. With a world-class infrastructure, visionary sustainability initiatives and no standing army, Costa Rica is a green, peaceful jewel of the region. Taking into account that more than a third of the country enjoys some form of environmental protection and there's greater biodiversity than the USA and Europe combined, it's a country that earns the superlative descriptions.

The Pure Life

And then you have the people. Costa Ricans (or Ticos as they refer to themselves) are very proud of their little slice of paradise, and are ever eager to welcome guests to sink into the easygoing rhythms of *pura vida* – the pure life – every bit as much of a catchy motto as it is an enduring mantra. With the highest quality of life in Central America and a fantastic tourism infrastructure, all the perfect waves, perfect sunsets and perfect beaches seem like the pure life indeed.

White-Water Rafting

3 So many rivers, so little time. But the dedicated adrenaline junkie could easily cover some heart-pounding river miles in the span of a few days in this compact little country. For those without the drive to do them all, pick a river, any river: Pacuare (p126), Reventazón (p126), Sarapiquí (p456). Any of the three are fun runs (though we're partial to the Pacuare), with rapids ranging from Class II to Class V, and all have stretches of smooth water that allow rafters to take in the luscious jungle scenery surrounding these river gorges.
Río Pacuare

Parque Nacional Manuel Antonio

4 Although droves of visitors pack Parque Nacional Manuel Antonio (p317) – the country's most popular (and smallest) national park – it remains an absolute gem. Capuchin monkeys scurry across its idyllic beaches, brown pelicans dive-bomb its clear waters and sloths watch over its accessible trails. It's a perfect place to introduce youngsters to the wonders of the rainforest, and splashing around in the waves you're likely to feel like a kid yourself. There's not much by way of privacy, but it's so lovely that you won't mind sharing.

RALPH HOPKINS / LONELY PLANET IMAGES ©

CHRISTER FREDRIKSSON / LONELY PLANET IMAGES ©

HOLGER LEUE / LONELY PLANET IMAGES ©

Parque Nacional Corcovado

5 Muddy, muggy and intense, the vast, largely untouched rainforest of Parque Nacional Corcovado (p382) is anything but a walk in the park. Here, travelers with a flexible agenda and a sturdy pair of rubber boots thrust themselves into the unknown and come out the other side with the story of a lifetime. And the further into the jungle you go, the better it gets: the country's best wildlife-watching, most desolate beaches and most vivid adventures lie down Corcovado's seldom-trodden trails. Green iguana

Montezuma

6 If you dig artsy-rootsy beach culture, enjoy rubbing shoulders with neo-Rastas and yoga freaks or have always wanted to spin fire, study Spanish or lounge on sugar-white coves, you'll find your way to Montezuma (p260). Strolling this intoxicating town and rugged coastline, you're never far from the rhythm and sound of the sea. From here you'll have easy access to the famed Cabo Blanco reserve (p267), and can take the tremendous hike to a triple-tiered waterfall. Oh, and when your stomach growls, the town has some of the best restaurants in the country.

Parque Nacional Tortuguero

7 Canoeing Parque Nacional Tortuguero's canals (p412) is a boat-borne safari, where thick jungle meets the water and you can get up close with shy caiman, river turtles, crowned night herons, monkeys and sloths. In the right season, under cover of darkness, watch the awesome, millenia-old ritual of turtles building nests and laying their eggs on the black-sand beaches of this national park. Sandwiched between extravagantly green wetlands and the wild Caribbean Sea, this is among the premiere places in Costa Rica to watch wildlife.

Zip Lining in the Rainforest Canopy

8 The wild-eyed, frizzy-haired happiness of a canopy tour is self-evident. Few things are more purely joyful than clipping into a high-speed cable, laced above and through the seething jungle canopy. This is where kids become little daredevils and adults become kids. Invented in Santa Elena, zip-lining outfits quickly multiplied, cropping up in all corners of Costa Rica. The best place to sample the lines is still Monteverde (p166), where the forest is alive, the mist fine and swirling, and the afterglow worth savoring. Santa Elena

Mal País & Playa Santa Teresa

9 Think tasty waves, creative kitchens and babes in board shorts and bikinis. It's no wonder that this rugged corner of the Peninsula de Nicoya, home to Mal País and Playa Santa Teresa (p268), has become one of Costa Rica's most life-affirming destinations. Here, the sea – perfect in color and temperature – is alive with wildlife. The hills are lush and dotted with stylish boutique sleeps and the road to Mal País is still rutted, ending in an authentic Tico fishing hamlet where you can cast away and score a dinner worthy of kings. Playa Santa Teresa

CHRISTIAN ÅSLUND / LONELY PLANET IMAGES ©

CASEY MAHANEY / LONELY PLANET IMAGES ©

Surfing

10 Costa Rica's east coast may move to the laid-back groove of Caribbean reggae, but the country's best year-round surfing is on the Pacific coast. It's home to a number of seaside villages where the day's agenda rarely gets more complicated than a scrupulous study of the surf report, a healthy application of sunblock and a few cold Imperial beers. With plenty of good breaks for beginners, and the country's most reliable rides (including perhaps the world's second-longest left-hand break, in Pavones – p393), Costa Rica has inexhaustible potential for surfers. Mal País

Wildlife-Watching

11 Monkeys and crocs, toucans and iguanas – Costa Rica is a thrill for wildlife enthusiasts. World-class parks, long-standing dedication to environmental protection, and mind-boggling biodiversity enable Costa Rica to harbor scores of rare and endangered species. Simply put, it's one of the best wildlife-watching destinations on the globe. In fact, visitors hardly have to make an effort; no matter where you travel in the country, the branches overhead are alive with critters galore, from lazy sloths and mischievous monkeys, to a brilliant spectrum of tropical birds. Capuchin monkeys

Playa Sámara

12 Some expat residents call Playa Sámara (p247) 'the black hole of happiness,' which has something to do with that crescent of sand spanning two rocky headlands, the opportunity to learn to surf, stand-up paddle board, surf cast or fly above migrating whales in an ultra-light, and the plethora of nearby all-natural beaches and coves. All of it is easy to access on foot or via public transportation, which is why it's becoming so popular with families who enjoy Sámara's palpable ease and tranquility.

Sarapiquí Valley

13 Sarapiquí (p456) rose to fame as a principal port in the nefarious old days of United Fruit dominance, before it meandered into agricultural anonymity, only to be reborn as a paddler's mecca thanks to the frothing serpentine mocha magic of its namesake river. These days it's still a paddling paradise, and it's also dotted with fantastic ecolodges and private forest preserves that will educate you about pre-Columbian life, get you into that steaming, looming, muddy jungle and introduce you to local wildlife up close.
Tirimbina Rainforest Center (p458)

Hot Springs

14 It may no longer creep down the mountainside, but beneath La Fortuna lava heats dozens of bubbling springs. Some of these springs are free, and any local can point the way. Others are, shall we say, embellished, dressed up, luxuriated. Take Tabacón Hot Springs (p135), set in the path of Volcán Arenal's 1975 eruption. It's a cheesy but still appealing set piece, what with its faux cliffs, Garden of Eden motif, and water that flows and pools at a steaming and healing 40°C (104°F).
Tabacón Hot Springs

Nosara

15 Nosara (p239) is a cocktail of international surf culture, jungled micro-climes and yoga bliss, where three stunning beaches are stitched together by a network of swerving, rutted earth roads that meander over coastal hills. Visitors can stay in the alluring surf enclave of Playa Guiones (p242) – where there are some fabulous restaurants and a drop-dead gorgeous beach – or in Playa Pelada (p244), which is as romantic as it is rugged and removed. One resident described the area as 'sophisticated jungle living,' and who wouldn't want more of that in their life? *Playa Guiones*

Kayaking in the Golfo Dulce

16 Getting out in Golfo Dulce (p388; the 'sweet gulf') brings hardy paddlers in contact with the abundant marine life in the bay – here dolphins play, whales breech and sparkling schools of tropical fish whiz by. Leaving the open water and navigating the maze of mangrove channels is another world completely, offering a chance to glide silently past herons, crested caracaras, snakes and sloths.

15

San José

17 The heart of Tico culture and identity lives in San José (p52), as do university students, intellectuals, artists and politicians. While not the most attractive capital in Central America, it does have some graceful neoclassical and Spanish-colonial architecture, leafy neighborhoods, museums housing pre-Columbian jade and gold, nightlife that goes on until dawn and some of the most sophisticated restaurants in the country. Street art – of both officially sanctioned and guerrilla varieties – add unexpected pops of color and public discourse to the cityscape. For the seasoned traveler, Chepe has its charms. Teatro Nacional (p55)

Coffee Plantations of the Central Valley

18 Take a little country drive on the scenic, curvy back roads of the Central Valley (p94), where the hillsides are a patchwork of varied agriculture and coffee shrubbery. If you're curious about that magical brew that for many makes life worth living, tour one of the coffee plantations and learn all about how Costa Rica's golden bean goes from plant to cup. A couple of the best places for a tour are Finca Cristina (p121) in the Valle de Orosi and Café Britt Finca (p115) near Barva.

19

20

MARTIN STRMISKA / ALAMY ©

Southern Caribbean

19 By day, lounge in a hammock, cruise by bike to snorkel off uncrowded beaches, hike to waterfall-fed pools and visit the remote indigenous territories of the Bribrí and Kèköldi. By night, dip into zesty Caribbean cooking and sway to reggaetón at open-air bars cooled by ocean breezes. The villages of Cahuita (p424) and Puerto Viejo de Talamanca (p432) – both outposts of this unique mix of Afro-Caribbean, Tico and indigenous culture – are the perfect, laid-back home bases for such adventures.
Puerto Viejo de Talamanca beach

Cerro Chirripó

20 The view from the rugged peak of Cerro Chirripó (p345), Costa Rica's highest summit – of wind-swept rocks and icy lakes – may not resemble the Costa Rica of the postcards, but the two-day hike above the clouds is one of the country's most satisfying excursions. A predawn hike holds the real prize: a chance to catch the fiery sunrise and see both the Caribbean and the Pacific in a full and glorious panoramic view.

Snorkeling the Nicoya Peninsula

21 Costa Rica has stunning wildlife on land, but its underwater world is equally captivating. Although a pricey trip out to the incomparable Isla del Cocos might break the budget, plunge into famous dive spots scattered around the northern section of the Nicoya peninsula (p212).

need to know

Currency
» The official unit is the Costa Rican colón, but US dollars (US$) are accepted everywhere.

Language
» Spanish and English

When to Go

- **Tamarindo** GO Nov–Apr
- **San José** GO Dec–Apr
- **Puerto Limón** GO Jan–Apr
- **Manuel Antonio** GO Dec–Feb
- **Puerto Jiménez** GO Feb–Mar, Sep–Oct

Tropical climate, rain year-round
Tropical climate, wet dry seasons

High Season
(Dec–Apr)
» 'Dry' season still sees some rain, but beach towns fill with domestic tourists.
» Accommodation should be booked well in advance; some places enforce two- or three-day minimum stays.

Shoulder
(May–Jul, Nov)
» Rain picks up and the stream of tourists starts to taper off.
» Roads are muddy, making off-the-beaten-track travel more challenging.

Low Season
(Aug–Oct)
» Rainfall is highest, but heavy rains bring swells to the Pacific, and the best surfing conditions.
» Rural roads can be impassable due to river crossings.

Your Daily Budget

Budget less than
US$40
» Dorm beds: US$8–15
» Eat at ubiquitous *sodas*; shop at markets; self-cater
» Hikes without a guide
» Travel via local bus

Midrange
US$40– 100
» Basic room with private bathroom: US$20–30 per day
» Eat at restaurants geared toward travelers for US$5–10
» Use efficient first-class bus companies such as Interbus

Top end over
US$100
» Luxurious lodges and hotels start at US$80
» Dine at international fusion restaurants
» Hire guides for wildlife-watching excursions
» Take short flights; rent 4WDs

Money

» ATMs ubiquitous, typically dispensing colones or dollars. Credit and debit cards widely accepted.

Visas

» Generally not required for stays of 30 or 90 days; tourist cards (typically valid for 90 days) are issued on inbound flights or at airport immigration.

Mobile Phones

» GSN and 3G systems available, but US-compatible ones require expensive international roaming; rental phones and prepaid SIM cards are cheap and widely available.

Driving

» Drive on the right; steering wheel is on the left side of the car.

Websites

» **Tico Times** (www.ticotimes.net) Online edition of Costa Rica's excellent English-language weekly newspaper.

» **Costa Rica Tourism Board** (www.visitcostarica.com) Official website of the Costa Rica Tourism Board (known as the ICT).

» **Lonely Planet** (www.lonelyplanet.com) Provides information on travel in Costa Rica, links to accommodations and traveling tips from the all-important Thorn Tree community forum.

Exchange Rates

Australia	A$1	₡523
Canada	C$1	₡506
Europe	€1	₡673
Japan	¥100	₡612
Mexico	MXN10	₡396
UK	£1	₡803
USA	US$1	₡506
US	$1	₡506

For current exchange rates see www.xe.com.

Important Numbers

Country code	☑506
International access code	☑011
International operator	☑00
Emergency	☑911
Costa Rica Board of Tourism	☑1-800-343-6332

Arriving in Costa Rica

» **Aeropuerto Internacional Juan Santamaria**

Bus – US$0.75; Alajuela–San José buses run frequently and will drop you off anywhere along Paseo Colón

Taxis – US$15–20; depart from official stand, about 20 minutes to the city

Rental car – Many rental-car agencies have desks in the airport

Car Rental vs Bus Travel

The early stage of planning a trip to Costa Rica quickly comes to a fork in the road: do you rent your own ride or get around the country via public transportation? Although car-rental agencies are ubiquitous – at every airport, city and even many of the smaller towns – deceptively cheap daily rates come with the unpleasant surprise of a mandatory insurance policy, which can double the price. Additionally, most off-the-beaten-track places worth exploring require a pricier 4WD vehicle for river crossings and rough roads, making the country's safe, cheap and reliable public bus system all the more appealing. In the end, the most affordable way to explore independently and see every corner of Costa Rica is a combination of long-distance bus travel and short-term car rental for excursions.

first time

Everyone needs a helping hand when they visit a country for the first time. There are phrases to learn, customs to get used to and etiquette to understand. The following section will help demystify Costa Rica so your first trip goes as smoothly as your fifth.

Getting Around

One thing that baffles most travelers visiting Costa Rica for the first time is the virtually non-existent street addresses. When you inevitably get lost and ask, many Ticos will offer directions using the relative distance from landmarks (soccer fields, radio towers). Confused? Get used to it; it's all part of the adventure.

Language

Spanish is the national language of Costa Rica, and knowing some very basic phrases is not only courteous but also essential, particularly when navigating through rural areas, interacting with park rangers and shopping at local markets. That said, a long history of North American tourists has made English the country's unofficial second language, and it's relatively easy to speak exclusively English while traveling here, particularly if you stick to heavily touristed areas and major cities. With the exception of basic *sodas* (inexpensive eateries), local buses, and shops catering exclusively to locals, travelers can expect bilingual menus, signs and brochures.

Booking Ahead

Booking ahead is rarely necessary for accommodations, with the notable exception of highest peak times – Semana Santa (Holy Week, the week preceding Easter) and the weeks surrounding Christmas and New Year. During low seasons – or the cleverly branded 'green season' – booking ahead via the internet will get travelers the lowest rates. It is essential to book wilderness lodges in advance any time of year, since it can be difficult (or impossible) to arrange transportation to their remote locations.

What to Wear

Although the coastal areas are hot and humid, calling for shorts and short sleeves, you'll want to pack a sweater and lightweight jacket for popular high-elevation destinations such as Volcán Irazú and Monteverde. If you plan to hike up Chirripó, bring lots of layers and a hat and gloves. Additionally, while hiking through the rainforest is often a hot and sweaty exercise, long sleeves and lightweight, quick-drying pants help keep the bugs away.

What to Pack

» Passport
» Phrasebook
» Swimsuit
» Digital camera
» Flip-flops
» Sunglasses
» Poncho
» Binoculars
» Bug repellent with DEET
» Refillable water bottle
» Field guide
» MP3 player
» Flashlight
» First aid kit
» Alarm clock
» Clothesline
» Sink stopper

Checklist

» Check the validity of your passport

» Check visa situation and government travel advisories

» Organize travel insurance

» Check flight restrictions on luggage and camping or outdoors equipment

» Check your immunization history

» Contact car insurance provider about foreign coverage

» If you plan to rent a car, bring a copy of your current insurance policy

Etiquette

» **Asking for Help**
Say *disculpe* to get someone's attention; *perdón* to ask for an apology.

» **Personal Space**
Don't be surprised if Ticos have fewer boundaries about personal space than what's customary in North America and Europe.

» **Visiting Indigenous Communities**
Ask permission to take photos, particularly of children, and dress more modestly than beachwear.

» **Surfing**
Novice surfers should be aware of 'dropping in' on more-experienced surfers and of swimmers in their path.

» **Hitchhiking**
Picking up hitchhikers in rural areas is common. If you get a ride from a local, offer a small tip.

Tipping

» **When to Tip**
Tips are uncommon and should be given only for exceptional service at top-end restaurants and hotels.

» **Restaurants**
Most restaurants add a 15% sales tax and 10% service fee, making tipping uncommon.

» **Taxis**
Optional, but many people round up to the nearest 100 colones or tip with a few coins.

» **Guides**
It is customary to tip tour guides US$1 to US$2 per person for good service.

Money

Both US dollars and Costa Rican colones are accepted everywhere, dispensed from ATMs across the country and used interchangeably. Euros will also be widely accepted as a form of payment at tourist-oriented shops and hotels, though usually with a poor exchange rate. The currency travelers use usually reflects the typical audience of the business: prices at tourist places are more commonly listed in US dollars; Costa Rican local services, buses and markets post prices in colones. There's no problem to spend only US dollars, if you're willing to accept an unfavorable, on-the-fly exchange rate; usually around ₡500 to the dollar. In such situations the change will usually be given in colones. With the exception of the smallest towns and shops in rural areas, credit and debit cards are accepted, as long as they have a Visa or MasterCard logo. Travelers checks are increasingly rare, and difficult to exchange except in banks and big cities.

what's new

For this new edition of Costa Rica, our authors have hunted down the fresh, the transformed, the hot and the happening. These are some of our favorites. For up-to-the-minute reviews and recommendations, see lonelyplanet.com/costa-rica.

Costaricapalooza

1 The Festival Imperial (p26) music festival started back up in March 2012 after a four-year hiatus, featuring headliners including the Flaming Lips, Björk and Thievery Corporation.

Osa Wild

2 This new community-oriented, sustainably run, tour agency (p365) gives travelers a chance to see the undiscovered Osa, by arranging family stays, local food tours and scientifically savvy visits to Parque Nacional Corcovado.

Costa Rica Surf Camp

3 Dominical has long been known as a surfing paradise and it's filled with surf instructors, but this new school is the best in class. We spent a couple weeks with their excellent local instructors.

Stadium Kickoff

4 With retractable roof and seating capacity for 35,000, the revamped Estadio Nacional de Costa Rica (p79) will primarily host soccer matches, but also heavy-hitters such as Pearl Jam, who played here on their 20th-anniversary tour.

Flutterby House

5 A few steps from the remote beaches of Parque Nacional Marino Ballena, this female-owned and -operated hostel (p330) espouses visionary sustainability practices, offers a couple tree houses and is a hosteller's dream come true.

Museo de Arte Costarricense

6 A complete renovation has made this museum (p61) sparkle. The highlight, of course, is the rotating exhibition of Costa Rican art, but another is the room-sized wraparound bas-relief depicting the country's history.

Rock-climbing in Cachi

7 One of the more easily accessible spots for sport-climbing is gaining popularity in the Orosi Valley. The basalt wall at Cachi (p124) has more than a dozen routes ranging in difficulty.

Papaya

8 The tapas and the view at Papaya (p272), Moana Lodge's brand-new restaurant, cantilevered high above the Mal País coast, are both magnificent.

Hot Springs Rio Negro

9 All natural and set in a meandering pocket of dry forest along the river near Parque Nacional Rincon de la Valle, Hot Springs Rio Negro (p198) is our favorite hot spring in the country.

Villa Deveena

10 In Playa Negra, Villa Deveena (p233) is brand-new and rocking with an incredible French kitchen. It makes its own goat cheese in its chef-operated dairy in the nearby hills.

if you like...

Beaches

Seemingly endless and lined by swaying palms, Costa Rica's beaches would take a lazy lifetime to explore thoroughly. Although few have the brilliantly white, sugary sand of Nicoya and Manuel Antonio, the wild beaches of both coasts have ample opportunities for a day of dreamy solitude.

Playa Manuel Antonio With mischievous monkeys, perfect sand and idyllic turquoise water, this beach alone is worth the national park admission fee (p317).

Playa Grande The nation's longest beach is good for endless strolling, and is a favorite of leatherback turtles and surfers alike (p220).

Playa Guiones Backed by lush vegetation, these gentle waves are ideal for swimming, surfing or just frolicking (p242).

Playa Negra This wild, pristine black-sand beach doesn't draw many surfers, making this Cahuita beach one of the best places in the country for swimming (p424).

Parque Nacional Marino Ballena Dreaming of spending the day on an isolated desert island? The long, rugged, coconut-strewn beaches of Ballena are ideal (p331).

White-water Rafting & Kayaking

With Costa Rica's ample waterways and excellent operators, the opportunities for rushing down frothing white-water rapids and coasting through mangrove channels will satisfy even the greatest thirst for adventure.

Ríos Pacuare and Reventazón Take on exciting runs of Class II–IV rapids on the country's best white water, which is best between June and October (p126).

Río Sarapiquí Finally making a comeback after losing its mojo due to the 2009 quake. It's a great place to learn how to kayak, as well (p456).

Golfo Dulce Lucky kayakers can paddle out with dolphins and explore sea caves (p388).

Canals of Tortuguero Excellent for kayaking through canals to get up close and personal with abundant birds and wildlife (p412).

Surfing

Costa Rica's perfect waves, long-standing surf culture and endless blue skies make it a world-class destination, whether you're wobbling to your feet on a longboard or shredding monster swells. Remember that the best Pacific swells are during the rainy season – perfect for surfers on a budget.

Dominical It's easy to see why so many foreigners show up to surf and can never can bring themselves to leave this place, an ideal destination for surf bums (p324).

Pavones One of the largest left-hand breaks on the planet draws the goofy-footed from near and far (p393).

Playa Sámara The beach breaks here are some of the country's best for learning. Those who master the game paddle out to reef breaks (p247).

Playa Grande Costa Rica's most accessible, reliable break draws hordes. Lucky it's so big that it never seems crowded (p220).

Salsa Brava Near Puerto Viejo, this place has the country's biggest waves; in December they get up to 7m tall (p433).

DAVID TIPLING / IMAGEBROKER ©

» Keen-billed toucan (p508)

Bird- & Wildlife-Watching

Even for those who don't know their snowy-bellied emerald from their grey-breasted wood wren, Costa Rica's birds are a thrill. Nearly 900 bird species fill Costa Rica's skies – more than in the entire United States and Canada combined.

Wilson Botanical Garden About 1000m above sea level, this private reserve attracts many specialty birds of southern Costa Rica, including some very rare high-altitude species (p353).

Península de Osa Although rare in the rest of the country, scarlet macaws frequently light up the skies around Puerto Jiménez and Parque Nacional Corcovado (p358).

Parque Nacional Los Quetzales In a bucolic mountain setting, this park is named for its banner attraction, the flamboyantly colored ceremonial bird of the Aztecs and Maya (p340).

Monteverde & Santa Elena Cloud Forest Reserves Keep your eyes peeled for the keel-billed toucan (p158).

Tortuguero Herons, kites, ospreys, kingfishers, macaws: the bird list is a mile long at this wildlife-rich park (p412).

Hiking

Rainforest trails and endless strolls down the beach, high-altitude mountains and cloud forest: the only way to see it all in Costa Rica is to don some boots and hit the trail.

Parque Nacional Chirripó Up and up and up: the trail to the very top of Costa Rica is a thrilling (chilly) adventure (p348).

Parque Nacional Corcovado The challenging trails that go through the park are not to be trifled with, but they provide a supreme look at the wonders of the rainforest, and offer a huge adventure (p384).

Monteverde cloud forest Utterly fantastic for day hikes, a walk through cloud-forest gorges passes amazing plant and animal life (p177).

Parque Nacional Volcán Tenorio The trails circumnavigate volcanoes and misty waterfalls. Add a few blue morpho butterflies for an ultimate sampler of Costa Rican scenery (p184).

Volcán Barva A little tough to get to, but the trip is worth the reward: crater lakes and quiet cloud forest (p401).

Luxury Spas & Resorts

Long gone are Costa Rica's rough-and-tumble days; nowadays travelers enjoy this country in the lap of luxury. These plush comforts are scattered throughout the country and many espouse standard-setting sustainability practices.

Florblanca On a sugary stretch of Pacific, Florblanca's 11 villas are in a luxurious league of their own, ideal for once-in-a-lifetime escapes (p270).

El Silencio Hanging at the edge of a canyon amid endless acres of rolling green, El Silencio is a sumptuous slice of Zen in the cloud forest (p110).

La Paloma Lodge A posh delight in Costa Rica's wildest corner, this chic jungle lodge is far off the grid (p379).

Hotel Villa Caletas Far out of the way atop a Pacific cliff, Caletas offers guests ultimate seclusion, personalized service and breathtaking Pacific sunsets (p285).

Poás Volcano Lodge Surrounded by trails at the edge of the Poás volcano, this boutique hotel is bedecked in rough timbers and volcanic rock (p104).

If you like... visiting indigenous communities
book a home stay with Osa Wild, a new tour organization that is deeply embedded in the communities of the Osa Peninsula and can arrange home stays in the rainforest.

Ecolodges

Although Costa Rica's amazing natural resources are at risk of being loved to death, Costa Rica's wealth of top ecolodges give visitors an opportunity to make a minimal impact without sacrificing creature comforts.

Casa Corcovado Jungle Lodge Osa's only top-certified ecolodge is far removed from civilization, just a steamy hike from the wilds of Corcovado (p382).

Villa Blanca Cloud Forest Hotel & Nature Reserve With the highest possible sustainability rating and a nightly movie screening, Villa Blanca offers plush, amenity-studded ecological digs (p112).

Arenas del Mar The best ecolodge near Manuel Antonio, this architectural stunner has private Jacuzzis overlooking the coast (p312).

Ecolodge San Luis By far the best ecolodge of the region, with the Monteverde Cloud Forest Reserve just outside the door (p181).

Rancho Naturalista This bird-watching lodge scores plenty of lofty credits for sustainability (p127).

Diving & Snorkeling

Although visibility varies greatly with the season and climate, Costa Rica's many small islands, caves and coastal rock formations are excellent for underwater exploration.

Isla del Cocos The only truly world-class dive spot in Costa Rica, the crystal waters surrounding this offshore island are filled with marine life. A week-long live-aboard stint makes this an experts-only outing (p396).

Isla del Caño Not ready to make the big trip out to Cocos? Caño has reliable visibility, sea turtles, barracudas and, if you're lucky, humpback whales (p382).

Bahía Salinas These shallow waters make for fun, easy, entry-level diving and, when the weather is right, colorful snorkeling (p206).

Playa Manzanillo In September and October this Caribbean beach has the best snorkeling in the entire country (p268).

Fishing

Although a venture into the open sea can be a pricey proposition, Costa Rica's sportfishing is the stuff of legend.

Golfo Dulce Year after year boats leaving from little Puerto Jiménez and Golfito return with fish that challenge world records. The Pacific Gulf Stream and mineral-rich Golfo Dulce make ideal conditions (p388).

Caño Negro An abundant population of tarpon and no-frills fishing ventures make this area a low-key option in the Caribbean (p468).

Quepos Plenty of captains lead fishing ventures into the waters off Quepos, which offer a shot at marlin and sailfish between late December and May (p304).

San Gerardo de Dota Trout-fishing in the clear upper regions of the Río Savegre is excellent. May and June is the time for fly-fishing in this unexpected alpine environment (p338).

Playa Grande Epic surf casting brings in big fish from rocks that get thrashed with surf (p220)

month by month

January

Every calendar year opens with a rush of visitors, as North American and domestic tourists flood beach towns to celebrate. January weather is ideal, with dry days and only occasional afternoon showers.

☆ Fiesta de Santa Cruz

Held in Santa Cruz, this festival centers around a rodeo and bullfights. It also includes the requisite religious procession, music, dances and a beauty pageant.

☆ Las Fiestas de Palmares

Ten days of beer drinking, horse shows and other carnival events take over the tiny town of Palmares. There's also a running of the bulls.

Fiesta de los Diablitos

Men wear carved wooden devil masks and burlap sacks and, after roaming from house to house for free booze, re-enact the fight between the indigenous people and the Spanish. Spoiler alert: in this one, the Spanish lose.

February

February is the perfect month to visit, with ideal weather and no holiday surcharges. The skies above the Nicoya are particularly clear, and it is the peak of turtle nesting season.

Fiesta Cívica de Liberia

A beauty pageant and carnival atmosphere enlivens Liberia at the end of February.

March

Excellent weather continues through the early part of March, though prices shoot up at the end of the month if it corresponds with Semana Santa, the week leading up to Easter, and North American spring break.

 Feria de la Mascarada

Every March the town is home to the famous Feria de la Mascarada, a tradition with roots in the colonial era, in which people don massive colorful masks (some of which weigh up to 20kg), and gather to dance and parade around the town square. Demons and devils are frequent subjects, but celebrities and politicians also figure in the mix (you haven't lived until you've seen a 6m-tall Celia Cruz). The festival is usually held during the last week of the month, but dates vary from one year to the next; inquire locally.

☆ Envision Festival

Held in Dominical during the first week of March, this is a festival with a new age bent, bringing together fire dancers, yoga and jam bands.

Día del Boyero

A colorful parade, held in Escazú, honors ox-cart drivers, and includes a blessing of the animals.

☆ Festival Imperial

Some 30,000 music fans fill the La Guácima outdoor venue in Alajuela, north of San José, for the country's biggest rock festival. Performers recently included TV on the Radio, Skrillex, Björk, LMFAO and the Flaming Lips.

April

Easter, and the preceding week, Semana Santa, can fall early in April, which makes beaches crowded and prices spike. Nicoya and Guanacaste are very dry and hot, with very little rain.

⭐ Día de Juan Santamaría

Commemorating Costa Rica's national hero, who died in battle against William Walker's troops in 1856, this week-long celebration includes parades, concerts and dances.

May

Wetter weather patterns begin to sweep across the country in May, which begins the country's low season and brings on discounted prices. Good bargains and reasonably good weather make it an excellent season for budget travel.

🍴 San Isidro Labrador's Day

An opportunity to taste the bounty of the surrounding region, this is one of the nation's largest agricultural fares.

June

The Pacific Coast gets fairly wet during June, though this makes for good surfing swells. The beginning of the so-called 'green season,' there are lots of discounted rates to be found.

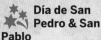 Día de San Pedro & San Pablo

Celebrations with religious processions are held in villages of the same name.

July

July is mostly wet, particularly on the Caribbean coast, but the month also occasionally enjoys a brief dry period that Ticos call *veranillo*, or summer. Expect rain, particularly late in the day.

🏃 Fiesta de la Virgen del Mar

Held in Puntarenas and Playa del Coco, this party involves colorful, brightly lit regattas and boat parades.

⭐ Día de Guanacaste

Celebrates the annexation of Guanacaste from Nicaragua. There's also a rodeo in Santa Cruz.

August

The middle of the rainy season doesn't mean that mornings aren't bright and sunny, and travelers who don't mind a bit of rain will find great deals on hotels and tour packages. This is a great month if you're visiting to surf big waves, as the rain brings swells.

⭐ La Virgen de los Ángeles

The patron saint is celebrated with an important religious procession from San José to Cartago.

September

The Osa Peninsula gets utterly soaked during September, which is in the heart of the rainy season and what Ticos refer to as the *temporales del Pacífico*. It is the cheapest time of year to visit the Pacific side.

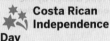 Costa Rican Independence Day

With events all over the country, Costa Rica's Independence Day is a fun party. The center of the action is the relay race that passes a 'Freedom Torch' from Guatemala to Costa Rica. The torch arrives at Cartago in the evening of the 14th, when the nation breaks into the national anthem.

October

Many roads become impassable as rivers swell and rain continues to fall in October, one of the wettest months in Costa Rica. Many of the lodges and tour operators are closed until November.

⭐ Día de la Raza

Columbus' historic landing on Isla Uvita has traditionally inspired a small carnival, with street parades, live music and dancing on October 12. The party was on hiatus for a few years but returned in 2009 to a small but enthusiastic turn out. It is unclear whether it will continue to be held. Inquire locally. During this time, book hotels in advance.

November

The weather can go either way in November. Some years it dries up a bit, others years see an extension of rain from *El Niño*. Access to Corcovado Park is very difficult after several continuous months of rain, though by the month's end the skies clear up.

 Día de los Muertos

Families visit graveyards and have religious parades in honor of the dead – a lovely and picturesque festival.

December

Although the beginning of the month is a great time to visit Costa Rica, with clearer skies and relatively uncrowded attractions, things really ramp up toward Christmas, when travelers need to make reservations well in advance.

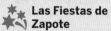 **Las Fiestas de Zapote**

If you're in the San José area between Christmas and New Year's Eve, this week-long celebration of all things Costa Rican (namely rodeos, cowboys, carnival rides, fried food and booze) annually draws in tens of thousands of Ticos to the bullring in the suburb of Zapote, just southeast of the city.

(Above) Traditional dance performance held on Independence Day (p27)
(Below) Drivers of oxcarts are honored during Día del Boyero (p26)

itineraries

Whether you've got six days or 60, these itineraries provide a starting point for the trip of a lifetime. Want more inspiration? Head online to lonelyplanet. com/thorntree to chat with other travelers.

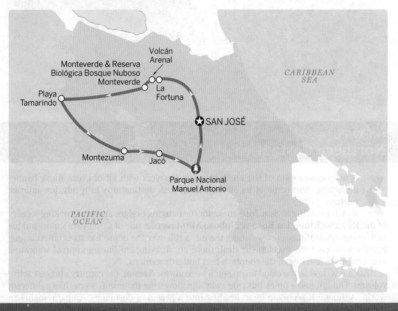

Two Weeks
Essential Costa Rica

> This is the trip you've been dreaming about: a romp through paradise with seething volcanoes, tropical parks and ghostly cloud forests.

From **San José**, beeline north to **La Fortuna**. After hiking the forest on the flanks of **Volcán Arenal**, soak in the area's hot springs. Then catch a boat across Laguna de Arenal, and a bus to **Monteverde**, where you might just encounter the elusive quetzal on a stroll through the **Reserva Biológica Bosque Nuboso Monteverde**.

It's time for the beach: head west to the biggest party town in Nicoya, **Playa Tamarindo**, and enjoy the ideal surf and rowdy nightlife.

Continuing south, go through **Montezuma** where you can connect via jet boat to **Jacó**, another town with equal affection for surfing and partying. Spend half a day on the bus down to Quepos, the gateway to **Parque Nacional Manuel Antonio**. A full day in the park starts with some jungle hikes and wildlife-watching and ends with a picnic and a dip in the park's perfect waters.

Two Weeks
Northern Costa Rica

> A deep exploration of the north presents travelers with all of Costa Rica's banner attractions and some of its off-the-beaten-path destinations in a tidy, low-mileage package.

After landing in **San José**, make for the hanging bridges and breathtaking scenery of the **Reserva Biológica Bosque Nuboso Monteverde**, one of Costa Rica's most unique and iconic destinations. Just watching the mists roll over the dense forests is entertaining, but the add-ons here sweeten the deal: there are dizzying zip lines and areal walkways, excellent hikes and one of the country's best butterfly gardens.

After a few days in the cloud forest you'll be ready for **Arenal**, the country's biggest active volcano. Though just a quick bus ride away, the glowering mountain seems like a different world. Although it seems to be in heading into a period of dormancy, Arenal remains an incredible sight. Another few hikes and you'll be ready for the area's hot springs.

Now, leave the tourists behind and head into the northern lowlands, an agricultural zone where real-life Costa Rica awaits. Community tourism initiatives have sprung up in this historically farm-based economy, with inviting ecolodges and family stays. After a couple days of connecting with easygoing Ticos, make for **La Virgen** to raft the county's wildest waters on the **Río Sarapiquí**.

With the remaining week, it's time to hit the beach. Catch a bus for **Playa Tamarindo**, to party with other travelers, sample some of the country's finest international cuisine and take a few surfing lessons. If you're here during turtle season, **Playa Grande** will host a horde of nesting leatherbacks; if you're not, the human action on the beach is an equally illuminating mating ritual.

You can either stay put or string together a series of southbound buses to visit one heavenly beach after the next: there's stunning sand and contemporary cuisine at **Playa Sámara** or legendary swells at **Mal País** and **Playa Santa Teresa**. Any of them would be excellent places to swim in warm Pacific waters and chill out on the beach. Wind down your trip with a bit of yoga at **Montezuma** and head back to San José via Jacó by jet boat and bus.

» (above) Hiking in the Reserva
Biológica Bosque Nuboso Monteverde
(p177)
» (left) Volcán Arenal (p145)

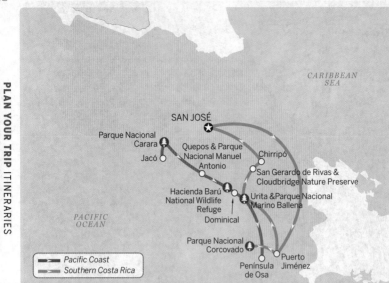

CARIBBEAN SEA

SAN JOSÉ

Parque Nacional Carara

Jacó

Quepos & Parque Nacional Manuel Antonio

Chirripó

San Gerardo de Rivas & Cloudbridge Nature Preserve

Hacienda Barú National Wildlife Refuge

Urita &Parque Nacional Marino Ballena

PACIFIC OCEAN

Dominical

Parque Nacional Corcovado

Puerto Jiménez

Península de Osa

Pacific Coast
Southern Costa Rica

Two Weeks
Pacific Coast Explorer

Kick things off in the resort town of **Jacó**, a scrappy, if cosmopolitan enclave of fine dining and raging nightlife. In case you need a reminder that you're still in Costa Rica, backtrack north up the coast to **Parque Nacional Carara**, home to large populations of enchanting scarlet macaws.

Heading south along the coast, drop in on **Quepos**, a convenient base for the country's most popular national park, **Parque Nacional Manuel Antonio**.

Here, the rainforest sweeps down to meet the sea, providing refuge for rare animals, including the endangered Central American squirrel monkey.

Continue on south – stopping to sample the roadside ceviche stands – and visit **Hacienda Barú National Wildlife Refuge** to look for sloth, or keep heading south to **Dominical** for more waves. For deserted beach wandering keep on to Uvita, where you can look for whales off **Parque Nacional Marino Ballena**.

From Uvita, you can either continue south to the far-flung **Península de Osa**, or head to San José.

Two to Three Weeks
Southern Costa Rica & Osa

Hand's down the best itinerary for adventurers. Either head down the Pacific coast or fly into **Puerto Jiménez**, which serves as the gateway to Osa. Here, you can spend a day or so kayaking the mangroves and soaking up the charm of this tiny town.

The undisputed highlight of Osa is **Parque Nacional Corcovado**, one of the country's best wildlife-watching spots. Spend a few days exploring the trails with backpack in hand; particularly well-equipped travelers can trek across the entire park.

Return to Puerto Jiménez and link up with the Uvita, where you wander empty beaches and surf a bit in the **Parque Nacional Marino Ballena**. Then, it's off to the mountains. Link together buses for **San Gerardo de Rivas**, where you can spend a day getting used to the altitude and hiking through the **Cloudbridge Nature Preserve**. End the trip with an exhilarating two-day adventure to the top of **Chirripó**.

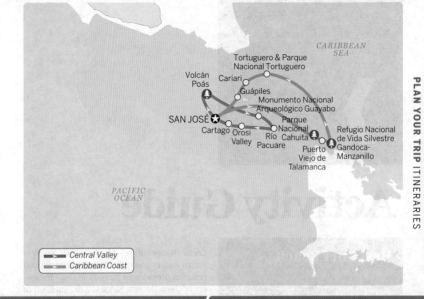

CARIBBEAN SEA

Tortuguero & Parque
Nacional Tortuguero

Volcán Poás   Cariari

Guápiles

Monumento Nacional
Arqueológico Guayabo

SAN JOSÉ

Cartago   Orosi
Valley

Parque
Nacional
Cahuita

Río
Pacuare

Refugio Nacional
de Vida Silvestre
Gandoca-
Manzanillo

Puerto
Viejo de
Talamanca

PACIFIC
OCEAN

Central Valley
Caribbean Coast

One to Two Weeks
Carribean Coast

Spanish gives way to English, and Latin beats change to Caribbean rhythms as you explore the 'other Costa Rica.'

Hop on the first eastbound bus out of **San José** for **Cahuita**, capital of Afro-Caribbean culture and gateway to **Parque Nacional Cahuita**. Get your fill of this mellow little village before moving on to **Puerto Viejo de Talamanca**, the Caribbean's center for nightlife, cuisine and all-round positive vibes.

From Puerto Viejo, rent yourself a good old-fashioned bicycle and ride to **Manzanillo**, from where you can snorkel, kayak and hike in the **Refugio Nacional de Vida Silvestre Gandoca-Manzanillo**.

For the adventurous at heart, grab a boat from Moín to travel the canal-lined coast to **Tortuguero**, where you can watch nesting green and leatherback turtles. Of course, the real reason you're here is to arrange a canoe trip through the mangrove-lined canals of **Parque Nacional Tortuguero**, Costa Rica's mini-Amazon.

After spotting your fill of wildlife, head back to San José via water taxi and bus through **Cariari** and **Guápiles**.

One Week
Central Valley

The central valley circuit is about sleeping volcanoes, strong cups of coffee and the spiritual core of the country. Since most tourists head toward Costa Rica's distant beaches, you'll enjoy mountain markets and colonial squares without the huge crowds.

Begin the scenic circuit of the region's gaping volcanoes by hiking the volcanic lakes and trails surrounding **Poás**, one of Costa Rica's most accessible glimpses into an active volcano. Move on to the **Monumento Nacional Arqueológico Guayabo**, the country's only significant archeological site, where visitors marvel at petroglyphs and a system of aqueducts.

With the geological and archeological wonders complete, rush the white water of the **Río Pacuare**, one of the country's best white-water runs, and some of the most scenic rafting in Central America.

Finally, swing south into the heart of the **Orosi Valley**, Costa Rican coffee country, and take the caffeinated 60km loop passing the country's oldest church and endless green hills. End this short circuit on a spiritual note at the country's grandest colonial temple, the Basílica de Nuestra Senora de Los Ángeles in **Cartago**.

Activity Guide

Best Surf Beach
Playa Tamarindo (p225)

Best Hike
Cerro Chirripó (p345)

Best Fishing
Bahía Drake (p375)

Best Dive Site
Isla del Cocos (p396)

Best Wildlife-Watching
Parque Nacional Corcovado (p382)

Best Rainforest for Families
Parque Nacional Manuel Antonio (p302)

Best White-Water
Río Pacuare (p126)

Costa Rica's miles of shoreline, endless warm waters and tally of national parks and reserves provides an incredible stage for lovers of the outdoors. Since the designation of the Reserva Natural Absoluta Cabo Blanco in 1963, Costa Rica has lured countless travelers in search of the pristine.

Despite all of the high-octane activities on offer, casual hiking and more intense trekking remain two of the country's most enduring outdoor activities. For the vast majority of travelers, Costa Rica equates with rainforest, and you're certain to encounter charismatic wildlife including primates, birdlife and butterflies galore. As first-time visitors quickly discover, no two rainforests are created equal, providing a constantly shifting palette of nature.

Of course, if you want to experience all that this country has to offer, you're going to have to get wet. Costa Rica proudly boasts some of the world's finest surfing, white-water rafting and kayaking. If those kinds of thrills don't suit you, don a mask, fins and snorkel, or pass the time with a rod and reel in hand.

In the end, what truly distinguishes Costa Rica from other competing destinations is the diversity and accessibility of outdoor experiences. While hard-core enthusiasts can seek out complete solitude in absolute wilderness, families and novices are equally well catered for. From jungle treks and beachcombing to rafting snaking rivers and surfing crashing waves – whatever you're looking for, Costa Rica has most definitely got it.

Hiking & Trekking

Whether you're interested in taking a walk in the park, or embarking on a rugged mountaineering circuit, the hiking opportunities around Costa Rica are seemingly endless, and nearly every visitor to the country will have a hike or trek on their agenda – whether they know it before they leave or not. With its extensive mountains, canyons, dense jungles, cloud forests and two coastlines, Costa Rica is one of Central America's best and most varied hiking and trekking destinations.

These hikes come in an enormous spectrum of difficulty. At tourist-packed destinations such as Monteverde and Santa Elena, trails are clearly marked, and even lined with cement blocks in parts. This is very appealing if you're traveling with the little ones, or if you're lacking navigational prowess. For long-distance hiking and trekking, there are lots more options in the remote corners of the country.

Opportunities for moderate hiking are also available in most parks and reserves, particularly once you leave the well-beaten tourist path. As this is Costa Rica, you can – for the most part – still rely on signs and maps for orientation, though it helps to have a bit of experience under your belt. Good hiking shoes, plenty of water and a confidence in your abilities will enable you to combine several shorter day hikes into a lengthier expedition. Tourist information centers at park entrances are great resources for planning out your intended route.

If you're properly equipped with the various camping essentials (tent, sleeping bag, air mattress etc), the country's longer and more arduous multiday treks are at your disposal. Costa Rica's top challenges are scaling Cerro Chirripó, traversing Corcovado and penetrating deep into the heart of La Amistad. While all three endeavors can be undertaken either solo or with trusted companions, local guides provide an extra measure of safety, and can help in identifying flora and fauna.

How to Make it Happen

If you're planning your trip around long-distance hiking and trekking, it's best to visit the country during the dry season (December to April). Outside this narrow window, rivers become impassable and trails are prone to flooding. In the highlands, journeys become more taxing in the rain, and the bare landscape offers little protection. And then there are the mosquitoes, which can be maddening if your hike is poorly timed.

Costa Rica is hot and humid: hiking in these tropical conditions can really take it out of you. Remember to wear light clothing that will dry quickly. Overheating and dehydration are the main sources of misery on the trails, so be sure to bring plenty of water and don't be afraid to stop and rest. Make sure you have sturdy, comfortable footwear and a lightweight rain jacket.

Unfortunately, readers occasionally write in with horror stories of getting robbed while on some of the more remote hiking trails. Although this is certainly not a common occurrence, it is always advisable to hike in a group for added safety. Hiring a local guide is another excellent way to enhance your experience, avoid getting lost and learn an enormous amount about the flora and fauna in your midst.

Some of the local park offices have maps, but this is the exception rather than the rule. If you are planning to do independent hiking on long-distance trails, be sure to purchase your maps in San José in advance.

TRANS-CONTINENTAL HIKE

With the right guide and a study pair of legs, hardcore hikers can attempt the 70km trek from the Caribbean to the Pacific. The journey takes anywhere from six to 16 days, traversing pristine rainforest and cloud forest, and scaling the continental divide in the Talamanca Mountain Range. Several outfitters run hikes that start at around $750 for one to three people, and the route that seems most often frequented has beginning and end points on the Pacific near Ujarrás. Those who feel up to Costa Rica's ultimate hiking challenge should contact the ATEC (p436), a community-based sustainable tourism outfit or **Coast to Coast Adventures** (📞2280-8054; www.ctocadventures.com), which can arrange a custom trip.

THESE BOOTS WERE MADE FOR WALKING

With its ample supply of mud, streams and army ants, hiking through Costa Rica's parks can be quite an adventure – particularly for your shoes. Footwear is a personal issue, but here are some options for keeping your feet happy in the jungle.

Do as the locals do and invest in galoshes (rubber boots), especially for the rainy season. Rubber boots are indestructible, protect you from snakes and ticks, provide excellent traction and can be easily hosed off at the end of the day. The downside of rubber boots is that they are not very comfortable. And while there isn't much support, the real comfort issue is that the rubber edge of the top of the boot can cause uncomfortable chafing. To avoid this, wear them with a pair of socks that are long enough to cover your calves. Still, they aren't perfect: river crossings guarantee that the boots will fill up with water at some point, and then your feet are wet for the rest of the day. You can buy big rubber boots at most any hardware store in the county. If you are larger than a size 44 – men's 10 in the US – consider buying them abroad. Price: approximately $6.

High-end sport sandals (like Chacos, Tevas or Crocs) are used by climbers to scramble up boulders to the starting points for climbing routes. These are great for crossing rivers, as the water runs right off them (and your feet). However, be aware that there are lots of creepy crawlies living in the rainforest, some of which might like to make lunch out of your toes, and sandals offer little protection. Price: $50 to $150.

If you are planning a long outing in the mountains, it's a good idea to invest in solid, waterproof hiking boots. You don't have to pay an arm and a leg for sturdy boots that offer strong support and keep your feet marginally dry. If you can't stand the idea of walking around with wet feet, consider tossing a pair of sandals into your pack too, and change your shoes for the river crossings. Price: $100 to $250.

A number of companies offer trekking tours in Costa Rica:

» **Osa Wild** (p365) Offers a huge variety of hikes in the Osa in partnership with a sustainability organization.

» **Costa Rica Trekking Adventures** (p349) Offers multiday treks in Chirripó, Corcovado and Tapantí.

» **Ocarina Expeditions** (☎2229-4278; www. ocarinaexpeditions.com) Naturalist-led treks in Corcovado and Chirripó, as well as volcano and cloud-forest hiking.

» **Osa Aventura** (☎2735-5670; www. osaaventura.com) Specializes in treks through Corcovado.

Surfing

Point and beach breaks, lefts and rights, reefs and river mouths, warm water and year-round waves make Costa Rica a favorite surfing destination. For the most part, the Pacific coast has bigger swells and better waves during the latter part of the rainy season, but the Caribbean cooks from November to May. Basically, there is a wave somewhere waiting to be surfed at any time of the year.

For the uninitiated, lessons are available at almost all of the major surfing destinations – especially popular towns include Jacó, Dominical and Tamarindo on the Pacific coast. For our money, the best value schools and lessons in the country are in Dominical. Surfing definitely has a steep learning curve, and can be potentially dangerous if the currents are strong. With that said, the sport is accessible to children and novices, though it's always best to inquire locally about conditions before you paddle out. Having trouble standing up? Here is a tip: long boards readily maintain their stability, even in heavy crashing surf.

Throughout Costa Rica, waves are big (though not Hawaii-big), and many offer hollow and fast rides that are perfect for intermediates. As a bonus, Costa Rica is one of the few places on the planet where you can surf two different oceans in the same day. Advanced surfers with plenty of experience under their belts can tackle some of the sport's most famous waves. The top ones include: world-famous Ollie's Point and Witch's Rock, off the coast of Parque Nacional Santa Rosa; Mal País and Santa Teresa, with a groovy scene to match the powerful waves; Playa Hermosa, whose bigger, faster curls attract a more determined (and experienced) crew of wave-chasers; Pavones, a legendary long left

Surfer's Map

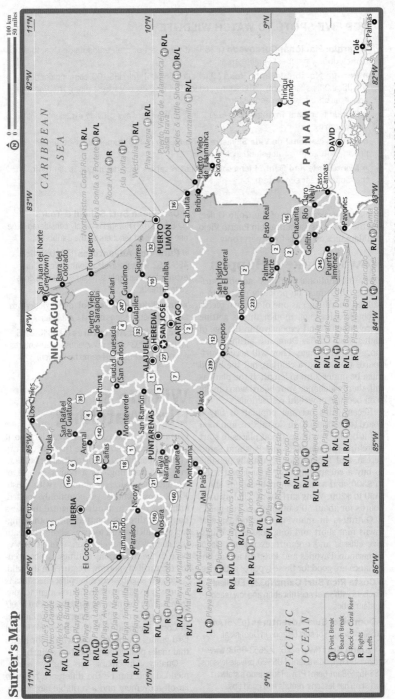

100 km
50 miles

CARIBBEAN SEA

PACIFIC OCEAN

NICARAGUA

PANAMA

Point Break
Beach Break
Rock or Coral Reef
R Rights
L Lefts

Ollie's Point
Potrero Grande
Witch's Rock
Peña Bruja
Playa Grande
Playa Tamarindo
Playa Langosta
Playa Avellanas
Playa Negra
Playa Junquillal
Playa Nosara
Garza
Camaronal
Playa Coyote
Playa Manzanillo
Mal País & Santa Teresa
Puntarenas
Puerto Caldera
Playa Doña Ana & Boca Barranca
Playa Tivives & Valor
Playa Escondida
Playa Jacó & Roca Loca
Playa Hermosa
Playa Esterillos-Oeste
Playa Esterillos-Este
Boca Damas
Quepos
Manuel Antonio
Playa El Rey
Matapalo
Dominical
Bahía Drake
Cabo Matapalo
Playa Pan Dulce
Backwash Bay
Playa Malapalo
Punta Banco
Zancudo
Pavones

TOP FIVE SPOTS TO WATCH WILDLIFE

» **Parque Nacional Corcovado** (p383) At the heart of the Península de Osa, this is the country's richest wildlife area.

» **Parque Nacional Santa Rosa** (tel, info 666 5051; full US$6.00, camping per person US$2.00; 8am-4pm; 4WD recommended) The tropical dry forest along the Pacific coast harbors a unique ecosystem.

» **Parque Nacional Tortuguero** (p412) Canals and waterways provide excellent bird-watching.

» **Refugio Nacional de Vida Silvestre Caño Negro** (p468) Expansive wetlands provide refuge for reptiles and avians alike.

» **Monteverde and Santa Elena** (p158)These reserves provide unique insight into the cloud-forest ecosystem.

across the sweet waters of the Golfo Dulce; and the infamous Salsa Brava in Puerto Viejo de Talamanca, which is for experts only.

How to Make it Happen

Most international airlines accept surfboards (they must be properly packed in a padded board bag) as one of the two pieces of checked luggage, though this is getting more difficult (and expensive) in the age of higher fuel tariffs. Domestic airlines offer more of a challenge. They will accept surfboards (for an extra charge), but the board must be under 2.1m in length. If the plane is full, there's a chance your board won't make it on because of weight restrictions.

Recently it's become popular to buy a board (new or used) in Costa Rica, and then sell it before you leave. Great places to start searching include Jacó, Mal País and Santa Teresa, and Tamarindo. It's usually possible to buy a cheap long board for about $250 to $300, and a cheap short board for about $150 to $200. Many surf shops will buy back boards for about 50% of the price you paid.

Outfitters in many of the popular surf towns rent short and long boards, fix dings, give classes and organize excursions. Jacó, Tamarindo, Pavones and Puerto Viejo de Talamanca are good for these types of activities.

» **Costa Rica Surf Camp** (p326) Excellent teachers with safety certification and low teacher-student ratios.

» **Dominical Surf Adventures** (p325) An excellent source of surf lessons in Dominical.

» **Iguana Surf** (Map p226; 2653-0613; www.iguanasurf.net; board rental US$20, private lessons US$45; 8am-6pm) Playa Tamarindo's stalwart surf shop has lessons, rentals and good tips.

» **Caribbean Surf School & Tours** (8357 7703) Hershel is widely considered to be one of the best teachers on the Caribbean.

» **Pura Vida Adventures** (in USA 415-465-2162; www.puravidaadventures.com) An excellent women-only surf camp that also does yoga retreats.

» **Van Dyke Surf School** (p434) Workshops and beginners lessons on the Caribbean.

» **Venus Surf Adventures** (8840-2365, in USA 800-793-0512; www.venussurfadventures.com) Has a six-day surf camp for women.

Wildlife & Bird-Watching

Costa Rica's biodiversity is legendary, so it should come as no surprise that the country offers unparalleled opportunities for wildlife- and bird-watching. As a bonus, people of all ages are already familiar with Costa Rica's most famous, yet commonly spotted, animals. You'll instantly recognize monkeys bounding through the treetops, sloths clinging to branches and toucans gliding beneath the canopy. Young children, even if they've been to the zoo dozens of times, typically enjoy the thrill of spotting creatures in the wild.

For the slightly older, keeping checklists is a fun way to add an education element to your travels. Want to move beyond the novice level? Check out your local bookstore before landing in Costa Rica and pick up some wildlife and bird guides – look for ones with color plates that make positive identification a cinch.

Quality binoculars are highly recommended and can be the difference between far-off movement and a veritable face-to-face encounter. For expert bird-watchers, a spotting scope is essential, and multipark itineraries will allow you to quickly add dozens of new species to your all-time list. Finally, it's worth pointing out that Costa Rica is brimming with wildlife at every turn, so always keep your eyes open and your ears peeled – you never know what's waiting for you just ahead!

How to Make it Happen

» **Aratinga Tours** (p341) Some of the best bird tours in the country are led by Dutch ornithologist Pieter Westra.

» **Birding on a Budget** (www.birdingonabudgetcr.com) A couple who are focused on setting up good-value birding tours for day trips, and to off-the-beaten path destinations.

» **Costa Rican Bird Route** (p463) Leads tours in the Estación Biológica la Selva.

Windsurfing & Kitesurfing

Laguna de Arenal is the nation's undisputed windsurfing (and kitesurfing) center. From December to April winds are strong and steady, averaging 20 knots in the dry season, often with maximum winds of 30 knots, and windless days are a rarity. The lake has a year-round water temperature of 18°C (64°F) to 21°C (70°F) with 1m-high swells.

For warmer water (but more inconsistent winds), try Puerto Soley in the Bahía Salinas.

White-Water Rafting & Kayaking

Since the birth of the ecotourism-based economy in the mid-1980s, white-water rafting has emerged as one of Costa Rica's top-billed outdoor pursuits. Ranging from family-friendly Class II swells to nearly unnavigable Class V rapids, Costa Rica's rivers offer highly varied white-water experiences.

First-time runners are catered for year-round, while seasoned enthusiasts arrive en masse during the wildest months from June through to October. There is also much regional variation, with gentler rivers located near Manuel Antonio along the central Pacific coast, and truly world-class runs along the Ríos Pacuare and Reventazón in the Central Valley. Since all white-water rafting in Costa Rica requires the presence of a certified guide, you will need to book all trips through a reputable tour agency.

River kayaking is not as popular as rafting, though it has its fair share of loyal fans. The tiny village of La Virgen in the northern lowlands is the unofficial kayaking capital of Costa Rica, and the best spot to hook up with other like-minded lovers of the sport. The Río Sarapiquí has an impressive variety of runs that cater to all ages and skill levels.

With 1228km of coastline, two gulfs and plentiful mangrove estuaries, Costa Rica is also an ideal destination for sea kayaking. This is a great way for paddlers to access remote areas and catch rare glimpses of birds and wildlife. Difficulty of access varies considerably, and is largely dependent on tides and currents.

How to Make it Happen

The months between June and October are considered to be the most exciting time for river rafting and kayaking, though some rivers offer good trips all year. Rafters and kayakers should bring sunblock, a spare change of clothes, a waterproof bag for a camera, and river sandals for foot protection. The

---

TOP FIVE SPOTS TO RAFT & KAYAK

» **Turrialba** (p126) Home to the country's most popular rafting rivers, the Pacuare and Reventazón.

» **La Virgen** (p456) The base town for rafting and kayaking on the Río Sarapiquí.

» **Manuel Antonio** (p317) A tourist mecca that offers family-friendly rafting year-round.

» **Parque Nacional Tortuguero** (p414) Boasts 310 sq km of wildlife-rich and kayak-friendly lagoons and canals.

» **Bahía Drake** (p377) Extensive mangrove patches are optimally explored by kayak.

» (above) Zip lining, Golfito (p388)
» (left) Snorkeling over a Costa Rican coral reef

government regulation of outfitters is shoddy, so ask lots of questions about your guide's water safety, emergency and medical training. If you suspect they're bluffing, move along. There are plenty of legit outfits.

River kayaking can be organized in conjunction with white-water rafting trips if you are experienced; sea kayaking is a popular activity year-round.

Aguas Bravas (2292-2072; www.aguas-bravas.co.cr) In La Virgen, this is the best outfitter on Costa Rica's best white water.

Pineapple Kayak Tours (p326) Exciting half-day kayak trips go through caves and mangroves channels.

Costa Rica Expeditions (2257-0766; www.costaricaexpeditions.com) This outfitter handles small groups and offers rafting trips that cater to foodies.

Exploradores Outdoors (p435) This outfit offers one- and two-day trips on the Ríos Pacuare, Reventazón and Sarapiquí.

Gulf Islands Kayaking (in Canada 250-539-2442; www.seakayak.ca) Tours on offer include five days of sea kayaking in Corcovado.

H2O Adventures (2777-4092; www.h2ocr.com) Arranges two- and five-day adventures on the Río Savegre.

Ríos Tropicales (p305) Can set up multi-day adventures on the Río Pacuare and two days of kayaking in Tortuguero.

Canopy Tours

The most vibrant life in the rainforest takes place at canopy level, but with trees extending 30m to 60m in height, the average human has a hard time getting a look at what's going on up there. You will find canopy tours everywhere in Costa Rica, and many of them will also have a zip line or two to whiz along for a small additional charge. The most elaborate facilities also have Superman cables (which allow you to fly like the Man of Steel) and Tarzan swings.

Some companies have built elevated walkways through the trees. SkyTrek (p147) near Monteverde and Rainmaker (p303) near Quepos are two of the most established operations in the country. A somewhat newer but equally popular operation is Actividades Arboreales near Santa María de Dota.

You can also take a ski lift–style ride through the tree tops, such as the Rainforest Aerial Tram (p402) near Braulio Carrillo or the smaller Monteverde Trainforest (p164) in Monteverde.

Diving & Snorkeling

The good news is that Costa Rica offers body-temperature water with few humans and abundant marine life. The bad news is that the visibility is low because of silt and plankton, and soft corals and sponges are dominant. If you are looking for turquoise waters and plenty of hard coral, head for Belize and Honduras.

However, if you're looking for fine opportunities to see massive schools of fish, as well as larger marine animals such as turtles, sharks, dolphins and whales, then you have arrived in exactly the right place. It's also worth pointing out that there are few places in the world where you can dive in the Caribbean and the Pacific on the same day, albeit with a good amount of effort and some advanced planning.

The Caribbean Sea is better for novice divers and snorkelers, with the beach towns of Manzanillo and Cahuita particularly well suited to youngsters. Puerto Viejo lays claim to a few decent sites that can be explored on a discovery dive. Along the Pacific, Playa del Coco and Isla del Caño up the ante slightly, offering a variety of sites for beginners and intermediates.

Isla del Cocos is the exception to the rule – this remote island floating in the deep Pacific is regarded by veteran divers as one of the best dive spots in the world. In order to catch a glimpse of the underwater world of Cocos, you'll need to visit on a liveaboard, and have some serious experience in your logbook.

How to Make it Happen

As a general rule, water visibility is not good during the rainy months, when rivers swell and their outflow clouds the ocean. At this time, boats to locations offshore offer better viewing opportunities.

The water is warm – around 24°C (75°F) to 29°C (84°F) at the surface, with a thermocline at around 20m below the surface where it drops to 23°C (73°F). If you're keeping it shallow, you can skin-dive (ie no wetsuit).

If you want to maximize your diving time, it's advisable to get diving accreditation beforehand. For more information, check out the **Professional Association of Diving Instructors** (PADI; in Canada 800-565-813, in Switzerland 52-304-1414, in USA 800-729-7234; www.padi.com), a nonprofit organization that provides diving insurance and emergency medical evacuation.

TOP FIVE SPOTS TO DIVE & SNORKEL

» **Playa del Coco** (p212) Home to manta rays, sharks and dozens of species of fish, all in large numbers.

» **Puerto Viejo de Talamanca** (p435) An emerging dive center that is good for snorkelers and novice divers.

» **Isla del Cocos** (p396) A truly world-class destination inhabited by an astonishing amount of marine life.

» **Cahuita and Manzanillo** (p435) Popular reefs that are good for snorkelers.

If you are interested in diving but are not accredited, you can usually do a one-day introductory course that will allow you to do one or two accompanied dives. If you love it, which most people do, consider getting certified, which takes three to four days and costs around $350 to $500.

Horseback Riding

Right across Costa Rica, you will inevitably find someone giving horseback-riding trips. Rates vary from $25 for an hour or two to more than $100 for a full day. Overnight trips with pack horses can also be arranged, and are a popular way of accessing remote destinations in the national parks. Riders weighing more than 100kg (220 lbs) cannot be carried by small local horses.

If you come across a good outfitter let us know (or give us the heads up on bad ones) by writing to Lonely Planet.

How to Make it Happen

The following companies organize horseback riding in Costa Rica:

» **Appaloosa Farms** (p147) Well-groomed horses take a four-hour trail to a hidden waterfall.

» **Sarapiquí Aguas Bravas** (☏2292-2072; www.aguas-bravas.co.cr) Horseback-riding day trips around Puerto Viejo de Sarapiquí and La Virgen.

» **Serendipity Adventures** (p43) Creates quality horseback-riding itineraries, including journeys to a Cabécar indigenous reserve.

Mountain Biking & Cycling

Although the winding, pot-holed roads and aggressive Costa Rican drivers can be a challenge, Costa Rica sees more and more

cyclists each year. There are numerous less-trafficked roads that offer plenty of adventure – from winding and scenic mountain paths with sweeping views to rugged trails that take riders through streams and past volcanoes. Cycling is on the rise in Costa Rica, and several Ticos have pedaled onto the international stage in recent years. The best long-distance rides are along the Pacific Coast's Interamericana, which has a descent shoulder and is relatively flat, and on the road from Montezuma to the Reserva Natural Absoluta Cabo Blanco on the southern Nicoya Peninsula.

Mountain biking has taken off in recent years and there are good networks of trails around Corcovado and Arenal, as well as more and more rides in the central mountains. You can rent mountain bikes in almost any tourist town, but the condition of the equipment varies greatly and most bikes are heavy, half-operable, dual-suspension monsters. For a monthly fee, **Trail Source** (www.trailsource.com) can provide you with information on trails all over Costa Rica and the world.

Most international airlines will fly your bike as a piece of checked baggage for an extra fee. Pad it well, because the box is liable to be roughly handled.

How to Make it Happen

Outfitters in Costa Rica and the USA can organize multiday mountain-biking trips around Costa Rica that cover stretches of highland and beach. Gear is provided on trips organized by local companies, but US outfitters require that you bring your own. If you try to see Costa Rica by the seat of a bicycle, be forewarned that the country's cycling shops are decidedly more geared toward utilitarian concerns. Bring any specialized equipment (including a serious lock) from home.

Numerous companies organize bike tours in Costa Rica.

» **Backroads** (☎800-462-2848, in USA 510-527-1555; www.backroads.com) Offers a variety of excursions, including a six-day cycling trip around Arenal and the Pacific coast.

» **Coast to Coast Adventures** (☎2280-8054; www.ctocadventures.com) Everything from short cycling excursions to 14-day coast-to-coast multisport trips.

» **Costa Rica Expeditions** (p41) Multisport itineraries including cycling, hiking, rafting and other adventures.

» **Lava Tours** (☎2281-2458; www.lava-tours.com) Reader-recommended tours include a bike ride (mostly downhill) from the Cerro de la Muerte to Manuel Antonio. Offers day trips, multiday packages and riding clinics.

» **MotoDiscovery** (☎830-438-7744, in USA 800-233-6564; www.motodiscovery.com) Organizes motorcycle tours through Central America, including an annual one from the Río Grande (known locally as Río Bravo del Norte) in Mexico to the Panama Canal.

» **Serendipity Adventures** (☎800-635-2325, 2558-1000, in USA 734-995-0111; www.serendipityadventures.com) Creates custom cycling itineraries to fit your schedule and your group.

» **Western Spirit Cycling** (☎in USA 800-845-2453; www.westernspirit.com) Offers a few different eight-day cycling itineraries.

Fishing

Sportfishing enthusiasts flock to both of Costa Rica's coasts for the thrill of reeling in mammoth marlins and supersized sailfish. Add dorado, wahoo and dolphin (the fish, not the mammal) to the list, and you can easily understand why the country has produced so many record-breaking catches. Of course, Costa Rica has an eco-image to maintain, which is why the vast majority of sportfishing companies encourage 'catch and release' practices in an effort to maintain existing fish populations.

The ocean is always open for fishing. As a general rule, the Pacific coast is best in June and July, though you'll get better fishing on the south coast then, while the Caribbean is best from September to November. Unless you have your own boat and tackle, you will need to book a trip through an operator.

Sportfishing is an expensive proposition, with baseline trips starting at several hundred dollars per outing. Assuming you have serious cash to burn, anyone can enjoy the thrill of getting a bite, though it definitely takes a bit of practice (and muscle) to reel in the big one. And, even if you're traveling with nonanglers, few people can resist the pleasure of an open-water cruise on a stylish fishing vessel.

For those on a more modest budget, there are several inland spots where you can hook freshwater fish. Finally, if you want to do as the locals do, try your hand at surf casting, which simply involves standing on a beach and casting a hook and line into the waves.

How to Make it Happen

Few airline restrictions will inhibit an angler from bringing their gear. Although solid catches come in year-round, there are seasonal restrictions on what types of fish you can catch. Typically, January and February are considered best for deep-sea fishing.

A good fishing resource is **Costa Rica Outdoors** (☎2282-6743, in USA 800-308-3394; www.costaricaoutdoors.com), a magazine available online or in hard copy that carries information on adventure travel, with a focus on fishing.

» **Discover Costa Rica** (☎257 5780, in USA 888-484-8227; www.discover-costa-rica.com) Offers six-day fishing packages; based in Quepos.

Travel with Children

Best Regions for Kids

Península de Nicoya
Excellent beaches and family-friendly resorts make this an ideal destination for families. This is a great place for kids (and their folks) to take surfing lessons.

Northwestern Costa Rica
Imagining fire flying out of the monstrous Volcán Arenal is thrilling for kids, as are the mysterious and ghostly cloud forests of Monteverde.

Central Pacific Coast
Easy trails lead past spider monkeys and sloths to great swimming beaches at Parque Nacional Manuel Antonio, a busy but beautiful piece of coastal rainforest.

Caribbean Coast
The whole family can snorkel all day at the relatively tranquil waters of Manzanillo or Cahuita and set out on a night adventure to see nesting turtles.

Costa Rica for Kids

Mischievous monkeys and steaming volcanoes, mysterious rainforests and palm-lined beaches – Costa Rica sometimes seems like a comic book reality. The perfect place for family travel, it is a safe, exhilarating tropical playland that will make a huge impression on younger travelers. The country's myriad adventure possibilities cover the spectrum of age-appropriate intensity levels. Additionally, the warm, family-friendly culture is extremely welcoming of little ones.

In addition to amazing the kids, this small, peaceful country has all of the practicalities that rank high with parents, such as an excellent transportation infrastructure, a low crime rate and a world-class healthcare system. But the reason to bring the whole family is the opportunity to share the country's unique experiences, like spotting a dolphin or sloth, slowly paddling a kayak through mangrove channels or taking a night hike in search of tropical frogs.

Children's Highlights

With its amazing landscapes and biodiversity, Costa Rica's family attractions largely remain an outdoor affair. It matters little which direction you travel; Costa Rica is an absolutely riveting country for kids.

Wildlife-Watching

Costa Rica's biggest attraction for children will undoubtedly be the abundant wildlife, which is nearly omnipresent from the moment the plane touches down. Even on the ride to the hotel, there's a chance of spotting the country's iconic blue morpho butterflies, a few sun-dazed iguanas or a flock of brightly colored tropical birds.

Those who get a little deeper by entering one of the country's national parks (particularly the crowded, but highly accessible trails of Parque Nacional Manuel Antonio) will find young wildlife-watchers face-to-face with a wondrous assortment of animals: keen-billed toucans and scarlet macaws, nesting leatherback turtles, troops of white-faced monkeys and a variety of technicolor tropical amphibians. There are lots of squeal-inducing creepy crawlies, like the oversize Hercules beetle, snakes and even some crocodiles – many are visible from a safe distance from the bridges crossing rivers. If you want to maximize your chances of spotting animals as well as learning about them, it's well worth hiring a certified guide, who can educate your family about these amazing creatures in their natural environment.

In addition to the parks, there seems to be a butterfly garden (or *finca de la mariposa*) in every other little town in the country. The best of the bunch is outside San José in Alajuela, where the tours are informative and the grounds are lovely. You can also find a number of exciting night hikes dedicated to spotting nocturnal animals around Quepos, Bahía Drake and Volcán Arenal. Many of the inland nature reserves and canopy walks can be extremely fascinating for young kids, and older kids with a thirst for adventure will love zooming through the trees on a zip line.

Beaches

» In general, the waters of the Caribbean are calmer and safer for swimming than those of the Pacific, but both coasts do have excellent swimming beaches.

» No matter how calm the water is, young swimmers should be supervised at all times and understand the dangers of riptides, which are particularly dangerous on the beaches at Dominical. Almost no beaches outside the major resorts have lifeguards.

» The best surf schools and camps are on the Península de Nicoya and all along the Central Pacific Coast.

» Many of the more experienced instructors have helped kids as young as five years old ride their first wave, though usually kids under 10 must be accompanied by a parent.

» Note that teaching surfing is a fairly casual line of work for some of the freelance instructors wandering around beachside communities, so inquire about water safety certification.

Other Family Adventures

» It is possible to wheel a stroller along the observation area at Parque Nacional Volcán Arenal, one of the few national parks that is accessible in this way.

» Extreme white-water rafting is best in the rainy season, but family-friendly rafting and 'safari trips' on the rivers happen year-round. The best Class I and II rapids for families are on the Río Sarapiquí.

» Check out water rafting on the Río Reventazón or Río Pacuare. Both rivers have sections with smoother runs that are perfect for families. Children must be at least nine years old, and even older for tougher runs.

Planning

Although Costa Rica is in the heart of Central America, it's a relatively easy place for family travel, making the nature of pre-departure planning more similar to North America or Europe than, say, Honduras. For an exhaustive number of travel suggestions for families, check out Lonely Planet's *Travel with Children*.

Before You Go

» Check immunizations about two months before traveling to make sure everyone in the family is up to date.

» Although malaria, yellow fever and other mosquito-borne illness are very uncommon in Costa Rica, consult your doctor to make sure immunizations are current. If you are traveling to Costa Rica from a country known for yellow fever, you may need to carry proof of immunization.

» Check validity of passports, which are required of the whole family.

» High seasons are particularly busy with families, so traveling around the North American spring break (which falls near the Costa Rican Easter week celebrations) or the week between Christmas and New Year requires the greatest amount of advance booking.

» Order good road maps if you are renting a car and topographical maps if you plan on serious hiking – neither are widely available in the country.

Costa Rica at Any Age

Infants & Toddlers

» If you're traveling with an infant, bring disposable diapers (nappies), baby creams or toiletries, baby aspirin and a thermometer from home, or stock up in San José. In rural areas, supplies may be difficult to find, though cloth diapers are more widespread.

» Strollers may help you get around high-end resorts, but are challenging to push around anywhere else in the country. Few national parks are set up to accommodate strollers. Consider investing in a quality hiking baby harness if you plan to spend much time in the parks.

Kids & Tweens

» Younger kids won't have a problem with the paths in most of Costa Rica's national parks, which are easy, short and well marked. Notable exceptions are Parque Nacional Corcovado, Parque Nacional Chirripó and Parque Nacional Amistad, which are more challenging to navigate.

» Although many surf schools allow for very young students, kids under 10 will likely have to take the class with a parent or guardian.

Teens

» Teenagers can take independent language or surfing lessons around the country, and during peak times, some surf schools offer classes for women and girls only.

» Consider more adventurous activities like hiking Parque Nacional Corcovado or summiting Chirripó.

Traveling in Costa Rica

» Because the entirety of Costa Rica is so reliably good for families, bringing the kids doesn't have to dictate where you'll go; it's safe to assume that most of the country that appeals to adults will also be alluring for kids.

» Although you will have to take some precautions to ensure the health and safety of little ones, Costa Rica's standards of safety are much more similar to North America and Europe than they are to other countries in Central America.

Getting There & Around

» Children under 12 receive a 25% discount on domestic-airline flights, while children under two fly free (provided they sit on a parent's lap).

» Children pay full fare on buses (except those under three years old).

» Single parents traveling with children may be asked for a notarized letter of permission from the other parent. It is rarely requested, but templates for such letters can be easily found online.

» Many lodges arrange shuttles to/from airports.

» Although many families opt to rent a car for part or all of their trip, Costa Rica's public transportation system is safe and relatively easy for families.

» Car seats for infants aren't always available at car-rental agencies, so bring your own or make sure you double (or triple) check with the agency in advance.

Family Accommodation

When it comes to accommodation in Costa Rica, families have a lot to choose from. From jungle ecolodges to beachside tents, you can find the type of accommodations your family needs at most tourist destinations. There are many rooms to accommodate families on a tight budget, and most midrange and top-end hotels have reduced rates for children under 12, provided the child shares a room with parents. Top-end hotels will provide cribs and usually have activities for children, swimming pools and play areas. Throughout this book, we have marked particularly family-friendly accommodations with this symbol: 🖼.

Eating with Kids

» Costa Rican cuisine is simple and hearty, if somewhat bland (beans and rice and grilled chicken or steak are omnipresent). The ubiquity of these dishes might be a bit dull for adults with adventurous appetites, but it makes it easier to cater to finicky young eaters.

» The volume of international travelers means that fast-food staples from home are commonly found.

» Special kids' meals are not normally offered in restaurants, though some fancy lodges will often offer them. However, most local eateries will accommodate two children splitting a meal or can produce child-size portions on request.

» If you're traveling with an infant, stock up on formula and baby food before hitting remote areas, and always carry snacks for long, remote drives – sometimes there are no places to stop for a bite.

» The tap water is safe to drink in Costa Rica.

» The hot weather requires lots of hydration. Kids might enjoy refreshing local drinks like *batidos* (fresh fruit shakes), either *al agua* (made with water) or *con leche* (with milk); coconut milk or *horchata* (cinnamon-spiked rice milk).

regions at a glance

San José

Museums ✓✓✓
Live Music ✓✓
Cuisine ✓✓✓

Old Gold & Upstart Art
Gritty, no-nonsense San José doesn't offer much in the way of architectural beauty, but it's the innards that count. In all of Costa Rica, this is the only place with a dense concentration of museums exhibiting everything from pre-Columbian gold frogs to the hottest multimedia installations by Costa Rica's contemporary artists.

Música en Vivo
As the cultural capital of Costa Rica, this is where you come to catch chamber music, international touring bands and up-and-coming local talent. The venerable Jazz Café is a solid place to start.

Cuisine Scene
Argentinian, vegetarian, Asian-fusion and classic French cuisine shine in superb San José venues. Some of the country's finest restaurants reside here, bringing a bit of diversity to *gallo pinto*–weary palates.

p52

Central Valley & Highlands

Volcanoes ✓✓
Rapids ✓✓✓
Countryside ✓✓

Volcanic Action
Volcanoes here range from wild and moderately active (Turrialba) to heavily trafficked (Poás), showing off ultramarine crater lakes and desolate, misty moonscapes.

White-Water Rush
World-class white water awaits on the Ríos Pacuare and Reventazón. The Pacuare, particularly, is worth a run for its thrilling rapids through a beautiful jungle gorge.

Wind & Dine
Costa Rica's picturesque highland countryside is often overlooked in favor of its beaches. Cows nibble contentedly along twisting mountain roads leading to villages with organic farmers markets and parks with psychedelic topiaries – perfect for picnics with local produce.

p94

Northwestern Costa Rica

Forests ✓✓✓
Ecolodges ✓✓✓
Waters ✓✓✓

Forests
Northwestern forests birthed the ubiquitous canopy tour. Studded with cathedral trees, which sprout dozens of species and shelter valuable watersheds; you'll be in awe of forests on volcanic slopes and along the wild coast.

Ecolodges
The sheer number of groovy, independently owned and operated ecolodges means you can choose from cute B&Bs to spectacular working *fincas* or biological stations ensconced in natural forest.

Waters
Stare into the placid waters of a vast artificial lake, lose yourself in aquamarine rivers, ride perfect lefts on wilderness beaches, or ride the wind on the most epic bay you've never heard of.

p130

Península de Nicoya

Tasty Surf ✓✓✓
Epic Dives ✓✓✓
Eats ✓✓✓

Tasty Surf
It's almost impossible to believe that there are so many waves on one spectacular, rugged peninsula. But, from the bottom to the top, there are countless perfect breaks to meet your needs.

Epic Dives
Don't expect Caribbean clarity or bath-water warmth, but if you do stride into the water you can expect mantas, bull sharks and schools of pelagics that will bend your brain.

Creative Local Eats
The creative kitchens that dot this intrepid coast source ingredients from local *fincas* and fishermen, and the dishes are prepared with passion and skill.

p209

Central Pacific Coast

Surfing ✓✓✓
Nature ✓✓✓
Beaches ✓✓

Surfing
From the pros-only Playa Hermosa to the beginner-friendly Dominical, the famous breaks of the Pacific coast bring blissful swells and tons of variety.

Manuel Antonio
Manuel Antonio, Costa Rica's smallest and most popular national park, is a kid-friendly, beach-lined delight. Sure, there are crowds of people, but at times they're outnumbered by monkeys, coati and tropical birds.

Deserted Beaches
It's a bit of a hike to get to Parque Nacional Marino Ballena, but those lucky few who find themselves on its empty beaches can scan the sparkling horizon for migrating whales.

p274

Southern Costa Rica

Chirripó ✓✓✓
Trout Fishing ✓✓
Culture ✓✓

Chirripó
Scaling the windswept peak of Chirripó is an exhilarating adventure into a wholly different Costa Rica from the one on the postcards. The view at sunrise from above the clouds is the brilliant highlight of this three-day excursion.

Trout Fishing
The high altitude valley cradling Parque Nacional Los Quetzales is more like the Alps than the tropics, but fishing the crystal clear rivers of the nearby San Gerardo de Dota is a refreshing break from beach.

Indigenous Communities
Traveling deep into Costa Rica's mountains allows you the chance to visit one of Costa Rica's endangered cultural treasures.

p334

Península de Osa & Golfo Dulce

Hikes ✓✓✓
Lodges ✓✓✓
Beach Towns ✓✓

Corcovado Hikes
Jaguars, jungle trails and wild things galore: this is among the world's most biologically intense patches of green. Hiking Corcovado national park is a sweaty, spine-tingling trip into the wonders of the tropical rainforest.

Jungle Lodges
Set deep in the wilderness around Bahía Drake, Osa offers jungle lodges in a wide variety of comforts – from rough-n-ready wilderness tent camps to secluded honeymooner ecolodges.

Remote Beach Towns
Once you get to the end of the road – literally – oceanside villages like Zancudo and Pavones are excellent places to chill, surf and unplug from the modern bustle.

p358

Caribbean Coast

Culture ✓✓✓
Wildlife ✓✓✓
Turtles ✓✓✓

Caribbean Flavor

Set apart geographically and culturally from the rest of Costa Rica, this coast has a distinct Afro-Caribbean flavor all its own. Taste it in the coconut rice, hear it the local *patois* and live it in super-chill Cahuita.

Wildlife-Watching

The waterlogged Caribbean coast teems with sloth, three of Costa Rica's four monkey species, crocodile, caiman, poison-dart frog, manatee, tucuxi dolphins and over 375 bird species.

Circle of Turtle Life

Turtle nesting is a serious business here. In Parismina and Tortuguero, the leatherback, green and hawksbill turtles return to their natal beaches to nest – a breathtaking experience.

p397

Northern Lowlands

Community ✓✓✓
Birds ✓✓✓
Paddling ✓✓✓

Community Tourism

This is where you'll discover real-life Costa Rica – on working *finca* homestays, tours through rainforest preserves, and on inky lagoons or mocha rivers with lifelong resident guides.

Birders Paradise

The humid swamps and, yes, hills of these lowlands are thick with forests and teeming with hundreds of species of birds from storks and egrets, to toucans and macaws.

Paddling & Floating

Whether you plan on paddling frothing white water shadowed by looming forest, wish to carve inland lakes by kayak, or just want to hop a motorboat to spot caimans or reel in tarpon, this is your Neverland.

p453

> Every listing is recommended by our authors, and their favourite places are listed first

> Look out for these icons:

 TOP CHOICE Our author's top recommendation   A green or sustainable option   **FREE** No payment required

On the Road

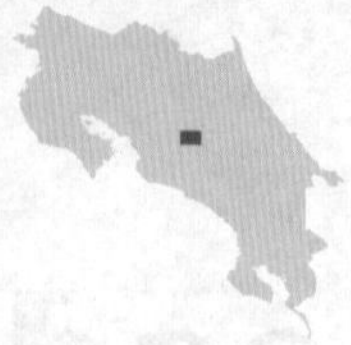

San José

POP GREATER METRO AREA: OVER 1.5 MILLION, CITY: 291,100 / 1170M

Best Places to Eat

» Park Café (p72)

» La Esquina de Buenos Aires (p70)

» Restaurante Tin-Jo (p70)

» Kalú Café & Food Shop (p70)

» Restaurant Whapin (p87)

Best Places to Stay

» Hotel Grano de Oro (p69)

» Hotel Aranjuez (p66)

» Mansión del Parque Bolívar Hotel (p67)

» Hotel Posada del Museo (p66)

» Hostel Pangea (p64)

Why Go?

San José is not a pretty city, what with the unremarkable concrete structures, clogged pedestrian arcades and fast-food monstrosities dominating its cityscape. And how delightful can a city really be when you're constantly dodging homicidal drivers, evading pickpockets and trying to tune out the cacophony of honking horns and ear-splitting reggaetón?

But once you get the hang of it, Chepe – as San José is affectionately known – quickly reveals its charms. Take your time poking around the more historic neighborhoods, where colonial mansions have been converted into contemporary art galleries, refined international restaurants and boutique hotels. Colorfully arresting murals and hipster buskers pop up on the most unexpected corners. And in its museums of gold and jade and national history lie all the layers of indigenous heritage, colonial past and great minds that made Costa Rica the environmental champion and military-free country we love today.

When to Go

Rainy season usually lasts from mid-April through December. The city's climate is considerably cooler than on the coasts, especially at night; daytime temps generally vary between 21°C to 27°C (70°F to 80°F). The best time to visit is around the Christmas holidays, when the Ticos' festive cheer reaches its height, with the Festival de Luz and Las Fiestas de Zapote being unmissable highlights. Otherwise, any season is good for exploring the capital's cultural attractions.

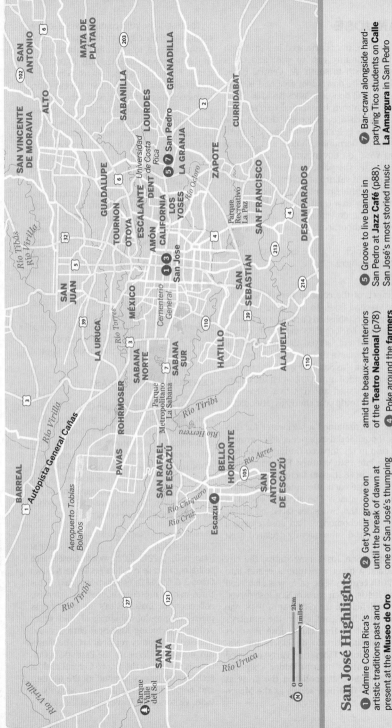

San José Highlights

1 Admire Costa Rica's artistic traditions past and present at the **Museo de Oro Precolombino y Numismática** (p54) and **Museo de Arte y Diseño Contemporáneo** (p58)

2 Get your groove on until the break of dawn at one of San José's thumping **nightclubs**

3 Take in a classical music performance after lingering amid the beaux-arts interiors of the **Teatro Nacional** (p78)

4 Poke around the **farmers markets** of Escazú, picking up locally grown and gourmet treats

5 Groove to live bands in San Pedro at **Jazz Café** (p88), San José's most storied music venue

6 Wander the quiet streets from **Barrio Amón** to **Los Yoses**

7 Bar-crawl alongside hard-partying Tico students on **Calle La Amargura** in San Pedro

8 Get a taste of Costa Rica's most sophisticated and diverse **culinary scene**

SAN JOSÉ

San José's center is arranged in a grid with avenidas running east to west and calles running north to south. Av Central is the nucleus of the downtown area and is a pedestrian mall between Calles 6 and 9.

The downtown has several *barrios* (districts), which are all loosely defined. The central area is home to innumerable businesses, bus terminals, hotels and cultural sites. West of downtown is La Sabana, named after the park, and just north of it is the elegant suburb of Rohrmoser. Further west is the affluent outer suburb of Escazú. Immediately east (and within walking distance) of the downtown area are the contiguous neighborhoods of Los Yoses and San Pedro.

You can pick up a free map of the city at the tourist office.

History

For much of the colonial period, San José played second fiddle to the bigger and relatively more established Cartago, a city whose origins date back to 1563 and which, during the colonial era, served as the provincial capital. Villanueva de la Boca del Monte del Valle de Abra – as San José was first known – was not founded until 1737, when the Catholic Church issued an edict that forced the populace to settle near churches (attendance was down).

The city remained a backwater for decades, though it did experience some growth as a stop in the tobacco trading route during the late 18th century. Following independence in 1821, rival factions in Cartago and San José each attempted to assert regional supremacy. The struggle ended in 1823 when the two sides faced off at the Battle of Ochomongo. San José emerged the victor and subsequently declared itself capital.

Despite San José's new status, the city remained a quiet agricultural center into the 20th century. The calm was shattered in the 1940s, when parts of San José served as a battlefield in the civil war of 1948, one of the bloodiest conflicts in the country's history. Out of that clash, José Figueres Ferrer of the Partido de Liberación Nacional (National Liberation Party) emerged as the country's interim leader – signing a declaration that abolished the army at the armory that now serves as the Museo Nacional.

The rest of the 20th century would see the expansion of the city from diminutive coffee-trading outpost to sprawling urban center. In the 1940s San José had only 70,000 residents. Today, the greater metro population stands at almost 1.6 million. Recent years have been marked by massive urban migration as Ticos (Costa Ricans) and, increasingly, Nicaraguans have moved to the capital in search of economic opportunity. As part of this, shantytowns have mushroomed on the outskirts, and crime is increasingly becoming a part of life for the city's poorest inhabitants.

The city remains a vital economic and arts hub, home to important banks, museums and universities – as well as the everyday outposts of culture: live music spaces, art centers, bookstores and the corner restaurants where *josefinos* (people from San José) gather to chew over ideas.

◉ Sights

San José is small and best explored on foot, joining locals along teeming sidewalks and pedestrian boulevards that lead to vintage theaters, crowded cafes, tree-shaded parks and some of the finest museums in Central America.

CENTRAL SAN JOSÉ EAST

Plaza de la Cultura PLAZA
(Map p60; Avs Central & 2 btwn Calles 3 & 5) For many Ticos, Costa Rica begins here. This architecturally unremarkable concrete plaza in the heart of downtown is usually packed with locals slurping ice-cream cones and admiring the wide gamut of San José street life: juggling clowns, itinerant vendors and cruising teenagers. It is perhaps one of the safest spots in the city since there's a police tower stationed at one corner.

Museo de Oro Precolombino y Numismática MUSEUM
(Map p60; ☏2243-4202; www.museosdelbanco central.org; Plaza de la Cultura, Avs Central & 2 btwn Calles 3 & 5; US$11; ◉9:15am-5pm daily) This three-in-one museum houses an extensive collection of Costa Rica's most priceless pieces of pre-Columbian gold and other artifacts, including historical currency and some contemporary regional art. The museum, housed underneath the Plaza de la Cultura, is owned by the Banco Central and its architecture brings to mind all the warmth and comfort of a bank vault. Security is tight; visitors must leave bags at the door.

SAN JOSÉ IN...

One Day

Begin with a peek inside the city's most beautiful building, the 19th-century Teatro Nacional (p55). Enjoy an espresso at the theater's atmospheric cafe (p71) before heading into the nearby Museo de Oro Precolombino y Numismática (p54) to peruse its trove of the country's pre-Columbian gold treasures. From here, stroll northeast through Parque Morazán to the Museo de Arte y Diseño Contemporáneo (p58), Central America's most prominent contemporary arts institution.

Take lunch on the terrace of Café Mundo (p70) or Kalú (p70). Afterwards, browse the shops of historic Barrio Amón, such as Kiosco SJO (p79), Galería Namu (p79) and eÑe (p79), ending with a happy-hour cocktail at El Morazán (p74).

Two Days

Start your second day in town with a primer on Costa Rican history at the Museo Nacional (p55), then explore the neighboring Mercado Artesanal (p79) for handicrafts. From here, go west on Av Central to the Catedral Metropolitana (p60), where *josefinos* still pack the pews for daily mass. Afterward, head northwest to the Mercado Central (p60) to shop for Costa Rican coffee, cigars and cheap eats.

In the evening, venture east to Los Yoses and San Pedro, where you'll find some of San José's best neighborhood eateries and bars, and the city's most esteemed venue for live music, the Jazz Café (p88).

Teatro Nacional NOTABLE BUILDING
(Map p60; 2221-5341; www.teatronacional.go.cr; Av 2 btwn Calles 3 & 5; admission US$7; 9am-4pm Tue-Sun) On the southern side of the Plaza de la Cultura resides the Teatro Nacional, San José's most revered public building. Constructed in 1897, it features a columned neoclassical facade that is flanked by statues of Beethoven and Calderón de la Barca, a 17th-century Spanish dramatist. The lavish marble lobby and auditorium are lined with paintings depicting various facets of 19th-century life. The most famous is *Alegoría al café y el banano*, an idyllic canvas showing coffee and banana harvests. The painting was produced in Italy and shipped to Costa Rica for installation in the theater, and the image was reproduced on the old ₡5 note (now out of circulation). It is clear that the painter never witnessed a banana harvest because of the way the man in the center is awkwardly grasping a bunch (actual banana workers hoist the stems onto their shoulders).

If you're looking to rest your feet, try the excellent onsite cafe (p71).

Across the street, also belonging to the national theater is the Museo Homenaje Joaquín García Monge (Map p60; 2259-9705; cnr Av 2 & Calle 5; 8am-4pm Mon-Fri), which features temporary exhibitions by contemporary Costa Rican and Central American artists.

Museo Nacional de Costa Rica MUSEUM
(Map p56; 2257-1433; www.museocostarica.go.cr; Calle 17 btwn Avs Central & 2; adult/child US$6/3; 8:30am-4:30pm Tue-Sat, 9am-4:30pm Sun) The Museo Nacional is located inside the old Bellavista Fortress, which served as the old army headquarters and saw fierce fighting (hence the pockmarks) in the 1948 civil war. It was here that President José Figueres Ferrer announced, in 1949, that he was abolishing the country's military.

The museum provides a quick survey of Costa Rican history, with exhibits of pre-Columbian pieces from ongoing digs, as well as artifacts from the colony and the early republic. Among the many notable pieces is the fountain pen that Figueres used to sign the 1949 constitution. Don't miss the period galleries in the northeast corner, which feature turn-of-the-20th-century furnishings and decor from when these rooms served as the private residences of the fort's various commanders.

Plaza de la Democracia PLAZA
(Map p60; Avs Central & 2 btwn Calles 13 & 15) Immediately west of the national museum is the stark Plaza de la Democracia, which was constructed by President Oscar Arias in 1989 to commemorate 100 years of Costa Rican democracy. Architecturally, the concrete

San José

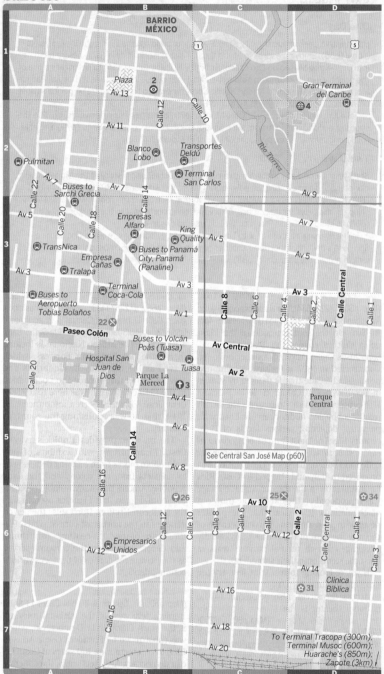

BARRIO MÉXICO

Plaza
Av 13
2

Calle 12

Calle 10

Av 11

Gran Terminal
del Caribe

4

Pulmitan

Blanco
Lobo

Transportes
Deldú

Calle 22

Av 7

Buses to
Sarchí Grecia

Av 7

Calle 14

Terminal
San Carlos

Río Torres

Av 9

Calle 20

Av 5

Calle 18

Empresas
Alfaro

King
Quality

Av 5

Av 7

Av 5

TransNica

Empresa
Cañas

Buses to Panamá
City, Panamá
(Panaline)

Calle 8

Calle 6

Calle 4

Calle 2

Calle Central

Calle 1

Av 3

Tralapa

Av 3

Av 3

Buses to
Aeropuerto
Tobías Bolaños

Terminal
Coca-Cola

Av 1

Av 1

22

Av 1

Paseo Colón

Buses to Volcán
Poás (Tuasa)

Av Central

Calle 20

Hospital San
Juan de
Dios

Tuasa

Av 2

Parque La
Merced

3

Parque
Central

Av 4

Calle 14

Av 6

See Central San José Map (p60)

Av 8

Calle 16

26

25

34

Av 10

Calle 12

Calle 10

Calle 8

Calle 6

Calle 4

Calle 2

Calle Central

Calle 1

Empresarios
Unidos

Av 12

Av 12

Av 14

Calle 3

Av 16

Clínica
Bíblica

31

Calle 16

Av 18

Av 20

To Terminal Tracopa (300m);
Terminal Musoc (600m);
Huarache's (850m);
Zapote (3km)

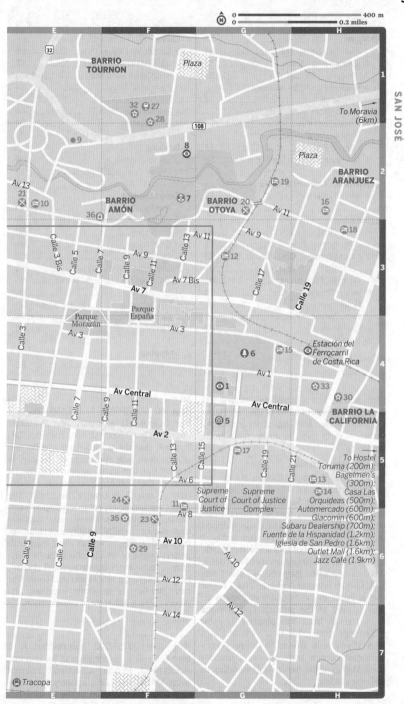

0 — 400 m
0 — 0.2 miles
N

BARRIO TOURNON

Plaza

32 27
28
9

108

8

To Moravia (6km)

Plaza

BARRIO ARANJUEZ

Av 13
21
10

BARRIO AMÓN

7

BARRIO OTOYA

20

19

Av 11

16

36

18

Calle 3 Bis
Calle 5
Calle 7
Calle 9
Av 9
Av 11
Calle 11
Calle 13

Av 11

Av 7 Bis

12

Av 9

Av 7

Parque España

Calle 17

Calle 19

Parque Morazán
Av 3

Av 3

Calle 3

6

15

Estación del Ferrocarril de Costa Rica

Av 1

Calle 7
Calle 9
Calle 11

Av Central

1

33

30

BARRIO LA CALIFORNIA

5

Av 2

Calle 13
Calle 15

17

Calle 19

Calle 21

To Hostel Toruma (200m);
Bagelmen's (300m);
Casa Las Orquideas (500m);
Automercado (600m);
Giacomin (600m);
Subaru Dealership (700m);
Fuente de la Hispanidad (1.2km);
Iglesia de San Pedro (1.6km);
Outlet Mall (1.6km);
Jazz Café (1.9km)

Av 6

13

14

Supreme Court of Justice

Supreme Court of Justice Complex

24

11
Av 8

35
23

29

Av 10

Calle 5
Calle 7
Calle 9

Av 10

Av 12

Av 10

Av 14

Av 12

Tracopa

San Jose

plaza is dull, but some of its elevated terraces provide decent views of the mountains surrounding San José (especially at sunset). On its western flank is an open-air crafts market (p79).

PARQUE ESPAÑA & AROUND

To the west of Parque España stands the recently remodeled Edificio Metálico (Map p60; cnr Av 7 & Calle 9), a century-old, two-story metal building that was prefabricated in Belgium. The structure was shipped piece by piece to San José and today it functions as a school and local landmark. On the Parque España's northeast corner is the Casa Amarilla (Map p60; Av 7 btwn Calles 11 & 13), an elegant colonial-style house that is home to the ministry of foreign affairs (closed to the public). The glorious ceiba tree in front was planted by John F Kennedy during his 1963 visit to Costa Rica. If you walk around to the property's northeast corner, you can see a graffiti-covered slab of the Berlin Wall standing in the rear garden.

Museo de Jade   MUSEUM
(Map p60; ☎2287-6034; 1st fl, Edificio INS, Av 7 btwn Calles 9 & 11; adult/child under 11yr US$8/free; ⊙8:30am-3:30pm Mon-Fri, 11am-3pm Sat) You will find the world's largest collection of American jade (pronounced 'ha-day' in Spanish) at this small museum on the 1st floor of the Instituto Nacional de Seguros (INS; National Insurance Institute). The pieces are varied: expect to see display cases cluttered with translucent jade carvings that depict fertility goddesses, shamans, frogs and snakes, as well as some incredible pottery (some of which reflects Maya influences), including a highly unusual ceramic head displaying a row of serrated teeth. The craftsmanship is generally excellent and pieces are in a fine state of conservation.

Museo de Arte y Diseño
Contemporáneo   MUSEUM
(Map p60; ☎2257-7202; www.madc.cr; Av 3 btwn Calles 13 & 15; admission US$3, Mon free; ⊙9:30am-5pm Mon-Sat) Commonly referred to as MADC, the Contemporary Art & Design Museum is housed in the historic Na-

tional Liquor Factory building, which dates from 1856. The largest and most important contemporary art museum in the region, MADC is focused on showing the works of contemporary Costa Rican, Central American and South American artists and occasionally features temporary exhibits devoted to interior design, fashion and graphic art.

Parque España PARK
(Map p60; Avs 3 & 7 btwn Calles 9 & 11) Surrounded by heavy traffic and flanked by MADC and the Museo de Jade, Parque España may be small, but it becomes a riot of birdsong every day at sunset when the local avian population comes in to roost. In addition to being a good spot for a shady break, the park is home to an ornate statue of Christopher Columbus that was given to the people of Costa Rica in 2002 by his descendants, commemorating the quincentennial of the explorer's landing in Puerto Limón.

Parque Morazán PARK
(Map p60; Avs 3 & 5 btwn Calles 5 & 9) To the southwest of the Parque España is Parque Morazán, named for Francisco Morazán, the 19th-century general who attempted to unite the Central American nations under a single flag. Once a notorious center of prostitution, the park is now beautifully illuminated in the evenings. At its center is the Templo de Música (Music Temple; Map p60), a concrete bandstand that serves as an unofficial symbol of San José.

BARRIO AMÓN
North and west of the Jade Museum lies this pleasant, historic neighborhood, home to a cluster of *cafetalero* (coffee grower) mansions constructed during the late 19th and early 20th centuries. In recent years, many of the area's historic buildings have been converted into hotels, restaurants and offices, making this a popular district for an architectural stroll. You'll find everything from art-deco concrete manses to brightly painted tropical Victorian structures in various states of upkeep. It is a key arts center.

Less than a block to the east of the Parque Nacional is the old train station to the Atlantic, the Estación del Ferrocarril de Costa Rica (Av 3 btwn Calles 17 & 23), which was built in 1908. Though the building is closed (it most recently housed a children's museum), it's nonetheless a remarkable example of tropical architecture, with swirling art nouveau–inspired beams and elaborate stonework all along the roofline.

One block to the west of the park is Jacob Karpio Galería (Map p60; ☎2257-7963; Av 1 btwn Calles 11 & 15; ☺10am-5pm Mon-Fri), the city's pre-eminent gallery, featuring established contemporary artists from around the region, including Priscilla Monge.

TEOR/éTica GALLERY
(Map p60; ☎2221-1051; www.teoretica.org; cnr Calle 7 & Av 11; admission by donation; ☺11am-6pm Tue-Sat, 11am-4pm Sun; 🖲) This contemporary art museum is the brick-and-mortar gathering space for the TEOR/éTica foundation, a nonprofit organization that supports Central American art and culture. Housed in a vintage mansion, each of its elegant rooms exhibits cutting-edge works by established and emerging figures from Latin America, such as Costa Rican artist Priscilla Monge, who is well known for her wry multimedia work.

Galería Andrómeda GALLERY
(Map p60; ☎2223-3529; andromeda@amnet.co.cr; cnr Calle 9 & Av 9; ☺10am-7pm Mon-Fri, 10:30am-5pm Sat) On Amón's southeastern edge, the smaller yet charming Galería Andrómeda is a free local art space featuring works by emerging artists, as well as a selection of literary magazines (in Spanish), among other publications.

Parque Nacional PARK
(Map p56; Avs 1 & 3 btwn Calles 15 & 19) One of the nicest of San José's green spaces is the Parque Nacional, a shady spot where retirees read newspapers and young couples smooch coyly on benches. At its center is the Monumento Nacional, a dramatic statue (erected in 1953) depicting the Central American nations driving out American filibuster William Walker. The park is dotted with myriad monuments devoted to key figures in Latin American history, including Cuban poet, essayist and revolutionary José Martí, Mexican independence figure Miguel Hidalgo and 18th-century Venezuelan poet and thinker Andrés Bello.

Across the street, to the south, stands the Asamblea Legislativa (Map p56) (Legislative Assembly), which also bears an important statue: this one a depiction of Juan Santamaría – the young man who helped kick the pesky Walker out of Costa Rica – in full flame-throwing action.

CENTRAL SAN JOSÉ WEST
Parque Central PARK
(Map p60; Avs 2 & 4 btwn Calles Central & 2) The city's central park is more of a run-down plaza than a park. At its center is a grandiose

Central San José

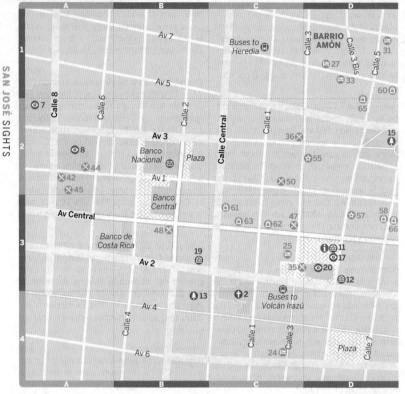

bandstand that looks as if it was designed by Mussolini: massive concrete arches support a florid roof capped with a ball-shaped decorative knob.

Catedral Metropolitana   CHURCH

(Map p60; Avs 2 & 4 btwn Calles Central & 1) To the east of the Parque Central is the Renaissance-style Catedral Metropolitana, built in 1871 after the previous cathedral was destroyed in an earthquake. The interiors, in keeping with the period, are graceful neoclassic, with colorful Spanish tile floors, stained-glass windows, and a Christ figure that was produced by a Guatemalan workshop in the late 17th century. On the north side of the nave, along the passage to the Capilla del Santisímo (Chapel of the Holy One), a recumbent Christ that dates back to 1878 draws devout Ticos, who arrive here to pray and deposit pleas scribbled on small slips of paper.

Teatro Melico Salazar   HISTORIC BUILDING

(Map p60; ☑2233-5424; www.teatromelico.go.cr; Av 2 btwn Calles Central & 2) On the north side of the Parque Central is this theatre, which was built in 1928 in a beaux-arts style. It is named after the well-known Costa Rican tenor Melico Salazar (1887–1950), who performed internationally (among other places, he sang at the Metropolitan Opera in New York City). The theater was the site of the 2002 presidential inauguration, and regularly hosts fine arts engagements.

Mercado Central   MARKET

(Map p60; Avs Central & 1 btwn Calles 6 & 8; ⊙6am-6pm Mon-Sat) Though *josefinos* mainly do their shopping at chain supermarkets, San José's crowded indoor markets retain an old-world feel. This is the main market, lined with vendors hawking everything from spices and coffee beans to *pura vida* souvenir T-shirts.

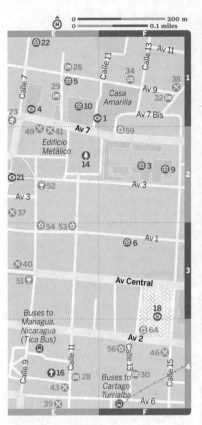

museum – actually two museums in one – is an excellent place to start. Housed in an old penitentiary built in 1909, it is part children's museum and part art gallery. Small children will love the hands-on exhibits related to science, geography and natural history, while grown-ups will enjoy the unusual juxtaposition of contemporary art in abandoned prison cells.

Spirogyra Jardín de Mariposas GARDENS
(Map p56; ☎2222-2937; www.butterflygardencr.com; Barrio Amón; adult/child US$7/3; ⊙8am-4pm; ☺; ☐to El Pueblo) Housing more than 30 species of butterfly – including the luminescent blue morpho – in plant-filled enclosures, this small butterfly garden is a great spot for kids. Visit in the morning to see plenty of fluttering. The garden is 150m east and 150m south of Centro Comercial El Pueblo, which can be reached on foot (about a 20- to 30-minute walk from downtown), by taxi or by bus.

LA SABANA

West of downtown, the bustle of the city's congested center gives way to private homes, condo towers and shopping areas chock-full of Ticos. At the heart of this district lies the sprawling Parque Metropolitano La Sabana, a popular recreation center – and a welcome patch of green amid the concrete of the capital.

Parque Metropolitano La Sabana PARK
(Map p64; ☎2284-8700) Known simply as Parque La Sabana, this 72-hectare green space at the west end of the Paseo Colón was once the site of the country's main airport. Today it is home to two museums, a lagoon, a fountain and a variety of sports facilities. It is also home to the Estadio Nacional de Costa Rica (p79) (Costa Rica National Stadium), where international and Division-1 soccer matches are played. During the day, it's a great place for a stroll, a picnic or a relaxed jog along its network of paths.

FREE **Museo de Arte Costarricense** MUSEUM
(Map p64; ☎2256-1281; www.musarco.go.cr; east entrance of Parque La Sabana; ⊙9am-4pm Tue-Sun) At the eastern entrance to the Parque La Sabana is the Museo de Arte Costarricense, in a Spanish-style structure that served as San José's main airport terminal until 1955. The newly remodeled museum features regional art and other exhibits.

Mercado Central Annex MARKET
(Map p60; Avs 1 & 3 btwn Calles 6 & 8) The Mercado Central Annex, and is less touristy than Mercado Central, and is crowded with butchers, fishmongers and informal counters dishing out typical Costa Rican *casados* (a set meal of rice, beans and cabbage slaw served with chicken, fish or meat).

Mercado Borbón MARKET
(Map p60; cnr Av 3 & Calle 8) The Mercado Borbón is more focused on produce, though it sells a bit of everything. (Be aware: the streets get sketchy around the Borbón.)

CENTRAL SAN JOSÉ NORTH

Museo de los Niños & Galería Nacional MUSEUM
(Map p56; ☎2258-4929; www.museocr.com; Calle 4, north of Av 9; adult/child US$2/1.50; ⊙8am-4:30pm Tue-Fri, 9:30am-5pm Sat & Sun; ☺) If you were wondering how to get your young kids interested in art and science, this unusual

Central San José

Museo de Ciencias Naturales La Salle MUSEUM
(Map p64; ☎2232-1306; http://lasalle.ed.cr/museo.php; Parque La Sabana; adult/child US$2/1.50; ☺7:30am-4pm Mon-Sat, 9am-5pm Sun; ☝) Found near the southwest corner of Parque La Sabana is the Museo de Ciencias Naturales La Salle, which has an extensive collection of dusty stuffed animals and minerals. The exhibit has definitely seen better days, and although some of the animals look like they're about to disintegrate, you would be hard pressed to find a more bizarre display of taxidermy. The museum is in the old Colegio La Salle (high school).

> **WORTH A TRIP**
>
> ## ZOO AVE
>
> San José does have its own zoo, Parque Zoológico Nacional Simón Bolívar (Map p56; ☑2233-6701; www.fundazoo.org; Av 11 btwn Calles 7 & 9; adult/child US$5/3; ☺9am-4:30pm daily; ⚐). But to see native birds and monkeys in a more naturalistic setting, check out the terrific Zoo Ave, outside of Alajuela. It's an easy day trip from San José and well worth the jaunt.

🏌 Activities

Golfers can reserve tee times at Parque Valle del Sol (p89), outside Escazú. If you want to swim with the kiddies and your hotel doesn't have a pool, head to the Ojo de Agua Springs (p99) in San Antonio de Belén, a popular swim spot for Tico families.

Parque Metropolitano La Sabana (☑2284-8700) has a variety of sporting facilities, including tennis courts, volleyball, basketball and baseball areas, jogging paths and soccer pitches. Pickup soccer games can be had on most days, though you'd better be good: Ticos can sink a drop shot by age seven. There is also an Olympic-sized swimming pool if you're a serious lap swimmer.

🕺 Courses

You can improve your dance moves on your own at Merecumbé, a chain of studios that will get you grooving to everything from salsa to waltz. Most courses are for locals, but some sessions are geared at foreign travelers. Schedules vary; call ahead.

The company has various studios, though, unfortunately, nothing downtown.

» Merecumbé Escazú (p89)

» Merecumbé San Pedro (☑2224-3531; 100m south & 25m west of the Banco Popular)

🗺 Tours

The city is small and easily navigable, but if you're looking for a walking tour that will guide you to key sites, there are plenty on offer.

Barrio Bird Walking Tours   WALKING TOUR
(☑8926-9867; www.toursanjosecostarica.com; tours $15-65) The knowledgeable and engaging Stacey Corrales shows visitors San José's famous and not-so-famous sights, providing history and insights on the city's architecture, murals and urban art. Specialized tours also cater to gourmands, photographers and bar-crawlers.

Costa Rica Art Tour   TOUR
(☑8359-5571, 2288-0896; www.costaricaarttour.com; per person US$125) This small outfit run by Molly Keeler organizes a recommended day tour that visits five different artist studios, where you can view (and buy) the work of local painters, sculptors, printmakers, ceramicists and jewelers. Lunch and hotel pickup is included in the price. Reserve at least one week in advance.

Swiss Travel Service   WALKING TOUR
(Map p56; ☑2282-4898; www.swisstravelcr.com) This long-standing agency offers a three-hour walking tour of San José that hits all the key sites.

🎉 Festivals & Events

Festival de Arte   ARTS FESTIVAL
Every even year, San José becomes host to the biennial citywide arts showcase that features theater, music, dance and film. It's held for two weeks in March. Keep an eye out for information in the daily newspapers.

Día de San José   RELIGIOUS FESTIVAL
(St Joseph's Day) On 19 March, San José marks the day of its patron saint with mass in some churches.

Festival de las Carretas   CULTURAL FESTIVAL
(Oxcart Festival) Takes place every November and is a celebration of the country's agricultural heritage. The highlight is a parade of oxcarts down Paseo Colón.

Festival de Luz   RELIGIOUS FESTIVAL
(Festival of Light) A month after Paseo Colón's oxcart parade is the Christmas parade, marked by an absurd amount of plastic 'snow.'

Las Fiestas de Zapote   CULTURAL FESTIVAL
(☺December 25 to January 1) If you're in the San José area between Christmas and New Year's Eve, this week-long holiday celebration of all things Costa Rican (namely

La Sabana

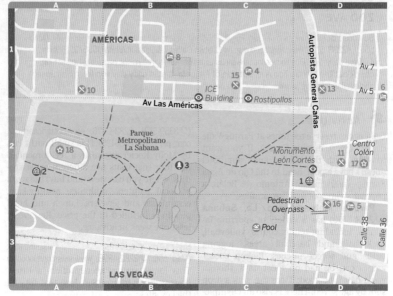

rodeos, cowboys, carnival rides, fried food and booze) annually draws in tens of thousands of Ticos to the bullring in the suburb of Zapote, just southeast of the city.

🛏 Sleeping

Accommodations in San José run the gamut from grim little boxes to luxurious boutique retreats. You'll find the cheapest sleeps in the city center, with nicer midrange and top-end spots clustered in more well-to-do districts such as Barrio Amón and La Sabana. Also worthwhile for their charm, safety and serenity are the adjacent neighborhoods of Los Yoses and San Pedro, which lie within walking distance from downtown.

For tonier options, the upscale suburb of Escazú – a 20-minute bus ride away – is a good choice. If you're flying into or out of Costa Rica from San José, you may find it more convenient to locate yourself in Alajuela, as the town is minutes from the international airport.

Reservations are recommended in the high season (December through April), in particular the two weeks around Christmas and Semana Santa (Holy Week, the week preceding Easter).

Hostels

The city overflows with hostels geared at backpackers. You'll have a bunk and a shared bathroom, but plan on bringing amenities such as soap, shampoo and towels. Many places are equipped with 21st-century goodies, however, like wi-fi and TV lounges. Some hostels also have affordable private rooms. All hotels listed below have hot-water showers.

For ease of use, all of San José's hostels are listed here, regardless of neighborhood. For some excellent alternatives, see the Los Yoses district.

TOP CHOICE **Hostel Pangea** HOSTEL **$**
(Map p60; ☎2221-1992; www.hostelpangea.com; Av 7 btwn Calles 3 & 3bis, Barrio Amón; dm $13-16, d with/without bathroom $40/32, ste $60-70; 🅿@🛜❄) This industrial-strength, Tico-owned hostel – 25 dorms and 25 private rooms – has been a popular 20-something backpacker hangout for years. It's not difficult to see why: it's smack in the middle of the city and comes stocked with a pool, a rooftop restaurant/lounge with stellar views, and a combination bar-movie theater furnished with beanbags and a stripper pole. Needless to say, this is a party spot. But the rooms are tidy, the mattresses firm and shared bathrooms enormous and clean. The

hostel's five suites have king-size beds and flat-screen TVs. Plus, there is free internet, free phone calls to North America, luggage storage and airport shuttles (from US$10).

Costa Rica Backpackers HOSTEL $
(Map p56; ☏2223-2406, 2221-6191; www.costarica backpackers.com; Av 6 btwn Calles 21 & 23; dm US$13, d without bathroom US$32; P@🛜⊛) This extremely popular hostel has 15 dormitories and 13 private double rooms spread over several structures that surround a spacious garden with hammocks and a freeform pool. Chill-out music completes the laid-back ambience, though you can always take things up a notch in the attached bar / restaurant or poolside bar. Rooms and shared bathrooms are basic but clean, and decorated with tropical-themed murals. There is a communal kitchen and TV lounge, as well as free luggage storage, internet access and pickups from San José bus stations.

Hostel Casa del Parque HOSTEL $
(Map p56; ☏2233-3437; www.hostelcasadelparque. com; cnr Calle 19 & Av 3; dm US$10, d with/without bathroom US$42/32; 🛜) A vintage art-deco manse from 1936 houses this quiet spot on the northeastern edge of Parque Nacional. Five large, basic private rooms (one with private bathroom) and one dormitory have parquet floors and simple furnishings. Take some sun on the plant-festooned outdoor patio, and take advantage of a shared kitchen and free wi-fi. The bilingual young owner, Federico Echeverría, is a good source of local dining information.

Gaudy's HOSTEL $
(Map p64; ☏2248-0086; www.backpacker.co.cr; Av 5 btwn Calles 36 & 38, Casa 3636; dm US$12, d with/without bathroom US$36/22; P@🛜) You'll find this homey hostel inside a sprawling modernist house in a residential area east of Parque La Sabana. Popular among shoestring travelers for years, it has 13 private rooms and two dormitories. The Colombian owners keep the design scheme minimalist and the vibe mellow; service is professional and the rooms well maintained. There's a communal kitchen, TV lounge, pool table and foosball, a courtyard strung with hammocks, as well as free internet.

Galileo Hostel
HOSTEL $

(Map p64; ☎2248-2094; www.hostelgalileo.com; cnr Calle 40 & Av 2; dm US$9-11, r without bathroom US$24-30; @🖵) In a vintage house east of Parque La Sabana, the snug, friendly Galileo Hostel has several dormitories and four private rooms with shared bath. The colorful dorms are tight but clean, and are the cheapest in town. There is free wi-fi, a communal kitchen, a small garden patio crowded with plants, as well as a friendly, cozy onsite bar. Bonus: the American owners host Sunday BBQs during the football season.

Mi Casa Hostel
HOSTEL

(Map p64; ☎2231-4700; www.micasahostel.com; Sabana Norte, 150m north of ICE Building; dm US$13, r with/without bathroom from US$32/25, all incl breakfast; 🅿@🖵) This converted modernist home in La Sabana has polished wood floors, vintage furnishings and half a dozen eclectic guest rooms to choose from (two of which are dormitories). One room is wheelchair-accessible. Mellow communal areas are comfortably furnished, and the shared kitchen is clean and roomy. There is a pleasant garden, where a tiny bar stocks cold beer for guests, and other perks include a pool table, free internet, and laundry service.

Homestays

Bells' Home Hospitality
HOMESTAY $$

(☎2225-4752; www.homestay-thebells.org; s/d incl breakfast US$30/50) This recommended agency is run by the bilingual Marcela Bell, who has operated the business for more than 20 years. She can arrange stays in more than a dozen homes around San José, each of which has been personally inspected. All are close to public transportation and travellers have sent only positive comments about these places. Note that there is a US$5 surcharge for one-night-only stays; dinner is available at an extra cost.

CENTRAL SAN JOSÉ EAST

Most of downtown's better sleeping options are located east of Calle Central, many of them in historic Victorian and art-deco mansions. Many of the top-end hotels accept credit cards.

TOP CHOICE Hotel Aranjuez
HOTEL $

(Map p56; ☎2256-1825; www.hotelaranjuez.com; Calle 19 btwn Avs 11 & 13; incl breakfast s/d from US$32/49, s/d without bathroom US$25/30; 🅿@🖵👪) This rambling hotel in Barrio Aranjuez consists of several nicely maintained vintage homes that have been strung together with connecting gardens and walkways. The 36 spotless rooms come in a variety of configurations, with lockboxes and cable TV. The hotel's best attribute, however, is the lush garden patio, where a legendary breakfast buffet is served every morning. Though the architecture can be a bit creaky and the walls thin, the service is efficient and the hotel is a solid, family-friendly option – it's so popular that there's now an annex half a block away. Annex rooms are of the generic apartment variety, sans wi-fi access but with the bounteous breakfast included. Credit cards accepted.

Hotel Posada del Museo
GUESTHOUSE $$

(Map p56; ☎2258-1027; www.hotelposadadelmuseo. com; cnr Calle 17 & Av 2; s $59-95, d $68-95; @🖵👪) This *posada* (country-style inn) is at a diagonal from the Museo Nacional, in a 1928 structure with a dramatic entrance that features a Juliet balcony overlooking the foyer. French doors line the entrances to each of the rooms (no two of which are alike), which are all named after Costa Rican birds and flowers.

SAN JOSÉ FOR CHILDREN

Chances are that if you're in Costa Rica on a short vacation you'll be headed out to the countryside fairly quickly. But if for some reason you're going to be hanging out for a day – or two or three – with your kids, here are a few activities to keep them busy.

The Museo de los Niños (p61) is a hit with children, who just can't keep their hands off the exhibits. Young nature-lovers will enjoy getting up close and personal with butterflies at the Spirogyra Jardín de Mariposas (p61) or checking out the exotic animals at the Parque Zoológico Nacional Simón Bolívar (p63).

If you're planning on spending more than a week in the city, note that many Spanish-language academies offer special custom-made lessons for teens. In addition, both the Teatro Eugene O'Neill (p88) and Teatro Fanal (p78) have children's theater groups. If your child is learning Spanish, this experience might make a vivid lesson.

ALFONSO PEÑA

Alfonso Peña is a born-and-bred *josefino* who edits the literary magazine *Matérika* (www.materika.org) and helps manage Galería Andrómeda (p59) in Barrio Amón.

What makes San José a compelling cultural center? Naturally, the city has incredible museums, such as the Museo de Arte y Diseño Contemporáneo (p58), the Teatro Nacional (p55), the Galería Nacional (p61) and TEOR/éTica (p59). But it goes beyond that. I've been a writer for 25 years and I'm constantly observing things. And San José is a city that wherever you go, there's something to see, from the architecture to the people on the street. Every visitor should consider it an absolute necessity to take a stroll through Barrio Amón. It's got these little streets that are full of magic. It's the oldest part of the city – there are houses here from the 19th century – and it's where much of our cultural life has taken place. This is where Costa Rican writers have tangled with issues like eroticism and crime and esoteric themes. There's so much to discover here. You just have to be willing to look for it.

Some rooms accommodate up to four people, making this a good spot for families. The amiable Argentine managers speak English, Spanish, French and Italian. Note to light sleepers: the hotel is adjacent to the train tracks. Credit cards accepted.

Mansión del Parque
Bolívar Hotel   BOUTIQUE HOTEL **$$$**
(Map p60; www.hotelparquebolivar.com; Av 9 btwn Calles 11 & 13; d $90-120, tr $120-125) Occupying a quiet nook in Barrio Otoya, this elegant new hotel offers five rooms that provide respite from city stress. The mansion's neoclassical architecture hints at the graceful decor inside, outfitted with polished wood floors, antiques and refined, locally made furniture. Breakfast is served on an upstairs terrace overlooking the back of Casa Amarilla, and the Italian management is friendly, knowledgeable and helpful. A gem in which to take refuge.

Hotel Don Carlos   HOTEL **$$**
(Map p60; 2221-6707; www.doncarloshotel.com; Calle 9 btwn Avs 7 & 9; incl breakfast s/d $70/80, s/d deluxe US$80/90; P@🛇🞲🏠) Built around an early 20th-century house that once belonged to President Tomás Guardia, this lovely Barrio Amón inn exudes a slightly campy colonial-era vibe. Thirty-three rooms are nestled around a pre-Columbian-themed sculpture garden with a sundeck, tables and a small pool (ideal for kids). All rooms come equipped with cable TV, lockbox and hair dryer. Don't miss the Spanish-tile mural, just outside the onsite restaurant, which beautifully depicts central San José in the 1930s. Credit cards accepted.

Kaps Place   GUESTHOUSE **$$**
(Map p56; 8647-7190, 2221-1169; www.kapsplace.com; Calle 19 btwn Avs 11 & 13; $25-50, d $45-60, tr $55-70, apt $85-125; P@🛇🏠) A colorful little guesthouse on a residential street in Barrio Aranjuez, Kaps Place has 24 small, homey rooms of various configurations spread over two buildings. Run by Karla Arias, this is decidedly a family place: expect to see kids playing in the yucca plant–filled courtyard or hopping on the trampoline. The spacious shared kitchen is immaculate, patios are strung with hammocks and the communal areas are wonderfully decorated in bright mosaics. There is free internet and Spanish, English and French are spoken.

Gran Hotel Costa Rica   HOTEL **$$$**
(Map p60; 2221-4000; www.granhotelcostarica.com; Calle 3 btwn Avs Central & 2; incl breakfast d standard/superior/deluxe $89/109/149, master ste/presidential ste $185/250; P🞲🞲@🛇) The city's first prominent hotel was constructed in 1930 and is recognized as a national landmark (John F Kennedy and soccer legend Pelé have both stayed here). Frequent renovations have kept the 107 rooms modern and comfortable, though they retain period touches such as brass bed frames and wood furnishings. Some of the units have wonderful views of the Teatro Nacional, and here and there are subtle architectural reminders of the hotel's history: exposed beams, molded ceilings and the dramatic entrance hall – lined with vintage photographs of San José. The hotel has an in-house restaurant and a popular terrace bar.

Casa Alfi HOTEL $
(Map p60; ☎ 2221-2102; www.casaalfihotel.com; Calle 3 btwn Avs 4 & 6; s/d/tr incl breakfast US$43/62/77 (incl tax); @ 📶) Steps from the Teatro Nacional, this simple two-story structure surrounds a bright covered courtyard around which nine guest rooms are located. The individually different rooms are simple but come equipped with TV, telephone, private bathroom and lockbox, and feature folk-art touches. It's a sleepy spot, despite being in the middle of the downtown hubbub. Credit cards accepted.

Cinco Hormigas Rojas B&B $
(Map p56; ☎2255-3412; www.cincohormigasrojas.com; Calle 15 btwn Avs 9 & 11; incl breakfast r US$40-60, f US$120; 🚭 📶) A one-of-a-kind B&B that is a veritable riot of plants – and everything else. Every nook and cranny of this six-room inn features a piece of art or embellishments crafted out of papier-mâché (toilet included). All of it is the vision of terrifically friendly, multilingual hippie chick Mayra Güell, who treats her guests to daily breakfasts featuring macrobiotic breads, fresh jams and juices and organic coffee. Reserve ahead, as drop-ins may go completely unnoticed.

Hotel Colonial HOTEL $$
(Map p60; ☎2223-0109; www.hotelcolonialcr.com; Calle 11 btwn Avs 2 & 6; s/d/ste incl breakfast US$58/68/98; P ❄ @ 📶 🏊) Guests at this 1940s Spanish-style inn are greeted by an intricately carved baroque-style carriage door and an arched poolside promenade. The 17 rooms are either whitewashed or painted an earthy shade of mustard yellow, with dark wood furnishings and bright bedspreads. Those on higher floors have sweeping views of the city and outlying mountains, while three of the ground-level rooms are wheelchair-accessible. Credit cards accepted.

Hotel Rincón de San José HOTEL $$
(Map p60; ☎2221-9702; www.hotelrincondesanjose.com; cnr Av 9 & Calle 15; s/d/tr/q incl breakfast US$60/72/90/115; @ 📶) Centered on three colonial-style houses in Barrio Otoya, this tidy spot, popular with couples and families, has 40 guest rooms – some of which are modern with bright linens and ceramic tile, while others are equipped with period-style pieces and polished wood floors. Breakfast is served in an attractive interior garden courtyard. Laundry service and luggage storage are available; credit cards are accepted.

Hotel Kekoldi HOTEL $$
(Map p60; ☎2248-0804; www.kekoldi.com; Av 9 btwn Calles 5 & 7; s/d/tr from US$57/69/79; 📶) The Kekoldi is set in an airy art-deco building in Barrio Amón. The hotel has 10 expansive, light-drenched rooms of various sizes, painted in light shades of pastel, and they come equipped with cable TV. Murals of beach landscapes adorn the common areas and there is also a garden for lounging. This is a relaxed spot, where English and German are spoken and credit cards accepted.

Hemingway Inn HOTEL $$
(Map p60; ☎2221-1804, 2257-8630; www.hemingwayinn.com; cnr Calle 9 & Av 9; incl breakfast s US$35-55, d US$40-60; 📶) This funky little spot in Barrio Amón has 17 rooms in a rambling *cafetalero* house dating to the 1920s. With a garden, shared kitchen and murals adorning the walls, the inn has a relaxed and friendly ambience. All of the rooms come with safes (US$3 per day) and each is simple, comfortable and unique. As a rare perk, pets can be accommodated with prior notice.

Hotel Santo Tomás HOTEL $$
(Map p60; ☎2255-0448; www.hotelsantotomas.com; Av 7 btwn Calles 3 & 5; d incl breakfast US$58-78; P 🚭 @ 📶 🏊) This stately early 20th-century colonial-style mansion is a Barrio Amón landmark that once belonged to the Salazar family of *cafetaleros*. Thirty rooms occupy the mansion itself and a newer annex in back. Mansion rooms are slightly frayed, with high ceilings and period furnishings, while newer rooms are equipped with brocaded bedspreads, modern bathroom, balcony and flat-screen TV. A garden courtyard contains a solarium, swimming pool, Jacuzzi and small open-air gym.

Raya Vida Villa GUESTHOUSE $$
(Map p56; ☎2223-4168; www.rayavida.com; Calle 15, off Av 11; s/d incl breakfast US$85/95, extra person US$20; P) This long-running B&B, housed in a secluded hilltop villa, reflects owner Michael Long's interest in art and antiques, dogs and cats. The house, built in the Spanish colonial style, has a patio with a fountain, a fireplace and a small garden, while an upstairs deck is a pleasant spot with city views. Five well-appointed rooms have polished wood floors, bright floral linens and expansive bathrooms, one of which has a whirlpool tub.

Casa Ridgway GUESTHOUSE $
(Map p56; 2233-2693, 2222-1400; www.amigos
paralapaz.org; cnr Calle 15 & Av 6bis; dm US$15, s/d
US$25/38, without bathroom US$22/34; P♿🐾🛜)
A small, peaceful guesthouse on a quiet side
street near the Supreme Court complex is
run by the adjacent Friends' Peace Center,
a Quaker organization promoting social
justice and human rights. The rooms are
immaculate, as are the shared showers and
communal kitchen. There is a small lounge,
and a lending library offers an extensive collection of books on Central American politics
and society. No smoking or alcohol is allowed, with quiet hours from 10pm to 6am.

Other good sleeping options to consider:

» **Casa Hilda** (Map p56; 2221-0037;
c1hilda@racsa.co.cr; Av 11 btwn Calles 3 & 3bis; s/d
US$20/30) Guesthouse run by the charming
Quesada family; has a natural spring in
center of house.

» **Costa Rica Guesthouse** (Map p56;
2223-7034; www.costa-rica-guesthouse.com; Av
6 btwn Calles 21 & 23; incl breakfast dm US$16, d
with/without bathroom from US$39/32; P@🛜)
Tranquil rooms in a house dating from 1904.

» **Hotel Fleur de Lys** (Map p60; 2257-2621,
2223-1206; www.hotelfleurdelys.com; Calle 13 btwn
Avs 2 & 6; incl breakfast s/d from US$88/96, junior
ste/master ste US$136/148; P♿@🛜) Pristinely
maintained, century-old Victorian mansion
near the train tracks; credit cards accepted.

LA SABANA & SURROUNDS

You'll find modern inns and vintage B&Bs
in the neighborhoods that surround Parque
Metropolitano La Sabana.

TOP CHOICE **Hotel Grano de Oro** BOUTIQUE HOTEL $$$
(Map p64; 2255-3322; www.hotelgranodeoro.
com; Calle 30 btwn Avs 2 & 4; d US$135-205, f/gar-
den/vista-del-oro ste US$215/265/385; P♿@🛜)
Hotel Grano de Oro is a favorite of honey-
mooners and it's not difficult to see why.
Built around a sprawling early 20th-century
Victorian mansion, this elegant inn has 40
demure 'Tropical Victorian' rooms furnished
with wrought-iron beds and rich brocade
linens. Several units maintain the hotel's
historic look while boasting private court-
yards with gurgling fountains. The lobby is
punctuated by a dramatic mahogany stair-
case and the public areas sparkle with fresh
tropical flowers and polished wood accents.
If you want to experience the Costa Rica of
a gilded age, this would be the place to do it.
The hotel is also home to the recommended
Restaurante Grano de Oro (p72).

Colours Oasis Resort HOTEL $$
(2296-1880, in USA & Canada 866-517-4390;
www.coloursoasis.com; Blvr Rohrmoser, cnr of El Tri-
angulo; d/ste from US$89/149; 🛜🏊) This long-
time gay and lesbian hotel in the elegant
Rohrmoser district (to the northwest of La
Sabana) is located in a sprawling Spanish
colonial–style complex. Here, rooms and
mini-apartments have paddle fans, modern
furnishings and impeccable bathrooms. Facilities include a TV lounge, mini-gym, pool,
sundeck and Jacuzzi – as well as an onsite
bar/restaurant, an ideal spot for an evening
cocktail. The helpful owners speak English
and Spanish and can offer all kinds of in-
sights on gay travel in the country.

Apartotel La Sabana HOTEL $$
(Map p64; 2220-2422; www.apartotel-lasabana.
com; 150m north of Rostipollos, Sabana Norte; d/
apt incl breakfast from US$60/75; P❄@🛜🏊👨)
This lovely, well-maintained apartment
complex has 32 units in various configura-
tions that draw long-term business travelers
as well as families. Apartments (with and
without kitchen) are decorated in neutral
tones and accented with wood furnishings
and folk art, plus the interior courtyard has
a nice pool. Service is attentive, and the
neighborhood is surprisingly quiet. Special
rates are available for weekly stays; credit
cards are accepted.

🖼 **Rosa del Paseo** HOTEL $$
(Map p64; 2257-3225, 2257-3258; www.rosadel
paseo.com; Paseo Colón btwn Calles 28 & 30; s/d/ste
from $75/85/90; P@🛜) Though it's right on
Paseo Colón, don't let the small facade fool
you: this sprawling Victorian mansion (built
in 1897 by the Montealegre family of coffee ex-
porters) reaches into an interior garden courtyard that provides a respite from city noise.
The hotel still maintains the original tile
floors and polished wood ceilings, as well as
antique oil paintings and sculptures. Rooms
are simple, with polished wood floors and
period-style furnishings. The garden, where
breakfast is served, is filled with heliconias
and bougainvilleas. Credit cards accepted.

✕ Eating

From humble corner stands dishing out
gut-filling *casados* to contemporary bistros
serving fusion everything, in cosmopolitan
San José you will find the country's best restaurant scene. Dedicated eaters should also
check out the dining options in Los Yoses
and San Pedro, as well as Escazú.

VOLUNTEERING IN SAN JOSÉ

For travelers who want an experience beyond vacation, there are dozens of not-for-profit organizations in San José that gladly accept volunteers.

» **Amerispan** (p106) Manages programs devoted to everything from animal rescue to women's education. In San José, there are opportunities to work in educational settings or with the elderly.

» **Central American Service Expeditions** (☑8839-0515; www.serviceexpeditions. net) A Costa Rican nonprofit that creates custom volunteer expeditions for families and teens, focused on sustainability. Around San José the group has helped build roads and day-care centers in unincorporated city slums.

» **GeoVisions** (☑in USA & Canada 877-949-9998; www.geovisions.org) An international nonprofit with school, hospital and orphanage-related placements.

» **Sustainable Horizon** (☑in USA & Canada 718-578-4020; www.sustainablehorizon. com) Arranges a wide variety of volunteer trips, including opportunities to help out at children's shelters.

» **United Planet** (☑in USA & Canada 800-292-2316; www.unitedplanet.org) For volunteers interested in health-, child- and elder-care fields.

» **Volunteer Abroad** (☑in USA & Canada 888-649-3788; www.volunteerabroad.ca) Among other options, it places volunteers in the children's hospital.

Top-end restaurants tend to get busy on weekend evenings; make a reservation.

CENTRAL SAN JOSÉ EAST

Long-standing neighborhood *sodas* (lunch counters) mix effortlessly with contemporary cafes and Asian-fusion eateries on San José's eclectic east side.

TOP CHOICE La Esquina de Buenos Aires ARGENTINE $$$
(Map p60; ☑2223-1909; http://laesquinadebuenos aires.com/; cnr Calle 11 & Av 4; mains US$10-30; ⊙11:30am-3pm & 6-11pm Mon-Fri, noon-11pm Sat & Sun; ☑) Spanish-tile floors, bright white linens and the sound of old tangos evoke the atmospheric bistros of San Telmo – making this one of the top spots in the city for a steak and a glass of Malbec. Also tasty are the housemade *empanadas* and the extensive selection of fresh pastas, including vegetarian options such as tender raviolis stuffed with mozzarella and fresh basil. There's a good South American–centric wine list, attentive service and flickering candlelight, making this an ideal place for a date. Reservations recommended; credit cards accepted.

Restaurante Tin-Jo ASIAN $$
(Map p56; ☑2221-7605; www.tinjo.com; Calle 11 btwn Avs 6 & 8; mains US$10-18; ⊙11:30am-3pm & 5:30am-10pm Mon-Thu, 11:30am-3pm & 5:30am-11pm Fri & Sat, 11:30am-10pm Sun; ☑) The interiors of this popular Asian standard-bearer are a riot of pan-Asian everything, just like the menu. Expect a wide range of fare from various regions – from *kung pao* shrimp to spicy tuna *maki* to *pad thai* – as well as an extensive vegetarian menu. Credit cards accepted.

Kalú Café & Food Shop CAFE $$
(Map p56; ☑2221-2081; www.kalu.co.cr; cnr Calle 7 & Av 11, Barrio Amón; mains US$11-18; ⊙11:30am-6pm Mon, 11:30am-9:30pm Tue-Sat; ☑) Sharing a sleek space with the **Kiosco SJO** (Map p56; ☑2258-1829; www.kioscosjo.com; cnr Av 11 & Calle 7; ⊙11am-6pm Mon, 11am-9:30pm Tue-Sat) design store, this style-conscious cafe is run by noted chef Camille Ratton. The menu is a global fusion of salads, sandwiches and pastas, such as homemade gnocchi cooked in Malbec with wild mushrooms (US$13). Whatever you do, don't miss dessert: their light and airy cheesecake (US$5), served with stewed fresh strawberries in balsamic, is mind-meltingly good.

Café Mundo ITALIAN $$$
(Map p60; ☑2222-6190; www.cafemundo.cr; cnr Av 9 & Calle 15, Barrio Otoya; mains US$8-34; ⊙11am-10:30pm Mon-Thu, 11am-11:30pm Fri, 5pm-12am Sat; ☑) Location. Location. Location. This longtime Italian cafe and expat favorite has it. Set on a sprawling terrace in a vintage Barrio Otoya mansion, it's a perfect spot to enjoy a glass of wine and good (if not earth-shattering) pizzas and pastas within sight of an outdoor fountain. The wine list is good and even includes a selection of bubbly Spanish cavas.

Alma de Café
CAFE $

(Map p60; ☎2233-2178; www.almadecafe.net; Plaza de la Cultura; mains US$4-10; ☺9am-7pm) One of the most beautiful cafes in the city, this atmospheric spot evokes early 20th-century Vienna. In other words, a perfect place to sip cappuccino, enjoy a crêpe or quiche and take in the lovely ceiling frescoes.

Café de los Deseos
CAFE $

(Map p56; ☎2222-0496; www.cafedelosdeseos.com; Calle 15 & Av 11, Barrio Otoya; US$4-10; ☺2-10pm Tue-Sat) Full of artsy young bohemians, Café de los Deseos offers up delicious visions for the eye as well as tasty *bocas* that include salads and individual pizzas. Smoothies, desserts, cocktails and other temptations round out the menu. The setting is cozy and colorful, its walls hung with the work of local artists and rooms adorned with beaded curtains, branches entwined with fairy lights and hand-painted tables. A lively but romantic spot for a bite and a glass of wine.

Restaurante La Criollita
COSTA RICAN $

(Map p60; ☎2256-6511; Av 7 btwn Calles 7 & 9; breakfast US$2.50, casados US$7; ☺7am-9pm Mon-Fri, 7am-4pm Sat) This homey local spot is popular with office types and dishes up a changing menu of simple Costa Rican specialties including stewed chicken and grilled fish. The setting is pleasant, the service efficient and you can accompany your meal with a glass of Chilean cabernet (US$4).

Restaurante Shakti
VEGETARIAN $

(Map p56; ☎2222-4475; cnr Av 8 & Calle 13; mains US$5-9; ☺7:30am-7pm Mon-Fri, 8am-6pm Sat; ☒) This informal neighborhood health-food outpost has simple, organic-focused cooking as well as freshly baked goods. Favorites include veggie burgers, along with various fish dishes, but most people arrive for the *casado* of the day – which is always vegetarian.

Huarache's
MEXICAN $

(☎2239-2828; Av 22 btwn Calles 5 & 7; mains US$3-6; ☺11am-11pm) This bustling Mexican restaurant on a nondescript block near Plaza Víquez (350m east of the Hospital de la Mujer) makes up for all the bland meals you've had in Costa Rica. Here you'll find fresh honest-to-goodness tacos, quesadillas, guacamole, tortilla soup and hot sauces that'll make you think you've died and gone to Mexico.

Vishnu
VEGETARIAN $

(Map p60; ☎2256-6063; www.vishnucr.com; Av 1 btwn Calles 1 & 3; mains US$4-11; ☺8am-7pm Mon-Fri, 9am-6pm Sat & Sun; ☒) You'll find a rainbow of fresh local produce, vegetable stews and well-rendered soy burgers at this informal chain of vegetarian cheapies. Most folks pile in for the inexpensive lunch specials, which generally include salad, fresh juice and dessert. There are a few vegan specialties as well. Vishnu has several branches dotted around downtown.

Café del Patio
CAFE $

(Map p56; ☎2221-2302; Calle 3 & Av 11; mains US$4-8; ☺noon-2pm Mon-Fri) Ensconced in the covered patio of Casa 927, this airy cafe incorporates historic charm with craftsy touches like flower arrangements made of recycled magazine pages. The weekday set lunch (US$7) is a fabulous deal, featuring fresh and simple cuisine slightly elevated from the ubiquitous *casado*. The ever-changing menu also features sandwiches, desserts and *empanadas* (turnovers stuffed with meat or cheese).

Don Wang
CHINESE $$

(Map p60; ☎2223-5925, 2223-6484; www.donwangrestaurant.com; Calle 11 btwn Avs 6 & 8; mains US$7-16; ☺11am-3pm & 5:30am-10pm Mon-Fri, 11am-11pm Sat, 11am-10pm Sun; ☒☒) This hopping Cantonese eatery is an ideal place for dim sum – served all day every day – as well as a long list of Chinese specialties, from stir-fried shrimp with cashews to *mu shu* vegetables (there are more than a dozen veggie dishes to choose from). Parents will love the children's play area in the corner – ideal for restless toddlers.

Nuestra Tierra
COSTA RICAN $$

(Map p60; ☎2258 6500; cnr Av 2 & Calle 15; mains US$10-28; ☺24hr; ☒) A taxidermied bull's head (and some pretenders) greet you at this country restaurant, where the theme is Costa Rican spit and sawdust. Cheery waiters deliver wooden platters piled with heaping *casados* to hordes of hungry tourists and Tico families seated at rustic picnic-style tables. Nuestra Tierra is a fine spot for lunch and sangria after a visit to the national museum.

A few other spots worth checking out:

» **Bar Morazán** (Map p60; ☎2222-4622; 2nd fl, Calle 7 btwn Avs 1 & 3; lunch casados US$5; ☺11am-2pm) Inexpensive *almuerzos ejecutivos* (set lunches) that you can enjoy under a mural of dogs playing poker.

» **El Patio del Balmoral** (Map p60; ☎2221-1700; www.elpatiodelbalmoral.com; Av Central btwn Calles 7 & 9; mains US$9-23; ☺6am-10:30pm, terrace bar 4pm-11pm) Upstairs seats on the terrace are best for taking in the air and pedestrian action over Av Central.

» **El Torito** (Map p60; ☎2256-0220; Av 7 btwn Calles 7 & 9; breakfast US$3, casados US$6; ☺7am-8pm) Informal cafe/bakery stocked with sweet and savory turnovers and fresh breads; also has reasonably priced lunch specials.

» **Restaurante 1930** (Map p60; ☎2221-4000; Plaza de la Cultura; mains US$12-30, espresso US$2; ☺24hr) This European-style cafe at Gran Hotel Costa Rica (p67) has a full menu; an excellent spot for coffee and people-watching.

Self-caterers can try:

» **Automercado** (Map p60; ☎2233-5511; www.automercado.co.cr; cnr Calle 3 & Av 3; ☺7am-9pm Mon-Sat, 8am-4pm Sun) Good selection of cheeses, produce, liquor, coffee and chocolate.

» **Perimercado** (Map p60; ☎2222-2252; Calle 3 btwn Avs Central & 1; ☺7am-9pm Mon-Sat, 8am-3pm Sun) An economical chain, conveniently located downtown.

CENTRAL SAN JOSÉ WEST

The city's hectic commercial heart has some of the cheapest eats in town.

Pastelería Merayo   BAKERY $
(Map p56; ☎2223-5758; Calle 16 btwn Paseo Colón & Av 1; pastries US$1-2; ☺Mon-Sat) This informal pastry shop has a wide variety of freshly baked, cavity-inducing goodies. The coffee is strong and it's a sweet way to pass the time if you're waiting for a bus at the Coca-Cola terminal.

Soda Castro   DESSERTS $
(Map p56; ☎2222-3452; Av 10 btwn Calles 2 & 4; mains US$3-6, sundaes US$5; ☺9am-9:30pm; ⚐) It's not in the best neighborhood, but this casual, six-decade-old Tico spot is a good place to feed the sweet tooth. You'll find sundaes and banana splits, but it's the house-made *paletas* (fresh fruit pops) that make this spot worth the walk. They come in a variety of seasonal flavors, including fantastically dreamy toasted coconut.

Q Café   CAFE $
(Map p60; ☎2221-0707; www.quecafe.com; 2nd fl, cnr Av Central & Calle 2; mains US$7-12; ☺8am-9pm Mon-Fri, 10am-8pm Sat & Sun) A sleek, monochromatic cafe with excellent views of the ornate Correo Central in the distance, this modern 2nd-story spot is perfect for coffee drinks (including delicious iced mocha) and pastries. Try the *empanadas,* which go well with the cafe's homemade hot sauce.

Mercado Central   MARKET $
(Map p60; Avs Central & 1 btwn Calles 6 & 8; ☺6:30am-6pm Mon-Sat) One of the cheapest places for a good lunch is at the Mercado Central, where you'll find a variety of *sodas* serving *casados*, tamales, seafood and everything in between. A good spot is **Mariscos Poseidon** (Map p60; Mercado Central Annex; mains US$4-8; ☺11am-6pm), a narrow, blue-and-yellow seafood joint run by the congenial Doris in the central market's northern annex, just off Av 1. The *ceviche mixto* appetizer (fish, shrimp and octopus marinated in lime juice) is tasty and cheap, as are the generous portions of seafood-studded rice. Afterwards, head across the street to the main market for dessert at **Helados de Sorbetera** (Map p60; ☎2256-5000; Mercado Central; frozen custard US$2-3; ☺10am-6pm), a century-old local favorite that serves up cinnamon-laced frozen custard. Do as the locals do and order *barquillos* (cylindrical sugar cookies) to accompany your icy treat.

LA SABANA & SURROUNDS

TOP CHOICE **Park Café**   EUROPEAN $$$
(Map p64; ☎2290-6324; 100m norte de Rostipollos, Sabana Norte; mains US$26-31; ☺noon-2pm & 7-9:30pm Tue-Sat) Built from scratch, though it looks deceptively like a restored historic building, the Park Café is an anomalous (and felicitous) fusion of antique shop and French restaurant. Michelin-starred chef Richard Neat offers an exquisite menu – crab ravioli with asparagus, artichoke and ginger sauce, for starters – and a carefully curated wine list. The backdrop, created by Neat's partner Louise French, is eclectically decorated and features antiques from India and Bali arranged in the garden courtyard and elegant interior.

Restaurante Grano de Oro   FUSION $$$
(Map p64; ☎2255-3322; www.hotelgranodeoro.com; Calle 30 btwn Avs 2 & 4; lunch mains US$12-25, dinner mains US$15-32; ☺7am-10pm) One of San José's top dining destinations is the stately, flower-filled restaurant at the Hotel Grano de Oro. Known for its Costa Rican–fusion cuisine, the menu is laced with unique specialties such as pork loin roasted in coffee

THE GALLO PINTO CONTROVERSY

No other dish in Costa Rica inspires Ticos quite like their national dish of *gallo pinto*, that ubiquitous medley of rice, beans and spices. You might even hear Costa Ricans refer to themselves as *'más Tico que gallo pinto'* (literally, 'more Costa Rican than *gallo pinto*.') Exactly what type and amount of this holy trinity makes up authentic *gallo pinto* is the subject of intense debate, especially since it is also the national dish of neighboring Nicaragua.

Both countries claim that the dish originated on their soil. Costa Rican lore holds that the dish and its iconic name were coined in 1930 in the neighborhood of San Sebastián, which is on the southern outskirts of San José. Nicaraguans claim that it was brought to the Caribbean coast of their country by Afro-Latinos long before it graced the palate of any Costa Rican.

The battle for the rights to *gallo pinto* doesn't stop here, especially since the two countries can't even agree on the standard recipe. Nicaraguans traditionally prepare it with small red beans, while Costa Ricans swear by black beans. And we're not even going to bore you with the subtle complexities of balancing cilantro, salt and pepper.

Nicaragua officially holds the world record for making the biggest ever pot of *gallo pinto*. On September 15, 2007, a seething vat of *gallo pinto* fed 22,000 people, which firmly entrenched Nicaragua's name next to *gallo pinto* in the *Guinness Book of World Records*. Costa Rica responded in 2009 by cooking an even more massive avalanche of the stuff, feeding a small crowd of 50,000. Though the event was not officially recognized as setting any records, that day's vat of *gallo pinto* warmed the hearts and bellies of many a proud Tico.

and seared duck crowned with caramelized figs. There is an encyclopedic international wine list (from US$25 per bottle), including half a dozen types of champagne and cava. For dessert, don't miss the coffee cream pie. Reservations recommended for dinner; credit cards accepted.

Machu Picchu PERUVIAN $$
(Map p64; ☎2222-7384, 2255-1717; www.restau rantemachupicchu.com; Calle 32 btwn Avs 1 & 3; mains US$8-22, children's menu US$6-9; ☺10am-10pm Mon-Sat, 11am-6pm Sun; 🛜🚷) This locally renowned Peruvian restaurant will do you right if you have a hankering for all things Andean. A popular spot for a leisurely Sunday lunch, it has an encyclopedic menu featuring tasty Peruvian classics such as *pulpo al olivo* (octopus in olive sauce), *ají de gallina* (a nutty chicken stew) and *causa* (chilled potato terrines stuffed with shrimp and avocado), among *many* other delicacies.

El Chicote STEAKHOUSE $$$
(Map p64; ☎2232-0936; www.elchicote.com; Av Las Américas, Sabana Norte; mains US$12-28; ☺11am-3pm & 6-10pm Mon-Fri, 11am-10pm Sat & Sun) A pleasant family spot that draws carnivores for long Sunday lunches, El Chicote grills up beefy sirloins in the middle of the restaurant and then serves them with black beans, fried bananas and steamy baked potatoes. If you don't do red meat, there are plenty of chicken and seafood options as well. There is also a six-page wine list, strong on Mediterranean and South American vintages (from US$7).

Soda Tapia FAST FOOD $
(Map p64; ☎2222-6734; www.sodatapia.com; cnr Av 2 & Calle 42; mains US$5-7, desserts US$3-4; ☺6am-2am Mon-Thu, 24hr Fri & Sat, 6am-midnight Sun; 🚷) An unpretentious '50s-style diner, this place is perpetually filled with couples and families noshing on grilled sandwiches and generous *casados*. If you have the nerve, try the monstrous 'El Gordo,' a pile of steak, onions, gouda cheese, lettuce and tomato served on Spanish bread. But save room for dessert: Tapia specializes in sundaes.

Las Mañanitas MEXICAN $$
(Map p64; ☎2256-5737; Calle 40 btwn Paseo Colón & Av 3; mains US$6-17; ☺11am-10pm Mon-Sat, noon-8pm Sun) You can get your Mexican fix at this charming garden restaurant that serves a variety of well-rendered specialties. It's the tacos that are tops: corn tortillas stuffed full of chicken, steak, sea bass or *carne al pastor* (spiced pork) – best when accompanied by one of the restaurant's refreshing margaritas.

Self-caterers can try:

» **Más X Menos** (Map p64; 2248-0968; www.masxmenos.co.cr; cnr Autopista General Cañas & Av 5; 7am-midnight Mon-Sat, 7am-9pm Sun) That's *'más por menos'* (more for less), in case you were wondering.

» **Palí** (Map p64; 2256-5887; www.pali.co.cr; Paseo Colón btwn Calles 24 & 26; 8:30am-7pm Mon-Thu, 8:30am-8pm Fri-Sat, 8:30am-6pm Sun) Good neighborhood supermarket.

🍷 Drinking

Whatever your poison, San José has plenty of venues to keep you lubricated. For many more drinking options, see the nearby neighborhoods of Los Yoses and San Pedro. The price of a beer will vary depending on the venue, but count on spending $2.50 and up. Take your ID; some places card everyone upon entering.

Note that some enterprising thieves have taken to lurking around popular spots, waiting to relieve drunken party people of their wallets. When leaving a bar late at night, keep your wits about you and take a taxi.

Good spots for people-watching include Café 1930 at the Gran Hotel Costa Rica (p67), El Patio del Balmoral (p72), overlooking the pedestrian walkway on Av Central, and Café de los Deseos (p71) in Barrio Otoya.

Bar Chavelona   BAR
(Map p56; 2221-6094; Av 10 btwn Calles 10 & 12; 5pm-5am) Nestled amid a row of auto body shops on the west side of town (in other words: take a taxi), this renowned bar, which dates back to 1927, was where Costa Rican author Carlos Luis Fallas (1909–66) once enjoyed happy hour in the company of the local intelligentsia. The bohemian atmosphere is long gone – replaced by an '80s decor that screams Duran Duran – but it remains a pleasant Tico spot for beer and *bocas* (savory bar snacks).

Bar Morazán   BAR
(Map p60; 2222-4622; 2nd fl, Calle 7 btwn Avs 1 & 3; 11am-2am) Decidedly local, in the heart of the San José tourist belt, this humble little bar has reasonably priced drinks, a sports-betting window, a stack of TVs displaying the games and a supersized mural of dogs playing poker. Awesome.

Centro Comercial El Pueblo   BAR
(Map p56; 2221-9434; www.centrocomercialelpueblo.com; Barrio Tournon; hours vary) This Spanish Mediterranean outdoor mall is a warren of bars, clubs and music venues. The proximity of one place to the next makes it ideal for a pub crawl and there is stringent security, which keeps the atmosphere generally safe (though it can get unruly in the wee hours). Things usually get going at about 9pm and shut down by 3am.

Chelle's   BAR
(Map p60; 2221-1369; cnr Av Central & Calle 9; 24hr) If you're drinking the night away with Ticos, you might find yourself here at 4am, clutching a cold one and telling people you just met that you love them. The greasy menu will help you soak up the booze.

El Morazán   BAR
(Map p60; 2256-5110; cnr Calle 9 & Av 3; cocktails US$5-7; noon-midnight) Facing Parque Morazán, this exposed-brick, Spanish tile-clad space dates back to 1904. Throughout its long life it has hosted all manner of historical figures (including Che Guevara, according to one account). It is a popular hangout among Chepe's young artsy set. In addition to beer, there is a full menu of classic cocktails and snacks. On some nights, there is live music.

Rapsodia   LOUNGE
(Map p64; 2248-1720; www.rapsodiacr.com; cnr Paseo Colón & Calle 40, Sabana Este; 11am-midnight Mon-Thu, 10pm-4am Fri-Sat) This hyperchic, see-and-be-seen lounge clad in stark black-and-white furnishings has a good list of cocktails and a menu of Mediterranean-inspired dishes and snacks. Guest DJs can often be found setting the mood.

☆ Entertainment

Pick up *La Nación* on Thursday for listings (in Spanish) of the coming week's attractions. The *Tico Times* 'Weekend' section (in English) has a calendar of theater, music and museum events. The free monthly magazine *San José Volando* is also a good guide to nightlife and cultural events.

Nightclubs

From thumping electronica to hip-hop to salsa, merengue and reggaetón, Chepe's clubs offer a wide variety of ways to get your groove on. Most spots open at around 10pm, but don't truly get going until after midnight. Admission charges vary (generally US$5 to US$10) depending on the location, the DJ and the night. Places come and go with alarming regularity, so ask around before heading out. The website Tico Party (www.ticoparty.com) keeps an up-to-date rundown of the latest spots (in Spanish).

For the trendiest nightspots, make your way to Escazú. Be safe: travel by taxi at night.

Complejo Salsa 54 y Zadidas CLUB
(Map p60; ☎8865-6919; Calle 3 btwn Avs 1 & 3) This vast 2nd-story club is a good place to shake it if you want to go Latin, playing a mix of merengue, salsa, cumbia and Latin swing. Be prepared to cut some serious rug here – the local dancers are expert *salseros*.

Club Vertigo CLUB
(Map p64; ☎2257-8424; www.vertigocr.com; Paseo Colón btwn Calles 38 & 40; ☉10pm-dawn) Located on the ground floor of a nondescript office tower, the city's premier club packs in Chepe's beautiful people with a mix of house, trance and electronica. Downstairs is an 850-person-capacity sweat-box of a dance floor, while upstairs you'll find a chill-out lounge lined with red sofas. Dress to the nines and note that admission charges can skyrocket on guest-DJ nights (from US$14).

Centro Comercial El Pueblo is dense with human activity on weekends. Clubs here come and go; here are a few standard-bearers.

» **Bar Twister** (Map p56; ☎2222-5746; Centro Comercial El Pueblo; ☉6pm-4am Wed-Sun) Catering to the Jaegermeister crowd; cavernous club with nightly DJs.

» **Ebony the Community** (Map p56; ☎2223-2195; Centro Comerical El Pueblo; ☉8pm-4am Wed-Sun) Sprawling disco spinning reggae, dancehall, hip-hop and reggaetón.

» **Tarrico** (Map p56; ☎2222-1003; ☉8pm-4am) Popular watering hole where hard-drinking *josefinos* pile in to play foosball and hit the dance floor.

Gay & Lesbian Venues

The city is home to Central America's most thriving gay and lesbian scene. As with other spots, admission charges vary depending on the night and location (from US$5 to US$10). Some clubs close on various nights of the week (usually Sunday to Tuesday) and others host women- or men-only nights; inquire ahead or check individual club websites for listings.

Many clubs are on the south side of town, which can get rough after dark. Take a taxi.

» **Bochinche** (Map p56; ☎2221-0500; www.bochinchesanjose.com; Calle 11 btwn Avs 10 & 12; ☉8pm-5am Wed-Sat) Club featuring everything from classic disco to electronica, as well as special themed nights.

» **Club Oh!** (Map p56; ☎2221-9341; www.clubohcostarica.com; Calle 2 btwn Avs 14 & 16; ☉from 9pm Fri & Sat) Massive dance club with attached lounge attracts a great mixed crowd; midnight drag shows every Friday.

» **La Avispa** (Map p56; ☎2223-5343; www.laavispa.co.cr; Calle 1 btwn Avs 8 & 10; ☉from 8pm Thu-Sat, from 5pm Sun) In operation for more than three decades, with pool tables and a boisterous dance floor; lesbian night twice a month.

» **Pucho's Nightclub** (Map p56; ☎2256-1147; www.puchosnightclub.com; cnr Calle 11 & Av 8; ☉Mon-Sat) Gay male outpost that's more low-rent (and significantly raunchier) than some others.

Cinemas

Many cinemas show recent Hollywood films with Spanish subtitles and an English soundtrack. Occasionally, films are dubbed over in Spanish (*hablado en español*) rather than subtitled; ask before buying a ticket. Movie tickets cost about US$4 to US$5, and generally Wednesdays are cheaper. Check newspaper listings or individual theater websites for schedules.

There are bigger multiplexes in Los Yoses and San Pedro, while the most modern theaters are in Escazú.

» **Cine Magaly** (Map p56; ☎2223-0085; www.ccmcinemas.com; Calle 23 btwn Avs Central & 1) Latest releases in a large theater.

» **Sala Garbo** (Map p64; ☎2222-1034; www.salagarbocr.com; cnr Av 2 & Calle 28) Art-house and classic films.

» **Teatro Variedades** (Map p60; ☎2222-6108; Calle 5 btwn Avs Central & 1) Dates from 1894, screening indie and Hollywood films.

Live Music

Centro Comercial El Pueblo (p74) has a number of spots featuring live Latin combos and rock bands – and everything in between. As with everything else at El Pueblo, these come and go like the tides. One long-standing space is **Los Balcones** (Map p56; ☎2221-4619; Centro Comercial El Pueblo; ☉Fri & Sat), which specializes in the socially conscious Latin American folk music known as *nueva trova*.

For a more upscale scene, try the 2nd-story bar at El Patio del Balmoral (p72), which hosts live bands on Thursday, Friday and Saturday nights, as well as the artsy El Morazán (p74). Otherwise, serious musical aficionados should head to the neighboring district of San Pedro, where Jazz Café (p88) serves as the city's pre-eminent live-music venue.

TRAVELIB COSTA RICA / ALAMY ©

KEITH LEVIT / ALAMY ©

1. Teatro Nacional (p55)
The lavish interior of San José's most revered public building.

2. Gran Hotel Costa Rica (p67)
This hotel, constructed in 1930, is a national landmark of Costa Rica.

3. Plaza de la Cultura (p54)
People-watch and feed the pigeons in the heart of downtown San José.

Gran Hotel Costa Rica

El Cuartel de la Boca del Monte LIVE MUSIC
(Map p56; ☑2221-0327; www.elcuartel.net; Av 1 btwn
Calles 21 & 23, Barrio California; ⊙11:30am-2pm
Mon-Fri, 6pm-midnight daily) Though not strictly
a live-music venue, this atmospheric old bar
with exposed brick walls has long drawn in
cheek-to-jowl crowds for live bands on most
nights (especially Fridays). It's popular with
university students, who arrive to flirt and
drink and various combinations thereof.

Theater

There's a wide variety of theatrical options in
San José, some in English. Local newspapers,
including the *Tico Times*, list shows. Most
theaters are not very large so performances
tend to sell out; get tickets as early as possible.

» **Auditorio Nacional** (Map p56; ☑2256-
5876; www.museocr.com; Museo de los Niños,
Calle 4 north of Av 9) Grand stage for concerts,
dance, theater and plays – and the site of
the Miss Costa Rica pageant.

» **Little Theatre Group** (☑8858-1446;
www.littletheatregroup.org) English-language
performance troupe that's been around
since the 1950s; see website for information
on performances.

» **Teatro Fanal** (Map p60; ☑2257-5524;
CENAC Complex, Calle 11 btwn Avs 3 & 7) Adjacent
to the contemporary art museum, this
company puts on Spanish-language works,
including children's theater.

» **Teatro La Máscara** (Map p60;
☑2222-4574; Calle 13 btwn Avs 2 & 6) Dance
performances and repertory theater.

» **Teatro Melico Salazar** (Map p60; ☑2233-
5424; www. teatromelico.go.cr; Av 2 btwn Calles
Central & 2) Restored 1920s theater with
regular music, theater, ballet and other
dance performances.

» **Teatro Nacional** (Map p60; ☑2221-5341;
www.teatronacional.go.cr; Calles 3 & 5 btwn Avs
Central & 2) Costa Rica's most important
theater stages plays, dance, opera, symphony,
Latin American music and more; its main
season runs from March to November.

Casinos

Gamblers will find casinos in several of the
larger hotels. Most are casual, but in the nicer
ones it's best to ditch the T-shirt in favor of a
button-down shirt in case there's a dress code.
Gents are advised that casinos are frequented
by prostitutes, so be wary if you're suddenly
the most desirable person in the room.

» **Casino Club Colonial** (Map p60; ☑2258-
2807; www.casinoclubcolonial.com; Av 1 btwn Calles
9 & 11; ⊙24hr) San José's most elegant casino.

» **Casino del Rey** (Map p60; ☑2257-7800;
www.delreyhotel.com; Hotel del Rey, cnr Calle 9 &
Av 1; ⊙24hr) Shocking-pink building offering
everything from roulette to slot machines
to what has to be the highest density of
prostitutes in the city.

TALK LIKE A TICO

San José is loaded with schools that offer Spanish lessons (either privately or in groups)
and provide long-term visitors to the country with everything from dance lessons to
volunteer opportunities. Many schools have been operating since at least 1998 and are
recommended by travelers.

Amerispan Study Abroad (☑in USA & Canada 800-879-6640; www.amerispan.com) A
variety of educational programs, as well as volunteer placements and medical Spanish.

Centro Cultural Costarricense Norteamericano (☑2207-7500; www.centro
cultural.cr; Calle 37 north of Av Central, San Pedro) A large school with Spanish courses,
though it operates mainly as an English school for Ticos.

Costa Rican Language Academy (☑2280-1685, in USA 866-230-6361; www.learn
-spanish.com; Calle Ronda, 175m west of San Pedro Mall, Barrio Dent) In addition to Spanish, it
offers cooking and dance.

Institute for Central American Development Studies (☑2225-0508; www.
icads.org; Curridabat) Month-long programs with or without homestays are combined
with lectures and activities focused on environmental and political issues.

Instituto Británico (☑2234-9054; www.institutobritanico.co.cr; west side of San Pedro
Mall, San Pedro) A good spot for teacher-training and corporate instruction.

Personalized Spanish (☑2278-3254; www.personalizedspanish.com; Tres Ríos) As the
name implies, private classes that cater to your needs.

Already speak Spanish? To truly talk like a Tico, check out the recently released app,
Costa Rica Idioms, available for the iPod, iPad and Android. It's quite basic but defines
local lingo and uses each term in a sentence. *Tuanis, mae!* (Cool, dude!)

Sports

Bullfighting is popular and fights are held seasonally in the southern suburb of Zapote over the Christmas period. Members of the public (usually drunk) are encouraged to participate in the action (the bull isn't killed in the Costa Rican version of the sport).

Estadio Nacional de Costa Rica STADIUM
(Map p64; ☎2284-8700; Parque Metropolitano La Sabana) International and national *fútbol* (soccer) games are played at the recently reconstructed Estadio Nacional. Located in Parque Metropolitano La Sabana since 1924 – in a structure that has hosted everyone from Pope John Paul II to football legend Pelé – the new stadium opened in March 2011 and now seats 35,000 spectators.

Shopping

Whether you're looking for indigenous carvings, high-end furnishings or a plastic howler monkey, San José has no shortage of shops, running the gamut from artsy boutiques to tourist traps stocked full of tropical everything. With the exception of markets, haggling is not tolerated in stores and shops. In touristy spots, keep an eye peeled for 'authentic' woodworks that have 'Made in Indonesia' stamped on the bottom.

For the country's finest woodcrafts, it is absolutely worth the trip to visit the Biesanz Woodworks (p93) workshop in Escazú.

TOP CHOICE **Galería Namu** HANDICRAFTS
(Map p60; ☎2256 3412; www.galerianamu.com; Av 7 btwn Calles 5 & 7; ⊙9am-6:30pm Mon-Sat, 1-5pm Sun Jan-Apr) This fair-trade gallery run by Aisling French does a great job of bringing together artwork and crafts from a diverse population of regional ethnicities. Here, you'll find a lovely array of Boruca masks, finely woven Wounaan baskets, Guaymí dolls, Bribrí canoes, Chorotega ceramics and Huetar carvings, as well as contemporary urban and Afro-Caribbean crafts. They can also help arrange visits to remote indigenous territories in different parts of Costa Rica. See their website for details.

Kiosco SJO ARTS & CRAFTS
(☎2258-1829; www.kioscosjo.com; cnr Av 11 & Calle 7, Barrio Amón; ⊙11am-6pm Mon, 11am-10pm Tue-Sat) With a focus on sustainable design by Latin American artisans, this sleek shop stocks handmade jewelry, hand-tooled leather boots and bags, original photography, artisanal chocolates, fashion and contemporary home decor by established regional designers. It's pricey, but rest assured that everything you find here will be of exceptional quality.

eÑe ARTS & CRAFTS
(Map p60; ☎2222-7681; laesquina13y7@gmail.com; cnr Av 7 & Calle 13; ⊙10am-6:30pm Mon-Sat) This hip little design shop across from the Casa Amarilla sells all manner of pieces crafted by Costa Rican designers and artists, including clothing, jewelry, handbags, picture frames, zines and works of graphic art.

La Casona MARKET
(Map p60; Calle Central btwn Avs Central & 1; ⊙9:30am-6:30pm Mon-Sat) Step right up to the number-one tourist trap in Chepe! What you give up in authenticity you'll make up for in convenience. Various stalls spread out over two floors stock T-shirts, banana-leaf paper journals and tree-frog stickers. Shop around as some quality crafts can be found.

Mercado Central MARKET
(Map p60; Avs Central & 1 btwn Calles 6 & 8; ⊙6am-6pm Mon-Sat) This is the best and cheapest place in the city to buy just about anything you'd want, whether that's a hammock (*Hecho en Nicaragua*), a *pura vida* T-shirt (Made in China), or a vast assortment of forgettable knickknacks. For something decidedly more Costa Rican, export-quality coffee beans and cigars can be bought at a fraction of the price you'll pay in tourist shops.

Mercado Artesanal MARKET
(Crafts Market; Map p60; Plaza de la Democracia, Avs Central & 2 btwn Calles 13 & 15; ⊙midmorning-sunset) A touristy open-air market that sells everything from handcrafted jewelry and Bob Marley T-shirts to elaborate woodwork and Guatemalan sarongs.

Rincón del Habano CIGARS
(Map p60; Calle 7 btwn Avs Central & 1; ⊙9am-6:30pm Mon-Fri, 9:30am-5:30pm Sat) You'll find a wide selection of cigars in this tiny decade-old shop that sells stogies from all over, including brands from Costa Rica, the Dominican Republic, Nicaragua and Cuba.

Bookstores

English-language magazines, newspapers, books and maps are widely available in shops throughout the city.
» **7th Street Books** (Map p60; ☎2256-8251; Calle 7 btwn Avs Central & 1; ⊙9am-6pm Mon-Sat, 10am-5pm Sun) Headquarters of all things English-language; also carries maps and music.

» Librería Lehmann (Map p60; ☎2223-1212; www.librerialehmann.com; Av Central btwn Calles 1 & 3; ☉8am-6:30pm Mon-Fri, 9am-5pm Sat, 11am-4pm Sun) Good selection of English-language books, guidebooks and topographic maps (upstairs).

» Librería Universal (Map p60; ☎2222-2222; www.universalcr.com; Av Central btwn Calles Central & 1; ☉8:30am-7pm Mon-Fri, 9am-6pm Sat, 9am-5pm Sun) Tiny selection of English-language books on 2nd floor; also has rack devoted to Costa Rican literature.

» Mora Books (Map p60; ☎8383-8385; www.morabooks.com; Calle 5 btwn Avs 5 & 7; ☉11am-7pm) Stuffed with used books in English, Spanish, French and German; best place in town to stock up, though hours are hit and miss.

ⓘ Information

Look for free copies of **San José Volando** (www.sanjosevolando.com), a monthly pocket-sized guide that has arts, food and other cultural listings in English. You can find it at art galleries, museums and better restaurants and hotels.

Cultural Centers

Various foreign institutions host film nights, art exhibits, theater, live music and academic conferences. Call ahead in January and February, when these spots tend to have limited hours.

» **Alianza Francesa** (☎2222-2283; www.afsj.net; cnr Calle 5 & Av 7) Has French classes, a small library and rotating art exhibits in a historic Barrio Amón home.

» **Centro Cultural de España** (☎2257-2919; www.ccecr.org; Rotonda del Farolito, Barrio Escalante) Offers a full roster of events, an audiovisual center and lending library.

» **Centro de Cine** (☎2223-2127, 2223-0610; www.centrodecine.go.cr; cnr Calle 11 & Av 9) Government-run film center holds festivals, lectures and events in outside venues; check website for current events.

Dangers & Annoyances

Though Costa Rica has the lowest crime rate of any Central American country, crime in urban centers such as San José is a problem. The most common offense is opportunistic theft (eg pickpockets and muggings). In the event that something of this nature were to happen, it's unlikely that you would be physically hurt, but it is nonetheless best to keep a streetwise attitude.

» Do not wear flashy jewelry.

» Keep your camera in your bag when you are not using it.

» Carry only as much cash as you'll need for the day.

» Unless you'll need it for official business, leave your passport in the hotel safe; a photocopy will suffice most of the time.

» Be wary of pickpockets at crowded events and the areas around bus stops.

» Never put your bag in the overhead racks on a bus.

» Do not walk around alone at night and stick to licensed taxis.

» If you are renting a car, always park it in a secure, guarded lot, and never leave anything in it.

» Men should be aware that prostitutes are known for their sleight-of-hand abilities, and that they often work in pairs.

Neighborhoods reviewed in this book are generally safe during the day, though you should be especially careful around the Coca-Cola bus terminal and the red-light district south of Parque Central, particularly at night. Be advised that adjacent neighborhoods can vary greatly in terms of safety; inquire locally before setting out.

Gridlocked traffic, gigantic potholes, noise and smog are unavoidable in San José. Most central hotels are victim to street noise, no matter how nice they are. Be skeptical of touts and taxi drivers who try to sell you tours or tell you that the hotel you've booked is a crime-infested bordello. Many of these folks will say anything to steer you to the places that pay them commissions.

TOURIST POLICE The establishment of a policía turística (tourism police) in 2007 has alleviated petty crimes against foreigners (you'll see them patrolling in pairs around San José). These officers can be helpful in the event of an emergency since most of them speak at least some English. But, if you find yourself the victim of a crime, you'll have to file a report in person at the **Organismo de Investigación Judicial** (☎2221-5337, 2222-1365; ☉9am-5pm Mon-Fri) in the Supreme Court of Justice building on the south side of downtown.

Emergency

» **Red Cross** (Cruz Roja Costarricense; ☎128, in San José 2542-5000; www.cruzroja.or.cr; Av 8 btwn Calles 14 & 16)

» **Traffic Police** (Policía de Tránsito; ☎2222-9245, 2222-9330; www.transito.go.cr)

Internet Access

Checking email is easy in San José, where cybercafes are more plentiful than fruit peddlers. Rates are generally US$.50 to US$1 per hour, though these days most hotels (even budget hostels) provide free internet access and wi-fi.

Laundry

Do-it-yourself laundry services are damn near impossible to find in San José. However, most hotels and hostels offer this service. Expect to pay anywhere from US$5 to US$12 for a load. High-end places may charge by the piece, which is generally more expensive.

Medical Services

For serious medical emergencies, head to **Hospital CIMA** (☎2208-1000, emergencies 2208-1144; www.hospitalcima.com; Los Laureles, San Rafael de Escazú) in Escazú.

» **Clínica Bíblica** (☎2522-1000, emergency 2522-1030; www.clinicabiblica.com; Av 14 btwn Calles Central & 1) The top private clinic downtown has 24-hour emergency room; doctors speak English, French and German.

» **Hospital La Católica** (☎2246-3000; www.hospitallacatolica.com; Guadalupe) Pricey clinic geared toward foreign medical-tourism patients.

» **Hospital San Juan de Dios** (☎2257-6282; cnr Paseo Colón & Calle 14) Free public hospital open 24 hours; expect long waits.

Money

ATMs that accept foreign bank cards are widely available in San José. Banks will exchange most foreign currencies and traveler's checks. Credit cards are widely accepted, though Visa tends to be preferred over MasterCard and American Express.

» **BAC San José** (☎2295-9797; www.bac.net; Av 2 btwn Calles Central & 1; ⊙9am-6pm Mon-Fri, 9am-1pm Sat)

» **BAC San José** (☎2295-9797; www.bac.net; Calle Central btwn Avs 3 & 5; ⊙8am-6pm Mon-Fri)

» **Banco de Costa Rica** (☎2233-7055; www.bancobcr.com; cnr Paseo Colón & Calle 40; ⊙9am-4pm Mon-Fri)

» **Banco de Costa Rica** (BCR; ☎2221-8143; www.bancobcr.com; cnr Calle 7 & Av 1; ⊙9am-4pm Mon-Fri)

» **Banco Nacional de Costa Rica Exchange House** (cnr Av Central & Calle 4; ⊙10:30am-6pm Mon-Fri, 8am-3:45pm Sat & Sun)

» **Citibank** (☎2257-6363; www.latinamerica.citibank.com/costarica/index.html; Av 1 btwn Calles Central & 1; ⊙9am-5pm Mon-Fri, 9am-noon Sat)

» **Scotiabank** (☎2221-8022; www.scotiabankcr.com; Calle 5 btwn Avs Central & 2; ⊙9am-5pm Mon-Fri)

Post

» **Correo Central** (Central Post Office; ☎2223-9766; www.correos.go.cr; Calle 2 btwn Avs 1 & 3; ⊙7:30am-5:30pm Mon-Fri, 7:30am-noon Sat)

Telephone

Local and international calls can be made from most public phones, which are all over town. You'll find banks of them on the west side of the Parque Central and around the Plaza de la Cultura. Many hotels also have public phones in their lobbies. Chip and Colibrí cards for these are sold at souvenir shops, newsstands and supermarkets. Telephone directories are usually available in hotels.

Tourist Information

» **Canatur** (Cámara Nacional de Turismo; ☎2234-6222; www.tourism.co.cr; Aeropuerto Internacional Juan Santamaría; ⊙8am-10pm) The Costa Rican National Chamber of Tourism has a small stand next to international baggage claim.

» **Instituto Costarricense de Turismo** (ICT; ☎2222-1090, in USA & Canada 866-267-8274; www.visitcostarica.com; Plaza de la Cultura, Calle 5 btwn Avs Central & 2) Government tourism office has handy free maps of San José and Costa Rica.

❶ Getting There & Away

San José is the country's transportation hub, and it's likely that you'll pass through the capital a number of times throughout your travels (whether you want to or not).

Air

AIRPORTS Two airports serve San José. There is an international departure tax of US$26 when leaving the country.

» **Aeropuerto Internacional Juan Santamaría** (☎2437-2400; www.aeris.cr) Handles international air traffic in its main terminal. Domestic flights, including those on Sansa, depart from the Sansa terminal.

» **Aeropuerto Tobías Bolaños** (☎2232-2820) In the San José suburb of Pavas, services domestic flights on NatureAir.

INTERNATIONAL AIRLINES The following have offices in San José. Airlines that service Costa Rica direct from the US are marked with an asterisk; they also have desks at the airport.

Air France (☎2220-4111; www.airfrance.com; Oficentro Ejecutivo La Sabana, 1st fl, Edificio 1; ⊙8am-noon & 1-5pm Mon-Fri)

American Airlines (☎2248-9010; www.americanairlines.co.cr; Centro de Servicio Sabana, Sabana Este; ⊙8am-6pm Mon-Fri, 8am-4pm Sat)

Avianca (☎2441-2776, 2441-2827; www.avianca.com; Aeropuerto Internacional Juan Santamaría; ⊙8am-5pm Mon-Fri)

Continental (☎2296-4911; www.continental.com; Aeropuerto Internacional Juan Santamaría; ⊙5am-noon & 2:30am-9:30pm)

COPA (☎2222-2672; www.copaair.com; 1st fl, Torre Mercedes Benz, cnr Calle 24 & Paseo Colón; ⊙8am-6pm Mon-Fri, 8am-noon Sat)

Cubana de Aviación (☏2221-6918, 2221-7625; www.cubana.cu; Calle 40 btwn Avs 2 & 4)

Delta (☏2256-7909; www.delta.com; 2nd fl, Edificio Torre Mercedes Benz; ⊙9am-1pm & 2-6pm Mon-Fri)

Grupo TACA (☏2299-8222; www.taca.com; cnr Calle 40 & Av Las Américas; ⊙8am-8pm Mon-Fri, 8am-5pm Sat, 9am-5pm Sun)

Iberia (☏2431-5633; www.iberia.com; Oficentro Tical, Alajuela; ⊙8am-noon & 1-5pm Mon-Fri)

United Airlines (☏2220-4844; www.united.com; Aeropuerto Internacional Juan Santamaría; ⊙8am-10pm Mon-Fri, 9am-1pm Sat)

CHARTER AIRCRAFT **Sansa** (☏2290-4100; www.flysansa.com) and **NatureAir** (☏2299-6000; www.natureair.com) offer charter flights from San José, as do the companies listed below. Most charters are small (three- to five-passenger) aircraft and can fly to any of the airstrips around Costa Rica. Each listing below indicates which San José airport the company operates from.

» **Aero Bell** (☏2290-0000; www.aerobell.com) Aeropuerto Tobías Bolaños

» **Aerotour** (☏2232-1248; www.aerotourcr.com) Aeropuerto Tobías Bolaños

» **Aviones Taxi Aéreo SA** (☏2431-0293, 2431-0160; www.aircharorcentralamerica.com) Aeropuerto Internacional Juan Santamaría

» **Viajes Especial Aéreos SA** (Veasa; ☏2232-1010, 2232-8043) Aeropuerto Tobías Bolaños

Bus

Bus transportation in San José can be bewildering. There are no public buses and no central terminal. Instead, lots of private companies operate out of stops scattered throughout the city. Many companies have no more than a stop (so pay the driver directly); some have a tiny office with a window on the street, while some operate from a terminal. The bigger stations service entire regions.

Bus schedules and prices change regularly. Download a useful but not always up-to-date PDF copy from the ICT website (www.visitcostarica.com; click on the 'General Info' link). Buses are crowded on Friday evening and Saturday morning and packed to the gills at Christmas and Easter.

For buses that run infrequently, it is advisable to buy tickets in advance. If you want to avoid hassle, book your travel through **A Safe Passage** (☏8365-9678; www.costaricabustickets.com), which can purchase bus tickets in advance for a small fee. They also arrange airport transfers.

BUS TERMINALS

Be aware that thefts are common in many bus terminals. Stay alert, keep your valuables close to you and don't stow anything important (such as passports and money) in the overhead racks or luggage compartment of a bus.

» **Gran Terminal del Caribe** (Calle Central, north of Av 13) A roomy station on the north end of town; central departure point for all buses to the Caribbean.

» **Terminal Coca-Cola** (Av 1 btwn Calles 16 & 18) A well-known, labyrinthine landmark; buses leave from the terminal and the four-block radius around it to points all over Costa Rica, including the Central Valley and the Pacific coast.

» **Terminal Musoc** (Av 22 btwn Calles Central & 1) On the south end of town; has buses to San Isidro and points north.

» **Terminal San Carlos** (cnr Av 9 & Calle 12) A small, rather decrepit terminal serving destinations in the north and northwest, such as Monteverde, La Fortuna and Sarapiquí.

INTERNATIONAL BUSES FROM SAN JOSÉ

International buses get booked up fast. Buy your tickets in advance – and take your passport.

CHANGUINOLA/BOCAS DEL TORO, PANAMÁ **Panaline** (☏2256-8721; cnr Av 5 & Calle 16) 10am; US$15; eight hours **Transportes Bocatoreños** (☏2227-5923; cnr Av 5 & Calle 16) 9am; US$10; six hours

DAVID, PANAMÁ **Tracopa** (☏2221-4214; Calle 5 btwn Avs 18 & 20) 7:30am & noon; US$25; nine hours

GUATEMALA CITY, GUATEMALA **Tica Bus** (☏2221-0006; www.ticabus.com; cnr Calle 9 & Av 4) 6am, 7:30am & 12:30pm; US$77; 48 hours

MANAGUA, NICARAGUA **King Quality** (☏2258-8834; www.king-qualityca.com; Calle 12 btwn Avs 3 & 5) 3am; US$44; eight hours Tica Bus (p82) 6am, 7:30am & 12:30pm; normal/executive US$26/38; nine hours **TransNica** (☏2223-4242; www.transnica.com; Calle 22 btwn Avs 3 & 5) 4am, 5am, 9am & noon; normal/executive US$27/37.50; nine hours

PANAMÁ CITY, PANAMÁ Panaline (p82) 1pm; US$25; 15 hours Tica Bus (p82) Noon & 11pm; normal/executive US$37/47; 15 hours

SAN SALVADOR, EL SALVADOR King Quality (p82) 3am; US$67; 48 hours Tica Bus (p82) 6am, 7:30am, 12:30pm & 11pm; normal/executive US$58/60; 48 hours

TEGUCIGALPA, HONDURAS King Quality (p82) 3am; US$65; 48 hours Tica Bus (p82) 6am, 7:30am & 12:30pm; US$47; 48 hours

DOMESTIC BUSES FROM SAN JOSÉ

TO THE CENTRAL VALLEY **Alajuela Tuasa** (Av 2 btwn Calles 12 & 14) Every 10 minutes from 4:30am to 10:45pm; US$1; 40 minutes

Cartago (Calle 13 btwn Avs 6 & 8) Hourly between 5:15am & 10pm; US$1.25; 40 minutes

Grecia (Av 5 btwn Calles 18 & 20) Every 20 minutes from 5:30am to 10pm; US$2; one hour

Heredia (Calle 1 btwn Avs 7 & 9) Every 10 minutes from 5am to 11pm; US$1; 20 minutes

Sarchí (Av 5 btwn Calles 18 & 20) 12:15pm, 5:30pm & 5:55pm Mon-Fri; US$2.25; direct, 1½ hours

Turrialba (Calle 13 btwn Avs 6 & 8) Hourly from 5am to 10pm; US$2.50; two hours

Volcán Irazú (Av 2 btwn Calles 1 & 3) 8am; round-trip US$5; two hours

Volcán Poás Tuasa (Av 2 btwn Calles 12 & 14) 8:30am; round-trip US$7; five hours

TO NORTHWESTERN COSTA RICA **Cañas Empresa Cañas** (☎2258-5792; Calle 16 btwn Avs 1 & 3) Departs 8:30am, 11:50am, 12:20pm, 1:40pm, 4:45pm & 6:15pm; US$5; 3¼ hours

Ciudad Quesada, San Carlos Autotransportes San Carlos (☎2255-4300; Terminal San Carlos) Hourly from 5am to 7:30pm; US$2.35; 2½ hours

La Fortuna (Terminal San Carlos) 6:15am, 8:30am & 11:30am; US$6; four hours

Liberia Pulmitan (☎2666-0458; Calle 24 btwn Avs 5 & 7) Hourly from 5am to 8pm; US$5; four hours

Monteverde/Santa Elena (Calle 12 btwn Avs 7 & 9) 6:30am & 2:30pm; US$7.50; 4½ hours; book ahead as this bus fills up quickly.

Peñas Blancas Transportes Deldú (☎2256-9072; www.transportesdeldu.com; Av 9 btwn Calles 10 & 12) 4am, 5am, 7am, 7:45am, 10:30am, 1:30am & 4pm; US$9; six hours

Tilarán Empresa Cañas (☎2258-5792; Calle 16 btwn Avs 1 & 3) 7:30am, 9:30am, 12:45pm, 3:45pm & 6:30pm; US$6.25; four hours. No 9.30am bus on Sunday.

TO PENÍNSULA DE NICOYA **Montezuma and Mal País** (Terminal Coca-Cola) 6am, 8am, 10am, noon, 2pm, 4pm & 6pm; US$13; six hours

Nicoya Empresas Alfaro (☎2256-7050; Av 5 btwn Calles 14 & 16) 6:30am, 10am, 1pm, 3pm & 5pm; US$5.40; five hours

Playa Bejuco Empresas Arza (☎2258-3883; Calle 12 btwn Avs 7 & 9) 6am & 3:30pm; US$8; 5½ hours. Buses stop on the street outside the Terminal San Carlos.

Playa del Coco Pulmitán (Calle 24 btwn Avs 5 & 7) 8am, 10am & 4pm; US$5.50; five hours

Playa Flamingo, via Brasilito Tralapa (Calle 20 btwn Avs 3 & 5) 8am, 10:30am & 3pm; US$9.35; six hours

Playa Nosara Empresas Alfaro (☎2256-7050; Av 5 btwn Calles 14 & 16) 6am; US$8; six hours

Playa Sámara Empresas Alfaro (☎2256-7050; Av 5 btwn Calles 14 & 16) 12:30pm; US$7.25; five hours

Playas Panamá and Hermosa Tralapa (Calle 20 btwn Avs 3 & 5) 3:25pm; US$9; five hours

Playa Tamarindo Empresas Alfaro (☎2256-7050; Av 5 btwn Calles 14 & 16) 11:30am & 3:30pm; US$9; five hours

Santa Cruz Empresas Alfaro (☎2256-7050; Av 5 btwn Calles 14 & 16) 6am, 10am, 1:30pm, 2pm, 3pm & 5pm; US$8.50; five hours

TO THE CENTRAL PACIFIC COAST **Dominical and Uvita Transportes Morales** (Terminal Coca-Cola) 6am & 3pm; US$5; seven hours

Jacó Transportes Jacó (☎2290-2922; Terminal Coca-Cola) 7:30am, 10:30am, 1pm, 3:30pm & 6:30pm; US$4; three hours

Puntarenas Empresarios Unidos (☎2222-8231; cnr Av 12 & Calle 16) every 40 minutes from 6am to 7pm; US$3.25; 2½ hours

Quepos/Manuel Antonio Transportes Morales (Terminal Coca-Cola) 6am, noon, 6pm & 7:30pm; US$7.25; four hours

TO SOUTHERN COSTA RICA & PENÍNSULA DE OSA **Ciudad Neily** Tracopa (p82) 5am, 10am, 1pm, 4:30pm & 6pm; US$10; eight hours

Golfito Tracopa (p82) 7am & 3pm; US$9.50; eight hours

Palmar Norte Tracopa (p82) 5am, 7am, 8:30am, 10am, 1pm, 2:30pm & 6:30pm; US$5.50; five hours

Paso Canoas, Panamá border crossing Tracopa (p82) 8:30am, 10:30am, 2:30pm, 7:30pm & 9pm; US$10; six hours

Puerto Jiménez Blanco Lobo (☎2221-4214; Calle 12 btwn Avs 9 & 11) 6am & noon; US$12; eight hours. This bus fills up quickly in high season; buy tickets in advance.

San Isidro del General Tracopa (p82) hourly from 5am to 6pm; US$4.50; three hours

San Vito Tracopa (p82) 6am, 8:15am, noon & 4pm; US$8.50; seven hours

TO THE CARIBBEAN COAST **Cahuita** Autotransportes Mepe (p84) 6am, 10am, 12pm, 2pm & 4pm; US$7.50; four hours

Cariari, for transfer to Tortuguero Empresarios Guapileños (Gran Terminal del Caribe) 6:10am, 9am, 10:30am, 1pm, 3pm, 4:30pm, 6pm & 7pm; US$3.25; 2¼ hours

Guápiles Empresarios Guapileños (Gran Terminal del Caribe) Hourly from 5:30am to 7pm; US$2.25; 1½ hours

Puerto Limón Autotransportes Caribeños (Gran Terminal del Caribe) Every 30 minutes from 5am to 7pm; US$5; three hours

Puerto Viejo de Talamanca Autotransportes Mepe (p84) 6am, 10am, 12pm, 2pm & 4pm; US$8.65; 4½ hours

Siquirres Líneas del Atlántico (Gran Terminal del Caribe) 6:30am, 8am, 9:30am, 11am, noon, 1pm, 3pm, 4pm, 5pm & 6pm; US$3.20; 1½ hours

Sixaola, Panama border crossing Autotransportes Mepe (p84) 6am, 10am, 2pm & 4pm; US$11; six hours

TO THE NORTHERN LOWLANDS **Los Chiles, Nicaragua border crossing** Autotransportes San Carlos (p83) 5:30am & 3:30pm; US$4.25; five hours

Puerto Viejo de Sarapiquí Autotransportes Mepe (Gran Terminal del Caribe) 6:30am, 7:30am, 10am, 11:30am, 1:30pm, 2:30pm, 3:30pm, 4:30pm & 6pm; US$3.20; two hours

TOURIST BUSES

Grayline (☑2220-2126; www.graylinecostarica.com) and **Interbus** (☑2283-5573; www.inter busonline.com) shuttle passengers in air-con minivans from San José to a long list of popular destinations around Costa Rica. They are more expensive than the standard bus service, but they offer door-to-door service and can get you there faster.

ⓘ Getting Around

Central San José frequently resembles a parking lot – narrow streets, heavy traffic and a complicated one-way system mean that it is often quicker to walk than to take the bus. The same applies to driving: if you rent a car, try to avoid downtown. If you're in a real hurry to get somewhere that is more than 1km away, take a taxi.

Getting Into Town

If traveling by bus, you'll arrive at one of several international bus terminals sprinkled around the western and southern parts of downtown. Some of this area is walkable provided you aren't hauling a lot of luggage and are staying nearby. But, if you're arriving at night, take a taxi, since most terminals are in dodgy areas.

Note that many taxi drivers in San José are commissioned by hotels to bring them customers, and the hotel scene is so competitive that drivers will say just about anything to steer you to the places they represent. Among other things, they will 'call' your hotel and a voice on the other end will tell you that they're fully booked. Be skeptical. Tell drivers firmly where it is you would like to go. And if you have concerns about where you have chosen to stay, ask to see a room before settling in for the night.

To & From the Airports

AEROPUERTO INTERNACIONAL JUAN SANTAMARIA International flights arrive at Aeropuerto Internacional Juan Santamaría in nearby Alajuela.

You can reserve a pickup with **Taxi Aeropuerto** (☑2221-6865; www.taxiaeropuerto.com), which charges a flat rate of between US$21 and US$30 for trips to and from most parts of San José. (These are a bright red-orange color.) You can also take a street taxi, but the rates may vary wildly. Plan on spending at least US$20 to US$25; more in heavy traffic.

Interbus (p84) runs an airport shuttle service that will pick you up at your hotel (US$15 per person), good value if you're traveling alone. The cheapest option is the **red Tuasa bus** (cnr Calle 10 & Av 2; ₡400) bound for Alajuela. Tell the driver that you're getting off at the airport (*Voy al aeropuerto, por favor*). Many hotels can also arrange for private airport pickup at reasonable rates.

From downtown, the drive to the airport can take anywhere from 20 minutes to an hour (more if you take the bus) – and vice versa. Plan accordingly.

AEROPUERTO TOBÍAS BOLAÑOS Buses to Tobías Bolaños depart every 30 minutes from Av 1, 250m west of the Terminal Coca-Cola. A taxi to the airport from downtown starts at about US$15. Interbus (p84) also has an airport shuttle service for US$15.

Bus

Local buses are useful to get you into the suburbs and surrounding villages, or to the airport. Most buses run between 5am and 10pm and cost in the vicinity of US$0.50 to US$0.75.

Buses from Parque La Sabana head into town on Paseo Colón, then go over to Av 2 at the San Juan de Dios hospital. They then go three different ways through town before heading back to La Sabana. Buses are marked Sabana–Estadio, Sabana–Cementerio or Cementerio–Estadio. These buses are a good bet for a cheap city tour. Buses going east to Los Yoses and San Pedro go back and forth along Av 2 and then switch over to Av Central at Calle 29. (These are easily identifiable by the big sign that says 'Mall San Pedro' on the front window.) The route starts at the corner of Av 2 and Calle 7, near Restaurante El Pollo Campesino.

Buses to the following outlying suburbs and towns begin from bus stops at the indicated blocks. Some places have more than one stop – only the main ones are listed here.

» **Escazú** Avenida 6 (Av 6 btwn Calles 14 & 16); Calle 16 (Calle 16 btwn Avs 1 & 3)

» **Guadalupe** (Av 3 btwn Calles Central & 1)

» **Pavas** (Av 1 btwn Calles 20 & 22)

» **Santa Ana** (Calle 16 btwn Avs 1 & 3)

Car

It is not advisable to rent a car just to drive around San José. The traffic is heavy, the streets narrow and the meter-deep curbside gutters make parking nerve-wracking. Also, break-ins are frequent and leaving a car – even in a guarded lot – might result in a smashed window and stolen belongings.

If you are renting a car to travel in Costa Rica, there are more than 50 car-rental agencies – including many of the global brands – in and around San José. Travel agencies and upmarket hotels can arrange rentals; you can also arrange rentals online and at the airport. Within Costa Rica, check the local yellow pages (under 'Alquiler de Automóviles') for a complete listing. Note that there is a surcharge of about US$25 for renting cars at Aeropuerto Internacional Juan Santamaría.

One excellent local option is **Wild Rider** (☎2258-4604; www.wild-rider.com; Paseo Colón btwn Calles 30 & 32; ☺8am-6pm), run by a charming pair of Germans. While their specialty is motorcycles, they have a fleet of about 40 small sports utility vehicles. Prices are very reasonable (from US$310 per week in high season), but reserve well in advance.

Motorcycle

Given the apparent homicidal nature of most San José drivers, renting a motorcycle to get around the city is recommended only for those who are truly qualified. Rentals are usually small and rates start at about US$50 per day for a 350cc motorcycle and climb from there. Plan on paying more than US$150 a day or more for a Harley.

Wild Rider (p85) rents sports bikes like the Honda XR-250 or the Suzuki DRZ-400S. Prices start at US$420 per week in high season (including insurance, taxes and helmets). They organize on- and off-road guided tours as well.

For Harleys, see **Harley Davidson Rentals** (☎2289-5552; www.mariaalexandra.com; cnr Calle 3 & Av 23) in Escazú.

Taxi

Red taxis can be hailed on the street day or night, or you can have your hotel call one for you. *Marías* (meters) are generally used, though a few drivers will tell you they're broken and try to charge you more – especially if you don't speak Spanish. (Not using a meter is illegal.) Make sure the *maría* is operating when you get in, or negotiate the fare up front. Short rides downtown cost US$2 to US$4. There's a 20% surcharge after 10pm that may not appear on the *maría*.

You can hire a taxi and a driver for half a day or longer if you want to do some touring around the area; for such trips, it is best to negotiate a flat fee in advance.

AROUND SAN JOSÉ

Over the years, as San José's urban sprawl has crawled up the hillsides of the Central Valley, the boundary lines have blurred between the heart of the city and the villages that encircle it. Here you will find a little bit of everything: from crowded slums filled with immigrant workers to stylish residential neighborhoods where modernist houses hide behind 3m-high walls. Within this belt, there are a number of areas that offer an appealing alternative to staying in the city proper.

Just a few hundred meters east of San José's downtown are the contiguous neighborhoods of Los Yoses and San Pedro, home to a number of embassies as well as the most prestigious university in the country, the Universidad de Costa Rica (UCR). To the west, about 7km away, is Escazú, where Americanized housing developments lie alongside old Tico homesteads. Looking for a more relaxing alternative to the urban grind? These areas are a great place to start.

Los Yoses & San Pedro

These two side-by-side neighborhoods may lie in close proximity, but their characters are each totally unique. Los Yoses is a charming residential district dotted with modernist structures, historic homes, cozy inns and chilled-out neighborhood eateries. San Pedro, on the other hand, which houses the university district, is more boisterous – brimming with bars, clubs and student activity. Both of these areas provide an enticing (and convenient) alternative to staying in San José.

Los Yoses and San Pedro are centered on a roundabout where Av Central meets the road to Zapote. The traffic circle is punctuated by the Fuente de la Hispanidad (a large fountain), which serves as an area landmark. To the west lies the district of Los Yoses; to the east, you'll find San Pedro, anchored by a small plaza and the Iglesia de San Pedro. About three blocks to the north of this point is the tree-lined campus of the UCR.

Most streets in Los Yoses and San Pedro are unnamed, and locals rely almost entirely on the landmark method to orient themselves. In Los Yoses, major area landmarks include the Subaru dealership, the old ICE building (El Antiguo ICE), the Spoon restaurant and the Mall San Pedro. In San Pedro, common points of reference include the old Banco Popular building (El Antiguo Banco Popular) and the Iglesia de San Pedro.

◉ Sights

For contemporary art, pay a visit to the lobby of the Hotel Milvia, which doubles as a noted gallery during daytime hours.

Museo de Insectos   MUSEUM
(Insect Museum; ☎2511-5318; www.miucr.ucr. ac.cr; US$2; ☺1-4:45pm Mon-Fri) This museum has an extensive collection of insects assembled by the Facultad de Agronomía at the

Universidad de Costa Rica. Curiously, it is housed in the basement of the music building (Facultad de Artes Musicales), a brutalist structure painted an incongruous shade of Barbie pink. It is claimed that this is the only insect museum of its size in Central America. The museum is signposted from the Iglesia de San Pedro.

🛏 Sleeping

Hotel Milvia B&B $$
(☎2225-4543; www.hotelmilvia.com; 250m east, 100m north and 100m east of Más X Menos, San Pedro; s/d/tr incl breakfast US$59/69/75; @🛜) This lovely Caribbean-style plantation building once served as the home of Ricardo Fernández Peralta, an artillery colonel who fought in Costa Rica's 1948 civil war. Nine eclectic rooms – some carpeted, others with shining wood floors, all dotted with bright pieces of art – surround a pleasant courtyard with a trickling fountain. An upstairs terrace provides incredible views of the mountains in the distance.

TOP CHOICE Hostel Toruma HOSTEL $
(☎2234-8186; www.hosteltoruma.com; Av Central btwn Calles 29 & 33, Los Yoses; dm/s/d US$13/35/55; P@🛜🏊) This graceful neoclassical home once belonged to José Figueres, the Costa Rican president who abolished the army and granted women the right to vote. In late 2009, the hotel completed a top-to-bottom makeover that preserved the Spanish-tile floors and left the facade's decorative friezes sparkling. While the Toruma contains four dormitories, it feels much more like an inn, with 17 large private rooms, each of which is equipped with a modern bathroom, a sofa, wi-fi and flatscreen TV. Upstairs, an internet lounge is dotted with bean bags; downstairs, a small poolside restaurant serves breakfast, light snacks and beer. It's a mellow spot, popular with chilled-out solo travelers, couples and young families – and one of the best budget deals in San José.

Casa Las Orquideas BOUTIQUE HOTEL $$
(☎2283-0095; www.lasorquideashotel.com; 75m west of Automercado, Los Yoses; dm/s/d incl breakfast from US$15/60/70; P🛜) Casa Las Orquideas offers a welcoming, cozy place to stay despite being located directly on the thoroughfare that is Av Central. It has quaint, homey rooms, some of which have low stone-walled shower stalls or hand-painted murals.

Hotel 1492 Jade y Oro B&B $$
(☎2256-5913; www.hotel1492.com; Av 1 btwn Calles 29 & 33, Barrio Escalante; d standard/deluxe incl breakfast US$70/80; P🛜) On a quiet side street, you'll find this intimate B&B in a Spanish-style house built in the 1950s by the Volio family. The rooms vary in size, but all are nicely accented, with Portuguese tilework and some original furnishings. Breakfast is served in a charming rear garden.

Hostel Casa Yoses HOSTEL $
(☎2234-5486; www.casayoses.com; Av 8 near Calle 41, Los Yoses; incl breakfast dm US$13, d with/without bathroom US$38/32; @🛜) A mellow spot, this nine-room Spanish Revival–style house from 1949 is perched on a hill that offers lovely views of the valley from the front garden. The 10 stylish and simple rooms (six of them dorms) are spotless, with wood floors and tiled hallways. There is a shared kitchen, a lounge with a pool table and foosball, and even an area for BBQs. The young Tico owners speak Spanish, English and French.

Hostel Bekuo HOSTEL $
(☎2234-1091; www.hostelbekuo.com; 325m west of Spoon, Los Yoses; dm US$11, d from US$29; 🛜) This restful spot feels more like a home than a hostel. The airy modernist structure has nine unique and colorful rooms (four of which are dormitories; one of which is reserved especially for women), as well as large tiled bathrooms, an expansive TV lounge dotted with bean bags, and an interior courtyard garden slung with hammocks. The shared kitchen is neat, comfortable and well equipped.

Hotel Le Bergerac BOUTIQUE HOTEL $$
(☎2234-7850; www.bergerachotel.com; Calle 35 btwn Avs Central & 8, Los Yoses; d standard/superior/deluxe/grande incl breakfast US$97/117/135/150; P@🛜) A whitewashed building contains a bright lobby accented with fresh flowers and 25 rooms that overlook a tropical garden at this Los Yoses standard-bearer. Though sizes and configurations vary, they are all comfortable and sunny, accented with wood floors and floral bedspreads, and equipped with immaculate bathroom, cable TV, telephone and safe. There is an onsite restaurant with a full bar.

Casa Agua Buena GUESTHOUSE $
(☎2280-3548; www.aguabuena.org/casabuena/index.html; San Pedro; r per week US$60-80) East of San Pedro, these ramshackle group houses are popular among international students and long-term travelers on tight

budgets. Accommodations consist of two simple peach-colored homes with rooms of various sizes, equipped with shared kitchen, washing machine and a lounge with cable TV. Some rooms share bathrooms.

✕ Eating

Succulent Turkish sandwiches, Caribbean-style *rondón* (seafood gumbo), steaming pizzas – you can find just about every type of food in the narrow streets of San Pedro and Los Yoses, including quaint neighborhood spots well off the tourist trail.

Self-caterers can try **Más X Menos** (☏2225-0636; Av Central, San Pedro; ☺7am-midnight Mon-Sat, 7am-9pm Sun) and **Automercado** (☏2225-0361; Av Central btwn Calles 39 & 41, Los Yoses; ☺7am-9pm Mon-Sat, 8am-8pm Sun), large, modern supermarkets that stock plenty of everything. The latter has a good selection of healthy items, including veggie burgers.

TOP CHOICE **Restaurant Whapin** CARIBBEAN $$ (☏2283-1480; www.whapincr.com; cnr Calle 35 & Av 13, Barrio Escalante; mains US$13-21; ☺8am-11pm Mon-Fri, 11:30am-11pm Sat) If you don't make it to the Caribbean, then absolutely make sure you eat here: an intimate corner spot painted Rasta red, yellow and green, and serving up spectacularly delicious meals. Enjoy a steamy bowl of *rondón* (seafood gumbo cooked in coconut milk), a plate of rice and red beans, or fish simmered in spicy coconut sauce. Don't forget the fried plantains and, in season, the crisp breadfruit. Wash it all down with *agua de sapo*, a zesty sweet ginger drink.

Olio MEDITERRANEAN $$ (☏2281-0541; cnr Calle 33 & Av 3, Barrio Escalante; tapas US$5-11, dishes US$11-18; ☺11:30am-1am Mon-Fri, 4pm-midnight Sat; ☏) This cozy, Mediterranean-flavored gastropub serves a long list of tempting tapas, including divine stuffed mushrooms *(hongos madrileños)*, goat-cheese croquettes and garlic shrimp. There are also more than 17 house-made pastas to choose from and a decent beer and wine list (bottles from US$2, by the glass from US$5). A romantic spot for a date, with conversation-worthy quirks of decor and beautiful patrons.

Sofía Restaurante Mediterraneo MEDITERRANEAN $$ (☏2224-5050; www.sofiamediterraneo.com; cnr Calle 33 & Av 1, Barrio Escalante; mains US$6-18;

☺10am-3pm Mon-Tue, 10am-11pm Wed-Sat, noon-5pm Sun ; ☏) A hidden gem, Sofía serves a variety of Turkish and Mediterranean specialties, including fresh hummus, dolmas, house-made tortellini, grilled lamb and a rotating selection of daily specials. Save room for their sweet, delicate baklava.

Giacomin BAKERY $ (☏2224-3463; www.pasteleriagiacomin.com; Av Central east of Calle 37, Los Yoses; pastries from US$1.30; ☺8am-noon & 2-7pm Mon-Fri, 8am-noon & 2-6:30pm Sat) Obscured by the Automercadeo parking lot is this 1960s pastry shop that *josefinos* swear is the best in town. Here you'll find delicious mushroom mini-pizzas, flaky croissants and what has to be Central America's best cinnamon roll (*arrollado de canela*). This in addition to petits-fours, cream puffs, truffles and all sorts of sweet dreaminess. The tranquil upstairs lounge and balcony are perfect for a sipping cappuccino and reading a book.

Pane e Vino PIZZERIA $ (☏2280-2869; www.paneevino.co.cr; 25m west & 10m south of Más X Menos, San Pedro; pizzas US$6.50-16; ☺5pm-midnight Mon-Sat, 5-10pm Sun; ☏) Delicate superthin-crust pizza comes in 90 different variations at this rustic San Pedro family spot, where you can satisfy your cravings for *salame picante* (pepperoni). The heaping bowls of pasta are a deal, including the delicious *pasta pane e vino*, penne in a light tomato sauce studded with artichokes and mushrooms. There is a decent selection of wine (from US$8).

Café Kracovia CAFE $ (☏2253-9093; www.cafekracovia.com; 50m north of the Law School at UCR; mains US$5-11; ☺7:30am-8pm Mon-Fri, 10am-8pm Sat; ☏) With several distinct spaces – a lower-lit, intimate downstairs; good light and laptops upstairs; and outdoor garden courtyard – this hip cafe has a spot for everyone. Sip espresso while you partake of the free wi-fi, or enjoy a little sunshine with your sandwich. Contemporary artwork, mosaic details and a distinct university vibe create an appealing ambience for lunching on well-prepared cafe eats: crêpes, wraps, pastries and salads. Look for the building's white arches across the highway from – no joke – Hooters.

Comida Para Sentir VEGETARIAN $ (☏2224-1163; 100m north of Iglesia de San Pedro; casados US$3.50-7; ☺10am-6pm Mon-Fri; ☏) This informal, bustling student spot serves an international menu of veggie everything including curried rice with cashews, vegetable *casado* and whole-grain sandwiches. Don't miss the *tardes de maíz* (afternoons of corn), from 3pm to 6pm, featuring delicious corn-based treats like *pupusas* and tamales.

Le Chandelier FRENCH $$$
(☑2225-3980; www.lechandeliercr.com; 100m west & 100m south of El Antiguo ICE, San Pedro; mains US$11-27; ☺11:30am-2pm & 6:30am-midnight Mon-Fri, 6:30am-midnight Sat) Whether you're sitting next to the fireplace or outside on the patio, it's hard to find a more romantic place than this two-decade-old Los Yoses outpost. Here, chef Claude Dubuis serves traditional French specialties (think duck *à l'orange*) with a few Costa Rican flourishes. Save room for the crêpes suzette for two (US$12).

Bagelmen's DELI $
(☑800-212-1314; www.bagelmenscr.com; cnr Av Central & Calle 33; breakfast US$2-4; ☺7am-9pm; ☎) It's not Brooklyn, but if you've been on the *gallo pinto* diet, you'll be glad to know that Bagelmen's offers decent bagels and free wi-fi.

🍷 Drinking

Calle 3, to the north of Av Central, is known as Calle La Amargura (Sorrow St). However, it should be called Calle de la Cruda (Street of Hangovers) because it has the highest concentration of bars of any single street in town, and many of these are packed with customers (mainly university students) even during daylight hours. Places come and go, but **Terra U** (50m north of Av Central), **Caccio's** (150m north of Av Central) and **Tavarúa** (across the street from Terra U) are longtime party spots. The area gets rowdy in the wee hours: watch out for drunks and pickpockets.

Río Bar BAR
(☑2225-8371; Av Central, west of Calle 43; ☺noon-midnight Sun-Tue, noon-2am Wed-Sat) Just west of the fountain, this large, popular bar with an upstairs lounge has live bands on some nights and flat-screen TVs showing the current game. Early in the evening it's a good spot to watch the rush-hour traffic crawl by in the company of an after-work crowd.

Tao LOUNGE
(☑2225-5696; Calle 41 btwn Avs Central & 8) A dimly lit lounge decorated with lots of Buddhas, this hip spot has fusion cocktails and decent

Vietnamese appetizers, including satay and spring rolls (from US$4). There may be a cover charge when guest DJs appear.

Un Lugar Resto-bar BAR
(☑2225-3979; Calle 33 btwn Avs 11 & 13, Barrio Escalante; ☺11am-2am Mon-Sat) This small wood-lined bar serves as a neighborhood hangout that draws artsy types and young professionals for cold beer and *bocas* (US$4 to US$7). This is a good spot for solo women travelers.

Roots Reggae Bar BAR
(☑2280-4964; Av 8, btwn Calle 43 & Spoon, Los Yoses; ☺5pm-midnight Tue-Sun) The dreadlocked set crowds this cool lounge bar, a sweet spot to get a beer and hang with reggae-loving locals.

☆ Entertainment

Jazz Café LIVE MUSIC
(☑2253-8933; www.jazzcafecostarica.com; 50m east of Antiguo Banco Popular; ☺6pm-2am) *The* destination in San José for live music, with a different band every night. Countless performers have taken to the stage here, including the legendary Cuban bandleader Chucho Valdés and Colombian pop star Juanes. Admission charges vary, but plan on spending about US$8 to see local groups.

Other venues for entertainment include:
» **Multicines San Pedro** (☑2283-5715, 2283-5716; www.ccmcinemas.com; 2nd fl, Mall San Pedro; admission US$5) Popular multiplex with 10 screens showing the latest Hollywood flicks.
» **Teatro Eugene O'Neill** (☑2207-7554; www.centrocultural.cr; Calle 37 north of Av Central, San Pedr-o) Shows performances sponsored by the Centro Cultural Costarricense Norteamericano.
» **Teatro de Bellas Artes** (☑2511-6733; www.teatro.ucr.ac.cr; San Pedro) Has a wide variety of programming, including works produced by the UCR fine-arts department.

🛍 Shopping

» **Mall San Pedro** (☑2283-7516; northwest of Fuente de la Hispanidad, San Pedro) Busy four-story mall (often used as a landmark) housing the Multicines, a food court, a video arcade and the usual mix of retailers.
» **Outlet Mall** (American Mall; cnr Av Central & Calle Central, San Pedro) Smaller, economical spot across from the Iglesia de San Pedro.

ℹ Information

There are dozens of internet cafes in the streets surrounding Calle La Amargura, so you will have no problem logging on. Rates begin at US$0.75 per hour.

» **Burbujas** (☑2224-9822; 150m east & 25m south of the Scotiabank; ☉9am-5pm Mon-Sat) Laundry service; about US$6 for a regular-sized load.

» **Post Office** (☑2253-4633; 150m south of Iglesia de San Pedro; ☉8am-noon & 1-5:30pm Mon-Fri)

» **Scotiabank** (☑2234-4888; Av Central btwn Calles 5 & 7; ☉9am-6pm Mon-Fri, 9am-1pm Sat) Changes cash and has a 24hr ATM.

» **TAM Travel** (☑2527-9700, in USA & Canada 877-826-8785; www.tamtravel.com; Calle 39 btwn Avs Central & 8) Airline ticketing, local travel and more.

ℹ Getting There & Away

From the Plaza de la Cultura in San José, take any bus marked 'Mall San Pedro.' A taxi ride from downtown will cost about US$5, depending on traffic. To get into San José, take one of the buses that make stops all along Av Central heading west into the city.

Escazú

You can find an unusual juxtaposition of gringo expats, moneyed aristocrats and old-world Tico village life in Escazú, this sprawling suburb climbing a steep hillside overlooking San José and Heredia. The area is really made up of three distinct adjoining neighborhoods: San Rafael de Escazú, Escazú Centro and San Antonio de Escazú.

At the bottom of the hill is San Rafael, which is one part Costa Rica, two parts USA, dotted with strip malls, top-end car dealerships, tract housing and chain restaurants. Escazú Centro retains an unhurried Tico ambience, where narrow streets are cluttered with shops, *sodas* and old-world taverns. At the top of the hill, the area around San Antonio remains almost entirely residential; it's a mix of humble rural homes, sprawling estates and spectacular views. The further you get up the hill, the more scarce public transportation becomes, so it's best to have your own vehicle.

Escazú's proximity to Pavas and Alajuela makes it a convenient place to stay if you want to be near San José's airports.

◉ Sights & Activities

Because this is a residential area, there's little in the way of tourist attractions – but if you're looking for a pleasant neighborhood to lodge and enjoy a leisurely meal, it's ideal. The best spot for a walk is the narrow, gridded streets of Escazú Centro, which at its heart contains a small park and the Iglesia Escazú (cnr Av Central & Calle Central). First built in 1799, it has been rebuilt many times due to regular earthquakes. The remodeled exterior isn't much to look at, but the stone-columned interior is pleasant, with a main altar covered in ceramic tiles and capped by a gilded baroque-style altar.

Golfers can hit the links at the Parque Valle del Sol (☑2282-9222, ext 219/218; www.vallesol.com; 1.7km west of HSBC Bank; 18 holes with a cart per person US$94; ☉6:30am-6pm Tue-Sun, 8am-6pm Mon) in the nearby suburb of Santa Ana. Or you can sharpen your salsa dance moves at Merecumbé Escazú (☑2289-4774, 8884-7553; cnr Av 3 & Calle Cortés).

✯ Festivals & Events

On the second Sunday of March, Escazú celebrates Día del Boyero, a celebration in honor of oxcart drivers. Dozens of boyeros from all over the country decorate traditional, brightly painted carts and form a colorful (if slow) parade.

⊨ Sleeping

Escazú is a stylish area with accommodations ranging from sleek boutique inns to homey B&Bs – but there's not much for the budget traveler. Street addresses aren't always given; call directly or check hotel websites for directions (which are invariably complicated).

TOP CHOICE **Posada El Quijote**   B&B $$
(☑2289-8401; www.quijote.cr; Calle del Llano, Bello Horizonte; d standard/superior/deluxe incl breakfast US$95/105/115; P☺❉☎) This Spanish-style *posada* on a hillside rates as one of the top B&Bs in the San José area. Standard rooms are simple yet homey, with wooden floors, throw rugs, cable TV and private hot-water bathrooms, while larger superior and deluxe units have either a small patio or a private terrace. All guests are invited to take a nip at the honor bar, and then relax on the outdoor patio while soaking up the sweeping views of the Central Valley.

Escazú

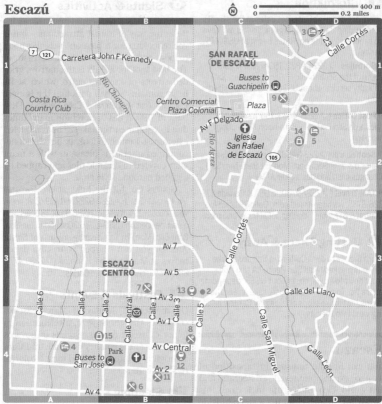

Costa Verde Inn
TOP CHOICE   INN $$

([☎]2228-4080; www.costaverdeinn.com; incl breakfast s/d/tr $55/65/75, d apt from $85; [P][@][🛜][🌊]) The sister lodge of the famous Manuel Antonio hotel, this homey stone inn is surrounded by gardens that contain a hot tub, a mosaic-tile swimming pool, a BBQ area and even a sundeck with wi-fi. Fourteen simple rooms of various sizes have king-sized beds, comfy rocking chairs and folk-art accents. Five apartments come with fully equipped kitchen. A generous Tico breakfast is served on the outdoor terrace. Weekly rates are available; credit cards accepted.

Casa de las Tías
                                                    B&B $$

([☎]2289-5517; www.hotels.co.cr/casatias.html; s/d/tr incl breakfast US$80/90/100; [P][➡][🛜]) In a quiet area of San Rafael, this yellow-and-turquoise Cape Cod–style house (complete with picket fence) has five immaculate, individually decorated rooms, all with private bathrooms. The house is adorned with crafts that owners Xavier and Pilar have picked up on their travels in Latin America, lending the place a cozy, intimate feel.

Casa Cristal
                                                    INN $$$

([☎]2289-2530; www.casacristalcr.com; Bello Horizonte; d incl breakfast US$130-225; [P][➡][❄][🛜][🌊]) This chic, whitewashed hotel is situated on what has to be the best piece of real estate in Escazú: at the end of a winding mountain road, on a hillside overlooking several dozen hectares of uninhabited parkland, with the twinkling lights of San José in the distance. There are eight individually decorated contemporary guest rooms (some with Jacuzzi tubs), most of which have floor-to-ceiling windows that allow for uninterrupted views of the Central Valley. Note that the hotel does not accept children under the age of 12.

Escazú

Boutique Hotel   B&B $$

(☎2288-6762; www.bedandbreakfastcr.com; Carretera John F Kennedy, 1km west of Costa Rica Country Club; d standard/junior/deluxe/ste incl breakfast US$90/95/115/125; P❄☎) This friendly, contemporary inn has five simple rooms with blond-wood floors; large, comfortable beds; painted sinks with folk-art motifs; mini-refrigerators and in-room coffeemakers. Two units come with air-con and two are wheelchair-accessible. A broad outdoor deck with pleasant views is stocked with rocking chairs for lounging.

Beacon Boutique Hotel   HOTEL $$$

(☎2228-3110; www.mybeaconescazu.com; Av Central btwn Calles 4 & 6; d incl breakfast US$129-299; P❄@☎☀) A stylish 27-room inn situated at the heart of Escazú Centro, the top-end Beacon Boutique comes stocked with all manner of luxury goodies: high thread-count linens, down comforters, king-sized beds, plush robes, in-room coffeemakers and even a pillow menu. Room decor is contemporary Spanish Mediterranean, with amenities such as an onsite gym, spa, wine bar and courtyard with a pool.

Villa Escazú   B&B $$

(☎2289-7971; www.hotels.co.cr/vescazu.html; d without bathroom incl breakfast US$50-65, 2-night minimum; P☎) This wood chalet with a wraparound veranda is surrounded by gardens and fruit trees. The two quaint, wood-paneled rooms feature local artwork, comfy couches and a shared bathroom. Breakfast is served on the outdoor balcony. A small, fully equipped studio and an apartment are also available for rent (from US$225 per week). Reserve well in advance.

Apartotel María Alexandra   HOTEL $$

(☎2228-1507; www.mariaalexandra.com; cnr Calle 3 & Av 23; d apt from US$80; P❄☎☀) This centrally located apartment-hotel in San Rafael has 15 clean, wood-paneled apartments with private bedroom, kitchen and laundry area – all of which channel a late-'70s *Brady Bunch* vibe. There is a sauna, mosaic-tile swimming pool and a small gym.

✖ Eating

Restaurante Cerutti   ITALIAN $$

(☎2228-4511; www.ceruttirestaurante.com; Calle Cortés, San Rafael; dishes US$11-25; ◷noon-2:30pm & 6:30am-11pm Mon-Sat; ☞) Pricey Cerutti delivers predictably top-notch Italian specialties, including fresh seafood and house-made pastas. The ravioli stuffed with ricotta and mushrooms is a local favorite, and you can't go wrong with the long list of delicious risottos. Credit cards accepted.

Chez Christophe   BAKERY $

(☎2228-2512; 75m south of Centro Comerical El Paco, San Rafael; ◷7am-7pm Tue-Sat, 8am-6pm Sun) If you have a hankering for a coffee éclair, croque monsieur or a plain (but transcendent) croissant, stop here and linger awhile. Waffles are reserved for Sundays only, but every other day of the week, this authentic French bakery offers freshly baked breads and pastries, as well as espresso and a full breakfast and lunch menu.

Buena Tierra   ORGANIC $

(☎2288-0342; buenatierra.organica@gmail.com; cnr Calle Central & Av 4; mains US$6-8; ◷9am-5:30pm Mon-Fri, 9am-2pm Sat; ☞) A cute and friendly organic cafe, Buena Tierra is a good place to detox. This airy little spot brings the outside in, with huge windows propped open and tree-trunk tabletops. All fruits, vegetables, rice and beans used in the restaurant are organic, while *batidos* (fruit shakes) are made with a choice of water, milk, goat's milk yogurt or almond milk. The cafe also organizes an organic farmers' market on Wednesday mornings.

La Casona de Laly COSTA RICAN $
(☎2288-5807; cnr Av 3 & Calle Central; bocas $2-5, mains $5-15; ☺11am-midnight Mon-Sat, 11am-6pm Sun) At the heart of Escazú Centro, this much-loved restaurant/tavern specializes in country-style Tico fare. Locals and expats alike pack the joint for cheap, lip-smacking *bocas,* ice-cold beers and a soundtrack of merengue accompanied by the cackling of the owner's pet birds, who inhabit the cages that line the entire west wall of the restaurant. Be sure to try the *dados de queso* (fried cheese cubes) – they are the best.

Soda Río de Janeiro COSTA RICAN $
(☎8811-5263; cnr Calle 1 & Av 2; mains US$5-6; ☺6am-6pm Mon-Sat) Located southeast of the Iglesia Escazú, this charismatic little *soda* decked out with bright-red tablecloths is frequently full. Typical Tico fare includes pork chops, chicken or fish accompanied by big jars of spicy, pickled vegetables. There's a tiny aquarium of angelfish that you can watch while you wait for a seat.

La Esquina Argentina ARGENTINE $
(☎2288-2811; cnr Av Central & Calle Cortés; dishes US$3-9; ☺7am-2pm Mon-Fri) This popular roadside stand sells piping-hot *empanadas,* smoked meats and tasty mashed potatoes. The outdoor patio is a good spot to linger over a cup of coffee.

Tiquicia COSTA RICAN $$
(☎2289-5839; www.miradortiquicia.com; bocas US$5-11, mains US$13-23; ☺noon-midnight Tue-Thu, noon-2am Fri-Sat, noon-9pm Sun) This long-running hilltop Tico restaurant serves up bounteous platters, in addition to live folk music on weekends. Without a doubt, it's a tourist trap – an expensive one – but you're not here to eat, you're here to admire the extravagant views of the Central Valley. The restaurant is 5km south of Escazú Centro on a paved road. It's tricky to find; call for directions or check the website for a map.

Self-Catering
On Saturdays, head to the farmers market along Av 2, just south of the park in Escazú Centro. There's also an organic farmers market on Wednesdays, featuring delectables such as cheese, honey and fish. It's 1km south of Paco, opposite the Red Cross building.

Self-caterers will find plenty of choice in Escazú's supermarkets, the best being the gigantic Automercado.

» **Automercado** (☎2588-1812; Atlantis Plaza, Calle Cortés, San Rafael; ☺7am-10pm Mon-Sat, 8am-9pm Sun)

» **Más X Menos** (☎2228-0954; Centro Comercial Escazú, Carretera John F Kennedy, San Rafael; ☺6:30am-midnight Mon-Sat, 6:30am-10pm Sun)

» **Supermercado Saretto** (☎2228-0247; San Rafael; ☺8am-8pm Mon-Sat, 9am-2pm Sun)

☕ Drinking
To sip fine vintages, visit the stylish ground-floor wine bar at the Beacon Boutique Hotel (p91) (7pm to midnight). For local flavor, nothing beats the La Casona de Laly (p92).

Centro Comercial Trejos Montealegre BAR
(Calle Cortés, San Rafael) This complex on the northern edge of San Rafael is a hot nightlife outpost. The scenesters start rolling in at 9pm and keep going until the wee hours. In San José, party places come and go quickly – inquire locally before setting out.

Taberna Arenas BAR
(☎2289-8256; cnr of Av Central & Calle 3; ☺from 4pm) This delightful, old-fashioned Tico bar is an Escazú institution. Arenas has good *bocas* and a wide selection of domestic and imported beers. Owner Don Israel is a true charmer, and has his photos with various heads of state on the walls, along with the agricultural implements that are de rigueur in any country bar.

The Pub BAR
(☎2288-3062; Av 3 btwn Calles 3 & 5; ☺from 11am) This small, friendly American-owned pub has a list of more than two dozen international beers, a dozen local brews and a selection of

THE FINE WOODCRAFTS OF BARRY BIESANZ

Located in the hills of Bello Horizonte in Escazú, the workshop of Biesanz Woodworks (☑2289-4337; www.biesanz.com; ⊗8am-5pm Mon-Fri, 9am-3pm Sat) is one of the finest woodcrafting studios in the nation, run by celebrated artisan Barry Biesanz. His bowls and other decorative containers are exquisite and take their inspiration from pre-Columbian techniques, in which the natural lines and forms of the wood determine the shape and size of the bowl. The pieces are expensive (from US$85 for a palm-size bowl), but they are unique – and so delicately crafted that they wouldn't be out of place in a museum.

shots with scary-sounding names like 'Test Tube Baby' and 'Anti-Freeze'. A greasy bar menu is available to soak up the damage.

☆ Entertainment

Cinemark   CINEMA
(☑2201-5050; www.cinemarkca.com; Multiplaza Escazú; admission US$5, Wed US$3) Shows first-run movies.

Jazz Café   LIVE MUSIC
(☑2288-4740; www.jazzcafecostarica.com; north side of Autopista Próspero Fernández; from US$6; ⊗from 7pm) Find a little aural satisfaction at the Jazz Café, the sister club of the San Pedro standard-bearer. The calendar features a mix of local and international bands. If you're coming from San José, take the exit immediately after the tollbooth.

Club Gaira   CLUB
(☑2290-2972; www.clubgaira.com; next to Ferretería EPA, San Rafael; admission varies; ⊗from 7pm) Escazú's new trendy, design-conscious club with a geometric-meets-tribal decor (zebra pelts and striped couches); has two bars, two dance floors and DJs spinning hip-hop, Latin and electronica.

The Centro Comercial Trejo Montealegre also has a number of dance spots.

🛍 Shopping

Atlantis Plaza   SHOPPING CENTER
(Calle Cortés, San Rafael) A symphony of brutal-looking steel is home to a small shopping center lined with boutiques, a bookstore, a supermarket and a range of eateries.

Multiplaza Escazú   SHOPPING CENTER
(www.multiplazamall.com; ⊗10am-8pm Mon-Sat, 10am-7pm Sun) Costa Rica's most stylish and massive shopping mall has everything you need (or don't). Of particular interest to campers is the Cemaco, a budget depart-

ment store that sells basic fishing and camping supplies, including propane gas for your portable stove. If you're coming from San José, the mall can be reached by taking any bus marked 'Escazú Multiplaza'.

Driftwood Books   BOOKS
(☑2288-0142; 2nd fl, cnr Calle 2 & Av Central; ⊗3-5pm Mon-Fri) A tiny second-story shop jammed with used, mostly English-language books, for sale or trade (two for one). It displays a collection of vintage bells.

ⓘ Information

» **Banco de Costa Rica** (Av Central btwn Calles Central & 1) A 24hr ATM.

» **Hospital CIMA** (p81) Affiliated with Baylor University Medical Center in the USA; one of the most modern hospitals in the greater San José metro area.

» **Scotiabank** (☑2288-0125; www.scotiabankcr. com; Carretera John F Kennedy; ⊗9am-6pm Mon-Fri, 9am-1pm Sat) Has a 24hr ATM; can exchange cash and traveler's checks.

ⓘ Getting There & Around

Frequent buses between San José and Escazú cost about US$0.75 and take about 25 minutes. All depart San José from east of the Coca-Cola Terminal or south of the Hospital San Juan de Dios. They take several routes: buses labeled 'San Antonio de Escazú' go up the hill to the south of Escazú and end near the Iglesia San Antonio de Escazú; those labeled 'Escazú Centro' end in Escazú's main plaza; others, labeled 'Guachipelín' go west on the Carretera John F Kennedy and pass the Costa Rica Country Club. All buses go through San Rafael.

For motorcycle rental, see Harley Davidson Rentals (p85), inside the Apartotel María Alexandra. Riders have to be more than 25 years of age and have a valid motorcycle driver's license. Rates start at US$150 per bike per day and include helmet, goggles and unlimited mileage (insurance and tax are not included).

Central Valley & Highlands

Best Places to Eat

» Xandari (p102)

» Finca Rosa Blanca (p115)

» Como en Casa (p102)

» Colbert Restaurant (p105)

» La Casona del Maíz (p106)

Best Places to Stay

» Poás Volcano Lodge (p104)

» Vista del Valle Plantation Inn (p106)

» El Silencio (p110)

» Orosi Lodge (p122)

» Turrialtico Lodge (p127)

Why Go?

It is on the coffee-cultivated hillsides of the Central Valley that you'll find Costa Rica's heart and soul. This is not only the geographical center of the country, but also its cultural and spiritual core. It is here that the Spanish first settled, here that coffee built a prosperous nation, here that picturesque highland villages still gather for centuries-old fiestas. It is also here that you'll get to fully appreciate Costa Rica's country cooking: artisanal cheeses, steamy corn cakes and freshly caught river trout.

Curvy mountain roads and cattle traffic force travelers to slow their roll. Quaint (and sometimes quirky) agricultural towns invite leisurely detours to farmers' markets and church processions, a refreshing break from the tourist-industrial complex on the coasts. But it's not all cows and coffee – world-class rapids, resplendent quetzals and close encounters with active volcanoes all show off the rich landscape in which Costa Rica's character is rooted.

When to Go

An elevated altitude and landlocked location mean that the Central Valley and Highlands are far more temperate than the coasts. Temps hover around 25°C (77°F) year-round, making the region a popular retreat for weekending *josefinos* (inhabitants of San José) seeking to escape the heat. During 'green' season, from June to December, afternoon showers are not uncommon, but the sun usually shines through after an hour or so of rain. This is also the high season for rafting, June through October being the best months.

History

As in other parts of the country, there is little in the historical record about the ethnicities that inhabited the Central Valley prior to the arrival of the Spanish. What is known is that the people of the area – largely the Huetar – practiced an animist religion, produced stone sculpture and clay pottery, and communicated in a Chibchan dialect that is now extinct. They also developed and maintained the ancient highland city of Guayabo – which is today the biggest and most significant pre-Columbian archeological site in the country.

European settlement in Costa Rica would not begin in earnest until 1563, when Juan Vásquez de Coronado founded the colonial capital of Cartago, what is today Costa Rica's oldest Spanish city. Over the next two centuries, Spanish communities would pop up in Heredia, San José and Orosi. Throughout this period, however, the area remained a colonial backwater, a checkerboard of Spanish farming communities and *indios bravos* (fierce Indians) who had not come under colonial dominion, and who practiced a largely itinerant agriculture.

It was only after independence, in the 1830s, that the area began to prosper with the expanded cultivation of coffee. The *grano de oro* (golden bean) transformed the country, providing the revenue to invest in urban infrastructure such as electricity and pavements, not to mention many baronial mansions. Coffee has since been overtaken as a key agricultural export by pineapples and bananas. But its legacy lives on, reflected in the culture, architecture and traditions of many highland towns.

ALAJUELA & THE NORTHERN VALLEY

Volcanoes shrouded in mist, undulating coffee *fincas* (plantations), bustling agricultural centers. The area around the provincial capital of Alajuela, 18km northwest of San José, seems to have it all – including Juan Santamaría International Airport, just 3km outside the city. The proximity to the airport makes this area a highly convenient transit point if you are entering or leaving the country here. For travelers seeking to avoid San José, it offers a good selection of local restaurants and accommodations.

Alajuela

POP 47,900

Costa Rica's second city is also home to one of the country's most famous figures: Juan Santamaría, the humble drummer boy who died putting an end to William Walker's campaign to turn Central America into slaving territory in the Battle of Rivas in 1856. A busy agricultural hub, it is here that farmers bring their products to market.

Alajuela is by no means a tourist 'destination.' Much of the architecture is unremarkable, the streets are often jammed and there isn't a lot to see here. But it's an inherently Costa Rican city, and, in its more relaxed moments, it reveals itself as such, where families have leisurely Sunday lunches and teenagers steal kisses in the park. It's also a good base for exploring the countryside to the north.

◉ Sights & Activities

ALAJUELA CITY CENTER

Parque Central   PARK
(Avs Central & 1 btwn Calles Central & 2) The shady Parque Central is a pleasant place to relax beneath the mango trees, or people-watch in the evenings.

Museo Juan Santamaría   MUSEUM
(☑2441-4775; www.museojuansantamaria.go.cr; Av 1 btwn Calles Central & 2; admission free; ⊙10am-5:30pm Tue-Sun) Situated in a century-old structure that has served as both a jail and an armory, the Museo Juan Santamaría chronicles the life and history of Juan Santamaría. A basic exhibit area contains vintage maps, paintings and historical artifacts related to the conflict that ultimately gained Costa Rica's independence. It also hosts rotating exhibitions and occasional performances in the small auditorium.

Cathedral   CHURCH
(Calle Central btwn Avs Central & 1) To the east of Parque Central is the 19th-century cathedral, which suffered severe damage in the 1991 earthquake. The hemispherical cupola is unusually constructed of sheets of red corrugated metal. Two presidents are buried here.

Iglesia La Agonía   CHURCH
(Calle 9 btwn Avs Central & 1) A Renaissance-inspired structure, built in 1941, houses the Iglesia La Agonía, a popular local spot for

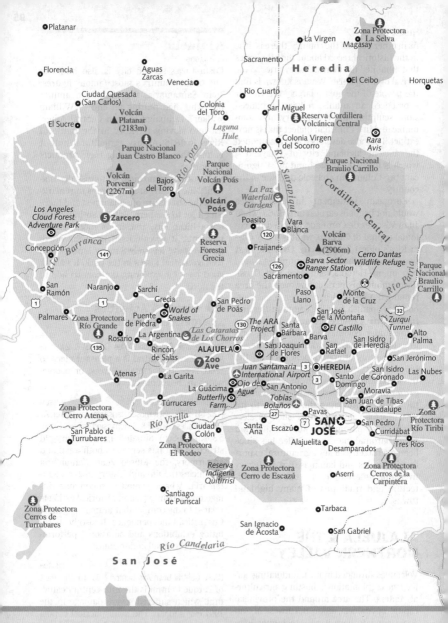

Central Valley & Highlands Highlights

1 Paddle for your life down the cascading rapids of the **Río Pacuare** or **Río Reventazón** (p126)

2 Peer into the mammoth craters and volcanic lakes of the area's volcanoes: **Irazú** (p120), **Poás** (p103) and **Turrialba** (p124)

3 Walk along the aqueducts and take in the still mystery of petroglyphs at Costa Rica's largest archaeological site, the pre-Columbian **Monumento Nacional Arqueológico Guayabo** (p128)

Limón

Parque Nacional Tortuguero

Cariari

Río Frio

0 ____ 20 km
0 ____ 10 miles

Santa Clara

Rainforest Aerial Tram

Quebrada González Ranger Station

Guápiles

Guácimo

Río Reventazón ❶

Zona Protectora Acuiferos Guacimo y Pococi ❹

Siquirres

Reserva Forestal Cordillera Volcánica Central ❹

Reserva Río Pacuare

Reserva Indígena Barbilla

Volcán Turrialba ❷

Parque Nacional Volcán Turrialba ❹

Parque Nacional Volcán Irazú

Volcán Irazú ❷

Santa Cruz

Lajas (Santa Teresita)

Parque Nacional Barbilla

Rancho Redondo

(219)

(230)

Tierra Blanca

San Gerardo

Pacayas

Monumento Nacional Arqueológico Guayabo ❸

Reserva Indígena Alto y Bajo Chirripó

Cot

(230)

Cervantes

Juan Viñas

Turrialba

Pavones

Catie & Adventure Education Center ❹

Río Pacuare ❶

Cartago ❻

(8)

Finca Cristina

Finca la Flor de Paraíso

Río Reventazón

La Suiza

Tuis

Tejar (10)

Presa de Cachí

Paraíso

Cachí

Lankester Gardens

Ujarrás

Lago de Cachí

Cartago

Moravia

Orosi ❹

Valle de Orosi

Zona Protectora Río Navarro y Río Macho ❹

Palomo

Río Navarro

Zona Protectora Cuenca del Río Tuis ❹

Río Sombrero

Tapantí

Purisil

Parque Nacional Tapantí-Macizo Cerro de la Muerte ❹

❹ Explore the wilderness, culture and coffee *fincas* of the beauteous **Valle de Orosi** (p120)

❺ Wind along scenic mountain roads to **Zarcero**

(p108), home of trippy topiary and organic farming

❻ Visit the country's most venerated religious relic at the **Basílica de Nuestra Senora de Los Ángeles** (p116) in Cartago

❼ Get to know macaws, margays and monkeys up close at **Zoo Ave** (p105), a wildlife rescue center

Alajuela

N 0 ___ 0 ___ 400 m
0 ___ 0.2 miles

Mass. The columned interiors are airy and graceful, with ornate wood altars and, interestingly, a main altar encrusted with a fluorescent crucifix (somehow, it works).

Parque Juan Santamaría — PLAZA

(Calle 2 btwn Avs 2 & 4) Two blocks south of Parque Central, Parque Juan Santamaría features a statue of the hero in action, flanked by cannons. Across the way, the **Parque de los Niños** has a more parklike scene going on, complete with playground equipment, chattering toddlers and canoodling teenagers.

AROUND ALAJUELA

ARA Project — WILDLIFE RESERVE

(8389-5811; www.thearaproject.org; Río Segundo de Alajuela; suggested per person donation US$20; by appointment) Richard and Margot Frisius founded this crucial and successful green and scarlet macaw breeding program in 1992. After Margot passed away in 2008, the nonprofit took a name change, but continues in the Frisius' vision to reintroduce macaws into the wild. The ARA Project offers volunteer opportunities at both the breeding center and release sites (from US$10 to US$23 per person per day, including accommodations).

Alajuela

See the website for details. Guided tours of the breeding center can be arranged by appointment. Three kilometers south of Alajuela, it's tricky to find; get directions.

Butterfly Farm   GARDENS
(📞2438-0400; www.butterflyfarm.co.cr; La Guácima de Alajuela; adult/4-11yr $19/12.50, with transportation from San José $40/25; ⏰tours 8:30am, 11am, 1pm & 3pm) Started in 1983, the Butterfly Farm opened as the first commercial butterfly farm in Latin America. In the wild it's estimated that less than 2% of caterpillars survive to adulthood, while breeders at the farm boast an astounding 90% survival rate. This ensures a steady supply of pupae for gardens, schools, museums and private collections around the world.

Entrance fees include a guided two-hour tour, with the option of transportation to and from hotels in San José, as well as combo tours. Find details and directions on its website.

Ojo de Agua Springs   SWIMMING
(📞2441-0655; San Antonio de Belén; admission US$1.50, children under 6 free; ⏰6am-4pm; 👶) About 6km south of Alajuela, this picturesque working-class water park gets packed on weekends with families from San José and Alajuela. Approximately 20,000L of water gush out from the spring each minute, powering a small waterfall and filling various pools (including an Olympic-sized lap pool complete with diving tower) and an artificial boating lake. From here, the water is piped down to the coast at Puntarenas, for which the springs are a major supplier of water.

From Alajuela, buses depart every half hour from the main terminal area on the southwest end of town; less frequently on weekdays. From San José, drivers can take the San Antonio de Belén exit off the Interamericana; Ojo de Agua is just past San Antonio.

🎓 Courses

For details about Spanish-language study, see Spanish Schools in the Central Valley (p106). To improve your dance moves, check out the class schedule at **Merecumbé** (📞2442-3536; www.merecumbe.net; Av 2 btwn Calles 8 & 10).

🎉 Festivals & Events

In the town that gave birth to Juan Santamaría, it would be expected that the anniversary of the **Battle of Rivas**, on April 11, would be particularly well celebrated. This momentous event is commemorated with civic events, including a parade and lots of firecrackers.

🛏 Sleeping

Since Alajuela is so close to the international airport, most hotels and B&Bs can arrange airport transfers for a small fee (or for free). If you are driving your own car it's worth remembering that many places in the city center don't have dedicated parking, there are many guarded lots available, however. Also, expect street noise to be a fact of life.

As in other spots, taxi drivers will try to steer you to places that pay them a commission. Remember: be skeptical, don't believe everything you hear and if you're unsure about where you've chosen to stay, ask to see a room.

A few of the budget hotels also offer dorm rooms. All top-end hotels accept credit cards, as do most mid-range spots.

TOP CHOICE Hostel Maleku
HOSTEL $

(☏2430-4304; www.malekuhostel.com; dm US$13, s/d without bathroom US$25/35, all incl breakfast; @) This sweet little backpackers' abode has spic-and-span rooms tucked into a vintage home on a quiet street, 50m west of Hospital San Rafael. There are also three private rooms, with shared bathrooms, a communal kitchen, a TV lounge and free internet. It's a wonderful, serene spot and the staff is very helpful. Free shuttles to the airport leave the hostel hourly starting at 5am.

TOP CHOICE Alajuela Backpackers Boutique Hostel
HOTEL $

(☏2441-7149; www.alajuelabackpackers.com; cnr Av 4 & Calle 4; dm US$15, s/d/tr US$38/48/60, s/d junior ste US$55/78; ❄@🛜) This four-story inn is more hotel than hostel, with private rooms and dorms surrounding a plant-draped atrium. Watch movies on the flat-screen TV in the beanbag lounge, or sip beers on the 4th-floor bar terrace and watch planes take off in the distance. Dorms house only four people per room, and each has its own bathroom. Junior suites have plasma TV and comfy king-sized bed. Credit cards accepted.

TOP CHOICE Xandari Resort Hotel & Spa
HOTEL $$$

(☏2443-2020; www.xandari.com; d villa US$230-315; P♿❄🛜♨) Overlooking the Central Valley, this romantic spot is the fanciful joint design of a Tico architect/designer couple. All rooms are villas, painted in tropical colors and tastefully but playfully decorated with folk art and hand-woven textiles; all include garden-view shower, mini-fridge and sitting area. The grounds offer more than 3km of trails for exploring, three pools, a Jacuzzi, a spa, an excellent gift shop and a restaurant specializing in organic local foods; and most of the staff are hired from the local village.

Hotel Los Volcanes
B&B $$

(☏2441-0525; www.hotellosvolcanes.com; Av 3 btwn Calles Central & 2; r standard US$35-60, superior US$46-75, all incl breakfast; P♿❄@🛜) This refurbished 1920s home has 15 rooms – from vintage units with wood floors, period-style furniture and clean, shared bathrooms, to contemporary rooms with flat-screen TV

and safe. There's also an enjoyable courtyard in the back, complete with gurgling fountain. The helpful Tico owners can arrange free airport drop-off at the end of your stay.

Hotel 1915
HOTEL $$

(☏2441-0495; www.1915hotel.com; Calle 2 btwn Avs 5 & 7; d US$65-100 incl breakfast; P❄@🛜) The exterior may not look like much, but step through the front door and you'll find yourself in a quaint 16-room inn built around a century-old home. Rooms have adobe walls, wood-beam ceilings and period-style furnishings, most also have a mini-fridge. The graceful living room has a stained-glass window, and many of the floors are clad in vintage Spanish tile. The lovely open-air lounge is a great space to chill.

Trapp Family Lodge
INN $$

(☏2431-0776; www.trappfam.com; r US$95, additional person US$15, child 3-11yr US$6, all incl breakfast; P@♨🛜👶) This highly recommended spot is the comfiest, most attractive option within reach of the airport landing strip. A bright, Spanish-style country inn houses 20 terra-cotta–tiled rooms with comfortable beds and a graceful hacienda vibe. The best units have balconies overlooking a lovely garden laced with bougainvillea and fig trees, and a pool. It's located 2km from the international airport; free airport transfers are provided.

🏄 Hotel Pacandé
HOTEL $

(☏2443-8481; www.hotelpacande.com; Av 5 btwn Calles 2 & 4; s & d US$30-55, tr US$45-70, all incl breakfast; P@) This popular, locally run option is very clean throughout, offering 10 large rooms with wood furnishings, folk-art touches and cable TV. Less expensive rooms share bathrooms. The outdoor breakfast nook is a great spot for a morning brew.

Hotel Cortéz Azul
HOTEL $

(☏2443-6145; hotelcortezazul@gmail.com; Av 5 btwn Calles 2 & 4; dm US$10, d with/without bathroom US$30/25; P🛜) The owner, Eduardo Rodríguez, is a local artist who displays his unique work throughout the property (check out the *Last Supper* mural). The hotel has 10 homey, clean rooms with polished wood floors, a common area and two kitchens.

🏄 Hotel Buena Vista
HOTEL $$$

(☏2442 8595; www.hotelbuenavistacr.com; d standard/deluxe/junior ste/villa incl breakfast US$100/120/145/180; P♿@🛜♨) About 5km north of

A BEACON FOR BOOK LOVERS

Book-a-holics rejoice! One of the best English-language bookstores in the country resides in Alajuela. Goodlight Books (☎2430-4083; www.goodlightbooks.com; Av 3 btwn Calles 1 & 3; ☺9am-6pm), managed by longtime expat Larry Coulter, offers a selection of over 9000 well-organized books (both used and new). He also keeps a worthwhile stock of difficult-to-find books on Costa Rica and the region, and there's a small array of volumes in Dutch and German. You will also find maps, guidebooks and a tiny cafe serving very tasty iced coffee.

The best part: the name. It was inspired by the Ernest Hemingway short story, *A Clean, Well-Lighted Place*.

Alajuela, this whitewashed Mediterranean-style hotel, perched on a mountaintop, has panoramic views of the nearby volcanoes. The best of the tastefully decorated, newly remodeled rooms have private balconies with valley views; five villas offer privacy along with wood-beamed ceilings, minibar and private balcony. A small trail leads from the hotel through a coffee *finca* and down to the main road.

Cala Inn B&B
HOTEL $

(☎2441-3219; www.hotelcalacr.com; Calle 2 btwn Avs 2 & 4; dm US$12, d with/without bathroom US$40/35, all incl breakfast; ☜) This small, modern eight-room spot overlooking Parque Juan Santamaría has spotless, simple parquet-floor rooms. The accommodation options vary in size and furnishings, from a dorm that sleeps four to a private room with king-sized bed. All share a kitchen and a cozy lounge with cable TV and foosball. Credit cards accepted.

Hotel Trotamundos
HOTEL $

(☎2430-5832; www.hoteltrotamundos.com; Av 5 btwn Calles 2 & 4; dm US$12, d with/without bathroom US$35/30, all incl breakfast; @) Though basic, the rooms here are clean and the service super-friendly. Three dorms and seven private units with cable TV – one with outdoor balcony facing the street – are nestled into a two-story house surrounding a small courtyard. There is a shared kitchen, public phones, free internet and a small communal area. Credit cards accepted.

Las Orquídeas Inn
HOTEL $$

(☎2433-7128; www.orquideasinn.com; s US$72-160, d US$82-170; P☺❀☜☎) On the road to San Pedro de Poás, this stately colonial-style structure houses 19 well-appointed rooms. Bright standard units with terra-cotta tile floors are decked out in rich textiles and situated steps away from a garden with

pool and Jacuzzi. Nicer suites come with polished wood floors, and some have great valley views.

Mango Verde Hostel
HOSTEL $

(☎2441-6330; mirafloresbb@hotmail.com; Av 3 btwn Calles 2 & 4; dm US$10, s/d US$15/25; @☜) This small, friendly hotel has nine basic rooms, though there's a decent-sized shared kitchen, a garden patio, plenty of hammocks and a lounge space.

Vida Tropical B&B
B&B $$

(☎2443-9576; www.vidatropical.com; Calle 3 north of Av 11; s/d incl breakfast US$45/60, additional person US$10, child under 12yr free; P@☜❀) In a quiet residential neighborhood, this Colombian-American–run house has five snug, simple guest rooms awash in bright murals (all but one share a bathroom). The well-tended backyard is perfect for catching some sun in a hammock, and laundry service is available. Rates include a free pick-up or drop-off at the airport.

Welcome to CR B&B
B&B $$

(☎2265-6563; www.welcometocr.com; d incl breakfast US$50; P@☜) The friendly Tico-American owners of this charming little place include airport pick-up or drop-off in the rate. Located about 5km east of the airport on the road to San Joaquín, it's a homey spot, with three double rooms with private bathroom and à la carte breakfast. They can book all manner of package tours.

Eating

For the cheapest meals, head to the enclosed Mercado Central (Calles 4 & 6 btwn Avs 1 & Central; ☺7am-6pm Mon-Sat). Self-caterers can stock up on groceries at the Palí (cnr Av 2 & Calle 10; ☺8am-8pm), MegaSuper (Av Central btwn Calles Central & 2; ☺8am-9pm) or Más X Menos (Av 1 btwn Calles 4 & 6; ☺7am-9pm Mon-Sat, 7am-8pm Sun).

Xandari
INTERNATIONAL $$$

(☑2443-2020; www.xandari.com; Xandari Resort Hotel & Spa; mains US$9-20; ☑) If you want to impress a date, you can't go wrong at this elegant restaurant with incredible views. The menu is a mix of Costa Rican and international, with plenty of vegetarian options. The restaurant utilizes the resort's homegrown organic produce, supplemented by locally grown organic produce whenever possible – making for tasty *and* feel-good gourmet meals.

Como en Casa
ARGENTINE $$$

(☑2441-7607; Plaza Real Alajuela; mains US$10-28; ☺11am-10pm Sun-Wed, to 11pm Thu-Sat; ☑) With its white tablecloths and festive atmosphere, this Argentinean grill is a popular weekend lunch spot, serving a comprehensive round-up of grilled meats and a strong selection of pastas (including vegetarian options). A good wine list is comprised mostly of Chilean and Argentinean vintages (about US$25 a bottle).

Jalepeños Central
MEXICAN $

(☑2430-4027; Calle 1 btwn Avs 3 & 5; mains US$3-8; ☺11:30am-9pm Mon-Sat) Run by an animated Colombian American from New York City, this popular Tex-Mex spot will introduce some much-needed spice into your diet. You'll also find Tico specialties, spit-roasted chicken and New York–style cheesecake.

Ceviche del Rey
PERUVIAN $$

(☑2440-0779; www.cevichedelreycr.com; Calle 2; mains US$5-18; ☺11am-11pm) It's worth the trek to the outskirts of town, north of Río Alajuela, for Peruvian food at this favorite family outpost. Expect Andean classics, such as fresh *ceviche* (seafood marinated in lime juice), the tender stir-fries known as *saltados* and even harder-to-find regional specialties such as *cabrito a la norteña* (stewed goat in cilantro) – but don't expect to find *cuy* (guinea pig).

Coffee Dreams Café
CAFE $

(☑2430-3970; cnr Calle 1 & Av 3; mains US$2-9; ☺8am-8pm Mon-Sat) For a variety of dishes along with the *típico* (traditional Costa Rican) eats, this adorable cafe is a reliably good place to dine or have a coffee accompanied by one of its rich desserts.

Diveno Natural
VEGETARIAN $

(☑2440-6723, 8703-0583; divenonatural@yahoo.com; Calle 3 btwn Avs 3 & 5; mains US$4-7; ☺7am-5pm Mon-Fri, 7am-9pm Sat, 11am-6pm Sun; ☑) Run by a friendly Adventist family, this bright, clean macrobiotic restaurant serves daily specials and a rotating selection of dishes that are always vegetarian. *Casados* (set meals) make use of soy-based mock meats, while fresh tamales and other specialties are often on the menu.

Café Las Delicias
CAFE $

(☑2440-3678; cnr Av 3 & Calle 1; dishes US$3-7; ☺8am-8pm Mon-Sat) A cute corner spot for cappuccino, iced coffee, chilled drinks, cheesecake and a highly yummy *pastelito de piña* (pineapple pastry).

La Mansarda
COSTA RICAN $$

(☑2441-4390; Calle Central btwn Avs Central & 2, 2nd fl; mains US$5-16; ☺11am-11pm) Grilled fish and chicken dishes are the specialty at this casual balcony restaurant overlooking the street. Save room for the *flan de coco* (coconut flan) or, better yet, a belt of Flor de Caña rum.

☆ Entertainment

The perennial Costa Rican soccer champions, Alajuela's own La Liga, play at the Estadio Morera Soto at the northeast end of town on Sundays during the *fútbol* (soccer) season. If you can't get tickets, stop by Cugini Bar & Restaurant (☑2440-6893; cnr Av Central & Calle 5; ☺noon-midnight Mon-Sat) where you can catch the game over a brew or tuck into a plate of hearty Italian-American pasta.

For beer and *bocas* (appetizers), the relaxed 4th-floor terrace bar at Alajuela Backpackers Boutique Hostel (p100) is the airiest spot in town. Otherwise, there's no shortage of dive bars and karaoke, if that's more your style.

ⓘ Information

Banco Nacional (Calle 2 btwn Avs Central & 1; ☺8:30am-3:45pm Mon-Fri) Centrally located ATM dispensing colones and US dollars.

Citibank (cnr Calle 2 & Av 6; ☺9am-5pm Mon-Fri, 9am-noon Sat) Has a drive-through and two ATMs.

Conexion (☑2431-2623; Calle 1 btwn Avs 3 & 5; per hr US$0.75; ☺8am-7pm Mon-Sat) Internet access, international calls and photocopying services.

Hospital San Rafael (☑2436-1000; www.hospitalsanrafael.sa.cr; Calle 4) Alajuela's new hospital, a three-story complex, 300m south of Av 10.

AWAY FROM SAN JOSÉ

For many visitors to Costa Rica, a night in San José is practically obligatory at the beginning or end of every trip. But if you have a car, you can instead arrange to stay at one of the following country inns. All lie within an hour's drive from the international airport – and all have incredible mountain scenery.

» Just outside Alajuela, Trapp Family Lodge (p100) and Xandari Resort Hotel & Spa (p100) have pastoral settings, 10 minutes from the airport.

» To the north, Poás Volcano Lodge (p104) and Poás Lodge (p104) are about 45 minutes to one hour from the airport.

» A 30-minute cruise along the Interamericana leads to Vista del Valle Plantation Inn (p106).

» The dreamy Finca Rosa Blanca (p115) will have you at less than 30 minutes from the airport check-in.

» Casa Amanecer (p111) in San Ramón is an easy 45-minute drive up the Interamericana.

» The drive to Villa Blanca Cloud Forest Hotel (p112) will take slightly over an hour, but the gorgeous scenery is worth the drive time.

Post Office (☑2443-2653; Av 5 btwn Calles Central & 1; ◷8am-5:30pm Mon-Fri, 8am-noon Sat)

Scotiabank (cnr Av Central & Calle 1; ◷8:30am-5pm Mon-Fri, 9am-1pm Sat) Has 24-hour ATM.

ⓘ Getting There & Away

Taxis (around US$7) go to the Juan Santamaría International Airport from central Alajuela.

There is no central bus terminal; instead, a number of small terminals and bus stops dot the southwestern part of the city. Note that there are two Tuasa terminals (east and west) right across the street from each other.

Atenas (Calle 10 btwn Avs Central & 2; US$1.25; 30 minutes) Departs half-hourly from 6am to 5:30pm Monday to Friday.

Butterfly Farm (cnr Av 2 & Calle 8; US$0.75; 30 minutes) Departs hourly from 8:30am to 7:30pm.

Heredia (☑2442-6900; Calle 8 btwn Avs Central & 1; US$0.75) Departs every 15 minutes from 5am to 10pm.

La Garita/Zoo Ave (Calle 10 btwn Av 2 & Central; US$0.50; 20 minutes) Departs half-hourly from 6am-5:30pm, Monday to Friday.

San José (Tuasa West) (Calle 8 btwn Avs Central & 1; US$1; 45 minutes) Departs every 10 minutes from 5am to 11pm.

San José via Juan Santamaría International Airport (Av 4 btwn Calles 2 & 4; Station Wagon; US$1; 45 minutes) Departs every 10 minutes 4am- midnight.

Sarchí (Calle 8 btwn Avs Central & 1; US$0.75; 30 minutes) Departs half-hourly from 5am through to 10pm.

Volcán Poás (Tuasa West) (☑2442-6900; Calle 8 btwn Avs Central & 1; US$7; 4½ hours round-trip) Departs around 9:15am, returns around 2:30pm.

Parque Nacional Volcán Poás

Just 37km north of Alajuela, via a winding and scenic road, is the most heavily trafficked national park in Costa Rica, Parque Nacional Volcán Poás (☑2482-2165; admission US$10; ◷8am-3:30pm). And for those who want to peer into an active volcano – without the hardship of hiking up to one – this is ideal. Volcán Poás (2704m) had its last blowout in 1953, which formed the enormous crater, measuring 1.3km across and 300m deep.

Poás offers visitors the wonderful opportunity to watch the bubbling and steaming cauldron belch sulfurous mud and water hundreds of meters into the air. There are two other craters, as well, one of which contains a striking sapphire-blue lake ringed by high-altitude forest.

The main crater at Poás continues to be active to varying degrees. In fact, the park was briefly closed in May 1989 after a minor eruption sent volcanic ash spouting more than 1km into the air, and lesser activity closed the park intermittently in 1995. In recent years, however, Poás has posed no imminent threat, though scientists still monitor it closely.

🏃 Activities

Hiking

From the visitors center, you will find a paved wheelchair-accessible path that leads to a crater lookout. Because of the toxic sulfuric-acid fumes that are emitted from the cauldron, visitors are prohibited from descending into the crater.

From the lookout, two trails branch out – to the right is Sendero Botos, to the left Sendero Escalonia. Sendero Botos is a short, 30-minute round-trip hike through dwarf cloud forest, which is the product of acidic air and freezing temperatures. Here you can wander and look at bromeliads, lichens and mosses clinging to the curiously shaped and twisted trees growing in the volcanic soil. Birds abound, especially the magnificent fiery-throated hummingbird, a high-altitude specialty of Costa Rica. The trail ends at Laguna Botos, a peculiar cold-water lake that has filled in one of the extinct craters.

Sendero Escalonia is a slightly longer trail through taller forest, which gets significantly less traffic than the other parts of the park. While hiking on the trail, look for other highland specialties, including the sooty robin, black guans, screech owls and even the odd quetzal (especially from February to April). Although mammals are infrequently sighted in the park, coyotes and the endemic montane squirrel are present.

👉 Tours

Many companies offer daily tours to the volcano, but these can be overpriced (US$40 to US$100) and you'll usually arrive at the volcano at around 10am – right when the clouds start rolling in. Also, readers complain that they're often rushed off the crater, though there always seems to be time for stopping at a souvenir store on the way back. As always, shop around and ask questions.

It's just as easy to visit the volcano using public transportation from San José or Alajuela. And, if you have two or more people in your group, the best deal is to rent a car or hire a taxi for the day and visit the volcano at your leisure.

🛏️ Sleeping & Eating

There is no camping or other accommodations inside the park itself.

ON THE ROAD TO POÁS

The road up to the park is lined with stands selling fruit, cheese and snacks – as well as countless touristy spots serving typical Tico fare – so you won't go hungry. Bring your own bottled water, though, as the tap water is undrinkable.

Poás Lodge   B&B $$

(☎2482-1091; www.poaslodge.com; 4km south of park entrance; d US$55-70, ste US$90, all incl breakfast; 🅿🛜) Five comfortable, contemporary rooms perched high on the slope of Poás all look onto stunning Central Valley views. Each room is different, but all include coffeemaker, satellite TV and comfortable beds. The roadside cafe has huge picture windows on three sides, through which you can watch fog swirling down the mountain or, on clearer days, down to the Nicoya Peninsula. Stop in for a cappuccino or seasonal specialty – the cafe uses organic and locally grown produce as much as possible.

Lagunillas Lodge   LODGE $$

(☎8959-0119, 8835-2899; www.lagunillaslodge.com; d US$30-35, d cabinas US$50) This lodge and farm is the closest accommodation to Volcán Poás, signposted about 2km before the park. While lodgings are basic, the family that operates it is charming. Rustic log *cabinas* offer stellar views, hot-water showers and heaters. Hiking trails and horseback rides are available. There's also a fish pond where you can catch your dinner, and a restaurant that will cook it up for you (from US$5). To get down its steep dirt road, 4WD is absolutely, positively required. Call ahead.

East of Poás

About 10km before the entrance to the national park, a winding, paved road heads east through Poasito, before arriving in the village of Vara Blanca, where it turns north and leads to the famed La Paz Waterfall Gardens. This is scenic, uncluttered countryside – the ideal place for a pleasant drive or to spend the night.

🔝 Poás Volcano Lodge   LODGE $$$

(☎2482-2194; www.poasvolcanolodge.com; 8.75km northwest of Fraijanes; d standard, US$100, junior ste US$130, master ste US$200-300, all incl breakfast; 🅿@🛜) Find contemporary class at this high-altitude dairy farm, where a dozen rooms combine rusticity and elegance in an idyllic rural setting. Several suites are decked out with either balcony or hot tub in a private garden, and all guests have access to several inviting common rooms, includ-

LA PAZ WATERFALL GARDENS

This garden and hotel complex is host to 3.5km of hiking trails and five scenic waterfalls, including the largest, **La Catarata de la Paz (Peace Waterfall)**. Visitors can also tour a butterfly conservatory, an aviary, an orchid display, a serpentarium and wildlife refuge that houses native cats of Costa Rica. It's an ideal spot for active seniors and small children (there are even special children's activities), since many of the trails are smooth and well maintained.

You can stay on-site at the Peace Lodge (☑2482-2100; www.waterfallgardens.com; La Paz Waterfall Gardens; d standard/deluxe/villa US$315/375/495, additional adult/child US$40/20; P 🛜 🌊 ♿), whose over-the-top rooms boast gorgeous valley views, private deck with Jacuzzi, fireplace and huge bathroom with another Jacuzzi tub. There's also a heated outdoor infinity pool, complete with heated waterfall.

ing a games room and a library. The property also maintains more than 3km of hiking trails offering views of the volcano – and all the way to Nicaragua – on clear days.

Colbert Restaurant   FRENCH $$
(☑2482-2776; www.colbert.co.cr; 6km east of Poasito; mains US$5-17; ☺noon-9pm Fri-Wed) At this charming French restaurant with lovely views, you'll find a chef who looks like he's straight out of Central Casting: Joël Suire is not only French, he is amply moustachioed and wears a toque. Naturally, the menu is loaded with traditional French items such as onion soup and house-made paté. A good wine list (bottles from US$16) is strong on vintages from South America and France.

❶ Information

Some 250,000 people visit the park annually, making Poás the most packed national park in the country; weekends get especially jammed. The best time to go is on a weekday in the dry season. In particular, arrive early in the morning before the clouds obscure the view. If the summit is cloudy, hike to the other craters and return to the cauldron later – winds shift and sometimes the cloud cover is blown away.

Near the entrance, there is a visitors center with a souvenir stand, a coffee shop, a small museum and informative videos that play hourly between 9am and 3pm.

Be advised that overnight temperatures can drop below freezing, and it may be windy and cold during the day. Also, Poás receives almost 4000mm of rainfall each year. Dress accordingly.

❶ Getting There & Away

Taxis to the park cost around US$50 from San José or US$30 from Alajuela. If you're driving, the road from Alajuela to the volcano is well signed.

From San José (US$7, five hours), Tuasa buses depart 8:30am daily from Av 2 between Calles 12 and 14, stopping in Alajuela at about 9:15am and returning at 2:30pm. Most of these buses also make a pit stop at one of the roadside restaurants along the way.

West to Atenas

From Alajuela, a narrow, paved highway leads 25km west to the lovely mountain town of Atenas. It's a nice day trip, with a perfect climate and a charming rural atmosphere.

LA GARITA

In an area that attracts scientists who research maize, it is not surprising that this town – spread out along the road that connects Alajuela to Atenas – is lined with restaurants whose specialty is corn: corn soup, cornbread, tamales and *chorreadas* (savory corn pancakes) to be exact. It's located 11km west of Alajuela and worth the pilgrimage if you are looking for good country eats. The road is dotted with little family-run establishments where you can sample these regional treats.

About 10km west of Alajuela, you'll find Zoo Ave (☑2433-8989; www.zooavecostarica.org; La Garita; adult/child US$15/4; ☺9am-5pm; P ♿), a well-designed animal park sheltering more than 115 species of birds on colorful, squawking display in a relaxing 14-hectare setting. The zoo houses all four species of Costa Rican monkey, wild cats, reptiles and other native critters, many of which are rescues. Though technically a zoo, it is also an important animal breeding center that aims to reintroduce native species into the wild; admission fees fund wildlife rescue, rehabilitation, release and conservation programs.

SPANISH SCHOOLS IN THE CENTRAL VALLEY

Unless otherwise noted, prices are given for five four-hour days of instruction, with/ without a week's homestay. Prices include two meals a day.

» **Adventure Education Center** (☑2556 4609; www.adventurespanishschool.com; US$460/325)

» **Amerispan** (☑in USA & Canada 800-879-6640; www.amerispan.com; US$730/555)

» **Centro Panamericano de Idiomas** (☑2265 6306; www.cpi-edu.com; US$510/360)

» **Finca la Flor de Paraíso** (☑2534 8003; www.la-flor.org; with homestay US$450)

» **Intensa** (☑2442-3843, in USA & Canada 866-277-1352; www.intensa.com; US$437/307) Also located in Heredia.

» **Intercultura** (☑2260-8480, in USA & Canada 866-978-6668; www.interculturacostarica. com; US$455/300)

» **Montaña Linda** (☑2533-3640; www.montanalinda.com; with accommodation US$240)

Continue west and the road slides over the Interamericana. Just north of the intersection, La Casona del Maíz (☑2433-5363; mains US$5-15; ⊘7am-9pm; ⊞) is usually jam-packed with families enjoying the spectacular Tico country cooking. The menu is heavy on the grilled meats and corn dishes, though there are veggie casados as well. The *chorreadas* are excellent, but don't leave without sampling the tasty corn soup, studded with sweet, fresh kernels, or the falling-off-the-bone pork ribs *(costillas de cerdo)*.

Buses (US$0.90, 30 minutes) run between Alajuela and La Garita, via Zoo Ave, every half-hour.

ATENAS

This small village, on the historic *camino de carretas* (oxcart trail) that once carried coffee beans as far as Puntarenas, is best known as having the most pleasant climate in the world, at least according to a 1994 issue of *National Geographic*. It's not too heavy on sights, but springtime is always in the air.

About 1km before the center of town, you'll see the Monumento al Boyero (Monument to the Oxcart Driver) on the north side of the road.

In town, the very appealing plaza is a pleasant, shady spot to enjoy a scoop of gelato from Gelly's (☑2455-0044; gellys.atenas@gmail. com; gelato US$1.50-3; ⊘2-7pm Mon, 11:30am-7pm Tue-Fri, 11:30am-8pm Sat-Sun; ⊜), the astroturf-carpeted gelatería on the plaza's west side.

On the eastern end of town, you'll find the typical Restaurant La Trocha del Boyero (☑2446-0533; casados US$5, mains US$6-13; ⊘11am-9pm Tue-Sun; ⊜⊞). Tico families pour into the pleasant outdoor deck on

weekends for fresh trout (in season) and heaping bowls of *chifrijo* (rice and beans with fried pork, corn chips and fresh tomato salsa). It is located on the main road to Alajuela, 300m east of the gas station, and 100m to the south. Look for a sign at the turnoff.

Only five minutes from town is the lovely hillside Vista Atenas B&B (☑2446-4272; www.vistaatenas.com; d/tr incl breakfast US$75/85, cabina/casita US$75/100; ⊜⊞). This bright and peaceful spot has beautiful valley views from the swimming pool, and the friendly managers are very helpful.

Half-hourly buses connect the village of Atenas to Alajuela and San José from 5:40am to 10pm. The area is quite spread out, however, and best navigated by car.

Northwest to Sarchí

To the northwest of Alajuela, the carefully cultivated hills are home to the picturesque agricultural towns of Grecia (22km), Sarchí (29km), Naranjo (35km) and Zarcero (52km) – among others – many of which are popular weekend getaways for *josefinos* in search of fresh mountain air.

ROSARIO AREA

From the Interamericana, near the road to Grecia, you'll see the well-signed turnoff for the Vista del Valle Plantation Inn (☑2450-0900, 2451-1165; www.vistadelvalle.com; d incl breakfast US$100-185; ⊞⊜@⊜⊞), adjoining the Zona Protectora Río Grande. Here you'll find 17 individually designed villas overlooking a forested gorge. Private trails lead to a 90m-high waterfall in the adjoining reserve, and the staff can arrange massages and horseback tours. There is also an open-air **restaurant** (mains US$10 to US$20) serving fine Costa Rican fusion cuisine.

Two kilometers west of the turnoff to Grecia, you'll find Tropical Bungee (☎8980-5757, bridge 2450-3434, office 2248-2212; www.bungee.co.cr; 1st/2nd jump US$75/35), where you can arrange to hurl yourself off the 80m-high bridge over the Río Colorado. It's easiest to make a reservation online.

GRECIA
POP 12,400

The village of Grecia – once named the 'Cleanest Little Town in Latin America' – is centered on a pleasant Parque Central (Central Plaza) that is anchored by one of the most charming churches in Costa Rica.

◎ Sights

Catedral de la Mercedes   CHURCH
At the heart of town you'll find the incredibly quaint Catedral de la Mercedes, a red metal structure that was prefabricated in Belgium and shipped to Costa Rica in 1897 – and resembles a gingerbread church. It has an airy nave, bright Spanish tile floors and a Gothic-style altar covered in marble.

World of Snakes   ZOO
(☎2494-3700; adult/child US$11/6; ☺8am-4pm) Grecia's premiere attraction lies 1.5km south of the bus station. It is a well-run breeding center focused on supporting endangered snake populations. More than 150 snakes (representing more than 50 species) are displayed in large cages. Informative tours are given in English, German or Spanish.

Rock Bridge   BRIDGE
A couple of kilometers to the south of Grecia, a bend in the road leads to an 18th-century rock bridge, which connects the hamlets of Puente de Piedra and Rincón de Salas. Locals say that the only other rock bridge like this is in China, and some tales have it that it was built by the devil. In 1994 it was declared a National Site of Historic Interest. With all that hype, don't be surprised that it's small. Ask for directions, as it's hard to find.

Las Cataratas de Los Chorros   WATERFALL
(admission US$5; ☺8am-5pm Tue-Sun) About 7km south of Grecia, toward Santa Gertrudis, are two gorgeous waterfalls and a swimming hole surrounded by picnic tables. It's a popular spot for weekending couples. Again, get detailed directions before setting out.

🍴 Sleeping & Eating

A Pali (☎2444-6696; ☺8am-7pm Mon-Thu, 8am-8pm Fri-Sat, 8am-6pm Sun) supermarket sits to the southeast of the church. Cheap eats can be found at the lunch counters and shops in the bus station, and a farmers market takes place north of town on Friday afternoons and Saturday mornings.

B&B Grecia   B&B $$
(☎2494-2573; www.bandbgrecia.com; s US$35-45, d US$45-55, additional person US$10, all incl breakfast; 🐾) This tiny B&B located 150m south of Parque Central maintains three spotless rooms, including one that comes with a Jacuzzi. The lovely owners Denny and Rachelle can help arrange area tours, and have created a relaxed, homey environment here.

Mangifera Hostel   HOSTEL $
(☎2494-6065; www.mangiferahostel.com; on the north side of Parque Central; dm/s/d US$12/17/28, d with bathroom US$34, all incl breakfast; P🐾) This cozy hostel feels instantly welcoming, with its wood floors and friendly ambience. It has only five rooms, two of which are dorms. There's a shared kitchen and small garden in the back. Laundry service is available.

Hotel Aeromundo   HOTEL $$
(☎2494-0094; www.hotelaeromundo.com; s US$40, d US$60-70, apt US$75-100, all incl breakfast; P🐾🐾) About 100m east of the cathedral, this tidy spot has 14 snug, carpeted rooms with cable TV surrounding an interior courtyard draped in plants. Three apartments are stocked with full kitchens. Credit cards accepted.

Café Delicias   CAFE $
(☎2494-2093; dishes US$2-5; ☺8am-7pm; 🐾) For rich coffee drinks and snacks – as well as free wi-fi – hit this enjoyable spot near the southwest corner of Parque Central.

❶ Information

The **Banco de Costa Rica** (south side of cathedral; ☺9am-4pm Mon-Fri) has a 24-hour ATM.

❶ Getting There & Away

The bus station is 300m west of the cathedral.

San José US$1, one hour, departs every 15 minutes from 5:30am to 8:30pm, half-hourly on weekends.

Sarchí, connecting to Naranjo US$0.50, 30 minutes, departs every 25 minutes from 5am to 8:30pm.

SARCHÍ
POP 3600

Welcome to Costa Rica's most famous crafts center, where artisans produce the ornately painted oxcarts and leather-and-wood furnishings for which the Central Valley is known. You'll know you've arrived because just about everything is covered in the signature geometric designs – even city hall. Yes, it's a tourist trap, but it's a pretty one. The town is stretched out along a road that weaves through hilly countryside.

Most people come in for an afternoon of shopping and call it a day, but if you have time on your hands, it is possible to meet different artisans and custom order a creation.

Sarchí is divided by the Río Trojas into Sarchí Norte and Sarchí Sur, and is rather spread out, straggling for several kilometers along the main road from Grecia to Naranjo. It's easiest to explore by private car.

In Sarchí Norte, you'll find the heart of the village, including a twin-towered **church**, some restaurants and *pulperías* (corner stores), and what is purported to be the **world's largest oxcart** (photo op!).

◉ Sights

Jardín Botánico Else Kientzler   GARDENS
(☎2454-2070; www.elsegarden.com; 400m north of soccer field, Sarchí Norte; adult/child US$15/10; ☺8am-4pm; ⊕) This well-tended botanical garden has 2km of trails winding through more than 2000 types of clearly labeled plants, including succulents, fruit trees, palms, heliconias and orchids. There's also a picnic area and an excellent playground, outfitted with sturdy multi-level climbing structures and even a zip line.

🛏 Sleeping & Eating

A great farmers market is held on Fridays behind Fábrica de Carretas Eloy Alfaro, where you can grab homemade snacks, *queso palmito* (a local cheese) and lots of produce.

Hotel Paraíso Río Verde   B&B $$
(☎2454-3003; www.hotelparaisorioverde.com; San Pedro de Sarchí; r US$30-40, bungalow US$60, all incl breakfast; P 🖥 🏊) Pickings are slim in town, but if you have your own wheels, this German-Tica–run B&B is the best place to stay in Sarchí. Located in the highland village of San Pedro de Sarchí, the property overlooks coffee plantations and vistas of volcanoes Poás, Barva and Irazú. Two private rooms are available in the main house, while the spacious bungalows (with kitchenette) afford a bit more privacy.

Cabinas Mandy   CABINA $
(☎8814-1555; 300m north of fire station, Sarchí Norte; s/d US$16/20; P) This small, basic budget option offers simple, well-kept rooms with cable TV and private hot shower.

Hotel Daniel Zamora   HOTEL $
(☎2454-4596; 50m north of soccer field, Sarchí Norte; d US$20-24; 🖥) On a quiet street in Sarchí Norte, the Zamora is an acceptable, basic spot. Seven tile-floor rooms have cable TV and private hot shower.

Las Carretas   COSTA RICAN $
(☎2454-1633; Sarchí Sur; mains US$7-14; ☺11am-9pm) One of the most popular spots for a lunch break is this family restaurant adjacent to the Fábrica de Carretas Joaquín Chavarrí, serving up *típico* cuisine. There's a bounteous Sunday buffet (US$12; from 11:30am to 3:30pm).

Super Mariscos   SEAFOOD $
(☎2454-4330; mains US$7-15; ☺11am-10pm Tue-Sun; 🖥) At a low-lying bend in the road in Sarchí Sur, Super Mariscos serves up good *ceviche*, fish tacos and seafood galore, as well as pasta and a few beef dishes. Everything comes with a side of fries and a smidgen of salad. To top off the dining experience, the otherwise nondescript decor features a fake shark busting out of one wall.

❶ Information

On the soccer field, about 100m south of the church, **Banco Nacional** (☺8:30am-3:45pm Mon-Fri) changes money.

❶ Getting There & Around

If you're driving from San José, from the Interamericana, take the signed exit to Grecia and from there follow the road north to Sarchí. If you're coming from the west, take the turnoff north to Naranjo, then head east to Sarchí.

Buses arrive and depart from Sarchí Norte.

Alajuela US$0.80, 30 minutes, departs half-hourly from 5am to 10pm.

Grecia US$0.80, 20 minutes, departs half-hourly from 5am-8:30pm.

San José US$2, 1½ hours, departs half-hourly between 5am and 10pm.

ZARCERO
POP 3800

North of Naranjo, the road winds for 20km until it reaches Zarcero's 1736m perch at the western end of the Cordillera Central. This is a gorgeous location: the mountains look as if they've been lifted from landscape paintings

SHOPPING SARCHÍ

Most travelers come to Sarchí for one thing only: *carretas*, the elaborate, colorfully painted oxcarts that are the unofficial souvenir of Costa Rica – and official symbol of the Costa Rican worker. In Sarchí, these come ready for the road (oxen sold separately) or in scaled-down versions. But the area produces plenty of other curios as well: leather-and-wood furniture (including those incredible rocking chairs that collapse for shipping), wood tableware and trinkets emblazoned with the colorful mandala-design popularized by *carretas*.

Workshops are usually open from 8am to 4pm daily; they accept credit cards and US dollars; and they can arrange international shipping for you. Following is a list of some of the most respected and popular spots, though with more than 200 vendors, it pays to shop around as prices and quality vary.

» **Coopearsa** (✆2454-4196, 2454-4050; www.coopearsa.com; 200m west of soccer field, Sarchí Norte) Kitsch-filled paradise of *carretas*, woodwork and painted feathers.

» **Fábrica de Carretas Eloy Alfaro** (✆2454-4131; 100m north of Palí supermarket, Sarchí Norte) The country's oldest workshop; produced the massive oxcart in Sarchí's main plaza.

» **Fábrica de Carretas Joaquín Chaverri** (✆2454-4411; Sarchí Sur) Oldest and best-known factory; watch artisans doing their meticulous work in the small studio in the back.

and the climate is famously fresh. But the real reason you're here is to see the country's most surreal shrubbery.

Parque Francisco Alvarado, in front of the blue Iglesia de San Rafael (built 1895), was just a normal plaza until the 1960s, when a gardener named Evangelisto Blanco suddenly became inspired to shave the ordinary, mild-mannered topiary into a bizarre series of drippy, abstract shapes. Over the years, these have morphed into fanciful chimeras, blobby dancing creatures and a double tunnel of melting arches. In other words, bring your camera.

Zarcero is a center for Costa Rica's organic-farming movement. You can find unusual varieties of pesticide-free goodies all over town, and the surrounding mountains are just perfect for an afternoon picnic. If there was ever a place where the roadside stands are worth it, this is it. Winding country lanes in the area are all lined with stands selling fresh cashews, honey, sweets and *queso palmito*, a locally made cheese with a delicate taste (and goes well with fresh tomatoes and basil).

If you brought your swimsuit, stop at **Piscinas Apamar** (✆2463-3674; www.apamar.org; 400m west of the park, on the road to Guadalupe; adult/child US$3/2.40; ⏰7am-3pm Mon-Fri, 8am-3pm Sat-Sun), on the road to Guadalupe (up the hill, behind the Musmanni), where there's a huge indoor swimming pool and several hot tubs.

Just north of the church is **Hotel Don Beto** (✆2463-3137; www.hoteldonbeto.com; d with/without bathroom US$35/25, tr US$45; P🖙), a comfortable spot that houses eight tidy rooms with hardwood floors – many come with private balcony. The helpful Tico owners can organize trips throughout the area, including excursions to the nearby Los Ángeles Cloud Forest Adventure Park or the Parque Nacional Juan Castro Blanco.

Hourly buses traveling between San José and Ciudad Quesada stop at Zarcero, though some buses may be full by the time they reach Zarcero, particularly on weekends. There are also buses from Alajuela, San Ramón and Grecia.

BAJOS DEL TORO
POP 250

A road snakes east out of Zarcero, through winding hillsides dotted with family farms, up into the lower reaches of the area's cloud-forest ecosystem. If you were looking for a little piece of Costa Rica where everybody knows everybody, then look no further. This 250-person town (full name: Bajos del Toro Amarillo) is rural idyll at its finest.

There are no banks or internet cafes. Bring all the cash you need. The following businesses are all listed in order as you drive into town.

LAS FIESTAS DE PALMARES

If you're around in mid-January, be sure to detour through Palmares for the rowdy annual **Las Fiestas de Palmares**. The 10-day, beer-soaked extravaganza features carnival rides, a *tope* (horse parade), fireworks, big-name bands, small-name bands, exotic dancers, fried food, *guaro* tents and the densest population of merry Ticos you've ever seen. It is one of the biggest events in the country – crowds can reach upwards of 10,000 people. For the other 355 days of the year, Palmares is a tumbleweed town, where life is centered on the ornate stained-glass church in the attractive, palm-fringed central plaza.

Sleeping & Eating

Bosque de Paz Rain/Cloud Forest Lodge & Biological Reserve LODGE $$$
(☏2234-6676; www.bosquedepaz.com; per person incl 3 meals US$116-168; P) This 1000-hectare reserve has more than 22km of trails in tropical old-growth forest, as well as a 12-room hacienda-style inn with a dozen whitewashed, terra-cotta tiled rooms with large windows that offer forest views. More significantly, the area is part of an important wilderness corridor between Parque Nacional Volcán Poás and Parque Nacional Juan Castro Blanco. Needless to say, bird-watching is a specialty. Vegetarian and vegan diets can be accommodated; rates are based on double occupancy. Advance reservations recommended.

TOP CHOICE **El Silencio** LODGE $$$
(☏2761-0301, reservations 2476-0303; www.elsilenciolodge.com; s/d incl 3 meals and 1 guided hike US$385/480; P🐾🛜) When it comes to absolute serenity, there are few places in Costa Rica that can beat this superbly designed mountain lodge that doesn't just talk the environmental talk but walks it as well. No earth was moved to construct the 16 simply but luxuriously designed *cabina* suites stocked with minibar, fireplace, rocking chair and private deck with Jacuzzi. In addition, there is a spa, 8km worth of trails (one of which leads to a stunning waterfall) and a health-conscious menu stocked with organic local foods and strong on vegetarian dishes. Most all of the charming, bilingual Tico staff hail from the region.

Soda Restaurante Nené COSTA RICAN $
(☏2761-1932; mains US$6-7; ☺8am-5pm) This small tourist complex has stocked tilapia and trout ponds where you can catch your own and then have it fried or grilled with garlic at the on-site *soda* (cheap, informal lunch counter). May be closed during the low season.

Hotel y Villas Bajo del Toro HOTEL $$
(☏2476-0696; r US$50; P) Four spacious ceramic-tile rooms have private balcony, rocking chair and views of a rushing river. Units sleep up to four and come equipped with hot-water bathroom, coffeemaker and mini-fridge. A small *soda* serves typical meals. This is a weekend spot, so prices may be flexible midweek.

Restaurante Típico Toro Amarillo COSTA RICAN $
(☏2761-1918; breakfast US$3-4, casados US$5-6; ☺6am-6pm) Down the street, in a circular wood building, you'll find this rustic country eatery – with a changing daily menu – run by a local women's cooperative. It has two tidy *cabinas* (double US$24) in the back, both with private bathroom and hot water.

❶ Getting There & Away

If driving north from the Interamericana through Zarcero, take a right immediately after the church and head north about 15km. The road is almost entirely paved but the last stretch is steep and rocky; 4WD is recommended. There are daily buses from Zarcero.

PARQUE NACIONAL JUAN CASTRO BLANCO

This 143-sq-km **national park** (admission US$10, camping per person US$3) was created in 1992 to protect the slopes of Volcán Platanar (2183m) and Volcán Porvenir (2267m) from logging. The headwaters for five major rivers originate here as well, making this one of the most important watersheds in the country.

The park is in limbo, federally protected but still privately owned by various plantation families – only those parts that have already been purchased by the government are technically open to travelers. As yet, there is almost no infrastructure at all for visitors, though there is a Minae office (☑2460-7600) in El Sucre, north of Zarcero, where you can pay fees for camping or day use. However, the office is frequently closed, and fees are rarely collected.

The park is most popular among anglers as each of the five rivers is brimming with trout. The lack of infrastructure and tourist traffic means that your chances of spotting rare wildlife (such as quetzals, black guans and curassow) are very high – but it also means that maintained trails are almost nonexistent. It is best to go with a guide, which can be arranged through tour agencies and hotels in the area.

SAN RAMÓN
POP 10,400

The colonial town of San Ramón is no wallflower in the pageant of Costa Rican history. The 'City of Presidents and Poets' has sent five men to the country's highest office, including ex-president Rodrigo Carazo, who built a tourist lodge a few kilometers to the north at the entrance to the Los Ángeles Cloud Forest.

◉ Sights

Iglesia de San Ramón   CHURCH
At the center of this charming agricultural town, you'll see the twin spires of the ash-gray Iglesia de San Ramón. The interiors are definitely worth checking out: it has a lovely baroque-style altar, Spanish-tile floors and neat rows of wood pews.

Parque Central   PLAZA
The best time to visit is on Saturday during the farmers market, when cheeses and chorizo are on display and the local ladies can be found shopping and gossiping.

Museo de San Ramón   MUSEUM
(☑2437-9851; admission free; ⊙9am-5pm Tue-Sat)
On the north side of the park, this museum maintains a few simple exhibits devoted to detailing life in Costa Rica during the colony and the early republic. The adjacent gallery shows rotating art exhibitions.

⌂ Sleeping & Eating

TOP CHOICE Casa Amanecer   B&B $$
(☑2445-2100; www.casa-amanecer-cr.com; s/d incl breakfast US$60/70; P⑤) Located a 10-minute drive northeast of San Ramón, on the road to Concepción, is this sleekly designed B&B run by Christopher and Luisa. Here you will find four graceful contemporary rooms with polished concrete floors, orthopedic beds and wonderful valley views. The owners put great effort into being environmentally conscious, from the veggie breakfasts to the biodegradable cleaning products. Additional meals, in-room massages (from US$30) and airport transfers (US$50 for up to four people) can be arranged with advance reservation.

Hotel La Posada   INN $$
(☑2445-7359; www.posadahotel.net; 400m north of the church; d standard/deluxe incl breakfast US$60/70; P✳@⑤) Well-maintained rooms at this pleasant inn surround a lush, plant-filled courtyard. They are somewhat baroque-looking, outfitted with massive, handcrafted beds that lie somewhere on the design continuum between Louis XIV and African safari. All have mini-fridge and cable TV; the more expensive units come with Jacuzzis and some are wheelchair-accessible.

La Paquereña   COLOMBIAN $
(☑2447-1364; 175m north of ICE building; mains US$3-9; ⊙7am-5pm Mon-Sat, 9am-2pm Sun) Cozy and rustic, with log walls and a vintage cast-iron kitchen tableau on an interior balcony, this friendly *soda* serves up *casados* with a Colombian twist, *salchipapas* (sausage and fries), sandwiches, and grilled fish and beef.

ⓘ Information

Banco de Costa Rica (300m west of Parque Central; ⊙9am-4pm) Has an ATM.
Banco Nacional (100m south of southwest corner of church; ⊙8:30am-3:45pm Mon-Fri, 9am-1pm Sat) Has an ATM that also dispenses US dollars.

ⓘ Getting There & Away

There are hourly buses to San José, as well as frequent buses to Ciudad Quesada via Zarcero. Buses depart from Calle 16 between Avs 1 and 3.

LOS ÁNGELES CLOUD FOREST ADVENTURE PARK

This private reserve (☑2289-6569; per person US$20-45; ⊙8am-4pm), 18km north of San Ramón, is centered on a lodge and dairy ranch that was once owned by ex-president Rodrigo Carazo. Some 800 hectares of primary and secondary forest have 11km of foot trails that lead to towering waterfalls and misty cloud forest vistas. The appeal of this cloud forest (adjacent to Monteverde) is that it is comparatively untouristed, which means you will have a good chance of observing wildlife (jaguars and ocelots have been spotted), and the bird-watching is fantastic.

Bilingual naturalist guides are available to lead hikes (per person US$30) and guided horseback-riding trips (per hour US$20). Alternatively, you can zip along the tree tops on the reserve's obligatory canopy tour (per person US$45).

A taxi to the reserve and hotel costs about US$15 from San Ramón, and the turnoff is well signed from the Interamericana.

🛏 Sleeping

TOP CHOICE Villa Blanca Cloud Forest Hotel & Nature Reserve   LODGE $$$
(✆2401-3800, in USA & Canada 877-256-8399; www.villablanca-costarica.com; d superior/deluxe/honeymoon US$189/210/235, additional person US$50, child under 6yr free; 🅿@🛜♨) Occupying a cloud forest aerie, this lodge underwent a major update in 2004 to its current gorgeous state. Thirty-five free-standing *casitas* (little houses) deliberately eschew TVs, but do have wi-fi, private terraces, minibar and safe. Certified at the highest level of sustainability, the lodge practices composting, recycling and energy usage policies. The lodge also houses a spa, yoga facility, games room, movie theater screening films nightly and a lovely restaurant, and staff can arrange hikes and other tours.

Tierras Enamoradas   LODGE $$$
(Lands in Love; ✆2447-9331; www.landsinlove.com; 32km from San Ramón to La Fortuna; d incl breakfast US$118, additional person US$22; 🅿🛜❄) This Israeli-run vegetarian lodge has eclectic rooms with bright floral motifs, a lounge, an outdoor swimming pool, pet hotel (US$20 per night) and a plethora of adventure activities, from a canopy tour to canyoning to horseback riding. The restaurant serves an international mix of (rather pricey) vegetarian and vegan dishes. It is colorfully and extremely well signposted.

HEREDIA AREA

Though microchips produced in Heredia have become one of Costa Rica's most important exports, the region also remains a vital coffee producer and a gateway to one of Costa Rica's largest swaths of highland forest, Parque Nacional Braulio Carrillo.

Heredia

POP 21,500

During the 19th century, La Ciudad de las Flores (the City of the Flowers) was home to a *cafetalero* (coffee grower) aristocracy that made its fortune exporting Costa Rica's premium blend. Today the historic center retains some of this well-bred air, with a leafy main square, and low-lying buildings reflecting Spanish-colonial architectural style.

Although only 11km from San José, Heredia is – in personality – at a remove from the grit and grime of the capital. Yet it still maintains a cosmopolitan vibe – largely due to the high-tech corporations that have settled amid the area's coffee *fincas*. In addition, the Universidad Nacional (National University) keeps things a touch bohemian, and on any afternoon, you're bound to find local bars and cafes abuzz with young folk idling away their time.

Heredia is also an excellent base from which to explore the little-visited Volcán Barva, within the Parque Nacional Braulio Carrillo.

◎ Sights

Iglesia de la Inmaculada Concepción   CHURCH
(east side of Parque Central) Built in 1797, this church facing a wide, pleasant Parque Central is still in use. The church's thick-walled, squat construction is attractive in a Volkswagen Beetle sort of way. The solid shape has withstood the earthquakes that have damaged or destroyed almost all the other buildings in Costa Rica that date from this time.

El Fortín   TOWER
(north of Parque Central) This 1867 guard tower is the last remaining turret of a Spanish fortress and the official symbol of Heredia. It's a national historic site, but because of its fragile state, its passageways are closed to the public.

Casa de la Cultura   MUSEUM
(✆2261-4485; cnr Calle Central & Av Central; admission free; ⊙hours vary) The Casa de la Cultura occupies a low-lying Spanish structure that dates back to the 18th century. The building at one point served as the residence of President Alfredo González Flores, who governed from 1913 to 1917. It is beautifully maintained and now houses permanent historical displays as well as rotating art exhibits.

Heredia

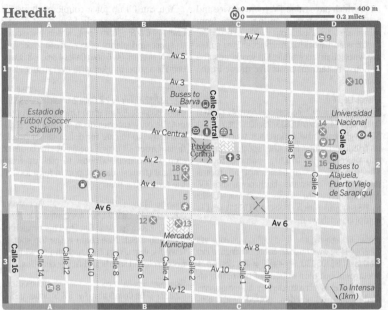

INBioparque · GARDENS

(☎2507-8107; www.inbioparque.com/en; 4km south of Heredia, Santo Domingo; adult/student/child US$23/17/13, parking US$3; ⏰8am-3pm Fri, 9am-4pm Sat-Sun; ♿) This excellent botanical garden is run by the non-profit National Biodiversity Institute (INBio), which catalogs Costa Rica's biodiversity and promotes its sustainable use. Visitors can admire native plants and animals in miniature versions of the country's various life zones, as well as visit farm animals, a butterfly garden and a model sustainable home. Children's theatre and multimedia shows run throughout the day, and the park is wheelchair-accessible. Last-admission times are listed here, but the park doesn't actually close until 5pm or 5:30pm. See the website for directions and additional information.

🛌 Sleeping

Hotel Chalet Tirol · INN $$$

(☎2267-6222; www.hotelchaleteltirol.com; 3km north of Castillo Country Club; d US$93-155, ste US$93-128, all incl breakfast ; P🛜) Northeast of Heredia, you'll find this charming hotel channeling the gingerbread quaintness of the Alps. (It was once covered in fake snow and used as a backdrop for a German beer advert.) The 25 suites and two-story chalets,

Heredia

all of which have cable TV, room service and a gorgeous mountain setting, range from minimalist to kitted out with extras like Jacuzzis and working fireplaces. Two suites are wheelchair-accessible. On weekends, the in-house restaurant hosts live music in the evenings.

Hotel Las Flores HOTEL $
(☎2261 8147; www.hotel-lasflores.com; Av 12 btwn Calles 12 & 14; s/d/tr US$13/25/40; P 📶) A bit of a walk from the action, but worth it for its friendly, homey feel, this spotless family-run place has 29 brightly painted rooms. The furnishings are basic, but all rooms have private hot-water bathroom and TV. An attached *soda* serves breakfast (US$2 to US$4) and lunch (US$3 to US$5) and is equipped with wi-fi.

Hotel Bougainvillea HOTEL $$$
(☎2244-1414; www.hb.co.cr; Santo Domingo; d incl breakfast US$105-130; P ⊖ @ 📶 ≋ 👪) Set on 4 hectares about 6km outside of town, this efficient hotel is surrounded by an expansive, well-manicured garden dotted with old-growth trees, stunning flowers and plenty of statuary. Eighty-two crisp, whitewashed rooms have balconies with views of mountains or city, and several private trails wind by the swimming pool and tennis courts, through forest and orchards. Credit cards accepted.

Hotel Valladolid HOTEL $$
(☎2260-2905; www.hotelvalladolid.net; cnr Calle 7 & Av 7; s/d incl breakfast US$75/87; P ❄ 📶) This business hotel on a quiet street has 12 bright, clean and business-like tiled rooms. They all have microwave, mini-fridge, bar, cable TV and private bathroom with hot water. The staff is quite helpful; credit cards accepted.

Hotel América HOTEL $$
(☎2260-9292; www.hotelamericacr.com; Calle Central btwn Avs 2 & 4; s/d incl breakfast US$60/70; @ 📶) Of the four hotels in this local chain, this is the best deal. It is centrally located just south of the church, and though unspectacular in design, it's clean and comfortable. Tile-floor rooms come equipped with cable TV, safe and fan.

Eating

In the grand tradition of university towns worldwide, Heredia offers plenty of spots for pizza slices and cheap vegetarian grub, not to mention one branch of every fast-food outlet imaginable.

You can fill up for a couple of thousand colones at the **Mercado Municipal** (Calle 2 btwn Avs 6 & 8; ⏲6am-6pm), which has *sodas* to spare and plenty of very fresh groceries. **Más X Menos** (Av 6 btwn Calles 4 & 6; ⏲8:30am-9pm) is a supermarket with everything else.

Espigas COSTA RICAN
(☎2237-3275; cnr Av 2 & Calle 2; breakfast US$6.50, mains US$4-8; ⏲7am-9pm) One of the only, if not the only, eateries open on Sunday, Espigas is the go-to cafe for delicious set breakfasts. Order sit-down meals at the counter, stop by the front window to pick up fresh *batidos* (fruit shakes) or pop in for a look at the tantalizing pastry case.

Vishnu Mango Verde VEGETARIAN $
(☎2237-2526; Calle 7 btwn Avs Central & 1; dishes US$3-7; ⏲8am-7pm Mon-Sat; 🖉) This branch of the famous San José chain is the top spot in town for vegetarian fare, including a wide array of colorful salads and filling *casados*.

Cowboy Steakhouse STEAKHOUSE $$
(☎2237-8719; Calle 9 btwn Avs 3 & 5; dishes US$4-15; ⏲5-11pm Mon-Sat) This yellow-and-red joint with two bars has patio seating and the best beef cuts in town. As the title suggests, steak is the focal point, making it a meat-lover's must. But the hearty salads and extensive list of *bocas* (savory bar snacks) are worth a nibble as well.

Drinking & Entertainment

With a thriving student body, there's no shortage of live music, cultural events and the odd happening. Stay aware: downtown Heredia can get a bit dodgy at nighttime.

The university district is hopping most nights of the week. **La Choza** (Av Central btwn Calles 7 & 9), **El Bulevar** (cnr Calle 7 & Av Central) and **El Rancho de Fofo** (Av Central btwn Calles 7 & 9) are three long-running watering holes.

After a few rounds of beers, the party really kicks off at the **Miraflores Discotheque** (cnr Av 2 & Calle 2), where locals groove to a mix of international beats.

Information

Hospital San Vicente de Paul (☎2562-8100; www.hsvp.sa.cr; Av 8 btwn Calles 14 & 16) Brand-new location at south end of town.

Internet Café (Av Central btwn Calles 7 & 9; per hr US$0.75; ⏲24hr)

Scotiabank (Av 4 btwn Calles Central & 2; ⏲8:30am-5pm Mon-Fri, 9am-1pm Sat) Has a 24-hour ATM dispensing US dollars.

❶ Getting There & Away

There is no central bus terminal, and buses leave from bus stops scattered around the southern part of town.

Alajuela US$0.80, 20 minutes, departs every 15 minutes from 6am to 10pm.

Barva US$0.65, 20 minutes, departs half-hourly from 5:15am to 11:30pm.

Puerto Viejo de Sarapiquí US$2.50, 3½ hours, departs at 11am, 1:30pm and 3pm.

San José US$0.90, 20 minutes, departs every 20 to 30 minutes from 4:40am to 11pm.

San José de la Montaña/Paso Llano for Volcán Barva Transportes del Norte; US$1, 1¼ hours, departs at 4:50am, 6:15am, 7:40am, 1pm and 5pm Monday to Friday.

Santa Bárbara US$0.70, 20 minutes, departs every 10 to 30 minutes from 5:15am to 11:30pm.

Barva

POP 6100

Just 2.5km north of Heredia is the historic town of Barva, a settlement that dates back to 1561 and which has been declared a national monument. The town center is dotted with low-lying 19th-century buildings and is centered on the towering Iglesia San Bartolomé, which was constructed in 1893. Surrounded by picturesque mountains, it just oozes colonial charm. The surrounding area was once popular with the Costa Rican elite: Cleto González Víquez (1858–1937), twice president of Costa Rica (he built the original National Library), was born and raised here. It's a perfect spot for a lazy afternoon stroll.

◉ Sights & Activities

Museo de Cultura Popular   MUSEUM
(☏2260-1619; Santa Lucía; admission US$3; ⊙10am-5pm Sun) Housed in a restored 19th-century farmhouse about 1.5km southeast of Barva, this tiny museum is run by the Universidad Nacional, exhibiting period pieces such as domestic and agricultural tools. It's best to reserve a tour ahead of time, when staff can arrange a hands-on visit.

Café Britt Finca   GUIDED TOUR
(☏2277-1600; www.coffeetour.com; adult with/without lunch US$37/20, student US$32/16; ⊙tours 9:30am & 11am; ⊕) The most famous coffee roaster in Costa Rica, Café Britt Finca offers a 90-minute bilingual tour of its area plantation that includes coffee tasting, a video presentation and a hokey stage play about

the history of coffee (small kids will likely dig it). More in-depth tours are available, as are packages including transport from San José; reserve ahead. Drivers won't be able to miss the *many* signs between Heredia and Barva.

✦ Festivals & Events

Every March the town is home to the famous Feria de la Mascarada, a tradition with roots dating back to the colonial era, in which people don massive colorful masks (some of which weigh up to 20kg), and gather to dance and parade around the town square. Demons and devils are frequent subjects, but celebrities and politicians also figure in the mix (you haven't lived until you've seen a 6m-tall Celia Cruz). The festival is usually held during the last week of the month, but dates vary; inquire locally.

⌂ Sleeping

TOP CHOICE Finca Rosa Blanca   INN
(☏2269-9392; www.fincarosablanca.com; d incl breakfast US$295-520; ᴘ@☏⛵) Set amid a stunning hillside coffee plantation just outside of Santa Bárbara, this honeymoon-ready, Gaudí-esque confection of suites and villas is cloaked in fruit trees that shade private trails. Thirteen sparkling white adobe rooms with wood-beam ceilings and private balconies are lavishly appointed; one tops a tower with a 360-degree view, reached by a winding staircase made from a tree trunk. Shower in an artificial waterfall, take a moonlit dip in the pool, have an organic citrus-coffee bath soak at the spa – or, better yet, dip into a *very* romantic dinner at the hotel's recommended restaurant (mains US$18-26), which serves locally focused dishes, such as mountain trout with sweet-corn ragout. Credit cards accepted.

❶ Getting There & Around

Half-hourly buses travel between Heredia and Barva (US$0.85, 20 minutes), picking up and dropping off in front of the church.

CARTAGO AREA

The riverbank setting of the city of Cartago was handpicked by Spanish Governor Juan Vásquez de Coronado, who said that he had 'never seen a more beautiful valley.' Cartago was founded as Costa Rica's first capital in 1563, and Coronado's successors endowed the city with fine colonial architecture.

However, as things tend to happen in Costa Rica, the city was destroyed during a 1723 eruption of the Volcán Irazú. Any remaining landmarks were toppled by the earthquakes in 1841 and 1910.

Although the city was relegated to backwater status when the seat of government moved to San José in 1823, the surrounding area, particularly the Orosi Valley, flourished during the days of the coffee trade. Today much of the region continues to be devoted to the production of coffee, among other agricultural products. And though Cartago no longer has the prestige of being a national capital, it nonetheless remains a vital commercial hub – not to mention the site of the most important religious monument in the country.

Cartago

POP 24,900

After the rubble was cleared, in the early 20th century, nobody bothered to rebuild Cartago to its former quaint specifications. As in other commercial towns, expect plenty of functional concrete structures. One exception is the bright white Basílica de Nuestra Señora de los Ángeles, which is visible from many parts of the city, standing out like a snowcapped mountain above a plain of one-story edifices.

The city is thrown briefly into the spotlight every August, when pilgrims from every corner of the country descend on the basilica to say their most serious prayers. The remainder of the year, Cartago exists mainly as a commercial and residential center, though the beauty of the surrounding mountains helps take the edge off modern life.

◉ Sights

Basílica de Nuestra Señora de Los Ángeles   CHURCH

(cnr Av 2 & Calle 16) The most important site in Cartago – and the most venerated religious site in the country – this basilica exudes airy Byzantine grace, with fine stained-glass windows, hand-painted interiors and ornate side chapels featuring carved wood altars. Though the structure has changed many times since 1635, when it was first built, the relic that it protects remains unharmed inside.

La Negrita (the Black Virgin) is a small (less than 1m tall), probably indigenous,

representation of the Virgin Mary, found on this spot on August 2, 1635 by a native woman. As the story goes, when she tried to take the statuette with her, it miraculously reappeared back where she'd found it. Twice. So the townspeople built a shrine around her. In 1824, she was declared Costa Rica's patron Virgin. She now resides on a gold, jewel-studded platform at the main altar. Each August 2, on the anniversary of the statuette's miraculous discovery, pilgrims from every corner of the country (and beyond) walk the 22km from San José to the basilica. Many of the penitent complete the last few hundred meters of the pilgrimage on their knees.

Las Ruinas de la Parroquia   RUIN

(Iglesia del Convento; cnr Av 2 & Calle 2) Las Ruinas de la Parroquia was built in 1575 as a shrine to St James the Apostle (Santiago, in Spanish), destroyed by the 1841 earthquake, rebuilt a few years later and then destroyed again in the 1910 earthquake. Today only the outer walls of the church remain, but 'the Ruins' are a pleasant spot for hanging out and people-watching – though legend has it that the ghost of a headless priest wanders the ground on foggy nights.

FREE Museo Municipal de Cartago   MUSEUM

(☑2550-4426; Av 6 btwn Calles 2 & 4; admission free; ◉9am-4pm Tue-Sun; ●) Occupying a former military barracks, this museum opened in 2010, bringing a little high-tech sophistication to historic preservation. It houses a digital library and a warren of galleries that feature a permanent collection as well as art and multimedia exhibitions and musical performances.

Elias Leiva Museum of Ethnography   MUSEUM

(☑2551-0895; Colegio Luis Gonzaga, Calle 3 btwn Avs 3 & 5; adult/student US$7/4; ◉7am-2pm Mon-Fri) For an insight into regional cultures, visit this museum, located in the basement of the Colegio Luis Gonzaga. It has a few small displays of pre-Columbian and colonial artifacts.

⌷ Sleeping & Eating

Lodging options are limited and your best bet for food is to stroll along Avs 2 and 4 downtown, where sodas and bakeries can be found. Self-caterers will find MegaSuper (Calle 3 btwn Avs 4 & 6; ◉7am-10pm) and Palí (Av 2 btwn Calles 4 & 6; ◉8:30am-7pm Mon-Thu,

A NATURAL EDUCATION

Immerse yourself in the Central Valley's rural culture with a stay at Finca La Flor de Paraíso (☎2534-8003; www.la-flor.org; ♿) outside Cartago. This not-for-profit organic farm operated by the Association for the Development of Environmental and Human Consciousness (Asodecah) has a recommended volunteer-work program that will allow you to get your hands dirty on projects related to agriculture, reforestation, animal husbandry and even medicinal-herb cultivation. There is also an on-site Spanish school.

The cost of the volunteer-work programs, including room and board (in simple wood *cabinas* and dormitories), is US$20 daily. Vacationers can arrange day trips (per person US$10) or overnight stays (US$50) – both of which include meals. Family rates are available; advance reservations necessary.

8:30am-7:30pm Fri-Sat, 8:30am-6pm Sun) supermarkets downtown, and fresh veggies and other items at the Mercado Central (cnr Av 1 & Calle 4; ⊙7am-6pm Mon-Sat).

Hotel Dinastía
HOTEL $

(☎2551-7057; Calle 3 near Av 6; r with/without bathroom US$20/15) The only budget option in town, this bare-bones spot has 27 aging rooms with thin walls. Rooms with private bathroom have hot water. It's located behind the bus station.

Los Ángeles Lodge
B&B $$

(☎2591-4169, 2551-0957; Av 4 btwn Calles 14 & 16; s/d incl breakfast US$35/50; P❄🛜) With its balconies overlooking the Plaza de la Basílica, this decent B&B stands out with spacious and comfortable rooms, hot showers and breakfast made to order by the cheerful owners.

La Puerta del Sol
COSTA RICAN $$

(☎2551-0615; Av 4 btwn Calles 14 & 16; mains US$6-10; ⊙8am-10pm Sun-Thu, 8am-midnight Fri-Sat) Located downstairs from Los Ángeles Lodge, this pleasant restaurant has been around since 1957 and serves myriad Tico specialties as well as burgers and sandwiches. Don't miss the vintage photos of Cartago displayed on the walls.

El Nido
BAKERY $

(☎2551-6957; Av 4 btwn Calles 10 &12; ⊙6am-7pm) Pick up a hunk of *dulce de leche* cake at the busy pastry counter, or sit down with a sandwich and espresso at this friendly neighborhood bakery and cafe.

🛍 Shopping

Bazar Mafalda
RELIGIOUS ITEMS

(☎2552-3592; Av 4 btwn Calles 12 & 14; ⊙9am-5pm) To the west of the church, this place stocks an interesting selection of rosaries,

scapulars and ex-votos – and, rather incongruously, soccer paraphernalia and nail polish.

Terra Mall
MALL

(☎2278-6970; Autopista Florencio del Castillo) On the main highway, about 8km west of Cartago in Tres Ríos, you'll find this massive mall, stocked with everything from a high-end multiplex to brand-name boutiques.

ℹ Information

Hospital Max Peralta (☎2550-1999; www.hmp.sa.cr; Av 5 btwn Calles 1 & 3) Emergency and medical services.

Internet Alta Velocidad (Calle 1 btwn Avs 1 & 3; per hr US$0.70; ⊙9am-7pm) At the back corner of the mini-mall.

Museo Municipal de Cartago (p116) Free Internet access.

Scotiabank (☎2591-9000; cnr Av 2 & Calle 2; ⊙9am-5pm Mon-Fri) Has 24-hour ATM.

ℹ Getting There & Away

Bus stops are scattered around town.

Paraíso & Finca la Flor de Paraíso US$1.25, 40 minutes, departs hourly from 7am to 10pm.

Paraíso & Lankester Gardens US$0.40, 20 minutes to Lankester Gardens, departs hourly from 7am to 10pm.

Orosi US$0.70, 40 minutes, departs half-hourly from 5:30am to 10pm Monday to Saturday.

San José US$0.85, 45 minutes, departs every 15 minutes until midnight.

Turrialba US$1.40, 1½ hours, departs every 45 minutes from 6am to 10pm weekdays, 8:30am, 11:30am, 1:30pm, 3pm and 5:45pm weekends.

Volcán Irazú US$6, five hours round-trip, departs Cartago around 8:30am, returns around 12:30pm.

JAN CSERNOCH / ALAMY ©

1. White-water rafting on the Río Pacuare (p126)

Rafting on the scenic Río Pacuare takes you through virgin rainforest and a series of spectacular canyons.

2. Parque Nacional Volcán Irazú (p120)

Irazú, from the indigenous word *ara-tzu*, (thunder-point), is the largest and highest (3432m) active volcano in Costa Rica.

3. Oxcart, Sarchí (p109)

Elaborate, colorfully painted oxcarts are the unofficial souvenirs of Costa Rica, and Sarchí is the place to get one.

4. Parque Nacional Volcán Poás (p103)

The varied scenery around this national park includes hillsides dotted with coffee plantations.

RICHARD CUMMINS / LONELY PLANET IMAGES ©

Parque Nacional Volcán Irazú

Looming on the horizon 19km northeast of Cartago, Irazú, which derives its name from the indigenous word *ara-tzu* (thunderpoint), is the largest and highest (3432m) active volcano in Costa Rica. In 1723 the Spanish governor of the area, Diego de la Haya Fernández, watched helplessly as the volcano unleashed its destruction on the city of Cartago (one of the craters is named in his honor). Since the 18th century, 15 major eruptions have been recorded.

One of the most memorable occurred in March of 1963, welcoming visiting US President John F Kennedy with a rain of volcanic ash that blanketed most of the Central Valley (it piled up to a depth of more than 50cm). During two years' worth of subsequent activity, agricultural lands northeast of the volcano were devastated, while clogged waterways flooded the region intermittently. In 1994 Irazú unexpectedly belched a cloud of sulfurous gas, though it quickly quietened down. At the time of research, the volcano was slumbering peacefully, aside from a few hissing fumaroles.

The national park was established in 1955 to protect 23 sq km around the base of the volcano. The summit is a bare landscape of volcanic-ash craters. The principal crater is 1050m in diameter and 300m deep; the Diego de la Haya Crater is 1000m in diameter, 80m deep and contains a small lake; and the smallest, Playa Hermosa Crater, is slowly being colonized by sparse vegetation. There is also a pyroclastic cone, which consists of rocks that were fragmented by volcanic activity.

☞ Tours

Tours are arranged by a variety of San José operators and cost US$40 to US$60 for a half-day tour, and up to US$100 for a full day combined with lunch and visits to sights such as the Lankester Gardens (p121) or the Orosi Valley.

Tours from hotels in Orosi (US$25 to US$40) can also be arranged – these may include lunch and visits to the basilica in Cartago or sights around the Orosi Valley.

✗ Eating

Restaurant 1910 COSTA RICAN $
(☏2536-6063; casados US$7; ⊙closed Mon; 🛜) On the road up to Irazú, 100m north of the Guayabo turnoff, this homey spot is worth a stop for lunch to see its collection of old photographs documenting the 1910 earthquake that completed the destruction of colonial Cartago. Expect a long list of Tico specialties, including fresh grilled river trout.

❶ Information

Pay admission and parking fees at the **ranger station** (☏2200-5025, in Cartago 2551-9398; park admission US$10, parking US$2.20; ⊙8am-3:30pm) at the park's entrance. There's a basic cafe and gift shop inside the park. Note that cloud cover starts thickening, even under the best conditions, by about 10am, about the same time as the bus rolls in. If you're on one of those buses, do yourself a favor and head straight for the crater. If you have a car, make an effort to arrive early and you'll likely be rewarded with the best possible views and an uncrowded observation area. The park is busiest on Sundays and holidays, when a line of cars up to 1km-long queues at the park entrance.

At the summit it is possible to see both the Pacific Ocean and the Caribbean Sea, but it is rarely clear enough. The best chance for a clear view is in the very early morning during the dry season (January to April). It tends to be cold and windy up here and there's an annual rainfall of 2160mm – come prepared with warm, rainproof clothes.

From the parking lot, a 200m trail leads to a viewpoint over the craters. While hiking, be on the lookout for high-altitude bird species, such as the volcano junco.

❶ Getting There & Away

The only public transportation (US$6) to Irazú departs from San José at 8am, stops in Cartago at about 8:30am and arrives at the summit around 10am. The bus departs from Irazú at 12:30pm.

If you're in a group, renting a car is the best deal: you can get to the park early and follow it up with a leisurely lunch overlooking the spectacular Orosi Valley at Sanchiri Restaurante (p121).

To get to the volcano, drivers can take Hwy 8 from Cartago, which begins at the northeast corner of the plaza and continues 19km to the summit. The road is well signed.

Valle de Orosi

This straight-out-of-a-storybook river valley is famous for its mountain vistas, hot springs, a lake formed by a hydroelectric facility, a truly wild national park and coffee – lots and lots of coffee. A 60km scenic loop (freshly paved in 2009) winds through a landscape of rolling hills terraced with shade-grown coffee plantations and expansive valleys dotted with pastoral villages. If you're lucky enough to have a rental car (or a good bicycle), you're in for a treat, though it's still possible to navigate most of the loop via public buses.

The loop road starts 8km southeast of Cartago in Paraíso, and then heads south to Orosi. At this point you can either continue south into Parque Nacional Tapantí-Macizo Cerro de la Muerte or loop back to Paraíso via Ujarrás.

PARAÍSO AREA

Though the village of Paraíso isn't all that its name implies, it does lead to the wonderful Orosi Valley beyond.

About 3km east of Cartago on the road to Paraíso, the University of Costa Rica runs the exceptional Lankester Gardens (☑2511-7939; www.jbl.ucr.ac.cr; adult/student US$7/5; ☺8:30am-4:30pm) (look for a faded pink monolith marking the turnoff). It was founded as a private garden by British orchid enthusiast Charles Lankester in 1917 and turned over to the university for public administration in 1973. Orchids are the big draw at this tranquil 11-hectare botanical garden, with more than 1100 at their showiest from March to May. This is one of the few places in the country where foreigners can legally purchase orchids to take home. There's also a Japanese garden, as well as bromeliad, palm, heliconia and other tropical gardens. Guided tours in English and Spanish can be arranged with prior reservation; the garden is wheelchair-accessible.

From Paraíso, the road north to Turrialba meanders 2km before arriving at Finca Cristina (☑2574-6426, in USA 800-355-8826; www.cafecristina.com; guided tour per person US$15; ☺by appointment only), an organic coffee farm. Linda and Ernie have been farming in Costa Rica since 1977, and a two-hour tour of their *microbeneficio* (miniprocessing plant) is a fantastic introduction to the processes of organic-coffee growing, harvesting and roasting.

Continuing a few kilometers down the road to Orosi, you'll hit Mirador Orosi (5km from Orosi; admission free; ☺8am-5pm), a scenic overlook complete with toilets, secure parking lot, and ample photo and picnic opportunities.

About 2km south of Paraíso, and 1km off the main road, you'll find Sanchirí Mirador & Lodge (☑2574-5454; www.sanchiri.com;

s/d incl breakfast US$66/82; Ⓟ), a delightful, family-run B&B that offers an excellent reason to break up a road trip. A dozen superclean, ceramic-tiled rooms with comfortable wood furnishings, and five slightly more rustic *cabinas,* look onto staggering vistas of Parque Nacional Tapantí-Macizo Cerro de la Muerte and Río Reventazón in the valley below. If you only need a lunch stop, the onsite restaurant (mains US$4-22; ☺7am-8pm) is a great choice for generous portions and even more extravagant views.

OROSI
4500

Named for a Huetar chief who lived here at the time of the conquest, Orosi charmed Spanish colonists in the 18th century with its perfect climate, rich soil and wealth of water – from lazy hot springs to bracing waterfalls. So, in the typical fashion of the day, they decided to take the property off Orosi's hands. Today the area remains picturesque – and is a good spot to revel in beautiful scenery and a small town atmosphere.

◉ Sights

Iglesia de San José Orosi   CHURCH
Orosi is one of the few colonial-era towns to survive Costa Rica's frequent earthquakes, which have thankfully spared the photogenic village church. Built in 1743, it is the oldest religious site still in use in Costa Rica. The roof of the church is a combination of thatched cane and ceramic tiling, while the carved wood altar is adorned with religious paintings of Mexican origin.

Museo de San José Orosi   MUSEUM
(☑2533-3051; admission US$1; ☺1-5pm Tue-Sat, 9am-5pm Sun) Adjacent to the Iglesia de San José Orosi is a small museum with interesting examples of Spanish-colonial religious art and artifacts, some of which date back to the 17th century.

⚥ Activities

The town is a perfect base from which to explore Parque Nacional Tapantí-Macizo Cerro de la Muerte, which offers excellent birdwatching and some lovely hikes, or to rock climb in nearby Cachi.

Aventuras Orosi   RAFTING
(☑8345-6368, 2533-4000; www.aventurasorosi.info; Motel Río, north side of hanging bridge; ☺9am-4pm) Operated by the charming Luis, who served as a guide for the venerable Río Tropicales rafting company for years, this small

CENTRAL VALLEY & HIGHLANDS VALLE DE OROSI

outfit can organize short, local rafting expeditions (US$40), tours of neighboring coffee *fincas* (US$30), and custom itineraries.

Montaña Linda LANGUAGE COURSE
(☎2533-3640; www.montanalinda.com; 300m south of plaza) One of the most affordable Spanish-language schools in the country; check the website for current prices and schedule.

THERMAL SPRINGS

Being in a volcanic region also means Orosi has the perks of thermal springs. Though not on the scale of the steaming-hot waters found near Fortuna, Orosi does offer a couple of nice modest pools with warm water. **Los Balnearios** (☎2533-2156; 25m from Orosi Lodge; admission US$3.60; ⏲7:30am-4pm Wed-Mon) has several pools, right in town, **Los Patios** (☎2533-3009; 1.5km south of Orosi; admission US$4; ⏲8am-4pm Tue-Sun) is a larger complex with a few more pools.

Sleeping & Eating

TOP CHOICE **Orosi Lodge** INN
(☎2533-3578; www.orosilodge.com; south of park, near entrance to Los Balnearios; d/tr US$55/65, d chalet US$85, additional person US$15; P) This quiet haven, run by a friendly German couple, has eight bright rooms with wood-beam ceilings and tile floors (one room is wheelchair-accessible). Each comes with a minibar, coffeemaker and free organic coffee – and most face a lovely garden courtyard with a fountain. A two-story, three-bedroom chalet sleeps up to five, with a master suite that offers incredible views of volcanoes Irazú and Turrialba. Delicious, wholesome breakfasts are US$7, and the homemade pastries are worth a stop; credit cards accepted.

Montaña Linda HOSTEL
(☎2533-3640; www.montanalinda.com; dm US$8.50, d US$30, s/d/tr without bathroom US$15/22/30, guesthouse s/d with bathroom US$30/35; P @) Two blocks south and three blocks west of the bus stop is this great, chilled-out budget option. Eleven tidy dorms and brightly accented private rooms surround a homey terrace with flowers and hammocks. Units all come with access to hot showers, and kitchen privileges are available for a small additional fee (US$1). Also available: a more upmarket guesthouse with rooms and private bathrooms; all share a kitchen.

Hotel Reventazón HOTEL
(☎2533-3838; d/tr US$40/50; P) A functional two-story cement structure with seven large, clean tile-floor rooms that come equipped with cable TV, hot water and fridge. More expensive units are bigger and have better views of the mountains and forest.

Panadería Suiza BAKERY $
(☎8706-6777; f.mosi@gmx.ch; 100m south of Banco Nacional; breakfast US$3-4; ⏲5:30am-5pm Tue-Sun) If you're up at the crack of dawn craving fruit and yogurt, you're in luck (unless it's a Monday)! Ebullient Swiss expat Franzisca serves breakfast, snacks and sandwiches at her corner shop, and is the baker of excellent pastries and whole-grain breads. She also rents bikes and provides local travel information.

Restaurante Coto COSTA RICAN $
(☎2533-3032; north side of park; mains US$5-24; ⏲8am-10pm) Established in 1952, this family-run eatery dishes out good *típico* food in a wood-beamed dining room with open-air seating. It's a great place to enjoy mountain views and the goings-on about town.

Information

Find more information on the area on the village website (www.orosivalley.com).

Banco Nacional (300m south of the park) has an ATM and changes money.

OTIAC (Orosi Tourist Information & Arts Café; ☎2533-3640; ⏲9am-4pm Mon-Sat;) Run by the multilingual Toine and Sara, two long-term residents, OTIAC functions as an information center, cafe, cultural hall and book exchange. They can help arrange tours and are a good source of information about volunteer and teaching opportunities. Find it 200m south of the park and one block west of the main road.

Getting There & Away

All buses stop about three blocks west of the *fútbol* (soccer) field; ask locally about specific destinations.

Cachí Dam & Ruinas US$0.60, 20 minutes, departs half-hourly from 6am to 9pm.

Cartago US$0.80, 40 minutes, departs every 45 minutes from 5am to 9pm.

PARQUE NACIONAL TAPANTÍ – MACIZO CERRO DE LA MUERTE

This 580-sq-km **national park** (admission US$10; ⏲8am-4pm) protects the lush northern slopes of the Cordillera de Talamanca, and has a rainy claim to fame: it is the wettest park in the country, getting almost 8000mm of precipitation a year. In 2000 it was expanded to include the infamous Cerro de la Muerte – otherwise known as the 'Mountain of Death.' This precipitous peak is the highest point on the Interamericana and the northernmost extent of *páramo*, a highland shrub and tussock grass habitat that's most commonly found in the Andes and is home to a variety of rare bird species.

Known simply as Tapantí, the park also protects wild and mossy country that's fed by, literally, hundreds of rivers. Waterfalls abound, vegetation is thick and the wildlife is prolific, though not always easy to see because of the rugged terrain.

🏃 Activities

WILDLIFE-WATCHING

Quetzals are said to nest on the western slopes of the valley, where the park information center is located. More than 300 other bird species have also been recorded in the park, including hummingbirds, parrots, toucans, trogons and eagles. The bird-watching opportunities here are legendary, as it's possible to spot a large variety of birds in a small area. Though rarely sighted due to the thick vegetation, monkeys, coatis, pacas, tayras and even pumas, ocelots and oncillas are present.

HIKING

Three signed trails lead from the information center, the longest of which is a steep 4km round-trip, while a well-graded dirt road that is popular with mountain bikers runs through the northern section of the national park. Tapantí is not open to backcountry hiking.

🛏 Sleeping & Eating

Kiri Mountain Lodge   LODGE
(☎8394-6286, 2533-2272; www.kirilodge.net; s/d incl breakfast US$24/45; 🅿) About 1km before the park entrance, Kiri has six rustic *cabinas* with private hot shower resting on 50 mossy hectares of land. Trails wind into the nearby Reserva Forestal Río Macho, which is adjacent to Tapantí and inhabited by much of the same wildlife. A restaurant specializes in trout, which can be caught in the well-stocked pond and then served up any way you like (casados US$7 to US$10; open 7am to 8:30pm).

Monte Sky   LODGE
(☎8382-7502, 2231-3536; www.intnet.co.cr/mon tesky; per person incl meals US$45; 🅿) Five

kilometers north of town, on the road to Tapantí, this 536-hectare private reserve teems with 290 bird species. There is a basic lodge and plenty of hiking trails. The folks at OTIAC in Orosi can help arrange overnight stays.

❶ Information

There is an **information center** (☎2200-0090; ⏲6am-4pm) near the park entrance – here, you can pick up a simple park map to a couple of trails leading to various attractions, including a picnic area, a swimming hole and a lookout with great views of a waterfall. Rainfall is about 2700mm in the lower sections but reaches almost 8000mm in some of the highest parts of the park, so make sure you pack rain gear. Fishing is allowed in season (April to October; permit required), but the 'dry' season (January to April) is generally considered the best time to visit.

❶ Getting There & Away

If you have your own car, you can take a bumpy gravel road (4WD recommended) from Purisil to the park entrance.

Buses are trickier. From Cartago, take an Orosi–Purisil bus (make sure it's going to Purisil; not all of them do). The bus can drop you 5km from the entrance. Inquire at OTIAC or Aventuras Orosi about guides and other transport options.

OROSI TO PARAÍSO

From Orosi, a loop road heads north and parallels the Río Orosi before swinging around the artificial Lago de Cachí. The lake was created following the construction of the Cachí Dam (the largest in the country), which supplies San José and the majority of the Central Valley with electricity. Buses run from Orosi to the dam and nearby ruins, though this stretch is best explored by car or bicycle – and it's worth exploring as this is beautiful countryside.

Sights here are all listed traveling north along the eastern shore of the lake, from Orosi around to Ujarrás. After Ujarrás, the road continues for a few more kilometers before looping back to Paraíso.

About 3km southeast of the dam, on the left-hand side of the road, the charming lakeside La Casona del Cafetal Restaurant (☎2577-1515, 2577-1414; www.lacasonadel cafetal.com; mains US$7-27; ⏲11am-6pm; 🐾) is situated in the middle of a coffee plantation and is especially popular with local families on buffet Sundays. Specialties include fresh river trout and coffee-laced desserts. There's a small playground, short trails and a lagoon with paddle boats for rent (in high season).

Across the main from La Casona is the turnoff to the mountaintop Cabañas de Montaña Piedras Albas (☎8883-6449, 2577-1462; www.cabinas.co.cr/costa_rica1.htm; 2.5km from central Cachí; cabinas US$70-80; P♨), an ideal place to really slow down. Bright wood cabinas come with kitchen, cable TV, and private deck with lake and mountain views, and there are private hiking trails. Private transportation is a must.

Another 2km along the main road and 1km south of the dam, is Casa del Soñador (Dreamer's House; ☎2577-1186, 2577-1021; admission free; ⊙8am-6pm), an artisanal woodworking studio run by Hermes Quesada, the son of renowned Tico carver Macedonio Quesada. Hermes maintains the *campesino* (peasant farmer) tradition of whittling gnarled coffee-wood branches into ornate religious figures and whimsical characters. His workshop displays sculptures of all sizes, with pieces available for purchase.

The road to Tucurrique forks off the main lake loop toward Escalada Cachí (☎2577-1974, 8867-8259; rockclimbingcachi@hotmail.com; 2km from fork; ⊙8am-4pm Sat-Sun, by appointment only Mon-Fri), a sport-climbing spot with routes of varying difficulty. The US$16 fee includes equipment rental, as much climbing as you can crank out, and a soak in its lovely river-diverted pool afterwards. Heed the roadside sign that recommends 4WD – if you don't think you or your rental 4WD can negotiate a supersteep track covered in marbles, park and hike down (and don't leave anything in your car). Call ahead.

Past the dam, you'll find the small village of Ujarrás at the bottom of a long, steep hill – a couple of shop signs with the word 'Ujarrás' tell you that you've arrived. Turn left at a sign for Restaurant La Pipiola to head toward the old village (about 1km), which was damaged by a flood in 1833 and abandoned.

Only the crumbling walls remain of Iglesia de Nuestra Señora de la Limpia Concepción (admission free; ⊙8am-4:30pm; ♨), a 1693 colonial stone church once home to a miraculous painting of the Virgin discovered by a local fisherman. According to lore, the relic refused to be moved, forcing clerics to build the church around it. In return the Virgin helped locals defeat a group of marauding British pirates in 1666. After floods and a few earthquakes, however, the painting conceded to move to Paraíso, leaving the ruins to deteriorate photogenically

in a rambling park. (Kids can let off some steam at the fantastic playground here.) Every year, usually on the Sunday closest to April 14, there's a procession from Paraíso to the ruins, where Mass, food and music help celebrate the day of La Virgin de Ujarrás. The church's grassy grounds are a popular picnicking spot on Sunday afternoons – but go in the middle of the week and chances are that you'll have them all to yourself.

After Ujarrás, the road continues for a few more kilometers before looping back to Paraíso.

TURRIALBA AREA

In the vicinity of Turrialba, at an elevation of 650m above sea level, the Río Reventazón gouges a mountain pass through the Cordillera Central. In the 1880s this geological quirk allowed the 'Jungle Train' between San José and Puerto Limón to roll through, and the mountain village of Turrialba grew prosperous from the coffee trade. Later, the first highway linking the capital to the coast exploited this same quirk. Turrialba thrived.

However, things changed by the early 1990s when the straighter, smoother Hwy 32 through Guápiles was completed and an earthquake shut down the railway for good. Suddenly, Turrialba found itself off the beaten path. Even so, the area remains a key agricultural center, renowned for its mountain air, strong coffee and Central America's best white-water rafting. To the north, the area is home to two important sites: the majestic Volcán Turrialba and the archeological site of Guayabo.

Turrialba

31,100

When the railway shut down in 1991, commerce slowed down, but Turrialba nonetheless remained a regional agricultural center, where local coffee planters could bring their crops to market. And with tourism on the rise in the 1990s, this modest mountain town soon became known as the gateway to some of the best white-water rafting on the planet. By the early 2000s, Turrialba was a hotbed of international rafters looking for Class-V thrills. For now, the Río Pacuare runs on, but its future is uncertain.

DAMNING THE RIVERS?

Considered one of the most beautiful white-water rafting rivers in the world, the wild **Río Pacuare** became the first federally protected river in Central America in 1985. Within two years, however, Costa Rica's national power company, the Instituto Costarricense de Electricidad (ICE), unveiled plans to build a 200m gravity dam at the conveniently narrow and screamingly scenic ravine of Dos Montañas.

The dam would be the cornerstone of the massive Siquirres Hydroelectric Project, which would include four dams in total, linked by a 10km-long tunnel. If built, rising waters on the lower Pacuare would not only flood 12km of rapids up to the Tres Equis put-in, but also parts of the Reserva Indígena Awari and a huge swath of primary rainforest where some 800 animal species have been recorded.

The project was intended to help ICE keep up with the country's rapidly increasing power demands (per capita consumption of energy in Costa Rica has grown more than 73% since 1975, according to the World Bank). But as the proposal moved from speculation to construction, a coalition of local landowners, indigenous leaders, conservation groups and, yep, white-water rafting outfits organized against it. (Rafael Gallo, of the Fundación Ríos Tropicales, the charitable arm of the venerable rafting company, was a key figure in this fight.)

The group filed for the first Environmental Impact Assessment (EIA) in the region's history – and won. The move required ICE to seek an independent study of the dam's environmental impact and economic feasibility, effectively stalling its construction. In the meantime, organizers were able to draw international attention to the situation. In 2005 residents of the Turrialba area held a plebiscite on the issue of the dam. Of the 10,000 residents polled, 97% gave the project a thumbs down – a resounding 'No.'

As a result of these efforts, the project has been shelved until 2016, and the lower part of the river is now protected as a forest reserve. But there is still talk of installing a dam further up the river. It's worth noting that the neighboring **Río Reventazón** has already lost a third of its Class-V rapids due to the first phase of the Siquirres Project. If you were thinking of going rafting in Costa Rica, the time to do it is now.

CENTRAL VALLEY & HIGHLANDS TURRIALBA

◉ Sights

Catie GARDENS
(Centro Agronómico Tropical de Investigación Center for Tropical Agronomy Research & Education; ☑2556-2700; www.catie.ac.cr/jardinbotanico; 3km east of Turrialba; admission US$10, guided tours US$25-50; ☉7am-4pm Mon-Fri, 8am-4pm Sat-Sun) Catie consists of 1000 hectares dedicated to tropical agricultural research and education. Agronomists from all over the world recognize this as one of the most important centers in the tropics. You need to make reservations for one of several guided tours through laboratories, greenhouses, a seed bank, experimental plots and one of the world's most extensive libraries of tropical-agriculture literature. Alternatively, pick up a map and take a self-guided walk.

☞ Tours

Plenty of operators offer either kayaking or rafting in the area.

» **Costa Rica Ríos** (☑in USA & Canada 888-434-0776; www.costaricarios.com) Week-long rafting trips must be booked in advance.

» **Explornatura** (☑2556-2070, in USA & Canada 866-571-2443; www.explornatura.com; Av 4 btwn Calles 2 & 4)

» **Río Locos** (☑2556-6035; www.whiteh2o.com)

» **RainForest World** (☑2556-0014; www.rforestw.com)

» **Tico's River Adventures** (☑2556-1231; www.ticoriver.com)

⌂ Sleeping

TURRIALBA

TOP
CHOICE **Casa de Lis Hostel** HOSTEL **$**
(☑2556-4933; www.hostelcasadelis.com; Av Central near Calle 2; dm US$10, d/tr/q US$40/45/50, without bathroom US$25/35/40; ☎) Just what Turrialba needed – a bright, new hostel right in the center of town. This sweet four-room place is spotless, with a fully equipped kitchen, roof terrace for enjoying volcano views, a small garden in the back and a distinctly friendly atmosphere. Inexpensive breakfasts (topping out at US$4) and laundry service are available.

WHITE-WATER RAFTING IN THE CENTRAL VALLEY

There are two major rivers in the Turrialba area that are popular for rafting – the Río Reventazón and the Río Pacuare. The following is a quick guide to the ins and outs (and ups and downs) of each.

Río Reventazón

This storied rock-lined river has its beginnings at the Lago de Cachí, an artificial lake created by a dam of the same name. It begins here, at 1000m above sea level, and splashes down the eastern slopes of the cordilleras to the Caribbean lowlands. It is one of the most difficult, adrenaline-pumping runs in the country, with more than 65km of rapids.

Tour operators divide the river into four sections between the dam and the take-out point in Siquirres.

» **El Carmen** A Class II float that's perfect for families.

» **Florida** The final and most popular segment is a scenic Class III with a little more white water to keep things interesting.

» **Pascua** Has 15 Class IV rapids and is considered to be the classic run.

» **Peralta** Rated Class V, this section is the most challenging; tours do not always run it due to safety concerns.

Water levels stay fairly constant year-round because of releases from the dam. There are no water releases on Sunday, however, and although the river is navigable, it's generally considered the worst day.

Río Pacuare

The Río Pacuare is the next major river valley east of the Reventazón, and has arguably the most scenic rafting in Costa Rica, if not all of Central America. The river plunges down the Caribbean slope through a series of spectacular canyons clothed in virgin rainforest, through runs named for their fury and separated by calm stretches that enable you to stare at near-vertical green walls towering hundreds of meters above.

» **Lower Pacuare** With Class II–IV rapids, this is the more accessible run: 28km through rocky gorges, past an indigenous village and untamed jungle.

» **Upper Pacuare** Also classified as Class III–IV, but a few sections can go to Class V, depending on conditions. It's about a two-hour drive to the put-in, after which you'll have the prettiest jungle cruise on earth all to yourself.

The Pacuare can be run year-round, though June to October are considered the best months to do so. The highest water is from October to December, when the river runs fast with huge waves. March and April is when the river is at its lowest, though it is still challenging.

Trips & Prices

A number of reputable national companies organize trips, as can agencies in Turrialba.

Day trips usually raft the Class II–IV Lower Pacuare or Class III segments of Río Reventazón, which both have easy-access put-ins. Other runs – such as the Upper Pacuare and Pascua segment of Reventazón – will require more time spent in a van. Multiday excursions with camping or lodge accommodations are offered by numerous companies.

For day trips (many of which originate in San José), you can expect to pay anywhere from US$85 to US$120 depending on the transportation, accessibility and amenities. It is generally less expensive to leave from Turrialba, and put-in on the Lower Pacuare or Class III segments of the Reventazón (from US$75). For two-day trips, prices vary widely depending on accommodations, but expect to pay US$195 to US$300 per person. Children must be at least nine years old for most trips, and older for the tougher runs.

Hotel Interamericano
HOTEL **$**

(📞2556-0142; www.hotelinteramericano.com; Av 1 near Calle 1; s/d/tr/q US$25/35/50/65, without bathroom US$11/22/33/44; P🖥️) On the south side of the old train tracks is this basic 22-room hotel, regarded by rafters as *the* meeting place in Turrialba. The showers are clean, the tiled rooms are bright, and Luis, the bilingual manager, is a gem of a human as well as a great source of local information.

Turrialba B&B
B&B

(📞2556-6651; akius@hotmail.com; Calle 1 north of Av 6; s/d/tr US$40/60/80; ❄️🖥️) This tranquil spot has clean, bright, well-appointed rooms, a cozy living-room area, a lovely garden patio equipped with a Jacuzzi and a library chock-full of travel guides on Latin America. There is also a shared kitchen and a small bar. Excellent value.

Hotel Wagelia
HOTEL

(📞2556-1566; www.hotelwageliaturrialba.com; Av 4 btwn Calles 2 & 4; s/d incl breakfast US$80/99; P❄️🖥️) Simple, modern and clean no-frills rooms come with cable TV and face a quiet, interior courtyard. A restaurant serves many Tico specialties, and the pleasant terrace bar is a good place for a drink and wi-fi.

AROUND TURRIALBA
There are some stellar hotels around the Turrialba area. All have private hot-water bathrooms, and can arrange tours and rafting trips.

TOP CHOICE Turrialtico Lodge
LODGE

(📞2538-1111; www.turrialtico.com; 8km east of Turrialba; d incl breakfast US$64-75; P🖥️) Off the highway to Siquirres, this Tico-run lodge has been owned and managed by the García family since 1968. There are 14 attractive, polished-wood-panel rooms in an old farmhouse that have paintings by local artists. Rooms in the reception building share a large terrace and sitting area, and a pleasant open-air restaurant (mains US$3 to US$15) serves up country cooking. Best of all are its fantastic, dramatic views.

Rancho Naturalista
LODGE

(📞2554-8101; www.ranchonaturalista.net; per person incl 3 meals US$145; P@) About 1.3km south of Tuis, a signed dirt road (4WD needed) leads to Rancho Naturalista, a small lodge set on 50 hectares of land that lies 900m above sea level – and attracts dedicated bird-watchers. There have been 433 species recorded in the area, more than 200 of them from the lodge balcony alone. Fifteen simple rooms are scattered around the main lodge or there are nicer separate *casitas*, with wood furniture, tile floors and a comfortable deck stocked with hammocks and rockers. Meals include organic produce grown on the grounds.

Casa Turire
LUXURY HOTEL **$$$**

(📞2531-1111; www.hotelcasaturire.com; d standard/ ste/master ste incl breakfast US$135/210/350, additional person US$25-55, child under 6yr free; P❄️@🖥️) From the highway, take the turnoff to La Suiza/Tuis, head south for 2km and you'll see signs leading to Casa Turire. An elegant three-story plantation inn, it has 16 graceful well-appointed rooms with high ceilings, wood floors and wrought-iron beds; a massive master suite comes with a Jacuzzi and excellent views of the coffee and macadamia-nut plantations in the distance. Spa services are available, there's a restaurant (dishes US$7 to US$33) and bar, and the helpful staff can arrange area activities such as horseback riding, bird-watching and kayaking on the on-site lake.

🍴 Eating

Sodas and bakeries abound. Self-caterers can find supplies at the well-stocked MegaSuper (cnr Calle 3 & Av 2)

Panadería La Castellana
BAKERY **$**

(📞2556-9090; www.lacastellanacr.com; cnr Calle 2 & Av 4; breakfast US$2.50-5, pizza US$8-13; ⏱️24hr) Whether it's pizza by the slice, *gallo pinto* (a common meal of blended rice and beans) and eggs or coffee and a pastry, La Castellana does it well and at all hours. It even offers half-orders for smaller appetites. Dine in, or pick up some whole-wheat bread or desserts for eats on the road.

Restaurant Betico Mata
BARBECUE **$**

(📞2556-8640; Hwy 10; gallos US$1.25-1.75; ⏱️ 11am-midnight, until later Sat & Sun) This carnivore's paradise at the south end of town specializes in *gallos* (open-faced tacos on corn tortillas) piled with succulent, freshgrilled meats including beef, chicken, sausage or pork, all soaked in the special house marinade. All go smashingly well with an ice-cold beer. The restaurant has a counter that faces the street – making it easy to park and pick up a snack if you're driving through town.

La Feria

(☎2556-5550; Calle 6 north of Av 4; casados US$5, mains US$4-11; ⊙11am-10pm Wed-Mon, 11am-2pm Tue; ✎) This unremarkable-looking eatery has friendly service and excellent, inexpensive home cooking. Try the *pollo a la milanesa,* a crisp chicken cutlet served with cucumber-yogurt dipping sauce.

❶ Information

There's no official tourist office, but most hotels and rafting outfits can organize tours, accommodations and transportation throughout the region.

Banco de Costa Rica (cnr Av Central & Calle 3; ⊙9am-4pm Mon-Fri) Has 24-hour ATM.

Cafe Internet (☎2556-4575; cnr Av 2 & Calle 4; per hr US$0.75; ⊙8am-8pm)

❶ Getting There & Away

A modern bus terminal is located on the western edge of town off Hwy 10.

San José via Paraíso & Cartago US$2.60, two hours, departs every 45 minutes from 5am to 6:30pm.

Siquirres, for transfer to Puerto Limón US$2.25, 1¾ hours, departs every 60 to 90 minutes from 6am to 6pm.

La Suiza & Tuis US$0.65,departs every 60 to 90 minutes from 7am to 10pm Monday through Saturday, every two hours on Sunday from 7am to 8:30am.

MONUMENTO NACIONAL ARQUEOLÓGICO GUAYABO

Nestled into a patch of stunning hillside forest 19km northeast of Turrialba is the largest and most important archaeological site in the country. Guayabo is composed of the remains of a pre-Columbian city that was thought to have peaked at some point in AD 800, when it was inhabited by as many as 20,000 people. Today visitors can examine the remains of old petroglyphs, residential mounds, an old roadway and an impressive aqueduct system – built with rocks that were hauled in from the Río Reventazón along a cobbled, 8km road. Amazingly, the cisterns still work, and (theoretically) potable water remains available on-site.

The settlement, which may have been occupied as early as 1000 BC, was mysteriously abandoned by AD 1400 and Spanish explorers left no record of ever having found the ruins. For centuries, the city lay largely untouched under the cover of the area's thick highland forest. But in 1968, archaeologist Carlos Aguilar Piedra of the University of Costa Rica began systematic excavations of Guayabo, finding polychromatic pottery and gold artifacts that are now exhibited at San José's Museo Nacional.

In 1973, as the site's importance became evident, Guayabo was declared a National Monument, with further protections set forth in 1980. The site occupies 232 hectares, most of which remains unexcavated. It's a small place – so don't go expecting Mayan pyramids.

⚒ Activities

WILDLIFE-WATCHING

The site currently protects the last remaining premontane forest in the province of Cartago, and although mammals are limited to squirrels, armadillos and coatis, there are good bird-watching opportunities here. Particularly noteworthy among the avifauna are the oropendolas, which colonize the monument by building sacklike nests in the trees. Other birds include toucans and brown jays – the latter are unique among jays in that they have a small, inflatable sac in their chest, which causes the popping sound that is heard at the beginning of their loud and raucous calls.

❶ Information

There's a small information and **exhibit center** (☎2559-1220; admission US$7; ⊙8am-3:30pm) that provides an overview of what the city may have once looked like. (The best archaeological pieces can be found at the Museo Nacional in San José.) Guided tours are not available, but the very well-maintained trails are well signed.

Camping (per person US$5) is permitted; services include flush toilets and running water. Average annual rainfall is about 3500mm, making dry season (January to April) the best time to visit – though it might still rain. Bring insect repellent; it gets mighty buggy.

❶ Getting There & Away

By car, head north out of Turrialba and make a right after the metal bridge. The road is well signed from there. It's mostly paved, but the last 3km of the drive is not; 4WD recommended.

Buses from Turrialba (US$0.85, one hour) depart at 11:15am, 3:10pm and 5:20pm Monday through Saturday and at 9am, 3pm and 6:30pm on Sunday. Buses travel from Guayabo to Turrialba at 5:15am, 7am, 12:30pm and 4pm Monday through Saturday; 7am, 12:30pm and 4pm on Sunday. You can also take a taxi from Turrialba (from US$16).

Parque Nacional Volcán Turrialba

This rarely visited active volcano (3328m) was named Torre Alba (White Tower) by early Spanish settlers, who observed plumes of smoke pouring from its summit. Since its last eruption in 1866, Turrialba has generally slumbered quietly. However, in January 2010, a small eruption rained a fine sprinkle of ash as far as 27km away. It was nothing major as far as eruptions go, but vulcanologists have been monitoring the situation carefully. More sulfuric gas and ash escaped from a new vent in January 2012, but the park remained open at the time of research.

Turrialba was declared a national park in 1955, and protects a 2km radius around the volcano. Below the summit, the park consists of mountain rainforest and cloud forest, dripping with moisture and mosses, full of ferns, bromeliads and even stands of bamboo. Although small, these protected habitats shelter 84 species of birds and 11 species of mammals.

If the summit is open, you can peer into the Central Crater to observe minor fumarole activity in the bubbling sulfurous mud. The West Crater, which had its last major eruption in 1866, is spewing clouds of sulfur and steam, and is therefore closed to the public. The smaller Eastern Crater lacks fumarole activity.

Although the craters are not nearly as dramatic as Poás or Irazú, the lack of infrastructure and tourists gives the summit a wild and natural feeling.

🏃 Activities

Hiking
From the end of the road, unmarked trails through montane forest lead to the Eastern Crater and the Central Crater. Be advised that the summit is not developed for tourism, so keep your distance from the craters and be especially careful along the edges – they are brittle and break easily.

From the rim there are views of Irazú, Poás and Barva volcanoes – weather permitting, of course.

🛏 Sleeping

Volcán Turrialba Lodge   LODGE $$
(☎2273-4335; www.volcanturrialbalodge.com; 14km northwest of Santa Cruz; s/d US$25/50; 🅿🛜) Accessible by 4WD only, this working cattle ranch truly gets you away from it all. Tidy, lemon-yellow *cabinas* are heated by wood stoves and contain full kitchens, and the area offers fantastic views of Volcán Turrialba. The staff can also organize hikes and horseback rides. Meals (US$3 to US$20) are typical country cooking, served in front of a blazing stove at the restaurant/lounge, where there is a TV, board games and a small bar. It gets chilly up here, so bring warm clothes.

❶ Information

At the time of research, there was neither a ranger station nor an admission fee, though there may be rangers at the summit. Because of the recent volcanic activity and its effect on road conditions, it's imperative to inquire locally about conditions before setting out and to inform someone of your plans. The average temperature is only about 15°C (59°F), so dress accordingly.

If it's closed, you can always admire the summit on the volcano's very own webcam at www. ovsicori.una.ac.cr/videoturri.html.

❶ Getting There & Away

The volcano is only about 15km northwest of Turrialba as the crow flies, but more than twice as far by car than foot. From the village of Santa Cruz (13km from Turrialba and connected via public buses), an 18km road climbs to the summit. The road is paved for the first 10km, and then becomes increasingly rough; 4WD is necessary. Note: an 'adventure park' has been established on the mountainside, but the road into the park continues past here, after it forks to the right.

You can also get a 4WD taxi from Santa Cruz for about US$30 each way.

Northwestern Costa Rica

Best Places to Eat

» Gingerbread (p151)

» Don Rufino (p142)

» Trio's (p174)

» Brisas del Lago (p153)

» Vista Copal (p208)

Best Places to Stay

» Rancho Margot (p148)

» Celeste Mountain Lodge (p185)

» Ecolodge San Luis & Research Station (p181)

» Mystica Resort (p153)

» Lucky Bug B&B (p152)

Why Go?

You've probably heard of northwestern Costa Rica's super-stars: misty cloud forests and that now-dormant volcano delivering old lava fields, a stunning lake and bubbling hot springs. Venture further and you'll discover aquamarine rivers, affordable ecolodges, magnificent waterfalls, grassy savanna, Costa Rica's second-biggest city, and the most epic bay you've never heard of, blessed with world-class wind and powdery sand. With a shiny new airport terminal, it's never been easier to explore the great northwest.

When to Go

The climate varies widely from the dry heat of Guanacaste to the swirling, ever present mist of Monteverde and, to a lesser extent, Arenal and Tenorio. It gets cool at night in the mountains – even during the dry season, so pack your bags accordingly. Guanacaste is Costa Rica's driest province, getting very little rain from November to April, when the winds bless (and blast) Bahía Salinas. Humpback whales migrate up the coast in September and October.

ARENAL ROUTE

If you've got your own wheels and a little time, take the road from Ciudad Quesada to the Arenal area – you are in for one beautiful ride. With the backdrop of Volcán Platanar, the road winding through this green, river-rich agrarian region passes through prosperous, quaint towns bright with bougainvillea. In front of you, if the weather cooperates, the resolute peak of Arenal will loom.

Past La Fortuna, the paved road (beware of potholes) hugs the north bank of Laguna de Arenal. On either side of the road, up the green slope and down on the lakeside, turnouts and driveways for lovely inns, kooky ersatz Austrian mini-villages, hip coffeehouses and eccentric galleries appear like pictures in a pop-up book. Scattered in between, you can't help but notice the real-estate signs offering lots for sale, but the area is bucolic and not overdeveloped, and each stop feels far enough away from the next to offer a sense of isolation.

Heading back around the western edge of the lake, you'll pass through the lakeside Nuevo Arenal and down to the pleasant mountain town of Tilarán before descending toward the Interamericana. Note that this route is also well served by public transportation.

Ciudad Quesada (San Carlos)

POP 29,900

The official name of this small city is Ciudad Quesada (sometimes abbreviated to 'Quesada'), but all the locals know it as San Carlos, and local buses often list San Carlos as the destination. It's long been a bustling ranching and agricultural center, known for its *talabaterías* (saddle shops), where a top-quality saddle can cost US$1000. Get a sense of that at Feria del Ganado (cattle fair and auction), which is held every April and accompanied by carnival rides and a *tope* (horse parade).

DON'T MISS

PARKS & RESERVES

Northwestern Costa Rica has a wealth of parks and reserves, ranging from little-visited national parks to the highlight on many visitors' itineraries, Monteverde.

» **Parque Nacional Guanacaste** (p204) One of the least-visited parks in Costa Rica. The land transitions between dry tropical forest and humid cloud forest.

» **Parque Nacional Palo Verde** (p189) Stay at the research station and take a guided tour to see some of the 300-plus bird species recorded in this rich wetland.

» **Parque Nacional Rincón de la Vieja** (p197) Peaceful, muddy isolation can be found at this national park just outside of Liberia, where bubbling thermal activity abounds.

» **Area de Conservacion Guanacaste** (p200) Access legendary surf, hike through the largest stand of tropical dry forest in Central America and visit a historical battle site.

» **Parque Nacional Volcán Arenal** (p145) Centered on the perfect cone of Volcán Arenal, the clouds will sometimes disperse, revealing the hulking giant.

» **Refugio Nacional de Vida Silvestre Bahía Junquillal** (p204) Another small, peaceful protected site, this refuge has a beach backed by mangrove swamp and tropical dry forest.

» **Reserva Biológica Bosque Nuboso Monteverde** (p177) Costa Rica's most famous cloud forest, Monteverde receives a steady stream of visitors without having lost its magic.

» **Reserva Biológica Lomas de Barbudal** (p190) If you're here in March, you might be lucky enough to catch the yellow blooms of the *corteza amarilla* tree in this tropical dry forest reserve.

» **Reserva Santa Elena** (p180) Slightly less crowded and at a higher elevation than Monteverde, this is also a good place to spot a quetzal.

Northwestern Costa Rica Highlights

1 Wake early to hike in the **Reserva Biológica Bosque Nuboso Monteverde** (p177) and **Reserva Santa Elena** (p131)

2 Satisfy your need for speed on windy **Bahía Salinas** (p206) with a kitesurfing course, or bronze on a deserted bay

3 Trek the circuit of waterfalls, thermal pools and volcanic vents of **Volcán Rincón de la Vieja** (p197)

4 Hike out to the otherworldly cerulean-blue waters of the **Río Celeste** at **Parque Nacional Volcán Tenorio** (p184)

5 Watch wildlife at Costa Rica's largest wetland sanctuary, **Parque Nacional Palo Verde** (p189)

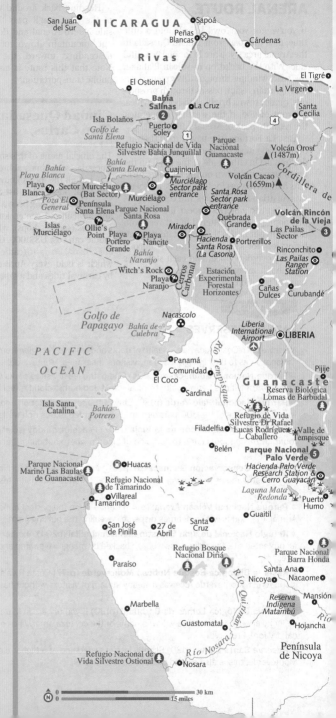

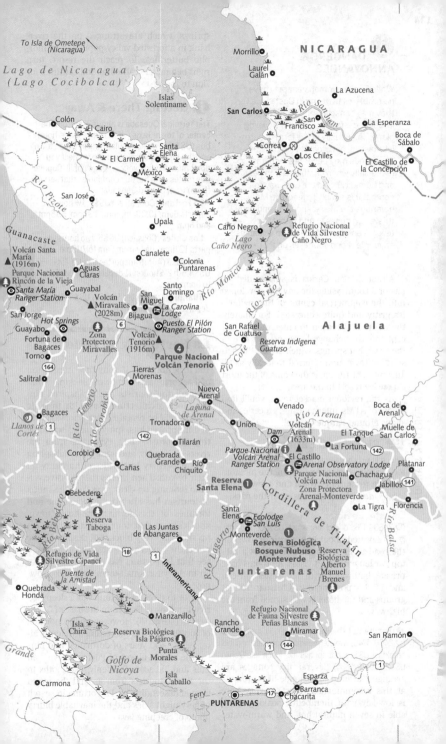

ⓘ DANGERS & ANNOYANCES

While foreign women generally have no problems traveling in Costa Rica, they may sense a whiff of machismo in Guanacaste, most often if traveling alone, and usually in the form of harmless hissing or catcalls. This constant annoyance may become exasperating (especially when combined with heat and humidity), and the best way to combat it is simply to ignore it. More nefarious are the pickpockets and bag thieves on buses to and from Monteverde and La Fortuna. Keep valuables at your feet and your eyes on them.

Although San Carlos is surrounded by pastoral countryside, the city has developed into the commercial center of the region – it's gritty and quite congested. Fortunately, there's no real reason to enter the city, except to either change buses or visit one of the area's hot springs, which are on the outskirts of town, and referred to locally as 'El Tucanito' (El Tucano is the name of the most expensive resort in the area).

As the regional market town, you'll find plenty of ATMs, internet cafes, groceries and shops around Parque Central.

⌾ Sleeping & Eating

There is no shortage of budget hotels and eateries around town. Apart from the plethora of chain restaurants, you'll find a few decent local *sodas* (cheap eateries) near the park.

Loma Verde Hotel HOTEL $$
(☎2460-1976; d incl breakfast US$60; P❄@ 🖥🐕) Located about 2km north of town on the road to Florencia, this hotel has a hilltop garden with great vistas. All rooms have private bathroom with hot water, air-con and TV. It's popular with Christian retreat groups and the hotel is well signed from the highway.

Termales del Bosque RESORT $$
(☎2460-4740; www.termalesdelbosque.com; d incl breakfast US$75, hot springs incl lunch adult/child US$21/19; P🖥🐕) Several airy cottages are arranged around the jungle-like grounds at this recommended resort. Luxury here is low-key with therapeutic soaking available in seven natural hot- and warm-water

springs, which are arranged on the riverbank in a forested valley populated by morpho butterflies. To reach the resort, turn right behind the cathedral and continue for 7km to the east.

ⓘ Getting There & Away

The Terminal Quesada is about 2km from the center of town. Taxis (US$1) and a twice-hourly bus (US$.50) make regular runs between town and the terminal. Walking there is fine if you don't mind hauling your luggage uphill. Popular bus routes (and the bus companies that service them) from Ciudad Quesada:

La Fortuna (Coopatrac) US$2; 1½ hours; departs 6am, 10:30am, 1pm, 3:30pm, 5:15pm and 6pm.

Los Chiles (Chilsaca) US$5; two hours; departs 12 times daily from 5am to 7:15pm.

San José (Autotransportes San Carlos) US$4.50; 2½ hours; 11 departures from 5am to 6pm.

Tilarán (Transportes Tilarán) US$5; 4½ hours; departs 6:30am and 4pm.

La Fortuna & Around

POP 10,000

You'll be forgiven if your first impression of La Fortuna is somewhat lacking, what with all the tourists and uninspired cinder block architecture. But with time its charms will be revealed. Here, horses graze in unimproved lots, spiny iguanas scramble through brush, sloth eyes peer from the riverside canopy, and sunny, eternal spring mornings carry just a kiss of humidity on their breath. Then there's that massive volcano looming on clear days. Yes, the influx of tourism has altered the face, fame and fortunes of this former one-horse town, and it's true that tour operators have set up shop on every block, but despite all the noise, the longer you linger, the more you'll see that La Fortuna has managed to retain an underlying, small-town *sabanero* (cowboy) feel.

Prior to 1968, La Fortuna was a sleepy agricultural town, 6km from the base of Cerro Arenal (Arenal Hill). However, on the morning of July 29, 1968, Arenal erupted violently after nearly 400 years of dormancy, and buried the small villages of Pueblo Nuevo, San Luís and Tabacón. Suddenly, like moths to the flame, tourists from around the world started descending on La Fortuna in search of fiery night skies and the inevitable blurry photo of creeping lava.

Since then, La Fortuna has served as the principal gateway for visiting Volcán Arenal, and it's still one of the top destinations for travelers in Costa Rica. However, be warned that the great mountain has stopped spewing its molten discharge, and there are no longer lava photo ops. But the mountain is still glorious, and the town is well connected by public transport to San José. Many travelers arrive from or head out to Monteverde via the scenic and unusual jeep-boat-jeep transfer, which is somehow jeep-less. If you have your own transport, consider staying at the Arenal Observatory Lodge or in the small town of El Castillo, as you'll be rewarded with fewer crowds and a more rustic vibe.

◉ Sights & Activities

Hot Springs

What's the consolation prize when you can no longer see lava creeping down the Arenal slopes? Why, hot springs, of course. You'll be glad to know that beneath La Fortuna the lava is still curdling and heating countless bubbling springs. There are several free hot springs in the area that any local can take you to. Of course, if you're after a more comfortable experience, consider one of the area's resorts.

Eco Thermales Hot Springs   HOT SPRING
(☑2479-8484; adult/child US$34/29; ☺10am-9pm; P☺⛟) A large forbidding gate leads to this recommended, reservation-only complex. Everything from the natural circulation systems in the pools to the soft, mushroom lighting is understated yet luxurious. Just 100 visitors per four-hour slot are welcomed at 10am, 1pm and 5pm. During the evening session, guests have the option to choose from one of three set dinner menus.

The Springs Resort & Spa   HOT SPRING
(☑2401-3313, in USA 954-727-8333; www.thespringscostarica.com; admission US$40; P☺) If you're looking for a luxurious hot springs experience, the Springs features 18 free-form pools with various temperatures, volcano views, landscaped gardens, waterfalls and swim-up bars, including a jungle bar with a waterslide. You can sleep (p141) here too.

Tabacón Hot Springs   HOT SPRING
(☑2519-1900; www.tabacon.com; day pass incl lunch or dinner adult/child US$85/40, evening pass incl dinner US$70/35; day pass without meals US$65/45; ☺10am-10pm; P☺) If a movie di-

rector ever needed a setting for a cheesy Garden of Eden dream sequence, Tabacón Hot Springs would be it. Here, broad-leaf palms, rare orchids and other florid tropical blooms part to reveal a 40°C (104°F) waterfall pouring over a (fake) cliff, concealing natural-esque caves complete with camouflaged cup holders. Lounged across each well-placed stone-like substance, overheated tourists of various shapes and sizes relax.

The spa, 14km west of La Fortuna, is actually on the site where a volcanic eruption ripped through in 1975, killing one local. The former village of Tabacón was destroyed in the 1968 eruption, killing 78. Don't, ahem, sweat it. The mountain is once again dormant. For now. (Insert spooky music here.)

Day Spas

Many top-end hotels have spas that are open to nonguests including **Tabacón Grand Spa Thermal Resort Lodge** (☑2256-1500; www.tabacon.com; d incl breakfast US$245-450; P☺✳@☺☺), the Springs Resort & Spa (p135) and Casa Luna Hotel & Spa (p142), among others.

El Sueño Spa   SPA
(☑2479-8261; Av Central; treatments US$20-75; ☺9am-9pm) This place offers massages, facials and reflexology treatments in a peaceful salon. It also sells volcanic mud so you can relive the spa experience at home.

Herrera Day Spa   SPA
(☑2479-9016; cnr Av Volcán & Calle 3; treatments US$45-110; ☺8:30am-noon, 1-6pm) Two hundred meters northeast of Parque Central, Herrera offers six varieties of massage, facials and full-body volcanic mud treatments.

Other Sights & Activities

There are some fun hiking trails in and around Parque Nacional Volcán Arenal (p146). Most of the trails are located on private nature reserves, none of which are free.

La Catarata de la Fortuna   WATERFALL
(US$10; ☺8am-5pm) You can glimpse the sparkling 70m ribbon of clear water that pours through a sheer canyon of dark volcanic rock arrayed in bromeliads and ferns with minimal sweat equity. But it's worth the climb down and out to see it from the jungle floor. Though it's dangerous to dive beneath the thundering falls, a series of perfect swimming holes with spectacular views tiles the canyon in aquamarine. Keep an eye on your backpack.

La Fortuna

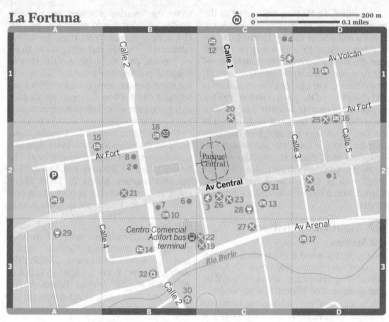

From the turnoff on the road to San Ramón, it's about 4km uphill to the falls. If you decide to walk up, you'll enjoy spectacular views of Cerro Chato as you hike through pastures and past the small hotels lining the road. You might appreciate a stop at Neptune's House of Hammocks (p144). You can also get to the waterfall on horseback or by car or taxi.

Cerro Chato   HIKING
The La Catarata de la Fortuna (p135) falls are the trailhead for this seriously strenuous five- to six-hour climb to the beautiful lake-filled volcanic crater that is Cerro Chato. Starting from here, you'll have to pay a US$10 fee for crossing the *finca* (farm) leading to Cerro Chato; a slightly cheaper (though you'll still pay a fee) and only slightly less physically taxing alternative would be to hike up the other side from Arenal Observatory Lodge (p145).

Festivals & Events

The big annual bash is Fiestas de la Fortuna, held in mid-February and featuring two weeks of Tico-rules bullfights, colorful carnival rides, greasy festival food, craft stands and unusual gambling devices. It's free, except for the beer (which is cheap)

and you'll have a blast trying to decide between the temporary disco with go-go dancers getting down to reggaetón or the rough and wild tents next door with live *ranchero* and salsa.

Tours

You could have someone blindfold you and spin you around on Av Central and chances are you'd manage to stumble right into a tour-operator's desk – unless a tout got a hold of you first. While exploding development in La Fortuna means there's a lot of healthy competition to be found, you'll need to shop around, compare prices and not buy your tour from some friendly dude on the street.

There's usually a two-person minimum for any trip, and groups can work out discounts in advance with most outfitters. If you don't want to deal with tour operators, most hotels can arrange trips for you, though you will probably be charged a US$5 per person commission. It's also becoming standard practice in La Fortuna to sell tourists pricey tours to distant destinations, such as Caño Negro. If you're turned off by the idea of public transportation, this is a fine option, though you'll save yourself a ton of money (and probably have a

La Fortuna

much better experience) if you actually go to these places on the local bus and then organize a tour upon arrival.

Although it's no longer erupting, Volcán Arenal is the big drawcard here, and you don't need a guide's help to take a hike into the upper reaches of the national park (by far the better option). Organized Arenal tours are available and are generally combined with a dip into the hot springs. Prices vary widely, but generally run US$25 to US$65 per person. Make sure your tour includes entry fees to the park and hot springs.

Canoa Aventura CANOEING
(☑2479-8200; www.canoa-aventura.com; full-day trip to Caño Negro incl breakfast & lunch US$131; ⊙6:30am-9:30pm) About 1.5km west of town on the road to Arenal, Canoa Aventura specializes in canoe and float trips led by bilingual naturalist guides. Most are geared toward wildlife- and bird-watching. Popular paddles include the full-day trip to Caño Negro.

Ecoglide CANOPY TOUR
(☑2479-7120; www.arenalecoglide.com; adult/student & child 5-12yr US$45/35; ⊙8am-4pm; 🔄) Opened in 2008, Ecoglide is the biggest canopy game in town, featuring 12 cables,

14 platforms and a 'Tarzan' swing. The dual-cable safety system provides extra security and peace of mind.

Arenal Paraíso Canopy Tours CANOPY TOUR
(☑2479-1100; www.arenalparaiso.com; adult/student & child US$45/35) Popular two-hour tours along 12 zip lines.

Canopy Los Cañones CANOPY TOUR
(☑2479-1000; www.canopyloscanones.com; US$45) Canopy Los Cañones has 15 cables from 50m to 500m long, over the rainforest.

Arenal Mundo Aventura CANOPY TOUR
(☑2479-9762; www.arenalmundoaventura.com; adult/child US$67/55) At this ecological park you can take a canopy tour over La Fortuna Waterfall (p135), go rappelling or horseback riding, and catch Maleku performances all in one spot.

PureTrek Canyoning CANYONING
(☑2479-1315, in USA 1-866-569-5723; www.pure trek.com; 4hr incl transportation & lunch US$98; ⊙7am-10pm) The reputable PureTrek leads guided rappels down four waterfalls, one of which is 50m high. It's located several kilometers west of town, on the road to Arenal Nayara Hotel & Gardens (p141). Children as young as five years old can participate, but there's no price break.

NORTHWESTERN COSTA RICA LA FORTUNA & AROUND

Around La Fortuna

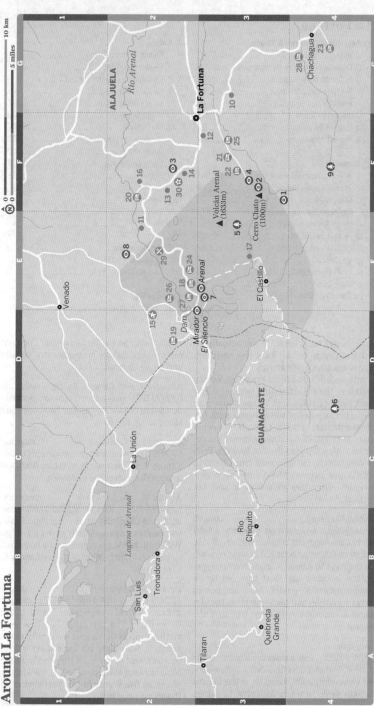

0
0 10 km
5 miles

ALAJUELA

Río Arenal

La Fortuna

Chachagua

23

28

10

12

25

21

3

16

22 4

14

30 2

13

20 Volcán Arenal 1

(1633m)

11 Cerro Chato

8 (1100m)

5

17

29 El Castillo

26 18 24

Venado 27 Arenal

15 7

Dam El Castillo

19 Mirador

El Silencio

6

GUANACASTE

La Unión

Laguna de Arenal

Río

Chiquito

San Luis

Tronadora

Quebrada

Grande

Tilarán

Around La Fortuna

Desafío Adventure Company RAFTING, HORSE RIDING
(☑2479-9464; www.desafiocostarica.com; Calle 2; horse tour to Arenal US$65; ◎6:30am-9pm) Desafío has the widest range of river trips in Fortuna, and offers paddling trips on the Ríos Balsa and, occasionally, the Sarapiquí.

It also offers horse riding treks to Volcán Arenal, adventure tours rappelling down waterfalls, and mountain bike expeditions. Look for the crenelated new building.

Wave Expeditions RAFTING, KAYAKING
(☑2479-7262; www.waveexpeditions.com; cnr Calle 2 & Av Fort; river trips US$65-85; ◎7am-9pm) A rafting shop in the center of town, Wave Expeditions runs the wild Toro and mellower Balsa. You can also run the smooth Arenal River on an inflatable kayak or pair a canopy zip-line tour with the rafting experience.

Aguas Bravas RAFTING, KAYAKING
(☑2479-7645; www.aguas-bravas.co.cr; safari float trip US$50, Class III/Class IV trips US$65/85; ◎7am-7pm) Aguas Bravas, 2km east of Fortuna, offers a gentle safari float trip on Peñas Blancas that's a good choice for families, plus Class III and IV trips.

Fortuna Mountainbike MOUNTAIN BIKING
(☑2479-7704; www.fortunamb.com; Calle 3; half-/full day US$10/15, tours US$67-96; ◎7am-5pm) This upstart mountain-biking outfitter of-fers a range of quality rentals, as well as a half-day, fully supported 26km ride on gravel roads to Lake Arenal, and full day tours that range from 36km to 85km in length and include lunch.

Aventuras Arenal TOUR
(☑2479-9133; www.arenaladventures.com; Av Central; ◎7am-8pm) Around for over 15 years, this outfit organizes a variety of local day tours on bike, boat and horseback.

Jacamar Tours HIKING
(☑2479-9767; www.arenaltours.com; Av Central; ◎7am-9pm) Recommended for its incredible variety of naturalist hikes. It's located on the ground level of Hotel Arenal Carmela (p141).

Sunset Tours TOUR
(☑2479-9800; www.sunsettourcr.com; Calle 2; ◎6:30am-9pm) Recommended for high quality tours with bilingual guides. It is also the local booking office for Nature Air.

🛏 Sleeping

There are loads of places to stay in town. If you're driving, consider staying on the pastoral road to Cerro Chato, a few kilometers south of town, where several appealing hotels have cropped up, or closer to the volcano in El Castillo.

In the low-season room rates plummet by as much as 40%.

IN TOWN

TOP CHOICE La Fortuna Backpackers   HOSTEL $

(☎2479-9700; www.fortunabackpackers.com; cnr Calle 5 & Ave Fort; dm/d US$10/25; P@☎) The best hostel in town is set in a humble peach tinted casa and blessed with a cutesy sky blue paint job. Rooms, private and dorms alike, are spotless and have new mattresses; the kitchen is large and updated; the shared bathroom is huge and there are ample activities on offer.

Gringo Pete's   HOSTEL $

(☎2479-8521; www.gringopeteshostel.com; Calle 7, 20m north of Av Arenal; dm US$7, r 20-24; P☎) A nice, original hostel with cubbyhole-sized private rooms and a large tiled dorm. There is an ant issue, but if you keep food out of your rooms, you'll be fine. Amenities include a communal kitchen, BBQ and a laundry service.

Arenal Backpackers Resort   HOSTEL $

(☎2479-7000; www.arenalbackpackersresort.com; Av Central; dm US$14, tents s/d US$25/35, d US$56; P✳@☎☲) Set out on its own, this self-proclaimed 'five-star hostel' with volcano views is among the cushier hostels in Costa Rica. Dorm rooms have private hot-water bathroom, and you'll sleep easy on the thick, orthopedic mattresses. Private rooms definitely cater to midrange travelers but they're worth the splurge. The newest budget accommodations option is the covered tent city; each raised tent contains a double air mattress and electricity. But the real draw is the landscaped pool with swim-up bar, where backpackers spend lazy days lounging with a cold beer. You'll be in a traveler's party bubble here. Not that there's anything wrong with that.

Cabinas Arsol   B&B $

(☎2479-9913; www.cabinasarsol.com; cnr Calle 5 & Av Volcán; s/d US$20/30; @) A recently refurbished, American-Tica–owned B&B with cramped and somewhat oddly situated rooms that also happen to have charms like pastel paint jobs and beamed ceilings. Beds are new, and digs are quite clean and come with cable TV and breakfast. There's an attached vegetarian cafe here, too.

La Choza Inn   INN $

(☎2479-9361; www.lachozahostel.com; Av Fort btwn Calles 2 & 4; incl breakfast dm US$8, d US$30-35; P@☎) This popular budget inn 100m west of Parque Central has a great variety

of rooms – from spotless doubles in a pink washed concrete section to airy, palm-wood dorm rooms. There's a well-stocked communal kitchen and an extremely personable staff, and it's consistently packed.

Arenal Hostel Resort   HOSTEL $

(☎2479-9222; www.paraisotropical.org; Av Central; dm/s/d US$14/44/52; P✳☎) A hotel under new, ambitious management. The lodge rooms sprinkled around the garden are spacious with stone floors. Upstairs rooms have balconies, and all have air-con. The dorm wasn't up and running when we visited, but should be open by the time you visit.

Mayol Lodge   LODGE $

(☎2479-9110; www.mayollodge.com; Av Arenal; d economy/standard US$27/37; P✳☎☲) It doesn't look like much, but the huge standard rooms are a steal with high, white-washed wooden ceilings, pastel paint jobs, Spanish-tiled floors, a balcony with volcano views, cable, and a lovely pool nestled over the riverside surrounded by trees.

Hotel Pepito's Place   HOTEL $$

(☎2479-9238; Calle 2; d US$50; P✳@☎) A quite cute, good value place with spotless air-con rooms (they have ceiling fans, too), tiled floors and beds dressed in tasteful quilts. There are lovely blooming flowers from the 2nd floor terrace.

Hotel Arenal Rabfer   HOTEL $$

(☎2479-9187; www.arenalrabfer.com; Calle 1; d from US$65; P✳@☎☲) Arguably the most architecturally appealing of the downtown options, with a striking shingled 2nd floor. Rooms, set up around a pebbled pool area and shady palm garden, are spacious with high slanted ceilings, although the interiors could use an update. Clearly the transformation is in mid-stride.

Hotel Las Colinas   HOTEL $$

(☎2479-9305; www.lascolinasarenal.com; Calle 1 btwn Avs Central & Arenal; s/d/tr incl breakfast from US$55/70/90; P✳@☎) The friendly owners of Las Colinas have completely remodeled this hotel, creating modern, airy rooms and a 2nd-story terrace with ample sun lounges and great views of the volcano. All rooms have similar amenities like cable TV and solar-generated hot water, but rates increase with room and bed space. Avoid the dark 1st floor and grab a bright room off the terrace.

Hotel Arenal Carmela
HOTEL **$$**

(☑2479-9010; www.hotelarenalcarmela.com; Av Central; s/d incl breakfast US$65/75; P✳@❀🛜🏊) A cute courtyard family hotel just off the main drag, with a kid-friendly pool and slender sun deck. And while they've crammed quite a few rooms into this small area, digs are modern, clean and have balconies.

Sleeping Indian Hostel
HOSTEL **$**

(☑2479-8431, 8843-7101; Av Fort; s/d US$25/30; 🛜) Ethnic insensitivities aside, this is a bright and cheery 2nd story hostel with six fan-cooled, tiled rooms with wooden beds and wi-fi. It's run by a mellow, sophisticated local who offers plenty of communal space accented by drums, handicrafts and rather inviting hammocks.

WEST OF TOWN

TOP CHOICE / **Hotel Campo Verde**
BUNGALOW **$$**

(☑2479-1080; www.hotelcampoverde.com; s/d $75/90) An absolutely darling family-owned property. Canary yellow wooden bungalows have vaulted beamed ceilings, two double beds, lovely drapes and chandeliers, and a sweet tiled patio blessed with two waiting rockers. Book the wooden bungalows furthest from the road at the foot of the mountain.

Erupciones Inn B&B
B&B **$$**

(☑2479-1400; www.erupcionesinn.com; d incl breakfast US$60-65; P✳) The colorful *cabinas* (cabins) at this quaint B&B off the highway and by the riverside, are adorned with ornamental tiles and windows facing the volcano. Some have vaulted, beamed ceilings, and each comes with its own private patio with chairs. It's 9km west of La Fortuna.

Arenal Nayara Hotel & Gardens
HOTEL **$$$**

(☑2479-1600; www.arenalnayara.com; r/ste incl breakfast US$232/350; P✳@🛜🏊) This intimate hotel has 24 *casitas* (cottages) with Asian-inspired architecture and minimalist decor. All rooms have exquisite furnishings and bedding, rich woods, flat-screen TV, DVD player, iPod dock, an outdoor shower and a private outdoor Jacuzzi where you can soak up views of Arenal volcano. The only thing missing are the hot springs. You'll have to leave the property for those.

Arenal Kioro
HOTEL **$$$**

(☑2479-1700; www.hotelarenalkioro.com; d incl breakfast US$446; P✳🛜🏊) The 53 all-suite rooms feature floor-to-ceiling windows with in-your-face volcano views, whirlpool tub,

balconies and floral decor. There are eight beautiful thermal hot-spring pools surrounded by lush gardens. Onsite amenities include a restaurant, gym and full-service spa.

Springs Resort & Spa
RESORT **$$$**

(☑2401-3313; www.springscostarica.com; d from US$435; P✳@🛜🏊🍴) Ok, so The Bachelor had one rather steamy private date here. And why not? After all, Arenal's swankiest hot springs property is set 4km from the highway amid *pueblo* (small town) pasture land and perched on a precipice with spectacular volcano and valley views. Rooms are plush with all of the four-star amenities. There are eight thermal pools and an indulgent, top-shelf spa as well as four restaurants, four bars and a private zoo. True, it is very much the American package-tourist scene, but it is lovely.

SOUTH OF TOWN
Just a few kilometers south of town, a mostly dirt road trundles to the base of Cerro Chato, and hotels now dot either side of it. Even further flung is the village of Chachagua, just 8km south along the road to San Ramón. Crisscrossed by local rivers, this authentic, agrarian, market *pueblo* is an antidote to the touristy brouhaha of La Fortuna.

Chachagua Rainforest Hotel
HOTEL **$$$**

(☑2468-1010; www.chachaguarainforesthotel.com; d incl breakfast from US$135; P⊖🛜🏊) This hotel is a naturalist's dream, situated on a private reserve that abuts the Bosque Eterno de Los Niños in Chachagua. Part of the property is a working orchard, cattle ranch and fish farm, while the rest is humid rainforest that can be accessed either through a series of hiking trails or on horseback. The cheaper rooms aren't really worth the splurge but for $10 extra you can have a spacious dark wood bungalow with wood floors, exquisite bathrooms and wide decks with a love seat and a rocker out front. There's a pool within the exquisitely lush grounds, as well as a restaurant that features food raised or grown on the premises. The 2km dirt road forking off the main road may require a 4WD in the rainy season.

Villas Josipek
CABINA **$**

(☑8812-2626, 2430-5252; www.costaricavillas josipek.com; per person US$25; P🏊) In the village of Chachagua, these immaculate, simple wooden cabins with volcano views are surrounded by private rainforest trails that penetrate the Bosque Eterno de Los Niños. All eight of the cabins have full kitchen, and the largest sleeps up to 12. There's a well-kept pool on the quiet, jungle-fringed property, and the family can arrange tours in the region.

Hotel Cerro Azul
HOTEL $$

(2479-7360; www.ranchocerroazul.com; d US$72; P✳❄☎) Nothing fancy here, just four cute, shingled cabins with decks overlooking the trees, the river and the volcano beyond. Think: simple, natural, beautiful, comfortable.

Catarata Eco-Lodge
LODGE $$

(2479-9522; www.cataratalodge.com; s/d incl breakfast US$63/74; P@❄☎≋) Well, they do recycle and don't automatically throw your linens in the wash every day; apart from that, the 'eco' of this lodge extends to simply caring about the environment. Still, digs are decent little (and we do mean little) Spanish-tiled and wood rooms set up in duplex pods with log columns and beamed ceilings. But it has a gorgeous setting at the base of Cerro Chato.

Casa Luna Hotel & Spa
HOTEL $$$

(2479-7368; www.casalunalodge.com; s/d incl breakfast US$125/135, spa treatments US$40-130; P✳@❄☎≋) The snazziest joint on this road, this terra-cotta floored, adobe-style lodge has sex appeal. Wooden doors open into elegant split-level duplexes with tiny private patios. It offers spa treatments and the pleasant pool area is edged with landscaped garden walkways leading to a groovy open-air lobby. It's 1.5km from the main road, on the right.

🍴 Eating

TOP CHOICE **Restaurant Don Rufino** STEAKHOUSE $$$

(2479-9997; www.donrufino.com; cnr Av Central & Calle 3; mains US$16-39; 10am-11pm) In almost every way this trendy, hopping indoor-outdoor bar and grill is light years ahead of the competition. In addition to the grilled meats, which include rib eye, filet, peppercorn tenderloin medallions, and a porterhouse with gorgonzola sauce, it trades in tilapia and crab risotto, offers a ginger-glazed grilled tuna, and a Bengali chicken in coconut curry. It even has a *tom yum* soup. In other words, this spot is anything but *tipica*. Tables book up with the well-coifed in high season. Break out the smell goods and reserve ahead.

Soda Ara
SODA $

(2479-7267; cnr Calle 5 & Av Fort ; mains US$4-8; 6am-7pm) A succulent smelling soda, with the usual greasy spoon *casados* (cheap set meals), roast meats and tasty breakfasts for a song. If you want fast *tipica* with flavor, belly up to the picnic tables or rustic lunch counter opposite the open kitchen.

Soda Viquez
SODA $

(2479-7133; cnr Calle 1 & Av Arenal; mains US$6-10; 7am-10pm) Insanely popular among travelers, this friendly spot takes *tipica* and adds something to it. It has a tasty, saucy steam table, but also makes chicken, beef and fish six different ways if you choose to order off the menu. Prices are reasonable, portions ample.

Soda La Parada
SODA $$

(2479-9547; www.restaurantelaparada.com; Av Central; mains US$5-19; 24hr) Facing Parque Central and all the street action, this popular *soda* does a brisk trade in, well, everything, from questionable pizzas to more reliable *tipica* including a steam table that is heavy with beans, roast chicken, boiled corn and pork skin. It's not uncommon to find all the long wooden tables packed.

La Cascada
RESTAURANT $$

(2479-9145; cnr Av Fort & Calle 1; mains US$6-26; 11am-late) This thatched-roof landmark has been around so long that the *palapa* (thatched palm) roof is almost as big an institution as the volcano it mimics. With a small bar it acquires a drinking crowd at night but tourists consider it a lunch and dinner option, too. It has all the roast and grilled meat dishes, pastas, sandwiches and three veggie options.

My Coffee
CAFE $

(2479-8749; Av Central; mains US$6-9; 8am-8pm; ☎) Doubtless, the best breakfast in town. Even if the lounge is a bit overdone, it's a cool concept spot where the coffee comes naturally filtered Tico-style and is fantastic. It offers omelets, eggs al gusto, French toast and pancakes.

Gecko Gourmet
DELI $

(2479-8905; cnr Calle 2 & Av Fort; mains US$4-8; 7am-3:30pm; ✍) Tired of *gallo pinto* and *casados*? Stop by this little deli for creative breakfasts such as banana pancakes, cream cheese-stuffed French toast, bagels and lox, or a breakfast burrito. But be warned, they have no stove so eggs are cooked in the microwave. How... organic? Nevertheless, it does have an intriguing lunch menu featuring a tasty *caprese* chicken sandwich, a roasted veggie wrap and more.

Flying Tomato Cafe VEGETARIAN $
(✉2479-9913; www.cabinasarsol.com; cnr Calle 5 & Av Volcan; mains US$3-5; ☺8am-9pm; ✈) An exclusively veggie kitchen, serving pasta, veggie burgers, stir-frys and soups, and the only place in Fortuna to offer soy milk for espresso drinks and *batidos* (fruitshakes). Hours can be iffy.

La Casa de la Hormiga SODA $
(Av Arenal; mains US$3-5; ☺6am-8pm) Locally beloved and set conveniently next door to the bus station, this open-air lunch counter is one of the quaintest, cheapest *sodas* in town. They do all the *casados*, as well as big breakfasts and burgers, too.

Lava Lounge RESTAURANT $$
(✉2479-7365; Av Central btwn Calles 4 & 2; mains US$8-12; ☺11am-10:30pm; 🕾✈) This hip, open-air restaurant is a breath of fresh air when you just can't abide another *casado*. There's pasta, fish, burgers, wraps, five kinds of tacos and excellent chips and guacamole. All of it brought to your picnic table beneath an elegantly lit *palapa* roof, by friendly waiters. It has live music every Wednesday and Sunday evening.

Restaurante Mirador Arenal
Steak House STEAKHOUSE $$$
(✉2479-1926; mains US$16-28; ☺10am-10pm; 🕾) There's more than a little cowboy kitsch at this old Sabanero steak barn. The waiters dress like cowboys and those portraits of horses and that desert landscape mural are so dreadful they're glorious. But there's some swank here, too, including good wine, leather tablecloths (may as well use the whole cow), and fine cuts of grass-fed beef. Carnivors should try the local Churrasco cut. It's located 8km west of La Fortuna.

Super Cristian 2 SUPERMARKET
(cnr Av Central & Calle 1; ☺7am-9pm) For groceries, stop by this well-stocked place on the southeast corner of Parque Central; there's another **Super Cristian 2** (corner Av Arenal and Calle 2) down by the river.

Mega Super SUPERMARKET $
(Av Arenal; ☺7am-9pm Mon-Sat, 7am-8pm Sun) Next to the bus terminal, this spacious super is a good place to visit before that long bus ride.

Drinking & Entertainment

Despite the tourist influx, La Fortuna unfortunately remains a cultural wasteland. Occasionally, cultural events are advertised on flyers posted on store windows, though entertainment in the area tends to be aimed at locals looking to get hammered and tourists conspiring to get loose.

Rockoco BAR
(Av Central; ☺5pm-3am) Easily the coolest new bar in Fortuna, what with its flayed magic bus facades embedded with booths, surfboard decor and graphed up Marilyn, Mona and Frida portraits on the back wall. The arced bamboo bar is wide and welcoming and it does burgers and cocktails, offers *shisha* pipes, and serves icy beer. What's not to love?

Volcán Look CLUB
(✉2479-9690; men cover charge US$4; ☺8pm-3am Wed-Sat) This club is reportedly Costa Rica's biggest discotheque outside of San José. It's about 5km west of town, though it's virtually abandoned except on weekends and holidays: don't bother showing up until after 11pm unless you want to dance *cumbia* alone.

El Establo BAR
(Calle 2; ☺5pm-2am Wed-Sat) La Fortuna's raucous *sendero* bar with an attached disco, fronts the bull ring and attracts an ever enthusiastic local following. The age demographic here expands from 18 to 88. That's almost always a good thing.

Cosechos JUICE BAR
(Calle 1 btwn Avs Central Arenal; drinks US$2-3.50; ☺10am-9pm) A branch of Costa Rica's favorite juice bar is tucked in across the street from Hotel Las Colinas, and it does wonderful alchemy with fruits and veggies, including an intriguing mango-strawberry-pineapple smoothie, a watermelon-passion-fruit milkshake, and the counter-intuitive but delicious watermelon-strawberry-lemon combo.

Shopping

Although there is no shortage of knickknack overload in La Fortuna's ubiquitous cheap touristy boutiques, quality capitalism is slim pickings. However, local artisans converge on the hippie restaurant/bar deluxe that is the Lava Lounge (p143) in the evening to display exquisite beaded, silver and braided bracelets, earrings and necklaces. They'll be lined up and waiting by the front door almost every night.

Neptune's House of Hammocks HOMEWARES (☑2479-8269; hammocks US$50-170) On the road to La Catarata de La Fortuna (p135), it sells soft drinks and hammocks (yes, cat-sized models are available) that you can try out while you take a breather.

❶ Information

Internet Access

Arenal Rocks Internet (☑8854-2898; Av Central; per hr US$1.20; ☺8am-11pm) Located under the Hotel Arenal Carmella.

Ciro Internet Café y Mas (☑2479-7769; Av Central; per hr US$1; ☺7am-6:30pm Mon-Fri, 8am-6:30pm Sat)

Expediciones (☑2479-9101; cnr Av Central & Calle 1; per 30/60min US$.80/1.20; ☺7am-9pm Mon-Sat) Most tour operators in town also provide internet access, but if you're not interested in hearing a sales pitch, there are no hassles here.

Laundry

Barbujas (☑2479-7115, 8910-7737; Calle 3 btwn Avs Central & Arenal; per kilo US$4; ☺8am-8pm) A friendly and reliable *lavanderia* in the center of town.

Lavandería La Fortuna (☑2479-9737; Calle 4; per 4kg US$8; ☺8am-9pm Mon-Sat; ❀) Friendly staff will wash, dry and fold while you surf the internet for free.

Medical Services

Centro Médico Arenal Vital (☑2479-7027; Calle 1; ☺24hr) Located in the Hotel Las Colinas building, this private clinic is open 24/7 and has English-speaking staff.

Clínica Fortuna (☑2479-9461; Calle 3 btwn Avs Volcán & Fort; ☺7am-10pm Mon-Thu, 7am-8pm Fri-Sun) Look for the hidden bust of US President John F Kennedy, unceremoniously propped next to a generator.

Money

BAC San José (☑2295-9797; cnr Av Fort & Calle 3) Can change travelers checks.

Banco de Costa Rica (☑2479-9113; Av Central)

Banco Nacional (☑2479-9355; cnr Calle 1 & Av Fort)

Banco Popular (cnr Av Central & Calle 5)

Post

Correos de Costa Rica (Av Fort; ☺8am-5:30pm Mon-Fri, 7:30am-noon Sat)

❶ Getting There & Away

Bus

All domestic buses stop at the Centro Comercial Adifort bus terminal (Av Arenal). The Tica Bus to Nicaragua (US$27) passes by El Tanque between 6:30am and 7am daily; to catch the bus you'll have to take an early taxi to El Tanque (15 minutes, US$12).

Keep an eye on your bags, particularly on the weekend San José run.

Ciudad Quesada (Auto-Transportes San José–San Carlos) US$1.60; one hour; six departures per day at 6:15am, 8:10am, 9:30am, 10:15am, 2:30pm, 4:45pm.

Monteverde US$3.60; six to eight hours; departs 8am (change at Tilarán at 12:30pm for Monteverde).

San José (Auto-Transportes San José–San Carlos) US$4.25; 4½ hours; departs 12:45pm and 2:45pm. Alternatively, take a bus to Ciudad Quesada and change to frequent buses to the capital.

Tilarán (Auto-Transportes Tilarán) US$2.60; 3½ hours; departs 8:30am and 5:30pm.

Jeep-Boat-Jeep

The fastest route between Monteverde-Santa Elena and La Fortuna is the sexy-sounding jeep-boat-jeep combo (US$12 to US$18, three hours) – the 'jeep' is actually a minivan with the requisite yellow 'turismo' tattoo. It's still a terrific transportation option and can be arranged through almost any hotel or tour operator in either town. The minivan from La Fortuna takes you to Laguna de Arenal, meeting a boat that crosses the lake, where a 4WD taxi on the other side continues to Monteverde. This is increasingly becoming the primary transportation between La Fortuna and Monteverde as it's incredibly scenic and well priced and it'll save you half a day of travel over rocky roads.

❶ Getting Around

Bicycle

Some hotels rent bikes to their guests, though Fortuna Mountainbike (p139) has the best maintained mountain and road bikes in town. Note that cycling after dark is illegal in La Fortuna.

The classic mountain-bike trip to La Catarata (about 7km from town) climbs to a fairly brutal, if nontechnical, last few kilometers, although we've heard stories of hardy pack-a-day smokers who've made it (just barely).

Car

La Fortuna is easily accessible by public transportation, but nearby attractions such as the hot springs, Parque Nacional Volcán Arenal and Laguna de Arenal demand internal combustion (walking). Luckily, you can rent cars in town.

Adobe Rent a Car (☑2479-7202; www.adobecar.com; Av Arenal; 4WD per day from US$70; ☺7am-7pm) The cheapest of La Fortuna's rental options. Cars and service are both quite reliable.

Alamo (☑2479-9090; www.alamocostarica.com; cnr Av Central & Calle 2; weekly rates from US$560; ☺7:30am-6pm)

Parque Nacional Volcán Arenal

Arenal was just another dormant volcano surrounded by fertile farmland from about AD 1500 until July 29, 1968, when huge explosions triggered lava flows that destroyed three villages, killing about 80 people and 45,000 cattle. The area was evacuated and roads throughout the region were closed. Eventually, the lava subsided to a relatively predictable flow and life got back to normal. Sort of.

Although it occasionally quieted down for a few weeks or even months, Arenal produced menacing ash columns, massive explosions and streams of glowing molten rock almost daily from 1968 until it all quite abruptly ended in 2010, leaving the alarmed local tourist industry to gasp and spew in its place. Still, any obituary on the Arenal area is quite premature given the fact that the volcano has retained its picture-perfect conical shape despite the volcanic activity, and there is still plenty of forest on its lower slopes and in the nearby foothills.

While the molten night views are gone for now (one never knows what lies beneath or beyond), this mighty mountain is still worthy of your time. Though clouds may shroud her at any time, there are several beautiful trails to explore, and even if it does rain and there is a chill in the air, you are just a short drive away from hot springs.

◉ Sights & Activities

Arenal was made a national park in 1995, and it is part of the Area de Conservación Arenal, which protects most of the Cordillera de Tilarán. This area is rugged and varied, and the biodiversity is high; roughly half the species of land-dwelling vertebrates (birds, mammals, reptiles and amphibians) known in Costa Rica can be found here.

Birdlife is rich in the park and includes such species as trogons, rufous motmots, fruitcrows and lancebills. Commonly seen mammals include howler monkeys, white-faced capuchins and surprisingly tame coatis (though it's tempting, don't feed wild animals).

Arenal Observatory Lodge RESEARCH STATION
(☑lodge 2479-1070, reservations 2290-7011; www.arenalobservatorylodge.com; day pass per person US$4, museum admission free; ℗) This Lodge was built in 1987 as a private observatory for the Universidad de Costa Rica. Scientists chose to construct the lodge on a macadamia-nut farm on the south side of Volcán Arenal due to its proximity to the volcano (only 2km away) and its relatively safe location on a ridge. Since its creation, volcanologists from all over the world, including researchers from the Smithsonian Institute in Washington, DC, have come to study the active volcano. Today, the majority of visitors are tourists, though scientists regularly visit the lodge, and a seismograph in the hotel continues to operate around the clock. The lodge is the only place inside the park where you can legally bed down.

Besides beds the lodge offers massages (from US$60), guided hikes and all the usual tours at good prices. There's an excellent trail network, including the leisurely Waterfall Trail (p145) and the challenging-but-worth-it Cerro Chato Trail (p145). You can swim in the pool, wander around the macadamia-nut farm or investigate the pine forest that makes up about half of the 347-hectare site. You can also rent horses for US$8 per hour.

Waterfall Trail HIKING
(www.arenalobservatorylodge.com; Arenal Observatory Lodge; day pass per person US$4) This scenic hike departing from the Arenal Observatory Lodge is an easy, 2km round-trip hike, which takes about an hour to complete. The terrain starts out flat then descends into a grotto where you'll find a thundering gusher of a waterfall that's about 40ft high. You'll feel the mist long before you see its majesty.

Cerro Chato Trail HIKING
(arenalobservatorylodge.com; Arenal Observatory Lodge; day use per person $4) The ultimate hike in the national park, the Cerro Chato Trail meanders through pasture before climbing quite steeply through remnant forest and into patches of virgin growth reaching into misty sky. Eventually the trail crests Cerro Chato, Arenal's dormant partner, and ends in a 1100m-high volcanic lake that is simply stunning. It will take between two to three hours each way, though the hike is only 8km round trip.

Sendero Los Heliconias HIKING
(☑2461-8499) From the ranger station (which has trail maps available) you can hike this 1km circular track, which passes by the site of the 1968 lava flow (vegetation here is slowly sprouting back to life). A 1.5km-long path branches off this trail and leads to an overlook.

FEELIN' HOT, HOT, HOT!

Volcanoes are formed over millennia as a result of the normal shifting processes of the earth's crust. For example, when oceanic crust slides against continental crust, the higher-density oceanic crust is pushed into a deep region of the earth known as the asthenosphere. This process, along with friction, melts the rocky crust to form magma, which rises through weak areas in the continental crust due to its comparatively light density. Magma tends to collect in a chamber below the earth's crust until increasing pressure forces it upward through a vent and onto the surface as lava. Over time, lava deposits can form large, conical volcanoes with a circular crater at the apex from which magma can escape in the form of gas, lava and ejecta.

Although our understanding of volcanoes has greatly progressed in the past few decades, scientists are still unable to predict a volcanic eruption with certainty. However, it is possible to monitor three phenomena – seismicity, gas emissions and ground deformation – in order to predict the likelihood of a volcanic eruption. Seismicity refers to the ongoing seismic activity that tends to accompany active volcanoes. For example, most active volcanoes have continually recurring low-level seismic activity. Although patterns of activity are difficult to interpret, generally an increase in seismic activity (which often appears as a harmonic tremor) is a sign that an eruption is likely.

Scientists also routinely monitor the composition of gas emissions as erupting magma undergoes a pressure decrease that can produce a large quantity of volcanic gases. For example, sulfur dioxide is one of the main components of volcanic gases, and an increasing airborne amount of this compound is another sign of an impending eruption. Finally, scientists routinely measure the tilt of slope and changes in the rate of swelling of active volcanoes. These measurements are indicators of ground deformation, which is caused by an increase in subterranean pressure due to large volumes of collecting magma.

Since Volcán Arenal is still considered by scientists to be active (despite recent appearance to the contrary) comprehensive monitoring of the volcano occurs frequently.

Sendero Las Coladas   HIKING
(2461-8499) This track branches off the Heliconias trail and wraps around the volcano for 2km past the 1993 lava flow before connecting with the Sendero Los Tucanes (US$4), which extends for another 3km through the tropical rainforest at the base of the volcano. To return to the car-parking area, you will have to turn back. You'll get good views of the summit on the way to the parking lot.

Sendero Los Miradores   HIKING
(2461-8499) From the park headquarters (not the ranger station) is the 1.3km Sendero Los Miradores, which leads down to the shores of the volcanic lake, and provides a good angle for volcano viewing.

Old Lava Flow Trail   HIKING
(2461-8499) Branching from Park Headquarters is this interesting and strenuous lower elevation trail. It follows the flow of the massive 1992 eruption, is 4km round trip and takes two hours to complete. If you want to keep hiking, combine it with the 1.8km El Ceibo trail (p146).

El Ceibo Trail   HIKING
(2461-8499) This scenic 1.8km trail, which leads through secondary forest and is accessed from Park Headquarters, can be combined with the Old Lava Flow Trail (p146) or completed on its own in about 80 minutes.

Arenal 1968   HIKING
(2462-1212; www.arenal1968.com; per person US$10; ⊙7am-10pm) Near the highway turnoff to the park, this new trail system is worth checking out. Arenal 1968, a private network of trails and lookouts along the original 1968 lava flow, is located 1.2km from the turnoff, just before the ranger station.

🛏 Sleeping & Eating

Arenal Observatory Lodge   LODGE $$$
(2290-7011, 2479-1070; www.arenalobservatory lodge.com; r $90-190; P🐕@🛜🏊) Set high on the Arenal slopes, this sensational, sprawling lodge has a variety of rooms spread throughout the property, five of which are wheelchair-accessible. Rates include a buffet breakfast and access to 6.5km of hiking trails. Rooms in the La Casona sector are about 500m away

in the original farmhouse. It now houses four rustic doubles sharing two bathrooms; there are volcano views from the house porch. Standard rooms, adjacent to the main lodge, were originally designed for researchers but have been renovated to acceptably plush standards. Smithsonian rooms, accessible via a suspension bridge over a plunging ravine, are the best and have the finest views. The White Hawk Villa, with a kitchen and several rooms, is perfect for groups.

The restaurant, though overpriced, has a good variety of international dishes and is decorated with jars of venomous snakes in formaldehyde. Yum?

ⓘ Information

The **ranger station** is on the western side of the volcano. Most people arrive as part of a group tour, but you can easily reach it independently. The ranger station complex includes an information center and parking lot. From here, trails lead 3.4km toward the volcano.

ⓘ Getting There & Away

To get to the ranger station by car, head west from La Fortuna for 15km, then turn left at the 'Parque Nacional' sign and take the 2km good dirt road to the entrance on the left side of the road. You can also take an 8am bus toward Tilarán (tell the driver to drop you off at the park) and catch the 2pm bus back to La Fortuna.

If you are heading to Arenal Observatory Lodge, continue driving on the dirt road. About 3km past the ranger station you will come to a small one-lane bridge and parking area; this was once a popular night lava-viewing spot. Shortly after you cross the bridge, you'll reach a fork in the road; left goes to Arenal Observatory Lodge and right goes to the village of El Castillo. Turn left and continue 2.6km to reach the lodge. You'll pay a US$2 entry fee at the front gate. This steep, hard-packed gravel and partially paved road is fine for most vehicles, but a 4WD is recommended.

A taxi from La Fortuna to either the lodge or to El Castillo will cost about US$30.

El Castillo

The tiny mountain village of El Castillo is a wonderful alternative to staying in La Fortuna – it's bucolic, reasonably untouristed (although there is a tight expat community), and has easy access to Parque Nacional Volcan Arenal. There are also some delightful accommodations options. It's best to have your own wheels out here, as buses don't serve this little enclave.

⊙ Sights & Activities

Kayak Lake Arenal   KAYAKING
(☑8721-0935, 2479-1079; per person with/without guide US$40/20) This American-owned kayak outfitter offers three-hour kayak rentals. Whether you choose to paddle with a guide or not, it's best to start early in the morning when bird activity is high, and before the wind kicks up.

El Castillo-Arenal Butterfly Conservatory   WILDLIFE RESERVE
(☑2479-1149; www.butterflyconservatory.org; adult/student US$14/10; ⊙8am-4pm) This conservatory has one of the largest butterfly exhibitions in Costa Rica, and raises all the butterflies and frogs on exhibit. Altogether there are six domed habitats, a ranarium, an insect museum, a medicinal herb garden, and an hour's worth of trails through a botanic garden and along the river. The center is always looking for a few good volunteers.

Arenal EcoZoo   ZOO
(☑2479-1059; www.arenalecozoo.com; adult/child US$16/10; ⊙8am-7pm) Meet 36 of the most dangerous snake species in the world, like Eliza, a 5m-long Burmese python, then handle and milk a venomous snake. The EcoZoo, more commonly known as El Serpentario, is also home to vibrant frogs, amphibious lizards, spiny iguanas, shy turtles, vengeful scorpions, hairy tarantulas and floating butterflies.

ⓖ Tours

SkyTrek   CANOPY TOUR
(☑2479-9944; www.skyadventures.travel; adult/child Sky Tram only US$42/29, Sky Walk only US$33/21, Sky Trek & Sky Tram US$73/46; ⊙7:30am-4pm) El Castillo's entry in the canopy tour category has zip lines (Sky Trek), a tram (Sky Tram) and a series of hanging bridges (Sky Walk). It's well run and safe, and visitors tend to leave smiling. It also offers night tours that begin at 5pm and must be reserved in advance

Appaloosa Farms   HORSE RIDING
(☑2479-1140; per person US$35) A fabulous horseback riding option. Tours depart from a working dairy aboard well-maintained horses. Your humble and knowledgable guide, Lelander Alvarez, will lead you on a four-hour tour through the rainforest to a hidden waterfall. Be sure to call to reserve at least a day ahead.

Finca Artesana TOUR

(☎8533-7902; unafinca@gmail.com; horse tour/ hiking tour per person US$25/20) Tomas and Hannah, the bakers and distillers (p149) of all things vinegary, spicy and sweet in El Castillo, have a *finca*, a lovely 45-minute hike from Rancho Margot. It's set within the national park, where they grow organic peach palm, hearts of palm and bananas, protected by 50 species of indigenous plants to keep pests at bay. Tomas leads the hiking tour, and that's the one you should do if you want to learn about a highly nutritious indigenous crop that local people lived off for generations, much like the Native Americans did with corn. There are over 200 varieties of peach palm. Some feed humans, others feed livestock, and still others give you an extremely hard, flexible wood, á la bamboo. Yes, Tomas would like to start a peach palm revolution.

Sleeping & Eating

Rancho Margot RESORT, LODGE $$$
TOP CHOICE

(☎8302-7318; www.ranchomargot.org; s/d bunk house US$90/150, bungalow US$152/230, lunch/ dinner $15/20; P🛜🏊) Rancho Margot, part resort lodge, part 152-hectare, self-sufficient organic farm, is downright cinematic. Set along the rushing Río Caño Negro, it's surrounded by rainforested mountains. Choose from tiny bunk house accommodations, or the far better bungalows with sweet mosaic-tiled washbasins, Spanish tiles, and a deck strung with a hammock blessed with views of hulking mountains, weeping jungle and that placid lake. Even the bungalows' tiled roofs are a sight to behold, sprouting with bromeliads. Day-trippers might be interested in visiting for the many activities on offer, including horseback riding, mountain biking, waterfall rappelling, kayaking, yoga and fishing. And there are hiking trails to a waterfall and nearby viewpoint. The one, oh so slight issue, is that staff are predominantly students and volunteers, which means that the level of professionalism can be hit and miss. However, reception staff are warm and on the ball, and most are English speaking. All meals are included in the room prices as is yoga and a complimentary ranch tour where you can see how this off-the-grid, sustainable organic ranch works. All other tours will cost you from US$35 to US$55 per person. Oh, and there is a full-service spa here, too.

Essence Arenal HOSTEL $

(☎2479-1131; www.essencearenal.com; dm/d US$14/28; P@🛜🏊) Perched on a 100-acre hilltop with incredible volcano and lake views, this 'boutique hostel' is the best cheap sleep in the Arenal region. The basic but clean rooms have orthopedic mattresses and hypo-allergenic pillows. Or you might enjoy a fine hippified tent, done up with plush bedding and wood furnishings? Martin, the resident Mexican shaman, ignites Saturday night sweat lodges on a nearby promontory, which are free for guests. Possibly the best reason to stay is the onsite restaurant, where you will participate in the loving preparation of vegetarian meals (US$10) that will delight even the most hardcore carnivore. It's not easy getting here without your own wheels, but it's well worth the trip. After crossing the bridge into El Castillo, turn left towards the Butterfly Conservatory and go 1km uphill; a 4WD is required. The hostel can arrange transportation from La Fortuna. English, French, Spanish and German are spoken.

Hummingbird Nest B&B B&B $$

(☎2479-1174, 8835-8711; www.hummingbirdnestbb. com; d incl breakfast US$75; P) At the entrance to town you'll see a small path that leads up the (steep) hill to one of our favorite B&Bs. Also known as Nido del Colibri, it's owned by a former Pan Am flight attendant and all-round world traveler who has found a small slice of paradise to call her own. Her quaint complex has two guest rooms with private hot showers, access to a fabulous communal kitchen, and enough frilly pillows to make you miss home. Soak the night away in a huge outdoor Jacuzzi in the garden. There's a two-night minimum.

Nepenthe HOTEL $$

(☎8892-5501, 8760-0412; Krisaray21@hotmail. com; s/d US$70/85; P❄🛜🏊) The highlight of the newest nest in El Castillo is the spectacular infinity pool overlooking the lake. Lodge-like rooms are simple, tiled numbers with colorful artisanal accents set in a gentle arc of a ranch-style building. There are hammocks on the patio and the Blue Lagoon spa (by appointment only, treatments from $35) comes highly recommended.

Cabinas La Tucanes HOTEL $

(☎2479-1076; s US$30-35, d US$40) Here you'll find huge bright and spotless rooms, with garish tiled floors, but you'll forgive that for this much space. They sleep up to three, have new beds, plush towels and hot water, and a sweet family runs it all. Pay $5 more for a great *tipica* breakfast. If you can, grab the top floor room which catches a nice breeze off the terrace.

Finca Artesana   DELI, BAKERY $
(☎8533-7902; unafinca@gmail.com) Meet Thomas and Hannah. He's Czech and makes the hot sauce and the vinegar; she's American and bakes the cookies and breads. Although you can find their creations throughout El Castillo, the fiery hot sauces and vinegars are cheapest at the source and made from peach palm, the ancient indigenous cash crop in Costa Rica. Breads and cookies are made to order. They sell their wares out of their house, just uphill from Essence Arenal in the heart of El Castillo.

Pizza John's Jardín Escondido   PIZZERIA $
(☎2479-1155; mains US$5-9; ⊘noon-9pm) On the road to Rancho Margot, look for the small sign leading to this pizzeria, which is hidden at the end of a grassy alley. The intimate, two-story structure is covered in graffiti scrawled by international visitors. Owner John DiVita of Los Angeles is lively and entertaining, with stories about his past life as a punk rocker and his escape from corporate America. He also cooks up an awesome pizza pie and delicious homemade ice cream. Follow it all up with some Zombie Coffee why don't you?

La Mesa de Mama   COSTA RICAN $
(☎2479-1954; mains US$6-9; ⊘7am-8pm) Sit down at the picnic tables for Mama's *tipica* home cooking. Serves cheap grilled fish, chicken and beef *casados*, and rice dishes with shrimp, squid or chicken. Mama does breakfast too.

Laguna de Arenal Area

About 18km west of La Fortuna you'll arrive at a 750m-long causeway across the dam that created Laguna de Arenal, an 88-sq-km lake and the largest in the country. A number of small towns were submerged during its creation, but the lake now supplies valuable water to Guanacaste, and produces hydroelectricity for the region. High winds also produce power with the aid of huge steel windmills, though windsurfers and kitesurfers frequently steal a breeze or two.

If you have your own car (or bicycle), this is one of the premier road trips in Costa Rica. The road is lined with odd and

elegant businesses, many run by foreigners who have fallen in love with the place, and the scenic views of lakeside forests and Volcán Arenal are about as romantic as they come. Strong winds and high elevations give the lake a temperate feel, and you'll be forgiven if you suddenly imagine yourself in the English Lakes District or the Swiss countryside.

But, things are changing – quickly. Gringo baby boomers, lured to the area by the eternal spring climate, are snapping up nearly every spot of land with a 'For Sale' sign on it. Some Ticos are not all that happy about the impending loss of their lakeside paradise, and, in fact, this part of the country doesn't actually feel much like Costa Rica at all. Still, it is nourishing to have Laguna Arenal in your life. Rain or shine, be it a quick and lively affair or one that lasts.

Most of the road is paved and in decent condition, though you'll find some big potholes. Buses run about every two hours, and hotel owners can tell you when to catch your ride.

DAM TO NUEVO ARENAL

This beautiful stretch of road is lined on both sides with cloud forest, and there are a number of fantastic accommodations strung along the way.

AROUND THE DAM

⊙ **Sights & Activities**

Forget for a moment that there are always ecological issues associated with dams and revel in the fact that this one created a lake that is rather magnificent. In the absence of wind the glassy surface reflects the volcano and surrounding mountains teeming with cloud forest. There are secluded bays and coves to explore and a forested island, too. You'll find a kayak concession usually set up on the west end of the dam, but take care because when the wind kicks it can be a bitch to make it back home, and be sure to wear sunblock even on cloudy days.

Puentes Colgantes de Arenal   FOREST
(Arenal Hanging Bridges; ☎2290-0469; www.hangingbridges.com; adult/student/child under 12yr US$25/22/free; ⊘7:30am-4:30pm) Unlike the fly-by view you'll get on a zip-line canopy tour, a walk through Puentes Colgantes de Arenal allows you to explore the rainforest and canopy from six suspended bridges and 10 traditional bridges at a more natural and peaceful pace. The longest swaying bridge

WORLD-CLASS WIND

Some of the world's most consistent winds blow across northwestern Costa Rica, and this consistency attracts wind riders. Laguna de Arenal is rated one of the best wind-surfing spots in the world and kitesurfers flock here too, especially from late November to April when Tico Wind (☑8813-7274, 2692-2002; www.ticowind.com; windsurf/kitesurf half-day US$50/58, full-day incl lunch US$85/86) sets up camp on the lake shore. It has state-of-the-art boards and sails, with equipment to suit varied wind conditions. First-timers should consider the 'Get on Board' package (US$120). Lessons are offered in English, Spanish, German, Italian and Portuguese. Beginner Kitesurf instruction ($480) is much more detailed and requires nine hours, but students will graduate International Kiteboarding Organization–certified and ready to cruise. The launch is located 15km west of Nuevo Arenal, about 400m after the Equus bar-restaurant. The entrance is by the big white chain link fence with 'ICE' painted on it. Follow the dirt road 1km to the shore.

Laguna de Arenal is also now attracting wakeboarders. Paradise Adventures Costa Rica (☑2479-8159, 8856-3618; www.paradise-adventures-costa-rica.com; per hr US$200), based in La Fortuna, has the latest wakeboarding equipment. Rates are for up to seven people including equipment, lessons and boat ride.

It gets a little chilly on Laguna de Arenal, and rentals usually include wet suits, as well as harnesses and helmet. For a warmer experience, head up to Bahía Salinas on Costa Rica's far northwestern coast. Resorts at that budding kitesurf mecca and drop dead gorgeous bay offer seasonal rentals and instruction. When the wind is right, riders insist that Salinas conditions wildly surpass even world class Laguna de Arenal. The seasons in Salinas are the same as for the lake.

is 97m long and the highest is 25m above the earth. All are accessible from a single 3km trail that winds through a tunnel and skirts a waterfall. Reservations are required for guided bird-watching tours (three hours, from 6am) or informative naturalist tours (9am and 2pm).

The bridges are easily accessible by car and well signed, though most tourists arrive on a package tour from La Fortuna. The Tilarán bus can drop you off at the entrance, but it's a 3km climb from the bus stop.

🛏 Sleeping & Eating

Arenal Lodge   LODGE $$$
(☑2290-4232; www.arenallodge.com; incl breakfast d standard/superior US$89/140, f US$167, junior ste US$175, chalet US$184; P❋⊠) If you want to stay in the area, Arenal Lodge is 400m west of the Laguna de Arenal, at the top of a steep 2.5km ascent, though the entire lodge is awash with views of Arenal and the surrounding cloud forest. Standard rooms are just that, but junior suites are spacious and tiled, and have wicker furniture, a big hot-water bathroom and a picture window or balcony with volcano views. The lodge also has a Jacuzzi, a billiards room, a sophisticated restaurant (mains US$8 to US$18), complimentary mountain bikes and private stables.

Lost Iguana Resort   RESORT $$$
(☑2479-1331, 2267-6148; www.lostiguanaresort.com; standard/deluxe r incl breakfast US$245/275; P❋@🛜⊠) This stylish and splashy tropical resort, just 1.5km from the dam, is set among lush rainforest and rushing streams and there are glorious volcano views. Even the standard rooms have private balconies looking out on Arenal, beds boasting Egyptian cotton sheets, flat screens with Apple TV, a terra-cotta wet bar, and an invaluable sense of peace and privacy. Of course they don't have a Jacuzzi tub or outdoor rain shower like the deluxe versions do. Reception and restaurant areas are romantic enough to appeal, even if leaving your cozy *casita* seems a tragedy.

UNIÓN AREA

The following attractions are listed in order of distance from the Laguna de Arenal dam.

You can't miss Hotel Los Héroes (☑2692-8013, 2692-8012; www.hotellosheroes.com; incl breakfast d with/without balcony US$65/55, tr/apt US$80/115; P⊠), a more than slightly incongruous alpine chalet 13.5km west of the dam. Large, immaculate rooms with wood paneling and hot-water bathrooms are decorated with wood furniture that may make Swiss-Germans a little homesick, particularly when viewing paintings of two-headed children in lederhosen. There are also two apartments (each sleeps up to five) with full kitchen, huge bathroom and balcony overlooking the lake. Facilities include a Jacuzzi, swimming pool and a church complete with Swiss chimes. The owners have even built a miniature train (US$11) that brings you up a hill to an underground station beneath the Rondorama Panoramic Restaurant (mains US$10 to US$20), a revolving dining room (seriously!) that's reportedly unique in Central America. There's also a hiking trail that is great for wildlife-watching.

Rates for the gorgeous cottages at La Mansion Inn Arenal (2692-8018; www. lamansionarenal.com; r/cottages incl breakfast US$175/200) include a champagne breakfast, fruit basket, welcome cocktail, canoe access and horse rides. They feature huge split-level rooms with loud paint jobs, private terraces, lake views, high ceilings and Italianate painted walls and arches. The cheaper rooms are almost as swank, and we actually like them a bit better. There's also an ornamental garden featuring Chorotega pottery, a fabulous infinity lap pool, and a formal restaurant (four-course dinner excluding wine US$22 to US$38) with a bar shaped like the bow of a ship. It's 15.5km west of the dam.

You'll see the psychedelic Boa Art Shop (8928-0262; www.boadesign.net; 9am-7:30pm) signs for several kilometers, and it's worth a stop for mind-melting totem poles with floating heads and hands, and engaging ceramic works made by Guanacaste artisans. Pieces are hewn from local clay and hand painted with natural paints alchemized from the same mud as the dish itself. All the wood sculptures are made from roots found in the lake. Incredibly, no varnish is used, only beeswax.

A serene, German-run escape, La Ceiba Tree Lodge (2692-8050; www.ceibatree-lodge. com; s/d US$63/84; P✴🛜) is 22km west of the dam and centered on a magnificent 500-year-old ceiba tree. Its five spacious, cross-ventilated Spanish-tiled rooms are entered through Maya-inspired carved doors and decorated with original paintings. There are rustic artifacts on the walls, a polished wood ceiling and epic views of Laguna de Arenal. The tropical gardens and utterly lovely dining/hangout area make this mountaintop spot a tranquil retreat from whatever ails you. It's one of the best value places on the lake.

Another accommodation option is Villa Decary B&B (2694-4330, in US or Canada 1-800-556-0505; www.villadecary.com; r/casitas incl breakfast US$109/164; P✴🛜🛏), an all-round winner with bright, spacious, well-furnished rooms, and two massive Cape Cod–style *casitas* that sleep up to four. The elegance extends from the clumps of slender palms to the delicious full breakfasts and, of course, to the fabulous hosts. Rooms have private hot showers, a queen and a double bed, and bright serape bedspreads and artwork. They also have balconies with excellent views of the woodland immediately below and the lake just beyond. The *casitas* have epic views from wide porches, and kitchenettes. Paths into the woods behind the house offer opportunities for bird- and wildlife-watching, and there's a good chance that howler monkeys will wake you in the morning. Guests can borrow binoculars and a bird guide to identify what they see. Decaray (named for a French botanist who discovered a new species of palm) also boasts one of the best collections of palm trees in Costa Rica. And by all means, pay your respects to Olivia, she is a goddess. It's 24.5km west of the dam, and 2km east of Nuevo Arenal.

Make absolutely sure to book dinner reservations at the Gingerbread Hotel & Restaurant (2694-0039, 8351-7815; www.ginger breadarenal.com; mains US$9-40; 5-9pm Tue-Sat, lunch by reservation only), one of the best restaurants in northwestern Costa Rica. You may even choose to stay at the charming boutique hotel built into the same stone house as the restaurant, but the thing here is the kitchen. With the freshest local fare providing the foundation for his weekly menus, Chef Eyal, the bigger than life Israeli who trained in Chicago and NYC, turns out transcendent meals and is choosy about his wine list, emphasizing top Chilean and Spanish vintners (wines US$30 to US$200). Portions are enormous and it's best to split and share. We loved the blackened tuna salad and the mushrooms smothered in creamy, parsley inflected gravy. It's big food that goes down smooth, and there's no pretension in this very cozy, out-of-the-way, lake-view dining room with walls covered in paintings by artists in the community. A word to the wise: do not pass up dessert. Come prepared – credit cards are not accepted, and don't be alarmed if Eyal, shouts, sweats, dances and raps along to Naughty by Nature. It happens.

Just before you reach Nuevo Arenal you'll pass a marina, where you can join Arenal Kayak (☑2694-4336; 2hr tour US$30) for a two-hour guided paddle on the lake. It also offers hotel pick-up free of charge.

NUEVO ARENAL

Although surrounded in aging *extranjero cultura* (expat culture), this two-horse town still feels very Tico. A rest stop for travelers heading to Tilarán and points beyond, it's certainly a pleasant (and cheap) place to spend the night. The tiny downtown also has a gas station, a Banco de Costa Rica and Banco Nacional (both with ATMs), Super-Compro and a bus stop near the park. They even have a rickety old *plaza del toros*.

The only good-sized town between La Fortuna and Tilarán, it's 27km west of the dam, or one hour drive from La Fortuna. In case you were wondering what happened to old Arenal, it's about 27m below the surface of Laguna de Arenal. In order to create a large enough reservoir for the dam, the Costa Rican government had to make certain, er, sacrifices, which ultimately resulted in the forced relocation of 3500 people. Today, the humble residents of Nuevo Arenal don't seem to be fazed by history, especially since they now own premium lakeside property.

🛏 Sleeping & Eating

Aurora Hotel HOTEL $
(☑2694-4243; r US$24; P@🖥🐕) You'd never know it from the street, but these rooms are rather sweet, spotless, spacious, wood cabin–like constructions with lovely lake views and vaulted beamed ceilings. It's one of the best deals on Laguna de Arenal. The attached restaurant does decent pizza. It's on the east side of the square.

Cabinas Catalina CABINA $
(☑8819-6793; d US$20; P) Across from the gas station are these sterile budget digs with ceiling fans and a breezy perch set back from the main drag. Rooms sleep up to three people.

Sunset Grill AMERICAN $
(☑2694-4557; www.sunsetgrillcostarica.com; mains US$5-9; ☉7am-11pm; 🖥) American owned and patronized, Sunset Grill does big breakfasts, burgers and Philly-style cheesesteaks. The attached internet cafe offers internet service (US$1 per hour), and it occasionally stays open until 2am, depending upon the bar crowd.

Moya's Place PIZZERIA $$
(☑2694-4001; mains US$6-12; ☉11am-10pm) A new and savory smelling pizza joint, it also does an assortment of wraps, pastas and salads, as well as a lovely fresh, stuffed trout steamed in banana leaf. It doesn't serve any alcohol.

Las Delicias SODA $
(☑8320-7102; mains US$4.50-11; ☉7am-9pm; 🖥) A cheap and cheerful *soda* near the top of the hill as you approach town. It has ample wooden table seating and does Western-style breakfasts, pasta dishes, quesadillas and grilled steaks on the cheap. But if you come here get a *casado*, that's what this place is known for.

Tom's Pan BAKERY $$
(☑2694-4547; mains US$9-16; ☉7:30am-5pm Mon-Sat; 🖥) Better known as 'the German bakery,' this slightly overrated landmark is a famous rest stop for road-trippers heading to Tilarán. Its breads, strudels and cakes are all homemade, and they also sell the *Costa Rica Travel Map* (US$15), the country's best road map, in its attached market.

NUEVO ARENAL TO TILARÁN

West and around the lake from Nuevo Arenal, the scenery becomes even more spectacular just as the road gets progressively worse. Tilarán is the next 'big' city, with a reasonable selection of hotels and restaurants, plus roads and buses that can take you to Liberia, Monteverde or beyond.

🛏 Sleeping & Eating

Blue Zone Spa B&B $$
(☑2694-4713; www.bluezonespa.com; d incl breakfast US$75; P🖥🐕) The sounds of nature will lull you to sleep at this intimate B&B on the banks of the rainforest-shaded Río Cote. Four simple, tiled rooms feature queen beds and creative bathrooms. The property was recently rebranded as a full-service spa, which is set downstairs. It offers facials, massages and body scrubs. Treatments range from US$75 to US$125.

Lucky Bug B&B B&B $$
(☑2694-4515; www.luckybugcr.net; r incl breakfast US$89-120; P🌀🖥🐕) Set on a rainforest lagoon, the bungalows at the Lucky Bug are not only blissfully isolated but feature unique art and decorative details by local artisans, including the owner's big-eyed, blonde triplets (aka the Kardashians by the Lake). Here are blond wood floors, wrought

iron butterflies, hand-painted geckos, mosaic wash basins and end tables. Each room is unique and captivating. There is also an on-site Caballo Negro Restaurant (mains US$8 to US$14) and the fabulously quirky Lucky Bug Gallery. Should you fall in love with a painting of a bug or something bigger, they can ship it for you. It's 3km west of Nuevo Arenal.

Ecolodge Andamaya
LODGE **$$**

(✆2694-4306; www.ecolodgecostarica.com; r/ cabin incl breakfast US$75/125; P❄🐾📶) This aging, environmentally friendly lodge has been done up with hip touches such as draped scarves, retro door numbers, and stylish floral motifs. Built in 1990 with an endowment from the World Bank, the hotel is committed to preserving its 250 hectares of primary forest and 50 hectares of secondary-growth forest. There are 14km of trails, and even if you don't stay here you can join one of its indigenous guides on a guided hike (per person US$20). Standard rooms with hot-water shower are in a handsome wood-and-stone lodge that has a large fireplace and billiards lounge, TV and a small library. There are also 14 larger cabins with picture windows. The views from here on clear days are simply spectacular, with Arenal looming like a siren above the deep blue lake. The onsite restaurant serves French cuisine. Go 4.5km west of Nuevo Arenal, then turn 3km down an unpaved road.

La Rana de Arenal
HOTEL **$$**

(✆2694-4031; www.hotel-larana-arenal.com; s/d incl breakfast US$30/45; P📶) Watch out for the hairpin turnoff at the driveway to La Rana, a quaint German-run spot with seven simple, comfortable rooms. The restaurant serves good international food (mains US$6 to US$11), with an emphasis on German cuisine, in an airy upstairs pub-style dining room. There are tennis courts on the property, and birding tours. It's 5.7km from Nuevo Arenal.

Surf Chalets
CABINA **$$**

(r incl breakfast US$60; P📶) This breezy, tumbledown, disorganized collection of basic wooden *cabinas* on a hill has a hippie-rasta-kitesurf feel, but there is elegance and allure here. The wooden rooms have Spanish-tiled floors and the property has a majestic perch. The turn-off is about 12.5km from Nuevo Arenal. Just before the speed bump, make a right turn uphill for 1km.

Mystica Resort
RESORT **$$**

(✆2692-1001; www.mysticacostarica.com; s/d incl breakfast US$85/100, villa US$145; ⊙noon-9pm; P@📶) About 15km west of Nuevo Arenal, this Mediterranean-style retreat has several comfortable, colorful rooms with Spanish-tiled floors, vibrant woven bedspreads, hot showers and a wide, inviting front porch with volcano views. Even if you're not staying here, it's a great place to stop for a wood-fired pizza (US$5 to US$14). Yoga ($11) and meditation classes are held in the fabulous sheltered hardwood yoga space overlooking a gurgling creek, and there's a tree-house healing center for Reiki and massage (spa treatments US$55 to US$60). Wait, we feel an 'om' coming on.

Volcano Brewing
HOTEL **$$**

(✆2653-1262, 2695-5050; www.volcanobrewing company.com; r US$60-75; P🍴❄🐾📶) Is it a brewery? A hotel? A kitesurf camp? Actually, the converted, lakefront Hotel Tilawa is all of the above, and more than living up to its legendary history among wind riders. The remodel was a stunner. Expect polished concrete floors, pastel paint jobs and high, slanted, dark wood ceilings. Upstairs rooms are cheaper, but that's because downstairs rooms come with kitchenettes, private patios and fireplaces. There's a pool and Jacuzzi and the restaurant's pub grub selections are scrawled on the chalkboard in true tavern style. Oh, and they brew three types of beer: a pale ale, a seasonal wheat beer and what they call a shandy. Think beer meets ginger ale meets lemonade.

Maverick's
BARBECUE **$$$**

(✆2694-4895; mains US$15-26; ⊙11am-8pm; 🐾) A somewhat obscure corner of the American barbecue palate is the Central California tradition known as Santa Maria barbecue, which is exactly what the Central Californian owners cook up here. In addition to burgers, dogs, and tender smoky chicken and ribs, they offer fresh grilled seafood on Thursday, Friday and Saturday nights, and that old Santa Maria staple: roast tri-tip. The dining patio views are sublime, but they'll pack your order to go, if you wish.

Café y Macadamia de Costa Rica
CAFE **$$**

(✆2692-2000; cafeymacadamia@yahoo.com; pastries & coffee US$2-4, mains US$6-13; ⊙8am-8pm; 📶) Pull over for a cup of coffee and maybe an elegantly prepared salad or Thai chicken curry, and leave room for a tasty pastry, all best savored along with the spectacular

SIEPMANN / IMAGEBROKER ©

MICHAEL FISCHER IMAGEBROKER ©

1. Parque Nacional Volcán Arenal (p145)

The picture-perfect conical shape of Volcán Arenal provides a great backdrop while hiking through the varied terrain of the surrounding area.

2. Parque Nacional Volcán Tenorio (p184)

The Catarata de Río Celeste is a waterfall that cascades 30m down into a fantastically aquamarine pool.

3. Reserva Biológica Bosque Nuboso Monteverde (p177)

Tropical butterflies are among the many kinds of wildlife you can spot in and around this biological reserve.

4. Tabacón Hot Springs (p135)

After a day's hiking visitors can relax at this spa, 14km west of La Fortuna.

DAMIAN TURSKI / LONELY PLANET IMAGES ©

views of Laguna de Arenal. The gigantic, wood-floored room and equally large outdoor terrace alone make it worth a stop to stretch your legs. It does pizza and pasta at dinner, and sells lovely beaded and carved jewelry. It's 10.5km west of Nuevo Arenal.

Equus Bar-Restaurant
TAVERN $$

(mains US$6-14; ⏰3-9pm Fri, 11am-2am Sat, 11am-9pm Sun) Set on its own little cove, this groovy tavern specializes in grilled meat plates and is perennially popular among wind riders looking to swap stories over an icy Imperial. There's a good mix of Tico and Western dishes, and on some nights there's live music. This is what passes for a night scene on the lake. It's 14.5km west of Nuevo Arenal.

Brisas Del Lago
SODA $$

(☎2695-3363; mains US$6-11; 🛜🍴) Simple Tico fare is done with panache at this dressed-up *soda*. They marinate chicken breasts in their own BBQ sauce, skewer Thai-style shrimp and sauce teriyaki chicken, and the garlic fish is sensational. To get here head toward Tilarán, then make a left at the T-junction toward the community of San Luis. Continue for 800m.

Tilarán

POP 8100

Near the southwestern end of Laguna de Arenal, the small town of Tilarán has a laid-back, middle-class charm – thanks to its long-running status as a regional ranching center. This tradition is honored on the last weekend in April with a rodeo that's popular with Tico visitors, and on June 13 with a *fiesta de toros* (Festival of the Bull) that's dedicated to patron San Antonio.

Situated on the slopes of the Cordillera de Tilarán, this little hub is a much cooler alternative (in climate and atmosphere) than, say, Cañas, and makes a pleasant stop between La Fortuna and Monteverde. Life unfurls immediately around the main plaza. Wander more than a block in any direction, and things get rather residential. Street signs are a new and limited resource.

Sleeping & Eating

Cheap meals can be found in the *mercado* (market) beside the bus terminal, or pop into the SuperCompro (⏰8am-8pm) for groceries; it's across from the park.

TOP CHOICE Hotel Cielo Azul
HOTEL $

(☎2695-4000; www.cieloazulresort.com; r US$20; 🅿✳🛜🏊♿) Found about 500m before town, coming from Nuevo Arenal, this hillside property has eight recently re-done rooms with newly tiled floors and bathroom. There is cable TV, the pool is lovely and it even has a spinning studio. This is Tilarán's best deal.

Hotel Tilarán
HOTEL $

(☎2695-5043; r with/without bathroom US$11/7; 🅿) As cheap as they come, rooms are tiny and cleanish, but you will hear the caged bird sing. If you can get one of the rooms toward the back, this is a decent budget choice on the west side of Parque Central. Its cute, almost retro *soda* (mains US$3 to US$6) is on the streetfront.

Hotel El Sueño
HOTEL $

(☎2695-5347; s/d US$20/30; 🅿) Near the bus terminal, this beautiful (in an ageing, baroque sort of way) hotel has antique decorated rooms set around a cheerful atrium, but it's worth splurging for the balcony, where you can bask in the faded glory.

Soda y Restaurante El Nilo
SODA $

(cnr Av 3 & Calle 1; meals US$6-8, empanadas US$1.50; ⏰7am-7pm) An oh-so-cute *soda* run by two ladies who fold the best chicken *empanadas* in town and craft delectable *casados* too. Meals are served on pressed tablecloths with local pottery mounted on the dining room walls.

Soda Mi Casita
SODA $

(mains US$3-6; ⏰6am-9pm Mon-Sat, 7am-2:30pm Sun) The most popular *soda* in town among locals, it does delectable plates of fried fish, grilled chicken and all the rice dishes and roast meats you'd expect. Grab one of the wooden tables facing the park.

ℹ Information

The city has several ATMs and two gas stations. Check email while waiting for your bus at **Cybercafé Tilarán** (☎2695-9010; per hr US$1.20; ⏰9am-10pm Mon-Sat), 25m west of the bus terminal.

ℹ Getting There & Away

Tilarán is usually reached by a 24km paved road from the Interamericana at Cañas. The route on to Santa Elena and Monteverde is unpaved and rough, though ordinary cars can get through with care in the dry season.

Buses arrive and depart from the terminal, half a block west of Parque Central. Be aware that Sunday afternoon buses to San José may be sold out by Saturday. The route between Tilarán and San José goes via Cañas and the Interamericana, not the Arenal–La Fortuna–Ciudad Quesada route. Regular services go to the following locations:

Cañas US$1; 30 minutes; departs 5am, 7am, 8am, 9am, 10am, 11:30am and 3:30pm.

La Fortuna US$5; three hours; departs 10am, 2:30pm and 4:30pm.

Nuevo Arenal US$1; 1¼ hours; departs 5am, 6am, 8am, 9am, 10am, 11am, 1pm, 2:30pm and 3:30pm.

Puntarenas US$4; two hours; departs 6am and 1pm.

San José (Auto-Transportes Tilarán) US$7; four hours; departs 5am, 7am, 9:30am, 2pm and 5pm.

Santa Elena/Monteverde US$3; 2½ hours; departs once daily at 12:30pm.

INTERAMERICANA NORTE

Despite Tico speed demons and lumbering big rigs, the Interamericana, which bisects the travel hub of Liberia, offers a wide-angle view of the region. The main artery connecting San José with Managua runs through kilometers of tropical dry forest and neat roadside villages to the open Guanacaste grasslands, where savanna vistas are broken only by windblown trees. Along the way, thin, earthen roads branch off and wander up the slopes of volcanoes shrouded in cloud forest, skirt hidden waterfalls and meander into vast estuaries that kiss pristine bays.

Costa de Pájaros

The 40km stretch of partially paved road between Punta Morales in the south and Manzanillo in the north is famous for its mangrove-lined shores, which attract countless varieties of birds (and birdwatchers). Once the most famous sight in the area, Isla Pájaros (Bird Island) lies less than 1km off the coast at Punta Morales, but has become difficult to reach. There are no facilities on the 3.8-hectare islet, which protects a rare colony of brown pelican. The only way to visit is to entice a local fisherman to buzz you out on his *panga*. Nothing formal is set up, and you'll need to be able to speak some Spanish to close the deal.

Popular with bird-watchers, La Ensenada Lodge (☏2289-6655; www.laensenada. net; per person US$38, meals US$7-14) is a remote 380-hectare *finca* and working cattle ranch, salt farm and papaya orchard. Rustic but comfortable wooden bungalows face the Golfo de Nicoya, have private bathrooms heated by solar panels and private patios with hammocks – perfect for watching sunsets (or birds). There's a pool, restaurant, tennis courts, a romantically rickety jetty and a terrific trail network that will allow you to explore a spectacular *finca*. It no longer buzzes guests to the Isla de Pajaros, but does offer mangrove tours (per person US$82), where you can glimpse dozens of bird species, caimans and crocs, as well as horseback tours (US$23) through the tropical dry forest.

Juntas

POP 5300

Las Juntas de Abangares is a small town on the Río Abangares that was the center of the gold-mining industry in the late 19th and early 20th centuries. Today it's simply a pleasant mountain market town, set in a verdant bowl, blessed with ample sunshine, and peopled with ranchers and farmers. Of course, it isn't thrilling, which is why most travelers don't hang long, but if you have wheels and it's starting to get dark, it's a good place to spend the night rather than attempting the muddy slip-and-slide commonly known as the road to Monteverde at night.

The town is centered on the Catholic church, which has some very nice stained glass. The small but bustling downtown is about 300m north of the church, with a Banco Nacional, several *sodas* and small markets. The Ecomuseo is 3km from the main road.

◉ Sights

Ecomuseo de las Minas de Abangares   MUSEUM

(☏2662-0310; adult/child US$4/1.75; ⊗8am-noon, 1:30-4pm Tue-Sun) OK, so the terms 'eco' and 'mining' don't mix well, but it's worth seeing the photographs and models depicting the old mining practices of the area. On the grounds are a picnic area and children's play area, and a good system of trails that skirt mining artifacts. There's also good birdwatching (and iguana-ing) along the trails, and monkeys are occasionally glimpsed.

Tours

Mina Tours TOUR
(☑2662-0753; www.minatours.com; day trips
from US$30; ☺8am-5pm Mon-Fri) Behind the
church, Mina Tours is a family-run tour outfit that can arrange transportation and offers several gold-themed tours, including of
the Ecomuseo and abandoned mines.

Sleeping & Eating

Cabinas y Restaurante Heliconias CABINA $
(☑2662-2260; s/d US$28/40; ☐❋) Set along
the river, this leafy property has 12 super
clean and spacious rooms with high beamed
ceilings, rustic wood furnishings, ceiling
fans and cable. It's the best sleep within
walking distance of the town center, and the
attached restaurant (mains US$5 to US$14)
specializes in roast meats including a smoky
BBQ pork. It's set 50m off the main road and
about 1km west of town as you approach
from the Interamericana.

**Restaurante y Cabinas
Mirador el Angel** CABINA $
(☑2693-8489, 8994-9452; r incl breakfast per person US$20; ☐) Halfway between Juntas and
Monteverde, a well-signed, steep dirt road
leads up to this hidden gem with amazing
views of the valley and Golfo de Nicoya. The
menu (mains US$2 to US$14) features terrific grilled fresh fish *casados*, plus burgers
and other fast food. The rustic cabins overlook the family's coffee plantation and have
private bathroom with hot water, TV and
balcony. Owners Angel and Concha are wonderfully hospitable, though little English is
spoken. It's located about 4km south of the
tiny village of San Rafael.

Pueblo Antiguo Lodge & Spa LODGE $
(☑2662-0033; www.puebloantiguo.com; r incl
breakfast US$38; ☐❋☷) This rustic getaway
rests on the lip of a wooded ravine next to
the Ecomuseo and its onsite hot springs,
swimming pool, Jacuzzi, sauna, nature
trails and restaurant ensure you will be suf-
ficiently soothed. Its 10 wooden lodge rooms
aren't fancy, but are very comfy, and there's
a good chance wildlife will appear on your
doorstep. The friendly staff arrange tours to
the nearby Ecomuseo and gold mines.

Restaurante Los Mangos RESTAURANT $$
(☑2662-0410; mains US$5-14 ; ☺11am-2am Tue-
Sun) The nicest restaurant in town is on the
main road and does your standard mix of
casados, *ceviche* and fried chicken. There

are touches of elegance here too, what with
polished concrete floors, a fresh coat of paint,
twirling ceiling fans and pressed tablecloths,
and it'll get you liquored at night.

Getting There & Away

Buses from Cañas (US$1, 45 minutes) depart
at 6:30am, 12:30pm and 3:30pm. Buses to San
José (US$3, three hours) depart at 6:30am and
10:45am. The bus terminal is two blocks east
of the main road, parallel to Parque Central and
next to the municipal market where there are
ample cheap eats. There are no buses to the
Ecomuseo, but a taxi will cost about US$8
one way.

Drivers should take the turnoff from the
Interamericana, 27km south of Cañas at a gas
station called **La Irma** (☑2645-5647), where
you can also catch buses between Liberia and
San José. Monteverde is 30km northeast from
Las Juntas on a mostly paved road; the last
12km are a rough dirt road, though it's passable
for normal cars in the dry season. From Juntas,
take your first left after the plaza, cross the
one-lane bridge, turn right and follow the signs
to Monteverde.

Monteverde & Santa Elena

Strung between two lovingly preserved
cloud forests is this slim corridor of civili-
zation, which consists of the Tico village of
Santa Elena and the Quaker settlement of
Monteverde. A 1983 feature article in *Na-
tional Geographic* described this unique
landscape and subsequently billed the area
as the place to view one of Central America's
most famous birds – the resplendent quet-
zal. Suddenly, hordes of tourists armed with
tripods and telephoto lenses started brav-
ing Monteverde's notoriously awful access
roads, which came as a huge shock to the
then-established Quaker community. In an
effort to stem the tourist flow, local com-
munities lobbied to stop developers from
paving the roads. And it worked. Today,
the dirt roads leading to Monteverde and
Santa Elena have effectively created a moat
around this precious experiment in sustain-
able ecotourism.

The cloud forests near Monteverde and
Santa Elena are one of Costa Rica's premier
destinations for everyone from budget back-
packers to well-heeled retirees. On a good
day, Monteverde is a place where you can
be inspired about the possibility of a world
in which organic farming and alternative
energy sources are the norm. On a bad day,

MISTY MICROCLIMES

When ecologists arrived in the area to investigate the cloud forests, they discovered that they are actually two different ecosystems that straddle both sides of the continental divide. In the Reserva Biológica Bosque Nuboso Monteverde, the warm, moisture-laden trade winds from the Caribbean sweep up the slopes of the divide where they cool and condense to form clouds. These clouds congregate over the Reserva Santa Elena, where the absence of trade winds means that the forests here are a few degrees warmer than in Monteverde. As a result, each ecosystem boasts several endemic species, most of which you probably won't be able to see. But you will notice that even medium sized trees in these forests can support 70 species of flowering plants including 40 orchid varietals. Many of the bromeliads and orchids get their nutrients from the air and mist that floats through and coats everyone and everything. Life is abundant, throbbing and palpable here.

Monteverde can feel like Disneyland in Birkenstocks and a zip-line harness. Take heart in the fact that the local community continues to fight to maintain the fragile balance of nature and commerce.

Driving from either of the Interamericana's first two turnoffs to the region, you'll first arrive in Santa Elena, a bustling community of budget hotels, restaurants and attractions. A road beginning at the northern point of the triangle leads to Juntas and Tilarán, with a turnoff to Reserva Santa Elena. From the westernmost point of the triangle (to the right as you enter town) you can access a scenic and heavily rutted 6km road to the Monteverde reserve. About 2km from Santa Elena, the neighborhood of Cerro Plano has a nucleus of cute businesses centered on Casem and the Monteverde Cheese Factory. Almost 5km from town, a turnoff leads down a steep 3km to the epic Ecolodge San Luis and the San Luis Waterfall.

⊙ Sights

Ecotourism is big business in Monteverde and Santa Elena, so it's unsurprising that there are a number of adventure-themed park attractions scattered around both towns. And if there's a certain critter you're itching to see, there are plenty of places where your view won't be obscured by all those pesky trees.

El Jardín de las Mariposas   ZOO
(Butterfly Garden; ☑2645-5512; www.monteverde butterflygarden.com; adult/student/children 12 & under US$9/7/3; ⊙9:30am-4pm) One of the most interesting activities is visiting the butterfly garden. Admission entitles you to a naturalist-led tour (in Spanish or English)

that begins with an enlightening discussion of butterfly life cycles and the butterfly's importance in nature. A variety of eggs, caterpillars, pupae and adults are examined. Visitors are taken into the greenhouses, where the butterflies are raised, and on into the screened garden, where hundreds of butterflies of many species are seen. The tour lasts about an hour.

Ranario   ZOO
(Frog Pond; ☑2645-6320; ranariomv@racsa.co.cr; adult/student & child US$12/10, adult combo US$18; ⊙9am-8:30pm) Monteverde's cloud forest provides a heavenly habitat for amphibians, which, if you're lucky, you'll see in the park. But at the Ranario about 25 species of Costa Rica's colorful array of frogs and toads reside in transparent enclosures lining the winding indoor-jungle paths. Sharp-eyed guides lead informative tours in English or Spanish, pointing out frogs, eggs and tadpoles with flashlights. Many resident amphibians are more active by night, so it's best to visit during the evening. The adult combo ticket includes admission to the butterfly garden (p159).

Serpentario   ZOO
(Serpentarium; ☑2645-6002; per person US$9; ⊙9am-8pm) Here you'll find about 40 species of snake, plus a fair number of frogs, lizards, turtles and other cold-blooded critters. Sometimes it's tough to find the slithering, venomous stars in their comfy, foliage-filled cages, but guides are available in Spanish or English for free tours.

Bat Jungle   ZOO
(☑2645-6566; adult/child US$11/9; ⊙9:30am-7:30pm) Learn about echolocation, bat-wing aerodynamics and other amazing facts about

Monteverde & Santa Elena

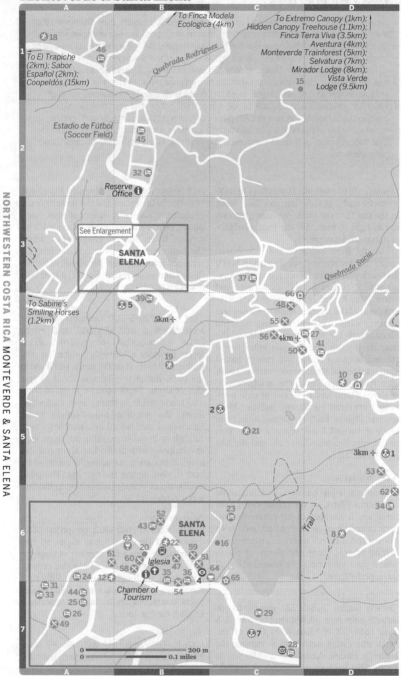

To Finca Modela
Ecologica (4km)

To Extremo Canopy (1km);
Hidden Canopy Treehouse (1.1km);
Finca Terra Viva (3.5km);
Aventura (4km);
Monteverde Trainforest (5km);
Selvatura (7km);
Mirador Lodge (8km);
Vista Verde
Lodge (9.5km)

To El Trapiche
(2km); Sabor
Español (2km);
Coopeldós (15km)

Quebrada Rodríguez

Estadio de Fútbol
(Soccer Field)

Reserve
Office

See Enlargement

SANTA
ELENA

Quebrada Sucia

To Sabine's
Smiling Horses
(1.2km)

5km

4km

3km

SANTA
ELENA

Iglesia

Chamber of
Tourism

Trail

0   200 m
0   0.1 miles

these (incredibly cute) flying mammals. The stellar Bat Jungle, a labor of love realized by biologist Richard Laval, has terrific exhibits including a free-flying bat habitat, beautiful sculptures and a lot of bilingual educational displays. The bats are most active during feeding times (9am, noon and 3pm). The Bat Jungle makes up part of the new **Paseo de Stella visitors center**, a modern hacienda that also houses a cafe specializing in Argentine chocolate, a museum of Monteverde history and an art gallery. The wide terrace is a wonderful spot to stop for coffee and a handmade truffle.

Jardín de Orquídeas GARDENS
(Orchid Garden; ☎2645-5308; www.monteverde orchidgarden.com; adult/child under 12yr US$10/ free; ⏰8am-5pm) This sweet-smelling garden has shady trails winding past more than 400 types of orchid organized into taxonomic groups. Included with admission are guided tours in Spanish and English, on which you'll see such rarities as *Plztystele jungerman-nioides*, the world's smallest orchid, and several others marked for conservation by the Monteverde Orchid Investigation Project.

Friends Meeting House COMMUNITY
(⏰meetings 9am Wed, 10:30am Sun) In 1949 four Alabama Quakers (a pacifist religious group also known as the 'Society of Friends') were jailed for their refusal to be drafted into the Korean War. Since Quakers are obligated by their religion to be pacifists, the four men were eventually released from prison. However, in response to the incarceration, 44 Quakers from 11 Alabama families left the USA and headed for (much) greener pastures, literally. The Quakers chose Monteverde (Green Mountain) for two reasons: a few years prior, the Costa Rican government had abolished its military and the cool, mountain climate was ideal for grazing cattle. Ensconced in their isolated refuge they adopted a simple, trouble-free life of dairy farming and cheese production. In an effort to protect the watershed above its 15-sq-km plot in Monteverde, the Quaker community agreed to preserve the mountaintop cloud forests.

Quakerism began as a breakaway movement from the Anglican Church in the 1650s, founded by the young George Fox, who in his early twenties heard the voice of Christ, and claimed that direct experience with God was possible without having to go through the sacraments. Today, this belief is

NORTHWESTERN COSTA RICA MONTEVERDE & SANTA ELENA

Monteverde & Santa Elena

commonly described by Quakers as the 'God in everyone,' and the Monteverde Quaker community continues to lead a peaceful lifestyle in the area and remain extremely active in the local community.

If you're interested in learning more about the Society of Friends, prayer meetings at the Friends Meeting House in Monteverde are held on Sunday at 10:30am and Wednesday at 9am. If you're willing to give at least a six-week commitment, there are numerous volunteer opportunities available. For more information, contact the Monteverde Friends School.

🏃 Activities

Don't forget your hiking boots, bug spray and a hat – there's plenty to do outdoors around here, including lots of action either on horseback or in the jungle.

Hiking

The best hikes are at the two cloud-forest reserves bookending the main road, Reserva Biológica Bosque Nuboso Monteverde and Reserva Santa Elena.

Bosque Eterno de los Niños HIKING
(Children's Eternal Forest; ☑2645-5003; www.ac mcr.org; ☺7:30am-5:30pm; adult/student day use US$8/5, guided night hike US$15/10, Estación Biológica San Gerardo all-inclusive US$40) If you've ever felt cynical about school children asking for money to save the rainforest, then you really must see what they purchased with all that spare change. Keep in mind, however, that this enormous 220-sq-km reserve, which dwarfs both the Monteverde and Santa Elena reserves, is largely inaccessible. The international army of children who paid the bills decided that it was more important to provide a home for local wildlife among the primary and secondary forest (and to allow former agricultural land to be slowly reclaimed by the jungle) than to develop a lucrative tourist infrastructure.

The effort has allowed for one fabulous trail that hooks into a system of unimproved trails that are primarily for researchers. The 3.5km Sendero Bajo del Tigre (Jaguar Canyon Trail) offers more open vistas than those in the cloud forest, so spotting birds tends to be easier. The reason is that a good portion of the surrounding area was clear-cut during the mid-20th century, though there has been significant regrowth since it was granted protected status. The resulting landscape is known as premontane forest, which is unique in Costa Rica as most things clear cut stay clear cut.

Make reservations in advance for the popular two-hour night hikes, which set off at 5:30pm. The Estación Biológica San Gerardo, reachable from a rather gnarly two-and-a-half hour trail from Reserva Santa Elena, is managed by Bosque Eterno de los Niños and has dorm beds for researchers and students, but you may be able to stay overnight with prior arrangements. If you're looking for a volunteer program, Children's Eternal is always looking for help.

Santuario Ecológico HIKING
(Ecological Sanctuary; ☑2645-5869; adult/student/child US$10/8/6, guided night tour US$15/12/10; ☺7am-5:30pm, guided night tours 5:30-7:30pm) Offering hikes of varying lengths, Santuario Ecológico has four loop trails (the longest takes about 2½ hours at a slow pace) through private property comprising premontane and secondary forest, coffee and banana plantations, and past a couple of waterfalls and lookout points. Coati, agouti and sloth are seen on most days, and monkey, porcupine and other animals are common. Bird-watching is also good. Guided tours are available throughout the day, but you'll see even more animals on the guided night tours.

Reserva Sendero Tranquilo HIKING
(Tranquil Path Reserve; ☑2645-5010; admission US$20; ☺tours 7:30am & 1pm) An 81-hectare private reserve, Reserva Sendero Tranquilo is located between the Reserva Biológica Bosque Nuboso Monteverde and the Río Guacimal. Trails here are narrow to allow for minimal environmental impact, and group size is capped at six people, which means you won't have to worry about chattering tourists scaring away all the animals. The trails pass through four distinct types of forest, including a previously destroyed area that's starting to bud again.

Sendero Valle Escondido HIKING
(Hidden Valley Trail; ☑2645-6601; day use US$5, night tour adult/child US$20/10; ☺7am-4pm) This trail begins behind Pensión Monteverde Inn and slowly winds through a deep canyon into an 11-hectare reserve. Compared to the more popular reserves, Valle Escondido is quiet during the day and fairly undertouristed, so it's a good trail for wildlife-watching. However, the reserve's two-hour guided night tour (at 5:30pm) is very popular, so it's best to make reservations in advance.

Cerro Amigos HIKING

Take a free hike up Cerro Amigos (1842m) for good views of the surrounding rainforest and, on a clear day, of Volcán Arenal, 20km away to the northeast. Near the top of the mountain, you'll pass by the TV towers for channels 7 and 13. The trail leaves Monteverde from behind Hotel Belmar and ascends roughly 300m in 3km. From the hotel, take the dirt road going downhill, then the next left. Note that this trail does not connect to the trails in the Monteverde reserve, so you will have to double back.

Catarata San Luis HIKING

(guided hike adult/child US$10/8.50) A popular (but strenuous) hike visits the Catarata San Luis, a gorgeous ribbon streaming in three tiers from the cloud forests into a series of swimming holes just screaming for a picnic. The distance from the parking area to the falls is only a few kilometers, but it's steeply graded downhill, and the rocky, muddy terrain can get very slick. It's important to go slow and turn back if it becomes too difficult. However, your efforts will be worth it as the waterfall is simply breathtaking. Alternatively, you may wish to join a guided hike to the falls, offered by the fantastic Ecolodge San Luis (p181). Hikes must be reserved at least a day in advance. And be warned, you may never want to leave the lodge.

Drivers will need a 4WD to ford the little river and climb the muddy road out. You can park (US$6 per car) at a private farm, which is next to the trailhead. Several horseback-riding companies offer excursions to the falls (US$50 per person), but note that much of the road is now paved and this is hard on the horses' knees. A taxi from town to the falls costs about U$15.

Santa Maria's Finca Agroturistica HIKING

(☑2645-6548; cafesanta06@hotmail.com; per person US$22) One of the new night hikes in the area, this two-hour walk departs at 5:30pm and offers possibilities of sloth, armadillo and snake sightings among other animals. It was just a year old at research time and already popular.

Canyoneering

The newest adrenalin-addled activity in town demands a bit more sweat and exertion from tourists than the canopy theme parks. Canyoneering is part rappelling, part bouldering and part hiking, there will be a bit of swimming involved too – and maybe even a zip line? You are in Costa Rica after all. Extremo Canopy (p166) offers a fun canyoneering tour that can be paired with a zip-line experience.

Finca Modelo Ecologica CANYONEERING

(☑2645-5581; www.familiabrenestours.com; US$45; ☺tours 8am,11am & 2pm) This 1200-hectare family *finca* offers a number of diversions, including two-hour dairy tours (US$15) and a similar perusal of its organic vegetable garden (US$25), but its *raison d'être* is their new two-hour canyoneering tour, which winds past six waterfalls and includes a 40m rappel down the largest of them all.

Hanging Bridges, Trams & Trains

OK, so you're too scared to zip through the canopy on a steel cable. Fear not: the makers of eco-fun have something special for you – hanging bridges and trams, the seemingly safer and slightly less expensive way to explore the tree tops.

Aventura (p166), Selvatura (p166) and Sky-Walk (owned by SkyTrek, p166) have systems of hanging bridges across which you can traipse and live out your Indiana Jones fantasies. There are subtle differences between all of them (some are fat, some are thin, some are bouncy, some are saggy), though you're going to enjoy the views of the canopy regardless of which one you pick. They're all priced around US$30 for adults and US$20 for students and children. The two forest reserves also have rather impressive hanging bridges.

SkyTram OUTDOORS

(☑2645-5238; www.skyadventures.travel; SkyWalk & SkyTram adult/student/children under 12 US$55/44/29) Owned by SkyTrek, SkyTram is a wheelchair-accessible cable car that leads you on a gentle ride through the cloud forest; tickets can only be purchased in conjunction with SkyWalk or SkyTrek.

Monteverde Trainforest SCENIC RIDE

(☑2645-5700; www.trainforest.com; adult/senior/student/child under 12yr US$50/40/35/free; ☑) Monteverde Trainforest is a miniature train system that travels 4 miles through the forest, penetrating one tunnel and crossing four bridges. The scenic railroad offers amazing views of Monteverde and Arenal lake and volcano. This is a great option for families with young children, as kids under 12 ride free. It's located 5km north of downtown Santa Elena, on the road to Reserva Santa Elena.

Horseback Riding

Until relatively recently this region was most easily traveled on horseback and, considering the roads around here, that's probably still true. Several operators offer the chance to test this theory with guided horseback rides ranging from two-hour tours to five-day adventures. Shorter trips generally run about US$15 per hour, while an overnight trek including meals and accommodations runs between US$150 and US$200.

Sabine's Smiling Horses HORSE RIDING
(②2645-6894, 8385-2424; www.horseback-riding-tour.com; waterfall tour US$50; ⊘depart 8am)
Run by Sabine, who speaks English, French, Spanish and German, Smiling Horses offers a variety of treks including a popular waterfall tour (three hours). Her horses are in great condition.

Desafío Adventure Company HORSE RIDING
(②2645-5874; www.monteverdetours.com) Does local treks for groups and individuals around town, day trips to San Luis Waterfall (US$60 including admission, six hours) and several multiday rides. This established outfitter will arrange rides to La Fortuna ($85), usually on the Lake Trail. The company also arranges white-water rafting trips on the Ríos Toro, Sarapiquí and others, and can help with transport and hotel reservations. Located next door to Morpho's Restaurant.

FREE **Mirador Lodge** HORSE RIDING
(②8702-4077, 2645-5354; www.miradorlodge.com)
This isolated cloud-forest lodge offers horseback tours as far as Arenal (US$70), starting from the lodge. If the weather and trail conditions are not perfect, they will arrange a taxi-boat-taxi transfer as an alternative.

⭐ Festivals & Events

The Monteverde Music Festival is held annually on variable dates from late January to early April. It has gained a well-deserved reputation as one of the top music festivals in Central America. Music is mainly classical, jazz and Latin, with an occasional experimental group to spice things up. Concerts are held on Thursday, Friday and Saturday, at different venues all over town and at the Monteverde Institute, which sponsors it. Some performances are free, but most events ask US$5 to US$15 – proceeds go toward teaching music and the arts in local schools.

📖 Courses

Centro Panamericano de Idiomas LANGUAGE
(CPI; ②2265-6306; www.cpi-edu.com; classes with/without homestay US$510/360; ⊘8am-5pm)
Specializes in Spanish-language education, with some courses geared toward teenagers, medical professionals and social workers.

Monteverde Institute COURSES
(②2645-5053; www.monteverde-institute.org; ⊘courses 1-10 weeks) A nonprofit educational institute that offers interdisciplinary courses in tropical biology, conservation, sustainable development and Spanish, among other topics. Courses are occasionally open to the public, as are volunteer opportunities in education and reforestation – check the website. Spanish classes start at $345 per week, with homestays with local families available for $20 a night. Longer courses include university-accredited programs for undergraduates and they emphasize tropical community ecology. Internships and volunteer opportunities are also available.

🌳 Tours

Monteverde Cheese Factory FACTORY
(La Lechería; ②2645-5522; adult/child US$10/8; ⊘tours 9am & 2pm Mon-Sat, store 7:30am-5pm Mon-Sat, 7:30am-4pm Sun) Until the upswing in ecotourism, Monteverde's number-one employer was this cheese factory, also called La Lechería (the Dairy). Started in 1953 by Monteverde's original Quaker settlers, the factory produces everything from a creamy Gouda to a very nice sharp, white cheddar, sold all over the country, as well as other dairy products such as yogurt and, most importantly, ice cream. Reservations are required for the two-hour tour of the factory.

Coffee Plantations

Coffee-lovers will be excited to find some of the finest coffee in the world right here. Late April is the best time to see the fields in bloom, while the coffee harvest (by hand) takes place from December to February. Any time is a good time to see how your favorite beverage makes the transition from ruby-red berry to smooth black brew. Advance reservations are required for all tours, which you can book directly by phone or through many hotels. Most charge about US$30 for adults, including transportation to the *fincas*.

Café Monteverde TOUR
(②2645-5901; www.monteverde-coffee.com; per person US$15; ⊘7:30am-6pm) Run by Cooperative Santa Elena, this highly recommended

NORTHWESTERN COSTA RICA MONTEVERDE & SANTA ELENA

tour takes visitors to *fincas* that use organic methods. Start by helping to pick perfect coffee beans, after which you'll be brought to the *beneficio* (coffee mill), where you can watch as the beans are washed and dried, roasted and then packed. Of course, you'll also get to taste the final product with a snack. The cafe itself offers free samples of six roasts, or buy some beans to take home.

Coopeldós
GUIDED TOUR
(☎2693-8441; www.coopeldos.com) This cooperative of 450 small and medium-sized organic coffee growers is Fairtrade-certified. One of its main clients is Starbucks. It's about halfway between Tilarán and Monteverde.

Don Juan Coffee Tour
GUIDED TOUR
(☎2645-7100; www.donjuancoffeetour.com; adult/child 6-12/ child under 6 US$30/12/free; ☺7am-4:30pm) Book this two-hour tour at their downtown shop near the SuperCompro.

El Trapiche
GUIDED TOUR
(☎2645-5834; www.eltrapichetour.com; per person $30; ☺10am & 3pm Mon-Sat, 3pm Sun) This traveller-recommended, family-run coffee plantation also grows sugar cane. Besides coffee, you can sample the area's other famous beverage, *saca de guaro*, a cane-based liquor. Reservations are recommended during high season.

Canopy Tours
Wondering where the whole canopy tour craze was born? Santa Elena is the site of Costa Rica's first zip lines, today eclipsed in adrenaline by the nearly 100 imitators who have followed, some of which are right here in town. You won't be spotting any quetzals or coatis as you whoosh your way over the canopy, and questions remain over the eco value of this type of pseudo-adventure tourism, but if you came to Costa Rica to fly, this is the absolute best place to do it.

Before you clip in, you're going to have to choose where, how fast, and how high you will soar – this is more challenging than you'd think. Much like the rest of Costa Rica, Monteverde works on a commission-based system, so be skeptical of the advice that you're given, and insist on choosing the canopy tour that you want. We provide basic information on the five major players in town, though it's good to talk to the friendly, unbiased staff at Pensión Santa Elena if you want the full scoop.

Aventura
CANOPY TOUR
(☎2645-6388; www.monteverdeadventure.com; per person US$45; ☺7am-4pm) Aventura has 19 platforms that are spiced up with a Tarzan swing, a 15m rappel and a Superman zip line that makes you feel as if you really are flying. Aventura's cables and hammock bridge are laced through secondary forest only. It's about 3km north of Santa Elena on the road to the reserve, and transportation from your hotel is included in the price.

Extremo Canopy
CANOPY TOUR
(☎2645-6058; www.monteverdeextremo.com; adult/child US$40, superman canopy ride US$5, tarzan swing $35; ☺8am-4pm) The newest player on the Monteverde canopy scene, this outfit runs small groups through secondary forest, and doesn't bother with extraneous attractions if all you really want to do is fly down the zip lines. There's a Superman canopy ride, allowing you to fly Superman-style through the air – the highest and most adrenaline-addled Tarzan swing in the area – and a bungee jump. One way or another, you will scream.

Original Canopy Tour
CANOPY TOUR
(☎2645-5243; www.canopytour.com; adult/student/child US$45/35/25; ☺7:30am-4pm) On the grounds of Cloud Forest Lodge, this is the fabled zip line route that started this adventure–theme park trend. These lines aren't as elaborate as the others, but with 14 platforms, a rappel through the center of an old fig tree and 5km of private trails worth a wander afterward, you can enjoy a piece of history that's far more entertaining than most museums.

Selvatura
CANOPY TOUR
(☎2645-5929; www.selvatura.com; adult/child US$45/30; ☺7:30am-4pm) One of the bigger games in town, Selvatura has 3km of cables, 18 platforms and one Tarzan swing over a stretch of incredibly beautiful primary cloud forest. In addition to the cables it has a hummingbird garden, a butterfly garden and an amphibian and reptile exhibition. The office is across the street from the church in Santa Elena.

SkyTrek
CANOPY TOUR
(☎2645-5238; www.skyadventures.travel; adult/student/child US$83/66/53; ☺7:30am-5pm) This very fast canopy tour consists of 11 platforms attached to steel towers that are spread out along a road and zoom over swathes of primary forest. We're talking speeds of up to 64km/h, which is probably why SkyTrek was the first canopy tour with a real brake system. The price includes admission to the SkyTram gondola and SkyWalk hanging bridges; cheaper packages are also available.

THE FABLE OF THE GOLDEN TOAD

Once upon a time, in the cloud forests of Monteverde, there lived the golden toad (*Bufo periglenes*), also known as the *sapo dorado*. Because this bright-orange, exotic little toad was often seen scrambling amid the Monteverde leaf litter – the only place in the world where it appeared – it became something of a Monteverde mascot. Sadly, the golden toad has not been seen since 1989 and is now believed to be extinct.

In the late 1980s, unexplained rapid declines in frog and toad populations all over the world spurred an international conference of herpetologists to address these alarming developments. Amphibians once common were becoming rare or had already disappeared, and the scientists were unable to agree upon a reason for the sudden demise of so many amphibian species in so many different habitats.

Several factors may be to blame for these declines, including the fact that amphibians breathe both with primitive lungs and through their perpetually moist skin, which makes them susceptible to airborne toxins. Their skin also provides little protection against UV light, which studies have shown can result in higher mortality rates to amphibian embryos and damaged DNA that in turn causes deformities. Pesticides also have been proven to cause deformities and hermaphroditism. And then there's the global issue of habitat loss. If all that didn't tell a bleak enough story, scientists have since discovered that the worldwide spread of chytridiomycosis disease (caused by the fungus *Batrachochytrium dendrobatidis*, in case you were wondering) has decimated amphibian populations everywhere.

According to the Global Amphibian Assessment, 30% of New World amphibians (1187 species) are currently threatened with extinction. In response to this dire statistic, an international coalition of zoos and wildlife conservation organizations have jointly established Amphibian Ark (www.amphibianark.org), an attempt to 'bank' as many species as possible in the event of further die-offs. We may never know what happened to the golden toad, but as one of the first warning signs that the ecosystem is off balance, its mysterious disappearance might have given a chance for survival – and a happy never-ending? – to other amphibian species.

🛌 Sleeping

During Christmas and Easter many hotels are booked up weeks in advance. January to April, and also in July, reservations are a good idea, though you can almost always find somewhere to stay. Note that Monteverde can get quite cool at night, so don't be surprised if your room doesn't have a fan, but squawk if it doesn't have a warm blanket. The rates listed reflect those during high season, but low-season rates can be as much as 30% to 40% lower.

TOP CHOICE **Pensión Santa Elena** HOSTEL $
(☏2645-6240, 2645-5051; www.pensionsanta elena.com; camping per person US$4, dm/s/d US$7/25/30, d without bathroom US$16-20, cabinas US$35-50; P@🛜🖥) This full-service hostel is a perennial favorite, located in central Santa Elena. Each room is different, with something to suit every budget and group. The best rooms are in the new annex building, which features little touches like superior beds, stone showers and iPod docks in every ·room (the speakers are hidden in the ceil-ing). Hostel amenities include hot showers, an internet cafe, shared kitchen and huge lounge, and free wi-fi, coffee and tea all day. The charming Costa Rican staff is fully bilingual (Spanish and English), and they offer the most unbiased tourist information in town.

TOP CHOICE **Hidden Canopy Treehouses** RESORT $$$
(☏2645-5447; www.hiddencanopy.com; incl breakfast & afternoon tea d garden rooms US$175-195, tree houses US$265-310; P🛏) The classiest spot in all of Monteverde, the American owner likes to call her unique boutique sleep: 'glam-ping,' but only the glam fits, because this stylish spot is a long way from camping. Hidden within 13 acres of private rainforest are four stilted wood-and-glass tree houses, each with a unique floor plan, decor and name. All feature a treetop balcony, luxurious bedding, private bathroom, waterfall shower, custom-made furniture and paintings by local artists, plus high-end amenities such as minibar, coffeemaker, hair dryer, and safe. The two-level Eden tree house has a fireplace, glass-enclosed Jacuzzi

and canopied bed – perfect for honeymooners. The Neverland tree house sleeps four and overlooks its own koi pond and has 1½ baths. There are two less-expensive rooms in the main house, where breakfast and sunset teas (you may opt for bubbly) are held.

Montelena Hostel
HOSTEL $

(2645-6549; http://www.minihostels.com/hostel/Montelena+Hostel; US$7-10; @♠) The cheapest sleep in Santa Elena and beloved by the backpacker brigade, Montelena is smack in the center of town on the main road (the bus practically drops you off on the doorstep). It has spacious tiled dorms, a few private rooms, and a communal kitchen too. It's above Tico y Rico.

Cabinas El Pueblo
HOSTEL $

(2645-6192; www.cabinaselpueblo.com; r with/without bathroom incl breakfast US$35/20; P@♠) This pleasant hostel run by an attentive Tico couple is one of Santa Elena's best value options. The price includes free breakfast, wi-fi and coffee or tea all day. The well-furnished rooms are bright and clean, if cramped, with firm mattresses and private hot-water showers. Some rooms also have a TV and fridge. You'll also find a fully equipped kitchen, balcony, garden and hammocks.

Monteverde Backpackers
HOSTEL $

(2645-5844; www.monteverdebackpackers.com/home.html; dm/s/d incl breakfast US$10/20/30; P@♠) Part of the Costa Rica Hostel Network, Monteverde Backpackers is smaller and more basic than the other cheapies, but it's clean and friendly, with wood-paneled rooms, comfy beds and some of the hottest, most powerful showers we've ever felt. You'll also find a communal kitchen, outdoor patio and TV lounge. Find Monteverde Backpackers on a hill just above Cabinas Vista al Golfo.

Hotel El Sueño
HOTEL $$

(2645-5021; www.hotelelsuenocr.com; s/d incl breakfast US$35/50; P♠) This friendly Tico-run hotel has huge wooden rooms with private hot showers. The pricier upstairs rooms are airier, though the best ones are toward the back. There's a great balcony with sweeping views of the area.

Cabinas Vista al Golfo
HOSTEL $

(2645-6321; www.cabinasvistaalgolfo.com; dm/s/d US$10/20/25; P♠▣) Rooms in this bright, kitschy lodge are well kept, the showers are hot and the owners will make you feel right at home. The upstairs balcony rooms ($5 extra)

have great views of the rainforest and, on a clear day, the Golfo de Nicoya. There's a small communal kitchen, and beds in a barn-like dorm sprinkled with beanbag chairs.

Camino Verde B&B
B&B $

(2645-5641; www.hotelcaminoverde.com; s/d US$25/40) Formerly known as Tina's Casitas, this well-loved travelers' nest offers an assortment of spacious, bright rooms on a rambling elf-like property. It's a quiet spot in a garden setting, and it may be a touch overpriced, but it's still a decent choice.

Hospedaje Pie Del Monte
HOTEL $

(8473-4120, 2645-6789; r US$20-25; P) This place has simple spotless rooms with Spanish tiles and queen beds, hot water and wi-fi just off the highway to Monteverde. There are also two larger cabin-like rooms with a full kitchen, but these are often booked, so call ahead.

Mar Inn B&B
B&B $

(2645-5279; www.monteverdemarinn.com; r incl breakfast US$40; P@♠▤) On a hill about 50m north of the high school, this family-run B&B is a great option, as the managers are welcoming and breakfasts filling. Wood-paneled rooms are rustic and airy with garish tiles, but you'll overlook that as the quiet location means a restful night's sleep. There's a communal kitchen and shared balcony where rocking chairs are oriented toward those lovely sunset views of Santa Elena and the Golfo de Nicoya.

Hotel El Tucan
MOTEL $

(2645-7590; r with/without bathroom US$12/25) If a wood-paneled lodge and cheap motel made sweet love they would conceive this cheapie. Rooms are clean and decent value though some suffer from late-night cigarette remorse. Rooms with shared bathrooms are tiny, but those with private porcelain are solid with queen beds and hot water.

Sloth Backpackers
HOSTEL $

(2645-5793; www.monteverdeslothbackpackers.com; per person US$14) A colorful, corrugated tin and cinder block hovel that is well priced and comes with friendly management and a peaceful, backroad location. Guests share communal bathrooms.

Hotel El Atardecer
HOTEL $

(2645-5462; atardecer@hotmail.com; s/d incl breakfast US$25/40; P♠) A cute and oft-overlooked family-run lodge that offers great value, spotless tiled rooms with high beamed ceilings and new bathroom tiles.

La Colina Lodge
LODGE $

(☑2645-5009; www.lacolinalodge.com; s/d US$20/35; P) This is the former Flor Mar, opened in 1977 by Marvin Rockwell, one of the area's original Quakers, who was jailed for refusing to sign up for the draft in 1949 and then spent three months driving down from Alabama. Nowadays, the gringo owners are as gracious and unpretentiously welcoming as the lodge itself. All of the rambling rooms on this peaceful property, frolicking with chickens and peacocks, are hand-painted in cheery colors with unique furniture and decor, and the kitchen and communal areas provide either shade or sun, and always a relaxed vibe. It is a bit ragged and worn down, with warped floors and doorways in some rooms.

Arco Iris Ecolodge
LODGE $$

(☑2645-5067; www.arcoirislodge.com; s US$30, d economy/standard/superior US$40/85/110; P@▣) This clutch of pretty cabins is on a little hill overlooking Santa Elena and the surrounding forests, and has the privacy and intimacy of a mountain retreat. The lodge features a system of private trails that wind throughout the property, including one that leads to a lookout point where you can see the Pacific on a clear day. There are different room sizes and styles to choose from, so you can either go rustic or live it up. Breakfast is an additional US$7. English, Spanish, German and French spoken.

Finca Terra Viva
LODGE $$

(☑2645-5454; www.terravivacr.com; d incl breakfast US$45, extra person US$5; P@⛟) A 300-acre working dairy *finca* surrounded by lush forest, 3.5km or so out on the road toward Reserva Santa Elena. It's a unique sleep that offer guests a typically Costa Rican rural experience. Kids love this place, which is teeming with cattle, horses, pigs and sheep. Each of the six rustic, wooden rooms sleeps up to four and has a private hot shower; a few free-standing *casitas*, fitted with kitchenette, are available for those who crave more privacy. Horseback riding tours (per person US$30) can be arranged, and you can try your hand at milking cows and making cheese at the organic dairy. It serves dinner for $7 per person, but doesn't provide lunch. Two-night minimum.

Quetzal Inn
LODGE $$

(☑2645-6076; www.quetzalinn.com; d with/without balcony US$45/40; P@▣) Up a quiet alley is this lovely little lodge. With wood-plank walls, high sloped ceilings and green surroundings, this family-run inn embodies the perfect combination of central location, thoughtfully designed accommodations and a personable, hospitable ambience. Rooms with balconies are slightly larger. An extra $5 will buy you breakfast in the morning.

Hotel Don Taco
HOTEL $$

(☑2645-5263; www.hoteldontaco.com; r/cabañas US$45/55; P) A rambling, dare we say almost craftsman-style, hotel on a hill above town. Older standard rooms are comfy enough but you can also opt for private *cabañas* with a Golfo de Nicoya view. Tiles are garish but management and their pets are sweet and attentive.

Mariposa B&B
LODGE $$

(☑2645-5013; vmfamilia@costarricense.cr; s/d incl breakfast US$45/55; P🛜) Just 1.5km from the Monteverde reserve, this friendly family-run place has quite nice rooms with terra-cotta floors and beamed ceilings, hot water, plush towels and a sweet Tico family to look after you. It's a great value, nestled into the forest with a little balcony for observing wildlife.

Rustic Lodge
LODGE $$

(☑2645-6256; www.monteverderusticlodge.com; r US$66; P✴@🛜) One of the better choices in the area, this new build has tree columns out front to give the wood lodge a more rustic appeal, but the spacious, spotless, updated rooms with beamed ceilings are why you're here.

Swiss Hotel Miramontes
HOTEL $$

(☑2645-5152; www.swisshotelmiramontes.com; s/d incl breakfast US$80/90; P) Just outside Santa Elena on the road to Juntas is this charming European-inspired retreat, well situated in a grove of pine trees and tropical flowers. Eight rooms of varying size come with fabulous hot-water bathrooms. Kids love the expansive landscaped grounds, with trails through the well-stocked orchid garden. The restaurant specializes in Swiss treats (mains US$4 to US$11) and, as this is a Swiss-run Costa Rican hotel, staff speak English, German, French and Spanish.

Hotel El Viandante
HOTEL $$

(☑2645-6475; www.hotelelviandante.com; d incl breakfast US$60; P@🛜⛟) Perched on a small but steep hill with views of the gulf, this small B&B is a great choice for families. It's not super fancy, but the 12 recently remodeled rooms have pinewood interiors with high ceilings, huge private bathroom with hot water and hair dryers, cable TV, orthopedic mattresses and baby cribs on request. Enjoy an American breakfast with a view from the top-floor lounge.

Cloud Forest Lodge
LODGE **$$**

(☎2645-5058; www.cloudforestlodge.com; s/d US$90/100; P@🛜) Spacious rooms at this hilltop lodge are spotless and have hot showers, but lack extras such as satellite TV. Instead, there are trails to walk, birds (and sometimes sloths) to be seen in the garden and surrounding cloud forest, and views of the Golfo de Nicoya. The uber-professional (you might even say, humorless) staff can arrange tours (they operate the Original Canopy Tour, p166) – including the area's only night canopy tour. It's a pleasant walk into town, but you'll probably need a car or a series of taxis to get around.

Los Pinos Cabañas y Jardines
LODGE **$$**

(☎2645-5252; www.lospinos.net; cabañas standard/junior ste/family US$65/85/125; P) Around the peaceful, forested gardens of this 9-hectare property, which once formed part of the family *finca,* are 14 free-standing *cabañas* which sleep two to six people. With plenty of space between them, each *cabaña* affords a sense of privacy and has a fully equipped kitchen and small terrace. It's a superb setting for those seeking a little solitude in easy walking distance of restaurants and shops around Cerro Plano. Though all of the *cabañas* are very comfortable and cozy, family rooms are the largest. Junior suites and family cabins are outfitted with hair dryers, cable TV and more upscale furnishings.

Hotel Claro de Luna
B&B **$$**

(☎2645-5269; www.clarodelunahotel.com; s/d incl breakfast US$60/70 ; P🛜) A kitschy but still tasteful choice, rooms are set in an aging Swiss-style chalet, but there is grace among the old bones. The downstairs rooms have faux-adobe walls, wood floors and furnishings with tasteful lighting and sweet bathrooms. Cash discounts of $10 are common.

Vista Verde Lodge
LODGE **$$**

(☎2200-5225; www.info-monteverde.com; d standard/superior incl breakfast US$68/75; P) When you really want to get away from it all, take the signed side road just east of Selvatura and head 2.5 rough kilometers (4WD only) to this remote, and a bit weather-beaten, lodge, where you'll fall asleep to the sounds of the surrounding rainforest. Wood-paneled rooms

with picture windows take in views of Volcán Arenal and beyond. Rooms in the new annex have queen beds and fabulous bath tubs and only cost an extra $7. There's also a great common area where you can unwind in front of the TV and warm your feet beside the fire. Some 4km of trails run through 64 hectares of primary and secondary forest.

Trapp Family Lodge
HOTEL **$$**

(☎2645-5858; www.trappfam.com; d superior/ste US$96/113, extra person US$17; P😃@🛜🐾) The closest lodge to the reserve entrance (just under 1km away) has 20 spacious rooms with high wooden ceilings, big bathrooms and fabulous views from picture windows (which overlook either gardens or cloud forest). Mountain suites come with TV and refrigerator, and are a bit larger. There's an elegant yet rustic restaurant (mains US$14 to US$19), a groovy wood bar and a sitting room with cable TV that's open till 10pm.

Hotel El Bosque
HOTEL **$$**

(☎2645-5221; www.bosquelodge.net; s/d incl breakfast US$45/62; P❄🛜) A decent array of tiled motel-like rooms with high beamed ceilings on a rambling property in Cerro Plano. It's quiet, laidback, leafy and affordable.

Ficus Sunset Suites
LODGE **$$**

(☎2645-5157; s/d from US$86/92; P❄@🛜) Set on the road out of Santa Elena, just before the highway, this new build has upscale, lodgelike rooms in a hilltop compound within walking distance from town.

Hotel Poco a Poco
HOTEL **$$$**

(☎2645-6000; www.hotelpocoapoco.com; s/d/tr incl breakfast US$102/113/124; P😃@🛜🏊) A short walk from Santa Elena will bring you to this funky property, which is adorned with ceramic mushrooms, tree frogs and other Costa Rican critters. Yellow-stucco rooms sleep three and there are some great perks – full bathtub, a heated and covered swimming pool, free wi-fi, cable TV and a DVD library (rental US$3) to dip into during those rainy nights. The best draw, however, is the excellent restaurant (mains US$7 to US$12), which is also open to the public and specializes in barbecue.

🍃 Hotel Belmar
HOTEL **$$$**

(☎2645-5201; www.hotelbelmar.net; standard/superior incl breakfast $102/130; P@🛜🏊) Despite being a 'real' ecoresort (the most unusual attraction is the onsite 'Biodigestor' used to create gas for cooking and heating), the

Swiss-style Hotel Belmar admirably doesn't flaunt this in its name. The gorgeous all wood rooms are definitely upscale, especially the top floor Superior varietal, which comes with king bed and lovely art-deco tiled balconies overlooking the cloud forest. The biggest bonus is right out back: the trailhead for Cerro Amigos. Amenities include a Jacuzzi, pool table, pond and great restaurant with tremendous views of cloud forest and the gulf.

Hotel Fonda Vela   LODGE $$$
(☑2645-5125; www.fondavela.com; d/junior ste US$135/180; P🐾@🐕🌊) With a convenient location near the Monteverde reserve, unique architectural styling, 14 hectares of trail-laced grounds and a private stable, this classy retreat is a sophisticated base for enjoying nature. Standard rooms are spacious and light, with wood accents and large windows; and the suites are among the nicest rooms in town, featuring wood ceilings, a bathtub, balcony and sitting room with huge TV. Many rooms are wheelchair-accessible.

El Establo Mountain Resort   HOTEL $$$
(☑2645-5110; www.hotelelestablo.com; d deluxe/ste incl breakfast US$250/325; P🐾@🌊) This is a seriously upscale lodge offering deluxe rooms with an orthopedic mattress, cable TV, fridge, safe and hair dryer, while the open-plan suites are A-frame lofts with private terraces. Some of the suites have Jacuzzi tubs facing wonderful views, while others have private flagstone terraces. Additional amenities include a spa, two indoor pools, two restaurants, hiking trails, and tennis and basketball courts. It's a steep hike to the best rooms, but the resort runs a shuttle on request.

🍴 Eating

Santa Elena has most of the budget kitchens in the area, but there's good eating throughout the Monteverde swirl.

The giant **SuperCompro** (☑2758-7351; ⊗7am-9pm) grocery store in Santa Elena has everything you could possibly need including organic produce. The tiny **Whole Foods Market** (⊗7:30am-5:30pm, no relation to the corporate-organic, global dominatrix) in Cerro Plano has a smaller selection, but profits are reinvested in the community (it's part of the Casem cooperative).

Taco Taco   MEXICAN $
(mains US$5-8; ⊗noon-8pm; 🐕) This brand new *taquería* offers tasty Tex-Mex tacos, burritos and quesadillas filled with shred-

ded chicken, slow-roasted short rib, pork *al pastor*, roasted veggies and battered mahi mahi.

Sabores   ICE CREAM $
(☑2645-6174; cones US$1-3.50; ⊗noon-8pm Wed-Mon; 🐕) This place serves Monteverde's own brand of ice cream, plus coffee and a variety of homemade desserts. It's the perfect place for a civilized scoop after a morning hike through primitive forest.

Donde Henry   CASADO $
(☑2645-6533; casados US$7; ⊗8am-9pm) A new cafeteria-style *casado* joint serving pick-and-mix *típica* to a devoted local following. Meals are large and tasty, if not magnificent. Grilled chicken breast, fish filet and roast pork are the common mains. Get it with beans, rice, and steamed or sautéed veggies and dowse it with two freshly made chili sauces.

La Carambola Art Cafe   CAFE $
(☑2645-5465; lacarambolacafe@gmail.com; mains US$6-12; ⊗11am-9pm; 🐕📶) A cute, bohemian new addition up the hill from town. It's owned by young, hip San José transplants serving something different from standard *típica*. Here you'll find 100% fruit smoothies, freshly made hummus and pita sandwiches packed with Indian or Thai spiced chicken, and ample vegetarian choices, too. Beer and wine is also served.

Cafe Chunches   CAFE $
(☑2645-5147; dishes from US$5; ⊗8am-7pm Mon-Fri, 8am-6pm Sat; 🐕) Owned by an American biologist, this bookstore and curio shop has expanded to include a loft cafe with the best breakfasts in town. It has bagels, egg dishes, excellent coffee and smoothies, too. There's also a reliable laundry service, and the bulletin board is a good source of information.

Stella's Bakery   BAKERY $
(☑2645-5560; mains US$2-6; ⊗6am-10pm) Step into the terra-cotta entry way and browse temptations such as cinnamon rolls, cherry pie or the decadent frosted brownies. That spanakopita looks lovely, too. It's all self service, except for the wine.

Tico y Rico   CAFETERIA $
(☑2645-5204; mains US$4-12; ⊗6:30am-9:30pm) A decent *típica* diner with ample greasy spoon breakfasts, and it has tasty chicken, beef and *pescado casados,* too.

A Sweet Slice of Madre Earth

To explore the Reserva Biológica Bosque Nuboso Monteverde (p177) is to arrive at the pinnacle of Costa Rica's continental divide. Here, the warm, humid trade winds from the Caribbean sweep up forested slopes where they cool and condense into clouds that congregate over the nearby Reserva Santa Elena (p180). What that means is a blast of swirling misty euphoria as you take in two forests rich in diversity and oxygen, where lichen-draped trees soar, exotic birds gossip and sing, and orchids and bromeliads bloom.

Life is abundant, throbbing and palpable here. But strangely, the slight temperature and topographical differences in the two forests means that each has their own unique ecosystem with several endemic species among the 70-odd species of flowering plants (including 40 orchid varietals). Many of the bromeliads and orchids get all their nutrients from the floating mist, so no tickling their exposed roots.

Most folks spend a half-day in either or both reserves. Santa Elena gets fewer visitors and can feel wilder, but Monteverde has that continental divide view. Afterwards you can linger in and around nearby Santa Elena or Monteverde – the latter sprouted from an American Quaker settlement that still thrives. In fact, the settlers who decamped here in the 1950s, in response to religious persecution at home, were the area's original conservationists. Visitors to the Friends Meeting House (p161) on worship days are always welcome. And if you can't bear to leave the forests at closing time, head to the magnificent Ecolodge San Luis and Research Station (p181) on Monteverde's western flank – a lush plateau that sheers into a virtual abyss. Here you can rub shoulders with visiting scientists, hike to the gushing Catarata San Luis (p164) and experience the forest in all its wild glory, day and night.

Clockwise from top left

1. Suspension bridge, Reserva Biológica Bosque Nuboso Monteverde 2. Birdlife, Reserva Biológica Bosque Nuboso Monteverde 3. Catarata San Luis

Restaurante Maravilla SODA $
(☎2645-6623; mains US$6-10; ⏰11am-9pm; ✎) Just about the cheapest and most authentic restaurant in Santa Elena, this charming *soda* serves typical Costa Rican specialties, including excellent meaty and vegetarian *casados*, pasta dishes and burgers. It can get crowded during lunch hour.

Trio's RESTAURANT $$
(☎2645-7254; mains US$7-17; ⏰lunch & dinner) A touch of class in sweet Santa Elena, this rather Ikea-chic dining room behind Super-Compro is perched in the trees and the menu also aims high. At first blush you may be shocked at how un-*tipica* it is. What with coconut curry, pork ribs slathered in guava barbecue sauce, chicken breasts stuffed with figs and goat cheese, and a Tico version of Cobb salad on the menu, but dishes deliver big time. Even the green salad is special – packed with avocado, hearts of palm and blessed with a passionfruit feta vinaigrette (yes, it works). The cocktails are tasty too, and for dessert there's an amazing looking mango split.

Café Caburé CAFE $$
(☎2645-5020; www.cabure.net; mains US$10-12; ⏰9am-8pm Mon-Sat; 📶) An Argentinean cafe set in the gorgeous Santa Fe–style lodge above the bat cave in Paseo de Stella (p161). It specializes in creative and delicious wraps, tortillas stuffed with chicken mole, chipotle rubbed steak, curried potatoes or lemon shrimp. The beef *empanadas* are fabulous, and there are some magnificent gourmet truffles too! Seriously, the chocolate here is high art.

Sofia RESTAURANT $$
(☎2645-7017; mains US$12-16; ⏰11:30am-9:30pm) Sofia has established itself as one of the best places in town with its Nuevo Latino cuisine – a modern fusion of traditional Latin American cooking styles. Think sweet-and-sour fig, roasted pork loin, plantain-crusted sea bass and shrimp with green mango curry. The ambience is flawless – soft lighting, hip music, picture windows, romantic candle settings, sloping wooden ceilings, pastel paintwork and potent cocktails to lighten the mood.

La Chimera RESTAURANT $$
(☎2645-6081; tapas US$4-10; ⏰11:30am-9:30pm) Latin-infused tapas such as fried calamari with green chili-coconut sauce, slow-cooked white beans and pork, and sea bass with passionfruit cream and spicy mango chutney, are complemented by an excellent wine list featuring robust Chilean reds and crisp whites. Dine alfresco on the trellis patio or in the groovy, burnt orange dining room. The cocktails rock. Skip dessert.

Musashi JAPANESE $$
(☎2645-7160; sushi US$5-8, rolls & mains US$5-18; ⏰11am-11pm Tue-Sun) Crave good sushi in the Tico rainforest? Look no further than this tiny restaurant in the heart of Santa Elena. Jesus, the Venezuelan owner, is a classically trained sushi chef, and his sushi boats are a good deal for groups. You'll also find other favorite Japanese dishes including teppanyaki, teriyaki and lunch bento box specials.

Johnny's Pizzería PIZZERIA $$
(☎2645-5066; www.pizzeriadejohnny.com; mains US$11-24; ⏰11:30am-10pm) Johnny's has been serving up wood-fired, thin-crust pizzas since 1993. We're partial to the original Traviesa with artichoke hearts, mushrooms, red onion and tomato sauce spiced with oregano, but the Monteverde sounds good too. Think: prosciutto, green olives and home-grown organic leeks. There's a warm and elegant atmosphere, and the tapas bar upstairs serves mussels, tortilla soup and mixed ceviche.

Sabor Español SPANISH $$
(☎2645-5387; saborespanola@hotmail.com; mains US$6-15; ⏰noon-9pm Tue-Su) She's from Barcelona. He's from Ibiza. And together, Heri and Montse have created one of the most authentic and lovely Spanish restaurants in Costa Rica. They specialize in paella, *papas bravas*, fresh fish, meats and chicken. Wash it down with some of the best sangria this side of the Atlantic. The ambience is rustic, intimate, super *tranquilo* and well worth the trip 2km north of downtown.

Pizzeria Natasha PIZZERIA $$
(☎2645-6919; US$9-17; ⏰11am-10pm) If you're nesting in Santa Elena and have a pizza itch, try this cheap joint below Restaurante Maravilla. It does a dozen thin crust pies including a Bolognese pizza, as well veggie, chicken and beef lasagna.

Restaurante El Campesino RESTAURANT $$
(☎2645-6883; mains US$6-20; ⏰11am-11pm) Relax beneath about 80 stuffed animals won from machines by the dexterous owner, who also serves up amazing *casados*, salads and a variety of sublime ceviche with a smile.

Morpho's Restaurant
RESTAURANT $$

(☎2645-5607; mains US$7-20; ⊙11am-9pm; 🐟🍴) This romantic downtown restaurant spices up typical Costa Rican food by adding gourmet flair. *Casados* feature a variety of European-influenced sauces (think sea bass in a fruity demiglaze), and are served with a traditional *batido* or a glass of wine. The menu also has a good variety of vegetarian dishes.

Tree House Restaurant & Café
CAFE $$

(☎2645-5751; mains US$7-18; ⊙11am-10pm; 🐟) Built around a half-century-old *higuerón* (fig) tree, this hip cafe serves up everything from BLTs to pizza to grilled tenderloin to seafood specials. It's a lively space to have a bite, linger over wine and occasionally catch live music.

Pizzería Tramonti
ITALIAN $$

(☎2645-6120; www.trimonticr.com; mains US$10-16; ⊙11:30am-9:30pm Mon-Sat) It's worth the trip to this lovely stone house if you hanker for authentic Italian, as the pizzas are baked in a wood-fired oven, and the pastas and seafood are consistently fresh. The atmosphere is relaxed yet romantic.

🍷 Drinking & Entertainment

Monteverde and Santa Elena nightlife generally involves a guided hike and nocturnal critters, but since this misty green mountain draws artists and dreamers, there's a smattering of regular cultural offerings. When there's anything going on you'll see it heavily advertised around town with flyers.

TOP CHOICE Bar Amigos
BAR

(☎2645-5071; www.baramigos.com; ⊙noon-3am) A disarming place because of its strange resemblance to one of those massive ski lodge bars, complete with picture windows overlooking the mountainside. But this is the one, consistent place in the area to let loose. There are DJs, karaoke, all the sports from the US and a billiard room downstairs.

La Taberna
LIVE MUSIC

(☎2645-4883; ⊙8pm-1am) Formerly Matae Cana, but with half the panache, this is the live music depot for rockers. We saw a Green Day tribute band play on Christmas Eve. It sometimes stays open till 3am. Look for the Matae Cana sign.

The Common Cup
CAFE

(coffee from US$2; ⊙7am-6pm; 🐟) A cute yet sophisticated coffee shop with its own roastery, the name betrays the fact that Heiner, the gentleman barista, crafts quite an uncommon cup of joe. Not simply because the coffee is gourmet and fabulous but because Heiner paints butterflies, monkeys, baby bears, hearts and leaves in the milky foam. All beans are locally grown and there are pastries, cakes, full breakfasts and wi-fi too.

Cafe Colibri
CAFE

(☎2645-7768; www.cafesantamarta.com; coffee drinks US$2; ⊙8am-5pm) There's a middling-to-unsatisfying cafe within the Monteverde reserve, but just outside the gates, Cafe Collibri (hummingbird cafe) is much better for coffee and cakes. The twin brothers who own the place make superb gourmet coffee from locally grown and roasted beans sourced from the family's *finca*, Santa Marta, where they offer coffee tours. They are also the head of a local cooperative export business funneling new cash flow to local growers.

Cosechas
JUICE BAR

(naturales & batidos US$1.50-3; ⊙7:30am-8pm) A storefront juice bar and alchemical wonderland of raw veggie and fruit juices. It serves creative *batidos* like strawberry-soursop or watermelon-passionfruit. Or slam down a chili ginger, celery, parsley, pineapple and carrot for a counter-intuitive zing of life.

🛍 Shopping

During our recent visit a very large, looming and ugly shopping mall had been built (but not yet occupied) on a hill overlooking Santa Elena. The road from Monteverde to Santa Elena has some great local galleries.

TOP CHOICE Luna Azul
JEWELRY

(☎2645-6638; lunaazulmonteverde@gmail.com; ⊙9am-6pm Mon-Sat) A super cute gallery with the best quality jewelry we saw in the entire area. It has soaps, some clothing racks, greeting cards, wood sculpture and macramé too, but jewelry is the thing. Crafted from silver, shell, crystals and turquoise, the work is stylish and stunning.

Hummingbird Gallery
HANDICRAFTS

(☎2645-5030; ⊙8:30am-5pm) This gallery just outside Monteverde reserve has exceptionally beautiful nature photography, watercolors, art by the indigenous Chorotega and Boruca people and, best of all, feeders that constantly attract several species of hummingbird. Great photo ops include potential hot shots of the violet sabrewing (Costa Rica's largest hummer) and the coppery-headed emerald, one of only three mainland birds endemic to Costa Rica. An identification board shows the nine species that are seen here. If you'd like a closer look, slides and photographs of the jungle's most precious feathered royalty (and other luminous critters) by renowned British wildlife photographers Michael and Patricia Fogden are on display.

Art House HANDICRAFTS
(Casa de Arte; ☎2645-5275; www.monteverdearthouse.com; ☉9am-6:30pm) Several rooms stuffed with colorful Costa Rican artistry is what you'll find at the Art House. There's jewelry, ceramic work, Boruca textiles and paintings. Though styles here differ quite a bit, it's at the crafts end of the artsy-craftsy spectrum, and it's a great place to find a unique local souvenir.

Alquima Artes HANDICRAFTS
(☎2645-5847; www.alquimaartes.com; ☉9am-5pm) Set in the Casem complex you'll find this cute gallery showcasing local artisans' jewelry, paintings and sculpture, and there's even raw honey for sale.

Aretsana En Madera JEWELRY
(☉9am-8pm) An apt name for this wood and jewelry craftsman live workspace. There's jewelry beaded and seeded, and wood sculpture of varying quality – some quite good. The proprietor/artist sells bags of seeds and beads if you're feeling creative.

Río Shanti HANDICRAFTS
(☎2645-6121; www.rioshanti.com; ☉11am-6pm; ☝) Many come for a spa treatment, massage (US$75 per hour) or yoga class for adults and children (US$12; be sure to call ahead for an appointment or schedule), but this calming space on the road into Monteverde also has a gallery stocked with handmade soaps, essentials oils, hand-painted tiles and woven blankets.

Casem HANDICRAFTS
(Cooperativa de Artesanía Santa Elena Monteverde; ☎2645-5190; www.casemcoop.org; ☉8am-5pm Mon-Sat, 10am-4pm Sun high season) Begun in 1982 as a women's cooperative representing eight female artists, today Casem has expanded to reportedly include almost 150 local artisans, eight of whom are men. Sadly, embroidered and hand-painted clothing, polished wooden tableware, handmade cards and other work make for an underwhelming selection. The best stuff is in the Sky Gallery upstairs.

❶ Information

Emergency
Police (☎2645-5127)

Internet Access
There is an abundance of internet cafes (per hour US$1 to US$2) in and around Santa Elena. Nearly all hotels and hostels are wired with wi-fi.

Medical Services
Consultorio Médico (☎8304-2121, 2645-7778; ☉24hr) Across the intersection from Hotel Heliconia.

Red Cross (☎2645-6128; ☉24hr) A hospital located just north of Santa Elena.

Vitosi (☎2645-5004; ☉8am-8pm Mon-Sat, 9am-8pm Sun) German-run pharmacy and department store, across from the Chamber of Tourism.

Money
Banco de Costa Rica (☎2645-5519; ☉8am-4pm Mon-Fri, 8am-noon Sat) 24hr ATM.

Banco Nacional (☎2645-5027; ☉8:30am-3:45pm) 24hr ATM in the new building behind the parking lot.

Banco Popular 24hr ATM.

Post
Correos de Costa Rica (☉8am-4:30pm Mon-Fri, 8am-noon Sat) Across from the shopping mall.

Tourist Information
Chamber of Tourism (☎2645-6565; www.monteverdecr.com; ☉8am-8pm) Operated by the local Chamber of Commerce, this office only promotes hotels and tour companies that pay the membership fee, so come in with the understanding that you'll get biased information.

Pensión Santa Elena (www.pensionsantaelena.com) A more objective option than the tourist office, even if you're not staying here. Talk to friendly hostel staff, who can also book tours, or, better yet, check out its comprehensive website.

❶ Getting There & Away

Bus
All buses stop at the **bus terminal** (☎2645-5159; ☉5:45am-11am & 1:30am-5pm Mon-Fri, to 3pm Sat & Sun) in downtown Santa Elena, where most of the budget digs are, and do not continue into Monteverde, so unless you fancy a walk, you'll need to switch to a taxi if that's where you plan to stay. On the trip in, keep an eye on your luggage, particularly on the San José–Puntarenas leg, as well as on the Monteverde–Tilarán run. Keep all bags at your feet and not in the overhead bin. Stories of theft and loss are legion.

Las Juntas US$2; 1½ hours; departs from bus station at 4:20am, 6am and 3pm. Buses to

Puntarenas and San José can drop you off in Las Juntas.

Managua, Nicaragua (Tica Bus) US$28; eight hours; a small shuttle bus (US$2) departs from the bus station at 6am and brings you to the Interamericana in Lagartos.

Puntarenas US$3; three hours; departs from the front of Banco Nacional at 4:20am, 6am and 3pm.

Reserva Monteverde US$1.20; 30 minutes; departs from the front of Banco Nacional at 6:15am, 7:20am and 1:20pm, returns at 6:45am, 11:30am and 2pm.

Reserva Santa Elena US$2; 30 minutes; departs from front of Banco Nacional at 6:30am, 8:30am, 10:30am and 12:30pm, returns at 11am, 1pm and 4pm.

San José (TransMonteverde) US$5; 4½ hours; departs the Santa Elena bus station at 6:30am and 2:30pm.

Tilarán, with connection to La Fortuna US$3; seven hours; departs from the bus station at 6am. This is a long ride as you will need to hang around for two hours in Tilarán. If you have a few extra dollars, it's recommended that you take the jeep-boat-jeep option to La Fortuna.

There's no direct bus to Cañas. Most people take a bus to Juntas, then transfer from there to frequent Interamericana-route buses for Cañas, Liberia and beyond.

Car

While most Costa Rican communities regularly request paved roads in their region, preservationists in Monteverde have done the opposite. All roads here are shockingly rough, and 4WD is necessary all year, especially in the rainy season. Many car-rental agencies will refuse to rent you an ordinary car during the rainy season if you admit that you're headed to Monteverde.

There are four roads from the Interamericana: coming from the south, the first turnoff is at Rancho Grande (18km north of the Puntarenas exit); a second turnoff is at the Río Lagarto bridge (just past Km 149, and roughly 15km northwest of Rancho Grande). Both are well signed and join one another about a third of the way to Monteverde. Both routes boast about 35km of steep, winding and scenic dirt roads with plenty of potholes and rocks to ensure that the driver, at least, is kept from admiring the scenery.

A third road goes via Juntas, which starts off paved, but becomes just as rough as the first two a few kilometers past town, though it's about 5km shorter. Finally, if coming from the north, drivers could take the paved road from Cañas via Tilarán and then take the rough road from Tilarán to Santa Elena.

There are now two gas stations open for business in the area.

Jeep-Boat-Jeep

The fastest route between Monteverde-Santa Elena and La Fortuna is a jeep-boat-jeep combo (around US$15 to US$25, three hours), which can be arranged through almost any hotel or tour operator in either town. A 4WD minivan takes you to Río Chiquito, meeting a boat that crosses Laguna de Arenal, where a van on the other side continues to La Fortuna. This is increasingly becoming the primary transportation between La Fortuna and Monteverde as it's incredibly scenic, reasonably priced and saves half a day of rough travel. Even if you may be confused as to why there are absolutely no jeeps involved in the process whatsoever.

❶ Getting Around

Bicycle

Hotel El Viandante is the only place in town that rents out mountain bikes (three hours/full day US$10/15). The price includes new Trek bikes, helmet, pump and water bottle. Guided bike tours (US$20 to US$50) to regional attractions are also available. That said, cycling in Monteverde–Santa Elena is not for the lighthearted beginner. The area is extremely hilly, rocky and muddy, and dominated by surprisingly high speed traffic. Be prepared.

Reserva Biológica Bosque Nuboso Monteverde

Here is a virginal forest dripping with mist, dangling with mossy vines, sprouting with ferns and bromeliads, gushing with creeks, blooming with life and nurturing rivulets of evolution. It is so moving that when Quaker settlers first arrived in the area, they agreed to preserve about a third of their property in order to protect this watershed. By 1972, however, encroaching squatters threatened its sustainability. The community joined forces with environmental organizations such as the Nature Conservancy and the World Wildlife Fund to purchase 328 hectares adjacent to the already preserved area. This was called the Reserva Biológica Bosque Nuboso Monteverde (Monteverde Cloud Forest Biological Reserve), which the Centro Científico Tropical (Tropical Science Center) began administrating in 1975.

In 1986 the Monteverde Conservation League (MCL) was formed to buy land to expand the reserve. Two years later it launched the International Children's Rainforest project, which encouraged children and school groups from all over the world to raise money to buy and save tropical rainforest adjacent to the reserve. Today the reserve totals 105 sq km.

The most striking aspect of this project is that it is the result of private citizens working for change rather than waiting around for a national park administered by the government. The reserve relies partly on donations from the public. As the underfunded Minae struggles to protect the national-park system, enterprises like this are more important than ever for maintaining cohesive wildlife corridors.

Visitors should note that some of the walking trails are very muddy, and even during the dry season (late December to early May) the cloud forest is rainy (hey, it's a rainforest – so quit bitching and bring rain gear, suitable boots and a smile). Many of the trails have been stabilized with concrete blocks or wooden boards and are easy to walk on, though unpaved trails deeper in the preserve turn sloppy during the rainy season.

Because of the fragile environment, the reserve allows a maximum of 160 people at any time. During the dry season this limit is almost always reached by 10am, which means you could spend the better part of a day waiting around for someone to leave. The best strategy is to get here before the gates open, or better (and wetter) to come during the off season, usually May through June and September through November.

There are a couple of important points to consider. If you only have time to visit either the Monteverde or Santa Elena reserve, you should know that Monteverde gets nearly 10 times as many visitors, which means that the infrastructure is better and the trails are regularly maintained, though you'll have to deal with much larger crowds. Also, most visitors come to Monteverde (and Santa Elena) expecting to see wildlife. However, both reserves cover large geographic areas, which means that the animals have a lot of space to move around and away from annoying humans. The trees themselves are primitive and alone worth the price of admission, though a lot has changed since the quetzal-spotting days of 1983. The animals have adapted to the increased tourist volume by avoiding the main trails, but most people who visit either reserve are more than satisfied with the whole experience.

🏃 Activities

Hiking

There are 13km of marked and maintained trails – a free map is provided with your entrance fee. The most popular of the nine trails, suitable for day hikes, make a rough triangle (El Triángulo) to the east of the reserve entrance. The triangle's sides are made up of the popular Sendero Bosque Nuboso (1.9km), an interpretive walk (booklet US$1 at the gate) through the cloud forest that begins at the ranger station, paralleled by the more open, 2km El Camino, a favorite of bird-watchers. The Sendero Pantanoso (1.6km) forms the far side of El Triángulo, traversing swamps, pine forests and the continental divide. Returning to the entrance, Sendero Río (2km) follows the Quebrada Cuecha past a few photogenic waterfalls.

Bisecting the triangle, the gorgeous Chomogo Trail (1.8km) lifts hikers to 1680m, the highest point in the triangle. Other little trails crisscross the region including the worthwhile Sendero Brillante (300m), with bird's-eye views of a miniature forest. However, keep in mind that despite valiant efforts to contain crowd sizes, these shorter trails are among the most trafficked in the country, and wildlife learned long ago that the region is worth avoiding.

The trail to the Mirador La Ventana (elevation 1550m) is moderately steep and leads further afield to a wooden deck overlooking the continental divide. To the west, on clear days you can see the Gulf of Nicoya and the Pacific. To the east you can see the Penas Blanca's valley and the San Carlos plain. Even on wet, cloudy days it's magical. Especially when the winds are howling and fine swirling mist washes over you in waves. All over these woods, in hidden pockets and secluded gullies, that mist collects into rivulets which gathers into threads that stream into a foaming *cascada*, visible from Sendero Cascada. From here the water pools, then forms into a gushing river, best glimpsed from Sendero Río or Sendero Chuecha. There's a 100m suspension bridge about 1km from the ranger station on Sendero Wilford Guindon. A mini Golden Gate suspended in the canopy, you can feel it rock and sway with each step.

There are also trails to three backcountry shelters that begin at the far corners of the triangle. Even longer trails, many of them less developed, stretch out east across the reserve and down the Peñas Blancas river valley to the lowlands north of the Cordillera de Tilarán and into the Bosque Eterno de los Niños. If you're strong enough and have the time to spare, these hikes are highly recommended as you'll maximize your chances of spotting wildlife, and few tourists venture beyond the triangle. But if you're serious about visiting the backcountry shelters, you should first talk to the park service as you will be dealing with rugged terrain, and a guide is highly recommended and at times essential. Also, backcountry camping and sleeping in these shelters is normally no longer allowed.

Wildlife-Watching

Monteverde is a bird-watching paradise and though the list of recorded species tops out at more than 400, the one most visitors want to see is the resplendent quetzal. The Maya bird of paradise is most often spotted during the March and April nesting season, though you may get lucky any time of year.

For those interested in spotting mammals, the cloud forest's limited visibility and abundance of higher primates (namely human beings) can make wildlife-watching quite difficult, though commonly sighted species (especially in the backcountry) include coatis, howler monkeys, capuchins, sloths, agoutis and squirrels (as in 'real' squirrel, not the squirrel monkey).

Tours

Although you can hike around the reserve on your own, a guide is highly recommended, and not just by us but by dozens of travellers who were inspired by their adventures to email Lonely Planet. The park runs a variety of guided tours: make reservations at least one day in advance. As size is limited, groups should make reservations several months ahead for the dry season and holiday periods. Guides speak English and are trained naturalists, and proceeds from the tours benefit environmental-education programs in local schools.

The reserve can recommend excellent guides for private tours. Costs vary depending on the season, the guide and where you want to go, but average about US$60 to US$100 for a half-day. Entrance costs may be extra, especially for the cheaper tours. Full-day tours are also available. The size of the group is up to you – go alone or split the cost with a group of friends.

Natural History Tours   NATURAL HISTORY
(☑2645-5122, reservations 2645-5112; tours excl entry fee US$17) The reserve offers guided

natural history tours at 7:30am daily, and on busy days at 8:30am as well. Participants meet at the Hummingbird Gallery, where a short 10-minute orientation is given. A half-hour slide show from renowned wildlife photographers Michael and Patricia Fogden is followed by a 2½- to three-hour walk. Once your tour is over, you can return to the reserve on your own, as your ticket is valid for the entire day.

Night Tours   WALKING TOUR
(incl entry fee with/without transportation US$20/17) The reserve offers recommended two-hour night tours at 7:15pm nightly. These are by flashlight (bring your own for the best visibility) and offer the opportunity to observe the 70% of regional wildlife that have nocturnal habits.

Bird-Watching Tours   BIRD-WATCHING
(5hr tour incl entry fee per person US$64) Guided bird-watching tours in English begin at Stella's Bakery at 6am, and usually see more than 40 species. There's a two-person minimum and six-person maximum. Longer tours go on by request at a higher fee, and usually more than 60 species are seen.

Sleeping & Eating

Mountain Lodge   LODGE $$$
(☑2645-5122; www.cct.or.cr; r with/without bathroom per person US$64/53) Near the Reserva Biológica Bosque Nuboso Monteverde park entrance is a mountain lodge with capacity for 47 people. It is usually used by researchers and student groups but are often available to tourists – make reservations. Prices include full board (three meals).

Backcountry Shelters   HUT $
(dm US$5) There are three backcountry shelters, with drinking water, showers, propane stoves and cooking utensils. You need to carry a sleeping bag, candles, food and anything else (like toilet paper) you might need. El Valle (6km, two hours) is the closest from the park entrance; Alemán Hut (8km, four hours) is near a cable car across Río Peñas Blancas; and Eladios Hut (13km, six hours) is the nicest, with separate dorm rooms and a porch. Trails are muddy and challenging, and the scenery mossy and green – and this may be the best way to appreciate the reserve. However, at research time reservations were hard to come by and normally only granted to visiting scientists. Still, it's worth enquiring at the park office.

Restaurant RESTAURANT $
(plates US$3-9; ⊙7am-4pm) There is a small restaurant at the entrance to the reserve, which has a good variety of sandwiches, salads and typical dishes.

ⓘ Information

The **visitors center** (☑2645-5122; www.cct.or.cr; park entry adult/student & child/child under 6yr US$17/9/free; ⊙7am-4pm) is adjacent to the reserve gift shop, where you can get information and buy trail guides, bird and mammal lists, and maps. The shop also sells T-shirts, beautiful color slides by Richard Laval, postcards, books, posters and a variety of other souvenirs, and rents out binoculars (US$10); you'll need to leave your passport. The annual rainfall here is about 3000mm, though parts of the reserve reportedly get twice as much. It's usually cool, with high temperatures around 18°C (65°F), so wear appropriate clothing.

It's important to remember that the cloud forest is often cloudy (!) and can even be, gasp, rainy, and the vegetation is thick – this combination cuts down on sound as well as vision. Also keep in mind that main trails in this reserve are among the most trafficked in Costa Rica. Some readers have been disappointed with the lack of wildlife sightings. Hire a guide and you'll see more.

The reserve is managed by the Centro Científico Tropical and supported by donations through the **Friends of Monteverde Cloud Forest** (www.friendsofmonteverde.org).

ⓘ Getting There & Away

Public buses (US$1.20, 30 minutes) depart the Banco Nacional in Santa Elena at 6:15am, 7:20am, 1:20pm. Buses return from the reserve at 6:45am, 11:30am and 4pm. You can flag down the buses from anywhere on the road between Santa Elena and the reserve – inquire at your hotel about what time they will pass by. Taxis are also available for around US$9.

The 6km walk from Santa Elena is uphill, but lovely – look for paths that run parallel to the road. There are views all along the way, and many visitors remark that some of the best birdwatching is on the final 2km of the road.

RESERVA SANTA ELENA

Though Monteverde gets all the attention, this exquisitely misty 310-hectare reserve (☑2645-5390, 2645-7107; www.reservasantaelena.org; adult/student US$14/7; ⊙7am-4pm) just a fraction of the size of that other forest, has plenty to recommend it. You can practically hear the canopy, draped with epiphytes, breathing in humid exhales as water drops on to the leaf litter and mud underfoot. The odd call of the three-wattled bellbird or low crescendo of a howler monkey punctuates the higher-pitched bird chatter.

While Monteverde Crowd...er...Cloud Forest entertains almost 200,000 visitors annually, Santa Elena sees fewer than 20,000 tourists each year, which means its dewy trails through mysteriously veiled forest are usually far quieter. It's also much less developed; plus, your entry fee is helping support another unique project.

This cloud-forest reserve was created in 1989 and opened to the public in March 1992. It was one of the first community-managed conservation projects in the country, and is now managed by the Santa Elena high school board and bears the quite unwieldy official name of Reserva del Bosque Nuboso del Colegio Técnico Profesional de Santa Elena. You can visit the reserve office (☑2645-5693; ⊙8am-4pm Wed-Fri) at the high school.

The reserve is about 6km northeast of the village of Santa Elena. This cloud forest is slightly higher in elevation than Monteverde, and as some of the forest is secondary growth, there are sunnier places for spotting birds and other animals throughout. There's a stable population of monkey and sloth, many of which can be seen on the road to the reserve. Unless you're a trained ecologist, the old-growth forest in Santa Elena will seem fairly similar in appearance to Monteverde, though the lack of cement blocks on the trails means that you'll have a much more authentic (note: muddy) trekking experience.

This place is moist and almost all the water comes as fine mist, and more than 25% of all the biomass in the forest are epiphytes – mosses and lichens – for which this place is a humid haven. Ten per cent of the species found here aren't be found in Monteverde, which is largely on the other side of the continental divide, but both are home to the quetzal. Remember rule No 407 of cloud forests: it's often cloudy.

There's a simple restaurant, coffee shop and gift store. Note that all proceeds go toward managing the reserve as well as to environmental-education programs in local schools. Donations are graciously accepted.

🏃 Activities

More than 12km of trails are open for hiking including four circular trails of varying difficulty and length, from 45 minutes (1.4km) to 3½ hours (4.8km) along a stable trail system. Unlike Monteverde, Santa Elena is not developed enough to facilitate backcountry hiking and at the time of writing it was not possible to overnight in the reserve.

If you have some extra time, there's a good volunteer program here – possible projects include trail maintenance, surveying, administration and biological research. You're expected to make at least a one-week commitment, and very basic dorm-style accommodations (no electricity and very cold showers) are available free to volunteers, though all but the most rugged will prefer a US$10-per-day homestay, including three meals. Although at times it's possible to simply show up and volunteer, it's best to contact the reserve in advance.

☞ Tours

The reserve offers guided tours (3hr tours excl admission per person US$15; ☺7:30am & 11:30am daily); try to make the earlier hike. Reservations are recommended during the dry season. The reserve can also arrange private tours for up to three people for US$75.

❶ Getting There & Away

A daily shuttle (US$2, 30 minutes) between the village of Santa Elena and the reserve departs from the Banco Nacional in town at 6:30am, 8:30am, 10:30am and 12:30pm, and returns at 11am, 1pm, 3pm and 4pm. A taxi from Santa Elena costs US$10 to US$12.

Ecolodge San Luis & Research Station

Formerly a tropical biology research station, this drop-dead gorgeous facility integrates academia with high-quality ecotourism and education. It's administrated by the University of Georgia and is Monteverde's best-kept secret. The 62-hectare campus is set on a cinematic, jade plateau with cloud forested mountains jack-knifing on three sides and keyhole sea views to the west where there is another stark drop-off. Adjoining the southern reach of the Monteverde reserve, much of the campus overlooks the Río San Luis. Its average elevation of 1100m makes it a tad lower and warmer than Monteverde, and bird-watchers have recorded some 230 species attracted by the slightly nicer weather. There's a working farm with tropical fruit orchards and a coffee harvest from November to March, and a number of trails into primary and secondary forest, including a trail to the Catarata San Luis (p164). Guides lead tours (adult/student US$10/8.50) to the triple-tiered 70m waterfall – these must be reserved in advance.

A variety of comfortable accommodations at the lodge (☎2645-8049; www.ecolodgesan luis.com; bungalows s/d US$79/144, r US$102/192) are available for anyone interested in learning about the cloud forest environment and experiencing a bit of rural Costa Rican life. Rooms are built into a long house with soaring beamed ceilings and a common balcony overlooking a forest teeming with monkeys and migratory birds, and the boiling river below. Rates include meals and most activities. There is a host of day and night hikes guided by biologists, as well as slide shows, seminars and horseback rides. They even have a spa. Discounts can be arranged for students, researchers, large groups and long stays.

The ecolodge also runs a resident naturalist volunteer program, though there is a preference for University of Georgia students and graduates, and a six-month commitment is required. The position entails leading a number of workshops and guided walks, as well as participating in development projects on the station and in the community. Training, room and board are provided. Yes, this is a special place to spend a few days/weeks/months/years.

From the main road between Santa Elena and Monteverde, it's a steep 3km walk from the signed road where the bus will drop you off. A 4WD taxi from town costs about US$15 each way, and the lodge can also arrange transportation from San José in advance.

Cañas

POP 25,500

If you're cruising north on the Interamericana, Cañas is the first town of any size in Costa Rica's driest province, Guanacaste. *Sabanero* culture is evident on the sweltering streets, where full-custom pickup trucks share the road with swaggering cowboys on horseback. It's a dusty, typically Latin American town, where almost everyone struts slowly and businesses shut down for lunch. It's all centered on the Parque Central and the decidedly atypical Catholic church.

Although you're better off basing yourself in livelier Liberia, Cañas is a good place to organize rafting trips on the nearby Río Corobicí or for exploring Parque Nacional Palo Verde. And if you need to stop for gas, it's worth a stroll; just don't leave valuables in the car.

◉ Sights & Activities

Though most visitors to Cañas simply use the town as a base for visits to nearby Parque Nacional Palo Verde or for rafting on the Río Corobicí, it's worth the trip just to see the Catholic church's psychedelic mosaics designed by famed local painter Otto Apuy. Sinewy vines and colorful starbursts that have enveloped the modern church's once-clean lines are enhanced by jungle-themed stained glass that's completely different from anything on offer at the Vatican. In the adjacent Parque Central, park benches and the pyramid-shaped bandstand are equally elaborate. The Plaza de Toros hosts bullfights in January and February.

Las Pumas   ZOO
(☑2669-6044; adult/child US$8/4; ⊙8am-4:30pm) This wild-animal shelter was started in the 1960s by the late Lilly Hagnauer, a Swiss environmentalist. It's the largest shelter of its kind in Latin America, housing big cats including pumas, jaguars, ocelots, jaguarundis and margays – plus a few deer, fox, monkeys, peccaries, toucans, parakeets and other birds that were either orphaned or injured. This is a labor of love. The shelter does not receive any government funding and relies on visitor admission and donations to survive. Volunteers are always welcomed, but you must make arrangements beforehand. The shelter is still operated by the Swiss Family Hagnauer, a local Cañas institution; Lilly's husband Werner manages Las Pumas, their daughter Verena runs Rincón Corobicí and Verena's son Dany runs Ríos Tropicales. Don't mention one to the other, family rivalries and whatnot.

Safaris Corobicí   RAFTING
(☑2669-6191; www.safaricorobici.com; Interamericana Km 193; 2hr per person US$42/30, 3hr birdwatching per adult/child under 14 yr US$48/35; ⊙departures 7am-3pm; ☑) Gentle rafting trips down the Río Corobicí can be booked at the office on the Interamericana about 4.5km north of Cañas. The emphasis is on wildlife observation rather than exciting whitewater rafting. The river is Class I–II (in other words, pretty flat) but families and naturelovers enjoy these trips. Swimming holes are found along the river. The company also offers one Class III/IV white-water trip (US$90) per day.

Ríos Tropicales   RAFTING
(☑2233-6455; www.rinconcorobici.com; ⊙departures 7am-3pm; ☑) The popular Ríos Tropicales offers Class I–II family 'float tours' including its popular two-hour, flora and fauna viewing tour (adult/child US$50/35). For the more adventurous, there are Class III–V white-water rafting trips on Río Tenorio that feature a death-defying 3.6m drop (US$90)! Ríos Tropicales operates out of the Rincón Corobicí restaurant.

🛏 Sleeping

TOP CHOICE Caña Brava Inn   HOTEL $$
(☑2669-1294; www.canabravainn.com; cnr Interamericana & Av 5; s/d US$45/60; P🅿❄🛜🏊) The newest and most upscale hotel in town has all the modern amenities including well-insulated rooms with flat-screen TV, wi-fi, huge comfy bedding and contemporary, dark wood furnishings. Pricier rooms have Jacuzzi. The hotel also houses an international restaurant, a small casino and the area's largest disco (open from 6pm to 1am, Wednesday to Saturday).

Hotel Capazuri   RESORT $$
(☑2669-6280; capazuri@racsa.co.cr; camping US$6, s/d US$30/45; P❄🏊) Inconveniently located about 2.5km northwest of Cañas on the Interamericana, this small, family-run Tico resort isn't a bad choice if you have wheels. Rooms are aging but still nice enough and most sleep three, with TV and private hot-water bathroom. There's also a festive onsite restaurant and a huge pool. The friendly management will also let you pitch a tent although it won't be the most magical camping experience of your life.

Cabinas Corobicí   HOTEL $
(☑2669-0241; cnr Av 2 & Calle 5; s/d US$18/20; P🛜) A quiet cheapie at the far end of town, this has some ghastly older rooms but the four rooms in the new building (um, you'll know where they are) have fresh tiles, crown mouldings, cable tv and wi-fi, and the area is fairly quiet at night.

Hotel Cañas   HOTEL $
(☑2669-5118; www.hotelcanascr.com; cnr Calle 2 & Av 3; s/d US$24/32; P🅿❄🛜☑) A professionally run collection of decent, tiled rooms with wooden beds, air-con and hot water, off the main drag. It's quiet, super clean and those potted (silk!) plants offer the illusion of nature. Portions in its popular restaurant (mains US$4 to US$10) are quite generous.

✕ Eating

Many of the restaurants in town shut down on Sunday, but luckily there's an enormous SuperCompro (⊗8am-8pm) right on the Interamericana and a Palí (Av 5 btwn Calles 4 & 2; ⊗8am-8pm) just around the corner.

TOP CHOICE Soda Los Antejitos   SODA $
(Av 3, btwn Calles Central & 1; casados with juice US$5; ⊗6:30am-7:30pm) A great local haunt, this white tiled *soda* is popular among locals for its fantastic *casados*. Even the steaks look divine here and the price is just as appetizing. The burgers, fish and sausage dishes look worthy of a leap, and it serves breakfasts too.

Hacienda La Pacífica   RESTAURANT $$
(☑2669-6050; www.pacificacr.com; mains US$8-24; ⊗6am-10pm) Once a working hacienda and nature reserve, this elegant restaurant is 4.5km north of Cañas on the Interamericana and is now part of a private hotel for researchers, and the odd tourist. Many of the ingredients are grown right here on experimental organic plots, including the only large-scale organic rice cultivation site in the country. The result are *tipica* meals, prepared and presented with taste and grace. The rooms (doubles US$90) are quite lovely too.

ℹ Information

You can find public phones, a post office, library, a Banco Nacional and Banco Popular with ATMs on the streets surrounding the Parque Central or along the Interamericana.

Emergency Clinic (☑2669-0092; cnr Av Central & Hwy 1; ⊗7am-4pm Mon-Fri) 24hr on-call service.

Internet Ciberc@ñas (☑2663-5232; Av 3 btwn Calles 1 & 3; per hr US$1; ⊗8am-9pm Mon-Sat, 2-9pm Sun) Has fast computers, air-con and, if you get here at 8:15am, two hours for the price of one.

Minae/ACT Office (☑2669-0533; Av 9 btwn Calles Central & 1; ⊗8am-4pm Mon-Fri) Has limited information about nearby national parks and reserves.

ℹ Getting There & Away

All buses arrive and depart from **Terminal Cañas** (⊗8am-1pm & 2:30-5:30pm) at the northern end of town. There are a few *sodas* and snack bars, and you can store your bags (US$0.50) at the desk. There's also a taxi stand in front.

Juntas US$0.80; 1½ hours; departs 9:20am, 2:20pm, 4:50pm and 6pm.

Liberia US$3; 1½ hours; departs 4:30am, 5:35am, 6:10am, 6:40am, 7:15am, 7:45am, noon, 1:30pm, 4:30pm and 5:30pm.

Puntarenas US$3; two hours; departs 6am, 9:20am, 10:30am, 11:30am, 12:30pm, 3:30pm and 4:30pm.

San José US$5; 3½ hours; departs daily at 4am, 4:50am, 6:15am, 8:50am and 12:10pm. There are two afternoon buses departing at 1:30pm and 5pm on Sunday only.

Tilarán US$1; 45 minutes; departs 6am, 8am, 9am, 10:30am, noon, 1:45pm, 3:30pm and 5:45pm.

Upala US$3; two hours; departs 4:30am, 6am, 8:30am, 11:15am, 1pm, 3:30pm and 5:15pm.

Puente La Amistad

About 23km south of Cañas on the Interamericana a turnoff leads 25km on Rte 18 to the Puente de la Amistad Costa Rica–Taiwan (Costa Rica–Taiwan Friendship Bridge). The 780m bridge spans the Río Tempisque and was built and financed by the Taiwanese government in 2003. The 'Friendship Bridge' has greatly reduced travel time to and from the beaches in Nicoya. It opened in 2003.

Long before you get here, you'll notice dozens of signs on the Interamericana advertising the best steakhouse in Guanacaste: Bar-B-Q Tres Hermanas (☑2232-6850; www.bbqtreshermanas.com; cnr Interamericana & Rte 18; mains US$7-18; ⊗11am-9pm; 🖗). Believe the hype! This local landmark's specialty is barbecue beef and pork ribs, marinated and slow cooked for eight hours. Kids will love the playground and noisy bull and monkey animatronics. Leave all boring vegetarian friends at home.

There is a small parking area and observation platform on the western side of the river so that you can admire and take photos (as the locals proudly do) of the bridge before you cross over.

Volcán Tenorio Area

Parque Nacional Volcán Tenorio, part of the Area de Conservación Arenal (ACA), is one of the highlights of northwestern Costa Rica. It's a cool, misty, magical place highlighted by cloud forests and that icy blue river that is Río Celeste, the region's namesake. The park entrance is located just north of Bijagua (pronounced 'bee-hag-gwa'), the only sizeable town in the Tenorio sphere. It has a few hotels, a Banco Nacional ATM, several small

LAS FIESTAS DE GUANACASTE

Guanacastecos love their horses almost as much as they love their fiestas. And what better way to get the best of both worlds than with a *tope* (horse parade), a mix of Western rodeo and country fair complete with cattle auction, food stalls, music, dancing, drinking and, of course, bull riding. In Costa Rica the bulls are never killed, so watching the insane helmetless, bareback, bucking bronco action is exciting and (usually) gore-free. Even better than watching the bull riding is the aftermath of the rider getting tossed, as it's fairly common for the local drunks and young machos to jump into the ring to act as volunteer rodeo clowns, which is simultaneously hilarious and stupefying.

Though the bull riding usually draws the biggest crowds, the main event is the *tope* itself, where you can see the high-stepping gait of the *sabanero* (cowboy), which demands endurance and skill from both horse and rider.

Topes are also a great place to catch the region's traditional dance, known as the *Punto Guanacasteco*. Perhaps the showiest aspect of the dance is the long, flowing skirts worn by the women. This skirt is meant to resemble an oxcart wheel, which is a traditional Costa Rican craft most often associated with the town of Sarchí. *Punto Guanacasteco* traditionally served as a means of courtship, and it's common for the dance to be frequently interrupted by young men who shout rhyming verses in order to try to win over a love interest. The dance and accompanying music are fast paced and full of passion, and they're similar to most other Central American styles.

Topes are a fairly common occurrence in Guanacaste, so ask a local about where one might be happening, or look out for posters. Generally, *topes* occur on Costa Rican civic holidays, though you can bet on finding big parties during Semana Santa (the week before Easter), the week between Christmas and New Year, and on July 25, the anniversary of Guanacaste's annexation.

sodas and bars, but no gasoline; the nearest gas pumps are in Upala or Cañas. If you have your own wheels, the park is a fairly long but certainly do-able day trip from Liberia or Cañas, but consider basing yourself in one of the area's fabulous mountain lodges and visiting both the Tenorio and Miravalles areas from there over two or three days.

A paved road 6km northwest of Cañas branches off the Interamericana and heads north to Upala, passing between Volcán Miravalles to the west and Volcán Tenorio (1916m) to the east.

PARQUE NACIONAL VOLCÁN TENORIO

They say when God finished painting the sky blue, he washed his paintbrushes in the Río Celeste. The heavenly blue river, waterfalls and lagoons of Parque Nacional Volcán Tenorio are among the most spectacular natural phenomena in Costa Rica, which is probably why the park is known to locals simply as, Rio Celeste.

Established in 1976, this magical 184-sq-km national park remains one of the most secluded and least-visited parks in the country due to the dearth of public transportation and park infrastructure. As a result, it

remains a blissfully pristine rainforest abundant with wildlife. Soaring 1916m above the cloud rainforest is the park's namesake, Volcán Tenorio, which actually consists of three peaked craters: Montezuma, Tenorio I (the tallest) and Tenorio II.

Your first stop will be the **Puesto El Pilón ranger station** (☑2200-0135; www.acaren altempisque.org; adult/child under 12 US$10/free; ⊙8am-4pm, last entry 2:30pm), which houses a small exhibit of photographs and dead animals. Pick up a free English or Spanish hiking map.

🏃 Activities

A well-signed trail begins at the ranger station parking lot and winds 1.5km through the rainforest until you reach an intersection. Turn left and climb down a very steep and slippery staircase to the Catarata de Río Celeste, a milky-blue waterfall that cascades 30m down the rocks into a fantastically aquamarine pool.

They were building a new waterfall trail at research time, so you may not have to retrace your steps, but you will have to climb back up to the main trail to continue 400m further to the Mirador, where, from the double-decker wooden platform, you'll get gorgeous views of Tenorio. Further on is the techni-colored Pozo Azul (Blue Lagoon). The trail loops around the lagoon 400m until you ar-rive at the confluence of rivers known as Los Teñidores (The Stainers). Here, two small rivers – one whitish blue and one brownish yellow – mix together to create the blueberry milk of Río Celeste.

For the final reward, continue 300m to the Aguas Termales (hot springs) to soak your weary muscles. This is the only place in the park where you're permitted to enter the water; bring your own towel and swim-suit. Plans for a circuit trail are afoot, but for now the trail ends here. Retrace your steps to return to the ranger station. Hiking to the volcano crater is strictly prohibited.

Allow three to four hours to complete the entire hike. It's about a 7km roundtrip, but parts of the trail are steep and rocky. And be-cause this is a rainforest, the trail can be wet and muddy almost year-round. Good hiking shoes or boots are a must. After your hike, you'll find an area to wash your footwear near the trailhead.

🛏 Sleeping & Eating

There are a few simple *sodas* in Bijagua, but you'll probably be eating at your lodge.

AROUND BIJAGUA

TOP CHOICE **Celeste Mountain Lodge** LODGE $$$
(☑2278-6628; www.celestemountainlodge.com; s/d/tr incl all meals US$150/180/215; P) One of the most innovative and sustainable hotels we've ever seen, Celeste Mountain Lodge is proof that one can be ecofriendly with-out giving up comfort or style. The French owner, Joels Marchel, moved to Canada and became one of Costa Rica's first and best in-ternational travel champions, booking count-less tour groups and families into dream Tico holidays for decades, all the while dreaming up the perfect jungle lodge. This is it, and the contemporary open-air hilltop lodge in the shadow of Volcán Tenorio is absolutely stun-ning. It was built in 2007 using ecofriendly materials such as recycled wood, plastic, old truck tires and coconut fiber. Lamps, sculp-tures and other decorative items are made of scrap metal. Hot water comes from solar power, and cooking gas is partially produced by kitchen waste. There's even an ingenious hot tub heated by burning salvaged wood. Nothing in the building was imported, ex-cept for Marchel. The self-proclaimed 'radi-cal' believes we all need to change the way we travel, including 'unplugging' on holiday,

so you won't find TVs, hair dryers or other gizmos here. But elegance is not spared in the slightest. The 18 rooms are four-star styl-ish with colorful accents, concrete tile floors and wooden shutters that open onto immo-bilizing volcano and jungle vistas (also visible from the hip common atrium). The property features labyrinthine gardens, a soccer pitch, and a 2km interpretive hiking trail laid with geotextile (no more muddy shoes!), which makes for soundless hiking in one of Costa Rica's prime bird-watching zones. The price includes all meals at the amazing organic restaurant and service is simply outstanding. The lodge is located at the end of a 3.5km-long, rough (4WD required) access road that begins at the northern end of Bijagua.

Tenorio Lodge LODGE $$$
(☑8886-5382, 2466-8282; www.tenoriolodge.com; s/d incl breakfast US$115/125; P✱@🛜) Locat-ed on a lush hilltop with amazing views of Volcán Tenorio, this lodge has some of the most romantic and private accommodations around. There are eight roomy bungalows, each containing two orthopedic beds (one king and one queen), private bathroom with solar-heated water, panoramic windows and balcony with volcano views. The gorgeous lodge has a lovely restaurant featuring a dai-ly changing dinner menu (but no lunch). On the 7-hectare property you'll find two ponds, a heliconia garden and two hot tubs to enjoy after a long day of hiking. It's located 1km south of downtown Bijagua.

Sueno Celeste B&B $$
(☑2466-8221; www.sueno-celeste.com; d US$75; P🛜🏊) This cute, funky B&B has a collec-tion of stylish bungalows with polished concrete floors, frilly bed linens, molded concrete rain showers, and beamed ceil-ings, scattered around a garden plot with Tenorio views. They sleep up to four and are tremendous value. There's even a small dipping pool and breakfast is served with home-baked bread.

Hotel El Cacao HOTEL $
(☑2466-8052; www.hotelcacaocr.com; s/d US$25/40) The best choice in Bijagua town is locat-ed 300m north of the main highway down a dirt road. Rooms are set in a freshly painted, canary yellow building and have new tiles, cable TV and wooden beds. There is plenty of deck seating with lovely views of Volcán Miravalles and tasteful patio decor includ-ing old milk cans and coffee grinders, and delicate, dangling ferns.

Posada La Amistad
HOMESTAY **$$**

(☑8978-2676, 8356-0285; www.posadarioceleste. com; r incl meals per person US$44; P) Posada la Amistad, aka China Verde (you'll see signs for both), is a homestay tucked into a rural ranching community, 1km northeast of the park entrance. Barnlike rooms are rustic but clean and fresh, with stone floors. Your stay includes a guide to the park (you will have to pay your own entry fee), and you must try the vine swing! It is truly an awesome ride. The owner, Wilber, is fabulous. He'll teach you about all the flora, birds and insects you see, and walk you through his pig pen, pineapple and noni fields, coffee and cacao groves, and herb garden where he cultivates ginger, lemongrass and mint.

Cabinas Piuri
HOTEL **$**

(☑8706-0617, 2479-8462; s/d incl breakfast US$30/40, planetarium room US$50; P⊞) A rather majestic entrance greets you 300m past the national park gates. Here you'll find a massive gushing fountain erupting against a gorgeous cloud forest backdrop. Cheaper rooms are set in bright pink longhouses with king beds, crown moldings, white tiled floors and canary yellow walls. Some are quite musty, so you'll have to sniff around. Or you can simply opt for the concrete, egg-shaped planetarium room, where logs have been embedded into walls sculpted with various animal totems. It's an original nest, to be sure. But the best part of this property is its perch on a gorgeous slice of the milky blue river. They have crafted stone dipping pools from the flowing river, but you may as well swim in the magnificent river itself. It's about 1km west of the park entrance.

Tenorio's Door
HOTEL **$**

(☑8306-6878; www.tenoriodoor.es.tl; d US$20 ; P) Family owned right in the rustic *pueblo* of El Pilon, walking distance to the park gates (and not much else), rooms are extremely basic with painted concrete floors and shower stalls, but linens are fresh and rooms do come with breakfast.

Rio Celeste Hideaway
HOTEL **$$$**

(☑2206-5114; www.riocelestehideaway.com; d incl breakfast US$249-299) An elegant address recently opened for business just 550m, and across a pedestrian-only bridge, from the park gate. This luxury property has huge, 90-sq-m thatched *casitas* with wood floors, pastel paint jobs, antique furnishings and flat-screen TVs, sprinkled among lush land-scaped grounds. To get here by car you must take Hwy 4 (read: not Hwy 6!) toward Upala and follow the signs west toward Santo Domingo, San Miguel and Parque Nacional Volcán Tenorio. You can't reach Rio Celeste Hideaway by car from Bijagua, although locals hold out hope that the road will go through one day soon.

La Carolina Lodge
LODGE **$$**

(☑2466-6393; www.lacarolinalodge.com; per person incl meals & horse rides US$75-90; P⊠) Flanked by a roaring river and tucked in the trees this gloriously rustic retreat. This isolated lodge is set on a working cattle ranch on the slopes of the volcano, and is highly recommended for anyone looking for a beautiful escape from the rigors of modern life. Amazing meals (organic beans, rice, fruits, cheeses, chicken and pork from the farm) are cooked over an outdoor wood-burning stove, and they are a treat – as is soaking in the wood-fired hot tub. Rooms with hot shower in the lovely all wood main house are basic, and the nicer, roomier cabins have more privacy and romance. Room rates include guided hikes in the national park, as well as horse rides in the surrounding countryside with visits to nearby hot springs and swimming holes. The lodge is about 1.3km west of the charming ranching hamlet of San Miguel.

❶ Getting There & Away

There are no direct buses to the national park. Buses between San José and Upala stop in Bijagua (US$8, four daily). Buses also run between Upala (US$1) and Cañas via Bijagua (US$1.25). Most lodges can pick you up in Bijagua.

There was a new national park shuttle available from Bijagua when we came through. It's US$10 roundtrip and leaves Bijagua at 8:40am, returning between 1pm and 2pm, depending upon client preference. Still, it's better to have your own wheels here.

Thanks to a new road, just completed in late 2011, you can now reach the national park directly from Bijagua. Follow the signs to Celeste Mountain Lodge and keep going for approximately 4km until you reach the park entrance. A 4WD is highly recommended.

About 5km north of Bijagua is the gravel road to San Miguel. Turning left at the San Miguel intersection will bring you to La Carolina Lodge (1.3km). The rough dirt road (4WD required) continues another 13km until it meets up with Hwy 4, the main Upala–Fortuna thoroughfare. Turning right will take you 4km down an even rougher road to the national park gate.

THE BACKROAD BETWEEN TENORIO AND MIRAVALLES

An epic backroad, 4WD track links Tenorio to Miravalles. This is useful for road trippers who wish to base in Tenorio and visit Miravalles for the day (an itinerary that we recommend highly). About 12km south of Bijagua make a right where you see a sign toward the *pueblo* of Río Chiquito. It's a rather small sign, and once you make the turn you'll be in the even smaller *pueblo* (OK, it's bigger than a road sign). The road narrows immediately and severely. Don't worry, there is no dead end. After fording a stream it goes crazy vertical. Shift into 4-low and grind up the 200m hill. At the top are marvelous vistas of the two mountains, acres of rangeland and the vast valley below. Then you'll go down again, ford another stream, navigate a steeper incline and be rewarded with massive views once more. By now you'll be in old Tico cattle country. Enjoy it. Within an hour you'll be dipping into hot springs. From Miravalles detour down the slope on paved roads toward the Interamericana, take in the Llano de Cortes Waterfall and return to the Río Celeste area via Hwy 6.

Volcán Miravalles Area

Volcán Miravalles (2028m) is the highest volcano in the Cordillera de Guanacaste, and although the main crater is dormant, the geothermal activity beneath the ground has led to its rapid development as a hot-springs destination.

Miravalles isn't a national park or refuge, but the volcano itself is afforded a modicum of protection by being within the Zona Protectora Miravalles. You can also take guided tours of the government-run Proyecto Geotérmico Miravalles, north of Fortuna, an ambitious project inaugurated in 1994 that uses geothermal energy to produce electricity, primarily for export to Nicaragua and Panama. It also produces about 18% of Costa Rica's electricity. A few bright steel tubes from the plant snake along the flanks of the volcano, adding an eerie, alien feel to the remote landscape. But the geothermal energy most people come here to soak up comes in liquid form. The hot springs are north of the tiny village of Fortuna de Bagaces (not to be confused with La Fortuna de Arenal or Bagaces). The sleeping options in the area aren't fabulous, so we suggest basing yourself in Tenorio and visiting the springs on a day trip, as the two mountains are linked by a rather glorious back road.

Activities

Thermo Manía
HOT SPRING

(2673-0233; www.thermomania.net; adult/child US$10/8; ⊗8am-10pm; @ 🛜 ♿) The biggest complex in the area has some Disney–Flintstone *queso* to it, but there are 11 thermal pools ranging from 36°C to 40°C, split into two areas. The upper pool complex is older, though it does have a swim up bar and waterslide. Much more tasteful are the five stone pools and sauna in the leafy lower sector. These are the best in the area, although all the pools could be a touch hotter. There's also a full spa (with private mud baths), playground, museum, soccer field and picnic tables. The busy restaurant-bar (mains US$4 to US$10) is housed in a 170-year-old colonial cabin furnished with museum-worthy period pieces. Guests who stay in the 26 log-cabin rooms (per person adult/child US$40/26) have free access to the pools during their stay, with TV and cold-water bathroom (neatly counterbalancing the lack of cold-water pools). Families love it here.

El Guayacán
HOT SPRING

(2673-0349; www.termaleselguayacan.com; adult/child 3-10 US$7/5; fumaroles tour US$2; 🛜♿) El Guayacán, whose hissing vents and mud pots (stay on the trail!) are on the family *finca*, lies just behind Thermo Manía. Seven thermal pools and one cold pool with a waterslide are flanked by clean, simple, cold-water *cabinas* (s/d US$30/60) brushed in loud colors. This unpretentious place has a mellow, family vibe to it. There's an on-site restaurant (mains US$4 to US$10) and it even has a hanging bridge in the nearby forest.

Yökö Termales
HOT SPRING

(2673-0410; www.yokotermales.com; adult/child US$4/3; ⊗7am-10pm; @🛜) Yökö has five hot springs ranging from 20°C to 35°C, and a larger pool with a small waterslide and waterfall, set in an attractive meadow at the foot of Miravalles. There's also a not-fit-for-humans 50°C pool boiling on the grounds.

The 12 canary tinted rooms (s/d incl breakfast US$40/75) are comfy with beamed and plywood ceilings that look unfinished. It's a decent, but not magical, sleeping option. Extra amenities include a Jacuzzi, sauna and a relaxed restaurant (mains US$2 to US$10) serving everything from burgers to filet mignon.

Termales Miravalles   HOT SPRING
(☎8357-8820, 8305-4072; adult/child US$4/3; ☑) For some local flavor, Termales Miravalles has two pools and a waterslide, and lies along a thermal stream. The owners have set up a small restaurant here and offer camping (US$6 per person) on the property. They're usually open on weekends year-round, and daily during high season. The access road is directly across from Yökö hot springs.

Centro de Aventuras   CANOPY TOUR
(☑camping, tours 2673-0469, mountain or horse tours 8765-3686, room reservations 2673-0233; www.volcanoadventuretour.com) Near the base of the volcano is Centro de Aventuras, which has a number of offerings including a canopy tour (adult/children US$40/30) and horseback riding (US$25 to US$70). The clean, brightly painted *cabinas* (d US$40 to US$50) have private hot-water bathroom and are centered on a pool that's fed by mountain spring water. This is a good place to inquire about local guides who can take you on independent full-day horseback and hiking tours to the summit of Miravalles (per person $70).

ⓘ Getting There & Away

Volcán Miravalles is 27km northeast of Bagaces and can be approached by a paved road that leads north of Bagaces through the communities of Salitral and Torno, where the road splits. From the left-hand fork, you'll reach Guayabo, with a few *sodas* and basic *cabinas*; to the right, you'll find Fortuna de Bagaces (so named as not to confuse it with La Fortuna, Bagaces overlap notwithstanding), with easier access to the hot springs. Both towns are small population centers, and are not of much interest to travelers. The road reconnects north of the two towns and continues toward Upala.

Buses (US$1.50, one hour) from Liberia to Guayabo or Aguas Claras (via Fortuna) depart at 6am, 9am, 11am and 2pm and pass by all the hot-spring entrances. Return buses to Liberia (via Guayabo) pass by the hot springs at about 2:30pm, 3:30pm and 4:30pm.

Bagaces
POP 4600

This small town is about 22km northwest of Cañas on the Interamericana, and is the headquarters of the Area de Conservación Tempisque (ACT; ☎2200-0125; ☺8am-4pm Mon-Fri), which, in conjunction with Minae, administers Parque Nacional Palo Verde, Reserva Biológica Lomas de Barbudal, and several smaller and lesser-known protected areas. The office is on the Interamericana opposite the signed main entry road into Parque Nacional Palo Verde. The office is mainly an administrative one, but sometimes rangers are available. Any buses between Cañas and Liberia can drop you off in Bagaces. If you're heading to Miravalles, there are hourly local buses to both Fortuna and Guayabo.

◉ Sights

Llanos de Cortés   WATERFALL
(by donation; ☺8am-5pm) If you have time to visit only one waterfall in Costa Rica, make it Llanos de Cortés. This beautiful hidden waterfall is located about 3km north of Bagaces; head north on the Interamericana, turn left on the dirt road after the Río Piedras bridge, then follow the bumpy road (4WD required) for about 1km, and turn right at the guarded gate where you'll make a donation (US$2 will do the job) in exchange for your admission. Proceeds help fund the local primary school. Continue down the dirt road about 300m to the parking area, then scramble down the short, steep trail to reach this spectacular 12m-high, 15m-wide waterfall, which you'll be able to hear from the parking lot. The falls drops into a tranquil pond with a white sandy beach that's perfect for swimming and sunbathing. Go 'backstage' and relax on the rocks behind the waterfall curtain, or shower beneath the lukewarm waters. We did see two daredevils pick their way among the boulders on the mossy rock wall to the top. It's quite risky though. On weekends this is a popular Tico picnic spot, but on weekdays you'll often have the waterfall to yourself.

Apart from a portable toilet, there are no services here except for the occasional vendor selling fruit and cold coconut water in the parking area. Although the lot is guarded, don't leave valuables exposed in your car. If you don't have a car, any bus trawling this part of the Interamericana can drop you at the turnoff, but you'll have to hike from there to the falls.

Parque Nacional Palo Verde

The 184-sq-km **Parque Nacional Palo Verde** (☑2524-0628; www.ots.ac.cr; adult/child under 12yr US$10/1; ⊘8am-4pm) is a wetland sanctuary in Costa Rica's driest province. It lies on the northeastern bank of the mouth of Río Tempisque, and at the head of the Golfo de Nicoya. All of the major rivers in the region drain into this ancient intersection of two basins, which creates a mosaic of habitats, including mangrove swamps, marshes, grassy savannas and evergreen forests. A number of low limestone hills provide lookout points over the park, and the park's shallow, permanent lagoons are focal points for wildlife.

The park derives its name from the *palo verde* (green tree), which is a small shrub that's green year-round and abundant within the park. The park is also contiguous in the north with the 73-sq-km Refugio de Vida Silvestre Dr Rafael Lucas Rodríguez Caballero and the Reserva Biológica Lomas de Barbudal, which, along with Parque Nacional Barra Honda, make up part of the Area de Conservación Tempisque, a large conservation area containing some of Costa Rica's last remaining strands of dry tropical forest. A recent addition to this project was Refugio do Vida Silvestre Cipancí, which protects the corridors linking the various parks from being clear cut by local farmers.

Palo Verde has the greatest concentrations of waterfowl and shorebirds in Central America, and over 300 different bird species have been recorded in the park. Birdwatchers come to see the large flocks of heron (including the rare black-crowned night heron), stork (including the endangered jabirú), spoonbill, egret, ibis, grebe and duck; and forest birds, including scarlet macaw, great curassow, keel-billed toucan, and parrots are also common. Frequently sighted mammals include deer, coati, armadillo, monkey and peccary, as well as the largest population of jaguarundi in Costa Rica. There are also numerous reptiles in the wetlands including crocodiles that are reportedly up to 5m in length.

The dry season, from December to March, is the best time to visit as flocks of birds tend to congregate in the remaining lakes and marshes and the trees lose their leaves, thus allowing for clearer viewing. However, the entire basin swelters during the dry season, so bring adequate sun protection. There are also far fewer insects in the dry season, and mammals are occasionally seen around the watering holes. Take binoculars or a spotting scope if possible. During the wet months, large portions of the area are flooded, and access may be limited.

🏃 Activities & Tours

To fully appreciate the size and topography of the park, it's worth organizing a boat trip down the Río Tempisque, a wide brown brackish river contained on either side by mangroves. Arrangements can be made through the Organization of Tropical Studies (OTS) or the Hacienda Palo Verde Research Station. Travelers also recommend the guided bird-watching tours that can be arranged through the Hacienda. Tour operators in San José and La Fortuna run package tours to Palo Verde, but you'll save money by arranging everything yourself.

You can also explore the park's seven maintained trails on your own. La Venda (2.1km) is the longest and runs adjacent to the lagoon. The best vegetation is visible from El Querque (650m), and La Jacana is a short (200m) trail elevated above the lagoon that birders love. No matter which trail you choose, know that it gets fiercely hot in the dry season, so carry ample water, a sun hat and avoid hiking around midday.

🛏 Sleeping & Eating

Overnight visitors should make reservations and must also pay the US$10 entry fee.

Camping (per person US$5) is permitted near the Hacienda Palo Verde Research Station, where toilets and hot-water showers are available. Meals and box lunches (US$7 to US$9) are available at the OTS research station by advance arrangement.

Hacienda Palo Verde Research Station LODGE
(☑2524-0607; www.ots.ac.cr; r incl meals per person US$38; ℙ🛜) Run by the OTS, Hacienda Palo Verde Research Station conducts tropical research and teaches university graduate-level classes. Researchers and those taking OTS courses get preference for dormitories with shared bathrooms. A few basic two- and four-bed rooms with shared bathrooms are also available. The research station is on a well-signed road 8km from the park entrance.

ⓘ Information

Your best source of information on the park is the Hacienda Palo Verde Research Station (p189).

ⓘ Getting There & Away

The main road to the entrance, usually passable to ordinary cars year-round, begins from a signed turnoff from the Interamericana, opposite Bagaces. The 28km gravel road has tiny brown signs that usually direct you when the road forks, but if in doubt, take the fork that looks more used. Another 8km brings you to the limestone hill, Cerro Guayacán (and the Hacienda Palo Verde Research Station), from where there are great views; 2km further are the Palo Verde park headquarters and ranger station. You can drive through a swampy maze of roads to the Reserva Biológica Lomas de Barbudal without returning to the Interamericana, but it's easy to lose your way. Follow the power lines overhead, and you'll be fine.

Buses connecting Cañas and Liberia can drop you at the ACT office in Bagaces, opposite the turnoff to the park. If you call the ACT office in advance, rangers *may* be able to pick you up in Bagaces. If you're staying at the Hacienda Palo Verde Research Station, the staff can also arrange to pick you up in Bagaces.

Reserva Biológica Lomas de Barbudal

The 26-sq-km Lomas de Barbudal reserve forms a cohesive unit with Palo Verde and protects several species of endangered trees, such as mahogany and rosewood, as well as the common and quite spectacular corteza amarilla. This tree is what biologists call a 'big bang reproducer' – all the yellow cortezes in the forest burst into bloom on the same day, and for about four days the forest is an incredible mass of yellow-flowered trees. This usually occurs in March, about four days after an unseasonal rain shower.

Nearly 70% of the trees in the reserve are deciduous, and during the dry season they shed their leaves as if it were autumn in a temperate forest. This particular habitat is known as tropical dry forest, and occurs in climates that are warm year-round, and have a prolonged dry season that lasts several months. Since plants lose moisture through their leaves, the shedding of leaves allows the trees to conserve water during dry periods. The newly bare trees also open up the canopy layer, enabling sunlight to reach ground level and facilitate the growth of thick underbrush. (Dry forests were once common in many parts of the Pacific slope of Central America, but little remains. They also exist north and south of the equatorial rainforest belt, especially in southern Mexico and the Bolivian lowlands.)

Lomas de Barbudal is also known for its abundant and varied wasps, butterflies, moths and other insects. There are about 250 different species of bee in this fairly small reserve – representing about a quarter of the world's bee species. Bees here include the Africanized 'killer' bees – if you suffer from bee allergies, this is one area where you really don't want to forget your bee-sting kit.

There are more than 200 bird species, including the great curassow, a chickenlike bird that is hunted for food and is endangered, as well as other endangered species including the king vulture, scarlet macaw and jabirú stork. Lomas de Barbudal is also home to a variety of mammal species, including the scene-stealing white faced capuchin, as well as some enormous crocodiles – you might want to leave your swimsuit at home.

ⓘ Information

At the reserve entrance, there's a small **information center** (🕿2671-1029; admission by donation; ⊙7am-4pm), though the actual reserve is on the other side of the Río Cabuyo, behind the museum. The infrastructure of the park, if you can even call it that, is not overly geared to tourists, though there are three hiking trails that radiate from the information center and cover 1.1km *in total*. A small map is provided. It is not possible to overnight in the park and backcountry hiking is not permitted.

ⓘ Getting There & Away

The turnoff to Lomas de Barbudal from the Interamericana is near the small community of Pijije, 14km southeast of Liberia or 12km northwest of Bagaces. It's 7km to the entrance of the reserve. The road is unpaved, but open all year – some steep sections may require 4WD in the rainy season. Buses between Liberia and Cañas can drop you at the turnoff to the reserve.

Liberia

POP 63,000

The sunny, rural capital of Guanacaste has long served as a transportation hub connecting Costa Rica with Nicaragua, as well as being the standard-bearer of Costa Rica's *sabanero* culture. Even today, a large part of the greater Liberia area is involved in ranching operations, but tourism is fast becoming a significant contributor to the economy. With an expanding international airport, Liberia is a much safer and surprisingly chilled-out alternative Costa Rican gateway to San José, which means more travelers are spending a night or two in this small but sweet college town, knitted together by corrugated tin fencing, mango trees and magnolias. And, though most of the historic buildings in the town center are a little rough around the edges and in desperate need of a paint job, the 'white city' is a pleasant one, with a good range of accommodations and services for travelers on all budgets. The streets in downtown Liberia are surprisingly well signed, a rarity in Costa Rica. Still, it's largely a launch pad for exploring Rincon de la Valle National Park and the beaches of the Península de Nicoya.

◉ Sights

Near the entrance of town, a statue (Av 25 de Julio) of a steely-eyed *sabanero*, complete with an evocative poem by Rodolfo Salazar Solórzano, stands watch over Av 25 de Julio, the main street into town. The blocks around the intersection of Av Central and Calle Central contain several of Liberia's oldest houses, many dating back about 150 years.

Parque Central   PARK
The somewhat shady but not particularly picturesque Parque Central frames Iglesia Inmaculada Concepción de María. The park is also the seasonal hangout of the Nicaraguan grackle, a tone-deaf bird that enjoys eating parrot eggs and annoying passers-by with its grating calls.

Iglesia Inmaculada
Concepción de María   CHURCH
(Parque Central) If this *iglesia* (church) doesn't cut it for religious splendor, walk six blocks northeast of the park along Avenida Central where you'll find the oldest church in town, popularly called La Agonía (though some maps show it with a different name – see below).

FREE Museo de Guanacaste   HISTORIC BUILDING
(cnr Av 1 & Calle 2; ⊗8am-4pm Jan 2–Dec 23) It's not much of a museum but Liberia's old city jail is definitely interesting. Depressing dorms and cells surround a barren concrete courtyard. Occasional student concerts are held here, and there are plans for an actual museum to be staged here...at some point.

La Agonía   CHURCH
(Av Central) Six blocks northeast of the park you'll find the oldest church in town, popularly called La Agonía (although maps show it as La Iglesia de la Ermita de la Resurección). It's a gloriously decrepit mud-and-brick relic, locked and closed to the public, but the adjacent park has become the de-facto skate park – complete with poured concrete ramps and charming local skate punks. Strolling to La Agonía and the surrounding (somewhat seedy) blocks makes for an interesting walk.

Africa Mía   WILDLIFE RESERVE
(⌂2666-1111; www.africamia.net; adult/child US$18/12, guided van tour US$30/24; ⊗8am-6pm) About 9km south of Liberia is a private wildlife reserve with free-roaming elephants, zebras, giraffes, ostriches and other animals. Splurge for the deluxe African Safari Wildlife Tour (adult/child US$65/55) in an open-top Hummer with a stop at a waterfall.

🛏 Sleeping

Liberia is at its busiest during the dry season – reservations are strongly recommended over Christmas, Easter, Día de Guanacaste and on weekends. During the wet season, however, most of the midrange and top-end hotels give discounts.

TOP CHOICE Bed & Breakfast El Punto   HOTEL $$
(⌂2665-2986; www.elpuntohotel.com; cnr Interamericana & Av 4; d with/ without airport pick up $97/80; P🅿❄@🛜🐾) This converted elementary school is now a chic loft hotel, and would definitely feel more at home in trendy Miami than in humble Guanacaste. The saturated tropical colors of the lofts manage to be understated and minimalist. All rooms have beautifully tiled bathroom, kitchenette, hammocks, free wi-fi and colorful modern art. The common area features low outdoor sofas and even crayons for the kids, and the young bilingual owner, Mariana, is charm personified. She hosts art openings in her adjacent gallery.

Posada de la Calle Real   HOTEL $$
(⌂2666-0626; cnr Calle Real & Av 4; r with bathroom US$60, without bath US$20-55; ⊗restaurant 11am-11pm; P🅿❄🛜🐾) Set in a lovingly restored 1938 *posada* this property has the most old-world class in Liberia. The two biggest and best rooms in the main house share a bath but they have wood floors, soaring wood-paneled ceilings, cable tv, and queen beds as well as two twins. You could sleep

Liberia

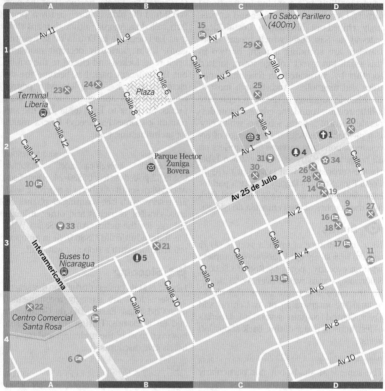

the whole family in here for just $55. The room in the main house with private bathroom is less lovely and costs a bit more. Smaller cheaper digs are also quite quaint, but they share a bathroom with restaurant customers, so it's worth spending a bit more. The attached restaurant serves pizzas and pastas (US$5 to US$16) on a wood patio dining area around a gorgeous backyard pool.

Hotel La Siesta   HOTEL $$
(☏2666-0606; lasiestaliberia@hotmail.com; Calle 4 btwn Avs 4 & 6; s/d incl breakfast US$40/50; ☺7am-6pm; P✳@☎☀) It doesn't look like much from the street, but this cute, fairly modern hotel has a series of spotless tiled rooms, with wi-fi, hot water and cable TV, set around an inviting pool. The grounds are lovingly looked after and it comes with a continental breakfast. Rooms upstairs are slightly larger. There's also an attached restaurant (meals US$5 to US$8), which is regarded by locals as having the best *casado* in town.

Hotel Los Angeles   MOTEL $
(☏2665-5900; Ave 7 btwn Calle 2 & 4; s/d US$24/40; P✳@☎) Bright and newly renovated, this boutique motel has tiled floors, wood-paneled ceilings, cable tv, wi-fi, and generally nicely appointed, spotless rooms. Management is friendly and warm, making it terrific overall value.

Hilton Garden Inn
Liberia Airport   HOTEL $$$
(☏2690-8888; www.hiltongardeninn.hilton.com; d US$149-219; P⊖✳@☎☀) Liberia's newest hotel looks and feels like it was engineered in the soulless business-hotel laboratory, and plopped from the sky in the middle of a vast, parched, would-be business-park savannah. But once you are through the gates and on the property, even skeptics will like its pleasantries, such as the pool, gym and tennis courts, in-room fridge, microwave, flat-screen TV, and free internet and wi-fi access. Most importantly, it's almost directly across

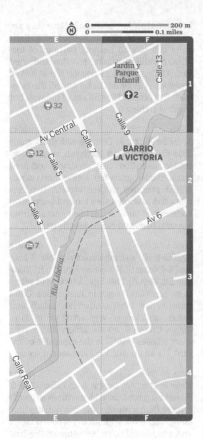

from the airport and there's a free shuttle. Perfect if you have an early-morning flight.

Hotel Casa Real HOTEL **$**

(☎2666-3876; Calle Central btwn Av 2 & 4; r $20; P🐾) The rooms are cramped but clean and well appointed with antiques and quilts. For the price this is one of the best downtown options.

Hotel Boyeros HOTEL **$$**

(☎2666-2529; www.hotelboyeros.com; cnr Interamericana & Av 2; d US$70; P🐾❄@🛜🏊🍴) The largest hotel in Liberia feels like a cross between a dude ranch and the Holiday Inn. Once proud rooms, arced around the pool on two floors, all have comfortable furnishings, air-con and cable TV, but they are aging quite conspicuously. There's also a 24-hour restaurant (mains US$9 to US$21), free wifi, pool with waterslide, kiddie pool and a shaded sitting area. Look for the sculpture of the *boyero* (oxcart driver) out front.

Hostal Ciudad Blanca HOTEL **$**

(☎2666-3962; Av 4 btwn Calles 1 & 3; s/d with fan US$30/40, with air-con US$35/45; P❄) One of Liberia's most attractive hotels is in a recently refurbished historic colonial mansion. Tree-shaded rooms have air-con, fan, cable TV, nice furnishings and private hot-water bathroom, although some smell of cigarettes. The charming little restaurant-bar across the street is perfect for a nightcap.

Hotel La Guaria
HOTEL $

(☏26660-0000; Av Central btwn Calle 3 & 5; r US$30; ᴾ✽🙖) This bright, reasonably up-to-date courtyard hotel offers really good value. It has clean rooms with air-con and wi-fi. There is a casino, so beware the sleaze factor, but it is a solid choice otherwise.

Hotel La Casona
HOTEL $

(☏2666-2971; casona@racsa.co.cr; cnr Calle Real & Av 6; r from US$13; ᴾ✽🙖) Quite basic but decent digs in a converted house in the center of town. Management is *tranquilo* and all rooms have cable tv and wi-fi.

Hotel Guanacaste
HOTEL $

(☏2666-0085; www.higuanacaste.com; cnr Calle 14 & Av 5; dm US$9, r US$12-20; ᴾ🙖) Affiliated with Hostels International, but nothing particularly special, digs are dingy but cheap with wi-fi and a solid in-house bus booking service to San José and Managua.

Hotel Liberia
HOTEL $

(☏2666-0161; www.hotelliberia.com; Calle Central btwn Avs Central & 2; dm US$10, r with/without bathroom US$12/20; ᴾ) Rooms here are ragged and worn, despite the nice entry way. More expensive rooms have chipped tiled floors, soaring ceilings, and are do-able, but steer clear of the gritty cheapies. Rooms are set around a courtyard and management is lovely.

La Posada del Tope
HOTEL $

(☏2666-3876; www.posadadeltope.com; Calle Real btwn Avs 2 & 4; r without bathroom per person US$10-18; ᴾ😴@🙖) A grungy little joint that is nothing if it isn't dingy, cheap and still somehow inviting. Yes, rooms are cramped, and could be cleaner, but somehow you'll still feel drawn to this converted mid-19th-century house. Gotta be that attractive wood floored lobby.

🍴 Eating

ᴛᴏᴾ CHOICE Copa de Oro
RESTAURANT $$

(☏2666-0532; cnr Calle Central & Av 2; mains US$5-16; ⊙11am-10pm Wed-Mon; 🙖🍴) Our favorite family restaurant is popular with locals and gringos alike. There's an extensive food and drink menu. The dish we loved best is the rice and seafood house specialty, *arroz copa de oro*, but the *casados* are excellent and there's a nice *ceviche* menu too.

El Pochote
RESTAURANT $$

(☏2665-7020; Barrio La Carreta, 150mts Sur de Hogar; dishes US$6-18; 🙖) *Chicharrónes* are the specialty of this house, and they are far more than just pork skin. Here they are beautiful, tender chunks of fried pork. Each order comes with heaping portions of tortillas, picadillos, frijoles, molidos and fried yuca. Oh, and the pork portion size is just as generous. A medium basket and all the sides feeds five people. It's a bit out of the way, but worth searching for.

Jauja
RESTAURANT $$

(☏2665-2061; cnr Av Central & 10th street; mains US$8-18; ⊙11am-1am; 🙖) A stylish, new indoor-outdoor bar and cafe serving wood-fired pizza, tender grass-fed steaks and wood-grilled, pounded chicken breasts. It serves pasta and seafood dishes too and burgers on home-baked buns. A solid new venture from a young, born-and-raised Liberia chef.

Café Liberia
ORGANIC $

(☏2665-1660; www.cafeliberia.com; Calle 8 btwn Avs 2 & 4; dishes US$1-7; ⊙8am-7pm Mon-Fri, 10am-6pm Sat; @🙖🍴) This hip historic spot offers tasty breakfasts, organic juices, rich Costa Rican coffee, fresh sandwiches, salads and crepes, and lots of vegetarian items. Plus, there's free wi-fi, an art gallery and a yoga space (classes US$15) in the expansive courtyard. It's an upscale local and tourist scene.

Rancho Dulce
SODA $

(Calle 0 btwn Avs Central & 2; mains US$2-6; ⊙breakfast, lunch & dinner) Sometimes a *casado* is more than a *casado*, and this outstanding, family-run *soda*, with groovy wooden tables and good *batidos*, serves some of the best amid shady *palapa* ambience.

Pan y Miel
BAKERY $

(☏2666-0718; Calle 2 btwn Avs 3 & 5; mains US$2-6; ⊙6am-6pm) The best breakfast in town can be had at this branch of the local bakery, which serves its excellent bread as sandwiches and French toast, as well as offering a buffet line with *casado* fixings, pastries and fresh fruit. There's a bakery-only branch, with tasty, flaky pineapple turnovers a block north of Parque Central.

Pizza Pronto
ITALIAN $$

(☏2666-2098; cnr Av 4 & Calle 1; mains US$8-17; ⊙11am-11pm) This very cute, old-world pizzeria, where the wood is stacked next to the smoking courtyard oven, keeps it romantic and simple – just pizza, pasta and salads... although we'll admit that the taco pizza does sound ambitious. Don't worry, you can choose from a long list of toppings and create your own.

Sabor Parillero — RESTAURANT $$

(☎2665-5983; Calle 0; mains US$5-18; ☺5pm-11pm Mon-Fri, 11am-11pm Sat & Sun) A hole-in-the-wall barbecue joint across from the cemetery with a spectacularly tender rib eye and cheap grilled meat *casados*. All the meat is grass-fed, and sourced from *fincas* within 20km. It's a bit out of the way, about 800m north of Parque Central, but you'll be glad to take the long walk home.

Restaurante El Pilon — RESTAURANT $

(Cnr Avs 5 & 7; ☎2665-5869; Calle 0, btwn Av 5 & Av 7; casados US$6; ☺7am-3pm) A great little find for fans of *casados*. This local diner serves seven *casados* daily featuring fresh *pescado*, *pollo*, steak, lamb and more. Relax around wooden tables in the cool, dark tiled dining room.

El Zaguán — RESTAURANT $$

(☎2666-2456; cnr Ave Central & Calle 1; mains US$7-14; ☺6am-10pm; ☏⬛) Located in a beautiful colonial building, this family-friendly restaurant has an extensive international menu specializing in meat including New York strip, filet mignon and burgers. You'll also find fish, pasta and rice dishes. The outdoor balcony is a great people-watching spot, which is a good thing because service is *muy despacio*.

Paso Real — SEAFOOD $$$

(☎2666-3455; Av Central btwn Calles Central & 2; mains US$9-20; ☺10am-10pm) An old standby, this 2nd floor fish house doesn't dole out ambience as much as it delivers tasty seafood dishes. The shrimp platters are particularly delectable, but all is fresh and flavorful. Portions are big enough to share.

Before you board that long bus ride, pick up cheap eats and fresh fruit and veggies at the traditional covered market (Ave 7 btwn Calles 8 & 10; ☺6am-7pm Mon-Sat, 6am-noon Sun) conveniently located next to Terminal Liberia. Or grab groceries at the SuperCompro (☎2758-7351; Av Central btwn Calles 2 & 4; ☺8am-8pm Mon-Fri, 8am-6pm Sat & Sun) or the humongous Maxi Bodega (Av 7 btwn Calles 8 & 10; ☺8am-10pm Mon-Sat, 8am-9pm Sun). Stop by Jumbo Supermercado (Plaza Santa Rosa) to load up on a good selection of international groceries including tahini, Argentinean wine and curry paste, before heading to the beach. They also have ample wine and liquor, and a savory lunch counter, forever feeding the ravenous herd on the cheap (*casados* US$4).

🍷 Drinking & Entertainment

Live music and dance performances are often held at the Parque Central gazebo and at the nearby La Gobernación (cnr Av Central & Calle Central), an old municipal building. Your best chance of seeing Punto Guanacasteco is to be in town for a *tope*.

Ciro's — BAR

(Calle 2 btwn Av 0 & 1; ☺11am-11pm) The newest and liveliest bar in Liberia belongs to this branch of the San José original. It's not much, just a handful of tables, a simple bar and doors that roll open onto the sidewalk. But the sound system rocks and the locals bring the party.

Bar Kasa — BAR

(Cnr Calle 0 & Av 6; ☺7pm-1am) Liberia is something of a college town, and this new hot spot is where the hipsters like to bend their collective elbow, laugh, conspire, debate and flirt, most evenings.

Liberia Supremacy — BAR

(Av 1 btwn Calles 5 & 7; ☺4pm-late Tue-Sun) A bit of Jamaica bleeds over into Liberia at this popular reggae bar decorated with posters of Bob Marley and Che. There's a friendly vibe, cheap beer, an extensive Mexican *bocas* (appetizers) menu and the most uncomfortable bar stools ever crafted.

Morales House — BAR

(☎2665-2490; cnr Av 1 & Calle 14; bocas US$3-7; ☺3pm-2am) A real Guanacaste *sabanero* hangout, this barnlike bar with cowboy motif has bulls' heads on the walls, blaring *ranchera* music and American sports on TV.

ℹ Information

Internet Access

Cyberm@nia (☎2666-7240; Av 1 btwn Calles 2 & Central; long-distance calls per minute US$0.30 ; ☺8am-10pm) With the friendliest staff ever, this spot is good for internet and cheap long-distance calls to most parts of the world. Though it is in need of some serious aromatherapy.

Planet Internet (☎2665-3737; Calle 0 btwn Avs Central & 2; per hr US$1; ☺9am-9pm) Has speedy machines in a spacious, frigidly air-conditioned room; also offers internet calls.

Medical Services

Hospital Dr Enrique Baltodano Briceño (☎2666-0011, emergencies 2666-0318) Behind the stadium on the northeastern outskirts of town.

Money

Most hotels will accept US dollars and may be able to change small amounts. Liberia probably has more banks per square meter than any other town in Costa Rica.

BAC San José (☑2666-2020; Centro Comercial Santa Rosa; ☺9am-6pm Mon-Fri, 9am-1pm Sat) Changes travelers checks; try this 24hr ATM if others won't accept your card.

Banco de Costa Rica (☑2666-2582; cnr Calle 0 & Av 1) 24hr ATM.

Banco Nacional (☑2666-0191; Av 25 de Julio btwn Calles 6 & 8; ☺8am-3:45pm Mon-Fri, 9am-1pm Sat) 24hr ATM.

Banco Popular (cnr Calle 12 & Av 25 de Julio) 24hr ATM.

Citibank (cnr Interamericana & Av 25 de Julio; ☺9am-6pm Mon-Fri, 9am-12:30pm Sat) 24hr ATM and changes money.

HSBC (Cnr Av 2 & Interamericana; ☺9m-6pm Mon-Fri, 9am-12:30pm Sat) 24hr ATM.

❶ Getting There & Away

Air

Since 1993 Aeropuerto Internacional Daniel Oduber Quirós (LIR), 12km west of Liberia, has served as the country's second international airport, providing easy access to beautiful beaches without the hassle of dealing with the lines and bustle of San José. In January, 2012, the sleek, mod new US$35 million terminal was unveiled, which should mean more flights serving a wider range of destinations.

There are no car-rental desks at the airport; make reservations in advance, and your company will meet you at the airport with a car. You will find a money-exchange, cafe, gift shops and a fantastic, inexpensive duty-free shop (but it's tucked away and hard to find – keep looking). Taxis to Liberia cost US$20. Downtown-based **Liberia Travel** (☑2666-4383; www.liberia travelcr.com; cnr Av 25 de Julio & Calle 6; ☺8am-6pm Mon-Fri, 8am-noon Sat) can help book flights worldwide.

At research time all airlines serving Liberia, including American Airlines, Continental, Delta, United and US Airways flew first to the USA – where international connections abound, but that should change soon.

NatureAir (☑International Airport Daniel Oduber Quiros 2668-1106, reservations 2299-6000; www.natureair.com) To/from San José, Fortuna, Tambor, Nosara and Tamarindo.

Sansa (☑International Airport Daniel Oduber Quiros 2668-1017, reservations 2290-4100; www.flysansa.com) To/from San José.

Bus

Buses arrive and depart from **Terminal Liberia** (Av 7 btwn Calles 12 & 14) and **Terminal Pulmi-**

tan (Av 5 btwn Calles 10 & 12). Routes, fares, journey times and departures are as follows:

Cañas US$2; 1½ hours; departs Terminal Liberia 5:30am, 6:30am, 7:30am, noon, 1:30pm, 4:30pm, 5:30pm, 6:45pm and 7:45pm. It's quicker to jump off the San José–bound bus in Cañas.

Guayabo de Bagaces US$3; one hour; departs Terminal Liberia 6am, 9am, 11am and 2pm.

La Cruz/Peñas Blancas US$2.50; 1½ to two hours; departs Pulmitan every hour from 5am to 6pm.

Managua, Nicaragua US$26; five hours; departs Pulmitan 7am, 8am and noon (buy tickets one day in advance). You can also flag down Nicaragua-bound buses on the Interamericana at McDonald's.

Nicoya, via Filadelfia & Santa Cruz US$2.25; 1½ hours; departs Terminal Liberia every 30 minutes from 3:30am to 9pm.

Potrero Bay, Playa Flamingo, Playa Brasilito US$3; 1½ hours; departs Terminal Liberia almost hourly from 3:30am to 9pm.

Playa del Coco US$1; one hour; departs Pulmitan every hour from 5am to 11am, then 12:30pm, 2:30pm and 6:30pm.

Playa Hermosa, Playa Panamá US$1.60; 1¼ hours; departs Terminal Liberia 4:30am, 4:40am, 4:50am, 7:30am, 11:30am, 1pm, 3:30pm and 5:30pm.

Playa Tamarindo US$2.75; 1½ to two hours; departs Terminal Liberia hourly between 3:50am and 6pm. Some buses take a longer route via Playa Flamingo.

Puntarenas US$3; three hours; eight buses from 5am to 3:30pm. It's quicker to jump off the San José–bound bus in Puntarenas.

San José US$6; four hours; 11 departures from Pulmitan from 4am to 8pm.

Car

Liberia lies on the Interamericana, 234km north of San José and 77km south of the Nicaraguan border post of Peñas Blancas. Highway 21, the main artery of the Península de Nicoya, begins in Liberia and heads southwest. A dirt road, passable to all cars in dry season (4WD is preferable), leads 25km from Barrio la Victoria to the Santa María entrance of Parque Nacional Rincón de la Vieja; the gravel road to the Las Pailas entrance begins from the Interamericana, 5km north of Liberia (passable to regular cars, but 4WD is recommended).

There are many rental-car agencies in Liberia (none of which have desks at the airport), rates can vary and you'll get steep discounts for rentals of a month or more. Most companies can arrange pickup in Liberia and drop-off in San José, though they'll charge you extra, and are based on Hwy 21 on either side of the airport.

Some companies will drop off your car in town upon request.

Adobe (☏2667-0608, in USA 866-767-8651; www.adobecar.com) One of the cheapest companies in Costa Rica.

Avis (☏2668-1196; www.avis.co.cr)

Budget (☏2436-2000, 2668-1024; www.budget.com)

Europcar (☏2667-0219; www.europcar.co.cr)

Hola (☏2667-4040; www.hola.net)

Mapache (☏2586-6363; www.mapache.com) Just 1km east of the airport.

Toyota Rent a Car (☏2258-5797, 2668-1212; www.toyotarent.com) Just 800m north of the airport.

VIP Car Rental (☏8941-1697, 8941-1691; www.vipcarrentaltours.com) Expect discount prices on well-maintained vehicles. It's not a kinder, gentler option, just the best value, and they'll meet you at your Liberia area hotel for drop-offs and pick-ups, although you may have to call and remind them.

Parque Nacional Rincón de la Vieja

Given its proximity to Liberia, this 141-sq-km national park feels refreshingly uncrowded and remote. Named after the active Volcán Rincón de la Vieja (1895m), the steamy main attraction, the park also covers several other peaks in the same volcanic range, including the highest, Volcán Santa María (1916m). The park exhales geothermal energy, which you can see in its multihued fumaroles, hot springs, bubbling and blooping ashy gray *pailas* (mud pots), and a young and feisty *volcancito* (small volcano). All of these can be visited on foot and horseback on well-maintained, but sometimes steep, trails.

The park was created in 1973 to protect a vital watershed that feeds 32 rivers and streams. Its relatively remote location means that wildlife, rare elsewhere, is out in force here, with the major volcanic crater a rather dramatic backdrop to the scene. Volcanic activity has occurred many times since the late 1960s, with the most recent eruption of steam and ash in 1997. At the moment, however, the volcano is gently active and does not present any danger – ask locally for the latest, as volcanoes do act up.

Elevations in the park range from less than 600m to 1916m, so visitors pass through a variety of habitats as they ascend the volcanoes, though the majority of the trees in the park are typical of those found in

dry tropical forests throughout Guanacaste. One interesting tree to look out for is the strangler fig, a parasitic species that covers the host tree with its own trunk and proceeds to strangle it by competing for water, light and nutrients. The host tree eventually dies and rots away, while the strangler fig survives as a hollow, tubular lattice. The park is also home to the country's highest density of Costa Rica's national flower, the increasingly rare purple orchid (Cattleya skinneri), locally known as *guaria morada*.

Most visitors to the park are here for the hot springs, where you can soak to the sound of howler monkeys overhead. Many of the springs are reported to have therapeutic properties, which is always a good thing if you've been hitting the *guaro cacique* a little too hard. Several lodges, just outside the park, provide access and arrange tours. You can also book transportation and tours from Liberia.

◎ Sights & Activities

Wildlife-Watching

The wildlife of the park is extremely varied. Almost 300 bird species have been recorded here, including curassow, quetzal, bellbird, parrot, toucan, hummingbird, owl, woodpecker, tanager, motmot, dove and eagle.

Insects range from beautiful butterflies to annoying ticks. Be especially prepared for ticks in grassy areas – long trousers tucked into boots and long-sleeved shirts offer some protection. A particularly interesting insect is a highland cicada that burrows into the ground and croaks like a frog, to the bewilderment of naturalists.

Mammals are equally varied; deer, armadillo, peccary, skunk, squirrel, coati and three species of monkey make frequent appearances. Tapir tracks are often found around the lagoons near the summit. Several wild cat species have been recorded here, including jaguar, puma, ocelot and margay, but you'll need patience and good fortune to observe one.

Hiking

A circular trail east of Las Pailas (about 3km in total) takes you past the boiling mud pools (Las Pailas), sulfurous fumaroles and a *volcancito*. About 350m west of the ranger station is the well-signed trail to Pozo Azul. Although the wooden stairs are decrepit and being reclaimed by jungle you can pick your way (carefully) alongside it to a marvelous river view and the stunning aquamarine swimming hole. Further away along the same trail are several waterfalls – the largest, Catarata La Cangreja, 5.1km west, is a classic, dropping 50m straight from a cliff into a small lagoon where you can swim. Dissolved copper salts give the falls a deep blue color. This trail winds through forest, past truly massive strangler figs, then on to open savannah spiked with yucca on the volcano's flanks, where you can enjoy views as far as the Palo Verde wetlands and the Pacific beyond. The slightly smaller Cataratas Escondidas (Hidden Waterfalls) are 4.3km west on a different trail and a bit higher on the slope.

The longest and most adventurous hike in the area is the 16km round-trip trek to the summit of Rincón de la Vieja and nearby Laguna de Jilgueros, which is reportedly where you may see tapirs – or more likely their footprints, if you are observant. The majority of this hike follows a ridge trail, and if it is windy and/or cloudy rangers will close it, as the trail is dotted with sulfurous hot springs and geysers, and hikers have been severely burned (and occasionally boiled) in the past. Even if it is open (which is rare) – come prepared for the weather.

From the Santa María ranger station, a trail leads 2.8km west through the 'enchanted forest' and past a waterfall to sulfurous hot springs with supposedly therapeutic properties. Don't soak in them for more than about half an hour (some people suggest much less) without taking a dip in the nearby cold springs, 2km away, to cool off. There's also a lovely 1.1km trail to the Catarata Bosque Encatnado, Santa María's best waterfall. If you cobble all the Santa María trails together you'll have a gorgeous 12km day hike.

Hot Springs & Spas

Hot Springs Rio Negro　　　　HOT SPRING
(www.guachipelin.com; per person US$10, massage per hr US$75; ⊙9am-5pm) Set in the dry forest along the Río Negro and owned and operated by Hacienda Guachipelín, this is our favorite commercial hot spring in northwestern Costa Rica. The six natural, stone-crafted hot pools are accessible by a lovely wooded trail, and set quite magically in the forest along the river. Those closest to the hanging bridge, on either side of the river, are the hottest, and top out at 40°C. It has a small snack bar and massages are available, but there's no electricity and no concrete. What you'll feel here is wind, water and heat. Admission comes with a short tour through the woods describing indigenous medicinal flora. To get here make the turn, 1km from the Las Pailas Ranger Station, toward Rincón de la Vieja Mountain Lodge and the Santa María sector. The hot springs will be on your right.

Simbiosis Spa　　　　SPA
(☑2666-8075; www.simbiosis-spa.com; admission US$15, massages & spa treatments US$30-75; ⊙9am-5:30pm) Under renovation when we visited and affiliated with Hacienda Guachipelín, this long-running spa reopened to the public in February, 2012. Expect volcanic mud baths, sauna, cold pool, showers and lounge chairs, all in a natural outdoor setting. You can also arrange massages and spa treatments on the spot, though it's recommended you reserve ahead.

Tours

All lodges can arrange a number of tours, including horseback riding (US$25 to US$35), mountain biking (US$10 to US$30), guided waterfall and hot-spring hikes (US$15 to US$25), rappelling (US$20 to US$50), rafting and tubing on the lesser-known Río Colorado (US$45 to US$60), hanging bridges (US$15 to US$20) and, everyone's favorite cash-burner, canopy tours (US$50). Rates vary depending on the season, and there are a number of package deals available. If you're staying in Liberia, it's possible to organize these activities in advance either through your hotel, or by contacting the lodges directly.

Hacienda Guachipelín　　　　GUIDED TOUR
(☑2666-8075; www.guachipelin.com) The area's most commercial lodge, it has a huge stable and offers horseback tours that skirt two different waterfalls (per person US$25 to US$35). There's also a canopy tour (adult/child 12 and under US$50/30) and Day Pass packages are on offer that include a horseback tour, a canopy flight, river tubing and a dip in the Río Negro hot springs (adult/child 12 and under US$85/75). You don't have to sleep here to play here.

Sleeping & Eating
LAS PAILAS SECTOR
Many hotels are a long way from any eateries, so you're stuck with paying for (often pricey) meals at your hotel restaurant. On the road to the park is an eclectic collection of lovely lodges that are worth considering if you've got your own wheels. Lodges are listed in order of proximity to the park gates.

HOTTEST SPOTS FOR THERMAL POOLS & MUD POTS

Costa Rica's volcano-powered thermal pools and mud pots provide plenty of good, clean fun for beauty queens and would-be mud wrestlers alike.

On the slopes of Volcán Rincón de la Vieja, Hot Springs Rio Negro (p198) has several pools in a transporting jungle setting.

While some hot spots around Arenal charge outrageous fees to soak in sparkly surrounds, Eco Thermales Hot Springs (p135) maintains its sense of elegance by limiting guest numbers.

The pinnacle of luxurious dirt exists in the remote heights of Rincón de la Vieja at Borinquen Mountain Resort & Spa (p200), where, if mineral mud is not your thing, you can opt instead for a wine or chocolate skin treatment.

Tico-run and family-friendly, Recreo Verde (p465) has several thermal pools, campsites, cabins, a large steaming warm pool and a seething jungle setting.

Rincón de la Vieja Mountain Lodge
LODGE $$
(☑8708-0238; www.hotelricondelavieja.com; standard s/d incl breakfast US$45/65, bungalows s/d US$65/75; P@☀) Closest to the Las Pailas entrance, this rustic hacienda is on 400 hectares of protected land in breezy horse country and has 34 spacious standard rooms, some with wildly painted walls or exposed-beam roofs, and even larger cottages with balconies. There's a small pond on the property and they can arrange horse and canopy tours nearby, as well. Staff here are utterly charming and it's just 3km from the park entrance.

Hacienda Guachipelín
HOTEL $$$
(☑2666-8075; www.guachipelin.com; s/d incl breakfast US$96/102 ; P❄@☀) On the road to Las Pailas, Hacienda Guachipelín is an appealing, 19th-century working cattle ranch on 12 sq km of primary and secondary forest, and has over 100 spacious, if simple, rooms and suites with private hot-water bathroom and porch. There is a garden-fringed pool, and guests are received at check-in with a welcome drink. The downside is that this place feels like a factory farm, catering largely to package-tour clientele who descend for organized horse tours, in-house canopy tours and guided hikes in the national park.

Rancho Curubandé Lodge
LODGE $$
(☑2665-0375; www.ranchocurubande.com; s/d incl breakfast US$52/64; P❄☀) Quite good value rooms, spotless and simple with beamed ceilings and wide common front porch lit by tasteful wrought iron chandeliers. They're set on a peaceful *finca* with horses for hire.

Canyon de la Vieja Adventure Lodge
LODGE $$
(☑2665-5928; www.thecanyonlodge.com; r US$97; P❄❄☀) Riverside rooms surround a *palapa* bar and pool, and the attractive accommodations are a comfortable place to crash after a day of adventure – including horse tours, tubing, rafting and canopy tours. There's a full-service spa on the property and a lovely 3km trail along the riverside.

El Sol Verde
CAMPGROUND $$
(☑2665-5357; www.elsolverde.com; campsites US$7, tent houses US$25, r US$48-69; P) The lovely Dutch couple here in Curubandé village offer three sweet Spanish-tiled, wood-walled rooms. Or consider bedding down in the camping area where there's a few wooden, tin-roof tent houses with bed and electricity, a shared outdoor kitchen and plenty of space to pitch your own tent.

Casa Rural Aroma de Campo
HOTEL $$
(☑2294-7100; www.aromadecampo.com; s/d incl breakfast US$49/75; P☀) A secluded sweet spot, this serene, epiphyte-hung, hammock-strung oasis has six elegantly designed rooms with polished hardwood floors, colorful wall art, mosquito nets and classy rural sensibility. Oh, and there's a pet parrot, too.

SANTA MARIA SECTOR & CANAS DULCES AREAS
North of the road to Las Pailas is another, nearly roadless flank of the park, accessible from the road that leads through the painfully cute *pueblo*, Canas Dulces (which has some *cabina* properties). This is where dramatic shark fin mountains draped in forest jut from pasture lands, and spectacular waterfalls thunder into valleys and bowls steaming with hot springs and scalding volcanic mud.

NORTHWESTERN COSTA RICA PARQUE NACIONAL RINCÓN DE LA VIEJA

Rinconcito Lodge
LODGE $$

(☎2200-0074; www.rinconcitolodge.com; standard s/d US$25/45, superior incl breakfast s/d US$38/60; P) Just 3km from the Santa María sector of the park, this recommended budget option has attractive, rustic cabins with private hot-water showers, and is surrounded by some of the prettiest pastoral scenery imaginable. Cheaper rooms are just as clean and fresh as the larger variety, but they're tiny. Since it primarily caters to budget travelers, it also offers inexpensive local tours throughout the national park and onto Miravalles, and shuttles travelers to and from Liberia (one way US$30). Best of all, it has its own 3km single-track trail direct to the Santa María sector of the national park, and a fabulous little kitchen. Standards are high all around.

Buena Vista Lodge
LODGE $$

(☎2690-1414; www.buenavistalodgecr.com; d incl breakfast US$88-99; P@☀♠) On the way to Borinquen, this lodge caters to package tourists big time, and for the price, rooms could be fancier and service a bit sweeter. Still, the hilltop location is magnificent and the views? *Muy buena*! Plus, it has spring-fed pools, a 400m-high mountain waterslide, canopy trail, hanging bridges, four restaurants, a herpetarium, great views, live entertainment and loads more activities to keep kids (and grown-ups) busy.

Borinquen Mountain Resort & Spa
RESORT $$$

(☎2690-1900; www.borinquenresort.com; d incl breakfast US$185-365; ⊘Anáhuac Spa 10am-6pm) If you want to splurge, wallow here. The most luxurious resort in the area features plush, fully air-conditioned bungalows with private deck, minibar and satellite TV. The onsite hot springs, mud baths and natural saunas are beautifully laid out and surrounded by greenery, but a treatment (US$55 to US$200) at the unbelievably modern, elegant Anáhuac Spa suspended over the river and steaming jungle, is the icing on this decadent mud pie.

ⓘ Information

Each of the two main entrances to the park has its own ranger station, where you sign in and get free maps. Most visitors enter through **Las Pailas ranger station** (☎2661-8139; www.acguanacaste.ac.cr; adult/child 6-12/child 5 yr and under US$10/1/ free; ⊘7am-5pm Tue-Sun, no entry after 3pm) on the western flank. Trails to the summit and the most interesting volcanic features begin here. The **Santa María ranger station** (☎2661-8139; adult/child 6-12 yr/child 5 yr and under US$10/1/free; ⊘7am-5pm daily, no entry past 3pm) to the east, is in the Hacienda Santa María, a 19th-century *rancho* with a small public exhibit that was reputedly once owned by US President Lyndon Johnson. It's closest to the sulfurous hot springs and also has an observation tower and a nearby waterfall.

ⓘ Getting There & Away

The Las Pailas sector is accessible via a good, 20km gravel road that begins at a signed turnoff from the Interamericana 5km north of Liberia; a private road is needed to reach the park and costs US$1.50 per person. The Santa María ranger station, to the east, is accessible via a rougher road beginning at Barrio La Victoria in Liberia. Both roads are passable to regular cars throughout the dry season, but a 4WD is required during the rainy season and is highly recommended at all other times (or it will take you twice as long). There's no public transportation, but any of the lodges can arrange transport from Liberia for around US$20 to US$30 per person each way (two or three people minimum). Alternately, you can hire a 4WD taxi from Liberia for about US$35 to Las Pailas, or US$65 to Santa María, each way.

To travel between the two sectors you needn't double back to Liberia. About 1km from the Las Pailas park entrance is the turn toward Rincón de la Vieja lodge, Río Negro hot springs, the Santa Maria Sector, and eventually San Jorge, Guayabo and Bagaces.

The road to Canas Dulces and beyond, toward Buena Vista Lodge and Borinquen Mountain Resort & Spa, is well-signed about 11.5km north of Liberia, where it intersects with the Interamericana.

Area de Conservacion Guanacaste

Among the oldest (established in 1971) and largest protected areas in Costa Rica, this sprawling 386-sq-km national refuge on the Península Santa Elena protects the largest remaining stand of tropical dry forest in Central America, some of the most important nesting sites of several species of sea turtle, and deep historical gravitas. Almost all of the worthy diversions can be found in a vast area known as the Santa Rosa Sector. Famous among Ticos as a national stronghold, Costa Rica has been invaded three times, and the enemy has always surrendered in Santa Rosa.

The best known of these events was the Battle of Santa Rosa, which took place on March 20, 1856, when the soon-to-be-self-declared president of Nicaragua, an uppity American named William Walker, invaded Costa Rica. Walker was the head of a group of foreign pirates and adventurers known as the 'Filibusters' that had already seized Baja and southwest Nicaragua, and were attempting to gain control over all of Central America. In a brilliant display of military prowess, Costa Rican President Juan Rafael Mora Porras guessed Walker's intentions, and managed to assemble a ragtag group of fighters that proceeded to surround Walker's army in the main building of the old Hacienda Santa Rosa, known as La Casona. The battle was over in just 14 minutes, and Walker was forever driven from Costa Rican soil.

Santa Rosa was again the site of battles between Costa Rican troops and invading forces from Nicaragua in both 1919 and 1955. The first was a somewhat honorable attempt to overthrow the Costa Rican dictator General Federico Tinoco, while the second was a failed coup d'état led by Nicaraguan dictator Anastasio Somoza. Today, you can still see Somoza's abandoned tank, which lies in a ditch beside the road just beyond the entrance to the park. However, the military history surrounding the park didn't end with Somoza, as Santa Rosa was later used as a staging point for the US military during the Sandinistas–Contra war.

Although the park was established mainly due to historical and patriotic reasons, in a surprising coincidence Santa Rosa has also become extremely important to biologists. Upon seeing its primordial acacia thorn trees and tall jaragua grass, first impressions of the park are likely to have you believe you've suddenly landed in the African savanna, though closer inspection reveals more American species of plants, including cacti and bromeliads. Santa Rosa is also home to Playa Nancite, which is famous for its *arribadas* (mass nesting) of olive ridley sea turtles that can number up to 8000 at a time!

However, the majority of travelers are here for one reason – the chance to surf the near-perfect beach break at Playa Naranjo, which is created by the legendary offshore monolith known as Witch's Rock (also known locally as Roca Bruja). The park is home to another break of arguably equal fame, namely Ollie's Point, which was immortalized in the film *Endless Summer II*, and is named after US Marine Lieutenant Colonel Oliver North. North is most famous for illegally selling weapons to Iran during the Reagan era, and using the profits to fund the Contras in Nicaragua. Ollie's Point refers to the nearby troop staging area that everyone but the US Congress knew about.

Difficult access means that most of the Santa Rosa sector is fairly empty, though it can get reasonably busy on weekends in the dry season when Ticos flock to the park in search of their often-hard-to-find history. And, unfortunately, those breaks can get busy in the dry season too. But in the wet months from July through December, particularly in September and October, you'll often have the park virtually to yourself.

The park's Sector Murciélago (Bat Sector) encompasses the wild northern coastline of the Península Santa Elena, and is not accessible from Santa Rosa. Here you'll find the isolated white-sand beach of Playa Blanca (no camping allowed) and the trailhead for the Poza el General watering hole, which attracts birds and animals year-round. The famed surf break, Ollie's Point in Playa Portero Grande, is in this sector of the park and can only be reached by boat from Playa del Coco or Tamarindo. Or you can do as Patrick and Wingnut did in *Endless Summer II* and crash-land your chartered plane on the beach (ahem, not actually recommended).

Sights & Activities

La Casona   HISTORIC BUILDING
(⊙8-11:30am, 1-4pm) Historic La Casona, the main building of the old Hacienda Santa Rosa, is near park headquarters in the Santa Rosa sector. Unfortunately, the original building was burnt to the ground by arsonists in May 2001, but was rebuilt in 2002 using historic photos and local timber. The boulder foundation is still authentic, and there are other 19th-century charms such as wagon wheels, a restored adobe kitchen and one prominently displayed yoke on the porch eaves, not to mention those fabulous old shade trees around the Casona corrals. Two hiking trails leave from behind the museum.

The battle of 1856 was fought around this building, and the military action, as well as the region's natural history, is described with wonderful new historical displays in English and Spanish. They detail the old gold rush route, William Walker's evil imperial plans, and the 20-day battle breakdown.

The arsonists were a local father-son team of poachers who were disgruntled at being banned from hunting here by park rangers. They were caught and sentenced to 20 years in prison for torching a building of national cultural and historical value. Unfortunately, poaching continues in the park since it's difficult for rangers to effectively patrol such a large area.

Wildlife-Watching

The wildlife is both varied and prolific, especially during the dry season when animals congregate around the remaining water sources and the trees lose their leaves. More than 250 bird species have been recorded, including the raucous white-throated magpie jay, unmistakable with its long crest of manically curled feathers. The forests contain parrot and parakeet, trogon and tanager, and as you head down to the coast, you will be rewarded by sightings of a variety of coastal birds.

Bats are also very common; about 50 or 60 different species have been identified in Santa Rosa. Other mammals you have a reasonable chance of seeing include deer, coati, peccary, armadillo, coyote, raccoon, three kinds of monkey, and a variety of other species – about 115 in all. There are also many thousands of insect species, including about 4000 moths and butterflies (just bring insect repellent).

Reptile species include lizards, iguanas, snakes, crocodiles and four species of sea turtle. The olive ridley sea turtle is the most numerous, and during the July to December nesting season tens of thousands of turtles make their nests on Santa Rosa's beaches. The most popular beach is Playa Nancite, where, during September and October especially, it is possible to see as many as 8000 of these 40kg turtles on the beach at the same time. The turtles are disturbed by light, so flash photography and flashlights are not permitted. Avoid the nights around a full moon – they're too bright and turtles are less likely to show up. Playa Nancite is strictly protected and entry is restricted, but permission may be obtained from park headquarters to observe this spectacle; call ahead.

The variety of wildlife reflects the variety of habitat within park boundaries. Apart from the largest remaining stand of tropical dry forest in Central America, habitats include savanna woodland, oak forest, deciduous forest, evergreen forest, riparian forest, mangrove swamp and coastal woodland.

Hiking

Near Hacienda Santa Rosa is El Sendero Indio Desnudo, an 800m trail with signs interpreting the ecological relationships among the animals, plants and weather patterns of Santa Rosa. The trail is named after the common tree, also called *gumbo limbo*, whose peeling orange-red bark can photosynthesize during the dry season, when the trees' leaves are lost (resembling a sunburned tourist... or 'naked Indian,' as the literal translation of the trail name implies). Also seen along the trail is the national tree of Costa Rica, the *guanacaste*. The province is named after this huge tree species, which is found along the Pacific coastal lowlands. You may also see birds, monkeys, snakes and iguanas, as well as petroglyphs (most likely pre-Columbian) etched into rocks along the trail.

Behind La Casona a short 330m trail leads up to the Monumento a Los Héroes and a lookout platform. There are also longer trails through the dry forest, including a gentle 4km hike to the Mirador, with spectacular views of Playa Naranjo, which is accessible to hikers willing to go another 9km along the deeply rutted road to the sea. The main road is lined with short trails to small waterfalls and other photogenic natural wonders.

On the road to Playa Naranjo, and about 8km from shore, you'll pass a trailhead for the Mirador Valle Naranjo trail. It's a short 600m hump to a viewpoint with magical Naranjo vistas.

From the southern end of Playa Naranjo, there are two hiking trails: Sendero Carbonal is a 5km trail that swings inland along the mangroves and past Laguna El Limbo where the crocs hang out; Sendero Aceituno parallels Playa Naranjo for 13km and terminates near the estuary across from Witch's Rock. There's also a 6km hiking trail that starts where the northern branch of the access road terminates – this leads to the biological research station at Nancite; you'll need prior permission to access this beach. You'll also need to park in Naranjo and walk the 3.5km back to the Sendero Nancite trailhead, from where it's an additional 7km to the secluded beach where there is no water source, so plan extensively and carefully or you will suffer.

Surfing

The surfing at Playa Naranjo is truly world-class, especially near Witch's Rock, a beach break famous for its fast, hollow 3m rights (although there are also fun lefts when it isn't pumping). Beware of rocks near the river mouth, and be careful near the estuary as it's a rich feeding ground for crocodiles during the tide changes. Oh, and by the way, the beach is stunning, with a sweet rounded boulder-strewn point to the north and shark fin headlands to the south. Even further south, Nicoya and Papagayo peninsular silhouettes reach out in a dramatic attempt to out do each other.

The surfing is equally legendary at Ollie's Point off Playa Portero Grande, which has the best right in all of Costa Rica with a nice, long ride, especially with a south swell. The bottom here is a mix of sand and rocks, and the year-round offshore is perfect for tight turns and slow closes. Shortboarding is preferred by surfers at both spots.

🛏 Sleeping & Eating

Campground CAMPGROUND
(per person US$2) There's a shady developed campground close to the park headquarters, with picnic benches, grills, flushing toilets and cold-water showers. Playa Naranjo has pit toilets and showers, but no potable water – bring your own, and don't expect complete solitude. People do love to camp there, and everyone shares one sandy flat basin, only moderately sheltered from gusty wind by thin trees.

Other camping areas in the park are undeveloped. There's a 25-person, two-night maximum for camping at Playa Naranjo. There's also a small campsite with pit toilets and showers near the ranger station in the Sector Murciélago, though you'll have to carry in your own food and water.

Research Station HOSTEL
(📞2666-5051; www.acguanacaste.ac.cr; dm US$15, meals US$6-7) Make reservations in advance to stay here; basic to grim eight-bed dorms have cold showers and electricity. Researchers get priority, but there's usually some room for travelers. Good meals are available in the *comedor*.

❶ Information

Access to the **Santa Rosa Sector park entrance** (📞2666-5051; www.acguanacaste.ac.cr; adults/child 6-12yr/5yr and under US$10/1/free, surfing surcharge US$15 ; ⊘8am-4pm) is on the west side of the Interamericana, 35km north of Liberia and 45km south of the Nicaragua border. From the entrance, it's another 7km to park headquarters, where you'll find the administrative offices, scientists' quarters, an

information center, three basic campgrounds, a museum and nature trail. This office administers the Area de Conservación Guanacaste (ACG).

From this complex, a very rough track leads down to Playa Naranjo, 12km away. Even during the dry season, this road is only passable to a high-clearance 4WD, and you must sign an eerie waiver at the park entrance stating that you willingly assume all liability for driving this road. The park requires you to be completely self-sufficient if you choose to undertake the trip, which means bringing your own water and knowing how to do your own car repair. The rangers simply don't have the resources to bail you out or perform vehicle repair if you get into trouble. During the rainy months (May to November) the road is open to hikers and horses but closed to all vehicles; if you want to surf here, it's infinitely easier to gain access to the beach by hiring a boat from Playa del Coco or Tamarindo, further south. Be aware that rangers can and will shut down Playa Nancite to visitors during the turtle nesting season.

The park's Sector Murciélago (Bat Sector) encompasses the wild northern coastline of the Península Santa Elena, and is not accessible from the main body of the park. Ollie's Point in Playa Portero Grande is in this sector of the park and can only be reached by boat from Playa del Coco or Tamarindo.

❶ Getting There & Away

The well-signed main park entrance can be reached by public transportation: take any bus between Liberia and the Nicaraguan border and ask the driver to let you off at the park entrance; rangers can help you catch a return bus. You can also arrange private transportation from the hotels in Liberia for about US$20 to US$30 per person round trip.

To get to the northern Sector Murciélago, continue north on the Interamericana past the entrance to the Santa Rosa sector for 10km and turn left once you pass through the police checkpoint. Continue on this road for a few more kilometers until you reach the village of Cuajiniquíl and then bear left. Continue on this road for another 15km, which will bring you past such historic sights as the former hacienda of the Somoza family (it's currently a training ground for the Costa Rican police) and the airstrip that was used by Oliver North to 'secretly' smuggle goods to the Nicaraguan Contras in the 1980s. Continue straight until you cross a river, then hang a right and keep going straight over two more rivers until you reach the village of Murciélago and the park entrance. You can camp at the Murciélago ranger station, or continue 12km on a dirt road beyond the ranger station to the remote bays and beaches of Bahía Santa Elena and Bahía Playa Blanca. A 4WD is a must, and even then the road may be impassable in the wet season. Also, signage is nonexistent.

Refugio Nacional de Vida Silvestre Bahía Junquillal

This 505-hectare wildlife refuge is part of the ACG, administered from the park headquarters at Santa Rosa. There is a ranger station (☑2666-5051; www.acguanacaste.ac.cr; adult/child 6-12yr/child 5yr & under US$13/5/free, camping per person US$2; ◷8am-5pm) in telephone and radio contact with Santa Rosa.

The quiet bay and protected beach provide gentle swimming, boating and snorkeling opportunities, and there are tropical dry forest and mangroves. Two short trails (totaling 1.7km) hug the coast and take the wandering visitor to a lookout for marine bird-watching in one direction, and to the mangroves in the other. Pelicans and frigate birds are seen, and turtles nest here seasonally. Volcán Orosi can be seen in the distance. This is a very popular campground among domestic tourists, and it's outfitted with brick grills and picnic tables at every site. Campers should note that during the dry season especially, water is at a premium and is turned on for only one hour a day. There are pit latrines.

There is no sign pointing the way from Cuajiniquíl. Once you enter town, continue for about 2km on the paved road and turn right onto a dirt road after you pass Super-Compro. Continuing 4km along the dirt road (passable to ordinary cars) brings you to the entrance of Bahía Junquillal. You'll know you're getting close when that glorious cobalt bay appears from out of nowhere on your left. From the entry post there is a sign pointing out the 700m dirt road leading to the beach, ranger station and camping area. If you miss the turn to the refuge you'll land in an estuary fishing village where stilted houses overlook a tidal channel, and several *sodas* serve fresh seafood. The refuge road is passable to all cars.

Parque Nacional Guanacaste

Opened on July 25, 1989 (Guanacaste Day), Parque Nacional Guanacaste is the newest part of the Área de Conservación Guanacaste and forms a protected nature corridor that now stretches from the Pacific to the Caribbean coast. The park is almost adjacent to the Santa Rosa Sector, separated by only the Interamericana. It's about 5km northwest of Parque Nacional Rincón de la Vieja, and one of the least-visited parks in the country because tourist access is highly restricted.

The 345 sq km of Parque Nacional Guanacaste are much more than a continuation of the lowland habitats found in Santa Rosa. In its lower western reaches, the park is indeed composed of the dry tropical rainforest characteristic of much of Guanacaste, but the terrain soon begins to climb toward two volcanoes – Volcán Orosi (1487m) and Volcán Cacao (1659m). Here the landscape slowly transitions to the humid cloud forest that's found throughout much of the highland Cordillera de Guanacaste. This habitat, which is similar in function to Parque Nacional Carara, provides a refuge for altitudinal migrants that move between the coast and the highlands. Thus the national park allows for the ancient migratory and hunting patterns of various animal species to continue as they have for millennia.

However, this ecosystem is more the domain of biologists than tourists (admission is by reservation only), and there are two active research stations within the borders of the park. In addition to observing animal migratory patterns, researchers are also monitoring the pace of reforestation as much of the park is composed of ranch land. Interestingly enough, researchers have found that if the pasture is carefully managed (much of this management involves just letting nature take its course), the natural forest will reinstate itself in its old territory. Thus, crucial habitats in the national park are not just preserved, but in some cases they are also expanded.

For information on visiting the park, contact the ACG headquarters (☑2666-5051; www.acguanacaste.ac.cr; adult/child US$10/1) in Parque Nacional Santa Rosa.

◉ Sights & Activities

Hiking trails in the national park are among the least developed in the entire country, and are principally used by researchers to move between each of the stations. It's advisable to talk to the staff before setting out on any of the hikes, as infrastructure in the park is almost nonexistent. If you have a relevant background in biology or ecology, volunteer positions are available, though it's best to contact ACG well in advance of your arrival.

Maritza Biological Station RESEARCH STATION
(☎2666-5051; www.acguanacaste.ac.cr; adult/child $10/1, dm US$15-20) This is the newest and most accessible station and has a modern laboratory. From the station, at 600m above sea level, rough trails run to the summits of Volcán Orosi and Volcán Cacao (about five to six hours). A better trail leads to a site where several hundred petroglyphs have been found that are chipped into volcanic rock. As with most indigenous sites in Costa Rica, little is known about the origins of the petroglyphs, although the area was believed to have been inhabited by the Chorotega.

To get here, turn east off the Interamericana opposite the turnoff for Cuajiniquíl. The station is about 17km east of the highway along a dirt road that may require a 4WD vehicle, especially in the wet season.

Pitilla Biological Station RESEARCH STATION
(☎2666-5051; adult/child US$10/1, dm US$15) This station lies on the northeast side of Volcán Orosi, which is on the eastern side of the continental divide. The surrounding forests around here are humid, lush and unlike anything you'll find in the rest of Guanacaste.

To get to the station, turn east off the Interamericana about 12km north of the Cuajiniquíl turnoff, or 3km before reaching the small town of La Cruz. Follow the paved eastbound road for about 28km to the community of Santa Cecilia. From here, a dirt road in truly terrible condition heads 11km south to the station – you'll need a 4WD year-round.

Sleeping & Eating

You can camp (per person US$2.50) near the stations, but there aren't any facilities.

If there's space, you may be able to reserve dorm-style accommodations at Maritza (p205) or Pitilla (p205) Biological Stations. The stations are quite rustic, with room for 30 people, and shared cold-water bathrooms. Meals are also available and should be arranged in advance.

La Cruz

POP 4800

La Cruz is the closest town to the Peñas Blancas border crossing with Nicaragua, and it's the principal gateway to Bahía Salinas, Costa Rica's premier kitesurfing destination. La Cruz itself is a sweet, gritty and fairly sleepy provincial town set on a mountaintop plateau, with lots of Tico charm (and barbed wire), and magical views of an epic wind-swept bay from nearly every corner. From here you can easily bus down to the white-sand beaches on Bahía Salinas.

Sleeping & Eating

La Cruz may possibly have the most *heladerías* (ice-cream shops) per capita in Costa Rica, for which you'll be glad when the mid-afternoon heat smites you. Pick up groceries at the neighboring Almacén Super Único and SuperCompro La Cruz, on the east side of the plaza. There are a handful of *sodas* scattered about town.

TOP CHOICE **Hotel La Mirada** HOTEL $
(☎2679-9702; www.hotellamirada.com; s/d US$27/40; P❄@) Despite the name, there are no views to speak of, but just off the Interamericana is the town's newest nest. Family-owned and lovingly cared for, rooms are a bit oddly laid out but super clean with beamed ceilings, cable TV and loft sleeping spaces for the kids. For the money, this is the best deal in town.

Amalia's Inn INN $
(☎2679-9618; s/d US$20/30; P❄⊛) The shared terra-cotta terraces at Amalia's have stupendous bay views. The white stucco house on a cliff isn't a bad place to spend the night, either – cozy, homey rooms are decorated with anything from white wicker to modular leather, each with private hot-water bathroom and air-con. The brick floors could use a mop, but the wooden ceilings are nice. Walls in the meandering house are hung with modernist paintings by Amalia's late husband Lester Bounds. Amalia's niece is now the lady of the house, and short of offering meals, she'll make you feel right at home.

Hotel Bella Vista HOTEL $
(☎2679-8050; r with/without bathroom US$16/12; P❄⊛) With a lovely mosaic-bottomed pool and breezy restaurant at the top of the hill, this Dutch-run hotel is a great place for a beer in the evenings. Rooms are laid out rather poorly so feel more stuffy than they are. In reality they are reasonably clean with wooden beamed ceilings and cable TV, and are fan cooled. Those on the second level get more light and have outstanding views.

HEADING NORTH OF THE BORDER

Peñas Blancas is a busy border crossing, open 6am to 8pm daily. You won't be charged to exit or enter Costa Rica, but entering and leaving Nicaragua costs US$10. Driving a car across the border is another $27, but most car-rental companies in Costa Rica won't allow you to cross borders; check before you sign your contract. Alternatively, leave your car in the 'no man's land' parking area between borders for $5 per day. Banks on either side will change local colones and córdobas for dollars but, inconveniently, not for each other. Independent money changers will happily make the exchange for you – at whatever rates they feel like setting.

The border posts are about 1km apart. Hordes of generally useless touts will offer to 'guide' you through the simple crossing – let them carry your luggage if you like, but agree on a fee beforehand. You'll also be charged US$1 to enter the state of Rivas. Should you have any hard currency left at this point, there's a fairly fabulous duty-free shop, with fancy makeup and lots of liquor, waiting for you in Sapoá, the Nicaraguan equivalent of Peñas Blancas.

Relax with your purchases on the 37km bus ride (US$1, 45 minutes), departing every 30 minutes, to Rivas. The city is a quiet transport hub, though its well-preserved 17th-century center is worth exploring (think a more run-down version of Granada without all the crowds).

If you're good at bargaining (and you will have to bargain hard), there will be a number of taxis waiting on the Nicaraguan side of the border to whisk you to Rivas (US$30).

Restaurante Goal SEAFOOD $$
(☑2679-9397; mains US$6-18; ⊙11am-10pm) Here's a local fish house abutting the soccer field with wooden tables and chairs, tasteful arches and beamed ceilings. It specializes in fish and shrimp dishes and has octopus too. Get a whole fish dinner, a filet, seafood soup, ceviche, jumbo shrimp, or lobster.

❶ Information

Changing money at the border post often yields a better exchange rate than in town.

Banco Nacional (☑2679-9296) At the junction of the short road into the town center; has a 24hr ATM.

Banco Popular (☑2679-9352) In the town center; has an ATM.

Cruz Roja (☑2679-9004, emergency 2679-9146) A small clinic just north of the town center on the road toward the border.

Café Internet (☑8838-8128, 2679-8190; per hr US$1; ⊙8am-7pm Mon-Sat)

❶ Getting There & Away

A **Transportes Deldú counter** (⊙7:30am-12:30pm & 1:30am-6pm) sells tickets and stores bags. To catch a TransNica bus to Peñas Blancas you'll need to flag a bus down on the Interamericana. Buses to the beaches depart from the bus terminal down the hill and around the corner from Hotel Bella Vista; a taxi to the beach costs US$16 to US$20.

Liberia (Transportes Deldú) US$2.50; 1½ hours; eight departures per day from 5:30am to 6:30pm. Alternatively, catch any San José–bound bus.

Peñas Blancas US$1; 45 minutes; 10 departures per day from 5am to 5:30pm.

Playa Jobó US$1.50; 30 minutes; departs at 8:30am, 11:15am, 2pm and 5pm.

San José via Liberia (Transportes Deldú) US$7; five hours; departs almost every hour.

Bahía Salinas

Bahía Salinas is not just the best place in all of Costa Rica for kitesurfing, it's also a stunning, under the radar destination even if you don't ride wind. Although giddy riders do shred beneath magnificent rainbows that arch over a wide and deep bay extending all the way to Nicaragua. The deconstructed nature of the destination – communities congregate on stunning, empty beaches clumped with tropical forests home to howler tribes, and linked by dirt roads – creates a *tranquilo* rural vibe . There are two massive residential developments in the works, with rumors of over 200 houses going in above magnificent Playa Jobó by 2014. You can already see the outline of a rather weighty footprint, and if these projects come to full fruition, Bahía Salinas won't be the same. Get here soon.

◉ Sights & Activities

A dirt road (normally passable to cars) leads down from the lookout point in La Cruz past the small coastal fishing community of Puerto Soley and out along the curve of the bay to the consistently windy beaches of Playa Papaturro, across from Blue Dream, and Playa Copal, the kiting vortex. It's an incredibly wide beige beach backed by scrubby *manzanillo* trees with views across the sea all the way to Nicaragua. It does get crazy windy here, so, though picturesque, it's not about beach combing. Copal is for launching kites and riding, and Papaturro is only a safe launch for advanced riders.

If wind isn't your thing, head around the point to Playa Jobó, a perfect, 300m-wide horseshoe of a bay with calm water and headlands sprouting with flowering trees, or Playa Rajada just beyond. Rajada is set on the southern most arm of Salinas. It's ruggedly gorgeous and although you can see open ocean from here, the tiny 200m bay is sheltered enough to be almost placid. In September and October, humpback whales often congregate off Playa Rajada. Boats can be rented in the village of El Jobó or at one of the local resorts to visit Isla Bolaños, a seabird refuge home to the endangered brown pelican (visits are restricted to April through November to avoid disturbing nesting seabirds). Or try contacting Frank Schultz (☑8827-4109; franksdiving@costaricense.co.cr; two tanks per person US$100-150, fishing trips for up to 4 people US$350), who also organizes fishing and diving trips to Isla Despense, Isla Caballo and Isla Murcielago with its resident bull sharks. Jose Piporro (☑2676-1171; fishing trips per hour US$50) is also an excellent local fishing guide and will take you out on hourly trips. He's based on the fishermen's beach, Playa Manzanillo.

Kitesurfing

Forget what you may have heard – Bahía Salinas has Costa Rica's best kitesurfing, which is why it is an internationally known mecca for riders between November and March, when the wind howls fairly consistently.

The shape of the hills surrounding the bay funnels the winds into a predictable pattern (though it can be gusty, ranging between 20 to 40 knots), and the sandy, protected beaches make this a safe place for beginners and experienced riders alike. It's important to remember that there are inherent dangers to kiting (namely the risk of losing a limb – yikes!), so seek professional instruction if you're not experienced. The Professional Air Sports Association (PASA) and the International Kiteboarding Organization (IKO) have set standards for beginner instruction. You'll need to take a nine-hour certification course to rent gear and safely go out on your own.

Kitesurf School 2000 KITESURFING
(☑8826-5221; www.bluedreamhotel; 9hr beginner course US$319, lessons per hr US$40) Kitesurf School 2000, the area's original kite shop, prefers you make reservations a couple of days in advance for two days of lessons or equipment rental (basic gear per day US$65). Italian, Spanish and English are spoken. There's also an excellent and incredibly swift repair service and it is IKO certified.

Bob's Cometa Copal KITESURFING
(☑2676-1192; www.islandsurf-sail.com; private lessons per hr US$50) Another reputable kitesurfing school, this seasonal shop is run by American Bob Selfridge, who not only offers kitesurfing lessons with PASA (Professional Air Sports Association) and IKO-certified instructors, but is himself an instructor, lifeguard and emergency medical technician. It's open November to June.

Kite House KITESURFING
(☑8370-4894; www.kiteboardingcostarica.com; lessons per hr US$45-50) The newest operation on the beach offers instruction and rentals on Playa Copal. Instructors speak French and English. They also run a bit of a flophouse (rooms from US$33) that isn't the best value, but feels like a slumber party.

🛏 Sleeping & Eating

Most hotels in Bahía Salinas offer transfers from San José or Liberia airports.

Blue Dream Hotel HOTEL $$
(☑8826-5221, 2676-1042; www.bluedreamhotel. com; dm US$17, standard s/d US$32/42, bungalow s/d US$36/46; ☉Sep-Jul; ℗❋@☞) Home base of Kitesurf School 2000, this friendly, groovy hotel looks out over Playa Papaturro from its terraced hillside, with simple, comfortable Spanish-tiled rooms at the top of the hill. Along with the hammock-strung garden, there's the Mediterraneo restaurant (open for breakfast, lunch and dinner) serving local and Mediterranean food,

all run by Italian kiteboarding instructor Nicola, the first instructor on the bay, and his charming staff. The shop also does rapid repairs.

Bob's Cometa Copal
CABINA $$

(☏2676-1192; www.kitesurfincostarica.com; cabinas US$45-65; P�](r)⛱) A seasonal operation with clean, colorful little feaux-dobe *cabinas* at the top of a hill with gorgeous views of the bay. *Cabinas* are quite sweet with Spanish tile, vaulted beamed ceilings and kitchenettes. In addition to organizing PASA and IKO certified kitesurfing lessons and rentals (lessons per hour US$50), Bob rents out gear, and his restaurant has the best kitchen on the bay.

Bolaños Bay Resort
HOTEL $$

(☏2676-1163; www.hotelbolanosbay.com; r with/ without sea views incl breakfast US$65/75; P⚡@(r)⛱♨) Basically a down-on-its-luck, three-star place with solid bones including an almost too dramatic *palapa* entry way, seaside pool and epic bay views. Yes, it looks and feels a bit ignored, but the rooms are quite cheery with polished concrete floors, flat screen TVs and whitewashed wood furnishings. It's not a bad option at this price.

Ecoplaya Beach Resort
HOTEL $$

(☏2676-1010; www.ecoplaya.com; s/d US$80/90, villas from US$130; P⊝⚡@⛱♨) There are things we love about Ecoplaya. The rooms are huge with sustainable teak furnishings, there are cool design elements like soaring, slanted ceilings and a floating beam,

and those views from 2nd floor rooms are epic. Though the beach is thin and gray, it's close to gorgeous Playa Jobó and, really, any vantage point on this bay is special. On the other hand, the restaurant is not so magical, and the grounds feel very much like a three-star package tour haunt.

Vista Copal
RESTAURANT $

(☏2676-1006; mains US$6-10; ⏱8am-10am, 5-9pm; (r)) A stunning octagonal, thatched wooden dining room with drop-dead gorgeous views and absurdly good food. We had a pan of fried fish filet that was perfectly cooked, scattered with garlic and herbs, and served with a lovely salad and black beans. The homemade chips and *habanero* salsa are ridiculous. Be judicious with the *habanero*. Other options include chicken with mustard sauce, spaghetti Bolognese and burgers. Whatever is on offer is displayed on the chalkboard. Think of it as the best kitesurf pub ever.

❶ Getting There & Away

Buses (US$1.50) along this road depart the La Cruz bus terminal to the village of Jabó at 5am, 8:30am, 11:15am, 2pm and 5pm. Buses from Jabó to La Cruz depart at 6am, 9:30am, noon, 3pm and 5:45pm. A taxi to the beaches costs about US$16 to US$20.

To get to Playa Jobó, take the road past Bolaños Bay Resort for about 2km. It dead ends at the beach. For Playa Rajada, double back to the main road and make a right (don't go toward La Cruz), and veer right again at the Mini Super in El Jobo; 3km later the road ends at the beach.

Península de Nicoya

Why Go?

You don't need an excuse to explore this wild peninsula, though there are plenty. Maybe you're here to sample sapphire waters that peel left and right, and curl into perfect barrels up and down the coast. Or you could always dive, snorkel, fish or paddle in the life-affirming Pacific that will enliven your soul. Afterward, burn days and nights hiking through jungle, spot nesting leatherbacks, or bound across rugged roads, fording rivers and navigating ridges with massive coastal views. Fear not. There's no shortage of groovy boutique nests, yoga studios and tasteful kitchens to nourish and shelter you between adventures. Point is, whether you've set aside days or weeks, your excuse matters a whole lot less than what you do with it.

Best Places to Eat

» Koji's (p271)

» Playa de los Artistas (p265)

» Restaurant Mary (p272)

» Cocolores (p265)

» Villa Deveena (p233)

» Rip Jack Inn (p221)

When to Go

The northern Península de Nicoya has one of the driest climates in Costa Rica, although rainfall does peak during the green season of September and October when swollen rivers make some regions impassable. But that's also when the peninsula is at its most lush and the roads and sky aren't nearly as dusty. It's when whales are migrating and prices are cheap. Yes, even wet season is glorious here.

Best Places to Stay

» Florblanca (p270)

» Moana Lodge (p272)

» Hotel Amor de Mar (p263)

» Refugio del Sol (p244)

» Las Avellanas Villas (p232)

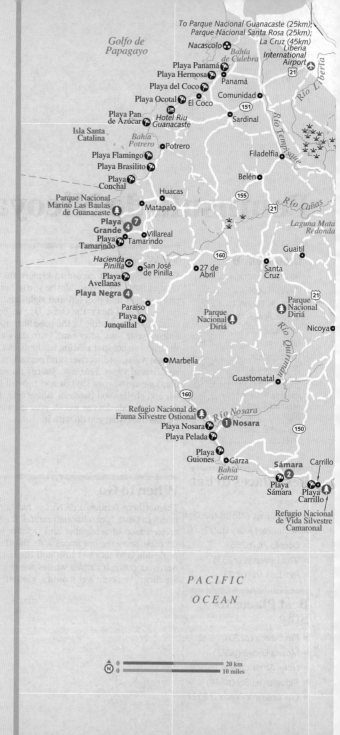

Península de Nicoya Highlights

① Catch the morning swell and perfecting afternoon *asanas* in **Nosara** (p239)

② Ford rivers and navigate the coastal 4WD tracks between **Samara** (p247) and **Santa Teresa** (p268)

③ Hike to the tip of the peninsula at **Reserva Natural Absoluta Cabo Blanco** (p267)

④ Surf luscious breaks at **Playas Grande** (p220) and **Negra** (p231)

⑤ Explore the pristine waters of **Mal País** (p268)

⑥ Sample **Koji's** (p271) sensational sushi in Santa Teresa

⑦ Glimpse the hulking **leatherbacks** on Playa Grande

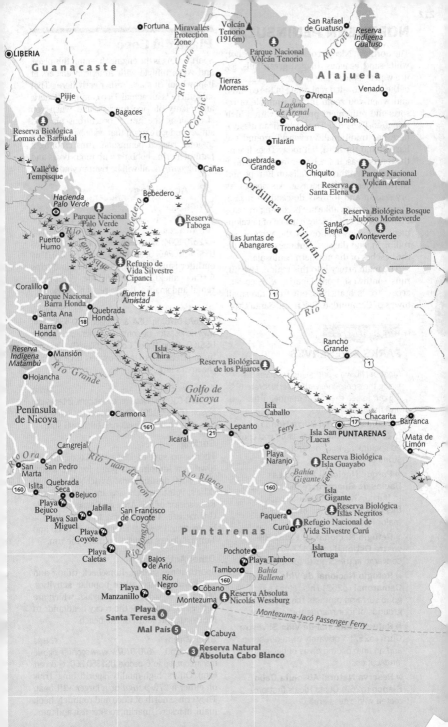

NORTHERN PENINSULA

The northern Nicoya coastline in a snapshot: white-sand beaches, rugged green hills, azure waters, stucco subdivisions. This is some of the most coveted real estate in the country, and when you zoom in, it's a jumble of resorts and retirement properties with a high gringo-to-Tico ratio. The Costa Rican lifestyle here has traditionally revolved around the harvest and the herd, but today Ticos live by the tourist season. Each year from December to April, when the snow falls on Europe and North America, Guanacaste experiences its dry season and tourists descend en masse. Ticos and expats alike are becoming increasingly aware of the tricky balance of development and conservation as the waves keep rolling in, and the sun continues to smile on the beaches of the northern peninsula.

The main artery into this region, Hwy 21, runs southwest from Liberia, with coastal access roads branching out from the small towns of Comunidad, Belén and Santa Cruz.

DON'T MISS

PARKS & RESERVES

Most of Nicoya's parks and reserves lie along the shoreline, with several stretching out to sea to protect marine turtles and their nesting sites.

» **Parque Nacional Barra Honda** (p237) Best in the dry season; you can go spelunking in underground limestone caves.

» **Parque Nacional Marino Las Baulas de Guanacaste** (p224) Crucial to the survival of the leatherback turtle, this park protects one of the turtle's major Pacific nesting sites.

» **Refugio Nacional de Fauna Silvestre Ostional** (p246) Olive ridleys converge in mass nestings at Ostional.

» **Refugio Nacional de Vida Silvestre Camaronal** (p252) This refuge has good surf and protects the nesting grounds of four marine turtle species.

» **Refugio Nacional de Vida Silvestre Curú** (p257) A privately owned reserve and an unexpected oasis of diverse landscapes.

» **Reserva Natural Absoluta Cabo Blanco** (p267) Costa Rica's first protected wilderness area.

Playa del Coco

Sport fishing is the engine that built this place, and you'll mingle with American anglers at happy hour (it starts rather early here). That said, there is an actual Tico community here, and plenty of Tico tourists, and when you stroll along the grassy beachfront plaza at sunset and gaze upon that wide bay sheltered by long, rugged peninsular arms cradling a natural marina bobbing with motorboats and fishing *pangas*, all will be right in your world.

Activities

Diving

Deep Blue Diving Adventures   DIVING, SNORKELLING
(☎2670-1004; www.deepblue-diving.com; 2 tanks US$79-110, PADI Open Water Course US$415) This outfitter runs two-tank local dives and trips further afield, which include equipment rental and snacks. It also rents bicycles.

Rich Coast Diving   DIVING
(☎2670-0176, in USA & Canada 800-434-8464; www.richcoastdiving.com; 2 tanks per person US$100, Open Water Course US$450) On the main street, this Dutch-owned dive shop is the area's largest.

Summer Salt   DIVING
(☎2670-0308; www.summer-salt.com; 2 tanks per person US$100-120) This friendly Swiss-run dive shop has professional, bilingual staff.

Surfing

There's no surf in Playa del Coco, but the town is a jumping-off point for two legendary surf destinations: Witch's Rock and Ollie's Point, which are inside the Santa Rosa sector of the Area de Conservacion de Guanacaste. The best way to reach them is by boat, and several surf shops in Coco and Tamarindo are licensed to make the run.

Other Activities

Sportfishing, sailing, horseback riding and sea kayaking are other popular activities. Many places will rent sea kayaks, which are perfect for exploring the rocky headlands to the north and south of the beach.

Blue Marlin   FISHING
(☎8828-8250, 2670-0707; www.sportfishingbluemarlin.com; up to 6 people US$350-860; ⊙depart 6am) Offers high-quality sportfishing trips on either a 27ft *panga* or a larger 42ft boat. They cruise north of Coco and routinely hook mahi, mackerel, marlin, rooster fish and tuna.

DIVERS DO IT DEEPER

The northern peninsula is one of the best and most easily accessible dive destinations in the country. Dives are made either around volcanic rock pinnacles near the coast, or from a boat further off at Isla Santa Catalina (about 20km to the southwest) or Isla Murciélago (40km to the northwest, near the tip of Península Santa Elena). Do not expect to see colorful hard coral, and the water can get chilly and visibility mediocre (9m to 15m, and sometimes up to 20m), but the sites make up for it with abundant marine life. Plenty of turtles and pelagics meander through, including mantas, sharks and whales, and you'll be lost in huge schools of smaller tropical fish.

Isla Santa Catalina and Isla Murciélago both host migrant manta rays from December to late April, and Murciélago is also known for its regular sightings of resident bull sharks. Divers also head to Narizones, which is a good deep dive (about 27m), while Punta Gorda is an easy descent for inexperienced divers.

If you haven't been scuba diving before, consider taking a 'Discovery Course,' which costs about US$145. If you're interested in getting your Open Water Diver certification, which allows you to dive anywhere in the world, a three- to four-day course is about US$420.

Papagayo Golf & Country Club GOLF
(2697-0169; www.papagayo-golf.com; 9/18 holes US$55/95, putting green US$6; 6:30am-5pm Tue-Sun) An 18-hole course located 10km southeast of Playa del Coco.

Festivals & Events

In late January the town hosts a **Fiesta Cívica**, with bullfights, rodeos, dancing and plenty of drinking. But the biggest festival in Coco is the **Fiesta de la Virgen del Mar**, celebrated in mid-July with a vivid religious-themed boat procession in the harbor and a horse pageant.

Sleeping

Budget lodgings primarily cater to Tico weekenders.

Casa Vista Azul BOUTIQUE HOTEL $$$
(2670-0678; www.hotelvistaazul.com; r incl breakfast US$90, apt per month US$500; P) This stunning boutique hotel has seven rooms, and an apartment in a somewhat incomplete (and moderately depressing) McMansion subdivision, on a cliff high above the coast. All nests have air-con and bathroom, are flooded with light and have wide-open ocean views. There's also a breezy rooftop dining area, and the owner can help arrange tours. To get here, head west off the main road, just south of Flor de Itabo, and follow the signs.

Cafe de Playa HOTEL $$$
(2670-1621, 2670-1471; www.cafedeplaya.com; d incl breakfast US$200; P@) Several elegant, but not huge, rooms at this beach club, adorned with gallery-worthy contemporary art, beamed ceilings, flat screens, marble baths and pebbled tile floors, look onto the circular pool and provide easy access to the beach, and beachfront restaurant. It's about 15 minutes' walk into the town center, but you may not feel the need to leave.

Toro Blanco HOTEL $$
(2670-1707; www.toroblancoresort.com; s/d US$40/70; P) This canary-yellow, three-story colonial-style building surrounds a courtyard with a lovely swimming pool. Apartments are outfitted with engraved headboards, wooden wardrobes, full kitchens, flat-screen TV, and private balcony or patio. Accents, like dangling lanterns, are quite elegant.

Cabinas Coco Azul CABINA $
(2670-0431; cabinascocoazul_cr@yahoo.com; d US$35; P) This two-story, white-and-brick building is the best of several budget *cabinas* located in a leafy gated complex behind the church. Rooms are sparkling clean and comfy with cold-water showers.

Hotel La Puerta del Sol HOTEL $$
(2670-0195; www.lapuertadelsolcostarica.com; d incl breakfast US$80; P@) A five-minute walk from town, this unpretentiously luxurious Mediterranean-inspired hotel has two large suites and eight huge pastel-color rooms with polished brick and concrete floors, each with its own private terrace. The well-manicured grounds have a glorious pool and a trellis-shaded gym.

Hotel Savannah
HOTEL $$

(☎2670-0367; d US$50; P❄❅🔊) A quiet and relaxed inn with small, basic, but immaculate tiled rooms in a shady longhouse. It's on a quiet side road, with a swimming pool, communal kitchen, barbecue grills and pleasant garden.

Ruby's Lodging
HOTEL $

(☎8932-9002; s/d US$30/40; P❄🔊) One of the best budget deals in town, this family-operated property offers basic but clean tiled rooms with cable, wi-fi and hot water. Management is warm and welcoming and long-term stays are available.

Laura's House B&B
B&B $$

(☎2670-0751; www.laurashousecr.com; s/d incl breakfast US$45/55; P❄❅🔊) The eight simple, spotless and reasonably spacious rooms at this homey B&B overlook a small pool and have cable TV. There's a friendly, family vibe and it is a short walk to the center of town.

Villa del Sol B&B
HOTEL $$

(☎2670-0085, in Canada 866-793-9523, in USA 866-815-8902; www.villadelsol.com; room US$70, studios US$90; P❄@🔊) This leafy, tranquil property, found 1km north of the town center, has a good mix of spotless, well-furnished rooms and studio apartments. The hotel is around 100m from the beach, which isn't as crowded at this end. Reserve ahead.

Hotel Mar & Mar
HOTEL $

(☎2670-1212; ⊙s/d US$20/40; P) A romantic beachfront hacienda with an all-wood upper floor and fan-cooled rooms downstairs, with ceramic tiled floors and beamed ceilings. Singles are clean but cramped. Double rooms are far better and worth the extra dosh. All have cold-water showers.

El Oasis Backpackers Hostel
HOSTEL $

(☎2670-0511; dm per person US$15 ; ❄@) Although there is a bouncer at this hostel, and a suspicious security deposit required (US$20; it is refundable), the digs are surprisingly bright. It's a co-ed dorm, sleeping 12 people with a kitchen, laundry facilities and cold-water showers, and it's set off the street in a garden plot.

Hotel Coco Palms
HOTEL $$

(☎2670-0367; www.hotelcocopalms.com; d from US$49; P❄@🔊) This popular low-key resort hotel has a variety of rooms including some apartments with kitchens. The hallways are light and airy with high ceilings, and double rooms are a fantastic deal with pastel accent wall and tasteful but fun bathroom tile. There's a pleasant outdoor deck and pool, and the small sushi bar (sushi US$5 to US$11) and bigger international restaurant keep guests well fed. But is the armed guard absolutely necessary?

🍴 Eating

For groceries, you can stock up at Coco Palms Supermercado (☎2670-0367; ⊙24hr), or the massive Auto Mercado (☎2670-2232; ⊙8am-8pm, 8am-9pm Fri & Sat) near the entrance of town.

La Vida Loca
TOP CHOICE
AMERICAN $

(☎2670-0181; mains US$4-9; ⊙11am-11pm) Across a creaky wooden footbridge on the south end of the beach is where you'll find this popular gringo hangout. They specialize in US-style comfort food such as burgers, nachos, meat loaf, chili dogs, clam chowder and more. It's also the best bar in town, hosting a monthly live music show with buffet (US$20).

Soda Teresita
SANDWICHES $

(☎2770-0665; sandwiches US$3-15; ⊙6:30am-8:30pm) On the west end of the soccer field, this popular *soda* is your best bet for a *torta* (sandwich), an array of breakfasts, as well as *ceviche* and all the grilled meats and fish dishes.

La Dolce Vita
PIZZERIA

(☎2670-1384; www.ladolcevitacostarica.com; mains US$9-18; ⊙8am-10pm) Set in the Pueblito Sur development, this is the local expat choice for wood-fired pizza in Playa Del Coco. The restaurant is lovingly set in a brick courtyard around a gurgling fountain, sprinkled with candlelit tables. They also do a range of pastas, a nice yellow fin tuna seared and drenched in a lime, caper, olive and cherry tomato sauce, and scald steaks and chops too.

Las Olas
SEAFOOD $$

(☎2670-2003; mains US$7-16; ⊙11am-10pm) Just north of the cramped commercial vortex on the main road, this is a dressed-up seafood *soda* with tablecloths, bamboo design accents, and recommended fresh seafood in the kitchen. The lounge area is quite cool, featuring molded concrete booths and dripping candles, whirling fans and a gurgling fountain.

Congo
CAFE **$$**

(☑2670-2135; mains US$6-8; ⊘8am-8pm Mon-Sat, 8am-6pm Sun; 🛜☑) Part cafe, part funky retail boutique, the interior is groovy with arced booths, rattan sofas and a deconstructed wood-and-granite coffee bar. They serve all the espresso drinks and an array of sandwiches and salads.

Restaurante Donde Claudio y Gloria
SEAFOOD **$$**

(☑2670-0256; www.dondeclaudioygloria.com; mains US$7-30; ⊘7am-9pm Sun-Thu, 7am-10pm Fri & Sat) Founded by Playa del Coco pioneers Claudio and Gloria Rojas, this casual, beachfront seafood restaurant has been a local landmark since 1955. It's a must for seafood-lovers, with such interesting dishes as spicy mahi in an almond, raisin and white-wine sauce. Be warned, service can be painfully slow, but the solid jazz soundtrack will keep you buoyant.

Citron
RESTAURANT **$$**

(☑2670-0942; www.cirtoncoco.com; mains US$11-16; ⊘5:30pm-10pm Mon-Sat) A high-end spot in the new Pacifica Shopping Mall. They do a nice tenderloin carpaccio and mixed *ceviche*, plate Catalonian sea bass with chard and have mouth-watering caramelized pork tenderloin. There's a good desert menu too.

Drinking

If you're looking for entertainment that doesn't involve drinking, you've come to the wrong town.

Beach Bums
BAR

(☑2670-0110; www.facebook.com/pages/Beach-Bums-Bar-Grill-Costa-Rica/157328027619427; ⊘11am-midnight; 🛜) A huge beach barn open to the sand and sea, blazed with graffiti murals, nailed down with a surfboard bar, icing the coldest beer in town. They have live music from 6pm to 9pm Wednesday to Saturday and on Sunday evenings.

La Vida Loca
BAR

(☑2670-0181; ⊘11am-2am) Keep the party moving at La Vida Loca, with live music on some weekends.

Zi Lounge
CLUB

(☑2670-1978; ⊘11:30am-2:30am; 🛜) A snazzy night spot, trying oh so hard to be Ibiza sleek, while stuck in a beer-drinking fishing port. Still, this bass-thumping outdoor mosh pit draped in bold tapestries is not unattractive. Thursday is ladies night.

ⓘ Information

The police station and a small **post office** are southeast of the plaza by the beach. The few people arriving at Playa del Coco by boat will find the **migración (immigration) office** across from Deep Blue Diving Adventures.

Banco Nacional South of the center on the main road into town, exchanges US dollars and traveler's checks.

BAC Bank (Pacífico Plaza) 24hr ATM

BCR Bank (⊘9am-4pm Mon-Fri) Changes US dollars. The ATM is operational from 5am to 10pm.

Cabinas Catarino (☑2670-0156; per hour US$2)

Main Post Office (⊘8am-noon & 1-5:30pm) Located near the entrance of town next to Flor de Itabo hotel.

ⓘ Getting There & Away

BUS All buses arrive and depart from the main terminal next to Immigration.

Filadelfia, for connection to Santa Cruz US$1; 45 minutes; departs 11:30am and 4:30pm.

Liberia US$1; one hour; departs seven times from 5:15am to 8pm.

San José (Pulmitan) US$8; five hours; departs 4am, 8am and 2pm.

CAR Note that there's no gas station in town; the nearest one is in Sardinal, about 7.5km inland from Playa del Coco.

TAXI A taxi from Liberia to Playa del Coco costs US$50. Taxis between Playa del Coco and Playas Hermosa or Ocotal will cost about US$20.

Playa Hermosa

The other Hermosa is not the legendary surf beach, but a rather lovely wide and languid sheltered bay, framed by headlands, sprinkled with coconut palms and *manzanillo*. Although it's only 5.5km (by road) north of Playa del Coco, and development is springing up rapidly along this entire coastline, Hermosa feels more dignified. Bill Beard's Diving Safaris (☑2672-1259; www.billbeardcostarica.com) has been scuba diving and snorkeling since 1970. Aqua Sport (☑2672-0050) offers kayaks for rent, fishing and snorkeling tours.

🛏 Sleeping

Do it the Tico way and camp for free under a few shady spots at the far southern end of the main beach.

Hotel Playa Hermosa
HOTEL **$$$**

(☑2672-0046; www.hotelplayahermosa.com; r from US$198; 🅿❄@🛜🏊) *Hermosa* (pretty) would be the simplest way to describe this lovely all-suite hotel, notched into the southern headland, with spectacular design elements such as exposed steel and thick limestone columns. All the well-appointed rooms ring a pool and beautifully landscaped garden. Get here via the first beach access road.

Hotel El Velero   RESORT $$
(☎2672-1017, 2672-0036; www.costaricahotel.net; d US$90; P✳🐕🏊) Just steps from the beach, this resort hotel has 22 spacious and fully equipped rooms decorated with woodwork, bamboo beds and colorful bedspreads, pastel accent walls, and granite washbasins. Ask for a seafront room on the second floor for maximum views.

Cabinas La Casona   CABINA $
(☎2672-0025; gaviotalouise@hotmail.com; s/d US$30/40; P) One block east of the beach, these seven cutesy, cozy *cabinas* with whitewashed rooms, small kitchenette, TV and hot-water bathroom are ideal for self-caterers.

Hotel Villa Bel Mar   HOTEL $$
(☎2672-0276; www.sevillaresort.es; s/d US$65/70; P✳🏊) A sweet Spanish-owned, beachfront inn with a pool that leads to a lawn that leads to the sand. Rooms are super clean and bright with colorful paint jobs, whimsical bathroom tile, cable TV, air-con and wi-fi.

Playa Hermosa Inn   HOTEL $$
(☎2672-0063; www.BandBonthebeach.com; s/d incl breakfast US$45/70; P✳🏊) Centered on a gigantic tree (horrifically pruned) and right on the beach, rooms have high beamed ceilings, two beds and a mini fridge. Cheaper digs are fan cooled and don't have sea views.

Iguana Inn   INN $
(☎2672-0065; s/d US$10/20; ✳) Set 100m back from the beach, this rambling bi-level inn has simple rooms, with lovely ceramic floors and coral paint jobs downstairs. Upstairs rooms are all wood and slightly larger.

✗ Eating & Drinking

Whether you're just passing through or spending the night, there are some nice kitchens here. Supplies are available at Mini Super Cenizaro, on the paved road into town.

Aqua Sport   COSTA RICAN $$
(☎2672-0050; mains US$9-23; ◷10am-10pm) In addition to kayak rental and tours they now have a tiki bar and fish house. Meals are

served in a dining room decorated with old buoys and conch shells. They keep it simple and typical in the kitchen with all the Tico dishes you've come to expect.

Restaurante Pescado Loco   SEAFOOD $$
(☎2672-0017; mains US$5-20; ◷1am-10pm) The 'Crazy Fish' serves up some of the freshest seafood around. We got excited about the *pulpo de gallego* (Galician octopus). The restaurant is parallel to the beach, north of the first access road.

Ginger   MEDITERRANEAN $
(☎2672-0041; plates US$5-12; ◷5-10pm Tue-Sun) If you're driving north, look toward the hills on the right and you'll see this stunner cantilevered into the trees. The chic ambience, which feels more like Ibiza than Costa Rica, is complemented by a gourmet list of Asian- and Mediterranean-inspired tapas.

❶ Getting There & Away

BUS Buses to Liberia and San José depart from the main road on the northern end of the beach and make a stop in Sardinal.

Liberia US$1; 1¼ hours; departs seven times from 5:30am to 7:30pm.

San José (Empresa Esquivel) US$9; six hours; departs 5am.

CAR If you're driving from Liberia, take the signed turnoff to Playa del Coco. The entire road is paved.

Further north of Hermosa, the main coastal road leads to the beaches along the Gulf of Papagayo. Playa Panama is right in the middle of the gulf with mangroves on one side and a placid bay that feels almost like a lake. In between are the rustic Playa Bonita and Playa Buena, which you can access with your own wheels and a bit of ingenuity.

TAXI A taxi from Liberia costs about US$20 and a taxi from Coco about US$15.

Playa Ocotal

Coming from the South, this is the last gasp of semi-rustica on the peninsula. The beach is gray and wooded, and the northernmost corner is quite picturesque. It's about 4km southwest of Playa del Coco by paved road, and aside from a few privately owned villas (which are mostly rented as vacation houses), there isn't an actual town here, though it's close enough to Coco for you to either drive or take a leisurely stroll here along the road. It's worth a trip simply to eat at Father Rooster's.

🏃 Activities

Rocket Frog Divers DIVING
(☎2670-1589; www.facebook.com/pages/Rocket
-Frog-Divers/253991077984154; 2 tanks US$80-125;
⊙7:30am-6:30pm) An awesome upstart dive
shop on the Los Almendros property, they hit
22 local dive sites and motor out to the Catalina Islands (two tanks US$125) to dive with
mantas. From May to November they make
the run to Isla Murcielagos to see bull sharks.

🛏 Sleeping & Eating

Los Almendros de Ocotal APARTMENT $$$
(☎2670-1744; www.losalmendrosrentals.com; studi-
os/apt/villas US$82/180/237; ❏✳@➳) Perched
on the hillside just above Playa Ocotal, these
studios and apartments are a great deal for
self-caterers. Studios sleep two, apartments
sleep four and villas sleep six. Some units
have a private pool and terrace.

Father Rooster Bar & Grill PUB $$
(☎2670-1246; www.fatherrooster.com; mains US$7-
14; ⊙11am-9:30pm) This gastropub by the sea
serves up a good variety of grilled and Tex-
Mex dishes, and you cannot beat the location – especially if you sit in the rockers on
the shaded wooden terrace or at tables under the palms sunk into the sand.

Beaches South of Playa Ocotal

Although they're next to one another, Playas
Danta, Pan de Azúcar, Potrero, Flamingo,
Brasilito and Conchal have relatively little
in common. The beaches range from gray
to white sand to crushed seashells, while the
range of development is also random.

Although it's tempting to take the 'road'
from Sardinal to Potrero, there's a reason
why locals call this route the 'Monkey Trail.'
The first 8km of gravel road leading to the
small town of Nuevo Colón is fine, but the
second half is pretty brutal, and should only
be tackled in dry season with a 4WD. The
Monkey Trail begins 5km west of El Coco;
turn right at the Castrol Oil sign and follow the signs for Congo Trail Canopy Tour
(☎2666-4422; US$65). At the 'T' intersection
in Nuevo Colón, turn left, bear left at the
fork and continue for 5km until you reach
Congo Canopy. From there, it's a hair-raising
6km drive to Bahía Potrero.

To avoid the rough roads, return to the
main peninsular highway from El Coco,
then head south through Filadelfia and on
to Belén (a distance of 18km), from where
a paved road heads 25km west to Huacas.
Take the road leading north until you hit the
ocean in Brasilito. Turn right and head north:
you'll pass Playa Flamingo and Bahía Potrero
before reaching Playa Pan de Azúcar. If you
make a left instead and head south, you will
end up at Playa Conchal. If you're into sea
kayaking, the proximity of the beaches to one
another makes for some great day trips.

PLAYA PAN DE AZÚCAR

Although buses stop at Potrero, those with
their own ride can head 3km north on a
recently paved road to 'Sugar-Bread Beach,'
which derives its name from the strip of
almost-white sand that's protected at both
ends by rocky headlands. This is one of the
most scenic stretches of road in all of northern Costa Rica, as dry rugged cliffs sheer
down into aquamarine coves sheltered by
off-shore islets. Difficult access and the lack
of cheap accommodations create an atmosphere of total seclusion, and the ocean here
is calm, clear and perfect for snorkeling.

Luxury at the Hotel Sugar Beach
(☎2654-4242; www.sugar-beach.com; d incl breakfast from US$132; ❏✳@➳➳) is simple and
understated. The 22 lovely rooms are entered via elaborately hand-carved wooden
doors. Deluxe rooms are larger and have
stunning ocean views. But the real reason
you're here is to slow down and linger on an
isolated beach. Overheard in the lobby.

PLAYA DANTA

Next door to Playa Pan de Azúcar is Playa
Danta, blessed with its own serene and rustic bay. At research time a multi-use luxury
development called Las Catalinas was nearing completion, which is bittersweet. Bitter
because nature loses again. Sweet because
Lola's (www.lascatalinascr.com; dishes US$8-
13; ⊙10am-5pm), the Avellanas classic, has
a baby sister right here on the beach with
slanted chairs, open kitchen and a brilliant
menu (the smoothies are sinful and that
poke is sensational).

Next door to Lola's is Pura Vida Ride
(☎2654-6137; www.puravidaride.com; kayak &
snorkeling tours 1/2 people US$60/90). They rent
kayaks, mountain bikes, snorkel sets and offer stand-up paddling lessons (one/two
people US$60/100) and rentals (per hour
US$20). Multi-day cycling trips and spe-
cialized kayak tours with English speaking
guides are also available. Gear is top notch,
and they serve espresso and gelato too.

Around the point is Playa Dantita, a blonde beach kissed by aquamarine waters. Just walk the narrow trail from the north end of Danta, up and over the point and down to the white sand. That beach and point also happen to have the best snorkeling in the area.

BAHÍA POTRERO

Separated from Playa Flamingo by a rocky headland, several undeveloped beaches are strung along this low-key bay. The black-sand beach is Playa Prieta, the gorgeous white-sand beach is Playa Penca, where stand up paddle (SUP) boarders ply the sheltered turquoise bay toward gleaming offshore islets, and Playa Potrero, the biggest, is in between.

There's a small fishing pueblo at Potrero, just beyond the northern end of the beach. This is where the bus line ends, so the beaches here don't get the weekend rush found at Brasilito. Further south in the center of the bay, the village of Surfside is home to a growing US and Canadian retirement village knitted into the tropical dry woodland.

In Potrero, the Casa del Sol strip mall has a small gringo-run Welcome Center (2654-5460; 9am-5pm Mon-Sat), where you can pick up free maps and brochures. Nearby on the road toward the Monkey Trail, Banco de Costa Rica has a 24-hour ATM.

Sleeping

Hotel Isolina HOTEL $$
(2654-4333; www.isolinabeach.com; d US$68; P❄@🛜🏊) These attractive yellow buildings are set back from the northern end of the beach. Rooms have hot showers, cable TV and air-con, while larger villas have two bedrooms and a fully equipped kitchen. Ole, the attached restaurant, serves up Spanish specialties like paella and steamed mussels.

Oki Doki B&B $$
(8645-9427, 2654-5543; s/d US$45/55; 🏊) On the road to Portrero from Surfside, they call it a B&B, but this place feels more like a boutique motel. Rooms have ceramic tile floors, high ceilings, mirrored head boards (not as bad as it sounds) and groovy paint jobs. There's a lovely pool area and garden too.

Bahía del Sol RESORT $$$
(2654-4671, 2224-7290; www.bahiadelsolhotel. com; d/ste incl breakfast from US$180/410; P❄@🛜🏊) With a prime beachfront location at Playa Potrero, this luxurious resort gets high marks for four-star laid-back el-

egance. Large, tiled rooms and suites have all the amenities and surround a garden and spa. Out front, the lawn leads to a beach peppered with *palapas*.

Eating & Drinking

The Shack AMERICAN $$
(2654-6038; mains US$5-17; 8am-11pm; 🛜) A fabulous diner set beneath a stilted tin roof twirling with ceiling fans. Come for breakfast when homemade bagels and sausages are served. Lunch and dinner feature Tex-Mex flavor. They do a lobster roll and pizzas too.

El Castillo RESTAURANT $
(8893-9603; mains US$6-10; noon-midnight; 🛜) Why not dine in a castle? This crenelated, stone wall, would-be Surfside tourist magnet is brand new and rather cool, thanks to that fabulous old tree dangling with vines in the foreground. Tico-owned, they specialize in small plates with big flavors, and strobe vintage music videos on their projection screen.

Las Brisas Bar & Grill RESTAURANT $
(2654-4047; mains US$5-12; 11am-10pm) Just off the northwest corner of the soccer field in Potrero, this popular beachfront bar has been a local favorite since 1950. Villagers pack the joint nightly for *bocas*, beers and brilliant sunsets. Wednesday is ladies' night.

ℹ Getting There & Away

BUS Many buses begin their route in Potrero on the southeast corner of the soccer field. Buses to Playa Flamingo often stop in Potrero but ask locally before setting out as not every bus goes all the way into Potrero.

Liberia US$2; two hours; departs 8am, noon and 3pm

San José (Tralapa) US$11; five hours; departs 2:45am, 9am and 2pm Monday to Saturday, and 9am and 2pm on Sunday.

Santa Cruz US$2; one hour; departs nine times per day from 5am to 10pm.

CAR The drive from here to Playa Pan de Azucar is one of the most scenic stretches of paved road in all of Northern Costa Rica.

PLAYA FLAMINGO

Anytime a once pristine slice of paradise sprouts McMansions and condo subdivisions, and gets stitched up with a network of roads (paved and otherwise), it becomes easy to point fingers and raise hell about what was and what now is. And, yes, Flamingo does feel like a developer's raunchy fantasy. But none of that changes the fact that this sugary, postcard-worthy white sand and shell beach is glorious. Kissed by a serene blue sea with the rugged keys of the Catalinas floating off in the distance, it attracts a local Tico scene along with package tourists. Nose the air if you must, but why not enjoy the place?

🏃 Activities

Flamingo Adventures ADVENTURE SPORTS
(📞2654-5648; www.flamingoadventures.com) This one stop adventure outfitter in La Plaza mall can get you into all sorts of action. Think: horseback, ATV, surf, kayak, fishing and much more.

🛏 Sleeping & Eating

Mariner Inn INN $
(📞2654-4081; marinerinn@hotmail.com; d US$34; 🅿✳@🖵) This harbor-view old-school inn is an incredible deal. Rooms are a bit old, but not too shabby. The dark wood beds are Ikea chic, the ceramic Spanish tile is lovely and there's a fresh coat of paint and cable too. Formerly a sailor's hang, the bar is fantastic.

Flamingo Beach Resort RESORT $$$
(📞2654-4444; www.resortflamingobeach.com; d from US$149; 🅿✳@🏊) The gaudy Flamingo is the granddaddy of the area's resorts. With 91 four-star rooms, tennis courts, a pool and a wide restaurant terrace, it sprawls along the beautiful beach.

Marie's DINER $$
(📞2654-4136; meals US$6-17; ◷6:30am-9:30pm) Set in the La Plaza complex, Marie's is something of an upscale, thatched diner. They do steak sandwiches and burgers, fish tacos, egg and Cesar salad, rotisserie chicken and Jacuzzi-sized margaritas.

Mar y Sol RESTAURANT $$$
(📞2654-4151; www.marysolflamingo.com; mains US$7-28; ◷4pm-10pm Wed-Mon) For a special night out you can't go wrong at this hilltop treasure with stunning panoramic sea and sunset views. It is run by the French-American Taulere family, including accomplished chef Jean-Luc. Come early and enjoy the spectacular sunset.

Angelina's RESTAURANT $$$
(📞2654-4839; mains US$17-30; ◷4-10pm) Set in La Plaza, the creative fusion menu gets rave reviews, but it's pricey. The artful, frugal traveler comes early for their killer happy hour menu featuring Asian chicken wings, mini pork sliders and a frozen mojito.

❶ Getting There & Away

AIR The closest airport is about 16km away by paved road at Tamarindo, and has regular scheduled flights.

BUS Buses depart from the traffic circle near the entrance of town and travel via Brasilito. Schedules change often, so ask locally about departure times as well as the best place on the road to wait for the bus.

Liberia US$2; two hours; departs 8am, noon and 3pm

San José (Tralapa) US$11; five hours; departs 2:45am, 9am and 2pm Monday to Saturday, and 9am and 2pm on Sunday.

Santa Cruz US$2; one hour; departs nine times per day from 5am to 10pm.

PLAYA BRASILITO

Underrated Brasilito has an authentic pueblo feel. There's a town square, a beachfront soccer pitch, a pink-washed cobble stone *iglesia* and a friendly local Tico community. All of which makes up for the beach, which has its (much) betters on either side. Still, it's just a short stroll along the sea to sugary Conchal.

The owner of La Casita de Pescado (p220) offers the area's best horse tours. The nearest ATM is in Playa Flamingo.

🛏 Sleeping

Tropical Fun Cabinas CABINA $
(📞2654-5519; www.diversiontropical.com; s/d US$35/40; 🅿✳🖵🏊) Here's an outstanding deal on clean, if cramped, tiled rooms with cable TV and hot-water showers. Guests have free use of snorkel gear and mountain bikes, and there's a communal barbecue set by a rather nice pool.

Hotel Brasilito $$
(📞2654-4237; www.brasilito.com; r with/without air-con US$49/25; 🅿✳🖵) On the beach side of the plaza, this recommended hotel offers simple, bright and clean rooms with wood floors and tiled baths. If it's available, splurge for the sea-view room. It has a private hammock-strung patio ideal for soaking up the sunset.

Hotel y Restaurante Nany HOTEL $$
(📞2654-4320; hotelnany.net; s/d US$50/60; 🅿✳@🖵🏊) Set well back from the road and shrouded in mango and palm trees, this impressive Tico-run property offers large, good-value rooms painted in cheerful tropical colors. They come with cable, air-con and their pool is salinated, so no chlorine here.

Conchal Hotel
HOTEL $$

(☎2654-9125; www.conchalcr.com; d incl breakfast US$96; P✳@🐕🏊) The nine rooms at this bougainvillea- and palm-dappled lodge are quite nice and spacious with dimpled ceramic tile floors, queen beds, slanted beamed ceilings and unique design touches such as swerving wooden desks.

Eating & Drinking

La Casita de Pescado
SEAFOOD $$

(☎2654-5171; mains US$4-20; ⏰9am-9pm) Set on either side of the sandy road to Conchal this beachfront, Tico-owned fish house has cheap yet delicious seafood. The affable owner also offers horse tours (per person US$35) through area mountains to a secluded bay.

Il Forno Restaurant
RESTAURANT $$

(☎2654-4125; mains US$6-18; ⏰12:30pm-9:30pm; 🚗) This recommended Italian restaurant is in a romantic garden and has thin-crust pizza, homemade pastas and risottos, and enough fresh eggplant dishes to keep vegetarians happy and healthy.

Happy Snapper
SEAFOOD $$

(☎2645-4413; mains US$7-21; ⏰8am-noon; 🛜🍴) Got kids? Bring the whole family down to this thatched seafood feedlot with a swimming pool (free for customers) and a huge grassy lounge area.

Don Brasilito's
RESTAURANT

(☎2654-5318; bocas US$3-5; 🛜) Set a block north of the square, this massive dive is popular with the gritty old-school tourist set who descend from early afternoon. The wall-less interior offers ample seating and they serve *ceviche*, burgers and Mexican food if you must.

❶ Getting There & Away

Buses to and from Playa Flamingo travel through Brasilito. There is a bus ticket office at the north end of Brasilito – look for the blue house with the 'Tralapa Agencia (⏰8am-noon & 1-6pm Mon & Wed-Sat, 8am-noon, 1-3pm Sun) sign.

PLAYA CONCHAL

Just 1km south of Brasilito is Playa Conchal, one of the most beautiful beaches on the peninsula. The name comes from the billions of *conchas* (shells) that wash up on the beach, and are gradually crushed into coarse sand. The shallows drift from an intense turquoise to sea-foam green deeper out, a rarity on the Pacific coast. If you have snorkeling gear, this is the place to use it.

On weekends, the beach is often packed with locals, tourists and countless vendors, but on weekdays during low season, Playa Conchal can be pure paradise. The further south you stroll, the wider, sweeter and more spectacular the beach becomes.

The easiest way to reach Conchal is to simply walk 15 minutes down the beach from Playa Brasilito. You can also drive along the sandy beach road, though you'll be charged US$2 to park.

With 285 hectares of property, including an over-the-top, free-form pool and a championship golf course, the all-inclusive **Westin Resort & Spa** (☎2654-3500; www.starwoodhotels.com; d all inclusive from US$812; P✳@🛜🏊) really does have everything you could ever want and is the only hotel in Conchal.

Playa Grande

From Huacas, the southwesterly road leads to Playa Grande (across the estuary from Tamarindo), a beach that's wide and gorgeous, famous among conservationists and surfers alike. By day, the offshore winds create steep and powerful waves, especially at high tide. By nighttime, an ancient cycle continues to unfurl as leatherback sea turtles bearing clutches of eggs follow the ocean currents back to their birthplace. The name fits, as the beach runs from the Tamarindo estuary for three miles, around a dome rock – with tide pools and superb surf fishing – and onto equally grand Playa Ventanas. The water is exquisite, warm, clear and charged with dynamic energy. Even confident swimmers should obey those riptide signs, however. People have drowned here.

Since 1991 Playa Grande has been part of the Parque Nacional Marino Las Baulas De Guanacaste, which protects one of the most important leatherback nesting areas in the world. Add it all up and you have an epic beach town that attracted a growing expat community and lures return visitors who can't get enough Grande.

🏃 Activities

Surfing is most people's motivation for coming to Playa Grande, and it is indeed spectacular. If you get rolled too hard and need a doctor, find the Playa Grande Clinic (☎2653-2767, 24 hr emergency 8827-7774) next to Kike's Place.

Frijoles Locos
SURFING

(☎8354-2044; www.frijoleslocos.com; 9am-5pm) On the road into town, the friendly Ian and Corynne Bean rent and sell surfboards (US$10 to US$20 per day), give lessons (US$45 for one person, US$60 for two people), and offer massage therapy in their day spa around back. They repair dings here too.

Playa Grande Surf Store
SURFING

(☎2652-9227; board rental per day US$12-15; ☺8am-7pm) They rent long and short boards.

Playa Grande Surf Camp
SURFING

(☎8870-4164; www.playagrandesurfcamp.com; board rental per day US$15-20) Gerry and his cohorts rent short or long boards, and show you how to ride 'em.

Playa Grande Surf School
SURFING

(☎2653-0952; www.micasahostel.com; board rental per day US$15, lessons per person US$40) Based out of Mi Casa Hostel, this well-run surf school offers board rentals and lessons.

🍴 Sleeping & Eating

Hotels are signposted from the main road into Playa Grande. Bring a flashlight for walking around at night.

TOP CHOICE La Marejada Hotel
BOUTIQUE HOTEL $$

(☎2653-0594, in USA & Canada 800-559-3415; www.hotelswell.com; r US$70; ✽🛜❄) Hidden behind a bamboo fence, this stylish boutique nest is the friendliest, most relaxing hotel in Playa Grande. The eight elegantly understated rooms have stone tile floors, rattan and wooden furnishings, and queen beds. The lovely owners, Carli and Gail, are attentive to your every need, and after a day of surfing, treat yourself to an in-house massage (per hour US$60). Carli will skillfully wring out all of your kinks.

Rip Jack Inn
INN $$

(☎2653-0480; www.ripjackinn.com; d US$90; P✽@❄) This comfy, convivial inn has a handful of clean, modern, artfully painted rooms, lovely floor lamps, and doublewide macramé hammocks on the front porch. They offer regular yoga classes (US$12, schedule varies by the season), and the upstairs open-air restaurant-bar features pork loin marinated in brown sugar and Worcestershire, mahi slathered in lime sauce, and flank steak dressed in whiskey and cream. The sushi chef spears his own catch and serves it up raw. Even the burger is masterful. It's easily the best kitchen on the *playa*.

Playa Grande Surf Camp
CABINA $

(☎8870-4164; www.playagrandesurfcamp.com; dm per person US$10, s/d US$35/45; P✽🛜❄) This great budget option has three thatched, A-frame *cabinas* with private, hammock-strung porches, just steps from the beach. There's also a dorm, surf lessons and board rentals.

El Manglar & Mi Casa Hostel
VILLA, HOSTEL $

(☎2653-0952; www.micasahostel.com; dm/r/villa US$15/40/70; P@✿🏄) Near the southern end of the beach this funky, friendly faux-dobe villa property is actually two hotels in one. Villas have private patios, an outdoor grill and a cute kitchen and living area. Rooms have slightly less space but are still stylish and there's a hostel with a dorm. All choices surround lush grounds in the Palm Garden Estates neighborhood.

Playa Grande Inn
INN $$

(☎2653-0719; www.playagrandeinn.com; r US$50; P✽🛜❄) This old standby has recently had a good scrubbing. In fact, she was exfoliated down to her handsome hardwood bones. Clean rooms are basic and only slightly rickety. There's a small pool, and the restaurant and bar area is particularly cool with fun chain link and paper lanterns. The restaurant (mains US$6 to US$14) is open in the evenings with pub grub highlights including tuna Carpaccio, quesadillas and good thin-crust pizzas.

Cantarana
INN $$

(☎2653-0486; www.hotel-cantarana.com; s/d US$70/95) Nestled in the semi-gated Palm Beach Gardens *barrio*, this lovely, intimate inn has a glittering pool, spacious rooms with stylish pastel paint jobs, gorgeous bathroom tile and private patios. Service is outstanding and the upscale restaurant (mains US$16 to US$30), which is open evenings and serves Mediterranean surf and turf, comes highly recommended.

Hotel Las Tortugas
HOTEL $$

(☎2653-0423; www.lastortugashotel.com; d US$90; P✽@❄) Grande's bad old granddad, Louis Wilson, the owner of this hotel, is a local hero as he was instrumental in helping to designate Playa Grande as a national park. The hotel is steps from the beach and was carefully designed to keep ambient light away from the nesting area, and to block light from development to the north. Spacious rooms have air-con and hot-water bathroom, black flagstone floors, and sweet front porches.

222

CHRISTER FREDRIKSSON / LONELY PLANET IMAGES ©

3

AARON MCCOY / LONELY PLANET IMAGES ©

CHRISTER FREDRIKSSON / LONELY PLANET IMAGES ©

1. Playa del Coco (p212)
Playa del Coco is one of many picturesque beaches along the northern Península de Nicoya.

2. Reserva Natural Absoluta Cabo Blanco (p267)
This idyllic beach setting is the reward for reaching the end of the reserve's hiking trail.

3. Playa Avellanas (p231)
The popular Playa Avellanas was made famous in the classic surf movie *Endless Summer II*.

4. Montezuma (p260)
Horseback is one way of taking in the rugged coastline around Montezuma.

Hotel Bula Bula
HOTEL $$$

(☎2653-0975; www.hotelbulabula.com; r incl breakfast US$120; P❄@🐕) Located a few hundred meters inland near the Tamarindo estuary, rooms aren't huge, but they're decorated with whimsical art and have beamed ceilings. Factor in the landscaped grounds, inviting pool, and sweet rattan rockers on the porch and it's a win. But one of the biggest draws is **the Great Waltini's**. This onsite restaurant serves burgers, sandwiches and fajitas at lunch and grilled seafood and steak dinners at night. Portions are massive, and so are the margaritas. You can arrange a boat across the river to Tamarindo from here, as well.

Kike's Place
RESTAURANT $

(☎2653-0834; www.kikesplacecr.com; mains US$4-10; ⊗7am-midnight) On the road into town, take note of Kike's (pronounced 'kee-kays'), the friendly local bar and restaurant where you can shoot pool, grind *ceviche* and let your hair down. There are live bands on Saturday night, and they have a handful of basic affordable rooms from US$20.

Cafe Del Pueblo
PIZZERIA $$

(☎2653-2315; mains US$10-18; ⊗5-9pm) Just east of town, and recommended by local foodies, this pizzeria also does homemade pasta and fresh seafood dishes too.

❶ Getting There & Away

There are no buses to Playa Grande. You can drive to Huacas and then take the paved road to Matapalo, followed by a rough dirt road to Playa Grande.

Alternatively, catch a boat across the estuary from Tamarindo to the southern end of Grande (around US$1 per person, from 7am to 4pm). From Playa Grande arrange your boat to Tamarindo at Hotel Bula Bula (p224). And if you want a scenic, quirky ride through the mangroves on your way to or from the boat, call the **Timbuktuktuk** (☎8519-0918; per person US$5).

Parque Nacional Marino Las Baulas De Guanacaste

Playa Grande is considered one of the most important nesting sites in the world for the *baula* (leatherback turtle). In 1991 the entire beach and adjacent land (700 hectares), along with 220 sq km of ocean, was designated Las Baulas National Marine Park (☎2653-0470; admission incl tour US$25; ⊗8am-noon & 1-5pm, tours 6pm-2am). This government act followed a 15-year battle between conservationists and various parties including poachers, developers and tour operators.

The ecosystem is primarily composed of mangrove swamp, ideal for caiman and crocodile, as well as numerous bird species, including the beautiful roseate spoonbill. Other creatures to look for when visiting are howler monkey, raccoon, coati, otter and a variety of crab. But, as is to be expected, the main attraction is the nesting of the world's largest species of turtle, which can weigh in excess of 400kg. Nesting season is from October to March, and it's fairly common to see turtles lay their eggs here on any given night. Of course, it might not be a leatherback. Chances of seeing one of these giants hover around 10%, while you are 95% sure to see a green or black turtle nest.

The leatherback is critically endangered and, despite increased conservation efforts, fewer leatherbacks are nesting on Playa Grande each year. In an effort to protect the dwindling population, park rangers collect eggs and incubate them to increase their chances of survival. Even so, sea turtles must hatch on the beach and enter the water by themselves, otherwise memory imprinting does not occur, and the hatchlings will never return to their birthplace to nest. It's estimated that only 10% of hatchlings survive to adulthood, though leatherbacks can live more than 50 years, and females lay multiple clutches of eggs during a single nesting season.

During the day, the beach is free and open to all, which is a good thing as the breaks off Playa Grande are fast, steep and consistent. At night, however, it is only possible to visit the beach on a guided tour, to ensure that nesting cycles may continue unhindered.

🏃 Activities

The park office (p224) is by the northern entrance to Playa Grande. Reservations for turtle-watching can be made up to seven days in advance, and they're highly recommended as there is limited space. You can show up without one, as there are frequent no-shows, though this is less likely on weekends and during the holiday season.

Many hotels and tourist agencies in Tamarindo can book tours that include transportation to and from Playa Grande, admission to the park and the guided tour. The whole package costs about US$45. If you don't have your own transportation, this is the best way to go.

The show kicks off anytime from 9pm to as late as 2am. You might only have to wait for 10 minutes before a turtle shows up, or you could be there for five hours. Bring a book or a deck of cards for entertainment. It could be a very long night – but well worth it.

Tourists are not allowed on the beach until the turtles have made it to dry sand. Guards with two-way radios will alert your guide, who will accompany you to a designated viewing area. Photography, filming or lights of any kind are prohibited to protect the turtles. Over the span of one to two hours, you can watch as the turtle digs its nest, lays about 80 to 90 silver shiny eggs and then buries them in the sand (while grunting and groaning).

If you're looking for a project, the park office usually accepts volunteers to monitor and catalog each nest.

Playa Tamarindo

Well, they don't call it Tamagringo for nothing. Tamarindo's perennial status as Costa Rica's top surf and party destination has made it the first and last stop for legions of tourists. It stands to reason, then, that this is the most developed beach on the peninsula with no shortage of hotels, bars and restaurants. Yet, despite its party-town reputation, Tamarindo is more than just drinking and surfing. It forms a part of the Parque Nacional Marino Las Baulas de Guanacaste, and the beach retains an allure for kids and adults alike. Foodies will find some of the best restaurants in the country. Families and students will appreciate the fierce competition that has kept lodging prices reasonably low. And Tamarindo's central location makes it a great base for exploring the northern peninsula.

Amazingly, there's no gas station here. For that, you'll have to drive 15 paved kilometers to Huacas, hang a right and go up the hill. The gas station is 4km ahead, on the right.

🏃 Activities

Sportfishing
There are more than 30 fishing outfitters offering a variety of tour packages. Prices vary wildly depending on boat size, but expect to pay at least US$250 for a half-day tour.

Surfing
Like a gift from the surf gods, Tamarindo is often at its best when neighboring Playa Grande is flat. The most popular wave is a medium-sized right that breaks directly in front of the Tamarindo Diria hotel. The waters here are full of virgin surfers learning to pop up. There is also a good left that's fed by the river mouth, but be advised that crocodiles are occasionally sighted here, particularly when the tide is rising (which is, coincidentally, the best time to surf), and there can be head-high waves in front of the rocks near Le Beach Club.

More advanced surfers will appreciate the bigger, faster and less crowded waves at Playa Langosta (on the other side of the point); Playas Avellanas, Negra and Junquillal to the south; and Playa Grande to the north.

A number of surf schools and tour operators line the main road in Tamarindo. Surf lessons are about US$45 for 1½ to two hours, and most operators will let you keep the board for a few hours beyond that to practice.

Kelly's Surf Shop   SURFING
(☏2653-1355; www.kellysurfshop.com; board rental per day/week US$15/90; ⊘9am-6pm) One of the very best surf shops in the area, they have a terrific selection of newish boards that they rent by the day or week, and have premium boards that cost a bit more.

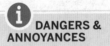

DANGERS & ANNOYANCES

Tamarindo has a growing drug and prostitution problem. Vendors openly ply their wares on the main road by the rotunda, and some bars can get rough at closing time. Theft is a problem. Leave your hotel room locked, use safes and don't leave valuables on the beach. If you're driving, never leave anything in your car.

There have also been a few murders and disappearances over the past several years in Tamarindo. Remember, although Costa Rica is by far the safest country in Central America, it's important to keep your wits about you. Travel in pairs. If you're alone, tell somebody where you're going. Don't get so wasted that you become vulnerable to crime or accident. Use common-sense precautions that you would practice anywhere.

Playa Tamarindo

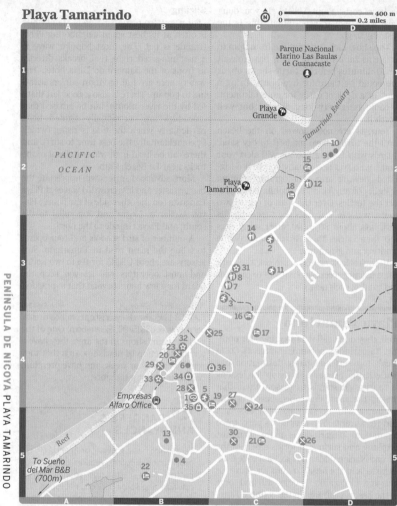

Matos Surf Shop   SURFING
(☏2653-0845; www.matossurfshop.com; board rental from US$10, lessons US$35; ☺lessons 9-11am & 2-4pm) The granddaddy of local surf shops is owned by an Uruguyan DJ-photo-entrepreneur. They offer lessons, and rent and sell boards at the cheapest rates in town.

Witch's Rock Surf Camp   SURFING
(☏2653 0239; www.witchsrocksurfcamp.com; ☺8am-8pm) Board rentals, surf camps, lessons and regular excursions to Witch's Rock and Ollie's Point are available, though they're pricey. Endless Summer surf legend, Robert August, shapes boards here.

Tsunami Surf   SURFING
(☏8887-0207, 2653-0280; board rental US$15, lessons 1/2 people US$45/50) Tsunami Surf rents good-quality boards, offers surf lessons, and arranges transport to and from Tamarindo.

Other Activities

Bike Shop   CYCLING
(☏2653-2136; cruisers/mountain bikes per day US$15/25) Next to Kelly's Surf Shop, this no-nonsense bike garage offers one of the best selections of cruisers and mountain bikes in Tamarindo.

Playa Tamarindo

Blue Trailz CYCLING
(☏2653-1705; www.bluetrailz.com; tours US$55-75; ⏰7am-7pm Mon-Sat) Blue Trailz are the local experts on mountain biking, distance cycling, bike tours and repairs. They also rent beach cruisers (two hours US$10, all day US$20).

Agua Rica Diving Center DIVING
(☏2653-0094, 8888-0225; www.aguarica.net; two tanks US$100) Italian-owned Agua Rica Diving Center, the area's scuba-diving expert, offers snorkeling and an assortment of dives in the Catalina Islands, including diving certification classes and trips to the Cocos Islands.

Hacienda Pinilla GOLF
(☏2680-3000; www.haciendapinilla.com; 9 holes/18 holes US$95/185) Just outside Tamarindo, near the village of San José de Pinilla, Hacienda Pinilla has a 7500-yard, par-72 course that was designed by noted architect Mike Young.

Estudio YOGA
(☏8346-8005; www.seryogastudio.com; US$15) There's a full schedule of daily yoga, tai chi and Pilates mat classes at this airy and bright studio on the top floor of Tamarindo plaza.

Tamarindo Tennis Club TENNIS
(☏2653-0898; www.facebook.com/tamarindo.tennis.club; court rental per person US$10; ⏰7:30am-5pm) If you're up for a game there are two well-maintained hard courts at this tiny tennis club on the property of a contemporary B&B.

🎓 Courses

Use your vacation time wisely by learning Spanish. There are several language schools in Tamarindo, all of which charge about US$420 to US$440 for a week-long intensive course (beginner to advanced), including 'homestay' accommodations with a Tico family. Most schools offer multiple-week discounts, and 'Spanish & Surf' packages that include language lessons, surf classes, accommodations and board rentals for about US$600 per week. Options include the following:

Coastal Spanish Institute (☎2653-2673; www.coastalspanish.com)

Wayra (☎2653-0359; www.spanish-wayra.co.cr)

☞ Tours

Boat tours, snorkeling trips and scooter rentals can be arranged through various tour agencies in town. Many also rent out equipment.

Parque Nacional Marina Las Baulas De Guanacaste office ECOTOUR
(☎2653-1687; tours to turtle nesting sites US$25) The official Tamarindo branch of the nearby national park, they book turtle-spotting night tours and offer daytime estuary tours. This is also where you'll grab a boat across the river to Playa Grande.

Papagayo Excursions BOAT TOUR
(☎2653-0254; tamarindobeach.net/papagayo) The longest-running outfitter in town organizes a variety of tours including visits to turtle-nesting sites.

Go Adventures TOUR
(☎2653-1563; www.goadventurescostarica.com; half day up to 6 people US$250) Go Adventures runs sportfishing trips on their own boat and also book transport, snorkeling and diving trips.

🛏 Sleeping

We constantly receive complaints about Tamarindo hotels, so choose wisely. Be mindful, most budget hotels have cold water only. Midrange options generally have hot-water bathrooms. The bulk of top-end hotels can arrange tours in the area, and accept credit cards. The rates given are high-season rates; low-season rates can be 25% to 40% lower.

TOP CHOICE La Oveja Negra HOSTEL $
(☎2653-0005; www.laovejanegrahostel.com; dm/d US$15/35; P@🛜) The hippest hostel in town has an international crowd. You'll like the super clean, tiled rooms; the funky art on the walls; and the groovy multihued sofa and open kitchen in the common areas. The only demerit: private rooms share baths. They offer board rentals and surf lessons (group/private US$30/45) too.

Tamarindo Backpackers HOSTEL $
(☎2653-4545; www.tamarindobackpackers.com; dm US$16, d with/without bath US$50/40; P🌀❄@🛜🏊) Hidden down a quiet cul-de-sac in a wooded, residential neighborhood, you'll find a fantastic hostel in a gorgeous yellow hacienda. The doubles with private baths are downright luxurious with high-end Spanish-tiled floors, beamed ceilings and fat flat-screens on the wall. The dorms are quite clean but otherwise just okay, but the common area includes lovely tropical gardens, a small pool and hammocks.

Blue Trailz Hostel HOSTEL $
(☎2653-1705; dm US$12, r US$55) Set right behind a surf shop, this immaculate and intimate hostel has two dorm rooms downstairs with air-con, new tile floors and kitchenette, and two identical private rooms upstairs that sleep up to four.

Beach House Tamarindo HOSTEL $
(☎2653-2848; www.beachhousetamarindo.com; dm incl breakfast US$13-15, r US$30; P@🛜) The only beachfront hostel, this drowsy, dreamy, friendly nest at the river mouth offers small, simple but clean dorm rooms with fan or air-con. There's a communal kitchen, living room, patio, balcony, immediate beach access and free breakfast. They have two private rooms as well.

Pura Vida Hostel HOSTEL $
(☎8747-8780; www.puravidahostel.com; dm/r US$12/35; ➡❄@🛜) Yes, the entryway does feel a bit prison blocky, what with all the razor wire, but inside the leafy compound are dorms and private rooms accented by hand-painted flourishes and mirrored mosaics. Private rooms have their own baths and management wants you to know that they promote energy healing and discourage partying. How... joyous... of... them.

Cabinas Marielos CABINA $$
(☎2653-0954, 2653-0141; www.cabinasmarieloscr.com; s/d US$40/55; P❄) One of the best deals in town, this underrated property has a variety of *cabinas* to fit every budget. All have firm beds, colorful patios, slanted beamed ceilings, speckled tile floors, and share a communal kitchen.

Hotel La Laguna del Cocodrilo HOTEL $$
(☎2653-0255; www.lalagunadelcocodrilo.com; d US$60-70, ste US$120; P❄🛜) A beachfront location blesses this charming French-owned hotel, with well-kept rooms overlooking

either the shady grounds or the ocean and estuary. Adjacent to a crocodile-filled lagoon (hence the name), the hotel opens onto a rocky garden that rolls to the sand.

15 Love
B&B $$

(☑2653-0898; www.15lovebedandbreakfast.com; d incl breakfast US$95) A self-proclaimed contemporary B&B, this white-washed, concrete, mod villa with weathered louvered accents overlooks a plunge pool and two hard courts and is within earshot of the sea. Interiors are quite stylish with polished concrete floors, high ceilings, floating beds and designer light fixtures.

Sueño del Mar B&B
B&B $$$

(☑2653-0284; www.sueno-del-mar.com; d US$195, casitas US$220-240; P❋@❂❆) This exquisite bed and breakfast on Playa Langosta is set in a stunning faux-dobe Spanish-style *posada*. The six rooms have four-poster beds, artfully placed crafts and open-air garden showers, while the romantic honeymoon suite has a wraparound window with sea views. There is private beach access beyond the pool and tropical garden, and a priceless, pervasive atmosphere of seclusion and beauty. To preserve it, no children are allowed.

La Palapa
HOTEL $$$

(☑2653-0362; www.lapalapatamarindo.com; d US$120; P❋❂) This intimate eight-room beachfront hotel offers loft beds, ocean views and big-screen TVs with DVD player. The terra-cotta–tiled floors lead to shaded terraces on the beach.

Hotel La Colina
APARTMENT $$$

(☑2653-0303; www.la-colina.com; apartments from US$125; P❋❂❆▥) Seek out this sprawling, leafy, kitschy spot, where all rooms are full apartments with kitchens, living areas and jaw-dropping views from private tiled patios. The three top-floor penthouse suites are simply massive with tiled floors; rattan furnishings; a full kitchen; two bedrooms; romantic, hand-painted murals on the walls and vaulted beamed ceilings.

El Jardín del Edén
HOTEL $$$

(☑2653-0137; www.jardindeleden.com; standard/ superior incl breakfast US$153/190; P❋@❂❆) On a hill overlooking Tamarindo, this luxurious French-run hotel has 36 exquisite rooms, each with a sitting area and private patio or balcony. There is a swim-up bar and gorgeous views from the pool deck.

✗ Eating

Tamarindo has some of the best restaurants in Costa Rica. But be prepared to pay – a cheap meal in this town is about as common as a nesting turtle. Super 2001 (⊙7am-9:30pm Mon-Sat, 8am-8:30pm Sun) and Super Compro (⊙8am-9pm Mon-Sun) are well stocked with international groceries.

Buon Apetito
ITALIAN $

(☑2653-0598; mains US$6-10; ⊙8am-9pm) An authentic Italian deli with imported meats and cheeses piled and served on home-baked ciabatta by the endearing Italian *madre* at the counter. She also does pizza, pasta and, ahem, gelato. These are the best sandwiches in Tamarindo. Grab one and munch on the beach.

El Casado del Carro
COSTA RICAN

(casados US$4-6; ⊙noon-2pm) Señora Rosaria has been delivering top-quality meat and chicken *casados* from her late-model Toyota hatchback for nine years. Her devoted Tico following lines up daily at noon, and she generally sells out by 2pm. You'll get your meal in a Styrofoam platter (nobody's *perfecto*) and it will usually include yucca or plantains, rice, chicken or beef, and some tasty black beans. Get yours with a squeeze of chili.

Longboards
AMERICAN $

(☑2653-0027; mains US$4-11 ; ⊙11am-10pm Thu-Tue) An American-style barbeque joint and expat favorite, with excellent pulled pork, ribs and beef brisket. Belly up to the surfboard-shaped tables and grind some proper barbeque.

Gil's Place
RESTAURANT $

(☑2653-2641; dishes US$3-8; ⊙7:30am-8:30pm) A Tamarindo classic thanks to *grandisimo* burritos stuffed with chicken, beef or fish, beans, and cheese. And if you crave burritos for breakfast, he does those too.

Felafel Bar
MEDITERRANEAN $

(☑2653-1268; mains US$5-8 ; ⊙9am-11pm) This new Mediterranean cafe serves all the faves, shwarma, falafel, tabbouleh, hummus and kebabs. And like any good shwarma joint they routinely (if not regularly) stay open into the wee smalls.

Nogui's
SEAFOOD $$

(☑2653-0029; mains US$8-22; ⊙11am-11pm) A fish shack with real Mediterranean charm, this fabulously romantic, wooden and stained-glass, tin-roof gem on the beach flaunts local seafood. Make a dinner reservation, or get sloshed at the bar with the occasionally rowdy (but not too rowdy) regulars.

Lazy Wave
SOUTH AMERICAN $$$

(☎2653-0737; meals US$8-25; ◎6-10pm Sat-Thu) Dine at a table if you must, but the best place to enjoy your meal and glass of wine is on the covered pavilion, where you can curl up amid pillows in cushy lounge chairs. If you're out to woo that hot thing you met last night, this hip nightspot, built around a huge tree, is a good place to start the evening. There's a solid wine list, good mix of cocktails and Asian- and Euro-influenced *bocas* as well as a full menu that offers everything from grilled lobster tails to mussels and escargot.

La Baula
PIZZERIA $$

(☎2653-1450; mains US$9-13; ◎5:30am-11pm; ⊕) By far the best pizza in Tamarindo – this casual open-air restaurant has real wood-fired pizzas, pastas and other Italian fare. It's also one of the most family-friendly restaurants in town, with a playground to keep the kids entertained.

Dragonfly Bar & Grill
RESTAURANT $$

(☎2653-1506; www.dragonflybarandgrill.com; mains US$10-16; ◎6-11pm Mon-Sat; 🖥) Dragonfly is a local favorite, not just for its refined menu, but also for its lovely tiki-bar atmosphere and the chic tent-like structure of the dining room. The menu has a fusion bent, featuring pork chops with chipotle-apple chutney and Thai-style crispy fish cake with curried corn. Linger a while over your wine and perhaps you can find room for a divine dessert.

Seasons
RESTAURANT $$$

(☎8368-6983; www.seasonstamarindo.com; mains US$15-18; ◎6-10pm Mon-Sat) Don't leave town without eating here. Israeli chef Shlomy serves innovative dishes with Mediterranean accents that change daily depending on availability of local ingredients. One of our favorite plates was the seared tuna in a chili marinade and honey glaze. Located at Hotel Arco Iris, the understated yet elegant open-air restaurant has indoor seating or romantic poolside tables. Reservations are recommended.

🍷 Drinking & Entertainment

On Tamarindo weekends, all you really have to do is follow the scene wherever it happens to go. Cruising the main drag has the festive feel of spring break, and nearly every bar hosts a ladies' night.

Aqua Disco
CLUB

(☎2653-2782; www.aquadiscoteque.com) Aqua Disco is the only real nightclub in Tamarindo. The best nights are Monday (ladies' night) and Saturday, when for a US$4 cover charge they have an open bar for two hours.

Sharky's
CLUB

(☎8729-8274; www.facebook.com/pages/Sharkys-Rock-n-Roll-Sports-Bar/100457196739718?sk=info; ◎6pm-2am) Sharky's, an indestructible concrete-floored dance hall, is a consistent choice especially on Saturday, when crowds spill out onto the street for the ladies' 80s night.

El Garito
LOUNGE

(◎5pm-2am) A new and oh-so-intimate lounge with seemingly divergent house and punk music cravings in Plaza Tamarindo.

Bar 1
BAR

(☎2653-2586; www.facebook.com/pages/BAR-1/88966320905?sk=info; ◎6:30pm-2am Thu-Tue) The classy Bar 1 is an open-air people-watching jewel. It's on the third floor at Plaza Tamarindo, and the sushi is recommended here too.

Le Beach Club
CLUB

(☎2653-0178; ◎11am-close) This place has beds and hammocks on the sand and DJs on Saturday. They also get an excellent sundowner crowd who drink, coo, giggle and swoon to throbbing club hits as the orb melts into the sea.

Pacifico
BAR

(www.facebook.com/people/Pacifico-Bar-Tamarindo/100001253258686?sk=info; ◎6pm-2am) Pacifico like to fancy themselves a dance club, but really they're a tropical dive bar with occasional live bands and DJs, and that's okay. Better in fact. Thursday is reggae night.

🛍 Shopping

Morena
CLOTHING

(☎2653-4539; Info@bikinishopcr.com; ◎10am-6pm) An exquisite cubbyhole bikini shop that also offers elegant silver and beaded jewelry, and lovely silk scarves. Worth seeking out for a retail therapy fix.

ℹ Information

Tourist information is available from any of the tour operators in town, your hotel and the **Tamarindo News** (www.tamarindonews.com).

BAC San José (☎2653-1617; Plaza Conchal; ◎8:30am-3:30pm) Has an ATM and exchanges US dollars and traveler's checks.

Backwash Laundry (per kg US$2; ⊘8am-8pm Mon-Sat) Get your filthy unmentionables washed, dried and folded.

Banco de Costa Rica (Plaza Conchal) 24hr ATM.

Centro Medico Tamarindo (☑2653-1974, emergency 8835-8074; ⊘24hr)

Internet Bakanos (per hour US$2.50; ⊘8am-10pm) On the second floor above an Italian deli, this office offers high-speed internet connections and international phone calls.

HSBC 24hr ATM.

❶ Getting There & Away

Air
The airstrip is 3km north of town; a hotel bus is usually on hand to pick up arriving passengers, or you can take a taxi. During high season, **Sansa** (☑2653-0012) has two daily flights to and from San José (each way US$111), while NatureAir (each way US$120) has three. All passengers must pay an additional US$3 departure tax. Some flights transit through Liberia.

Bus
Buses for San José depart from the Empresas Alfaro office behind the Babylon bar. Other buses depart across the street from Zullymar Hostel. It's possible to get to Montezuma or Mal País and Santa Teresa by bus for about US$11 total, but it will take all day and multiple changes: take the 5:45am bus to Liberia, bus to Puntarenas, ferry to Playa Naranjo, bus to Cobano and bus to Montezuma or Mal País.

Liberia US$3; 2½ hours; departs 13 times per day from 4:30am to 6:30pm.

San José US$11; six hours; departs 5:30am and 2pm. Alternatively, take a bus to Liberia and change for frequent buses to the capital.

Santa Cruz US$2; 1½ hours; departs 6am, 9am, noon, 2pm, 3pm and 4pm.

Car & Taxi
By car from Liberia, take Hwy 21 to Belén, then Hwy 155 via Huacas to Tamarindo. If you're coming from the southern peninsula, drive just past Santa Cruz, turn left on the paved road to 27 de Abril, then northwest on a decent dirt road for 19km to Tamarindo. These routes are well signed.

A taxi to or from Santa Cruz costs about US$30, and US$50 to or from Liberia. Alternatively, consider a minibus shuttle service. **Tropical Tours** (☑8849-8569, 2640-1900; www.transportation-costarica.com) offers door-to-door service to Montezuma and Mal País (US$42 per person, five hours). **Tamarindo Shuttle** (☑2653-2626, 2653-4444; www.tamarindoshuttle.com) services the Aeropuerto Internacional Daniel Oduber Quiros in Liberia (US$20 per person, 1½ hours), and will pick you up or drop you off at your hotel of choice.

❶ Getting Around
Boats on the northern end of the beach can be hired to cross the estuary for daytime visits to the beach at Playa Grande at the National Park station (p228). The ride is US$1 per person and run from about 7am to 5pm.

Many visitors arrive in rental cars. If you get here by air or bus, you can rent bicycles and dirt bikes in town. There's no gas station, but you can buy expensive gas from drums at the hardware store near the entrance to town. (It's cheaper to fill up in Santa Cruz or at the gas station in Huacas.) Rent wheels with **Hola Rent a Car** (☑2653-2000; www.hola.net), **Alamo** (☑2653-0727; www.alamocostarica.com) or **Mapache Rent a Car** (☑2586-6300, reservations, San Jose 2586-6363; www.mapache.com).

Playas Avellanas & Negra

These popular surfing beaches were made famous in the surf classic *Endless Summer II*, and Playa Avellanas is still an absolutely stunning, pristine sweep of pale golden sand. Backed by mangroves in the center and two gentle hillsides on either end, there's plenty of room for surfers and sunbathers to have an intimate experience even when there are lots of heads in town. The wave here is decent for beginners and intermediate surfers. Little Hawaii is the powerful and open-faced right featured in *Endless Summer II*, while Beach Break barrels at low tide. Still, advanced surfers get bored here.

Playa Negra is also undeniably romantic. Though the sand is a bit darker and the beach is broken up by rocky outcrops, those gorgeous dusty back roads link tidepools of expat shredders who picked this place to exist (and surf) peacefully. Though there isn't much local soul here, it's still a stunning nook blessed by a world-class right that barrels. Further south is (hush hush) Playa Tortuga, an epic break for advanced surfers only. The waves are best between April and November, but start getting good in March.

The beaches begin 15km south of Tamarindo. To get here backtrack from Tamarindo 5km to the village of Villareal, and turn right onto the dirt road. This road gets progressively worse and usually requires a 4WD. If you're not coming from Tamarindo, head west on the paved highway from Santa Cruz, through 27 de Abril to Paraíso, then follow the signs. While you're at the beach, be absolutely certain that nothing is visible in your car as professional thieves operate in this area.

WHAT TO DO IF YOU'RE CAUGHT IN A RIPTIDE

Riptides account for the majority of ocean drownings, though a simple understanding of how these currents behave can save your life. Rip currents are comprised of three parts: the feeder current, the neck and the head. The feeder current consists of rapidly moving water that parallels the shore. When this water reaches a channel, it switches direction and flows out to sea, forming the neck of the rip. This is the fastest-moving part of the riptide, and can carry swimmers out to sea at a speed of up to 10km/h. The head is formed past the breakers where the current quickly dissipates.

If you find yourself caught in a riptide, it's important to conserve your energy and not to panic and fight the current – this is the principal cause of drownings. It's impossible to swim directly back to shore. Instead, tread water and let yourself be swept out past the breakers. Once you're in the head of the rip, you can swim parallel or diagonally to the shore until you're out of the channel, then swim back to shore with the waves.

Rip currents usually occur on beaches that have strong surf, and there are indicators, such as the brownish color on the surface of the water that is caused by swept-up sand and debris. If you're ever in doubt about the safety of a beach, inquire locally about swimming conditions. Remember, rips are survivable as long as you relax, don't panic and conserve your energy.

Part of the Playa Negra Hotel complex, **Playa Negra Surf Shop** (☑2652-9298; www.playanegra.com; board rental per day US$20; ☺8am-5pm) rents boards and sells T-shirts, sunglasses and other beach accessories. **Café Playa Negra** (☑2652-9351; www.playanegracafe.com; ☺7am-9pm) has a laundry service (US$7 per load) and internet access (US$2 per hour).

🛏 Sleeping & Eating

PLAYA AVELLANAS

Options for sleeping and eating in Playas Avellanas tend to be rather spread out.

TOP CHOICE Las Avellanas Villas APARTMENT $$
(☑8821-3681, 2652-9212; www.lasavellanasvillas.com; s/d/tr/q US$55/65/75/85; P✴☎) Stunningly designed, these four *casitas* have polished concrete floors, a bedroom and living area linked by wooden bridges, open-air showers, and large windows looking out onto front and back terraces. They have full kitchens, and the grounds are just 300m from the beach at the northern end of Avellanas.

Mauna Loa Surf Resort BUNGALOW $$
(☑2652-9012; www.hotelmaunaloa.com; d US$80; P✴☎☎✿) This hip and pleasant Italian-run spot is a great place for families, with a secure location that's a straight shot to the beach. Paths lead from the pool area through a well-tended garden to attractive pod-like bungalows with pastel-brushed walls, and swaying hammocks on their terrace. They offer discounts for stays of three nights or more.

Rancho Elena CAMPGROUND $
(☑2652-9058; camping per person US$6) Your hostess is the fabulous *madre* Elena who will gladly cook for you when she isn't in her rocker out the front of her fabulous shack, which abuts a rocky stretch of lonely *playa* at the southern edge of Avellanas. It's quite a place to camp with a crew of friends.

Casa Surf GUESTHOUSE $
(☑2652-9075; www.casa-surf.com; per person US$10; P) Look for the 'Casa Surf' across from Cabinas Las Olas, and pull over – if not for espresso and banana bread, then for a clean, quiet place to stay among the rambling shredder set. This place has five simple rooms with shared bathroom and a full kitchen. They also offer bike rentals (US$7 per day) and surfboard rentals (US$10 to US$15 per day).

Cabinas Las Olas BUNGALOW $$
(☑2652-9315; www.cabinaslasolas.co.cr; d US$90; P✴☎☎) On the road from San José de Pinilla into Avellanas, this pleasant hotel is set on spacious grounds only 200m from the beach. Ten airy, individual bungalows have shiny woodwork, stone detailing, hot-water showers and private decks. There's a restaurant (mains US$5 to US$30), and a specially built boardwalk leads through the mangroves down to the beach (good for wildlife-spotting). Kayaks and boards are available for hire.

Lola's on the Beach CAFE $$
(☑2652-9097; meals US$8-13; ☺10am-5pm Tue-Sun) Lola's, a mod and hauntingly stylish beach cafe, is the place to hang out. Mini-

malist slanted wood chairs are planted in the sand beneath thatched umbrellas, and the tree stump bar overlooks a gorgeous open kitchen where the beachy cuisine includes an epic tuna poke, an overstuffed spicy grilled chicken pita, papaya salad and classic Dutch-style fries. The smoothies are likewise terrific, and then there is Lola, herself. Don't be coy; the lady pig-queen of Avellanas deserves your love.

PLAYA NEGRA

Cabinas Del Mar CABINA $
(☑8829-0531, 2652-9279; d/tr US$20/30) Large, tiled-roof *cabinas* sleep up to three and have beamed ceilings, full kitchens, hammocks on the porch and a porchside grill, and are within earshot of the sea. The property is also home to the tastefully small-scale Marvel Bikini Company. To get here take the left fork on your way to Playa Negra and follow the Marvel Bikini signs.

Kontiki HOSTEL $
(☑2652-9117; www.kontikiplayanegra.com; dm/r US$15/20; P🐾) Along the road from Avellanas, this low-key place run by a splendid young couple has a rambling collection of tree-house dorms and private rooms on stilts that are frequented by both surfers and howlers. In the middle of it all is a rickety pavilion where guests swing in hammocks.

Café Playa Negra HOTEL $$
(☑2653-4360, 8818-9092; www.cafeplayanegra. com; d with air-con/without incl breakfast US$65/55; P❄@🐾🏊) These stylish, minimalist digs, upstairs from the cafe, have polished concrete floors and elevated beds dressed with colorful bedspreads. There's a groovy shared deck with plush lounges, and the downstairs cafe (mains US$7 to US$13) is open for breakfast, lunch and dinner (closing in between) and serves tasty Peruvian-fusion fare. When the DJ rocks the spot it feels like an upscale island dance hall.

Hotel Playa Negra BUNGALOW $$$
(☑2652-9134; www.playanegra.com; s/d/villas US$90/100/115-140; P❄🐾🏊) This sweet compound of thatched circular bungalows, slung with front porch hammocks, is steps from a world-class surf break. Each cabin has a queen-sized bed, two single beds, and a bathroom with roomy hot-water showers. There's also a thatched-roof international restaurant (mains US$8 to US$16) and a surf shop with internet access (US$3 per

hour). The newest and best bungalows are furthest from the beach. Closer models look a bit weather beaten. They host regular yoga classes in a beachside pavilion.

Villa Deveena RESTAURANT $$$
(☑2653-2328; www.villadeevena.com; mains US$18-28; ⊙restaurant 7am-9pm; 🐾) Like a beautiful sunset or a Da Vinci painting, the French chef at this boutique, family-run villa property, off the main Negra drag, is spoken about in hushed tones by local *extranjeros* up and down the coast. And truth be told, the entire Balinese-themed property is worthy of praise, including those swish bungalows (double US$95) set around a gorgeous, glittering pool. But it's the food that's on another level. Think mahi baked with preserved lemon and rosemary, slow braised shortrib, duck confit, and lobster ravioli. Patrick Jamon, the former executive chef at LA's famed Regency Club where he cooked for Fortune 500 CEOs and a handful of presidents, even makes his own goat cheese from his herd in the hills.

❶ Getting There & Away

The new daily bus to Playa Avellanas departs Santa Cruz's Terminal Diria at 12:30pm (US$1.50, 1½ hours), passing by most of the hotels and restaurants of note. The bus to Santa Cruz departs at 5:30am.

Two daily buses to Playa Negra leave Santa Cruz at 6am and 8am; the bus for Santa Cruz departs at 1:30pm from the V on the main road (US$1.50, 1½ hours).

Playa Junquillal

Hard to pronounce and almost as difficult to find, Junquillal (say 'hoon-kee-yal') is a 2km-wide gray-sand wilderness beach that's absolutely stunning and mostly deserted. There's a dome boulder to the south that crumbles into a jutting rock reef and beyond that is a vast, 200-hectare estuary carved by the Rio Nanda Mojo. To the north is a narrow rise of bluffs sprouting clumps of palm trees. Sunsets are downright surreal with blinding golds, molten oranges and shocking pinks. The sea does swirl with fierce rip currents, however, and when it gets big, surfers descend from Negra. But even when surf isn't high, it's dangerous out there and drownings do happen. Don't let kids or even intermediate swimmers venture out alone.

Olive ridley turtles nest in Junquillal from July to November, with a peak from August to October, though in smaller numbers than at the refuges; Junquillal is also an important nesting site for leatherbacks. Though it is not officially protected, conservation groups have teamed up with local communities to protect the nesting sites and eliminate poaching. For more information seek out Vida Verde Azul (☑8718-2267). They have an office in the southern end of town. Local environmentalist, and owner of El Castillo Divertido (☑8351-5162, 2658-8428; www.castillodivertido.com; per person US$25), Silvia Hector, offers kayaking tours through the mangroves along the Rio Nanda Mojo.

With far more Tico locals than tourists, Junquillal has an inviting authenticity unique on the northern peninsula. The nearest town is 4km inland at Paraíso, which has a few local *sodas* and bars. Accommodations are spread out along the beach.

🛏 Sleeping & Eating

TOP CHOICE Mundo Milo Ecolodge   BUNGALOW $$
(☑2658-7010; www.mundomilo.com; d US$60-70; P🗗❄) Dutch owned, and easily the most creative nest, here you can choose from a fan-cooled African-style bungalow with a soaring sky-lit, bamboo ceiling, zebra and giraffe patterned accents, a full kitchen and private patio; or one of their more conventional, but still stylish, air-conditioned bungalows. The pool is an artful arc overlooking the dry tropical woodland, with monkeys howling, birds chanting and waves crashing in the distance. The restaurant (mains US$10 to US$14) has a tribal feel and serves seared tuna, tender and juicy tenderloin and a sea bass in coconut sauce.

Hotelito Sisisi   VILLA $$
(☑8376-2284, 2658-7118; www.hotelitosisisi.com; d US$59-80) On the road into Junquillal this bougainvillea-shrouded villa looms. Guests stay in the rust colored tiled *cabinas* nestled in the lush palm garden. All are brand new and lovely with beamed ceilings, exquisite bathroom tile, king beds, flat-screen TVs, mini fridge and time-sucking front porches.

Casas Pelicano   BUNGALOW $$
(☑2658-8228; www.casaspelicano.cr; d US$55; ❄) A marvelous, if intimate, collection of bungalows nestled in a cliffside garden above the sea. Rooms are simple but ample and the terrazzo framed pool is lovely. Bungalows have full kitchens. Reserve ahead.

El Castillo Divertido   HOTEL $
(☑8351-5162, 2658-8428; www.castillodivertido.com; d US$40; P) On a hilltop you'll find the entrance to this funky, colorful faux-dobe lodge, decked out with crenelated walls and carved and molded masks. The hotel's rooftop bar has panoramic views. Tiled rooms are clean and have hot showers, and the owner offers kayaking tours through the nearby estuary.

Hotel Iguanazul   HOTEL $$$
(☑2658-8124; www.hoteliguanazul.com; d US$102, d all-inclusive US$178; P❄@🗗❄) Gorgeously perched on the bluffs, rooms aren't fabulous but they are set in a number of canary yellow, three-star, stand-alone *casitas* on the palm-shaded lawn overlooking the swirling, thrashing sea. Management offers an all-inclusive option and arranges kayaking and snorkeling tours.

Plumita Pacífica   APARTMENT $$
(☑2658-7125; www.plumitapacifica.com; d US$75; P🗗) When all you need is your sweetie and a secluded palm-fringed beach, these isolated apartments are the answer. There are two modern apartments, each with a fully equipped kitchen, queen bed, iPod dock, beach-front patio and a hot-water shower big enough for two. And just steps from your front door, the desolate beach has hammocks, picnic tables and an outdoor shower.

Hotel Tatanka   PIZZERIA $$
(☑2658-8426, in USA & Canada 800-498-0824; www.hoteltatanka.com; pizza US$9-13; @) Ten ranch-style rooms (single/double US$60/80) with hot-water bathrooms have rustic wooden furnishings. There's an inviting pool, as well, but you're here for their succulent, open-air pizzeria that serves authentic wood-fired pies in the evenings.

Aside from the hotel restaurants, your best option for cheap eats is to head to nearby Paraíso, though there a few small spots on the beach, including the locally popular Bar y Restaurant Junquillal (dishes US$4-7).

❶ Getting There & Away

Buses depart from Junquillal to Santa Cruz (US$2, 1½ hours) at 5:30am, 6am, 9am, noon and 4pm; you can catch the bus anywhere along the main road. Buses from Santa Cruz's Terminal Diria to Junquillal depart at 7:30am, 10:30am and 2:30pm.

If you're driving, it's about 16km by paved road from Santa Cruz to 27 de Abril, and another smooth 17km into town.

From Junquillal, it's possible to drive 35km south to Nosara via the legendary surf spot of Marbella. However, this is a rough road for 4WD only and may be impassable in the rainy season. There are no gas stations on the coastal road and little traffic, so ask before setting out. It's easier to reach beaches south of Junquillal from Nicoya.

A taxi from Santa Cruz to Junquillal costs about US$50.

Santa Cruz

A stop in Santa Cruz, a *sabanero* (cowboy) town typical of inland Nicoya, provides some of the local flavor missing from foreign-dominated beach towns. Unfortunately, there aren't any attention-worthy sights, so most travelers' experience of Santa Cruz consists of changing buses and buying a mango. However, the town is an important administrative center in the region, which gives it a healthy middle-class appeal, and serves as a good base for visiting Guaitil.

About three city blocks in the center of Santa Cruz burned to the ground in a devastating fire in 1993. An important landmark is a vacant lot-looking field known as Plaza de Los Mangos, which was once a large grassy square with three mango trees. Soon after the fire the attractive and shady Parque Bernabela Ramos opened 400m south of Plaza de Los Mangos.

Festivals & Events

Rodeos gather during the Fiesta de Santa Cruz in the second week in January, and on July 25 for Día de Guanacaste, when you can check out the *sabaneros*, admire prize bulls and drink warm beer and enjoy blaring *ranchero* tunes.

Sleeping & Eating

There are countless cheap *sodas* and Chinese diners in town.

La Calle de Alcalá HOTEL $$
(2680-0000; s/d US$61/84; P❄🛜🏊) With its stucco arches and landscaped garden around a pool, this inn gets points for design and proximity to the bus station (it's one block due east of the terminal). Carved wooden doors open into tiled rooms with hair dryers and rattan furnishings. Rooms are a bit small for the price, however, and some are musty.

Hotel La Pampa HOTEL $$
(2680-0586; s/d US$50/60; P❄) A good midrange option, this L-shaped peach-tinted hotel 50m west of the Plaza de Los Mangos isn't all that inspiring from the outside, but the rooms are clean and modern, wired with wi-fi and cable TV.

Casa Fonda RESTAURANT $$
(2680-4949; mains US$7-15; ⊙6am-10pm) This rather swish for Santa Cruz spot is decked out with local pottery, wrought iron and planter boxes, and is something of a middle-class local hang. They do upscale *tipica*, espresso drinks and a good looking seafood pasta.

ⓘ Information

Kion, on the southwest plaza corner, is a Wal-Mart–style department store selling English-language newspapers and more. There's a gas station off the main intersection with the highway, and one ATM and at least two internet cafes facing Plaza de Los Mangos. Change money at **Banco de Costa Rica** (2680-3253), three blocks north of Plaza de Los Mangos.

ⓘ Getting There & Away

Santa Cruz is 57km from Liberia and 25km south of Filadelfia on the main peninsular highway. A paved road leads 16km west to 27 de Abril, from where dirt roads continue to Playa Tamarindo, Playa Junquillal and other beaches.

DON'T MISS

GUAITIL

An interesting excursion from Santa Cruz is the 12km trip by paved road to the small artisanal potter community of Guaitil. Attractive ceramics are made from local clays, using earthy reds, creams and blacks in pre-Columbian Chorotega style. Ceramics are for sale outside the potters' houses and also in San Vicente, 2km beyond Guaitil by unpaved road. If you ask, you can watch part of the potting process, and local residents would be happy to give you a few lessons for a small price.

Take the main highway toward Nicoya and then follow the signed Guaitil road to the left, about 1.5km out of Santa Cruz. This road is lined by yellow corteza amarilla trees and is very attractive when they bloom in April. Unreliable buses (US$.60, 45 minutes) arrive from Santa Cruz every two hours from dawn to dusk on weekdays and until 2pm on Saturday. However, a round-trip taxi should only cost about US$20, depending on how long you stay.

Some buses depart from Terminal Tralapa on the north side of Plaza de Los Mangos. For Empresas Alfaro buses, buy tickets at the Alfaro office, 200m south of the plaza, but catch the bus on the main road north of town.

Liberia (La Pampa) US$2; 1½ hours; departs every 30 minutes from 4:10am to 8:40pm.

Nicoya (La Pampa) US$1; one hour; departs every 30 minutes from 4:50am to 10:30pm.

San José US$10; 4½ hours; seven buses from 4:30am to 5pm (Tralapa); eight buses from 3am to 4:30pm (Empresas Alfaro).

Local buses leave from Terminal Diria 400m east of the plaza. The schedules fluctuate constantly, so ask around.

Bahía Potrero, via Playa Brasilito & Playa Flamingo US$3; one hour; departs 19 times per day.

Playa Junquillal US$2; 1½ hours; departs 7:30am, 10:30am and 2:30pm.

Playa Tamarindo US$2; 1½ hours; departs every hour until 7pm.

CENTRAL PENINSULA

Long the political and cultural heart of Guanacaste, the inland region of the central peninsula looks and feels palpably more 'Costa Rican' than the beach resorts of the northern coast. Over generations, the dry tropical forest has been cut down to make way for the *sabaneros'* cattle, but stands of forest remain, interspersed between *fincas* and coastal villages, sometimes backing stretches of wild, empty beaches. Though the areas around Sámara and Nosara are developing slowly, most foreigners who are drawn to the rugged coastline are active in its conservation. So it remains rife with secluded beaches, small villages, and endless possibilities for getting 'off the map.'

Hwy 21 snakes through the higher elevations of the interior, from the population center of Santa Cruz down through Nicoya, where sinuous Hwy 150 branches through the forest toward Sámara.

Nicoya

A hub between the beaches and ranches, the big cities and *pueblitos*, come here for a blast of Tico time. Truckers, road trippers and locals converge around a grid, packed with commerce and crowned with a gorgeous *iglesia* that makes the leafy Parque Central worth a loiter. Now, that's not necessarily an argument to linger more than a night. Nicoya is by no means fabulous. Just real.

Situated 23km south of Santa Cruz, and a good base for exploring Parque Nacional Barra Honda, Nicoya was named after a Chorotega chief who welcomed Spanish conquistador Gil González de Ávila in 1523 (a gesture he regretted). In the following centuries, the Chorotega were wiped out by the colonists, though the distinctive facial features of the local residents are a testament to their heritage.

⊙ Sights

Iglesia de San Blas   CHURCH
(⊙mass 6pm Mon & Fri, 7am Tue, 7am & 7pm Thu) In Parque Central, the colonial Iglesia de San Blas dates back to the mid-17th century. Appealingly peaceful, with an old brick floor and crumbling stone walls, it's under continuous restoration, but it can be visited when mass is not in session.

🎊 Festivals & Events

The town goes crazy for Día de Guanacaste, on July 25, so expect plenty of food, music and beer in the plaza to celebrate the province's annexation from Nicaragua. The Festival de La Virgen de Guadalupe is one of the most unique festivals in Costa Rica.

🛏 Sleeping & Eating

Most sleeping options have cold showers.

Super Compro (Av 1) and Palí supermarkets provide food and supplies for self-caterers. There are also a number of cheap *sodas* in the *mercado* that are good for a quick bite.

Hotel Jenny   HOTEL $
(⊅2685-5050; cnr Calle 1 & Av 4; s/d US$20/30; P⊛🅿🛜) It ain't Shangri La, but rooms are bright enough, clean enough, air-conditioned, have cable TV, and are a damned decent value. Try to get one in the cooler, darker halls rather than the noisier ones facing the street.

Hotel Chorotega   HOTEL $
(⊅2685-5245; Calle Central; r US$18; P⊛🛜) Next to the Río Chipanzo in a quiet residential neighborhood, and run by a pleasant family that keeps small, dark, bare-bones rooms clean and neat.

Cafe Daniela   SODA $
(⊅2686-6148; Calle 3; mains US$4-7; ⊙7am-9pm; 🅿) A popular new *soda*, they have appetizing *tipica* bites. Think: gallo pinto in the morning, and fish, beef, chicken and veggie *casados* too. They even have a mixed salad. All served in bright tiled environs.

Nicoya

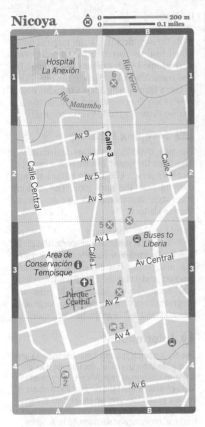

⊙ Sights

1 Iglesia de San Blas	A3

🛏 Sleeping

2 Hotel Chorotega	A4
3 Hotel Jenny	B4

⊗ Eating

4 Cafe Daniela	B3
5 La Castallena Pananderia	B3
6 Palí Supermarket	B1
7 Super Compro	B2

Hospital La Anexión (☏2685-5066) The main hospital on the peninsula is north of town.

Net Seasons (Av 2; per hr US$1; ◷9am-10pm; ☎) Swift internet access in air-conditioned environs across from the plaza.

❶ Getting There & Away

Most buses arrive at and depart from the **bus terminal** southeast of Parque Central.

Liberia US$2.25; 2½ hours; departs every 30 to 60 minutes from 3:30am to 10pm.

Playa Naranjo, connects with ferry to Puntarenas US$3; three hours; departs 5am, 9am, 1pm and 5pm.

Playa Nosara US$2; 2½ hours; departs 4:45am, 10am, 1pm, 3pm and 5:30pm Monday to Saturday. On Sundays buses depart at 10:30am, 1pm, 3pm and 4:30pm.

Sámara US$2; two hours; 13 buses per day from 5am to 9pm.

San José, via Liberia (Empresas Alfaro) US$7.50; five hours; departs five times daily.

San José, via Puente La Amistad (Empresas Alfaro) US$7; four hours; departs 10 times from 3am to 5pm Monday to Saturday and five times on Sunday.

Santa Ana, for Barra Honda US$1; one hour; departs 11am and 4pm Monday to Saturday.

Other buses for Santa Cruz, Filadelfia and Liberia depart every 30 minutes from 3:50am to 8:30pm from the terminal northeast of the park.

La Castallena Pananderia   CAFE **$**
(☏2675-3227; Calle 3; sandwiches US$3; ◷5am-8pm; ☎) In addition to their countless fresh baked loaves and goodies, they do espresso drinks and fresh pressed beef, ham and chicken sandwiches on their airy crunchy baguettes. It's the ideal picnic supply depot on your way to Barro Honda.

❶ Information

Area de Conservación Tempisque (ACT; ☏2685-5667; Av Central; ◷8am-4pm Mon-Fri) The office of the ACT can help with accommodations and cave exploration at Parque Nacional Barra Honda.

Banco de Costa Rica (Calle Central; ◷8:30am-3pm Mon-Fri) Exchanges US dollars.

Banco Popular (Calle 3; ◷9am-4:30pm Mon-Fri, 8:15am-11:30am Sat) Exchanges US dollars. It also has a 24hr ATM at Hospital La Anexión.

Parque Nacional Barra Honda

Situated about halfway between Nicoya and the mouth of the Río Tempisque, this 23-sq-km national park protects a massive underground system of caverns composed of soft limestone, carved by rainfall and erosion over a period of about 70 million years. Speleologists have discovered more than 40 caverns, some reaching as far as 200m deep, though to date only 19 have been fully explored. There have also been discoveries of pre-Columbian remains dating to 300 BC.

Stalagmites, stalactites and a host of beautiful formations have, ahem, evocative names such as fried eggs, organ, soda straws, popcorn, curtains, columns, pearls, flowers and shark's teeth. However, unlike caverns found elsewhere, Barra Honda is not developed for wide-scale tourism, which means that they feel less like a carnival attraction and more like a scene from Indiana Jones. So, don your yellow miner's hat and sturdy boots, and be prepared to get down and dirty.

◉ Sights & Activities

Parque Nacional Barra
Honda Caverns
CAVES

(☎2659-1551, tour reservations 8662-4714; adult/child US$10/1; ☉ trails 8am-4pm, caverns 8am-1pm) You can only explore the caves with a guide from the Asociación de Guías Ecologistas de Barra Honda, which can be arranged at the ranger station. A guide charges about US$36 per person, US$52 for two, not including park admission. The descent involves ladders and ropes, so you should be reasonably fit and must be at least 12 years old.

The only cave with regular access to the public is the 41m-deep La Terciopelo, which has the most speleothems – calcite figures that rise and fall in the cave's interior. The best known of these is El Órgano, which produces several notes when lightly struck. Scientists and visitors must obtain permits to enter other caves. These include Santa Ana, the deepest at 161m; Trampa (Trap), 110m deep with a vertical 52m drop; Nicoya, where early human remains were found; and Pozo Hediondo, or Fetid Pit. It's a cave, not a cavern, famous for its more than 5000 resident bats, which create mountainous piles of guano. Walk the 2km from the park gate to the cavern's mouth or opt for a ride in a 4x4. Tours to the caverns on foot last about four hours. Only groups of five people or less can enter the caverns and they cannot be entered after 1pm.

Wildlife Watching
While wildlife-watching underground, you'll have the chance to see such fun-loving creatures as bats, albino salamander, blind fish and a variety of squiggly invertebrates. On the surface, howler and white-faced monkeys, armadillo, coati, kinkajou and white-tailed deer are regularly spotted, as are striped hog-nosed skunk and anteater.

Hiking
The Barra Honda hills have a few hiking trails through deciduous, dry tropical forest which lead to waterfalls (in the rainy season) adorned with calcium formations. It's also possible to hike 3.5km to the top of Cerro Barra Honda, which has a mirador with a view of Río Tempisque and Golfo de Nicoya. You won't need a guide to hike the trails.

🛏 Sleeping & Eating

The vast majority of visitors arrive on day trips from the beach, but there is a camping area (per person US$2) with bathrooms and showers near the park gate. The station's dorm-style accomodations are no longer open to visitors.

Hotel Las Cavernas
HOTEL $

(☎2659-1574; per person with air-con/fan US$25/18; P❋☎) Located just outside the park gates. Not many folks stay here, but it's up and running and there is a pool and a restaurant. Rooms have a fresh coat of paint and concrete floors, and the mountain location is splendid. You will hear the howlers' roar.

ℹ Information

The dry season is the only time that tourists are allowed to enter the caves, though the hiking is fine at any time of year. Always carry several liters of water and let the rangers know where you are going. Two German hikers died at Barra Honda in 1993 after getting lost on a short hike – they had no water and succumbed to dehydration. Sneakers or, preferably, boots are necessary if you intend to go caving.

The ranger station in the southwest corner of the park takes the admission fee, provides information and arranges guides. It's best to call and arrange your guide at least the day before. Plan to arrive early to tour the caverns, as tours last three to four hours and you'll need to be out of the caverns by 1pm.

ℹ Getting There & Away

The easiest way to get to the park is from Nicoya. No buses go directly to the park; however, buses to Santa Ana (1km away) will get you close. These leave Nicoya at 11:15am and 4pm Monday to Saturday. Return buses leave Santa Ana at noon and 4:30pm. There are no buses on Sunday. The better option is to take a taxi from Nicoya, which will cost about US$20 round-trip. You can arrange for your driver to pick you up at a specified time.

If you have your own vehicle, take the peninsular highway south out of Nicoya toward Mansión and make a left on the access road leading to

Puente La Amistad. From here, continue another 1.5km and make a left on the signed road to Barra Honda. The dirt road will take you to the village of Barra Honda then wind to the left for another 6km, passing Santa Ana, before ending at the national park gate. The road is clearly marked, and there are several signs along the way indicating the direction of the park. After the village of Barra Honda, the road is unpaved, but in good condition. However, there is no telling what the next rainy season will do, so ask locally before setting out.

If you are coming to the park from Puente La Amistad, you will see the access road to Barra Honda signed about 16km after leaving the bridge. From this point, follow the above directions.

Nosara Area

Nosara is a cocktail of international surf culture, stunning back-road topography, jungled microclimates, moneyed expat mayhem and yoga bliss. It effortlessly recalls Malibu, Oahu's North Shore and Byron Bay, Australia, while remaining completely its own – only in Costa Rica – incarnation. Here, three stunning beaches are stitched together by a network of swerving, rutted earth roads that meander over coastal hills and kiss the coast just west of the small Tico village of Nosara. From the south, the first beach you'll come to is Playa Garza, still a sleepy Tico fishing village with an arc of pale brown sand and headlands on either side of the rippling bay. Fishing boats bob 100m from shore and there's a point break to the Northside. There are a few *cabinas* and *sodas* here too and lots of sand space with precious few tourists.

But there's a reason the majority of visitors descend on Playa Guiones. It's quite simply a slice of raw nectar. A wide generous undeveloped arc of marbled sand, with a few pebbles and shells mixed in, excellent beach breaks and plenty of space. It's a place for surfers, surf dogs and surf babies. You will see unmanned strollers lodged in the wet sand at low tide.

Playa Pelada, just north, is rough and rugged, dry and less endowed with surfers and luxury, which could be viewed as a luxury in itself. Things feel at once a touch spookier and more profound in Pelada. Of course, this beach lacks surf, but does have those sheared-away boulders tumbling into a foaming sea, two alluring beachside restaurants and a fishing village intimacy Guiones lacks.

Inland are remnant pockets of luxuriant vegetation that attracts birds and wildlife. The area has seen little logging, partly because of the nearby wildlife refuge. There are a few hundred foreigners living permanently in the Nosara area (mainly North Americans), the majority of them keen on protecting the rainforest. One resident described the area as 'sophisticated jungle living,' and indeed blending retirement with conservation is an interesting experiment. However, Ticos remain hostile to development, mainly because land prices have been driven through the roof in just under a decade.

For visitors, Nosara is a laid-back surf haven that caters to midrange tourists, but there are dorms here too, and you can definitely gut it out on a budget. The area is spread out along the coast and a little inland (making wheels a necessity). Nosara village, where you'll find supplies and gas, and the airport, are 5km inland from the beach. The main areas with accommodations, restaurants and beaches are Playa Pelada to the north and Playa Guiones to the south. There are many unidentified little roads, which makes it hard to get around if you don't know the place – look for hotel and restaurant signs, and ask for help. Log on to Nosara Travel's website (www.nosaratravel.com/map.html) for a handy map.

🏃 Activities

Miss Sky
CANOPY TOUR

(☏2682-0969; www.missskycanopytour.com; adult/child 5-12 US$65/45; ⊘office 7am-5pm) Miss Sky has brought a canopy tour to Nosara, with a total length of 11,000m above a pristine, private reserve. The zip lines don't go from platform to platform, but from mountainside to mountainside, and have double cables for added safety. Your top speed will be about 45kph. Tours leave twice daily, at 8am and 2pm. The morning tour is slightly longer.

Reserva Biológica Nosara
HIKING

(☏2682-0035; www.lagarta.com; US$6, guided nature walks US$15) The private 35-hectare reserve behind the Lagarta Lodge has trails leading through a mangrove wetland down to the river (five minutes) and beach (10 minutes). This is a great spot for birdwatching, and there's a good chance you'll see some reptiles as well (look up in the trees as there are occasionally boa constrictors here). Non-guests can visit the reserve for self-guided hikes or guided nature walks.

The Undiscovered Nicoya

When it comes to beautiful beaches, Península de Nicoya has been blessed with an embarrassment of riches. Notoriety and development have not been spread equally among them, which means there are hidden nooks and coves that remain overlooked and, at least for now, unexploited.

Playa Penca

1 Playa Penca (p218) is the kind of unexpected find that appears out of nowhere. A gleaming jewel of a beach that's immediately captivating.

Playas San Miguel & Coyote

2 Too often overlooked, this pair of virgin beaches (p253) has a certain rustic elegance, and nesting olive ridley turtles bring eco gravitas.

Playa Carrillo

3 White sand framed by granite, backed by jungle. What's not to love? It can be busy with Ticos on weekends and holidays, but otherwise it's empty and sweet (p251).

Playa Pan de Azúcar

4 A stretch of jaw-dropping raw coastal beauty, a jigsaw of rugged cliffs and pristine coves (p217).

Playa Junquillal

5 Beachcombing meets the wilderness at this stunning and mostly deserted beach (p233) with a 200-hectare estuary just beyond.

Clockwise from top left
1. Playa Penca 2. Playa Coyote 3. Playa Carrillo

Tica Massage
SPA

(2682-0096; www.ticamassage.com; US$35-65; 9am-6pm) After a hard day of surfing, treat yourself to a (totally legit) spa treatment at Tica Massage, across from Casa Tucan in the Heart of Nosara Wellness Center. Consider the invigorating Hawaiian-style Lomi Lomi massage.

Stand Up Paddle Nosara
KAYAKING

(2682-1418; www.theyogahousecostarica.com) Nosara's original SUP outfitter, located at Yoga House, runs tours, rentals and lessons, and offers a range of kayak trips through a third entity, Drifters Kayaking, which is the same company as the other two. Confused yet? Just call them. You'll have fun.

Playa Guiones
SURFING

Check out Playa Guiones for the best beach break in the Central Peninsula, especially when there is an offshore wind. Although the beach is usually full of surfers, there are fortunately plenty of take-off points.

Coconut Harry's
SURFING

(2682-0574; www.coconutharrys.com; board rental per day US$15-20, lessons US$45; 7am-5pm) At the main intersection in Guiones, this surf shop offers private lessons, board rental (including stand-up paddle boards), and they even rent snorkels and fins.

Nosara Surf Shop
SURFING

(2682-0186; www.nosarasurfshop.com; board rental per day US$15-20, surf lessons per hour US$40; 7am-6pm) They rent surfboards, repair dings and arrange surf lessons and tours.

El Punto
SURFING

(2682-1081; www.surfocostarica.com; board rental per day US$15-20, lessons per hour US$40, bike rental per day US$10; 8am-6pm) Across the street from Kaya Sol, Tico-owned El Punto is a highly recommended surf shop that offers lessons and rents boards and bicycles.

Nosara Yoga Institute
YOGA

(2682-0071, toll-free 866-439-4704; www.nosarayoga.com) In the hills near Playa Guiones is the famous Nosara Yoga Institute. Regular classes are open to the public, but they also hold workshops, retreats and instructor training courses for beginning and advanced students in a beautiful jungle setting.

Yoga House
YOGA

(2682-1418, 2682-0289; www.theyogahousecostarica.com; per class US$10) An inviting, professional, nurturing yoga space tucked behind Cafe de Paris in the Guiones area, they offer a Surfers Class at 12:30, geared to soothe and stretch the upper body, and a terrific, passive but still challenging Yin Yoga class that smooths out kinks in your faschia and demands surrender.

Pilates Nosara
YOGA

(2682-0096; www.pilatesnosara.com; per person US$10) Set in the Heart of Nosara Wellness complex is this upstart studio, offering Pilates mat and Power Yoga classes. Check their website for an up-to-date class schedule.

Nosara Wellness
YOGA

(2682-0360; www.nosarawellness.com; per class US$10, private sessions from US$60) A wellness studio in Playa Pelada that, in addition to their offerings of massage, Pilates and sports rehab, acupuncture and dance classes, offers something called Aerial Yoga. It involves slings and hammocks and various compromising positions.

Blue Spirit
YOGA

(2656-8300; www.bluespiritcostarica.com) This new, plush yoga retreat center is less for travelers passing through and more for folks looking to take a week-long workshop with name yogis. Shiva Rea and Krishna Das are just two international luminaries who passed through in 2012.

Turtle-Watching

Most hotels in the area can arrange guided tours to Refugio Nacional de Fauna Silvestre Ostional, where you can watch the mass arrivals of olive ridley turtles.

Sleeping & Eating

Prices outside of high season can be 20% lower or better.

PLAYA GUIONES

TOP CHOICE 4 You Hostel
HOSTEL $

(2682-1316; www.4youhostel.com; dm/semi-private/private US$18/25/35; P @) A fantastic new hostel close to the Guiones action. The high-end minimalist design makes this evolutionary flop house (read: dorm) feel luxurious. Within the dorms are three semi-private pods which have walls that don't quite reach the soaring ceiling, hence the semi-private category. And there was one fully private bungalow at research time, with more to come.

TOP SPOTS FOR A SPECTACULAR SMOOCH

The Península de Nicoya is blessed with endless romantic beaches, but if you're looking for a dramatic backdrop for that cinematic kiss, here's where to set the scene.

» Head to Papaya Restaurant at Moana Lodge (p272) in Mal País for breakfast or sunset with a view.

» Take a sunset stroll on the perfectly arced and desolate Playa Junquillal (p233).

» Wake up early and hike up to the Montezuma Waterfall (p263).

» Book a bungalow at romantic El Pequeño Gecko Verde (p248), canoodle over cocktails followed by a sunset stroll on the secret beach, Playa Izquierda.

» Pack a *pincin* and hike to the beach at the end of the world, or, you know, the peninsula at Reserva Natural Absoluta Cabo Blanco (p267).

Kaya Sol   HOSTEL $$

(☎2682-1459; www.kayasol.com; dm US$13, d US$45-90; 🛜🏊) The heart of this sprawling surfer-and-seeker retreat is the dorm-style accommodations. The shared bathrooms are spotless and the pool, with waterfall shower, is perfect for cooling off. There are also a few rooms and private cabins with hot-water bathroom in the back of the property. The restaurant serves American-style food, and the bar is the place to hang out at night. It's down the road from the Mini Super Delicias.

Casa Tucan   HOTEL $$

(☎8611-7954; r US$75; P🌸@🛜🏊) Charming, laid back and locally owned, sweet rooms have high-beamed ceilings, new tasteful bathroom tile, wooden beds, minifridge, cable TV, an inviting pool and friendly restaurant bar. They even rent a nice selection of boards on the cheap to guests (per day US$5 to US$10).

Gilded Iguana   HOTEL $$

(☎hotel 2682-0245, restaurant 2682-0259; www.thegildediguana.com; r US$50-75; P🌸🏊) Down the second access road to Guiones, this longstanding hotel for anglers and surfers has well-furnished, tiled rooms of varying sizes, with hot-water bathroom and refrigerator, that sleep three. The tasty restaurant (mains US$9 to US$14) serves generous platters of fish tacos, chicken parmigiana, fajitas and seafood specials, and the attached bar is a popular gringo hangout with live music on Tuesday and Saturday nights. Reserve your table well in advance.

Café de Paris   HOTEL $$

(☎2682-0087, 2682-1035; www.cafedeparis.net; d US$90; P🌸@🛜🏊) This pleasant hotel is located at the corner of the main road and the first access road that leads to Playa Guiones.

Splashy modern loft rooms are set in one shingled longhouse. Some have wood floors, others polished concrete, all have rain showers, molded concrete wash basins and ample style. Accents like glass-floored lofts and floating stairs are worth seeing. The bakery/restaurant turns out heavenly pastries.

Casa Romántica   HOTEL $$

(☎2682-0272; www.casa-romantica.net; d incl breakfast with/without air-con US$95/70; P🌸@🛜🏊) Right next to Playa Guiones, rooms aren't fancy and some have funky layouts with odd corners, but the best of the bunch have high beamed ceilings, wood furnishings, views of the manicured gardens surrounding the pool, and management is always warm and sweet. The small restaurant (mains US$6 to US$18) features international cuisine including Greek salads, pastas and even veggie burgers.

🌿 Harmony Hotel   HOTEL $$$

(☎2682-4114; www.harmonynosara.com; d/bungalow US$280/330; P🌸@🛜🏊) Okay, this place is nice and the 14 bungalows and 10 rooms are scattered around a lush monkey-patrolled garden, with private access to the beach, but at these prices we expect more from bungalows that are no doubt spacious but with dated bathroom fixtures, and worn wooden decks. The service is fabulous, they have a sustainability ethos, and the bar area is exquisite. The rooms just need a refresher.

L'Acqua Viva Hotel & Spa   HOTEL $$$

(☎2682-1087, Canada toll-free 1-877-216-0181, US toll-free 1-888-273-1977; www.lacquaviva.com; r US$205, ste US$310-525; P🌸🛜🏊) A bit of Bali in Nosara, L'Acqua Viva is one of the most luxurious hotels in the central peninsula. Inside and out, the property is simply stunning, with water, wood and bamboo features throughout. The open-air restaurant and funky lounge bar are the best in town. The 36 contemporary rooms are decorated in minimalist style with all the five-star amenities you'd expect. Yet we do have one major complaint: the location. It abuts the main Nosara road, and it's too far from the beach.

Robin's INTERNATIONAL $

(☎2682-0617; mains US$4-7; ☺8am-5pm Mon-Sat, 10am-4pm Sun; ☎☏) Perfectly suited to the health-conscious yogis and surfers who live in and visit Nosara, Robin prepares (you'll see her working in the kitchen) a welcome menu of salads, wraps and sandwiches on homemade, whole-wheat foccacia. She also has a worthy raw menu including 'living' pad thai and maki rolls, and veggie quesadillas with gluten-free tortillas, organic kale and roasted peppers. But if you must indulge your sweet tooth, get the ice cream. It too is homemade and sublime.

Rosi's Soda Tica SODA $

(☎2682-0728; mains US$3-6; ☺8am-3pm Mon-Sat) Next to Marlin Bill's on the main highway, this is the only *soda* in Guiones and it's a damn good one. They keep it simple with a few sandwiches, salads, *casados*, and gallo pinto in the morning. All are served in airy, cheerful environs.

Beach Dog Café CAFE $

(☎2682-1293; www.facebook.com/beachdogcafe; dishes US$6-9; ☺8am-3pm daily, 8am-10pm Wed & Sat; ☎☏) Just steps from the beach, this groovy cafe has tasty breakfasts (dig that banana bread French toast) and a lunch menu that includes quesadillas, a variety of sandwiches, and uber popular fish tacos. The smoothies are exceptional here, and in addition to wi-fi, they offer free international calls to the US and Canada. They're steps from the sand.

Marlin Bill's SEAFOOD $$$

(☎2682-0548; www.facebook.com/pages/Marlin-Bills-Restaurant/343540496705?sk=info; meals US$11-25; ☺11am-10 Mon-Sat) Across the main road from the Guiones swirl, this is your granddad's fish house, which makes it all the more satisfying. Grab lunch here (the menu is cheaper), though it's worth the coin anytime for a hearty filet of fresh grilled tuna, prepared simply and perfectly, and a slab of that creamy key lime pie.

Mini Super Delicias del Mundo SUPERMARKET

(☎2682-0291; ☺8:45am-1pm & 2:30am-6:15pm Mon-Sat) Stock up on groceries at the Mini Super Delicias del Mundo near Kaya Sol; the bulletin board advertises local events and job openings.

Organico SUPERMARKET

(☺7:30am-7pm Mon-Sat, 9am-5pm Sun) Attention Whole Foods addicts, let this be your methadone. Here you'll find a healthy helping of organic fruits and veg, exotic and local spices, almond and soy milk and a fair amount of goods that are not organic in the slightest (we're looking at you, Cup O'Noodles). But they have bulk nuts and dried fruit and enough organic goods that it qualifies. There's a deli, and a wine and liquor selection too. It's on the highway south of Marlin Bill's.

PLAYA PELADA

TOP CHOICE Refugio del Sol LODGE $$

(☎8561-6211; www.refugiodelsol.com; s/d with kitchenette US$50/55, s/d without kitchenette US$35/45; ℗❄☎) This rustic lodge is decked out with ceramic tiled floors, beamed ceilings, artisanal crafts and wood furnishings, candles and lanterns, and other soulful touches that make it feel like home. Rooms open onto a wide L-shaped patio strung with hammocks, and the gorgeous young Italian couple who own it make tasty Italian food for guests every night, and are generous of heart. Plus, it's just a short stroll to the sand.

Almost Paradise VILLA $

(☎2682-0172; www.almostparadise-costarica.com; dm/r $13/45) An aging, somewhat decrepit villa, with latter-day charm. Though it is falling apart in a few places, the all-wood rooms are airy and comfy with magnificent views. The restaurant is open for lunch and dinner and is worthy of a sunset beverage, for sure. Okay, so there is more than a hint of youth culture angst in this rusty old joint. But, hey, you're in a surf town. Goes with the territory.

Lagarta Lodge LODGE $$

(☎2682-0035; www.lagarta.com; s/d US$75-105/80-110; ℗@☎) North of Pancho's Resort, a road dead-ends at this six-room hotel, a recommended choice high on a steep hill above the private 50-hectare Reserva Biológica Nosara. Bird-watching and wildlife-spotting conditions are good here. Large rooms have high ceilings, hot showers and a small private patio or balcony. The balcony restaurant (mains US$9 to US$22) is worth a visit just for the spectacular views of the river, mountains, sea and sunset, though the rotating menu of international and Tico specialties is equally appealing.

Pancho's Resort
BUNGALOW $$

(☑2682-0591; www.panchosresort.com; bungalows US$65-135; P❋@☎☀) On the main road between Playa Pelada and Nosara village, this large property has it all: a supermarket, a popular Mexican restaurant (mains US$8 to US$12) and eight comfortable bungalows sleeping three to seven people. They have attractive tiled floors, high ceilings, hot-water bathroom, loft and kitchenette. To top it off, Pancho and his bilingual family are all incredibly nice.

Villa Mango B&B
B&B $$

(☑2682-1168; www.villamangocr.com; d incl breakfast US$89; P☀) Set high on a hillside with views of both bays, you can't help but relax at this tiny B&B in the trees. Rooms have a Mediterranean flair, are quite spacious and feel much more like a boutique hotel than a B&B. Bathrooms are especially lovely with rustic touches. Breakfasts are huge, and while there's a pool on the property, you can also take a short stroll down to an isolated stretch of beach.

La Luna
INTERNATIONAL $$

(☑2682-0122; www.facebook.com/pages/LA-LUNA/187210908478; dishes US$6-24; ☉8am-10pm) On the beach, to the right of Hotel Playas de Nosara, you'll find this impressive stone building that houses a trendy restaurant/bar and art gallery. The eclectic menu has Asian and Mediterranean flourishes, and the views (and cocktails) are intoxicating. Call ahead for reservations.

Olga's Bar & Grill
RESTAURANT $$

(☑8848-0706; www.facebook.com/Olgas.Bar.Grill. Nosara; mains US$7-16; ☉10am-10pm) A few hundred meters to the north of La Luna, on a separate side road, lies the *other* beachfront restaurant on Pelada, where the hilarious bombastic Olga serves tasty *tipica* (though she is an expat) and comes up with creative concoctions like a briny shrimp and mussel soup and more traditional grinds, like Baja-style fish tacos. Your meal will be served in a wonderful white washed *palapa* with unbroken sea views, and the salsa soundtrack rocks.

🍸 Drinking & Entertainment

There are a few places to bend the elbow in the village of Nosara. Near the soccer field is Tropicana, which is a great place for showing off your salsa moves. The bar at Kaya Sol (p243) has a popular ladies' night on Monday, regular live music and is always a good vibe. Bar Banana, south of Guiones on the main highway, rocks on Saturday (ladies' night) and Thursday (reggae night). The popular bar at Casa Tucan (p243) attracts a slightly older crowd for live music on Wednesday and Sunday.

Honali Beach House
CLUB

(☑2682-5051; www.facebook.com/pages/Honali-Beach-House/133762260006245?sk=info; mains US$6-9; ☉11am-midnight) The new hot spot is a mod, molded concrete-and-glass clubhouse in a wooded corner of Guiones. You'll find outdoor billiard tables, cushioned wood stump seating and a dangling blue surfboard sign declaring 'Land of Honali' in mirrored lettering. They serve all manner of pub grub and *casados*, and though none of the design is in terribly good taste, who cares? It's a club! By the beach! Let loose!

ℹ️ Information

There are two gas stations in Nosara village, but only one was open during our visit. Oddly there is no laundry service available in the beach areas of Nosara. You may inquire at your hotel or hostel, but not all of them are happy to clean your dirties either.

That strange concrete lotus flower that peaks above the trees and is visible from both beaches is the tumbledown remains of Hotel Las Playas Nosara, and is a good place for a surreptitious photo shoot if not a beach getaway. It looks almost... haunted.

Banco Popular (☑2682-0011, 2682-0267; ☉9am-3pm Mon-Fri) Changes US dollars and traveler's checks, and gives cash advances on Visa cards only; the ATM also only accepts Visa cards.

Nosara Travel (☑2682-0300; www.nosaratravel.com; ☉9am-3pm Mon-Fri) In Playa Guiones, this office books air tickets, arranges car rentals and books hotel reservations or vacation homes.

Nosaranet & Frog Pad (☑2682-4029, 2682-4039; www.thefrogpad.com; per hr US$4; ☉9am-7pm Mon-Sat, 10am-6pm Sun) The going rates for internet use are pretty astronomical in Nosara. The Frog Pad also has used books for sale, and rents out DVDs, bikes (per day US$10) and surfboards (per day US$15).

Police (☎2682-0317) Next to the Red Cross and post office on the southeast corner of the soccer field in Nosara village center.

Seekret Spot (☎2682-1325; per hr US$4; ⏱10am-6:30pm Wed-Mon) Internet access and international phone calls. Located on the main road to Playa Pelada. Oh, and it's an Italian-owned gelateria, too.

① Getting There & Away

Air

Both Sansa and NatureAir have one daily flight to and from San José for about US$111 to US$120 each way.

Bus

Local buses depart from the *pulpería* (corner grocery store) by the soccer field. Traroc buses depart for Nicoya (US$2, two hours) at 5am, 5:30am, 7am, noon and 3pm. There's no 5:30am bus on Sundays. Empresas Alfaro buses going to San José (US$9, five to six hours) depart from the pharmacy by the soccer field at 12:30pm. To get to Sámara, take any bus out of Nosara and ask the driver to drop you off at 'la bomba de Sámara' (Sámara gas station). From there, catch one of the buses traveling from Nicoya to Sámara.

Car

From Nicoya, a paved road leads toward Playa Sámara. About 5km before Sámara (signed), a windy, bumpy (and, in the dry season, dusty) dirt road leads to Nosara village (4WD recommended). It's also possible to continue north (in the dry season), to Ostional, Junquillal and Paraíso, though you'll have to ford a few rivers. Ask around before trying this in the rainy season, when Río Nosara becomes impassable.

There are a handful of rental car agencies in the Nosara area, including **Economy Rent a Car** (☎2299-2000; www.economyrentacar. com) next to Marlin Bill's in Guiones and **Alamo** (☎2242-7733; www.alamocostarica.com) in the Playa Pelada area.

Refugio Nacional de Fauna Silvestre Ostional

This 248-hectare coastal refuge extends from Punta India in the north to Playa Guiones in the south, and includes the beaches of Playa Nosara and Playa Ostional. It was created in 1992 to protect the *arribadas*, or mass nesting of the olive ridley sea turtles, which occurs from July to November with a peak from August to October. Along with Playa Nancite in Parque Nacional Santa Rosa, Ostional is one of two main nesting grounds for this turtle in Costa Rica.

The olive ridley is one of the smallest species of sea turtle, typically weighing around 45kg. Although they are endangered, there are a few beaches in the world where ridleys nest in large groups that can number in the thousands. Scientists believe that this behavior is an attempt to overwhelm predators.

Prior to the creation of the park, coastal residents used to harvest eggs indiscriminately (drinking raw turtle eggs is thought to increase sexual vigor). However, an imaginative conservation plan has allowed the inhabitants of Ostional to continue to harvest eggs from the first laying, which are often trampled by subsequent waves of nesting turtles. By allowing locals to harvest the first batches, the economic livelihood of the community is maintained, and the villagers in turn act as park rangers to prevent other poachers from infringing on their enterprise.

Rocky Punta India at the northwestern end of the refuge has tide pools that abound with marine life, such as sea anemone, urchin and starfish. Along the beach, thousands of almost transparent ghost crabs go about their business, as do the bright-red Sally Lightfoot crabs. The vegetation behind the beach is sparse and consists mainly of deciduous trees, home to iguanas, crabs, howler monkeys, coatis and many birds. Near the southeastern edge of the refuge is a small mangrove swamp where there is good bird-watching.

🏃 Activities

Mass arrivals of nesting turtles occur during the rainy season every three or four weeks and last about a week (usually on dark nights preceding a new moon), though it's possible to see turtles in lesser numbers almost any night during nesting season. In the dry season, a fitting consolation prize is the small number of leatherback and green turtles that also nest here. Many of the upmarket hotels and tour operators in the region offer tours to Ostional during nesting season, though you can arrange with local guides to visit independently. Contact the Association Guias Locales (☎2682-0428) in the center of Ostional town across from Soda La Plaza.

Surfers catch some good lefts and rights here just after low tide, though this stretch of sea is notorious for strong currents and isn't suitable for swimming unless you're

TRACKING TURTLES

Since 1997 Programa Restauracíon de Tortugas Marinas (Pretoma|Marine Turtle Restoration Program; www.pretoma.org) has collaborated with locals to monitor turtle-nesting activity and operate hatcheries. Members of the community are hired as field assistants, and environmental education activities are held with the children in town. The project also involves tagging, measuring and protecting nesting turtles, which has resulted in a drastic reduction in poaching levels.

At the time of writing, Pretoma was operating projects in Playa Caletas, Playa San Miguel, Playa Corozalito (on the central Pacific coast) and Punta Banco, near the border with Panama. For more information on volunteering, visit the website.

green and have flippers. But there is 5km of unbroken beach here, sprinkled with driftwood and swaying with coconut palms.

🛏 Sleeping & Eating

Camping (per person US$3) is permitted behind the centrally located Soda La Plaza, which has a portable toilet available for use. The *soda* is open for breakfast, lunch and dinner.

Ostional Turtle Lodge　　　　LODGE $
(☑2682-0131; www.surfingostional.com; r with/without air-con per person US$15/20) A great two-room guesthouse with well-appointed tiled rooms with high ceilings and lovely mosaic baths. Their coup de grace is the exquisite yoga rancho strung with hammocks, backed by mangroves, overlooking pasture land and within earshot of the sea.

Albergue Ecoturismo Arribadas　　HOTEL $
(☑8816-9815; www.arribadas.com; per person incl breakfast US$20) A new cheapie but goodie, located in the center of town. Spotless rooms have high slanted ceilings, new tile and private baths. They help arrange turtle tours as well.

Brovilla Resort Hotel　　　　LODGE $$
(☑8519-6059; www.brovillaresorthotel.com; r/villa incl breakfast US$60/135; [P][✱][🖥][🛜][⛱]) In the hills, 2km north of town, the area's original ecolodge languished neglected until 2011 when a Minnesota family revived the place. Rooms are actually wood-and-stone cabins with stone showers, ceiling fans, and sliding doors opening to magnificent sea views. Concrete villas have flagstone accents, new built-in cabinetry and loft bedrooms, and and are fully equipped with inviting kitchens and satellite TV. Some of the lodge buildings are swathed in murals, and banisters are crusted in seashells giving it a kitschy feel. The delicious *palapa*-style restaurant

is open from Thursday to Tuesday and has a circle bar and an Italian chef (mains US$9 to US$24). Good marks all around.

ℹ Getting There & Away

Ostional village is about 8km northwest of Nosara village. During the dry months there are two daily buses from Santa Cruz (times change, so ask around), but at any time of the year the road can get washed out by rain. Hitchhiking from Nosara is reportedly easy.

If you're driving, take a 4WD as a few rivers need to be crossed. From the main road joining Nosara beach and village, head north and cross the bridge over the Río Nosara. At a T-junction 2km after the bridge, take the left fork (which is signed) and continue on the main road north to Ostional, about 6km away. There are several river crossings on the way to Ostional, so ask locally about conditions before setting out.

Beyond Ostional, the dirt road continues on to Marbella before arriving in Paraíso, northeast of Junquillal. Be careful and ask before attempting this drive and use a 4WD.

Playa Sámara

Is Samara the black hole of happiness? That's what more than one expat has said after stopping here on vacation and never leaving. And perhaps it is more than the sum of its parts? Because on the surface it's just an easy-to-navigate beach town with barefoot, three-star appeal, and a crescent-shaped strip of pale-gray sand spanning two rocky headlands. Not spectacular, just safe, mellow, reasonably developed, easily navigable on foot and accessible by public transportation. The sea is also rather calm. Not surprisingly, you'll find it's popular with vacationing Tico and foreign families and backpackers, who enjoy Samara's palpable ease and tranquility. But be careful, the longer you stay the less you'll want to leave.

If you've got some extra time and a 4WD, explore the hidden beaches north of Sámara such as Playa Barrigona, equally famous for its pristine beach as for its celebrity resident, Mel Gibson.

Activities

Experienced surfers will probably be bored with Sámara's inconsistent waves, though beginners will have a blast.

Pato Surf School
SURFING
(☎8336-5105, 8761-4738; www.samarabeach.com/patosurfschool/index; board rental per hour US$4, lessons semi-private/private US$30/50) Set right on the beach, Pato offers inexpensive and quality board rental, and beginner surf instruction.

C&C Surf School
SURFING
(☎2656-0590; cncsurfsamara.webs.com; board rentals per day US$16, lessons semi-private/private US$30/40; ◷8am-8pm) A great choice, offering private and semi-private lessons; the fee includes another hour of board rental afterwards, and the school donates 10% from every surf lesson to a local children's school and a turtle conservation project. It also rents kayaks and surfboards and arranges a variety of tours and trips throughout Costa Rica.

Wing Nuts
CANOPY TOUR
(☎2656-0153; adult/child US$60/40) The local zip-line operator's 10 platforms are located on the eastern outskirts of town off the main paved road.

Flying Crocodile
SCENIC FLIGHTS
(☎2656-8048; www.flying-crocodile.com; flights 20/30/60-minutes US$110/150/230, lessons per hour US$200) Several kilometers west, in Playa Buenavista, the Flying Crocodile offers ultralight flights and lessons.

Pura Vida Dive Center
DIVING
(☎8523-0043; www.puravidadive.com; 2-tank dive incl equipment US$100) There are 25 dive sites within a 20-minute boat ride from Samara, where you can see dozens of fish, blooming rock reefs, and, if you're lucky, hammerheads. You'll need three divers to make a trip. The shop is located across from Posada Matilori, about 100m east of the main road.

Courses

Centro de Idiomas Intercultura
LANGUAGE COURSE
(☎2260-8480, 2656-0127; www.samaralanguageschool.com; courses per week with/without home-

stay US$455/300) Has a campus right on the beach. Language courses can be arranged with or without a family homestay.

Sleeping

Budget options generally have cold-water showers; go midrange and more than likely you'll get hot water.

TOP CHOICE El Pequeño Gecko Verde
BUNGALOW $$
(☎2656-1176; www.gecko-verde.com; d from $90; P❄🐾🏊) A hidden slice of heaven, contemporary and beautifully decorated bungalows have beds dressed in plush linens, artisanal carvings on the walls, a private terrace with hammock and outdoor dining area, plus our favorite feature – an outdoor stone shower. Onsite amenities include a saltwater swimming pool with waterfall, a lush garden and a fabulous open-air restaurant and bar. Behind the property, a 400m jungle trail and steep cement staircase lead to a secret beach that doesn't appear on any map – Playa Izquierda, a stunning cove backed by high cliffs with amazing sunset views.

Hostel Mariposas
HOSTEL $
(☎8703-3625; www.hostelmariposas.com; dm US$15, d with/without bath US$38/35; 🐾) The best hostel in town is down a dirt road on the way to the language school. It's got wooden rooms and dorms, plenty of swaying hammocks, paper lantern lighting and a communal kitchen, and it's just 60m from the sand.

Casa Paraiso
GUESTHOUSE $
(☎2656-0741; sabinasalvatore@hotmail.com; s/d US$30/40) Here's a lovely little guesthouse brushed in deep blues and inviting pastels with high ceilings and comfy beds. It's not spectacular, but it is spotless and offers really good value.

Hotel Playa Samara
HOTEL $
(☎2656-0190; per person weekday/weekend US$15/30; 🐾) The digs are cheap and not all that tasty, but they aren't bad either with high wooden ceilings, private baths, queen beds and new fans to cool your engines. Plus, it's just steps from the sand.

Camping Cocos
CAMPGROUND $
(☎2656-0496; camping per person US$6) On the eastern edge of the beach, this attractive site has well-maintained facilities but can sometimes be absolutely packed. After 10pm, it's quiet time.

La Mansion B&B
B&B **$**

(☏2265-9151; www.samarabeach.com/lamansion; s/d US$40/50; 🛜) Here's a white-washed concrete hacienda on a quiet street, twirling with fans, bursting with colorful knick-knacks and mounted with more than a few crucifixes. There's loads of charm here and rooms are spacious and bright, plus the breakfast is huge. Bathrooms are shared.

Hotel Matilori
HOSTEL **$**

(☏2656-0984; posadamatilori@racsa.co.cr; dm/s/d US$$15/20/25; P🛜🛜) A terrific value hostel with wooden dorm rooms that sleep four in the newer annex and private rooms in the main house that share baths. Guests have use of a spotless updated kitchen, and ownership speaks French, Spanish and English and is quite endearing. It's on a quiet side street close to the beach.

Tico Adventure Lodge
LODGE **$$**

(☏2656-0628; www.ticoadventurelodge.com; d US$50; P🛜🛜🛜) The US owners are proud of the fact that they built this lodge without cutting down a single tree, and they have every reason to be – it's stunning. Nine double rooms with bathroom and wood accents aren't big or particularly bright, but they're surrounded by lush vegetation and old-growth trees. Cheaper weekly and monthly rates are available.

Hotel Casa Valeria
HOTEL **$**

(☏2656-0511; casavaleria_af@hotmail.com; s/d with shared bath US$25/30, r with private bath US$50-70; P🛜) Here's a cheery beachside guesthouse with reasonable prices, hammocks in the garden and comfy public spaces on a sweet slice of beach. Some rooms are bigger than others, and those with private bath that sleep up to four are a steal. It's about 100m east of the main road. They only accept cash.

Samara Inn
INN **$$**

(☏2656-0482; www.hotelsamarainn.com; s/d US$55/80; P🛜🛜🛜🛜) A large, lovingly designed lodge with tiled rooms that are basic but have nice touches like glass doors, groovy shower curtains, porcelain bowl sinks, and dark wood furniture. The pool is gorgeous and the property is set behind the grassland with unbroken views to the sea from your breakfast table.

Hotel Giada
HOTEL **$$**

(☏2656-0132; www.hotelgiada.net; d US$65; P🛜🛜🛜🛜) A cute Italian-themed place with canary yellow, sponge painted rooms in

a hacienda huddled between two pools. It's in the center of town so it ain't quiet, but the colorful African art and leafy landscape offer plenty of charm. Rooms aren't huge but they are bright, and have bamboo desks and ceramic tile. They offer US$10 discounts for cash payment.

Las Ranas
LODGE **$$**

(☏2656-0609; www.samarabeach.com/lodgelasranas/index; d US$95-115; 🛜) A new-build stucco lodge with a king's location. We're talking nearly 180 degrees of ocean vistas from the restaurant, pool and upper rooms. And those rooms are a step above from the usual three-star noise you'll see in Samara. There are canopy beds, granite tile floors, balconies and soaring beamed ceilings. It's just east of town, and you'll need wheels to nest here.

Sámara Tree House Inn
BUNGALOW **$$$**

(☏2656-0733; www.samaratreehouse.com; bungalows incl breakfast US$85-130; P🛜@🛜🛜) These five stilted tree houses for grown-ups are so appealing that you might extend your stay. Fully equipped kitchens have pots hanging from driftwood racks, huge windows welcome light and breezes, and hammocks are hung underneath the raised bungalows. Even the bathroom tile is gorgeous.

Villas Pepitas
APARTMENT **$$$**

(☏2656-0747; www.villaspepitas.com; apt from US$110; P🛜@🛜) On the west side of town, just before crossing the river, these cheery, well-appointed apartments are perfect for couples or families. Expect full kitchens, rustic wood furnishings and plenty of patio and living space to make you feel at home on this blooming Mediterranean-style garden property. It's quiet on this road, but just a short walk into town and to the beach.

✖ Eating

Self-caterers can stock up on supplies at Super Sámara Market, east of the main road, or the smaller Super La Amistad on the main road by the beach.

Ahora Si
VEGETARIAN **$$**

(☏2656-0741; Sabinasalvatore@hotmail.com; mains US$5-11; 🛜🛜) A Venetian-owned, vegetarian restaurant and all-natural cocktail bar, they do smoothies with coconut milk; gnocchi with nutmeg, sage and smoked cheese; soy burgers and yucca fries; wok stir-fries; and thin-crust pizzas too. All served on a lovingly decorated tiled patio.

Lo Que Hay
RESTAURANT **$**

(☎2656-0811; tacos US$2, meals from US$6; ☺7am-late) Brand new and already rocking, this beachside *taqueria* and pub strobes ball games on the big screen, offers four delectable taco fillings (fish, chicken, beef or pork), and mains like blackened fish, slow roasted pork and beef fajitas. The grilled avocados stuffed with *pico de gallo* are money, and the bar crowd sips into the wee smalls.

Restaurante Jardín Marino
SODA **$$**

(☎2656-0934; mains US$6-16; ☺7am-10pm) A tin roof, open-air tiled *soda* on the main road leading to the beach, serving *tipica* and a few Western forays like pasta and burgers. The food won't change your life, but it will satisfy.

Gusto
ITALIAN **$$**

(☎2656-2219; www.gustocostarica.com; dishes mains US$7-24) An Italian-fusion place with homemade pasta, three types of fish Carpaccio, generous Thai beef and tuna salads, and an assortment of meat, chicken and fish dishes, including a wasabi cream tuna, miso steak and spaghetti with lobster! The pasta is made fresh and there are the usual saucy suspects: arrabiata, puttanesca, pesto, and carbonara. The room elegantly flickers with candles and is draped with silky linens, the pebbled concrete floor is swirled with floral motifs. It's located downtown.

Kaibella
THAI **$$**

(☎8722-2394, 2656-2352; dishes US$4-12; ☺6-9pm; ☝) Hidden in the uninspiring environs of the Central Comercial Shana, this Canadian-owned Thai kitchen crafts crispy spring rolls, scallops in green curry, a nutty massaman beef curry and pad thai. The food is not terrifically authentic, but there is a lot of fresh flavor and ample vegetarian eats. If only it didn't take 45 minutes to cook a curry. Take out is available.

Al Manglar
ITALIAN **$$**

(☎2656-0096; mains US$8-18; ☺5pm-10pm; ☝) This thatched-roof, open-air restaurant serves excellent gnocchi and ravioli, and the pizzas are perfect. It's tucked on a side street behind El Lagarto.

Casa Esmeralda
SODA **$$**

(☎2656-0489; mains US$6-17; ☺noon-9:30pm Mon-Sat) A favorite with locals, it's a dressed-up soda with table clothes, faux adobe walls, and tasty salads, pastas, meat, chicken and fish dishes. The *arroz con camarones* comes highly recommended.

El Lagarto
RESTAURANT **$$$**

(☎2656-0750; www.ellagartobbq.com; mains US$11-70; ☺10am-11pm; ☝) Grilled meats are the big draw at this beachfront alfresco restaurant studded with old trees. Watching the chefs work their magic on the giant wood-fired oven is part of the fun. Wash it all down with the biggest margaritas you've ever seen. It's touristy and pricey, but a worthy splurge.

Gusto Beach Sporting Club
$$

(☎2656-0252; www.gustocostarica.com; mains US$8-17 ; ☝) One of the better restaurants in town now has a beach club too. They do the pastas and an array of grilled meat and fish dishes in hip beach environs punctuated by an occasionally mind-numbing drum-and-bass soundtrack. On the bright side, they have lockers, beach tennis and volleyball, wi-fi and more.

🍷 Drinking & Entertainment

Lo Que Hay (p250) lures a gringo crowd and keeps it rocking deep into the night.

La Vela Latina
BAR

(☎2656-2286; www.facebook.com/pages/Beach-Bar-La-Vela-Latina/211409918292?sk=info; ☺11am-midnight; ☝) La Vela Latina, among the beach bars and restaurants that congregate south of the main road, serves pub grub and sushi (we can't vouch for it), but you're here for the buckets of icy beers, perfectly blended cocktails, sangria, and, ahem, their ample Gypsy Kings collection.

Bar Olas
BAR

(☺noon-late) If you'd like to settle in for an evening of beers with the locals, check out Bar Olas on the north end of the beach. This archetypal seafront dive makes almost no effort – even the beer should be colder – but they're open early, serve late and drinks are cheap.

Bar Arriba
BAR

(www.facebook.com/SamarArriba; ☺5:30pm-2am) The poshest bar in town is Bar Arriba, a Spanish-run party place where the lighting is sufficiently dim and red, the flat screen strobes, the sound system thumps Spanish alt rock and club hits, and they pour Flor de Cana, Havana Club and Ron Zacapa. As the name suggests, it's located on the second level of the Centro Comercial Shana.

🔒 Shopping

Numerous vendors sell crafts and hand-made jewelry at stands along the main road.

Galería Dragonfly　　　　HANDICRAFTS
(📞2656-0964; ⊙10am-9pm) A woven hemp and leather gallery of hippie art, jewelry and accessories, only some of which will lose its appeal after the THC subsides in your system. But there is love and warmth here.

Marea Surf Shop　　　　SPORTS
(📞2656-1181; ⊙7am-6pm) Part cafe, part downtown surf shop, they don't rent gear but they have top-quality tees, hats, board shorts and boards for the buying and the shopkeeper steams a fine espresso.

ℹ️ Information

Surf the excellent www.samarabeach.com to get the skinny on Sámara.

Banco Nacional (📞2656-0086; ⊙9am-5pm Mon-Fri) Change money at this bank next to the church; there's also an ATM.

Banco Costa Rica (⊙9am-4pm Mon-Fri, 24hr ATM) Just off the main road and across from the cell tower and soccer field, they change foreign currency and there's an ATM.

Internet Sámara (📞2656-1102; per hr US$2; ⊙9am-1pm, 3-9pm) On the main road next to Bar Arriba.

Post Office (⊙8am-noon & 1:15am-5:30pm Mon-Fri) Located in the same building as the police station, on the main road where it meets the beach.

Sky Net Tours (📞2656-0920; www.samara-tours.com; per hour US$2; ⊙9am-9pm) Formerly the Samara Travel Center, this extremely helpful place has an internet cafe, and can book flights and Interbus tickets and arrange tours. It also rents bicycles (per day US$10), scooters (per day US$30), and motorcycles (per day US$35).

Sámara Laundry (📞2656-3000; per kg US$2.50; ⊙8am-6:30pm Mon-Sat) Laundry service located on the main road, in the Century 21 building, two blocks up from the beach.

ℹ️ Getting There & Away

The beach lies about 35km southwest of Nicoya on a paved road. No flights were operating out of the Samara airport (PLD) at research time.

BUS Empresas Alfaro (⊙7:30am-1pm, 1:30am-5pm) has a bus to San José (US$8, five hours) that departs at 4:30am and 8:30am. All buses depart from the main intersection just south of Entre Dos Aguas B&B. Buy your San José bus tickets at the Alfaro office behind Bazar d'Liss on the main intersection in town.

Traroc buses to Nicoya (US$2.50, two hours) depart hourly from 5:30am to 6:30pm from the *pulpería* by the soccer field; there's a more limited schedule on Sunday.

Playa Carrillo

About 4km southeast of Sámara, Carrillo is a wide, arcing beach with clean white sand, cracked granite headlands and a jungle backdrop. On weekends and holidays, the palm-fringed boulevard is lined with cars and the beach crowded with Tico families.

The little town is on a hillside above the beach and attracts a trickle of surfers working their way down the coast, as well as schools of American sportfishers chasing billfish. About 200m east of the beach, **La Selva** (📞2656-2236; adult/child US$8/5; ⊙8am-7pm) is a small wildlife refuge and botanical garden with monkeys, iguanas, alligators, coatis and other critters. Night tours depart at 5:30pm.

🏄 Activities

Kingfisher Sportfishing　　SPORTFISHING
(📞2656-0091; www.costaricabillfishing.com) A well-known local outfit, offering half- and full-day excursions from US$600.

Surf Casting

You don't have to drop big bucks to catch some nice-sized fish – do as the Ticos do and try your hand at surf casting. Most hotels and tour outfitters can set you up for a few dollars.

Surfing

Surfing here is better than at nearby Playa Sámara, though it's nothing great. Mid- to high tide is when you can catch decent waves.

TOURS

Carrillo Tours　　　　TOUR
(📞2656-0543; www.carrillotours.com; ⊙8am-7pm) On the road up the hill, Carrillo Tours organizes snorkeling, dolphin-watching, kayaking, horseback riding and trips to Palo Verde.

Popo's Surf Camp　　SURFING, KAYAKING
(📞2656-0086; www.camaronal.com; river trips per person US$35, Isla Chora trips per person US$55) This old standby offers surf lessons and kayak tours along the river and all the way out to Isla Chora aboard expedition-style kayaks. Tours operate with a minimum of two guests.

🛏 Sleeping & Eating

Most hotels are at the eastern end of the beach on a hill. The beach is a five- to 10-minute walk down from places.

La Tropicale
TOP CHOICE · BUNGALOW $$
(☎8884-9471, 2656-0159; www.samarabeach.com/latropicale; d US$60; ✦❋🕸🗙) Across from La Selva is a fun, funky, fabulous inn that has ramshackle charm and plenty of hip touches. Rooms are actually stand-alone bungalows draped with lovely linens and blessed with gorgeous screened baths that feel more outside than in. They also have larger houses with full kitchens that sleep four.

Cabinas El Colibrí
CABINA $$
(☎2656-0656; www.cabinaselcolibri.com; d incl breakfast US$60; ✦❋🕸🗙🐾) These Argentine-run cabinas are huge with vaulted beamed ceilings, hammocks on the porch, cable TV, wi-fi and hot water. Mini-apartments with kitchenette are the same price but don't include breakfast. Cabinas El Colibrí is a relaxed and comfortable spot, and you'll be well fed at the attached steak house, which is open for dinner and serves traditional Argentine *parrilladas* (grilled meats), *empanadas*, as well as fresh grilled tuna.

Puerto Carrillo Hotel
HOTEL $$
(☎2656-1104; r US$50; ✦❋🕸🗙) A dozen or so comfy, three-star caliber rooms are arced around an inviting pool at this low-key spot popular with Tico families. Rooms are spotless with high ceilings and a splash of color, and are terrific value.

Casa Buenavista
B&B $$
(☎2656-0385; www.samarabeach.com/casabuenavista; d incl breakfast US$65; ✦🕸) A sweet Italian couple runs this two-room B&B. Every basic but homey room here has its own hot-water bathroom, porch and entrance, there's also a small shaded yoga terrace in the garden, and they offer high-quality shiatsu massage (per hour US$35). It's in town, 350m from the beach. Reserve ahead.

Popo's Surf Camp
CABINA $$
(☎2656-0086; www.camaronal.com; d US$60) Here's an inviting huddle of aging but attractive, two-story wooden *cabinas* overlooking the river. They have full kitchens and are set in town just above the beach.

Carrillo Club
CABINA $$
(☎2656-0316; www.carrilloclub.com; d incl breakfast from US$75; ✦❋🕸) This pretty yellow inn on the hillside has a clutch of comfortable, attractive, if aging *cabinas* with a private terrace, full kitchen and hot-water bathroom. There's a pool with ocean views, and the beach is a short walk downhill. Taking breakfast on the big front terrace is a treat, with beautiful, expansive views of Playa Carrillo below.

❶ Getting There & Away

Sansa flights were no longer servicing the airstrip just northwest of the beach at research time. Some Traroc buses from Nicoya to Sámara continue on the well-paved road to Playa Carrillo; check with the driver first.

Islita Area

The coast southeast of Playa Carrillo remains one of the peninsula's most isolated and wonderful stretches of coastline, mainly because it's largely inaccessible and lacking in accommodations. But if you're willing to tackle rugged roads or venture down the coastline in a sea kayak (or possibly on foot), you'll be rewarded with abandoned beaches backed by pristine wilderness and rugged hills.

There are a few small breaks in front of the Hotel Punta Islita, where you'll find a gorgeous cove punctuated with that evocative wave-thrashed boulder that is Punta Islita. At high tide the beach narrows, but at low tide it is wide and as romantic as those vistas from above. Another good beach and point break lies north of Punta Islita at Playa Camaronal, a charcoal gray stretch of sand strewn with driftwood and sheltered by two headlands. This beach also happens to be a protected nesting site for leatherback, olive ridley, hawksbill and black turtles, and is officially known as Refugio Nacional de Vida Silvestre Camaronal (⊙8am-6pm).

Playas Corzalito and Bejuco to the south of Punta Islita are both backed by mangrove swamps, and offer good opportunities for bird- and wildlife-watching.

Also worth a visit is the small town of Islita, which is home to the Museo Islita (⊙8am-4pm Mon-Sat), an imaginative contemporary art house crusted with mosaic murals, and featuring carvings and paintings that adorn everything from houses to tree trunks. This project was organized by Hotel Punta Islita, which sells local art in its gift shop and invests proceeds in the community.

🛏 Sleeping & Eating

You can camp on the beaches (without facilities) if you have a vehicle and are self-sufficient.

Hotel Punta Islita RESORT $$$
(☑2656-2020; www.hotelpuntaislita.com; d incl breakfast from US$330, casitas from US$528; P❄@🛜🏊) This luxury resort serves as an example of how to ethically operate a hotel. In addition to organizing community arts projects, they sponsored the construction of various public buildings, including a new church. The hotel is on a hilltop, and has 51 fully equipped rooms with staggering ocean views; spend up for a suite (with a private outdoor Jacuzzi). The infinity pool and surrounding grounds are simply stunning; they have a full-service spa, a beach club with a sunken pool bar and lounges on a rolling lawn, and good waves in the sheltered bay. Staff will arrange any tour you desire.

Restaurante Kimbute SODA $$
(☑2656-1394; mains US$4-18; ⊙noon-9:30pm) The only indie shingle in town, it's a rather preppy *soda* with timber tabletops set under a few broad thatched umbrellas. The *ceviche* gets good marks and their *casados* are quite nice too.

1492 Restaurant INTERNATIONAL $$$
(☑2661-4044; mains US$14-28; ⊙7am-10pm; 🛜) The movie *1492* was shot on location in Punta Islita, and some of the props adorn the restaurant. The cuisine here, which is a fusion of Costa Rican and international food, is top quality – and the view is superlative.

❶ Getting There & Away

Air

NatureAir and Sansa each fly once daily between San José and Punta Islita (one way around US$120). The resort offers private charters in their own plane to Liberia (US$195) and San José (US$850) for up to five people.

Bus

The closest you can get to Islita by bus is to take one of Empresa Arza's two daily buses from San José that go through San Francisco de Coyote and on to Playas San Miguel and Bejuco. Keep in mind, though, that from Bejuco there is still a long uphill hike to Islita – and hitchhiking is almost impossible due to the lack of traffic.

Car

Although Punta Islita is less than 10km by road southeast of Playa Carrillo, the coastal 'road' is wicked and requires some river crossings that are impossible in the wet season. The 'easiest' route heads inland on the paved road from Playa Carrillo to the village of Estrada. When you come to the fork in the road, bear left. At the T-intersection in Santa Marta, turn right onto the gravel road to Islita. At the next T-intersection, you can turn right on the rough but decent dirt road to reach Islita (11km), or left to reach Playas San Miguel and Coyote via San Pedro, Cangrejal and Bejuco.

Playas San Miguel & Coyote

Just south of Playa Bejuco are arguably two of the most beautiful and least visited beaches in Costa Rica. Playa San Miguel is a desolate and beautiful beach buffeted by a hulking granite headland and backed by elegant coconut palms. There's a no-name bar at the end of the road, on the beach. Playa Coyote, to the south, is likewise a wilderness beach, but at high tide much of the fine, silver-gray sand gets swallowed up. San Miguel and Coyote serve as nesting grounds for olive ridley turtles.

There are no coastal villages to speak of, though a number of in-the-know foreigners have settled in the area and have built accommodations near the shoreline. The nearest village is San Francisco de Coyote, which is 4km inland and has a few small *sodas*, *cabinas* and an internet cafe. For a good online map of the area, visit www.nicoyapeninsula.com/coyote/map.php.

◎ Sights & Activities

You can surf crowd-free beach breaks off San Miguel, particularly when the tide is rising. At Coyote there is an offshore reef that can be surfed at high tide. If swimming, you are advised to take precautions as the surf can pick up, and there are not many people in the area to help you in an emergency. If you have your own sea kayak, these beaches (as well as nearby Islita) are perfect for coastal exploration.

Mike's Jungle Butterfly Farm GARDENS
(☑8719-1703, 2655-8070; junglemike@live.com; tours adult/child 12 & under US$20/10; ⊙9am-3pm Mon-Sat) Mike's beautiful mountainside property includes a lovely butterfly garden. He'll give you a tour if you make reservations in advance, and you can camp here too.

🛏️ Sleeping & Eating

You can camp on both beaches if you're self-sufficient, as there are no services.

Jungle Mike's Butterfly
Farm & Cottages
CABINA $$

(📞8719-1703, 2655-8070; junglemike@live.com; camping per person US$5, r US$65) American-Tico owned and set just outside Pueblo Nuevo, this place has two cute *cabinas* on a hill overlooking a sublime stretch of coast, and they are a steal. They sleep four, have peaked beamed ceilings, flaunt gorgeous mosaic motifs in the kitchen area, and open onto massive patios with drop-dead gorgeous views of the Pacific and verdant mountains on all sides. You can also camp at Mike's butterfly rancho.

Hotel Arca de Noé
HOTEL $$

(📞8352-9320, 2655-8065; dm US$10, d incl breakfast US$70; P❄🌐🏊) Found inland from the beach, this pleasantly landscaped, critter-friendly complex has 10 attractive doubles with a private hot-water shower and air-con. They aren't the best value rooms on the peninsula but are plenty comfortable. Plus, the owners grow their own fruits and herbs.

Flying Scorpion
HOTEL $$

(📞2655-8080; http://escorpionvolador.com; s/d incl breakfast US$45/55, apt from US60, houses US$80-200; P❄🌐) Turn right at the Blue Pelican and continue on the dirt road along the beach for a few hundred meters to find this mellow inn with a handful of clean, very comfortable rooms with new teak beds and an assortment of eclectic folk art. It has direct beach access for long days of surfing, and you'll be happy to come back to the bar/restaurant's homemade bread, pasta and ice cream. Run by an amiable couple and their pack of Weimaraners, this is a great spot to zone out for a few days or weeks.

Casa Caletas
RESORT $$$

(📞2655-1271; www.casacaletas.com; d incl breakfast US$140; P❄🏊) Down at the end of the road before turning toward Mal País, this beautiful boutique resort sits on the bank of the Río Coyote in Punta Coyote, and feels blissfully isolated. There's an airy restaurant (mains US$7 to US$14), cushy rooms and an infinity pool overlooking the river and ocean. The beach is accessible by crossing the river or via trails, and the hotel can arrange horseback rides, kayaking and fishing

trips. To get here, take the road from San Francisco de Coyote toward Mal País and follow the signs for the hotel.

Rhodeside Bed & Breakfast
and Espresso Bar
B&B $$

(📞2655-8006; www.rhodesidebedandbreakfast. com; d US$60; P❄🌐) An American-owned coffee shop and B&B on the hillside between San Miguel and Pueblo Nuevo. The iconoclastic owners do exquisite espresso drinks (from locally sourced beans) and delicious breakfasts. They also have quaint, spotless, tiled rooms with hot water and lovely patio views.

Pizza Tree
PIZZERIA $$

(📞2655-8063; pizzas US$9-12 ; ⏰noon-10pm; 🐾) As you head north, after you pass the turn to Playa Coyote and are almost into San Miguel proper you'll come across a fantastically whimsical tree-house pizzeria in Javillal. Italian-owned and operated, they serve crispy thin-crust pizzas and foccacia prepared in a wood-fired brick oven.

Cafe Sante
CAFE $

(dishes US$6-10; ⏰10am-4pm Mon-Fri) This cheery new spot is set in the quaint crossroads town of San Francisco de Coyote. They serve espresso, sandwiches and salads but are only open for lunch during the week.

ℹ️ Getting There & Away

BUS **Empresa Arza** (📞2650-0179) has two daily buses from San José that cross the Golfo de Nicoya on the Puntarenas ferry and continue through Jicaral to San Francisco de Coyote, and on to Playas San Miguel and Bejuco. Buses depart San José at 2:30am and 1pm, pass through San Francisco de Coyote at about 10:30am and 9pm, and arrive at Playa San Miguel at noon and 10pm. Return buses leave Bejuco at 12:30pm and 10:30pm, pass through Playa San Miguel at around 1pm and 11:45pm, and San Francisco de Coyote at 2:30pm and midnight. This service is sketchy in the rainy season and the trip may take longer if road conditions are bad.

SOUTHEASTERN PENINSULA

Word has spread about the hippie-chic outpost of Montezuma and the miles of surf breaks in Santa Teresa-Mal País – which manages to be dusty, real and glamorous.

During the dry season, packs of international surfers and wanderers arrive hungry for the wild beauty and soul-stirring waters on either side of the peninsula. In between, and at the very southern tip of the Península de Nicoya, lies the first natural reserve in Costa Rica. It used to require hours of sweaty bus rides and sluggish ferries from the mainland to access this tropical land's end, but these days there are more roads and regular shuttles, making Cabo Blanco an easy day trip from either base. But if you have the time and money, embrace the gritty arduous drive down the rugged southeastern peninsula, which includes several river crossings, and two low-tide beach traverses before you reach Mal País, just north of the reserve, and head back into the muddy jungle, and climb over one more steep pass to the park gates.

Playa Naranjo

This tiny village next to the ferry terminal is nothing more than a few *sodas* and small hotels that cater to travelers either waiting for the ferry or arriving from Puntarenas. There really isn't any reason to hang around, but if you do get stuck at the port for a night, the better of Playa Naranjo's two hotels is just 400m away on their own deep green cove. Hotel Oasis del Pacifico (☑8850-7186; r US$46; P❄☀❄) has a pool in the center of leafy palm-studded grounds, and their rooms are huge, airy, tiled affairs and are plenty clean and comfortable. There's no restaurant, but a collection of *sodas* sit 200m away close to the port.

❶ Getting There & Away

All transportation is geared to the arrival and departure of the Puntarenas ferry, so don't worry – if one is running late, the other will wait.

Boat

The **Coonatramar ferry** (☑2661-1069; www.coonatramar.com; adult/child/bicycle/motorcycle/car US$2/1/4/6/18) to Puntarenas departs daily at 8am, 12:30pm, 5:30pm and 9pm, and can accommodate both cars and passengers. The trip takes 1½ hours. If traveling by car, get out and buy a ticket at the window, get back in your car and then drive on to the ferry. You cannot buy a ticket on board. Show up at least an hour early on holidays and busy weekends, as you'll be competing with a whole lot of other drivers to make it on.

Bus

Buses meet the ferry and take passengers on to Nicoya (US$3, three hours). Departure times are (approximately) 7am, 10:50pm, 2:50pm and 7pm. Regular buses journey from Paquera to Montezuma, though there are none that go southeast from here.

Car & Taxi

It's possible to get to Paquera via a scenic, rugged and steep but passable road over three inland ridges with magical vistas of Bahía Gigante. A 4WD is recommended, especially in the rainy season when there are rivers to cross. The only public transportation is 4WD taxi, which costs about US$40.

Islands near Bahía Gigante

The waters in and around the isolated Bahía Gigante, 9km southeast of Playa Naranjo, are studded with rocky islets and deserted islands. Since there is no public transportation here, and a 4WD is a necessity almost year-round, the area feels very quiet and unhurried. However, travelers are drawn here for its range of activities, namely sportfishing, snorkeling, diving and kayaking, which can all be arranged through hotels and travel agencies from Paquera to Montezuma.

ISLA SAN LUCAS

The largest island in Bahía Gigante (just over 600 hectares) is about 5km off the coast from Playa Naranjo, and from a distance seems like a beautiful desert island. However, the 'Island of Unspeakable Horrors' has a 400-year history as one of the most notorious jails in Latin America. The island was first used by Spanish conquistadors as a detention center for local tribes in the 16th century. In 1862 the job of warden was inherited by the Costa Rican government, which used the island to detain political prisoners until 1992.

Visitors can expect to see the 100-year-old overgrown remains of the prison. Although there are still guards living on the island, their primary purpose is to discourage poachers, which means travelers are usually permitted to wander freely through the prison grounds and even camp on the island.

ISLA GIGANTE

In the middle of Bahía Gigante is the 10-hectare Isla Gigante, which is shown on most maps as Isla Muertos (Island of the Dead) because it is home to a number of Chara burial sites (and is believed by locals to be haunted).

ISLA GUAYABO, ISLAS NEGRITOS & LOS PÁJAROS

This cluster of islands was recently established as a biological reserve to protect the nesting seabird populations, including the largest breeding colony of brown pelicans found in Costa Rica. No land visitors are allowed except researchers with permission from the park service. However, the reserves can be approached by boat, and the bird populations are plainly visible from the ocean.

ISLA TORTUGA

Isla Tortuga, which consists of two uninhabited islands just offshore from Curú, is widely regarded as the most beautiful island in Costa Rica. The white-sand beaches feel like baby powder under your toes, there are gargantuan coconut palms overhead, and the coral reef is perfect for snorkeling. Unfortunately, Tortuga receives heavy boat traffic from tour operators from Montezuma and Jacó, but if you visit during the week in low season it can be magical.

☞ Tours

Most travelers arrange tours either through the hotels listed here or with an operator in Montezuma or Jacó. However, this is one region where independence (and language skills) can make for a good adventure – enquire locally to find out if someone who has a boat is willing to take you where you want to go for a reasonable price. Turismo Curú (p256), in Paquera, offers a variety of low-key itineraries to the islands.

Calypso Tours   BOAT TOUR
(☎2256-2727; www.calypsocruises.com; tours from US$139) The most luxurious island excursion is with Calypso Tours. The company transports passengers to Isla Tortuga in a luxurious 21m motorized catamaran. It's all flash with a couple of outdoor Jacuzzis, an underwater viewing window, and a kayaking option. It's not a bad deal considering that the price includes transportation from San José, Jaco, Manuel Antonio or Monteverde, food and drinks.

❶ Getting There & Away

There is no public transportation in the area. The dirt road from Playa Naranjo to Paquera requires a 4WD for most of the year.

Paquera

The tiny village of Paquera is about 25km by road from Playa Naranjo and 4km from the ferry terminal. Paquera is more of a population center than Playa Naranjo, though there's little reason to stay here longer than you have to.

Cabinas & Restaurante Ginana   CABINA $
(☎2641-0119; s/d/tr US$24/36/40; ⓟ✳@☎✲) There are a number of *cabinas* in the village, though this is the best option, with 28 simple and clean tiled rooms. Their quality restaurant (dishes US$3 to US$6) turns out tasty seafood in tiled *palapa* environs, if you need a bite to eat before getting on the ferry.

❶ Information

Banco Popular (⊙8:15am-4pm), on the side street, can change US dollars and traveler's checks. On the main road, across from the gas station, you'll find **Turismo Curú** (☎2641-0004; www.curutourism.com; ⊙8am-9pm), operated by the knowledgeable Luis Schutt of the Curú refuge. Luis offers a tour that combines a visit to Curú and a snorkeling trip to Isla Tortuga for US$30 per person (a great deal!). They also run dive trips (two tanks US$100) to Isla Tortuga, and offer internet access (per hour US$2) in their Paquera office.

❶ Getting There & Away

All transportation is geared to the arrival and departure of the Puntarenas ferry. If either is running late, the other will wait.

Boat

Ferry Naviera Tambor (☎2641-2084; www.navieratambor.com; adult/child/bicycle/motorcycle/car US$1.65/1/4.50/7/23) leaves daily at 6am, 9am, 11am, 2pm, 5pm and 8pm. The trip takes about an hour. Buy a ticket at the window, reboard your car and then drive onto the ferry; you can't buy a ticket on board. Show up at least an hour early on holidays and busy weekends. The terminal contains a *soda* where you can grab a bite while waiting for the boat.

Bus

Buses meet passengers at the ferry terminal and take them to Paquera, Tambor and Montezuma. The bus can be crowded, so try to get off the ferry fast to get a seat.

Most travelers take the bus from the terminal directly to Montezuma (US$3, two hours). Many taxi drivers will tell you the bus won't come, but this isn't true. There are no northbound buses.

COSTA RICAN WILDCAT CONSERVATIONISTS

Since 1992 Programa para la Conservación de Felinos (Profelis; Feline Conservation Program) has taken care of confiscated felines that were given to the center by the Ministerio del Ambiente y Energía (Minae; Ministry of Environment and Energy). The project concentrates on smaller felines, including the margay, ocelot and jaguarundi, and aims to rehabilitate and, when possible, reintroduce animals to the wild. In addition, a large component of the program involves the environmental education of the public.

Profelis is headquartered in Hacienda Matambú, a private wildlife reserve in San Rafael de Paquera, about 5km west of Paquera. Volunteers are sought after, especially those who have experience in either keeping animals or veterinary science. For more information on volunteering, visit www.grafischer.com/profelis or contact Profelis (☏2641-0646, 2641-0644; www.grafischer.com/profelis).

Taxi

Getting several travelers together to share a taxi is a good option since the ride will take half as long as the bus. The ride to Montezuma is about US$12 per person, and to Mal País it's about US$20 – provided you can get enough people together.

A 4WD taxi to Playa Naranjo costs about US$40 for up to four people.

Refugio Nacional de Vida Silvestre Curú

Situated at the eastern end of the peninsula and only 6km south of Paquera, the tiny, 84-hectare Refugio Nacional de Vida Silvestre Curú (☏2641-0100; www.curuwildlife refuge.com; day fee adult/child 3-11/2 & under US$10/5/free; ⊗7am-3pm) holds a great variety of landscapes, including dry tropical forest, semi-deciduous forest and five types of mangrove swamp. The rugged coastline is also home to a series of secluded coves and white-sand beaches that are perfect for snorkeling and swimming. The entrance to the refuge is clearly signed on the paved road between Paquera and Tambor (it's on the right-hand side). Day visitors can show up anytime during operating hours and pay the day fee to hike the 17 well-marked, easy to moderate trails, or join a variety of tours – from horseback riding and kayaking through the estuary to snorkeling and guided hikes. Local fauna includes deer, three types of monkey, agouti and paca, and three species of cat. Iguana, crab, lobster, chiton, shellfish, sea turtle and other marine creatures scurry on the beaches and in the tide pools. Bird-watchers have recorded more than 232 bird species.

Camping is not allowed in the reserve, though there are six rustic cabinas (r per person US$60, meals US$10) with private cold showers. Stays must be arranged in advance either through the Turismo Curú office in Paquera, or at the reserve's entrance.

Playas Pochote & Tambor

These two mangrove-backed, gray-sand beaches are protected by Bahía Ballena, the largest bay on the southeastern peninsula, and are surrounded by small fishing communities. In the past 15 years, the area has slowly developed as a resort destination, but for the most part, Pochote and Tambor are mellow authentic Tico beaches, providing plenty of opportunities for hiking, swimming, kayaking and even whale watching.

The beaches begin 14km south of Paquera, at the mangrove shrouded, fishing pueblo of Pochote, and stretch for about 8km southwest to Tambor. They're divided by the narrow estuary of the Río Pánica, where you'll find two seafood *sodas* on the Pochote side, overlooking the river. Tambor is the area's access point. It should also be said that there is one rather conspicuous all-inclusive mega-resort in the Tambor area. Hotel Playa Tambor has a convention center and golf course, but once you're in the pueblo, you won't even know it's there.

🏃 Activities

Both beaches are safe for swimming, and there are occasional whale sightings in the bay. The gentle waters also make this a good spot for kayaking, and Curú's hiking trails are just down the road.

Surfing the Peninsula

Ever since longtime Tamarindo (p225) resident and surf legend Robert August started riding waves all those decades ago, surfers have descended to this rugged peninsula in search of the perfect wave. Many stayed. Hence the tourist and expat boom which has yielded some truly epic beach towns.

One of our favorite places in all of Costa Rica, Playa Grande (p220) is across the river and a world away from Tamarindo. It doubles as a national park (p224) that protects leatherback turtle nesting grounds, which means the wide beach, which rambles for miles, is damn near pristine. The wave shapes up beautifully with head high sets year-round, and the local expat residents have opened up some truly tasty kitchens and comfy inns.

At the other end of the peninsula, Mal País and Santa Teresa (p268) continue to be favored by young, hip and sexy surfers from northern Europe to southern Argentina. Here, too, the beach is long and the swell is scarily consistent, which means you can generally find some space of your own – particularly if you drive just a bit north to Playa Hermosa or Manzanillo. There's a wonderful farm-to-table movement happening here, Mal País is stunning fishing harbor, and a visit to the nearby Reserva Natural Absoluta Cabo Blanco (p267) is a must.

In between, hit Nosara (p239) for consistent surf and a welcome cloud of hippie-chic comfort, then venture further north to Playa Negra (p231), where the surf can swell big and gnarly. Or move on to nearby Playa Avellanas (p231), an understated yet elegant place to nest within reach of white-sand beaches and a break kind to beginners, despite its *Endless Summer II* pedigree. To dodge the crowds, consider a shoulder- or wet-season trip or befriend a local and seek out the still-hidden waves tucked between all the big names.

Clockwise from top left
1. Surfing at Mal País 2. Beach at Mal País
3. Playa Guiones (p242), Nosara

🛌 Sleeping

🏄 Cabinas Cristina
CABINAS $

(☎2683-0028; r US$30-44; [P][❄][?]) Just 50m from the beach, and across from Tambor's rather romantically ramshackle Victorian church, this old standby has simple and spotless rooms, and a small but tasty home-style restaurant. The owners are warm and welcoming and offer valuable travel tips. Room price varies with size and amenities.

Tambor Tropical
BOUTIQUE HOTEL $$$

(☎2365-2872; www.tambortropical.com; ste incl breakfast US$185-210; [P][?][≋]) Romantically set on the beach amid a palm-fringed garden, Tambor Tropical is a lovely boutique hotel with stunning architecture. The 12 roomy, hexagonal suites all have dark wood interiors, full kitchen, wet bar and private veranda. There's no air-con but the ocean breeze will keep you cool on all but the hottest days. You'll pay slightly more for a second-story room.

H & B Cabinas
CABINAS $$

(☎2683-0025; s/d US$40/50) Just over the hill from the beach in Tambor, rooms are clean with tiled floors, crown moldings and wooden walls. Rooms range in size and those in back are quieter and decent value.

❶ Getting There & Away

The airport is just north of the entrance to Hotel Barceló Playa Tambor. Hotels will arrange pickup at the airport for an extra fee. Between them, Sansa and NatureAir (one way/round-trip from US$83/168) have up to 10 daily flights to and from San José. There's a **Budget** (☎2436-2030, 2683-0500; www.budget.co.cr; ☺8am-6pm Mon-Sat, 8am-4pm Sun) car rental shingle 4km from the Tambor airport. They have a free shuttle to and from the 'terminal'.

Paquera–Montezuma buses pass through here.

Cóbano

Cóbano has two gas stations, a post office, clinic, pharmacy, three supermarkets and Banco Nacional (☎2642-0210; ☺8:30am-3:45pm Mon-Fri, 9am-1pm Sat), making it the only real 'city' (it's barely a town) in the southeastern peninsula. There are a few hotels and restaurants, but there's no reason to stay since Montezuma is only 7km away.

Paquera–Montezuma buses pass through here, and a 4WD taxi to Montezuma costs about US$12.

Montezuma

Montezuma is an immediately endearing beach town that demands you abandon the car, stroll, swim and, if you are willing to stroll even further, surf. The warm and wild ocean, and that remnant, ever-audible jungle, has helped this rocky nook cultivate an inviting, boho vibe. Typical tourist offerings, such as canopy tours, do a brisk trade here, but you'll also bump up against Montezuma's internationally inflected, artsy-rootsy beach culture in yoga classes, volunteer corps, festivals, veggie-friendly dining rooms, and neo-Rastas hawking uplifting herbs. No wonder locals lovingly call this town 'Montefuma.' It's not perfect. The lodging is particularly poor value, and the eateries can be that way too (though there are some absolute gems). But in this barefoot *pueblo*, which unfurls along several kilometers of rugged coastline, you're never far from the rhythm and sound of the sea, and that is a beautiful thing.

◉ Sights & Activities

Picture-perfect white-sand beaches are strung along the coast, separated by small rocky headlands, offering great beachcombing and ideal tidepool contemplation. Unfortunately, there are strong rip tides, so inquire locally before going for a swim.

The beaches in front of the town are nice enough, but the best beach is just north of Cocolores, where the sand is powdery and sheltered from big swells. This is your glorious sun-soaked crash pad, and the further northeast you walk the more solitude you'll find. The water's shade of teal is immediately nourishing, the temperature is perfect and it's clean enough to attract wildlife. We saw two big rays at the water's surface. During low tide, the best snorkeling is at Playa Las Manchas, 1km west of downtown. There's great surf if you're willing to walk the 7km up the coast to Playa Grande, or if you head south about 3km to Playa Cedros. Because of the town's carefree boho feel, topless and (sometimes) nude sunbathing have become de rigueur on some beaches. No one is likely to say anything if you choose to bare your wares, but keep in mind that many residents find it disrespectful.

Proyecto Montezuma
VOLUNTEERING

(☎8314-0690; www.proyectomontezuma.com) Kerri Bowers and César Benavides from

Montezuma

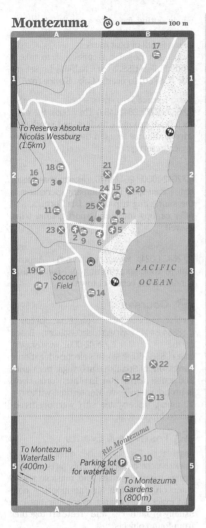

To Reserva Absoluta
Nicolás Wessburg
(1.5km)

PACIFIC

OCEAN

Soccer
Field

Río Montezuma

To Montezuma
Waterfalls
(400m)

Parking lot
for waterfalls

To Montezuma
Gardens
(800m)

Montezuma

Activities, Courses & Tours
1 Cabo Blanco Travellers B2
2 Devaya Yoga...A3
3 La Escuela del Sol A2
4 Montezuma EcoTours.........................A2
   Montezuma Yoga..................... (see 12)
5 Proyecto Montezuma...........................B3
6 Sun Trails A3
   Zuma Tours ....(see 6)

Sleeping
7 Cabinas Flory.......................................A3
8 Cabinas Mar y Cielo B2
9 El Sano Banano A3
10 Hotel Amor de Mar B5
11 Hotel El Jardín A2
   Hotel El Tajalin............................(see 3)
12 Hotel Los Mangos B4
13 Hotel Lucy B4
14 Hotel Lys A3
   Hotel Moctezuma ....(see 5)
15 Hotel Pargo Feliz.................................B2
16 Luna Llena A2
17 Luz de Mono B1
18 Montezuma Pacific A2
19 Pensión Jenny A3

Eating
   Bar Restaurante Moctezuma ......(see 5)
20 Cocolores..B2
21 Orgánico..B2
22 Playa de los Artistas B4
23 Puggo's...A3
24 Soda La Naranja...................................B2
   Soda Monte El Sol.......................(see 6)
25 Vaca Loca A2

Drinking
   Chico's Bar...................................(see 12)

Proyecto Montezuma run an innovative volunteer program that not only gives to the community, but also fosters cultural exchange, pays fair wages to its employees and gifts you something for donating your time and energy. You can choose the project in which you'd like to participate, such as teaching local classes or removing trash from the beach and jungle (privileges that you will pay for). Or you can simply sign up for a sustainable adventure tour or surf lessons (two hours US$40) in and around Montezuma. Check out their website for details.

Montezuma Bike Tours   CYCLING
(☏8871-1540; www.montezumabiketours.com; per person US$38-60) The Peninsula's top mountain-bike outfitter has a Montezuma address. Rides range in terrain and difficulty and last up to four hours, taking in hidden beaches, waterfalls and rugged mountains, and spanning from 14km to 17.8km in length. They even offer a full moon ride.

Montezuma Gardens   GARDENS
(☏2642-1317, 8888-4200; www.montezumagar dens.com; adult/student/child US$8/6/4; ⊙8am-4pm) About 1km up the hill toward Cóbano, alongside the waterfall trail, you can take a tour through this lovely lush *mariposario*

(butterfly garden) and nursery where the mysterious metamorphoses occur. You'll learn about the life cycles and benefits of a dozen local species, of which you'll see many colorful varieties. There's also a B&B (rooms US$70 to US$90) here.

Sun Trails CANOPY TOUR
(☑2642-0808; www.suntrailsadventures.com; US$40; ☺office 8am-8pm) After you've flown down nine zip lines, this 2.5-hour canopy tour winds up with a hike down – rather than up – to the waterfalls; bring your swimsuit. Book at the Sun Trails office in town, where you'll also have internet access (per hour US$2).

Reserva Absoluta Nicolás Wessburg HIKING
Inland from Montezuma is a private conservation area that was the original site of Nicholas Olof Wessburg and Karen Mogensen's homestead. Although the reserve is closed to visitors, you can either hike or go horseback riding along its perimeter – tours can be arranged through operators in town or at the Los Caballos Nature Lodge finca (p265).

Devaya Yoga YOGA
(☑8833-5086; www.devayayoga.com; per class US$12; ☺classes 8:30am & 4pm) A studio smack in the middle of town, above Montezuma Expediciones, they offer morning and evening classes.

Montezuma Yoga YOGA
(☑8704-1632; www.montezumayoga.com; per person US$14; ☺classes 9:30am Mon-Fri, 5pm Mon, Wed & Fri, 6pm Sun) Anusara-inspired instruction, which pairs Iyengar alignment principles with a Vinyasa flow, is available in a gorgeous studio kissed by ocean breezes, lit by paper lanterns, sheltered by a peaked tin roof held up by natural contoured timbers, on the Hotel Los Mangos (p264) property.

☞ Tours

Tour operators around town rent everything from snorkeling gear to body boards and bikes. Prices vary depending on the season, and it pays to shop around. They can also arrange speed-boat transfers to Jacó as well as private shuttle transfers.

The most popular tour is a boat trip to Isla Tortuga (p256), which costs around US$50 and should include lunch, fruit, drinks and snorkeling gear. Although the island is certainly beautiful, travelers complain that the whole outing feels like a tourist circus, especially during high season when the entire island is full of boat tours.

Another popular excursion is to take a guided hike (US$55) or a half-day horseback ride (US$60) to nearby Cabo Blanco (p267).

Cabo Blanco Travellers TOUR
(☑8835-0270, 2642-1439) They book the daily Jacó boat, ground transfers, and snorkeling trips and horse tours in the two nearby biological reserves.

Montezuma EcoTours TOUR
(☑2642-1000, 2642-0467; montezumaecotours. com; ☺8am-9pm) This company specializes in the snorkeling trip out to Isla Tortuga, and offer canopy tours and sport fishing trips, as well.

Zuma Tours TOUR
(☑2642-0024; www.zumatours.net) Another canopy tour, sport fishing and Isla Tortuga vendor in the center of town.

☞ Courses

La Escuela del Sol DANCE, LANGUAGE COURSE
(☑8884-8444; www.laescueladelsol.com) Based at the El Tajalin (☑2642-0061; www.eltajalin. com; r US$62-80; ❄🐾📶), this electic educational vortex offers Spanish, surf, yoga, fire dance and scuba instruction. In other words, there is no excuse to leave Montezuma without a bilingual, underwater, surf warrior, dreadlocked hippie soul.

⚑ Festivals & Events

Festival de Arte Chunches de Mar ARTS
(www.chunchesdemar.com) This arts festival brings together artists and musicians who camp on the beach for one month – note that exact dates change every year, but it is usually in January – and create art together from found objects.

Montezuma International Film Festival FILM
(www.montezumafilmfestival.com) Usually held in early November, this is a great excuse to celebrate the arts in Montezuma before high season kicks in.

⛁ Sleeping

MONTEZUMA
The high season gets crowded, though with so many hotels dotting such a small town you're bound to find something even if you have to search for it. More importantly, Montezuma is a town distinguished by

THE MONTEZUMA WATERFALL

A 20-minute stroll south of town takes you to a set of three scenic waterfalls. The main attraction is to climb the second set of falls and jump in. Despite the warning sign, countless people do this every day, and about half a dozen people have died in the process.

The first waterfall has a good swimming hole, but it's shallow and rocky and not suitable for diving. From here, if you continue on the well-marked trail that leads around and up, you will come to a second set of falls. These are the ones that offer a good clean leap (from 10m up) into the deep water below. To reach the jumping point, continue to take the trail up the side of the hill until you reach the diving area. Do not attempt to scale the falls. The rocks are slippery and this is how almost all the ill-fated jumpers have perished. From this point, the trail continues up the hill to the third and last set of falls. These are not safe for jumping. However, there is a rope swing that will drop you right over the deeper part of the swimming hole (just be sure to let go on the out-swing!).

A lot of travelers enjoy the thrill, but indulge at your own risk. To get there, follow the main Montezuma road south out of town and then take the trail to the right after Hotel La Cascada, past the bridge. You'll see a clearly marked parking area for visitors (US$2 per car), and the trailhead.

poor value lodging, so it does make sense to book a good room ahead of time. Note that some hotels have a three-night minimum during Christmas and Easter weeks.

Camping is technically illegal on the beaches, but there is a small, shaded camp ground with bathrooms (200m away) and cold-water showers only a 10-minute walk north of town on the beach. It's got a communal ethos, and there's no charge for space. Kick in for meals and all will be groovy.

There are a sprinkling of long-term rentals and boutique three-star hotels above Montezuma off the road to Cabano, all of which are only suitable if you have wheels.

TOP CHOICE Hotel Amor de Mar   B&B $$
(☑2642-0262; www.amordemar.com; d US$50-100, houses US$250; ꟼ❋) An absolutely lovable German-owned bed and breakfast with 11 unique rooms replete with exquisite touches like natural timber–framed mirrors, organic lanterns, and rocking chairs on a terrace laced with fishing netting and dotted with hundreds of potted plants. Then there's the palm-dappled lawn that rolls out to the tide pools and the Pacific beyond. In a town distinguished by overpriced, poor-value lodging this place is the best there is. They also have two exquisite private beach villas that sleep six and eight respectively.

Luna Llena   HOSTEL $
(☑2642-0390; www.lunallenahotel.com; dm US$10, d US$35-50; ꟼ) On the northern edge of town on a hilltop overlooking the bay is this delightful German-US–run budget option that's terrific value. There's an inviting dorm and 12 private rooms in a variety of sizes and prices, all with mosquito net, fan and safe large enough to fit a laptop. Rooms closer to the road are cheaper. There are two fully equipped kitchens, a BBQ grill and a breezy communal lounge, strung with rattan chair-swings, and blessed with stunning ocean views. Reserve ahead because this place is popular.

Hotel Pargo Feliz   CABINA $
(☑2642-0064; d US$35-45; ❋) The best budget deal in town – you can't beat the location of these beachfront *cabinas* in the heart of Montezuma. Simple but clean rooms have fan, bathroom and free wi-fi. The communal balcony and garden terrace have relaxing hammocks with sea views, and at night the surf will lull you to sleep. You'll pay more for an upstairs room.

Hotel Lucy   GUESTHOUSE $
(☑2642-0273; dm/d US$10/35; ꟼ) This beachside pensión is popular with shoestring travelers, and was the first budget place to open in town. It's an excellent deal, with hammocks, tables and chairs on the shared terraces overlooking a rocky beach glistening with tide pools. Ask for a room upstairs – the ocean views and verandas make all the difference.

Cabinas Flory   CABINA $
(☑2642-0648; d US$30; ꟼ❋) Our favorite cheapie is this cheery place, family-owned

and pure Tico, with hippie tapestries hanging from the eaves and a funky sky-blue and jungle mural paint job. All wood rooms are huge with fabulous shutters and standing fans. The affable owner rents rooms by the night and month (a steal at US$400). She does laundry too.

Hotel Lys
HOTEL $

(☎2642-1404; www.hotellysmontezuma.net; s with shared bath US$15, d with/without bath US$30/40; P@🛜) The first thing you'll see at this beachside budget hotel is the magic bus, collecting dust opposite the massive squatter campsite. The place is Tico-owned but run by a charming Huntington Beach refugee poet, who doubles as the chef. The rooms at Hotel Lys aren't huge or fancy but they are worthy value and there's the party-time hostel vibe you've come to know and love. Get a taste of it at their regular family dinners (US$10 per person). They don't take room reservations. It's first-come, first-served here.

Hotel Los Mangos
HOTEL $$

(☎2642-0076; www.hotellosmangos.com; d with/without bathroom US$65/35, tr bungalows US$95; P❄️) This is a charming hotel offering bright, clean orange-and-blue doubles with shared hot-water bathrooms in the main building and bungalows with private bathrooms scattered around the mango-dotted gardens. There is also a gorgeous wooden pavilion near the base of the hills where daily yoga classes are held.

El Sano Banano
BOUTIQUE HOTEL $$

(☎2642-0638; www.ylangylangbeachresort.com; d US$75; P❄️@🛜❄️) A well-run boutique hotel in the center of town. Although their many businesses take up an entire city block, they have just 12 prim and comfortable rooms; you'll need to check in here for the Ylang-Ylang Beach Resort (p265) too. Although the baked goods look appetizing, the attached restaurant is way overpriced for simple dishes – 12 bucks for a *casado*? But it's worth showing up in the evening when the restaurant shows nightly films for US$6 minimum consumption.

Cabinas Mar y Cielo
CABINA $$

(☎2642-0261; ground floor/top-floor d US$40/50; P❄️🛜) Simple, basic but clean rooms with air-con and fridge, set on a rocky headland off the main road near Chico's Bar. They overlook a lovely palm and flower garden and a sweet slice of sea.

Hotel El Jardín
CABINA $$

(☎2642-0548; www.hoteleljardin.com; d US$85-95, casas US$115; P❄️🛜❄️) This hillside hotel has 15 luxurious stained-wood *cabinas* of various sizes and amenities (some have a stone bathroom and ocean views). The grounds are landscaped with tropical flowers and lush palms, and there's a pool and Jacuzzi for soaking your cares away. They even have a humble spa, making it quite a nice little three-star resort.

Luz de Mono
LODGE $$

(☎2642-0090; www.luzdemono.com; standard/ste incl breakfast US$60/80; P🛜❄️) A stone lodge built into a lush inlet of remnant jungle, the upstairs rooms have high palm-beamed ceilings, wood furnishings, cable TV, and new tile throughout, but the downstairs standard rooms aren't worth the cash. They don't have air-con but ceiling fans keep you cool, and there's a lovely pool area.

Montezuma Pacific
GUESTHOUSE $$

(☎2642-0204; r US$45-65; P❄️🛜) A small, tucked-away property worth considering, rooms in this older atrium-style guesthouse won't wow you, but the mosaic mix-match tile is cool and all rooms have aircon, mini-fridge, cable TV and security boxes. Plus, the owner is a charming gentleman. More expensive rooms are larger and sleep three.

Hotel Moctezuma
HOTEL $

(☎2642-0058; s/d US$30/40; P❄️🛜) Great deal on all wood rooms overlooking the southern beach. It's above the main junction so it's not exactly silent, but rooms are clean with wide terraces, air-con, ceiling fans and wi-fi. And they frequently have vacancies when lesser joints are full.

Pensión Jenny
GUESTHOUSE $

(☎8835-3114; r without bathroom per person US$20) This lovely white-and-blue country house north of the soccer field is a bit removed from the action, which makes it a good, basic but clean option if you want a quiet night's sleep.

AROUND MONTEZUMA

Anamaya
RESORT $$$

(☎2642-1289; www.anamayaresort.com; per week from US$1,045) Self-billed as a mind, body and soul retreat, Anamaya's perch is pretty damn special. Set on a hilltop with ocean panoramas and remnant weeping jungle on all sides, this environment is certainly dramatic enough to spark enlightenment, if only for heartbeat. The narrow but ample yoga space – their *raison d'etre* – floats off the main house and has that insane aforementioned view. As does the adjacent infinity pool. Primarily geared for week-long yoga retreats, they will open their 12 stylish shingled *cabinas* for nightly hotel guests when space permits.

Los Caballos Nature Lodge　　LODGE $$
(☏2642-0124; www.naturelodge.net; d incl breakfast US$70-100; P❋❄🐾) North of Montezuma on the road to Cóbano, this 16-hectare ranch is adjacent to the Reserva Absoluta Nicolás Wessburg. The lodge has 12 simple but elegant rooms in a lovely hacienda, beautifully landscaped, with a pool deck blessed with ocean and woodland views. The Canadian owner prides herself on having some of the best looked-after horses in the area, and there are great opportunities here for riding on the trails around the reserve. There's also a spa offering a variety of wellness treatments. You can rent bikes, go hiking, or splash around the infinity pool. It's 3km from the town center.

Ylang-Ylang Beach Resort　　RESORT $$$
(☏2642-0636;　www.ylangylangresort.com; standard/ste/ bungalow incl breakfast & dinner US$205/245/275; ❋❄) About a 15-minute walk north of town along the beach you'll find a collection of beautifully appointed rooms, suites and polygonal bungalows. The lush four-star property contains a palm-fringed swimming pool, yoga center, gourmet organic restaurant and spa. The bar is one of the best places in town to enjoy a sunset cocktail, and their tasty kitchen, Paz En El Mundo, slices top-quality sushi. Oh, and you can't actually drive here, though staff will pick you up in their custom beach cruisers from El Sano Banano.

🍴 Eating

Self-caterers should head to the **Super Montezuma** for fresh food.

[TOP CHOICE] **Playa de los Artistas**　INTERNATIONAL $$
(☏2642-0920;　www.playamontezuma.net/playa-delosartistas; mains US$9-13; ⊙noon-9pm Mon-Sat) This artfully decorated beachside spot is the most adored and romantic restaurant in town and one of the very best on the peninsula. The international menu with heavy Mediterranean influences changes daily depending on locally available ingredients, though you can always count on fresh sea-

food roasted in the wood oven and presented impeccably. We had a superb oven-roasted tuna shank smothered in olive oil, diced tomatoes and onions that was pink in the middle and perfectly crisp at the skin. Pair it with something fine from their wine list or choose among half-dozen international beers on offer.

Cocolores　　MEDITERRANEAN $$
(☏2642-0348; mains US$9-22; ⊙4:30am-9:30pm Tue-Sun) One of the best restaurants in Montezuma, beachside Cocolores has a pleasant, thatched-roof patio for candlelit dinners. The menu focuses on Tico-Mediterranean fusion. The curry and coconut shrimp with spicy mango chutney is divine as are the mahi mahi fajitas and their five flavors of spaghetti. Prices aren't cheap but portions are ample. Don't miss it.

Soda La Naranja　　SODA $
(☏2390-6250; mains US$6-12; ⊙7:30am-9pm Mon-Sat; ✍) Get your tasty *tipica casados* here. They also do 14 different fruit juices, crepes and *gallo pinto* at breakfast, burgers and veggie burgers, kebabs and all manner of seafood.

Soda Monte El Sol　　SODA $
(☏8849-4962; mains US$5-14; ⊙7am-9pm) A cute hole-in-the-wall *soda* that does all the *tipica* dishes, tasty and affordable *casados*, pasta, burgers and a variety of juices and smoothies. All is served on pressed tablecloths in a humble dining room touched with grace. It gets packed at lunch.

Vaca Loca　　CAFE $
(mains US$6-9; ⊙7am-6pm Mon-Fri, 7am-10pm Sat, 8am-6pm Sun) A very cute new cafe with one long, built-in, wrap-around booth. It's Italian owned, and she does meatball subs and plates, chicken Milanese, chicken parmigiana, and assorted salads and fish tacos.

Puggo's　　MIDDLE EASTERN $$
(☏2642-0308; mains US$7-20; ⊙noon-11pm) A locally beloved restaurant decorated like a Bedouin tent that specializes in Middle Eastern cuisine including falafel, hummus, kebabs, and aromatic fish, which they dress in imported spices and herbs and roast whole. Cap it off with a strong cup of Turkish coffee.

Bar Restaurante Moctezuma　　MEDITERRANEAN $$
(☏2642-0058; mains US$4-23; ⊙7:30am-11pm; 🛜📶) An unapologetically Mediterranean restaurant overlooking the sea, where they

steam mussels and clams, broil Spanish-style octopus, slice smoked fish Carpaccio, crush and spice gazpacho soup, grill shrimp, lobster and fish filet and even serve burgers and chicken sandwiches. It's usually packed.

Orgánico ORGANIC $$
(www.montezumabeach.com/cafe-organico; mains US$7-11; ⊗8am-9pm; ✐) When they say 'pure food made with love,' they mean it – this healthy cafe turns out nine vegetarian or vegan dishes including spicy Thai burgers, a *sopa azteca* with tofu, burritos, falafel, smoothies and other meat-free treats you can feel good about. But they do meat dishes, like spaghetti Bolognese, too. Whaddaya want? They're Italian. They have live music almost nightly, including an open-mic session on Monday nights.

🍷 Drinking & Entertainment

If you're not down for drinks, you can stop by El Sano Banano (p264) to check out which movie is screening that night.

Chico's Bar BAR
(⊗11am-2am) A sprawling complex of bars, tables, beach chairs and a wide dance floor. It can get loud, especially on Thursday which is reggae night. If you can score a table outside, it can be sort of romantic, but the bar area seems to be a magnet for local cougars, which, depending on your viewpoint, may not be a bad thing. Bar-keeps are well stocked with all manner of spirits, and these old weathered bones are built to withstand a hurricane.

ℹ️ Information

The only ATM in town is a BCR *cajero* located across from Chico's Bar. The nearest full-service bank is in Cóbano. For money exchange, tour operators in town will take US dollars, euros or traveler's checks. Expect to pay a heavy commission.

El Parque (☎2642-0164; per kg US$2, bikes/scooters/ATVs per day US$10/40/75; ⊗7am-8pm) The best place in town to get your laundry done. It also rents bikes, scooters, and ATVs.

Librería Topsy (☎2642-0576; ⊗ 8am-4pm Mon-Fri, 8am-noon Sat) Has US newspapers and magazines, and a large lending library with mostly used books in several languages. They accept trade-ins but don't offer straight swaps.

Sun Trails (☎2642-0808; www.suntrailadventures.com; per hr US$2; ⊗8am-8pm)

ℹ️ Getting There & Away

Boat

A fast passenger ferry connects Montezuma to Jacó in an hour. At US$40 or so, it's not cheap, but it'll save you a day's worth of travel. Boats depart at 9:30am daily and the price includes van transfer from the beach to the Jacó bus terminal. Book in advance from any tour operator. Dress appropriately; you will get wet.

Bus

Buses depart Montezuma from the sandy lot on the beach, across from the soccer field. Buy tickets directly from the driver. To get to Mal País and Santa Teresa, go to Cóbano and change buses.

Cabo Blanco via Cabuya US$1.50; 45 minutes; departs 8:15am and 4:30pm.

Cóbano US$1; 30 minutes; departs every two hours from 8am to 8pm.

Paquera US$3; 1½ hours; departs 5:30am, 8am, 10am, noon, 2pm and 4pm.

San José US$14; six hours; departs 6:15am and 2pm.

Car & Taxi

During the rainy season the stretch of road between Cóbano and Montezuma is likely to require a 4WD. In the village itself, parking can be a problem, though it's easy enough to walk everywhere.

A 4WD taxi can take you to Mal País (US$70) or Cóbano (US$12).

Montezuma Expeditions (www.montezumaexpeditions.com) Operates private shuttles to San José (US$45), La Fortuna (US$50), Tamarindo (US$45) and Sámara (US$45).

Cabuya

This tiny, bucolic village is populated by a community of Ticos and expats, and unfurls along a rugged dirt road about 7km south of Montezuma. Although it is a hidden gem, ideal for those looking to chill, it's rather bereft of interesting sights, aside from the Cabo Blanco reserve. But it is worth visiting the cemetery, which is on Isla Cabuya and can only be reached when a natural land bridge appears at low tide. Here you'll find a few modest graves marked by crosses, but make sure you keep an eye on the tides!

From Montezuma, the first hotel you'll come to is **El Ancla Del Oro** (☎2642-0369; www.hotelelancladeoro.com; s/d US$15/25, cabinas US$35-45; P🐾). Recently reopened by a Dutch couple, it's quite a cute budget habitat with wood-paneled, simple but super clean rooms with private baths. Their stand-alone, A-framed *cabinas* are more secluded but less spacious. If you rent one of these, however, you will see howlers and white-faced monkeys from bed. Next, you'll find the Belgian-owned Hotel Celaje (☎2642-0374; www.celaje.com; s/d incl breakfast US$78/90; P✷@☂☎✉), which has a collection of cute, spacious A-frame, thatched bungalows that sleep four, and are set on a sublime palm-dappled slice of shore and open onto a nice pool and Jacuzzi.

Turning down the signed side road, you'll find the Howler Monkey Hotel (☎2642-0303; www.howlermonkeyhotel.com; s/d US$30/60; P☂✉), and more large A-frame bungalows with kitchenettes. They're clean and comfortable, and the place is right on a slice of very quiet, rocky beach. The friendly Irish owner rents bikes, ATVs and kayaks.

For everything else, make a pit stop at Café El Coyote (☎2642-0354; www.montezumarestcafeelcoyote.com; mains US$5-11; @). The owners serve pizza, seafood and veggie meals, arrange taxis to and from Montezuma and Mal Pais, and offer internet access. Panadería Cabuya (☎2642-1184; mains US$3-17; ☺6:30am-8pm Mon-Sat, 6:30am-6pm Sun; ☎) is a local landmark serving fresh bread and pastries, strong coffee and a stellar menu. Think: blackened tuna *casados* and absurdly good pita sandwiches that are piled with chicken or ham or cheese, and require a knife and fork! The cookies alone (um, they're the size of your hand) are worth your attention.

Reserva Natural Absoluta Cabo Blanco

Just 11km south of Montezuma is Costa Rica's oldest protected wilderness area. Cabo Blanco is comprised of 12 sq km of land and 17 sq km of surrounding ocean, and includes the entire southern tip of the Península de Nicoya. The moist microclimate on the tip of the peninsula fosters the growth of evergreen forests, which are unique when compared with the dry tropical forests typical of Nicoya. The park also encompasses a number of pristine white-sand beaches and offshore islands that are favored nesting areas for various bird species.

The park was originally established by a Danish/Swedish couple, the late Karen Mogensen and Nicholas Olof Wessburg, who settled in Montezuma in the 1950s and were among the first conservationists in Costa Rica. In 1960 the couple was distraught when they discovered that sections of Cabo Blanco had been clear-cut. At the time, the Costa Rican government was primarily focused on the agricultural development of the country, and had not yet formulated its modern-day conservation policy. Karen and Olof were instrumental in convincing the government to establish a national park system, which eventually led to the creation of the Cabo Blanco reserve in 1963. The couple continued to fight for increased conservation of ecologically rich areas, but, tragically, Olof was murdered in 1975 during a campaign in the Península de Osa. Karen continued their work until her death in 1994, and today they are buried in the Reserva Absoluta Nicolás Wessburg, which was the site of their original homestead.

Cabo Blanco is called an 'absolute' nature reserve because prior to the late 1980s visitors were not permitted. Even though the name hasn't changed, a limited number of trails have been opened to visitors, but the reserve remains closed on Monday and Tuesday to minimize environmental impact.

🏃 Activities

Wildlife-Watching

Monkey, squirrel, sloth, deer, agouti and raccoon are usually present, and armadillo, coati, peccary and anteater are occasionally sighted.

The coastal area is known as an important nesting site for the brown booby, mostly found 1.6km south of the mainland on Isla Cabo Blanco (White Cape Island). The name 'Cabo Blanco' was coined by Spanish conquistadors when they noticed that the entire island consisted of guano-encrusted rocks. Seabirds in the area include the brown pelican and the magnificent frigate.

Hiking

From the ranger station, the Sendero Sueco (Swedish Trail) leads 4.5km down to a wilderness beach at the tip of the peninsula, while the Sendero Danes (Danish trail) is a spur that branches from Sendero Sueco and reconnects a kilometer later. So, you can make this small 2km loop and stay in the woods, or take on the considerably more difficult and much more rewarding hike to the cape, heading down one way and taking the other path back up. Be advised that the trails can get very muddy (especially in the rainy season), and are fairly steep in certain parts – plan for about two hours in each direction.

PENÍNSULA DE NICOYA RESERVA NATURAL ABSOLUTA CABO BLANCO

The wide, sandy pebble beach at the end of the trail is magnificent. It's backed by jungle, sheltered by two rugged headlands including one that stretches out into a rock reef with island views just off-shore. The water is striped turquoise at low tide, but the cool currents still make for a refreshing dip. Visibility isn't always great for snorkeling but you may want to bring a mask anyway. Driftwood is smooth, weathered, and piled haphazardly here and there. There are even picnic tables and a grill, if you care to get ambitious. Simply put, it is a postcard, and frankly a must do. Leave the beach by 2pm to get out before the park closes.

ℹ️ Information

The **ranger station** (☎2642-0093; admission adult/child under 12yr US$10/1; ☺8am-4pm Wed-Sun) is 2km south of Cabuya at the entrance to the park, and trail maps are available. It is not possible to overnight in the park, though there are plenty of options in nearby Cabuya or Montezuma. Bring drinks and snacks as there is no food or water available.

The average annual temperature is about 27°C (80°F) and annual rainfall is some 2300mm at the tip of the park. Not surprisingly, the trails can get muddy, so it's best to visit in the dry season, from December to April, and start your hike early before it gets too steamy.

ℹ️ Getting There & Away

Buses (US$1.50, 45 minutes) depart from the park entrance for Montezuma at 9am and 4pm. A taxi from Montezuma to the park costs about US$16.

During dry season, you can drive (4WD required) for 7km from Cabuya to Mal País via the stunningly scenic Star Mountain Rd, so called because it passes by the Star Mountain Eco Resort.

Mal País & Santa Teresa

Get ready for tasty waves, creative kitchens and babes in board shorts and bikinis, because the southwestern corner of Península de Nicoya has all that and more. Which is why it's become one of Costa Rica's most life-affirming destinations. Here, the sea is alive with wildlife and is almost perfect when it comes to shape, color and temperature. The hills are dotted with stylish boutique sleeps and sneaky good kitchens run by the occasional runaway, top-shelf chef. Sure, there is a growing ribbon of mostly expat development on the coastline, but the hills are lush and that road is still rutted earth (even if it is intermittently sealed with aromatic vats of molasses). The entire area unfurls along one coastal road that rambles from Santa Teresa in the north through Playa El Carmen – the area's commercial heartbeat, terminating in the authentic Tico fishing hamlet of Mal País. The whole region is collectively known to Ticos as Mal País.

The road from Cóbano meets the beach road next to Frank's Place, on the western side of the peninsula. To the left (south) lies Mal País and to the right (north) is Santa Teresa. Dead ahead is the beach at Playa El Carmen. In the dry season you can take the 4WD road from Montezuma via Cabuya, which terminates in Mal Pais village. A left turn brings you to the southernmost point of the main drag – the Mal Pais fishing harbor.

🏃 Activities

Surfing is the be all and end all for most visitors to Mal País, but the beautiful beach stretches north and south for kilometers on end, and many accommodations can arrange horseback-riding tours and fishing trips. Or find the fishing harbor in Mal País and arrange your own fishing tour. It does help to speak some Spanish, however.

Surfing

The following beaches are listed from north to south.

About 8km north of the Playa El Carmen intersection, Playa Manzanillo is a combination of sand and rock that's best surfed when the tide is rising and there's an off-shore wind.

The most famous break in the area is at Playa Santa Teresa, and it's fast and powerful. This beach can be surfed at virtually any time of day, though be cautious as there are scattered rocks. To get here take the lane just north of La Lora Amarilla from the main road. The beach down the alley from Casa Zen is our favorite. White and powdery, it's great for swimming and surfing, as a small cove is protected by rock reefs on both sides.

Playa El Carmen, downhill from the main intersection, is a good beach break that can also be surfed anytime. The beach is wide and sandy and curls into successive coves, so it makes good beachcombing and swimming terrain too.

The entire area is saturated with surf shops, and competition has kept the prices low. This is a good place to pick up an inexpensive board, and you can probably get most of your money back if you sell it elsewhere. Most of the local shops also do rentals and repairs, and may clue you into secret surf spots.

Alex Surf Shop
SURFING

(☑8786-9676, 2640-0364; board rental per day US$12-20, ATVs per day US$80) Rent or buy a board here, or take a lesson. They rent ATVs too, and are found just 250m north of the intersection.

Jobbie's Surf Shop
SURFING

(☑8703-4048; www.surfjobbie.com; board rental half-day/full-day US$15/20, lessons private/semi-private US$55/45) Kooky local Canuck Josh (aka 'Jobbie') is a brand in and of himself, and he gives surfing lessons from his well-run shop in Playa El Carmen.

Shithole
SURFING

(☑8994-7068; board rental per day US$10; ☺8am-5:30pm) The Shithole, aka Surf Hole, is named after the local break of the same name. But even they are slightly confused, as they have signs for both clean and dirty iterations. It really is just one rickety but dependable surf shop with good boards for rent and sale on the cheap. It's 200m north of the main intersection.

Nalu Surf School
SURFING

(☑2640-0714, 2649-9391; board rental half-/full-day US$6/12, lessons per person US$40; ☺lessons 8:30am & 10:30am) A popular, long-running surf school. They rent boards by the half and full day, and offer daily lessons, with a price break for a three-lesson package.

Kina Surf Shop
SURFING

(www.kinasurfcostarica.com; lessons per person US$45, board rentals per day US$12-20; ☺9am-5pm Mon-Sat, 10am-4pm Sun) A terrific, efficient surf shop near the break in Santa Teresa. Lessons for beginner, intermediate and advanced surfers are available and last 90 minutes.

Al Chile Surf Shop
SURFING

(☑2640-0959; board rental per day US$10, lessons per person US$40) Set in front of Hostal Brunela, they have some of the best prices in town.

Freedom Ride
SURFING

(☑2640-0521; rental half-/full-day US$25/35, lessons per person US$50; ☺9am-6pm) A stand up paddle (SUP) place with sharp, English-speaking management, set in Mal Pais prop-

er. They offer full and half-day rentals, and two-hour SUP lessons too. Lessons should be arranged in advance.

Yoga

Yoga naturally complements surfing, and if you haven't been in the water for a while, the stretching can be the perfect antidote to sore flippers.

Casa Zen
YOGA

(☑2640-0523; www.zencostarica.com; per person US$8) Offers three- to seven-day yoga retreats; the instructor here teaches a variety of styles, from Ashtanga to Vinyasa.

Horizon Yoga Hotel
YOGA

(☑2640-0524; www.horizon-yogahotel.com; per person US$10; ☺classes 9am Mon-Sat, 11am Mon-Thu, 5pm Fri & Sun) Offers two classes daily, in a serene environment overlooking the ocean.

🛏 Sleeping & Eating

Frank's Place occupies the corner of the main intersection in Playa El Carmen; this is also where shuttles will drop you off and pick you up. Entries are listed in order of their proximity to the main Playa El Carmen intersection.

SANTA TERESA

Pura Vida Mini Hostel
HOSTEL $

(☑8879-9084, 2640-0912; www.minihostelsanteresa.com; dm US$11-13, r US$35; P✳@☎⏚) If you favor a funky party pit over a secluded, pristine hideaway, you can (barely) sleep here among the gap-year refugees and drunken international interlopers. Rooms in the main house have accordion divider doors while the thatched *casitas* by the pool feel a bit more secure. But let's be honest, you ain't here for security or sterility. There's a communal kitchen overlooking the pool and the thatched bungalows have air-con. Management books tours and offers surf and bike rentals (per day US$6).

Tranquilo Backpackers
HOSTEL $

(☑2640-0589; www.tranquilobackpackers.com; dm US$11, r with/without baths US$35/30; P✳@☎) This is our favorite hostel in the area. Rooms and dorms are set in an airy faux-dobe lodge with wrought-iron windows and polished concrete floors. Downstairs dorms sleep up to six, while private rooms upstairs are sizable and open onto a wide, breezy terrace. It's about 800m north of the Playa Carmen intersection.

Horizon Yoga Hotel
HOTEL $$$

(☑2640-0524; www.horizon-yogahotel.com; d US$124; P❋@❄❅) A stunning terraced property on the Santa Teresa hillside with a range of rooms including villas that sleep up to five and have private pools. A better choice, however, are the stilted bamboo bungalows. They have hammock-strung decks with massive 180-degree ocean views, which are the same views as those at the nearby tea house that plays jazz, offers veggie bites and smoothies, as well as their own special herbal tea blend. Replete with fountains and profound beauty, this is barefoot elegance at its best.

Brisas Del Mar
SEAFOOD $$

(☑2640-0941; mains US$14-18; ⊗4-10pm Tue-Sun) Begin with a mango-passion fruit bellini on this gorgeous poolside dining patio at the otherwise non-descript Hotel Buenos Aires. The view is sensational and the day's dishes are written in colorful hues on blackboards, emphasizing fresh seafood. Get yours cooked Moroccan style, tossed with linguini, blackened, sauced or curried. If you enjoy bold flavors you will love it here.

Chicken Joe's
BARBEQUE $

(☑2640-1111; ⊗mains US$7; ❄❆) A Peruvian-owned roadside chicken shack that also happens to prepare fine ceviche. The chicken is tasty with its tight, caramelized, garlicky skin and moist meat. Pair it with yucca fries and the chef's transcendent pineapple barbecue sauce. There's a reason that the town's best chefs frequently lunch here.

Wavetrotter
HOSTEL $

(☑2640-0805; dm/r US$15/40) A simple but classy new hostel with all-wood dorms upstairs that overlook a barn-like interior. There are private rooms in the garden and they rent boards ($10) and repair dings too.

Funky Monkey Lodge
BUNGALOW $$

(☑2640-0272; www.funky-monkey-lodge.com; dm/d US$17/80; P❋@❄) Up the hill from Tuanis, this funky hostel-cum-lodge is situated at the top of a natural-rock hill, and has sweet, rustic-style bungalows built out of bamboo. Each has an open-air shower, and shares a communal kitchen. It's Argentinian owned, and a fun and friendly choice.

Don Jon's
BUNGALOW $

(☑2640-0700; www.donjonsonline.com; dm/d US$16/45; P❋❄) This friendly spot offers several rustic teak bungalows that are quite creative and appealing, and attractive Spanish-tiled dorms with high-beamed ceilings. There's a communal kitchen and the onsite restaurant serves burritos, tacos and sandwiches.

Zwart Cafe
CAFE $

(☑2640-0011; mains US$4-8; ⊗7am-5pm; ❄) Zwart may mean black in Dutch, but this shabby-chic, artist-owned gallery and cafe is all white (or mostly, damn dust!). You'll love the surf-inspired technicolor canvasses, the lively outdoor patio and popular breakfasts including three flavors of crepes and two varieties of French toast. At lunch it's all about the burritos. There's a dynamite used bookstore here too.

Canaima Chill House
APARTMENT $$

(☑8371-5680; www.hotel-canaima-chill-house.com; d US$60-100; P❄❅) The name fits because that's exactly what this eight-room boutique hotel is. Spanish run, the 'rooms' are actually incredibly stylish bamboo loft apartments with kitchens, stone grotto showers, polished concrete floors and wide indoor-outdoor living rooms with a hanging bamboo bed outside and platform bed inside. Guests share the Jacuzzi and plunge pool off the sunken bean-bag lounge. It's set in the hills, 500m from the main road, so you'll want to have wheels.

Cuesta Arriba
HOSEL $$

(☑2640-0607; www.cuestaarribahostel.com; incl breakfast dm with bathroom US$18, s/d US$55/65; P❋❄❅) Up a hill and across from one of Santa Teresa's best surf breaks, this is a thinking person's hostel attracting an older, more polished crowd. Each bright, colorful room sleeps six and has a hot-water bathroom and creative mosaic tile embellishments. There's a big, beautiful kitchen area and a breezy wood-floored terrace upstairs with a TV and DVD player. It also has boards for rent, laundry service, free breakfast and secure parking. There are hammocks in the garden and lots of places to lounge, and the vibe is happy and relaxed. The bus from San José terminates 100m south of the hostel.

Florblanca
VILLAS $$$

TOP CHOICE

(☑2640-0232; www.florblanca.com; villas incl breakfast US$350-800; P❋@❅) Truly in a class of its own, these 11 romantic villas are scattered around three hectares of land next to a pristine white-sand beach. Indoor-outdoor spaces are flooded with natural light and replete with design details, such as an open-air bathroom and sunken indoor-outdoor living area. Complimentary yoga and Pilates classes are offered, as are free use of bikes, surfboards and snorkeling equipment. Their tour desk is innovative and will create personalized and adventurous itineraries (think: spear-fishing and lobster diving) you won't find elsewhere. Their sensational restaurant, Nectar (mains US$11 to US$24), is open to the public and is highly recommended for its innovative, seasonal, farm fresh Latin American cuisine. If they have it, order the seared sesame-crusted tuna drizzled in jalapeño-ponzu sauce. Treatments at their Spa Bambu are addictive and open to the public, as well. Children under 13 are not allowed.

TOP CHOICE **Koji's** SUSHI $$
(2640-0815; dishes from US$5; 5:30am-9:30pm Wed-Sun) Koji Hyodo's sushi shack in nearby Playa Hermosa is a twinkling beacon of fresh raw excellence. The atmosphere and service are superior, of course, but his food is a higher truth. The grilled octopus is only barely fired and sprinkled with sea salt. There's a sweet crunch to his lobster sashimi, sliced trace-paper thin and sprinkled with fresh ginger. The tuna rivals even Hawaiian sushi houses (and that's saying something), and all of his signature rolls melt and spark with creative spice. Between bites sip one of two local microbrews on tap. There are generally bar seats available, but if you want a table, book ahead. They're located 2km north of Florblanca. If you cross the bridge, you've gone too far.

PLAYA CARMEN

Frank's Place HOTEL $$
(2640-0096, 2640-0155; www.franksplacecr.com; economy s/d US$25/40, standard s/d US$55/75, superior s/d US$65/95; P❄@🖤💺) Coming into town from Cóbano the first place you'll see is this historic surfer outpost, but Frank has grown up, and this is no longer the backpackers' paradise it once was. Standard tiled rooms have air-con and cable TV, economy rooms share baths. Superior rooms are quite large and have all the creature comforts. The free-form pool, whirlpool and restaurant are great places to hang out and get the latest surf report.

Artemis Café RESTAURANT $$
(2640-0579; www.artemiscafe.com; mains US$7-14 ; 7am-2:30am; 🖤) They have a menu to satisfy any homesick *extranjero*, with steak

frites, oven-roasted turkey or pastrami sandwiches, cheese plates, and heaping Western breakfasts. There's also a groovy lounge scene at night with DJs spinning cool tracks and occasional live music.

Pizzeria Playa Carmen PIZZERIA $$
(2640-0110; mains US$8-23; 11am-9pm) Playa Carmen's most conspicuous pizza joint is this splashy restaurant right on the *playa*, which makes it ideal for sundowners. They do every conceivable sandwich and pasta you can imagine, but get the pizza. That's what they're known for.

Casa Azul HOTEL $$
(2640-0379; www.hotelcasaazul.com; s/d US$60/70, ste & casa US$125-350) About 100m from the intersection, right on the beach, this fabulous electric-blue house looms over the garden, a pool and the waves just beyond. The downstairs rear room is the most economical. It isn't huge, but it's attractive with ceramic tile floors, wrought-iron bed and plenty of light. The top-floor flat is one huge suite that sleeps five and has epic ocean views. The secluded garden *casa* has a private patio with sea views, and sleeps three.

MAL PAÍS

The Place BUNGALOW $$
(2640-0001; www.theplacemalpais.com; d incl breakfast US$60, bungalows US$90-120; P❄🖤💺) This hipster euro-flavored spot feels like a dance party could break out at any moment, what with the electronica soundtrack and cushy blood-red lounges and day beds by the pool. Cheaper rooms are air-conditioned and have a hot-water bathroom, but it's absolutely worth it to splurge on the more expensive bungalows – each one is creatively decorated according to a different theme. The owners can arrange surfing lessons and tours, and the small restaurant serves Mediterranean-style seafood by candlelight in the evenings.

Blue Jay Lodge BUNGALOW $$
(2640-0089; www.bluejaylodgecostarica.com; d incl breakfast US$58; P💺) These charming stilted bungalows are built along a forest-covered hillside, each with its own hot-water bathroom and a huge, screened-in veranda with hammocks. They sleep three, and though they're a bit on the rustic side, the luxury is in their spaciousness and openness to the dramatic surroundings. Book the Pizote bungalow if you can. The lodge is 200m from the beach.

Restaurante y Cabinas Caracoles SODA $
(☎8788-7790; Morajose41@yahoo.es; mains US$4-13, r US$45-100; 🛜🅿) The lone *soda* on this end of the coast. They serve *típica*, crafted in a cute tiki bar *cocina*, on timber tables in a garden that rolls onto the rocky beach. They do all the usual chicken, beef and seafood dishes, as well as sandwiches and salads. But the location is the thing.

Pachamama HOTEL $$
(☎2640-0195; www.pacha-malpais.com; teepee US$10, bungalows and houses US$60-125) There are a range of accommodations on this sweet earth-loving property. You can have a faux-dobe bungalow with a kitchenette and lovely shady front porch, a wicked two story house that sleeps five, with a romantic wooden loft, or you can crash in a three-story teepee and use a communal outdoor kitchen. All choices are romantic and recommended. They rent boards to guests.

La Hacienda B&B CABINA $
(☎2640-0067; www.lahaciendamalpais.com; r US$90; breakfast US$5; 🅿❄🛜❄) Bed down in one of the rust-tinted stone and concrete *cabinas*, or choose one of two fabulous lodge rooms attached to the main house. Try to book the one on the pool deck, with its sunken floor, lovely local art and natural timber-beamed ceiling. Management is from Cape Cod. She's a massage therapist, and he's a terrific fisherman and surfer. They rent boards to guests (per day US$10), and he does kayak fishing tours (per person $20) too.

Camping Elimar CAMPGROUND $
(per person US$4) Set on a stunning slice of rocky coastline is this humble family-run campsite where a pebble beach rolls onto a rock reef that becomes tide pools. There's ample shade and flat ground where you can pitch your tent, and a shared grill, showers, bathrooms and electricity.

TOP
CHOICE **Moana Lodge** BOUTIQUE HOTEL $$$
(☎2640-0230; www.moanalodge.com; r US$100, stes US$225-260) A simply stunning boutique property etched into the wooded hillside above Mal País. Standard rooms are all-wood garden cottages, decked out with African art, and close to the pool and reception. The massive two-room, wood-sided junior suites are magnificent. Cantilevered so high they have 180-degree views of the coast, there are wood floors throughout, rain showers inside and outside, a wet bar, cable TV, wi-fi, and sliding glass door entry to both rooms revealing that mighty view. Their new, top-shelf tapas bar, Papaya (☎2640-0230; www.moanalodge.com; tapas US$6-9), shares that stunning perch.

TOP
CHOICE **Restaurant Mary** INTERNATIONAL, ORGANIC $$
(☎2640-0153; mains US$7-17; ⏱5:30am-10pm Thu-Tue) Hidden in plain sight in Mal País village, this charming restaurant with polished concrete floor, wood oven, pool table and chalkboard menu has a tremendous reputation among local expats and international foodies alike, and deservedly so. They offer delicious pizzas and tasty menu staples like tacos and fresh salads. But their specials are sensational. Think: Thai lobster tails drizzled with raw honey, a lamb po'boy, and seafood chowder. Even dessert is fabulous (do not sleep on the bread pudding). Their secret? They use only fresh, organic ingredients from local farms and fishermen.

🍷 Drinking & Entertainment

Kika LIVE MUSIC
(⏱6pm-2am) An otherwise rather charmless Argentine-owned tiki bar whose *raison d'être* is the local punk-rock-ska cover band that performs on Thursday and Saturday nights, and attracts a lively crowd. Good band, bad band? Don't think too hard, rockers, there's music in the air!

FREE **La Lora Amarilla** BAR
(⏱7pm-2am) The town's enormous concrete hangar of a dive bar is perfectly situated a stone's throw from Kika (p272), making for an easy flow between both on Thursday (reggae-dub night) and Saturday nights.

Rocamar
(☎2640-0250; ⏱noon-9pm; 🛜) Tucked away on the sand deep in Santa Teresa is this beach lounge that has become a popular local expat hang at sunset. There's a thatched dining area (meals US$8 to US$16), timber tables and beanbags stuck in the sand, and hammocks slung in the trees, all perfectly positioned for sunset.

❶ Information

Next door to Frank's Place, **Banco de Costa Rica** (⏱9am-4pm Mon-Fri) has a 24hr ATM. Directly across the street at the Centro Comercial Playa El Carmen, you'll find a branch of

Banco Nacional (☎2640-0598; ⊙1-7pm) that can change US dollars and has an ATM.

You can find internet access all over Mal País, but for a start, try Frank's Place (p271) on the main intersection.

There are several grocery stores along the coast. The largest is **Super La Hacienda** (⊙7am-8pm), located 100m north of Cuesta Arriba hostel. The closest gas station is 2km up the Cóbano road from Playa Carmen.

A useful website for local info is www.mal pais.net.

❶ Getting There & Around

All buses begin and end at Ginger Café, 100m south of Cuesta Arriba hostel; you can flag the bus down anywhere along the road up to Frank's Place, at which point buses turn left and head inland toward Cóbano.

A new direct bus from Mal País to San José via the Paquera ferry departs at 6am and 2pm (US$13, six hours). Local buses to Cóbano (US$2, 45 minutes) depart at 7am, 11:30am, 2pm and 6:30pm.

A taxi to or from Cóbano costs approximately US$32. Taxis between Mal País, Playa Carmen and Santa Teresa range from US$4 to US$8. A taxi to the ferry in Paquera is US$55.

Montezuma Expeditions (☎2642-0919; www.montezumaexpeditions.com; CentroComercial Playa El Carmen) organizes shuttle-van transfers to San José, Tamarindo or Sámara (US$45), plus La Fortuna and Monteverde (US$50).

There's a **Budget** (☎2640-0500; www.budget.co.cr; ⊙8am-6pm Mon-Sat, 8am-4pm Sun) rental car shingle in Playa Carmen next to Banco Nacional. They also rent cars from their Tambor airport location. There's an **Alamo** (☎2242-7733; www.alamocostarica.com; ⊙7:30am-5:30pm) office at Frank's Place. More than a few local expats get around on four wheels. It's not the most economical way to go, but ATVs do fit the road conditions rather well. **Quad Point** (☎8707-5978, 2640-0965; per day US$70) is one of a handful of ATV rental depots near the Playa Carmen intersection.

Central Pacific Coast

Best Places to Eat

» Agua Azul (p313)

» Roadside ceviche stands,
Costenara Sur (p322)

» Soda Nanyoa (p327)

» Cevicheria El Dorado (p307)

» Citrus (p333)

Best Places to Stay

» Perla de Pacifico (p279)

» Flutterby House (p330)

» Wide Mouth Frog
Backpackers (p305)

» Posada Del Sol (p326)

» Sonidos del Mar (p292)

Why Go?

Stretching from the rough-and-ready port of Puntarenas to the tiny town of Uvita, the central Pacific coast is home to both wet and dry tropical rainforests, sun-drenched sandy beaches and a healthy dose of wildlife. On shore, national parks protect endangered squirrel monkeys and scarlet macaws, while offshore waters are home to migrating whales and pods of dolphins.

With so much biodiversity packed into a small geographic area, it's no wonder the coastal area is often thought of as Costa Rica in miniature. Given its close proximity to San José and the Central Valley and highlands, and its well-developed system of paved roads, the region is a favorite weekend getaway for domestic and international travelers.

While threats of unregulated growth and environmental damage are real, it's also important to see the bigger picture, namely the stunning nature that first put the central Pacific coast on the map.

When To Go

West of the Cordillera Central, rains fall heavily between April and November. The hillsides are particularly lush and green during this time, while in summer (December to March) little rain falls, leaving the countryside dry and barren-looking.

History

Prior to the tourism boom in Costa Rica, the central Pacific coast – particularly the Quepos port area – was historically one of the country's largest banana-producing regions. However, in response to the 1940 banana blight that affected most of Central America, the United Fruit Company (also known as Chiquita Banana) introduced African palms to the area. Native to West Africa, these palms are primarily cultivated for their large, reddish fruits, which are pressed to produce a variety of cooking oils.

Although the banana blight finally ended in the 1960s, the palm plantations were firmly entrenched and starting to turn a profit. Since palm oil is easily transported in tanker trucks, Quepos was able to close its shipping port in the 1970s, which freed up resources and allowed the city to invest more heavily in the palm oil industry. In 1995 the plantations were sold to Palma Tica, which continues to operate them today. With the exception of commercial fishing and tourism, the palm oil plantations serve as the primary source of employment in the Quepos area.

In more recent years, this stretch of the Pacific has grown increasingly popular with the package-holiday crowd, as it's quite easy – particularly for North Americans – to squeeze in a one-week retreat and be back to work on Monday. Unable to resist the draw of paradise, a good number of baby boomers nearing retirement have relocated to warmer climes.

This demographic shift has been facilitated by the Costa Rican government's decades-old policy of offering tax incentives and legal residence to foreigners who buy property or start businesses and enterprises in the country. Foreign investment has thus far blessed this region with vitally needed economic stimuli, though the rising cost of living has priced a significant percentage of local Ticos out of the market.

A sparkling new marina at Quepos has brought in a larger volume of tourists visiting Costa Rica on yachts and cruise ships, and several exclusive high-end gated communities continue to attract an even greater number of wealthy immigrants. Things are indeed changing quickly along this stretch of coastline, though it's difficult to imagine that the authenticity of the coastal fishing villages, agricultural plantations and protected areas could ever be lost.

Parks & Reserves

The central Pacific coast is home to a number of parks and reserves, including the most visited national park in Costa Rica.

» **Hacienda Barú National Wildlife Refuge** (p323) A small reserve that encompasses a range of tropical habitats and is part of a major biological corridor that protects a wide range of species.

» **Parque Nacional Carara** (p281) Home to 400 different species of birds, including the rare scarlet macaw, which is amazingly a commonly sighted species in the park.

» **Parque Nacional Manuel Antonio** (p317) The pristine beaches, rainforest-clad mountains and wildlife never fail to disappoint in this, Costa Rica's most touristed national park.

» **Parque Nacional Marino Ballena** (p331) A vitally important marine park, and is the country's premier destination for both whale- and dolphin-watching.

❶ Getting There & Around

The best option for exploring the coast in depth is to have your own form of private transportation. With the exception of a few odd unpaved stretches of dirt off the main highways, the central Pacific coast has some of the country's best roads.

Major cities and towns along the coast, such as Puntarenas, Jacó, Quepos, Dominical and Uvita, are serviced by regular buses. Generally speaking, public transportation is frequent and efficient, and is certainly more affordable than renting a car.

Both **NatureAir** (www.natureair.com) and **Sansa** (www.flysansa.com) service Quepos, the base town for accessing Manuel Antonio. Prices vary according to season and availability, though you can expect to pay less than US$75 for a flight from San José or Liberia.

PUNTARENAS TO QUEPOS

The northern reaches of the central Pacific coast extend from the maritime port of Puntarenas, a historic shipping hub that has fallen on harder times, to the booming town of Quepos, which is a gateway to Parque Nacional Manuel Antonio. In between are vast swaths of forested hillsides and wilderness beaches, which together protect large concentrations of remarkable wildlife. However, the local spotlight is fixed firmly on the surf city of Jacó, which plays host to a colorful cast of characters.

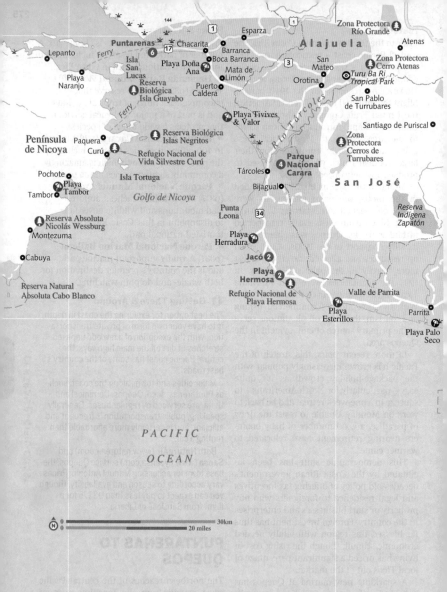

Central Pacific Coast Highlights

1 Watch troops of monkeys, lazy sloths and gliding brown pelicans at **Parque Nacional Manuel Antonio** (p317)

2 Ride the waves (or learn how) on the beaches of **Jacó** (p288), **Playa Hermosa** (p296) and **Dominical** (p324)

3 Stop at a roadside *ceviche* stand along the **Costanera**

Sur (p322) for the country's freshest fish

4 Listen to squawking pairs of rare scarlet macaws flying overhead at **Parque Nacional Carara** (p281)

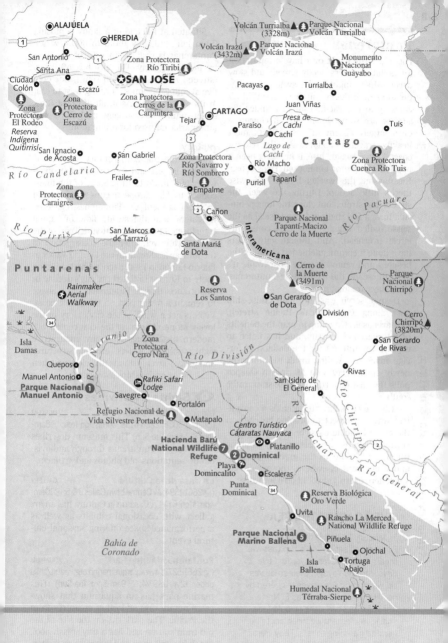

5 Scan the horizon for pods of breaching humpback whales from the deserted beaches of **Parque Nacional Marino Ballena** (p331)

6 Unearth the ramshackle historic charms (and stay in the region's coziest hotel) in **Puntarenas** (p278)

7 Get a guided animal-spotting tour at the **Hacienda Barú National Wildlife Refuge** (p323)

Puntarenas

Port cities the world over have a reputation for polluted waters, seedy streets and slow decay, which might be a traveler's first impression of little Puntarenas, Costa Rica's gateway to the Pacific. But just under the surface are some down-to-earth charms – ones largely absent in Costa Rica's most heavily traveled regions. As the closest coastal town to San José, it has long been a popular escape for landlocked Ticos (Costa Ricans) on the weekend, but otherwise there's little action. During the week the streets that stretch out along the long peninsula have a feel that's as lackadaisical as the scissor-tailed frigate birds that constantly circle overhead. And though city elders have done a commendable job cleaning the beaches and renovating the boardwalk, it's hard to escape the feeling that Puntarenas' glory days are long past.

Despite serving as the main cruise-ship port along Costa Rica's Pacific stretch, Puntarenas is struggling to reap the benefits of international tourism, and has failed to capture the interest (or the dollars) of foreign investors. Adding insult to injury, the newly opened Pez Vela Marina in Quepos pulls the vast majority of cruise-ship traffic south.

Still, the city's ferry terminal is a convenient way to connect to pristine beaches on the central Pacific coast or to southern Nicoya. While most travelers are only stopping through en route to the greener pastures and bluer seas elsewhere, those who get stuck here overnight could do a lot worse.

FIVE AGAINST THE SEA

In January 1988 five fishermen from Puntarenas set out on a trip that was meant to last seven days. Just five days into the voyage, their small vessel was facing 9m waves triggered by northerly winds known as El Norte. Adrift for 142 days, they would face sharks, inclement weather, acute hunger and parching thirsts. They were finally rescued – 7200km away – by a Japanese fishing boat. The book *Five Against the Sea* by US reporter Ron Arias recounts in gripping detail the adversities they faced and how they survived.

Situated at the end of a sandy peninsula (8km long but only 100m to 600m wide), Puntarenas is just 110km west of San José by paved highway. The city has 60 calles (streets) running north to south, but only five avenidas (avenues) running west to east at its widest point. As in all of Costa Rica, street names are largely irrelevant, and landmarks are used for orientation.

History

Prior to the mid-20th century, Puntarenas was the largest and most significant open-water port in Costa Rica. Some of the finest coffees to fill European cups were carried to the continent on Puntarenas-registered freighters, and the steady flow of capital transformed Puntarenas into the 'Pearl of the Pacific.' However, after the construction of the railway leading from the Central Valley to Puerto Limón in 1890, a more direct shipping route to Europe initiated the city's decline in importance, though Puntarenas did manage to remain a major port on the Pacific coast. Visitors get a whiff of the city's glory in the lovely stone church at the city center, but modern history has left many unattractive sights: polluted waters, eroding structures and tacky souvenir stands that close up when the hulking cruise ships leave port.

◎ Sights & Activities

Museo Histórico Marino MUSEUM
(☑2661-5036, 2256-4139; admission free; ◎8am-1pm & 2-5pm Tue-Sun) This museum describes the history of Puntarenas through audiovisual presentations, old photos and artifacts.

La Casa de la Cultura GALLERY
(☑2661-1394; Av Central btwn Calles 3 & 5; ◎10am-4pm Mon-Fri) La Casa de la Cultura has an art gallery with occasional exhibits as well as a performance space offering seasonal cultural events.

Puntarenas Marine Park AQUARIUM
(☑2661-5272; www.parquemarino.org; adult/child under 12yr US$7/4; ◎9am-5pm Tue-Sun) This marine park has an aquarium that showcases manta rays and other creatures from the Pacific. The park sits on the site of the old train station and has a tiny splash pool, snack bar, gift shop and information center.

Paseo de los Turistas BEACH
(Tourists' Stroll) You can stroll along the beach or the aptly named Paseo de los Turistas (Tourist's Stroll), a pedestrian boulevard stretching along the southern edge of town. Cruise ships

make day visits to the eastern end of this road, and a variety of souvenir stalls and *sodas* (informal lunch counters) are there to greet passengers. On weekend nights, this is the place to knock back beers and find the party.

Tours

Tour operators will greet passengers disembarking from cruise ships. Quality and price are highly variable, but a few come highly recommended.

Calypso Island Cruises BOAT TOUR
(800-887-1969, 2256-2727; www.calypsocruises. com; Av 3, near Calle 9) This long-established, top-class, gringo-owned catamaran makes day trips to Tortuga's brilliant white beaches (adult/teen/child US$139/119/75). Trips come with a picnic lunch, fresh fruit, snacks and booze. It also operates Puntarenas' only fine dining establishment, El Shrimp Shack.

Odyssey Day Tours ADVENTURE TOUR
(8319-1315, 2635-0628; www.odysseytourscr.com; Av 4;) Diego and Alvaro, a pair of friendly bilingual brothers, host a variety of customizable day tours, and come with a slew of excellent recommendations. Costa Rica's full suite of adventures are on offer: white-water rafting and trips to local canopy walks and nearby national parks. Located in front of the cruise ship dock.

Festivals & Events

Puntarenas is one of the seaside towns that celebrates the Fiesta de La Virgen del Mar (Festival of the Virgin of the Sea) on the Saturday closest to July 16. Fishing boats and elegant yachts are bedecked with lights, flags and decorations and sail around the harbor, seeking protection from the Virgin as they begin another year at sea. There are also boat races, a carnival, and plenty of food, drinking and dancing.

Sleeping

There's no shortage of accommodations in Puntarenas, though a slew of the very cheapest ones ones cater to the clientele that want to pay by the hour. Also, high humidity and lots of rain makes even the most upscale options muggy, so make sure there's a fan.

TOP CHOICE Perla de Pacifico B&B $
(2661-6860; cnr Av 3 & Calle 3; d from US$35;) This elegant 1920s open-air bayside mansion has been restored with immaculate care, offering a glimpse into Puntarenas' old glory. There are only two rooms for rent, both of which have modern bathrooms and access to a wraparound porch – the perfect place to watch the fishing boats come in. In the evening guests may join gregarious German expat Michael, who will occasionally fire up the brick oven, share a drink and blast a few jazz records. It's near Parque Victoria.

Cabinas Joyce CABINA $$
(2661-4290, 8706-9101; cnr Calle 4 & Av 2; s US$20, d US$40-60;) This is the very best option near the bus station, a spotless little joint of tiled rooms overseen with a hawkish eye by the cantankerous, if lovable, Joyce.

Hotel Cabezas HOTEL $
(2661-1045; Av 1 btwn Calles 2 & 4; s/d from US$20/25;) This no-nonsense budget option is an excellent choice. Pastel-painted rooms have functional overhead fans and screened windows, which means you'll sleep deeply without needing air-con. This hotel is safe and secure, although you certainly shouldn't leave your valuables strewn about.

Costa Rica Yacht Club HOTEL $$
(2661-0784; www.costaricayachtclub.com; s/d incl breakfast from US$75/85, villas with air-con US$175;) Some 3km east of downtown, in Cocal at the narrowest portion of the peninsula, this yacht club caters to both local and foreign yachters as well as the public. Rooms at the club are surprisingly plain – with terra-cotta tiled floors. The modern villas can easily accommodate a group.

Gran Hotel Imperial HOTEL $$
(2661-0579; Paseo de los Turistas btwn Calles Central & 2; s/d from US$25/40;) Well situated near the bus stations, this dilapidated and rickety wooden structure still manages to retain a little old-world charm. Cavernous rooms (some with a spacious balcony) are cool and clean, and have subtle colonial flourishes, such as wooden furniture and dated paintings, to help set the atmosphere. A beer cooler of Imperial (Costa Rica's favorite beer) greets you when you enter.

Hotel Tioga HOTEL $$
(2661-0271; www.hoteltioga.com; Paseo de los Turistas btwn Calles 17 & 19; d deluxe/executive incl breakfast from US$80/90;) Opened in 1959, this is the most established hotel in Puntarenas, where prices vary according to the room. It's worth spending a few extra dollars for the larger ones, which have sweeping views of the sea.

Double Tree Resort by Hilton Puntarenas HOTEL $$$
(☑2663-0808; http://doubletree.hilton.com; all-inclusive packages per person from US$290, child under 12yr free; P❋@☎☕♨) A family-friendly option that gets top billing for its enormously curvaceous swimming pool, immense offering of water sports and around-the-clock entertainment, this all-inclusive resort is boasting a fresh new look and a new name to boot. While there are certainly nicer beaches down the coastline, there is excellent value to be had here, especially if you book in advance through the internet.

✖ Eating

The freshest, cheapest food is available in the stands and *sodas* near the Palí supermarket and Central Market. This is also the stomping grounds of a motley mix of sailors, drunks and prostitutes, but the scene is raffish rather than dangerous – during the day at least. There are more *sodas* along the Paseo de los Turistas between Calles Central and 3, but most of the sit-down options in this area are loaded with *turistas* (tourists) and overpriced.

Despite Puntarenas' surprisingly large (though largely unseen) population of Chinese fishermen, the fare at the Chinese restaurants is a greasy disappointment.

Self-caterers can head to the Palí supermarket (Calle 1 btwn Avs 1 & 3) or the Central Market, where you can find cut-to-order tuna steaks for a pittance.

La Casona SOUTH AMERICAN $
(cnr Av 1 & Calle 9; casados US$5-12) This bright-yellow house is marked with a small, modest sign, but it's an incredibly popular lunch spot, attracting countless locals who jam onto the large deck and into the interior courtyard. Portions are heaped, and soups are served in bathtub-sized bowls – bring your appetite.

El Shrimp Shack SEAFOOD $$
(☑2661-0585; Av 3 btwn Calles 7 & 3; US$9-18; ☺9am-7pm) Perhaps the most upscale dining in Puntarenas, the menu focuses on shrimp dishes in a variety of preparations (curried, grilled, deep-fried) and the dining room features brightly polished wood floors, palms and views of the harbor.

Restaurante Kaite Negro SEAFOOD $
(☑2661-2093; cnr Av 1 & Calle 17; dishes US$6-12) On the north side of town, this rambling restaurant is popular with locals, and serves good seafood and a good variety of tasty

bocas (appetizers). If you really want to see the place swinging, the open-air courtyard comes to life on weekends with live music and all-night dancing.

La Yunta Steakhouse STEAKHOUSE $$
(☑2661-3216; Paseo de los Turistas btwn Calles 19 & 21; meals US$6-20) A favorite with the cruise-ship crowd, this long-running steakhouse has professional service (bow ties!), a tiered veranda overlooking the boardwalk and ocean and impressive portions of well-prepared tender meat. The menu is rounded out by seafood.

🍷 Drinking & Entertainment

Entertainment in the port tends to revolve around boozing and flirting, though occasionally there's a more highbrow offering at La Casa de la Cultura. On the weekends, follow crowds of Ticos to the countless bars lining Paseo de los Turistas.

El Oasis del Pacífico BAR
(cnr Paseo de los Turistas & Calle 5) A popular spot with a lengthy bar and a warehouse-sized dance floor.

Capitán Moreno's DANCE
(cnr Paseo de los Turistas & Calle 13) A time-honored spot for shaking some booty, with a huge dance floor right on the beach.

❶ Information

The major banks along Av 3, to the west of the market, exchange money and are equipped with 24-hour ATMs.

Puntarenas Tourism Office (Catup; ☑2661 2980; ☺8am-5pm Mon-Fri; ☎) Opposite the pier on the 2nd floor above Bancrédito. It closes for lunch.

❶ Getting There & Away

Boat

Car and passenger ferries bound for Paquera and Playa Naranjo depart several times a day from the **northwestern dock** (Av 3 btwn Calles 31 & 33). (Other docks are used for private boats.) If you are driving and will be taking the car ferry, arrive at the dock early to get in line. The vehicle section tends to fill up quickly and you may not make it on. In addition, make sure that you have purchased your ticket from the walk-up ticket window before driving onto the ferry. You will not be admitted onto the boat if you don't already have a ticket.

Schedules change seasonally (or even at whim), and can be affected by inclement weather. Check with the ferry office by the dock for any changes. Many of the hotels in town also have up-to-date schedules posted.

To Playa Naranjo (for transfer to Nicoya and points west), **Coonatramar** (☎2661-1069; www.coonatramar.com) has daily departures at 6am, 10am, 2:30pm and 7:30pm. The cost for a regular car is about US$37. Passenger tickets cost about US$2.

To Paquera (for transfer to Montezuma and Mal País), **Ferry Peninsular** (☎2641-0118) also has several daily departures between 9am and 8:30pm and charges US$18 for a passenger car and US$1.70 for a passenger.

Bus

Buses for San José depart from the large navy-blue building on the north corner of Calle 2 and Paseo de los Turistas. Book your ticket ahead of time on holidays and weekends. Buses for other destinations leave from across the street, on the beach side of the Paseo.

Jacó US$2; 1½ hours; departs 5am, 11am, 2:30pm and 4:30pm.

Quepos US$4; 3½ hours; departs 5am, 8am, 11am, 12:30pm, 2:30pm and 4:30pm.

San José US$3; 2½ hours; departs every hour from 4:15am to 9pm, stopping en route at the Alejula airport.

Santa Elena, Monteverde US$3; 2½ hours; departs 1:15pm and 2:15pm.

❶ Getting Around

Buses marked 'Ferry' run up Av Central and go to the ferry terminal, 1.5km from downtown. The taxi fare from the San José bus terminal in Puntarenas to the northwestern ferry terminal is about US$2.

Buses for the port of Caldera (also going past Playa Doña Ana and Mata de Limón) leave from the market about every hour and head out of town along Av Central.

Around Puntarenas

The road heading south from Puntarenas skirts along the coastline, and a few kilometers out of town you'll start to see the forested peaks of the Cordillera de Tilarán in the distance. Just as the port city fades into the distance, the water gets cleaner, the air crisper and the vegetation more lush. At this point, you should take a deep breath and heave a sigh of relief – the Pacific coastline gets a whole lot more beautiful as you head further south.

About 8km south of Puntarenas is Playa San Isidro, the first 'real' beach on the central Pacific coast. Although it is popular with beachcombers from Puntarenas, surfers prefer to push on 4km south to Boca Barranca, which some say is the third-longest left-hand surf break in the world. Conditions here are best at low tide, and it is possible to surf here year round. However, be advised that there isn't much in the way of services out here, so be sure that you're confident in the water and seek local advice before hitting the break.

Just beyond the river mouth is a pair of beaches known as Playa Doña Ana and El Segundo, which are relatively undeveloped and have an isolated and unhurried feel to them. Surfers can find some decent breaks here too, though, like Playa San Isidro, they are more popular for Tico beachcombers on day trips from Puntarenas, especially during weekends in the high season. There are snack bars, picnic shelters and changing areas, and supervised swimming areas.

The next stop along the coast is Mata de Limón, a picturesque little hamlet that is situated on a mangrove lagoon, and locally famous for its bird-watching. If you arrive during low tide, flocks of feathered creatures descend on the lagoon to scrounge for tasty morsels. Mata de Limón is divided by a river, with the lagoon and most facilities on the south side.

A major port on the Pacific coast is Puerto Caldera, which you pass soon after leaving Mata de Limón. There aren't any sights here, and the beach is unremarkable unless you're a surfer, in which case there are a few good breaks to be had here (though be careful as the beach is rocky in places).

Buses heading for the Caldera port depart hourly from the market in Puntarenas, and can easily drop you off at any of the spots described here. If you're driving, the break at Boca Barranca is located near the bridge on the Costanera Sur (South Coastal Hwy), while the entrance to Playa Doña Ana and El Segundo is a little further south (look for a sign that says 'Paradero Turístico Doña Ana'). Also, the turnoff for Mata de Limón is located about 5.5km south of Playa Doña Ana.

Parque Nacional Carara

Straddling the transition between the dry forests of Costa Rica's northwest and the sodden rainforests of the southern Pacific lowlands, this national park is a biological melting pot of the two. Acacias intermingle with strangler figs, and cacti with deciduous kapok trees, creating heterogeneity of habitats with a blend of wildlife to match. It's not the biggest, not the wildest and not the most beautiful, but the significance of this national

GARABITO

The area encompassed by Parque Nacional Carara was once home to a legendary indigenous hero, a local *cacique* (chief) named Garabito. Commanding a vast area from the Golfo de Nicoya to the Central Valley, he led a fierce struggle against the Spanish in the mid-16th century.

At the time, a favorite tactic of the Spanish conquistadors throughout Latin America to weaken native resistance was to turn tribes against each other and decapitate the tribal leadership – literally. Although each story has grisly variations, the fate of captured *caciques* often involved public humiliation at a show trial, brutal torture and decapitation. Sometimes, the heads of *caciques* would be mounted and displayed.

Garabito was a different story. The popular chieftain constantly disrupted the Spanish establishment in the Pacific region and, in 1560, Guatemalan high command dispatched a military force to arrest him. Garabito, who claimed to have never spent two nights in the same bed, eluded capture, but the Spanish managed to seize his wife, Biriteka, as a hostage. Garabito countered by having one of his followers dress up as the chieftain and allow himself to be captured. While the camp celebrated catching who they thought was Garabito, the real Garabito escaped with his wife. The ruse is a celebrated victory of Costa Rica's indigenous underdogs, but eventually Garabito, too, had to accept defeat at the hands of the Spanish. Senior in years and lacking the support which had fueled his earlier series of indigenous rebellions, Gabarito surrendered in the 1570s, and was even baptized as a Christian.

park cannot be understated. Surrounded by a sea of cultivation and livestock, it is one of the few areas in the transition zone where wildlife finds sanctuary. The park can easily be explored in half a day's expedition.

Carara is also the famed home to one of Costa Rica's most charismatic bird species, the scarlet macaw. While catching a glimpse of this tropical wonder is a rare proposition in most of the country, macaw sightings are common at Carara. And, of course, there are more than 400 other avian species flitting around the canopy, as well as Costa Rica's largest crocodiles in the waterways – it's best to leave your swimming trunks at home!

Situated at the mouth of the Río Tárcoles, the 52-sq-km park is only 50km southeast of Puntarenas by road or about 90km west of San José via the Orotina highway. During our last visit the visitor center visible from the road was a half-remodeled mess, though there were murmurs of a renovation.

The dry season from December to April is the easiest time to go, though the animals are still there in the wet months. March and April are the driest months. Rainfall is almost 3000mm annually, which is less than in the rainforests further south. It's fairly hot, with average temperatures of 25°C (77°F) to 28°C (82°F), but it's cooler within the rainforest. An umbrella is important in the wet season and occasionally needed in the dry months. Make sure you have insect repellent.

Dangers & Annoyances

Increased tourist traffic along the Pacific coast has unfortunately resulted in an increase in petty theft. Vehicles parked at the trailheads are routinely broken into, and although there may be guards on duty, it is advised that drivers leave their cars in the lot at the Carara ranger station and walk along the Costanera Sur for 2km north or 1km south. Alternatively, park beside Restaurante El Cocodrilo.

Sadly, armed robberies, which in the past were unheard of outside San José, have been reported both along the trails and on the peripheries of the park. Police presence in the area has subsequently increased, but there is no substitute for your own vigilance. Whenever possible, travel in a group, don't carry unnecessary valuables and, if things do take a turn for the worse, never resist or try to fight off a mugger.

◉ Sights

With the help of a hired guide, it's possible to visit the archaeological remains of various indigenous burial sites located within the park, though they're tiny and unexciting compared to anything you might see in Mexico or Guatemala. At the time of the Europeans' arrival in Costa Rica, these sites were located in an area inhabited by an indigenous group known as the Huetar (Carara actually means 'crocodile' in the Huetar language). Unfortunately, not much is known about this group, as little cultural evidence was left behind. Today the few remaining Huetar are confined to several small villages in the Central Valley.

If you're driving from Puntarenas or San José, pull over to the left immediately after crossing the Río Tárcoles bridge, also known as Crocodile Bridge. If you scan the sandbanks below the bridge, you'll have a fairly good chance of seeing as many as 30 basking crocodiles. Although they're visible year round, the best time for viewing is low tide during the dry season. Binoculars will help a great deal.

Crocodiles this large are generally rare in Costa Rica as they've been hunted vigorously for their leather. However, the crocs are tolerated here as they feature prominently in a number of wildlife tours that depart from Tárcoles. And of course, the crocs don't mind as they're hand-fed virtually every day.

🏃 Activities

Wildlife-Watching

The most exciting bird for many visitors to see, especially in June or July, is the brilliantly patterned scarlet macaw, a rare bird that is common to Parque Nacional Carara. Its distinctive call echoes loudly through the canopy, usually moments before a pair of these soaring birds appear against the blue sky. If you're having problems spotting them, it may help to inquire at the ranger's station, which keeps tabs on where nesting pairs are located.

Dominated by open secondary forest punctuated by patches of dense, mature forest and wetlands, Carara offers some superb bird-watching. More than 400 different species of birds inhabit the reserve, though your chances of spotting rarer species will be greatly enhanced with the help of an experienced guide. Some commonly sighted species include orange-billed sparrow, five kinds of trogon, crimson-fronted parakeet, blue-headed parrot, golden-naped woodpecker, rose-throated becard, gray-headed tanager, long-tailed manikin and rufous-tailed jacamar (just to name a few!).

Birds aside, the trails at Carara are home to several mammal species, including red brocket, white-tailed deer, collared peccary, monkey, sloth and agouti. The national park is also home to one of Costa Rica's largest populations of tayra, a weasel-like animal that scurries along the forest floor. And, although most travelers aren't too keen on stumbling upon an American crocodile, some truly monstrous specimens can be viewed from a safe distance at the nearby Crocodile Bridge.

According to the park rangers, the best chance of spotting wildlife is at 7am, when the park opens.

Hiking

Some 600m south of the Crocodile Bridge on the left-hand side is a locked gate leading to the **Sendero Laguna Meándrica** trail. This trail penetrates deep into the reserve and passes through open, secondary forest and patches of dense, mature forest and wetlands. About 4km from the entrance is Laguna Meándrica, which has large populations of heron, smoothbill and kingfisher. If you continue past the lagoon, you'll have a good chance of spotting mammals and the occasional crocodile, though you will have to turn back to exit.

SCARLET MACAWS

With their shocking bright-red bodies, blue-and-yellow wings, long red tail and white face, the scarlet macaw (Ara macao) is one of the most visually arresting birds in the neotropical rainforest. It also mates for life and can live up to 75 years. Flying across the forest canopy in pairs, squawking like an old married couple, there are few birds in Costa Rica with such character, presence and beauty.

Prior to the 1960s, the scarlet macaw was distributed across much of Costa Rica, though trapping, poaching, habitat destruction and the increased use of pesticides devastated the population. By the 1990s the distribution was reduced to two isolated pockets: the Península de Osa and Parque Nacional Carara.

Fortunately, these charismatic creatures are thriving in large colonies at both locales, and sightings are virtually guaranteed if you have the time and patience to spare. Furthermore, despite this fragmentation, the World Conservation Union continues to evaluate the species as 'Least Concern,' which bodes well for the future of this truly emblematic rainforest denizen.

Another 2km south of the trailhead is the Carara ranger station (admission US$10; ⊘7am-4pm) – get there via the Sendero Laguna Meándrica trail – where you can get information and enter the park. There are bathrooms, picnic tables and a short nature trail. Guides can be hired for US$20 per person (two minimum) for a two-hour hike.

About 1km further south are two loop trails. The first, Sendero Las Araceas, is 1.2km long and can be combined with the second, Sendero Quebrada Bonita (another 1.5km). Both trails pass through primary forest, which is characteristic of most of the park.

🛏 Sleeping & Eating

Camping is not allowed, and there's nowhere to stay in the park. As a result, most people come on day trips from neighboring towns and cities such as Jacó.

Restaurante El Cocodrilo   LATIN AMERICAN $
(☑2661-8261; mains US$5-12; ⊘6am-8pm) Located on the north side of the Río Tárcoles bridge, this is the nearest place to get a decent meal. It has inexpensive, filling meals, and is extremely popular with travelers stopping to check out the crocodiles. If you're nervous about leaving your car at the trailhead, there is secure parking here in a guarded lot.

ℹ Getting There & Away

Any bus traveling between Puntarenas and Jacó can leave you at the park entrance. You can also catch buses headed north or south in front of Restaurante El Cocodrilo. This may be a bit problematic on weekends, when buses are full, so go midweek if you are relying on a bus ride. If you're driving, the entrance to Carara is right on the Costanera and is clearly marked.

Tárcoles & Around

The small, unassuming town of Tárcoles is little more than a few rows of houses strung along a series of dirt roads that parallel the ocean. As you'd imagine, this tiny Tico town isn't much of a tourist draw, though the surrounding area is perfect for fans of the superlative, especially if you're interested in seeing the country's tallest waterfall and some of its biggest crocodiles. Here, hikers penetrate virgin forest in search of remote swimming holes and ample wildlife, while aspiring crocodile hunters can get an up-close view of these exquisite predators.

About 2km south of the Carara ranger station is the Tárcoles turnoff to the right (west) and the Hotel Villa Lapas turnoff to the left. To get to Tárcoles, turn right and drive for 1km, then go right at the 'T' junction to the village.

◉ Sights & Activities

Catarata Manantial de Agua Viva   WATERFALL
(☑8831-2980; admission US$20; ⊘8am-3pm) A 5km dirt road past Hotel Villa Lapas leads to the primary entrance to the Catarata Manantial de Agua Viva, which is a 200m-high waterfall, claimed to be the highest in the country. From here, it's a steep 3km hike down into the valley, though there are plenty of benches and viewpoints where you can rest. Be sure to keep an eye out for the beautiful (but deadly) poison-dart frog as well as the occasional scarlet macaw. The falls are more dramatic in the rainy season when they're fuller, though the serene rainforest setting is beautiful any time of year. At the bottom of the valley the river continues through a series of natural swimming holes where you can take a dip and cool off. A camping area and outhouse are located at the bottom. Local buses between Orotina and Bijagual can drop you off at the entrance to the Parque Nacional Carara.

Jardín Pura Vida   GARDENS
(☑2637-0346; admission US$20; ⊘8am-5pm) Some 2km up the road from Catarata Manantial de Agua Viva is the 70-hectare Jardín Pura Vida in the town of Bijagual. This private botanical garden offers great vistas of Manantial de Agua Viva cascading down the side of a cliff, and there are some easy but altogether pleasant hiking trails. There is a small restaurant on the grounds, and you can also arrange horseback riding and tours through the area. As with getting to the Catarata Manantial de Agua Viva, local buses between Orotina and Bijagual can drop you off at the entrance to the Parque Nacional Carara. At the time of writing the Jardín was up for sale, so its future is uncertain.

☞ Tours

This area is known for crocodile-watching tours, and travelers anywhere near this part of the coast will be bombarded with advertisements and flyers for them. Although it will be hard for adrenaline junkie to resist, these tours have a dubious impact on the natural habitat of the magnificent animals who lurk in the mudflats of the Río Tárcoles.

Although they are definitely a spectacle to behold, it's frustrating to watch the crocodiles being hand-fed by the tour guides. If you do visit the crocodiles on a tour, ask a lot of questions and do your part to encourage responsible interaction with the animals. Tours usually cost US$25 per person for two hours.

Both Crocodile Man (☎2637-0771; www.crocodilemantour.com) and Jungle Crocodile Safari (☎2637-0338; www.junglecrocodilesafari.com) have offices in Tárcoles. The tours leave from town or you can arrange to be picked up at your hotel.

🛏 Sleeping & Eating

🏝 Hotel Villa Lapas   RESORT $$$

(☎2221-5191; www.villalapas.com; all-inclusive r from US$130; P❋🤫🏊🐾) Located on a private reserve comprising both secondary rainforest and expansive tropical gardens, this all-inclusive eco resort is a classy retreat with a particularly Costa Rican flavor. With a modest number of rooms housed in an attractive Spanish colonial–style lodge, guests can unwind in relative comfort in between guided hikes, bird-watching trips, canopy tours and the obligatory soak in the infinity pool. There's an onsite zip line and a (admittedly kitschy) 'Santa Lucia Town,' which has a couple of souvenir shops and a chapel that hosts numerous weddings.

❶ Getting There & Away

There are no buses to Tárcoles, but any bus between Puntarenas and Jacó can leave you at the entrance. If you're driving, the entrance to the town is right on the Costanera Sur and is clearly marked. If you're staying at Hotel Villa Lapas, it's possible to arrange a pick-up from either San José or Jacó with an advance reservation.

Playa Herradura Area

Until the mid-1990s, Playa Herradura was a rural, palm-sheltered beach of grayish-black sand that was popular mainly with campers and local fishermen. In the late 1990s, however, Herradura was thrown into the spotlight when it was used as the stage for the movie *1492*. Rapid development ensued, resulting in the construction of one of the most high-profile hotels in the country, namely the Los Sueños Resort & Marina.

While parts of the beach today look like one giant gravel pit, Playa Herradura represents one possible future for the central Pacific coast. Sprawling complexes of condos and high-rise apartments are slowly encircling the bay and snaking up the mountainside, while the marina boasts rows of luxury yachts and sportfishing vessels. Although opinionated detractors of Playa Herradura are quick to lob insults, there are some truly world-class hotels on the beach and high up in the surrounding mountains that are worth seeking out.

🛏 Sleeping & Eating

You have to pay to play in Playa Herradura, so consider moving further down the coast to Jacó if you're not prepared to bunk down in the top-end price bracket.

TOP CHOICE / Hotel Villa Caletas   BOUTIQUE HOTEL $$$

(☎2637-0505; www.hotelvillacaletas.com; r US$178-470; P❋🤫🏊) Although the views of the Pacific are amazing, what makes the hotel truly unique is its fusion of architectural styles, incorporating elements as varied as tropical Victorian, Hellenistic and French colonial. The ultraexclusive accommodations are located on the tiny headland of Punta Leona, perched high on a dramatic hillside at the end of a serpentine driveway adorned with cacti and Victorian lanterns. Each room is sheltered in a tropical garden and surrounded by dense foliage that gives the appearance of total isolation. The interiors of the rooms are individually decorated with art and antiques, but nothing is nearly as magnificent as the views you'll have from your room. There is also a French-influenced restaurant, a striking infinity pool and a private 1km trail leading down the hillside to the beach.

Los Sueños Resort & Marina   RESORT $$$

(☎2630-9000; www.lossuenosresort.com; r from US$410; P❋🤫@🏊🐾) This is the US$40 million hotel, marina and condo project that completely transformed this once-secluded bay into one of Costa Rica's most exclusive destinations. The centerpiece of the project is a 250-berth yacht marina that unfolds onto a lush golf course, upscale shopping center, resort hotel and ultraelite residential development. The entire Spanish colonial complex is a five-star class act from check-in to checkout, but its mass-market approach lacks the intimacy and personality found at Villa Caletas.

1. Parque Nacional Carara (p281)
The brilliantly patterned scarlet macaw is a highlight of Parque Nacional Carara.

2. Jacó (p288)
Strolling the beach promenade in Jacó, a bustling spot for partying and surfing.

3. Parque Nacional Manuel Antonio (p317)
Iguanas are ubiquitous at this national park.

4. Parque Nacional Manuel Antonio (p317)
Go for a swim at one of the park's idyllic beaches.

Zephyr Palace
BOUTIQUE HOTEL $$$

(☎2637-0505; www.zephyrpalace.com; r US$550-1500; P🅿✳@🛜🏊) Need more proof that Costa Rica is experiencing some monumental changes? Welcome to the Zephyr Palace, the sister hotel (and pet project) of Villa Caletas. While the older sibling woos guests with subtle notes of elegance and sophistication, Zephyr whops them over the head with unchecked hedonism. At this veritable marble palace, individually decorated theme rooms that wouldn't look out of place in Las Vegas evoke the splendor of ancient Rome, pharaonic Egypt and Asia. There are only seven rooms, but the Imperial Suite has a secret passage way leading to a subterranian meeting room.

Jimmy T's Provisions
SELF-CATERING $

(☎2637-8636; Los Sueños Marina; ⊙9am-6pm) For foodies looking to self-cater in style, Jimmy T is something of a godsend. His small store on the docks of the Los Sueños Marina might cater mostly to the yachting set, but it's stacked floor to ceiling with organic, imported and rare food. Italian cheeses, grass-fed meat, Asian foods? It's a dream come true for travelers who love to cook.

❶ Getting There & Away

The Herradura turnoff is on the Costanera Sur, about 6km after the Costanera Sur leaves the edge of the ocean and heads inland. From here, a paved road leads 3km west to Playa Herradura. There are frequent local buses (US$2.25, 20 minutes) connecting Playa Herradura to Jacó.

Jacó

Few places in Costa Rica generate such divergent opinions and paradoxical realities as Jacó. Partying surfers, North American retirees and international developers laud Jacó for its devil-may-care atmosphere, bustling streets and booming real-estate opportunities. Ecotourists, marginalized Ticos and loyalists of the 'old Costa Rica' absolutely despise the place for the *exact* same reasons.

Jacó was the first town on the central Pacific coast to blow up from tourist development, and despite ups and downs over the years, it remains a major draw for backpackers, surfers, snowbirds and city-weary *josefinos* (inhabitants of San José). But, for all its comfortable tourist infrastructure, all the guests trampled a wide path. Although working-class Tico neighborhoods are in near proximity, open-air trinket shops and tour operators line the tacky main drag which, at night, is given over to a safe but somewhat seedy mix of binge-drinking students, weed-slinging surfers and scantily clad working girls.

While Jacó's ramshackle charm is not for everyone, the surfing is excellent, the restaurants and bars are cosmopolitan and the nightlife can be a throbbing, exciting adventure. And although the US-style cityscape of strip malls and gated communities may be off-putting to some, it's impossible to deny the things that put this place on the map in the first place: the sweeping beauty of the beach, the constantly excellent waves and the lush tropical surroundings.

Playa Jacó is about 2km off the Costanera, 3.5km past the turnoff for Herradura. The beach itself is about 3km long, and hotels and restaurants line the road running just inland. The areas on the northern and southern fringes are the most tranquil and attractive, and are the cleanest.

Note that in an effort to make foreign visitors feel more at home, the town has placed signs with street names on most streets. These names are shown on the map, but the locals continue to use the traditional landmark system.

History

Jacó has a special place in the hearts of Ticos as it is the quickest oceanside escape for landlocked denizens of the Central Valley. Many Ticos recall fondly the days when weekend shuttle buses would pick up beach-seekers in the city center and whisk them away to the undeveloped Pacific paradise of Jacó. With warm water, year-round consistent surf, world-class fishing and a relaxed, beachside setting, it was hard to believe that a place this magical was only a short bus ride away from San José.

The secret got out in the early 1990s when Canadians on package tours started flooding Jacó, though for the most part tourism remained pretty low-key. Things picked up a bit in the late 1990s when surfers and anglers the world over started visiting Costa Rica en masse, though Jacó remained the dominion of Central Valley Ticos looking for a little fun and sun. However, things changed dramatically as soon as retiring baby boomers in search of cheap property began to colonize this once tiny Costa Rican beach town.

In only a few years' time, Jacó became the most rapidly developing town (some would argue city) in all of Costa Rica. Plots

Jacó Center

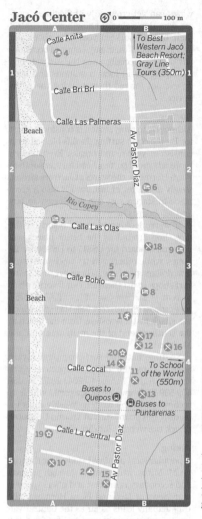

Calle Anita

To Best
Western Jacó
Beach Resort;
Gray Line
Tours (350m)

Calle Bri Brí

Calle Las Palmeras

Beach

Av Pastor Díaz

Río Copey

Calle Las Olas

Calle Bohío

Beach

To School
of the World
(550m)

Calle Cocal

Buses to
Quepos

Buses to
Puntarenas

Calle La Central

Av Pastor Díaz

Jacó Center

Activities, Courses & Tours

of land were subdivided, beachfronts were cleared, hillsides were leveled and almost overnight Jacó became the exclusive enclave of moneyed expats. Ticos were happy that development brought coveted Western institutions such as paved roads and fast-food restaurants, but as the initial flash of cash and glitz started to fade, some began to wonder if they had inadvertently sold the doormat beneath their feet.

Jacó's future is anything but certain. Optimists point out that the town is simply experiencing growing pains, and argue that drugs and prostitution have subsided with the town's increasingly stable infrastructure. Pessimists are quick to retort that wealth attracts opportunism, especially of the illicit kind, and that the problems in Jacó are just getting started.

Regardless of which camp you fall into, one thing is for certain: all of Costa Rica is casting a watchful eye on Jacó, and will ultimately point to the city as either an example of development gone awry, or a success story of wealth creation.

Dangers & Annoyances
First, let's clear up some common misconceptions: Jacó bills itself as a fun-in-the-sun and family-friendly holiday destination, and – for the most part – this is absolutely true. Tourist infrastructure here is among the best in the country, and all around the greater Jacó area you can expect some high-quality service for your money.

Furthermore, even though it's often stereotyped as a wild party destination for young surfers and retired cruisers, Jacó is also proud to equally cater to families and young children. If you're traveling with little ones, Jacó is safe and fun for all ages.

Aside from occasional petty crime such as pickpocketing and breaking into locked cars, Jacó is certainly not a dangerous place by any stretch of the imagination. However, the high concentration of wealthy foreigners and comparatively poor Ticos has resulted in a thriving sex and drugs industry. To be fair, the local council has done an admirable job cleaning things up in recent years, and these vices are not as public as they once were. But this is not to say that Jacó is squeaky clean, by any account.

Jacó is the epicenter of Costa Rica's thriving prostitution scene. Assuming the working girl is over 18 (which is not always a given), prostitution is legal in Costa Rica, but travelers who wish to explore this dark corner of Costa Rican nightlife should carefully consider the health and safety risks and myriad social impacts.

🏃 Activities

Swimming
Jacó is generally safe for swimming, though you should avoid the areas near the estuaries, which are polluted. Be advised that the waves can get crowded with beginner surfers who don't always know how to control their boards, so keep your wits about you and stay out of their way. Riptides occasionally occur, especially when the surf gets big, so inquire about local conditions and keep an eye out for red flags marking the paths of rips.

Surfing
Although the rainy season is considered best for Pacific coast surfing, Jacó is blessed with consistent year-round breaks. Even though more advanced surfers head further south to Playa Hermosa, the waves at Jacó are strong, steady and a lot of fun. Jacó is also a great place to start a surf trip as it's easy to buy and sell boards here.

If you're looking to rent a board for the day, shop around as the better places will rent you a board for US$15 to US$20 for 24 hours, while others will try to charge you a few dollars per hour. There are too many surf shops to list them all. Our favorite place to rent is Carton Surf Shop (☎2643-3762; www.cartonsurfboards.com; Calle Madrigal), which is a shack just a few steps from the beach at the southern end of the main drag on Calle Madrigal.

Six-time national surf champion Álvaro Solano runs the highly respected Vista Guapa Surf Camp (☎2643-2830, in USA 409-599-1828; www.vistaguapa.com), which is recommended by readers. Weekly rates including full board start at around US$1000. Check the website for directions.

Hiking
A popular local pastime is following the trail up Mt Miros, which winds through primary and secondary rainforest and offers spectacular views of Jacó and Playa Hermosa. The trail actually leads as far as the Central Valley, though you only need to hike for a few kilometers to reach the viewpoint. Note that the trailhead is unmarked, so ask a local to point it out to you.

Horse Riding
Be wary of winging it here; unfortunately, readers have reported incidents of horse abuse in Jacó and visitors will see malnourished and mistreated animals on offer near the beach.

Discovery Horseback Tours   HORSE RIDING
(☎8838-7550; www.horseridecostarica.com; rides from $65) Nearby beach and rainforest rides are available through Discovery Horseback

---

GOING TOPLESS?

Though it's the cultural norm in several corners of the globe, going topless is heavily frowned upon in Costa Rica. This, of course, shouldn't be surprising, as more than two-thirds of Ticos are practicing Catholics. Sure, if you bare it all the guys on the beach will hoot and holler, but remember that families often frequent Costa Rican beaches. If the temptation to get a little extra sun is too much to bear, be considerate and move to an isolated stretch of sand.

Just for the record, there is one place in the central Pacific where topless sunbathing is sometimes tolerated, namely La Playita in Manuel Antonio. However, a new hotel development has ended this nudie tradition, and those who bathe in the buff risk a stern warning from police.

JACÓ FOR CHILDREN

Jacó has long been on the radar screens of Tico families looking to swap the congestion of San José for the ocean breezes of the central Pacific coast. Therefore, you'll find that your children are very well cared for in Jacó, and there is enough on offer to keep even those with the shortest attention spans amused for days on end.

Families flock to the beach in Jacó, and compared with more famed surfing destinations up and down the coast, the waves here are modest. As with any water-based activities, the usual amount of parental watch is required, though young children can safely splash about on most days. However, strong surges often accompany ill weather, so it's always best to survey the scene and inquire locally about conditions.

Beyond the beach you'll find a grocery list of activities on offer in Jacó, and a good number of operators offer discounts for young children.

There is a tremendous diversity of accommodations in the Jacó area, and aside from the more backpacker-oriented youth hostels and the upmarket boutique hotels, the vast majority welcome children. Smaller, more intimate B&B types are good for maintaining a comfortable, familial atmosphere, while larger resorts have a range of child-friendly amenities on offer. If possible, book in advance if you need to reserve child beds or have other special requests. Hotels with outdoor pools can save the day, especially when the mercury starts to rise.

Eating out in Jacó with kids is a breeze, since nearly all of the places in town offer English menus and/or have English-speaking staff, and there are plenty of familiar takeout options. Fruit smoothies are an excellent way to keep your children properly hydrated and happy.

Tours, a highly recommended outfit run by an English couple who offer an extremely high level of service and professionalism.

Kayaking

Kayak Jacó Costa Rica Outriggers KAYAKING
(☑8869-7074, 2643-1233; www.kayakjaco.com; 2hr tour US$70) This reliable company facilitates kayaking and sea-canoeing trips that include snorkeling excursions to tropical islands, in a wide variety of customized day and multiday trips. This outfit does not have an office in Jacó – though you might see them set up in Playa Agujas 250m east of the beach. Still, it's best to either phone or email in advance.

Hang Gliding

HangGlide Costa Rica SCENIC FLIGHTS
(☑2643-4200; www.hangglidecr.com; from US$100) HangGlide Costa Rica will pick you up in Jacó and shuttle you to an airstrip south of Playa Hermosa where you can tandem-ride in a hang glider or fly in a three-seat ultralight plane. There's no office in town.

Spas

Serenity Spa SPA
(☑2643-1624; Av Pastor Díaz) East of Calle Bohio, Serenity Spa offers the full range of spa services. Open by appointment.

✍ Courses

School of the World LANGUAGE COURSE
(☑2643-1064; www.schooloftheworld.org; 1–4 week packages US$525-1680) This popular school and cultural studies center offers classes in Spanish, surfing, art and photography. The impressive building and activities center also houses a cafe and art gallery. Rates include kayaking and hiking field trips and onsite lodging. Spanish and surfing are the most popular programs. See the website (under About) for directions.

☞ Tours

Tours around the area include visits to Parque Nacional Carara (from about US$50) as well as longer-distance trips around the country. Another popular destination is Isla Damas – you can organize tours here or in Quepos, further south. Isla Damas is not technically an island, but the tip of a pointed mangrove forest that juts out into a small bay just south of Parrita. During high tide, as the surrounding areas fill with water, this point becomes an island – offering an incredible opportunity for bird- and other wildlife-watchers. Boating tours can be arranged from Jacó for around US$70 per person, but more avid adventurers can opt for a sea-kayaking expedition with several operators that work with local hotels.

Virtually every shop, hotel and restaurant in town books tours, as Jacó operates on a lucrative commission-based system. As you'd imagine, it's hard to know who is greasing whose palms and who is running tours, though usually it works out. Still, you shouldn't book anything through touts on the streets, and if an offer from a vendor seems too good to be true, then most likely it is.

In Jacó there are also a handful of competing companies offering similar package canopy tours.

Gray Line Tours TOUR
(☑2220-2126; www.graylinecostarica.com; Best Western Jacó Beach Resort, Av Pastor Díaz) Gray Line Tours is one long-standing agent that receives good reviews. It books tours throughout the country as well as private intercity transportation.

Waterfalls Canopy Tour ADVENTURE SPORTS
(☑2632-3322; www.waterfallscanopy.com; tours from US$86) Because of its huge suite of different packages (including nocturnal zip-line rides), this is the most highly recommended company. Like its competitors, it doesn't have formal offices in Jacó but you'll see third-party vendors along the main drag who will assist with a booking for a small commission. If you are pinching every penny you should contact the company directly, or have your accommodations do so for you.

Vista Los Sueños
Canopy Tour ADVENTURE SPORTS
(☑8898-3741, 8342-3683; www.canopyvistalos suenos.com; tours from US$80; ☺tours 8am, 10am, 1pm & 3pm) The longest zip-lines in the area belong to this company, which offers 14 cables accessed by tractor cart though the lush hillside.

🛏 Sleeping

Jacó has hosted a variety of tourists for years, and there's a wide spread of places to lay your head. From spare concrete-block dives with little more than a bed and a fan to spendy upscale resorts with full amenities, there's a lot to choose in just a few blocks.

The center of town, with its many bars and discos, can mean that noise will be a factor in where you choose to stay. The far northern and southern ends of town have more relaxed and quieter accommodations.

Budget hotels are scattered around the Jacó area, though there are frequent reports about petty theft and sometimes a few extra dollars affords the peace of mind that comes with a secure room.

Jacó is chockablock with midrange hotels – there are a number of places that have a certain *je ne sais quoi*, while still offering safety, security and comfortable surroundings to slightly more discerning travelers.

Although the town has slowly inched more upscale, the Global Economic Crisis saw many proposed top-end resorts and hotel developments abruptly halted. In the meantime, however, there are a number of all-inclusive-style resorts, and a few boutique hotels and luxurious guesthouses.

Reservations are highly recommended on weekends in the dry season and become critical during Easter and the week between Christmas and New Year's Eve.

The rates given are high-season rates, but low-season rates could be as much as 30% to 40% lower. If you plan on a lengthy stay (more than five days), ask about long-term rates.

TOP CHOICE **Sonidos del Mar** GUESTHOUSE $$$
(☑2643-3924, 2643-3912; www.sonidosdelmar. com; Calle Hidalgo; house US$250; ⓟ🅰@🤖🐾) Howard and Lauri, a South African-American couple, will welcome you to their guesthouse as if you were family. And when you see their house, you'll wish you were! Set within a mature garden at the bend of a river, 'Sounds of the Ocean' may be one of the most beautiful guesthouses in Costa Rica. Lauri is a skilled artist and a collector who has lovingly filled each room with original paintings, sculptures and indigenous crafts. The house itself is impeccable, incorporating stylistic elements such as vaulted Nicaraguan hardwood ceilings and black, volcanic-rock showers. Guests have free use of kayaks and surfboards, and the beach is only 50m away. Full spa services are also available. The house can accommodate up to six people, and cheaper weekly and monthly rates are available.

La Comita CABINA $
(☑2643-3615; Av Pastor Díaz; d without bathroom US$31, with bathroom, fan and air-con US$53; ⓟ🅰🤖) Private, simple and situated just out of earshot of the booming nightlife and near Calle Bohío, La Comita is the best budget option for those seeking a private room. You park within the secure gate, and guests laze in hammocks in front of each room,

which range from basic bargains without bathrooms to ones with cable television and air-con. The French–Canadian expat who has run the place for years will offer good suggestions about where to find the local action and how to avoid the tourist traps.

Hotel Mar de Luz
HOTEL **$$**

(☏2643-3259; www.mardeluz.com; Av Pastor Díaz; d/tr/q incl breakfast US$78/98/118; 🅿✸❄@ 🛜✷👪) This adorable little hotel with Dutch-inspired murals of windmills and tulips, between Calles Las Palmeras & Las Olas, has tidy and attractive air-conditioned rooms that are perfect for a little family fun in the sun. Since it can be difficult sometimes to appease the little ones, the friendly Dutch owners (who also speak Spanish, English, German and Italian) offer two swimming pools, several BBQ grills and plenty of useful information on how to best enjoy the area. The owners are also extremely committed to fighting drugs and prostitution in Jacó, and are at the forefront of an admirable campaign to clean up the city.

Cabinas Antonio
CABINA **$**

(☏2643-3043; cnr Av Pastor Díaz & Bulevar; d US$39; 🅿✷👪) Something of an institution among shoestringers and local Tico families, this clutch of cabins at the northern end of Jacó is one of the best deals in town. Basic rooms are uninteresting at best, but they are clean and cozy, and come with private cold shower and cable TV. And, of course, when you're just steps from the surf, it's hard to be too fussy about your surroundings.

Clarita's Beach Hotel and Sports Bar and Grill
HOTEL **$$**

(☏2643-3327; www.claritashotel.com; s/d from US$70/80; 🅿✸@🛜✷) The three most important rules in the real-estate business are location, location and location. If you subscribe to this mantra, Clarita's beachfront location at the western end of Bulevar is difficult to top. Basic rooms with cutesy flourishes are modestly priced, especially if you can sleep easy with just a fan at night, while more expensive rooms come with 'luxuries,' such as hot-water shower, cable TV and air-con. The attached sports bar and grill is a fun and friendly open-air joint that serves up your typical beer and nachos fare.

AparHotel Vista Pacífico
APARTMENT **$$**

(☏2643-3261; www.vistapacifico.com; d incl breakfast from US$68; 🅿🔄@🛜✷) Located on the crest of a hill off Bulevar just outside Jacó,

this Canadian-run hotel is an absolute gem that is worth seeking out. The views of the coastline from here are phenomenal, particularly at sunset when you'll have panoramic vistas of a fiery sky, and the mountaintop location also means that it's a few degrees cooler (and a whole lot quieter) than neighboring Jacó. Homey rooms of varying sizes and shapes cater to all budgets, and are made all the better by the warm and caring hosts. There is even a BBQ pit where you can grill up some killer eats while chatting with other guests.

Docelunas
BOUTIQUE HOTEL **$$$**

(☏2643-2277; www.docelunas.com; Costanera Sur; d/junior ste incl breakfast US$140/160; 🅿🔄✸@ 🛜✷) Situated in the foothills across the highway, 'Twelve Moons' is a heavenly mountain retreat consisting of only 20 rooms sheltered in a pristine landscape of tropical rainforest. Each teak-accented room is intimately decorated with original artwork that's available for purchase, and the luxurious bathrooms feature double sinks and bathtubs. Yoga classes are given daily, there's a full spa which uses the hotel's own line of beauty products, and you can dip in a free-form pool that's fed by a waterfall. The open-air restaurant serves everything from marlin *ceviche* (raw but well-marinated seafood) to vegan delicacies. To reach the hotel, make a left off the Costanera between the two entrances for Playa Jacó.

Hotel de Haan
HOSTEL **$$**

(☏2643-1795; www.hoteldehaan.com; Calle Bohío; dm/d from US$19/48; 🅿@🛜✷) This Dutch-Tico outpost is one of the top budget bets in town, and is perennially popular with backpackers from around the world. Rooms are tiled, and steamy hot-water showers (dorms have shared bathrooms) are clean and secure. There's also a shared kitchen with fridge, a pool and free internet around the clock. Plus, you can meet fellow travelers on the upstairs balcony and swap travel stories over a few cans of Imperial until the wee hours of the morning.

Hotel Poseidon
HOTEL **$$$**

(☏2643-1642; www.hotel-poseidon.com; Calle Bohío; d from US$105; 🅿✸@🛜✷) It's hard to miss the huge Grecian wood carvings that adorn the exterior of this small European-run hotel. On the inside, sparkling rooms are perfectly accented with stylish furniture and mosaic tiles, though the highlight of the property is the elegant open-air restaurant that specializes in fresh fish – it's one of the best spots in town. There's a pool with a convenient swim-up bar, as well as a small Jacuzzi for getting to know your neighbors.

Villas Estrellamar   VILLA $$
(☑2643-3102; www.estrellamar.com; s/d US$75/85, 1-/2-bedroom villas US$85/100; P❄@✶🐾) While the spacious rooms of the Estrellamar, at the eastern end of Calle Las Olas, are certainly good value considering they boast a massive bathroom and private balcony, it really is worth paying the small bit of extra cash for your own personal villa. Depending on the size of your party, you can choose from one- and two-bedroom villas that have a full kitchen and plenty of space for stretching out after a day at the beach or a night on the town. Regardless of which accommodations option you choose, be sure to take a relaxing swing in the hammock pavilion, and keep an eye out for the huge iguanas that live on the grounds and feed off the mango tree.

Camping El Hicaco   CAMPGROUND $
(☑2643-3004; Calle Hicaco; campsites per person US$5; P) The only proper campground in town: there are picnic tables, bathrooms and a lockup for gear, though its proximity to the bars and clubs means you might not get much shut-eye. Don't leave valuables in your tent as theft is a big problem here.

Hotel Copacabana   HOTEL $$
(☑2643-1005; www.copacabanahotel.com; Calle Anita; r/ste from US$95/159; P❄@✶🐾) This three-story resort hotel gets good marks for offering a variety of rooms and suites to meet the size and needs of your party. Fairly modern standard rooms are well priced considering the hotel's convenient beachfront location and rich offerings of amenities, including an attractive pool and hot tub. Of course, the hotel really packs in the value with its larger suites that come equipped with a well-stocked kitchenette and spacious private balcony from where you can get a personal view of the Pacific sunset.

Best Western Jacó Beach Resort   HOTEL $$$
(☑2643-1000; www.bestwestern.com; Av Pastor Díaz; r from US$141; P❄@✶🐾🏃) Despite whatever preconceived notions you may have about the Best Western, this particular establishment in the famous US chain is the original full-service beach resort in Jacó. That said, dark and dingy rooms are certainly showing their age, despite impressive grounds, convenient beach access and the laundry list of resort activities. Although gringos often prefer to bed down in some of the newer top-end resorts, the Best Western does attract a loyal Tico-family following. If you're planning on spending the night here, it pays to check for internet specials. Located between Bulevar and Calle Ancha.

✗ Eating

The quality of fare in Jacó is high, and aside from the Quepos and Manuel Antonio area, the city proudly boasts the most eclectic offering of international cuisine on the central Pacific coast. While the vast majority of eateries cater primarily to Western palates, there are still a few local spots that have weathered the storm of change.

It's worth pointing out that hours can fluctuate wildly, especially in the rainy season when many shops close sporadically, so it's best to eat early.

Los Amigos   MEXICAN $$
(☑2643-2961; cnr Av Pastor Díaz & Calle Pops; mains US$6-12; ☺noon-11pm Sun-Thu, to 1am Fri & Sat; ➋✶🐾) The English menu at Los Amigos announces a motley mix of Mexican and Thai food, lunch wraps and snacks that cater to North American tastes. Sounds like gringo central, right? Perhaps it is, but it fits perfectly in Jacó, and the pre-party atmosphere, wi-fi and cranked air-con feels just right. The food is nothing to write home about, but it comes in big portions and all the imports on the long beer list are a godsend for those who crave hops.

Soda A Cachete   CAFE $
(☑8633-1831; Av Pastor Díaz; meals US$4-8; ☺7am-5pm) Although many of the local sodas have been pushed out by gringo palates, this little place survives through its loyal following of local surfers, who drop by for huge, excellent breakfasts and set lunches. A few bucks will get you rice, beans, a fish or meat dish of the day and some juice. It's across from the Red Cross.

Tsunami Sushi   JAPANESE $$
(☑2643-3678; Av Pastor Díaz; meals US$7-15; ☺5-10pm Sun-Thu, to 1am Fri) If you've got a hankering for raw fish, don't miss Tsunami, a modern and lively restaurant north of Calle Cocal, which serves up an exquisite assortment of sushi, sashimi and California rolls. Pacific sport fish – dolphinfish, tuna and wahoo – are the freshest rolls.

Wok
CHINESE $

(☏2643-6168; Av Pastor Díaz; mains US$4-8; ☺11:30am-10pm Mon-Sat) The Wok's pan-Asian menu is reliably good – especially the stir-fries and the ribs (only available on Wednesdays) – and it stays open late. The scattered tables facing Jacó's main street also provide primo people-watching. It's next to Budget Rent-a-Car.

Hotel Poseidon Restaurant
SEAFOOD $$$

(☏2643-1642; Calle Bohío; mains US$10-30) This is one of the most sophisticated restaurants in town, and the specialty here is fresh seafood served up with Asian flare. Sauces are inventive, the staff is professional and the atmosphere is upscale yet relaxing. A good bet for top-quality food and refined European-style dining that consistently receives good marks from travelers.

El Hicaco
SEAFOOD $$$

(☏2643-3226; Calle Hicaco; mains US$10-20) This oceanside spot brims with casual elegance and is regarded as one of the finer dining experiences in Jacó. Although the menu is entirely dependent on seasonal offerings, both from the land and the sea, the specialty of the house is seafood, prepared with a variety of special sauces highlighted by Costa Rica's tropical produce.

Lemon Zest
FUSION $$$

(☏2643 2591; Av Pastor Díaz; mains US$15-20; ☺5-10pm Mon-Sat; ☎🖪) Chef Richard Lemon (a former instructor at Le Cordon Bleu Miami) wins ample accolades for Jacó's most swish menu. The menu's roster of upscale standards – shrimp and penne; seared duck in blackberry sauce; grilled tuna – might lack a creative concept, but they're carried out with due sophistication in a dining room of soft light and modern paintings. Plus, the drinks menu is excellent. It's just south of Más x Menos Supermarket.

Rioasis
PIZZERIA $$

(cnr Calle Cocal & Av Pastor Díaz; pizzas US$9-13; ☺noon-midnight) There's pizza, and then there's *pizza* – this much loved pizzeria definitely falls into the latter category, especially since there are more than 30 different kinds of pies on the menu. Of course, considering that each one emerges from an authentic wood-fired oven, and is topped with gourmet ingredients from both Costa Rica and abroad, you really can't go wrong here.

Bar Restaurante Colonial
TAPAS $

(cnr Av Pastor Díaz & Calle Bohío; mains US$6-10; ☺10am-midnight) Centered on a large bar facing the alfresco table settings, this breezy tapas-style bar and restaurant is perfect for some light noshing followed up by a crafted cocktail or two. Fast-food staples are balanced out by local seafood options, while signature drinks make excellent use of regional liquors and fresh fruit juices.

Taco Bar
MEXICAN $$

(Calle Pops; meals US$6-12; ☺8am-6pm) A one-stop shop for Mexican, seafood, salads and smoothies. Get your drink in the gargantuan 1L sizes, or your greens at the salad bar featuring more than 20 different kinds of exotic and leafy combinations. And, of course, there's the obligatory fish taco, which may be one of the planet's greatest food combinations.

Más X Menos
SELF-CATERING $

(Av Pastor Díaz; ☺8am-9pm Mon-Fri, to 10pm Sat, 7am-9pm Sun) This Western-style supermarket has an impressive selection of fresh produce, and local and international culinary items.

🍺 Drinking & Entertainment

Jacó isn't the cultural capital of Costa Rica, it's where people go to get hammered and party the night away. There are numerous raging bars and dance clubs that cater to good times–seeking expats and travelers, but choose carefully if you're going to hit the nightlife, as a good portion of the scene in Jacó revolves around prostitution. Gentlemen's clubs are dotted around town, so be sure to check things out a bit. They're as easy to spot as they are hard to stomach; just look for the crowd of male snowbirds and scantily clad Tica 20-somethings.

Clarita's Beach Hotel and Sports Bar and Grill
SPORTS BAR

Part hotel and part watering hole, this sports bar and grill at the western end of Bulevar sets the table with ample pub grub, and quenches the thirst with copious draft beers. Sports fans will appreciate being able to catch the game on the big screen (and be served by a waitstaff dressed up in cheerleader outfits). On Saturday afternoons, a trio of codgers sets up in the corner to amble through Costa Rican folk songs, calypso versions of Bob Marley favorites and several beers.

Le Loft
DANCE DJ

(Av Pastor Díaz) The Loft is Jacó's sleekest nightlife offering and makes a good addition to the beach clubs and girly bars with some much needed urban sophistication. Live DJs spin essential mixes while glam-aspiring customers do their best to look beautiful and act fabulous. There's a calendar of special events and a balcony perch where travelers take in the action on the street below.

Disco La Central
DANCE

(Calle La Central) This unintentionally retro disco sets the volume at 11 (whether or not there's anyone on the dance floor), though it's an old-timer on the Jacó scene that still draws in a strong local following. Very much an after-hours spot, Disco La Central doesn't really get going until the restaurants and bars have emptied out, sending inebriated patrons out in search of flashing lights and heavy bass.

ⓘ Information

Jacó is relatively expensive and during the high season it's jam-packed with tourists, so reservations are recommended, especially around the winter holidays.

There's no independent tourist information office, though several tour offices will give information. Look for the free monthly *Jaco's Guide*, which includes tide charts and up-to-date maps, or go to www.jacoguide.com. The free monthly magazine *Central Pacific Way* has information on tourist attractions up and down the coastline. For cash, there are ATMs everywhere, though the best rates (and longest lines) will be found at the big branches, like Banco Popular.

ⓘ Getting There & Away

Air

NatureAir (www.natureair.com) and **Alfa Romeo Aero Taxi** (www.alfaromeoair.com) offer charter flights. Prices are dependent on the number of passengers, so it's best to try to organize a larger group if you're considering this option.

Boat

The jet-boat transfer service that connects Jacó to Montezuma is, far and away, the most efficient to connect the central Pacific coast to the Península de Nicoya. The journey across the Golfo de Nicoya only takes about an hour (compared to about seven hours overland), though at US$40 it's definitely not cheap. (For a small extra fee you can bring a bicycle or surfboard.) The bonus? Sometimes travelers see dolphins along the ride. Several boats leave daily from Playa Herradura, 2km north of town. Reservations are required and can be made at most tour

operators in town (the most consistent daily departure is at 10:45am). It's a beach landing, so wear the right shoes.

Bus

Buses for San José stop at the Plaza Jacó mall, north of the center. The bus stop for other destinations is opposite the Más x Menos supermarket. (Stand in front of the supermarket if you're headed north; stand across the street if you're headed south.) The departure times listed here are approximate since buses originate in Puntarenas or Quepos. Get to the stop early!

Puntarenas US$1.75; 1½ hours; departs 6am, 9am, noon and 4:30pm.

Quepos US$1.75; 1½ hours; departs 6am, noon, 4:30pm and 6pm.

San José US$4; three hours; departs 5am, 7:30am, 11am, 3pm and 5pm.

ⓘ Getting Around

Getting around in Jacó is easy on foot; strolling the length of town in flip flops takes about 20 minutes.

Bicycle & Scooter

Several places around town rent out bicycles, mopeds and scooters. Bikes can usually be rented for about US$3 to US$5 an hour or US$8 to US$15 a day, though prices change depending on the season. Mopeds and small scooters cost from US$25 to US$50 a day (many places ask for a cash or credit-card deposit of about US$200).

Car

There are several rental agencies in town, so shop around for the best rates.

Budget (☏2643-2665; Plaza Jacó Mall; ⊙8am-6pm Mon-Sat, to 4pm Sun)

Economy (☏2643-1719; Av Pastor Díaz; ⊙8am-6pm) South of Calle Ancha.

Taxi

Taxis to Playa Hermosa from Jacó cost between US$8 and US$13. To arrange for a pick-up, call **Taxi 30-30** (☏2643-3030), or negotiate with any of the taxis along Av Pastor Díaz.

Playa Hermosa

While newbies struggle to stand up on their boards in Jacó, a few kilometers south in Playa Hermosa seasoned veterans are thrashing their way across the faces of some truly monster waves. Regarded as one of the most consistent and powerful breaks in the whole country, Hermosa serves up serious surf that commands the utmost respect. Of course, you really need to know what you're doing in these parts – huge waves and strong riptides are unforgiving, and countless surfboards here have wound up shattered to pieces and strewn about on the shoreline. Still, even if you're not a pro, the vibe here is excellent, the surfers are chilled out and the beach lives up to its name.

There are several places on the Pacific Coast that have names that translate to 'Pretty Beach' in Spanish, though none is more deserving than this lovely 10km-long strip of grey sand. It has seen significant investment in recent years: billed as an upscale alternative to Jacó, the shore sports a couple of brand-new upmarket hotels and notably more upscale visitors, but in comparison with neighboring Jacó and Playa Herradura, the development is modest. For the time being, Hermosa is very much a slow-paced beach town edged by the Costanera Sur and the surf-washed shores of the Pacific.

Activities

Surfing
Most of the adrenaline-soaked action takes place at the northern reaches, where there are no less than half a dozen clearly defined beach breaks. These have tons of power and break very near the shore, particularly in the rainy season between May and August. Conditions are highly variable, but you can expect the maximum height to top out around high tide. Swell size is largely dependent on unseen factors such as current and offshore weather patterns, but when it gets big, you'll know. At times like these, you really shouldn't be paddling out unless you have some serious experience under your belt. Playa Hermosa is not for beginners, and even intermediate surfers can get chewed up and spat out here. To watch the action, park at the small road by the Backyard Hotel and wander out to the beach.

Yoga
Vida Asana Retreat Center   YOGA
(✆2643-7108; www.vidaasana.com) High in the hills above Playa Hermosa lies this retreat, which offers fully customizable packages combining yoga, surfing and healthy organic meals. Advanced reservations are highly recommended, and prices are dependent on the size of your party, the season and the extent of requested instruction. The accommodations are breezy, rustic and set amid lush jungle.

Festivals & Events
If you don't think you can hack it with the aspiring pros, you might want to give the surf on this beach a miss. However, consider stopping by in August when local and international pro surfers descend on Hermosa for the annual surf competition. Dates vary, though the event is heavily advertised around the country, especially in neighboring Jacó.

Sleeping
The highway is the only road, and the bulk of accommodations are just off it. While there aren't proper addresses to speak of, everything is clustered along an easily identifable stretch unofficially known as 'Playa Hermosa Village.' Note that rates vary wildly depending on season, demand and the whim of the proprietor. They're also negotiable.

TOP CHOICE Tortuga del Mar   LODGE $$
(✆2643-7132; www.tortugadelmar.net; r US$75, studios from US$85; P✷@🛜🏊) Top-end accommodations with a recession-proof midrange price tag, this newish lodge is sheltered amid shady grounds, and comprises of just a handful of rooms housed in a two-story building. Tropical modern is the style at hand, making excellent use of local hardwoods to construct lofty ceilings that catch every gust of the Pacific breezes. The larger studios are spacious and even feature mini kitchenettes that make self-catering a real possibility within this budget bracket.

Cabinas Las Olas Hotel   HOTEL, CABINA $$
(✆2643-7021; www.lasolashotel.com; r US$45-75, ranchos US$100, skybox US$100; P✷@🏊) This distinctive three-story A-frame building is home to an awesome 'skybox room,' a teak-accented, ocean-facing penthouse where you can fall asleep and wake up to the sounds of the surf and watch surfers shred. If heights aren't your thing, you can also rent one of several beachside *ranchos* (small houses) that come equipped with kitchenette and sleep several people comfortably. Alternatively, budget travelers can snag a cheap but cheerful room in the main house, which has spartan rooms and bunks. At the time of writing, the management was in the early stages of a huge expansion that would add an upmarket hotel and timeshare.

Backyard Hotel   HOTEL $$$
(✆2643-7011; www.backyardhotel.com; r/ste from US$135/200; P✷@🛜🏊) The quality linens and mattresses here have substantially raised the bar for accommodations in Playa Hermosa. In addition, the proximity of the accompanying Backyard Bar makes this

boutique hotel ideal if you want to be in the heart of the (admittedly limited) action – but maddening if you don't. Despite the mix and match of modern furniture, little touches like hair dryers, alarm clocks and in-room mini bar are worthy attempts at going upmarket, but the real bonus is that there's space to stretch out – each tiled room has a private outdoor sitting area, which overlooks the beach or the hills.

Cabinas Las Arenas
CABINA $$

(☑2643-7013; www.cabinaslasarenas.com; s/d/tr/q US$37/49/55/62; P❄@☎) Las Arenas caters to the backpacking surfer crowd by sticking to the basics in an effort to keep prices on the low side. It's a great place to meet travelers. The property comprises 10 cabins that can each sleep up to four, providing tremendous bang for your buck if you're traveling in a group. The premises are also home to a restaurant, surf supply shop and a small beach BBQ pit.

Cabinas Brisa del Mar
CABINA $

(☑2643-2076; http://cabinasbrisadelmar.com; s/d/tr US$25/40/45; P❄@) If your wallet is looking a bit thin these days, consider bunking down at this Floridian-run crash pad, which is decidedly more budget-friendly than the vast majority of options in Hermosa. Brisa del Mar has a few rooms of varying sizes with air-con, private hot shower and cable TV, as well as a communal kitchen where you can self-cater. If the surf is looking too small (or too big!), you can pass the time on the basketball court or with a few games of table tennis.

Costanera
B&B $$

(☑2643-2042; www.costaneraplayahermosa.com; r from US$55; P❄) For a bit of European flair, this well-priced Italian-run B&B has a very sophisticated ambience. Five rooms of various sizes and shapes have vaulted wooden ceilings and beachfront terraces, each offering a fair degree of privacy and intimacy. Of course, the undisputed highlight of these accommodations is the authentic handmade pasta and rich Italian sauces served at the onsite restaurant each evening.

Terraza del Pacífico
HOTEL $$$

(☑2643-3222; www.terrazadelpacifico.com; r/ste from US$115/175; P❄@☎❄🏊) Although its a bit worn at the edges, this granddaddy of top-end hotels at the northern end of town is a good option for families, located on prime beachfront overlooking some killer

breaks. With Spanish colonial accents and tiled-floor rooms throughout, the establishment draws upscale surfers and moneyed San José weekenders. Assuming you can prise yourself away from the beach, there's a whole list of impressive amenities on offer, including a pool with swim-up bar.

✗ Eating & Drinking

Backyard Bar
BREAKFAST $

(☑2643-7011; meals US$5-10; ☺noon-late; ☎) A proper eatery unlike any that Hermosa has previously known, the Backyard Bar's expansive menu reaches beyond the usual surfer fare and serves a good fried-egg breakfast. As the town's de facto nightspot, the Backyard Bar occasionally hosts live music, and heavy pours at happy hour every night of the week. Depending on the season and the night, the scene here is a crap shoot – one night there's a booming sound system and a pair of trashy go-go dancers, the next it's a bunch of retired surfers nursing beers – but if you stay in Playa Hermosa a visit is inevitable.

Jungle Surf Café
CAFE $

(meals US$4-9; ☺7am-9pm) If you're looking for a quick bite between sets, this terminally laid-back cafe is a local institution that offers everything from burritos to kebabs, though locals swear by the seriously gourmet fish tacos. There is also a small bar decorated with the obligatory surf paraphernalia that makes for a refreshing place to have a sundowner after a long day of thrashing about in the waves.

❶ Getting There & Away

Located only 5km south of Jacó, Playa Hermosa can be accessed by any bus heading south from Jacó. Frequent buses running up and down the Costanera Sur can easily pick you up, though determined surfers can always hail a taxi (with surf racks) or stick out a thumb if there is a rush.

Since Jacó serves as the regional transportation hub, see the Jacó section (p296) for detailed information on getting there and away.

Playa Esterillos

If it's possible for you to stretch your budget for a night or two, try the Alma De Pacífico (☑2778-7070; www.xandari.com; villa US$295-440; P❄@☎), a visually stunning resort that is aiming to put Playa Esterillos on the map. There is no shortage of attractive resorts along this stretch of the Pacific, but what makes this one so unique is the incredible architectural scheme. Each individually designed villa encompasses a range of intriguing design elements including wooden-lattice ceilings, sheer walls of glass framing private gardens, concrete-poured furniture done up with custom leatherwork and impossibly intricate mosaic tile work. As if all of this wasn't enough to make you postpone your onward travel plans, there is also an onsite restaurant specializing in gourmet and organic healthy fare, as well as an immaculate palm-fringed infinity pool that faces the crashing surf.

The long-standing Pélican Hotel (☎2778-8105; www.pelicanhotelcr.com; r from US$45; P✿❄🔋🐾♿) hits a sweet spot on this part of coast: it's affordable, safe and homey, and on a dreamy stretch of the Pacific. The rooms are a bit rustic (creaky wooden floors, no TVs) but are warmly lit with wooden lamps and open to balconies that overlook a small tiled pool. Only steps away from the surf, guests can take in sunsets over the waves from a hammock, borrow the long board or splash around in the waves. The only catch? Its fairly isolated so visitors' only eating option is the onsite restaurant, which is a bit spendy. Another option is Montery Del Mar Hotel (☎2778-8787; www.monterey-delmar.com; Playa Esterillos Este; d from US$130), which has more elegant gardens, a better restaurant and more spacious grounds but a bit less character.

At the opposite end of the budget spectrum is the lovable clutch of spare *cabinas* at Holly's High Tide (☎2778-8831, in USA 530-214-6341; www.facebook.com/Hollyshightide; Esterillos Este; campsite/s US$10/15; P@🔋🐾). The setup couldn't be more blissfully disconnected: it's just a few basic cabins near a lovely stretch of water, which share a bathroom and a small cooking area under a pavilion. Apart from a handful of amiable surfers and a friendly dog, the place is pretty quiet. Located off a dirt road and by a yellow fence, the sunsets and surf here are the attractions, and this is one of the best budget joints to unplug on the whole coast.

Parrita & Around

A bustling town on a river of the same name, Parrita is home to a tremendous palm oil–processing plant. If the wind is blowing right, the plant can be smelled from several kilometers away, though the odor is somewhat pleasant if you're a fan of fried foods. Although palm oil doesn't perhaps have the immediate recognition of olive oil, the product finds its way into just about everything from chocolate bars and french fries, to baked goods and snack foods.

While you're rolling through the area, a glimpse of the day-to-day maintenance of the palms is fascinating. To keep them free of insects, workers clear growth on the forest floor and apply poison to the trunks. To encourage fruit growth and provide easy access to the pod the fronds are regularly clipped. Pods are then transported to processing plants where the fruits are separated and pressed. Huge big-rig trucks stacked full of reddish fruit come flying down this relatively poor stretch of the Costanera Sur – be careful on the road out there!

The primary reason for visiting Parrita is to visit Playa Palo Seco, a quiet, unhurried black-sand beach located near mangrove swamps that provides good opportunities for bird-watching. A 6km dirt road connects the eastern edge of town to the beach. Another popular excursion is to visit Isla Damas, which is actually the tip of a mangrove peninsula that becomes an island at high tide. Most people arrive here on package tours from Jacó or Quepos, though you can hire a boat to take you to and from the island.

If you're looking to stay on Playa Palo Seco, Beso del Viento B&B (☎2779-9674; www.besodelviento.com; s/d/q US$87/112/136; P🐾) is a lovely place that has modest but comfortable apartments at the standard of a charming independent European inn. Each room has a tiled bathroom, elegant decor and access to fully stocked kitchen and breezy grounds. The French owners are fantastic cooks, and they go out of their way to make guests feel like family. Kayaks, bikes and horses can be rented if you're interested in exploring this off-the-beaten-path area. But the real attraction is a chance to enjoy a deserted stretch of the coast at a high level of classy comfort.

Parrita is about 40km south of Jacó, and can be reached by any bus heading south from Jacó. After Parrita, the coastal road dips inland through more palm-oil plantations on the way to Quepos.

Reserves of the Central Pacific Coast

Costa Rica's best road trip follows the Costanera Sur, along a string of fantastic natural parks. With wet and dry tropical forests and long beaches, these parks are alive with brightly colored birds, curious monkeys and a veritable army of iguanas – all of which show off the country's stunning biodiversity.

Rancho La Merced National Wildlife Refuge

1 Surrounding Parque Nacional Marino Ballena on the southern part of the central Pacific coast, this former cattle ranch has excellent horse trails, primary and secondary forest and miles of mangrove channels (p330).

Parque Nacional Marino Ballena

2 It's appropriate that this lovely, relatively quiet national park (p331) is shaped like a whale's tail; from the beaches it's possible to spot the migrating giants as they swim near shore.

Hacienda Barú National Wildlife Refuge

3 Excellent trails and naturalist-led hikes make this the best bird-watching spot on the central Pacific coast (p323). And just in case spotting rare tropical birds doesn't thrill you, there's also a zip line.

Catarata Manantial de Agua Viva

4 With macaws overhead this picture-perfect jungle waterfall drops 183m from one swimmable pool to the next. It's best during the rainy season, when the flows are full (p284).

Clockwise from top left
1. Rancho La Merced National Wildlife Refuge
2. Parque Nacional Marino Ballena 3. Hacienda Barú National Wildlife Refuge

PARQUE NACIONAL MANUEL ANTONIO & AROUND

As visitors find themselves along this small outcropping of land that juts out into the Pacific, the air becomes heavy with humidity, scented with thick vegetation and alive with the call of birds and monkeys, making it suddenly apparent that *this* is the tropics. The reason to come here is the stunning Parque Nacional Manual Antonio, one of the most picturesque bits of tropical coast in Costa Rica. If you get bored of cooing at the baby monkeys that scurry in the canopy and scanning for birds and sloths, the turquoise waves and perfect sand provides endless entertainment. However, there's no pretending that Manuel Antonio is anyone's secret – despite being the smallest of Costa Rica's national parks, it is also one of the most popular. Little Quepos, the once sleepy fishing and banana village on the park's perimeter, has rapidly ballooned with this tourism-based economy (although it is admirably clinging to its roots despite ongoing socioeconomic transformation), and the road leading from Quepos to the park is overdeveloped. However, the rainforested hills sweeping down to the sea and the blissful beaches make the park a stunning destination worthy of the tourist hype.

Note that, for purposes of clarity, we've divided our coverage into four sections: Quepos proper (the area's only proper small city), the road from Quepos to Manuel Antonio, the tiny Manuel Antonio Village and the national park itself.

Quepos

Located just 7km from the entrance to Manuel Antonio, the small, busy town of Quepos serves as the gateway to the national park, as well as a convenient port of call for travelers in need of goods and services. Although the Manuel Antonio area was rapidly and irreversibly transformed following the ecotourism boom, Quepos has largely retained an authentic Tico feel, particularly when you get out of the middle of town. Exuding an ineffable charm that is absent from so much of the central Pacific, Quepos still has glimmers of traditional Latin America, even while being a heavily traveled stop on the tourist-packed gringo trail.

While most visitors to the Manuel Antonio area prefer to stay outside Quepos, accommodations are generally cheaper and better in town, though you will need to organize transportation to both the national park and the beaches. Quepos can be an appealing place to stay, especially since it's home to a burgeoning restaurant scene that belies its small size and is also home to one of the country's best hostels. Quepos is gridded with easy-to-walk streets, which provides the opportunity to interact with the friendly locals, who have thus far weathered the storm of change with cheerfulness and optimism.

Downtown Quepos is a small checkerboard of dusty streets that are lined with a mix of local- and tourist-oriented shops, businesses, markets, restaurants and cafes. The town loses its well-ordered shape as

---

X MARKS THE SPOT

Locals have long believed that a treasure worth billions and billions of dollars lies somewhere in the Quepos and Manuel Antonio area, waiting to be discovered. The legend was popularized by English pirate John Clipperton, who befriended the coastal Quepoa during his years of sailing to and from the South Pacific. Clipperton's belief stemmed from a rumor that in 1670 a number of Spanish ships laden with treasure escaped from Panama City moments before it was burned to the ground by Captain Henry Morgan. Since the ships were probably off-loaded quickly to avoid being raided at sea, a likely destination was the San Bernadino de Quepo Mission, which had a strong loyalty to the Spanish crown.

John Clipperton died in 1722 without ever discovering the legendary treasure, and the mission closed permanently in 1746 as most of the Quepoa had succumbed to European diseases. Although the ruins of the mission were discovered in 1974, they were virtually destroyed and were long since looted. However, if the treasure was indeed as large as it's described in lore, it is possible that a few gold doubloons could still be lying somewhere, waiting to be unearthed.

RAINMAKER AERIAL WALKWAY

Rainmaker is a privately owned rainforest that offered the first aerial walkway through the forest canopy in Central America. Although its star has faded a bit, the place is still regarded as one of the region's best. From its tree-to-tree platforms there are spectacular panoramic views of the surrounding primary and secondary rainforest, as well as occasional vistas out to the Pacific Ocean. The reserve is also home to the full complement of tropical wildlife, which means that there are myriad opportunities here for great bird-watching as well as the occasional monkey sighting. The trips are often completed by a swim in a natural pool at the base of a waterfall.

Tours with naturalist guides leave hotels in Manuel Antonio and Quepos daily except Sunday; reservations can be made at most hotels or by calling the Rainmaker office (✆in Quepos 2777-3565, in USA 540-349-9848; www.rainmakercostarica.org). A self-guided trip through the aerial walkway costs only US$15 per person (kids are free!) and for US$35 a guide is included. Bird-watching and amphibian and reptile tours (US$90) are also on offer. Binoculars are invaluable for watching wildlife, as are water and sun protection for staying hydrated and sunburn-free.

Rainmaker also offers opportunities for volunteers to participate for two weeks to one month in one of the four departments needed to run and preserve the project. There are also opportunities to work with local schools and various community outreach programs. Contact staff for more information regarding fees and placements.

From the parking lot and orientation area, visitors walk up a beautiful rainforest canyon with a pristine stream tumbling down the rocks. A wooden boardwalk and series of bridges across the canyon floor lead to the base of the walkway. From here, visitors climb several hundred steps to a tree platform, from which the first of six suspension bridges spans the treetops to another platform. The longest span is about 90m, and the total walkway is about 250m long. At the highest point you are some 20 stories above the forest floor.

In addition, there are short interpretive trails that enable the visitor to identify some of the local plants, and some long and strenuous trails into the heart of the 20-sq-km preserve. Keep your eye out for poison-dart frogs, which are very common along the trails!

A large colorful sign marks the turnoff for Rainmaker on the Costanera Sur at the northern end of Pocares (10km east of Parrita or 15km west of Quepos). From the turnoff, it is 7km to the parking area.

it expands outward, but the sprawl is kept relatively in check by the mountains to the east and the water to the west.

Southeast of the town center is the brand-new Pez Vela Marina, a shimmering jewel of architectural prowess that – to be frank – seems a bit out of place in drowsy Quepos. In 2010 the marine slips opened up to the public with much fanfare, though it will still be a few years before the construction is fully complete. The next phase was supposed to include residential communities, shopping complexes and boutique hotels, which could eventually reshift the town's orientation, but the Global Economic Crisis seems to have slowed development.

History

The town's name was derived from the indigenous Quepoa, a subgroup of the Brunka (Boruca), who inhabited the area at the time of the Spanish conquest. As with many indigenous populations across the region, the Quepoa were quickly decimated by newly introduced European diseases. By the end of the 19th century no pure-blooded Quepoa were left, and the area proceeded to be colonized by farmers from the highlands.

Quepos first came to prominence as a banana-exporting port in the early 20th century, though a huge bout of banana blight in the mid-20th century decimated the industry. African oil palms, which currently stretch toward the horizon in dizzying rows around Quepos, soon replaced bananas as the major local crop, though unfortunately they generated a lot less employment for the locals.

The future, on the other hand, is looking bright for locals as foreign visitors are coming to the Manuel Antonio area by the boatload, and more people means more

Quepos

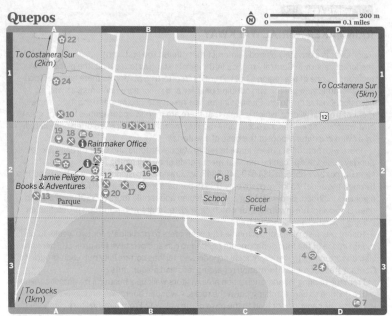

Map labels:
To Costanera Sur (2km)
To Costanera Sur (5km)
Rainmaker Office
Jamie Peligro Books & Adventures
Parque
School
Soccer Field
To Docks (1km)

jobs in the area's rapidly expanding tourism industry. The opening of the Pez Vela Marina may also have profound effects on this humble town, though questions of sustainability and the need for balanced growth continue to be fiercely debated in the local media.

Dangers & Annoyances

The town's large number of easily spotted tourists has attracted thieves. In response, the Costa Rican authorities have greatly increased police presence in the area, but travelers should always lock hotel rooms and never leave anything in their cars. The area is far from dangerous, but the laidback atmosphere shouldn't lull travelers into a false sense of security, and it's best to walk in a group or take a taxi while heading home from the bars at night.

In addition, women should keep in mind that the town's bars attract rowdy crowds of plantation workers on weekends. So walking around town in your swimsuit will most certainly garner the wrong kind of attention.

Note that the beaches in Quepos are polluted and not recommended for swimming. Go over the hill to Manuel Antonio instead, where there are some of the most dreamy waters in all of Costa Rica.

Activities

Diving

The dive sites are still being developed in the Quepos and Manuel Antonio area, though the following operators have both been recommended by readers. The dive sites are away from the contaminated beaches, so water pollution is not a problem when diving.

Oceans Unlimited DIVING, SNORKELING
(2777-3171, in USA 407-385-6598; www.scubadivingcostarica.com) This shop takes its diving very seriously, and runs most of its excursions out to Isla Larga and Isla del Caño, which is south in Bahía Drake (connected through a two-hour bus trip south). It also has a range of specialized PADI certifications and regular environmental awareness projects that make it stand out from the pack. The shop is near the southeast corner of the football field, on the road to Manuel Antonio.

Sportfishing

Sportfishing is big here, and offshore ventures are said to be best from December to April, when sailfish are being hooked. By and large this is a high-dollar activity; expect to pay upwards of US$1000 to hire a boat for the day. If you want to shop around a bit, make for the Pez Vela Marina and ask around – the office is in touch with a number of local captains.

Quepos

Bluefin Sportfishing   FISHING
(☑2777-1676, 2777-2222; www.bluefinsportfishing.
com) Across from the soccer field, this outfitter does excellent fishing trips. It also offers
a laundry list of other tours.

White-Water Rafting

h2o Adventures   ADVENTURE TOUR
(☑2777-4092; www.riostropicales.com) The ven-
erable Costa Rican rafting company Ríos
Tropicales has an office in Quepos called
h2o Adventures. Rates for class III and IV
rapids runs start at US$67 in the low season.
In summer they are US$82.

Tours

There are numerous reputable tour operators in the Quepos area but the scene can
be a bit beguiling because of the abundance
of third-party booking agents who work on
commission. The best way to arrange a tour
is through your hotel or hostel. People also
give glowing reviews to tours booked out
of the foreign-language bookstore called
Jaime Peligro (p308).

Iguana Tours   ADVENTURE TOUR
(☑2777-2052; www.iguanatours.com) With tours
that leave for destinations all over the
central Pacific coast, this adventure-travel
shop offers reputable river rafting, sea kayaking, horseback riding, mangrove tours
and dolphin-watching excursions. It's no
fly-by-night operation – it's been around
since '89 – and has a proven commitment
to ecotourism principles.

Sleeping

Staying in Quepos offers a cheaper alternative to the sky-high prices at many lodges on
the road to Manuel Antonio. It can also be
more convenient, as all the banks, supermarkets and bus stops are in Quepos. Still, those
who save a bit here on a room may have to
spend it on taxi rides to the park. Reservations are recommended during high-season
weekends and are necessary during Easter
and the week between Christmas and New
Year's Eve.

TOP
CHOICE **Wide Mouth Frog
Backpackers**   HOSTEL $
(☑2777-2798; www.widemouthfrog.org; dm US$11,
r with/without bathroom & fan US$50/40;
@ 🛜 🛏 🐕) Friendly, secure and ideally outfitted for travelers of all stripes – it's a bit
hard not to crow about this backpacker outpost, one of the best hostels in the country.
Brightly tiled rooms with a variety of price
points are situated around an inviting pool
where backpackers catch rays before hitting
the communal kitchen and sharing stories
over dinner. There's a TV lounge with a free
DVD rental library and wi-fi, a couple of
lazy dogs padding around the place and an
intimidating fellow watching the place after
hours. The perfect staging area for Manuel
Antonio, here travelers can fill up on free
breakfast before hitting the national park,
and return home to divvy up a cold six pack.
At the time of writing there were designs on
a rooftop yoga room, which would ice the
cake.

QUEPOS FOR CHILDREN

The entire Quepos and Manuel Antonio area is one of Costa Rica's leading family-friendly destinations. With beaches and rainforest in close proximity – not to mention a healthy dose of charismatic wildlife – the region can enchant young minds regardless of their attention spans.

You'll find that most families with children congregate in the hotels and resorts lining the Quepos–Manuel Antonio Rd, but this is more due to accommodations density than other factors. In fact, the appeal of Quepos for children is that there is plenty to explore beyond the hotel walls, which can give parents a bit of fresh air and breathing room.

All in all, the town's excellent restaurant scene is kid-friendly, and the local Ticos in town are very welcoming to little ones. And finally, while you're not exactly on the beach or up in the forest, it's just a short and uneventful ride out to Manuel Antonio if the kids need an idyllic day on the beach.

Hotel Sirena HOTEL $$
(2777-0572; www.lasirenahotel.com; s/d/tr incl breakfast US$60/75/85; P✳︎🛜🏊) This intimate boutique hotel is a welcome and warm addition to the Quepos scene, and is easily the best midrange option in town. Amid the bustle of Quepos' rough-and-ready street scene, the Sirena's whitewashed walls, soft pastel trims and aromatherapy offer a slice of breezy Mediterranean serenity. The halls are perfectly accented with potted plants and original art, and are highlighted by a quaint tiki bar overlooking a tranquil swimming pool. In their rooms, guests enjoy crisp white linens, air-conditioning, cable and a mini-fridge. Rooms upstairs get much better light.

La Foresta Nature Resort ECOLODGE $$$
(2777-3130; www.laforestanatureresort.com; ste/bungalow/villa from US$118/146/280; P✳︎@🏊🐾) This resort hotel (formerly known as Rancho Grande) is located out of the action on the road to the Quepos airport. Crisscrossed by hiking and horseback-riding trails, the property has a butterfly garden and a small zip line, making it good for families who need a lot of room to run around. Still, the luxury here is low-key, and most definitely not in the same league as some of the posh places found further out along the Quepos–Manuel Antonio Rd. But if you're looking for bucolic ambience without having to sacrifice customer service, it's a reliable option.

Best Western Hotel Kamuk HOTEL $$$
(2777-0379; www.kamuk.co.cr; r from US$99; P✳︎@🏊🐾) Forget that this upmarket Quepos stalwart bears the Best Western brand; in reality the Hotel Kamuk is a surprisingly refreshing historic building that provides great value. The chain standard ensures professional service from check-in to checkout, though past reception, the hotel is anything but American in ambience. The core of the hotel is a winding wooden staircase that fans out to breezy hallways adorned with colonial flourishes. Rooms are a bit on the small side, but you can always head to the attractive pool or Western-style restaurant if you want a bit more breathing space. If you're planning on staying here, check the internet as discount rates are sometimes available. Even if you're not staying here, the smoky casino on the ground floor can be a riot, particularly with the waggish cast of working girls and fishermen – all pressing their luck in different ways.

Hotel Villa Romántica HOTEL $$$
(2777-0037; www.villaromantica.com; s/d from US$68/98; P✳︎@🏊🐾) A short walk southeast from the town center brings you to this peaceful garden oasis, which is overflowing with verdant greens and tropical flowers. If you're looking for a compromise between the convenience of staying in Quepos and the intimate proximity to nature found in Manuel Antonio, this is an excellent choice. The rooms themselves are designed to be light and open, which is a nice departure from the cloistered feel found at many other midrange spots.

🍴 Eating

For food, Quepos has the best of all worlds – tons of cheap local eats are just around the corner from polished places with menus that cater to tourist hordes. Visitors who decide to stay on the road to Manuel Antonio or nearer the park won't have anywhere near the quality or diversity of food options accessible by foot right at the center of little Quepos.

If you want to go local, you can't go wrong with the mercado central (Central Market; ☺hours vary), a vast complex in the center of town that hosts budget-friendly *sodas* and cafes and fruit and vegetable vendors. There are too many good *sodas* at the *mercado* to mention them all, so just sniff it out, look over the daily specials and follow the crowd. There's also a weekly farmers market (☺5-10pm Fri) near the waterfront on Friday nights where you can pick up locally made bread, yogurt and fresh fish.

TOP
CHOICE Cevicheria El Dorado   CEVICHE $
(☎8942-2625; meals US$5; ☺11am-9pm Mon-Sat) There's nothing to it – a tinny radio playing Costa Rican pop, a few well-worn stools and a couple of friendly ladies behind the counter – but locals seek out this tiny *ceviche* joint for amazing dishes of fresh affordable fish dressed in citrus and cilantro (coriander) and sided with a few cooked plantains. The selection changes with the seasonal catch, but the price always stays low.

Soda Como Bien   CAFETERIA $
(☎2777-2550; mains US$3-6; ☺7:30am-4pm Mon-Sat) A discussion about which is the best of the *mercado's sodas* can quickly become contentious, but little Como Bien, in the northeast corner of the market, is among the best on the whole coast. The daily rotation of delicious cafeteria options might include fresh fish in a tomato citrus sauce, *olla de carne* (beef soup with rice) or chicken soup, but everything is fresh, the ladies behind the counter are friendly and the burly portions are a dream come true for hungry shoestringers. If you're just looking for something quick before or after a big bus ride, pick up one the fresh *empanadas* (turnovers).

Café Milagro   CAFE $
(meals US$5-8; ☺6am-10pm Mon-Fri; 🛜) Serving some of the country's best cappuccino and espresso, this is a great place to perk up in the morning – try the *perezoso* (meaning 'lazy' or 'sloth'), which is a double espresso poured into a large cup of drip-filter coffee. Or, if you want to simply relax and read the English-language newspapers that are available, you can indulge in a baked good or a freshly made deli sandwich.

Bohemia Café   CAFE $
(☎2774-0109; meals US$5-10; ☺9am-9pm Mon-Sat; 🛜) The decor is a bit loud – it's a mess of colors and animal print – but this little spot draws a pleasant mix of travelers who tend to clack away on their keyboards or wolf down decent burritos and cheap smoothies. For upscale dishes it does pan-international dishes with tropical flair, such as mahimahi with coconut and pineapple.

Escalofrío   ITALIAN $
(gelato $2, meals US$6-11; ☺Tue-Sun; 🛜) Here you'll find more than 20 different flavors of gelato, which may just be the perfect way to beat the tropical heat. There is also a spacious alfresco seating area where you can sample other Italian treats including espressos and cappuccinos as well as an assortment of pizzas (which come from a lovely wood-fired oven) and pastas. It also has a deli across the street where travelers can get sandwiches with imported Italian meats and cheeses to take into Manuel Antonio.

Tropical Sushi   JAPANESE $$
(meals US$9-15; ☺5-11pm) Quepos has gone cosmopolitan: for authentic Japanese (yes, the sushi chef is from Japan!), try this colorfully decorated restaurant, which packs in the hostel crowd for all-you-can-eat specials (US$20). If you're a purist, you can stick to the tuna sashimi spreads, though it's worth venturing out a bit and sampling some of the local Costa Rican–style rolls.

Monchados   CARIBBEAN $$
(dishes US$8-15; ☺5pm-midnight) Although the food is inconsistent, this is something of a Quepos institution among gringos. The long-standing Mex-Carib spot offers traditional Limón-style dishes and Mexican standards. Food here is eclectic, innovative and never bland, a theme that is also reflected in the vibrant decorations and fairly regular live music.

Super Mas   SUPERMARKET $
(☎2777-1162; ☺7am-8pm Mon-Sat; 🛜) Don't mistake this market for your average supermarket: the wondrous aisles of Super Mas have an astonishing array of imported goods, fresh bread and liquor.

🍸 Drinking & Entertainment
Nightlife in Quepos has a good blend of locals and travelers, and it's cheaper than anything you'll find in the Manuel Antonio area. If you are looking for something a bit more sophisticated, however, it's easy enough to jump in a taxi. Keep in mind that the nightclub scene here starts very late, so don't even think about finding the action before 10pm.

Dos Locos BAR
(☎2777-1526; ⊙7am-11pm Mon-Sat, 11am-10pm Sun) This popular Mexican restaurant is the regular watering hole for the local expat community, and sometimes serves as a venue for the occasional live band. It opens onto the central cross streets of town and its fun for people-watching and cheap Imperials. It has an English-language trivia night every Thursday.

El Gran Escape BAR
(☎2777-0395; ⊙6am-11pm) A fisher-friendly bar and restaurant that is good for cold beer, warm pub grub and some light-hearted chit-chat about the one that got away.

Sargento García BAR
(☎2777-2960; ⊙9am-9pm) This stars-and-stripes tribute bar may be a bit heavy on the Americana for some, but look no further if you're craving a Budweiser and some big-screen sports. On Wednesday nights it offers free salsa dancing classes at 8pm.

Republik Club CLUB
(cover charge for men US$3; ⊙6:30pm-2:30am) Republik hosts the most reliable party in central Quepos, and it has some kind of drink special nearly every night if you arrive before 10pm. (Of course, the place is pretty lonely at that hour.) Later, the volume gets loud, the drinks become more pricey and things tend to career out of control. Depending on the night it can be a excellent place to party, though ladies with a strong constitution and a taste for adventure should go on Thursday, when they can drink free most of the night.

Musik CLUB
The decor of this futuristically themed place (white plastic furniture and lasers) is a bit heavy-handed, but the centrally located club has theme nights, requisite (dangerously cheap) ladies' specials and a molar-rattling sound system. When the place is empty, get a corner seat on the balcony to watch the action unfold on the streets below. It's above a Century 21 office.

Discoteca Arco Iris CLUB
(⊙10pm-late) An industrial-sized discotheque just north of town that brings out the locals with thumping dance beats. Don't even think of coming here early; you'll be drinking alone. There's a cover of about US$6 every night to dissuade the riffraff.

Casino CASINO
(⊙slot machines 11am-6pm, all games 6pm-4am) If you feel like putting your cash on the line, there's a small but suitable casino at the Best Western Hotel Kamuk, but the scene gets a bit seedy.

ℹ Information

The photocopied city guide available at Wide Mouth Frog is completely in tune with the happenings in town, and, if you stay there, it's a handout worth hanging on to. Aside from it, the latest happenings are listed in *Quepolandia*, a free English-language monthly magazine that can be found at many of the town's businesses. Both Banco de San José and Coopealianza have 24-hour ATMs on the Cirrus and Plus systems. Other banks will all change US dollars and traveler's checks.

The best source of books for travelers within miles is **Jaime Peligro** (☎2777-7106; www.queposbooks.com; ⊙9:30am-5:30pm Mon-Sat), a bookstore that has a complete selection of local guides, literature in a number of languages and tons of local information.

ℹ Getting There & Away
Air
Both **NatureAir** (www.natureair.com) and **Sansa** (www.sansa.com) service Quepos, which is the base town for accessing Manuel Antonio. Prices vary according to season and availability, though you can expect to pay a little less than US$75 for a flight from San José or Liberia. Flights are packed in the high season, so book (and pay) for your ticket well ahead of time and reconfirm often. The airport is 5km out of town, and taxis make the trip for a few thousand colones (do not pay more than US$8), depending on traffic.

Bus
All buses arrive at and depart from the busy, chaotic main terminal in the center of town. If you're coming and going in high season, buy tickets for San José in advance at the **Transportes Morales ticket office** (☎2777-0263; ⊙7-11am & 1-5pm Mon-Sat, 7am-1pm Sun) at the bus terminal.

Jacó US$1.50; 1½ hours; departs 4:30am, 7:30am, 10:30am and 3pm.

Puntarenas US$4.25; 3½ hours; departs 8am, 10:30am and 3:30pm.

San Isidro de El General, via Dominical US$4; three hours; departs 5:30am, 11:30am and 1:30pm.

San José (Transportes Morales) US$7 to US$8; four hours; departs 5am, 8am, 10am, noon, 2pm, 4pm and 7:30pm.

Uvita, via Dominical US$8; 4½ hours; departs 10am and 7pm.

ⓘ Getting Around

Bus

Buses between Quepos and Manuel Antonio (US$0.35) depart roughly every 30 minutes from the main terminal between 6am and 7:30pm, and less frequently after 7:30pm. The last bus departs Manuel Antonio at 10:25pm. There are more frequent buses in the dry season.

Car

A number of American car-rental companies operate in Quepos; reserve ahead and reconfirm to guarantee availability.

Alamo (☑2777-3344; ⊙7:30am-noon & 1:30am-5:30pm)

Taxi

Colectivos (shared taxis or minibuses) between Quepos and Manuel Antonio will usually pick up extra passengers for a few dollars. A private taxi will cost a few thousand colones. Call **Quepos Taxi** (☑2777-0425, 2777-0734) or catch one at the taxi stand south of the market. The trip between Quepos and the park should cost about US$15. At night there is an abundance of private taxis; have the front desk of your hotel call one.

Quepos to Manuel Antonio

Sure, the park itself is a natural wonder, but the road to it is an overdeveloped mess. The serpentine road that links Quepos to Manuel Antonio is lined with hotels and tour operators, and the roadside is lined with tourists in flip flops.

From the Quepos waterfront, the road swings inland for 7km before reaching the beaches of Manuel Antonio Village and the entrance to the national park. This route passes over a number of hills awash with picturesque views of forested slopes leading down to the palm-fringed coastline.

This area is home to some of Costa Rica's finest hotels and restaurants, though navigating the area without a car is challenging. While shoestringers and budget travelers are catered for, this is one part of the country where those with deep pockets can bed down and dine out in the lap of luxury.

Note that the road to Manuel Antonio is steep, winding and very narrow. Worse, local bus drivers love to career through at high velocities, and there are almost no places to pull over in the event of an emergency. At all times you should exercise caution and drive and walk with care, especially at night. Be particularly aware of pedestrians.

⊙ Sights & Activities

Fincas Naturales   FARM

(☑2777-0850; www.wildliferefugecr.com; adult/child US$15/8; ⊙8am-4pm; 🖝) Situated just across the road from Hotel Sí Como No, this private rainforest preserve and butterfly garden breeds about three dozen species of butterfly – a delicate population compared to the menagerie of lizards, reptiles and frogs that inspire gleefully grossed-out squeals from the little ones. Among the many tours is a cool sound-and-light show at night (US$35 per person), enabling visitors to see the insect markings that glow in ultraviolet light.

Serenity Spa   SPA

(☑2777-0777, ext 220; www.sicomono.com; Hotel Sí Como No) After a day's activities you can relax at the Serenity Spa, a good place for couple's massages, sunburn-relief treatments, coconut body scrubs and tasty coffee. It offers a strangely appetizing exfoliant made from crushed rice, ginger and lime. Open by appointment.

Amigos del Río   RAFTING

(☑2777-1084; www.adventuremanuelantonio.com) Amigos del Río runs white-water rafting trips for all skill levels on the Ríos Savegre and Naranjo. Prices vary depending on the size of the party and the nature of your trip.

🛏 Sleeping

The Quepos–Manuel Antonio Rd is heavily skewed towards ultra-top-end hotels, but plenty of noteworthy midrange accommodations and excellent budget hostels are hidden along the way. High-season rates are provided throughout this section, though it's worth knowing that low-season rates can be as much as 40% lower. Reservations are an absolute must for busy weekends and holiday seasons. Although the sleeping options along the Quepos–Manuel Antonio Rd are closer to the park than those in Quepos, many of them will still require a taxi or a long walk along the busy road to reach the park.

⌖ Vista Serena Hostel   HOSTEL $$

(☑2777-5162; www.vistaserena.com; ⊙3-/4-bed dm US$13/15, bungalow without bathroom US$50; 🅿@) In an area that is hopelessly overpriced, it's a relief to find such a great budget hostel. Perched scenically on a quiet hillside, this memorable spot allows guests to enjoy spectacular ocean sunsets from a hammock-filled terrace and strum the communal

Manuel Antonio Area

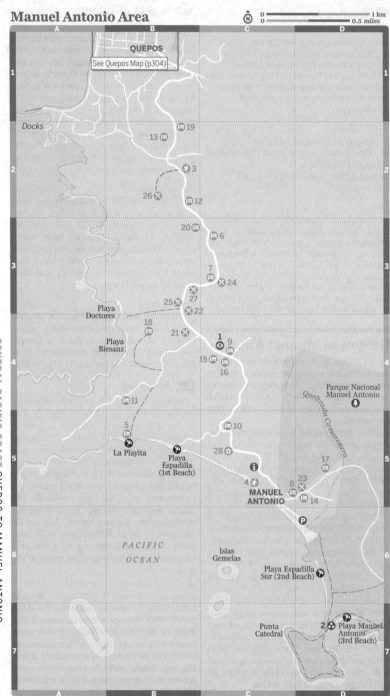

QUEPOS
See Quepos Map (p304)

Docks

Playa Doctores

Playa Biesanz

La Playita

Playa Espadilla (1st Beach)

PACIFIC OCEAN

Islas Gemelas

Parque Nacional Manuel Antonio

Quebrada Camaronera

MANUEL ANTONIO

Playa Espadilla Sur (2nd Beach)

Punta Catedral

Playa Manuel Antonio (3rd Beach)

Manuel Antonio Area

guitar. A short trail hike through local farmland leads to a remote wilderness beach. The spick-and-span white-tiled dorms have shared bathrooms, a communal kitchen and a TV lounge, though there are private bungalows for couples who want a bit more privacy. Sonia and her son Conrad, the helpful Tico owners, speak fluent English, and are commendable for their efforts in assisting countless travelers.

Makanda by the Sea   VILLA $$$
(②2777-0442; www.makanda.com; studio/villa incl breakfast from US$265/400; P❋@🛜🏊) Comprising of just six villas and five studios, Makanda has an unmatched air of intimacy and complete privacy. Villa 1 (the largest) will take your breath away – one entire wall is open to the rainforest and the ocean. The other villas and studios are air-conditioned and enclosed, though they draw upon the same minimalistic, Eastern-infused design schemes. The grounds are also home to a beautiful infinity pool and Jacuzzi, both offering superb views out to sea, as well as a series of flawless Japanese gardens that you can stroll through and reflect on the beauty of your surroundings. And, if you're still not impressed, you can access a private beach by taking the 552 steps down the side of the mountain – bliss!

Backpackers Manuel Antonio   HOSTEL $
(②2777-2507; www.backpackersmanuelantonio. com; dm incl breakfast US$12, d without bathroom US$35; 🛜) This locally owned hostel has a fresh paint job, a very sociable vibe and a good location – relatively near the entrance of the park and walking distance from a good grocery store and bakery. The dorms are clean and secure and there's a grill and pool out back. Larger rooms, with a bunk and double bed, are good for families. It's in front of the football field.

Hotel Costa Verde   HOTEL $$$
(②2777-0584; www.costaverde.com; efficiency/ studio from US$115/149, Boeing 727 fuselage home US$500; P❋@🛜🏊) This collection of rooms, studios and – believe it or not – a fully converted Boeing 727 fuselage occupies a lush, tropical setting that is frequented by regular troops of primate visitors. Efficiency units are attractively tiled, and face the encroaching forest, while slightly more expensive studios have full ocean views. But the real kicker here is the airplane–tree house hybrid, which gives new life to a previously decommissioned Boeing. The fuselage has been completely retrofitted with wooden paneling, and now houses two bedrooms, a fully functional master bathroom, and a chandelier-lit

SAVING THE SQUIRREL MONKEY

With its expressive eyes and luxuriant coat, the *mono tití* (Central American squirrel monkey) is a favorite of the four Costa Rican monkey species. It is also in danger of extinction as there are roughly only 1500 of these animals left in Manuel Antonio, one of its last remaining native habitats.

Unfortunately, the area's constant threat of overdevelopment is one of the animal's greatest threats. To remedy this problem, a conservation project known as Saving Mono Tití (www.savingmonotiti.com) is taking bold measures to prevent further decline. This coalition of organizations is helping to create a sustainable wildlife corridor between Parque Nacional Manuel Antonio and the Zona Protectora Cerro Nara in the northeast.

To achieve this aim, they are reforesting the Río Naranjo, a key waterway linking the two locations. More than 10,000 trees have already been planted along 8km of the Naranjo. This not only has the effect of extending the monkeys' habitat, but also provides a protected area for other wildlife to enjoy. Scientists at the Universidad Nacional de Costa Rica have mapped and selected sites for reforestation, and business owners in the area as well as private donations support the project financially.

balcony that branches off the wing. When toucans flit by the cockpit, it's a bit surreal. The owners of Hotel Costa Verde were also the masterminds behind El Avión bar.

Hotel Sí Como No   HOTEL $$$
(☎2777-0777; www.sicomono.com; r US$230-290, ste US$305-340, child under 6yr free; P❋@ 🏊⭐♿) This flawlessly designed hotel is an example of how to build a resort while maintaining environmental sensibility. Buildings are insulated for comfort and use energy-efficient air-con units; water is recycled into the landscape, and solar-heating panels are used to heat the water. No surprise here that the Sí Como No is one of only four hotels in the country to have been awarded five out of five leaves by the government-run Certified Sustainable Tourism campaign. Eco-friendliness aside, the hotel is also gorgeous and packed full of family-friendly amenities. The rooms themselves are accented by rich woods and bold splashes of tropical colors, and feature enormous picture windows and sweeping balconies – you'll never feel closed off from the surrounding rainforest and distant ocean. The hotel has two pools (one with a slide for kids, one for adults only, both with swim-up bars), two solar-heated Jacuzzis, a health spa, a THX movie theater and two excellent restaurants.

Arenas del Mar   BOUTIQUE HOTEL $$$
(☎2777-2777; www.arenasdelmar.com; r US$330-600; P❋@🏊⭐) This visually arresting hotel and resort complex is consistently shortlisted among Costa Rica's finest upscale hotels. Despite the extent and breadth of the grounds, there are only 40 rooms, which ensures an unmatched degree of personal service and privacy. It has won numerous ecotourism awards since its inception, and was designed to incorporate the beauty of the natural landscape. In short, the overall effect is breathtaking, especially when you're staring down the coastline from the lofty heights of your private open-air Jacuzzi.

Hotel Las Tres Banderas   HOTEL $$
(☎2777-1871; www.hoteltresbanderas.com; d/ste/ apt US$80/120/250; P❋@🏊⭐♿) This welcoming roadside inn is owned by a Polish-born US citizen who lives in Costa Rica – hence the very appropriate moniker, *tres banderas* (three flags). Fourteen doubles and three suites are spacious affairs with imported tiles and local woods and, while some could use a bit of air, they all come with a porch where guests can relax in leather-crafted rocking chairs and look for sloths in the forest behind the property. Dinner is often prepared on an outdoor grill and guests congregate to dine together around the deep central pool, which lends a communal flourish to the property.

Mimo's Hotel   HOTEL $$
(☎2777-2217; www.mimoshotel.com; d/ste from US$75/105; P❋@🏊♿) Run by a delightful Italian couple, this whitewashed and wood-trimmed hotel has spacious, clean, terra-cotta tiled rooms that are lit up with bright, colorful murals. The property is connected by lovely stone paths, bringing guests to the palm-fringed swimming pool,

a glowing Jacuzzi and restaurant serving Italian-influenced dishes. The owners speak half a dozen languages, and have a wealth of knowledge about Costa Rica.

BaBaLoo Inn HOTEL **$$**
(☎2777-3461; www.babalooinn.com; d standard/ king US$90/202; ❲P❳❲❊❳❲❤❳) This US-run establishment offers standard rooms with private balcony overlooking a lush, tropical garden. However, we're partial to the larger king rooms featuring dramatic ocean views, a comfortable sitting area, oversized beds and shower, a small kitchenette and enough space for a family of four. All rooms come with small extras, like a fully stocked minibar and DVD player, which means that there is plenty to do on a rainy day.

Hotel Casitas Eclipse HOTEL **$$$**
(☎2777-1738, 2777-0408; www.casitaseclipse.org; r/ste/casitas from US$140/190/330; ❲P❳❲❊❳❲@❳❲❤❳❲❤❳) The soothing curves of this architecturally arresting, pure-white complex hint at the beauty within. The hotel consists of nine attractive, split-level houses spread around three swimming pools. The bottom floor of each house is an enormous junior suite, while the upper floor is a standard room with private terrace. These have a separate entrance but a staircase (with lockable door) combines the two and, *voilà*, you have a sumptuous *casita* (apartment) sleeping five.

Hotel La Mariposa BOUTIQUE HOTEL **$$$**
(☎2777-0355; www.lamariposa.com; r US$215-450, ste US$450; ❲P❳❲❊❳❲@❳❲❤❳❲❤❳) This internationally acclaimed hotel was the area's first luxury accommodations option, so unsurprisingly it snatched up the best view of the coastline. Fifty-plus pristine rooms of various sizes are elegantly decorated with hand-carved furniture – big spenders should check out the penthouse suite, which has a Jacuzzi on the terrace facing the sea. This hotel was listed in the book *1000 Places to See Before You Die*, principally for the immaculate gardens and world-class views that hug every corner of the property.

Hotel Mono Azul HOTEL **$$**
(☎2777-2572; www.monoazul.com; r US$40-65, child under 12yr free; ❲P❳❲❊❳❲@❳❲❤❳❲❤❳❲❤❳) This is a great family option, as the entire hotel is decorated with animal murals and rainforest paraphernalia, not to mention the three pools and games room. You'll also sleep well at night knowing that your money is going to a good cause. The Mono Azul is home to 'Kids

Saving the Rainforest' (KSTR), started by two local schoolchildren who were concerned about the endangered *mono tití* (Central American squirrel monkey). Many of these adorable critters were run over on the narrow road to the national park, or electrocuted on overhanging electrical cables, so KSTR purchased and erected monkey 'bridges' across the road (you can see them, often in use, as you head to the park). Ten percent of hotel receipts are donated to the organization.

✗ Eating & Drinking

Many hotels listed previously have good restaurants open to the public. As with sleeping venues, eating and drinking establishments along this stretch are skewed upmarket. Reservations are recommended on weekends, holidays and during the busy dry season.

There are more eating options in the surrounding area in Quepos and Manuel Antonio Village.

TOP CHOICE Agua Azul INTERNATIONAL **$$**
(☎2777-5280; meals US$7-18; ⏰11am-10pm Thu-Tue) Perched on the 2nd floor with uninterrupted ocean views, Agua Azul is a killer lunch spot on this stretch of road – perfect for early morning park visitors who are heading back to their hotel. The breezy, unpretentious open-air restaurant is renowned for its 'big ass burger'. But the burger is only the beginning of satisfying menu choices. Selections like the panko-crusted catch of the day or seared tuna on tequila lime cucumber salad are executed with artful precision.

Kapi Kapi Restaurant FUSION **$$$**
(☎2777-5049; meals US$15-40) While there is some stiff competition for the title of best restaurant in the Manuel Antonio area, this Californian creation raises the bar on both quality and class. Kapi Kapi, which is a traditional greeting of the indigenous Maleku people, welcomes diners with soft lights, earthy tones and soothing natural decor, which perfectly frame the dense forest lying just beyond the perimeter. The menu is no less ambitious, spanning the globe from America to Asia, and making several pivotal stops along the way. Pan-Asian–style seafood is featured prominently on the menu, and brought to life with Continental-inspired sauces, while South American wines and Costa Rican coffees complete this globetrotting culinary extravaganza.

Restaurante Gato Negro MEDITERRANEAN $$
(☎2777-0408; Hotel Casitas Eclipse; dishes US$9-16) An elegant yet subdued dinner spot that specializes in Mediterranean cuisine, the 'Black Cat' serves up traditional standards, such as homemade pastas and assorted antipasto spreads, alongside more inventive Costa Rican–influenced tapas-style dishes. The bar also bustles during the busy dry season, drawing in lovers of crafted cocktails and chilled wines.

Café Milagro CAFE $$
(breakfast US$4-6, sandwiches US$4-7; ☎) The sister cafe of the one in Quepos is an obligatory stop on the way to the park for exquisite coffee – pure black gold. Breakfast and sandwiches are well priced and filling, and patrons can grab them en route to the trails or linger at the wooden tables out front to watch the world go by.

Restaurante Barba Roja MEXICAN $$
(☎2777-0331; meals US$7-20; ⊙4-10pm Mon, 10am-10pm Tue-Sun) A long-standing Manuel Antonio area institution, the Barba Roja offers an excellent mix of US standards with a bit of Mexican flair. After a long day on the trails, recoup over a heaping bowl of nachos and a smooth but potent margarita. On weekends, bring your dancing shoes as the Barba Roja transforms into a discotheque once the sun drops below the horizon.

🌿**Claro Que Sí** ORGANIC $$
(☎2777-0777; Hotel Sí Como No; meals US$8-15) A casual, family-friendly restaurant that passes on pretension without sacrificing on quality, Claro Que Sí proudly serves organic and locally sourced food items that are in line with the philosophy of its parent hotel, Sí Como No. Guilt-free meats and fish are expertly complemented with fresh produce, resulting in flavorful dishes typical of both the Pacific and Caribbean coasts.

Le Papillon EUROPEAN $$$
(☎2777-0355; Hotel La Mariposa; lunch US$10-20, dinner US$20-40) The featured restaurant at Manuel Antonio's landmark luxury hotel is perfectly perched to take in the daily sunset over the vast expanse of the Pacific Ocean. As you'd imagine, you're paying for the view at this world-class institution, though when the sun dips below the horizon and lights up the sky, you'll stop caring about the price. The food is largely continental cuisine that takes advantage of Costa Rica's rich bounty of fresh seafood and tropical produce – if you're trying to keep to your budget, the lunch menu is a good deal.

Ronny's Place BURGERS, SEAFOOD $$
(☎2777-5120; mains US$6-14; ⊙noon-10pm) Head 800m west from the main drag on the well-marked dirt road opposite Manuel Antonio Experts – it's worth the trip for the view alone. Ronny, the bilingual Tico owner, has made his rest stop a favorite of locals and travelers alike. The menu delivers big burgers and fresh seafood, and its washed down with excellent sangria. And while the food might be unspectacular, the views are insane: two pristine bays and primitive jungle on all sides. While plenty of places along this stretch of road boast similar views, the location just off the beaten path, down the rough, cow-lined road, makes Ronny's feel like a secret find.

Super Joseth SELF-CATERING $
(☎2777-2960; ⊙7am-9pm, from 8am Sun) Although it's a godsend for self-caterers, Super Joseth is a place that's reflective of its location – a bit pricy, stocked for foreign travelers and very busy. It has a full selection of booze (Campari?), sunblock and upscale picnic goods.

El Avión BAR
(☎2777-3378; mains US$6-14; ☎🍴) This unforgettable airplane bar-restaurant was constructed from the body of a 1954 Fairchild C-123. Here's where the story gets interesting – allegedly, the plane was purchased by the US government in the '80s for the Nicaraguan Contras, but never made it out of its hangar in San José because of the ensuing Iran-Contra scandal that embroiled Oliver North and his cohorts in the US government. (The plane is lovingly referred to as 'Ollie's Folly.') In 2000 the enterprising owners of El Avión purchased it for the surprisingly reasonable sum of US$3000 and carted it piece by piece to Manuel Antonio. It now sits on the side of the main road, where it looks as if it had crash-landed into the side of the hill. It's a great spot for a beer, guacamole and a Pacific sunset, and in the evenings during the dry season there are regular live music performances.

☆ Entertainment

Sí Como No Cinema CINEMA
(☎888-742-6667; www.sicomono.com; Hotel Sí Como No; ⊙8:30pm) This 45-seat theater shows a fun rotation of popular American movies. If you spend US$10 at the hotel's restaurant or bar, admission is free.

QUEPOS TO MANUEL ANTONIO FOR CHILDREN

The Quepos to Manuel Antonio stretch of road is home to the lion's share of accommodations and restaurants in these parts, and you will see plenty of vacationing families wherever you go. But it's worth pointing out that many of the high-end boutique hotels and upscale eateries are not always very welcoming of babies and young children. Assuming, however, that you avoid anything with obvious over-the-top glitz and glamour, your children will be well catered for at many of the establishments covered in this section.

A word of caution: driver visibility is limited along parts of the narrow, steep and winding road, particularly during low-light and foul-weather conditions. If you find yourself walking along the road (there is no shoulder), keep a close eye on your children at all times, and warn them to be careful of passing cars. Likewise, always drive carefully, and return the favor by keeping an eye out for pedestrians.

❶ Getting There & Away

A good number of visitors who stay in this area arrive by private or rented car. The public bus from Quepos will let you off anywhere along the road.

Manuel Antonio Village

As you travel the road between Quepos and Parque Nacional Manuel Antonio, the din from roaring buses, packs of tourists and locals hunting foreign dollars becomes increasingly loud, reaching its somewhat chaotic climax at Manuel Antonio Village, whose beer advertisements and barkers have inched right up to the gates of the park. Hordes descend on this tiny oceanside village at the entrance to one of the country's most celebrated tourist destinations. Don't show up all bright-eyed and bushy-tailed, expecting deserted beaches and untouched tropical paradise. Higher primates tend to be the most frequently sighted species, especially during the congested dry season when tour groups arrive en masse.

While it can be difficult at times to have a quiet moment to collect your thoughts, the environs here really do look as glossy and polished as the travel brochures suggest. And, when troops of monkeys climb down from the forest canopy to the tropical sands, you really can get up close and personal with some marvelous wildlife. So, in short, the moral is to arrive in Manuel Antonio with some realistic expectations, though more often than not, you're going to have a memorable visit.

◉ Sights & Activities

Body boards and kayaks can be rented all along the beach at Playa Espadilla. White-water rafting and sea kayaking are also popular in this area. Don't worry about finding a place to rent equiptment; they'll find you. The possibility for good snorkeling in the area is nearly nonexistent due to crowded waters and the low visibility of the Pacific waters.

Playa Espadilla BEACH
There's a good beach, Playa Espadilla, near the entrance to the Parque Nacional Manuel Antonio, though you need to be wary of rip currents. There are some lifeguards working at this beach, though not at the other beaches in the area.

La Playita BEACH
At the far western end of Playa Espadilla, beyond a rocky headland (wear sandals), is one of Costa Rica's most famous gay beaches and a particular draw for young men. For years it was also one of Costa Rica's only nude beaches, but the nearby construction of a big hotel seems to have ended that tradition, and those who bathe in the buff have been known to suffer police harassment. The beach is inaccessible one hour before and after the high tide, so time your walk well. Also, don't be fooled – you do not need to pay to use the beaches as they're outside the park.

Manuel Antonio Surf School SURFING
(☏2777-4842; www.masurfschool.com) If you're looking to surf, the gentle ankle-slappers here are perfect for getting your sea legs. Manuel Antonio Surf School has a kiosk on the beach. As with any surf lessons on the beach, the quality of instructors varies a lot. Be sure to check whether the price comes with a couple of extra hours of board rental.

Planet Dolphin CRUISE
(☏2777-2137; www.planetdolphin.com; Cabinas Piscis) Steve Wofford at Planet Dolphin offers dolphin- and whale-watching tours; starlight

GAY GUIDE TO MANUEL ANTONIO

For jet-setting gay and lesbian travelers from the world over, Manuel Antonio has long been regarded as something of a dream destination. Homosexuality has been decriminalized in Costa Rica since the 1970s – a rarity in all-too-often machismo-fueled conservative Central America – and a well established gay scene blossomed in Manuel Antonio soon after. Gay and lesbian travelers will find that it's unlike any other destination in the country.

It's not hard to understand why Manuel Antonio first started attracting gay travelers, especially since the area is stunningly beautiful, and has long attracted liberal-minded and tolerant individuals. There is also a burgeoning artist community and a sophisticated restaurant scene.

Sights & Activities

During the daylight hours, the epicenter of gay Manuel Antonio is the famous La Playita, a beach with a long history of nude sunbathing for gay men. Alas, the days when you could sun in the buff are gone, but La Playita still is widely regarded as a playful pick-up scene for gay men on the prowl.

Sleeping

A significant number of hotels in the Manuel Antonio area advertise themselves as being gay-friendly and even the ones that don't are unlikely to discriminate. Of course, if you want to enjoy the freedom and peace of mind that comes with staying at exclusively gay accommodations, book a room at the gay-owned and operated Hotel Villa Roca (www. villaroca.com; r incl breakfast from $350; P@🛜🔥), a collection of brightly whitewashed rooms and apartments situated around a central pool and sundeck. The expansive view from the pool takes in an uninterrupted view of the water and rocky offshore islands. This is also the place to catch incredible sunsets.

Eating & Drinking

The Manuel Antonio area has always been proud to host one of the most sophisticated and cosmopolitan restaurant scenes on the central Pacific coast. While there are no exclusively gay restaurants and bars, there are a few with particularly good gay-oriented events. Barba Roja (p314) is a reliably good restaurant with a gay scene on Sunday nights and Liquid (⏰9pm-3am Tue & Thu-Sun), a nightclub near the bottom of the hill, is a good place for young gay guys to party. After enough deceptively strong, colorful cocktails the dance floor is a blast. It has theme parties every night of the week and a raucous annual 'Mr Liquid' competition.

---

sailing cruises are also available. Prices vary depending on the size of your group and your itinerary. The cruises sometimes leave out of the Pez Vela Marina in Quepos.

🛏 Sleeping & Eating

The village of Manuel Antonio is the closest base for exploring the national park, though the selection of eating and sleeping options is not as varied as in Quepos proper or the Quepos to Manuel Antonio stretch of road. It's also completely overrun with foreigners.

Backpackers Paradise Costa Linda　　　　　　　　　HOSTEL $
(☎2777-0304; www.costalinda-backpackers.com; dm or r without bathroom per person from US$10; P✳@🛜) While it's most definitely not in the same class as competing hostels in Que-

pos and on Quepos–Manuel Antonio Rd, this shoestringers' crash pad is decent enough for a night or two, especially considering the rock-bottom prices. The beachside location is excellent, and the small garden cafe serves up some satisfying comfort food (meals US$5 to US$9), but the rooms lack personality and style, and are in desperate need of an update.

Hotel Playa & Cabinas Espadilla　　　　　　HOTEL, CABINA $$$
(☎2777-0416, 2777-0903; www.espadilla.com; cabins/r from US$100/165; P✳🛜🔥👣) Two properties in one: the hotel is centered on a large swimming pool and tennis courts, but the rooms are fairly bland considering the hefty price tag. The cabins are very affordable, however, and while they're a bit worn

for wear, you have access to all the facilities at Hotel Playa. There are certainly swisher properties up the road en route to Quepos, but you can't beat the convenience that comes with staying here.

La Posada BUNGALOW **$$$**
(2777-1446; www.laposadajungle.com; bungalows US$125-225; P✳☎) Your private jungle bungalow can accommodate you and several of your friends, though you might have some furry visitors as – quite literally – you're on the edge of the national park. From the comfort of your fully equipped home away from home, which is jam-packed with modern amenities, including a fully stocked kitchen, you can view wildlife as it scurries across your front yard (or across your rooftop in the middle of the night!).

Hotel Vela Bar & Restaurant SEAFOOD **$**
(2777-0413; www.velabar.com; meals US$6-13; @☎) Hotel Vela is primarily known for its justifiably famous thatched-roof bar and restaurant, which serves up some of the freshest seafood in the area. However, the hotel is also a surprisingly affordable spot to post up for a night or two – rooms here are fairly basic, but it's hard to beat the price (single/double US$43/55) considering that you can literally wake up, have your morning coffee and stroll over to the entrance to the Parque Nacional Manuel Antonio.

❶ Information

La Buena Nota (2777-1002), at the northern end of Manuel Antonio village, serves as an informal tourist information center. It sells maps, guidebooks, books in various languages, English-language newspapers, beach supplies and souvenirs; it also rents out body boards. You can inquire here about guesthouses available for long-term stays. Look for a free copy of the English-language *Quepolandia,* which details everything to see and do in the area. If you're looking for a quick online overview, visit www. www.manuelantonio.net.

❶ Getting There & Away

Buses depart Manuel Antonio for San José (US$7 to US$9, four hours) at 6am, 9:30am, noon and 5pm. These will pick you up in front of your hotel if you are on the road to flag them down, or from the Quepos bus terminal, after which there are no stops. Buy tickets well in advance at the Quepos bus terminal. This bus is frequently packed and you will not be able to buy tickets from the driver. Buses for destinations other than San José also leave from the main terminal in Quepos.

Parque Nacional Manuel Antonio

A place of swaying palms and playful monkeys, spakling blue water and riotous tropical birds, Parque Nacional Manuel Antonio (2777-0644; park entrance US$10; ⊙7am-4pm Tue-Sun) embodies Costa Rica's postcard charms. It was declared a national park in 1972, preserving it (with just minutes to spare) from being bulldozed and razed to make room for a coastal development project. Although Manuel Antonio was enlarged to its present-day size of 16 sq km in 2000, it is still the country's smallest national park. Space remains a premium, and as this is one of Central America's top tourist destinations, you're going to have to break free from the camera-clicking tour groups and actively seek out your own idyllic spot of sand.

MONKEY BUSINESS

There are a number of stands on the beach that cater to hungry tourists, though everything is exuberantly overpriced and of dubious quality. Plus, all the food scraps have negatively impacted the monkey population. Before you offer a monkey your scraps consider the following risks to their health:

» Monkeys are susceptible to bacteria transmitted from human hands.

» Irregular feeding will lead to aggressive behavior as well as create a dangerous dependency (picnickers in Manuel Antonio suffer downright intimidating mobs of them sometimes).

» Bananas are not their preferred food, and can cause serious digestive problems.

» Increased exposure to humans facilitates illegal poaching.

It should go without saying: don't feed the monkeys. And, if you do happen to come across someone doing so, take the initiative and politely ask them to stop.

That said, Manuel Antonio is absolutely stunning, and on a good day, at the right time, it's easy to convince yourself that you've died and gone to a coconut-filled paradise. The park's clearly marked trail system winds through rainforest-backed tropical beaches and rocky headlands, and the views across the bay to the pristine outer islands are unforgettable. As if this wasn't enough, add a ubiquitous population of iguanas, howlers, capuchins, sloths and squirrel monkeys.

◉ Sights & Activities

Hiking & Swimming

After the park entrance, it's about a 30-minute hike to **Playa Espadilla Sur** and **Playa Manuel Antonio**, the park's idyllic beaches, which is where most people spend a good part of their time in the park. There will be numerous guides leading clusters of groups along the flat hike, so a bit of eavesdropping will provide solo shoestring travelers an informal lesson on the many birds, sloths and monkeys that can be observed along the way. Eventually, the obvious, well-trodden trail veers right and through forest to an isthmus separating Playas Espadilla Sur and Manuel Antonio. This is also where there's a park ranger station and information center (its hours are random, but we've yet to see it open, so be pleasantly surprised if it is staffed).

Geography fun fact: this isthmus is called a *tombolo* and was formed by the accumulation of sand between the mainland and the peninsula beyond, which was once an island. Along this bridge are the park's two amazing beaches, Playa Manuel Antonio, on the ocean side, and the slightly less-visited (though occasionally rough) Playa Espadilla Sur, which faces Manuel Antonio Village. With their turquoise waters, shaded hide-outs and continual aerial show of brown pelicans, these beaches are dreamy.

At its end, the isthmus widens into a rocky peninsula, with a thick forest in the center. Several informal trails lead down the peninsula to near the center of it, the Punta Catedral. If you bushwhack your way through, there are good views of the Pacific Ocean and various rocky islets that are bird reserves and form part of the national park. Brown boobies and pelicans nest on these islands.

At the western end of Playa Manuel Antonio you can see a semicircle of rocks at low tide. Archaeologists believe these were arranged by pre-Columbian indigenous people to function as a turtle trap. (Turtles would swim in during high tide, but when they tried to swim out after the tide started receding, they'd be trapped by the wall.) The beach itself is an attractive one of white sand and is popular for swimming. It's protected and safer than the Espadilla beaches.

Beyond Playa Manuel Antonio, if visitors return towards the trail from the entrance of the park, the trail divides and leads deeper into the park. The lower trail is steep and slippery during the wet months and leads to the quiet Playa Puerto Escondido. This beach can be more or less completely covered by high tides, so be careful not to get cut off. The upper trail climbs to a lookout on a bluff overlooking Puerto Escondido and Punta Serrucho beyond – a stunning vista. Rangers reportedly limit the number of hikers on this trail to 45.

The trails in Manuel Antonio are well marked and heavily traversed, though there are some quiet corners near the ends of the trails. Off-trail hiking is not permitted without prior consent from the park service.

Watch out for the manchineel tree *(Hippomane mancinella)* – it has poisonous fruits that look like little crab apples, and the sap exuded by the bark and leaves is toxic, causing the skin to itch and burn. Warning signs are prominently displayed beside examples of this tree near the park entrance.

Wildlife-Watching

Increased tourist traffic has taken its toll on the park's wildlife as animals are frequently driven away or – worse still – taught to scavenge for tourist handouts. To its credit, the park service has reacted by closing the park on Monday and limiting the number of visitors to 600 per day during the week and 800 per day on weekends and holidays.

Even though visitors are funneled along the main access road, you should have no problem seeing animals here, even as you line up at the gate. White-faced capuchins are very used to people, and normally troops feed and interact within a short distance of visitors; they can be encountered anywhere along the main access road and around Playa Manuel Antonio.

You'll probably also hear mantled howler monkeys soon after sunrise and, like capuchins, they can be seen virtually any-

TOP PICKS: KIDDY FUN IN MANUEL ANTONIO

» Buy a wildlife picture book, and make a game out of spotting animals.

» Teach your kids how to read a map and use a compass to navigate.

» If your older children have an adventurous streak, take them rafting.

» Cool off by splashing in the gentle surf at Playa Manuel Antonio.

» When in doubt, even the fussiest of tykes love playing in the sand.

where inside the park and even along the road to Quepos – watch for them crossing the monkey bridges that were erected by several local conservation groups.

Coatis can be seen darting across various paths and can get aggressive on the beach if you're eating. (Perhaps warranting their nickname of hog nosed coon). Three-toed and two-toed sloths are also common in the park. Guides are extremely helpful in spotting sloths as they tend not to move around all that much.

However, the movements of the park's star animal and Central America's rarest primate, namely the Central American squirrel monkey, are far less predictable. These adorable monkeys are more retiring than capuchins, and though they are occasionally seen near the park entrance in the early morning, they usually melt into the forest well before opening time. With luck, however, a troop could be encountered during a morning's walk, and they often reappear in beachside trees and on the fringes of Manuel Antonio Village in the early evening.

Offshore, keep your eyes peeled for pantropical spotted and bottle-nosed dolphins, as well as humpback whales passing by on their regular migration routes. Other possibilities include orcas (killer whales), false killers and rough-toothed dolphins.

Big lizards are also something of a featured sighting at Manuel Antonio – it's hard to miss the large ctenosaurs and green iguanas that bask along the beach at Playa Manuel Antonio and in the vegetation behind Playa Espadilla Sur. To spot the well-camouflaged basilisk, listen for the rustle of leaves along the edges of the trails, especially near the lagoon.

Manuel Antonio is not usually on the serious bird-watchers' trail of Costa Rica, though the bird list is respectable. The usual suspects include the blue-gray and palm tangers, great-tailed grackles, bananaquits, blue dacnises and at least 15 different species of hummingbirds. Among the regional endemics you should look out for are the fiery-billed aracaris, black-hooded antshrikes, Baird's trogons, black-bellied whistling-ducks, yellow-crowned nightherons, brown pelicans, magnificent frigate birds, brown boobies, spotted sandpipers, green herons and ringed kingfishers.

White-Water Rafting & Kayaking

While not as popular as Turrialba, Manuel Antonio is something of an emerging white-water rafting and sea-kayaking center. Although you shouldn't expect the same level of world-class runs here as in other parts of the country, there are certainly some adrenaline kicks to be had. For the best packages, see the activities section in Quepos (p305).

☞ Tours

Hiring a guide costs US$25 per person for a two-hour tour. The only guides allowed in the park are members of Aguila (a local association governed by the park service), who have official ID badges, and recognized guides from tour agencies or hotels. This is to prevent visitors from getting ripped off and to ensure a good-quality guide. Aguila guides are well trained and multilingual (French-, German- or English-speaking guides can be requested). Visitors report that hiring a guide virtually guarantees wildlife sightings.

❶ Information

Visitors must leave their vehicles in the parking lot near the national park entrance; the charge is US$3, but there have been reader reports of break-ins and thefts. Note that the road here is also very narrow and congested, so it's suggested that you leave your car at your hotel, and take an early morning bus to the park entrance instead, then simply walk in.

The park entrance is a few meters south of the rotunda. Count your change carefully as tourists have complained about being shortchanged. Here you can hire naturalist guides to take you into the park; see Tours, above, for more information.

Parque Nacional Manuel Antonio

There's good reason that Manuel Antonio (p317) is Costa Rica's most popular national park: this stunning green gem has excellent beaches, accessible trails and lots of wildlife. It can be crowded, but at times it seems like the monkeys outnumber the people.

Although not as untamed as some of Costa Rica's other parks, Manuel Antonio's light hiking makes a good primer on the tropical rainforest environment. Here, you spend a leisurely morning navigating trails and scanning the canopy for wildlife before spending dreamy afternoons picnicking under swaying beach palms and swimming in the turquoise Pacific. The day ends as sundown sets the horizon ablaze and dinner is served at a cliffside restaurant. This is the Costa Rica you've been dreaming about.

WILDLIFE CHECKLIST

» **White-faced capuchin monkeys**
Often seen near the beach; keep your eyes peeled for adorable babies.

» **Mantled howler monkeys** You'll likely hear these beasts before you spot them; their call makes an iconic soundtrack to Costa Rica's rainforest.

» **Squirrel monkeys** These tiny monkeys, which often live in groups of between 20 and 75, are absolutely adorable.

» **Sloths** Two-toed and three-toed varieties can be seen lazing about in Manuel Antonio's canopy.

» **Toucans** These memorable birds of paradise are among the park's 180 winged species.

» **Black spiny-tailed iguanas (ctenosaurs)** They might lazily pose for your camera but they're the fastest-running lizards on earth.

Clockwise from top left
1. Squirrel monkey (p312) 2. Beach time, Parque Nacional Manuel Antonio 3. Suspension bridge, Parque Nacional Manuel Antonio

ANDRES POVEDA ON COSTA RICAN PRIDE

The founder of the Costa Rican Hostel Network has spent the last several years raising the bar for Costa Rica backpackers.

What does it mean to be Costa Rican? To understand this, all you need to do is spend some time hanging out with us Costa Ricans, or, as we prefer to call ourselves, Ticos. I think one of the most infectious qualities of Ticos is that we don't think too much about the future, and instead prefer to have a great time and simply enjoy the moment. You know, almost immediately upon arriving in this country, travelers are greeted with the words *pura vida,* which really is a catch-all phrase for Ticos. Although it directly translates as 'pure life,' *pura vida* really is a philosophy of living that all of us strive to uphold.

What is the best way for travelers to experience Costa Rica? The great thing about this country is that it has a youthful spirit, so you don't have to be 18 or 21 to have a good time here. In Costa Rica the great social equalizer is beer, so all you have to do is grab a bottle and just interact with the people around you.

To reach the entrance, you'll have to wade through the Camaronera estuary, which can be anywhere from ankle- to thigh-deep, depending on the tides and the season. However, in an impressive display of opportunism, there are boaters here to transport you 100m for the small fee of about US$1.

The ranger station and **national park information center** (☎2777-0644) is just before Playa Manuel Antonio. Drinking water is available, and there are toilets, beach showers, picnic tables and a refreshment stand. There is no camping and guards will come around in the evening to make sure that no one has remained behind. The information center keeps woefully unpredictable hours.

The beaches are often numbered – most people call Playa Espadilla (outside the park) '1st beach,' Playa Espadilla Sur '2nd beach,' Playa Manuel Antonio '3rd beach,' Playa Puerto Escondido '4th beach' and Playa Playita '5th beach.' Some people begin counting at Espadilla Sur, which is the first beach in the park, so it can be a bit confusing trying to figure out which beach people may be talking about. Regardless, they're all equally pristine, and provide ample opportunities for swimming or restful sunbathing.

The average daily temperature is 27°C (80°F) and average annual rainfall is 3875mm. The dry season is not entirely dry, merely less wet, so you should be prepared for rain (although it can also be dry for days on end). Make sure you carry plenty of drinking water, sun protection and insect repellent. Pack a picnic lunch if you're spending the day.

ⓘ Getting There & Away

The entrance and exit to Parque Nacional Manuel Antonio lies in Manuel Antonio Village.

QUEPOS TO UVITA

South of Quepos, the well-trodden central Pacific tourist trail begins to taper off, evoking the feel of the Costa Rica of yesteryear – surf shacks and empty beaches, roadside *ceviche* vendors and a little more space. Intrepid travelers can have their pick of any number of deserted beaches and great surf spots. The region is also home to the great bulk of Costa Rica's African palm oil industry, which should be immediately obvious after the few dozen kilometers of endless plantations lining the sides of the Costanera.

Rafiki Safari Lodge

Nestled into the rainforest, with a prime spot right next to the Río Savegre, the Rafiki Safari Lodge (☎2777-5327, 2777-2250; www.rafikisafari.com; s/d/ste incl all meals US$203/350/400, child under 5yr free; ℗@ 🕸🐾🏊❄) combines all the comforts of a hotel with the splendor of a jungle safari – all with a little bit of African flavor. The owners, South African expats who have lived in the area for years, have constructed 10 luxury tents on stilts equipped with modern bathroom, private porch and electricity. All units are screened in, allowing you to see and hear the rainforest without actually having creepy-crawlies in your bed. There's a spring-fed pool with a waterslide and ample opportunity for horseback riding, bird-watching (more than 350 species have been identified), hiking and white-water rafting. And of course, South Africans are masters on the *braai* (BBQ), so you know that you'll eat well alongside other guests in the *rancho*-style restaurant. This place makes for a great three-day stay; it's too remote to warrant the transport for only one night but guests exhaust all the activities on offer after three days.

The entrance to the lodge is located about 15km south of Quepos in the small town of Savegre. From here, a 4WD dirt road parallels the Río Savegre and leads 7km inland, past the towns of Silencio and Santo Domingo, to the lodge. However, if you don't have private transportation, the lodge can arrange all of your transfers, with advanced reservations.

Matapalo

For years, Matapalo has been off most travelers' radar screens, though without good reason as this palm-fringed, gray-sand beach has some truly awesome surf. With two river-mouth breaks generating some wicked waves, Matapalo is recommended for intermediate to advanced surfers who are comfortable dealing with rapidly changing conditions. As you might imagine, Matapalo is not the best beach for swimming as the transient rips here are about as notorious as they come.

The first hotel you'll see after turning off the Costanera is the German-run El Coquito del Pacífico (☏8384-7220, 2787-5028; www.elcoquito.com; bungalows from $65; P❋❄), which consists of a small batch of bungalows highlighted by their beaming whitewashed walls and rustic furnishings. The entire complex is attractively landscaped with shady gardens of almond and mango trees, and centered on an open-air bar and restaurant serving up the obligatory traditional German specialties.

Dreamy Contentment (☏2787-5223; www.dreamycontentment.com; r/bungalow/house US$25/75/200; P❋) is the best choice, a Spanish-colonial property with impressive woodworking and towering trees throughout. The bungalows are equipped with functional kitchenettes, though the real star attraction is the main house, which has the kitchen of your dreams, a beachfront veranda and a princely bathroom complete with hot tub. For those on a budget, there are basic but reasonably conformable backpacker rooms that put you in front of the surf without having to dig too deep.

At the end of the road you'll find the Bahari Beach Bungalows (☏2787-5014; www.baharibeach.com; cabins/tents US$55/105; P❄) with luxury safari-style beachfront tents and a small clutch of cabins. All of the tents are fully furnished and have electricity, tiled bathroom with hot shower, hand-painted sink and ocean views. The cabins, across the road, are also beautifully decorated and come ornamented with fresh flowers. There's a pool overlooking the ocean, a spa and a restaurant featuring continental cuisine.

Buses between Quepos and Dominical can drop you off at the turnoff to the village; from there it's a couple of kilometers to the beach.

Hacienda Barú National Wildlife Refuge

Located on the Pacific coast 3km northeast of Dominical on the road to Quepos, this wildlife refuge (☏2787-0003; www.hacienda baru.com; admission US$6, each extra day US$2, guided tours US$20 to US$60) forms a key link in a major biological corridor called 'the Path of the Tapir.' It comprises more than 330 hectares of private and state-owned land that has been protected from hunting since 1976. The range of tropical habitats that may be observed here include pristine beaches, riverbanks, mangrove estuaries, wetlands, selectively logged forests, secondary forests, primary forests, tree plantations and pastures.

This diversity of habitat plus its key position in the Path of the Tapir biological corridor accounts for the multitude of species that have been identified in Hacienda Barú. These include 351 birds, 69 mammals, 94 reptiles and amphibians, 87 butterflies and 158 species of trees, some of which are more than 8.5m in circumference. Ecological tourism provides this wildlife refuge with its only source of funds with which to maintain its protected status, so guests are assured that money spent here will be used to further the conservation of tropical rainforest.

There is an impressive number of guided tours (US$20 to US$60) on offer. You can experience the rainforest canopy in three different ways – a platform 36m above the forest floor, tree climbing and a zip line called 'the Flight of the Toucan.' In addition to the canopy activities, Hacienda Barú offers bird-watching tours, hiking tours, and two overnight camping tours in both tropical rainforest and lowland beach habitats. Hacienda Barú's naturalist guides come from local communities and have lived near the rainforest all of their lives. Even if you don't stop here for the sights, the onsite store carries an excellent selection of specialist titles for bird-watchers.

For people who prefer to explore the refuge by themselves, there are 7km of well-kept and marked, self-guided trails, a bird-watching tower, 3km of pristine beach, an orchid garden and a butterfly garden.

The Hacienda Barú Lodge (d $65-75, extra person $10, child under 10yr free) consists of six clean, two-bedroom cabins located 350m from Barú beach. The red-tiles, roofed, open-air restaurant serves a variety of tasty Costa Rican dishes (restaurant meals US$6 to US$10).

The Quepos–Dominical–San Isidro de El General bus stops outside the hacienda entrance. The San Isidro de El General–Dominical–Uvita bus will drop you off at the Río Barú bridge, 2km from the hacienda office. A taxi from Dominical costs about US$5.

If you're driving, the El Ceibo gas station, 50m north of the Hacienda Barú Lodge, is the only one for a good distance in any direction. Groceries, fishing gear, tide tables and other useful sundries are available, and there are clean toilets.

Dominical

Dominical hits a real sweet spot with the travelers who wander up and down its rough dirt road with a surfboard under arm, balancing the day's activities between intense adrenaline rush of riding perfect waves and the lazy swing of a hammock. And although some may decry the large population of expats and gringos who have hunkered down here, proud residents are quick to point out that Dominical recalls the mythical 'old Costa Rica' – the days before the roads were all paved, and when the coast was dotted with lazy little towns that drew a motley crew of surfers, backpackers and affable do-nothings alike. Dominical has no significant cultural sights, no paved roads and no chain restaurants, and if you're not here to learn to surf or swing in a hammock it might not be the place for you.

But the overall picture is a bit more complex, especially since Dominical is starting to stretch its legs, seeking to attract more than the college-aged and shoestringer sets. The completion of the Costanera Sur, which runs right by town, is facilitating the spread of development further south along the coast, which has brought along with it an intense wave of foreign investment. At the time of writing they were building another, taller cell tower that promised – gasp! – reasonable internet connections and there were even rumors that they might pave the road. In the meantime, however, Dominical remains the sort of place where it's best to just slow down, unwind and take things as they come.

The Costanera Sur bypasses the town entirely; the entrance to the village is immediately past the Río Barú bridge. There's a bone-rattling main road through the village, where many of the services are found, and a parallel road along the beach. For the most part, development remains low-key. The few roads around the village are still dusty and potholed, and forests – not fast-food outlets – front the majority of the beach.

Dangers & Annoyances

Waves, currents and riptides in Dominical are very strong, and there have been drownings in the past. Watch for the red flags (which mark riptides), follow the instructions of posted signs and swim at beaches that are patrolled by lifeguards. If you're smart, this is no problem, but people die here every year.

Also, Dominical attracts a heavy-duty party crowd, which in turn has led to a burgeoning drug problem.

◉ Sights & Activities

Dominical owes its fame to its seriously sick point and beach breaks, though surf conditions here are variable. There is a great opportunity to learn surfing in the white-water beach breaks, but beware of getting in too deep, as you can really get trashed out here if you don't know what you're doing. If you're just getting started, stay in the white water or make for the nearby Playa Dominicalito, which is a bit is tamer.

Centro Turístico
Cataratas Nauyaca   WATERFALL
(☎2787-0198, 2771-3187; www.cataratasnauyaca.com; ⊛) Just north of the turnoff for Dominical is the junction for San Isidro de El General – if you turn left towards San Isidro de El General and travel for about 10km, you'll

BATTLING THE BLOOD SUCKERS

Whether you call them skeeters, mozzies or midges, everyone can agree that fending off mosquitoes is one of the most annoying parts of traveling in the tropics. Although the scientific evidence surrounding effective mosquito-bite prevention is circumstantial at best, the following is a list of road-tested combat strategies for battling the blood-suckers.

» Wear socks, long trousers and a long-sleeved shirt, especially at dusk when mosquitoes feed.

» Eat lots of garlic (not recommended if you're traveling with your significant other).

» Fill your room with the smoke of the ever-present burnable Costa Rican mosquito coils.

» Invest in a good-quality mosquito net, preferably one that has been chemically treated.

» Never underestimate the power of spraying yourself with DEET.

see an entrance to the right that leads to this tourist center. This Costa Rican family-owned and -operated center is home to a series of wonderful waterfalls that cascade through a protected reserve of both primary and secondary forest.

There's no vehicle access within the center, but you can hire horses for a guided ride to two waterfalls that plunge into a deep swimming hole. With advance notice, a tour can be arranged, including the guided ride, swimming and country meals with the local family. Tours leave at 8am, take six to seven hours and cost US$60 per person. Accommodations in Dominical can also arrange tours to the falls.

Parque Reptilandia ZOO
(☑2787-8007; www.crreptiles.com; adult/child US$10/1; ◉9am-4:30pm) A worthwhile diversion is the aptly named Parque Reptilandia, located 10km outside of Dominical in the town of Platanillo. If you're traveling with kids who love slick and slimy reptiles, or you yourself just can't get enough of these prehistoric creatures, don't miss the chance to get face to face with Costa Rica's most famous reptiles. The animal park is home to everything from alligators and crocodiles to turtles and poison-dart frogs. Our favorite section is the viper section, home to such infamous critters as the deadly fer-de-lance. For an added bonus, stop by on Friday for feeding time – we promise you won't be disappointed.

Bamboo Yoga Play YOGA
(☑2787-0229; www.bambooyogaplay.com) The salty old guard might roll their eyes at Bamboo Yoga Play – a studio which offers classes in yoga, dance and 'artful warrior coaching' – but the sessions offer a welcome new (new agey) addition to Dominical's surf-dominated offerings. Sofiah Thom, the primary teacher, leads the classes in honeyed tones and occasionally puts on spectacular fire-dancing shows. It has several tidy accommodations for people interested in yoga-intensive stays.

Dominical Surf Adventures RAFTING, SURFING
(☑2787-0431; www.dominicalsurfadventures.com; ◉8am-5pm Mon-Sat, 9am-3pm Sun) A bit of an adventurer's one-stop shop, visitors can book white-water trips, kayaking, snorkel and dive trips and surf lessons from this humble little desk on the main drag. Rafting trips start at US$80 (for runs on the Class II and III Guabo) and include a more gnarly run on the Río Coto Brus' Class IV rapids. Thankfully, there's no hustling sales pitch.

⚡ Courses

Adventure Spanish School LANGUAGE COURSE
(☑2787-0023, in USA & Canada 800-237-2730; www.adventurespanishschool.com) This school runs one-week Spanish-language programs starting at US$400, without homestay. Private lessons are available, as are discounts for longer periods of study.

☞ Tours

Dominical has emerged as a jumping-off point for trips to Parque Nacional Marino Ballena and, further south, Parque Nacional Corcovado. Get details at Southern Expeditions (☑2787-0100; www.southernexpeditionscr.com) at the entrance to the village. The staff can also organize trips to the Guaymí

LEARNING TO SURF IN DOMINICAL

Altough Dominical attracts some serious surfers and the waves can be gnarly, the quality of surf instruction here is among the best and most affordable in the country. For beginners who need lots of time and attention, the two most important questions to ask are about the ratio of students to instructors and if rates include board rental. There are scores of shops and instructors who offer services with a wide range of quality; the following come highly recommended.

Costa Rica Surf Camp (☑8812-3625, 2787-0393; www.crsurfschool.com; Hotel Diu Wak; individual lessons from $40, all inclusive packages per week from $1050) This fantastic, locally owned surf school prides itself on a 2:1 student-to-teacher ratio, teachers who have CPR and water-safety training and years of experience. The amiable owner, Cesar Valverde, runs a friendly, warm-hearted program.

Sunset Surf (www.sunsetsurfdominical.com) Operated by Dylan Park, who grew up surfing the waves of Hawaii and Costa Rica, Sunset offers a variety of packages (including one for women only). It has a 3:1 student-to-instructor ratio and Park is an excellent instructor.

indigenous reserve near Boruca (inland), and all tours can be individually customized to meet your interests. Dominical Surf Adventures (p325) also has a suite of tours. Another excellent day trip is on offer from **Pineapple Kayak Tours** (☑2787-0302; www.pineapplekayaktours.com), which runs a thrilling four-hour tour out to the beautiful Ventanas Caves.

✱ Festivals & Events

Envision Art, Music and Sacred Movement Festival   ART, MUSIC
(www.envisionfestival.com) This new event brings four days of alternative art, music, fire dancing, dreadlocks and DJs to sleepy Dominical in early March. Attendees set up camp in a field behind Bamboo Yoga Play.

🛏 Sleeping

Dominical proper is home to the majority of the area's budget accommodations, while midrange and top-end places are popping up on the outskirts of town. The rates given here are for high season, but low-season rates could be up to 30% to 40% lower. Note that there are additional accommodations options in the nearby mountaintop village of Escaleras. Although most of the year Dominical has an unflappably laid-back vibe, the place goes bananas over the holidays, when Ticos from around the country flock to the coast. Travelers on the thinnest of shoestrings can probably get away with camping on the beach, but the local police are likely to move you along after a few days.

IN TOWN

TOP CHOICE Posada Del Sol   HOTEL **$**
(☑2787-0082; d from US$25; ▣🛜📶) There are only five rooms at this charming, secure, tidy little place, but if you score one, consider yourself lucky (no advance reservations are taken). Posada Del Sol hits the perfect price point and has basic comforts – hammocks outside each room, a sink to rinse out your salty suit and a clothesline to dry it. It's no place to party (it's a short stroll to the beach or to the bars in town) but the warm-hearted, watchful proprietor, Laticia, makes the place so inviting. Single travelers should check out the tiny single in the back – a great deal.

Tortilla Flats   CABINA, HOTEL **$**
(☑2787-0033; r US$25-40; ▣✳) This popular budget hotel contains 20-odd rooms of varying shapes and sizes, mostly filled by surfers and young North American travelers ready to party at the bar (which can be loud). The rooms are scattered throughout several buildings just a few steps from the beach, and they come in a spread of budget levels, though all have hot showers. The best feature is the hammock-strung patio and terrace on the 2nd floor.

Hotel DiuWak   HOTEL **$$**
(☑2787-0087; www.diuwak.com; r US$75-120, ste US$140-160; ▣✳@🛜❄📶) This proper resort complex offers low-key luxury and is easily the most cush place in town. The grounds surrounding the waterfall-fed pool are palm-fringed, which makes for relaxing days of idle laziness, and there are some great on-

site amenities, including a bar, restaurant, fitness center and health spa. Inquire about the size of the room as some are larger than others, and can easily accommodate you and a few of your friends.

Cabinas San Celemente CABINA $
(☑2787-0158; s US$10, d US$25-40; P❄️🛜) Backpackers, beach bums and surfers gravitate to this classic Dominical spot, which is right near the water and has a variety of different options – some of them sparkling from a recent upgrade, others as basic as can be. Budget-conscious travelers can choose from either shiny wooden *cabinas* or simple dorm rooms at the adjacent Dominical Backpackers Hostel.

Antorchas Camping CAMPGROUND $
(☑2787-0307; campsites per person US$5, dm US$10; P) Just a few meters from the beach, this campground is one of the most secure in town, though you should still be extremely diligent about locking up your valuables in the provided lockers. Campers can take advantage of basic amenities, including cold showers and a shared kitchen, while more finicky shoestringers can bed down in spartan dorms for a few extra dollars a night.

Domilocos HOTEL $$
(☑2787-0244; www.domilocos.com; r US$50; P❄️@🏊) This Italian-owned property is a solid midrange option, with Mediterranean-inspired grounds, an attractive swimming pool lined with potted plants and one of the town's best restaurants, ConFusione. Fairly ordinary rooms with solid beds and bamboo furniture are nothing to write home about, but they're definitely a step up in comfort from the budget hotels.

AROUND DOMINICAL

Albergue Alma de Hatillo B&B B&B $$
(☑8850-9034; www.cabinasalma.com; r US$65; P❄️@🛜🏊) One of the most loved B&Bs on the entire Pacific coast, this hidden gem is run by Sabina, a charming Polish woman who has legions of dedicated fans the world over. If you're looking for a quiet base from which to explore the Dominical area, this tranquil spot is home to immaculate cabins spread among several hectares of fruit trees. Guests rave about the organic produce on offer at Sabina's restaurant, as well as the daily yoga classes in her open-air studio. Alma de Hatillo is located about 6km north of town along the Constanera Sur.

Hotel Villas Río Mar HOTEL $$
(☑2787-0052; www.villasriomar.com; bungalows US$75-95, ste US$130-140; P❄️🛜🏊) Just beyond the edge of town, a sign points under the bridge to this property about 800m from the village. Here you'll find a few dozen polished-wood bungalows, each with a private hammock-strung terrace, as well as a handful of luxury suites that accommodate small groups. Río Mar also functions as a miniresort, offering a pool, Jacuzzi, tennis court, equipment rental, restaurant and bar.

Cascadas Farallas LODGE $$$
(☑2787-8378; www.waterfallvillas.com; ste/villas from US$125/225; P❄️@🛜🏊) Although it's a bit outside Dominical proper, this spiritual retreat is located beside a series of cascading waterfalls. Balinese-style suites and villas are decked out from floor to ceiling with Zen-inducing Asian art, and regular yoga and meditation sessions help guests seek peace and tranquility. To reach the property, take the San Isidro de El General fork (just north of the Dominical turnoff) for 3km, and look out for the Balinese dragon banners marking the entrance.

Hotel y Restaurante Roca Verde HOTEL $$
(☑2787-0036; www.rocaverde.net; r US$85; P❄️@🛜🏊🚶) Overlooking the beach about 1km south of town, this US-owned hotel has common spaces with tile mosaics, festive murals and rock inlays. The 12 tropical-themed rooms are starting to show their age, but are comfortable places to unwind. Still, the real action takes place in the festive communal areas, which include an open-air bar and infinity pool. Occasionally, the hotel turns into a theater when local theater groups and dancers perform in the hotel lobby. It also hosts one of the most raucous party nights on Saturday.

✗ Eating & Drinking

The restaurant scene in Dominical is of a high standard, catering mostly to foreign guests. The town also loves to party, though the scene changes from night to night. Maracutú hosts lots of live music and DJs; the late-night scene unfolds at San Clemente on Friday and Hotel y Restaurante Roca Verde on Saturday.

Soda Nanyoa COSTA RICAN $
(mains US$3-7) In a town that caters to gringo appetites with inflated price tags, Nanyoa is a gratifying find: an authentic, moderately priced, better-than-most Costa Rican *soda*.

The big pinto breakfasts and fresh-squeezed juice are ideal after a morning session on the waves, and at night it lets patrons bring their own beer from the grocery across the street. All are enjoyed in a pleasant open-air dining area.

Chapy's Healthy Subs & Wraps   DELI $
(☑2787-0283; meals US$5-10; ☺9am-3pm Mon-Sat; ☑🐾) With crunchy wraps and thick, grilled veg sandwiches stacked high on homemade focaccia, Chapy's is a vegetarian's dream come true. As healthy as they are delicious, the sandwiches can be dressed in spicy hummus and homemade sauces. If you need a lunch to grab and go, this place has the best stuff in town.

San Clemente Bar & Grill   BREAKFAST $
(meals US$5-12; ☺9am-midnight) Near the center of village away from the beach, this classic Dominical watering hole is decorated with broken surfboards on the walls and serves up big breakfasts and Tex-Mex dishes. It's also one of the more popular places around to drink with like-minded travelers from around the world.

ConFusione   TAPAS $$$
(meals US$11-24; ☺3-11:30pm) Though the Italian-Latin fusion made this one of Dominical's top dining rooms (it's the only place in town with table linens *and* a full bar), it has recently overhauled the menu with an emphasis on small plates and tapas. You can stick to classics from the peninsula such as penne pasta and flatbread pizzas, stay local with freshly caught seafood and aged tenderloin, or strike a healthy balance – authentic gelato with tropical fruits. Of the small plates, the baby shrimp in brandy and cheese sauce is a rich and decadent delight.

Maracutú   ITALIAN $$
(meals US$6-12; ☑) The self-proclaimed 'world-music beach bar and Italian kitchen' serves up an eclectic culinary offering that is highlighted by some delicious vegetarian and vegan fare. Each night of the week it features a different genre of music, which is mostly live.

Tortilla Flats   BAR
Right on the beachfront, the newly expanded Tortilla Flats has become the de facto place for surfers to enjoy session beers and tacos after a morning in the water. Its open-air atmosphere is pleasant, the surf videos on the televisions are on a continuous loop and the staff is friendly.

❶ Information
There are no banking facilities in town – the only ATM is up on the highway – but San Clemente Bar & Grill will exchange traveler's checks. There's a postal service upstairs in the same small shopping center.

❶ Getting There & Away
Bus
Buses pick up and drop off passengers along the main road in Dominical.

Quepos US$6; three hours; departs 7:30am, 8am, 10:30am, 1:45pm, 4pm and 5pm.

Uvita US$1.20; one hour; departs 4:30am, 10:30am, noon and 6:15pm.

Taxi
Taxis to Uvita cost US$10 to US$20, while the ride to San Isidro de El General costs US$25 to US$35, and US$55 to US$65 for Quepos. Cars accommodate up to five people, and can be hailed easily in town from the main road.

Escaleras
Escaleras, a small community scattered around a steep and narrow dirt loop-road that branches off the Costanera, is famed for its sweeping views of the coastline and the crashing surf. Of course, if you want to make it up here, you're going to need a 4WD to navigate one of the country's most notoriously difficult roads. Needless to say, the locals weren't kidding when they named the place *escaleras* (staircase). Aside from the scenic views, travelers primarily brave the road to either have a relaxing mountain retreat in any of the places listed in this section, or to catch a 'Movie in the Jungle'.

The first entrance to Escaleras is 4km south of the San Isidro de El General turnoff before Dominical, and the second is 4.5km past the first one. Both are on the left-hand side of the road and poorly signed.

One of the first places you'll come to along the main road is the Bella Vista Lodge (☑3888-0155, in USA 800-909-4469; www.bellavistalodge.com; r/cabins incl breakfast $45/75; Ⓟ), a remote farm owned by long-time resident Woody Dyer. The lodge itself is in a revamped farmhouse (surrounded by a balcony providing superb ocean views) that contains four shiny-wood rooms with private, solar-heated shower. The grounds are also home to a two-storied private cabin with a full kitchen and living room and enough space to comfortably

MOVIES IN THE JUNGLE

Every Friday and Saturday night a Minnesotan-born expat named Toby invites locals and travelers to watch his favorite flicks, high on the hillside in Escaleras – one of the most magical regular events on the entire Pacific coast. Cinema Escaleras (☑2787-8065; www.moviesinthejungle.com) is built on a hilltop with panoramic views of jungle-fronted coastline and features state-of-the-art projection equipment and surround sound. The film selection and programming choices are witty and fun, often including a short film, old news film or silent short before the featured presentation. Films are shown every Friday at 6pm, with a potluck dinner and breathtaking sunset preceding the screening at 5pm. Of course there's popcorn, too – from a 1950s air popper. To get to the cinema, follow the first entrance to Escaleras a few hundred meters up the mountain and look for a white house on the left-hand side (this is only advisable with a 4WD). Note that a small donation is requested to pay for the projector bulbs. The films shown on Friday are in English; every other Saturday there are selected showings in Spanish.

accommodate six. Rates include breakfast or an evening snack of beer and chips, and there are tasty home-cooked meals (and pies!) available. If you don't have a 4WD, Woody will pick you up in Dominical for a small fee.

About 1km further up the Escaleras road, Villa Escaleras (☑8823-0509, in USA 773-279-0516; www.villa-escaleras.com; villa for 4/6/8 people US$240/280/320; P❄@🖵🌊) is a spacious four-bedroom villa accented by cathedral ceilings, tiled floors, colonial furnishings and a palatial swimming pool. Twice-weekly maid service and a wrap-around balcony awash with panoramic views make the setting complete. If you're planning on staying here long-term, inquire about discounted weekly and monthly rates.

Located on a different access road that's 1.2km south of the first entrance is Pacific Edge (☑2787-8010; www.pacificedge.info; cabins/bungalows from US$60/85; P❄🖵🌊). The owners are a worldly North American–British couple who delight in showing guests their slice of paradise. Four cabins are perched on a knife-edge ridge about 200m above sea level, while larger family-friendly bungalows accommodate up to six and come with fully stocked kitchen. Of course, if you're not one for cooking, there is a wonderful onsite restaurant specializing in international cuisine.

Escaleras is best accessed by private vehicle, though any of the accommodations listed previously can arrange a pick-up service with advance notice. If you're coming for Movies in the Jungle, a taxi from Dominical shouldn't cost more than US$10.

Uvita

Just 17km south of Dominical, this little hamlet is really nothing more than a loose straggle of farms, houses and tiny shops, though it should give you a good idea of what the central Pacific coast looked like before the tourist boom. Uvita does, however, serve as the base for visits to Parque Nacional Marino Ballena, a pristine marine reserve famous for its migrating pods of humpback whales, in addition to its virtually abandoned wilderness beaches. Uvita Dream (www.uvitadream.com) is an excellent site with an interactive map to help you get the lay of the land.

The area off the main highway is referred to locally as Uvita, while the area next to the beach is called Playa Uvita and Playa Bahía Uvita (the southern end of the beach). The beach area is reached through two parallel roads that are roughly 500m apart – they make a C-shape connecting back to the road. The first entrance is just south of the bridge over the Río Uvita and the second entrance is in the center of town. At low tide you can walk out along Punta Uvita, but ask locally before heading out so that the rising water doesn't cut you off.

◉ Sights & Activities

Uvita is a perfect base for exploring Costanera Sur, which is home to some truly spectacular beaches that don't see anywhere near the number of tourists that they should attract. Then again, perhaps this is a good thing as you'll have plenty of space to sprawl out and soak up the sun without having to worry about someone stealing your beach chair.

Surfers passing through the area tend to push on to more extreme destinations further south, though there are occasionally some swells at Playa Hermosa (not the same one that is just south of Quepos) to the north and Playa Colonia to the south. However, if you've just come from Dominical, or you're planning on heading to Pavones, you might be a bit disappointed with the mild conditions here. If you're a beginner, this can be a good place to practice.

Reserva Biológica Oro Verde FOREST

(☎2743-8072, 8843-8833) A few kilometers before Uvita you'll see a signed turnoff to the left on a rough dirt road (4WD only) that leads 3.5km up the hill (look over your shoulder for great views of Parque Nacional Marino Ballena) to this private reserve. It's on the farm of the Duarte family, who have lived in the area for more than three decades. Two-thirds of the 150-hectare property is rainforest, and there are guided hikes, horseback-riding tours and bird-watching walks. Tour prices are variable.

Rancho La Merced National Wildlife Refuge WILDLIFE RESERVE

(☎2771-4582; www.rancholamerced.com; d incl full board per person US$80) A few kilometers before Uvita, opposite the turnoff to Oro Verde, is this 506-hectare national wildlife refuge (and former cattle ranch) with primary and secondary forests and mangroves lining the Río Morete. Here you can take guided nature hikes, horseback-riding tours to Punta Uvita and bird-watching walks. You can also stay at La Merced in a 1940s farmhouse, which can accommodate up to 10 people in double rooms of various sizes. Tour prices vary.

🛏 Sleeping & Eating

The main entrance to Uvita leads inland, east of the highway, where you'll find a number of eating and sleeping options. More guesthouses, *sodas* and local businesses are along the disorderly, bone-jarring dirt roads that surround the edges of the park.

🏠 Flutterby House HOSTEL $

(www.flutterbyhouse.com; camping/dm/treehouse/d US$6/12/15/from 30; ⓟ@⚡♠) Is it possible to fall in love at first sight with a hostel? If so, the ramshackle collection of colorful *Swiss Family Robinson*-style tree houses and dorms at Flutterby has us head over heels. Run by a pair of beaming Californian sisters, the hostel is friendly, fun and well situated within a short stroll of Marino Ballena's beaches. They rent out boards and bikes, sell beer for a pittance, have a tidy, open-air communal kitchen and employ downright visionary sustainability practices. If it wasn't enough, the optional nightly dinner (with a pull of veggies from the local farmer's market or the onsite edible garden) is *dee*-licious. Follow the signs from the main highway; it's near the south entrance gate of the park.

🏠 Cascada Verde HOSTEL $$

(☎2743-8191; www.cascadaverde.org; shared loft per person US$12, dm/d US$12/45; ⓟ) About 2km inland and uphill from Uvita, this organic permaculture farm and holistic retreat attracts legions of dedicated alternative lifestylers for good reason – it's a peaceful place to connect with nature and meditate. Accommodations are basic and somewhat exposed to the elements, though there is ample outdoor communal space for yoga and quiet meditation (the upstairs space has a lovely distant view of the ocean), and you'll sleep deeply at night if you've spent any time here working on the farm. Cascada Verde is also home to a restaurant that serves vegetarian and raw-food specialties, which take advantage of produce grown on the property. A taxi here costs about US$4 from the highway area.

Cabinas Los Laureles CABINA $

(☎2743-8235; www.cabinasloslaureles.com; campsites US$10, s/d from US$20/25; ⓟ⚡♠) This pleasant, locally run spot has eight rooms that are set in a beautiful grove of laurels. If you're looking for a bit of local flavor and authentic Costa Rican hospitality, this is a good choice. The friendly and accommodating family can arrange horseback rides, boat tours and any other activities you might be interested in. The larger *cabinas* in back are particularly inviting for families who might want a little extra space to stretch out.

Bungalows Ballena BUNGALOW $$$

(☎2743-8543; www.bungalowsballena.com; apartments/bungalows US$115/230; ⓟ⚡⚡♠) These fully outfitted apartments and stand-alone bungalows are an excellent mid-market option for families and large groups. All have kitchens, wi-fi and satellite television. The place is outfitted for kids – there's a playground and big, welcoming pool in the shape of a whale's tail.

Tucan Hotel   HOSTEL, CAMPGROUND **$**

(☑2743-8140; www.tucanhotel.com; tents/hammocks/treehouse per person US$6; 🅿❄@🛜) Located 100m inland from the main highway, this is a most popular hostel for international travelers passing through Uvita. There is a variety of accommodations to suit all budgets, from simple tents and hammocks to dorms, private rooms and the lofty tree house. Even though the beach is right down the road, most guests get tangled up in the evil clutches of the hammock movie theater, a spectacular creation that needs to be treated with respect unless you want to defer your future travel plans.

Five Senses   FUSION **$$**

(☑8713-8767; meals US$8-20; ⊗Thu-Sun, with seasonal variations) Around the glow of a bonfire and breeze from the west, diners enjoy the newest fine-dining option on this stretch of coast. Five Senses' menu is international fusion with a strong local bent – chili chicken, artful stir-fries, snapper in garlic sauce – and the vibe is relaxed and romantic.

❶ Getting There & Away

Most buses depart from the two sheltered bus stops on the Costanera in the main village.

San Isidro de El General US$1.25; two hours; departs 6am and 2pm.

San José US$5; five hours; departs 5:15am and 2:15pm.

Parque Nacional Marino Ballena

This stunner of a marine park ($10) protects coral and rock reefs surrounding Isla Ballena. Despite its small size, the importance of this area cannot be overstated, especially since it protects migrating humpback whales, pods of dolphins and nesting sea turtles, not to mention colonies of seabirds and several terrestrial reptiles.

Although Ballena is essentially off the radar screens of most coastal travelers, this can be an extremely rewarding destination for beach-lovers and wildlife-watchers. The lack of tourist crowds means that you can enjoy a quiet day at the beach in near solitude – something that is not always possible in Costa Rica. And, with a little luck and a bit of patience, you just might catch a glimpse of a humpback breaching or a few dolphins gliding through the surf.

◉ Sights & Activities

The beaches at Parque Nacional Marino Ballena are a stunning combination of golden sand and polished rock. All of them are virtually deserted and perfect for some peaceful swimming and sunbathing. And the lack of visitors means you'll have a number of quiet opportunities for good bird-watching.

From the ranger station you can walk out onto Punta Uvita and snorkel (best at low tide). Boats from Playa Bahía Uvita to Isla Ballena can be hired for up to US$45 per person for a two-hour snorkeling trip, though you are not allowed to stay overnight on the island.

If you're looking to get under the water, Mystic Dive Center (☑2788-8636; www.mystic divecenter.com) is a PADI operation that offers scuba trips in the national park.

There is also some decent surfing near the river mouth at the southern end of Playa Colonia.

Wildlife-Watching

Although the park gets few human visitors, the beaches are frequently visited by a number of different animal species, including nesting seabirds, bottle-nosed dolphins and a variety of lizards. And from May to November, with a peak in September and October, olive ridley and hawksbill turtles bury their eggs in the sand nightly. However, the star attraction are the pods of humpback whales that pass through the national park from August to October and December to April.

Scientists are unsure as to why humpback whales migrate here, though it's possible that Costa Rican waters may be one of only a few places in the world where humpback whales mate. There are actually two different groups of humpbacks that pass through the park – whales seen in the fall migrate from Californian waters, while those seen in the spring originate from Antarctica.

🛏 Sleeping

The park is home to a free campground just 300m from the entrance, which has toilets and showers but no electricity. Keep in mind that the campground is not secure, so do not leave any valuables lying around inside your tent. As such, the vast majority of travelers prefer to stay in nearby Uvita or Ojochal, and visit the marine park on a day trip.

ℹ Information

Heading southeast from Punta Uvita, the park includes 13km of sandy and rocky beaches, mangrove swamps, estuaries and rocky headlands. All six kinds of Costa Rican mangrove occur within the park. There are coral reefs near the shore, though they were heavily damaged by sediment run-off from the construction of the coastal highway. Entrance is at the **ranger station** (☎2743-8236; admission US$6; ☉dawn-dusk) in Playa Bahía Uvita, the seaside extension of Uvita.

ℹ Getting There & Away

Parque Nacional Marino Ballena is best accessed from Uvita or Ojochal, either by private vehicle or a quick taxi ride; inquire at your accommodations for the latter.

Ojochal Area

Beyond Uvita, the Costanera Sur follows the coast as far as Palmar, approximately 40km away. This route provides a coastal alternative to the Interamericana, as well as convenient access to points in the Península de Osa. En route, about 15km south of Uvita, you'll pass the tiny town of Ojochal, which is on the inland side of the highway.

Ojochal also serves as a convenient base for exploring nearby Parque Nacional Marino Ballena, and there are plenty of accommodations here to choose from. Unlike slowly growing places like Uvita or Dominical, Ojochal's tourism infrastructure has sprung up rapidly (even though it's small, there are loads of vacation rentals, menus in English and sundry gringo comforts), which is both a blessing and a curse.

Just north of Ojochal, about 14km south of Uvita, is the wilderness beach of Playa Tortuga, which is largely undiscovered and virtually undeveloped, but it's home to some occasional bouts of decent surf.

🛏 Sleeping

There's not much of a nucleus to Ojochal and most of the sleeping and eating options are spread out along the Costanera Sur.

Lookout at Playa Tortuga   BOUTIQUE HOTEL **$$**
(☎2786-5074; www.hotelcostarica.com; d US$78-99; P☀@⚡☒) A signed turnoff on the eastern side of the road just after Km 175 leads to this beautiful hilltop sanctuary, where you'll find a dozen brightly painted rooms awash in calming pastels. The grounds are traversed by a series of paths overlooking the beaches below,

but the highlight is the large deck in a tower above the pool. Here you can pursue some early morning bird-watching, or perhaps better yet, indulge in some late-afternoon slothful lounging. It also has a wood-fired BBQ, excellent for grilling a fresh catch.

Hotel Villas Gaia   CABINA **$$**
(☎8382-8240; www.villasgaia.com; r from US$80; P@⚡☒💦) Along the beach side of the road is this beautifully kept collection of shiny wooden cabins with shaded porches, set in tranquil forested grounds. There is also an excellent restaurant serving a wide variety of international standards, as well as a hilltop pool (excellent for kids) where you can swim a few laps while enjoying the panoramic view of Playa Tortuga. The beach itself is a pleasant 20-minute hike along a dirt path that winds down the hillside.

Finca Bavaria   BOUTIQUE HOTEL **$$**
(☎8355-4465; www.finca-bavaria.de; s/d from US$64/74; P⚡☒) This quaint German-run inn comprises a handful of pleasing rooms, some in their own stand-alone cottages, with wood accents, bamboo furniture and romantic mosquito net–draped beds. The lush grounds are lined with walkways and hemmed by forest, though take in sweeping views of the ocean from the hilltop pool. And, of course, there's plenty of great German beer served by the stein. Look for the signed dirt road on the inland side of the road just beyond La Cusinga.

🌿 La Cusinga   ECOLODGE **$$$**
(☎2770-2549; www.lacusingalodge.com; Finca Tres Hermanas; s/d US$124/156; P) About 5km south of Uvita, this beachside ecolodge is powered by the hydroelectric energy provided by a small stream, and centered on a working organic farm. It's a relaxing place to unplug – in place of televisions there are yoga classes. Accommodations are in natural-style wooden and stone rooms with terra-cotta tiled floors and crisp white linens. Its location is excellent, with access to hiking, bird-watching, snorkeling and swimming in the national park. The resturant offers a savory, sustainable menu of upcale Costa Rican rural dishes that includes locally raised chicken, fresh seafood and organic produce.

Diquis El Sur   B&B **$$**
(☎2786-5012; diquiscostarica.com; r per day/week from US$55/330; P☀@⚡☒💦) In Ojochal proper, this French–Canadian-run bed and

breakfast is a home away from home, by the night or by the week. Accommodations are in a variety of fairly modest rooms that are priced by amenities, though all have kitchenettes conducive to self-catering. An interesting side fact: the property is named after the 'Diquis Spheres,' which are pre-Columbian stone balls that were rumored to have come from Atlantis. They are currently being displayed in the courtyard of the Museo Nacional de Costa Rica in San José.

Eating

The best eating options are located in the town of Ojochal itself; advance reservations are recommended as they command strong local followings. If you're continuing south and into something more casual, make sure to stop for fish at the side of the road – these are the southern-most roadside *ceviche* stands.

TOP CHOICE Citrus INTERNATIONAL $$$
(2786-5175; meals US$10-30; 11am-10pm Tue-Sat) With its fresh, bright, Moroccan-inspired flavors Citrus is a standout, even among the excellent choices within strolling distance. Offering New World dishes that are heavily influenced by Southeast Asian and north African culinary traditions (fish with ginger and green onions, a spicy lamb burger, plus a killer flourless French chocolate cake), and benefiting from its candlelit riverside location, Citrus welcomes patrons with flair and bravado.

Restaurante Exótica INTERNATIONAL $$$
(2786-5050; dishes US$10-30; 3-9pm Mon-Sat) While rural Ojochal isn't exactly a hot spot of cosmopolitan urbanity, this phenomenal gourmet restaurant certainly sets a high benchmark. The nouveau French dishes each emphasize a breadth of ingredients brought together in masterful combinations. Some of the highlights include oil-drizzled fish carpaccio, wild-duck breast topped with tropical-fruit tapenades and homemade desserts. With more than a decade in the business, yet only nine tables for diners to choose from, this is an intimate culinary experience that is certainly worth seeking out.

Getting There & Away

Daily buses between Dominical and Palmar can drop you off near any of the places described here. However, given the infrequency of transportation links along this stretch of highway, it's recommended that you explore the area by private car.

Southern Costa Rica

Best Places to Eat

» Casa Botania (p354)

» Pizzería Restaurante
Lilliana (p355)

» Kahawa Café &
Restaurante (p340)

» Cocolisos Truchero (p344)

» Soda La Terminal (p342)

Best Places to Stay

» Casa Mariposa (p344)

» Savegre Hotel de Montaña (p339)

» Monte Azul: Boutique Hotel + Center for Art & Design (p344)

» Crestones Base Lodge (p349)

» Casa Botania (p354)

Why Go?

Wild, vast and largely unexplored, southern Costa Rica is cut through the middle by the jagged range of the Cordillera de Talamanca and buttressed by agricultural lowlands that produce edible exports. If you're over Costa Rica's well-oiled tourism machine or burned out by beaches, welcome: this region is rugged, undeveloped and frosted by high-altitude chill.

For thrill-seekers, southern Costa Rica packs a punch with the country's highest peak, Cerro Chirripó (3820m), and Central America's wildest swath of protected land, the incomprehensibly vast Parque Internacional La Amistad. And while Monteverde is the country's most iconic cloud forest, southern Costa Rica offers equally mystical environments, including the heavenly Cloudbridge Nature Preserve.

In a country where only distant echoes of pre-Columbian influence remain, this is home to Costa Rica's visible indigenous presence. Large populations of Bribrí, Cabécar and Brunka live high in the mountains, clinging to traditions amid the changing tides of modernity.

When to Go

Like the rest of the country there are seasonal variations in rainfall, but southern Costa Rica gets as soaked with rain as some of the coastal regions do. Due to elevation, much of the region can be very chilly at night. The best time for serious bird-watching (particularly if you want to see a quetzal) is between November and May. The week leading up to Easter and Christmas season is also high season, mostly due to Ticos looking to escape the city for the mountains.

History
Costa Rica's indigenous population was almost entirely wiped out through both the direct and indirect effects of colonization. Spanish conquistadors eventually gave way to Catholic missionaries, though the end result was the same, namely the complete disruption of pre-Columbian life in the New World.

Even as late as the 20th century, indigenous groups were actively excluded from the Spanish-dominated society and pushed to the fringes. In fact, citizenship was not granted to the indigenous population until 1949, and reservations were not organized until 1977. In the last three decades, indigenous groups have been allowed to engage in their traditional languages and customs.

Still, an increasing number of indigenous youths find themselves unable to subsist on their ancestral lands, and many shed native traditions in favor of employment in the agricultural sector. Others have turned to the tourism sector for work, though as a population, economic gains have been modest.

Climate
Given its geographic diversity, the climate varies considerably throughout the southern zone. In the lowlands, it remains hot and humid year-round, with marked rainfall from mid-April through mid-December. In the highlands, however, you can expect much cooler temperatures year-round (getting as low as 4°C or 40°F at times).

Parks & Reserves
The parks and reserves of southern Costa Rica offer great opportunities for wildlife-watching and hiking.

» **Cloudbridge Nature Preserve** (p343) A tiny private reserve on the slopes of Cerro Chirripó that is operated by two New Yorkers, and is the site of an ongoing reforestation project.

» **Parque Internacional La Amistad** (p356) This enormous bi-national park is shared with Panama and protects a biological corridor of incredible ecological significance.

» **Parque Nacional Chirripó** (p345) Home to Costa Rica's highest and most famous peak, Cerro Chirripó, which on a clear day offers views of both the Pacific and the Caribbean.

» **Parque Nacional Los Quetzales** (p340) Costa Rica's newest national park is extremely rich in birdlife and offers a good chance of spotting the quetzal in all its resplendent glory.

» **Reserva Biológica Dúrika** (p350) This private reserve within Parque Internacional La Amistad is home to an independent, sustainable community committed to conservation.

ⓘ Getting There & Around
Because of complicated, frequently changing bus schedules, it's best to have your own 4WD ride if you want to explore the region in depth. That said, it's fairly easy to connect via bus to departure points for Amistad and Chirripó. Note that addresses in this part of the country are virtually non-existent, and the numbered posts along the Carretera Interamericana are used to locate things. Those numbers count the kilometers from San José.

Major towns in the southern zone are serviced by regular buses, though public transportation can get sporadic once you leave these major hubs.

NatureAir (www.natureair.com) and **Sansa** (www.sansa.com) service Palmar, which is a jumping-off point for the southern zone. Prices vary according to season and availability, but usually you can expect to pay a little less than US$75 for a flight from San José or Liberia.

THE ROAD TO CHIRRIPÓ
Traveling south from San Jose, the road to Parque Nacional Chirripó passes through gorgeous countryside of redolent coffee plantations and cool, misty cloud forests. The first major area of interest is the Zona Santa or 'Saint's Zone,' a collection of highland villages that famously bear sainted names: San Pablo de León Cortés, Santa María de Dota, San Marcos de Tarrazú, San Cristóbal Sur and San Gerardo de Dota. Further south in the Valle de El General, family-run *fincas* (farms) dot the fertile valley, though the action tends to center on San Isidro de El General, southern Costa Rica's largest town and major transportation hub.

Santa María & Valle de Dota
Centered on a grassy soccer field and surrounded by lavish plantations, Santa María de Dota is a picturesque Costa Rican town that merits at least a quick stop if you're driving (on bus, the detour would likely take a whole day). It's a sleepy place where mist rolls across the mountains and coffee production is the economic lifeblood. It seems as if the Coopedota processing facility employs half the town.

Southern Costa Rica Highlights

1 Shiver atop Costa Rica's tallest peak to watch the sunrise from **Cerro Chirripó** (p345)

2 Seek out the brightly colored quetzal and fish for trout in **Parque Nacional Los Quetzales** (p340)

3 Connect hiking to mountain waterfalls, milk a goat and learn about rainforest medicine at **Reserva Biológica Dúrika** (p350)

4 Hike through the ethereal cloud forest of **Cloudbridge Nature Preserve** (p343)

5 Go completely off the grid for a DIY adventure in pristine **Parque Internacional La Amistad** (p356)

6 Get a history lesson at the Reserva Indígena Boruca's vibrant **Fiesta de los Diablitos** (p351)

7 Hook a trout in the rushing river in **San Gerardo de Dota** (p338)

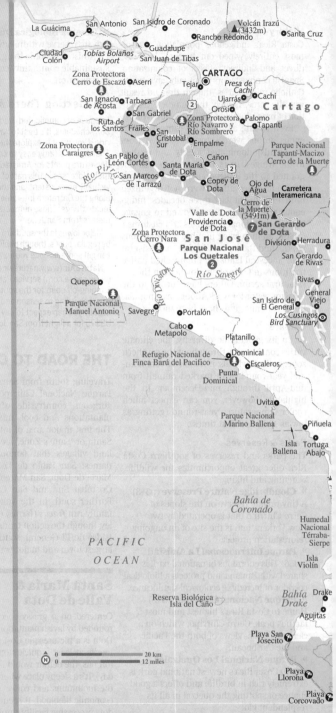

Coopedota (☎2541-2828; www.coopedota. com) can give you the complete picture of where your caffeine fix comes from: the Coffee Experience is a half-day tour (US$10) that takes guests to an organic coffee farm, visits the production facility and offers tastings. The cofounder and manager of the cafe previously won third place in a national barista competition and is locally famous for her signature coffee drinks.

Those who linger in the area should spend the night at El Toucanet Lodge (☎2541-3131; www.eltoucanet.com; s/d from US$55/71; P), a lovely country lodge that is perched at 1850m and offers seven rustic hardwood cabins with wonderful views of Valle de Dota. The Flintstones-style hot tub is an excellent place to recover from the day's activities. To reach the lodge, drive east from Santa María or turn off the Interamericana at Km 58.

Those traveling south on the Interamericana can cool their heels at Café de los Santos (Interamericana Km 52; ☺7:30am-6:30pm Mon-Fri, to 5:30pm Sat). When the weather is cool, a steaming cup of rich, brightly flavored high-altitude arabica coffee is ideal. The cafe also turns out fancy espresso drinks and buttery pastries for a few thousand colones. The gas station at this intersection is the last one before San Isidro de El General.

Most drivers from San José take the Interamericana south to Empalme, almost 30km from Cartago. Just south of the station a signed turnoff leads west on a paved road and turns to Santa María (10km away), San Marcos de Tarrazú (7km beyond) and San Pablo (4km further). Six daily buses (US$4, 2½ hours) connect these towns to San José.

San Gerardo de Dota

San Gerardo de Dota is unlike any other place in Costa Rica – a bucolic mountain town run through by a clear, rushing river and surrounded by forested hills that more resemble the alps than the tropics. It's set deep within a mountain valley; the air is crisp and fresh, and chilly at night, and orchard-lined Savegre basin hosts high-altitude species that draw bird-watchers from around the world. The elusive and resplendent quetzal is such a celebrity in these parts that in 2005 the national government demarcated a national park in its honor.

Visiting the national park is largely a self-organized, DIY affair since it has no permanent infrastructure, but the town of San Gerardo provides easy access to the trailheads and offers a wide assortment of tourist lodges. In stunning contrast to Costa Rica's famous tropical regions, San Gerardo de Dota is a charmer, well worth seeking out for a quiet couple days of fresh mountain air.

History

The banks of the Río Savegre were long protected by the steep flanks of the Talamanca mountains, prohibiting settlement in this area. It wasn't until 1952 that Efrain Chacón and his brothers – driven by drought – came south from Copey de Dota, and established a farm on the western slopes of Cerro de la Muerte.

In the early days, they planted typical subsistence crops but soon brought in dairy cattle, stocked the streams with trout and planted orchards. Trout attracted anglers from San José, while the fruit trees (along with the abundant wild avocado trees) attracted the resplendent quetzal.

Quetzals are spotted frequently every April and May (during breeding season) and are fairly common throughout the rest of the year.

🏃 Activities

Sportfishing

The trout-fishing in the Río Savegre is excellent: May and June is the time for fly-fishing and December to March for lure-fishing. A number of trout farms surround the village as well.

Bird-watching & Hiking

The best place to go bird-watching and hiking in the area is Parque Nacional Los Quetzales. Unfortunately there are no information facilities for tourists in the park, so inquire at the lodges in San Gerardo before you set out. You can hire local guides through the hotels. Travelers who wish to do extensive hiking in the area are advised to collect maps before they arrive.

🛌 Sleeping & Eating

Note that many of the lodges offer dinner with their accommodation and have access to the Parque Nacional Los Quetzales.

Dantica Lodge & Gallery   LODGE $$$
(☎8352-2761; www.dantica.com; r/ste from US$142/180; P✳@🛜) Definitely the most elegant place in San Gerardo, if not the whole

TALAMANCA TROUT FISHING

While most sportfishers flock to the coast for a big catch, the crystal-clear waters and the cool air of the cloud forest make for a hypnotic, tranquil setting, and the fish – here, rainbow trout – are no less tasty.

The trout here are not endemic. Supposedly, they were first introduced to Central American rivers by the US military in Panama and the healthy fish made their way north into Costa Rican waters.

In order to maintain healthy populations, fishers are strongly encouraged to limit stream fishing to catch-and-release. If you want to take home your trout for dinner, fish in one of the local spring-fed ponds, which are well stocked with 30cm to 50cm trout. Success is guaranteed and you just pay for what you take home (about US$4 per kilogram). This is a great option for kids and folk with poor fishing karma.

» **Finca Madreselva** (☏2224-6388) A popular local fishing spot that is home to a well-stocked trout pond and hiking trails – good for a full day of fun.

» **Pesca Deportiva Río Blanca** (☏2541-1816, 2541-1818) Near Santa María de Dota, this is another local spot that is popular among Tico families.

» **Ranchos La Isla** (☏2740-1038) Borrow equipment to fish in the river and ponds, then bring your catch back and have the staff fry it up for dinner.

» **Savegre Hotel de Montaña** (☏2740-1028) This lodge provides equipment and guides for fly-fishing in the Río Savegre, or you can fish in the picturesque pond and pay for what you catch.

---

southern zone, this upscale lodge consists of lovely natural wood and stone cabins and beautiful Colombian artwork. The modern comforts – leather sofas, plasma TVs, Jacuzzis and track lighting – are nice, but the stunning vistas over the cloud forest are the biggest appeal. Romantic breakfasts are served on guests' private terraces. A nature reserve complete with private trails is just steps away, as well as a spa where you can pamper yourself after hiking. If the price tag is a bit steep, stop by for the gallery's collection of art from all over Latin America.

Cabinas El Quetzal — CABINA $$
(☏2740-1036; www.cabinaselquetzal.com; d incl breakfast & dinner from US$60; P 🅿 🅐) This simple cluster of four family-run *cabinas* (cabins) has an elegantly homespun feel. The included meals are lovingly prepared (naturally, fresh trout is on offer) and the riverside setting is a tranquil perch from which to take in the fresh air. The rooms are simple and without frills (tile floors, small sitting areas, no televisions), but they're clean, comfortable and stocked with a pile of blankets in the likely event of a chilly night. (Some even have a wood-burning stove.) There's tons of space for little ones to run around and also a small playground.

Savegre Hotel de Montaña — LODGE $$$
(☏2740-1028; www.savegre.co.cr; s/d/ste incl 3 meals US$125/179/254; P @ 🅐) Set on a 160-hectare orchard and reserve, this famous lodge has been owned and operated by the Chacón family since 1957. It's now something of a Costa Rican institution, especially among bird-watchers keen to catch a glimpse of the quetzal. The edges of the grounds are lined with avocado trees, the favorite perch of the bird of paradise. The suites are gorgeous: wrought-iron chandeliers hang from the high wooden ceilings, while rich wooden furniture surrounds a stone fireplace. Its also has a roster of professional guides and an onsite spa.

Ranchos la Isla &
Restaurante Los Lagos — CAMPGROUND $
(☏2740-1038; campsites per person US$5; P) If you're heading to Chirripó and are geared up for a little bit of camping, this attractive property offers a handful of campsites on metal-roofed platforms alongside a small river. The accommodating Chinchilla families also go all out to make sure their guests are entertained by guiding hikes to nearby waterfalls in the hope of spotting the elusive quetzal. If you're looking for a hot meal, the onsite restaurant is a modest affair serving up wholesome, country-style *casados* (cheap set meals, usually served at lunchtime; US$4 to US$6).

La Comida Típica Miriam COSTA RICAN **$**
(☎2740-1049; meals US$5-10; ◷6am-8pm) One of the first places you will pass in San Gerardo (about 6km from the Interamericana) is the cozy house advertising *comida típica* (literally, 'typical meals'), regional specialities. Eating is almost like receiving a personal invitation to dine in a Tico home: the food is delicious and abundant and the hospitality even more so. Miriam also rents a few cabins (US$35) in the woods behind the restaurant, which are a modest but comfortable place to spend a night or two.

Kahawa Café & Restaurante CAFE **$**
(☎2740-1051) With an ideal riverside location, brightly polished wood tables and sparkling fish tanks filled with trout, this is an excellent little place to grab a bite after hiking in the park. There's a small boutique onsite.

❶ Getting There & Away

The turnoff to San Gerardo de Dota is near Km 80 on the Interamericana. From here, the dirt road descends 8km to the village. The road is very, very steep: take it slow if you're in an ordinary car. Buses between San José and San Isidro de El General can drop you at the turnoff.

Parque Nacional Los Quetzales

Formerly known as Reserva Los Santos, Parque Nacional Los Quetzales officially became a national park in 2005. Spread along both banks of the Río Savegre, at an altitude of 2000m to 3000m, Los Quetzales covers 50 sq km of rainforest and cloud forest lying along the slopes of the Cordillera de Talamanca.

The lifeblood of the park is the Río Savegre, which starts high up on the Cerro de la Muerte and feeds several mountain streams and glacial lakes before pouring into the Pacific near the town of Savegre. Although relatively small, this region is remarkably diverse – the Savegre watershed contains approximately 20% of the registered bird species in Costa Rica.

True to the park's new name, the resplendent quetzal is here, along with the trogon, hummingbird and sooty robin. Avians aside, the park is home to endangered species including jaguars, Baird's tapirs and squirrel monkeys. The park is also home to premontane forests, the second-most endangered life zone in Costa Rica.

The park has no facilities for tourists aside from a small ranger station (☎2200-5354; admission US$10; ◷ 8am-4pm), which collects fees. From here, a modest network of bird-watching trails radiates into the forest. All the lodges around San Gerardo de Dota organize hiking and bird-watching tours.

The park is bordered by the Interamericana; the entrance is just past Km 76. Any bus along this route can drop you off at the ranger station, though most people arrive in a private car or coach.

Cerro de La Muerte

Between Empalme and San Isidro de El General, the Interamericana reaches its highest point along the famed Cerro de la Muerte (3491m). The 'Hill of Death' received its grizzly moniker before it was paved, but it's still a white-knuckle drive, snaking the fog-shrouded spine along a path riddled with blind corners, masochistic bus drivers and hair-raising cliffs. The upside? Travelers who catch a small break in the fog will enjoy exquisite panoramic views of the Cordillera de Talamanca.

Cerro de la Muerte marks the northernmost extent of the *páramo,* a highland shrub and tussock grass habitat typical of the southern zone. This Andean-style landscape is rich in wildlife and is home to many of the same species found in the nearby Parque Nacional Chirripó. The area is also part of the Parque Nacional Tapantí-Macizo Cerro de la Muerte, which offers even more opportunities for hiking and bird-watching.

🛏 Sleeping & Eating

Note that addresses along this part of Costa Rica are nonexistent. The following are listed by their Km distance marker.

TOP CHOICE **Bosque del Tolomuco** B&B **$$**
(☎8847-7207; www.bosquedeltolomuco.com; Interamericana Km 118; d from US$65; P⊛🖏🐾) Named for the sly tayra (tree otter) spotted on the grounds, this cutesy B&B is run by a lovely, chatty Canadian couple. There are four spacious, light-filled cabins, the most charming of which is the secluded 'Hummingbird Cabin.' The grounds offer 5km of hiking trails, ample opportunities to indulge in bird-watching and some magnificent views of Los Cruces and Chirripó. A made-

MEETING YOUR MAKER

Although the treacherous drive across the Cerro de la Muerte might offer ample opportunities to meet your maker, look to the heavens at Km 104 for the towering statue of Christ, perched precariously on the edge of a cliff above.

to-order gourmet dinner is also available with advance notice. Day hikers who want to stretch their legs and get off the road can hike the network of trails for $2.

Mirador de Quetzales   HOTEL **$**
(☑8870-6027, 2200-4185; www.elmiradordequetzales.com; Interamericana Km 70; cabins per person incl 2 meals US$50; ℗) About 1km west of the Interamericana, this excellent budget option has painted wood walls and colorful curtains and, importantly, electric heaters. Prices also include an early-morning 'quetzal walk' – the bright beauties reside in these forested hills year-round, but sightings are virtually guaranteed between November and April. You can wander its system of trails for a small fee (US$6).

Mirador Vista del Valle   LODGE **$**
(☑8836-6193, 8384-4685; www.valledelgeneral.com; Interamericana Km 119; s/d US$41/47; ℗) Aptly named, the 'View of the Valley Lookout' boasts a windowed restaurant offering panoramic views that perfectly complement local specialities such as fried trout, and fresh-brewed coffee. Below the restaurant, cabins built entirely from cultivated wood are brightened by colorful indigenous tapestries.

❶ Getting There & Away

Frequent buses running between San José and San Isidro de El General can drop you off at any of the lodges listed here.

San Isidro de El General

With a population of only 45,000, San Isidro de El General is little more than a sprawling, utilitarian town at the crossroads between some of Costa Rica's prime destinations. Still, the strolling lovers and teenage troublemakers give the town square some charm, as does its unexpectedly lively bar scene.

'El General' is the region's largest population center and major transportation hub. If you're traveling to the southern Pacific beaches or Chirripó, a brief stop is inevitable. Some accommodations options just outside the town environs are worthy destinations in their own right.

And – a curious footnote! – the women of San Isidro de El General are widely regarded as Costa Rica's finest. It must be the fresh mountain air and strong coffee!

The heart of San Isidro is the network of narrow streets clustered around the Parque Central. An uncharacteristic but nevertheless impressive neo-Gothic cathedral lords over the eastern end.

☞ Tours

Aratinga Tours   BIRD-WATCHING
(☑2574-2319; www.aratinga-tours.com) Pieter Westra runs this highly recommended company and specializes in bird tours in his native Dutch, but he is fluent in English, Spanish and many dialects of bird. His website provides an excellent introduction to bird-watching in Costa Rica. He is based at Talari Mountain Lodge. Inclusive 2-week tours start at US$1800, though shorter and less expensive trips can be arranged by appointment.

✯ Festivals & Events

Agricultural Festival   AGRICULTURE
(☺1st week of Feb; 👫) This fair is a chance for local farmers to strut their stuff – and that they do, by taking over the central square with fresh flowers, fruits of the region and culinary delights. There are also bullfights and livestock competitions.

⌷ Sleeping

Options in San Isidro proper serve as one-night crash pads of varying levels of style and sophistication, while options outside the town generally have more character and warrant a longer stay.

IN TOWN

TOP CHOICE **Hotel Chirripó**   HOTEL **$**
(☑2771-0529; www.hotelchirripo.com; Av 2 btwn Av Central & Calle 1; s/d from US$17/23; ℗⑳) Let's put it bluntly: if you're traveling through town, weary and on a budget, this is *the* choice. Popular with discerning budget travelers, this centrally located hotel is a two-minute stroll from the bus station and filled with bare, whitewashed rooms that

San Isidro de El General

0 —————— 200 m
0 —————— 0.1 miles

San Isidro de El General

Sleeping
1 Hotel Chirripó B2
2 Hotel Los Crestones A3
3 Thunderbird Hotel & Casino A1

Eating
4 Kafe de la Casa A1
5 Mercado Central A2
6 Restaurant/Bar La Cascada A2
7 Soda La Terminal A2
8 Supermercado Central A2

are barren but utterly dirt- and grime-free. A few flowering plants and a festive mural in the lobby brighten otherwise monastic surroundings. The larger rooms have air-con and cable television for a few extra dollars.

Hotel Los Crestones   HOTEL $
(☏2770-1200, 2770-1500; www.hotelloscrestones.com; cnr Calle Central & Av 14; s/d from US$40/50; P❋❋🖤) This sharp motor court is decked with blooming flowerboxes and climbing vines outside – indeed a welcome sight to the road-weary traveler. Inside, functional rooms feature modern furnishings and fixtures, which are made all the better by the attentive staff who keep this place running efficiently.

Thunderbird Hotel & Casino   HOTEL $$
(☏2770-6230; www.hoteldiamantereal.com; cnr Av 3 & Calle 4; standard/luxury r US$40/60; P❋@🖤) 'Executive Elegance' is the boast of this upscale business hotel (which used to be the Hotel Diamante Real). After a series of upgrades it's surprisingly swish. The quarters are brightly painted and fitted with shiny black-lacquer furniture. There's a small casino downstairs where you can drink for free while feeding the slots.

AROUND SAN ISIDRO

Talari Mountain Lodge   LODGE $$
(☏2771-0341; www.talari.co.cr; Rivas; s/d US$49/72; P🖤❋) This secluded mountain lodge exudes an incredible amount of charm, as do the Dutch-Tica couple who run the place. They are ever-accommodating, also offering arrangements for treks to Chirripó and customized bird-watching tours – Pieter Westra of Aratinga Tours in San Isidro is their son. Accommodations are in simple wooden cabins on the edge of the forest. To get here, drive 7km south of San Isidro on the road from San Gerardo de Rivas.

Finca Ipe   HOMESTAY $
(www.fincaipe.com; 2-bedroom house rental per week/month from US$300/900; P) Located approximately 20km west of San Isidro, this self-sufficient, sustainable organic farm draws a group of devoted staff and volunteers who experiment with holistic medicine and permaculture. Those who want to roll up their sleeves and volunteer time and energy get a dorm bed, clean sheets and all the seasonal produce you can stomach, for about US$400 a month.

🍴 Eating & Drinking

The center of town is filled with locals; cheap, filling food; and bars.

Soda La Terminal   FAST FOOD $
(meals US$3-5; ⏰7am-7pm) This is an excellent place to wolf down a *casado* after a day of bus travel. Everything appears from behind the counter piping hot, sided with fresh salads, savory pinto (Costa Rica's famous rice and beans staple) and in big portions. Between 10am and 3pm there's a terrific deal in the US$2 special.

Kafe de la Casa   CAFE $
(Av 3 btwn Calles 2 & 4; meals US$6-13; ⏰7am-8pm) Set in an old Tico house, this bohemian cafe features eclectic artwork, an open kitch-

en and breezy garden seating. The menu has excellent breakfasts, light lunches, gourmet dinners and plenty of coffee drinks.

Restaurant/Bar La Cascada RESTAURANT **$**
(☑2771-6479; cnr Calle 2 & Av 2; dishes US$5-10; ⊗11pm-late) On an open 2nd-floor corner spot right in the heart of town, this pleasant, spacious restaurant brings in local businesspeople all day and transforms into a happening nightspot. Massive plasma screens blast music videos, and an extensive menu of pub grub attracts local youth and travelers for sessions of beer-addled, back-slapping cultural exchange.

Those watching their colones closely should head for the inexpensive *casados* in the Mercado Central (Central Market; Av 4 btwn Calles Central & 2), or the Supermercado Central (Av 6 btwn Calles Central & 2; ⊗7am-9pm Mon-Sat, 8am-2pm Sun), one block south.

❶ Getting There & Away

Bus

In San Isidro the local bus terminal is on Av 6 and serves nearby villages. Long-distance buses leave from points near the Interamericana and are frequently packed, so buy tickets early. Note that buses heading south to Golfito or Ciudad Neily will go through Palmar Norte.

FROM TRACOPA TERMINAL

You will find **Tracopa bus terminal** (☑2771-0468) on the Interamericana, just southwest of Av Central.

Neily US$7; four hours; departs 4:45am, 7:30am, 12:30pm, 3pm, 4pm, 4:30pm, 7pm

Palmar Norte US$4; two hours; departs 4:45am, 7:30am, 12:30pm, 3pm, 4pm, 4:30pm, 5:30pm, 6:30pm, 7:30pm, 9:30pm

Paso Canoas US$6; five hours; departs 8:30am, 10:30am, 2:30pm, 4pm, 7:30pm, 9pm

San José US$4.25; three hours; departs 7:30am, 8am, 9:30am, 10:30am, 11am, 1:30pm, 4pm, 5:45pm, 7:30pm

San Vito US$4.25; three hours; departs 5:30am, 9:30am, 11am, 2pm, 2:45pm, 5:45pm

FROM TERMINAL QUEPOS

Terminal Quepos (☑2771-2550) is on the side street south of the Tracopa terminal.

Dominical US$3.70; 2½ hours; departs 7:30am, 9am, 5:30pm

Palmar Norte US$4; three hours; departs 6:30am, 3pm

Palmar Norte/Puerto Jiménez US$6; five hours; departs 6:30am, 3pm

Quepos US$4; three hours; departs 7am, 1:30pm

Uvita US$1.60; 1½ hours; departs 8:30am, 4pm

FROM OTHER BUS STOPS

The following buses originate in San Isidro.

Buenos Aires (Gafeso) US$1.50; 1 hour; departs hourly 5am to 5pm from north of Terminal Quepos

San Gerardo de Rivas (for Parque Nacional Chirripó) US$1.60; 1½ hours; departs from the local terminal on Av 6 at 9:30am, 2pm, 6:45pm

Taxi

A 4WD taxi to San Gerardo de Rivas will cost between US$25 and US$30. To arrange one, it's best to inquire through your accommodations.

San Gerardo de Rivas

If you have plans to climb Chirripó, you're in the right place – the tiny, tranquil town of San Gerardo de Rivas is at the doorstep of the national park. This is a place to get supplies, a good night's rest and a hot shower before embarking on the trek.

Although hikers are keen to press on to the park as quickly as possible, the logistics of getting up the mountain and the infrequent bus schedule will almost certainly require a night in San Gerardo before the hike, the night after or both. Luckily, the boulder-strewn Río Chirripó and bird-filled alpine scenery make it a beautiful place to linger. Those who don't have the time or energy to summit Chirripó have lovely, less difficult hikes in the Cloudbridge Nature Preserve.

The road to San Gerardo de Rivas winds its way 22km up the valley of the Río Chirripó. The road is paved for the first 10km or so until the town of Rivas (note that this town is different from San Gerardo de Rivas). After Rivas, it gets bumpy, narrow and steep. The 'center' of San Gerardo de Rivas consists of the soccer field and the *pulpería* (corner grocery store) opposite. Otherwise, there's not much here – just the family farms and *cabinas* strung along the road and the river.

◉ Sights & Activities

TOP CHOICE **Cloudbridge Nature Preserve** NATURE PRESERVE
(☑in USA 212-362-9391; www.cloudbridge.org; admission by donation; ⊗sunrise-sunset) About 2km past the trailhead to Cerro Chirripó

you will find the entrance to the mystical, magical Cloudbridge Nature Preserve. Covering 182 hectares on the side of Cerro Chirripó, this private reserve is an ongoing reforestation and preservation project spearheaded by New Yorkers Ian and Genevieve Giddy. A network of trails traverses the property, which is easy to explore independently. Even if you don't get far past the entrance, you'll find two waterfalls, including the magnificent Catarata Pacifica. Volunteer reforestation and conservation opportunities are listed on the reserve's website.

Cocolisos Truchero
FISHING

(2742-5023; ⊘arrive before 4pm; 🚶) Five hundred meters down the hill from the middle of town is this lovely little trout farm, operated by the Marin family. If you're hanging out the day before or after a trip into the park, a perfect afternoon can be made out of sitting by the trout pools and taking in the celebrated orchid collection. Naturally, the fish is the best part; matronly Garita puts together a homemade feast of trout and home-cooked sides for US$5.

Thermal Hot Springs
HOT SPRINGS

(2742-5210; Herradura; admission US$5; ⊘7am-5pm) About 2km north of San Gerardo above the ranger station the road forks; take the left fork and walk for about 1km on a paved road for these hot springs. Turn right and take the rickety suspension bridge over the river. A switchback trail will lead you another 1km to a house with a *soda* (inexpensive eatery), which is the entrance to the springs.

🛌 Sleeping & Eating

Most options are situated along the narrow road running parallel to the river. The majority rent equipment (sleeping bags, air mattresses, cooking stoves etc), though supplies are limited and quality varies. The services on hand reflect the fact that many Chirripó-bound travelers are young, ready to rough it and on a shoestring budget. Many hotels and *cabinas* allow camping for a small fee.

TOP CHOICE 🏠 Casa Mariposa
HOSTEL $

(2742-5037; www.hotelcasamariposa.net; dm/s/d US$13/17/32; 🅿@) Just a short walk from the entrance of the park, this adorable lodge is built into the side of the mountain and has a warm, glowing atmosphere. Traveler-

oriented details – warm clothes to borrow for the hike, laundry service, assistance with booking Chirripó lodge – make it ideal. In the evening, guests gather around the wood stove in the communal living room to read, plan hikes, and welcome weary hikers returning from the summit. There's a tidy kitchen, a hammock-slung lookout on the roof and a stone soaking tub. There's only space for 15 guests, so advance booking is recommended.

🏠 Monte Azul: Boutique Hotel + Center for Art & Design
BOUTIQUE HOTEL $$$

(2742-5222; www.monteazulcr.com; Rivas; r from US$259; 🅿🛜🚶) Exposed beams and brightly colored furniture, fine linens and bold art – the luxurious and elegant Monte Azul single-handedly boosts the quality of accommodations within a stone's throw of Chirripó. Set on a private 125-hectare reserve, the luxury riverfront suites have tasteful contemporary art, small kitchens, luxury mattresses and linens, and custom-designed furniture. It's a class act from start to finish (guests are met with fresh, local fruit and cheese when they check in). The gourmet restaurant offers international fusions using organic produce from its garden. Note that this place is in the village of Rivas, which is down the mountain from San Gerardo de Rivas.

Cabinas y Restaurante El Descanso
CABINA, HOTEL $

(2742-5061; www.hoteleldescansocr.com; campsites per person US$5; r per person with/without bathroom $30/15; 🅿@🛜) This quaint and quiet homestead, run by the accommodating Elizondo family, is an excellent budget choice. The simple, spare cell-like single rooms on the ground floor are a fine option, although brighter, more spacious ones on the 2nd floor come with bathroom and balcony for a few dollars more. The onsite restaurant dishes out simple, good meals. Transportation to the park entrance for trekkers is included in the rate and the family also organizes tours and a guiding service.

🏠 Hotel de Montaña El Pelícano
HOTEL $

(8382-3000; www.hotelpelicano.net; r/cabins from US$30/72; 🅿@🛜) About 300m below the ranger station, this simple, functional budget lodge has a collection of spartan but spotless rooms that overlook the river valley. The highlight of the property is the gallery of the owner, a late-blooming artist who sculpts whimsical wood pieces.

El Urán Hotel y Restaurante   HOSTEL $

(☎2742-5003; www.hoteluran.com; dm/s/d US$10/25/35; P🛜) Just 50m below the trailhead, this no-nonsense youth hostel is something of an institution for hikers heading to/from Chirripó. Budget-friendly rooms are fine for a restful snooze, while the onsite restaurant, grocery store and laundry facility all cater to the shoestring set.

Río Chirripó Retreat   HOTEL $$

(☎2742-5109; www.riochirripo.com; Canaán; r per person incl 3 meals from US$120; P@🛜🏊) About 1.5km below the ranger station, in Canaán, this upscale lodge is centered on both a beautiful yoga studio overlooking the river, and a vast open-air, Santa Fe–style communal area. You can hear the rush of the river from eight secluded cabins, where woven blankets and stenciled walls evoke the southwest USA. Grounds include hiking trails, a heated swimming pool and a hot tub with sweeping mountain views.

❶ Information

The Chirripó **ranger station** (Sinac; ☎2200-5348; ☺6:30am-noon & 1-4:30pm) is about 1km below the soccer field on the road from San Isidro. Stop by early to check for availability at Crestones Base Lodge (p349), and to confirm and pay fees before setting out. The Base Lodge holds 10 first-come-first-served beds, which can be reserved only the day prior to arrival.

❶ Getting There & Away

Arriving via public transportation requires a connection through San Isidro. Buses to San Isidro depart from the soccer field at 5:15am, 11:30am and 4pm (US$1.60, 1½-2 hours). Any of the hotels can call a taxi for you.

Driving from San Isidro, head south on the Interamericana and cross Río San Isidro south of town. About 500m further on, cross the unsigned Río Jilguero and take the first, steep turn up to the left, about 300m beyond the Jilguero. Note that this turnoff is not marked.

The ranger station is about 18km up this road from the Interamericana. The road is paved as far as Rivas but beyond that it is steep and graveled. It is passable (although stressful) for ordinary cars in the dry season, but a 4WD is recommended. If you are driving past the village of San Gerardo de Rivas, to Albergue Urán or to Cloudbridge Nature Preserve, you will need a 4WD.

PARQUE NACIONAL CHIRRIPÓ

Costa Rica's mountainous spine runs the length of the country in four distinct cordilleras (mountain ranges), of which the Cordillera de Talamanca is the highest, longest and most remote. While most of the Talamanca highlands are difficult to access, Costa Rica's highest peak, Cerro Chirripó, at 3820m above sea level, is the focus of popular Parque Nacional Chirripó. Of course, while Chirripó is the highest and most famous summit in Costa Rica, it is not unique: two other peaks inside the park top 3800m, and most of the park's 502 sq km lies above 2000m.

Like a tiny chunk of the South American Andes, Parque Nacional Chirripó's rocky high-altitude features are an entirely unexpected respite from the heat and humidity of the rainforest (it's downright cold at night). Above 3400m, the landscape is *páramo*, which is mostly scrubby trees and grasslands, and supports a unique spectrum of highland wildlife. Rocky outposts punctuate the otherwise barren hills, and feed a series of glacial lakes that earned the park its iconic name: Chirripó means 'eternal waters.'

The bare *páramo* contrasts vividly with the lushness of the cloud forest, which dominates the hillsides between 2500m and 3400m. Oak trees (some more than 50m high) tower over the canopy, which also consists of evergreens, laurels and lots of undergrowth. Epiphytes – the plants that grow up the trunks of larger trees – thrive in this climate. However, the low-altitude cloud forest is being encroached upon by agricultural fields and coffee plantations in the areas near San Gerardo de Rivas.

The only way up to Chirripó is by foot. Although the trekking routes are long and challenging, watching the sunrise from such lofty heights, literally above the clouds, is an undeniable highlight of Costa Rica. You will have to be prepared for the cold – and at times wet – slog to the top, though your efforts will be rewarded with some of the most sweeping vistas that Costa Rica can offer. The vast majority of travelers visit Chirripó over three days: one to get to San Gerardo de Rivas to secure permits, one to hike to the Crestones Base Lodge and one to summit the peak and return to San Gerardo. An extra day of day hiking at the top is advisable for those who really wish to soak up the amazing sights.

1. Parque Nacional Los Quetzales (p340)
A waterfall on the Río Savegre, the lifeblood of this national park.

2. Parque Nacional Chirripó (p345)
There's an amazing diversity of flora and fauna to be found at Parque Nacional Chirripó.

3. Parque Nacional Chirripó (p345)
The 3820m summit of Cerro Chirripó is the highest point in Costa Rica.

4. Fiesta de los Diablitos (p351)
A performer of the Danza de los Diablitos (dance of the little devils), held during the festival.

The dry season (from late December to April) is the most popular time to visit Chirripó. February and March are the driest months, though it might still rain. On weekends, and especially during holidays, the trails can get a bit crowded with Tico hiking groups. The park is closed in May, but the early months of the rainy season are still good for climbing as it usually doesn't rain in the morning. In any season, temperatures can drop below freezing at night, so warm clothes (including hat and gloves), rainwear and a three-season sleeping bag are necessary. In exposed areas, high winds seem even colder. The ranger station in San Gerardo de Rivas is a good place to check on the weather conditions.

The maps available at the ranger station are serviceable for the major trails. Getting highly detailed topographical maps of the region is difficult, though some bookstores in San Jose, including 7th Street Books, stock them occasionally. If you know your trip will include a lot of time on Chirripó's less-traveled regions, order maps in advance through www.cartographic.com.

Activities

Wildlife-watching

The varying altitude means an amazing diversity of fauna in Parque Nacional Chirripó. Particularly famous for its extensive birdlife, the national park is home to several endangered species, including the harpy eagle (the largest, most powerful raptor in the Americas) and the resplendent quetzal (especially visible between March and May). Even besides these highlights, you might see highland birds including the three-wattled bellbird, black guan and tinamou. The Andean-like *páramo* guarantees volcano junco, sooty robin, slaty finch, large-footed finch and the endemic volcano hummingbird, which is found only in Costa Rica's highlands.

In addition to the prolific birdlife, the park is home to some unusual high-altitude reptiles, such as the green spiny lizard and the highland alligator lizard. Mammals include puma, Baird's tapir, spider monkey, capuchin and – at higher elevations – Dice's rabbit and the coyotes that feed on them.

Although spotting rarer animals is never a guaranteed proposition, here are a few tips to maximize your chances: pumas stick to the savanna areas and use the trails at dawn and dusk to move about; Baird's tapirs gravitate to various highland lagoons, mainly in the rainy season, so stake out the muddy edges at dawn or dusk if you see recent tracks; at nighttime, coyotes can be seen feeding at the rubbish bins near Crestones Base Lodge.

Hiking
CLIMBING CHIRRIPÓ

The park entrance is at San Gerardo de Rivas, which lies 1350m above sea level; from here the summit is 2.5km straight up! A well-marked 16km trail leads all the way to the top and no technical climbing is required. It would be nearly impossible to get lost.

The amount of time it takes to get up varies greatly – it can take as little as five and as many as 14 hours to cover the 10km from the trailhead to the hostel, depending on how fit you are: the recommended departure time is 5am or 6am. The trailhead lies 50m beyond Albergue Urán in San Gerardo de Rivas (about 4km from the ranger station). The main gate is open from 4am to 10am to allow climbers to enter; no one is allowed to begin the ascent after 10am (although it is unlikely that a fast-moving latecomer would be turned away). Inside the park the trail is clearly signed at every kilometer.

The open-sided hut at Llano Bonito, halfway up, is a good place for a lunch break. There is shelter and water, but it is intended for emergency use, not overnight stays.

TOP PICKS: ONLY IN CHIRRIPÓ

While Costa Rica's national parks stretch from valley floor to mountaintop, only in Chirripó can you do the following:

» Lord it over the Costa Rican landscape while standing at the country's highest point.

» Spot highland endemics including the volcano hummingbird and green spiny lizard.

» Catch glimpses of both the Caribbean and the Pacific in a single panoramic gaze.

» Zip up the sleeping bag just as the mercury drops below the freezing point.

» Experience a slice of the Andes without ever leaving Central America.

ⓘ DAY HIKING CHIRRIPÓ

Although it might be possible to leave San Gerardo de Rivas, summit Chirripó and return to town in a single day, don't do it. It would be an utterly exhausting slog for even the most fit hikers, and nearly guarantee returning in the dark over the muddiest parts of the trail.

If you don't have the time, consider a long day hike in the Cloudbridge Nature Preserve.

About 6km from the trailhead, the Monte Sin Fe (which translates as 'Mountain Without Faith'; this climb is not for the faint of heart) is a preliminary crest that reaches 3200m. You then enjoy 2km with gravity in your favor, before making the 2km ascent to the Crestones Base Lodge at 3400m.

Reaching the hostel is the hardest part. From there the hike to the summit is about 5km on relatively flatter terrain (although the last 100m is very steep): allow at least two hours if you are fit, but carry a warm jacket, rain gear, water, snacks and a flashlight just in case. From the summit on a clear day, the vista stretches to both the Caribbean Sea and the Pacific Ocean. The deep-blue lakes and the plush-green hills carpet the Valle de las Morenas in the foreground. It's recommended to leave the base camp at 3am to arrive in time to watch the sunrise from the summit – a spectacular experience.

A minimum of two days is needed to climb from the ranger station in San Gerardo to the summit and back, leaving no time for recuperation or exploration. It is definitely worthwhile to spend at least one extra day exploring the trails around the summit and/or the Base Lodge.

OTHER TRAILS

Most trekkers follow the main trail to Chirripó and return the same way, but there are several other attractive destinations that are accessible by trails from the base camp. This will require at least another day and real topographical maps. An alternative, longer route between the base lodge and the summit goes via Cerro Terbi (3760m), as well as Los Crestones, the moonlike rock formations that adorn many postcards. If you are hanging around for a few days, the glorious, grassy Sabana de los Leones is a popular destination that offers a stark contrast to the otherwise alpine scenery. Peak-baggers

will want to visit Cerro Ventisqueros (3812m), which is also within a day's walk of Crestones. These trails are fairly well maintained, but it's worth inquiring about conditions before setting out.

For hard-core adventurers, an alternative route is to take a guided three- or four-day loop trek that begins in the nearby village of Herradura and spends a day or two traversing cloud forest and *páramo* on the slopes of Fila Urán. Hikers ascend Cerro Urán (3600m) before the final ascent of Chirripó and then descend through San Gerardo. This trip requires bush camping and carrying a tent. Costa Rica Trekking Adventures (☎2771-4582; www.chirripo.com) can make arrangements for this tour.

🛏 Sleeping & Eating

The only accommodations in Parque Nacional Chirripó are at Crestones Base Lodge (Centro Ambientalista el Parámo; dm US$10), which houses up to 60 people in dorm-style bunks that have serviceable vinyl-coated matresses. The basic stone building has a solar panel that provides electric light for limited hours and sporadic heat for showers. Amazingly, it also has wi-fi. All crude comforts – sleeping bags, cooking stoves blankets and the like – should be rented in San Gerardo de Rivas, where they're ubiquitous.

Reservations are absolutely necessary at Crestones Base Lodge. Independent travelers will find it's virtually impossible to make reservations before arriving in Costa Rica. In-country, it's fairly easy to get a reservation through the Minae (☎2771-3155; aclap@sinac.go.cr) in San Isidro or at the ranger station directly. Payment is required to confirm the reservation. If you reserve in advance you must present your reservation and payment confirmation at the ranger station in San Gerardo de Rivas on the day before you set out.

Fortunately, the lodge reserves 10 spaces per night for travelers who show up in San Gerardo and are ready to hike on the following day. This is far and away the more practical option for most travelers. Even though there is no certainty that there will be space available on the days you wish to hike, local lodge owners say that showing up immediately when the ranger station opens is almost guaranteed to work. Space is at a premium during holiday periods and on weekends during the dry season. The ranger station opens at 6:30am – the earlier you arrive, the more likely you will be able to hike the following day.

Crestones Base Lodge provides drinking water, but no food. Hikers must bring all of their own provisions.

Camping is allowed only at a special designated area near Cerro Urán – not at Crestones or anywhere else in the park.

ℹ Information

It is essential that you stop at the Chirripó **ranger station** (Sinac; ☎2200-5348; ☉6:30am-noon & 1-4:30pm) at least one day before you intend to climb Chirripó so that you can get a space at the mountaintop hostel and pay your park entry fee (US$15 for two days, plus US$15 for each additional day). Space at the hostel is limited, so arrive early – first thing in the morning – to inquire about space on the following day. Even if you have a reservation, you must stop here the day before to confirm (bring your reservation and payment confirmation). You can also make arrangements here to hire a porter (a fixed fee of US$60 for up to 15kg of luggage) or to store your luggage while you hike. The hike is popular with Tico hikers and busiest the dry weeks before Easter. Although the trails are well marked, they can be a muddy mess.

ℹ Getting There & Around

Travelers connect to the trails via the mountain village of San Gerardo de Rivas, which is also home to the ranger station. See details under San Gerardo de Rivas for directions on how to get here. From opposite the ranger station, in front of Cabinas El Bosque, there is free transportation to the trailhead at 5am. Also, several hotels offer early-morning trailhead transportation for their guests.

THE ROAD TO LA AMISTAD

From San Isidro de El General, the Interamericana winds its way southeast through glorious geography of rolling hills and coffee and pineapple plantations backed by striking mountain facades, towering as much as 3350m above. Along this stretch, a series of narrow, steep, dirt roads lead to some of the country's most remote areas – some nearly inaccessible due to the prohibitive presence of the Cordillera de Talamanca. But it's worth enduring the thrilling road for the chance to visit Parque Internacional La Amistad, a true wilderness of epic scale.

Reserva Biológica Dúrika

A perfect example of sustainable tourism in action, the 75-sq-km Reserva Biológica Dúrika is home to a small but thriving community of about 100 Ticos and resident foreigners who are committed to local conservation, natural medicine and the preservation of indigenous culture. Since the late 1980s Dúrika has opened its arms to any travelers interested in their inspiring social experiment. Its beautiful location, community spirit and programs make it an excellent way to connect to this corner of the country.

Tours of the farm demonstrate the principles and processes of organic agriculture that Dúrika employs, such as fertilizer made from chili peppers. Guests can also arrange short hikes into the reserve, daylong forays to the Cabécar indigenous village of Ujarrás, and/or multiday treks. Travelers with a strong interest in indigenous cultures or medicinal plants should inquire about visits that focus on traditional healing methods.

Those who stay on the farm have a variety of excellent day hikes to check out local waterfalls (which fuel the community's hydroelectric power) and otherwise exploring the grounds. There are simple dorms (US$12) and candlelit cabins (per person from US$45). As an added bonus, rates include organic vegetarian meals made from locally grown foods. Reservations and information are available from the Fundación Dúrika office (☎2730-0657; www.durika.org) in Buenos Aires.

Although it is possible to drive to Dúrika in a 4WD, the office in Buenos Aires can arrange transportation to the reserve and watch over your car while you're staying at the reserve. This is a highly recommended option as the road out to the reserve is extremely challenging and potentially dangerous, especially if there has been heavy rainfall as the drive along the narrow road edges along the side of a canyon and can be terrifying.

Reserva Indígena Boruca

The picturesque valley of the Río Grande de Térraba cradles several mostly indigenous villages that comprise the reserve of Brunka (Boruca) peoples. At first glance it is difficult to differentiate these towns from typical Tico villages, aside from a few artisans selling their handiwork. In fact, these towns hardly cater to the tourist trade, which is one of the main reasons why traditional Brunka life has been able to continue without much distraction.

Be sensitive when visiting these communities – dress modestly, avoid taking photographs of people without asking permission, and respect the fact that these living communities are struggling to maintain traditional culture amid a changing world.

History

Historians believe that the present-day Brunka have evolved out of several different indigenous groups, including the Coto, Quepos, Turrucaca, Burucac and Abubaes, whose territories stretched all the way to the Península de Osa in pre-Columbian times. Today, however, the entire Brunka population is largely confined to the small villages of Rey Curré, which is bisected by the Carretera Interamericana, and Boruca, 8km north.

Festivals & Events

Fiesta de los Diablitos CULTURAL
A three-day Brunka event that symbolizes the struggle between the Spanish and the indigenous population. Sometimes called the Danza de los Diablitos, or 'dance of the little devils,' the culmination of the festival is a choreographed battle between the opposing sides. Villagers wearing wooden devil masks and burlap costumes play the role of the natives in their fight against the Spanish conquerors. The Spaniards, represented by a man in a bull costume, get whipped by branches and lose the battle. (There's a lot of homemade corn-based alcohol involved.) This festival is held in Boruca from December 31 to January 2 and in Curré from February 5 to 8.

Fiesta de los Negritos RELIGIOUS
Lesser-known than the Fiesta de los Diablitos, this festival is held during the second week of December to celebrate the Virgin of the Immaculate Conception. Traditional indigenous music (mainly drumming and bamboo flutes) accompanies dancing and costumes.

Sleeping & Eating

Although the little dirt streets of these towns have almost no structured tourism other than basic craft stalls, simple meals are available and travelers can find rooms to rent by inquiring locally. A good local resource for sorting out accommodation is Mileni Gonzalez (2730-5178; laflordeboruca@gmail.com).

Bar Restaurante Y Cabinas Boruca CABINAS $
(2730-2454; Boruca; per person from US$10; P) The only regular place to stay in the area is at the Tico-owned Bar Restaurante Boruca, which consists of five basic rooms. For a few dollars you can also camp around back with your own tent.

Shopping

The Brunka are celebrated craftspeople and their traditional art plays a leading role in the survival of their culture. While most people make their living from agriculture, some indigenous people have begun producing fine handicrafts for tourists. The tribe is most famous for its ornate masks, carved from balsa or cedar, and sometimes colored with natural dyes and acrylics. Brunka women also use pre-Columbian backstrap looms to weave colorful, natural cotton bags, placemats and other textiles. These crafts are not widely available elsewhere in the country.

Information

Rey Curré (usually just labelled 'Curré' on maps) is about 30km south of Buenos Aires, right on the Interamericana. Drivers can stop to visit a small **cooperative** (9am-5pm Mon-Fri, 2-5pm Sat) that sells handicrafts. In Boruca, local artisans post signs outside their homes advertising their handmade balsa masks and woven bags. Exhibits are sometimes on display in the informal museum, a thatch-roof *rancho* 100m west of the *pulpería*. The community operates an excellent website with historical information and more at www.boruca.org or tune in locally to 88.1 FM, a community radio station.

Getting There & Away

Buses (US$3.15, one hour) leave the central market in Buenos Aires at noon and 3:30pm daily, traveling to Boruca via a very poor dirt road. The bus returns the following morning, which makes Boruca difficult for a day trip relying on public transportation. A taxi from Buenos Aires to Boruca is about US$30.

Drivers will find a better road that leaves the Interamericana about 3km south of Rey Curré – look for the sign. In total, it's about 8km to Boruca from Rey Curré, though the going is slow, and a 4WD is recommended.

Palmar

At the intersection of the country's two major highways, this unremarkable village is a transportation hub that serves as a gateway to the Osa peninsula and Golfo Dulce. Although the town also serves as an important banana-growing center, for the average traveler there is little reason to spend any more time here than it takes to get off the plane or change buses. Quite simply, it's a hot, dusty and altogether uneventful place.

Palmar is actually split in two – to get from Palmar Norte to Palmar Sur, take the Interamericana southbound over the Río Grande de Térraba bridge, then take the first right beyond the bridge. Most facilities are in Palmar Norte, clustered around the intersection of the Carretera Interamericana and the Costanera Sur (Pacific Coast Hwy), while Palmar Sur is the locale of the airstrip.

Sleeping & Eating

You'll not want to linger in Palmar, but if you miss a connection you may find yourself spending the night.

Galería Namu (p79) can arrange local tours of the Boruca area, which include homestay, hiking to waterfalls, handicraft demonstrations and storytelling. These cost US$65 person/per day, and include meals, but not transportation to the village itself, which is relatively simple to work out by bus via Buenos Aires. Visit their website for more details.

Self-caterers will want to visit the Supermercado Térraba (Transportes Térraba bus stop) before heading to the Osa, as shopping opportunities are limited in Bahía Drake. The Panadería Palenquito (Tracopa bus stop) is a useful breakfast spot if you are catching an early-morning bus.

Brunka Lodge HOTEL $
(☎2786-7489; www.brunkalodge.com; r/ste US$50/75; ❄@🕸🏊) This is undoubtedly the most inviting option in Palmar Norte. Sun-filled, clean-swept bungalows are clustered around a swimming pool and a popular, pleasant open-air restaurant, and all rooms have hot-water bathrooms, cable TV and high-speed internet connections. The suite is particularly nice, as it has a private entrance to the pool.

❶ Getting There & Away

Air

Departing from San José, **NatureAir** (www.natureair.com) and **Sansa** (www.sansa.com) have daily flights to the Palmar airstrip. Prices vary according to season and availability, though you can expect to pay around US$100 to/from San José.

Taxis meet incoming flights and charge up to US$8 to Palmar Norte and US$15 to US$30 to Sierpe. Otherwise, the infrequent Palmar Norte–Sierpe bus goes through Palmar Sur – you can board it if there's space available.

Bus

Buses to San José and San Isidro stop on the east side of the Interamericana. Other buses leave from in front of Panadería Palenquito or Supermercado Térraba a block apart on the town's main street. The bus ticket office is inside the Palenquito.

Neily (Transportes Térraba) US$16; 1½ hours; departs 5am, 6am, 7am, 9:30am, noon, 1pm, 2:20pm, 4:50pm

San Isidro (Tracopa) US$4; three hours; departs 8:30am, 11:30am, 2:30pm, 4:30pm

San José (Tracopa) US$5.75; five hours; departs 5:25am, 6:15am, 7:45am, 10am, 1pm, 3pm, 4:45pm

Sierpe US$1.40; one hour; departs 4:30am, 7am, 9:30am, 11:30am, 2:30pm, 5:30pm

Neily

Although it is Southern Costa Rica's second-largest 'city,' Neily has retained the friendly atmosphere of a rural town, much like neighboring Palmar. There's not much of a reason to stay here unless you're resting up or recovering from the trip from Panama. At just 50m above sea level, steamy Neily serves as a regional transportation hub and agricultural center, and is decidedly lacking in tourist appeal.

Neily is located on the west bank of the Río Corredor, on the north side of the Interamericana. From here the Interamericana continues 17km to Panama, while Rte 16 makes a beeline north to the attractive mountain village of San Vito.

To the south, the lowlands are carpeted in the banana and palm plantations of the Valle de Coto Colorado, and in the north, the Fila Costeña is the source of spectacular mountain scenery.

There is a Banco Coopealianza (⏰8am-3pm Mon-Fri), just southwest of the *mercado* (market), that has a 24-hour ATM on the Cirrus network.

If you stay the night here, there's are plenty of budget dives, but only one good option, Hotel Andrea (☎2783-3784, 2783-

3715; www.hotelandreacr.com; across from Central Market; d without/with AC $37/46; P✆❀@ ☎🏠). Paths of terra-cotta tiles are brightly scrubbed, leading guests through the maze of yellow buildings to cool, whitewashed rooms. The heavy-handed Romanesque columns might look a bit like Caesar's Palace (the Las Vegas one), but the rooms are good value and very secure, and all have Adirondack chairs outside their doors for guests to enjoy the sun. There's even a nice restaurant onsite, one of the best in Neily, which serves pancakes and honey, omelets, fresh fish and steaks, among other things. Dinner is about US$10.

❶ Getting There & Away

Air

Departing from San José, **NatureAir** (www.natureair.com) and **Sansa** (www.sansa.com) have daily flights to the Neily airstrip. Prices vary according to season and availability, though you can expect to pay around US$100 to/from San José.

Bus

The following buses leave from the main terminal on the east side of town, which is attached to a *mercado* with a clutch of busy *sodas*:

Airport US$0.50; 30 minutes; departs 7:30am, 9:15am, 11:30am, 1:15pm, 3:15pm, 5:30pm, 6pm

Dominical US$4.10; three hours; departs 6am, 11am, 2:30pm

Golfito US$1.65; 1½ hours; departs hourly 6am to 7:30pm

Palmar US$1.65; 1½ hours; departs 4:45am, 9:15am, noon, 12:30pm, 2:30pm, 4:30pm, 5:45pm

Paso Canoas US$0.75; 30 minutes; departs every half-hour 6am to 6pm

Puerto Jiménez US$4; three hours; departs 7am, 2pm

San Isidro US$7; six hours; departs 7am, 10am, 1pm, 3pm

San José US$11; eight hours; departs 4:30am, 5am, 8:30am, 11:30am, 3:30pm

San Vito US$3; two hours; departs 6am, 7:30am, 9am, noon, 1pm, 4pm, 5:30pm

Zancudo US$4; three hours; departs 9:30am, 2:15pm

Taxi

Taxis with 4WD wait at the taxi stand southeast of the park. The fare from Neily to Paso Canoas is about US$8, but note that negotiation for prices is par for the course along the busy borderland.

Paso Canoas

The main port of entry between Costa Rica and Panama is like most border outposts the world over – hectic, slightly seedy and completely devoid of charm. As you might imagine, most travelers leave Paso Canoas with little more than a passing glance at their passport stamp.

Báncredito (⊘8am-4:30pm), near the Costa Rican Migración and Customs (⊘6am-11pm), changes traveler's checks and there is an ATM near the border. Rates for converting excess colones into dollars are not good, but they will do in a pinch. Colones are accepted at the border, but are difficult to get rid of further into Panama.

The **Instituto Panameño de Turismo** (☎2727-6524; ⊘6:30am-9:30pm), in the Panamanian immigration post, has information on travel to Panama. If you are arriving in Costa Rica, you'll find sparse tourist information at the Costa Rican Tourist Information office in Costa Rican Migración and Customs.

The hotels in Paso Canoas aren't particularly inviting, but **Cabinas Romy** (☎2732-2873; r from US$12) will do if necessary. Set around a pleasant courtyard, shiny rooms are decked with pastel-colored walls, wooden doors and floral bedspreads, which add a surprising bit of warmth to an otherwise drab town.

Tracopa buses leave for San José (US$12, six hours) at 4am, 7:30am, 9am and 3pm. The **Tracopa bus terminal** (☎2732-2201), or window really, is north of the border post, on the east side of the main road. Sunday-afternoon buses are full of weekend shoppers, so buy tickets as early as possible. Buses for Neily (US$1.35, 30 minutes) leave from in front of the post office at least once an hour from 6am to 6pm. Taxis to Neily cost about US$6 and to the airport about US$8.

Wilson Botanical Garden

Covering 12 hectares and surrounded by 254 hectares of natural forest, **Wilson Botanical Garden** (☎2773-4004; www.esintro.co.cr; Las Cruces Biological Station; admission US$8, guided tours half-/full-day US$18/24; ⊘7am-5pm Mon-Fri, 8am-5pm Sat-Sun) lies about 6km south of San Vito. This world-class garden was established by Robert and Catherine Wilson in 1963 and thereafter became internationally known for its collection.

In 1973 the area came under the auspices of the Organization for Tropical Studies (OTS) and today the well-maintained garden – part of Las Cruces Biological Station – holds more than 1000 genera of plants from about 200 families. Species threatened with extinction are preserved here for possible reforestation in the future.

The gardens are well laid out, many of the plants are labeled and a trail map is available for self-guided walks, featuring exotic species such as orchids, bromeliads and medicinal plants. The gardens are very popular among bird-watchers, who look for a number of rare species.

If you want to stay overnight at the botanical gardens, make reservations well in advance: facilities often fill with researchers. Accommodations are in comfortable cabins (singles/doubles including meals US$98/184) in the midst of the gorgeous grounds. The rooms are simple, but they each have a balcony with an amazing view.

Buses between San Vito and Neily pass the entrance to the gardens. Take the bus that goes through Agua Buena, as buses that go through Cañas Gordas do not stop here.

San Vito

Although the Italian immigrants who founded little San Vito in the 1850s are long gone, this hillside village proudly bears traces of their legacy in linguistic, cultural and culinary echos. As such, the town serves as a base for travelers in need of a steaming plate of pasta and a good night's sleep before descending into the deep wilderness.

The proximity of the town to the Reserva Indígena Guaymí de Coto Brus means that indigenous peoples pass through this region (Guaymí enclaves move back and forth undisturbed across the border with Panama). You might spot women in traditional clothing – long, solid-colored *pollera* dresses trimmed in contrasting hues – riding the bus or strolling the streets.

Tucked in between the Cordillera de Talamanca and the Fila Costeña, the Valle de Coto Brus offers some glorious geography, featuring the green, rolling hills of the coffee plantations backed by striking mountain facades, towering as much as 3350m above. The principal road leaves the Interamericana at Paso Real (near Rey Curré) and follows the Río Jaba to San Vito, then continues south to rejoin the Interamericana at Neily.

This winding mountain road (paved, but poorly maintained) offers spectacular scenery and a thrilling ride.

◉ Sights

About 3km south of town, Finca Cántaros (☎2773-3760; www.fincacantaros.com; admission $4, campsites per person $8; ⊗9:30am-5pm Tue-Sun; ▣) is a recreation center, campground and reforestation project. The 10 hectares of grounds – which used to be coffee plantations and pasture land – are now a lovely park with garden trails, picnic areas and a dramatic lookout over the city. The reception is housed in a pretty, well-maintained cabin that contains a small but carefully chosen selection of local and national crafts. You can take a self-guided hike to Laguna Zoncho and picnic at one of the small shelters, which is a good perch for watching rare birds and a nice view of the surrounding hills.

⌖ Sleeping & Eating

In addition to the following accommodations options, camping is available at Finca Cántaros.

TOP CHOICE Casa Botania   B&B $$

(☎2773-4217; www.casabotania.com; d from US$55; ▣✳⚲) This, the freshest B&B in the region, is exquisitely run by a Belgian–Tico couple and located 5km south of town on the road between the Wilson Botanical Garden and San Vito. It hits every note with pitch-perfect elegance, from the modern, brightly adorned rooms, to the library of bird-watching guides, to the gourmet meals, which are served on a polished deck overlooking the steaming foliage of the valley below. If you don't stay, book a dinner reservation; the three-course, locally sourced, ever-changing menu of smart European-touched Costa Rican fare wins raves.

Hotel El Ceibo   HOTEL $$

(☎2773-3025; s/d from US$36/52; ▣✳⚲) The best option in town – though fairly subdued by any account – is El Ceibo, conveniently located about 100m west of the main intersection, in a private, secure cul-de-sac. Here you can sleep easy in simple but functional rooms (some with balconies that have forest views, all with fans and nice little touches, like reading lamps) and dig into some authentic Italian pastas and wines in the skylit dining room.

RAINFOREST MEDICINE

Indigenous groups use tropical flowers, herbs and plants to treat all kinds of illnesses, from diabetes to a slipped disk. Here are a few of our favorites, courtesy of Paradise Tropical Garden:

» Most doctors treat stomach ulcers with antibiotics, but natural-medicine connoisseurs recommend the seeds from the spiny red annatto pod. Remove the seeds from the pod and wash away the red paste. You can eat the seeds straight from the pod, or dry them and grind them into your food.

» The leaves of the avocado tree are said to cure high blood pressure. Just boil them for three minutes and let them steep for another three. Strain the murky drink and store it in the fridge. Beware: this brew is a diuretic.

» If you suffer from a slipped disk, you might try this natural remedy, made from the bracts of the beautiful red plume ginger *(Alpinia purpurata)*, which is bountiful in the rainforest. The bracts are the small leaves at the base of the bloom. Pull them off the stem of the ginger and stuff as many as you can fit into a small bottle, then fill the bottle with rubbing alcohol. Let it sit for three days, before rubbing this tincture onto your sore back. This remedy should ease your pain within a few days.

If you would like to learn more, pay a visit to the Paradise Tropical Garden (☑2789-8746; www.paradise-garden.travelland.biz; Río Claro; admission by donation; ☺6am-5pm with one day's advance notice), where Robert and Ella Beatham have created a wonderfully sensual introduction to tropical fruits and rainforest remedies that they call the 'Tropical Fruit See, Smell, Taste & Touch Experience.' Besides this interactive display, visitors learn about the production of African palm oil and how it came to be the dominant crop of this region following the collapse of the banana industry. Robert and Ella are wonderful hosts, but you should call a day in advance if you want their full attention. The gardens are located just west of the town of Río Claro – follow the Interamericana for 1km, cross the Río Lagarto and turn right at the end of the bridge. From here, the garden is just 200m beyond.

Cabinas Rino   CABINA $
(☑2773-3071; s/d from US$12/20; ℗🐾) This 2nd-floor hotel is located above a block of shops on the main road, though it's fairly well insulated from the street noise below. Basic rooms with whitewashed walls are reasonably clean and comfortable, and staff are polite and courteous.

Pizzería Restaurante Lilliana   PIZZERIA $
(www.ilprosciuttolerici.com; pizzas US$4-9; ☺10:30am-10pm) This great spot for Italian fare offers more than a dozen different kinds of pizza, all of which are made from scratch and a sight more authentic than most of the pies in the country. The lovely mountain views and old-world environs make this a pleasant place to spend an afternoon.

❶ Information

If you're planning on heading to Parque Internacional La Amistad, San Vito is home to the **Minae parks office** (☑2773-3955; Calle 2 btwn Avs 4 & 6; ☺9am-4pm), which can help you get your bearings before heading to the national park.

❶ Getting There & Away

Air

Alfa Romeo Aero Taxi (www.alfaromeoair.com) offers charter flights to San Vito from Puerto Jiménez and Golfito – prices vary according to the number of people and season. The airstrip is 1km east of town.

Bus

The main **Tracopa bus terminal** (☑2773-3410) is at the northern end of the main street.

San Isidro US$4.24; three hours; departs 6:45am, 1:30pm

San José US$9; seven hours; departs 5am, 7:30am, 10am, 3pm

A local bus terminal at the northwest end of town runs buses to Neily and other destinations.

Neily US$0.65; 30 minutes; departs 5:30am, 7am, 7:30am, 9am, 11am, noon, 2pm, 5pm

Río Sereno US$1.60; 1½ hours; departs 7am, 10am, 1pm, 4pm

Car

The drive north from Neily is a scenic one, with superb views of the lowlands dropping away as the road winds up the hillside. The paved road is steep, narrow and full of hairpin turns. You can also get to San Vito from San Isidro via the Valle de Coto Brus – an incredibly scenic and less-used route with fantastic views of the Cordillera de Talamanca to the north and the lower Fila Costeña to the south.

PARQUE INTERNACIONAL LA AMISTAD

The 4070-sq-km Parque Internacional La Amistad is an enormous patch of green sprawling across the borders of Panama and Costa Rica (hence its Spanish name La Amistad, 'Friendship'). This is by far the largest protected area in Costa Rica. Standing as a testament to the possibilities of international cooperation and environmental conservation, the park was established in 1982 and declared a Unesco World Heritage Site just eight years later. It then became part of the greater Mesoamerican Biological Corridor, which protects a great variety of endangered habitats. Its cultural importance is also signifigant as it includes several scattered indigneous reserves.

Sound like an exciting place to visit? Well, not so fast. The vast majority of the park is high up in the Cordillera de Talamanca, and remains virtually inaccessible. Although there's no shortage of hiking and camping available for intrepid, independent travelers at lower altitudes, tourist infrastructure within the park is virtually nonexistent. If you play it by the book, trekkers are limited to specific areas, and strongly encouraged (in some places required) to make use of local guides. If you don't play it by the book, it's unlikely that anyone will notice.

While tourists flock to Costa Rica's better-known parks in the hopes of having an eco-adventure, La Amistad is truly as rugged as it comes. Tackling this pristine, potentially treacherous environment is no easy task, but La Amistad is brimming with possibilities for hard-core wilderness exploration – if your fear of growing old in an urban jungle drives you to explore verdant ones, you'll find none wilder on the planet.

The primary jumping-off point by which visitors lauch into the deepest parts of the park is the tiny mountain town of Altamira, 25km northwest of San Vito. There are four other official entrances to the park: one near Buenos Aires, one near Helechales, and two near San Vito. Still, the Estación Altamira is the only year-round, staffed facility.

Getting here is rough and confusing due to the terrible roads and lack of good maps. A bone-jarring 21km dirt road departs Hwy 237 at the small rest stop town of Guácimo (marked on some maps as Las Tablas). You'll pass through El Carmén before making a sharp turn uphill for the Altamira station.

🏃 Activities

Hiking

Of the few visitors who come here to hike, most leave from the Altamira ranger station. The first trail, Los Gigantes del Bosque, is a short 3km circuit that is named for the 40m trees along the way. Signposts in Spanish provide simple explanations of some of the flora, and the trail is an easy means of seeing some ancient rainforest. It passes two lookout points, one on the edge of the primary forest, and the other overlooking the rural landscape outside the park. The trail is marked, but it is not well maintained. Normally the loop takes two hours.

The longest trail (approximately 20km) – known as the Valle del Silencio – departs from the Altamira ranger station, and winds its way through pristine and hilly primary forest before ending up at a camping area and refuge at the base of Cerro Kamuk (3549m). The walk takes anywhere from eight to 12 hours, provided you are in very good physical condition. It is spectacular, and traverses one of the most isolated areas in all of Costa Rica, but a local guide is required to make the journey.

Contact the association of guides, Asoprola (⌀2743-1184; www.actuarcostarica.com) in Altamira to inquire about these arrangements. Rates vary depending on the size of your party and your intended course. Visit the organization's excellent website, which has detailed information about all the hikes.

Visiting Indigenous Groups

Besides the massive environmental preservation efforts of the park, La Amistad is also unique for its cultural preservation; the park is home to five different indigenous reservations for the Cabécar and Bribrí groups. These tribes originally inhabited lands on the Caribbean coast (and many still do), but over the past century they have migrated west into the mountains and as far as the Pacific coast. It is possible to visit the Cabécar via the Reserva Biológica Dúrika and the Bribrí though organizations in Puerto Viejo.

The reserves see relatively few independent foreign visitors (especially who aren't there doing missionary or volunteer work) and as a result the Cabécar and Bribrí tend to view tourists with deep curiosity. Although the unforgiving habitat in which they live has shaped societies that are tough and resilient, the Cabécar and Bribrí are known for their hospitality.

Of course, you should still make an effort to respect the sensibilities of your hosts. Although modern sensibilities have connected these villages with the outside world, they are still conservative societies, and it's recommended that you cover up as a sign of respect.

Additionally, most villagers will be happy to pose for a photo, but always ask before snapping away, to respect the dignity of the subject. Generally, people are not asked to pay for a photo, though it's best to ask your guide what is expected from you.

Tourism has a long way to develop in the region, which is one reason why a visit to a Cabécar or Bribrí village is so refreshing.

Wildlife-Watching

Although most of Parque Internacional La Amistad is inaccessible terrain high up in the Talamanca, the park is home to a recorded 90 mammal species and more than 400 bird species. The park has the nation's largest population of Baird's tapirs, as well as giant anteaters, all six species of neotropical cats – jaguar, puma (mountain lion), margay, ocelot, oncilla (tiger cat) and jaguarundi – and many more common mammals.

Bird species (49 unique) that have been sighted – more than half of the total in Costa Rica – include the majestic but extremely rare harpy eagle. In addition, the park protects 115 species of fish, 215 different reptiles and amphibians, as well as innumerable insect species.

🛏 Sleeping & Eating

All of the ranger stations, including Altamira, have camping facilities (per person US$6). There are basic hostels (per person US$10 to US$12) at Santa María de Pittier and at the base of Cerro Kamuk. These camps and hostels offer drinking water and toilets, and – in the case of Altamira – electricity. All food and supplies must be packed in and out.

Asoprola (p356) also runs a small, simple lodge and can make arrangements for lodging in local homes in the village of Altamira for a resonable fee (usually US$10 to US$15 per person). For an intimate look

at the lives of people living on the fringes of the rainforest, there is no better way than to arrange a homestay. Besides the options listed here, see the Reserva Biológica Dúrika, which is contained within the borders of the park.

Soda y Cabinas La Amistad   CABINA $
(☎2743-1080; r per person US$12; P) West of Santa María de Pittier, in the village of El Carmen, this place has simple cabins with cold-water showers. The cabins are useful if you want one last night's rest before heading in or out of the park.

Estación Altamira   RANGER STATION $
(☎2730-9846; camping per site US$6, dorm bed US$6; ⊙8am-4:30pm) This, the primary ranger station for La Amistad, has a camping area and small dorm. Compared with many of the digs in the area, the TV lounge and common area make it relatively swish. Relatively.

ⓘ Information

Limited information is available at local Minae offices – **San Isidro** (Sinac; ☎2771-3155, 2771-4836, 2771-5116; aclap@sinac.go.cr; Calle 2 btwn Avs 2 & 4; ⊙8am-noon & 1-4pm Mon-Fri), San Vito (p355) – but generally speaking they're minimally helpful.

To make reservations to camp or to stay in a refuge, it's better to call the park headquarters at **Altamira** (☎2200-5355; park fee per person per day US$7) directly. This is the best-developed area of the park, with a camping area, showers and drinking water, electric light and a lookout tower. A group of paratoxonomists studying insects in this area has created a small display of butterflies and moths.

The thickly forested northern Caribbean slopes and southern Pacific slopes of the Talamanca are protected in the park, but it is only on the Pacific side that ranger stations are found.

ⓘ Getting There & Away

If you have a tight schedule, a 4WD drive and steely nerves are required to get around this area – the buses are unreliable, the roads are terrible and things run on a very flexible schedule. To reach Altamira, you can take any bus that runs between San Isidro and San Vito and get off in the town of Guácimo (often called Las Tablas). From Guácimo buses depart at noon and 5pm for El Carmen; if the road conditions permit, they continue 4km to the village of Altamira. From the village of Altamira, follow the Minae sign (near the church) leading to the steep 2km hike to the ranger station.

Península de Osa & Golfo Dulce

Best Places to Eat

» Rancho Grande (p390)

» Jade Luna (p368)

» Soda Veleria (p368)

» Pizzamail.it (p368)

» Rancho Grande (p390)

Best Places to Stay

» Cabinas Murillo (p378)

» Tiskita Jungle Lodge (p394)

» Yoga Farm (p394)

» Esquinas Rainforest Lodge (p391)

» Lapa Ríos (p370)

Why Go?

Sure, it's difficult to get here, but the remote southwestern corner of the country is regarded as Costa Rica's most picturesque, pristine and exciting turf. Although much of the rainforest in Costa Rica is protected, no other region can offer the extent of wildlife found in Osa. In Corcovado, it's possible to see all four native species of monkey in the canopy overhead, while otherwise rare animals such as Baird's tapir can be spotted regularly. Indeed, the Osa peninsula is striking evidence that the beauty of the rainforest is worth saving.

Beyond Corcovado, the Osa peninsula captivates travelers with abandoned wilderness beaches, world-class surf and opportunities for rugged exploration. In a country where adventure is all too often downgraded and packaged for tourist consumption, Osa is the real deal. Simply put, it's a place for travelers with youthful hearts, intrepid spirits and a yearning for something truly wild.

When to Go

Although, as a rainforest, it's always wet here, it absolutely pours between October and December. Storms can make the roads impassable and the travel tough. This can be a bit maddening, particularly if you are traveling overland to Corcovado. If you come during this time, bring lots of dry socks! The upside to the rainy season? It's also the best time of year for swells, making for killer surfing. If you're traveling here independently a 4WD is an absolute necessity at any season, as river crossings are inevitable.

History

While the Guaymí were the earliest inhabitants of the Osa, the vast majority of the peninsula was never populated or developed by Ticos (Costa Ricans). In fact, because of the remoteness of the region, commercial logging was never a threat until the early 1960s.

Although this tumultuous decade saw the destruction of much of Costa Rica's remaining primary forests, Osa was largely spared. By 1975, however, international companies were greedily eyeing the peninsula's timber and gold. Fortunately, these ambitions were halted when researchers petitioned President Daniel Oduber to establish a national park.

In recent years the peninsula has attracted the attention of wealthy foreigners, who have snatched up some prime real estate, but there's hope that development will be more sustainable in this part of the country, particularly since there is a vested interest in keeping the peninsula green.

Climate

Though both are wet, the Osa peninsula has a rainy season and a dry season. During the rainy season (mid-April to mid-December) the amount of precipitation is astounding, with most months boasting more than 500mm. Even in the dry season, better described as the 'less rainy season,' expect a good downfall now and again.

Parks & Reserves

As the country's premier ecotourism destination, the Península de Osa has a plethora of parks, reserves and wildlife refuges. There seems to be a park around every corner – the following list is only the beginning.

» **Humedal Nacional Térraba-Sierpe** (p374) Approximately 330 sq km of protected mangrove wetlands.

» **Parque Nacional Corcovado** (p382) Osa's shining crown jewel, and one of Costa Rica's last true wilderness areas.

» **Parque Nacional Isla del Cocos** (p395) Visually stunning, utterly pristine and – by far – the country's most remote and difficult spot to access.

» **Parque Nacional Piedras Blancas** (p391) One of the last remaining stretches of lowland rainforest in the country.

» **Reserva Biológica Isla del Caño** (p382) A tiny marine and terrestrial park in Bahía Drake that is a popular destination for snorkelers, divers and biologists.

» **Reserva Forestal Golfo Dulce** (p362) On the northern shore of Golfo Dulce, this is an important biological corridor for migrating wildlife.

Dangers & Annoyances

The greatest annoyance in Osa is the difficult environment, particularly in Parque Nacional Corcovado. Trails are generally well marked but it can be difficult going at times, especially if you're not confident at navigating trails. Also, crossing the rivers that through the park create their own hazards, especially in the rainy season. Medical help is very far away – if you get lost out here, you have a serious problem.

If you're unsure about facing these challenges, it's recommended that you explore Corcovado either as part of an organized tour or with the help of a local guide. Hiring a knowledgeable guide will also provide up-to-date information on potential hazards, and it provides safety through numbers.

By and large, animals are not much of a problem in Corcovado. Sure, areas of Corcovado are also prime territory for the deadly fer-de-lance snake, but the chance of getting bitten is remote. Sure, there are big cats, but they are virtually invisible. According to guides, the most dangerous animal encounters are with grunting packs of peccaries – hairy, half-sized, wild pigs. One or two of them will scamper away, but when they travel in large packs (sometimes up to 200 large!) they can be aggressive and dangerous. The guides' advice in the unlikely event of an encounter is to climb a tree.

Although they don't carry Lyme disease, ticks are everywhere in Corcovado. In reality, they're nothing more than a nuisance, though you'd be wise to bring a good pair of tweezers. If you're not traveling with a buddy, a pocket mirror will also help, as these little buggers have a habit of turning up in some rather uncomfortable places.

ℹ Getting There & Around

Getting to Osa demands one of two things: lots of patience or a chartered flight. Given the reasonable cost of flights, the best option for exploring the peninsula is to fly in if your time is limited. If you choose to drive, you'll need 4WD, a spare tire, a whole day to get here from San Jose and steely nerves: roads in Osa are extremely poor, as most of the peninsula is still off the grid. Getting in and out via public transportation is possible, but slow going.

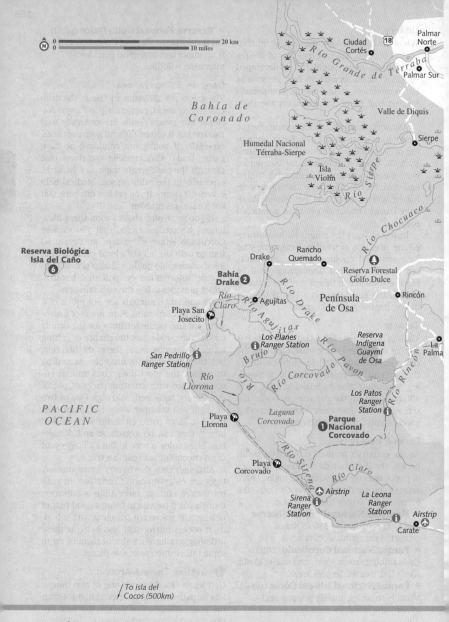

Península de Osa & Golfo Dulce Highlights

① Go deep into the rainforest jungle of **Parque Nacional Corcovado** (p382), the country's premier wilderness experience

② Explore the dense jungles that fringe the crystalline waters of **Bahía Drake** (p375)

③ Catch a ride on the world's longest left break at the slow-paced surfing paradise of **Pavones** (p393)

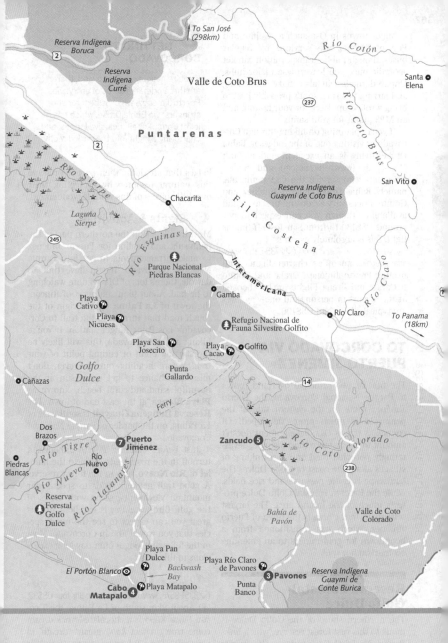

Map Labels

To San José
(298km)

Río Cotón

Reserva Indígena
Boruca

Valle de Coto Brus

Santa
Elena

Reserva
Indígena
Curré

237

Río Coto Brus

Puntarenas

San Vito

Río Sierpe

Chacarita

Reserva Indígena
Guaymí de Coto Brus

Fila Costeña

Laguna
Sierpe

245

Río Esquinas

Interamericana

Río Claro

Parque Nacional
Piedras Blancas

Gamba

Río Claro

To Panama
(18km)

Playa
Cativo

Playa
Nicuesa

Refugio Nacional de
Fauna Silvestre Golfito

Golfito

14

Playa San
Josecito

Playa
Cacao

Golfo
Dulce

Punta
Gallardo

Cañazas

Ferry

Río Coto Colorado

Dos
Brazos

Puerto
Jiménez

Zancudo

Río Tigre

Río
Nuevo

238

Piedras
Blancas

Río Nuevo

Río Platanares

Reserva
Forestal
Golfo
Dulce

Bahía de
Pavón

Valle de Coto
Colorado

Playa Pan
Dulce

Playa Río Claro
de Pavones

El Portón Blanco

Backwash
Bay

Pavones

Reserva Indígena
Guaymí de
Conte Burica

Cabo
Matapalo

Playa Matapalo

Punta
Banco

Legend

④ Watch the sun rise over the Golfo Dulce and set over the Pacific from the deserted beaches on **Cabo Matapalo** (p369)

⑤ Loaf around **Zancudo** (p392) for a slice of the 'Old Costa Rica' of surfer lore

⑥ Hike or paddle through the mangrove forests of **Reserva**

Biológica Isla del Caño (p382)

⑦ Gear up for the hike and meet other travelers in **Puerto Jiménez** (p364), a jungle town with a Wild West vibe

Major towns in Osa such as Golfito and Puerto Jiménez are serviced by regular buses, though public transportation can get sporadic once you leave these major hubs. Unpaved roads can also make for a long and jarring bus ride, so it's probably best to bring a rolled-up fleece for your bottom and an MP3 player for your sanity.

If you're planning on hiking through Corcovado or visiting one of the lodges in Bahía Drake, flying is an excellent option. Both **NatureAir** (www.natureair.com) and **Sansa** (www.sansa.com) service the Osa peninsula, namely Bahía Drake, Puerto Jiménez and Golfito. Prices vary according to season and availability, though you can expect to pay around US$130 to/from San José. If time is tight, this is absolutely worth it.

Alfa Romeo Aero Taxi (☎2735-5353; www.alfaromeoair.com) offers charter flights connecting Puerto Jiménez, Drake and Golfito to Carate and Sirena. Flights are best booked at the airport in person, and one-way fares are typically less than US$100.

TO CORCOVADO VIA PUERTO JIMÉNEZ

The first of two principal overland routes to Parque Nacional Corcovado, the Puerto Jiménez route on the eastern side of the peninsula is much more 'developed.' Of course, as this is Osa, development doesn't amount to much more than a single, devastatingly potholed road and a sprinkling of villages along the coast of Golfo Dulce. The landscape is cattle pastures and rice fields, while the Reserva Forestal Golfo Dulce protects much of the inland area. The largest settlement in the area is the town of Puerto Jiménez, which has transitioned from a boomtown for gold miners to an emerging ecotourism hot spot.

Reserva Forestal Golfo Dulce

The northern shore of the Golfo Dulce is home to this vast forest reserve, which links Parque Nacional Corcovado to the Parque Nacional Piedras Blancas. This connecting corridor plays an important role in preserving the biodiversity of the peninsula, and allowing the wildlife to migrate to the mainland. Although much of the reserve is not easily accessible, there are several area

ℹ GETTING TO CORCOVADO

If you're heading to Corcovado, there are three primary routes of entry: via Puerto Jiménez, which is best for shoe-stringers; via Bahía Drake, which has a lot of upmarket all-inclusive lodges; and chartering a flight into the park directly.

lodges that are doing their part to preserve this natural resource by protecting their own little pieces of this wildlife wonderland.

⊙ Sights & Activities

Most travelers skip the northern part of the peninsula and beeline for Puerto Jiménez to make arrangements to get into Parque Nacional Corcovado. If you have time to dawdle, there's lots of DIY wildlife-watching to be had. About 9km southeast of Rincón, the town of **La Palma** is the origin of the rough road that turns into the trail to Corcovado's Los Patos ranger station. If you're hiking across Corcovado, this will likely be the starting point or ending point of your trek. Before heading out, however, don't miss the chance to get some sun at the beautiful sand-and-coral beach, known as **Playa Blanca**, at the east end of town. The **Reserva Indígena Guaymí** is southwest of La Palma, on the border of Parque Nacional Corcovado.

Just before entering Puerto Jiménez, a turnoff in the road leads 16km to the hamlet of **Río Nuevo**, also in the forest reserve. A good trail network leads to spectacular mountain viewpoints, some with views of the gulf. Bird-watching is excellent in this area: you can expect to see the many species that you would find in Corcovado. Most of the following lodges offer day-long excursions in this area.

🌿 **Finca Köbö**   FARM
(☎8351-8576; www.fincakobo.com; 3hr tour US$32; ♿) About 8km south of La Palma, the Tico-run Finca Köbö is a chocolate-lover's dream come true (in fact *köbö* means 'dream' in Guaymí). The 50-hectare *finca* (farm) is dedicated to organic cultivation of fruits and vegetables and – the product of choice – cacao. Tours in English give a comprehensive overview of the life cycle of cacao plants and the production of chocolate (with degustation!). More than half of the territory is dedi-

cated to protecting natural ecosystems, and experimenting with different methods of reforestation. To really experience the beauty and vision of this *finca,* you can stay in simple, comfortable teak cabins (single/double US$35/66, meals US$8 to US$13), with lovely open-air bathrooms and quality linens. Those who stay longer can hike the surrounding forest tails and speak with local farmers.

🛏 Sleeping

Many of the accommodations along the northern part of the peninsula are lovely, but isolated – great for honeymooners who want to get away, not too exciting for others. Backpackers tend to move past all the following and head to Puerto Jiménez. Note that accommodations are also available at Finca Köbö.

TOP CHOICE **Danta Corcovado Lodge** LODGE **$$**
(☑8378-9188, 8819-1860; www.dantalodge.com; cabins per person US$70/119; 🅿🛜) Take note: if you're attempting a through-hike of Cor-

covado that starts or ends at the Los Patos ranger station, this sustainable, locally owned lodge is an ideal stopover. Conveniently located midway between the Los Patos station and La Palma, this low-key lodge is set on the *finca* of the congenial Sanchez family, who are talented artists. Rustic wood cabins are painted in warm hues and furnished with handcrafted pieces. The highlight of the lodge, however, is the family's traditional wood stove, which fires up some delicious, home-cooked meals. They will also give you a ride to the trailhead.

Bosque del Río Tigre ECOLODGE **$$$**
(☑8824-1372, in Puerto Jiménez 2735-5062, in USA 888-875-9453; www.osaadventures.com; s/d US$135/155, 4-day package per person from US$528; 🅿) On the edge of the Reserva Forestal Golfo Dulce, in the midst of a 13-hectare private reserve, this off-the-beaten-track ecolodge is a bird-watcher's paradise, and a place that's fancy without being pretentious. Four well-appointed guest rooms and one private, open-air *cabaña* (cabins) have huge

---

GUAYMÍ

The earliest inhabitants of Costa Rica's far southern corner were the Guaymí, or Ngöbe, who migrated over generations from neighboring Panama. The Guaymí inhabit indigenous reserves in the Valle de Coto Brus, the Osa peninsula and southern Golfo Dulce, though they retain some seminomadic ways and are allowed to pass freely over the border into Panama. This occurs frequently during the coffee-harvesting season, when many Guaymí travel to work on plantations.

The Guaymí have been able to preserve – to some degree – their customs and culture, and it is not unusual to see women wearing traditional dress. These vibrant, solid-color *pollera* dresses hang to the ankles, often trimmed in contrasting colors and patterns. Unlike other indigenous groups, the Guaymí still speak their native language and teach it in local schools.

The Guaymí traditionally live in wooden huts with palm roofs and dirt floors, although most families have now upgraded to wooden houses on stilts. However, they still live off the land, cultivating corn, rice and tubers, while fruit and palmitos grow in the wild.

The Guaymí reserves are largely inaccessible, which may be one reason why the culture persists. However, as tourism filters into the furthest corners of the country, there is a growing interest in indigenous traditions and handicrafts, and this demand may actually encourage their preservation. But the reserves are also at a precipitous point – without proper management and community participation, an influx of tourists (and tourist dollars) can also lead to cultural dilution.

The best way to visit the reserve is through Tamandu Lodge (☑8821-4525; www.tamandu-lodge.com; r per person $55), which is run by the Carreras, a Guaymí family. This unique lodge provides a rare chance to interact directly with an indigenous family and experience firsthand the Guaymí lifestyle. This is hands-on stuff: gather crabs and fish with palm rods; hunt for palmito or harvest yucca; learn how to prepare these specialties over an open fire. Accommodations are in rustic, wooden houses, built on stilts with thatch roofs. Home-cooked meals are included in the price. A member of the Carrera family will meet you in La Palma, from where it is a two-hour journey on horseback to the lodge – getting there is half the fun!

windows for viewing the feathered friends that come to visit. In case you want to brush up on your taxonomy, the lodge contains a library well stocked with wildlife reference books. Refer to Travel Information on its website for directions.

Villa Corcovado RESORT $$$
(☎8817-6969; www.villacorcovado.com; s/d incl meals US$385/770; P✳☎☀) Rincón seems an unlikely setting for a top-of-the-line resort, but you'll understand when you glimpse the 30 hectares of exquisite, unspoiled rainforest and the magnificent unobstructed vista of the Golfo Dulce. Eight light-filled, luxurious villas have private porches, wood-beamed ceilings and hardwood floors, and classy, contemporary decor. Gourmet meals (included) feature organic produce straight from the garden; you can request yours packed in a picnic to enjoy on a nearby deserted beach.

Suital Lodge LODGE $$
(☎8826-0342; www.suital.com; s/d/tr US$45/66/74) Lots of love has gone into the construction of this tiny clutch of *cabinas* on the northern shores of Golfo Dulce. It's situated on 30 hectares of hilly, forested property (not a single tree has been felled), and guests can take advantage of a network of trails that winds through the property and down to the beach. It's 15km northeast of Rincón.

❶ Getting There & Away

The easiest way to travel the eastern coast of the peninsula is by car. Otherwise, frequent buses ply the sole road between La Palma and Puerto Jiménez (US$0.50, 30 minutes).

Puerto Jiménez

With its ramshackle charms – a small airstrip, a fishing harbor, a few good *sodas* (cheap lunch counters) and a soccer field – Puerto Jiménez is something of a natural wonder in itself. Sliced in half by the swampy, overgrown Quebrada Cacao, and flanked on one side by the emerald waters of the Golfo Dulce, this untamed environment is shared equally by local residents and wildlife. While walking through the dusty streets of Port Jim (as the gringos are wont to call it), it's not unusual to spot scarlet macaws roosting on the soccer field, or white-faced capuchins swinging in the treetops adjacent to the main street.

Then again, it's not too hard to understand why Puerto Jiménez is brimming with wildlife, mainly because the town lies on the edge of Parque Nacional Corcovado. As the preferred jumping-off point for travelers heading to the famed Sirena ranger station, the town is a great place to organize an expedition, stock up on supplies, eat a hot meal and get a good night's rest before hitting the trails.

Indeed, Puerto Jiménez is known as the 'big city' in these parts, and here you'll find the region's largest and most diverse offering of hotels, restaurants and other tourist services. But don't be mistaken. Port Jim is very much a close-knit community at its core, and its small-town charm and languid pace are surprisingly infectious. While it is understandably difficult to resist the pull of the deep jungle just beyond, consider putting the brakes on and lingering here for a few days.

The compact, gridded and easily walkable 'downtown' is located to the west of the Río Platanares, which feeds a modest estuary and mangrove forest before reaching the Golfo Dulce. On the east side are the headquarters for Parque Nacional Corcovado and the airstrip. There is also a tiny access road leading to Playa Platanares, which is lined with a few upmarket properties.

History

Although it appears on maps dating to 1914, Puerto Jiménez used to be little more than a cluster of houses built on a mangrove swamp. With the advent of logging in the 1960s and the subsequent discovery of gold in the local streams, Jiménez became a small boomtown. The logging industry still operates in parts of the peninsula, but the gold rush has quietened down in favor of the tourist rush.

Even so, the town has a bit of a frontier feel, particularly in the low season, when locals huddle the local bars to wait out the downpour. Now, instead of gold miners descending on its bars on weekends, it's outdoors types who come to have a shot of *guaro* (local firewater) and brag about the snakes, sharks and alligators they've tousled with.

◎ Sights & Activities

Even though Corcovado is the central attraction, there are plenty of other diversions. Boat tours around the Golfo Dulce are also increasingly popular. The all-day outing often includes a mangrove tour, snorkeling excursion and dolphin-watching. Remember that it is illegal to swim with the dolphins,

DAY TRIPPER

You've got a free day in Port Jim and you don't want to hang around town? Here's what you can do:

» Take a trip to meet a local farmer or learn about rainforest medicine with Osa Wild (p365).

» Catch a wave and you're sittin' on top of the world. Check out the point break at Playa Pan Dulce in Cabo Matapalo (p369).

» Indulge your sweet tooth. See (and taste) where chocolate comes from at Finca Köbö (p362).

» Slow down and get some sun. Have a picnic on the deserted wilderness beach of Playa Blanca (p362).

despite your guide's best intentions. These outings are typically booked either through your accommodations, or by simply stopping by the waterfront and chartering your own boat and captain. As such, rates are variable depending on the nature of your trip.

Herrera Gardens &
Conservation Project   GARDENS
(☑2735-5267; admission US$5, 2hr guided tour US$15; ⊙6am-5pm) On the east side of the airstrip, Herrera Gardens and Conservation Project is a 250-acre reserve with beautiful botanical gardens. This innovative, long-term reforestation project offers an ecologically and economically sustainable alternative to cattle-grazing. Visitors can explore the 5km of garden trails or 15km of well-marked forest trails. Guided tours focus on birding, botany or even tree climbing! Stop by Jagua Arts & Crafts (☑tel, info 2735-5267; ⊙8am-5pm) (near the airstrip) to buy a map or arrange your tour.

Playa Platanares   BEACH
About 5km east of town, the secluded – and often deserted – Playa Platanares is excellent for swimming, sunning and recovering from too much adventure. The nearby mangroves of Río Platanares are a paradise for kayaking and bird-watching.

☞ Tours

Puerto Jiménez has a mess of tour operators, taxi drivers and barkers hungry for the tourist dollar. Ask lots of questions and choose carefully.

[TOP CHOICE] **Osa Wild**   ECOTOUR
(www.osawildtravel.com; Rte 245, downtown Puerto Jimenez; ecotours day tours from US$17) Get out a pen and underline this twice: Osa Wild is the way to connect with Corcovado park and Osa. Although it's a relatively young outfit,

it's just what the area so desperately needed: a resource for travelers to connect with community-oriented initiatives that go to the heart of the real Osa through homestays, farm tours and sustainable local cultural exchanges. Of course it also offers the more typical stuff like kayaking tours and guided trips through Corcovado (in fact Ifi, who's running the show, is a university-trained biologist and the best guide we've met in the region), but its focus on sustainability, environmental protection and community development leave it in a league of its own. It also sets up volunteer programs and rents tents and stoves for trips into the park. Amazing!

Aventuras Tropicales   ADVENTURE TOUR
(☑2735-5195; www.aventurastropicales.com) A Tico-run operation that offers all sorts of tropical adventures. It's southeast of the centre, on the way to Playa Platanares. Some of their most popular excursions include snorkeling and kayaking tours of the mangroves, which start at about $60 per person for half a day.

Escondido Trex   CANOEING, KAYAKING
(☑2735-5210; www.escondidotrex.com; Restaurant Carolina) Specializes in kayak tours, including mangrove paddles, night paddles, sunset tours and kayak-snorkel combos.

Osa Sportfishing   FISHING
(☑2735-5675; www.costa-rica-sportfishing.com; Restaurant Carolina) Transplanted Florida fishers who organize sportfishing vacations and dolphin- and whale-watching on the 50ft double-decker *Delfin Blanco*.

🛏 Sleeping

Puerto Jiménez is fairly quiet at most times of the year, though reservations are always a good idea on weekends and during busy

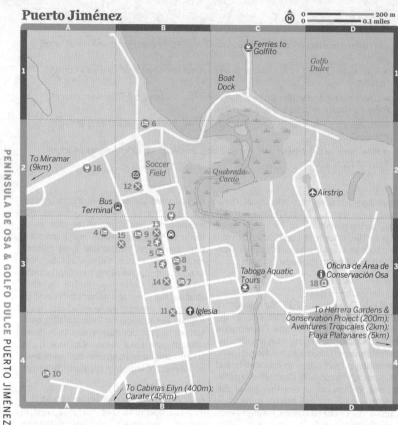

Puerto Jiménez

To Miramar (9km)

To Cabinas Eilyn (400m); Carate (45km)

Ferries to Golfito

Boat Dock

Golfo Dulce

Soccer Field

Quebrada Cacao

Bus Terminal

Airstrip

Taboga Aquatic Tours

Oficina de Área de Conservación Osa

To Herrera Gardens & Conservation Project (200m); Aventures Tropicales (2km); Playa Platanares (5km)

Iglesia

holiday times. Unlike other destinations in the Osa peninsula, backpackers and shoe-stringers are well catered for, and you'll find the greatest diversity of accommodations at the budget and midrange levels. Top-end options also abound, although they tend to be located on the outskirts of town.

Cacao Monkeys
CABINA $$

(☎2735-5248; www.cacaomonkeys.com; d incl breakfast US$60; P🅟🛜) On the fringes of downtown on a chocolate farm, this new joint has a set of five brightly painted wooden *cabinas,* each of a unique design, and an excellent riverside cafe (meals US$8). One *cabina* has a small kitchen, two are set up with a double and two single beds for families, and all have shiny hardwood floors and porches. It's a good option for families as it is a bit away from the noise of town and there's loads of wildlife right out the door.

Cabinas the Corner
HOSTEL $

(☎8362-8150; www.jimenezhotels.com/cabinas thecorner; dm/d US$10/12; P🛜) While this spare budget crash pad provides little more than a bed in a fan-cooled room for the night, the Corner is kept admirably clean and secure, and resultantly has a growing legion of devoted fans. Sure, when it pours, the corrugated metal roof sounds like a riot, but it'll do just fine if all you need is a bit of shut-eye before heading out to Corcovado, and this is as good a place as any to link up with other potential trekkers, form an expedition party and stock up on invaluable local advice. There's even a communal fridge where guests can store some cold ones. It's opposite the bus station.

Cabinas Back Packers
HOTEL $

(☎2735-5181; d with/without AC US$32/20) Puerto Jiménez has a burden of riches with budget digs, but this is among the best of the bunch – it's squeaky clean, relatively

Puerto Jiménez

quiet, situated directly next to the *colectivo* (collective car/truck) station leading to the park and just a bit out of the town, so you'll get a good night's sleep. There's a number of different options in a range of ammenities – some even have a television. It rents tents and camping gear and there's even a brightly tiled kitchen, available for a US$5 fee.

Cabinas Jiménez CABINA $$
(2735-5090; www.cabinasjimenez.com; s/d from US$35/50; P✸@) The efforts of the recent change in ownership are evident at this long-standing clutch of cabins. All of the rooms have jungle scenes painted on the walls, with underwater murals in the hot-water bathrooms. Refrigerators and safes are practical, while such details as carved wooden furniture, woven textiles and batik curtains add an elegant flair. The pricier rooms have fantastic views of the lagoon.

Iguana Lodge HOTEL $$$
(2735-5205; www.iguanalodge.com; casitas per person US$155, villas US$450; P✸) This luxurious lodge fronting Playa Platanares has the most architecturally alluring cabins in the area: four two-story bungalows have huge breezy decks, bamboo furniture, orthopedic beds draped in mosquito netting and lovely stone bathrooms with garden showers. Rates include three delectable meals a day: the creative cuisine is a highlight. If you're traveling in a large group, consider renting the three-room Villa Villa Kula, a charming tropical colonial house with a fully stocked kitchen.

Cabinas Oro Verde HOTEL $
(2735-5241; r per person US$15) Simple and central: this is what a solid budget hotel should be. Rooms are clean, if a little musty, and the bars on the windows are not pretty, but at least you know the place is safe. All in all, this is a good place to stumble back to late at night, but don't be surprised if you're woken up in the morning by early-bird shoppers. The best rooms are in front, with a terrace overlooking the street.

Cabinas Carolina CABINA $
(2735-5696; d with/without air-con US$40/35; ✸) The lack of windows makes this low-priced stalwart feel something like a concrete prison, but at least it's got air-con and a central location. The attached *soda,* Restaurant Carolina, is a Jiménez institution, so even if you're looking for something in a higher price bracket, don't miss the stellar *casados* (set meals) on offer here.

Cabinas Marcelina HOTEL $$
(2755-5286; Rte 245, Puerto Jimenez; d with/without air-con US$50/45; P✸) Marcelina's place is a long-standing favorite among budget travelers looking for a peaceful night of sleep. The concrete building is painted salmon pink and is surrounded by blooming trees, lending it a homey atmosphere that invites good dreams. Rooms have modern furniture, fluffy towels and tile bathrooms, which are certainly a welcome sight at this price range. It's near the Catholic church in downtown Puerto Jiménez.

Cabinas Eilyn CABINA $
(2735-5465; d incl breakfast with/without air-con US$40/35; P✸) Hospitality is a family affair at these quiet quarters on the edge of town. High ceilings, tile floors and a comfy porch enhance the decor of the four cozy *cabinas* that are attached to the Tico owners' home. Breakfast is a home-cooked meal of hearty *gallo pinto* (rice and beans) and fresh fruit.

PUERTO JIMÉNEZ FOR CHILDREN

Compared to Bahía Drake, the alternative access point for Parque Nacional Corcovado, Puerto Jiménez is much more family-friendly, mostly because of the wider range of goods and services. The simple fact that you're 'on-the-grid' can be very comforting to parents. Of course, Port Jim doesn't attract as many families as some of the more mainstream tourist destinations along the Central Pacific Coast and in the Nicoya peninsula, though children will nevertheless be well catered for here.

The wide range of sleeping listings gives you choice when it comes to comfort, quality and the all-important price. As a disclaimer, most of the budget options in town have some rough edges, but regardless of where you stay, there are plenty of activities on the roster.

✕ Eating

The restaurant scene in Puerto Jiménez is surprisingly subdued considering all the tourist traffic passing through. While there is no shortage of cheap *sodas* serving up typical Tico staples, for slightly fancier fare your options are much more limited.

TOP CHOICE Soda Veleria   SODA $
(Rte 245, Puerto Jiménez; mains US$3-8) Clean, cute and smack-dab in the middle of town, this *soda* is a dream – the kind of place you know is good because the local government workers all pile in at lunch. The heaping, fresh *casados* change daily and are delivered with fresh, homemade tortillas and sided with fresh fruit. Add sweet, considerate, quick service and Veleria is short-listed among our favorite *sodas* in all of Costa Rica.

Jade Luna   ICE CREAM $
(⊙10am-5pm) A glance at the tastes of the day – boutiquey, inventive flavors like dark chocolate bacon and key lime – and Jade Luna might seem a bit out of place in Port Jim, but the locally sourced, organic flavors are heaven after a sweaty hike in the park. Look for the stand along main street.

Pizzamail.it   PIZZERIA $$
(pizzas US$9-18; ⊙4-10:30pm; 🔊) Sure, most Costa Rican pizza are fairly pathetic affairs and it doesn't instill lots of confidence when you see a restaurant named after a website. Still, all doubts will be cast aside when a server at Pizzamail.it brings out the pie: a thin-crust, wood-fired piece of Italy in the middle of the jungle. From its small patio diners can watch squawking macaws in the trees over the soccer pitch. *Bellissimo!*

Restaurant Carolina   SOUTH AMERICAN $
(dishes US$3-8) This is the hub in Puerto Jiménez. Expats, nature guides, tourists and locals all gather here for food, drinks and plenty of carousing. The food is famous locally and the fresh-fruit drinks and cold beers go down pretty easily on a hot day.

Super Noventa y Sies   SELF-CATERING
(⊙9am-6pm) Stock up on food items, bug repellent and other necessities here.

🍷 Drinking

Juanita's   BAR
(⊙5pm-2am) You can get decent Mexican food at Juanita's, but it's more popular for the margaritas. One block south of the soccer field, just east of Rte 245.

Iguana Iguana   BAR
(⊙4pm-midnight) Iguana Iguana, at the cabins of the same name, is a popular watering hole, especially on weekends when the locals join in the action. On Rte 245, just west of downtown Puerto Jiménez.

ℹ Information

Oficina de Área de Conservación Osa (Osa Conservation Area Headquarters; 📞2735-5580; ⊙8am-noon & 1-4pm Mon-Fri) Information about Corcovado, Isla del Caño, Parque Nacional Marino Ballena and Golfito parks and reserves. Make reservations here to camp in Corcovado. It's on the east side of downtown, opposite the airstrip.

Banco Nacional de Costa Rica (⊙8:30am-3:45pm Mon-Fri) Due to completely inscrutable bureaucracy, money orders for the park must be purchased at this, the Banco Nacional de Costa Rica. It's opposite the church.

ℹ Getting There & Around

Air

NatureAir (www.natureair.com) and **Sansa** (www.sansa.com) have daily flights to/from San José; one-way flights are approximately US$130.

Alfa Romeo Aero Taxi (📞8835-3325, 2735-5178; www.alfaromeoair.com) has light aircraft (three and five passengers) for charter flights to Golfito, Carate, Drake, Sirena, Palmar Sur, Quepos and Limón. Prices are dependent on the number of passengers, so it's best to try to organize a larger group if you're considering this option. Sometimes, if there's already a trip planned into the park, this can be as low as US$60 per person.

Bicycle

Rent a bike at **Ciclo Corcovado** (☑2735-5429; per half-day US$8; ☺8am-5pm).It's located just east of Rte 245, on the north end of downtown.

Boat

Two passenger ferries travel to Golfito (US$6, 1½ hours), departing at 6am, noon and 2pm daily. Note that these times are subject to change; in this part of the country, schedules often fall prey to the whims of the captain.

A better option than chugging away on the ferries is to hire a private water taxi to shuttle you across the bay. You will have to negotiate, but prices are generally reasonable, especially considering that you'll be free of having to rely on the ferry. Fortunately, waters in the Golfo Dulce are sheltered and generally calm, though it's still good to have a reasonable degree of faith in the seaworthiness of both your captain and his ship before you set out.

Taboga Aquatic Tours (☑2735-5265) runs water taxis to Zancudo for about US$50. You can also hire a boat from Ronnie, a salty captain who charges about US$360 for a day for tours of the bay. Ask for him at the marina or try him on 8628-7550.

Bus

Most buses arrive at the peach-color terminal on the west side of town. All of these pass La Palma (23km away) for the eastern entry into Corcovado.

San Isidro US$7; five hours; departs 1pm.

Neily US$5; three hours; departs 5:30am and 2pm.

San Isidro de El General US$7; five hours; departs 1pm.

San José, via San Isidro de El General (Autotransportes Blanco Lobo) US$12; eight hours; departs 5am and 11am.

Car & Taxi

Colectivo Transportation (☑8837-3120, 8832-8680; Soda Deya) runs a collective truck service to Cabo Matapalo (1½ hours, US$6) and Carate (3 hours, US$10) on the southern tip of the national park. Departures are from Soda Deya at 6am and 1:30pm, returning at 8:30am and 4pm.

Otherwise, you can call and hire a 4WD taxi from **Taxi 348** (☑8849-5228; taxicorcovado@

racsa.co.cr) or from the **Central Taxi Center** (☑2735-5481). Taxis usually charge up to US$80 for the ride to Carate, up to US$50 for the ride to Matapalo, and more than US$100 for the overland trek to Drake.

You can also rent a vehicle from **Solid Car Rental** (☑2735-5777).

Cabo Matapalo

Matapalo isn't so much a village as it is a loose string of buildings at the the the tip of the Osa peninsula and the entrance to Golfo Dulce, almost completely obscured by jungle. It lies just 17km south of Puerto Jiménez, but this heavily forested and beach-fringed cape is a vastly different world, and can be very hard to reach. A network of trails traverses the foothills, which are uninhabited except for migrating wildlife from the Reserva Forestal Golfo Dulce. Along the coastline, miles upon miles of beaches in pristine wilderness are virtually empty, except for handfuls of surfers in the know.

Although facilities in this remote corner are extremely limited, Cabo Matapalo is home to a number of luxurious lodges that cater to travelers searching for peace and seclusion. Of course, it's hard to feel lonely out here given the breadth of animals about: scarlet macaw, brown pelican and all breeds of heron are frequently sighted on the beaches, while four species of monkey, sloth, coati, agouti and anteater roam the woods.

From the Puerto Jiménez–Carate road, the turnoff for Cabo Matapalo is on the left-hand side, through a crumbling white cement gate (called 'El Portón Blanco').

Those who intended to surf their way down the country will find expert waves at Playa Pan Dulce. The best swell is from the south and it can be surfed at all tides. Sometimes, they reach double-overhead height.

⟲ Tours

Psycho Tours   ADVENTURE TOUR
(Everyday Adventures; ☑8353-8619; www.psychotours.com) Naturalist Andy Pruter runs Psycho Tours, which offers high-adrenaline adventures in Cabo Matapalo. His signature tour is tree climbing (US$55 per person): scaling a 60m ficus tree, aptly named 'Cathedral.' Also popular – and definitely adrenaline inducing – is waterfall rappelling

(US$85) down cascades ranging from 15m to 30m. For the tamer of heart, excellent three- to four-hour guided nature walks (US$45) tap into Andy and his staff members' extensive knowledge base.

🛏 Sleeping

This area is off the grid, so many places do not have electricity around the clock or hot water. Reservations are recommended in the dry season (mid-December to mid-April). Prices given are high-season rates; prices include three meals, unless otherwise stated.

TOP CHOICE Lapa Ríos   LODGE $$$
(☑2735-5130; www.laparios.com; road to Carate, Km 17; s/d US$470/720; ℗😎) A few hundred meters beyond El Portón Blanco along the road to Carate, this top-notch all-inclusive wilderness resort combines the right amount of luxury with a rustic, tropical ambience. Scattered over the site are 16 spacious, thatched bungalows, all decked out with queen-sized beds, bamboo furniture, garden showers and private decks with panoramic views. An extensive trail system allows exploration of the 400-hectare reserve, while swimming, snorkeling and surfing are at your doorstep. As one of the select few hotels in Costa Rica to earn five leaves in the government-run Certified Sustainable Tourism program, Lapa Ríos also serves as a living classroom. If you need substantial proof that ecotourism can be a profitable and successful vehicle for ensuring wilderness preservation and empowering local communities with increased economic opportunities, look no further.

Ojo del Mar   BUNGALOW $$$
(☑2735-5531; www.ojodelmar.com; s/d incl breakfast from US$65/110; ℗) Tucked in amid the windswept beach and the lush jungle, this is a little plot of paradise. The six beautifully handcrafted bamboo bungalows are entirely open-air, allowing for all the natural sounds and scents to seep in (thatch roofs and mosquito nets provide protection from the elements). Solar power provides electricity in the *casa grande* (main house). Hammocks swing from the palms, while howler monkeys swing above. Rates include breakfast, but Niko – co-owner and cook – also serves an excellent, all-organic dinner. Look for this gem on the road to Carate, just before the Buena Esperanza Bar.

Ranchos Almendros   CABINA $$$
(Kapu's Place; ☑2735-5531; http://home.earthlink.net/~kapu/; r per person from US$$100; ℗) This is the end of the line on Cabo Matapalo, where the road stops pretending and turns into a sandy beach path. The property includes three cozy *cabañas* that are equipped with solar power, large screened windows, full kitchens and garden showers. As per the name, 'Almond Tree Ranch' is part of an ongoing project dedicated to the reforestation of Indian almond trees to create habitat for the endangered scarlet macaw.

El Remanso Lodge   LODGE $$$
(☑2735-5569; www.elremanso.com; road to Carate, Km 18; s/d from US$180/300; ℗😎) Set on 56 hectares of rainforest, El Remanso is a tropical paradise. Constructed entirely from fallen tropical hardwoods, the secluded, spacious and sumptuous cabins have shiny wood floors and beautifully finished fixtures. Several units have folding French doors that open to unimpeded vistas of the foliage and the ocean in the distance.

🍴 Eating & Drinking

Most hotels and lodges also have small shops that sell snacks and drinks and all the high-end places have options to include all meals. If you're planning on hiking, be sure to stock up on lots of fresh water as well as your favorite form of trail mix – once you're out in the woods or on the beach, options are decidedly limited.

Buena Esperanza Bar   BAR
(☑2735-5531; road to Carate; meals US$5-15; ⏱9am-midnight) About 1km before El Portón Blanco, you'll find a tropical hangout called the Buena Esperanza Bar, a festive, open-air bar on the east side of the road. The limited menu includes lots of sandwiches and vegetarian items, plus a full bar. It's Cabo Matapalo's only place to eat or drink, and so often attracts a decent crowd of locals, resident expats and tourists. There's even a disco ball.

ℹ Getting There & Away

If you are driving, a 4WD is highly recommended – even in the dry season – as roads frequently get washed out. There are several shallow rivers to cross on the way here. Otherwise, the transport *colectivo* will drop you here; it passes by at about 6:30am and 2pm heading to Carate, and 10am and 5:30pm heading back to Jiménez. A taxi will come here from Port Jim for about US$30.

Carate

If you make it all the way here, congratulations. A bone-rattling 45km south of Puerto Jiménez, this is where the dirt road rounds the peninsula and comes to an abrupt dead end. There's literally nothing more than an airstrip and a *pulpería* (corner store). Carate is nothing to see by itself, but it is the southwestern gateway for anyone hiking into Sirena ranger station in Parque Nacional Corcovado.

A handful of recommended wilderness lodges in the area make a good night's rest for travelers heading to/from Corcovado. The ride from Puerto Jiménez to Carate is also an adventure in itself as the narrow, bumpy dirt road winds its way around dense rainforest, through gushing rivers and across windswept beaches. Birdlife and other wildlife are prolific along this stretch: keep your eyes peeled and hang on tight.

🛏 Sleeping & Eating

Many places in Carate don't have 24-hour electricity or hot water. Reservations are recommended in the dry season – communication is often through Puerto Jiménez, so messages may not be retrieved every day. High-season rates are quoted; prices are per person, including three meals, unless otherwise stated. For shoestringers, the best option is to camp in the yard in front of the *pulpería*. The owner is a surly old guy who will charge you about US$5 a day to camp in his yard.

West of Carate is the national park, so if you're planning on hiking into Corcovado, you must be self-sufficient from here on out. The *pulpería* is the last chance you have to stock up on food and water.

🌿 **La Leona Eco-Lodge**   ECOLODGE $$$
(☎2735-5704; www.laleonaecolodge.com; s/d from US$95/180; P☒) On the edge of Parque Nacional Corcovado 2km west of the *pulpería*, this friendly lodge offers all the thrills of camping, without the hassles. Sixteen comfy forest-green tents are nestled between the palm trees, with decks facing the beach. All are fully screened and comfortably furnished; solar power provides electricity in the restaurant. Behind the accommodations, 30 hectares of virgin rainforest property offer opportunities for waterfall hiking, horseback riding and wildlife-watching.

Lookout Inn   HUT $$$
(☎2735-5431; www.lookout-inn.com; r per person from US$115; P@☒) A deep wilderness retreat, Lookout Inn has comfortable quarters with mural-painted walls, hardwood floors, beautifully carved doors and unbeatable views. Accommodations are in 'tiki huts,' which are open-air, A-frame huts accessible only by a wooden walkway winding through the giant joba trees (prime bird-watching territory). Behind the inn, 360 steps – known as the 'Stairway to Heaven' – lead straight up the side of the mountain to four observation platforms and a waterfall trail. And here's an interesting twist: if you don't spot a scarlet macaw during your stay, your lodging is free!

Luna Lodge   LODGE $$$
(☎in USA 888-409-8448, 8380-5036; www.lunalodge.com; s/d US$120/210; P) A steep road goes through the Río Carate and up the valley to this enchanting mountain retreat, located about 2km north of the *pulpería*. Taking full advantage of the vista, the high-roofed, open-air restaurant is a marvelous place to indulge in the delights of the gardens and orchards on the grounds. Seven spacious, thatch-roof bungalows each have a huge garden shower and private patio. The open-air meditation studio is nothing less than inspirational.

❶ Getting There & Away

NatureAir (www.natureair.com) and **Alfa Romeo Aero Taxi** (www.alfaromeoair.com) offer charter flights. Prices are dependent on the number of passengers, so it's best to try to organize a larger group if you're considering this option. If you're with others, the rate can be as low as US$60.

Transportation Colectivo (US$13; ⊙3 hours) departs Puerto Jiménez for Carate at 6am and 1:30pm, returning at 8:30am and 4pm. Note that the *colectivo* often fills up on its return trip to Puerto Jiménez, especially during the dry season. Arrive at least 30 minutes ahead of time or you might find yourself stranded.

Alternatively, catch a taxi from Puerto Jiménez (US$80). If you are driving, you'll need a 4WD – even in the dry season as there are a couple of river crossings. Assuming you don't have valuables in sight, you can leave your car at the *pulpería* (per night US$5) or at any of the tented camps along the road (with prior arrangements) and hike to La Leona station (1½ hours).

IMAGEBROKER / LONELY PLANET IMAGES ©

1. Parque Nacional Isla del Cocos (p395)

Some of the world's best diving can be found off the Isla del Cocos.

2. Pavones (p393)

This southernmost point of Costa Rica is a legendary surf destination.

3. Bahía Drake (p375)

This bay was named after Sir Francis Drake, who visited the area in March 1579.

DAVE AND SIGRUN TOLLERTON / ALAMY ©

TO CORCOVADO VIA BAHÍA DRAKE

One of the principal overland routes to Parque Nacional Corcovado, the Bahía Drake route starts in the Valle de Diquis, near the town of Sierpe, at the northern base of the Península de Osa. From here, the valley stretches west to the basin of the Río Grande de Térraba and south to Sierpe, from where the Río Sierpe flows out to Bahía Drake. Although most travelers make a direct route between Sierpe, Drake and Corcovado park, those who take the slow route may also take in the Humedal Nacional Térraba-Sierpe, a vast reserve that protects an amazinsg array of jungle swampland and overgrown mangroves. Where shoestringers can rough it overland via Puerto Jiménez, this route in is a bit better for folks who want to explore the jungle with a few more comforts.

Sierpe

This sleepy village on the Río Sierpe is the gateway to Bahía Drake, and if you've made a reservation with any of the jungle lodges further down the coast, you will be picked up here by boat. Beyond its function as a transit point, there is little reason to spend any more time here than it takes for your captain to arrive, though fortunately you won't have to if you time the connection right.

The Centro Turístico Las Vegas (⊘6am-10pm), next to the boat dock, is a catch-all place for tourist information, distributing a wide selection of maps and brochures. It also offers internet access and serves a broad range of food to waiting passengers.

If you get stuck for the night, the only real accommodations option in town is Hotel Oleaje Sereno (☎2786-7580; www.hoteloleaje sereno.com; s/d from US$45/70; ℙ❋). This surprisingly nice little motel has a prime dockside location overlooking the Río Sierpe, and is home to pleasant rooms with wood floors, sturdy furniture and crisp, mismatched linens. The open-air restaurant is one of Sierpe's most welcoming, with linen tablecloths and lovely river views. You can safely and conveniently lock your car in its nearby lot for US$6 a night.

Scheduled flights and charters fly into Palmar Sur, 14km north of Sierpe. If you are heading to Bahía Drake, your lodge will make arrangements for the boat transfer.

If for some reason things go awry, there is no shortage of water taxis milling about, though you will have to negotiate to get a fair price. Buses to Palmar Norte (US$6, 30 minutes) depart from in front of Pulpería Fenix at 5:30am, 8:30am, 10:30am, 12:30pm, 3:30pm and 6pm. A taxi to Palmar costs about US$30.

Humedal Nacional Térraba-Sierpe

The Ríos Térraba and Sierpe begin on the southern slopes of the Talamanca mountains and flow toward the Pacific Ocean. Once near the sea, however, they form a network of channels and waterways that weave around the country's largest mangrove swamp. This river delta comprises the Humedal Nacional Térraba-Sierpe, which protects approximately 330 sq km of wetland and is home to red, black and tea mangrove species. The reserve also protects a plethora of birdlife, especially waterbirds such as herons, egrets and cormorants.

The Térraba-Sierpe reserve has no facilities for visitors, though lodges can organize tours to help you explore the wetlands.

🛏 Sleeping

Unless you're in Sierpe for an all-inclusive bird-watching escape, it's best to press on to Drake.

Veragua River House   B&B $$
(☎2788-1460; www.hotelveragua.com/en; r from US$55; ℙ❋) This memorable bed and breakfast is centered on a Victorian-style river house that is hidden behind blooming hibiscus and shady fruit trees. Inside are inviting common areas decked out with antique furnishings and original artwork, and there is even a mock period library, a pool table and a discrete plunge pool. Guests stay in the four garden bungalows, which feature hand-painted tiles that are the work of the talented owner. The B&B is 3km north of Sierpe along the road to Palmar, and can easily be reached by car. If you don't have private transportation, ring the lodge and arrange for a pick-up.

🍴 Sábalo Lodge   LODGE $$$
(☎2770-1457; www.sabalolodge.com; r per person from US$125) Accepting only a dozen guests at a time in order to maximize the chance of getting up close and personal with wildlife,

FLOATING FOREST

As many as seven different species of *manglar* (mangrove) thrive in Costa Rica. Comprising the vast majority of tropical coastline, mangroves play a crucial role in protecting it from erosion. Mangroves also serve as a refuge for countless species of animals, especially fish, crab, shrimp and mollusks, and as a sanctuary for roosting birds seeking protection from terrestrial predators.

Mangroves are unique among plants in that they have distinct methods for aeration (getting oxygen into the system) and desalination (getting rid of the salt that is absorbed with the water). Red mangroves, which are the most common species in Costa Rica, use their web of aboveground prop roots for aerating the plant's sap system. Other species, such as the black mangrove, have vertical roots that stick out above the mud, while buttonwood mangroves have elaborate buttresses.

The most amazing feature of the mangrove is its tolerance for salt, which enables the plant to thrive in brackish and saltwater habitats. Some species, such as the Pacific coast black mangrove, absorb the salinated water, then excrete the salt through their leaves and roots, leaving behind visible crystals. Other species filter the water as it is absorbed – the mangrove root system is so effective as a filter that the water from a cut root is drinkable!

Despite their ecological importance, mangrove habitats the world over are being increasingly threatened by expanding human habitats. Furthermore, mangrove wood is an easily exploitable source of fuel and tannin (used in processing leather), which has also hastened their destruction. Fortunately in the Humedal Nacional Térraba-Sierpe, this fragile yet vitally important ecosystem is receiving the respect and protection that it deserves.

this highly personalized lodge receives much love from our readers. Guests are treated to a variety of activities, including guided hikes, horseback riding and ocean kayaking, and a portion of your accommodation fee helps to fund a local school. The lodge is accessible only by boat, and transportation from Sierpe is included in the package price.

Río Sierpe Lodge LODGE $$$
(☎2253-5203, 8384-5595; www.riosierpelodge. com; 3-day package incl meals & tours per person from US$305) The Río Sierpe's namesake lodge is nestled in this remote spot near where the river meets the sea. Breezy rooms with hardwood floors overlook the waterways that wind through the Sierpe delta, while hiking trails radiate from the lodge into the surrounding primary forest. Transportation from Sierpe is included in the price as the lodge is accessible only by boat.

Bahía Drake

As one of the Costa Rica's most isolated destinations, Bahía Drake is a veritable Lost World filled with tropical landscapes and abundant wildlife. In the rainforest canopy, howlers greet the rising sun with their haunting bellows, while pairs of macaws soar between the treetops, filling the air with their cacophonous squawking. Offshore in the bay itself, schools and pods of migrating dolphins flit through turquoise waters.

Of course, one of the reasons why Bahía Drake is brimming with wildlife is that it remains largely cut off from the rest of the country. With little infrastructure beyond dirt roads and the occasionally used airstrip, most of the area remains off the grid. However, Bahía Drake is home to a number of stunning wilderness lodges, which all serve as ideal bases for exploring this veritable ecological gem. And of course, if you're planning on visiting Sirena ranger station in Corcovado, you can trek south along the coastline and enter the park at San Pedrillo ranger station, though this route is long and difficult and, at the time of research, closed due to overgrown trails. If you're visiting the area on a shoestring, the best bet is to stay in Agujitas.

The shores of Bahía Drake are home to two settlements: Agujitas, a tiny town of 300 residents spread out along the southern shore of the bay, and Drake, a few kilometers to the north, which is little more than a few houses alongside the airstrip.

Bahía Drake & Around

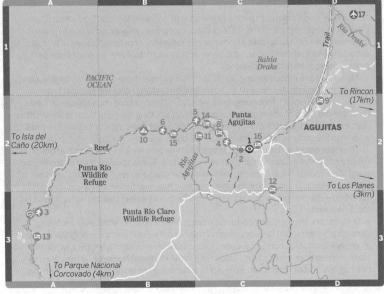

Agujitas is a one-road town (and not a very good road at that). It comes south from Rincón and past the airstrip in Drake. At the T, the right branch dead-ends at the water, where the **pulpería** (grocery store), **clinic** and **school** constitute the heart of Agujitas; the left branch heads out of town southeast to Los Planes. From the eastern end of Agujitas, a path follows the shoreline out of town. A swinging, swaying pedestrian bridge crosses the Río Agujitas to Punta Agujitas. From here, the trail picks up and continues south along the coast, all the way to Parque Nacional Corcovado.

The only way to get around the area is by boat or by foot. Fortunately, both forms of transportation are also recreation, as sightings of macaws, monkeys and other wildlife are practically guaranteed.

History

The bay is named for Sir Francis Drake himself, who visited this area in March 1579, during his circumnavigation in the *Golden Hind*. History has it that he stopped on the nearby Isla del Caño, but locals speculate that he probably landed on the continent as well. A monument at Punta Agujitas, located on the grounds of the Drake Bay Wilderness Resort (currently undergoing a remodel), states as much.

Activities

Hiking

All of the lodges offer tours to Parque Nacional Corcovado, usually a full-day trip to San Pedrillo ranger station (from US$85 to US$150 per person), including boat transportation, lunch and guided hikes. Indeed, if you came all the way to the Península de Osa, it's hard to pass up a visit to the national park that made it famous.

Some travelers, however, come away from these tours disappointed. The trails around San Pedrillo station attract many groups of people, which inhibit animal sightings. Furthermore, most tours arrive at the park well after sunrise, when activity in the rainforest has already quietened down.

Considering their hefty price tag, these tours are not necessarily the most rewarding way to see wildlife. The lodges strongly encourage their guests to take these tours (because they are obviously moneymakers), but you have other options.

The easiest and most obvious one is the long coastal trail that heads south out of Agujitas and continues about 10km to the border of the national park. Indeed, a determined hiker could make it all the way to San Pedrillo ranger station on foot in three to four hours (make sure you reserve a spot

Bahía Drake & Around

at the ranger station if you intend to spend the night). At the time of research, rangers were strongly discouraging this route as it was overgrown. From here, you might make the coastal route south to wildlife-rich Sirena ranger station, but river crossings and long stretches in the sun make this difficult, and rangers discourage it.

In addition to Corcovado, other popular day trips include nearby Playa San Josecito, a stunningly remote beach. Additional nearby options include Punta Río Claro Wildlife Refuge (also called the Marenco Rainforest Reserve), which can be accessed from the Río Claro trail or from Playa San Josecito.

Swimming & Snorkeling

About 20km west of Agujitas, Isla del Caño is considered the best place for snorkeling in this area. Lodges offer day trips to the island (US$80 to US$100 per person), usually including the park fee, snorkeling equipment and lunch, and a guided island hike in the afternoon. The clarity of the water and the variety of the fish fluctuate according to water and weather conditions: it's worth inquiring before dishing out the cash for a tour.

There are other opportunities for snorkeling on the coast between Agujitas and Corcovado. Playa San Josecito attracts scores of colorful species, which hide out among the coral reef and rocks. Another recommended spot is Playa Las Caletas, just in front of the Corcovado Adventures Tent Camp, and Playa Cocalito, a small, pretty beach that is near Agujitas and is pleasant for swimming and sunbathing.

Scuba Diving

Isla del Caño is one of Costa Rica's top spots for diving, with attractions including intricate rock and coral formations and an amazing array of underwater life, teeming with colorful reef fish and incredible coral formations. Divers report that the schools of fish swimming overhead are often so dense that they block the sunlight from filtering down.

While the bay is rich with dive sites, a local highlight is undoubtedly the Bajo del Diablo (Devil's Rock), an astonishing formation of submerged mountains that attracts an incredible variety of fish species, including jack, snapper, barracuda, puffer, parrotfish, moray eel and shark.

A two-tank dive runs from US$120 to US$150 depending on the spot, or you can do an open-water course for US$350 to US$450. Most of the upscale lodges in the area either have on-site dive centers or can arrange trips and courses through a neighboring lodge.

Kayaking & Canoeing

A fantastic way to explore the region's biodiversity is to paddle through it. The idyllic Río Agujitas attracts a huge variety of birdlife and lots of scaly reptiles. The river conveniently empties out into the bay, which is surrounded by hidden coves and sandy beaches ideal for exploring in a sea kayak. Paddling at high tide is recommended because it allows you to explore more territory. Most accommodations in the area have kayaks and canoes for rent for a small fee.

Sportfishing

Bahía Drake claims more than 40 fishing records, including sailfish, marlin, yellowfin tuna, wahoo, cubera snapper, mackerel and roosterfish. Fishing is excellent year-round, although the catch may vary according to the season. The peak season for tuna and marlin is from August to December.

PENÍNSULA DE OSA & GOLFO DULCE BAHÍA DRAKE

Sailfish are caught year-round, but experience a slowdown in May and June. Dorado and wahoo peak between May and August. Other species are abundant year-round, so you are virtually assured to reel in something. Many lodges can arrange fishing excursions, but you need to be prepared to pay heavily – half-/full-day excursions cost around US$600/1000.

Dolphin- & Whale-Watching

Bahía Drake is rife with marine life, including more than 25 species of dolphin and whale that pass through on their migrations throughout the year. This area is uniquely suited for whale-watching: humpback whales come from both the northern and the southern hemispheres to calve, resulting in the longest humpback whale season in the world. Humpbacks can be spotted in Bahía Drake year-round (except May), but the best months to see whales are late July through early November.

Several of the lodges are involved with programs that protect and preserve marine life in Bahía Drake, as well as programs that offer tourists a chance for a close encounter. Tours generally cost about US$100 per person. Note that since 2006, it is no longer legal to swim along with dolphins.

Canopy Tours

Original Canopy Tour OUTDOORS
(☑8371-1598; admission US$55; ☺8am-4pm) At Hotel Jinetes de Osa, the Original Canopy Tour has nine platforms, six cables and one 20m-observation deck from where you can get a new perspective on the rainforest. Tours take two to three hours.

☞ Tours

Corcovado Expeditions BOAT TOUR
(☑8818-9962; www.corcovadoexpeditions.net) Offers competitively priced tours to Corcovado and Isla del Caño, as well as a wide variety of specialty hikes including unique excursions to look for rare tropical birds and poison-dart frogs. The office is located between the clinic and the school.

Night Tour ECOTOUR
(☑8382-1619;www.thenighttour.com;toursUS$35; ☺7:45am-10pm) Tracie the 'Bug Lady' has created quite a name for herself with this fascinating nighttime walk in the jungle. Tracie is a walking encyclopedia on bug facts, and not just the boring scientific detail – one of her fields of research is the

military use of insects! Participants use night-vision scopes as an added bonus. Make reservations well in advance.

🛏 Sleeping & Eating

This area is off the grid, so many places do not have electricity. Reservations are recommended in the dry season (mid-December to mid-April).

While budget and midrange options are available, accommodations in Bahía Drake are heavily skewed toward the top end. But you can expect tremendous quality and service for your dollars, especially as you ascend the price ladder. Those on a tight budget should stay in Agujita, where there are several spare backpacker-oriented places.

High-season rates are quoted; prices include three meals, unless otherwise stated. Stand-alone eating options are virtually nonexistent in this part of the peninsula.

Most hotels and lodges also have small shops with snacks and drinks.

All of the midrange and top-end accommodations listed in this section provide transportation (sometimes free, sometimes not) from either Agujitas or the airstrip in Drake with prior arrangements.

For other accommodations, check out the stretch of coastline from Bahía Drake to Corcovado.

[TOP CHOICE] Cabinas Murillo CABINA $
(☑2256-2748; www.drakecorcovadocabins.com; per person with/without bay view US$20/15) Hands down the best value at the lower end of the budget range, this family-run place has simple, tidy rooms that are right in the middle of Drake. It's the rooms up on the hillside that are the best, though: for only a few dollars more guests get a balcony overlooking the entire bay, perfect for whale-watching.

Aguila de Osa Inn LODGE $$$
(☑2296-2190; www.aguiladeosa.com; s/d 2-night package US$623/1048) On the east side of the Río Agujitas, this swanky lodge consists of roomy quarters with shining wood floors, cathedral ceilings and private decks overlooking the ocean. The vast centerpiece of the lodge, however, is the comfortable yet elegant open-air *rancho* (small house-like building), which serves signature cocktails and innovative snacks. Diving and sportfishing charters are available to guests, as are significant discounts if you extend your stay beyond two nights.

Drake Bay Rainforest Chalet   CABINA $$$
(☎8382-1619; www.drakebayholiday.com; 3-/4-/5-/6-/7-day package per person from US$1150/1275/1400/1525/1650) Set on 18 hectares of pristine rainforest, this jungle getaway is a remote, romantic adventure. Huge French windows provide a panoramic view of the surrounding jungle, enjoyed from almost every room in the house. Sleeping quarters have a king-sized bed with giant mosquito net, flanked by a luxurious tile bathroom with a sunken shower and a decadent two-person hot tub. In an innovative twist on luxury, the Moroccan-themed kitchen is fully stocked for self-catering, though chef service is available for the culinarily impaired.

Pura Vida Drake Bay   CABINA $
(☎8720-0801; www.puravidadrakebay.com; d US$20; ☎) This economical option in the middle of town is a great bet for shoestringers who are entering the park via Bahía Drake. The owner, Martina, offers a few fan-cooled rooms and has a wealth of infomation about boat rides. She also can arrange a variety of tours into the park and the on-site *soda* is one of the best options in town.

Finca Maresia   BUNGALOW $$
(☎8832-6730; www.fincamaresia.com; s/d US$28/40, standard/superior bungalow US$85) After traveling the world for more than 20 years, the owners of this absolute gem of a hotel decided to settle down in their own veritable slice of paradise. Here amid a large *finca* that stretches across a series of hills, Finca Maresia beckons to shoestringers and budget travelers alike by offering a combination of low prices, high value and good design sense. All seven rooms overlook lush environs, and play a near-continuous audio track of jungle sounds. Beyond the show-stopping natural setting, the good taste of the owners is evident as you walk from room to room and view the transition from modernist glass walls to Japanese-style sliding rice-paper doors.

Hotel Jinetes de Osa   HOTEL $$$
(☎2236-5637, 8371-1598, in USA 800-317-0333; www.costaricadiving.com; s/d from US$66/110) Ideal for divers, the reasonably priced Jinetes de Osa boasts a choice bayside location that is literally a few steps from the ocean – you can sip your morning coffee from your hotel room while staring out across the bay. Jinetes also has a canopy tour, as well as one of the peninsula's top PADI (Professional Association of Diving Instructors) dive facilities, which means that guests have plenty of adrenaline-soaked activities on the roster. In fact, true diving aficionados would balk at staying elsewhere, especially since discount packages with full equipment rental are always available.

Cabinas El Mirador Lodge   CABINA $$
(☎8836-9415; www.miradordrakebay.com; per person from US$80; P☎) High on a hill at the northern end of Agujitas, El Mirador (Lookout Point) lives up to its name, offering spectacular views of the bay from its eight cozy cabins – catch the sunset from the balcony, or climb to the lookout that perches above. The hospitable Vargas family ensures all guests receive a warm welcome, as well as three square meals a day of hearty, home-cooked Costa Rican fare.

La Paloma Lodge   LODGE $$$
(☎2239-7502; www.lapalomalodge.com; 3-/4-/5-day package per person from US$1100/1245/1390; ☎) Perched on a lush hillside, this exquisite lodge provides guests with an incredible panorama of ocean and forest, all from the comfort of the sumptuous, stylish quarters. Rooms have shiny hardwood floors and queen-sized orthopedic beds, draped in mosquito netting, while shoulder-high walls in all the bathrooms offer rainforest views while you bathe. Each room has a large balcony (with hammock, of course) that catches the cool breeze off the ocean.

ⓘ Information

It's not easy to visit Bahía Drake if you're a backpacker since only a few shoestring options exist in Agujitas. Also, supplies, food and just about everything else are shipped in, which is reflected in local prices. However, Bahía Drake is one destination where parting with a bit of cash can greatly improve the quality of your experience.

ⓘ Getting There & Away
Air

Departing from San José, **NatureAir** (www.natureair.com) and **Sansa** (www.sansa.com) have daily flights to the **Drake airstrip**, which is 2km north of Agujitas. Prices vary according to season and availability, though you can expect to pay around US$130 to/from San José.

Alfa Romeo Aero Taxi (☎2735-5353; www.alfaromeoair.com) offers charter flights connecting Drake to Puerto Jiménez, Golfito, Carate and Sirena. Flights are best booked at the airport in person, and one-way fares are typically less than US$100.

Most lodges provide transportation to/from the airport, which involves a jeep or a boat or both, but advance reservation is necessary.

Boat

Unless you charter a flight, you'll arrive here by an exhilarating boat ride through mangrove channels and the ocean. It's one of the true thrills of visiting the area. Boats travel along the river through the rainforest and the mangrove estuary. Captains then pilot boats through tidal currents and surf the river mouth into the ocean. All of the hotels offer boat transfers between Sierpe and Bahía Drake with prior arrangements. Most hotels in Drake have beach landings, so be sure to wear appropriate footwear.

If you have not made advance arrangements with your lodge for a pick-up, you can always grab a private water taxi in Sierpe for a negotiable price.

Bus & Car

A rough dirt road links Agujitas to Rincón, from where you can head south to Puerto Jiménez or north to the Interamericana. A 4WD is absolutely necessary for this route, especially from June to December, as there are several river crossings. The most hazardous crossing is the Río Drake, and locals fish many a water-logged tourist vehicle out of the river. Even high-clearance 4WD vehicles have difficulty.

Once in Agujitas, you will likely have to abandon your car as most places are accessible only by boat or by foot. As theft or vandalism is always a very real possibility in Costa Rica, you should park your car in a secure place, and pay someone to watch it for a few days. There are several small *pulperías* where the management would be happy to watch over your 4WD for a nice tip.

If you are hiking through Parque Nacional Corcovado but you want to avoid the arduous San Pedrillo trail, you can hire a 4WD vehicle to La Palma (US$50 to US$75) and start the hike there. In theory, a bus also goes to La Palma, departing Drake at 4am during the dry season only, but it's best to inquire locally as it's not reliable.

Hiking

From Bahía Drake, it's a four- to six-hour hike along the beachside trail to San Pedrillo ranger station at the north end of Corcovado. If you are heading into the park, try to arrange reservations to camp at the ranger stations in advance through the office (p368) in Puerto Jiménez. Camping at this station isn't all that popular, so it's unlikely you'll be turned away due to lack of space. This part of the trail to San Pedrillo is open (with just the part from San Pedrillo to Sirena closed).

Bahía Drake to Corcovado

This craggy stretch of coastline is home to sandy inlets that disappear at high tide, leaving only the rocky outposts and luxuriant rainforest. Virtually uninhabited and undeveloped beyond a few tourist lodges, the setting here is magnificent and wild. If you're looking to spend a bit more time along the shores of Bahía Drake before penetrating the depths of Parque Nacional Corcovado, consider a night or two in some of the country's most remote accommodations.

The only way to get around the area is by boat or by foot, which means that travelers are more or less dependent on their lodges.

◉ Sights & Activities

A public trail follows the coastline for the entire spectacular stretch, and it's excellent for spotting wonderful wildlife. Among the multitude of bird species, you're likely to spot (and hear) squawking scarlet macaw, often traveling in pairs, and the hooting chestnut-mandible toucan. White-faced capuchin and howler monkeys inhabit the treetops, while eagle-eyed hikers might also spot a sloth or a kinkajou.

Scenic little inlets punctuate this entire route, each with a wild, windswept beach. Just west of Punta Agujitas, a short detour off the main trail leads to the picturesque Playa Cocalito (p377), a secluded cove perfect for sunning, swimming and body surfing. With no lodges in the immediate vicinity, it's often deserted. Playa Las Caletas (p377), in front of the Corcovado Adventures Tent Camp, is excellent for snorkeling.

Further south, the Río Claro empties out into the ocean. Water can be waist-deep or higher and the current swift, so take care when wading across. This is also the start of the Río Claro trail, which leads inland into the 400-hectare Punta Río Claro Wildlife Refuge (formerly known as the Marenco Rainforest Reserve) and passes a picturesque waterfall along the way. Be aware that there are two rivers known as the Río Claro: one is located near Bahía Drake, while the other is inside Corcovado near Sirena station.

South of Río Claro, the Playa San Josecito (p377) is the longest stretch of white-sand beach on this side of the Península de Osa. It is popular with swimmers, snorkelers and sunbathers, though you'll rarely find it crowded.

POISON DARTS & HARMLESS ROCKETS

Traversed by many streams and rivers, Corcovado is a hot spot for exquisitely beautiful poison-dart frogs. Two species here, the granular poison-dart frog and the Golfo Dulce poison-dart frog, are Costa Rican endemics – the latter occurs only in and around Corcovado. A search of the leaf litter near Sirena ranger station readily turns up both species, as well as the more widespread green and black poison-dart frog.

You might also find some other members of the family that have one important difference: they're not poisonous! Called rocket frogs because of their habit of launching themselves into streams when disturbed, they are essentially poison-dart frogs without the poisonous punch.

The difference is likely in their diets. Poison-dart frogs have a diet dominated by ants, which are rich in alkaloids, and are thought to give rise to their formidable defenses. Rocket frogs also eat ants but in lower quantities, and rely instead on their astounding leaps to escape predation. They also lack the dazzling warning colors of their toxic cousins.

From here you can access another private reserve, La Selva. A short, steep climb leads from the beach to a lookout point, offering a spectacular view over the treetops and out to the ocean. A network of trails continues inland, and eventually connects La Selva to the Río Claro reserve. Be advised that La Selva does not have any facilities: the trails are not labeled; there is no water or maps; you'll likely meet nobody along the way. If you choose to continue past the lookout point, make sure you have food, water and a compass.

The border of Parque Nacional Corcovado is about 5km south of here (it takes three to four hours to hike the entire distance from Agujitas to Corcovado). The trail is more overgrown as it gets closer to the park, and in the months after the rainy season it can close completely. Ask a lot of questions at the ranger station before embarking on this difficult route.

Sleeping & Eating

Reservations are recommended in the dry season (mid-December to mid-April). High-season rates are quoted; prices include three meals, unless otherwise stated. Many places in this area don't have electricity (pack a flashlight) or hot water. Stand-alone eating options are virtually nonexistent in this part of the peninsula.

With prior arrangements, all of the accommodation places listed in this section provide transportation (free or for a charge) from either Agujitas or the airstrip in Drake.

If you are putting the trip together on your own, you can get supplies in town; there are a couple small shops selling canned goods and snacks. Anything more elaborate will have to be brought in with you.

TOP CHOICE **Las Caletas Lodge** LODGE $$$
(☑8381-4052, 8326-1460; www.caletas.cr; r per person from US$70; @☎) This adorable little hotel is set on the picturesque beach of the same name and consists of five cozy wooden cabins that are awash with sweeping views. The Swiss–Tico owners are warm hosts who are passionate about environmental sustainability, and provide solar and hydroelectric power around the clock. The most economical way to stay is in your own tent; the lodge has covered camping platforms.

Guaria de Osa LODGE $$$
(☑2235-4313, in USA 510-235-4313; www.guaria deosa.com; per person US$100) Cultivating a new-age ambience, this Asian-style retreat center offers yoga, tai chi and all kinds of massage, along with the more typical rainforest activities. The lovely grounds include an ethnobotanical garden, which features exotic local species used for medicinal and other purposes. The architecture of this place is unique: the centerpiece is the Lapa Lapa Lounge, a spacious multistory pagoda, built entirely from reclaimed hardwood.

Proyecto Campanario CAMPGROUND $$$
(☑2258-5778; www.campanario.org; 4-day package per person US$475) Run by a former Peace Corps volunteer, this biological reserve is more of an education center than a tourist facility, as evidenced by the dormitory, library and field station. Behind the main facility, five spacious platform tents with

'garden' bathrooms offer a bit more privacy and comfort. Ecology courses and conservation camps are scheduled throughout the year, but individuals are also invited to take advantage of the facilities. The whole place is set on 150 hectares of tropical rainforest, which provides countless opportunities for exploration and wildlife observation. For information on arranging transportation to get here, contact the lodge directly.

Corcovado Adventures
Tent Camp　　　　　CAMPGROUND $$$

(☑8384-1679; r per person from US$80; 🐾) Less than an hour's walk from Drake brings you to this rugged family-run spot. It's like camping but comfy: spacious, walk-in tents are set up on covered platforms and fully equipped with sturdy wood furniture. Twenty hectares of rainforest offer plenty of opportunity for exploration, and the beachfront setting is excellent for water sports.

Casa Corcovado Jungle Lodge　　LODGE $$$

(☑2256-3181, in USA 888-896-6097; www.casa corcovado.com; 3-day package per person from US$895; 🐾) A spine-tingling boat ride takes you to this luxurious lodge on 175 hectares of rainforest bordering the national park. Each bungalow is tucked away in its own private tropical garden, and artistic details including antique Mexican tiles and handmade stained-glass windows make the Casa Corcovado one of this area's classiest accommodation options. Guests can also stretch their legs at any time on the lodge's extensive network of trails, which pass a number of watering holes. On site, the Margarita Sunset Bar lives up to its name, serving up 25 different 'ritas and great sunset views over the Pacific. Discounts are available for longer stays.

❶ Getting There & Away

Boat

All of the hotels offer boat transfers between Sierpe and Bahía Drake with prior arrangements. If you haven't made advance arrangements with your lodge for a pick-up, grab a private water taxi in Sierpe for a negotiable price.

Hiking

From Bahía Drake, it's a four- to six-hour hike along the beachside trail to San Pedrillo ranger station at the north end of Corcovado. Note that this trail can be impassable and overgrown depending on the season. If you're heading into the park, make sure you have reservations to camp at the ranger stations.

Reserva Biológica Isla del Caño

The centerpiece of this biological reserve is a 326-hectare island that is the tip of numerous underwater rock formations. Along the rocky coastline, towering peaks soar as high as 70m, which provide a dramatic setting for anyone who loves secluded nature.

The submarine rock formations are among the island's main attractions, drawing divers to explore the underwater architecture. Snorkelers can investigate the coral and rock formations along the beach right in front of the ranger station. Fifteen different species of coral have been recorded, as well as threatened species that include the Panulirus lobster and the giant conch. The sheer numbers of fish attract dolphins and whales, which are frequently seen swimming in outer waters. Hammerhead sharks, manta rays and sea turtles also inhabit these waters.

A steep but well-maintained trail leads inland from the ranger station. Once the trail plateaus, it is relatively flat, winding through evergreen forest to a lookout point at about 110m above sea level. These trees are primarily milk trees (also called 'cow trees' after the drinkable white latex they exude), believed to be the remains of an orchard planted by pre-Columbian indigenous inhabitants. Near the top of the ridge, there are several pre-Columbian granite spheres. Archaeologists speculate that the island may have been a ceremonial or burial site for the same indigenous tribes.

Camping is prohibited, and there are no facilities except a ranger station by the landing beach. Most visitors arrive on tours arranged by the nearby lodges; admission is US$10 per person, plus a US$4 additional charge for divers, although this fee is usually included in your tour price.

PARQUE NACIONAL CORCOVADO

Famously labeled by *National Geographic* as 'the most biologically intense place on earth,' this national park is the last great original tract of tropical rainforest in Pacific Central America. The bastion of biological diversity is home to Costa Rica's largest population of scarlet macaws, as well as countless other endangered species, including Baird's tapir, the giant anteater and the world's largest bird of prey, the harpy eagle. Corcovado's amazing biodiversity has long attracted a devoted stream of visitors who descend from Bahía Drake and Puerto Jiménez to explore the remote location and spy on a wide array of wildlife.

History

Because of its remoteness, Corcovado remained undisturbed until loggers invaded in the 1960s. The destruction was halted in 1975 when the area was established as government-administered parklands. In the early days park authorities had limited personnel and resources to deal with illegal clear-cutting, poaching and gold mining, the latter of which was causing severe erosion in the park's rivers and streams. By 1986 the number of gold miners had exceeded 1000, which promptly caused the government to evict them (and their families) entirely from the park.

Illegal logging has all but subsided, primarily since tourism has led to an increased human presence in the park. Furthermore, a coalition of organizations – including Conservation International, the Nature Conservancy and the World Wildlife Fund – have banded together to help organize and fund the park's antipoaching units.

Since 2003 Corcovado has – much to the chagrin of Minae (the Ministry of Environment and Energy) – remained stagnant on the 'tentative list' of Unesco World Heritage Sites. While no official disclosure has been released as to the reason behind the park's perennial failure to achieve recognition, local media speculates that mismanagement, poor funding and the inability to control illegal poaching may be contributing factors.

🏃 Activities

Wildlife-Watching

The best wildlife-watching in Corcovado is at Sirena, but the coastal trails have two advantages: they are more open, and the constant crashing of waves covers the sound of noisy walkers. White-faced capuchin, red-tailed squirrel, collared peccary, white-nosed coati and northern tamandua are regularly seen on both of the following trails.

On the less-traveled San Pedrillo–Sirena trail, Playa Llorona is a popular nesting spot for marine turtles, including leatherback, olive ridley and green turtles. Nesting turtles attract ocelot, jaguar and other predators, though they are hard to spot. While planning to make this hike, inquire with rangers as this trail can be closed seasonally when it gets overgrown.

Both coastal trails – the San Pedrillo–Sirena trail and the Carate–Sirena trail – produce an endless pageant of birds. Pairs of scarlet macaws are guaranteed, as the tropical almond trees lining the coast are a favorite food. The sections along the beach shelter mangrove black hawk by the dozens and numerous waterbird species.

A BEGINNER'S GUIDE TO PARQUE NACIONAL CORCOVADO

There are two major centers where tourists tend to organize their expeditions: Bahía Drake and Puerto Jiménez. Both of these areas are home to hotels, lodges and tour operators.

Each area has its own draw, though Puerto Jiménez is better for independent travelers and those on a budget, since it's connected via public transportation almost all the way to the Sirena ranger station, where most of the wildlife action happens. Bahía Drake has most elegant all-inclusive options along the coast and is much more remote. Most through-hikes start or end in Puerto Jiménez.

If you start the trek from Bahía Drake, you can hike to the San Pedrillo ranger station or take a boat to Sirena (the latter of these is a common option for the all-inclusive lodges). If you start the trek from Puerto Jiménez, you bus or taxi to Carate and hike to Sirena, or arrange for transport to La Leona or Los Patos ranger station, both of which are good bases for accessing Sirena.

A third option for accessing the park is to fly direct to the airstrips in either Carate or Sirena. This option is a bit more expensive, but it can be a huge time-saver if you're dealing with a time-crunched itinerary.

Be advised that if you're planning on sleeping in Corcovado, you must register in advance with the park office (p368) in Puerto Jiménez. This can be done either in person, by phone or often through your tour operator.

PENÍNSULA DE OSA & GOLFO DULCE PARQUE NACIONAL CORCOVADO

The Los Patos–Sirena trail attracts lowland rainforest birds such as great curassow, chestnut-mandibled toucan, fiery-billed aracari and rufous piha. Encounters with mixed flocks are common. Mammals are similar to those near coastal trails, but Los Patos is better for primates and white-lipped peccary.

For wildlife-watchers frustrated at the difficulty of seeing rainforest mammals, a stay at Sirena ranger station is a must. Baird's tapirs are practically assured – that is a statement that can be made at few other places in the world. This endangered and distant relative of the rhinoceros is frequently spotted grazing along the airstrip after dusk. Sirena is excellent for other herbivores, particularly red brocket (especially on the Los Platos–Sirena trail) and both species of peccary. Agouti and tayra are also common.

Jaguars are spotted very rarely, but have been seen near the airstrip in the early hours of the day. At night look for kinkajou and crab-eating skunk (especially at the mouth of the Río Sirena). Ocelot represents your best chance for observing a cat but, again, it's difficult.

Corcovado is the only national park in Costa Rica with all four of the country's primate species. Spider monkey, mantled howler and white-faced capuchin can be encountered anywhere, while the Los Platos–Sirena trail is best for the fourth and most endangered species, the Central American squirrel monkey. Sirena also has fair chances for the extremely hard-to-find silky anteater, a nocturnal animal that frequents the beachside forests between the Río Claro and the station.

The Río Sirena is a popular spot for American crocodile, three-toed sloth and bull shark.

Hiking

Paths are primitive and the hiking is hot, humid and insect-ridden, but the challenge of the trek and the interaction with wildlife at Corcovado are thrilling. Hiring a local

CORCOVADO WILDLIFE

As one of the most biologically intense places on earth, Parque Nacional Corcovado is absolutely teeming with wildlife. Just to get you excited for the trek ahead, we've prepared a few top picks for the best (and worst) of Corcovado wildlife.

Lucky to See

» **Jaguar** These elusive felines sit at the top of nearly everybody's rainforest wish list, though you're going to need an incredible amount of luck to spot one in the wild.

» **Ocelot** Of Corcovado's feline predators, these medium-sized cats are the most spotted – they're largely ground-lovers, and tend to stick to the trails.

» **Tapir** You don't have to wish very hard to spot these lumbering giants at Sirena station, though their commonness in Corcovado isn't a true reflection of the general population figure.

Lucky Not to See

» **Fer-de-lance** Known as a *terciopelo* in Costa Rica, the true bushmaster of Corcovado is not to be toyed with.

» **Bullet ant** Sitting alongside the tarantula hawk wasp as one of most pain-inducing biting insects, these enormous ants are best given a wide berth and a lot of respect.

» **Ticks** Approaching megalithic sizes in Corcovado; it's inevitable that you're going to pick up a few dozen, but hopefully they'll stick to where the sun does shine.

Pushing Your Luck

» **Crocodile** One of nature's oldest and most efficient predators, the crocodile is an amazing sight to behold, given that you're on the land and they're mostly in the water.

» **Peccary** Something akin to a tropical boar, these surly swine are best observed from the lofty heights of a tree, allowing you to view their antics from a safe distance.

» **Army ant** The infamous insect army can be heard crunching its way through the forest, so you'd be wise to give them the right of way.

Hiking in Parque Nacional Corcovado

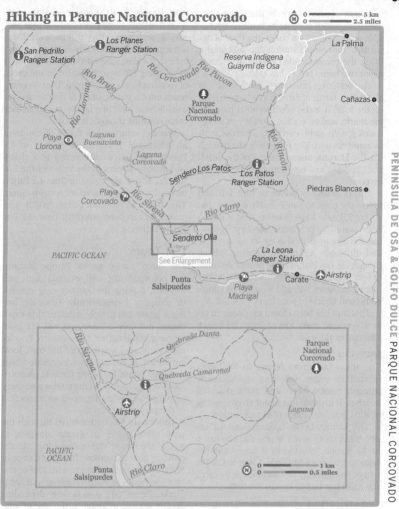

guide – to help spot wildlife and avoid getting lost – is highly recommended. Otherwise, travel in a small group. Carry plenty of food, water and insect repellent. And always verify your route with the rangers before you depart.

The most popular route traverses the park from Los Patos to Sirena, then exits the park at La Leona (or vice versa). This allows hikers to begin and end their journey in or near Puerto Jiménez, offering easy access to La Leona and Los Patos. The trek between Sirena and San Pedrillo is difficult, both physically and logistically.

Hiking is best in the dry season (from December to April), when there is still regular rain but all of the trails are open. It's still muddy, but you won't sink quite as deep.

SIRENA TO SAN PEDRILLO & LOS PLANES

The route between Sirena and San Pedrillo/Los Planes is the longest trail in Corcovado. The vast majority of this hike is along the beach, which means loose sand and little shade – grueling, especially with a heavy pack. One local guide recommends starting this hike at night in order to avoid the hot sun.

Another tricky factor is the three river crossings, which become difficult or impossible at high tide. As a result, the time of departure from Sirena station depends on the tides; the recommended departure time is about two hours before low tide.

The first river crossing – Río Sirena – is about 1km north of Sirena. The largest river on the hike, it is the neighborhood hangout for sharks and crocodiles, and it can sometimes spawn swift currents, so cross with extreme caution. The final river, the cascading Río Llorona, marks the end of the beach trail, and lies just before the trail splits and diverges.

Hikers generally prefer to turn left and follow the coast to San Pedrillo, a route that covers 23km in 10 to 15 hours, and is awash with stunning beachside scenery. Following the coastline is also easier to navigate and ultimately safer than heading inland, though the Los Planes route is most definitely less trafficked and more wild. Detouring inland, however, will add a couple of kilometers (and hours) to your hike.

This trail has been closed randomly in recent years, so make lots of inquiries before attempting the hike.

SIRENA TO LA LEONA

The 16km hike from Sirena to La Leona is another sizzler, following the shoreline through coastal forest and along deserted beaches. It involves one major river crossing at Río Claro, just south of Sirena station.

The journey between Sirena and La Leona takes six or seven hours. You can camp at La Leona; otherwise, it takes another hour to hike the additional 3.5km to Carate, where you can stay in a local lodge or catch the collective taxi to Puerto Jiménez.

SIRENA TO LOS PATOS

The route to Los Patos goes 18km through the heart of Corcovado, affording the opportunity to pass through plenty of primary and secondary forest. The trail is relatively flat for the first 12km. You will hike through secondary forest and wade through two river tributaries before reaching the Laguna Corcovado. From this point, the route undulates steeply (mostly uphill!) for the remaining 6km. One guide recommends doing this hike in the opposite direction – from Los Patos to Sirena – to avoid this exhausting, uphill ending. Near Los Patos, a lovely waterfall provides a much-needed shower at the end of a long trek.

The largest herds of peccary are reportedly on this trail. Local guides advise that peccary sense fear, but they will back off if you act aggressively. Alternatively, if you climb up a tree – about 2m off the ground – you'll avoid being bitten or trampled in the event of running into a surly bunch. Hint: peccary herds emit a strong smell of onions, so you usually have a bit of a heads-up before they come crashing through the bush.

You can camp at Los Patos, or continue an additional 14km to the village of La Palma. This four-hour journey is a shady and muddy descent of the valley of the Río Rincón. If you are traveling from La Palma to Los Patos, be prepared for a steep climb. The Danta Corcovado Lodge (p363) also makes an excellent overnight near the Los Patos station.

☞ Tours

The main routes across Parque Nacional Corcovado are well marked and well traveled, making the journey easy enough to complete independently. However, hiring a guide can greatly enhance this experience, not only because you will not have to worry about taking a wrong turn. Besides their intimate knowledge of the trail, local guides are amazingly knowledgeable about flora and fauna, including the best places to spot various species. Many guides also carry telescopes, allowing for up-close inspection of the various creatures.

Guides are most often hired through the park office (p368) in Puerto Jiménez, at any of the ranger stations heading into the park, or near the airstrip in either Carate or Sirena. You can also inquire with tour operators and hotels in Puerto Jiménez and Bahía Drake. Prices vary considerably depending on the season, availability, the size of your party and the type of expedition you want to arrange. In all cases, you will need to negotiate a price includes of park fees, meals and transportation.

Because of inconsistency, it's difficult to recommend a particular agency or guide as things change quickly in this part of the country. Additionally, reports from travelers detailing life-changing and life-threatening experiences in Corcovado are common, which means that this is one destination where it pays to put the book down and trust your gut.

Professionalism is best assessed by using your common sense – simply put, ask yourself whether or not this is the kind of person you would trust your life with. Professional guides are also usually outfitted with modern and well-maintained gear, and are quick to reassure travelers of the length and breadth of their experience.

On that note, the final factor in choosing a guide is park knowledge. No matter how many guidebooks you've read or maps you've studied, Corcovado can be a tricky place to access. Before choosing your guide, talk to them about your intended route, and be sure that they are knowledgeable about the trek ahead.

🛏️ Sleeping & Eating

Camping costs US$4 per person per day at any station; facilities include potable water and latrines. Sirena station has a covered platform, but other stations have no such luxuries. Remember to bring a flashlight or a kerosene lamp, as the campsites are pitch black at night. Camping is not permitted in areas other than the ranger stations.

Simple dormitory lodging (US$15) and meals are available at Sirena station only. Here, you'll find a vinyl mattress and simple bunk beds. We have had reports that this station had a bed-bug problem, so camping on one of the platforms is recommended. The station serves excellent meals (breakfast costs US$20, dinner is US$25). Other than that, you're on your own. Food and cooking fuel have to be packed in, so reserve as far in advance as possible through the Oficina de Área de Conservación Osa (p368) in Puerto Jiménez. Scientists and researchers working at the Sirena biological station get preference over travelers for accommodations and meals, but if you secure a reservation, you will be taken care of.

Otherwise, campers must bring all their own food. Note that ranger stations face a challenge with trash disposal, so all visitors are required to pack out all of their trash.

❶ Information

Information and maps are available at the **Oficina de Área de Conservación Osa** (☏2735-5580; park fee per person per day US$10; ⊙8am-noon & 1-4pm) in Puerto Jiménez. Contact this office to make reservations for lodging and meals at all of the ranger stations and to pay your park fee. Be sure to make these arrangements a few days in advance as facilities are limited, and they do fill up on occasion in the dry season.

Park headquarters are at Sirena ranger station on the coast in the middle of the park. Other ranger stations are located on the park boundaries: San Pedrillo station in the northwest corner on the coast; the new Los Planes station on the northern boundary (near the village of the same name); La Leona station in the southeast corner on the coast (near the village of Carate); and Los Patos ranger station in the northeast corner (near the village of La Palma).

Always check with rangers before setting out about trail conditions and possible closures (especially during the wettest months, from June to December).

❶ Getting There & Away

From Bahía Drake

From Bahía Drake, you can walk the coastal trail that leads to San Pedrillo station (about four hours from Agujitas), or any lodge can drop you here as a part of their regular tours to Corcovado. Alternatively, you can consider heading inland to the Los Planes station, though this is a longer, more heavily forested route. The route from San Pedrillo to Sirena is tough going – if it is open at all. During the time of research, just after the rainy season, the trail was overgrown and closed, though rangers expect it to reopen in the dry season.

You can also charter a boat to San Pedrillo (US$80 to US$125) or Sirena (US$135 to US$180). If you have a car, most hotels and lodges along Bahía Drake can watch over it for you for a few dollars a day.

From La Palma

From the north, the closest point of access is the town of La Palma, from where you can catch a bus or taxi south to Puerto Jiménez or north to San José.

Heading to Los Patos, you might be able to find a taxi to take you partway; however, the road is passable only by 4WD vehicles (and not always), so be prepared to hike the 14km to the ranger station. The road crosses the river about 20 times in the last 6km. It's easy to miss the right turn shortly before the ranger station, so keep your eyes peeled.

If you have a car, it's best to leave it with a hotel or lodge in La Palma instead of traversing the route to Los Patos, though it certainly is an adventure. Furthermore, once in Los Patos, there is no reliable place to park your car while trekking in the park.

From Carate

In the southeast, the closest point of access is Carate, from where La Leona station is a one-hour, 3.5km hike west along the beach.

Carate is accessible from Puerto Jiménez via a poorly maintained, 45km dirt road. This journey is an adventure in itself, and often

BAIRD'S TAPIR PROJECT

The Baird's Tapir Project (http://savetapirs.org) has been studying the populations of Baird's tapir around Sirena station since 1994 in the hope of enhancing conservation efforts. Scientists use radio telemetry (that's radio collars to us) to collect data about where the tapirs live, how far they wander, whom they associate with and how often they reproduce. So far, several dozen tapirs around Sirena are wearing collars, which allows scientists to collect the data without disrupting the animals.

Sirena station is an ideal place to do such research, because there is no pressure from deforestation or hunting, which gives researchers the chance to observe a healthy, thriving population. The animals' longevity and slow rate of reproduction mean that many years of observation are required before drawing conclusions.

So, what have we learned about these river rhinos so far? The nocturnal animals spend their nights foraging – oddly, they prefer to forage in 'disturbed habitats' (like along the airstrip), not in the dense rainforest. They spend their days in the cool waters of the swamp, out of the hot sun. Tapirs are not very social, but a male–female pair often shares the same 'home range,' living together for years at a time. Scientists speculate that tapirs may in fact be monogamous – who knew these ungainly creatures would be so romantic!

allows for some good wildlife-spotting along the way. A 4WD *colectivo* travels this route twice daily for US$10. Otherwise you can hire a 4WD taxi; prices depend on the size of your party, the season (prices increase in the rainy months) and your bargaining skills.

If you have your own car, the *pulpería* in Carate is a safe place to park for a few days, though you'll have some extra peace of mind if you tip the manager before setting out.

By Air

Alfa Romeo Aero Taxi (2735-5353; www. alfaromeoair.com) offers charter flights connecting Puerto Jiménez, Drake and Golfito to Carate and Sirena. Flights are best booked at the airport in person, and one-way fares are typically less than US$100. Note that long-term parking is not available at any of these locations, so it's best to make prior arrangements if you need to leave your car somewhere.

GOLFO DULCE

While Golfo Dulce is less celebrated than the Península de Osa, an increasing number of travelers are making the arduous journey in search of the world's longest left-hand break at Pavones. The region is also home to Parque Nacional Piedras Blancas, a stunning tract of rainforest that used to be part of Corcovado, and still protects the same amazing biodiversity. This far corner of Costa Rica is also home to significantly large indigenous populations, which live in the Reserva Indígena Guaymí de Conte Burica near Pavones.

Golfito

A rough-and-ready little city with a long and sordid history, Golfito is a ramshackle port that stretches out along the Golfo Dulce. The town was built on bananas – the United Fruit Company moved its regional headquarters here in the '30s. In the 1980s, declining markets, rising taxes, worker unrest and banana diseases forced the company's departure.

In an attempt to boost the region's economy, the federal government built a duty-free facility, the so-called Zona Americana, in Golfito. This surreal shopping center attracts Ticos from around the country, who descend on the otherwise dying town for 24-hour shopping sprees. Unless you count this shopping center, Golfito has no attractions whatsoever. And as charmless as it is by day, by night the place is home to surly ex-military men, boozy yachters, prostitutes and goons.

Still, as the largest town in Golfo Dulce, Golfito is a transportation hub for hikers heading to Corcovado, surfers heading to Pavones and sportfishers. Although it's unlikely that you'll want to stick around for any longer than you have to, there is a certain charm to the crooked buildings and long-faded facades of Golfito. Plus, the verdant slopes of the Refugio Nacional de Fauna Silvestre Golfito surround the town, providing a picturesque backdrop to the crumbling buildings.

The southern part of town is where you find most of the bars and businesses, including a seedy red-light district. Nearby is the so-called Muellecito (Small Dock), from where the daily ferry to Puerto Jiménez departs. The northern part of town was the old United Fruit Company headquarters, and it retains a languid, tropical air, with its large, veranda-decked homes. Now, the Zona Americana is home to the airport and the duty-free zone.

◎ Sights

Refugio Nacional de Fauna Silvestre Golfito
OUTDOORS

(☑MINAE Office in Golfito 2775 2620; park fee US$10) The small, 28-sq-km reserve encompasses most of the steep hills surrounding Golfito, though it's poorly publicized and easy to miss. It was originally created to protect the town's watershed, though it also protects a number of rare and interesting plant species. It is home to several cycads, which are 'living fossils,' and are regarded as the most primitive of plants. The reserve also attracts a variety of tropical birds, four species of monkey and several small mammals.

There are no facilities for visitors, save a gravel access road and a few poorly maintained trails, but for those who don't have the time or ability to hike in Corcovado, it provides a quick alternative. About 2km south of the center of Golfito, a gravel road heads inland, past a soccer field, and winds 7km up to some radio towers (Las Torres) 486m above sea level. This access road is an excellent option for hiking, as it has very little traffic.

A very steep hiking trail leaves from Golfito, almost opposite the Samoa del Sur hotel. A somewhat strenuous hike (allow about two hours) will bring you out on the road to the radio towers. The trail is easier to find in Golfito than at the top.

Finally, there are several trails off the road to Playa Cacao. Hikers on these routes will be rewarded by waterfalls and views of the gulf. However, the trails are often obscured, so it's worth asking locally about maps and trail conditions before setting off.

Playa Cacao
BEACH

Just a hop, skip and a jump across the bay, this small beach offers a prime view of Golfito stretched out along the coast, with the rainforest as a backdrop. If you're stuck in Golfito for the day, Playa Cacao is perhaps the most appealing spot from which to enjoy the old port. To reach the beach, catch a water taxi from Golfito for around US$12 per person. You can also get to Playa Cacao by walking or driving about 6km along a dirt road west and then south from the airport – a 4WD is recommended.

⚓ Activities

Sportfishing & Yachting

Golfito is home to several full-service marinas that attract coastal-cruising yachters. If you didn't bring your own boat, you can hire local sailors for tours of the gulf at any of the docks. You can fish year-round, but the best season for the sought-after Pacific sailfish is from November to May.

Banana Bay Marina
FISHING

(☑2775-0255; www.bananabaymarina.com) Charters can be arranged, and a full day of all-inclusive fishing starts at around US$750.

⌁ Sleeping

Note that the area around the soccer field in town (not far east of the Muellecito) is Golfito's red-light district, so you'd be wise to spend a few more dollars and stay elsewhere. Domestic tax-free shoppers are required to spend the night in Golfito, so hotel rooms can be in short supply on weekends and during holiday periods.

Casa Roland Marina Resort
RESORT $$$

(☑2775-0180; www.casarolandgolfito.com; d from US$192; P❋@☎☒) A brand-new construction in the Zona Americana, the Casa Roland is now Golfito's most swish hotel, and primarily caters to duty-free shoppers looking for an amenity-laden base. You can expect to find all the usual top-end standards including a swimming pool, restaurants and bars, tennis courts and a health spa, as well as a few extras such as a movie theatre and a casino. Rooms themselves lack the character typically found at this price range, but they're by far the most comfortable in town.

Cabinas y Marisquería Princesa de Golfito
CABINA $

(☑2775-0442; s/d US$15/25; ☎) If you get stuck in Golfito and you're watching your budget, this cozy little red-roofed house is the best option. The rooms aren't too fancy – they have fans and tile floors, firm beds and mismatched linens – but it is safe, homey and secure. Plus, if you're on your way in or out of one of the nearby parks, it has a laundry service for a small fee. The cabinas are located in the southern part of town, on Rte 14. Look for them on the bay side.

Samoa del Sur HOTEL **$**
(☎2775-0233, 2775-0264; www.samoadelsur.com; r from US$40; P❋@🅿🏊) This French-run facility offers handsome lodgings that are outfitted with tiled floors, stylish wood furniture and thick towels. The bar, with its huge dome ceiling, is a popular spot in the evenings, when guest congregate to throw darts and a big-screen television blasts music videos. The on-site swimming pool might be a bit run down, but you can watch the yachts roll in and out of the harbor while doing laps. It's near the Muellecito.

✗ Eating & Drinking

The small, walkable district of the Pueblo Civil has about a dozen *sodas* of reputable quality.

Restaurante Buenos Días BREAKFAST **$$**
(meals US$5-10; ⏱6am-10pm; P) Rare is the visitor who passes through Golfito without stopping at this cheerful spot opposite the Muellecito. Brightly colored booths, bilingual menus and super-convenient location ensure a constant stream of guests – whether for an early breakfast, a typical Tico *casado* or a good old-fashioned burger.

Rancho Grande COSTA RICAN **$**
(meals US$7-12) About 3km south of Golfito, this rustic, thatched-roof place serves country-style Tico food cooked over a wood stove. Margarita, the Tica owner, is famous for her *patacones* (fried plantain chips). Her hours are erratic, so stop in during the day to let her know you're coming for dinner.

8° Latitude BAR
(meals US$6-12) Northwest of the soccer field, this popular expat bar is frequented by Americans who divide their time between sportfishing and boozy gossip. Its laid-back and friendly atmosphere makes it the perfect place to tipple a few and listen to fish tales.

ⓘ Information

Immigration Office (☎2775-0423; ⏱8am-4pm) Situated away from the dock, in a 2nd-floor office above Soda Pavas.

Port Captain (☎2775-0487; ⏱7:30am-11am & 12:30pm-4pm Mon-Fri) Opposite the large Muelle de Golfito (where yachters check in when arriving).

ⓘ Getting There & Away

Air
The airport is 4km north of the town center near the duty-free zone. **NatureAir** (www.natureair.com) and **Sansa** (www.sansa.com) have daily flights to/from San José. One-way tickets are approximately US$100.

Boat
There are two main boat docks for passenger service: the **Muellecito** is the main dock in the southern part of town. There is a smaller dock north of the Muelle Bananero (opposite the **ICE building**) where you'll find the **Asociación de Boteros** (Abocap; ☎2775-0357), an association of water taxis that can provide service anywhere in the Golfo Dulce area.

Two passenger ferries travel to Puerto Jiménez from the Muellecito (US$6, 1½ hours), departing at 6am and 10am daily. Note that these times are subject to change; in this part of the country, schedules often fall prey to the whims of the captain.

A better option than chugging away on the ferries to Puerto Jiménez is to hire a private water taxi to shuttle you across the bay. You'll have to negotiate, but prices are usually between US$20 and US$30 a person (sometimes with US$50 minimum).

The boat taxi for Zancudo (US$6, 45 minutes) departs from the dock at Samoa del Sur hotel at noon, Monday through Saturday. The return trip is at 7am the next day (except Sunday). If you're staying at a coastal lodge north of Golfito and you've made prior arrangements for transportation, the lodge will pick you up at the docks.

Bus
Most buses stop at the depot opposite the small park in the southern part of town.

Neily US$1.30; 1½ hours; departs hourly from 6am to 7pm.

Pavones US$5; three hours; departs 10am and 3pm. This service may be affected by road and weather conditions, especially in the rainy season.

San José, via San Isidro de El General (Tracopa) US$11; seven hours; departs from the terminal near Muelle Bananero at 5am and 1:30pm.

Zancudo US$5; three hours; departs 1:30pm.

ⓘ Getting Around

City buses and collective taxis travel up and down the main road of Golfito. Although the payment system seems incomprehensible to anyone else but the locals, it shouldn't cost you more than a few coins.

Parque Nacional Piedras Blancas

Formerly known as Parque Nacional Esquinas, this national park was established in 1992 as an extension of Corcovado. Piedras Blancas has 120 sq km of undisturbed tropical primary rainforest, as well as 20 sq km of secondary forests, pasture land and coastal cliffs and beaches.

As one of the last remaining stretches of lowland rainforest on the Pacific, Piedras Blancas is also home to a vast array of flora and fauna. According to a study conducted at the biological station at Gamba, the biodiversity of trees in Piedras Blancas is the densest in Costa Rica, even surpassing Corcovado.

🏃 Activities

Wildlife-Watching

Because Piedras Blancas is so remote and so little visited, it is the site for several ongoing animal projects, including the reintroduction of scarlet macaws with the hopes of establishing a self-sustaining population, as well as the reintegration of wild cats like ocelot and margay, which were confiscated from private homes. Look for all of the wildlife that you might see in Corcovado: big cats and all four species of monkey, herds of collared and white-lipped peccary, crocodiles, various species of poison-dart frogs (including the endemic Golfo Dulce poison-dart frog) and more than 330 species of bird.

🛏 Sleeping

TOP CHOICE Esquinas Rainforest Lodge LODGE **$$$**
(📞2741-8001; www.esquinaslodge.com; s/d/tr incl meals US$150/240/300; P⊛) This lodge was founded by the nonprofit Rainforest of the Austrians, which was also vital in the establishment of Piedras Blancas as a national park. Now, surrounded by the primary and secondary rainforest of the park, Esquinas is integrally connected with the community of Gamba, employing local workers and reinvesting profits in community projects. Accommodations at Esquinas Lodge are in spacious, high-ceilinged cabins with ceiling fans and private porches. The lodge's extensive grounds comprise a network of well-marked trails and a welcoming stream-fed pool. By offsetting development with tree planting, it has become 100% carbon neutral. Gamba is 8km north of Golfito and 6km south of the Interamericana.

❶ Information

Parque Nacional Piedras Blancas does not have facilities for visitors. However, it is possible to access the park from the Esquinas Rainforest Lodge in Gamba, as well as any of the coastal lodges lining the beaches north of Golfito.

❶ Getting There & Away

Piedras Blancas is best accessed from the Esquinas Rainforest Lodge, which has an extensive trail network on-site and can easily arrange guided hikes deeper into the park. If you don't have your own transportation, any bus heading north from Golfito can drop you off at the lodge.

If you're staying at any of the coastal lodges north of Golfito, you can inquire about transportation to/from the park as well as guided hikes into the interior.

Playas San Josecito, Nicuesa & Cativo

Idyllic deserted beaches, backed by the pristine rainforest of Parque Nacional Piedras Blancas, define the northeastern shore of the Golfo Dulce. The appeal of this area is only enhanced by its inaccessibility: part of the charm is that very few people make it to this untouched corner of Costa Rica. If you're looking for a romantic retreat or a secluded getaway, all of the lodges along this stretch of coastline are completely isolated and serve as perfect spots for quiet reflection.

🏃 Activities

The beaches along this stretch are excellent for swimming, snorkeling and sunning. Lodges also provide kayaks for maritime exploration. Hiking and wildlife-watching opportunities are virtually unlimited, as the lodges provide direct access to the wilds of Piedras Blancas. Miles of trails lead to secluded beaches, cascading waterfalls and other undiscovered attractions.

🛏 Sleeping

If you're planning on staying at any of the lodges listed here, advance reservations via the internet are strongly recommended, especially since it can be difficult to contact them by phone.

All of these lodges are extremely isolated and are accessible only by boat – you can expect a beach landing, so make sure you're wearing the right kind of shoes! Prices include three meals per day and transportation to/from either Golfito or Puerto Jiménez.

Playa Nicuesa Rainforest Lodge LODGE $$$
(☎2735-5237, in USA 866-348-7610; www.nicuesa
lodge.com; s/d from US$225/380) Nestled into
a 65-hectare private reserve, this lodge is
barely visible from the bay. The rustic, natu-
ral accommodations are beautifully deco-
rated with canopied beds and indigenous
textile spreads; private hot-water bathrooms
have garden showers. Meals are served in
a thatched *rancho* featuring a sparkling,
polished-wood bar. Electricity is provided by
solar power, but the lodge usually uses can-
dlelight to conserve energy and enhance the
romantic atmosphere.

Dolphin Quest LODGE $$
(☎2775-8630, 2775-0373; www.dolphinquestcosta
rica.com; s/d campsites US$30/55, cabins US$60/
100, houses US$70/120) This jungle lodge offers
a mile of beach and 280 secluded hectares
of mountainous rainforest. Three round,
thatched-roof cabins and one large house are
on 2 hectares of landscaped grounds. Meals –
featuring organic ingredients from the garden – are served in an open-air pavilion near
the shore. To get here, arrange transportation
from the docks with Dolphin Quest; the hotel
is reachable only by private boat.

❶ Getting There & Away

All of the lodges offer boat transportation from
Puerto Jiménez and/or Golfito by prior arrange-
ment, though you can always grab a water taxi if
plans go awry.

Zancudo

Occupying a slender finger of land that juts
into the Golfo Dulce, the tiny village of Zancudo is about as laid-back a beach destination as you'll find in Costa Rica. On the west
side of town, gentle, warm Pacific waters lap
onto black sands, and seeing more than a
handful of people on the beach means it's
crowded. On the east side, a tangle of mangrove swamps attracts birds, crocodiles and
plenty of fish, which in turn attract fishers hoping to reel them in. Unlike nearby
Pavones, an emerging surf destination, Zancudo is content to remain a far-flung village
in a far-flung corner of Costa Rica.

🏃 Activities

The main activities at Zancudo are undoubtedly swinging on hammocks, strolling on
the beach and swimming in the aqua-blue
waters of the Golfo Dulce. Here, the surf is
gentle, and at night the water sometimes
sparkles with bioluminescence – tiny phos-
phorescent marine plants and plankton that
light up if you sweep a hand through the
water. The effect is like underwater fireflies.

The mangrove swamps offer plenty of opportunities for exploration: birdlife is prolific, while other animals such as crocodile,
caiman, monkey and sloth are also frequently spotted. The boat ride from Golfito gives
a glimpse of these waters, but you can also
paddle them yourself: rent kayaks from any
of the accommodations listings following.

Zancudo is a base for inshore and offshore fishing, river fishing (mangrove snapper, snook and corbina) and fly-fishing. The
best sportfishing is from December to May
for sailfish and May to September for snook,
though many species bite year-round. Trips
can be arranged through any of the accommodations listed here.

🛏 Sleeping & Eating

TOP CHOICE Coloso Del Mar CABINA $
(www.coloso-del-mar.com; d with/without view
US$45/40; P🖥) Rocky, a lazy, lovable dog,
pads around the grounds of this, our favorite
beachfront property in Zancudo. It's the little
things that make Coloso stand out – match-
ing sheets, shiny hardwood floors and coffeemakers. Of course, it also has an ideal
location just steps from the surf.

Au Coeur du Soleil CABINA $$
(www.aucoeurdusoleil.com; d US$45) There are
only a couple rooms here, but both are
brightly painted and lovingly maintained,
with fans, big windows and a central BBQ.
The French host is warm and gregarious and
he offers guests the use of bikes for cruising
around town.

Cabinas Sol y Mar CABINA $
(☎2776-0014; www.zancudo.com; campsites per
person US$3, cabins US$25-50; P@🖥) This
popular place offers various budget lodging
options: smallish economy dwellings that
are further from the water, larger standard
units with a shared terrace overlooking the
beach, and private deluxe units with fancy
tile showers and unobstructed ocean views.
Even if you're not staying here, the open-air
restaurant and thatched bar is a Zancudo
favorite.

Oceano CABINA $$
(☎2776-0921; http://bestcostaricavacations.com;
r US$79; P) With its back to the beach, this

friendly little Canadian-run inn has just two rooms, both spacious and airy with wood-beamed ceilings, tile bathrooms and quaint details such as throw pillows and folk art. The open-air restaurant is also inviting for dinner or drinks, especially if the sea has been kind to the local fishermen.

El Coquito
COSTA RICAN $

(meals US$7-8; ⊘7am-8pm Sun-Wed, later Thu-Sat) Bright, cheerful and right in the middle of Zancudo's main drag, this *soda* is a charmer. It offers a filling *casado* for US$7 of fresh fish, rice and fruit, and the *licuado* (smoothies) are magically refreshing after the long, dusty ride into town. On weekends the adjoining space transforms into a nightclub, with booming music and dancing.

ⓘ Information

Zancudo consists of one dirt road, which leads from the boat dock in the north, past the lodges that are strung along the shore, and out of town south toward Pavones. There is no bank in town and very few places accept credit cards, so bring your cash from Golfito.

ⓘ Getting There & Away

Boat

The boat dock is near the north end of the beach on the inland, estuary side. A water taxi to Golfito (US$6, 45 minutes) departs from this dock at 7am, returning at noon, Monday through Saturday. Inquire locally, however, as times are subject to change, though you can always find a local boat captain willing to take you for a negotiable price.

Bus

A bus to Neily leaves from the *pulpería* near the dock at 5:30am (US$5, three hours). The bus for Golfito (US$5) leaves at 5am for the three-hour trip, with a ferry transfer at the Río Coto Colorado. Service is erratic in the wet season, so inquire before setting out.

Car

It's possible to drive to Zancudo by taking the road south of Río Claro for about 10km. Turn left at the Rodeo Bar and follow the signs across the newly constructed bridge. From there, 30km of poorly maintained dirt road gets you to Zancudo.

Pavones

Home to what is reportedly the longest left-hand surf break on the planet, Pavones is a legendary destination for surfers the world over. As this is Costa Rica's southernmost

point, you'll need to work hard to get down here. However, the journey is an adventure in its own right, especially since the best months for surfing coincide with the rainy season.

Although the village remains relatively off the beaten path, both foreigners and Ticos are transforming Pavones from its days as a relative backwater. Still, the development here is progressing slowly and sustainably, which means that the palm-lined streets are still not paved, the pace of life is slow and the overall atmosphere remains tranquil.

The name Pavones is used to refer to both Playa Río Claro de Pavones and Punta Banco, which is 6km south.

The road into Pavones comes south and dead-ends at the Río Claro, which is where you'll find a small soccer field. About 200m to the east, a parallel road crosses the Río Claro and continues the 6km to Punta Banco.

⊙ Sights

Tiskita Jungle Lodge
FARM

(☑in San José 2296-8125; www.tiskita-lodge.co.cr; guided hike US$15) Set on a verdant hillside between Pavones and Punta Banco, Tiskita Jungle Lodge consists of 100 hectares of virgin forest and a huge orchard, which produces more than 100 varieties of tropical fruit with origins from all over the world. Trails wind through surrounding rainforest, which contains waterfalls and freshwater pools suitable for swimming. The combination of rainforest, fruit farm and coastline attracts a long list of birds. About 300 species have been recorded here. The fruit farm is particularly attractive to fruit-eating birds such as parrot and toucan. The forest is home to more reticent species such as yellow-billed cotinga, fiery-billed aracari, green honeycreeper and lattice-tailed trogon. The owners – personable conservationists and conversationalists Peter and Elizabeth Aspinall – or their son usually guide hikes. Reservations are recommended.

🏃 Activities

Surfing

Pavones is one of Costa Rica's most famous surf breaks – when the surf's up, this tiny beach town attracts hordes of international elite. Conditions are best with a southern swell, usually between April and October.

However, because Pavones is inside Golfo Dulce, it is protected from many swells so surfers can go for weeks without seeing any waves.

Pavones has become legendary among surfers for its long left. Some claim it is the world's longest, offering a two- or three-minute ride on a good day. Legend has it that the wave passes so close to the Esquina del Mar Cantina that you can toss beers to surfers as they zip by.

When Pavones has nothing (or when it's too crowded), head south to Punta Banco, a reef break with decent rights and lefts. The best conditions are at mid- or high tide, especially when there's swells from the south or west.

Yoga

TOP CHOICE Yoga Farm YOGA
(www.yogafarmcostarica.org) A unique and welcome addition to Pavones, this retreat has simple, clean rooms with wood bunk bed (dorm/room per night US$43/50, per week US$260/300), three vegetarian meals that are prepared primarily with ingredients from the organic garden, and daily yoga classes that take place in an open-air studio overlooking the ocean. It is a sweaty 15-minute walk from Rancho Burica in Punta Banco: take the road going up the hill to the left, go through the first gate on the left and keep walking up the hill.

🛏 Sleeping

PLAYA RÍO CLARO DE PAVONES

Riviera Riverside Villas VILLA $$
(☑8823-5874; www.pavonesriviera.com; s/d US$85/90; P☀🛜) This clutch of exclusive villas in Pavones proper offers fully equipped kitchens, cool tile floors and attractive hardwood ceilings. Big shady porches overlook the landscaped gardens, which offer a degree of intimacy and privacy found at few other places in town.

Cabinas Mira Olas CABINA $
(☑8393-7742; www.miraolas.com; r US$30-45; P🛜) This 4.5-hectare farm is full of wildlife and fruit trees, and cabins to suit all tastes. The 'rustic' cabin, incidentally, boasted the first flush toilet in Pavones, though it's quite different from the 'jungle deluxe,' a beautiful, open-air lodging with a huge balcony and elegant cathedral ceiling. To find Mira Olas, turn off at the fishing boats and follow the signs up the hill. It's behind the newly constructed cell tower.

PUNTA BANCO

Tiskita Jungle Lodge LODGE $$$
(☑in San José 2296-8125; www.tiskita-lodge.co.cr; s/d from US$155/275; P@🛜☀) Set amid extensive gardens and orchards, this lodge is arguably the most beautiful and intimate in all of Golfo Dulce. Accommodations are in a clutch of stunning wooden cabins accented by stone garden showers that allow you to freshen up while you go bird-watching. Daily rates include fresh home-cooked meals and guided walks. Reservations must be made in advance as the lodge fills up quickly. Even if you're not spending the night here, stop by for a guided tour of the property.

Cabinas La Ponderosa CABINA $$
(☑8824-4145, in USA 954-771-9166; www.cabinas laponderosa.com; r US$60-200; P☀🛜) Housed on six lovely landscaped hectares, these cozy cabins are tenderly cared for by Marshall and Angela McCarthy, who have spent years living in their adopted home of Pavones. The common lounge offers all kinds of entertainment, including a table-tennis table and a massive video library, but the real appeal of staying here is the warm hospitality of the McCarthys.

Rancho Cannatella GUESTHOUSE $$
(☑2776-2251; s/d US$25/45; ☀) Two kilometers south of Pavones, this adobe *rancho* is operated by the perenially shirtless Joseph Robertston, an expat who lives to surf and paddleboard the turquoise waves right outside across the road. There's a small pool, heated by the sun, and four tidy rooms for rent. The best deal is the little spartan wooden cabin in back, which has a kitchenette.

Rancho Burica HOSTEL $
(www.ranchoburica.com; r per person US$8-22; P) This friendly Dutch-run outpost is literally the end of the road in Punta Banco. All rooms have bathrooms and fans, while the pricier ones have mosquito-netted beds and attractive wood furniture. Hammocks interspersed around the property offer ample opportunity for chilling out. It's not the cleanest and the staff have incurable slacker syndrome, but it's a great place to party with other travelers. Reservations are not accepted: 'Just show up…like everyone else does.'

🍴 Eating & Drinking

As many of the places to stay in Pavones come with a refrigerator and burner, it's worth stocking up a bit at the centrally located market.

Café de la Suerte
CAFE $

(meals US$4-9; 🖋) Simple breakfasts, omelets and light veggie dishes dominate the menu here, all light fare to be washed down with a tropical-fruit smoothie.

Esquina del Mar Cantina
BAR

A Pavones institution that has great views of the left break, this is where you should grab a drink after your last ride. Meals are available for US$3 to US$9.

ℹ Information

Pavones has no bank or gas station, so make sure you have plenty of money and gas prior to arrival.

ℹ Getting There & Away

NatureAir (www.natureair.com) and **Alfa Romeo Aero Taxi** (www.alfaromeoair.com) offer charter flights. Prices are dependent on the number of passengers, so it's best to try to organize a larger group if you're considering this option.

Two daily buses go to Golfito (US$5, three hours). The first leaves at 5:30am and departs from the end of the road at Rancho Burica (but you can pick it up at the bus stop opposite the Riviera); the second leaves at 12:30pm from the Esquina del Mar Cantina. Buses from Golfito depart at 10am (to Pavones) and 3pm (to Punta Banco via Pavones) from the stop at the Muellecito.

A 4WD taxi will charge about US$65 from Golfito, though you can also take a water taxi for about the same price. If you're driving, follow the directions to Zancudo and look for the signs to Pavones.

PARQUE NACIONAL ISLA DEL COCOS

Even though it's a tiny speck of green amid the endless Pacific, the Isla del Cocos looms large in the imagination of the adventurer: jagged mountains and tales of treasure, a pristine and isolated ecosystem filled with wildlife and some of the world's best diving. Remember the opening shot of *Jurassic Park,* where the helicopter sweeps over a tropical island? That was here.

Isla del Cocos is around 500km southwest of the mainland in the middle of the eastern Pacific. As it's the most far-flung corner of Costa Rica, you'll have to pay through the nose to get here, though few other destinations in the country are as wildly exotic and visually arresting.

As beautiful as the island may be, its terrestrial environs pale in comparison to what lies beneath. Named by PADI as one of the world's top 10 dive spots, the surrounding waters of Isla del Cocos harbor abundant pelagics including one of the largest known schools of hammerhead sharks in the world.

Since the island remains largely uninhabited and is closed to overnight visitors, visits require either a private yacht or, more realistically, a liveaboard dive vessel. While nondivers are certainly welcome to make the trip, it pays to have some significant underwater experience in your logbook – sites around Isla del Cocos are as challenging as they are breathtaking.

History

In 1526 Spanish explorer Joan Cabezas stumbled on Isla del Cocos, though it wasn't noted on maps until its second discovery by French cartographer Nicolas Desliens in 1541. In the centuries that followed, heavy rainfall attracted the attention of sailors, pirates and whalers, who frequently stopped by for fresh water, coconuts and fresh seafood.

Between the late 17th and early 19th centuries, Isla del Cocos became a way station for pirates who are rumored to have hidden countless treasures here. The most famous was the storied Treasure of Lima, a trove of gold and silver ingots, gold laminae scavenged from church domes and a solid-gold, life-sized sculpture of the Virgin Mary. 'X marks the spot,' right? Not really. More than 500 treasure-hunting expeditions have found only failure.

In fact, in 1869 the government of Costa Rica organized an official treasure hunt. They didn't find anything, but the expedition resulted in Costa Rica taking possession of the island, a treasure in itself.

Settlers arrived on the island in the late 19th and early 20th centuries, though their stay on Isla del Cocos was short-lived. However, they did leave behind domestic animals that have since converted into feral populations of pigs, goats, cats and rats – all of which threaten the natural wildlife.

◉ Sights

Even though this is the turf of hard-core divers, making landfall and exploring is worth the time and effort. Need a second opinion? The famous oceanographer and diving guru Jacques Cousteau famously dubbed Cocos 'the most beautiful island in the world.'

Rugged, heavily forested and punctuated by cascading waterfalls, Cocos is ringed and transected by an elaborate network of trails. The highest point is at **Cerro Iglesias** (634m), where you can soak up spectacular views of the lush, verdant island and the deep blue Pacific.

Note that visitors to the island must first register with the park rangers, though your tour company will most likely make all the necessary arrangements well in advance.

Activities

Diving

The diving is excellent, and is regarded by most as the main attraction of the island. But strong oceanic currents can lead to treacherous underwater conditions, and Isla del Cocos can be recommended only to intermediate and advanced divers with sufficient experience.

The island has two large bays with safe anchorages and sandy beaches: Chatham Bay is located on the northeast side and Wafer Bay is on the northwest. Just off Cocos are a series of smaller basaltic rocks and islets, which constitute some of the best dive sites.

Isla Manuelita is a prime spot, home to a wide array of fish, ray and eel. Shark also inhabit these waters, including huge schools of scalloped hammerhead as well as whitetips, which are best spotted at night. Dirty Rock is another main attraction – a spectacular rock formation that harbors all kinds of sea creatures.

Wildlife-Watching

Because of its remote location, Isla del Cocos is the most pristine national parks in the country and one of Costa Rica's great wildlife destinations. Since the island was never linked to the Americas during its comparatively short geological history, Cocos is home to a very large number of rare endemic species.

Heading inland from the coastal forests up to the high-altitude cloud forests, it is possible to find around 235 unique species of flowering plants, 30% of which are found only on the island. This incredible diversity of flora supports more than 400 known species of insects. Sixty-five endemics, as well as a striking range of butterflies and moths, are included in this count. Scientists believe that more remain to be discovered.

Of the 87 recorded species on the island and neighboring rocks, the most pronounced are the aquatic birds: brown and red-footed booby, great frigatebird, white tern and brown noddy. There are also three terrestrial endemics, namely the Cocos cuckoo, Cocos flycatcher and Cocos finch.

The island's marine life is equally varied, with 18 species of coral, 57 types of crustacean and abundant fish, sea turtles, rays, dolphins and sharks. The scalloped hammerhead shark receives top billing, especially since it often schools in the hundreds.

Tours

Even the most fiercely independent travelers will likely have to join a tour to visit Cocos. Liveaboard dive operators, which mostly dock their vessels in Puntarenas, offer guided excursions to the island. Diving and food are included in the tour prices listed, but daily park fees are not.

Undersea Hunter DIVING
(☏2228-6613, in USA 800-203-2120; www.under seahunter.com) Offers 10-/12-day land and sea expeditions with room for 14 to 18 people from US$5045 per person.

Okeanos Aggressor DIVING
(☏in USA 866-653-2667; www.aggressor.com) Offers eight-/10-day land and sea expeditions with room for 22 from US$3335/3735 per person.

Sleeping

While visitors are permitted to make landfall on Cocos during the day, you must return to the boat at night to sleep.

Information

In order to protect the conservation status of the island, all visitors must apply for a permit at the **Área de Conservación de la Isla del Cocos** (Acmic; ☏2258-7350) in San José. However, unless you're sailing to the island on a private boat, tour operators will make all the necessary arrangements for you.

Getting There & Away

With advance reservations, both of the tour companies listed earlier will arrange transfers from either San José or Liberia to Puntarenas, which is the embarkation/disembarkation point for the tour.

Caribbean Coast

Best Places to Eat

» Cha Cha Cha (p430)

» Stashu's con Fusion (p441)

» Selvin's Restaurant (p448)

» La Pecora Nera (p446)

» Maxi's Restaurant (p449)

Best Places to Stay

» Rana Roja (p416)

» Tortuga Lodge & Gardens (p416)

» Playa Negra Guesthouse (p427)

» Hotel Pura Vida (p437)

» Costa Rica Tree House Lodge (p447)

Why Go

While the sunny climate and easy accessibility of the Pacific have paved the way (literally) for development on that rich coast, the Caribbean side has languished in comparison. The same rain-drenched malarial wildness that thwarted the first 16th-century Spaniards from settling here also isolated this region for centuries afterward. Thus, its culture – influenced by indigenous peoples and West Indian immigrants – blended slowly and organically and is distinctly different from the rest of Costa Rica. It still takes a little more effort to travel here to see the nesting turtles of Tortuguero, raft the Río Pacuare or dive the reefs of Manzanillo. Life is more rugged and rustic on this coast, allowing wildlife to thrive. And it's well worth tasting its unique flavors: the *rondón* (spicy seafood gumbo), the lilt of patois, and the uncrowded stretches of black-sand beaches.

When to Go

As evidenced by the spectacularly lush greenery in this region, there's no traditional 'dry season.' It rains throughout the year, though less in February and March and September and October – this latter period conveniently coinciding with when the rest of the country is getting soaked. Surfers, note: the biggest swells hit the southern Caribbean from December to March. Turtle-nesting season runs from March to October. January to June and September to December are best for sportfishing, although fishing is good year-round in the northern Caribbean.

Caribbean Coast Highlights

1 Canoe the jungle canals of **Tortuguero** (p412) in search of caiman, river otter and night heron

2 Surf, sample the culinary scene, laze on the beach and party in **Puerto Viejo de Talamanca** (p432)

3 Visit cacao and iguana farms at the **indigenous villages** (p444) around Bribrí

4 Chill out in rustic bliss in **Cahuita** (p424) and soak up its Caribbean Creole culture

5 Overdose on the dangerous cuteness of baby sloths at **Aviarios del Caribe** (p421)

6 Snorkel the teeming reefs off end-of-the-road **Manzanillo** (p448)

7 Volunteer to protect **endangered sea turtles**

8 Navigate a 4WD over pothole craters and hike through cloud forest to the summit lagoons of **Volcán Barva** (p401)

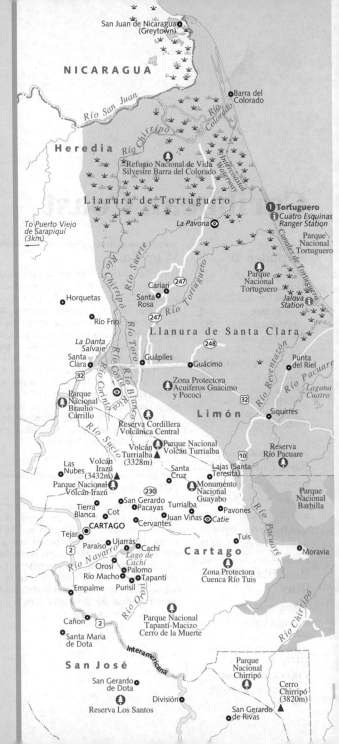

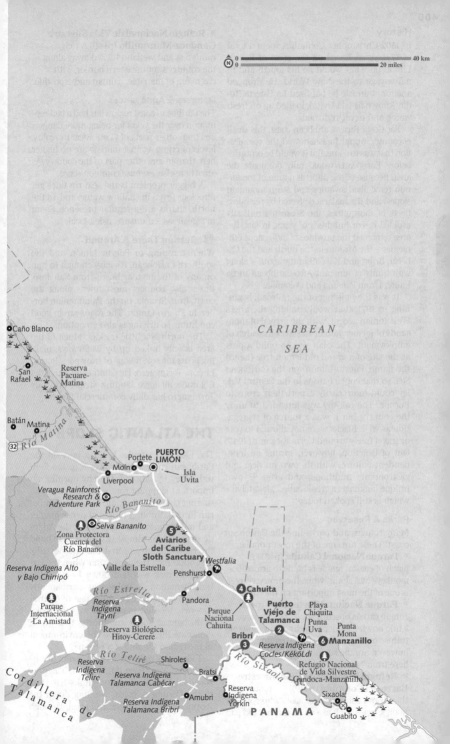

CARIBBEAN

SEA

Caño Blanco

San Rafael

Reserva Pacuare-Matina

Batán   Matina

Río Matina

THE ATLANTIC

32

Portete

PUERTO LIMÓN

Moín

Isla Uvita

Liverpool

Veragua Rainforest Research & Adventure Park

Río Bananito

Selva Bananito

Zona Protectora Cuenca del Río Bano

Aviarios del Caribe Sloth Sanctuary

5

Westfalia

Reserva Indígena Alto y Bajo Chirripó

Valle de la Estrella

Penshurst

Río Estrella

Reserva Indígena Tayni

Cahuita

4

Reserva Biológica Hitoy-Cerere

Pandora

Puerto Viejo de Talamanca

Parque Nacional Cahuita

Playa Chiquita

Parque Internacional La Amistad

2

Punta Uva

Punta Mona

Bribrí

3

Manzanillo

6

Río Telire

Shiroles

Reserva Indígena Cocles/KéköLdi

Reserva Indígena Telire

Bratsi

Río Sixaola

Reserva Indígena Talamanca Cabécar

Refugio Nacional de Vida Silvestre Gandoca-Manzanillo

Cordillera

Amubri

Reserva Indígena Yorkín

Sixaola

Reserva Indígena Talamanca Bribrí

de

Talamanca

PANAMA

Guabito

History

In 1502 Christopher Columbus spent a total of 17 days anchored off the coast of Puerto Limón on what would be his fourth and final voyage to the New World. He dropped anchor at an isle he baptized La Huerta (today known as Isla Uvita), loaded up on fresh water, and never returned.

For Costa Rica's Caribbean coast, this small encounter would foreshadowed the colonization that was to come. But it would be centuries before Europeans would fully dominate the area. Because of the difficult nature of the terrain (croc-filled swamps and steep mountain slopes) and the malaria delivered by relentless fleets of mosquitoes, the Spanish steadfastly avoided it. For hundreds of years, in fact, the area remained the province of indigenous ethnicities – the Miskito in the north and the Cabécar, Bribrí and Kèköldi in the south – along with a mix of itinerant Afro-Caribbean turtle hunters from Panama and Colombia.

It was the building of the railroad, beginning in 1871, that would solidify the area's West Indian accent, with the arrival of thousands of former Jamaican slaves in search of employment. The plan was to build a port at the site of a grand old lemon tree (hence the name, Puerto Limón) on the Caribbean Sea, so that coffee barons in the Central Valley could more easily export their crops to Europe. The railway was intended to unify the country, but it was a source of segregation as well. Blacks were not allowed to vote or travel freely around Costa Rica until 1949. Out of isolation, however, sprung an independent culture, with its own musical and gastronomic traditions, and even its own unique language, a creole called Mekatelyu – which is still spoken today.

Parks & Reserves

Many refuges and parks line the Caribbean coast. These are sme of the most popular:

» **Parque Nacional Cahuita** (p431) A patch of coastal jungle is home to armadillos, monkeys and sloths, while the protected reef is one of the most important on the coast.

» **Parque Nacional Tortuguero** (p412) Jungle canals obscure snoozing caimans, while howler, spider and capuchin monkeys traipse overhead. The star attraction, however, are the sea turtles, which nest here from March to October.

» **Refugio Nacional de Vida Silvestre Barra del Colorado** (p419) A remote park that draws fishing enthusiasts who come to hook species such as snook, tarpon and gar.

» **Refugio Nacional de Vida Silvestre Gandoca-Manzanillo** (p449) A rich rainforest and wetland tucked away along the country's southeastern border, with rivers full of manatee, caiman and crocodile.

Dangers & Annoyances

The Caribbean coast region has had a bad reputation over the years for being more dangerous than other parts of Costa Rica. In reality, levels of crime against tourists are no higher here than in any other part of the country. As anywhere else, exercise common sense.

A bigger problem is the sea: rip tides get ferocious (even in shallow water) and, in the north, sharks are a regular presence. Swim in safe areas – if unsure, ask a local.

❶ Getting There & Around

When traveling to Puerto Limón and the southern Caribbean, it's easy enough to hop on any of the regular buses from San José. Buses also connect most towns along the coast, from Sixaola, on the Panamanian border, to Puerto Limón. The roads are in good condition, so driving is also an option.

The north is a little trickier. Much of the area is only linked up by waterways, making boats the sole means of transport. Puerto Limón, Tortuguero, Parismina and Barra del Colorado all have landing strips, but only Tortuguero has daily commercial flights.

THE ATLANTIC SLOPE

The idea was simple: build a port on the Caribbean coast and connect it to the Central Valley by railroad, thereby opening up important shipping routes for the country's soaring coffee production. Construction began in 1871, through 150km of dense jungles and muddy mountainsides along the Atlantic slope. It took almost two decades to build the railroad, and the first 30km reportedly cost 4000 men their lives. But when the last piece of track was laid down in 1890, the transformation it unleashed permanently changed Costa Rica (and the rest of Central America, for that matter). It was the dawn of the banana boom, an industry that would dominate life, politics and the environment in the region for almost a century.

Today, the railroad is no longer. An asphalt highway (Hwy 32) – through Parque Nacional Braulio Carrillo – links San José to the Caribbean coast, winding down the foothills of the Cordillera Central, through agricultural plantations to the swampy lowlands around Limón. Likewise, banana production is not as mighty as it once was, supplanted in many areas by pineapples and African oil palms.

Parque Nacional Braulio Carrillo

Enter this underexplored national park and you will have an idea of what Costa Rica looked like prior to the 1950s, when 75% of the country's surface area was still covered in forest: steep hills cloaked in impossibly tall trees are interrupted only by cascading rivers and canyons. It has an extraordinary biodiversity due to the range of altitudes, from steamy 2906m cloud forest alongside Volcán Barva to lush, humid lowlands on the Caribbean slope. Its most incredible feature, however, is that this massive park (the size of New York's Rhode Island) is only 30 minutes north of San José.

Founded in the 1970s, Braulio Carrillo's creation was the result of a unique compromise between conservationists and developers. At the time, the government had announced a plan to build a new highway that would connect the capital to Puerto Limón. Back then, San José's only link to its most important port was via a crumbling railway or a slow rural road through Cartago and Turrialba. The only feasible route for the new thoroughfare was along a low pass between the Barva and Irazú volcanoes – an area covered in primary forest. Conservationists were deeply worried about putting a road (and any attendant development) in an area that served as San José's watershed. So a plan was hatched: the road would be built, but the 400 sq km of land to either side of it would be set aside as a national park. Thus, in 1978, Parque Nacional Braulio Carrillo was born.

Activities

Wildlife-Watching
Bird-watching in the park is excellent, and commonly sighted species include parrots, toucans and hummingbirds; quetzals can be seen at higher elevations, primarily in the Barva sector. Other rare but sighted birds include eagles and umbrella birds.

Mammals are difficult to spot due to the lush vegetation, though deer, monkeys and *tepezcuintle* (paca, the park's mascot) are frequently seen. Jaguars and ocelots are present but rare.

Hiking
From Zurquí, there is a short, steep 1km trail that leads to a viewpoint. You can also follow the Sendero Histórico, which follows the crystal-clear Río Hondura to its meeting point with the Río Sucio (Dirty River), the yellow waters of which carry volcanic minerals.

From Quebrada González, you can follow the 2.8km Sendero La Botella (about 90 minutes) past a series of waterfalls into Patria Canyon. There are several other unmarked trails that lead through this area, including a few places where you are permitted to camp, though there are no facilities.

Keep an eye out for the distinctive Gunnera plants, which quickly colonize newly exposed parts of montane rainforest. The huge leaves can protect a person from a sudden downpour – hence the plant's nickname *sombrilla de pobre* (poor man's umbrella).

CLIMBING VOLCÁN BARVA
Climbing Volcán Barva is a strenuous five-hour round-trip adventure along a reasonably well-maintained trail. Because of its relative inaccessibility, there is a good chance you will be alone. Begin from the western entrance of the park, north of Heredia. From there a signed track climbs to the summit. Trails are often muddy, and you should be prepared for rain any time of the year.

The trail leads to two lagoons – Lagos Barva and Copey – at the volcano's summit, and several spur trails lead to waterfalls and other scenic spots along the way.

Camping is allowed at basic campsites (per person US$3) near the ranger station; bring your own drinking water.

Volunteering
Cerro Dantas Wildlife Refuge VOLUNTEERING (www.cerrodantas.com) Near Monte de la Cruz, in the Barva sector, the Cerro Dantas Wildlife Refuge is an education facility that is always seeking volunteers to help out with administrative, maintenance and research duties. Contact the organization through its website.

ℹ Information
There have been reports of thefts from cars parked at entrances to the trails, as well as an armed robbery inside the park. Don't leave your car parked anywhere along the main highway. And as a general rule, you should always register at a station before setting out on a hike and, when possible, arrange for a guide.

RAINFOREST AERIAL TRAM

The brainchild of biologist Don Perry, a pioneer of rainforest canopy research, the Rainforest Aerial Tram (2257-5961; www.rainforestrams.com; adult/student & child US$55/28, full-day tour with lunch & guided hike US$99/56; ⊞) carries visitors to the heights of the forest canopy in a gondola. The 2.6km ride takes 40 minutes each way, affording unusual plant-spotting and bird-watching opportunities. The fee includes a knowledgeable guide, which is helpful since the dense vegetation can make observing animals difficult. A variety of other tours, as well as zip lining, are also available. Book online or in its San José office (Map p60; 2257-5961; reservations.cr@rainforestadventure.com; Av 7 btwn Calles 5 & 7; ⏰9am-5pm Mon-Fri).

The most popular hiking areas can be accessed from the San José–Guápiles highway. At the southern end of the park, 19km northeast of San José, is the **Zurquí ranger station** (2268-1039, 2268-1038; admission US$8; ⏰8am-4pm), while the **Quebrada González station** (2261-2619; admission US$8; ⏰7am-4pm) is at the northeast corner, 22km past the Zurquí tunnel. At both, you'll find guarded parking lots, toilets and well-marked trails.

People who want to climb Volcán Barva on a day trip or camp overnight can stop by the **Barva Sector ranger station** (2266-1883; admission US$8; ⏰7am-4pm), in the southwest of the park, 3km north of Sacramento. There are also two remote outposts, El Ceibo and Magasay, in the extreme northwest corner.

Temperatures can fluctuate drastically, and annual rainfall can be as high as 8000mm. The best time to go is the 'dry' season (January to April), but it is liable to rain then, too. Bring warm clothing, wet-weather gear and good hiking boots.

ⓘ Getting There & Away

Both the Zurquí and Quebrada González stations are on Hwy 32 between San José and Guápiles. Frequent buses between the two cities can drop you off at these, but pick-up on the road is dangerous and difficult.

The Barva station can be reached by following the decent paved road north from Heredia through Barva and on to San José de la Montaña, Paso Llano and Sacramento, where a signed, 4WD-only trail leads 4km north to the entrance. It is not advisable to drive this stretch in rainy season as the road is a mess of car-swallowing potholes.

Public buses from Heredia (Calle 1, between Avs 4 and 6; US$0.80) depart at 6:30am, noon and 4pm on weekdays; 6:45am, 11am and 4pm on weekends. For a day trip, it's best to take the earliest buses. Make sure you're catching a bus that goes all the way to Paso Llano, or you'll be left more than 15km from the park's entrance.

El Ceibo and Magasay can be accessed via rough roads from La Virgen.

Guápiles & Around

POP 20,200

A pleasant and decidedly nontouristy (if not terribly scenic) lowland agricultural town, Guápiles lies at the base of the northern foothills of the Cordillera Central. It serves as a transportation center for the Río Frío banana-growing region and also makes a convenient base from which to explore Parque Nacional Braulio Carrillo – a 20-minute drive away – or to organize excursions to Tortuguero.

The center of town is about 1km north of Hwy 32. The two major streets are one way, running parallel to each other. Most of the services are on the loop that these streets make through the busy downtown.

⊙ Sights & Activities

Jardín Botánico Las Cusingas GARDENS
(2382-5805; guided tour US$6; ⏰by appointment) This sprawling, 20-hectare botanical garden has more than 80 medicinal species, 80 orchid species and 30 bromeliad species. There are several easy trails for walking, as well as courses, research projects and a library on offer. From the main highway, turn north at Soda Buenos Aires, then go 4km by rough road to the signed entrance.

⨳ Sleeping

GUÁPILES

Hotel Country Club Suerre HOTEL $$
(2713-3000, 2710-7551; www.suerre.com; s/d US$75/95, each additional person US$20; ⓟ⊙❄🛜🏊) Just 1km north of the Servicentro Santa Clara, this business resort has a bland Holiday Inn vibe, but the 98 rooms are spacious and tidy, and the grounds meticulously maintained. There's a restaurant, casino, Olympic-sized pool, gym, shaded tennis courts and children's play area.

Hotel y Cabinas Wilson HOTEL **$**

(☏2710-2217; d with/without air-con US$18/15, tr with air-con US$30; P❄) This slightly musty, reasonably clean spot has 24 rooms with cool-water showers. Get a room in the back to avoid street noise. To get here from the main highway, turn north at the road west of Burger King. The hotel will be about 300m in, on your right, on a broad commercial street.

AROUND GUÁPILES

Casa Río Blanco B&B B&B **$$**

(☏2710-4124; www.casarioblanco.com; d/tr/q incl breakfast US$65/80/90; P) This rustic inn, run by the personable Annette and Herbie, has four little wood cabins on a 2-hectare hillside above the Río Blanco. It is blessedly devoid of niceties such as cable TV and wi-fi. Late-night entertainment consists of listening to frogs croak and watching the lightning

THE TROUBLED LEGACY OF BANANAS

The banana. Nothing embodies the tumultuous history of Latin America – and its complicated relationship to the United States – quite like this common yellow fruit. It is the crop that has determined the path of current affairs in more than one Central American nation. It is the sobriquet used to describe corrupt, dictatorial regimes – 'the banana republic.' Bananas are a symbol of frivolity, the raw material for Carmen Miranda hats and Busby Berkeley dance numbers. (Want to blow your mind? Look up 'The Lady with the Tutti Frutti Hat' from the 1942 musical flick, *The Gang's All Here* – it's a hallucinogenic panorama of dancing bananas.)

It was in Costa Rica, interestingly, where the idea of bananas as an industry was born. Imported from the Canary Islands by sailors during the colonial period, the fruit had long been a basic foodstuff in the Caribbean islands. But it was 19th-century railroad baron Minor Keith who turned it into a booming international business. After building the railroad between San José and Limón, Keith proceeded to carpet vast swaths of Central America in bananas. Over the course of the 20th century, the company he founded – United Fruit – would become an integral part of the region's economies and a behind-the-scenes puppet master in its political systems. (For a highly readable history on this topic, pick up *Bananas: How the United Fruit Company Shaped the World*, by journalist Peter Chapman.)

Part of the reason bananas became a continent-wide crop boils down to profit and biology. Bananas – a fruit afflicted with a high rate of spoilage – require a vast economy of scale (and cheap labor) to be profitable. It's also an inordinately delicate fruit to cultivate, partly because bananas are clones. The fruit doesn't grow from seeds; its propagation requires that a cutting be taken from an existing plant and put into the ground. This makes them incredibly vulnerable to illness – what kills one banana, kills all bananas. Entire networks of plantations can be devastated by fungus, such as the diseases that swept through Costa Rica's southern Caribbean coast in the 1910s and '20s.

Over the years, this weakness has led growers to turn to a veritable arsenal of chemicals to protect their crops. This, in turn, has taken a toll on both the environment and the workers who spray them, some of whom have been rendered sterile by powerful fungicides such as DBCP (now banned). Groups of workers in various countries have filed numerous lawsuits against fruit companies and chemical manufacturers – and won – but these victories are generally short-lived. Even when Central American courts rule in workers' favor, it is practically impossible for plaintiffs to secure payouts. One suit has made it to the US legal system, but has been derailed by questions about evidence, gathering.

There have been some attempts at growing bananas organically, but those efforts are not enough – and according to some experts, will never be enough – to replace the intense agribusiness that currently supplies the world with its fourth major foodstuff, after rice, wheat and milk. Costa Rica likes to think of itself as a country of coffee producers, a nation built on the work of humble, independent farmers. But the fact is that bananas remain the country's number-one agricultural export – as they have been for decades. They are an inextricable part of the country's DNA. And, unless everyone suddenly starts putting sliced apples into their cereal, that likely won't change any time soon.

WORTH A TRIP

EARTH UNIVERSITY

Several kilometers east of the main Guácimo turnoff on Hwy 32 (east of Guápiles), you'll arrive at the main entrance to EARTH (Escuela de Agricultura de la Región Tropical Húmeda; 🗹2713-0248, ext 5002; www.earth.ac.cr; guided tours per person US$25). This innovative not-for-profit university attracts students from all over the world to research sustainable agriculture in the tropics. The curriculum integrates various academic disciplines with plenty of hands-on activities at onsite greenhouses and biological labs. Travelers can visit the facilities on guided tours, which must be arranged at least one week in advance.

bugs. The inn secretes a private trail leading down to the river and a spectacular swimming hole. Call ahead for reservations; additional meals (including vegetarian options) can be arranged. From Hwy 32, go 7km west of Guápiles, turn south onto the dirt road immediately west of the Río Blanco bridge, and follow the rocky road for 1km.

La Danta Salvaje   LODGE $$$
(🗹2750-0012; www.ladantasalvaje.com; 4-night package per person US$225) West of Guápiles, a 45-minute 4WD trip and three-hour hike will take you 800m above sea level to this 410-hectare rainforest reserve in a critical buffer zone adjacent to Parque Nacional Braulio Carrillo. The rustic lodge hosts small groups for four days of hiking in the jungle, splashing around in swimming holes and spotting spider monkeys, tapirs and silky anteaters. Prices include three meals a day and guided hikes. Reservations must be made in advance.

✗ Eating

Deleites   BAKERY $
(pastries US$1.50-3; ⊙6am-7:30pm Mon-Sat, 7am-6:30pm Sun) This attractive, well-stocked bakery sells cookies, cakes, bread and even cappuccino. You'll find it along the main north–south road in the center of town, 100m west of Hotel y Cabinas Wilson.

Soda Buenos Aires   COSTA RICAN $
(🗹2710-1768; Hwy 32; mains US$3-7; ⊙9am-9pm Mon-Sat) Situated 1km west of Guápiles on the south side of the main highway, this popular *soda* (cheap, informal lunch counter) comes highly recommended for its fish dishes.

El Rubio   COSTA RICAN $
(🗹2710-2323; mains US$3.50-10) The clutter of pick-up trucks out front is a clue that you have stumbled onto this popular family eatery. It offers a wide selection of grilled fish and roasted meats. And there is a good selection of *bocas* (savory bar snacks), including

our favorite: *chifrijo*, a pile of rice and pinto beans studded with fried pork and capped with fresh tomato salsa and corn chips. On the road east of Burger King, go 100m north, then 100m east on the dirt road.

Más X Menos   SUPERMARKET
(⊙7am-9pm Mon-Sat, to 8pm Sun) This huge supermarket is 200m north of the bus terminal.

❶ Getting There & Away

The modern bus terminal, complete with eateries and **internet cafe** (⊙5:30am-8:30pm), is about 200m north of the main highway from the western Burger King turn-off.

Cariari (Guapileños) US$1; 20 minutes; departs every 15 minutes from 6am to 10pm.

Puerto Limón via Guácimo & Siquirres (Tracasa) US$3.55; two hours; departs hourly from 6am to 7pm.

Puerto Viejo de Sarapiquí (Guapileños) US$3.35; 45 minutes; departs at 5:30am, 8am, 9am, 10:30am, noon, 1:15pm, 2:30pm, 4pm, 5pm and 6:30pm.

San José (Guapileños) US$2.30; 1¼ hours; departs every 30 minutes from 6:30am to 7pm.

Cariari
POP 14,100

Due north of Guápiles, Cariari is a blue-collar, rough-around-the-edges banana town. Most travelers make their way quickly through here, en route to Tortuguero. If that's you, Cariari is your last opportunity to get cash.

There's a gas station and a branch of Banco de Costa Rica (⊙9am-4pm Mon-Fri), opposite San José bus terminal, with a 24-hour ATM on the Cirrus system.

If you get stranded, spend the night at Hotel El Trópico (🗹2767-7186; d with/without air-con US$30/24; 🅿✳🛜) on the main road (300m north of Terminal Caribeño), which has 15 tidy rooms and an onsite restaurant (open 7am to 10pm).

❶ Getting There & Away

Buses from San José and Guápiles have a regular service to Cariari. Note that Cariari has two terminals: the one serving San José (known as the *estación nueva* – new station) is at the southern end of town, while the one serving Guápiles and Caribbean destinations is about five blocks to the north, just west of the main road. This latter station is known as the *estación vieja* (old station) or Terminal Caribeño.

For transfer to Puerto Limón, take a bus to Guápiles and then transfer to one of the regular hourly buses to Limón.

To reach Tortuguero, you will have to take a bus to the dock at La Pavona from the *estación vieja*. From here, you can transfer to one of several boat services that make multiple daily trips to Tortuguero.

Guápiles (*estación vieja*) US$0.80; 20 minutes; departs every 20 minutes from 5:30am to 7pm.

La Pavona for boat transfer to Tortuguero (*estación vieja*) US$2; one hour; departs at 6am, 11:30am and 3pm.

San José (*estación nueva*) US$2.50; three hours; departs at 9am, 10:30am, 1pm, 3pm, 4:30pm, 6pm and 7pm.

If you are driving, the turnoff for the paved road to Cariari is about 1km east of Guápiles, at the Servicentro Santa Clara. Drivers heading to Tortuguero can leave cars at the guarded parking by the boat dock on the Río Suerte in La Pavona (about 30km north of Cariari).

To get to La Pavona, take the main road north out of Cariari, through Campo Dos and Cuatro Esquinas. At Abastecidor Palacio, make a left. It is generally well-signed. Casa Marbella in Tortuguero has posted a very helpful map of the exact route on its website at http://casamarbella.tripod.com/id10.html.

Siquirres

POP 18,800

The steamy lowland town of Siquirres has long served as an important transportation hub. It sits at the intersection of Hwy 32 (the main road that crosses the Atlantic slope to Puerto Limón) and Hwy 10, the old road that connects San José with Puerto Limón via Turrialba.

Even before the roads were built, it was a significant location – for it was in Siquirres in the early 20th century that the lines of segregation were drawn. At the time, blacks were barred from traveling west of here without special permission. So any train making its way from Limón to San José was required to stop here and change its crew: black conductors and engineers would change places with their Spanish counterparts and the train would continue on its route to the capital. This ended in 1949, when a new constitution outlawed racial discrimination.

Today Siquirres still marks the place where Costa Rica takes a dip into the Caribbean – and not just geographically. This is where Costa Rican *casados* (set meals) give way to West Indian *rondón*, where Spanish guitar is replaced with the strains of calypso, and where Costa Rica's inherently *mestizo* (mixed ancestry) race gives way to Afro-Caribbean features.

There is little reason to stop in Siquirres, unless you're heading to Parismina – in which case this is a good spot to find banking, internet and telephone services. (Tip: buy phone cards here; they aren't sold in Parismina.) For purposes of orientation, the Siquirres church – a highly recognizable round building – is located to the west side of the soccer field.

If you need somewhere to crash for the night, head 1km northeast of the park to Centro Turístico Las Tilapias (☏2768-9293; d with/without air-con US$55/45; 🅿✹🛜🐾), also known as 'Chito's Place.' Sadly, the star of this show, a 50-year-old, one-eyed crocodile named Pocho, died in 2011. But it still has 17 clean-but-basic rooms perched above a man-made lagoon, as well as a restaurant and bar. Get a taxi to take you (or to lead you, if you're driving) as it's quite hard to find.

Sodas and bakeries are plentiful in town.

Banco de Costa Rica (⊙9am-4pm), 100m north of the park, has a 24-hour ATM on the Cirrus network. Café Net Caribe (per hr US$0.65; ⊙8am-8pm Mon-Sat, 8am-6pm Sun), north of the park, across from Importadora Monge, on the 2nd floor, has a dozen terminals with decent connections.

❶ Getting There & Away

There are two principal bus terminals in town. At the corner terminal on the east side of the park, you'll find the following buses:

Guápiles US$1.25; 45 minutes; departs every 45 minutes 6:30am to 7:30pm.

Limón US$1.65; 1½ hours; departs almost hourly 6:30am to 10pm.

San José US$3.20; 1½ hours; departs almost hourly 5am to 6pm.

On the north side of the park, an L-shaped station has buses to Turrialba (US$1.25, 45 minutes, almost hourly 5:30am to 6:30pm).

WORTH A TRIP

VERAGUA RAINFOREST RESEARCH & ADVENTURE PARK

Nestled into the foothills of the Cordillera de Talamanca, this sprawling rainforest adventure park (☎2296-5056; www.veraguarainforest.com; adult with/without zip-line tour US$89/55, child with/without zip-line tour US$65/45; ▣) has guided tours of the forest along elevated walkways and maintained trails, as well as an aerial tram, a reptile vivarium, an insectarium, and hummingbird and butterfly gardens. And what would it be without a zip-line canopy tour? Many of the attractions are wheelchair-accessible – a good way of exploring nature if traveling with an elderly person or small children. To get here, take the signed turnoff south from Hwy 32 at Liverpool, 12km west of Puerto Limón.

To Parismina

At the L-shaped station on the park, you'll find buses to Caño Blanco, for transfer by boat to Parismina. **Caño-Aguilar** (☎2768-8172) operates the route to Caño Blanco (US$2, two hours, weekday departures at 4:15am, noon and 3:15pm, weekend departures at 7am, noon and 3:15pm). At Caño Blanco, you'll transfer to a water taxi (US$2) that makes the 10-minute trip to Parismina. (Take small change to pay the boatman.) There is a small restaurant with bathrooms by the dock.

Note: the Caño Blanco bus gets crowded. Get to the station early to buy your ticket and join the queue at least 15 minutes before the scheduled departure time.

Puerto Limón

POP 58,500

The biggest city on Costa Rica's Caribbean coast, the birthplace of United Fruit and capital of Limón Province, this hard-working port city sits removed from the rest of the country. Cruise ships deposit dazed-looking passengers between October and May. Around here, business is measured by truckloads of fruit, not busloads of tourists, so don't expect any pampering.

A general lack of political and financial support from the federal government means that Limón is not a city that has aged gracefully. It is a grid of dilapidated buildings, overgrown parks and sidewalks choked with street vendors. Crime is a problem: the city, distressingly, has as many homicides annually as San José – even though San José has five times the population. It's worth noting, however, that most of this violence is related to organized crime and does not affect travelers. Despite its shortcomings, Limón can be a compelling destination for adventurous urban explorers.

History

Until the 1850s, the most frequent visitors to Limón were pirates, who used the area's natural deep-water bays as hideouts. At the time, the country's main port was in Puntarenas, on the Pacific, but when the railroad arrived in the late 19th century, Limón blossomed into a full-blown trade hub. The city ultimately served as the key export point for the country's newest agribusiness: bananas.

Beginning in 1913, a series of blights shut down many Caribbean *fincas* (farms) and a large portion of the area's banana production moved to the southern Pacific coast. Afro-Caribbean workers, however, couldn't follow the jobs as they were forbidden to leave the province. Stranded in the least-developed part of Costa Rica, many turned to subsistence farming, fishing or managing small-scale cacao plantations. Others organized and staged bloody strikes against United Fruit. Fed up with the status quo, Limón provided key support to José Figueres (a Costa Rican revolutionary) during the 1948 civil war. This act was rewarded the following year when the new president enacted a constitution that granted blacks full citizenship and the right to work and travel freely throughout Costa Rica.

Even though segregation was officially dismantled, Limón continues to live with its legacy. The province was the last to get paved roads, the last to get electricity (areas to the south of the city weren't on the grid until the late 1970s) and the region has chronically higher crime and unemployment rates than the rest of the country. However, there have been some improvements in recent years. A police crackdown in 2009 led to a slight reduction in crime and, that same year, the government launched a US$80 million investment project to help revitalize the city's aging infrastructure. The most significant impact of this investment had been on the port at Moín, which at the time of writing was being approved for a massive upgrade to a container port. This will doubtless bring major change to the region, though how that manifests itself remains to be seen.

◉ Sights & Activities

Limón itself has no beach, but Playa Bonita, 4km northwest of town, has a pleasant, sandy beach.

Experienced surfers might want to hit Isla Uvita, the wild green rock that lies 1km offshore and is blessed with one of the country's most powerful lefts, a punishing reef break. The island is a 20-minute boat ride from Limón's main port at Moín.

Parque Vargas   PARK
The city's waterfront centerpiece won't ever win best in show, but its decrepit bandstand, paths and greenery are surprisingly appealing, all shaded by palms and facing the docks.

Avenida 2   STREET
Heading inland from Parque Vargas, Avenida 2 is the pedestrian mall that caters to the cruise-ship traffic. Keep an eye out for vendors selling home-burned CDs by local hip-hop and reggaetón bands; you can also expect to see CDs by Los Trinitarios, a Limón band that has been fusing calypso and salsa since the '70s.

☞ Tours

Tortuguero Wildlife Tours   BOAT TOUR
(☎2798-7027, 2758-2534; www.tortuguero-wildlife.com) This agency, run by the personable William Guerrero, organizes a variety of tours.

For other tour options in town, contact **Coopetortuguero** (☎2798-7029, 8865-2190, 8834-0072; coopetortuguero@gmail.com), an association of area guides.

🎊 Festivals & Events

Festival Flores de la Diáspora Africana (Late August) A celebration of Afro-Caribbean culture. While it is centered on Puerto Limón, the festival sponsors events showcasing African heritage throughout the province and San José.

Día de la Raza (Columbus Day; October 12) Columbus' historic landing on Isla Uvita has traditionally inspired a small carnival, with street parades, live music and dancing. During this time, book hotels in advance.

🛏 Sleeping

Limón offers nothing remotely upscale, but you'll find nicer hotels at nearby Playa Bonita.

Park Hotel   HOTEL $$
(☎2798-0555; www.parkhotellimon.com; Av 3 btwn Calles 1 & 2; s/d standard US$52/72, superior US$58/82, deluxe US$70/98; P❋❋@) Downtown Limón's most attractive hotel has 32 rooms in a peach-colored building that faces the ocean. Tiled rooms are tidy and sport clean bathrooms with hot water. Superior rooms have ocean views while the deluxe ones come with private balconies. The hotel also houses the swankiest restaurant in the town center. Credit cards are accepted.

Hotel Miami   HOTEL $
(☎2758-0490; hmiamilimon@yahoo.com; Av 2 btwn Calles 4 & 5; s/d US$26/33, with air-con US$35/46; P❋@) For its location on the main drag, this clean, mint-green place feels surprisingly serene, especially in the rooms in back. All 34 tidy rooms are equipped with cable TV and fan. Rooms with air-conditioning have hot water. Welcoming staff, common balconies overlooking the street and secure setup add up to the best value in town.

Hotel Acon   HOTEL $$
(☎2758-1010; cnr Av 3 & Calle 3; s/d US$41/57; ❋❋) The '60s-style modernist building is in a ramshackle state, but the place is generally clean. The 39 rooms are basic: bare linoleum floors and aged wood furnishings, some with creaky air-con units, though all have hot-water bathrooms.

✗ Eating

TOP CHOICE **Caribbean Kalisi**

Coffee Shop   CARIBBEAN $
(☎2758-3249; Calle 6 btwn Avs 3 & 4; mains from US$5; ⊘7:30am-7:30pm Mon-Fri, 8am-7:30pm Sat, 8am-5pm Sun) Belly up to the cafeteria-style counter at this friendly family spot and cobble together a plate of coconut rice, red beans and whatever's cooking that day – typically a wide variety of fabulous Caribbean meat and veggie dishes.

El Faro   INTERNATIONAL $$
(☎2758-4020; Barrio Santa Eduviges; mains US$7-17; ⊘11am-11pm; 🚗) High on a hill overlooking Limón, El Faro enjoys 270-degree views over city and sea and is best enjoyed

Puerto Limón

0 200 m
0 0.1 miles

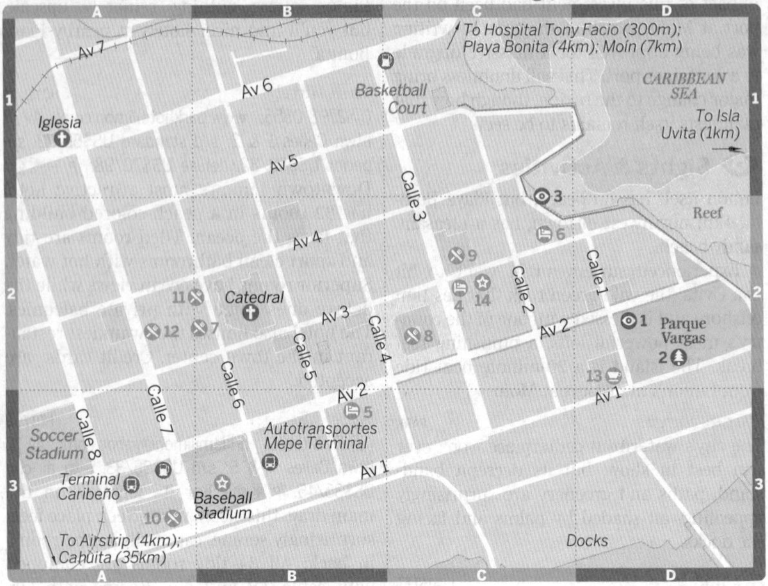

before all daylight has faded away. It's a festive local special-occasion spot, catering to tastes ranging from buffalo wings to 'Tico tenderloin' to whole fried snapper; the kids' menu proffers simple stuff like pasta with cheese.

Taquería y Antojería Yenori MEXICAN $
(☎2758-8294; Calle 7 btwn Avs 3 & 4; mains US$4-10; ⏰9am-9pm) This cute little Mexican joint serves tacos and *casados*. You have to ring the bell to get buzzed in, where you'll find clean tables, chilled soda and blaring air-con.

Restaurant Bionatura VEGETARIAN $
(☎2798-7474; Calle 6 btwn Avs 3 & 4; mains US$5-8; ⏰8am-5:30pm Mon-Sat; 🅥) In a town where everything seems to be deep-fried, this restaurant shines for its focus on healthy vegetarian cuisine, including fresh fruit salads, veggie burgers and *bistek de soya* (soy steak) *casados*.

Find cheap eats at the *sodas* in the **central market** (Av 2 btwn Calles 3 & 4; ⏰6am-8pm Mon-Sat). You can get groceries at the large **Más X Menos** (cnr Av 3 & Calle 3; ⏰8am-9pm), or at the **Palí** (cnr Calle 7 & Av 1; ⏰8am-7pm Mon-Thu, 8am-7:30pm Fri & Sat, 8:30am-6pm Sun) next to the Terminal Caribeño.

Drinking & Entertainment

No one in Limón need ever go thirsty. Bars by Parque Vargas and a few blocks west are popular hangouts for coastal characters: banana workers, sailors, ladies of the night, entrepreneurs, boozers, losers and everyone else. The standard warnings for solo women travelers go double here. (If you feel like having a beer, hit a restaurant.) This is a lousy town for getting drunk – keep your wits about you.

El Crucero CAFE
(☎2758-7003; cnr Calle 1 & Av 1; ⏰8am-6:30pm Mon-Sat) Kick back with an iced espresso and let the cross-breeze cool you at this corner cafe facing Parque Vargas and the docks. Delectables include muffins, smoothies and savory scones, with coffee brought to you by Café Britt.

Aquarius DJ
(Av 3 btwn Calles 2 & 3; ⏰8pm-2am) Inside Hotel Acon, this long-running disco spins salsa, reggaetón and pop on different nights.

Information

Though police presence has ramped up noticeably, pickpockets can be a problem, particularly in the market and along the **sea wall**. In

Puerto Limón

◎ **Sights**

▣ **Sleeping**

⊗ **Eating**

◉ **Drinking**

◉ **Entertainment**

addition, people do get mugged here, so stick to well-lit main streets at night, avoiding the sea wall and Parque Vargas. If driving, park in a guarded lot and remove everything from the car.

If you're traveling onward to Parismina or Tortuguero, Limón will be your last opportunity to get cash (and phone cards, for the Parismina-bound).

There's an internet cafe in the Autotransportes Mepe Terminal.

Banco de Costa Rica (⌨2758-3166; cnr Av 2 & Calle 1) Exchanges US dollars and has an ATM.

Hospital Tony Facio (⌨2758-2222) Serves the entire province of Limón. It's northeast of the center.

Post office (Calle 4 btwn Avs 1 & 2; ⊙9am-4pm)

Scotiabank (cnr Av 3 & Calle 2; ⊙9am-5pm Mon-Fri, 9am-1pm Sat) Exchanges cash and traveler's checks and has a 24-hour ATM dispensing US dollars.

❶ Getting There & Away

Puerto Limón is the transportation hub of the Caribbean coast.

Air

The airstrip is about 4km south of town. There are no regularly scheduled flights, but you can charter a flight to San José through **Nature Air** (www.natureair.com).

Boat

Cruise ships dock in Limón, but most boats providing transportation use the port at Moín, about 7km west of Limón.

Bus

Buses to and from San José, Moín, Guápiles and Siquirres arrive at **Terminal Caribeño** (Av 2 btwn Calles 7 & 8) on the west side of the baseball stadium.

Guápiles (Tracasa) US$4; two hours; departs almost hourly 5am to 6pm.

Moín, for boats to Tortuguero (Tracasa) US$0.60; 20 minutes; departs hourly 5:30am to 6:30pm.

San José (Autotransportes Caribeños) US$5.50; three hours; departs almost hourly 5am to 7pm.

Buses to points south all depart from **Autotransportes Mepe Terminal** (⌨2758-1572; Calle 6 btwn Avs 1 & 2), on the east side of the stadium.

Bribrí & Sixaola US$5.50; three hours; departs hourly between 5am and 7pm.

Manzanillo US$4.50; two hours; departs at 5:30am, 6am 10:30am, 3pm and 6pm Monday to Friday.

Puerto Viejo de Talamanca via Cahuita US$3.20; 1½ hours; departs almost hourly 5am to 7pm.

Around Puerto Limón

PLAYA BONITA

While not the finest beach in the Caribbean, Playa Bonita offers sandy stretches of seashore and good swimming convenient to Limón. Surfers make their way to Bonita for its point/reef break, which makes for a powerful (and sometimes dangerous) left. Any Limón–Moín bus will drop you off at these places.

▣ Sleeping & Eating

The road between Limón and Moín is home to some good accommodations that are much more attractive than anything in Limón proper.

Oasys del Caribe BUNGALOW $
(⌨2795-0024; oasysdelcaribe@ice.co.cr; s/d/f with air-con US$35/40/60, without air-con US$30/35/50; ❘P❘❄❘❀❘) About 3km northwest of Limón, on the inland side of the road, these cozy pink bungalows are decorated with lace curtains and bamboo furniture. The small pool is a huge perk, as this place does not have beach access.

Hotel Maribú Caribe
BUNGALOW **$$**

(☎2795-2553, 2795-2543; www.maribu-car ibe.com; s/d/f incl breakfast US$68/78/112; P❄✿❋) About 3km northwest of Limón, on the ocean side, is this 56-room hilltop hotel with spacious thatch-roofed, white-stucco bungalows dotting a well-maintained garden. Rooms come equipped with cable TV and minifridge. A popular onsite restaurant – with incredible water views – dishes out Costa Rican and Mediterranean specialties.

Hotel Playa Bonita
HOTEL **$$**

(☎2795-1670; www.hotelplayabonita.com; s/d standard US$42/60, executive US$60/80; P❄@❋) This seaside hotel has simple, whitewashed rooms and an ocean-view restaurant serving everything from burgers to jumbo shrimp. It's 2.5km from the entrance to the docks at Moín.

Reina's
SEAFOOD **$**

(☎2795-0879; mains US$7-14; ⊙10am-10pm) Situated right on the beach, Reina's has loud music, good vibes and plenty of *mariscos* (seafood) and *cerveza* (beer) on the menu.

MOÍN

This is Puerto Limón's main transportation dock, where you can catch a boat to Parismina or Tortuguero.

❶ Getting There & Away

The journey by boat to Tortuguero can take anywhere from three to five hours, depending on how often the boat stops to observe wildlife (many tours also stop for lunch). Indeed, it is worth taking your time. As you wind your way through these jungle canals, you are likely to spot howler monkeys, crocodiles, two- and three-toed sloths and an amazing array of wading birds, including roseate spoonbills.

Schedules for these tourist boats exist in theory only and change frequently depending on demand. If the canal is blocked by water hyacinths or logjams, the route might be closed altogether. If you're feeling lucky, you can just show up in Moín in the morning and try to get on one of the outgoing tour boats. But you are better off reserving in advance, particularly during slower seasons when boats don't travel the route on a daily basis. Call ahead for departure times and reservations. Fares to Tortuguero generally cost US$35 to US$40 one way, and about US$25 to Parismina.

Asociación de Boteros de los Canales de Tortuguero (Abacat; ☎8360-7325) Regular service to Tortuguero.

Caribbean Tropical Tours (☎8371-2323, 2798-7027; wguerrerotuca@hotmail.com) Run by master sloth-spotter William Guerrero and his wife; ideal for leisurely rides to Tortuguero.

Moín–Parismina–Tortuguero Water Taxi (☎2709-8005; one way US$35) Reservations essential, especially for stops in Parismina.

Tropical Wind (☎8313-7164, 8327-0317, 2798-6059) Almost-daily shuttles in high season.

Viajes Bananero (☎8833-1066, in San José 2222-8973) Regular (though not daily) trips to Tortuguero.

Tracasa buses to Moín from Puerto Limón (US$0.60, 20 minutes) depart from Terminal Caribeño hourly from 5:30am to 6:30pm. Get off the bus before it goes over the bridge. If driving, leave your car in a guarded lot in Limón.

NORTHERN CARIBBEAN

Running north–south along the country's waterlogged eastern shore, the Canales de Tortuguero (Tortuguero Canal) serves as the liquid highway that connects Puerto Limón to the lush lowland settlements to the north: Parismina, Tortuguero and Barra del Colorado. This is the wettest region in Costa Rica, a network of rivers and canals that are home to diminutive fishing villages and slick sportfishing camps, raw rainforest and all-inclusive resorts – not to mention plenty of wading birds and sleepy sloths.

Most significantly, the area's long, wild beaches serve as the protected nesting grounds for three kinds of sea turtles. In fact, more green turtles are born here than anywhere else. Much of the region lies only a 30-minute flight from San José – but it nonetheless can feel like the end of the earth.

Parismina

If you want to get a sense of what Costa Rica's Caribbean coast was like prior to the arrival of mass tourism, this tiny coastal fishing village, wedged between the Canales de Tortuguero and the Caribbean Sea, is an excellent spot to explore. Bereft of zip lines, 4WD adventure tours and wi-fi everything, it's the sort of place where old men play dominoes on their front porches and kids splash in muddy puddles in the road.

Sportfishing is the traditional tourist draw here. (The top tarpon season runs from January to mid-May, while snook are caught from September to November.) But a smattering of travelers also arrive to see and protect endangered sea turtles. Leatherback turtles nest on the beach between late February and early October, with the peak season in April and May. Green turtles begin nesting in June, with a peak in August and September. Hawksbills are not as common, but they are sometimes seen between February and September.

In addition, every year around July 16, fishers and local boat captains have a small waterborne procession in honor of the Virgen del Carmen, the patron saint of sailors.

🏃 Activities

Asociación Salvemos
Las Tortugas de Parismina VOLUNTEERING
(ASTOP/Save the Turtles of Parismina; ☑2710-7703, 2798-2220; www.parisminaturtles.org; ⊘2-4pm Mar-Oct) ASTOP is a grassroots turtle-protection organization employing former poachers as 'turtle guides.' It has built a guarded turtle hatchery to deter poachers and thieves. Travelers can volunteer as turtle guards to patrol the beaches alongside local turtle guides. Volunteers have to pay a US$30 registration fee, in addition to a daily US$27 lodging fee that includes training, accommodations with a local family and three meals daily. A three-night minimum is required.

ASTOP also organizes homestays (per night with three meals US$27) and offers internet access (per hour US$3), and can arrange horseback-riding trips, bike rentals, turtle-watching tours (per person US$20), wildlife-viewing excursions by boat, and farm and heliconia-garden tours in Caño Blanco.

Barrita SWIMMING
A 15-minute walk south of town brings you to the jungle-fringed freshwater lagoon called Barrita. From the Catholic church, head toward the beach and hang a right at the airstrip, then follow the path until it opens out onto the beach and (croc-free!) lagoon.

You can rent kayaks for US$10 per day at Carefree Ranch or Iguana Verde to explore the canals and their denizens.

🛏 Sleeping & Eating

Green Gold Ecolodge LODGE $$
(☑8647-0691, 8697-2322; www.greengoldecolodge. vpweb.ca; dm adult/child incl 3 meals US$50/30) About 3km south of the dock, this simple lodge, steps from the beach and surrounded by 36 hectares of jungle. This solar- and generator-powered retreat is run by the charming (and bilingual) Jason and Juliana. It's basic – expect dorm beds in screened-in upstairs rooms, a shared open-air kitchen and shared bathrooms – but it's comfortable for what it is: an authentic rainforest hideaway. Jason leads tours of all kinds, and the area is rife with as much wildlife as in Tortuguero, but hardly any people. Walk in from the village, or arrange for a truck ride from town (US$10 one way); advance reservations recommended.

Carefree Ranch CABINA $
(☑8909-8922, 2710-3149; r per person US$10) Opposite the Catholic church on the southern end of town, this clapboard house – bright yellow with green trim – has nine tidy rooms and an inviting, broad front porch. In Parismina, it's about as quaint as things get. Meals are available for an additional charge.

Iguana Verde CABINA $
(☑8765-1280, 2758-6400; s/d US$15/25) Set around a small garden courtyard in the middle of town, three tidy rooms have bathrooms and a shared screened patio. The attached *soda* is a great place to watch life meander by.

Parismina Gamefish Lodge CABINA $
(☑8971-1756, 2758-5456; r per person with/without air-con US$20/10; ✷) Across from Iguana Verde in the middle of town, this spot has six simple, tiled rooms surrounding a garden lined with hammocks. The beds are firm and the tiled rooms are spacious.

Soda Rancho La Palma COSTA RICAN $
(☑2798-0259; casados US$6; ⊘6am-7pm Mon-Sat) Right next to the dock, no-nonsense doña Amelia serves up fresh and tasty *casados*. She also keeps the small plaster statue of the Virgin that is paraded during the annual boat procession in July.

Don Alex at the hardware store, about 300m north of the dock, has camping and basic huts (US$6 to US$7; high season only), with access to showers and bathrooms.

Caribbean Tarpon Lodge (☎2798-0964, in USA 888-341-5525; www.caribbeantarponlodge.com; 5-day/4-night package per person US$1700-2500) and Río Parismina Lodge (☎2229-7597, in USA 210-824-4442, in USA 800-338-5688; www.riop.com; 5-day/4-night package per person US$2800; ☺☒) organize package sport-fishing expeditions from the USA.

ℹ Information

There are no banks or post offices in Parismina. Credit cards and traveler's checks are not accepted, so make sure you bring plenty of cash. While the village has a couple of pay phones, no one in town sells phone cards – bring your own. You can find internet access at ASTOP.

ℹ Getting There & Away

Parismina is only accessible by boat or chartered flight, and the only regular service is to Caño Blanco (for transfer to Siquirres).

To get to Caño Blanco, take one of the water taxis (US$2) that leave from the Parismina dock at 5:30am, 1:30pm and 4:30pm on weekdays, and at 9am and 1:30pm on weekends. Buses will be waiting at the dock to continue the journey to Siquirres (US$2), where you can find onward transport.

To travel to Puerto Limón (via Moín) or Tortuguero, it is simple enough to secure a seat on one of the tourist boats that travel between the two destinations, provided you reserve in advance. Note that it may take 24 to 48 hours to secure transportation (around US$25), as Parismina is not a regular stop. Call one of the boat companies in Moín directly, or ask doña Amelia at Soda Rancho La Palma to help you book.

Parque Nacional Tortuguero

'Humid' is the driest word that could truthfully be used to describe Tortuguero, a 311-sq-km coastal park that serves as the most important breeding ground of the green sea turtle. With an annual rainfall of up to 6000mm in the northern part of the park, it is one of the wettest areas in the country. In addition, the protected area extends into the Caribbean Sea, covering about 5200 sq km of marine habitat. In other words, plan on spending quality time in a boat.

The famed **Canales de Tortuguero** are the introduction to this park. A north–south waterway created to connect a series of lagoons and meandering rivers in 1974, this engineering marvel allowed inland navigation between Limón and coastal villages in something sturdier than a dugout canoe. Regular flights service the village of Tortuguero – but if you fly, you'll be missing half the fun. The leisurely taxi-boat ride, through banana plantations and wild jungle, is equal parts recreation and transportation.

Most visitors come to watch sea turtles lay eggs on the wild beaches. The area attracts four of the world's eight species of sea turtle, making it a crucial habitat for these massive reptiles. It will come as little surprise, then, that these hatching grounds gave birth to the sea turtle–conservation movement. The Caribbean Conservation Corporation, the first program of its kind in the world, has continuously monitored turtle populations here since 1955. Today green sea turtles are increasing in numbers along this coast, but the leatherback, hawksbill and loggerhead are in decline.

The area, however, is more than just turtles: Tortuguero teems with wildlife. You'll find sloths and howler monkeys in the treetops, tiny frogs and green iguanas scurrying among buttress roots, and mighty tarpons and endangered manatees swimming in the waters.

🏃 Activities

Turtle-Watching

Most female turtles share a nesting instinct that drives them to return to the beach of their birth (natal beach), in order to lay their eggs. (Only the leatherback returns to a more general region, instead of a specific beach.) During their lifetimes, they will usually nest every two to three years and, depending on the species, may come ashore to lay eggs 10 times in one season. Often, a turtle's ability to successfully reproduce depends on the ecological health of this original habitat.

The female turtle digs a perfect cylindrical cavity in the sand using her flippers, and then lays 80 to 120 eggs. She diligently covers the nest with sand to protect the eggs, and she may even create a false nest in another location in an attempt to confuse predators. She then makes her way back to sea – after which the eggs are on their own. Incubation ranges from 45 to 70 days, after which hatchlings – no bigger than the size of your palm – break out of their shells using a caruncle, or temporary tooth. They crawl to the ocean in small groups, moving as quickly as possible to avoid dehydration and predators. Once they reach the surf, they must swim for at least 24 hours to get to deeper water, away from land-based predators.

Because of the sensitive nature of the habitat and the critically endangered status of some species, tours to see this activity are highly regulated. So as to not alarm turtles as they come to shore (a frightened turtle will return to the ocean and dump her eggs), tour groups gather in shelter sites close to the beach and a spotter relays a turtle's location via radio once she has safely crossed the high-tide mark and built her nest. At this time, visitors can then go to the beach and watch the turtle lay her eggs, cover her nest and return to the ocean. Seeing a turtle is not guaranteed, but licensed guides will still make your tour worthwhile with the wealth of turtle information they'll share. By law, tours can only take place between 8am and midnight. Some guides will offer tours after midnight; these are illegal.

Visitors should wear closed-toe shoes and rain gear. Tours cost US$20 (a flat rate established by the village), which includes the purchase of a US$4 sticker that pays for the patrols that help protect the nesting sites from scavengers and looters. Nesting season runs from March to October, with July and August being prime time. The next best time is April, when leatherback turtles nest in small numbers. Flashlights and cameras are not allowed on the beach.

Other Wildlife-Watching

More than 300 bird species, both resident and migratory, have been recorded in Tortuguero – a bird-watchers' paradise. Due to the wet habitat, the park is especially rich in waders, including egrets, jacanas, 14 different types of heron, as well as species such as kingfishers, toucans and the great curassow (a type of jungle peacock known locally as the *pavón*). The great green macaw is a highlight, most common from December to April, when the almond trees are fruiting. In September and October, look for flocks of migratory species such as eastern kingbird, barn swallows and purple martins. The Caribbean Conservation Corporation conducts a biannual monitoring program, in which volunteers can help scientists take inventory of local and migratory species.

Certain species of mammals are particularly evident in Tortuguero, especially mantled howler monkeys, the Central American spider monkey and white-faced capuchin. If you've got a good pair of binoculars and a good guide, you can usually see both two- and three-toed sloths. In addition, normally

Around Tortuguero

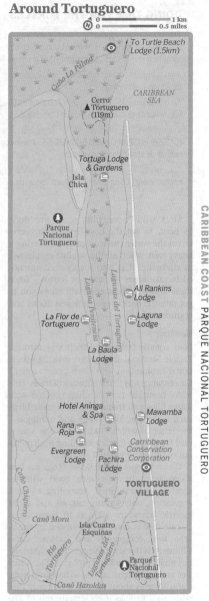

shy neotropical river otters are reasonably habituated to boats. Harder to spot are timid West Indian manatees. The park is also home to big cats such as jaguars and ocelots – but these are savvy, nocturnal animals whose sightings are very rare.

DOING TIME FOR THE TURTLES

There are many opportunities for volunteers to help protect sea turtles and the numerous other creatures that inhabit the Caribbean coast. In most cases, organizations require a minimum commitment of a week. A few options:

Asociación Salvemos Las Tortugas de Parismina (p411) Small, locally run organization in Parismina.

Asociación Widecast (☎in San José 8818-2543; www.widecast.org) Grassroots NGO that has volunteer opportunities in Cahuita and north of the Río Pacuare rivermouth.

Canadian Organization for Tropical Education and Rainforest Conservation (☎2709-8052, in Canada 905-831-8809; www.coterc.org) Canadian not-for-profit with a research station in Tortuguero.

Caribbean Conservation Corporation (☎2709-8091, in USA 800-678-7853; www.cccturtle.org) Long-time organization with a research station in Tortuguero.

Most wildlife-watching tours are done by boat. To get the best from Tortuguero, be on the water early or go out following a heavy rain, when all the wildlife comes out to sunbathe. It is also highly recommended to take tours by canoe or kayak – since these smaller, silent craft will allow you to get into the park's less trafficked nooks and crannies.

Boating

Four aquatic trails wind their way through Parque Nacional Tortuguero, inviting waterborne exploration. Río Tortuguero acts as the entrance way to the network of trails. This wide, beautiful river is often covered with water lilies and frequented by aquatic birds such as herons, kingfishers and anhingas – the latter of which is known as the snakebird for the way its slim, winding neck pokes out of the water when it swims.

Caño Chiquero and Caño Mora are two narrower waterways with good wildlife-spotting opportunities. According to park regulation, only kayaks, canoes and silent electric boats are allowed in these areas (a rule that is constantly violated by many area tour companies and lodges). Caño Chiquero is thick with vegetation, especially red guácimo trees and epiphytes. Black turtles and green iguanas like to hang out here. Caño Mora is about 3km long but only 10m wide, so it feels as if it's straight out of *The Jungle Book*. Caño Harold is actually an artificially constructed canal, but that doesn't stop the creatures – such as Jesus Christ lizards and caimans – from inhabiting its tranquil waters.

Canoe rental and boat tours are available in Tortuguero village.

Hiking

Behind Cuatro Esquinas station, El Gavilán Land Trail is the only public trail through the park that is on solid ground. Visitors can hike the muddy, 2km out-and-back trail that traverses the tropical humid forest and follows a stretch of beach. Green parrots and several species of monkey are commonly sighted here. The short trail is well marked. Rubber boots are required (for rent at hotels and near the park entrance).

ⓘ Information

Park headquarters is at **Cuatro Esquinas** (☎2709-8086; admission US$10; ⓧ5:30am-6pm with breaks for breakfast & lunch), just south of Tortuguero village. This is an unusually helpful ranger station, with maps, information and access to a 2km-loop nature trail. Wear boots: it's muddy, even in the dry season.

Jalova Station (ⓧ6am-6pm) is on the canal at the south entrance to the national park, accessible from Parismina by boat. Tour boats from Moín often stop here for a picnic; you will find a short nature trail, bathroom, drinking water and rudimentary camping facilities that may or may not be open (and may or may not be flooded).

ⓘ Getting There & Away

The park is a short walk from the village of Tortuguero (the most common entry point) and also accessible by boat from Parismina.

Tortuguero Village

Located within the confines of Parque Nacional Tortuguero, accessible only by air or water, this bustling little village with strong Afro-Caribbean roots is best known for attracting hordes of sea turtles (the name Tortuguero means 'turtle place') – and the hordes of tourists who want to see them. While the peak turtle season is in July and August, the park and village have begun to attract travelers year-round. Even in October, when the turtles have pretty much returned to the sea, caravans of families and adventure travelers arrive to go on jungle hikes and to canoe the area's lush canals.

◎ Sights & Activities

Volunteering

Caribbean Conservation Corporation   VOLUNTEERING
(CCC; ☎2709-8091, in USA 800-678-7853; www. cccturtle.org; admission US$1; ◷10am-noon & 2-5pm Mon-Sat, 2-5pm Sun) About 200m north of Tortuguero village, the CCC operates a research station that has a small visitor center and museum. Exhibits focus on all things turtle-related, including a video about the history of local turtle conservation.

CCC also runs a highly reputable environmental volunteer program, recommended by none other than National Geographic. During nesting season, volunteers can assist with turtle tagging and egg counts, and during bird-migration seasons, help with mist-netting and point-counts. Volunteer fees start at US$1440 per week and include bunk-house accommodations, all meals, first and last nights' hotel room in San José and transport to and from the capital.

Canadian Organization for Tropical Education and Rainforest Conservation   VOLUNTEERING
(Coterc; ☎2709-8052, in Canada 905-831-8809; www.coterc.org; admission free) This not-for-profit organization operates the Estación Biológica Caño Palma, 7km north of Tortuguero village. This small biological research station houses a diminutive museum that contains, among other things, an impressive collection of skulls. From here, a network of trails wind through the surrounding rainforest. Coterc is surrounded on three sides by water, so you'll have to hire a boat to get here.

The group also runs a volunteer program, in which visitors can assist with upkeep of the station and ongoing research projects, including sea-turtle and bird monitoring and plant-diversity inventories. Volunteer fees start at US$200 and include accommodations in dormitory buildings and three meals per day. A two-week minimum commitment is required. Call ahead to arrange a visit.

Boating & Canoeing

Signs all over Tortuguero advertise boat tours and boats for hire. This is obviously the best way to explore the surrounding waterways. See the list of recommended companies and guides in Tours below. Our advice: for optimum wildlife-spotting: forego the motors (the noise scares off wildlife) and opt for a guided tour by canoe.

Numerous area businesses rent kayaks and canoes; inquire locally.

Hiking

A number of trails extend from the village into the national park and around Coterc. Inquire at the agencies listed in Tours below for guided tours. Note: night hiking in the national park is not allowed.

☞ Tours

Guides have posted signs all over town advertising their services for canal tours and turtle walks. The **Tortuguero Info Center** (☎2709-8055; tortuguero_info@racsa.co.cr) can provide information. Going rates are about US$20 per person for a two-hour turtle tour, and US$15 for a two-hour hiking or boat excursion.

Barbara Hartung   BOAT TOUR
(☎8842-6561, 2709-8004; www.tinamontours.de) Trained zoologist offers hiking, canoe, cultural and turtle tours in German, English, French or Spanish.

Castor Hunter Thomas   BOAT TOUR
(☎8870-8634; castorhunter.blogspot.com; Soda Doña María) Excellent local guide who has led hikes, turtle tours and canoe tours for over 20 years.

Daryl Loth   BOAT TOUR
(☎2709-8011, 8833-0827; safari@racsa.co.cr) Canadian-born naturalist (formerly of Coterc) offers supersilent electric motorboat trips, turtle tours and guided hikes.

Chico   BOAT TOUR
(☎2709-8033; Cabinas Miss Miriam) His hiking and canoe tours receive rave reviews.

🛏 Sleeping

If you're unsure about where you've decided to stay, ask to see a room before putting any money down.

TORTUGUERO VILLAGE

There is a wide range of budget and midrange options here. Lodgings on the northern half of town are quieter.

TOP CHOICE Casa Marbella
B&B $$

(☎8833-0827, 2709-8011; casamarbella.tripod.com; s US$35-60, d US$40-65, extra person US$10, all incl breakfast; @🛜) Owned by naturalist Daryl Loth, this charming B&B manages to be wonderfully serene while also being in the middle of it all. Ten simple whitewashed rooms have good lighting and ceiling fans, as well as superclean bathrooms. Hearty breakfasts (think fresh pancakes with tropical fruit) are served on a lovely canal-side deck. It's opposite the Catholic church.

Hotel Miss Junie
CABINA $$

(☎2709-8102; www.iguanaverdetours.com; s/d standard US$45/50, superior US$55/60, all incl breakfast) Miss Junie's place is set on wide grounds, shaded by palm trees and strewn with hammocks and wooden armchairs. Spotless, wood-paneled rooms in a nicely kept tropical plantation–style building are tastefully decorated with wood accents and bright bedspreads. Upstairs rooms share a breezy balcony overlooking the canal. Credit cards accepted. It's at the northern end of the main road.

Cabinas Princesa Resort
CABINA $

(☎2709-8131; princesaresort08@yahoo.com; r per person with/without breakfast US$20/15; 🏊) Of the three Princesa hotels scattered about town, this oceanfront spot is the best. A clapboard structure with 23 basic wood-and-concrete rooms faces an open garden with two pools (one for children). An onsite restaurant serves Caribbean-Tico cuisine. It's 50m east of El Gavilán hardware store.

La Casona
CABINA $

(☎2709-8047, 2709-8092; s/d US$18/25, d with kitchenette US$35; 🛜) Ten cute cement rooms with rustic touches surround a garden at this family-run spot. Three units have kitchenettes with hot plates. It has a pleasant restaurant that serves Italian meals, and the managers can help arrange tours. Credit cards accepted. It's on the north side of the soccer field.

Cabinas Miss Miriam II
CABINA $

(☎8873-2671, 2709-8107; s/d US$20/30; 🛜) This beachside branch of Miss Miriam's budget *cabinas* has clean tiled rooms, firm mattresses and hot water. Rooms surround a small garden courtyard, and there's an onsite *soda* and free wi-fi. It's south of the soccer field, 25m east of the Adventist church.

Cabinas Tortuguero
CABINA $

(☎8622-8137, 2709-8114; cabinas_tortuguero@yahoo.com; s/d without bathroom US$10/16, s/d/tr US$20/25/30) Inland from the Tienda Bambú food shop, you'll find 11 brightly painted bungalows surrounding a tidy garden at this popular Tico-run budget spot. Rooms are clean and there are hammocks for lounging. It's 200m north of the park entrance.

Cabinas Beyetty
CABINA $

(☎8332-3304, 2709-8207; beyetty@hotmail.com; s/d US$15/20; @) Eight basic-but-neat cement-box rooms make up the offerings at this small family-run spot 75m south of the elementary school.

NORTH OF THE VILLAGE

Most of the lodges north of the village cater to high-end travelers on package deals, though most will accept walk-ins (er, boat-ins) if they aren't full. Rates include all meals and are based on double occupancy; credit cards are accepted; exception noted.

TOP CHOICE Rana Roja
LODGE $$

(☎8824-5758, 2709-8260; www.tortuguerorana roja.com; per person US$60; 🛜🏊) This Tico-run spot offers one of the best-value options in the area. Small, earth-colored cabins – all with private terraces and rockers – are connected by elevated walkways. The units are immaculate, with tile floors, hot showers and awesome jungle views. Free kayaks are available onsite and guests can make use of the turtle-shaped swimming pool at the neighboring Evergreen Lodge, just a couple of meters away.

Tortuga Lodge & Gardens
LODGE $$$

(☎2257-0766, 2521-6099; www.costaricaexpeditions.com/tortuga-lodge; 2-night package per adult/child US$528/304; 🏊) Tortuguero's most elegant lodge, operated by Costa Rica Expeditions, is set amid 20 hectares of private gardens. Here you'll find a serene environment, as well as 27 demure rooms that channel a 19th-century safari vibe. Units are accented with creamy linens, handmade textiles, vintage photos and broad terraces that invite lounging. The grounds come equipped with private trails, a pool and a bar-restaurant – both riverside. An all-around excellent choice.

Pachira Lodge
LODGE $$$

(☎2256-6340, 2257-2242; www.pachiralodge.com; 2-night package per adult/child US$289/100; 🛜🏊) A sprawling compound set on 5 hectares of land, this 88-room hotel is a popular family spot, with pristine, brightly painted clapboard bungalows and rooms that sleep up to four. (There are even cribs and children's beds.) All have private terraces, mini-fridge and safe – and there's a turtle-shaped pool, in addition to the region's only zip line (US$30).

Mawamba Lodge   LODGE $$$
(☎2709-8181; www.mawamba.com; 2-night package per adult US$285, adult/child superior US$423/212; ☎☎) With pool tables, foosball, a mosaic swimming pool, and butterfly and frog gardens, this is one of the most tricked-out lodges around. Rooms are simple, wood-paneled affairs with firm beds, good fans and roomy bathrooms with hot water. All are fronted by wide verandas with hammocks and rocking chairs. Packages include several tours.

Laguna Lodge   LODGE $$$
(☎2272-4943, 2709-8082; www.lagunatortuguero. com; 2-night package per person from US$250; ☎☎) This expansive lodge, liberally decorated with gorgeous mosaic art and trim, has 110 graceful rooms with high ceilings and wide decks lined with Sarchí-made leather rocking chairs. It also has a restaurant, two bars (canal-side and poolside), a massage room, soccer pitch and a Gaudí-esque reception area.

All Rankins Lodge   BUNGALOW $$$
(☎2758-4160, 8815-5175; allrankinstours@hotmail. com; 2-night package per person US$220) Run by Tortuguero native Willis Rankin Jr, this simple spot by the airport has 14 basic, wood bungalows with bathrooms and electric showers. The house restaurant dishes up fresh Caribbean cooking, right on the river. Rankin can arrange tours of all kinds. Credit cards not accepted.

📷 Turtle Beach Lodge   LODGE $$$
(☎2248-0707, after hours 8837-6969; www.turtle beachlodge.com; 2-night package per adult/child US$288/110; @☎) The northernmost lodge, located about 8km north of the village, is flanked on either side by beach and river. It is surrounded by 70 hectares of tropical gardens and rainforest. Spacious wood cabins have terra-cotta tile floors, hardwood furniture and huge screened windows to let in the breeze. You can explore the grounds on the network of jungle trails, or lounge around the turtle-shaped pool or the thatch-roofed hammock hut.

Hotel Aninga & Spa   LODGE $$$
(☎2256-6340, 2257-2242; www.aningalodget ortuguero.com; 2-night package per adult/child US$289/100; ☎☎) One of the trio of lodges run by the Pachira Group, the Hotel Aninga & Spa is a 1km boat ride north of the village. Nonguests can make appointments for spa treaments here.

Evergreen Lodge   LODGE $$$
(☎2709-8213; 2-night package per adult/child US$289/100; ☎☎) The Evergreen Lodge is the third of the Pachira lodges north of Tortuguero, with a more rustic, less resorty feel than its counterparts. It's on the south end of Laguna Penitencia.

La Baula Lodge   LODGE $$$
(☎8951-8951, 2709-8041; www.labaulalodge.com; 2-night package per person US$396; @☎☎) This laid-back, long-running lodge has an unpretentious atmosphere, though it could stand a minor makeover. The outdoor dining area features live Latin music on the weekends.

La Flor de Tortuguero   LODGE $$$
(☎2767-0395, 2767-0393; www.hotelflordetortu guero.com; 2-night package per person US$289; ☎☎) Under new management and undergoing gradual renovation at the time of writing, this lodge is in a lovely, wild location on Laguna Penitencia.

🍴 Eating

One of Tortuguero's unsung pleasures is the cuisine: the homey restaurants lure you in from the rain with steaming platters of Caribbean-style food.

Wild Ginger   FUSION $$
(mains US$10-30; ☉noon-9pm) This new beachfront standout is a fantastic addition to village dining options. Well-balanced fusion cuisine utilizes fresh ingredients and includes filet mignon with tamarind sauce and spaghetti carbonara. Leave room for dessert. It's 150m north of the elementary school.

Miss Junie's   CARIBBEAN $$
(☎2709-8029; mains US$9-14; ☉7-9am, 11:30am-2:30pm & 6-9pm) Tortuguero's best-known restaurant grew from a personal kitchen to a full-blown restaurant and lodge. Local specialties on the menu include chicken, fish, and whole lobster cooked in flavorful Caribbean sauces, with coconut rice and beans. It's at the northern end of the main road.

Soda Doña María COSTA RICAN **$**

(✆8870-8634; dishes US$3-6; ⏰7am-8pm) Recover from a hike in the park at this riverside *soda*, serving fresh *jugos* (juices), burgers and *casados*. It's about 200m north of the park entrance.

La Casona ITALIAN **$**

(casados US$6, mains US$6-12; ⏰7:30am-11am & 1:30am-8:30pm; ✐) La Casona serves a variety of Italian specialties, including a well-rendered lasagna made with hearts of palm. It's on the north side of the soccer field.

Miss Miriam's CARIBBEAN **$**

(mains US$4-16; ⏰8am-8pm) This little place dishes out huge plates of flavorful local food, like its well-spiced Caribbean chicken. The extensive menu is displayed above the kitchen (ask for prices). It's on the north side of the soccer field.

Budda Cafe EUROPEAN **$**

(pizzas US$7-9, dishes US$7-18; ⏰11am-9pm; ✐) This cafe on the main road keeps a hipster vibe with ambient club music on the sound system and 'om' symbols stenciled everywhere. It's a lovely setting for excellent pizzas, cocktails and crepes (savory and sweet). Grab a table over the canal outside for a prime view of the yellow-bellied flycatchers zipping over the canal. Credit cards accepted.

Dorling Bakery BAKERY **$**

(pastries from US$1, breakfast US$4-5; ⏰5am-7pm) Supersweet homemade banana bread, lemon cake and other pastries get you even more wired when combined with a shot of espresso. Therefore, it's the perfect (and only) option at 5am for a bite before an early-morning canal tour.

Super Morpho SELF-CATERING

(6:30am-9pm Mon-Sat, 8am-8pm Sun) Self-caterers can pick up basic groceries at the Super Morpho *pulpería* (corner store).

🍸 Drinking & Entertainment

La Taberna Punto de Encuentro BAR

(⏰11am-11pm) Adjacent to the Super Bambú *pulpería*, this popular tavern is mellow in the afternoons, but draws the party people after dark with cold beer and blaring reggaetón. The highlight, however, is the life-sized statue of Jar Jar Binks.

La Culebra CLUB

(⏰8pm-close) Next to the public dock in the center of town, this bright-purple nightclub –

Tortuguero's one and only – plays thumping music and serves beer and *bocas* right on the canal.

ℹ️ Information

Competition for business is fierce in Tortuguero and relentless touts often sell tourists less-than-stellar services. Many so-called 'guides' are unlicensed, others downright unprofessional. Go with recommended guides – and licensed guides, for turtle tours.

The community's website, **Tortuguero Village** (www.tortuguerovillage.com) is a solid source of information, listing local businesses and providing comprehensive directions on how to get to Tortuguero.

There are no banks or ATMs in town and only a few businesses accept credit cards, so bring all the cash you'll need. Internet connections can be iffy, especially during heavy rains.

Beyetty Internet (Cabinas Beyetty; per hr US$4; ⏰8:30am-9pm) Two vintage machines and a friendly proprietor.

Tortuguero Info Center (✆2709-8055; tortuguero_info@racsa.co.cr; per hr US$4; ⏰8am-7pm) Independent information center that sells Sansa airline tickets and provides internet access; may be closed in slower seasons. It's across from the Catholic church.

ℹ️ Getting There & Away

Air

The small airstrip is 4km north of Tortuguero village. Both **NatureAir** (✆2299-6000; www.natureair.com) and **Sansa** (✆2290-4100; www.flysansa.com) have daily flights to and from San José (the one-way flight takes 30 minutes). Charter flights land regularly here as well.

Bus & Boat

Tortuguero is accessible by boat from Cariari or Moín.

During the peak of the turtle-nesting season, we recommend purchasing your tickets at least one day in advance. Many of the information centers in Tortuguero sell these. If you are traveling to San José, you are best off taking a 6am boat because bus connections are better earlier in the day.

Getting to Tortuguero is not difficult; there are a number of companies that offer bus-boat transport service from Cariari to Tortuguero (via La Pavona) several times a day. But competition among rival transportation agencies is fierce, and some will say anything to get your fare – including telling you that they're the only transportation option in town. Don't believe the hype.

FROM SAN JOSÉ

Take the 6:10am, 9am or 10:30am bus to Cariari (three hours) from the Gran Terminal del Caribe in San José. In Cariari, you will arrive at a bus station at the southern end of town (known as the *estación nueva*). From here, walk or take a taxi 500m north to the *estación vieja* (old station), otherwise referred to as the Terminal Caribeño.

PUBLIC TRANSPORTATION FROM CARIARI

The cheapest option is by public transportation on **Clic Clic** (☎8844-0463, 2709-8155) or **Coopetraca** (☎2767-7137, 2767-7590), both of which charge US$5 per person for bus-boat service from the *estación vieja* all the way to Tortuguero. For these two options, the bus service will be the same, but the boat service will be different. Bring colones, as they may not accept US dollars. Buses depart Cariari at 6am, 9am, 11:30am and 3pm.

If you choose Clic Clic, buy only the bus ticket to La Pavona (US$2); if you choose Coopetraca, you'll buy the combined bus-boat ticket (US$5) up front. After a ride through banana plantations, you will arrive at the Río Suerte, where a number of boat companies will be waiting at the dock. (Get ready to be solicited.) If you're riding with Clic Clic, you will pay the remainder of your fare (US$3) to the boatman. Boats depart daily at 7:30am, 1pm and 4:30pm.

PRIVATE TRANSPORTATION FROM CARIARI

For a more expensive private service, there is **Viajes Bananero**, which has an office inside the San José bus terminal in Cariari. Buy your boat ticket here (US$10). From this same point, you will then take a bus (US$1.20) to its proprietary boat dock. Bus departure times are at 11:30am and 2pm. If you are traveling in a group, Bananero can arrange custom pick-ups. For private service, you will need to reserve ahead.

PRIVATE TRANSPORTATION FROM MOÍN

Moín–Tortuguero is primarily a tourist route, and while boats ply these canals frequently, there isn't a scheduled service. **Tropical Wind** (☎8313-7164, 8327-0317, 2798-6059; per person one way US$30) and **Viajes Bananero** (☎2709-8005; per person one-way US$35) are two Tortuguero-based agencies that make the run regularly; both of these can stop in Parismina (one way US$25). Likewise, you can always call the companies operating out of Puerto Limón, since they frequently have boats in the area. Note: it may take 24 to 48 hours to secure transportation – especially in the low season.

Package Tours

If you prefer to leave the planning to someone else, package tours take care of everything from the moment your plane lands in San José. Costs vary widely depending on accommodations and transportation.

Exploradores Outdoors (☎2222-6262; www. exploradoresoutdoors.com)

ⓘ WARNING

There have been reports of thefts on buses plying the route between Cariari and La Pavona. Keep important belongings with you and stash your cash in several places. Likewise, be wary of 'guides' that solicit you for tours on the bus – many of these folks aren't always who they claim to be.

Jungle Tom Safaris (☎2221-7878; www. jungletomsafaris.com)
Riverboat Francesca Nature Tours (☎2226-0986; www.tortugurocanals.com)

Barra del Colorado

At 904 sq km, including the frontier zone with Nicaragua, Refugio Nacional de Vida Silvestre Barra del Colorado, or 'Barra' for short, is the biggest national wildlife refuge in Costa Rica. It is also one of the most remote – more so since Costa Rica's commercial airlines suspended service to the area in 2009. This means that the only way to get to Barra is via local bus-boat transportation from Cariari or charter flight from San José.

The area has long been a favorite of sportfishers who arrive to hook gar, tarpon and snook. But those who aren't into fishing will be rewarded with incredible landscape. The Ríos San Juan, Colorado and Chirripó all wind through the refuge and out to the Caribbean Sea – through a soggy wetland habitat made up of marshes, mangroves and lagoons. Here, you'll find West Indian manatees, caimans, monkeys, tapirs and three-toed sloths, plus a riotous bird population that includes everything from keel-billed toucans to white hawks. There are countless species of waterbird.

The northern border of the refuge is the Río San Juan, the border with Nicaragua (many local residents are Nicaraguan nationals). This area was politically sensitive during the 1980s, due to the Nicaraguan conflict. Today, however, it is possible to journey north along the Río Sarapiquí and east along the Río San Juan, technically entering Nicaragua. While Costa Ricans have right of use, foreign travelers should carry a passport and US$10 when out fishing.

The village of Barra del Colorado lies near the mouth of the Río Colorado and is divided by the river into Barra del Norte and

Barra del Sur. The airstrip is on the south side, but more people live along the north side. The area outside the village is swampy and there are no roads; travel is almost exclusively by boat.

Activities

Fishing is the bread and butter of area lodges, and anglers go for tarpon from January to June and snook from September to December. Fishing is good year-round, however, and other catches include barracuda, mackerel and jack crevalle, all inshore; or bluegill, *guapote* (rainbow bass) and machaca in the rivers. There is also deep-sea fishing for marlin, sailfish and tuna, though this is probably better on the Pacific. Dozens of fish can be hooked on a good day, so 'catch and release' is an important conservation policy of all the lodges.

All of the lodges can also organize custom wildlife-watching excursions along mangroves, lagoons and canals (from US$40).

Sleeping & Eating

From the airport, only Tarpon Land Lodge and Río Colorado Lodge are accessible on foot. Other lodges will have a boat waiting when you arrive with prior reservation.

Tarpon Land Lodge   CABINA $
(☑8607-4484, 8818-9921; tarponlandlodge@hotmail.com; r US$30, r with sportfishing, meals & lodging US$300; ❄) The only budget option in Barra. Situated right next to the airstrip, a brightly painted building has worn wood rooms with private hot showers. An adjacent restaurant and bar is a local gathering spot and a good place for fish *casados* (mains from US$5).

Río Colorado Lodge   LODGE $$$
(☑2232-4063, in USA 800-243-9777; www.riocoloradolodge.com; d per person with/without fishing US$495/120; ❄) Built in 1971, this 18-room lodge is housed in a rambling tropical-style building connected by covered walkways. Rooms are breezy and there is a pool table, an outdoor deck with satellite TV and afternoon happy hours. Situated within walking distance of the landing strip, it attracts a local crowd at the bar, which has earned it a reputation as a 'party lodge.' Rates include meals.

Silver King Lodge   LODGE $$$
(☑2794-0139, in USA 877-335-0755; www.silverkinglodge.com; 3-day package per person from US$2500; ❄@❄) This excellent sportfishing lodge caters to couples and families. Huge

hardwood rooms have cane ceilings, colorful tapestries and lots of amenities. Outside, covered walkways lead to a large swimming pool. Bounteous meals are served buffet-style and an open-air bar whips up tropical drinks. Rates are all-inclusive.

Information

A couple of *pulperías* and a souvenir shop alongside the landing strip sell basic food supplies and dry goods. There is a public phone and patchy internet access. The Servicio de Parques Nacionales (SPN) maintains a small **ranger station** (refuge admission US$10, 60-day freshwater fishing license US$30; ◷6am-6pm) west of the village, in Barra del Sur. However, there are no facilities here. Bring exact change to pay for your entry fee as the rangers rarely have change.

Getting There & Away

It is possible to charter a boat from Tortuguero (prices range from around US$50 to US$100, depending on gas prices, season and number of passengers). Otherwise, most folks get here on air charters arranged by the individual lodges.

SOUTHERN CARIBBEAN

The southern coast is the heart and soul of Costa Rica's Afro-Caribbean community. Jamaican workers arrived in the middle of the 19th century to build the railroad and then stayed on to serve as labor for United Fruit. After the banana industry began its decline in the 1920s, government-mandated segregation kept the black community here. For more than eight decades, they existed independently of the rest of Costa Rica, managing subsistence farms, speaking English and Mekatelyu, eating spicy Caribbean gumbos and swaying to the beat of calypso. Although the racial borders fell in 1949, the local culture still retains its unique traditions.

Also in this area, to the interior, are some of the country's most prominent indigenous groups – cultures that have managed to remain intact despite several centuries' worth of incursions, first from the Spanish, later from the fruit industry and currently from the globalizing effects of tourism. They principally inhabit the Cocles/Kèköldi, Talamanca Cabécar and Bribrí indigenous territories.

Naturally, this fascinating cultural bubble wouldn't remain isolated forever. Since the 1980s the southern coast has seen the arrival of surfers, backpackers and adventurous families on holiday – many of whom have

GETTING TO SAN JUAN DE NICARAGUA

If you are planning to head further into Nicaragua, you can make arrangements with your lodge for a water taxi (per person US$60) to take you to the border town of San Juan del Norte – now called San Juan de Nicaragua (or Greytown). It's a tranquil village, with few services but an interesting history. At various times over the centuries, it has been under the control of Miskito people, Spanish colonists, British troops and even US Marines. Much of it was destroyed during the Contra-Sandinista conflict of the 1980s.

This is a little-used border crossing, however, so don't make the trip without first checking in with Costa Rican immigration officials in **San José** (☎2299-8001) or **Puerto Limón** (☎2798-2097). Barra del Colorado does not have an immigration office of its own, so you might have to secure an exit stamp prior to arriving there.

In San Juan, Río Indio Lodge (☎2231-4299, 2220-3594; www.therioindiolodge.com; d per person incl meals US$168; @☎) has 34 spacious polished-wood rooms, a restaurant and bar. Fishing is the forte, but you can also go hiking or kayaking.

San Juan is linked to the rest of Nicaragua by irregular passenger boats sailing up the Río San Juan to San Carlos, on the Lago de Nicaragua.

---

stayed, adding Italian, German and North American inflections to the cultural stew. For the traveler, it is a rich and rewarding experience – with lovely beaches to boot.

Reserva Biológica Hitoy-Cerere

One of the most rugged and rarely visited reserves in the country, Hitoy-Cerere (☎2795-3170; admission US$6; ⊗8am-4pm) is only about 60km south of Puerto Limón. The 99-sq-km reserve sits on the edge of the Cordillera de Talamanca, characterized by varying altitudes, evergreen forests and rushing rivers. This may be one of the wettest reserves in the parks system, inundated with 4000mm to 6000mm of rain annually.

Naturally, wildlife is abundant. The most commonly sighted mammals include gray four-eyed opossums, tayras (a type of weasel), and howler and capuchin monkeys. There are plenty of ornithological delights as well (with more than 230 avian species), including keel-billed toucans, spectacled owls and the green kingfisher. And, you can hardly miss the Montezuma oropendola, whose massive nests dangle from the trees like twiggy pendulums. The moisture, in the meantime, keeps the place hopping with various species of poison-dart frog.

The reserve is surrounded by some of the country's most remote indigenous reserves, which you can visit with a local guide.

Although there is a ranger station at the reserve entrance with bathrooms, there are no other facilities nearby. A 9km trail leads south to a waterfall, but it is steep, slippery and poorly maintained. Jungle boots are recommended.

❶ Getting There & Away

By car (4WD recommended) from Puerto Limón, head south to Penshurst. Just south of the Río Estrella bridge, head west on the signed road to Valle de la Estrella. Another sign at the bus stop sends you down a good dirt road about 15km to the reserve.

By public transportation, catch a bus from Puerto Limón to Valle de la Estrella. From the end of the bus line (Fortuna/Finca 6) you can hire a taxi to take you the rest of the way and pick you up at a prearranged time (from US$35).

Aviarios del Caribe Sloth Sanctuary

About 10km northwest of Cahuita, this wildlife sanctuary (☎2750-0775; www.slothsanctuary.com; tour adult/child US$25/15; ⊗8am-5pm) sits on an 88-hectare property bordering the Río Estrella. Here, proprietors Luis Arroyo and Judy Avery help injured and orphaned sloths, providing travelers with an opportunity to see these unique animals up close. (Irrefutable fact: there is nothing cuter than a baby sloth.) Though many of the rehabilitated sloths remain on the grounds – animals orphaned at a very young age don't have the skills to return to the wild – Luis and Judy have been successful at releasing more than 80 of them back into area forests.

Volunteer opportunities may be available; check the website for updates.

1. Puerto Viejo de Talamanca (p432)

Puerto Viejo de Talamanca is a mix of chilled-out beaches and hedonistic partying.

2. Rainforest Aerial Tram (p402)

Visitors can view the flora and fauna of the rainforest canopy during this unique gondola ride.

3. Parque Nacional Tortuguero (p412)

With more than 300 bird species, this national park is a bird-watcher's paradise.

4. Puerto Viejo de Talamanca (p432)

Laid-back bungalows are among the accommodations options here.

A STAY IN THE FOREST: SELVA BANANITO

On the edge of Parque Internacional La Amistad, this rustic family-run farm and lodge (☑8375-4419, 2253-8118; www.selvabananito.com; per person from US$130, per person 2-night package from US$432, all incl 3 meals daily; P) is composed of 12 hilly sq km ideal for tree climbing, waterfall rappelling, hiking and horseback riding. Above all, this is an environmentally conscious spot: the Stein family employs solar energy and uses biodegradable soaps and cleaning products. Cabins are all crafted from recycled hardwoods and constructed Caribbean-style, on stilts, for optimum ventilation.

Rates are based on double occupancy. Packages include transfers from San José, as well as a waterfall tour, horseback riding and a tree-climbing lesson. If you are driving yourself, note that the route requires river crossings; it's for 4WD only. Detailed driving directions are posted online.

Cahuita

POP 600

Even as tourism has mushroomed on Costa Rica's southern coast, Cahuita has managed to hold onto its laid-back Caribbean vibe. The roads are made of dirt, many of the older houses rest on stilts and chatty neighbors still converse in Mekatelyu. A graceful black-sand beach and a chilled-out demeanor hint at a not-so-distant past, when the area was little more than just a string of cacao farms.

Cahuita proudly claims the area's first permanent Afro-Caribbean settler – a turtle fisherman named William Smith, who moved his family to Punta Cahuita in 1828. Now his descendants, along with those of so many other West Indian immigrants, run the backyard eateries and brightly painted bungalows that hug this idyllic stretch of coast.

Situated on a pleasant point, the town itself has a waterfront, but no beach. For that, most folks make the jaunt to Playa Negra or into neighboring Parque Nacional Cahuita.

◉ Sights & Activities

Tree of Life   GARDENS
(☑8610-0490, 2755-0014; www.treeoflifecostarica.com; adult/child US$12/6, guided tour US$15; ⊙9am-3pm Nov–mid-Apr, daily tour 11am Jul-Aug, closed mid-Apr–Jun & Sep-Oct) This wildlife center and botanical garden 2km west of town on the Playa Negra road rescues and rehabilitates animals, while also promoting conservation through education. Among the animals in residence, there's a kinkajou, a pair of peccaries, sloths and monkeys. It's possible to volunteer here; see the website for information.

Mariposario de Cahuita   GARDENS
(☑2755-0361; admission US$10; ⊙8:30am-3:30pm Mon-Fri, to noon Sat; ♦) Stroll around the fountain-filled grounds of this butterfly farm and admire the local residents, including many friendly caterpillars. Descriptions are posted in several languages; guided tours are available. It's located just off of Hwy 36.

Playa Negra   BEACH
At the northwest end of Cahuita, Playa Negra is a long, black-sand beach flying the *bandera azul ecológica*, a flag that indicates the beach is kept to the highest ecological standards. This is undoubtedly Cahuita's top spot for swimming and is never crowded. When the swells are big, this spot also has an excellent beach break for beginners.

Playa Blanca   SWIMMING
At the entrance to the national park. A good option for swimming.

☞ Tours

Snorkeling, horseback riding, chocolate tours and visits to nearby indigenous territories are standard offerings.

Willie's Tours   TOUR
(☑2755-1024, 8917-6982; www.willies-costarica-tours.com; ⊙8am-noon & 3-7pm Mon-Sat) A full-service tour agency that can also arrange further-flung tours and transport.

Centro Turístico Brigitte   HORSE RIDING
(☑2755-0053; www.brigittecahuita.com; Playa Negra) Does it all, but specializes in horseback-riding tours; check website for tour and accommodation packages. Located 300m west and 50m south of the plaza.

Cahuita Tours   TOUR
(☑2755-0000, 2755-0101; www.cahuitatours.com) One of the most established agencies in town.

Mister Big J's TOUR
(☎2755-0353, 8887-4695; ☺7am-6pm) Offers the usual range of tours.

Roberto's Tours FISHING
(☎8396-9864, 2755-0117) Specializes in sport-fishing tours *and* has a restaurant for cooking up your catch.

🛏 Sleeping

There are two general areas to stay in Cahuita: the town center (which can be a little noisy), or north of town along Playa Negra. If you're roaming between Playa Negra and the center at night, it's best not to walk and especially not alone.

CENTER

TOP CHOICE **Bungalows Aché** BUNGALOW **$$**
(☎2755-0119; www.bungalowsache.com; bungalows US$40-50; P🖂) In Nigeria, Aché means 'Amen,' and you'll likely say the same thing when you see these spotless octagonal bungalows nestled into a delightful garden bordering the national park. The three charming, polished wood cabins have bright red-and-white linens and come stocked with a lockbox, minifridge, kettle and private decks with hammocks.

Alby Lodge BUNGALOW **$$**
(☎2755-0031; www.albylodge.com; d/tr/q US$50/55/60; P🖂) This fine German-run lodge on the edge of the park has spacious landscaped grounds that attract howler monkeys and birds. Four raised bungalows are spread out, allowing for plenty of privacy. High ceilings, mosquito nets and driftwood details make for pleasant jungle decor. A common *rancho* (thatched gazebo) has excellent communal kitchen facilities.

Hotel La Casa de las Flores HOTEL **$$**
(☎2755-0326; www.lacasadelasfloreshotel.com; d incl breakfast US$80, additional person US$15; P✳🖂) This bright Italian-owned spot has 10 large, sleek contemporary rooms (one of which is wheelchair-accessible) equipped with spacious bathrooms, cable TV and efficient air-con. The close proximity to Coco's, however, puts you within thumping distance of the bar's well-endowed speakers. Credit cards accepted.

Cabinas Jenny CABINA **$$**
(☎2755-0256; www.cabinasjenny.com; d/tr downstairs US$27/33, upstairs US$44/50; P) A stone's throw from the advancing waves are these neat, tidy rooms. Upstairs is best, with units that have wood detailing and ocean views,

as well as mosquito nets, coffeemakers and toaster ovens. Call in advance to make sure that somebody is here when you arrive.

Cabinas Secret Garden CABINA **$**
(☎8772-1846, 2755-0581; koosiecosta@live.nl; dm US$9, s/d US$15/25; P@🖂) This tiny Dutch-run place with a lush garden has five tiled units with fans, mosquito nets and hot-water showers in cubicle-style bathrooms. One dorm has five beds. It's on the road leading southwest from the national park entrance.

Ciudad Perdida BUNGALOW **$$**
(☎2755-0303; www.ciudadperdidaecolodge.com; d standard/house incl breakfast US$95/115; P✳🖂) Bordering the national park, this eco-conscious lodge offers cute one- and two-room, candy-colored wood bungalows in a landscaped garden. All include hammocks, ceiling fans, refrigerators and safe boxes. One house has a Jacuzzi, three have kitchens and all have cable TV. Credit cards accepted.

Kelly Creek Hotel CABINA **$$**
(☎2755-0007; www.hotelkellycreek.com; s/d US$50/55, extra person US$10; P🖂) Just outside the entrance to the national park, you may be serenaded by the dulcet squawks of the resident parrot; draw closer and find four graceful, tropical *cabinas* with high ceilings, cream-colored linens and mosquito nets. Paintings by local artists adorn the reception area, and the onsite restaurant (open from 6:30pm Monday to Saturday) serves up paella for two (US$15).

Spencer Seaside Lodging CABINA **$**
(☎2755-0027; s/d downstairs US$16/26, upstairs US$20/30; P) Rooms at this long-time, locally owned spot are basic but big – and the seaside setting can't be beat. Upstairs units have better views, as well as a shared terrace strung with hammocks.

Hotel Cabinas Vaz CABINA **$**
(☎2755-0218; hotelvaz@gmail.com; d with/without air-con US$40/35; P✳@🖂🏊) The first hotel you'll see as you walk into town from the bus station is this motor-court–style structure surrounding a gravel courtyard and a pool. Built in a tropical style, it houses 21 fairly spacious rooms with wood furnishings, bright ceramic tiles, cable TV and plenty of daylight. A terrific deal.

Siatami Lodge BUNGALOW **$$**
(☎2755-0374, reservations 2573-4746; www.siatami.com; s/d/tr/q US$65/72/82/100; P) This

Cahuita

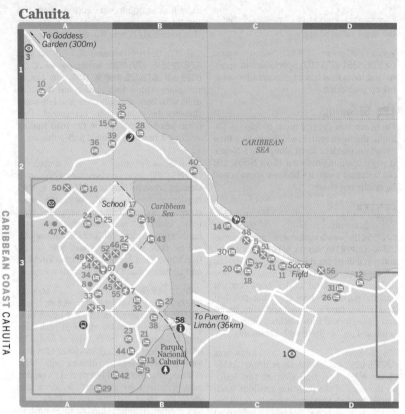

lodge, at a tranquil spot on the edge of Parque Nacional Cahuita, is ideal for families, as the 10 casas (houses) are fully equipped with two bedrooms, living space and kitchen. From each, a terrace overlooks a large private garden. With rainforest all around, this the next best thing to staying in the park itself.

Cabinas Safari 1
CABINA **$**

(☎2755-0405; www.cabinassafari.com; s/d/tr/q US$20/25/35/45; **P**@) Seven cheerful, tiled rooms come with floral linens, bathrooms, private decks and hammocks. The vibe is chilled and safe at this colorful spot. Find it on the same block as the Parque Central as you head north toward the beach.

Cabinas Arrecife
CABINA **$**

(☎2755-0081; www.cabinasarrecife.com; s/d/tr US$25/30/40; **P**🛜🌀) Tiled rooms at this oceanfront spot are basic but comfortable, with polished wood ceilings and fans. Tico

breakfasts (US$5) are available, as is a fully equipped shared kitchen. A tiny pool makes up for the lack of a beach.

Cabinas Riverside
CABINA **$**

(☎8893-2252; d with/without kitchen US$25/20; **P**) Efficient service and clean rooms are what you'll find at this tidy nine-room inn near Kelly Creek that is lined with hammocks and Adirondack chairs. Simple rooms have mosquito nets and hot stone showers.

Cahuita National Park Hotel
HOTEL **$$**

(☎2755-0244; hotelnationalpark03@gmail.com; s/d /tr/q US$40/45/55/65; **P**⟳🌀🛜) Try to get one of the huge, if bare, rooms with excellent ocean views. It's at the national park entrance.

Cabinas Smith 1 & 2
CABINAS **$**

(☎2755-0068; s/d/tr older r US$12/16/21, s/d/ tr/q newer r US$25/31/36/46; **P**🌀) Clean rooms in a quiet part of town, spanning two properties.

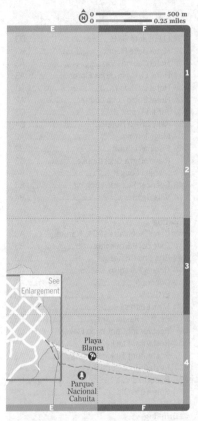

N 0 — 500 m
0 — 0.25 miles

See Enlargement

Playa Blanca

Parque Nacional Cahuita

PLAYA NEGRA

TOP CHOICE **Playa Negra Guesthouse** BUNGALOW $$

(✆2755-0127; www.playanegra.cr; d US$60-75, cottage US$95-140; P✿) This beautiful Caribbean-style plantation house, with several freestanding storybook cottages (equipped with full kitchens), is meticulously decorated and maintained. Guest rooms are painted sherbety colors and feature charming tropical accents, such as colorful mosaics in the bathrooms and cozy wicker lounge chairs on the private decks. Every unit has a minifridge and coffeemaker; there is a barbecue and honor bar, plus a lovely free-form pool set into a well-manicured garden dotted with fan palms. A winner all around. Credit cards accepted. Find it 200m west of the soccer field.

Piscina Natural CABINA $$

(✆2755-0146; piscinanaturalcr.hotels.officelive.com; d/tr US$40/50; P) This gem of a spot lies about 1km northwest of the soccer field along the main road. Run by inimitable Cahuita native Walter, it's a self-proclaimed 'Caribbean Paradise,' and rightfully so. Painted cement rooms are comfortable and come equipped with bathrooms. What makes this chilled-out little place so special are the lush grounds and the natural pool amid the rocks. There is a huge shared kitchen and an outdoor lounge studded with intriguing driftwood sculptures.

Magellan Inn INN $$$

(✆2755-0035; www.magellaninn.com; d with fan/air-con US$85/108, d deluxe US$130, all incl breakfast; P✿✿) An elegant little oasis in a very peaceful location, this very comfortable inn has six spacious rooms with rustic wood furnishings, firm mattresses and private terraces with hammocks. It also has a refined, open-air bar that overlooks a beautifully landscaped garden and pool. It's located along the road that branches off towards the Hotel Suizo Loco Lodge.

El Encanto B&B B&B $$

(✆2755-0113; www.elencantocahuita.com; s/d US$65/75, studio/ste/house US$95/125/220, all incl breakfast; P✿) This charming French-owned B&B, only about 200m west of downtown Cahuita, is set into lovingly landscaped grounds that are dotted with easy chairs and hammocks. Demure bungalows have high ceilings, tile floors and firm beds draped in colorful textiles. The studio and the beach house both have fully equipped kitchens. Credit cards accepted.

Villa Delmar CABINAS $

(✆2755-0375, 2755-0392; www.villadelmarcr.com; d US$18-25; P) In an out-of-the-way spot close to the national park, the Villa Delmar has a great deal for the price, with shared kitchen and laundry service.

Cabinas Brisas del Mar CABINAS $

(✆2755-0011; d US$30; P) Quiet spot near the water; small, fully equipped apartment available.

Hotel Belle Fleur CABINAS $

(✆8986-8413, 2755-0283; www.hotelbellefleur. com; s/d US$20/25, s/d with air-con US$27/32; P✿) Has potential, under new ownership; near entrance to park.

Cabinas Surfside CABINAS $

(✆2755-0246; evadarling1930@yahoo.com; s/d/tr US$20/25/30; P) Basic rooms face a grassy garden; run by a friendly local family. It's near the school.

Cahuita

Coral Hill Bungalows BUNGALOW $$$
(☑2755-0554, 2755-0479; www.coralhillbungalows.com; d/tr incl breakfast US$110/125 ; ◈) Heading away from Cahuita, hang a left at the Reggae Restaurant to find your way to Coral Hill Bungalows. Five immaculate bungalows are done up in tropical decor: wood floors, bamboo furniture, mosquito nets and hand-painted ceramic details; the porches sport hammocks and leather rocking chairs. Luxuries include pillow-top mattresses, fresh flowers and full breakfasts served by your gracious hosts.

Cabinas Algebra BUNGALOW $
(☑2755-0057; www.cabinasalgebra.com; bungalows US$20-35; ℗◈) This long-time German-run place has three cabins conveying a rustic *Swiss Family Robinson* vibe. Each of the cozy units is crafted from wood and strung with hammocks. An onsite restaurant serves Tico food, including veggie options on request. It's a 2km trek out of town, but the owners will come pick you up in town (for free!) if you call in advance. A solid, family-friendly budget choice.

Cabinas Tito BUNGALOW $
(☑8880-1904, 2755-0286; www.cahuita-cabinas-tito.com; d with/without hot water US$25/20, additional person US$8; ℗) Surrounded by extensive tropical gardens and banana plants, this charming spot offers seven brightly painted *casitas*. Just 200m outside of Ca-

huita down the small side road, the very clean units here are quiet and furnished in wicker, with mosquito nets and jungle accents.

Centro Turístico Brigitte
CABINA $

(☏2755-0053; www.brigittecahuita.com; s/d/tr US$35/40/50, s without bathroom US$15; P@☞) The well-signed Centro Turístico Brigitte is down the turnoff at the Reggae Restaurant. A couple of cute, basic wood *cabinas* are painted in bright colors and come with or without kitchens. Brigitte also offers surfboard and bike rentals, arranges tours and has an onsite restaurant. Credit cards accepted.

Cabinas Iguana
CABINA $$

(☏2755-0005; www.cabinas-iguana.com; d bungalow US$40-100, d without bathroom US$25; P☞☒) Set back from the beach on the road marked by the Reggae Restaurant, several bungalows are nestled into the lushly forested grounds. Simple wood cabins of various sizes have ceramic tile floors and beds with mosquito nets.

Cabinas Nirvana
CABINA $$

(☏2755-0110; www.nirvanalodge.com; d US$35-60, additional person US$10; ☞☒) The seven *cabinas* here come in a variety of arrangements at this lush garden spot surrounding a pool. A couple of units have kitchens, one has air-con and one has a broad veranda. You'll find it along the same turnoff marked by the Reggae Restaurant; credit cards accepted.

Bluspirit
BUNGALOW $$

(☏2755-0122; www.bungalowsbluspirit.com; s/d/tr US$40/50/60; P) Three small but delightful blue A-frame cabins are lined up on a pleasant stretch of rocky, waterfront property just 100m along the road to Playa Negra. They each have a thatch-roofed porch – hung with a hammock, of course – for maximum breeze-catching.

Bungalows Malú
BUNGALOW $$

(☏2755-0114; bungalowmalu@gmail.com; s/d/tr/q US$57/69/75/82; P✳☞☒) Seven stone bungalows, all with differing arrangements and amenities, surround an open-air *rancho* and a sunken pool with waterfall. Cabin floors are lined with an earthy terra-cotta tile and immaculate showers are crafted from stone. About 1km west of Cahuita, this is a perfect spot for families, with good beach access. Credit cards accepted.

Hotel La Diosa
CABINA $$

(☏2755-0055, in USA 800-854-7761; www.hotelladiosa.com; s US$60-95, d US$70-105, all incl breakfast; P✳☞☒) Set amid a tropical garden about 2.5km west of Cahuita, La Diosa has 10 spacious, cheery tiled cabins furnished with blond-wood headboards and chairs; some feature Jacuzzi tubs with views. There's a hardwood yoga studio, meditation space and a swimming pool.

Hotel Suizo Loco Lodge
BUNGALOW $$$

(☏2755-0349; www.suizolocolodge.com; s/d US$80/110, ste US$135, all incl breakfast; P☞☒) Ten immaculate, whitewashed bungalows have king-sized beds and folk-art decor at this family-friendly spot (cribs available). All units come equipped with safe, mini-fridge, solar-heated showers and small, private terraces. The perfectly landscaped grounds contain an impressive mosaic-tile pool with a swim-up bar. This serene lodge sits on the road forking off the main Playa Negra road about 2km out of Cahuita.

Atlántida Lodge
CABINA $$

(☏2755-0115; www.atlantida.cr; s/d standard US$45/55, deluxe US$72/80; P✳☒) Attractive grounds in central Playa Negra.

Goddess Garden
LODGE $$$

(☏2755-0055, in USA & Canada 800-854-7761; www.thegoddessgarden.com; d 5-night all-inclusive packages US$1320-1450; P☞☒) This place is situated at the end of the Playa Negra road, and is geared toward groups and retreats of up to 100 people, with yoga and event space.

Chalet Hibiscus
BUNGALOW $$

(☏2755-0021; www.hotels.co.cr/hibiscus.html; s/d/tr US$45/55/65, chalets US$60-140; P☞☒) These chalets about 2km west of Cahuita sleep six to 10 people; shared spaces include a pool and pool table.

Jardín Tropical
CABINAS $

(☏8811-2754; www.jardintropical.ch; d US$30, 2-bedroom house US$45; P) Basic, high-ceilinged *casitas* set in an overgrown garden down the Reggae Restaurant road.

Atiuhac
BUNGALOW $$

(☏2755-0651; www.atiuhac.com; d incl breakfast US$70, additional person US$25; P) About 3km beyond Cahuita on a small path branching off the main Playa Negra road, this rustic ecolodge suits those looking to commune with the jungle.

✗ Eating

CENTER

TOP CHOICE **Cha Cha Cha** — INTERNATIONAL $$

(☎8394-4153; mains US$9-20; ⊙noon-10pm Tue-Sun; 🍴) In a corner veranda of an old house, this attractive expat favorite is adorned with the chef's artwork and offers sophisticated world cuisine. Exquisite sauces star in dishes from filet mignon with wild mushrooms and truffle oil to mussels in Dijon sauce. Plenty of vegetarian options feature as well. Evocatively named cocktails, like the Dulce Amor (Sweet Love), made with starfruit and *guaro* (a local firewater made with sugarcane), are highly worthwhile, as are the decadent desserts.

Restaurant La Fé — SEAFOOD $$

(dishes US$7-30; ⊙7am-11pm) Chef and owner Walter, a Cahuita native, serves up tall tales and tasty meals at this reasonably priced spot. There's a laundry list of Tico and Caribbean items, but the main draw is anything doused in the restaurant's spicy-delicious coconut sauce.

Cafe Chocolatte 100% Natural — INTERNATIONAL $

(dishes US$3-11; ⊙6:30am-2pm Mon-Fri) There's no better place in Cahuita to greet the morning with a cup o' joe or unwind in the afternoon with a refreshing *jugo*. Hearty sandwiches on homemade whole-grain bread are perfect for beach picnics at the national park.

Restaurante Coral Reef — SEAFOOD $$

(☎2755-0133; mains US$6-21; ⊙11:30am-10pm) This place attracts fish-lovers, who arrive for steaming portions of seafood stew served in a pleasant 2nd-story balcony overlooking the main drag. The place gets packed, especially in high season (make a reservation).

Miss Edith's — CARIBBEAN $$

(☎2755-0248; mains US$5-24; ⊙7am-8pm; 🍴) This long-time local restaurant serves a slew of Caribbean specialties – including jerk chicken and potatoes stewed in garlic – and a number of vegetarian options. It's a famed spot that sometimes rests on its laurels, but when it's on, it's awesome.

El Girasol — ITALIAN $$

(☎2755-1164; mains US$9-22; ⊙noon-10pm) A newcomer to the Cahuita dining landscape, this authentic Italian spot is already receiving raves from its local countryfolk. Homemade pasta and bread, rich soups and antipastos, and traditionally prepared Italian fare are a welcome change of pace.

Cocoricó — FUSION $

(US$4-13; ⊙4-10pm Mon-Thu, noon-10pm Sat & Sun) Sweet spot for pizza and a movie (nightly).

Restaurant Caribbean Flavor — CARIBBEAN $

(mains US$4-12; ⊙7:30am-9pm Wed-Mon) As advertised!

Restaurant Típico Cahuita — CARIBBEAN $

(mains US$4-11; ⊙8am-last customer) Spacious spot serving local food, from *casados* to lobsters.

Café del Parquecito — COSTA RICAN $

(breakfast US$4-6; ⊙6am-3pm & 6pm-close) Five words: crepes stuffed with tropical fruit.

Roberto's — SEAFOOD $

(dishes US$5-18; ⊙7am-10pm) Open-air, sand floor and fresh seafood.

PLAYA NEGRA

Near Playa Negra, you can also head to Restaurant Bananas at Cabinas Algebra or Centro Turístico Brigitte for good breakfasts.

Sobre Las Olas — SEAFOOD $$

(☎2755-0109; pastas US$11-13, mains US$11-25; ⊙noon-10pm Wed-Mon; 🍴) Cahuita's top option for waterfront dining (an ideal spot for a date) is only a 300m walk out of town. It is owned by a lively Tico-Italian couple who serve a variety of Mediterranean-influenced specialties.

Chao's Paradise — CARIBBEAN $$

(☎2755-0480; seafood mains US$7-15; ⊙11am-11pm) Follow the wafting smell of garlic and simmering sauces to this highly recommended Playa Negra outpost that serves fresh catches cooked up in spicy 'Chao' sauce. The open-air restaurant-bar in central Playa Negra has a pool table.

Reggae Restaurant — CARIBBEAN $

(mains US$4-10; ⊙7-11am & noon-9pm) Exuding a friendly, laid-back vibe, this *soda* serves Caribbean-style standards, from basic *casados* to the house specialty, shrimp in coconut milk. In the central section of Playa Negra, this place also has facilities for camping (per person US$3), plus some comfortable cabins (US$20 to US$30).

🍺 Drinking

Low-key Cahuita is home to one insanely loud drinking hole: Coco's Bar (⊙noon-last man standing). You can't miss it at the main intersection, painted Rasta red, gold and green and cranking the reggaetón up to 11. On some nights (usually on weekends) there is also live music. For a quieter ambience, try one of the mellower bars right across the street.

Along Playa Negra, Chao's Paradise and Jardín Tropical are both good spots for a beer.

ℹ Information

The town's helpful website, www.cahuita.cr, has lodging and restaurant information, including pictures of many of the spots listed here. It also has a 'Cahuita Cam' showing live shots of Playa Blanca.

Willie's Tours (p424) has internet access. For internet access in Playa Negra, visit Centro Turístico Brigitte (p424). Mister Big J's (p425) has laundry service.

Banco de Costa Rica (◉9am-4pm Mon-Fri) At the bus terminal; has an ATM.

Internet Palmer (per hr US$2; ◉9am-8pm) Internet access and *cabinas*.

Supermercado Safari (◉7am-9pm Mon-Sat) Changes US and Canadian dollars, euros and traveler's checks at a steep commission.

ℹ Getting There & Away

All public buses arrive and depart at the bus terminal about 200m southwest of Parque Central.

Bribrí/Sixaola US$3.50; two hours; departs hourly from 6am to 7pm.

Puerto Limón (Autotransportes Mepe) US$5.10; 1½ hours; departs 6am, 9:30am, 10:45am, 1:45pm and 6:15pm. (These times are approximate because these buses originate in Manzanillo. Get there early just in case.)

Puerto Viejo de Talamanca US$1.25; 30 minutes to one hour; departs 6:15am, 6:45am, 11:15am, 3:45pm and 6:45pm.

San José (Autotransportes Mepe) US$8.25; four hours; departs 7am, 8am, 9:30am, 11:30am and 4:30pm.

ℹ Getting Around

The best way to get around Cahuita – especially if you're staying out along Playa Negra – is by bicycle. In town, rent bikes at Mister Big J's. At Playa Negra, bikes are available at Centro Turístico Brigitte for similar prices.

Parque Nacional Cahuita

This small park – just 10 sq km – is one of the more frequently visited national parks in Costa Rica. The reasons are simple: the nearby town of Cahuita provides attractive accommodations and easy access; more importantly, the white-sand beaches, coral reef and coastal rainforest are bursting with wildlife.

Declared a national park in 1978, Cahuita is typical of the entire coast (very humid), which results in dense tropical foliage, as well as coconut palms and sea grapes. The area includes the swampy Punta Cahuita, which juts into the sea between two stretches of sandy beach. Often flooded, the point is covered with cativo and mango trees and is a popular hangout spot for birds such as the green ibis, yellow-crowned night heron, boat-billed heron and the rare green-and-rufous kingfisher.

The dark Río Perezoso (Sloth River) bisects Punta Cahuita and sometimes prevents hiking between the ranger stations since it serves as the discharge for the swamp that covers the point.

Red land and fiddler crab live along the beaches, attracting mammals such as crab-eating raccoons and white-nosed coatis. White-faced capuchins, southern opossums and three-toed sloths also live in these parts. The mammal you are most likely to see (and hear) is the mantled howler monkey, which makes its bellowing presence known. The coral reef represents another rich ecosystem that abounds with life.

🏃 Activities

Hiking

An easily navigable 8km coastal trail leads through the jungle from Kelly Creek to Puerto Vargas. At times the trail follows the beach; at other times hikers are 100m or so away from the sand. At the end of the first beach, Playa Blanca, hikers must ford the Río Perezoso. Inquire about river conditions before you set out: under normal conditions, this river can be thigh-deep at high tide. During periods of heavy rain, it is often too dangerous to cross.

The trail continues around Punta Cahuita to the long stretch of Playa Vargas. It ends at the southern tip of the reef, where it meets up with a road leading to the Puerto Vargas ranger station. From the ranger station, it is another 1.5km along a gravel road to the park entrance. From here, you can hike back to Cahuita along the coastal highway, or you can catch a ride going in either direction.

Swimming

Almost immediately upon entering the park, you'll see the 2km-long Playa Blanca stretching along a gently curving bay to the east. The first 500m of beach may be unsafe for swimming but beyond that, the waves are generally gentle. (Look for green flags

Parque Nacional Cahuita

marking safe swimming spots.) The rocky Punta Cahuita headland separates this beach from the next one, Playa Vargas. It is unwise to leave clothing or other belongings unattended when you swim.

Snorkeling

Parque Nacional Cahuita contains one of the last living coral reefs in Costa Rica. While the reef represents some of the area's best snorkeling, it has incurred damage over the years from earthquakes and tourism-related activities. In an attempt to protect the reef from further damage, snorkeling is only permitted with a licensed guide. The going rate for one person is about US$30.

You'll find that conditions vary greatly, depending on the weather and other factors. In general, the drier months in the highlands (from February to April) are best for snorkeling on the coast, as less runoff results in less silt in the sea. Conditions are often cloudy at other times.

Volunteering

Though not renowned as a sea-turtle destination, Cahuita's beaches are nonetheless an important habitat for several breeds. Asociación Widecast (☑in San José 8818-2543; www.latinamericanseaturtles.org; volunteer fee per day US$50) has volunteering opportunities

for those interested in assisting on in-water research projects and various conservation-related activities. Reserve in advance.

It's also possible to volunteer at Tree of Life (p424) wildlife rescue center, on the road to Playa Negra.

🍴 Eating

Boca Chica   COSTA RICAN **$**
(☑2755-0415; meals US$7-20; ⊙9am-6pm) After the long, hot hike through the jungle, you may think you are hallucinating when you see Boca Chica, a small, whitewashed family recreation center, at the end of the road. It's not a mirage, just a well-placed bar and eatery, run by a charming Italian owner, offering cold *jugos*, homemade pasta, and Tico and Caribbean specialties.

ℹ️ Information

The **Kelly Creek ranger station** (☑2755-0461; admission by donation; ⊙6am-5pm) is convenient to the town of Cahuita, while 1km down Hwy 36 takes you to the well-signed **Puerto Vargas ranger station** (☑2755-0302; admission US$10; ⊙8am-4pm Mon-Fri, 7am-5pm Sat & Sun).

You do not have to pay the full admission fee if you enter at Kelly Creek. The park service is habitually underfunded, and fees do provide an important source of income. Tourist dollars support education, conservation and maintenance programs.

Cacao Trails

Halfway between Cahuita and Puerto Viejo de Talamanca in Hone Creek, this botanical garden and chocolate museum (☑2756-8186; www.cacaotrails.com; Hone Creek; guided tour US$25; ⊙7am-4pm) has a couple of small museums devoted to indigenous and Afro-Caribbean culture, a lush garden bursting with bromeliads and heliconias, as well as an onsite chocolate factory where cacao is processed in traditional ways. Two-hour tours include a visit to all of these spots, plus a hike to a nearby organic farm. Additional expeditions allow for further exploration by kayak on the adjacent Río Carbón. Any bus between Cahuita and Puerto Viejo can drop you at the entrance. This is a great outing for kids.

Puerto Viejo de Talamanca

There was a time when the only travelers to the little seaside settlement once known as Old Harbor were intrepid surfers who padded around the quiet, dusty streets, board under arm, on their way to surf Salsa Brava. That, certainly, is no longer the case. This burgeoning party town is bustling with tourist activity: street vendors ply Rasta trinkets and Bob Marley T-shirts, stylish eateries serve global fusion everything and intentionally rustic bamboo bars pump dancehall and reggaetón. The scene can get downright hedonistic, attracting dedicated revelers who arrive to marinate in ganja and *guaro*.

Despite that reputation, Puerto Viejo nonetheless manages to hold on to an easy charm. Stray a couple of blocks off the main commercial strip and you might find yourself on a sleepy dirt road, savoring a spicy Caribbean stew in the company of local families. Nearby, you'll find rainforest fruit farms set to a soundtrack of cackling birds and croaking frogs, and wide-open beaches where the daily itinerary revolves around surfing and snoozing. So, chill a little. Party a little. Eat a little. You've come to just the right place.

◉ Sights

Finca La Isla Botanical Garden FARM
(☑2750-0046; www.costaricacaribbean.com; self-guided/guided tour US$5/10; ☺10am-4pm Fri-Mon) To the west of town is a working tropical farm where the owners have been growing organic pepper, cacao, tropical fruits and ornamental plants for more than a decade. Part of the farm is set aside as a botanical garden, which is also good for bird-watching and for wildlife observation (look for sloths, poison-dart frogs and toucans). The informative guided tour includes admission, fruit tasting and a glass of fresh juice to finish, or you can buy a booklet (US$1) and take yourself on a self-guided tour.

Jungles of Talamanca FARM
West of Puerto Viejo, the Jungles of Talamanca is actually a small tropical nursery and cacao *finca*. This Bribrí family welcomes visitors to its home, where you can see cacao toasted over an open fire, then hand-ground into delicious chocolate or rich cocoa butter. Nutmeg, black pepper or cinnamon, all grown onsite, may be added. The resulting product is truly decadent – it's amazing that something so luscious comes from such humble origins. This place is 4km out of town, on the road to Bribrí; look for the sign just past the clinic.

🏃 Activities

Surfing

Breaking on the reef that hugs the village is the famed Salsa Brava, a shallow break that is also one of the country's most infamous waves. It's a tricky ride – if you lose it, the waves will plow you straight into the reef – and definitely not for beginners. **Salsa**

SAVING TALAMANCA

In April 2012, more than 70 businesses and homeowners in Cahuita and Puerto Viejo were shocked to receive notices that they were in violation of the 1977 Maritime Zone Law. The law deems that land within 50m of the high-tide line is public domain and thus off-limits for development. An additional 150m beyond that is considered a buffer zone and allows for limited development. The government-issued notices informed these local residents that they were required to demolish their buildings, at their own expense, by November 2012.

Though the Costa Rican government can move at a torpid pace, these notices sent shockwaves throughout the area as two large hotel properties were actually destroyed, on government order, in 2011 (the resulting rubble being left to rot in the jungle for more than a year afterwards). The sudden news is being met with strong protest from locals who are rallying to save the soul of their unique communities in the Talamanca canton. Residents are currently exploring the legal options open to them to prevent massive damage to the environment that the maritime law ostensibly protects.

It's no secret that this chilled-out stretch of Caribbean coastline has long been coveted by developers who see luxury resorts, marinas and big tourism bucks in its future. At the time of writing, it's unclear whether the future will bring demolition for further development or whether local residents will win a stay of execution – but, for the moment, the coast is clear.

Puerto Viejo de Talamanca

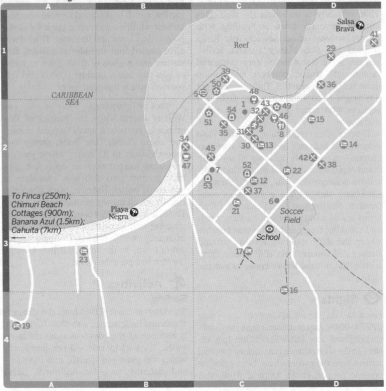

Brava offers both rights and lefts, although the right is usually faster. Conditions are best with an easterly swell.

For a softer landing, try the beach break at **Playa Cocles** – where the waves are almost as impressive and the landing far less damaging. Cocles is about 2km east of town. Conditions are usually best early in the day, before the wind picks up.

Waves in the area generally peak from November to March, and there is a surfing miniseason from June to July. From late March to May, and in September and October, the sea is at its calmest.

Several surf schools around town charge about US$50 for two hours of lessons. Stands around town rent boards from about US$20 per day.

Caribe Surf   SURFING
(☎8878-1739, 8357-7703) Lessons by super-smiley surf instructor, Hershel, widely considered the best teacher in the town.

Van Dyke Surf School   SURFING
(☎2750-0620; Hotel Puerto Viejo) Run by Kurt Van Dyke, founding father of the surf scene in Puerto Viejo.

ATEC (p436) and Aventuras Bravas (p436) can also arrange lessons.

Swimming

The entire southern Caribbean coast – from Cahuita all the way south to Punta Mona – is lined with unbelievably beautiful beaches. Just northwest of town, Playa Negra offers the area's safest swimming.

Southeast of town you will find some gems – stretches of smooth white sand, fringed by jungle and ideal for surfing, body surfing and, when the swell is low, swimming. **Playa Cocles** (2km east of town), **Playa Chiquita** (4km east), **Punta Uva** (7km east) and **Manzanillo** all offer post-card-perfect beach paradises. Swimming conditions vary greatly, however, and the surf can get dangerous. Riptides and power-

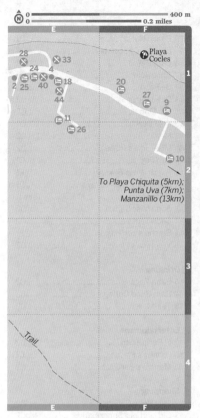

ful undertows can be deadly. Inquire at your hotel or with local tour operators about conditions before setting out.

Snorkeling

The waters from Cahuita to Manzanillo are protected by Costa Rica's only two living reef systems, which form a naturally protected sanctuary, home to some 35 species of coral and 400 species of fish, not to mention dolphins, sharks and, occasionally, whales. Generally, underwater visibility is best when the sea is calm.

Just south of **Punta Uva**, in front of the Arrecife restaurant, is a decent spot for snorkeling, when conditions are calm. The reef is very close to the shore and features include stunning examples of reindeer coral, sheet coral and lettuce coral. The reef at **Manzanillo** is also easily accessible. Most of the dive companies offer snorkeling trips for about US$35 to US$55 per person.

Diving

Divers in the southern Caribbean will discover upward of 20 dive sites, from the coral gardens in shallow waters to deeper sites with amazing underwater vertical walls. Literally hundreds of species of fish swim around here, including angelfish, parrotfish, triggerfish, shark and different species of jack and snapper.

Reef Runner Divers DIVING
(☎2750-0480; www.reefrunnerdivers.net; 1-/2-tank dive US$65/90; ☺8am-6pm) If you are not certified, you can use a temporary license for US$75 or spring for the full PADI certification for US$335.

Hiking

The immediate vicinity of Puerto Viejo is not prime hiking territory: the proximity of the Parque Nacional Cahuita and the Refugio Nacional de Vida Silvestre Gandoca-Manzanillo means that most trekkers will head to these protected areas to look for toucans and sloths.

Independent hikers can follow the town's most southerly road, which goes past the soccer field and the Cashew Hill Jungle Cottages. Once out of the village, the road dwindles to a path and leads straight up into the hills.

White-Water Rafting

Exploradores Outdoors RAFTING
(☎2750-2020; www.exploradoresoutdoors.com; 1-day trip incl 2 meals & transportation from US$99) This outfit offers one- and two-day trips on the Ríos Pacuare, Reventazón and Sarapiquí. Staff can pick you up and drop you off in either Cahuita, Puerto Viejo, San José or Arenal, and you're free to mix and match your pick-up and drop-off points. It has an office in the center of town.

🎓 Courses

Spanish School Pura Vida LANGUAGE COURSE
(☎2750-0029; www.spanishschool-puravida.com) Located at the Hotel Pura Vida, this company offers everything from private hourly tutoring (from US$18) to intensive five-hour-a-day sessions (from US$350 per week).

👉 Tours

Tour operators generally require a minimum of two people on any excursion. Rates are per person, but they may be discounted for larger groups.

Puerto Viejo de Talamanca

Activities, Courses & Tours
1	ATEC	C2
2	Aventuras Bravas	E1
3	Exploradores Outdoors	C2
4	Gecko Trail Adventures	E1
5	Reef Runner Divers	C1
6	Spanish School Pura Vida	C3
7	Terra Venturas	C2
8	Van Dyke Surf School	C2

Sleeping
9	Agapi	F1
10	Blue Conga Hotel	F2
11	Bungalows Calalú	E1
12	Cabinas Guaraná	C2
13	Cabinas Larry	C2
14	Cabinas Tropical	D2
15	Casa Verde	D2
16	Cashew Hill Jungle Cottages	C3
17	Coco Loco Lodge	C3
18	Coconut Grove	E1
19	El Pizote	A4
20	Escape Caribeño	F1
21	Hostel Pagalú	C3
	Hotel Puerto Viejo	(see 8)
	Hotel Pura Vida	(see 6)
22	Jacaranda Hotel & Jungle Garden	C2
23	Kaya's Place	A3
24	Lizard King Resort	E1
25	Lotus Garden	E1
26	Monte Sol	E2
27	Rocking J's	F1

Eating
28	Amimodo Caribe Restaurant	E1
29	Beach Hut	D1
30	Bread & Chocolate	C2
31	Café Viejo	C2
32	Chile Rojo	C2
33	De Paso	E1
34	Dee-Lite	B2
35	Flip Flop	C2
36	Koki Beach	D1
37	MegaSuper	C2
38	Miss Lidia's Place	D2
39	Pan Pay	C1
40	Puerto Viejo Bakery	E1
41	Restaurant Salsa Brava	D1
	Soda Mirna	(see 1)
42	Soda Miss Sam	D2
43	Soda Tamara	C2
44	Stashu's con Fusion	E1
45	Veronica's Place	C2

Drinking
46	Baba Yaga	C2
47	Dam Good Coffee	B2
48	Tex-Mex	C2

Entertainment
49	El Parquecito	C2
50	Johnny's Place	C1
51	Maritza's Bar	C2

Shopping
52	Lulu Berlu Gallery	C2
53	Old Harbour Supermarket	C2
54	Organic Market	C2

ATEC HIKING
(Asociación Talamanqueña de Ecoturismo y Conservación; ☎2750-0191, 2750-0398; www.ateccr.org; ☺8am-9pm) This highly reputable not-for-profit organisation promotes sustainable tourism by working with local guides and supporting local communities. Hiking, horseback riding and canoe trips involve bird-watching and visiting indigenous territories and local farms. Depending on the activity, half-day excursions start at about US$20 and go up to US$600 for month-long raptor-counting volunteer stints. The office is in the center of town.

Aventuras Bravas TOUR
(☎2750-2000, 2750-0626, 8849-7600; www.aventurasbravas.com) With offices in town and at Rocking J's hostel, this company works largely as a booking agent arranging almost every tour imaginable. Popular activities include kayak trips (US$25), rafting excursions (US$75) and canopy tours (US$55).

Gecko Trail Adventures TOUR
(☎2756-8412, in USA & Canada 415-230-0298; www.geckotrail.com) This is a full-service agency arranging local tours, but also transportation, accommodations and tours throughout Costa Rica. Find it 250m east of Puerto Viejo on the road to Playa Cocles.

Terra Venturas TOUR
(☎2750-0750; www.terraventuras.com; ☺8am-7pm) Offers overnights in Tortuguero (US$139 to US$209), as well as the usual local tours. Plus, it has its very own 23-platform, 2.1km-long

canopy tour (US$55), complete with Tarzan swing. The office is on the main road through Puerto Viejo, on the western end of town.

🛌 Sleeping

Puerto Viejo has a little bit of everything. All budget spots have private hot-water bathrooms unless otherwise stated. Note that rates are generally discounted slightly when paid in cash.

TOP CHOICE Hotel Pura Vida   HOTEL $

(📞2750-0002; www.hotel-puravida.com; s/d/tr without bathroom US$28/32/42, s/d/tr US$34/38/48; P🛜) Though this place has budget prices, the atmosphere and amenities are solidly mid-range. Ten breezy, immaculate rooms, clad in polished wood, bright linens and ceramic tile floors, make up this homey Chilean-German run inn on a quiet street opposite the soccer field. (Unit 6 is best, offering incredible views of town right from the solar-heated shower.) Alongside a lovingly tended garden, you'll find a serene lounge with easy chairs and hammocks. Simple breakfasts, light snacks and chilled beers are available at an additional charge. A great spot for couples; credit cards accepted.

TOP CHOICE Banana Azul   LODGE $$

(📞2750-2035; www.bananaazul.com; s/d from US$74/79, d ste US$149, all incl breakfast; P🛜🏊) Removed from town, this wonderful hotel sits at the edge of a blissfully tranquil black-sand beach. Rooms are all done up in the finest jungle chic: shining wooden floors, white linens, mosquito nets and private decks with views – as well as graceful touches such as bromeliads in the showers. An onsite restaurant-bar serves meals and sensational cocktails. Bikes, body boards and snorkeling gear are available for rent, and beach access is steps away. No children under 16; credit cards accepted.

Blue Conga Hotel   B&B $$

(📞2750-0681; www.bluecongacr.com; d/tr/q incl breakfast US$70/85/95; P🛜) This graceful B&B about 1km east of town has 10 simple rooms in a tropical-style building, all of which are named after local flora. Airy units have high ceilings, clerestory windows, canopy beds with mosquito nets, handcrafted lamps and private terraces. Breakfast is served in a large open-air *rancho* in the garden, which is a lovely place for lounging. Credit cards accepted.

Escape Caribeño   BUNGALOW $$

(📞2750-0103; www.escapecaribeno.com; s/d/tr garden view US$70/75/85, ocean view US$80/85/95; P❄@🛜) Charming Italian owners keep 14 spick-and-span bungalows with spotless bathrooms, some on the beach side and others in the garden across the road, 500m east of town toward Playa Cocles. More expensive units are in lovely Caribbean-style structures with stained-glass shower stalls, but all have stocked minifridges, cable TV, fans and hammocks. Breakfast is available with advance reservation. Credit cards accepted.

SALSA BRAVA

One of the biggest breaks in Costa Rica, Salsa Brava is named for the heaping helping of 'spicy sauce' it serves up on the sharp, shallow reef, continually collecting its debt of fun in broken skin, boards and bones. The wave makes its regular, dramatic appearance when the swells pull in from the east, pushing a wall of water against the reef, in the process generating a thick and powerful curl. There's no gradual build up here: the water is transformed from swell to wave in a matter of seconds. Ride it out and you're golden. Wipe out and you'll rocket headfirst into the reef. In his memoir, *In Search of Captain Zero*, surfer and screenwriter Allen Weisbecker describes it as 'vicious.' Some mordant locals have baptized it 'the cheese-grater.'

Interestingly, this storied wave helped turn Puerto Viejo into a destination. More than 30 years ago, the town was barely accessible. But that did not dissuade dogged surfers from the bumpy bus rides and rickety canoes that hauled them and their boards on the week-long trip from San José. They camped on the beach and shacked up with locals, carbo-loading at cheap *sodas*. Other intrepid explorers – biologists, Peace Corps volunteers, disaffected US veterans looking to escape the fallout of the Vietnam War – also materialized during this time, helping spread the word about the area's luminous sunsets, lush rainforests and monster curls. Today Puerto Viejo has a fine paved road, global eateries and wi-fi. The fierceness of Salsa Brava, however, remains unchanged.

Turtles of the Caribbean

One of the most moving experiences for visitors to the Caribbean coast is turtle-watching on its wild beaches. Witnessing the return of a massive turtle to its natal beach and its laborious nesting ritual feels both solemn and magical. Four species of sea turtle nest along the Caribbean coast: the green, leatherback, hawksbill and loggerhead, all of which are endangered or threatened.

Because of the sensitive habitat and critically endangered status of some species, turtle-nesting tours are highly regulated. Groups must be accompanied by licensed guides, who ensure that the turtles are able to lay their eggs in peace and that other nests are left undisturbed. Nesting season runs from March to October, with July and August being the most active period for green turtles. April is another good month, when leatherback turtles arrive.

Since it takes many years for sea turtles to mature and reproduce, their populations are quite vulnerable to environmental hazards such as pollution and poaching. Thus, conservation efforts are crucial to their survival – these efforts include guarding hatchlings from predators and providing incentives for local communities to protect turtles and their eggs. Volunteer opportunities are plentiful along the Caribbean coast, with tasks ranging from beach patrols, data collection and tagging to remove eggs to hatcheries and hatchling release.

Turtle-watching tours can be arranged through ATEC (p436) in Puerto Viejo, ASTOP (p411) in Parismina, and by licensed guides in Tortuguero village (p415). To volunteer, contact one of the organizations listed on p414; note that most organizations require the minimum commitment of a week.

Clockwise from top left
1. Hawksbill turtle 2. Green sea turtles 3. Leatherback turtle

Cabinas Guaraná
CABINA $

(2750-0244; www.hotelguarana.com; s/d/tr/q US$33/41/51/58; P@?) Amid a riotous tropical garden in town, 10 brightly painted concrete *cabinas* are decorated with wooden furniture and colorful folk tapestries, and each one comes with a small private terrace with hammock. There is a spacious shared kitchen and a vertigo-inducing tree house that offers spectacular sea views. This place is excellent value; credit cards are accepted.

Casa Verde
CABINA $$

(2750-0015; www.cabinascasaverde.com; s/d without bathroom from US$40/46, s/d/tr/q US$62/78/95/109; P?✆) Tiled walkways wind through gardens with 17 tidy rooms, each with high ceilings, stained wood furniture, folk-art touches and private terraces with hammocks. Cheaper rooms are more basic, but the shared bathrooms shine. A pool and hot tub – encrusted with rock formations – are straight out of *Fantasy Island*. Credit cards accepted.

Cashew Hill Jungle Cottages
BUNGALOW $$$

(2750-0256, 2750-0001; www.cashewhilllodge.co.cr; cottages US$90-150; P?✆) Set on a lush hillside studded with pre-Columbian-style statuary, the seven cottages at this lovely jungle spot are bright, colorful and comfortable. The wood houses are painted in vivid shades and come with full kitchens, loft-style sleeping areas and charming rustic touches such as shell-encrusted sinks. All of the units have private decks or patios stocked with comfy chairs and hammocks, while one two-bedroom cabin offers exquisite ocean views. It's a bit of a trek south of town, but it's worth it. Credit cards accepted.

Jacaranda Hotel & Jungle Garden
CABINA $

(2750-0069; www.cabinasjacaranda.net; s/d/tr/q from US$25/35/40/45; P@?) In a blooming garden intersected by mosaic walkways, this neat spot near the soccer field has 15 simple wood *cabinas* with lockboxes, spotless ceramic tile floors and murals of flowers. There is yoga and massage available onsite, as well as a shared kitchen and a garden patio for lounging. Credit cards accepted.

Lotus Garden
HOTEL $$

(2750-0232; www.lotusgardencr.com; d US$65-90; P✳?✆) Infusing a little Kyoto into Puerto Viejo just 200m east of town, the nine large, stone-lined suites at this inn come with king-sized four-poster beds,

cable TV, air-con, lockbox, Jacuzzi tubs, gobs of Asian textiles and Japanese names such as 'Shogun.' Several smaller doubles have simple decor and ceiling fans. To complete the mood, there's the recommended Lotus Garden Restaurant.

Cabinas Tropical
CABINA $

(2750-0283; www.cabinastropical.com; s/d US$38/42, d with air-con US$48; P✆✳✳?) Ten spacious rooms – decorated with varnished wood and shiny tiles – surround a primly landscaped garden on the eastern end of town. The comfortable quarters are just part of the appeal: biologist owner Rolfe Blancke leads excellent bird-watching hikes at dawn (per person US$60, minimum three people, breakfast provided).

Coco Loco Lodge
BUNGALOW $$

(2750-0281; www.cocolocolodge.com; d US$57-69, d bungalow US$63-75; P@?) You'll find various accommodations at this quiet Austrian-run hotel. The most charming of these are the palm-thatched bungalows, equipped with shining wood floors, minifridge and coffeemakers. All of these have private terraces with hammocks, offering views of the expansive garden. Credit cards accepted.

Agapi
HOTEL $$

(2750-0446; www.agapisite.com; d standard US$69-81, d/q ste US$120/150; P✳?✆) In a prime seaside location along the road to Playa Cocles, this sweet 18-room spot with a lovingly tended garden is run by a friendly Greek-Tica couple. Simple units vary in size and configuration, from wood-paneled cabins to spacious apartments with ocean views. There's a pool, Jacuzzi and kiddie pool. Breakfast and bicycle rental are available for an additional charge. Credit cards accepted.

Kaya's Place
INN $

(2750-0690; www.kayasplace.com; s/d without bathroom US$20/30, d with/without ocean views US$45/35; P?) This small, friendly inn just west of town has 17 snug, basic rooms, some of which share cool-water showers. A few units are rather dim, though the ones facing the garden are airy. A 2nd-floor lounge is filled with hammocks and offers prime ocean views. Bikes are available for rent; credit cards accepted.

Lizard King Resort
CABINA $$

(2750-0614; www.lizardkingresort.com; s/d US$35/45, d with air-con US$75; P✳?✆) Just

> ## HOSTEL LOWDOWN
>
> Of the two best hostels in town, choose to party down or peace out.
>
> Rocking J's (☎2750-0657; www.rockingjs.com; camping per person US$6-8, hammock US$7, dm US$11, d US$26, 3-4 person, ste US$60-70; [P][⊙]), Puerto Viejo's grooviest hostel and 'hammock hotel' is owned by the charismatic, mischievous 'J,' who organizes full-moon parties and drinking games. Consequently, good times, good vibes and new friends await here. The accommodations are basic: tight rows of tents and hammocks, snug dorms and private doubles share rickety showers in an environment brightened by an explosion of psychedelic mosaics. Surfboards, snorkels and bikes are available for rent and, in addition to an onsite restaurant and bar, there's also a music studio/survival bunker made from reclaimed shipping containers. Credit cards accepted.
>
> If peace is more your speed, Hostel Pagalú (☎2750-1930; www.pagalu.com; dm US$11, d with/without bathroom US$30/25; [P][⊙]) offers a break from the party. Super clean, contemporary, airy dorms and half a dozen private doubles are painted white with polished-wood accents. Niceties include large lockers, charging stations for MP3 players and reading lamps installed above each bunk. Private doubles are spacious (one is wheelchair-accessible) and there is a shared, open-air kitchen and a quiet lounge with tables and hammocks. In addition, the owners supply spring water on an honor system – enabling you to refill your reusable plastic bottles. Reservations not accepted; it's first-come, first-served.

outside the center of town, this two-story wooden lodge houses several simple rooms surrounding a pool in the quiet courtyard. Since all rooms have latticework near the ceiling for air circulation, it's more private upstairs. The in-house restaurant serves Mexican food, and the atmosphere is serene.

Hotel Puerto Viejo CABINA $
(☎2750-0620; www.thehotelpuertoviejo.com; dm US$10, r per person without bathroom US$10; [P][@][⊙]) No shoes, no shirt, no problem. This crash pad administered by surfer Kurt Van Dyke has a warren of 68 wooden rooms in the middle of town, some of which sleep up to eight. Units are basic but clean and come equipped with strong fans and bathrooms that run on recycled rainwater. Onsite, you'll find an huge shared kitchen and a chilled-out bar where the talk is all about waves. Rates go down with a stay of more than three nights. Credit cards accepted.

Bungalows Calalú BUNGALOW $$
(☎2750-0042; www.bungalowscalalu.com; s/d/tr US$35/45/50, d/tr/q with kitchen and air-con US$60/70/80; [P][✳][⊙][≋]) Family-friendly bungalows set in a tropical garden with a waterfall-fed pool.

Coconut Grove INN $
(☎2750-0093; www.coconutgrovepuertoviejo.com; s/d US$33/38, s/d without bathroom US$23/28; [P][⊙]) Just east of town, this basic spot is homey and rustic.

Monte Sol CABINA $
(☎2750-0098; www.montesol.net; d with/without bathroom US$30/25, d/q bungalows with kitchen US$45/65; [P][@][⊙]) Clean, basic *cabinas* in a quiet locale east of town have tile floors, mosquito nets and hammocks.

Cabinas Larry CABINA $
(☎2750-0964; s/d US$20/26; [P][⊙]) Bright, clean, safe, locally run budget spot downtown.

El Pizote CABINA $$
(☎2750-0227; www.elpizotelodge.com; d/tr/q US$63/79/93, bungalows with/without air-con from US$109/79; [P][✳][≋]) Good family spot in a peaceful garden setting west of town.

🗡 Eating

With the most diverse and impressive restaurant scene on the coast, Puerto Viejo has the cure for *casado* overkill.

TOP CHOICE **Stashu's con Fusion** FUSION $$
(☎2750-0530; meals US$7-18; ⊙5-10pm Thu-Tue; [✎]) Stroll 250m out of town toward Playa Cocles to this romantic candlelit patio cafe serving up creative fusion cuisine that combines elements of Caribbean, Indian, Mexican and Thai cooking. Steamed spicy mussels in red-curry sauce and tandoori chicken in coconut are just a couple of standouts. Excellent vegetarian and vegan items round out the menu. Owner and chef Stash Golas is an artist inside the kitchen and out. Do not miss.

Beach Hut
FUSION **$$**

(☑2750-0895; mains US$8-18; ⊙noon-midnight) With sand between your toes and Salsa Brava views before you, this place only gets better when the platter of seared tuna arrives at your table, encrusted with black pepper, crushed chilis and sesame seeds, all doused – alongside mandolin-thin slices of zucchini, wild mushroom and red onion – in an eyes-rolling-back-in-your-head soy marinade. Oh...where were we? Right: at the Beach Hut.

Bread & Chocolate
BREAKFAST **$**

(☑2750-0723; breakfast US$3-7; ⊙6:30am-6:30pm Tue-Sat, to 2:30pm Sun; ✎) Ever had a completely homemade PB&J (ie bread, peanut butter *and* jelly all made from scratch)? That and more can be yours at this dream of a gluten-lover's cafe in the center of town. Coffees are served in individual French presses; mochas come unconstructed so you have the pleasure of mixing your own homemade chocolate, steamed milk and coffee; and everything else – from the gazpacho to the granola – is lovingly and skillfully made in-house.

Veronica's Place
VEGETARIAN **$**

(☑2750-0263; www.veronicasplacepv.com; dishes US$4-7; ⊙8am-9pm Sun-Thu, to 4pm Fri; ✎) This delightful vegetarian cafe along the main road through town offers fresh, healthy interpretations of Caribbean food, using fresh fruits and vegetables, as well as soy products. Veronica rents *cabinas,* has a macrobiotic health-food store onsite and runs a volunteer work exchange on her organic farm.

Soda Mirna
CARIBBEAN **$**

(mains US$5-8; ⊙noon-10pm) This humble little *soda* on the main road offers excellent people-watching and tasty Caribbean-style dishes. Try the smoked pork chops with marinated onions or the zesty stewed chicken served with rice and beans – and whatever you do, don't forget to sample the fiery homemade hot sauce.

Chile Rojo
ASIAN **$$**

(☑2750-0025; mains US$6-15; ⊙Thu-Tue noon-11pm; ✎) Monday nights at this Asian fusion spot mean the all-you-can-eat (and quite decent) sushi and Asian buffet. Any other night of the week, this trendy 2nd-story spot offers excellent views of the main drag, and the sushi bar opens around 7:30pm. The cuisine is truly pan-Asian, running the gamut from tabbouleh to tikkas to Thai curries.

Pan Pay
BAKERY **$**

(☑2750-0081; dishes US$3-6; ⊙7am-7pm) This popular corner spot on the beachside road in town is excellent for strong coffee, fresh baked goods and hearty wedges of fluffy Spanish omelet served with crisp tomato-bread. There are sandwiches and other light meals, but it's thoughts of its flaky chocolate croissants that make us want to jump out of bed in the morning.

Puerto Viejo Bakery
BAKERY **$**

(pastries US$1-4, sandwiches US$7-10; ⊙7am-7pm) East of town on the road to Playa Cocles, perfect whole-grain breads and baguettes are baked daily for your picnic requirements. Menu items tend toward the simply wholesome, from the yogurt with fruit and granola to made-to-order sandwiches. But decadence is also well represented, in the form of flaky French pastries and rich cakes, or the brioche French toast.

Restaurant Salsa Brava
SEAFOOD **$$**

(☑2750-0241; mains US$9-20; ⊙noon-10pm) Specializing in fresh seafood and open-grill cooking, this popular spot is the perfect end-of-day cocktail stop – hit happy hour between 5pm and 7pm and you'll also catch two-for-one mojitos (US$6) for sunset overlooking the Salsa Brava surf break.

Amimodo Caribe Restaurant
ITALIAN **$$**

(☑2750-0257; meals US$9-29; ⊙4-10pm Mon-Thu, noon-10pm Fri-Sun; ✎) Listen to the waves crash at this local Italian favorite just east of town, where you can chow down on pizzas and homemade pasta dishes such as lobster spaghetti (US$29). A cheaper 'surfing menu' (US$7) features carb-heavy specialties: fish-and-chips or chicken-fried steak with rice.

Koki Beach
LATIN AMERICAN **$$$**

(☑2275-0902; www.kokibeach.com; meals US$11-26; ⊙2pm-midnight Wed-Sun; ☎) Reminiscent of Miami Beach, this sleek spot cranks reggae-lite and sports colorful Adirondack chairs that face the ocean from an elevated wooden platform on the east end of town. There's a decent selection of Peruvian-inflected *ceviches* (seafood marinated in lemon or lime juice, garlic and seasonings), meat and seafood dishes, but slim pickings for vegetarians.

Café Viejo
ITALIAN **$$$**

(☑2750-0817; www.cafeviejo.net; mains US$10-35; ⊙6pm-1am Wed-Mon) This pricey, sceney Mediterranean lounge and restaurant gets good marks for fresh pastas, tasty pizzas and fancy cocktails. The upscale, romantic ambience makes it a safe bet for important dates – and its location right on the main drag makes for excellent people-watching.

Dee-Lite   ICE CREAM $
(gelato US$2-3; ⏰10am-8:30pm) After disembarking from a bus, head for Dee-Lite (along the beach road) and cool off with an authentic gelato – our favorite flavor is Smack.

De Paso   EUROPEAN $
(mains US$4-15; ⏰11am-10pm) Surprisingly inexpensive good eats in a roadside hideaway just east of town.

Flip Flop   INTERNATIONAL $
(☑2750-2031; mains US$4-9; ⏰noon-10pm Mon-Sat) A little Caribbean, a little Thai, and more good grub in the regions between – all in central Puerto Viejo.

Soda Tamara   COSTA RICAN $
(☑2750-0148; breakfast US$3-6, seafood mains US$8-10; ⏰7am-10pm) With its signature red, green and yellow paint job, this is a popular spot to grab breakfast and watch the village wake up. During the day seafood is the specialty, but don't miss out on the moist coconut bread. Yum!

Find groceries at the local Old Harbour Supermarket (⏰6:30am-8:30pm) or the incongruous chain-store MegaSuper (⏰8am-7pm). Don't miss the weekly organic market (⏰6am-6pm Sat), when area vendors and growers sell snacks typical of the region.

Excellent places for Caribbean cooking are Soda Miss Sam (☑2750-0108; dishes US$2-16; ⏰9am-9pm), now run by Miss Glenda, and Miss Lidia's Place (☑2750-0598; dishes US$2-20; ⏰9am-9pm), both reasonably priced local favorites that dish up plenty of spicy coconut sauce. Both ladies have been around for years, pleasing the palates of locals and tourists alike.

🍷 Drinking

Tex-Mex   BAR
(⏰6am-2am) A rowdy open-air bar on the main road through town that has live music, pool tables and movies on big screens playing most nights. Mint-heavy mojitos and Bloody Marys made with fresh tomato juice make this a popular place.

Baba Yaga   BAR
(☑8388-4359) Go to this downtown spot on Tuesday for ladies' night, Sunday for reggae night.

Dam Good Coffee   CAFE
(espresso US$2; ⏰8am-4pm; 🛜) For a caffeine fix before a long bus ride, grab an espresso across the street from the beachside bus stop.

☆ Entertainment

Jungle Internet plays outdoor movies on the street on most nights after sunset. Pop in during the day to find out what's playing.

Maritza's Bar   LIVE MUSIC
(☑2750-0003) This nonfancy local spot down by the beach has regular live bands and DJs that play reggae, rock and salsa, and all the funky beats in between.

Johnny's Place   MUSIC
(⏰1pm-3am) This is a central, beachside institution, where DJs spin reggaetón, hip-hop and salsa to a mix of locals and travelers who take up the dance floor and surround the late-night beach bonfires outside.

El Parquecito   LIVE MUSIC
(⏰7pm-midnight) This pleasant outdoor lounge on the east end of town features jamming weekend bands that play reggae and calypso classics – among many other things.

🛍 Shopping

Makeshift stalls clutter the main road, selling knick-knacks and Rasta-colored accoutrements aplenty.

Lulu Berlu Gallery   ARTS & CRAFTS
(☑2750-0394; ⏰9am-9pm) Lulu Berlu Gallery, tucked off the main road in central Puerto Viejo, carries folk art, one-of-a-kind clothing and mosaic mirrors, among many other locally made items.

ℹ Information

Unfortunately, a cottage industry of drug dealers has become a permanent part of the landscape in Puerto Viejo. In fact, it can get quite aggressive. Be firm if you're not interested. And be aware that, though the use of marijuana (and harder stuff) is common in Puerto Viejo, it is nonetheless illegal.

As in other popular tourist centers, theft can be an issue. Stay aware, use your hotel safe, and if you are staying outside of town it is best not to walk alone late at night. Likewise, the town has a number of independent touts offering all manner of travel services. Choose your accommodations carefully and take tours from recommended agencies and guides.

INDIGENOUS COMMUNITIES IN THE SOUTHERN CARIBBEAN

The area is home to a number of thriving indigenous communities, many of which can be visited by travelers. Brush up on a little local knowledge first:

Bribrí & Cabécar

At least two indigenous groups occupied the territory on the Caribbean side of the country from pre-Columbian times. The Bribrí tended to inhabit lowland areas, while the Cabécar made their home high in the Cordillera de Talamanca. Over the last century, members of both ethnic groups have migrated to the Pacific side. But many have stayed on the coast, intermarrying with Jamaican immigrants and even working in the banana industry. Today the Bribrí tend to be more acculturated, while the Cabécar are more isolated.

The groups have distinct languages (which are preserved to some degree), though they share similar architecture, weapons and canoe style. They also share the spiritual belief that the planet – and the flora and fauna contained within it – are gifts from Sibö, (God). *Taking Care of Sibö's Gifts*, by Juanita Sánchez, Gloria Mayorga and Paula Palmer, is a remarkable record of Bribrí oral history.

Visiting Indigenous Communities

There are reserves on the Caribbean slopes of the Cordillera de Talamanca, including the Talamanca Cabécar territory (which is more difficult to visit) and the Bribrí territory, where locals are more equipped to handle visitors. ATEC (p436) organizes trips from Puerto Viejo.

The most interesting destination is Yorkín, in the Reserva Indígena Yorkín. While you are there, you can meet with a local women's artisan group, Mujeres Artesanas Stibrawpa, which offers demonstrations in roof thatching, cooking and basket-weaving. It's a rewarding trip, well worth the time and effort to get there (day trips US$70; overnights US$90).

Alternatively, you can visit the larger, modern village of Shiroles, about 20km west of Bribrí, where you can observe and participate in local chocolate production (half-day trip US$35). Half-day trips (US$20) also visit an iguana farm on the Kèköldi territory (this is a tiny ethnicity related to the Bribrí).

Note: it is not recommended to visit these territories independently. Not only are many spots difficult to reach, but in most cases villages do not have the infrastructure to accommodate streams of tourists. Of course, remember to be respectful – these are people's private homes and workspaces, not tourist attractions.

The websites **Green Coast** (www.greencoast.com) and **Puerto Viejo** (www.puertoviejosatellite.com) have information on lodging, eating and activities in the area. ATEC (p436) has internet access and reliable information on local tours and activites.

Banco de Costa Rica (⊘9am-4pm Mon-Fri) ATM sometimes runs out of cash on weekends.

Café Rico (☎2750-0510; caferico.puertoviejo@yahoo.com; laundry per kilo US$2; ⊘8am-4pm; ☏) Free cup of excellent coffee while you do laundry; also wi-fi, book exchange and rentals of bikes, boards and snorkeling gear.

Jungle Internet (☎2750-2086, 2750-2003; www.junglec.com; per hr US$3; ⊘8am-11pm) Internet access.

ⓘ Getting There & Away

All public buses arrive and depart from the **bus stop** along the beach road in central Puerto Viejo. **Grayline** (☎2220-2126; www.grayline costarica.com) runs a private daily bus service departing Puerto Viejo at roughly 2pm bound for San José (US$44). Reserve ahead.

Bribrí/Sixaola US$2.90; 30/90 minutes; departs every hour from 6:30am to 7:30pm.

Cahuita/Puerto Limón US$3.20; 30/90 minutes; departs roughly every hour from 5:30am to 7:30pm.

Manzanillo US$0.85; 30 minutes; departs 6:45am, 7:15am, 11:45am, 4:15pm and 7:15pm.

San José US$9.50; five hours; departs 9am, 11am and 4pm.

ⓘ Getting Around

A bicycle is a fine way to get around town, and pedaling out to beaches east of Puerto Viejo is one of the highlights of this corner of Costa Rica. You'll find rentals all over town.

Tienda Marcos (☎2750-0303; bicycles per day US$5; ⊘8:30am-5pm)

Tuanis Bike Rental (bicycles per half/full day US$4/6; ⊘7am-6pm)

Puerto Viejo to Punta Uva

A 13km road winds east from Puerto Viejo, through rows of coconut palms, alongside coastal lodges and through lush lowland rainforest before coming to a dead end at the sleepy town of Manzanillo. The road was paved for the first time in 2003, dramatically shortening the amount of time it took to drive or cycle the route. The weather and buses, however, have since done a number on the tarmac and it is now an extravaganza of crater-sized potholes. (Take your time driving, unless you want to lose an axle.)

If you want to stay close to Puerto Viejo while having access to a nice beach, Playa Cocles has a good mix of isolation and amenities, offering a wide variety of places to stay and eat. After that, the pickings get thin until you get closer to Punta Uva, where you'll find a cluster of lodges and restaurants – as well as one of the prettiest beaches in the region.

Buses heading from Puerto Viejo to Manzanillo will drop you at any of these places along the way.

◉ Sights

Jaguar Centro de Rescate WILDLIFE REFUGE
(☑2750-0710; www.jaguarrescue.com; admission US$15; ⊘tours 9:30am & 11:30am Mon-Sat) Named in honor of its original resident, this wildlife rescue center in Playa Chiquita now focuses mostly on sloths and monkeys. Founded by Spanish zoologist Encar and her partner Sandro, an Italian herpetologist, the center rehabilitates orphaned, injured and rescued animals for reintroduction into the wild whenever possible. Volunteer opportunities are available with a three-week minimum commitment.

🏃 Activities

The region's biggest draws involve surf, sand, wildlife-watching and attempts to get a decent tan between downpours. **Playa Cocles** is known for its great surfing and organized lifeguard system, which helps offset the dangers of the frequent riptides, while **Punta Uva** features the best and safest beaches for swimming.

Punta Uva Dive Center DIVING
(☑2759-9191; www.puntauvadivecenter.com; 1-/2-tank dives from US$65/75) At the first turn-off into Punta Uva.

Crazy Monkey Canopy Tour ADVENTURE TOUR
(☑2759-9057; Almonds & Corals Lodge, Punta Uva; per person US$40; ⊘8am-2pm) Call ahead to reserve.

🛏 Sleeping & Eating

All of the following places are listed from west (Puerto Viejo) to east (Punta Uva). Accommodations have hot water, unless otherwise noted. Note that some restaurants may have reduced hours or close down entirely during the low season.

PLAYA COCLES

A broad stretch of white-sand beach lies just 1.5km east of Puerto Viejo, offering proximity to the village and its many restaurants, but plenty of peace and quiet, too.

Cabinas El Tesoro CABINA $
(☑2750-0128; www.cabinaseltesoro.com; dm US$15, d/tr/q from US$40/55/85; ᴘ❄☀@🌐) Located right on the beach break at Playa Cocles, these 12 clean, simple *cabinas* have tile floors, queen beds and cable TV. Tidy dorms sleep up to four. You'll also find bikes and surfboards for rent; surf lessons are available and take place just across the road. The small open-air bar hosts grooving live music jams on Wednesdays. Credit cards accepted.

La Isla Inn CABINA $$
(☑2750-0109; www.laislainn.com; d with/without air-con US$85/60; ᴘ❄☀🌊) Opposite the lifeguard tower at the main hub of the beach lies this efficient wooden lodge with 12 expansive rooms, all of which are equipped with safes, cable TV and handmade wood furnishings crafted from the slightly curved outer boards that are discarded during lumber processing. Credit cards accepted.

Hotel Totem LODGE $$
(☑2750-0758; www.totemhotelresort.com; d with/without air-con US$75/65, junior ste/2-room ste US$90/110, additional person US$20, all incl breakfast; ᴘ❄☀🌊) This smartly decorated 20-room inn is set back into a tropical garden. Rooms are decked out with bamboo furnishings, folk art and spotless bathrooms with earth-toned tiles. Nicer suites (one of which is wheelchair-accessible) are even roomier. Has a surf shop, board rentals and an attached Italian restaurant. Credit cards accepted.

Cariblue BUNGALOW $$$
(☑2750-0518, 2750-0035; www.cariblue.com; d standard/deluxe/superior US$95/115/125, additional person US$30, all incl breakfast; ᴘ❄☀@🌐🌊)

Set in lovely gardens (with labeled plants for the botanically curious), the bungalows at this popular family spot have hardwood accents, bright linens and private decks equipped with hammocks and easy chairs. There is a pool table, an open-air lounge and a lovely mosaic pool, complete with swim-up bar. Credit cards accepted.

Cabinas Garibaldi
CABINA $

(☑2750-0101; d/tr US$30/40, d with kitchenette US$40; ℗) A basic surfer crash pad – and the cheapest stay in the area – offers a row of clean *cabinas* that share a porch with sea views. The waves are right across the street.

Azánia Bungalows
BUNGALOW $$

(☑2750-0540; www.azania-costarica.com; d incl breakfast US$90, additional person US$20; ℗@⊠) Ten spacious but dark thatch-roofed bungalows are brightened up by colorful linens at this charming inn set on landscaped jungle grounds. Nice details include woven bedspreads, well-designed bathrooms and wide-plank hardwood floors. A free-form pool and a hot tub nestle into the greenery, and there's an Argentine restaurant and bar. Credit cards accepted.

La Costa de Papito
BUNGALOW $$

(☑2750-0080; www.lacostadepapito.com; d incl breakfast US$84-89, additional adult/child US$15/5; ℗☎) Relax in rustic comfort in the sculpture-studded grounds at this popular Cocles outpost, which has wood and bamboo bungalows decked out with hand-carved furniture, stone bathrooms straight out of *The Flintstones* and roomy porches draped with hammocks. The onsite Que Rico Papito Restaurant serves Italian-influenced specialties, while the rustic, palm-thatched Indulgence Spa (☑2720-0536; 1hr massage US$59; ⊙11am-6pm Mon-Sat) offers massage and spa treatments.

El Tucán Jungle Lodge
CABINA $$

(☑2750-0026; www.eltucanjunglelodge.com; s/d/tr incl breakfast US$38/50/60; ℗☎) Only 1km off the road, this jungle retreat feels miles from anywhere – making it ideal for birdwatchers. Four superclean wooden *cabinas*, on the banks of the Caño Negro, have bright linens and share a broad patio with hammocks. The welcoming German owners organize walks in the area.

Le Cameleon
LUXURY HOTEL $$$

(☑2750-0501; www.lecameleonhotel.com; d from US$200; ℗❋☎⊠) Ambitiously, this contemporary boutique hotel chose gleaming white as the dominant aesthetic in these tropical environs. Its 23 all-white, air-conditioned rooms are enlivened by colorful throw pillows and stocked with all the requisite high-end goodies and services. A restaurant-lounge serves cocktails and fusion cuisine, and while it's not on the beach, its private beach club keeps patrons plied with lounge chairs and cold drinks. Credit cards accepted.

⟨TOP CHOICE⟩ La Pecora Nera
ITALIAN $$$

(☑2750-0490; mains US$11-30; ⊙5pm-late Tue-Sun; ☎) If you splurge for a single fancy meal during your trip, do it here. A lovely, candle-lit patio off the main road is home to this romantic eatery run by Tuscan-born Ilario Giannoni. It serves deftly prepared Italian seafood and pasta dishes, as well as unusual offerings such as the delicate *carpaccio di carambola:* transparent slices of starfruit topped with shrimp, tomatoes and balsamic vinaigrette. There is an extensive wine list (from US$16 a bottle), but you can't go wrong with the well-chosen and relatively inexpensive house wines. The restaurant has also branched out to a more casual spot next door, Gatta Ci Cova (sandwiches US$6-11, mains US$8-11; ⊙noon-10pm Tue-Sun; ☎), where you can grab panini and drinks.

PLAYA CHIQUITA

It isn't exactly clear where Playa Cocles ends and Playa Chiquita begins, but conventional wisdom applies the name to a series of beaches 4km to 6km east of Puerto Viejo.

Villas del Caribe
HOTEL $$

(☑2233-2200, 2750-0202; www.villasdelcaribe.com; d standard/junior US$75/100, junior villa/villa US$110/135, all incl breakfast; ℗❋☎) Lovely, brightly painted rooms at this resort have comfortable beds, sitting areas and roomy bathrooms with Spanish tile. Junior villas also come with kitchenettes, while the two-story villas have ocean views, king-sized beds, kitchens and BBQ. All have private decks with hammocks. Credit cards accepted.

Aguas Claras
BUNGALOW $$

(☑2750-0131; www.aguasclaras-cr.com; 1-/2-/3-room cottages from US$70/130/220; ℗@) Five tropical Victorian cottages painted in bright candy colors and edged in lacy woodwork sit tucked amid the trees on the beach side of the road. All cottages have fully equipped kitchens and tons of romantic charm.

Miraflores Eco-Lodge
B&B **$$**

(☎2750-0038; www.mirafloreslodge.com; d with/without bathroom US$60/50, d with kitchen US$75-95, all incl breakfast; **P@**☎) A variety of rooms are spread out over a couple of structures at this simple, homey spot run by long-time resident Pamela Carpenter, an expert on botany and medicinal plants. (Check out the garden labyrinth.) Upstairs rooms in the main house are best, with garden views. A small open-air lounge has a library.

Tierra de Sueños
BUNGALOW **$$**

(☎2750-0378; www.tierradesuenoslodge.com; cabins with/without kitchen US$135/95, all incl breakfast; **P**) True to its name, this dreamy little garden lodge is home to several adorable wood bungalows with mosquito nets and private decks. The very quiet, tropical atmosphere is complemented by a lack of internet access or wi-fi.

Playa Chiquita Lodge
CABINA **$$**

(☎2750-0062; www.playachiquitalodge.com; s/d incl breakfast US$60/70; **P**☎) Eight brightly painted wooden *cabinas* are slightly worn, and the water pressure is iffy, but there's a broad deck hung with hammocks facing the garden. This hotel has direct beach access via a beautiful 200m walk through the forest. Credit cards accepted.

Shawandha Lodge
BUNGALOW **$$$**

(☎2750-0018; www.shawandhalodge.com; d incl breakfast US$120, additional person US$25; **P✳@**☎☀) This upscale lodge has 13 private, spacious and uniquely nature-themed bungalows painted in earth tones and equipped with large mosaic-tiled bathrooms. A meticulously maintained thatched *rancho* serves as an open-air lounge, and there's a French-Caribbean restaurant. A private path across the road leads to the beach. Credit cards accepted.

Jungle Love Garden Café
CAFE **$**

(☎2750-0162; www.junglelovecafe.com; meals US$7-14; ⏱5-9:30pm Tue-Sun; ☑) American bohemian meets the Caribbean at this popular porch-front cafe that serves fusion dishes and an eponymous Jungle Love Milkshake, a very grown-up blend of Bailey's, *guaro* and local ice cream. The menu has veggie options and vegan items can be prepared on request. There are only eight tables; reserve ahead.

C&J Juice Joint
CAFE **$**

(☎2750-0904; www.candjcostarica.com; **P**☑) A small market and juice joint (freshly juiced veggies and fruit, sans water or sugar) also has a handful of clean, wood *cabinas* on offer at wallet-friendly rates (single/double US$15/25).

PUNTA UVA

Punta Uva is known for the region's most swimmable beaches, each lovelier than the next. To find the turnoff to the point (about 7km east of Puerto Viejo), look for the Punta Uva Dive Center sign.

Costa Rica Tree House Lodge
TOP CHOICE
BUNGALOW **$$$**

(☎2750-0706; www.costaricatreehouse.com; d US$200-390, extra person US$50; **P**) For adventurers who like their lodgings rustic and whimsical, this is the place for you. Five *casitas* of various sizes dot four jungle-filled hectares, including a literal 'tree house' – a two-story cabin built around the base of a living sangrillo tree. All are open-air and come equipped with mosquito nets, kitchens, BBQs and spacious decks with easy chairs and hammocks. Each unit has a private path that leads to a small white-sand beach. Proceeds support an iguana breeding program; credit cards accepted.

Casa Viva
BUNGALOW **$$$**

(☎2750-0089; www.puntauva.net; d per night/week from US$100/600; **P✳**☎) Enormous, well-constructed, fully furnished hardwood houses, each with tiled shower, kitchen and wraparound veranda, are set on a property that fronts the beach – an ideal spot in which to chill out in a hammock and observe the local wildlife.

Korrigan Lodge
BUNGALOW **$$**

(☎2759-9103; www.korriganlodge.com; d incl breakfast US$90; **P**) Four beautiful wood and concrete bungalows are topped with thatched roofs and nestled into a patch of lush jungle. All units have minibar, safe, modern bathrooms and private terraces with hammocks, plus all guests have access to free bikes. Breakfast is served in an open-air *rancho* surrounded by gardens. Credit cards accepted.

El Colibrí Lodge
CABINA **$$**

(☎2759-9036; www.elcolibrilodge.com; d/tr incl breakfast US$65/85, 2-bedroom house US$150; **P**) Perfect for couples and small families, there are four gracious, well-tended rooms with private terraces at this lovely, locally run spot nestled into the rainforest – ideal for wildlife-watching. Breakfast is served on the terrace or in the privacy of your room. A 300m trail winds through the rainforest to the beach.

🍃 **Almonds & Corals Lodge**   BUNGALOW **$$$**
(☎2759-9056, 2271-3000; www.almondsandcorals.com; s/d US$235/300, s/d master ste US$315/400, additional child/adult from US$50/93, all incl breakfast & dinner; P@🖨) Buried deep in the woods, this long-time luxury spot popular with honeymooners has 24 wood suites with four-poster beds, Jacuzzi tubs and private patios with hammocks. Rooms are screened in, making them comfortable, but you'll still be able to enjoy the nightly serenade of insects and frogs. Meals are served family-style in an open-air dining room. Credit cards accepted.

TOP CHOICE **Selvin's Restaurant**   CARIBBEAN **$$**
(☎2750-0664; mains US$7-15; ☺8am-8pm Wed-Sun) Selvin is a member of the extensive Brown family, noted for their charm, and his place is considered one of the region's best, specializing in shrimp, lobster, a terrific *rondón* and a succulent chicken *caribeño* (chicken stewed in a spicy Caribbean sauce).

Arrecife Restaurant   CARIBBEAN **$**
(☎2759-9200; www.arrecifepuntauva.net; mains US$7-15; ☺8am-10pm) Located on the second turn-off into Punta Uva, this popular beachside restaurant is great for a beer in the shade; the food is OK. It also rents a few basic tiled *cabinas* (doubles US$50).

🛍 **Shopping**

Echo Books & Chocolate Lounge   BOOKS
(www.echobookscostarica.com; ☺11am-dark Wed-Sun; 🛜) Admittedly, Echo Books is a strange place for a bookstore – buried in the jungle off the main road – but this tiny store has a decent selection of used paperbacks and new books, and the added lure of luscious homemade chocolate.

Manzanillo

The chill village of Manzanillo has long been off the beaten track, even since the paved road arrived in 2003. This little town remains a vibrant outpost of Afro-Caribbean culture and has also remained pristine, thanks to the 1985 establishment of the Refugio Nacional de Vida Silvestre Gandoca-Manzanillo, which includes the village and imposes strict regulations on regional development.

Activities are of a simple nature, *in* nature: hiking, snorkeling and kayaking are king. (As elsewhere, ask about riptides before heading out.) Other than that, you may find the occasional party at the locally renowned Maxi's bar and restaurant at the end of the road, which is the end of the line (where buses arrive).

🏄 **Activities**

Aquamor Talamanca Adventures   SNORKELING
(☎2759-9012, 8835-6041; www.greencoast.com/aquamor.htm) Rents snorkel gear and kayaks. There's a Coral Reef Information Center here. Hours vary; call ahead.

🍽 **Sleeping & Eating**

Most Manzanillo hotels have hot water. Two good family-operated *sodas* for cheap, tasty *casados* are Mi Rinconcito Alegre (casados US$5; ☺8am-8pm), right across from Aquamor, and Soda Miskito (casados US$5; ☺7am-9pm), which is decorated with lamps and greenery.

Cabinas Manzanillo   CABINA **$**
(☎8839-8386, 2759-9033; r US$35; P🛜) Run by the ever-helpful Sandra Castillo and Pablo Bustamante, these eight *cabinas* on the western end of town are so clean, you could eat off the tile floors. Cheery rooms have big beds, industrial-strength ceiling fans and spacious bathrooms. There's also a shared kitchen. From Maxi's, travel 300m along the main road toward Punta Uva, then make a left onto the dirt road leading back into town. Do not confuse this with the dilapidated beachside Hotel Manzanillo.

Cabinas Bucus   CABINA **$**
(☎2759-9143; www.costa-rica-manzanillo.com; s/d/tr US$25/35/45; P🛜) Four tidy, brightly painted tiled rooms in a two-story mustard-yellow structure have mosquito nets and private bathrooms, all sharing a small kitchen. Find it just beyond Cabinas Manzanillo. Omar, one of the co-owners, is one of Manzanillo's top guides.

Cabinas Something Different   CABINA **$**
(☎2759-9014; d from US$35; P) In town about 200m south of the main beach road, you'll find 18 simple *cabinas* named after local fauna. Rooms have minifridges and the welcoming owners can help organize tours.

Congo Bongo   BUNGALOW **$$$**
(☎2759-9016; www.congo-bongo.com; d/tr/q US$145/170/195, per week US$870/1020/1170; P) On the road to Punta Uva, you'll find

six charming wooden cottages set in a reclaimed cacao plantation (now dense forest). They offer fully equipped kitchens and plenty of living space, including open-air terraces and strategically placed hammocks that are perfect for spying on the wildlife. A network of trails leads through the 6 hectares of grounds to the beautiful beach.

TOP CHOICE Maxi's Restaurant CARIBBEAN $$
(mains US$5-42, lobster from US$18; ⊙6am-close; 🖼) Manzanillo's most famous restaurant attracts travelers from all over for large platters of tender grilled seafood, whole red snappers (*pargo rojo*), steaks and Caribbean-style lobsters (expensive and not necessarily worth it). Despite the tourist traffic, it's still a wonderful seaside setting for a meal and a beer. And the bar can get hopping on weekends, with live music and DJs. Maxi's also has clean *cabinas* (US$35 to US$50) for rent – right next to the bar.

🛈 Information

Casa de Guías (📞2759-9064) Opposite the Ministry of Environment and Energy (Minae) office on the way into town; provides information on local guides.

🛈 Getting There & Away

Buses from Puerto Viejo to Manzanillo (US$0.85, 30 minutes) depart at 6:45am, 7:15am, 11:45am, 4:15pm and 7:15pm. They return to Puerto Viejo at 5am, 7am, 8:30am, 12:45pm and 5:15pm. These buses all continue to Puerto Limón (US$3.20, 2½ hours) for onward transfers.

Refugio Nacional de Vida Silvestre Gandoca-Manzanillo

This little-explored refuge, called Regama for short, protects nearly 70% of the southern Caribbean coast, extending from Manzanillo all the way to the Panamanian border. It encompasses 50 sq km of land plus 44 sq km of marine environment. The peaceful, pristine stretch of sandy white beach is one of the area's main attractions. It's the center of village life in Manzanillo, and stretches for miles in either direction – from Punta Uva to Punta Mona in the east. Offshore, a 5-sq-km coral reef is a teeming habitat for lobsters, sea fans and long-spined urchins.

Other than the village itself, and the surrounding farmland areas (grandfathered when the park was created in 1985), the wildlife refuge is composed largely of rainforest. Cativo trees form the canopy, while there are many heliconias in the undergrowth. A huge, 400-hectare swamp – known as Pantano Punta Mona – provides a haven for waterfowl, as well as the country's most extensive collection of holillo palms and sajo trees. Beyond Punta Mona, protecting a natural oyster bank, is the only red mangrove swamp in Caribbean Costa Rica. In the nearby Río Gandoca estuary there is a spawning ground for Atlantic tarpon, and caimans and manatees have been sighted.

The variety of vegetation and the remote location of the refuge attract many tropical birds; sightings of the rare harpy eagle have been recorded here. Other birds to look out for include the red-lored parrot, the red-capped manikin and the chestnut-mandibled toucan, among hundreds of others. The area is also known for incredible raptor migrations, with more than a million birds flying overhead during autumn.

Despite the idyllic nature of the environment, there has been some political squabbling between the Minae (the government agency that administers the national parks in Costa Rica) and some local businesses over the management of the refuge. Some local operators are trying to get the village excluded from the confines of the refuge – which would open the door to increased development in the area. (In fact, unapproved constructions have already materialized – some within 50m of the high-tide line, a zone in which construction is prohibited by national law.) Others oppose it. It will likely take years – and armies of lawyers – to sort the mess out.

🏃 Activities

Hiking

A coastal trail heads 5.5km east out of Manzanillo to **Punta Mona**. The first part of this path, which leads from Manzanillo to Tom Bay (about a 40-minute walk), is well trammeled and clearly marked and doesn't require a guide. Once you pass Tom Bay, however, the path gets murky and it's easy to get lost, so ask about conditions before you set out or hire a guide. It's a rewarding walk – with amazing scenery, as well as excellent (and safe) swimming and snorkeling at the end.

Another, more difficult, 9km trail leaves from just west of Manzanillo and skirts the southern edges of the Pantano Punta Mona, continuing to the small community of Gandoca. This trail isn't commonly walked, as most people access Punta Mona and Gandoca from the park entrance at the refuge's northern edge, located on the road to Sixaola. If you want to hike this, be sure to hire a guide.

Snorkeling & Diving

The undersea portion of the park cradles one of two living coral reefs in the country. Comprising five different types of coral, the reefs begin in about 1m of water and extend 5km offshore to a barrier reef that local fishers have long relied on and researchers have only recently discovered. This colorful undersea world is home to some 400 species of fish and crustacean. **Punta Mona** is a popular destination for snorkeling, though it's a trek so you may wish to hire a boat. Otherwise, you can snorkel offshore at **Manzanillo** at the eastern end of the beach (the riptide can be dangerous here; inquire about conditions before setting out). Also check out the Coral Reef Information Center at Aquamor Talamanca Adventures (p448).

Conditions vary widely, and clarity can be adversely affected by weather changes.

Kayaking

You can explore some of the area's waterways by kayak, available from Aquamor Talamanca Adventures (per hour US$5). Paddle out to the reef, or head up the Quebrada Home Wark, in the west of the village, or the tiny Simeon Creek, at the east end of the village. These are short paddles – ideal if you've got kids.

Dolphin-Watching

In 1997 a group of guides in Manzanillo identified tucuxi dolphins, a little-known species previously not found in Costa Rica, and began observing their interactions with the bottlenose dolphins. A third species – the Atlantic spotted dolphin – is also common in this area. This unprecedented activity has attracted the attention of marine biologists and conservationists, who are following these animals with great interest. Learn more about this work through the Talamanca Dolphin Foundation (☑2759-0612, 2759-0715; www.dolphinlink.org), a nonprofit dedicated to the study and preservation of local dolphin populations.

ATEC (p436) organizes full-day dolphin-watching tours (US$95).

Turtle-Watching

Marine turtles – especially leatherback but also green, hawksbill and loggerhead – all nest on the beaches between Punta Mona and the Río Sixaola. Leatherbacks nest from March to July, with a peak in April and May. Local conservation efforts are under way to protect these nesting grounds since the growth of the area's human population has led to increased theft of turtle eggs.

During turtle season, no flashlights, beach fires or camping are allowed on the beach. All tourists must be accompanied by a local guide to minimize the disturbance to the nesting turtles.

☞ Tours

You could explore the refuge on your own, but without a guide you'll likely miss out on the refuge's incredible diversity of medicinal plants, exotic birds and earthbound animals. Most guides charge US$35 per person for a four- to five-hour trek, depending on the size of the group. Ask around at Maxi's or at the Casa de Guías.

Recommended local guides include Florentino Grenald (☑8841-2732, 2759-9043), who used to serve as the reserve's administrator; Omar (☑2759-9143; Cabinas Bucus) and Abel Bustamante (☑2759-9043).

ATEC (p436), Aquamor Talamanca Adventures (p448) and Casa De Guías (p449) offer tours of the area.

🛏 Sleeping & Eating

🌿 **Punta Mona** CABINA $$

(☑8321-8788; www.puntamona.org; dm US$45, s with/without bathroom US$75/55, all incl 3 organic meals; @) Five kilometers southeast of the village, you'll find this organic farm and retreat center that is an experiment in permaculture design and sustainable living. Covering some 40 hectares, it grows more than 200 varieties of edible fruits and veggies, which comprise about 90% of the huge vegetarian meals that are included in the daily rate. Check the website for myriad volunteer opportunities here. To arrange accommodations and transportation, email ahead of your visit.

❶ Information

An excellent photo book on the area, with commentary in Spanish and English, is *Refugio Nacional de Vida Silvestre Gandoca-Manzanillo* by Juan José Puccí, available locally.

Minae (☏2759-9100; ⏰8am-noon & 1-4pm) is located in the green wooden house as you enter town, and generally has trail maps of the refuge.

Aquamor Talamanca Adventures and **Casa de Guías** (☏2759-9064) are also good sources of information on what to do in the park.

Bribrí

This bustling, no-stoplight town in the foothills of the Cordillera de Talamanca lies at a bend in the paved road that connects Cahuita to Sixaola and the Panama border. The village is primarily an agricultural center and a spot for nearby indigenous communities to take care of errands; most travelers just pass through on their way to the border or local tours.

From Bribrí, a 34km road – mostly paved – takes the traveler to the border.

◎ Sights & Activities

You can inquire about tours to indigenous villages at Restaurant Bribrí.

Studio of Fran Vázques　　　　　GALLERY
(☏2751-0205) On the road to Bribrí, just north of the Sixaola turnoff, find the studio of this self-taught folk painter whose colorful acrylic landscapes are well known in Puerto Viejo and San José. Look for the brightly painted sign outside a small one-story house. Call ahead to visit, as hours vary.

Aiko-logi　　　　　　　WILDLIFE RESERVE
(☏2750-2084, 8997-6869; www.aiko-logi-tours.com; day tour incl transport & lunch US$60, overnight stay per person incl meals US$99) Nestled into the Cordillera de Talamanca, 2km outside the village (just beyond the Volio waterfall), is a private 135-hectare reserve centered around the site of what was once a small *finca*, on a piece of land fringed with dense primary rainforest. It's an ideal spot for bird-watching, hiking and splashing around in crisp, clean swimming holes. Day tours from Puerto Viejo and Cahuita can be arranged, as can overnight stays at Aiko-logi's tent platform. Reserve ahead.

🛏 Sleeping & Eating

There are a few basic lodging options, a supermarket and the requisite Musmanni bakery. Accommodations tend to fill up on market days (Monday and Tuesday).

Cabinas El Piculino　　　　　CABINA $
(☏2751-0130; d with/without air-con US$35/25; 🅿✱) Connected to the great soda (casados US$5; ⏰Mon-Sat) run by the same family, this spotless place has 22 clean, simple brightly

---

GETTING TO GUABITO & BOCAS DEL TORO, PANAMA

Welcome to Costa Rica's most entertaining border crossing! An old railroad bridge that spans the churning waters of the Río Sixaola connects Costa Rica with Panama amid a sea of agricultural plantations. Oversized buses and trucks also ply this route – so, if you're lucky, you'll get to watch one of these vehicles clatter along the wood planks as pedestrians scatter to the edges to let them pass.

From here, most travelers make for Bocas del Toro in Panama, a picturesque archipelago of jungle islands that is home to lovely beaches and endangered red frogs, and is easily accessible by regular water taxis from the docks at Almirante.

The border is open 7am to 5pm (8am to 6pm in Guabito, Panama, which is an hour ahead of Costa Rica), though one or both sides may close for lunch at around 1pm. At the entrance to the bridge, on the right-hand side, get your exit stamp at Costa Rica immigration office (☏2754-2044). Once over the bridge, stop at Panama immigration office on the left-hand side to get your passport stamped and purchase a tourist card for US$3. Personal cars (not rentals) can cross here. Note that if you aren't carrying proof of onward travel out of Panama, you will be 'required' to purchase a US$14 bus ticket out, conveniently sold on the road below.

Guabito has no hotels or banks, but in a pinch you can exchange colones at the market across the street. From the border, half-hourly buses (US$1, one hour) run to Terminal Piquera in Changuinola, where you can transfer to one of the frequent buses to Almirante (US$1.45, 45 minutes) for the water taxi. Alternatively, from Guabito you can take a collective taxi (per person US$10, one hour) straight to Almirante. From this point, hourly water taxis (per person US$5, 25 minutes) make the trip to Bocas del Toro between 6:30am and 7pm.

painted rooms with private hot showers; all have TV and most have air-con. There's a pleasant *rancho* in between the two establishments. Credit cards are accepted.

Restaurante Bribrí
COSTA RICAN **$**

(🖉2751-0044; casados US$4, mains US$5; ☺8am-6pm Mon-Sat) Run by the helpful Carlos and Miriam, this busy restaurant serves *casados*, chicken with rice, fried plantains and *gallos* (an open-faced taco). But it's also an excellent place to ask about tours to indigenous villages, where local guides lead hikes and boat rides through the area's jungle and rivers.

Restaurante Kaya Chökök Miàs Miàs
CARIBBEAN **$**

(casados US$3-7, mains US$3-9; ☺7am-4pm Mon-Fri) A pleasant 2nd-story terrace restaurant located near the Banco Nacional, this place serves up superdelicious cooking, including the delectably carnivorous 'Arroz Kaya' (US$5), a steaming pile of fried rice studded with bacon, ham, chicken and steak, and served with salad and fried plantains. Don't miss the pickled chili vegetables, just the thing for clearing your sinuses.

ℹ Information

Banco Nacional (☺8:30am-3:45pm) Changes US dollars. It's 100m north of the bus stop.

Internet Veloz (per hr US$1; ☺8am-6pm) Upstairs from the bus stop.

ℹ Getting There & Away

Buses arrive and depart hourly from in front of Restaurante Bribrí.

Puerto Limón, via Cahuita US$3.85; three hours; departs hourly from 6am to 7pm.

San José US$10.60; 5½ hours; departs 6:30am, 8:30am, 10:30am and 3:30pm.

Sixaola US$1.65; 30 minutes; departs hourly from 6am to 8pm.

Sixaola

POP 1800

This is the end of the road – literally. A bumpy tarmac leads to an old railroad bridge over the Río Sixaola that serves as the border crossing into Panama. Like most border towns, Sixaola is hardly scenic: it's an extravaganza of dingy bars and roadside stalls selling rubber boots.

Sixaola is centered on the optimistically named Mercado Internacional de Sixaola, a gravelly square where you can find taxis and a handful of *sodas*. The market is about two blocks from the border crossing.

There's no good reason to stay in Sixaola, but if you get stuck, head for safe, clean Cabinas Sanchez (🖉2754-2105; r US$15). From the border, head down the lower road, which is lined with sodas, and walk about 100m to the tunnel on the left. After exiting the underpass, walk another 100m to find the *cabinas*.

The bus station is one block north of the border crossing, on the east side of the main drag. Buses to either San José (US$11.60, six hours, departs 6am, 8am, 10am and 3pm) or Puerto Limón (US$3.30, three hours, departs hourly from 5am to 6pm) all stop at Bribrí and Cahuita.

Northern Lowlands

Why Go?

Venture onto the wild rivers and into the tropical jungle of the northern lowlands and you will discover real-life Costa Rica, where agricultural commerce and ecological conservation converge as a work in green progress. Stretching from the borderlands of Nicaragua, across the Cordillera Central, banana, sugarcane and pineapple *fincas* roll across humid plains. Community tourism lives and breathes here creating added revenue for a historically farm-based economy. You can fish for tarpon, spot a macaw in the wild, paddle into roaring rapids, and cruise inky lagoons all with lifelong resident guides, then nest in lodges that double as private rainforest preserves. You can even learn how to milk a cow at a family dairy during a homestay. When the tourist hoards gets you down, make your way here for a refreshing blast of rural realism, and an invigorating dose of wild beauty.

Best Places to Eat

» Rancho Magallanes (p459)

» Restaurante La Casona (p461)

» La Terazza (p472)

» Soda Marinero (p472)

When to Go

In the northern lowlands the dry season runs from April to November, but the lush jungles surrounding the rivers in the region, such as the Río Frío and the Río Sarapiquí, receive rainfall at almost any time of year. December is the peak rafting season on the Sarapiquí and the wetter it is, the better your run.

Best Places to Stay

» Chilamate Rainforest Eco Retreat (p459)

» Sarapiquís Rainforest Lodge (p458)

» Rara Avis (p464)

» Albergue El Soccoro (p464)

» Hotel de Campo Caño Negro (p470)

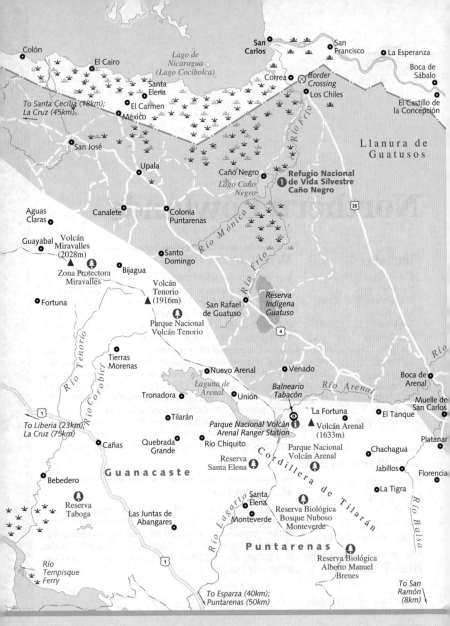

Northern Lowlands Highlights

① Explore the lagoons of **Refugio Nacional de Vida Silvestre Caño Negro** (p468) to take a gander at spoonbills or a stab at tarpon

② Raft through the jungle on the **Río Sarapiquí** (p456)

③ Experience the spectacular beauty and down-home grace of **Albergue El Soccoro** (p464), our favorite homestay in Costa Rica

455

CARIBBEAN
SEA

N 0 —————— 20 km
0 —————— 10 miles

El Castillo

④ **Río San Juan**

N I C A R A G U A

Alajuela

Llanura de
Guatusos

Laguna del
Lagarto Lodge

Refugio Nacional de
Vida Silvestre
Mixto Maquenque

Trinidad

Refugio Nacional
de Vida Silvestre
Barra del Colorado

Boca
Tapada

San Carlos

Río Toro

② **Río Sarapiquí**

Río Tres Amigos

Río Pital

Laguna
Astillero

H e r e d i a

Selva Verde Lodge;
Aventuras del Sarapiquí;
Chilamate Rainforest
Eco Retreat

Chilamate

(250)

Rancho
Magallenas

Bajos de
Chilamate

Puerto Viejo
de Sarapiquí

Pital

(162)

La Quinta de
Sarapiquí
Lodge

Zona Protectora

La Selva

⑤

**Tirimbina
Rainforest
Centre**

Río Chirripó

L i m ó n

(4)

La Virgen

**Sarapiquís
Rainforest
Lodge**

⑥

Heliconia Island

Cariari

Aguas
Zarcas

(140)

Venecia **⑦**

Río
Cuarto

(126)

Reserva
Cordillera
Volcánica
Central

Estación
Biológica
La Selva

Horquetas

Ciudad Quesada
(San Carlos)

(4)

San Miguel

Laguna
Hule

Sueño
Azul Resort

Río Frío

Parque Nacional
Juan Castro Blanco

Cariblanco

③ **Albergue El
Socorro**

Rara Avis

(4)

Santa
Clara

Guápiles

(32)

Bajos
del Toro

Volcán
Poás
(2704m) ▲

Parque Nacional
Volcán Poás

Catarata
La Paz

Parque
Nacional
Braulio
Carrillo

Río Puerto Viejo

Vara
Blanca

To San
José
(26km)

Río puerto Viejo

To Puerto
Limón (80km)

④ Keep your eyes peeled
for crocs and sloths as you
float along the **Río San Juan**
(p463) at the Nicaraguan
border

⑤ Explore the ruins around
the **Sarapiquís Rainforest
Lodge** (p458)

⑥ Traipse the suspension
bridges of **Tirimbina
Rainforest Center** (p458)

⑦ Check out bustling
Venecia (p465), a cute
middle-class hamlet where
you can sleep in a castle and
dip into hot springs

THE SARAPIQUÍ VALLEY

This flat, steaming stretch of *finca*-dotted lowlands was once part of the United Fruit Company's vast banana holdings. Harvests were carried from plantations to Puerto Viejo de Sarapiquí where they were shipped down river on boats destined for North America. In 1880 a railway connected rural Costa Rica with the port of Puerto Limón, and Puerto Viejo de Sarapiquí became a backwater. Although it's never managed to recover its faded glory, the river again shot to prominence as one of the premier destinations in Costa Rica for kayakers and rafters in the 1990s, until a devastating 2009 earthquake altered the river's natural course and chased off the tourist dollar. But the rapids are once again tasty, the paddlers trickling back, and there are a number of stellar lodges in the region that feature rainforest trails, suspension bridges, pre-Columbian ruins and chocolate tours.

La Virgen

Tucked into the densely jungled shores of the wild and scenic Río Sarapiquí, La Virgen was one of a number of small towns that prospered during the heyday of the banana trade. Although United Fruit has long since shipped out, the town remains dependent on their nearby pineapple fields, and they still lean on that river. For over a decade, La Virgen was the premier kayaking and rafting destination in Costa Rica. Dedicated groups of hard-core paddlers spent happy weeks running the Río Sarapiquí. But a tremendous 2009 earthquake and landslide altered its course and flattened La Virgen's tourist economy. Some businesses folded, others relocated to La Fortuna. But independent kayakers are starting to come back and there are now three river outfitters offering exhilarating trips on Class II to IV waters. Although there are cheap digs in town, consider staying in one of the more luxurious lodges just nearby.

◎ Sights & Activities

Serpentario ZOO
(☑2761-1059; adult/student & child US$8/6; ☺9am-5pm) Get face-to-face with 50 different species of reptile and amphibian, including a poison-dart frog, an anaconda and the star attraction, an 80kg Burmese python.

White-Water Rafting & Kayaking
The Río Sarapiquí isn't as wild as the white water on the Río Pacuare near Turrialba, though it will get your heart racing and the dense jungle that hugs the riverbank is lush and primitive. You can run the Sarapiquí year-round, but December offers the biggest water. The rest of the year, the river fluctuates with rainfall. The bottom line is, if it's been raining, the river will be at its best. Where once there were nearly a dozen outfitters in La Virgen, now there are three. All offer roughly the same Class II to IV options at similar prices.

Sarapiquí Outdoor Center RAFTING
(☑8322-5597, 2761-1123; www.costaricaraft.com; per person Class III/IV US$65/85, guided kayak trips US$120-150) Here is your local paddling authority. In addition to offering its own rafting excursions, it offers kayak rental (per day US$45) and instruction and is the head of the local tourism association. Indie paddlers should check in here for up-to-date river information.

Hacienda Pozo Azul Adventures ADVENTURE SPORTS
(☑2761-1360, in USA & Canada 877-810-6903; www.pozoazul.com; tours US$42-80, combo tours US$80-122; ⊕) Hacienda Pozo Azul Adventures specializes in adventure activities, including horseback-riding tours, a canopy

> **DON'T MISS**
>
> ## PARKS & RESERVES
>
> Several notable refuges and parks are found in the northern lowlands, offering opportunities for low-key, crowd-free boat tours and wildlife-watching.
>
> **» Parque Nacional Braulio Carrillo** (p462) Ecolodges in the Sarapiquí area can arrange rainforest tours and have accommodations at the northern end of Braulio Carrillo.
>
> **» Refugio Nacional de Vida Silvestre Caño Negro** (p468) The lagoons of Caño Negro attract a wide variety of birds year-round, though prime time for bird-watchers is between January and July.
>
> **» Refugio Nacional de Vida Silvestre Mixto Maquenque** (p463) Though there isn't much in the way of infrastructure at this refuge, local lodges can take you into this remote rainforest.

tour over the lush jungle and river, rappelling, and assorted river trips. Or indulge in any combination thereof. It is the most polished and best funded tour concession in the area, and ideal for families. The Adventure Center is in La Virgen town.

Aventuras del Sarapiquí RAFTING
(✆2766-6768; www.sarapiqui.com; river trips US$55-80) A highly recommended outfitter, Adventuras del Sarapiquí offers: mountain biking; canopy, hiking and horseback tours; and a variety of river trips. It is set just out of town on the main highway in Chilamate.

Inflatable Duckies KAYAKING
(✆8760-3787, 2761-0095; tours from US$65; ☺departs 9:30am & 1:30pm) This brand new concession offers beginners kayak instruction in inflatable kayaks, which allow for a fun paddle even when the river is low. Two trips daily. Reserve ahead.

Other Activities

Sarapiquí Eco Observatory BIRD-WATCHING
(✆2761-0801; www.eco-observatory.com; self-guided adult/student 9-16/ under 8 US$15/8/free, guided tours from US$20; ☺7am-5pm) La Virgen's newest attraction is an American-owned private preserve that uses bird feeders to attract critters, which translates into epic photo ops, but also calls the 'eco' moniker into question. Nevertheless, there are 200 species of bird on this 4-hectare reserve, laced with trails that run through secondary forest all the way down to the Río Sarapiquí.

🛏 Sleeping & Eating

Bar & Cabinas El Río BUNGALOW $
(✆2761-0138; r with fan/air-con US$15/20; P❄) About 1km from Pozo Azul at the southern edge of town, these seven A-frame bungalows have tiled floors, clean hot-water bathrooms and TV. About 100m further down the steep hill is the lovely open-air Bar El Río, on rough hewn stilts high above the river.

Cabinas El Bosque CABINA $
(✆2761-0204; r US$10) Basic but sparkling new cabinas set off the main highway, 1km from town. Rooms are set in little square houses with fan, new tile and sweet window treatments.

Hacienda Pozo Azul Adventures BUNGALOW $$
(✆2761-1360; www.haciendapozoazul.com; d luxury tent US$92; P@🛜🏊) Located near the south end of La Virgen, Pozo Azul features luxurious 'tent suites' scattered on the edge of the tree line, all on raised polished-wood platforms and dressed with luxurious bedding and mosquito nets. At night the frogs and wildlife sing you to sleep as raindrops patter on the canvas roof. Pozo Azul also boasts a restaurant-bar in town for lunch and dinner (mains US$6 to US$14), with a riverside veranda.

Restaurante y Cabinas Tía Rosita SODA $
(✆2761-1125, 2761-1032; www.restaurantetiarosita.com; meals US$2-6; ☺breakfast, lunch & dinner; P🛜) Tía Rosita is the most highly recommended *soda* (lunch counter) in La Virgen, with excellent *casados* (set meals) and Costa Rican–style *chiles rellenos* (stuffed fried peppers). The family also rents several *cabinas* (single/double US$10/15) with private hot shower, TV, fan and plenty of breathing space, about 100m down the road. There's an onsite internet cafe (US$0.60 per hour).

Restaurante Mar y Tierra RESTAURANT $
(✆2761-1603; mains US$4-11; ☺8am-10pm) La Virgen's favorite fine dining (but still very relaxed) option is this comfortable seafood and steak restaurant that's popular with both locals and travelers.

ℹ Information

Most of La Virgen's businesses are strung along the highway, including a gas station, a **Banco Nacional** (✆2212-2000) with 24-hour ATM, and a couple of small supermarkets.

ℹ Getting There & Away

La Virgen lies on Hwy 126, about 8km from San Miguel to the south, and 17km from Puerto Viejo de Sarapiquí to the northeast. Buses originating in San José, San Miguel or Puerto Viejo de Sarapiquí make regular stops in La Virgen. If you're driving, the curvy road is paved between San José and Puerto Viejo de Sarapiquí, though irregular maintenance can make for a bumpy ride.

La Virgen to Puerto Viejo de Sarapiquí

This scenic stretch of Hwy 126 is home to a few lovely, popular ecolodges. However, if you're the kind of traveler that scrapes together a few hundred colones every morning to buy a loaf of bread from Palí supermarket, fear not, as these places do allow nonguests to see their unusual attractions and private trails for a small fee. Even better, arrange a homestay with the farming families in nearby Linda Vista through the Chilamate Rainforest Eco Retreat (p459). Any bus between La Virgen and Puerto Viejo de Sarapiquí can drop you off at the entrances, while a taxi from La Virgen (or Puerto Viejo for Selva Verde) will cost from US$8 to US$10.

Sarapiquís Rainforest Lodge   LODGE $$$
(☎2761-1004; www.sarapiquis.org; d US$117; P☎✳@) About 2km north of La Virgen, Sarapiquis Rainforest Lodge is a unique ecolodge run in conjunction with the Centro Neotropico Sarapiquism, which aims to foster sustainable tourism by educating guests about environmental conservation and pre-Columbian culture. The complex consists of *palenque*-style thatched-roof buildings modeled after a 15th-century pre-Columbian village, and contains a clutch of luxuriously appointed rooms with huge solar-heated bathroom and private terrace. Guests rave about the variety of exhibits and attractions located on the grounds.

It's worth stopping by just to visit the Alma Ata Archaeological Park, Museum of Indigenous Cultures and Sarapiquís Gardens (www.sarapiquis.org; self-guided adult/child 4-16yr US$8/4, with guide adult/child 4-16yr US$15/8; ⊙9am-5pm). The archaeological site is estimated to be around 600 years old, and is attributed to the Maleku. Currently about 70 small stone sculptures marking a burial field are being excavated by Costa Rican archaeologists who have revealed a number of petroglyphs and pieces of pottery. Although the site is modest, and definitely not comparable in size or scope to other Central American archaeological sites, it's one of the few places in Costa Rica where you can get a sense of its pre-Columbian history.

The Museum de Culturas Indigenas (MCI) chronicles the history of the rainforest (and of human interactions with it) through a mixture of displays and videos. It also displays hundreds of indigenous artifacts. The gardens boast the largest scientific collection of medicinal plants in Costa Rica.

An onsite restaurant (mains US$8 to US$24) serves meals incorporating fruits, vegetables, spices and edible flowers used in indigenous cuisine, many of which are grown on the premises.

Tirimbina Rainforest Center WILDLIFE RESERVE
(☎2761-1579; www.tirimbina.org) A working environmental research and education center, Tirimbina Rainforest Center also provides tours (US$22 to US$25) and accommodations (double including breakfast US$63) for visitors. The 345-hectare private reserve and the nearby Centro Neotrópico Sarapiquís are connected by two suspension bridges, 267m and 117m long. Halfway across, a spiral staircase drops to an island in the river. Tirimbina reserve has more than 9km of trails, some of which are paved or wood-blocked. There are also several guided tours on offer including birdwatching, frog and bat tours, night walks and a recommended chocolate tour, which lets you explore a working cacao plantation and learn about the harvesting, fermenting and drying processes. Child and student discounts are available. Tirimbina is about 2km north of La Virgen.

La Quinta de Sarapiquí Lodge   LODGE $$$
(☎2761-1052; www.laquintasarapiqui.com; d US$120; P✳☎) About 5km north of La Virgen, this pleasant family-run lodge is on the banks of the Río Sardinal, which branches off from the Sarapiquí. The lodge has covered paths through the landscaped garden connecting thatched-roof, hammock-strung rooms. All have a terrace, ceiling fan, natural wood vanity and private hot shower. You can also get meals in the open-air restaurant (mains US$9 to US$15).

Activities at the lodge include swimming in the pretty pool or river (there's a good swimming hole nearby), fishing, boat trips and bird-watching, and you can spend time in the large butterfly garden or hike the 30-minutes' worth of trails through secondary forest accessible from the hotel. There's also a full-service spa.

Collin Street Bakery
Pineapple Plantation   FARM
(☎tours 2761-1700; www.collinstreet.com; ⊙tours 8am, 10am & 3pm Mon-Fri) You won't find any bread at Collin Street Bakery (its name reflects the ownership). Instead, you'll discover the sweetest, most delicious pineapples, grown right here at the world's largest organic pineapple plantation (although there are plenty of conventional pineapples grown here too). Collin Street offers tours (adult/student/child US$22.50/18.40/15.20) through its 1400 hectares of pineapple fields plus the processing and packing plant that ships 38 million pineapples a year. This is more than a *finca*, it's a city complete with worker housing, a medical clinic and a football field. The interesting but pricey

tour must be reserved 48 hours ahead, and ends with nibbles of fresh pineapple, and pineapple cake, washed down with a piña colada. The plantation is located 2km north of La Quinta and is well signed from the highway.

Rancho Magallanes
RESTAURANT $

(☎2766-5606; chicken US$3-12; ◷10am-10pm) Rancho Magallanes is a sweet roadside restaurant with a wood-burning brick oven where they roast whole chickens. Birds are halved or quartered, and served quite simply with tortillas and banana salsa. The skin is crispy and garlicky. Meat melts off the bone. You can dine with the truckers by the roadside oven or in the more upscale riverside dining area.

Selva Verde Lodge
LODGE $$$

(☎2761-1800, in USA & Canada 800-451-7111; www.selvaverde.com; s/d incl breakfast US$113/131, bungalow s/d US$130/160) In Chilamate, about 7km west of Puerto Viejo, this former *finca* is now an elegant lodge that protects over 200 hectares of rainforest. Guests can choose to stay at the river lodge, which is elevated above the forest floor on wooden platforms, or in a private bungalow, quietly tucked away in the nearby trees. Wood-floored rooms have private hot shower, screened windows, in-room safe and, of course, your very own hammock.

There are three walking trails through the grounds and into the premontane tropical wet forest. The two self-guided trails take 45 minutes and two hours to complete respectively, but the longest trail leads into primary forest and must be guided. You can either get a trail map and/or hire a bilingual guide (US$15 per person) from the lodge. Even lodge guests must pay the premium to enjoy the primary forest. There's a medicinal and butterfly garden. Various boat tours on the Río Sarapiquí are also available, from rafting trips to guided canoe tours. The lodge's Italian kitchen, La Terazza (mains US$7 to US$9) has wood-fired pizza, chicken masala, veal, beef, fish and pasta dishes too.

TOP CHOICE Chilamate Rainforest Eco Retreat
LODGE $$

(☎2766-6949; www.chilamaterainforest.com; dm US$30, s/d incl breakfast US$76/96) Founded in 2009 by Sarapiquí native Davis Azofeifa and his Irish-Canadian wife Meghan Casey, Chilamate is the most exciting lodge in the area.

The young couple spent three years building this oasis of beauty and warmth on 20 hectares of secondary forest.

The five large solar-powered cabins are basic but full of character, with comfy hand-crafted furniture, private bathroom, fan and traditional architectural style that provides natural air-cooling. Out the back, the bunkhouse has 12 dorm beds with shared bathroom and kitchen, perfect for groups or those on a tight budget. Other resort amenities include a fabulous stone bar, restaurant, and laundry facilities. Davis and Meghan have two young children, so the resort is naturally quite child-friendly. Covered flat walkways allow you to move between buildings in the complex without ever getting wet (after all, this is the rainforest!).

Behind the cabins, 6km of paths wind through the jungle, where you might spot sloths, monkeys, toucans, frogs, snakes and more. The resort provides rubber boots for sloshing through the jungle. It also offers an incredible array of tours, from horseback riding to homestays (per person including meals US$25) with one of 15 farming families living in nearby Linda Vista. Visiting biologists have been known to lecture in the outdoor classroom, and the retreat is affiliated with Earth University, so it does get student groups. There are discounts of up to 15% for stays of more than three days. With haunting howlers and canoodling toucans seemingly around every bend, and the river close by, this is a place to relax and recharge.

Puerto Viejo de Sarapiquí & Around

At the scenic confluence of Ríos Puerto Viejo and Sarapiquí, Puerto Viejo de Sarapiquí was once the most important port in Costa Rica. Boats laden with fruit, coffee and other commercial exports plied the Sarapiquí as far as the Nicaraguan border, then turned east on the Río San Juan to the sea. Today, it is simply a gritty palm-shaded market town. But there's grace here too, evidenced by the cute tiled benches and archways along the shopping district adjacent to the soccer field. There's also educational innovation. The local polytechnic high school offers students advanced tourism, ecology and agriculture degrees. The school even has its own reserve, laced with trails. Visitors, meanwhile, can choose from any number of activities in the surrounding area such as bird-watching, rafting, kayaking, boating and hiking. Migración (immigration office) is near the small wooden dock, sometimes avoided by visiting Nicaraguans who share the river with local fishers and visiting birders.

There is no dry season, but from late January to early May is the 'less wet' season. On the upside, when it rains here there are fewer mosquitoes.

Activities

Taking the launch from Puerto Viejo to Trinidad, at the confluence of the Ríos Sarapiquí and San Juan, provides a rich opportunity to see crocodiles, sloths, birds, monkeys and iguanas sunning themselves on the muddy riverbanks or gathering in the trees. This river system is a historically important gateway from the Caribbean into the heart of Central America, and it's still off the beaten tourist track, revealing rainforest and ranches, wildlife and old war zones, deforested pasture land and protected areas. There is one basic guest house in Trinidad where you can stay overnight.

**Associacion de Turismo
Rural Ruta Los Heroes**   BOAT TOUR
(☎2766-5858; 90min tour per person US$20; ☺8am-3pm) If you don't wish to go all the way to Trinidad, the pink building near the dock is a boat-captain cooperative. Together, they offer a variety of river tours including those with ecological and historical emphasis, but it's often closed in low season. If it is closed when you're here, negotiate directly with the captains you find at the dock. **Oscar Lao** is one trusted captain who offers fair prices and has a new boat. You can call him directly on ☎8365-3683.

Souvenir Rio Sarapiqui   RAFTING
(☎2766-6727; www.aguas-bravas.co.cr; class II/III per person US$50, Class III/IV per person US$100; ☺9am-5:30pm) Aguas Bravas no longer maintains an office in the Sarapiquí area, but it does run the river, and the owner of this souvenir shop books guests on Aguas Bravas rafts. They leave three times daily at 9am, 11am and 3pm, with two different trips available.

Lago Jalapa   HIKING, CANOEING
(☎8817-0452, 8317-2436; www.lagojalapa.com; per person US$20-45) The newest grassroots ecotourism effort in the area combines short hikes with an hour-long canoe trip on a lake about 8km from town. It gets excellent reviews from travelers but its administration is weak. Staff don't always answer phones and prices can vary depending on the day, plus guides speak no English. Still, it is a local business and worth looking into because Lago Jalapa is a stunning lake in the Refugio de Vida Silvestre, surrounded by forest teeming with wildlife. It even offers overnight kayaking and camping trips.

Sleeping

This stretch of jungle boasts quite a range of accommodations, from budget bunks in town designed for local long-term plantation workers, to several extraordinary lodges on the outskirts.

Cabinas Laura   CABINA $
(☎2766-6316; s/d US$20/24; P❄☎) A sparkling new and quiet choice on the road to the pier. Rooms are simple with new tile, wood furnishings and cable TV.

Mi Lindo Sarapiquí   HOTEL $
(☎2766-6281; s/d US$26/36; P❄@) On the south side of the soccer field, rooms here are simple but spacious and clean, have hot showers and ceiling fans. The onsite restaurant is slightly pricey (mains US$4 to US$16), though it offers some of the freshest seafood in town.

Posada Andrea Cristina B&B   CABINA $
(☎2766-6265; www.andreacristina.com; s/d incl breakfast US$32/52; P☎) About 1km west of the center, this recommended B&B has eight quaint cabins in its garden, each with a colorful paint job, stone tile, high beamed ceilings, hot water and outdoor table and chairs. It's situated on the edge of the forest, so there are plenty of opportunities for bird-watching while you sit outside and eat breakfast.

Hotel Gavilán   HOTEL $$
(☎2234-9507; www.gavilanlodge.com; d US$70; P❄☎☀) Sitting on a 100-hectare reserve about 4km northeast of Puerto Viejo, this former cattle *hacienda* is cozy, quaint and a bird-watching haven. Each of the spacious rooms has a pastel paint job, big hot-water shower and fan; all rooms have porches, some with river views. It is popular among a young, fashionable European crowd. The grounds feature 5km of private

trails and charming management arranges 90-minute guided bird-watching tours upon request.

Hotel Ara Ambigua   HOTEL **$$**
(☎2766-7101; www.hotelaraambigua.com; d incl breakfast with/without air-con US$70/60; P❋ @☲) About 1km west of Puerto Viejo near La Guaíra, this countryside retreat offers bright tiled rooms that are well equipped with private hot-water shower and cable TV. The real draws are the varied opportunities for wildlife-watching – you can see poison-dart frogs in the *ranario* (frog pond), caim-ans in the small lake, and birds that come to feed near the onsite **Restaurante La Casona**.

Hotel El Bambú   HOTEL **$$**
(☎2766-6005; www.elbambu.com; r standard/superior incl breakfast US$55/64; P❋☎☲) Set opposite the soccer field, rooms are huge and equipped with air-con and hot water. There's a big, inviting pool and a popular restaurant open to the main road. Spring for one of the quieter deluxe rooms out back, whose raised platform paths take you through the trees. Some rooms smell musty. Be choosy.

Eating

Most of the lodgings in and around Puerto Viejo have onsite restaurants or provide meals. There are several *sodas* in Puerto Viejo de Sarapiquí, a **Palí supermarket** (◷8am-9pm) at the west end of town, and the local Super Sarapiquí on the way to the port.

Soda Judith   SODA **$**
(mains US$2-5; ◷6am-7pm) The excellent Soda Judith, one block off the main road, is where early risers can grab some brewed coffee and a big breakfast or an *empanada* (turnover stuffed with meat or cheese) to start their day.

Bar y Restaurante Real Sarapiquí   CHINESE
(☎2766-5590; mains US$3-8 ; ◷7:30am-10pm) A popular local Chinese greasy spoon decorat-ed with Christmas lights and Chinese fans emblazoned with *caballos*. Call it multi-culti kitsch. It does roast quarter-chicken plates, fried rice, *wonton* soup, chow mein and all the noodle dishes. It's 150m east of Hotel El Bambu on the same side of the street.

Restaurante La Casona   RESTAURANT **$$**
(☎2766-7101; www.hotelaraambigua.com; meals US$8-16; ◷8am-10pm) At the Hotel Ara Am-bigua, this place is particularly recommend-ed for its oven-baked pizza and typical, home-made cuisine served in an open-air *rancho*.

❶ Information

Banco Popular (☎2766-6815) Has an ATM and changes money.

Banco de Costa Rica At the entrance of town; has ATM.

Cruz Roja (☎2766-6212) Provides medical care.

Gecko.Net (☎2766-7007; per hr US$1; ◷8:30am-7pm Mon-Fri, 9am-6pm Sun) Across from Cruz Roja, is the newest and fastest internet access in town.

❶ Getting There & Around

Puerto Viejo de Sarapiquí has been a transpor-tation center longer than Costa Rica has been a country, and is easily accessed by paved major roads from San José, the Caribbean coast and other population centers. There is a taxi stop across from the bus terminal, and they'll take you to the nearby lodges and Estación Biológica La Selva for US$5 to US$10.

Boat

The small port has a regular service to the small ranching outpost of Trinidad just across the Río San Juan from Nicaragua. Boats to Trinidad depart at 2pm and return the following morning at 5am and cost US$10 per person. You can also arrange transportation anywhere along the river (seasonal conditions permit-ting) from here through independent boat captains. A 90-minute river tour costs about US$20 per person (minimum two people). Serious voyages to Tortuguero (US$800) or Barra del Colorado (US$600) are mind-blowing yet somehow monotonous adventures that include space for five on board. To get to the dock, make a right from the main road at Banco Nacional and follow it until it ends.

Bus

Right across from the park, the **bus terminal** (☎2233-4242; ◷5am-7pm) sells tickets and stores backpacks (US$1) for a few hours, but not overnight. Local buses run hourly between La Virgen and Puerto Viejo de Sarapiquí from 6am to 8:15pm. The 30-minute trip costs about US$1.

Guápiles (Empresarios Guapileños) US$2; one hour; departs 5:30am, 6:45am, 7:10am, 9:40am, 10:30am, 12:10pm, 2:30pm, 3:45pm, 4:45pm and 7pm.

San José (Autotransportes Sarapiquí & Em-presarios Guapileños) US$2.50; two hours; departs 5am, 5:15am, 5:30am, 7am, 8am, 9:30am, 11am, 11:30am, 1:30pm, 3pm and 5:30pm.

SOUTH OF PUERTO VIEJO DE SARAPIQUÍ

South of Puerto Viejo de Sarapiquí, plantations line Hwy 4 and sprawl all the way to the marshes and mangroves of the Caribbean coast. To the west, the rugged hills of the Cordillera Central mark the northeastern boundary of Parque Nacional Braulio Carrillo. Most travelers on this scenic stretch of highway are either heading to the Caribbean coast or to the Central Valley. However, some are pulling off the road to visit the working research center Estación Biológica La Selva, the world-class botanical garden called Heliconia Island, or Rara Avis, one of the most isolated lodges in Costa Rica.

About 12 smoothly paved kilometers from Puerto Viejo de Sarapiquí is the village of Horquetas, around which you'll find the turnoffs for Heliconia Island and Rara Avis. From Horquetas it's another 15km to Hwy 32, which connects San José to the Caribbean coast and bisects Parque Nacional Braulio Carrillo on the way to San José.

Estación Biológica La Selva

Not to be confused with Selva Verde Lodge in Chilamate, Estación Biológica La Selva (☎2524-0607, 2766-6565; www.ots.ac.cr; s/d US$98/184 incl 3 meals & guided half-day tour; ℗) is a working biological research station equipped with laboratories, experimental plots, a herbarium and an extensive library. The station is usually teeming with scientists and students researching the nearby private reserve. La Selva does welcome drop-ins, though it's best to phone ahead and reserve your accommodations. Rooms are simple but comfortable, and rates include meals and guided hikes.

La Selva is operated by the Organization for Tropical Studies (OTS; ☎2524-0607; www.ots.ac.cr), a consortium founded in 1963 to provide leadership in the education, research and wise use of tropical natural resources. Twice a year OTS offers a grueling eight-week course open mainly to graduate students of ecology, along with various other courses and field trips that you can apply for.

The area protected by La Selva is 16 sq km of premontane wet tropical rainforest, much of which is undisturbed. It's bordered to the south by the 476-sq-km Parque Nacional Braulio Carrillo, creating a protected area large enough to support a great diversity of life. More than 886 bird species have been recorded here, as well as 120 mammal species (including 70 species of bat), 1850 species of vascular plant (especially from the orchid, philodendron, coffee and legume families) and thousands of insect species – with 500 types of ant alone.

🏃 Activities

Reservations are required for three-hour guided hikes (US$32, departing 8:30am and 1pm daily) with a bilingual naturalist guide. You'll head across the hanging bridge and into 57km of well-developed jungle trails, some of which are wheelchair-accessible. Unguided hiking is forbidden, although you'll be allowed to wander a bit after your guided tour. Make reservations for the popular guided bird-watching hikes, led at 5:45am and 7pm, depending on demand. Profits from these walks help to fund the research station.

No matter when you visit La Selva, it will probably be raining. Bring rain gear and footwear that's suitable for muddy trails. Insect repellent and a water bottle are also essential.

❶ Getting There & Away

Public buses between Puerto Viejo and Río Frío/Horquetas can drop you off 1km from the entrance to La Selva. It's about 4km from Puerto Viejo, where you can catch a taxi for around US$5 to US$7.

Sueño Azul Resort

Adventure-oriented tour groups make up the majority of guests at Sueño Azul (☎2764-1213; www.suenoazulresort.com; superior/junior ste US$124/143), a top-end adventure lodge upon a hill. It has an on-again off-again yoga retreat program and the secluded bamboo yoga platform is lovely, but that's one small, ephemeral slice of the business. Its perch on the stunning confluence of the Rios Sarapiquí and San Rafael, and vast property are the main draws. Here's a place with its own suspension bridge, canopy tour and waterfall. There is an enormous stable of gorgeous horses if you fancy a ride, as well as hiking trails and hot tubs, a pool, bar and a huge tiled patio replete with leather rockers. Rooms are huge with terra-cotta floors, log beds and river views, though some can smell musty.

A GREEN-GREEN SITUATION

The gorgeous green plumage, electric-blue wing tips and red forehead of the great green macaw (*Ara ambiguus*) have long attracted collectors of exotic birds. The illegal sale of just one macaw can fetch several thousand dollars, despite the fact that the species' nervous personality causes them to fare poorly in captivity. International trade has depleted the population though, fortunately, the great green macaw is protected by the Convention on International Trade in Endangered Species (Cites).

In addition to illegal poaching, deforestation also threatens the great green macaw. The northern lowlands have suffered from heavy deforestation in recent years due to the demand for increased agricultural and pasture land. Furthermore, the *almendro* tree (*Dipteryx panamensis*), whose nut provides 90% of the macaw's diet and whose high hollows are far and away the preferred nesting tree for breeding pairs, is highly sought after as a luxury hardwood. Extensive logging of the *almendro* has severely cut back potential nesting sites, and as a result the great green macaw is endangered. It's estimated that Costa Rica's population is as low as 200, with as few as 30 breeding pairs left.

But all is not lost! A coterie of nonprofit organizations and government agencies established the San Juan–La Selva Biological Corridor (www.greatgreenmacaw.org/BiologicalCorridor), which aims to protect existing green macaw populations as well as other species in the area. The corridor bridges the gap between the Reserva Cordillera Volcánica Central, Refugio Nacional de Vida Silvestre Barra del Colorado, Parque Nacional Tortuguero and the Indio-Maíz, Punta Gorda and Cerro Silva reserves in Nicaragua. Eventually, the hope is that all of these protected areas will form a Mesoamerican biological corridor that will stretch from Mexico through Central America.

In 2005 the Refugio Nacional de Vida Silvestre Mixto Maquenque (www.cct.or.cr/informacion-refugio-nacional-maquenque) was officially declared by then-president Abel Pacheco. Owing to this victory, Maquenque now protects an estimated 6000 species of vascular plant, 139 mammals, 515 birds, 135 reptiles and 80 amphibians. And as a 'mixed-use' wildlife refuge, the first of its kind in Costa Rica, it allows human residents to continue living and working within the boundaries of the refuge. However, most of the refuge's approximately 500 sq km, which are privately owned, are now bound to certain regulations, such as the drastic reduction of activities such as logging. So where does this leave the residents, who depend on forestry and agriculture for subsistence?

Enter the Costa Rican Bird Route (www.costaricanbirdroute.com), a project initiated by the nonprofit Rainforest Biodiversity Group in partnership with several other nonprofit organizations. The Costa Rican Bird Route has been working with and educating communities within these protected areas to help create viable and sustainable ecotourism opportunities, as economic alternatives to habitat-destructive agriculture and logging. While promoting locally owned lodges throughout the region, the Costa Rican Bird Route is also helping to establish new, community-based ecolodges from Río San Juan to Parque Nacional Braulio Carrillo. The hope is that green tourism – a field in which Costa Rica shines – will not only be more financially beneficial to these poor communities, but will also be salvation for the great green macaw.

Heliconia Island

This self-proclaimed 'oasis of serenity' is arguably the most beautiful garden in all of Costa Rica. Heliconia Island (☎2764-5220; www.heliconiaisland.com; self-guided/guided tours US$10/18; P) is a masterpiece of landscape architecture that was started in 1992 by New York City native Tim Ryan, a former professor of art and design. Today, this 2.3-hectare island overlooking the Río Puerto Viejo is owned by Dutch couple Henk and Carolien, and is home to more than 80 varieties of heliconia, tropical flowers, plants and trees. The grounds are a refuge for 228 species of bird (hummingbirds are the sole pollinators of heliconias). There are also resident howler monkeys, river otters, sloths and a few friendly dogs that will greet you upon arrival.

Henk and Carolien will guide you through the property, showing off a number of memorable plants including the Madagascar traveling palm, rare hybrids of heliconia found only on the island, and the *Phena-kospermum guyannense* (Phenomenal sperm), a unique flowering plant native to Guyana. They also own swatches of secondary forest on either side of the garden, which offers a wild forest buffer and attracts wildlife. The admission fee is waived for overnight guests, who stay in immaculate raised cabins with stone floors, hot-water showers and breezy balconies.

Heliconia Island is about 5km north of Horquetas, and there are signs along the highway pointing to the entrance. When you arrive at the entrance, park your car, walk across the metal bridge and turn left on the island to reach the gardens.

Rara Avis

When they say remote, they mean remote: this private reserve (☑2200-4238, 2764-1111; www.rara-avis.com; s/d incl meals US$85/150), which comprises 13 sq km of high-altitude tropical rainforest, is accessible only to overnight guests willing to make the three-hour tractor ride (seriously!) up a steep, muddy hill to get there.

The private reserve borders the eastern edge of Parque Nacional Braulio Carrillo and has no real dry season. Bird-watching here is excellent, with more than 350 documented species, while mammals including monkeys, coatis, anteaters and pacas are often seen. Visitors can use the trail system alone, or on guided hikes.

The accommodations, although lovely, are rustic – most don't have electricity, though the kerosene lamps and starry skies are unforgettable. Room prices, which include all meals, transportation and a guided hike, seem high, but it's because of the remote location – you, the groceries and the guides all have to be hauled up that mountain from Horquetas.

Since getting here is time-consuming and difficult, a two-night stay is recommended. The bus to Puerto Viejo de Sarapiquí leaves San José (about US$2, 1½ hours) from the Guápiles-Limón terminal at 6:30am, and you'll need to get off at Horquetas. Here, you'll embark on the famed three-hour tractor ride. You can also arrange to be taken by horseback, which requires hiking the last 3km yourself. There's a long list of items (from head lamps to mud boots) that you'll need to bring to make your stay as comfortable as possible. See the website for details.

HWY 126 TO SAN MIGUEL

Curving up the slopes of the Cordillera Central, Hwy 126 leaves behind the bustle of Heredia and Alajuela and leads to the foot of Volcán Poás before descending again into pastureland. This is *campesino* (farmer) country, where the plodding hoofbeat of cattle is about the speed of life, as the hard-to-spot rural speedbumps will remind you if you take those curves too quickly. You're off the beaten track now, and if you're self-driving, you may as well linger, because there are few Costa Rican corners quite this beautiful and unheralded.

Albergue El Soccoro (☑8927-0764; www.albergueelsocorro.com; per person incl meals US$70; P@) is 9km from San Miguel, 1000m above sea level, on a plateau surrounded by a magnificent knife's edge of mountains, tucked between the Cerro Congo and Volcan Poas. The owner was born and raised a rancher here, but in 2009 a massive earthquake struck the Vara Blanca area, destroying the road from Vara Blanca to San Miguel along with their home and dairy. This wonderful family rebuilt the ranch from scratch and incorporated a tourism component. Guests stay in one of three cozy, spotless A-framed cabins, from which you can explore 4km of trails in primary and secondary rainforest. There is also a working dairy. Kids (and grown-ups) can milk the cows. There are buffalo and horses to ride, and the *madre* cooks fine meals. There's even internet access.

Coming from the south, you'll cross a bridge over Rio La Paz, about 8km north of Vara Blanca, on a hairpin bend; to your left you will find an excellent view of the absolutely spectacular Catarata La Paz. Several other waterfalls may also be seen, particularly on the right-hand side (if you are heading north) in the La Paz Valley, which connects to the Sarapiquí Valley.

SAN MIGUEL TO LOS CHILES

The route from San Miguel to Muelle de San Carlos is trimmed by papaya plantations and jungles, and winds through the mountains in a series of hairpin turns. But just as the patchwork of *fincas* and wildflowers gives way to sugarcane, the road opens to a long, straight and steaming-hot stretch across the lowlands to Caño Negro and Los Chiles, a straightforward trip by riverboat to Nicaragua.

Venecia & Around

The westbound road traces the northern limits of the Cordillera Central as flowering vines scramble down the mountains and threaten to overtake the road. In the distance, the northern lowlands appear as a patchwork quilt of cane fields and rice paddies. The road momentarily straightens out as it enters the affluent rural town of Venecia, 14km west of San Miguel. There's a lively square and a maze of almost suburban streets stretching into the surrounding, and only recently tamed, hills. Still, the town passes by in a heartbeat as the road continues its dizzying wind toward Muelle de San Carlos.

If you're looking to break up the driving, what better place to spend the night than Venecia's famous 'medieval castle', **Torre Fuerte Cabinas** (☑2472-2424; s/d US$24/28; P❋☎), behind the big church. It's a sweet kitschy hotel, family-run, with lots of homey touches like silk flowers and plants. It's a perfect roadside cheapie. And yes. There's a turret.

Tucked behind what feels like Venecia's last tame subdivision, about 3km from downtown, and set 700m down a dirt road in a seething rainforest is **Recreo Verde** (☑2472-1020; www.recreoverde.com; adult/child US$6/4). The draw here is the mineral baths. They have three pools: two hot (although we use that term loosely) and one cold. All three are set just above the roaring river. The more crude-looking pool is the warmest. Sit under those PVC showers and let the heat rain down. There are a few short hiking trails here as well, a campground, and spacious polished-wood cabins that sleep five with a full kitchen and have a pair of rockers on the porch, along with a hammock.

Halfway between San Miguel and Venecia is the hamlet of Río Cuarto, from where an unpaved road heads southeast past a beautiful waterfall near Bajos del Toro, through Parque Nacional Juan Castro Blanco, and on to Zarcero.

Boca Tapada Area

Don't bother venturing out here if Tico time ticks you off; the rocky roads and lack of signage (even less than usual!) could mean a few unintended detours. On the roads that pass pineapple fields and packing plants, your fellow travelers will be commuting *caballeros* (cowboys) and *campesinos* (farmers) going about their day-to-day business. And at the end of the road, you'll be rewarded with a luxuriant bit of rainforest replete with frog- and rare birdsong, and an inkling of the symbiosis that can happen when humans make the effort. Local lodges offer rainforest tours into the Refugio Nacional de Vida Silvestre Mixto Maquenque.

🛏 Sleeping & Eating

TOP
CHOICE **Maquenque Eco-Lodge**   LODGE $$$
(☑2479-8200; www.maquenqueecolodge.com; r US$96/119; P☀) Opened in 2009, this lodge is located on 60 hectares with easy access to the Refugio Nacional de Vida Silvestre Mixto Maquenque. The 14 unique bungalows overlook a lagoon, the tropical garden has a lovely swimming pool, and there's also an onsite bar and restaurant. The lodge offers bird-watching, boating, night hikes and horseback-riding tours in the Maquenque refuge, as well as transfers from San Jose and La Fortuna.

Laguna del Lagarto Lodge   LODGE $$
(☑2289-8163; www.lagarto-lodge-costa-rica.com; s/d/tr US$51/70/80; P) This environmentally sensitive, German-run lodge is surrounded by 13 sq km of rainforest and is a legend among bird-watchers. Most of the 500-hectare 'grounds' of the lodge is jungle, some of which is swamp, and as a result the area's 10km of trails can get quite mucky. Canoes are available to explore the surrounding lagoons, where caimans dwell and Jesus Christ lizards make tracks across the water's surface. Horseback-riding trips and boat tours along the Nicaraguan border can be arranged. Some of the area's big trees have been cut in recent years, which means the place is not as well ensconced in virgin forest as it once was, but it's still lovely and wild and you do get up close and personal with wildlife.

Simple screened rooms have private bathroom and fan and share large, hammock-strung verandas. Package tours include transportation from San José, all meals and guided tours. Otherwise, breakfast is US$6, lunch US$8 and dinner US$15. Room rates are a bit high, but they include an afternoon guided hike through the jungle and a nighttime caiman-feeding walk. The lodge is about 9km from Boca Tapada.

NORTHERN LOWLANDS VENECIA & AROUND

ℹ Getting There & Away

If you're driving, getting to Boca Tapada is an adventure in itself. The nearest town of note is Pital, north of Aguas Zarcas. After passing through Pital, turn right after the church on the right and soccer field on the left, and continue through the village of Veracruz. At the Del Huerto pineapple packing plant, hang a left and continue along the paved road. About 10km later, where the pavement ends, turn right at the intersection. When you come to the gas station, turn right again and follow the signs for Mi Pedacito del Cielo to Boca Tapada.

Buses from San José (US$4, 2½ hours) depart from the Atlántico Norte terminal for Ciudad Quesada hourly from 5am to 7:30pm, with a connection to Boca Tapada (US$2, 1½ hours) where the lodges can pick you up by prior request.

Muelle de San Carlos

This small crossroads village is locally called Muelle. It was once an important dock (hence the name, and remnant shipping infrastructure) as it's the most inland spot from which the Río San Carlos is navigable. These days it's in sugarcane country and is a rest stop for truckers and travelers.

Tourists tend to stop for photo ops at Centro Turistica Las Iguanas, just before the bridge, where countless iguanas like to hang out in the bamboo above the river. The place itself serves forgettable tourist fare and souvenirs. Other than that, the main tourist activity in Muelle is pulling over to have a look at the map. A 24-hour gas station lies at the intersection of Hwy 4 (which connects Ciudad Quesada and Upala) and Hwy 35 (running from San José to Los Chiles). From Hwy 4 you can easily catch Hwy 32, the main artery serving the Caribbean coast.

🛏 Sleeping & Eating

Most of the budget digs are trucker crash pads, which means they can get rowdy and we can't wholeheartedly suggest them. But they do exist if you feel like giving them a go.

There are a number of *sodas* and a small supermarket on the road toward Los Chiles that will do if you're looking for your *casado* fix. However, one recommended spot is Restaurant-Bar La Subasta (☑2467-8087; mains US$3-11; ☺11am-11pm), which overlooks a bullpen and is bustling with hungry *campesinos*. It has an expansive menu of local dishes, and it's a great spot for a cold beer. Nearby Patanal, just south of town, is a ranching and sugarcane farming community sprinkled with steakhouses.

La Iguana Azul   BUNGALOW $
(☑2462-1115; d US$30) This old hacienda has some moldering charm. Set among spider palms, the cottages offer plenty of light and doors open right onto the riverside. Sheets are crisp and the restaurant is tasty. The best deal in town, all things considered. It's on the road to Los Chiles.

Tilajari Resort Hotel   RESORT $$$
(☑2462-1212; www.tilajari.com; d incl breakfast from US$96; P☺❄@🍴🏊) This former country club turned luxury resort has well-landscaped grounds overlooking the Río San Carlos, and offers an impressive number of tours and activities. Comfortable, well-appointed rooms have aged a bit, (um, the '80s called and want that bathroom vanity back) but they are spotless, spacious and accented with wood details. A few of the rooms and private trails are wheelchair-accessible. Other amenities include a lovely pool area, racquetball and tennis courts, a restaurant, sauna, spa and butterfly garden, plus access to the neighboring 400-hectare private rainforest reserve with several trails. The resort is 800m west of the intersection at Muelle, on the road to Ciudad Quesada.

Los Chiles

Seventy kilometers north of Muelle on a smooth, paved road through the sugarcane, and just three rutted kilometers south of the Nicaraguan border, lies the sweltering farming and fishing town of Los Chiles. The humid lowland village, arranged with dilapidated grace around a ragged soccer field and along the unmanicured banks of the leisurely Río Frío, is almost charming by border-town standards, sex workers and foreboding 'import-export' types notwithstanding. It was originally settled by merchants and fisherfolk who worked on the nearby Río San Juan, much of which forms the Nicaragua–Costa Rica border. In recent history, Los Chiles served as an important supply route for the Contras in Nicaragua, and was home to a strong US military presence throughout the 1980s.

Gringo traffic is on the rise in Los Chiles as it's a great base for enjoying the scenic water route to Caño Negro, and an early-morning excursion by small motorized boat is an adventure in itself. The second big draw is the scenic route to Nicaragua, a one-hour boat ride across the border that is becoming increasingly popular among foreign tourists. Crossing the border via the river is a relaxing, hassle-free way to go. Although the road continues past Los Chiles to Nicaragua, this border post is closed. The police patrolling this line in the sand are heavily armed and extremely bored, so don't waste your time and energy trying your luck there.

☞ Tours

Los Chiles is a convenient base to organize your tours to Caño Negro. You'll be able to get on the river early, which means you'll probably see more wildlife than folks being shuttled in from La Fortuna and San José. The port is also a good jumping-off point for exploring the islands of Lago de Nicaragua (Lake Nicaragua), and if you miss the early boat, private transportation to San Carlos in Nicaragua is available.

Just head to the dock where you can hire boat captains to take you up the lovely, chocolaty Río Frío during the dry season and all the way into Lago Caño Negro during the rainy season, as well as to San Carlos, Nicaragua, if necessary. Three- to four-hour trips cost about US$50 to US$90 for a small group, depending on the size and type of boat.

🛏 Sleeping & Eating

Accommodations in town are surprisingly limited, though most people aren't too keen on sticking around. There's a **Palí** (Av 1 & Calle 1) two blocks north of the bus stop, and the local **Supermercado Carranza** (Av 0 & Calle 2) on the west side of the soccer field to meet all of your grocery and bakery needs.

Hotel Wilson Tulipán　　　HOTEL $
(☑2471-1414; Ave 0 & Calle 4; r from US$24; P❄❄@☎) Three years later and still in the midst of remodeling, brand new rooms are set in a somewhat strange, ghost-town motel environs. They don't look remotely lived in, but the ubercheesy digs are fresh and clean with cable TV, and it's right down the road from the boats to Nicaragua. There are older but still comfortable rooms in the main building too, but those get plenty of night noise from the lively bar and restaurant (mains US$5 to US$8), which flaunts tasty seafood *tipica* and bad behavior.

Soda Juanita　　　SODA $
(☑2471-1607; mains US$2-6; ☺6am-6pm) Right next to the dock this cheery, bright-green *soda* serves tasty *casados*, the usual deep-fried fast foods, *batidos* (fruit shakes) and coffee. Seating at the counter or at one of the thatched tables makes a sweet spot to watch the world go by and await your boat to Nicaragua.

Restaurante El Parque　　　RESTAURANT $
(☑2471-1090; cnr Calle 2 & Av 0; mains US$4-7; ☺6am-9:30pm) This popular spot faces the plaza and has some of the best eats in town, and it's open early if you're looking to get your coffee fix before setting out on the river.

Soda Pamela　　　SODA $
(mains US$1-5; ☺6am-7pm) Here's a bright pink-and-green treat adjacent to the bus terminal with tasty *empanadas*, savory fried chicken plates and good coffee and *naturales*. The staff speaks English and is extremely helpful.

ℹ Information

The last stretch of paved road along Hwy 35 is home to a few restaurants, the post office and a gas station. If you continue north past Los Chiles on the rutted dirt road, you'll find yourself in the dusty no-man's-land en route to a border crossing you won't be allowed to use.

Drivers will want to hang a left (west) off the highway when you see the sign for Pali grocery store, to reach the town center and docks of the Río Frío. Most services are located along this road. The **bus terminal** is tucked behind Soda Pamela on Av 1.

The **docks** are located about 1km west of the bus terminal. If you're going by foot from the bus terminal, turn right onto the main street, walk one block past Cruz Roja, turn left, then make an immediate right downhill onto Av 0 to the waterfront. Before hopping on the boat to Nicaragua, you need to stop at Immigration, across the street from Hotel Tulipán.

Banco Nacional (☑2212-2000; Av 1 btwn Calles 0 & 1) Close to the central park and soccer field, changes cash and traveler's checks and has a 24-hour ATM.

Cruz Roja (Red Cross; ☑2471-1037, 2471-2025; cnr Calle 2 & Av 1; ☺24hr) On the west side of the plaza if you need basic medical assistance or supplies.

Internet.com (☑2471-1515; Av 0 btwn Calles 0 & 1; 8am-7pm; ☺per hr US$1) Get online.

Post office (☺8am-noon & 1-5:30pm Mon-Fri) One block west of the bus station.

❶ Getting There & Away

Drivers usually get here via Hwy 35 from Muelle, along about 70 paved, straight kilometers where you're likely to get passed by big-rig drivers with lead feet. Skid marks and reptilian road kill do break up the beautiful monotony of orange groves, sage-blue pineapple fields and dense sugarcane plantations. More scenic, if a little harder on your chassis, is the decent dirt road running for 50km from Upala, through Caño Negro, passable for normal cars throughout the dry season.

Regular boat transportation is limited to quick shuttles across the Nicaraguan border (US$10 to US$12) and various day trips throughout the region. Boats across the border leave daily at 12:30pm and 3:30pm, but get here early because space is limited and immigration lines are long. In addition to the boat fees, you'll need to pay a US$1.10 departure tax.

All buses arrive and leave from the terminal behind Soda Pamela, near the intersection of Hwy 35. Timetables are flexible, so play it safe and inquire locally.

Ciudad Quesada US$2.25; two hours; departs 12 times daily from 4:30am to 6pm.

San José US$6; six hours; departs 5:15am and 3pm.

Upala via Caño Negro US$4; 2½ hours; departs 5am, 2pm and 4:30pm.

Refugio Nacional de Vida Silvestre Caño Negro

This remote, 102-sq-km refuge has long lured anglers seeking that elusive 18kg snook, and birders hoping to glimpse rare waterfowl. During the dry season water levels drop, concentrating the birds (and fish) in photogenically (or tasty) close quarters. From January to March, when migratory birds land in large numbers, avian density is most definitely world class.

The Río Frío defines the landscape – south of the main Caño Negro dock it's a table-flat, swampy expanse of marsh and lagoon that is similar in appearance, if not size, to other famous wetlands such as the Florida Everglades or the Mekong Delta. North of town, it's a slender river that carves looming forest. During the wet season, the river breaks its banks to form one immense 800-hectare lake, and then contracts during the dry months from January through April, when water levels drop to the point where the river is barely navigable. By April it has almost completely disappeared – until the May rains begin. This cycle has proceeded

---

GETTING TO SAN CARLOS, NICARAGUA

Although there's a 14km dirt road between Los Chiles and San Carlos, Nicaragua, using this crossing requires special permission generally reserved for federal employees. Most regular folk go across by boat on the Río Frío, which is easily arranged in Los Chiles. You must first get an exit stamp in your passport at Immigration (the migración; ☏2471-1233; Calle 4 & Av 0; ☺8am-noon & 1:30am-4pm), about 100m east of the dock and directly across the street from Hotel Tulipán. If you are coming from Nicaragua, you must make Immigration your first stop.

Regular boats (US$10 to US$12, 90 minutes) leave Los Chiles at 12:30pm and 3:30pm daily, with extra boats at 11am and 2:30pm if demand is high. The early boat costs US$12, the late boat costs US$10. Boats leave San Carlos for Los Chiles at around 10:30am and 4pm, with extra boats scheduled as needed. Of course, the Nicaragua–Costa Rica border is not known for its reliability, so confirm these times before setting out. Nicaragua charges a US$7 entry fee and US$2 exit fee. Los Chiles municipality charges a US$1.10 exit and entry fee; after getting your passport stamped at Immigration, walk down to the docks and pay the exit fee at the yellow Recaudador Municipal office. Reverse this procedure if you are arriving here from Nicaragua.

Your boat will make a stop at the actual border post about halfway through the trip; note the psychedelic 'camouflage' paint job on the building where your friendly, gun-wielding Nicaraguan border personnel are based.

When you hit the confluence of the Río San Juan, consider keeping your fingers and toes in the boat as there are river sharks (seriously!). Sharks are one of several euryhaline species that are able to survive in both fresh- and saltwater conditions. Every year, sharks that have been tagged by scientists in the Caribbean Sea are later found swimming in Lake Nicaragua. Although the rapids of the Río San Juan are a deterrent for most species of marine fish, sharks are apparently able to negotiate the river without problems, and presumably head for fresh water in search of food.

THE WEEPING FOREST

Extensive deforestation of the Caño Negro area began in the 1970s in response to an increase in population density and the subsequent need for more farmland. Although logging practices were allowed to proceed in the area for almost two decades, the government took action in 1991 with the creation of the Refugio Nacional de Vida Silvestre Caño Negro. Since its creation, Caño Negro has served as a safe habitat for the region's aquatic and terrestrial birds, and has acted as a refuge for numerous migratory birds.

However, illegal logging and poaching have continued around the perimeter of the park, and wildlife has accordingly suffered. In the last two decades, one-time residents of the park, including ocelots, manatees, sharks and macaws, have vanished. Tarpon and caiman populations are decreasing, and fewer migratory birds are returning to the park each year. Additionally, anglers are reporting record lows in both the size and number of their catches.

Satellite images show that the lake is shrinking each year, and that water levels in the Río Frío are dropping rapidly. It's difficult to say with certainty what is causing these changes, though the farms surrounding Caño Negro require extensive irrigation, and sugarcane is nearly 10 times as water-intensive as wheat.

Locals are extremely worried about the stability of the park as entire communities are dependent on fishing and tourism for their survival. In response to the growing need to regulate development in the region, area residents have formed a number of organizations aimed at controlling development in the northern lowlands. If you want to support the Caño Negro community, book your tour in town and spend your tourist dollar locally.

without fail for millennia, and the small fishing communities that live around the edges of the reserve have adapted to each seasonal nuance.

Thanks to improved roads, dozens of tour operators are now able to offer relatively inexpensive trips to Caño Negro from all over the country. However, you don't need them to explore the river. It's much more intriguing to rent some wheels, navigate the rutted road into the rural flat lands and book a tour with a local guide through their cooperative right in the center of Caño Negro town. You'll save a lot of money and have a much better time. You can also bus to Caño Negro from Los Chiles rather easily. This puts money directly in the hands of locals and encourages communities in the area to protect wildlife.

🏃 Activities

Caño Negro is regarded among bird-watchers as one of the premier destinations in all of Central America. During the dry season, the sheer density of birds in the park is astounding, and you'll be impressed with the number and variety of different species that inhabit the park. At last count 365 species of bird lived here at least part of every year. In the winter months, migratory duck congregations can be enormous, and very well represented groups include six species of kingfisher, herons, cormorants, three types of egret, ibises, rails, anhingas, roseate spoonbills, toucans and storks. The refuge is also the only reliable site in Costa Rica for the olivaceous cormorant, Nicaraguan grackle and lesser yellow-headed vulture.

Conspicuous reptiles include the spectacled caiman, green iguana and striped basilisk. Howler monkeys, white-faced capuchins and two-toed sloths are common and, despite increasing incursions from poachers, pumas, jaguars and tapirs have been recorded here in surprising numbers.

Caño Negro is also home to an abundance of river turtles, which were historically an important part of the Maleku diet. Prior to a hunt, the Maleku would appease the turtle god, Javara, by fasting and abstaining from sex. If the hunt was successful, the Maleku would later celebrate by feasting on smoked turtle meat and consuming large quantities of *chicha*, a spirit derived from maize. And, well, they probably had some sex too.

Mosquitoes in Caño Negro are damn near prehistoric. Bring bug spray, or suffer the consequences.

TOP WATERWAYS FOR WILDLIFE-WATCHERS

Head to some of the following waterways for an up-close glimpse of the local wildlife.

» Whether you're resting between the rapids or traveling up to Trinidad, keep your eyes peeled for somnolent sloths or mud-covered caimans as you float up the Río Sarapiquí (p456).

» Wake up early to savor a quiet view of breakfasting birds on the lagoons of Caño Negro (p469).

» Not only is the Río Frío (p469) the kinder, gentler border crossing into Nicaragua, but you'll see trees filled with howler monkeys, and caimans on the riverbanks along the way.

» Lodges in the Boca Tapada area can get you on the Río San Carlos (p466), where the slow flow near the Río San Juan affords good opportunities for bird-watching.

☞ Tours

Caño Negro is not as difficult to access as it once was, and you'll have a much better experience if you avoid the tour operators and head directly to the park. Hiring a local guide is quick, easy and full of advantages – you'll be supporting the local economy, you will have more privacy when you're out on the water and, of course, there's the satisfaction of doing things independently. **Real Tour** (☎2471-1621; Real.tour@hotmail.com; 1hr tour US$40, 2-3hr tour US$60, 4hr tour US$70; ⊙8am-4pm) is well-signed, set right in the center of town, and is the local guide cooperative. If, for some reason, the office is closed, you can also find local guides hanging around the nearby dock. Guides typically offer two- to three-hour tours and charge US$60 for up to three people, which is incredibly reasonable and arguably one of the best deals in the country. For a bit more cash you can add in a one-hour turtle and butterfly tour. You will also need to pay for your entrance fee into the refuge (adult/child US$10/1) at the Real Tour office, which also has free internet and wi-fi available.

Although afternoon tours are possible, it's far better to overnight in Caño Negro and start your tour as early in the morning as possible, when wildlife is still active. We suggest launching at 6am. Folks staying in town basically have the refuge to themselves at daybreak, with boat-trippers from Puerto Viejo de Sarapiquí and Los Chiles arriving by 9am.

If you're looking to do a little sportfishing, it's best to organize your trips through one of the lodges in the park. Seasonal fishing licenses, valid for two months, can be arranged through the lodges or at the ranger station for US$34. You will need a photocopy of your passport and a small photo.

🛏 Sleeping & Eating

TOP CHOICE Hotel de Campo

Caño Negro   HOTEL $$

(☎2471-1012; www.hoteldecampo.com; s/d incl breakfast US$75/85; ⊙restaurant 7:30am-9:30pm; P☀☲) Set in an orchard of mango and citrus trees next to one of Caño Negro's lagoons, this Italian-Tico-run hotel is a fisherman's paradise. You can rent any combination of boats, guides (who speak English, Spanish, French and Italian), kayaks (four hours US$20) and fishing equipment here at the well-stocked tackle shop. And after angling for gargantuan tarpons all day, relax in little ceramic-tiled *casitas* with vaulted beamed ceilings, a ceiling fan, air-con and tasteful bedding and window treatments. There's also a pool and an extremely stylish restaurant (mains US$8 to US$14) with gushing fountains, natural timber columns and wood slab tables, timber beamed ceilings and twirling fans. The meals rock and the coffee is a gift from God. There's also a fantastic gift shop with both new production wood and ceramic sculpture – and some fabulous antique Guanacaste pottery and sculpture on display, but those ain't for sale!

Kingfisher Lodge   CABINA $

(☎2471-1116; www.kingfisherlodgecr.com; s/d from US$25/50; P) These rustic *cabinas* are about 400m from the town center, and there is a variety of rooms to accommodate travelers of all budgets. They're owned and operated by the Sequera brothers, who are recommended refuge guides and boat captains, and you can also arrange horseback riding here. Stop by the pink house with the sign advertising '*cabinas*' to check in or have a look.

Caño Negro Natural Lodge   LODGE **$$**
(📞2265-3302; www.canonegrolodge.com; d incl breakfast US$90/119; P❄🐕📶🏊) Perched on land that becomes a virtual island in the Río Frío during the rainy season, this lodge is surprisingly upscale considering its remote location. Well-appointed rooms have hot showers, glass-bowl sinks, wood furnishings, air-con and satellite TV. The friendly staff can arrange all your trips while you relax in the pleasant pool or Jacuzzi, or stroll the leafy grounds that have a bit of golden bamboo mixed in among the native trees. The onsite restaurant, *Jabirú* (mains US$9-16; ⏱7am-9pm), is open to the public and has wi-fi.

Soda La Palmera   SODA **$**
(📞2471-1045; mains US$3-12; ⏱6am-9pm) Right at the entrance to the refuge, this pleasant *soda* serves Tico standards and fresh fish, including your personal catch of the day.

ℹ Information

Caño Negro refuge is part of the Area de Conservación Arenal–Huetar Norte and is accessible primarily by boat. Close to the park entrance (that'd be the dock) is the tiny community of Caño Negro, which has no banks or gas stations. All visitors to the park must go to the **Real Tour** (📞2471-1621; park entry adult/child under 12yr US$10/1; ⏱8am-4pm) office to pay the park entrance fees. It's also where you can book a local guide. It's best to arrange an early-morning boat the day before.

The **Minae office and ranger station** (📞2471-1309; ⏱8am-4pm), located about 150m behind (north) the green-and-pink *pulpería* (corner grocery store), no longer offers service to tourists. For years rumors have swirled that all park offices, research labs and revamped accommodations were scheduled to move to the new Estación Biológica Caño Negro, located 6km north of the church at the end of the gravel road past the radio tower. It may be worth checking in at the ranger station to see if basic accommodations at the new station are up and running.

ℹ Getting There & Away

The village of Caño Negro and the entrance to the park lie on the rough road connecting Upala and Los Chiles, which is passable to all cars during the dry season. However, this road is frequently washed out during the rainy season, when a 4WD is required. Coming from Los Chiles it can be difficult to find the turn to Cano Negro as there is no sign. It's right before the big cell tower. If you get to Escuela Los Angeles you've passed it. Even coming from Muelle de San Carlos it is tough to find because there is just one faded sign on the right that indicates: 'Cano Negro 19km'.

There are three buses per day to Los Chiles (US$2) and Upala (US$2.50). Both buses stop at Real Tour and circle the village square at approximately 6am, 3pm and 5:30pm; ask around as this schedule changes frequently.

During the rainy season and much of the dry season, you can catch a boat (US$17) here from Los Chiles as well. This is becoming increasingly popular, especially as more travelers are crossing into and out of Nicaragua on the Río Frío.

Upala

Hey, a Tico town with no tourists! Just 9km south of the Nicaraguan border in the northwestern corner of the northern lowlands, Upala is a small *ranchero* town with a bustling market and plenty of tasty *sodas* that serve a widespread community of some 15,000 people. It's a center for the area's cattle and rice industries; most visitors are Costa Rican businesspeople who come to negotiate for a few dozen calves or a truckload of grain, and though it is a somewhat convenient public transit stopover between the Volcan Tenorio area and Caño Negro, there's not much of a reason to spend the night.

🛏 Sleeping

Cabinas Maleku   CABINA **$**
(📞2470-0142; d with fan/air-con US$10/12; P❄) Still the best option in town, the rooms wrap around a gravel parking area and have tasteful bedding, cable TV and hot water. Patios have mosaic tile, hand-painted Sarchí-style wooden chairs, and plenty of potted plants. It's a cheerful cheapie, for sure. Air-con rooms are slightly larger. There's an attached *soda* too.

Hotel Upala   HOTEL **$**
(📞2470-0169; Hotelupala@live.com.ar; s/d US$16/24; P) Despite the hip signage here, this long-running hotel is no great shakes, but it is reasonably clean and comes with polished tiled floors, cable TV and cold water showers.

✗ Eating

The busy market, just behind the bus terminal, opens early with several nice *sodas* dishing up good *gallos* (tortilla sandwiches), *empanadas* and just about everything else. There are also a few Chinese restaurants and produce vendors.

Soda El Oasis   SODA $
(meals US$5; ⊙6am-9pm) If you're here to catch a bus, this sweet spot just on the other side of the terminal, only 25m from the metal bridge, has a delicious and fresh steam table with grilled and sauced meats, steamed veggies, and rice and beans all at the ready.

Soda Marinero   SODA $
(🖉2470-3838; meals US$5; ⊙6am-9pm) Marinero is another cute market *soda*, clean and popular, with a steam table featuring shredded pork in chili sauce, two kinds of chicken, tasty black beans and salad. They do all the grilled *casados*, and fried chicken to go. It's 60m south of the metal bridge.

La Terazza   RESTAURANT $$
(🖉8514-1563; mains US$6-13; ⊙7am-11pm) If you're after more sophisticated eats and environs pay a visit to this 2nd-story, polished wood, wagon wheel of a bar and grill. In addition to three flat-screen TVs and all the ball games, La Terazza offers grilled pork *chuleta* plates, chicken brochettes, beef fajitas as well as whole fried-fish dinners.

❶ Getting There & Away

Upala is connected to the Interamericana north of Cañas by Hwy 6, an excellent paved road, and also to La Fortuna and Laguna de Arenal by the somewhat more potholed Hwy 4.

A rough, unpaved road, usually passable by all types of cars, skirts the Refugio Nacional de Vida Silvestre Caño Negro on the way to Los Chiles, the official border crossing with Nicaragua.

The bus terminal is right off the park; a **ticket booth** (⊙4:30am-5:15am, 7:30am-1pm & 6:45am-8pm Mon-Sat) has information and can store bags for about US$1. Taxis congregate just outside the bus terminal. The following buses depart from Upala:

Los Chiles, via Caño Negro US$2; two hours; departs 5am, 11am and 4pm.

San José, via Cañas US$4; five hours; departs 4:30am, 5:15am and 9:30am.

San Rafael de Guatuso Area

The small town of Guatuso (San Rafael on some maps) is 19km northeast of Nuevo Arenal and 40km east of Fortuna (not to be confused with the town of La Fortuna), and is the main population center of this predominantly agricultural area. Although the town itself is rather humble and sleepy, it's a decent base for exploring the fantastic Venado Caves. The area is also home to the few remaining Maleku, one of Costa Rica's indigenous groups. You can visit their nearby *palenques* (indigenous settlements) from here.

◉ Sights

Venado Caves   CAVE
(🖉2478-8008; adult/child under 12yr US$20/12; ⊙9am-4pm, last admission 2pm) About 4km south of Venado (Spanish for 'deer') along a good dirt road, the caves are a popular rainy-day attraction that can be organized as a day trip from La Fortuna, San José and other cities for US$50 to US$80 per person (including transportation and lunch). Or visit with your own car (bus service is inconvenient).

The caves were discovered by chance in 1945 when a farmer fell through a hole in the ground and found himself in an underground chamber surrounded by stalactites (hanging tight to the ceiling) and stalagmites (that might reach the ceiling...got it?). The exploration that followed uncovered an eight-chamber limestone labyrinth which extends for almost 3km. The cavern system, composed of soft, malleable limestone, was carved over the millennia by a series of underground rivers.

The caves get rave reviews from folks fond of giant spiders, swarms of bats and eyeless fish. A guide takes you through the caves, including a few tight squeezes, pointing out various rock formations and philosophizing about what they sort of look like.

Drop-ins are welcome, but it's best to make reservations so you don't need to wait around for a group. You're provided with a guide (some speak English), lights, helmets and showers afterward. You'll definitely want to bring a change of clothes. There's a small onsite *soda*, and a few restaurants in Venado, but no lodging.

We don't recommend coming by bus; the 'early' bus from Ciudad Quesada drops you off at a steep 4km slog to the cave entrance at about 2pm, too late to make the last admis-

A BRIEF HISTORY OF THE MALEKU

The Maleku (colloquially referred to as the Guatuso) are one of the few remaining indigenous groups in Costa Rica. Historically, they were organized into 12 communities scattered around the Tilarán-Guanacaste range and the Llanura de San Carlos. Although their numbers dwindled following the arrival of Spanish colonists, the population survived relatively intact until the early 20th century. With the invention of the automobile, the US rubber industry started searching for new reserves to meet the increasing demand for tires. With the aid of Nicaraguan mercenaries, industry representatives scoured Central America for stable rubber reserves, which were found on Maleku-inhabited land. The resulting rubber war virtually wiped out the population, and confined survivors to a handful of communities. Today, the Maleku number around 400, and live in the three *palenques* (settlements) of Sol, Margarita and Tonjibe.

As is the situation with most indigenous groups in Costa Rica, the Maleku are among the poorest communities in the country, and they survive by adhering to a subsistence lifestyle. Their diet revolves around corn and the *tipuisqui* root, a traditional food source that grows wild in the region. Fortunately, since the Maleku have a rich artisan tradition, they are able to earn a small income by selling traditional crafts to tourists. Although their modern crafts primarily consist of pottery, jewelry, musical instruments and other small trinkets that are desirable to tourists, historically they were renowned for their impressive jade work and arrow craftsmanship.

The Maleku are also famous for their unique style of clothing made from *tana:* tree bark that has been stripped of its outer layer, soaked in water and then pounded thin on wooden blocks. After it has been dried and bleached in the sun, it can be stitched together like leather, and has a soft texture similar to suede. Although it's rare to see modern Maleku wearing anything other than Western-style clothing, *tana* articles are often offered for sale to tourists.

Despite being small in number, the Maleku have held on to their cultural heritage, perhaps more than any other indigenous group in Costa Rica. This is especially evident in their language, which is one of the oldest in the Americas and linguistically distinct from the Amazonian and Maya dialects. Today, the Maleku still speak their language among themselves, and a local radio station, Radio Sistema Cultural Maleku, airs daily programs in the Maleku language. The Maleku have also maintained their ceremonial traditions, such as the seasonal custom of crying out to Mother Nature for forgiveness through ritualistic song and dance.

As with all indigenous reservations in Costa Rica, the Maleku welcome tourists, as craft sales are vital to their survival. You can access the *palenques* via Route 143, though it's best to inquire locally for directions as the roads are poorly maintained and unsigned. While you're at the *palenque*, please be sensitive to their situation and buy a few small craft. If you can, you might also consider bringing small, useful gifts such as pencils, pens and paper, for the schools.

sion into the caves. A taxi from San Rafael de Guatuso costs US$30 to US$40. If you're driving, the caves are well signed from Hwy 4.

🛏 Sleeping & Eating

There are several clean, basic *cabinas* in San Rafael de Guatuso, sometimes used on a long-term basis by farm workers, and a good selection of *sodas* and stores.

TOP CHOICE Cabinas Los Almendros CABINA $
(☏8887-0495; s/d US$17/20; P❄🛜) A cute family-run motel with well looked-after rooms blessed with a fresh coat of paint, air-con and cable. Bedding and window treatments are lovely, and each room is named after a different jungle beast or bird, complete with wooden sculpture. Set on the outskirts of town, this is easily the best choice in the area.

Cabinas Cristal CABINA $
(☏2464-0016; s/d US$20/24; P@🛜) This is a handful of clean pastel-brushed and tiled rooms in a tin-roof, atrium-style complex that includes an internet cafe (per hour US$1). Nothing fancy but they'll do for a night.

Soda La Zuyapa
SODA $

(meals US$4; ⏱6am-8pm) Recommended by locals as the best *soda* in this humble town, it does *casados* that are very un-*tipica* and come with noodles and potato salad unless you request otherwise. There are also burgers and fried chicken (which is excellent), and the black beans are also very good. There's even fresh pressed carrot juice – though it's usually diluted with orange juice.

ⓘ Getting There & Away

Guatuso lies on Hwy 4, about 40km from both Upala, to the northwest, and Muelle de San Carlos, to the southeast. Buses leave about every two hours for either Tilarán or Ciudad Quesada, some of which continue to San José. Ciudad Quesada is the most frequent destination.

Understand
Costa Rica

population per sq km

COSTA RICA   UNITED STATES   CANADA

ｉ ≈ 2 people

Costa Rica Today

Weathering the Economic Storm

Even despite the economic tumult that has rocked the world since 2008, Costa Rica's economy has remained remarkably stable thanks to consistently growing returns on tourism. Tourism now outpaces both agriculture and industry for the biggest slice of the economy. If you're concerned about the availability of an English menu, take note: North Americans now account for nearly half the country's 2.2 million annual tourists.

Aside from tourism, the country's principal agriculture exports include pineapples, coffee, fruits and plants, while industrial exports include microchips, construction materials, fertilizer and medical equipment.

Poverty levels have been kept in check for more than 20 years by strong welfare programs. Although approximately 21% of the populace lives below the poverty line – up 5% since 2008 – beggars are few and far between, and you won't see the street kids you see in other Latin American capitals. In fact, a good system of social services has made panhandling and begging extremely rare in Costa Rica.

Foreign investors continue to be attracted by the country's political stability, high education and well-developed tourism infrastructure. In recent years, while the American investment has been checkered, Costa Rica's most promising international economic partner has become China. China has made a number of large investments in the country's infrastructure in recent years, including a 2012 $1.7 billion investment to modernize an oil refinery on the Caribbean, and the shiny new Estadio Nacional de Costa Rica, the nation's largest sporting venue, which was financed entirely by the Chinese government and completed in 2011.

Laura Chinchilla Miranda, Costa Rica's first female president, has made economic stability a large focus since being reelected in 2010. While in office she has made major efforts to encourage Canadian investment and in 2011 she made a highly publicized tour through Asia to strengthen economic ties to the region.

» Population: 4.25 million

» Adult literacy: 96%

» Population living below the poverty line: 21%

» Annual carbon-dioxide emissions per person: 1.85 tons

» Year projected for countrywide carbon neutrality: 2021

Faux Pas

Topless Sunbathing It isn't appropriate for women to bathe topless in public areas, and can be offensive to your hosts. The first warning from police may be gentle, but the second can result in a ticket.

'La hora Tica' Don't be put off if your local host views an appointment as more of a ballpark suggestion for when to meet.

Gringo Media

» *Tico Times* – Costa Rica's biggest English-language newspaper is high quality, though news and views are often geared toward the expat community (www.ticotimes.com).

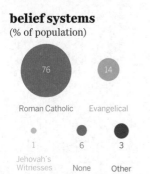

belief systems
(% of population)

76 Roman Catholic

14 Evangelical

1 Jehovah's Witnesses

6 None

3 Other

if Costa Rica were 100 people

94 would be white & *mestizo*
3 would be black
1 would be Chinese
1 would be Amerindian
1 would be other

Narcotrafficking

Security Minister Janina Del Vecchio's report from April 2012 was bleak: the violent drug trade of Costa Rica's neighbors had crossed its borders. Once only a bridge for the drug flow between South and North America, Costa Rica is becoming a storage and trading center for drug cartels. Between 2009 and 2012 authorities seized over 90 tons of cocaine – smuggled most colorfully in frozen sharks, surfboards and containers of wigs. After years on the sideline Costa Rica has finally entered the drug war.

With Mexican drug cartels moving in to control the northbound flow of cocaine, Costa Rica's proudly peaceful society is challenged by criminal forces that have long plagued Central America. Mexico's Sinaloa cartel has been in Costa Rica for years, but the presence of new rivals threatens a new battlefield for violent regional drug wars.

Most drugs are seized on the InterAmericana and in the Pacific (the Puntarenas bay is a graveyard of Coast Guard–seized ships), but relatively unguarded borders and no army makes the nation an ideal trafficking hub.

While Ticos grapple with the darkening storm, travelers will find the drug trade remains largely invisible, aside from a few more police checkpoints along the highways. Still, the Costa Rican government's increased attention to the drug problem makes it all the more foolish for visitors to attempt to purchase illegal drugs.

Aside from the conversational evergreens (namely *fútbol*, the weather and Latin American soap operas), Ticos often return to three hot topics: the lingering fallout from the Global Economic Crisis of 2008, the increasingly disruptive drug trade and balancing environmental protection with economic -development.

Contemporary Media Landscape

Although satellite television, multiplex cinema and imported radio defines Costa Rica's media landscape, there are a number of strong print newspapers in the country including the excellent daily, *La Nación*. Although Costa Rica's 1835 law guaranteeing freedom of the press is the oldest such law in Central America, outlets are limited and coverage tends to be cautious, largely due to years of *desacato,* an insult law, which allows public figures to sue journalists if their honor has been 'damaged'.

Wired Costa Rica

» Radio Dos – Broadcasting across the country on 99.5, Radio 2 spins an amazing selection of AM radio hits from the 1970s US charts.

» Population using the Internet: 43.7%
» Costa Rica's internet connectivity is the best in Central America.

» Although Google is Costa Rica's number one web destination, the top ten includes three sports gambling websites.

The 2001 assassination of radio journalist Parmenio Medina gave reporters another reason not to dig too deep. Medina was the host of a popular investigative program called *La Patada* (The Kick). Shortly before broadcasting a series on financial irregularities at a now-defunct Catholic radio station, Parmenio Medina was shot dead outside his home in Heredia. In 2007 the gunmen, in addition to a prominent businessman who ordered the hit, were sentenced to 35 years in prison after the country's longest-ever trial. Six other men were acquitted, while the other alleged mastermind, a Catholic priest, was acquitted of murder but found guilty of fraud.

Though libel and slander laws historically put the burden of proof on reporters, a defamation case against José Luis Jiménez Robleto, a reporter with the San José daily *Diario Extra,* was challenged in the nation's highest court and changed libel laws in 2010.

While journalists and free speech advocates celebrated the death of the *desacato* law, it remains only one obstacle to the nation's Byzantine libel, defamation and slander laws. In a surprising difference from most other developed democracies, Costa Rica's defamation laws are considered criminal, not civil, so journalists can be jailed if convicted. While not common, the historical shadow of *desacato* still shades press outlets through these laws, leaving Costa Rica yet in need of a truly independent and free press.

The recent growth in internet users has outpaced other countries in the region. In 2010 there were 2.2 million internet users. The World Bank's 2013 projections suggest that half the country's population will be connected.

Top Travel Lit

» *Green Dreams: Travels in Central America* (Stephen Benz) An astute analysis questioning the impact of visitors on the region.

» *Around the Edge* (Peter Ford) A story of traveling the Caribbean coast.

» *Green Phoenix* (William Allen) An absorbing account about conserving the Guanacaste rainforest.

» *Naturalist in Costa Rica* (Dr Skutch) An enchanting memoir and natural history guide.

» *Travelers' Tales Central America* (eds Larry Habegger and Natanya Pearlman) A collection of essays from writers including Paul Theroux.

History

Like many Central American countries, Costa Rica's history is drawn with a fairly loose sketch during the reign of its pre-Columbian tribes, whose cities were largely lost under the unrelenting creep of jungle foliage. But since the European 'discovery' of the New World, the country's history has been shaped by foiled conquistadors, monolithic fruit companies and indigenous rebellion that have familiar overtones throughout the region. It is in the mid-20th century that Costa Rica made a radical departure from the standard Central American playbook by abolishing its army, diversifying its economy and partnering with the international community to develop a world-class infrastructure. Toward the end of the last century, Costa Rica shone brightly on the world's stage thanks to leaders who helped negotiate peace in neighboring regions, a stable and healthy economic development and the growth of one of the world's most environmentally friendly governments.

Lost Worlds of Ancient Costa Rica

The coastlines and rainforests of Central America have been inhabited by humans for at least 10,000 years, but ancient civilizations in Costa Rica are largely the subject of speculation. It is thought that the area was something of a backwater straddling the two great ancient civilizations of the Andes and Mesoamerica. On the eve of European discovery some 500 years ago, an estimated 400,000 people were living in today's Costa Rica, though sadly our knowledge about these pre-Columbian cultures is scant. What wasn't destroyed by Spanish colonization was overgrown by jungle, and most traces of indigenous Costa Ricans simply disappeared.

Unlike the massive pyramid complexes found throughout other parts of Latin America, the ancient towns and cities of Costa Rica (with the exception of Guayabo) were loosely organized and had no centralized government or ceremonial centers. However, tales of lost cities still survive

TIMELINE

11,000 BC
The first humans occupy Costa Rica and populations quickly flourish due to the rich land and marine resources found along both coastlines.

1000 BC
The Huetar power base in the Central Valley is solidified following the construction and habitation of the ancient city of Guayabo, which is continuously inhabited until its mysterious abandonment in AD 1400.

100 BC
Costa Rica becomes part of an extensive trade network that moves gold and other goods and extends from present-day Mexico down though to the Andean empires.

PRE-COLUMBIAN COSTA RICA

The early inhabitants of Costa Rica were part of an extensive trading zone that extended as far south as Peru and as far north as Mexico. The region hosted roughly 20 small tribes, organized into chiefdoms with a permanent leader, a *cacique,* who sat atop a hierarchical society that included shamans, warriors, toilers and slaves.

Adept at seafaring, the Carib dominated the Atlantic coastal lowlands, and served as a conduit of trade with the South American mainland. In the northwest, several tribes were connected to the great Mesoamerican cultures. Aztec religious practices and Maya jade and craftsmanship are in evidence in the Península de Nicoya, while Costa Rican quetzal feathers and golden trinkets have turned up in Mexico. In the southwest, three chiefdoms showed the influence of Andean indigenous cultures, including coca leaves, yucca and sweet potatoes.

There is also evidence that the language of the Central Valley, Huetar, was known by all of Costa Rica's indigenous groups, which may be an indication of their power and influence. The Central Valley is home to the only major archaeological site uncovered in Costa Rica, Guayabo.

Thought to be an ancient ceremonial center, Guayabo once featured paved streets, an aqueduct and decorative gold. Here, archaeologists uncovered exquisite gold ornaments and unusual life-size stone statues of human figures, as well as distinctive types of pottery and *metates,* stone platforms that were used for grinding corn. Today the site consists of little more than ancient hewed rock and stone, though Guayabo continues to stand as testament to a once-great civilization of the New World.

Still a puzzle, however, are the hundreds of hand-sculpted, monolithic stone spheres that dot the landscape of the Diquis Valley in Palmar and the Isla del Caño. Weighing up to 16 tons and ranging in size from a baseball to a Volkswagen, the spheres have inspired many theories: an ancient calendar, extraterrestrial meddling or pieces of a giant game.

in the oral histories of Costa Rica's indigenous communities and there is hope among archaeologists that a great discovery lies in waiting. Considering that so much of the country consists of inaccessible mountains and rainforests, perhaps these dreams aren't so fanciful.

Heirs of Columbus

On his fourth and final voyage to the New World in 1502, Christopher Columbus was forced to drop anchor near present-day Puerto Limón after a hurricane damaged his ship. While waiting for repairs, Columbus ventured into the verdant terrain, and exchanged gifts with hospitable and welcoming chieftains. He returned from this encounter, claiming to have seen 'more gold in two days than in four years in Española.'

1522	1540	1562	1563
Spanish settlement develops in Costa Rica, though it will be several decades before the colonists can get a sturdy foothold on the land.	The Kingdom of Guatemala is established by the Spanish, and includes much of Central America – Costa Rica, Nicaragua, Honduras, El Salvador, Guatemala and the Mexican state of Chiapas.	Spanish conquistador Juan Vásquez de Coronado arrives in Costa Rica under the title of governor, determined to move the fringe communities of Spanish settlers to the more hospitable Central Valley.	The first permanent Spanish colonial settlement in Costa Rica is established in Cartago by Juan Vásquez de Coronado, who chooses the site based on its rich and fertile volcanic soils.

Columbus dubbed the stretch of shoreline from Honduras to Panama as Veraguas, but it was his excited descriptions of *costa rica,* the 'rich coast,' that gave the region its lasting name. At least, that is how the popular story goes.

Anxious to claim its bounty, Columbus petitioned the Spanish Crown to have himself appointed governor. But by the time he returned to Seville, his royal patron Queen Isabella was on her deathbed, which prompted King Ferdinand to award the prize to Columbus' rival, Diego de Nicuesa. Although Columbus became a very wealthy man, he never returned to the New World, and died in 1506 after being worn down by ill health and court politics.

To the disappointment of his *conquistador* (conqueror) heirs, his tales of gold were mostly lies and the locals were considerably less than affable. Nicuesa's first colony in present-day Panama was abruptly abandoned when tropical disease and warring tribes decimated its ranks. Successive expeditions launched from the Caribbean coast also failed as pestilent swamps, oppressive jungles and volcanoes made Columbus' paradise seem more like a tropical hell.

A bright moment in Spanish exploration came in 1513 when Vasco Núñez de Balboa heard rumors about a large sea and a wealthy, gold-producing civilization across the mountains of the isthmus – almost certainly referring to the Inca empire of present-day Peru. Driven by equal parts ambition and greed, Balboa scaled the continental divide, and on September 26, 1513, he became the first European to set eyes upon the Pacific Ocean. Keeping up with the European fashion of the day, Balboa immediately proceeded to claim the ocean and all the lands it touched for the king of Spain.

The thrill of discovery aside, the conquistadors now controlled a strategic western beachhead from which to launch their conquest of Costa Rica. In the name of God and king, aristocratic adventurers plundered indigenous villages, executed resisters and enslaved survivors throughout the Nicoya peninsula. However, none of these bloodstained campaigns led to a permanent presence as intercontinental germ warfare caused outbreaks of feverish death on both sides. Since the area was scarce in mineral wealth and indigenous laborers, the Spanish eventually came to regard it as the 'poorest and most miserable in all the Americas.'

New World Order

It was not until the 1560s that a Spanish colony was firmly established in Costa Rica. Hoping to cultivate the rich volcanic soil of the Central Valley, the Spanish founded the village of Cartago on the banks of the Río Reventazón. Although the fledgling colony was extremely isolated,

The origin of Earth – according to Bribrí and Cabécar creation myth – is the subject of the beautifully illustrated story *When Woman Became Sea* by Susan Strauss.

Visit World Mysteries at www.world-mysteries.com/sar_12.htm for an investigation of Costa Rica's mysterious stone spheres.

» Parque Nacional Volcán Poás (p103)

ALFREDO MAIQUEZ / LONELY PLANET IMAGES ©

1737

The future capital of San José is established, sparking a rivalry with neighboring Cartago that will eventually culminate in a civil war between the two dominant cities.

1821

Following a unanimous declaration by Mexico on behalf of all of Central America, Costa Rica finally gains its independence from Spain after centuries of colonial occupation.

it miraculously survived under the leadership of its first governor, Juan Vásquez de Coronado. Some of Costa Rica's demilitarized present was presaged in its early colonial government: prefering diplomacy over firearms to counter the indigenous threat, Coronado used Cartago as a base to survey the lands south to Panama and west to the Pacific, and secured deed and title over the colony.

Though Coronado was later lost at sea in a shipwreck, his legacy endured: Costa Rica was an officially recognized province of the Viceroyalty of New Spain (Virreinato de Nueva España), which was the name given to the viceroy-ruled territories of the Spanish empire in North America, Central America, the Caribbean and Asia.

For roughly three centuries, the Captaincy General of Guatemala (also known as the Kingdom of Guatemala), which included Costa Rica, Nicaragua, Honduras, El Salvador, Guatemala, and the Mexican state of Chiapas, was a loosely administered colony in the vast Spanish empire. Since the political and military headquarters of the kingdom were in Guatemala, Costa Rica became a minor provincial outpost that had little if any strategic significance or exploitable riches.

The Last Country the Gods Made, by Adrian Colesberry, is a collection of essays and photographs, providing an overview of Costa Rican history, geography and society.

As a result of its status as a swampy, largely useless backwater, Costa Rica's colonial path diverged from the typical pattern in that a powerful landholding elite and slave-based economy never gained prominence. Instead of large estates, mining operations and coastal cities, modest-sized villages of smallholders developed in the interior Central Valley. According to national lore, the stoic, self-sufficient farmer provided the backbone for 'rural democracy' as Costa Rica emerged as one of the only egalitarian corners of the Spanish empire.

Equal rights and opportunities were not extended to the indigenous groups and as the Spanish settlement expanded, the local population decreased dramatically. From 400,000 at the time Columbus first sailed, the population was reduced to 20,000 a century later, and to 8000 a century after that. While disease was the main source of death, the Spanish were relentless in their effort to exploit the natives as an economic resource. Central Valley groups were the first to fall, though outside the valley several tribes managed to survive a bit longer under forest cover, staging occasional raids. However, as in the rest of Latin America, repeated military campaigns eventually forced them into submission and slavery.

Fall of an Empire

Spain's costly Peninsular War with France from 1808 to 1814 – and the political turmoil, unrest and power vacuums that the conflict caused – led Spain to lose all its colonial possessions in the first third of the 19th century.

April 1823

The Costa Rican capital officially moves to San José after intense skirmishes with the conservative residents of Cartago, who take issue with the more liberal longings of the power-hungry *josefinos*.

December 1823

The Monroe Doctrine formerly declares the intentions of the USA to be the dominant imperial power in the western hemisphere despite protests from European powers.

» House of Congress in the capital, San José (p52)

THE LITTLE DRUMMER BOY

You may notice, during your travels through the countryside, statues of a drummer boy from Alajuela named Juan Santamaría. He is one of Costa Rica's most beloved national heroes.

In April 1856 the North American mercenary William Walker and his ragtag army attempted to invade Costa Rica during an ultimately unsuccessful campaign to conquer all of Central America. He had already managed to take control of Nicaragua, taking advantage of the civil war that was raging there. It didn't take him long after that to decide to march on Costa Rica, though Costa Rican President Juan Rafael Mora Porras guessed Walker's intentions and managed to recruit a volunteer army of 9000 civilians. They surrounded Walker's army as they lay waiting in an old hacienda (estate) in present-day Parque Nacional Santa Rosa. The Costa Ricans won the battle and Walker was forever expelled from Costa Rican soil. During the fighting, Santamaría was killed while daringly setting fire to Walker's defenses – and a national legend was born.

In 1821 the Americas wriggled free of Spain's imperial grip following Mexico's declaration of independence for itself as well as the whole of Central America. Of course, the Central American provinces weren't too keen on having another foreign power reign over them, and subsequently declared independence from Mexico. However, all of these events hardly disturbed Costa Rica, which learned of its liberation a month after the fact.

The newly liberated colonies pondered their fate: stay together in a United States of Central America, or go their separate national ways. At first, they came up with something in between, namely the Central American Federation (CAF), though it could neither field an army nor collect taxes. Accustomed to being at the center of things, Guatemala also attempted to dominate the CAF, alienating smaller colonies and hastening its demise. Future attempts to unite the region would likewise fail.

Meanwhile, an independent Costa Rica was taking shape under Juan Mora Fernández, first head of state (1824–33). He tended toward nation-building, and organized new towns, built roads, published a newspaper and coined a currency. His wife even partook in the effort by designing the country's flag.

Life returned to normal, unlike in the rest of the region where post-independence civil wars raged on. In 1824 the Nicoya-Guanacaste region seceded from Nicaragua and joined its more easygoing southern neighbor, defining the territorial borders. In 1852 Costa Rica received its first diplomatic emissaries from the USA and Great Britain.

1824	1856	1889	1890
The Nicoya-Guanacaste region votes to secede from Nicaragua and become a part of Costa Rica, though the region's longing for independence from both countries continues to this day.	Costa Rica puts a damper on the expansionist aims of the war hawks in the USA by defeating William Walker and his invading army at the epic Battle of Santa Rosa.	Costa Rica's first democratic elections are held, a monumental event given the long history of colonial occupation, though blacks and women were prohibited by law to vote.	The construction of the railroad between San José and Puerto Limón is finally completed despite years of hardships and countless deaths due to accidents and such diseases as malaria and yellow fever.

Coffee Rica

In the 19th century, the riches that Costa Rica had long promised were uncovered when it was realized that the soil and climate of the Central Valley highlands were ideal for coffee cultivation. Costa Rica led Central America in introducing the caffeinated bean, which transformed the impoverished country into the wealthiest in the region.

When an export market was discovered, the government actively promoted coffee to farmers by providing free saplings. At first Costa Rican producers exported their crop to nearby South Americans, who processed the beans and re-exported the product to Europe. By the 1840s, however, local merchants had already built up domestic capacity and learned to scope out their own overseas markets. Their big break came when they persuaded the captain of HMS *Monarch* to transport several hundred sacks of Costa Rican coffee to London, percolating the beginning of a beautiful friendship.

The Costa Rican coffee boom was on. The drink's quick fix made it popular among working-class consumers in the industrializing north. The aroma of riches lured a wave of enterprising German immigrants to Costa Rica, enhancing the technical and financial skills in the business sector. By century's end, more than one-third of the Central Valley was dedicated to coffee cultivation, and coffee accounted for more than 90% of all exports and 80% of foreign-currency earnings.

The coffee industry in Costa Rica developed differently from the rest of Central America. As elsewhere, there arose a group of coffee barons, elites that reaped the rewards for the export bonanza. But Costa Rican coffee barons lacked the land and labor to cultivate the crop. Coffee production is labor-intensive, with a long and painstaking harvest season. The small farmers became the principal planters. The coffee barons, instead, monopolized processing, marketing and financing. The coffee economy in Costa Rica created a wide network of high-end traders and small-scale growers, whereas in the rest of Central America, a narrow elite controlled large estates, worked by tenant laborers.

Coffee wealth became a power resource in politics. Costa Rica's traditional aristocratic families were at the forefront of the enterprise. At midcentury, three-quarters of the coffee barons were descended from just two colonial families. The country's leading coffee exporter at this time was President Juan Rafael Mora Porras (1849–59), whose lineage went back to the colony's founder Juan Vásquez de Coronado. Mora was overthrown by his brother-in-law, after the president proposed to form a national bank independent from the coffee barons. The economic interests of the coffee elite would thereafter become a priority in Costa Rican politics.

In the 1940s children in Costa Rica learned to read with a text that stated: 'Coffee is good for me. I drink coffee every morning.'

COFFEE

1900	1914	1919	1940
The population of Costa Rica reaches 50,000 as the country begins to develop and prosper due to the increasingly lucrative international coffee and banana trades.	Costa Rica is given an economic boost following the opening of the Panama Canal. The canal was forged by 75,000 laborers, many thousands of whom died during construction.	Federico Tinoco Granados is ousted as the dictator of Costa Rica in one of the few episodes of brief violence in an otherwise peaceful political history.	Rafael Ángel Calderón Guardia is elected president and proceeds to improve working conditions in Costa Rica by enacting minimum-wage laws as well as an eight-hour day.

Banana Empire

The coffee trade unintentionally gave rise to Costa Rica's next export boom – bananas. Getting coffee out to world markets necessitated a rail link from the central highlands to the coast, and Limón's deep harbor made an ideal port. Inland was dense jungle and insect-infested swamps, which prompted the government to contract the task to Minor Keith, nephew of an American railroad tycoon.

The project was a disaster. Malaria and accidents churned through workers as Tico recruits gave way to US convicts and Chinese indentured servants, who were in turn replaced by freed Jamaican slaves. To entice Keith to continue, the government turned over 3200 sq km of land along the route and provided a 99-year lease to run the railroad. In 1890 the line was finally completed and running at a loss.

Keith had begun to grow banana plants along the tracks as a cheap food source for the workers. Desperate to recoup his investment, he shipped some bananas to New Orleans in the hope of starting a side venture. He struck gold, or rather yellow. Consumers went crazy for the elongated finger fruit. By the early 20th century, bananas surpassed coffee as Costa Rica's most lucrative export and the country became the world's leading banana exporter. Unlike in the coffee industry, the profits were exported along with the bananas.

Costa Rica was transformed by the rise of Keith's banana empire. He joined another American importer to found the infamous United Fruit Company, soon the largest employer in Central America. To the locals, it was known as *el pulpo*, 'the octopus' – its tentacles stretched across the region, becoming entangled with the local economy and politics. United Fruit owned huge swathes of lush lowlands, much of the transportation and communication infrastructure and bunches of bureaucrats. The company drew a wave of migrant laborers from Jamaica, changing the country's ethnic complexion and provoking racial tensions. Amazingly, you can still see the marks that *el pulpo* left on Costa Rica – look for the rusting train tracks and a locomotive engine in Palmares.

For details on the role of Minor Keith and the United Fruit Company in lobbying for a CIA-led coup in Guatemala, pick up a copy of the highly readable *Bitter Fruit* by Stephen Schlesinger and Stephen Kinzer.

Birth of a Nation

The inequality of the early 20th century led to the rise of José Figueres Ferrer, a self-described farmer–philosopher and the father of Costa Rica's unarmed democracy. The son of Catalan immigrant coffee planters, Figueres excelled in school and went to MIT, in Boston, to study engineering. Upon returning to Costa Rica to set up his own coffee plantation, he organized the hundreds of laborers on his farm into a utopian socialist community, and appropriately named the property La Luz Sin Fin, 'The Struggle Without End.'

1940s

José Figueres Ferrer becomes involved in national politics and opposes the ruling conservatives. Figueres' social-democratic policies and criticism of the government angers the Costa Rican elite and President Calderón.

1948

Conservative and liberal forces clash, resulting in a six-week civil war that leaves 2000 Costa Ricans dead, many more wounded and destroys much of the country's fledgling infrastructure.

RAMON PRECIADO / ALAMY ©

» Statue of José Figueres Ferrer in San José

In the 1940s Figueres became involved in national politics as an outspoken critic of President Calderón. In the midst of a radio interview in which he badmouthed the president, police broke into the studio and arrested Figueres. He was accused of having fascist sympathies and was banished to Mexico. While in exile he formed the Caribbean League, a collection of students and democratic agitators from countries all over Central America, who pledged to bring down the region's military dictators. When he returned to Costa Rica, the Caribbean League, now 700 men strong, went with him and helped protest against the powers that be.

When government troops descended on the farm with the intention of arresting Figueres and disarming the Caribbean League, it touched off a civil war. The moment had arrived: the diminutive farmer–philosopher now played the man on horseback. Figueres emerged victorious from the brief conflict and seized the opportunity to put into place his vision of Costa Rican social democracy. After dissolving the country's military, Figueres quoted HG Wells: 'The future of mankind cannot include the armed forces.'

As head of a temporary junta government, José Figueres Ferrer enacted nearly a thousand decrees. He taxed the wealthy, nationalized the banks and established a modern welfare state. His 1949 constitution granted full citizenship and voting rights to women, African-Americans, indigenous groups and Chinese minorities. Today Figueres' revolutionary regime is regarded as the foundation of Costa Rica's unarmed democracy.

Thirty-three out of 44 Costa Rican presidents prior to 1970 were descended from just three original colonizing families.

The American Empire

Throughout the 1970s and '80s, the sovereignty of the small nations of Central America was limited by their northern neighbor, the USA. Big sticks, gunboats and dollar diplomacy were instruments of a Yankee policy to curtail socialist politics, especially the military oligarchies of Guatemala, El Salvador and Nicaragua.

In 1979 the rebellious Sandinistas toppled the American-backed Somoza dictatorship in Nicaragua. Alarmed by the Sandinistas' Soviet and Cuban ties, fervently anticommunist President Ronald Reagan decided it was time to intervene. Just like that, the Cold War arrived in the hot tropics.

The organizational details of the counterrevolution were delegated to Oliver North, an eager-to-please junior officer working out of the White House basement. North's can-do creativity helped to prop up the famed Contra rebels to incite civil war in Nicaragua. While both sides invoked the rhetoric of freedom and democracy, the war was really a turf battle between left-wing and right-wing forces.

1949	1963	1987	2000
Hoping to heal its wounds and chart a bold new future, the temporary government enacts a new constitution abolishing the army, desegregating the country, and granting women and blacks the right to vote.	Reserva Natural Absoluta Cabo Blanco at the tip of the Nicoya peninsula becomes Costa Rica's first federally protected conservation area through the efforts of Swedish and Danish conservationists.	President Oscar Arias Sánchez wins the Nobel Peace Prize for his work on the Central American peace accords, which brought about greater political freedom throughout the region.	At the start of the new millennium, the population of Costa Rica tops four million, though many believe the number is far greater due to burgeoning illegal settlements on the fringes of the capital.

Under intense US pressure, Costa Rica was reluctantly dragged in. The Contras set up camp in northern Costa Rica, from where they staged guerrilla raids. Not-so-clandestine CIA operatives and US military advisors were dispatched to assist the effort. A secret jungle airstrip was built near the border to fly in weapons and supplies. To raise cash for the rebels, North allegedly used his covert supply network to traffic illegal narcotics through the region.

The war polarized Costa Rica. From conservative quarters came a loud call to re-establish the military and join the anticommunist crusade, which was largely underwritten by the US Pentagon. In May 1984 more than 20,000 demonstrators marched through San José to give peace a chance, though the debate didn't climax until the 1986 presidential election. The victor was 44-year-old Oscar Arias Sánchez, who, despite being born into coffee wealth, was an intellectual reformer in the mold of Figueres, his political patron.

Once in office, Arias affirmed his commitment to a negotiated resolution and reasserted Costa Rican national independence. He vowed to uphold his country's pledge of neutrality and to vanquish the Contras from the territory. The sudden resignation of the US ambassador around this time was suspected to be a result of Arias' strong stance. In a public ceremony, Costa Rican school children planted trees on top of the CIA's secret airfield. Most notably, Arias became the driving force in uniting Central America around a peace plan, which ended the Nicaraguan war and earned him the Nobel Peace Prize in 1987.

In 2006 Arias once again returned to the presidential office, winning the popular election by a 1.2% margin, and subsequently ratifying the controversial Central American Free Trade Agreement (Cafta).

Prior to his re-election, President Oscar Arias Sánchez founded the Arias Foundation for Peace and Human Progress; on the web at www.arias. or.cr.

2006	2007	2010	2011
Nobel laureate Oscar Arias Sánchez is elected president for the second time on a pro-Cafta (Central American Free Trade Agreement) platform despite winning by an extremely narrow margin.	A national referendum narrowly passes Cafta. Opinion remains divided as to whether opening up trade with the USA will be beneficial in the long run for Costa Rica.	Costa Rica elects its first female president, National Liberation Party candidate Laura Chinchilla.	Central American drug wars encroach on Costa Rica's borders, and the country is listed among the USA's list of major drug trafficking centers.

The Tico Way of Life

Pura Vida

'Pura vida' – pure life – is more than just a slogan that rolls off the tongues of Tico (Costa Rican inhabitants) and emblazons souvenirs; in the laid-back tone with which it's constantly uttered, the phrase is a true mantra for the way of life here. Maybe the essence of the pure life is better lived than explained, but hearing *'pura vida'* again and again while traveling across this land – as a greeting, a stand-in for goodbye and an acknowledgement of thanks – it's clear that the concept is deep within the country's DNA.

The living seems particularly pure when Costa Rica is compared with its Central American neighbors such as Nicaragua and Honduras; there's little poverty, illiteracy or political tumult, the country is crowded with ecological jewels and has high standards of living. What's more, Costa Rica has flourished without an army for the past 60 years. The sum of the parts makes for a country that's an oasis of calm in a corner of the world that has been continuously degraded by warfare. And though the Costa Rican people are justifiably proud hosts, a compliment to the country is likely to be met simply with a warm smile and an enigmatic two-word reply: *pura vida*.

Daily Life in Costa Rica

With the lack of war, long life expectancy and a relatively sturdy economy, Costa Rica enjoys the highest standard of living in Central America. For the most part, Costa Ricans live fairly rich and comfortable lives, even by North American standards.

As in many of the places in Latin America, the family unit in Costa Rica remains the nucleus of life. Families socialize together and extended families often live near each other. When it's time to party it's also largely a family affair; celebrations, vacations and weddings are a social outlet for rich and poor alike, and those with relatives in positions of power – nominal or otherwise – don't hesitate to turn to them for support.

Given this mutually cooperative environment, it's no surprise that life expectancy in Costa Rica is almost the same as in the USA (most Costa Ricans are more likely to die of heart disease or cancer, instead of the childhood diseases that plague developing nations). A socialized health-care system and proper sanitation account for these positive statistics, as do a generally stress-free lifestyle, tropical weather and a healthy diet – the *pura vida*.

Still, the divide between rich and poor is broad. The middle and upper classes largely reside in the capital city, San José, as well as in the

For Costa Rican news in English, check out the weekly *Tico Times* at www.ticotimes.net or the tabloid *Inside Costa Rica* at www.insidecostarica.com.

NICA VS TICO

Ticos (inhabitants of Costa Rica) have a well-deserved reputation for friendliness, and it's a rare occurence for travelers of any sex, race or creed to experience prejudice in Costa Rica. However, it's unfortunate and at times upsetting that the mere mention of anything related to neighboring Nicaragua is enough to turn an average Tico into a stereotype-spewing anti-Nico (note that the term 'Nica' is used by some Ticos in a somewhat derogatory manner, so watch your language). Despite commonalities in language, culture, history and tradition, Nica-versus-Tico relations are at an all-time low, and rhetoric (on both sides) of *la frontera* (the border) isn't likely to improve anytime soon.

Why is there so much hostility between Nicas and Ticos? The answer is as much a product of history as it is of misunderstanding, though economic disparities between both countries are largely to blame.

Though Nicaragua was wealthier than Costa Rica as recently as 25 years ago, decades of civil war and a US embargo quickly bankrupted the country, and today Nicaragua is the second-poorest country in the western hemisphere (after Haiti). For example, the 2009 CIA World Factbook lists the GDP per capita purchasing power parity of Costa Rica as US$10,900, while Nicaragua is listed at only US$2800. The main problem facing Nicaragua is its heavy external debt, although debt-relief programs implemented by the International Monetary Fund (IMF) and the free-trade zone created by the Central American Free Trade Agreement (Cafta) are both promising signs for the future.

In the meantime, however, Nica families are crossing the border in record numbers, drawn to Costa Rica by its growing economy and impressive education and health systems. However, immigration laws in Costa Rica make it difficult for Nicas to find work, and the majority end up living in shantytowns. Also, crime is on the rise throughout Costa Rica, and though it's difficult to say what percentage is actually attributable to Nica immigrants, some Ticos are quick to point the finger.

It's difficult to predict whether or not relations will improve between both countries, although current signs are fairly negative. Costa Rica, whose civil guard is better funded than many countries' militaries, has a bad habit of being caught on the Río San Juan with a patrol boat of combat troops. Nicaragua, on the other hand, recently passed a law requiring all visiting Ticos to be in possession of a valid visa. As with all instances of deep-rooted prejudice, the solution is anything but clear.

---

major centres of the Central Valley highlands (Heredia, Alajuela and Cartago), and enjoy a level of comfort similar to their economic brethren in Europe and the USA. City dwellers are likely to have a maid, a car or two and, for the lucky few, a second home on the beach or in the mountains.

The home of an average Tico is a one-story construction built from concrete blocks, wood or a combination of both. In the poorer lowland areas, people often live in windowless houses made of *caña brava,* a local cane. For the vast majority of *campesinos* (farmers) and *indígenas* (people of indigenous origin), life is harder than in the cities, poverty levels are higher and standards of living are lower than in the rest of the country. This is especially true along the Caribbean coast, where the descendants of Jamaican immigrants have long suffered from a lack of attention by the federal government. However, although poor families have few possessions and little financial security, every member assists with working the land or contributing to the household, which creates a strong safety net.

As with the rest of the world, globalization is having a dramatic effect on Costa Ricans, who are increasingly mobile, international and intertwined in the global economy – for better or for worse. These days, society is increasingly geographically mobile – the Tico who was

The expression *matando la culebra* (meaning 'to be idle,' literally 'killing the snake') originates with *peones* (expendable laborers) from banana plantations. When foremen would ask what they were doing, the response was *'¡Matando la culebra!'*

born in Puntarenas might end up managing a lodge on the Península de Osa. And, with the advent of better-paved roads, cell phone coverage, and the increasing presence of North American and European expats (and the accompanying malls and big box stores), the Tico family unit has become subject to the changing tides of the wider global society.

Women in Costa Rica

By the letter of the law, Costa Rica's progressive stance on women's issues makes the country stand out among its Central American neighbors. A 1974 family code stipulated equal duties and rights for men and women. Additionally, women can draw up contracts, assume loans and inherit property. Sexual harassment and sex discrimination are also against the law, and in 1996 Costa Rica passed a landmark law against domestic violence, one of the most progressive in Latin America. With growing roles in political, legal, scientific and medical fields, Costa Rica has been home to some historic firsts; in 1998, both vice presidents (Costa Rica has two) were women and in February 2010 Arias Sánchez' former vice president, Laura Chinchilla, became the first female president.

Still, the picture of sexual equality is much more complicated than the country's bragging rights might suggest. A thriving legal prostitution trade has fueled illicit underground activities such as child prostitution and the trafficking of women. Despite the cultural reverence for the matriarch (Mothers Day is a national holiday), traditional Latin American machismo is hardly a thing of the past and antidiscrimination laws are rarely enforced. Particularly in the countryside, many women maintain traditional societal roles: raising children, cooking, and running the home.

In conjunction with two indigenous women, Paula Palmer wrote *Taking Care of Sibö's Gifts*, an inspiring account of the intersection between the spiritual and environmental values of the Bribrí.

Sports

From the scrappy little matches that take over the village pitch to the breathless exclamations of 'goal!' that erupt from San José bars on the day of a big game, no Costa Rican sporting venture can compare with *fútbol* (soccer). Every town has a soccer field (which usually serves as the most conspicuous landmark) where neighborhood aficionados play in heated matches.

The *selección nacional* (national selection) team is known affectionately as La Sele. Legions of rabid Tico fans still remember La Sele's most memorable moments in history, including an unlikely showing in the quarterfinals at the 1990 World Cup in Italy and a solid (if not long-lasting) performance in the 2002 World Cup. More recently, La Sele's failure to qualify for the 2010 World Cup led to a top-down change in leadership and the reinstatement of one-time coach Jorge Luis Pinto, a Colombian coach who has had mixed results on the international stage. In general, Pinto seems to be a good fit for the team's ferocious young leaders, including record-setting scorer Álvaro Saborío, goalkeeper Keylor Navas, striker Rolando Fonseca and forward Bryan Ruiz.

Get player statistics, game schedules and find out everything you ever needed to know about La Sele, the Costa Rican national soccer team, at www.fedefutbol.com.

With such perfect waves, surfing is growing in popularity among Ticos. Costa Rica annually hosts numerous national and international competitions that are widely covered by local media.

Bullfighting is also popular, particularly in the Guanacaste region, though the bull isn't killed in the Costa Rican version of the sport. More aptly described, bullfighting is really a ceremonial opportunity to watch an often tipsy cowboy run around with a bull.

Costa Rican Arts

Literature

Costa Rica has a relatively young literary history and few works of Costa Rican writers or novelists are available in translation. Carlos Luis Fallas (1909–66) is widely known for *Mamita Yunai* (1940), an influential novel that took the banana companies to task for their labor practices. Carlos Luis Fallas remains a very popular writer among the Latin American left.

Carmen Naranjo (1928–) is one of the few contemporary Costa Rican writers who has risen to international acclaim. She is a novelist, poet and short-story writer who also served as ambassador to India in the 1970s, and a few years later as Minister of Culture. In 1996 she was awarded the prestigious Gabriela Mistral medal from the Chilean government. Her collection of short stories, *There Never Was a Once Upon a Time,* is widely available in English. Two of her stories can also be found in *Costa Rica: A Traveler's Literary Companion.*

José León Sánchez (1930–) is an internationally renowned memoirist of Huetar descent from the border of Costa Rica and Nicaragua. After being convicted for stealing from the famous Basílica de Nuestra Señora de los Angeles in Cartago, he was sentenced to serve his term at Isla San Lucas, one of Latin America's most notorious jails. Illiterate when he was incarcerated, Sánchez taught himself how to read and write, and clandestinely authored one of the continent's most poignant books: *La isla de los hombres solos* (called *God Was Looking the Other Way* in the translated version).

Music & Dance

Although there are other Latin American musical hotbeds of more renown, Costa Rica's central geographical location and colonial history resulted in a varied musical culture that incorporates elements from North and South America and the Caribbean islands.

San José features a regular lineup of domestic and international rock, folk and hip-hop artists, but you'll find that the regional sounds also survive, each with their own special rhythms, instruments and styles. For instance, the Península de Nicoya has a rich musical history, most of it made with guitars, maracas and marimbas. The traditional sound on the Caribbean coast is calypso, which has roots in the Afro-Carib slave culture.

Popular dance music includes Latin dances, such as salsa, merengue, bolero and *cumbia.* Guanacaste is also the birthplace of many traditional dances, most of which depict courtship rituals between country folk. The most famous dance – sometimes considered the national dance – is the *punto guanacasteco.* What keeps it lively is the *bomba,* a funny (and usually racy) rhymed verse, shouted out by the male dancers during the musical interlude.

Painting & Sculpture

The visual arts in Costa Rica first took on a national character in the 1920s, when Teodórico Quirós, Fausto Pacheco and their contemporaries began painting landscapes that differed from traditional European styles, depicting the rolling hills and lush forest of Costa Rican countryside, often sprinkled with characteristic adobe houses.

The contemporary scene is more varied and it is difficult to define a unique Tico style. Several individual artists have garnered acclaim for their work, including the magical realism of Isidro Con Wong, the surreal paintings and primitive engravings of Francisco Amighetti, and the mystical female figures painted by Rafa Fernández. The Museo de Arte

THE TICO WAY OF LIFE

ALFONSO CHASE

Although he is yet untranslated, poet Alfonso Chase is a Fulbright scholar and a contemporary literary hero. In 2000 he won the nation's highest literary award.

The most comprehensive and complete book on Costa Rican history and culture is *The Ticos: Culture and Social Change in Costa Rica* by Mavis, Richard and Karen Biesanz.

y Diseño Contemporáneo in San José is the top place to see this type of work, and its permanent collection is a great primer.

Many art galleries are geared toward tourists and specialize in 'tropical art' (for lack of an official description): brightly colored, whimsical folk paintings depicting flora and fauna that evoke the work of French artist Henri Rousseau.

Folk art and handicrafts are not as widely produced or readily available here as in other Central American countries. However, the dedicated souvenir hunter will have no problem finding the colorful Sarchí oxcarts that have become a symbol of Costa Rica. Indigenous crafts, which include intricately carved and painted masks as well as handwoven bags and linens, are also widely available.

Landscapes & Ecology

The Land

Despite its diminutive size – at 51,000 sq km it is slightly smaller than the USA's West Virginia – Costa Rica's land is an explosion of Technicolor contrasts and violent contradictions. On one coast are the breezy skies and big waves of the Pacific. Only 119km away lie the muggy and languid shores of the Caribbean. In between there are active volcanoes, alpine peaks and crisp high-elevation forest. Few places on earth can compare with this little country's spectacular interaction of natural, geological and climatic forces.

The vibrancy of its natural resources has also made Costa Rica something of a comeback kid: the deforestation here in the early 1990s was among the worst in Latin America. Today the country is a global leader in tropical conservation. Now in charge of an exemplary system of well-managed and accessible parks, Costa Rica is perhaps the best place in the world to experience rainforest habitats, while its stunning natural landscape brings tourists in increasing numbers. Ready for a tour?

The Pacific Coast

Start by twisting and turning around the endless gulfs, sandy peninsulas and deserted bays of the Pacific, some 1016km long. Rugged, rocky headlands give way to classic white- and black-sand beaches bedecked with palms. Strong tidal action creates an excellent habitat for waterbirds, a dramatic crash of surf and some exquisite surfing.

Two major peninsulas hook out into the Pacific along the coast: Nicoya in the north and Osa in the south. Although they look relatively similar from space, on the ground they could hardly be more different. Nicoya is one of the driest places in the country and holds some of Costa Rica's most developed tourist infrastructure; Osa is wet and rugged, run through by wild, seasonal rivers and rough dirt roads that are always under threat from the creeping jungle.

Just inland from the coast, the landscapes of the Pacific lowlands are a narrow strip of land backed by mountains. This area is equally dynamic, ranging from dry deciduous forests and open cattle country in the north, to misty, mysterious tropical rainforests in the south.

Central Costa Rica

Move just a bit inland from the Pacific coast and you immediately ascend the jagged spine of the country: the majestic Cordillera Central in the north and the rugged, largely unexplored Cordillera de Talamanca in the south. Continually being revised by earthquakes and volcanic activity, these mountains are part of the majestic Sierra Madre chain that runs north through Mexico.

A land of active volcanoes, clear trout-filled streams and ethereal cloud forest, these mountain ranges generally follow a northwest to southeast line, with the highest and most dramatic peaks in the south near the Panamanian border. The highest in the country is the rugged, windswept 3820m peak of Cerro Chirripó.

In the midst of this powerful landscape, surrounded on all sides by mountains, are the highlands of Meseta Central – the Central Valley. This fertile central plain, some 1000m above sea level, is the agricultural heart of the nation and enjoys abundant rainfall and mild temperatures. It includes San José and cradles three more of Costa Rica's five largest cities, accounting for more than half of the country's population.

> Michael Crichton's book *Jurassic Park* is set on Isla del Cocos. In it, he refers to Ticos as 'Ticans.'

The Caribbean Coast

Cross the mountains and drop down the eastern slope and you'll reach the elegant line of the Caribbean coastline – a long, straight 212km along low plains, brackish lagoons and waterlogged forests. A lack of strong tides allows plants to grow right over the water's edge along coastal sloughs. Eventually, these create the walls of vegetation along the narrow, murky waters that characterize much of the region. As if taking cues from the slow-paced Caribbean-influenced culture, the rivers that rush out of the central mountain take on a languid pace here, curving through broad plains toward the sea.

Compared with the smoothly paved roads and popular beaches of the Pacific coast, much of the land here is still largely inaccessible except by boat or plane. The best access points for travelers are the Parque Nacional Tortuguero and the Barra del Colorado National Wildlife Refuge, which both allow intimate visits to this little-discovered border between land and sea.

The Geology

If the near proximity of all this wildly diverse beauty makes Costa Rica feel like the crossroads between vastly different worlds, that's because it is. Part of the thin strip of land that separates two continents with vastly different wildlife and topographical character and right in the middle of the world's two largest oceans, it's little wonder that Costa Rica boasts such a colorful collision of climates, landscapes and wildlife.

> The world-famous Organization for Tropical Studies runs three field stations and offers numerous classes for students seriously interested in tropical ecology. See www.ots.ac.cr.

Costa Rica's geological history began when the Cocos Plate, a tectonic plate that lies below the Pacific, crashed headlong into the Caribbean Plate, which is off the isthmus' east coast. At a rate of about 10cm every year, it might seem slow by human standards, but the collision was a violent wreck by geological standards, creating the area's 'subduction zone' that is rife with geological drama. The plates continue to collide, with the Cocos Plate pushing the Caribbean Plate toward the heavens and making the area prone to earthquakes and ongoing volcanic activity (Arenal, one of the world's most active volcanoes, is in Costa Rica's north).

But despite all the violence underfoot, these forces have blessed this country with some of the world's most beautiful and diverse tropical landscapes.

Out on a Reef

Compared with the rest of the Caribbean, the coral reefs of Costa Rica are not a banner attraction. Heavy surf and shifting sands along most of the Caribbean coast produce conditions that are unbearable to corals. The exceptions are two beautiful patches of reef in the south which are protected on the rocky headlands of Parque Nacional Cahuita and Refugio Nacional de Vida Silvestre Gandoca-Manzanillo.

These diminutive but vibrant reefs are home to more than 100 species of fish and many types of coral and make for excellent snorkeling and diving. Countless damselfish, sergeant majors, parrot fish and surgeonfish gather to feed on abundant marine algae, while predatory barracuda come to prey on the fish. Gandoca-Manzanillo is a famous nesting ground for four species of sea turtle. Even better, turtle volunteers have been patrolling these beaches since 1986 to prevent poaching, and turtle populations are doing really well thanks to their efforts.

Unfortunately, the reefs themselves are in danger due to sediment washing downriver from logging operations, and toxic chemicals that wash out of nearby agricultural fields, factors that have been curbed by the government but which persist. Also, a major earthquake in 1991 lifted the reefs up as much as 1.5m, stranding and killing large portions of this fragile ecosystem. More recently, climate change has led to warmer water in the Caribbean, which puts the reefs at greatest peril – scientists released a report in 2008 that found over half of the Caribbean reefs were dead from increased temperatures.

So far the coral reefs of Costa Rica have been largely overlooked, but with these threats hanging over them, there's little time to lose.

Wildlife

Nowhere else in the world are so many types of habitats squeezed into such a tiny area, and Costa Rica's wildlife has been comingling species from different continents for millennia. In terms of number of species per 10,000 sq km, Costa Rica tops the list of countries, at 615 species, compared with a wildlife-rich country such as Rwanda that has 596, or the comparatively impoverished USA with its 104 species. This simple fact alone (not to mention the ease of travel and friendly residents) makes Costa Rica the premier destination for nature lovers from all over the world.

The large number of species in Costa Rica is also due to the relatively recent appearance of the country. Roughly three million years ago Costa Rica rose from the ocean, and formed a land bridge between North and South America. As species from these two vast biological provinces started to mingle, the number of species essentially 'doubled' in the area where Costa Rica now sits. For a detailed look at Costa Rica's animals, look to the Wildlife Guide (p507).

Flora

Simply put, Costa Rica's floral biodiversity is mind-blowing – close to 12,000 species of vascular plants have been described in Costa Rica, and the list gets more and more crowded each year. Orchids alone account for about 1400 species.

The diversity of habitats created when this many species mix is a wonder to behold – one day you're canoeing in a muggy mangrove swamp, and the next day squinting through bone-chilling fog to see orchids in a montane cloud forest. Jump on a bus and in a short ride you'll be fighting your way through the vines of a tropical rainforest. Sure, everyone loves Costa Rica's celebrated beaches, but travelers would be remiss to visit the country without seeing some of Costa Rica's most distinctive plant communities, including rainforests, mangrove swamps, cloud forests and dry forests.

Experiencing a tropical forest for the first time can be a bit of a surprise for visitors from North America or Europe, who are used to temperate forests with little variety. Such regions are either dominated by conifers, or have endless tracts of oaks, beech and birch. Tropical forests, on the other hand, have a staggering number of species – in Costa Rica,

The tale of the green turtle's rebound in Tortuguero is told in two popular books by Archie Carr: The Windward Road: Adventures of a Naturalist on Remote Caribbean Shores and The Sea Turtle: So Excellent a Fishe.

LANDSCAPES & ECOLOGY

Carol Henderson's Field Guide to the Wildlife of Costa Rica is a handy all-in-one resource.

BIODIVERSITY

for example, almost 2000 tree species have been recorded. If you stand in one spot and look around, you'll see scores of different plants, and if you walk several hundred meters you're likely to find even more.

RAINFOREST

The dense, humid, vibrant mystery of the tropical rainforest connects acutely with a traveler's sense of adventure. These forests, far more dense with plant life than any other environment on the planet, are leftover scraps of the prehistoric jungles that once covered the continents. Standing in the midst of it and trying to take it all in can be overwhelming: tropical rainforests contain over half of the living organisms known on earth. Naturally, this riotous pile-on of life requires lots and lots of water – it typically gets between five and six *meters* of water annually.

Classic rainforest habitats are well represented in parks of the southwest corner of Costa Rica or in mid-elevation portions of the central mountains. Here you will find towering trees that block out the sky, long looping vines and many overlapping layers of vegetation. Large trees often show buttresses, winglike ribs that extend out from their trunks for added structural support. And plants literally climb atop other plants, fighting for a bit of sunlight. The most impressive areas of primary forest – a term designating completely untouched land that has never been disturbed by humans – exist on the Península de Osa.

CLOUD FOREST

Visiting the unearthly terrain of a cloud forest is a highlight for many visitors; there are amazing swaths of it in Monteverde, along the Cerro de la Muerte and below the peaks of Chirripó. In these regions, fog-drenched trees are so thickly coated in mosses, ferns, bromeliads and orchids that you can hardly discern their true shapes. These forests are created when humid trade winds off the Caribbean blow up into the highlands, cool and condense to form thick, low-hanging clouds. With constant exposure to wind, rain and sun, the trees here are crooked and stunted.

Cloud forests are widespread at high elevations throughout Costa Rica (such as the Parque Nacional Chirripó area) and any of them warrant a visit. Be forewarned, however, that in these habitats the term 'rainy season' has little meaning because it's always dripping wet from the fog – a cloud forest often hovers around 100% humidity.

TROPICAL DRY FOREST

Along Costa Rica's northwest coast lies the country's largest concentration of tropical dry forest – a stunningly different scene than the country's wet rainforests and cloud forests. During the dry season many trees drop their foliage, creating carpets of crackling, sun-drenched leaves and a sense of openness that is largely absent in other Costa Rican habitats. The large trees here, such as Costa Rica's national tree, the guanacaste, have broad, umbrella-like canopies, while spiny shrubs and vines or cacti dominate the understory. At times, large numbers of trees erupt into spectacular displays of flowers, and at the beginning of the rainy season everything is transformed with a wonderful flush of new green foliage.

This type of forest was native to Guanacaste and the Península de Nicoya, though it suffered generations of destruction for its commercially valuable lumber. Most was clear-cut or burned to make space for ranching. Guanacaste and Santa Rosa national parks are good examples of the dry forest and host some of the country's most accessible nature hiking.

The National Biodiversity Institute is a clearinghouse of information on both biodiversity and efforts to conserve it; see www.inbio.ac.cr.

The tallest tree in the rainforest is usually the silk-cotton tree, or the ceiba. The most famous example is a 70m elder in Corcovado.

THE ESSENTIAL RAINFOREST

After a decade or so of political tumult, the concept of climate change has been transformed from crackpot theory to genuine scientific fact, and these days it's difficult to find someone who doesn't acknowledge that humans have negatively influenced the health and sustainability of the planet. As developing nations continue to modernize, global carbon emissions rise and evidence of the greenhouse effect can be felt across the planet – in melting glaciers, warming seas and extreme weather patterns.

One of the only protections against the continued rise of carbon dioxide (CO_2) levels remains the protection of tropical rainforest. Tropical rainforests limit the greenhouse effect of global warming by storing carbon and hence reducing the amount of CO_2 in the atmosphere – they act as a 'carbon sink.' Although the best defense against climate change is rapidly being destroyed the world over, the fight to protect rainforest has become an issue of wide global concern. In an example of the interconnectedness of environments, scientists have found that the deforestation of Latin American rainforests is affecting global ecosystems, such as the Sahel in Africa, where desertification has increased as deforestation in Latin America increases.

As rainforest land continues to be cut, the stakes become ever higher. In 2004, scientists made an announcement following a 20-year study in the Amazon, claiming the world's tropical forests may become less able to absorb CO_2. In some areas of the forest scientists discovered that bigger, quicker-growing species were flourishing at the expense of the smaller ones living below the forest canopy. Since plant growth is dependent upon CO_2, the team hypothesized that the bigger plants in tropical rainforests were getting an extra boost from rising levels of global emissions.

Human destruction of natural habitats, unbridled economic development, pollution and climate change all threaten the vast biological diversity of Costa Rica's rainforest. Reversing the tides is a difficult proposition given the world's growing human population, and a costly venture. In 2012 the chief of the United Nations Convention on Biological Diversity announced that maintaining the current level of biodiversity would cost US$300 billion a year, about 10 times more money than is currently being spent on conservation efforts.

MANGROVES

Found along brackish stretches of both coasts, mangrove swamps are a world unto themselves. Growing on stilts out of muddy tidal flats, five species of trees crowd together so densely that no boats and few animals can penetrate them. Striking in their adaptations for dealing with salt, mangrove trees thrive where no other land plant dares tread and are among the world's most relentless colonizers. The mangrove seeds are heavy and fleshy, blooming into flowers in the spring before falling off to give way to fruit. By the time the fruit falls, it has covered with spiky seedlings that anchor in the soft mud of low tides. In only 10 years, this seedling has the potential to mature into an entire new colony.

Though often thought of as mosquito-filled backwaters, mangrove swamps play extremely important roles in the ecosystem. Not only do they buffer coastlines from the erosive power of waves, they also have high levels of productivity because they trap nutrient-rich sediment and serve as spawning and nursery areas for innumerable species of fish and invertebrates. The brown waters of mangrove channels – rich with nutrients and filled with algae, shrimp, crustaceans and caimans – form tight links in the marine food chain and are best explored in a kayak, early in the morning.

There are miles of mangrove channels along the Caribbean coast, and several patches of mangrove on the Pacific, near Bahía Drake.

Costa Rica's national tree is the guanacaste, commonly found on the lowlands of the Pacific Slope.

1

1. Refugio Nacional de Vida Silvestre Gandoca-Manzanillo (p449)
Visitors can snorkel in the clear Caribbean waters of this little-explored refuge.

2. Reserva Biológica Bosque Nuboso Monteverde (p177)
Waterfalls gush through this biological reserve.

3. Parque Nacional Volcán Arenal (p145)
Volcán Arenal looms large in this national park.

4. Playa Carrillo (p251)
Popular Playa Carrillo is a wide, arcing beach with clean white sand and a jungle backdrop.

COSTA RICA'S EASTER BLOSSOM

Among Costa Rica's 1400 species of orchids, the *guaria morada (Cattleya skinneri)* is celebrated with special reverence. Blooming around the time of Lent and Easter, this gorgeous orchid with dense clusters of lavender-rose flowers is prominently displayed on altars and in homes and churches everywhere in Central America. In the old days these flowers grew liberally on the walls and roofs of old houses and courtyards, where they added a special charm. However, this ancient custom fell by the wayside and they are no longer a common sight.

In honor of its links to history and tradition, the orchid was chosen as Costa Rica's national flower in 1937. Unfortunately, the plant's amazing popularity has resulted in wild populations being harvested without restraint, and an alarm was raised in 2004 that it could become extinct in the wild without immediate action. Hopefully, the orchid's numbers will begin to increase again, because although it is easy to grow commercially, no quantity of orchids in a greenhouse can replace the flowers found in the wild forests of Costa Rica.

Fauna

Though tropical in nature – with a substantial number of tropical animals such as poison-dart frogs and spider monkeys – Costa Rica is also the winter home for more than 200 species of migrating birds that arrive from as far away as Alaska and Australia. Don't be surprised to see one of your familiar backyard birds feeding alongside trogons and toucans. Birds are one of the primary attractions for naturalists, who scan endlessly for birds of every color, from strawberry-red scarlet macaws to the iridescent jewels called violet sabrewings (a type of hummingbird). Because many birds in Costa Rica have restricted ranges, you are guaranteed to find different species everywhere you travel.

Visitors will almost certainly see one of Costa Rica's four types of monkeys or two types of sloths, but there are an additional 230 types of mammals awaiting the patient observer. More exotic sightings might include the amazing four-eyed opossum or silky anteater, while a lucky few might spot the elusive tapir, or have a jaguarundi cross their path.

The extensive network of national parks, wildlife refuges and other protected areas are prime places to spot wildlife.

If you are serious about observing birds and animals, the value of a knowledgeable guide cannot be underestimated. Their keen eyes are trained to notice the slightest movement in the forest, and they recognize the many exotic sounds. Most professional bird guides are proficient in the dialects of local birds, greatly improving your chances of hearing or seeing these species.

No season is a bad season for exploring Costa Rica's natural environment, though most visitors arrive during the peak dry season when trails are less muddy and more accessible. An added bonus of visiting between December and February is that many of the wintering migrant birds are still hanging around. A trip after the peak season means fewer birds, but this is a stupendous time to see dried forests transform into vibrant greens and it's also when resident birds begin nesting.

Endangered Species

As expected in a country with unique habitats and widespread logging, there are numerous species whose populations are declining or in danger of extinction. Currently, the number-one threat to most of Costa Rica's endangered species is habitat destruction, followed closely by hunting and trapping.

Dr Alexander Skutch is famous for the *Guide to the Birds of Costa Rica*, but he also wrote several other contemplative books about his feathered friends, including *A Naturalist in Costa Rica* and *The Minds of Birds*.

Two-toed sloths descend from the trees once every two weeks to defecate.

Costa Rica's four species of sea turtles – olive ridley, leatherback, green and hawksbill – deservedly get a lot of attention. All four species are classified as endangered or critically endangered, meaning they face an imminent threat of extinction. While populations of some species are increasing, thanks to various protection programs along both coasts, the risk for these *tortugas* is still very real.

Destruction of habitat is a huge problem. With the exception of the leatherbacks, all of these species return to their natal beach to nest, which means that the ecological state of the beach directly affects that turtle's ability to reproduce. All of the species prefer dark, undisturbed beaches, and any sort of development or artificial lighting (including flashlights) will inhibit nesting.

Hunting and harvesting eggs are two major causes of declining populations. Green turtles are actually hunted for their meat. Leatherbacks and olive ridleys are not killed for meat, but their eggs are considered a delicacy – an aphrodisiac no less. The hawksbill turtles are hunted for their unusual shells, which are sometimes used to make jewelry and hair ornaments. Of course, any trade in tortoise-shell products and turtle eggs and meat is illegal, but a significant black market exists.

The legendary resplendent quetzal – the bird at the top of every naturalist's must-see list – teeters precariously as its home forests are felled at an alarming rate. Seeing a noisy scarlet macaw could be a bird-watching highlight in Costa Rica, but trapping for the pet trade has extirpated these magnificent birds from much of their former range. Although populations are thriving in the Península de Osa, the scarlet macaw is now extinct over most of Central America, including the entire Caribbean coast.

National Parks & Protected Areas

The national-park system began in the 1960s, and has since been expanded into a National Conservation Areas System with an astounding 186 protected areas, including 32 national parks, eight biological reserves, 13 forest reserves and 51 wildlife refuges. At least 10% of the land is strictly protected and another 17% is included in various multiple-use preserves. Costa Rican authorities enjoy their claim that more than 27% of the country has been set aside for conservation, but multiple-use zones still allow farming, logging and other exploitation, so the environment within them is not totally protected. The most amazing number might be the smallest of all: Costa Rica's parks are safe haven to approximately 5% of the world's wildlife species.

Travelers may also be surprised to learn that, in addition to the system of national preserves, there are hundreds of small, privately owned lodges, reserves and haciendas (estates) that have been set up to protect the land, and many of these are well worth visiting. Many of these are owned by longtime Costa Rican expats who decided that this country was the last stop down their journey along the 'gringo trail' in the 1970s

LANDSCAPES & ECOLOGY

The seven species of poison-dart frog in Costa Rica are beautiful to look at but have exceedingly toxic skin secretions that cause paralysis and death.

MACAWS

While the female scarlet macaw sits on her nest, the male regurgitates food for her to eat, and later does the same for their chicks.

LOOK BUT DON'T JUMP IN

Swimming with dolphins has been illegal since 2006, although shady tour operators out for a quick buck may encourage it at the expense of the animals. Research indicates that in some heavily touristed areas, dolphins are leaving their natural habitat in search of calmer seas. When your boat comes across these amazing creatures of the sea, do not jump into the water. From the comfort of the boat you can have an awe-inspiring and longer-lasting experience (the dolphins and whales usually swim away quickly when humans are in the water, but they might stay and swim around a boat indefinitely). And more importantly, you won't disturb the peace of these gentle giants.

and '80s. The abundance of foreign-owned protected areas is a bit of a contentious issue with Ticos. Although these are largely nonprofit organizations with keen interests in conservation, they are private and often cost money to enter.

Although the national-park system appears glamorous on paper, the national conservation body (Sinac; Sistema Nacional de Areas de Conservación) still sees much work to be done. A report from several years ago amplified the fact that much of the protected area is, in fact, at risk. The government doesn't exactly own all of this land – almost half of the areas are in private ownership – and there isn't a budget to buy it. Technically, the private lands are protected from development, but there have been reports that many landowners are finding loopholes in the restrictions and selling or developing their properties, or taking bribes from poachers and illegal loggers in exchange for access to their lands.

On the plus side is a project by Sinac that links national parks and reserves, private reserves and national forests into 13 conservation areas. This strategy has two major effects. First, these so-called megaparks allow greater numbers of individual plants and animals to exist. Second, the administration of the national parks is delegated to regional offices, allowing a more individualized management approach in each area. Each conservation area has regional and subregional offices delegated to provide effective education, enforcement, research and management, although some regional offices play what appear to be only obscure bureaucratic roles.

Although many of the national parks were expressly created to protect Costa Rica's habitats and wildlife, a few parks preserve other resources such as the country's foremost pre-Columbian ruins at Monumento Nacional Arqueológico Guayabo, an important cave system at Parque Nacional Barra Honda and a series of geologically active and inactive volcanoes in several parks and reserves.

Most national parks can be entered without permits, though a few limit the number they admit on a daily basis and others require advance reservations for accommodations within the park's boundaries (Chirripó, Corcovado and La Amistad). The average entrance fee to most parks is US$10 per day for foreigners, plus additional fees for overnight camping where permitted.

Most parks in the country have a ranger station of some kind, and though these are largely administrative offices for the park with few formal services for travelers, it is worth dropping in if you plan to deeply explore the park. The *guardeparques* (park rangers) know the parks inside and out and can offer tips on trail conditions, good camping spots and places to see wildlife. Naturally, these conversations will be most helpful if you speak Spanish.

With Costa Rican parks contributing significantly to both national and local economies through the huge influx of tourist money, there is little question that the country's healthy natural environment is important to its citizens. In general, support for land preservation remains high because it provides income and jobs to so many people, plus important opportunities for scientific investigation.

Environmental Issues

Costa Rica's environmental issues are as unique (and occasionally dizzying) as the landscape itself. No other tropical country has made such a concerted effort to protect the environment and in 2012 Costa Rica was ranked one of the top five nations in the world for its overall environmental performance in a study published by Yale and Columbia universities. At the same time, as the global leader in the burgeoning ecotourism economy, Costa Rica is proving to be a case study in the

For maps and descriptions of the national parks, go to www.costarica-nationalparks.com.

Hunting and harvesting of sea turtle eggs – a once-popular working-class bar snack – has decimated their populations. Due to deforestation it is also best to avoid products made from tropical hardwoods if you're uncertain of the origin.

POPULAR PROTECTED AREAS

NAME	FEATURES	WILDLIFE	WHEN TO VISIT
Parque Nacional Cahuita	easily accessible hiking, beach walking and snorkeling	monkeys and marine life	year-round
Parque Nacional Chirripó	Costa Rica's highest summit, cloud-forest trekking	diverse animal and plant life at varying altitudes	dry season (Jan-Mar), closed May
Parque Nacional Corcovado	vast, remote rainforest with giant trees	jaguars, scarlet macaws and tapirs	avoid rainy season (May-Nov)
Parque Nacional Manuel Antonio	beach walking and wildlife-watching	diverse monkey species	avoid peak holidays
Parque Nacional Santa Rosa	dry forest with guanacaste (the national tree), hiking and wildlife-watching	monkeys, peccaries and coatis	dry season (Jan-Mar)
Parque Nacional Tortuguero	beach walking and sea turtle egg-laying	sea turtles, sloths, manatees and crocodiles	turtle season, check with park for details
Reserva Biológica Bosque Nuboso Monteverde	world-famous cloud forest and bird-watching	resplendent quetzals and other rare birds	avoid peak holidays
Reserva NaturalAbsoluta Cabo Blanco	beach walking and bird-watching	monkeys and sea birds	year-round

pitfalls and benefits of ecological tourism, and the pressures of over-population, global climate change and dwindling natural resources have made Costa Rica a case study in the urgency of environmental protection.

Deforestation

Sometimes, when the traffic jams up around the endless San José sprawl, it is hard to keep in mind that this place was once covered in a lush, unending tropical forest. Tragically, after more than a century of clearing for plantations, agriculture and logging, Costa Rica lost about 80% of its forest cover before the government stepped in with a plan to protect what was left. Through its many programs of forest protection and reforestation, 52% of the country is forested once again – a stunning accomplishment.

Despite protection for two-thirds of the remaining forests, cutting trees is still a major problem for Costa Rica, especially on private lands being cleared by wealthy landowners and multinational corporations. Even within national parks, some of the more remote areas are being logged illegally because there is not enough money to hire guards to enforce the law.

Apart from the direct loss of tropical forests and the plants and animals that depend on them, deforestation leads directly or indirectly to a number of other severe environmental problems. Forests protect the soil beneath them from the ravages of tropical rainstorms; after deforestation much of the topsoil is washed away, lowering the productivity of the land and silting up watersheds and downstream coral reefs.

CAVES

The fabulous limestone caves of Parque Nacional Barra Honda were formed in the remains of ancient coral reefs after they were uplifted out of the ocean.

Cleared lands are frequently planted with a variety of crops, including Costa Rica's main agricultural product, bananas, the production of which entails the use of pesticides as well as blue plastic bags to protect the fruit. Both the pesticides and the plastic bags end up polluting the environment as well.

Because deforestation plays a role in global warming, there is much interest in rewarding such countries as Costa Rica for taking the lead in protecting their forests. The USA has forgiven millions of dollars of Costa Rica's debt in exchange for increased efforts to preserve rainforests. The Costa Rican government itself sponsors a program that pays landowners for each hectare of forest they set aside, and has petitioned the UN for a global program that would pay tropical countries for their conservation efforts. Travelers interested in taking part in volunteer projects that can help protect Costa Rica's trees should look to volunteer opportunities in conservation and forestry.

For further information about volunteering in Costa Rica, see the Directory (p529).

Tourism

The other great environmental issue facing Costa Rica comes from the country being loved to death, directly through the passage of more than two million foreign tourists a year, and indirectly through the development of extensive infrastructure to support this influx. For years resort hotels and lodges continued to pop up, most notably on formerly pristine beaches or in the middle of intact rainforest. Too many of these projects were poorly planned, and necessitate additional support systems, including roads and countless vehicle trips, with much of this activity unregulated and largely unmonitored.

Another concern was that hotels and lodges are simply dumping wastewater into the ocean or nearby creeks rather than following expensive procedures for treating it. With an official estimate that only 4% of the country's wastewater is treated, and with thousands of unregulated hotels in operation, there's a good chance that some hotels and lodges aren't taking care of their waste.

It is worth noting, however, that many private lodges and reserves are also doing some of the best conservation work in the country, and it's really inspiring to run across homespun efforts to protect Costa Rica's environment spearheaded by hardworking families or small organizations tucked away in some forgotten corner of the country. These include projects to boost rural economies by raising butterflies or native flowers, efforts by villagers to document their local biodiversity, or amazingly resourceful campaigns to raise funds to purchase endangered lands.

The Refugio Nacional de Vida Silvestre Curú (p257), Tiskita Jungle Lodge (p393) in Pavones, and Rara Avis (p464) near Puerto Viejo de Sarapiquí are but a few examples. Costa Rica is full of wonderful tales about folks who are extremely passionate and generous in their efforts to protect the planet's resources

Sustainable Travel
HOW TO KNOW IF A BUSINESS IS REALLY ECOFRIENDLY
Ecotourism and 'green travel' are big business in Costa Rica, and sometimes it can seem like every hotel, restaurant, souvenir stall and ATV tour operator is claiming to be a friend to Mother Earth. Navigating the minefield of jargon – 'green,' 'sustainable,' 'low carbon footprint,' 'ecofriendly' – can be daunting. Since sustainable travel and 'ecotourism' have no universal guidelines, when booking your trip here are some things to look for in an ecofriendly business:

Few organizations are as involved in building sustainable rainforest-based economies as the Rainforest Alliance. See the website for special initiatives in Costa Rica: www.rainforest-alliance.org.

Green Phoenix, by science journalist William Allen, is an absorbing account of his efforts, alongside scientists and activists, to conserve and restore the rainforest in Guanacaste.

RAINFOREST

A WHOPPER OF A PROBLEM

Although there is a long history of deforestation in Costa Rica, massive clear-cutting of the rainforests (particularly in Guanacaste) intensified during the 1970s. Currently, there is much debate regarding the causes of this wide-scale deforestation, but research suggests that a shift in governmental philosophy likely sparked the event. Specifically, national policies were implemented at the time that promoted increased land use relating to agriculture, wood production, pastureland creation and improved transit infrastructure. It is argued that these initiatives were aimed at speeding up the country's economic development, especially in response to the decrease in the international demand for Costa Rican coffee.

Clearly, development is a double-edged sword as it's impossible to argue that the philosophies of the 1970s did not in fact improve the quality of life in Costa Rica. Today, Guanacaste is one of the richest provinces in Costa Rica, and the country as a whole is often regarded as the gem of Central America. Quality of life for those in Costa Rica is among the highest in Latin America, and Ticos have never had to starve like their neighbors to the north and south. However, cattle ranchers in Costa Rica produce an abundance of meat, much of which is destined for the international fast-food market. Thus the devastation of the rainforest is not solely a product of national improvement.

The body of evidence supporting these claims is astounding, and consists of everything from court testimonials to recorded data on imports and exports. Officially, most fast-food companies maintain that they are in favor of rainforest preservation, and that they do not use hamburger meat of foreign origin in their products. However, although imported beef is only a small portion of the total meat consumed in the USA, this accounts for a significant percentage of Central American beef production. One documented problem is that when Central American beef arrives at a US point of entry, it is often marked as 'US inspected and approved,' which disguises the origin of the product. Furthermore, since the meat in a single burger can be derived from multiple cows, it's difficult to verify that a product is in fact free of foreign beef.

As a consumer, it's virtually impossible to ensure that you're not eating beef that's been raised on recently deforested areas, aside from boycotting the major fast-food retailers. In late 2007 Costa Rica approved the Central American Free Trade Agreement (Cafta), which took effect on January 1, 2009. The law reduced tariffs on beef exports. Several fast-food companies have started adopting healthier menus (though much of this is attributable to recent declines in profits). In the meantime, researchers in Costa Rica are hard at work investigating the natural processes of reforestation.

» At the bare minimum, an ecofriendly business should have obvious recycling programs, effectively manage its wastewater and pollutants, and use alternative energy systems and natural illumination.

» A high rating from a legitimate sustainability index; in Costa Rica, the government-sactioned Certificado para la Sostenibilidad Turística (CST; www.turismo-sostenible.co.cr) offers a 'five-leaf' rating system. The top classification currently has fewer than two dozen hotels. Factors considered by the CST include physical-biological parameters, infrastructure and services, which includes management practices; external clients' practices; and socioeconomic environment, including interaction with local communities. Its website has a complete directory.

» Partnership with environmental conservation programs, education initiatives or regional or local organizations that work on solving environmental problems.

» A majority of its employees from the local population, associating with locally owned businesses, providing places where local handicrafts can be displayed for sale, serving foods that support local markets, and using local materials and products in order to maintain the health of the local economy.

AFFORDABLE & SUSTAINABLE LODGING

Although most of Costa Rica's proudly sustainable digs come with a high price tag, these hotels offer visionary sustainability practices for those on a budget:

» Flutterby House (p330)

» Casa Mariposa (p330)

» Punta Mona (p450)

» Rancho Margot (p148)

FIVE WAYS TO SAVE THE RAINFOREST

Although much ado has been made over the years of 'saving the rainforest,' a few simple, easy gestures can add up to help lessen the impact on this delicate landscape.

» **Plant a tree** At Selva Bananito Lodge (p424) on the Caribbean coast, you can help reforest a former banana plantation.

» **Work in the local community** Spend part of your trip with community-led grassroots organizations such as the Fundación Corcovado (p530), dedicated to preserving one of Costa Rica's last true frontiers, Parque Nacional Corcovado.

» **Drink organic, shade-grown coffee** Organic coffee-growing avoids the use of chemical pesticides and fertilizers, minimizing their environmental impact and ensuring the survival of old-growth forests.

» **Say no to beef** The number-one reason for forest clearing in Central America is to feed cows, mostly for export. Consider grass-fed beef, which is better for your health and better for the environment.

Adrian Forsyth has written several colorful children's books about the rainforest, including *Journey Through a Tropical Jungle* and *How Monkeys Make Chocolate.*

» **Give your green** Money talks, especially when it's in the hands of sustainable tour operators like Osa Wild (p365).

» **Bring it home** Sustainability practices that protect Costa Rica are just as urgent at home. Take the inspiration to protect the rainforest home with you.

TRAVELING GREEN

Don't love Costa Rica's landscape to death. The impact of visiting such an ecologically rich and sensitive environment can be lessened if travelers remember a few basic actions.

» **Buy carbon offsets** One round-trip flight between New York and San José produces over one ton of CO_2 emissions.

» **Drink tap water** Fill your bottle from a rainwater-collection system, and purify natural water sources while hiking. Reuse bottles.

» **Recycle** When you arrive in a new town, ask around to see if there are any recycling programs. If a system is in place, spread awareness among your fellow travelers.

» **Pick up garbage** While walking along a beach or a trail, pick up any garbage you see – your actions might inspire others.

» **Respect the land** Stick to the trails as this reduces the erosion caused by human transit. Likewise, don't damage plants, and always observe wildlife from a distance.

» **Don't feed animals** Feeding animals interferes with their natural diets and makes them susceptible to bacteria transferred by humans or pesticides contained within fruit.

Costa Rica Wildlife Guide

Birds »
Reptiles & Amphibians »
Land Mammals »
Marine Animals »
Insects »

Humpback whale, Parque Nacional Marino Ballena (p331)

CLAUDE HUOT / ALAMY ©

Birds

Bird-watchers delight: Costa Rica's amazing biodiversity includes approximately 850 species of bird, including six endemic species – the country holds a greater variety of birds than Europe, North America or Australia.

With their dark bodies, yellow chests and brilliant beaks, toucans are classic rainforest birds; six species are found in Costa Rica. Huge bills and vibrant plumage make species such as the chestnut-mandibled toucan and the keel-billed toucan hard to miss – they are common across the country. Listen for the keel-billed's song: a repetitious 'carrrick!' at dusk.

Of the 16 parrot species in Costa Rica, none is as spectacular as the scarlet macaw. Unmistakable for its large size, bright-red body, blue-and-yellow wings, long red tail and white face, it's common in Parque Nacional Carara (p281) and the Península de Osa (p358). Macaws have long monogamous relationships and can live 50 years.

The most dazzling bird in Central America, the quetzal holds great cultural importance and was once of great ceremonial significance for the Aztecs and the Maya. Look for its bright-blue mohawk, red breast and long green tail at high elevations and near Parque Nacional Los Quetzales (p340). Quetzals love to feed on young avocados, which they swallow whole and later spit out the seed.

The descriptively named roseate has a white head and a distinctive spoon-shaped

CHRISTER FREDRIKSSON / LONELY PLANET IMAGES ©

BEST BIRD-WATCHING PARKS

» Parque Nacional Carara (p281)
» Wilson Botanical Garden (p353)
» Parque Nacional Corcovado (p382)
» Parque Nacional Los Quetzales (p340)

Clockwise from top left
1. Keel-billed toucan 2. Scarlet macaws 3. Quetzal

bill, and feeds by touch. It swings its open bill back and forth, submerged underwater, until it feels food and then snaps the bill shut. It's the only pink bird in Costa Rica, common around the Península de Nicoya and along Pacific lowlands. On the Caribbean side, look for the roseate at the Refugio Nacional de Vida Silvestre Caño Negro (p468).

The cute little blue-gray tanager is always seen in pairs and is the ubiquitous songbird of tropical woodlands and gardens. There are 42 species of tanager in the country – many are brightly colored and all have bodies that are about the size of an adult fist. Look for them everywhere except at high elevation. Their common name in Costa Rica is *viuda*, meaning widow.

Nicknamed the 'Jesus bird', the northern jacana has long, thin toes that enable it to walk on top of aquatic plants, appearing to walk on water. You'll see them countrywide at low elevations and marshes. At first glance the dark, brownish-black body appears relatively nondescript, but when disturbed the bird stretches its wings to reveal startling-yellow feathers.

The distinctive black frigate bird, with an inflatable red throat pouch, is large, elegant and streamlined. It makes an acrobatic living by aerial piracy, harassing smaller birds into dropping their catch, then swooping in to steal their meal midair. They are common along both coasts, where they can be seen circling above the water.

More than 50 species of hummingbird have been recorded – and most live at high elevations. The largest is the violet sabrewing, with a striking violet head and body with dark-green wings.

Reptiles & Amphibians

More than half of the 220 species of reptiles in Costa Rica are snakes, though only a couple are deadly. Of the 160 species of amphibian, frogs and toads garner the most attention, as early-warning indicators of climate change.

The bright-green basilisk lizard is notable for the huge crest running the length of its head, body and tail. Common along watercourses in lowland areas (particularly around Golfo Dulce), it has the appearance of a small dinosaur.

The stocky green iguana is regularly encountered draping its 2m-long body across a branch over water. Despite their enormous bulk, iguanas are incessant vegetarians, and prefer to eat young shoots and leaves. You'll see them just about everywhere in Costa Rica.

The unofficial symbol of Costa Rica, the red-eyed tree frog has red eyes, a green body, yellow and blue side stripes, and orange feet. Despite this vibrant coloration, they're well camouflaged in the rainforest, and rather difficult to spot. They are widespread apart from the Península de Nicoya, which is too dry for them. You'll have a particularly good chance of seeing them at La Selva biological station (p462).

Among the other scaly beasts you may encounter are crocodiles, who can be seen from Crocodile Bridge (p283), on the Central Pacific coast, poison-dart frogs, which were used to poision indigenous arrowheads, and the green spiny lizard, which lazes on fenceposts of the Nicoya Peninsula. Two more you'll likely avoid are the the fer-de-lance pit viper, which lives in agricultural areas of the Pacific and Caribbean slopes, and the eyelash pit viper, which lives in low-elevation rainforest parks.

Clockwise from top left
1. Green spiny lizard 2. Red-eyed tree frog
3. Eyelash pit viper

VENOMOUS CREATURES

Note that bites from any of these are exceptionally rare and nonlethal.

» **Bark scorpion** A little jab from this common brown variety is painful but not lethal.

» **Vampire bat** After anticoagulant saliva inhibits blood clotting, these bats lick up their dinner.

» **Roadguarders** A bite from this large brown snake of the northwest can cause vomiting, headache and bleeding, but won't kill.

» **Yellow-bellied sea snake** Though no deaths have been recorded, a bite from this bi-colored sea snake attacks the nervous system.

» **Tarantula hawk** This wasp packs a wallop that kills tarantulas, though only stings humans when provoked.

3

Land Mammals

A wild selection of land mammals inhabit Costa Rica's multitudinous biomes, but the rainforest has the stars: fierce predators, crafty prey, and more than a few playful primates.

Costa Rica is home to the brown-throated three-toed sloth and Hoffman's two-toed sloth. Both are 50cm to 75cm in length, with stumpy tails, and tend to hang motionless from branches, or slowly progress upside down along a branch toward leaves, their primary food. Look for them in Parque Nacional Manuel Antonio (p317).

The spider monkey is named for its long and thin legs, arms and tail, which enable it to pursue an arboreal existence in forests near Monteverde. They swing from arm to arm through the canopy, and can hang supported just by their prehensile tail.

The king of Costa Rica's big cats, the jaguar is extremely rare, shy and well camouflaged, so the chance of seeing one is virtually nonexistent (the best chance is in Parque Nacional Corcovado, p382). They do have large territories, however, so you may see their prints or droppings, or even hear their roar – a sound more like a series of deep coughs.

The loud vocalizations of a male mantled howler monkey can carry for more than 1km even in dense rainforest, and will echo through many of the nation's national parks including La Selva, Corcovado, Santa Rosa and Monteverde. This crescendo of noise is one of the most characteristic and memorable of all rainforest sounds.

The small and inquisitive white-faced capuchin monkey has a prehensile tail that is typically carried with the tip coiled and one is likely to steal your lunch near the Volcán Arenal or Parque Nacional Manuel Antonio. Capuchins occasionally descend to the ground, where food such as corn and even oysters is part of their diet.

Clockwise from top left
1. White-faced capuchin monkey 2. White-nosed coati
3. Jaguar

RALPH HOPKINS / LONELY PLANET IMAGES ©

CHRISTER FREDRIKSSON / LONELY PLANET IMAGES ©

The adorable, diminutive squirrel monkey travels in small- to medium-sized groups during the day, squealing or chirping noisily and leaping and crashing through vegetation in search of insects and fruit. They live only along the Pacific and are common in Parque Nacional Manuel Antonio and the Península de Nicoya.

The white-nosed coati is a frequently seen member of the raccoon family, but is brownish and longer, slimmer and lighter than your average raccoon. Its most distinctive feature is a long, mobile, upturned whitish snout with which it snuffles around in search of food.

While the bristly, stinky little white-lipped and collared peccary might not be the Península de Nicoya's most glorious predator, large families of them (which can number in the hundreds) pose a very real threat to hikers through Parque Nacional Corcovado. They move in large groups and are mostly silent, until a provocation starts them woofing and clacking their teeth together.

Little more than 1m in length, the ocelot has a short tail and a pattern of many beautiful rosettes. Though it is the most common of the Costa Rican wild cats, it is very shy and rarely seen. It lives in and around farmland, dry and wet forests and throughout Costa Rica.

Baird's tapir, a large pudgy, pig-like browsing mammal, has a characteristic prehensile snout and lives deep in tropical forests of the Península de Nicoya. Although humans rarely encounter them, past hunting and slow reproduction rates have pushed the species to the edge of extinction.

Marine Animals

Costa Rica has one of the most biologically diverse marine ecosystems in the world and an astounding variety of marine animals. Deepwater upwellings are constant year-round, making these waters extremely productive and creating ideal viewing conditions at any season.

The smallest of Costa Rica's sea turtles, the little olive ridley is easy to love – it has a heart-shaped shell. They nest during the rainy season, and between September and October they'll arrive in huge numbers at Ostional beach (p246) in the Guanacaste province. They are legendary for their synchronized nesting, as 200,000 of the turtles emerge from the sea during a short period of a few days.

In a few of the rivers, estuaries and coastal areas on the Caribbean, you may catch a glimpse of the endangered West Indian manatee, a large marine mammal (up to 4m long and weighing 600kg) that feeds primarily on aquatic vegetation. Although a 2010 United Nations report on the animal affirms sightings have steadily increased over the years, it has been in peril since the 1990s, when only 100 animals were counted in the country.

Migrating whales, which arrive from both the northern and southern hemispheres, include orca, blue and sperm whales, and several species of relatively unknown beaked whale. Humpback whales are commonly spotted along the Pacific coast by tour boats. The best place to see them is in Bahía Drake (p375).

Divers are relatively likely to encounter the whale shark, the world's biggest fish, in the waters off Reserva Biológica Isla del Caño (p382), the Golfo Dulce (p358) or Isla del Cocos (p395). While these creatures can certainly post some impressive stats – some reach 6m long and over 2 tonnes, adult

Clockwise from top left
1. Hammerhead shark 2. Olive ridley turtles
3. Bottle-nosed dolphin

males have been known to live 70 years – the majestic sharks are not dangerous for divers.

With wings that can reach 7m, the elegant manta ray is common in the warm Pacific waters and can be seen when diving off the coast of Guanacaste and around the Bat and Catalina islands. Sometimes you don't have to don a wetsuit to see them either – very fortuitous visitors might catch one jumping from the waves, which is thought to be a sign of play.

Bottle-nosed dolphins are year-round residents in Costa Rica, and quite common. These charismatic cetaceans are among the most intelligent animals on the planet, and have been observed exhibiting complex sociocultural behaviors.

Keep a lookout for them on the boat ride to Drake: they sometimes chase the water taxis across the bay.

The massive 360kg leatherback sea turtle is much, much bigger than the olive ridley, and distinguished by its soft, leathery carapace, which has seven ridges. It nests on the Pacific beaches of the Osa and Nicoya peninsulas. Sadly, many die each year from eating plastic bags, which they mistake for jellyfish, a key part of their diet.

Aptly named, the intimidating hammerhead shark has a unique cephalofoil that enables it to maneuver with incredible speed and precision. Scuba divers can see enormous schools of hammerheads around the remote Isla del Cocos..

Insects

No fewer than 35,000 species of insect have been recorded in Costa Rica, yet it's estimated by entomologists that thousands more remain undiscovered.

The blue morpho butterfly flaps and glides along tropical rivers and through openings in the forests. When it lands, the electric-blue upper wings close, and only the mottled brown underwings become visible, an instantaneous change from outrageous display to modest camouflage. This is something of a national icon, and you'll likely see it on either coastal slope, away from the cities.

Easily identified by its enormous size and hairy appendages, the Costa Rican red tarantula is an intimidating arachnid that can take down a mouse, but it is completely harmless to humans. Similar to party people who descend on Costa Rica's beach towns, they are usually most active at night while foraging and seeking mates.

Several butterflies in Costa Rica display wings with large circles to imitate the eyes of predators as a form of protection. The owl butterfly is notable for its purple forewings and appears at dusk and dawn on the northwest Pacific coast.

Just turn on your flashlight while visiting one of Costa Rica's old-growth forests and you might draw out the Hercules beetle, one of the largest bugs in the world, a terrifying-looking but utterly harmless scarab beetle that can be as big as a cake plate. Fun fact: it can carry over 100 times its own body weight.

Below
Blue morpho butterfly

Survival Guide

Directory A–Z

Accommodations

Accommodations come at every price and comfort level: from luxurious ecolodges and sparkling all-inclusive resorts to backpacker palaces and spartan rooms with little more than a bed and four cinderblock walls. The variety and number of rooms on offer means that advance booking is not usually mandatory.

Rates provided are for the high- or dry-season, generally between December to April. Many lodges lower their prices during the low or rainy season, from May to November. Prices change quickly in Costa Rica, so view prices as approximations. Expect to pay a premium during Christmas, New Year and Easter week (Semana Santa). Prices are inclusive of tax and given in US dollars, which is the preferred currency for listing rates in Costa Rica. However, colones are accepted everywhere, and are usually exchanged at current rates without an additional fee.

A sales and tourism tax of 16.3% is added to all room fees. We have attempted to include taxes in the prices listed here. Paying with a credit card sometimes incurs additional fees, and note that many hotels charge per person, rather than per room – read rates carefully.

The term *cabina* (cabin) is a catch-all for Costa Rican hotels that can define wide range of prices and amenities – from very rustic to very expensive.

Apartments & Villas

The network of long-term rentals has grown dramatically in recent years. These can be an excellent option for families, as they typically include kitchens and several bedrooms. The following networks of rental apartments are peer-reviewed and cover a spectrum of prices, sophistication and amenities. They are throughout the country.

Airbnb Costa Rica (www.airbnb.com/costa-rica)

Escape Villas (www.villascostarica.com) Has high-end villas across Costa Rica, though most are near Manuel Antonio. They are suitable for families and honeymooners looking for luxury.

Vacation Rentals By Owner (VRBO) (www.vrbo.com) This worldwide network of vacation rentals by owner has hundreds of properties listed in Costa Rica.

B&Bs

Almost unknown in the country prior to the ecotourism boom, the B&B phenomenon has swept through Costa Rica in the past two decades, primarily fueled by the increasing number of resident European and North American expats. Generally speaking, B&Bs in Costa Rica tend to be midrange to top-end affairs. You can find B&Bs listed in the *Tico Times* and on the following websites:

BedandBreakfast.com (www.bedandbreakfast.com/costa-rica.html)

Costa Rica Innkeepers Association (www.costaricainnkeepers.com)

Pamela Lanier's Worldwide Bed and Breakfasts Directory (www.lanierbb.com)

Camping

» Camping on Costa Rica's coasts is not legal, but it is widely tolerated. Many local families camp at the beach during the holidays.

» Most major tourist destinations have at least one campsite and if not, most budget hotels outside San José accommodate campers

BOOK YOUR STAY ONLINE

For more accommodations reviews by Lonely Planet authors, check out http://hotels.lonelyplanet.com. You'll find independent reviews, as well as recommendations on the best places to stay. Best of all, you can book online.

RESERVING BY CREDIT CARD

» Some pricier hotels will require confirmation of a reservation with a credit card. Before doing so, note that some top-end hotels require a 50% to 100% payment upfront when you reserve. This rule is not always clearly communicated.

» In most cases advance reservations can be canceled and refunded with enough notice. Ask the hotel about its cancellation policy before booking. It is often easier to make the reservation than to unmake it.

» Many hotels charge a hefty service fee for credit card use.

» Have the hotel fax or email you a confirmation. Hotels often get overbooked, and if you don't have confirmation, you could be out of a room.

on their grounds. Although these usually include toilets, cold showers and basic self-catering facilities (a sink and a BBQ pit), they can be crowded and noisy.

» In most national parks campsites are usually of excellent quality and are rigorously cleaned and maintained by staff. As a general rule, you will need to carry in all of your food and supplies, and carry out all of your trash.

» Theft is a major concern for campers. Camp in a group if possible. If not, don't leave anything in the tent unattended.

» Don't camp near riverbanks, which are prone to flooding and home to snakes.

» Mosquito netting and repellent with DEET are often essential.

Hostels

Although there are still a handful of Hostelling International (HI) hostels left in Costa Rica, the backpacker scene has gone increasingly up-market. Compared to other destinations in Central America, hostels in Costa Rica tend to be fairly expensive, though the quality of service and accommodations is unequaled. Expect to pay between US$10 to US$15 for a dorm bed.

Hotels

It is always advisable to ask to see a room – and a bathroom – before committing to a stay, especially in budget lodgings. Rooms within a single hotel can vary greatly.

Price Ranges
BUDGET

» Budget accommodation in the most popular regions of the country are competitive and need to be booked well in advance during the high season.

» The cheapest places generally have shared bathrooms, but it's still possible to get a double with a bathroom for US$25 in towns off the tourist trail.

» On the top end of the budget scale, rooms will frequently include a fan and bathroom with hot water.

» Hot water in showers is often supplied by electric showerheads, which will dispense hot water if the pressure is kept low.

» Most budget hotels also have a few midrange options with more amenities, including AC and televisions.

» Wireless internet is increasingly available at budget accommodation, particularly in popular tourist destinations.

MIDRANGE

» Midrange rooms will be more comfortable than budget options, and will generally include a bathroom with gas-heated hot water, a choice between fans and air-con, and cable or satellite TV.

» Most midrange hotels have wireless internet, though often it is limited to the area near reception or the office.

» Many midrange places offer tour services, and will have an onsite restaurant or bar and a swimming pool or Jacuzzi.

» Many hotels in this price range offer kitchenettes or even full kitchens.

TOP END

» This price bracket includes many ecolodges, all-inclusive resorts, and business and chain hotels, in addition to a strong network of intimate boutique hotels, remote jungle camps and upmarket B&Bs.

» Top-end places in Costa Rica adhere to the same standards of quality and service as similarly priced accommodation in North American and Europe.

PRICE RANGES

The following price ranges refer to a standard double room with bathroom in high season. Unless otherwise stated a combined tourism and sales tax of 16.3% is included in the price.

$ less than $40
$$ $40–100
$$$ more than $100

» The staff at hotels of this category will likely speak English.

» Many lodgings in this category include amenities such as hot-water bath tubs, private decks, satellite TV and air-con as well as concierge, tour and spa services.

» A typical breakfast is usually gallo pinto (literally 'spotted rooster'), a stir-fry of rice and beans. This national breakfast dish is usually served with eggs, cheese or natilla (sour cream).

Business Hours

» **Restaurants** Usually open from 7am and serve dinner until 9pm, though upscale places may open only for dinner. In remote areas, even the small *sodas* (inexpensive eateries) might open only at specific meal times.

» **Government Offices** Typically open between 8am and 5pm Monday to Friday, but often close between 11:30am and 1:30pm.

» **Banks** Hours are variable, but most are open at least from 9am to 3pm Monday to Friday.

» **Shops** Most are open from 8am to 6pm Monday to Saturday.

» Unless otherwise stated, count on sights, activities and restaurants to be open daily.

Climate

Costa Rica's diverse landscapes as well as its geographical position create a number of varied climates all in close proximity to each other. The highlands are cold, the cloud forest is misty and cool, and San José and the Central Valley get an 'eternal spring'. Both the Pacific and Caribbean coasts are pretty much sweltering year-round, although they are rainier from May to November.

Customs Regulations

» All travelers over the age of 18 are allowed to enter the country with 5L of wine or spirits and 500g of processed tobacco (400 cigarettes or 50 cigars).

» Camera gear, binoculars, and camping, snorkeling and other sporting equipment are readily allowed into the country.

» Dogs and cats are permitted entry providing they have obtained both general health and rabies vaccination certificates.

» Pornography and illicit drugs are prohibited.

Discount Cards

Note that discount cards are not universally accepted at museums and parks.

» **Costa Rica Card** (www.costaricacard.org; individual/couple/family US$30/40/60) Gives hotel and restaurant discounts through an affiliated network. Must be picked up in-country and used with photo ID.

» **ISIC Student Identity Card** (www.isic.org; US$20-30 depending on origin country) Discounts on museum and tour fees for full-time students.

» **International Student Exchange** (ISE; www.isecard.com; US$25) Discounts on museums and tour fees for full-time student between 12 and 26 years old.

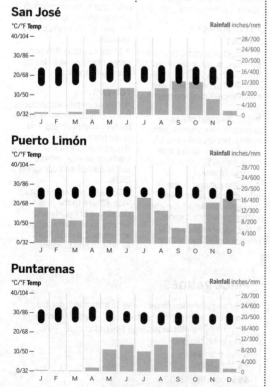

San José

°C/°F Temp — Rainfall inches/mm

Puerto Limón

°C/°F Temp — Rainfall inches/mm

Puntarenas

°C/°F Temp — Rainfall inches/mm

Electricity

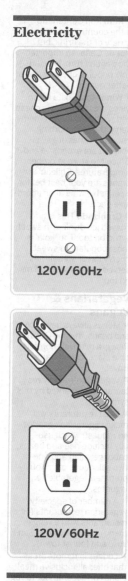

120V/60Hz

120V/60Hz

Embassies & Consulates

Mornings are the best time to go to embassies and consulates. Australia and New Zealand do not have consular representation in Costa Rica; their closest embassies are in Mexico City. Most countries are represented in San José.

Canada (☏2242-4400; www. canadainternational.gc.ca; Oficentro Ejecutivo La Sabana, 3rd fl, Edificio 3, Sabana Sur) Behind La Contraloría.

France (☏2234-4167) On the road to Curridabat, 200m south and 50m west of the Indoor Club.

Germany (☏2290-9091; 8th fl, Torre La Sabana, Sabana Norte) Two blocks west of ICE building.

Guatemala (☏2283-2555; Curridabat) Casa Izquierda, 500m south and 30m west of Pops.

Honduras (☏2291-5147; Urbanización Trejos Montealegre) About 100m west of Banca Promérica, Escazú.

Israel (☏2221-6444; 11th fl, Edificio Centro Colón, Paseo Colón btwn Calles 38 & 40)

Italy (☏2234-2326; cnr Av Central & Calle 41)

Mexico (☏2257-0633) About 250m south of the Subaru dealership, Los Yoses.

Netherlands (☏2296-1490; Oficentro Ejecutivo La Sabana, 3rd fl, Edificio 3, Sabana Sur) Behind La Contraloría.

Nicaragua (☏2283-8222; Av Central 2540 btwn Calles 25 & 27, Barrio La California)

Panama (☏2281-2442) Head 200m south and 25m east from the *antiguo higuerón* (old fig tree), San Pedro.

Spain (☏2222-1933; Calle 32 btwn Paseo Colón & Av 2)

Switzerland (☏2221-3229; 10th fl, Edificio Centro Colón, Paseo Colón btwn Calles 38 & 40)

UK (☏2258-2025; 11th fl, Edificio Centro Colón, Paseo Colón btwn Calles 38 & 40)

USA (☏2519-2000; http://cos tarica.usembassy.gov; Carretera a Pavas) Opposite Centro Comercial del Oeste.

Food

Traditional Costa Rican staples, for the most part, are very basic, somewhat bland and frequently described as comfort food. The diet consists largely of rice and beans. Food is not heavily spiced, unless you're having traditional Caribbean-style cuisine.

Tourist districts offer a wide selection of international food, and often international chefs. The most popular foreign food in Costa Rica (at least among the Ticos) is Chinese. Many restaurants serve *arroz cantonés* (fried rice).

Along the coast seafood is plentiful. Fish is often fried, but may also be grilled or blackened.

Tap water is safe to drink in Costa Rica.

Staples & Specialties

» **Bocas** A menu of cheap fried snacks, often served in a bar to accompany beer.

» **Casado** An inexpensive set lunch, usually of rice, black beans, meat, plantain and a small salad. An extremely popular *casado* is the ubiquitous *arroz con pollo*, which is chicken and rice usually dressed up with grains, vegetables and a good mix of mild spices.

» **Ceviche** While not traditional Tico fare, ceviche is on most menus, and usually contains octopus, tilapia, dorado and/or dolphin (the fish, not Flipper). Raw fish is marinated in lime juice with chilies, tomatoes and herbs. Served chilled, it is a delectable way to enjoy fresh seafood.

» **Empanadas** Corn turnovers stuffed with ground meat, chicken, cheese or sweet fruit.

PRICE RANGES

The following price ranges refer to a standard meal. Unless otherwise stated tax is included in the price.
$ less than $9
$$ $9–15
$$$ more than $15

PRACTICALITIES

» **Emergency** The local tourism board, **Instituto Costarricense de Turismo** (ICT; ☎2222-1090, in USA & Canada 866-267-8274; www.visitcostarica.com; Plaza de la Cultura, Calle 5 btwn Avs Central & 2), is located in San José and distributes a helpful brochure with up-to-date emergency numbers for every region. Dialing 911 will contact emergency services and an English-speaking operator, though response time is slow.

» **DVDs** DVDs in Costa Rica are region 4.

» **Weights & Measures** Costa Ricans use the metric system for weights, distances and measures.

» **Power** While Costa Rica uses a 120V/60Hz power system that is compatible with North American devices, power surges and fluctuation are frequent.

» **Gallo Pinto** The 'spotted rooster' is the national dish and consists of savory rice and black beans. It comes in various levels of fanciness and is served with scrambled eggs and fruit. Even at its most basic it is filling and cheap.

» **Olla de Carne** A traditional, filling meat stew, filled with a variety of squash (including the chayote, a local pear-shaped vegetable).

» **Patacones** Fried green plantains cut in thin pieces.

» **Sauces** Salsa Lizano is the most popular sauce in the country and is often poured over *gallo pino* or meat dishes. It's the Tico version of Worcestershire sauce. Tabasco, or vinegar-based hot sauce of some variety, is also available on demand.

» **Tamales** Steamed cornmeal surrounds a filling of meat and vegetables. These are popular at Christmas time.

Drinks

» **Coffee** The most popular beverage in the country. Traditionally, it is served strong and mixed with hot milk to taste, also known as *café con leche*. Most drinkers get *café negro* (black coffee) and for those who want a little milk, you can ask for *leche al lado* (milk on the side). Many trendier places serve cappuccinos and espressos, and milk is nearly always pasteurized and safe to drink.

» **Batidos** Fresh fruit drinks (like smoothies) made either *al agua* (with water) or *con leche* (with milk). The array can be mind-boggling and includes mango, papaya, *piña* (pineapple), *sandía* (watermelon), *melón* (cantaloupe), *zarzamora* (blackberry), *zanahoria* (carrot), *cebada* (barley) and *tamarindo* (fruit of the tamarind tree).

» **Pipas** Green coconuts that have a hole macheted into the top of them and a straw for drinking the 'milk' – a very refreshing and filling drink.

» **Agua Dulce** Sugarcane water or boiled water mixed with brown sugar.

» **Horchata** Found mostly in the countryside, it is a sweet drink made from rice milk and flavored with cinnamon.

» **Beer** Imperial is the most ubiquitous beer sold, recognized by the eagle-crest logo. Pilsen, another pilsen, has a higher alcohol content. Bavaria produces a lager and Bavaria Negro, a delicious full-bodied dark beer.

» **Guaro** A colorless alcohol distilled from sugarcane and usually consumed by the shot.

» **Rum** Ron Centenario is the country's excellent variety of the drink, but Flor de Caña, an imported Nicaraguan rum, is justifiably popular, cheaper and of better quality.

» **Wine** Most Costa Rican wines are cheap, taste cheap, and will be unkindly remembered the next morning. Imported wines are available but are expensive and difficult to store at proper temperatures. Chilean brands are your best bet for a palatable wine at an affordable price.

» **Granizado** This is a shaved ice drink with sweet syrup on top. The 'kola' is most popular – a sweet cherry flavor sometimes served with condensed milk on top.

Vegetarians & Vegans

» Menus always have rice and beans, making Costa Rica is a relatively comfortable place for vegetarians to travel.

» Vegetarian-friendly restaurants are marked by this symbol: ☑

» Most restaurants will make vegetarian *casados* on request, which usually include rice and beans, cabbage salad and one or two selections of variously prepared vegetables or legumes.

» A number of specialty vegetarian restaurants (or restaurants with a veggie menu) can be found in San José and tourist towns.

» Lodges in remote areas that offer all-inclusive meal plans can accommodate vegetarian diets with advance notice.

» Vegans, macrobiotic and raw food–only travelers will have a tougher time as there are fewer outlets accommodating those diets. If you intend to keep to your diet, it's best to choose a lodging where you can prepare food yourself.

Gay & Lesbian Travelers

In Costa Rica, the situation facing gay and lesbian travelers is better than most Central American countries and there are some areas of the country – particularly Quepos and Manuel Antonio park – that have been gay vacation destinations for two decades.

Homosexual acts between two consenting adults (aged 18 and over) are legal; though you should note that travelers may still be subject to the laws of their own country in regard to sexual relations. Still, most Costa Ricans are tolerant of homosexuality only at a 'don't ask, don't tell' level.

Since 1998 there have been laws on the books to protect 'sexual option' and discrimination is generally prohibited in most facets of society, including employment. And though the country is becoming increasingly more gay-friendly with the cultural currents of the rest of the world, this traditional culture has not always been quick to adopt equal protection. Legal battles to recognize same-sex partnerships have been a hot topic in the country since 2006 and were a major point of contention in the 2010 presidential race. Current President Laura Chinchilla Miranda opposes gay marriage but has voiced support for legal recognition of same-sex couples.

Same-sex couples are unlikely to be the subject of harassment, though public displays of affect might attract unwanted attention. The undisputed gay and lesbian capital of Costa Rica is Manuel Antonio. The monthly newspaper *Gayness* and the magazine *Gente 10* (in Spanish) are both available at gay bars in San José. There are a number of other resources for gay and lesbian travelers.

Agua Buena Human Rights Association (☎2280-3548; www.aguabuena .org) This noteworthy non-profit organization has campaigned steadily for fairness in medical treatment for people living with HIV/AIDS in Costa Rica. In Spanish.

CIPAC (☎2280-7821; www. cipacdh.org) The leading gay activist organization in Costa Rica. In Spanish.

International Gay & Lesbian Travel Association (IGLTA; ☎954-776-2626, in USA 800-448-8550; www. iglta.org) Maintains a list of hundreds of travel agents and tour operators all over the world.

Toto Tours (☎773-274-8686, in USA 800-565-1241; www. tototours.com) Gay-travel specialists who organize regular trips to Costa Rica, among other destinations.

Health

Before You Go

» Get necessary vaccinations four to eight weeks before departure.

» Ask your doctor for an International Certificate of Vaccination (otherwise known as the 'yellow booklet'), which will list all the vaccinations you've received. This is mandatory for countries that require proof of yellow-fever vaccination upon entry.

» A list of medical evacuation and travel insurance companies can be found on the website of the **US State Department** (www.travel. state.gov/medical.html).

» Worldwide travel insurance is available at www.lonely planet.com/travel_services. You can buy, extend and claim online anytime – even if you're already on the road.

In Costa Rica

AVAILABILITY & COST OF HEALTH CARE

» Good medical care is available in most major cities, but may be limited in rural areas.

» For an extensive list of physicians, dentists and hospitals visit http://us embassy.or.cr.

» Most pharmacies are well supplied and the pharmacists are licensed to prescribe medication. A handful are open 24 hours. If you're taking any medication on a regular basis, make sure you know its generic (scientific) name, since many pharmaceuticals go under different names in Costa Rica.

INFECTIOUS DISEASES

» **Dengue Fever (Breakbone Fever)** Dengue is transmitted by aedes mosquitoes, which often bite during the daytime and are usually found close to human habitations, often indoors. Dengue is especially common in densely populated, urban environments. It usually causes flulike symptoms including fever, muscle aches, joint pains, headaches, nausea and vomiting, often followed by a rash. Most cases resolve uneventfully in a few days. There is no treatment for dengue fever except taking analgesics such as acetaminophen/paracetamol (Tylenol) and drinking plenty of fluids. Severe cases may require hospitalization for intravenous fluids and supportive care. There is no vaccine. The key to prevention is taking insect protection measures.

» **Hepatitis A** The second most common travel-related infection (after traveler's diarrhea). It's a viral infection of the liver that is usually acquired by ingestion of contaminated water, food or ice, though it may also be acquired by direct contact with infected persons. Symptoms may include fever, malaise, jaundice, nausea, vomiting and abdominal pain. Most cases resolve without complications, though hepatitis A occasionally causes severe liver damage. There is no treatment. The vaccine for hepatitis A is extremely safe and highly effective.

» **Leishmaniasis** This is transmitted by sand flies, and most cases occur in newly cleared forest or areas of secondary growth. The highest incidence is in Talamanca. It causes slow-growing ulcers over exposed parts of the body. There is no vaccine. To protect yourself from sand flies, follow the same precautions as for mosquitoes.

» **Malaria** Malaria is very rare in Costa Rica, occurring only occasionally in rural parts of the Limón Province. It's transmitted by mosquito bites, usually between dusk and dawn. Taking malaria pills is not necessary unless you are making a long stay in the province of Limón (not Puerto Limón). Protection against mosquito bites is most effective.

» **Traveler's Diarrhea** Tap water is safe and of a high quality in Costa Rica, but when you're far off the beaten path it's best avoid tap water unless it has been boiled, filtered or chemically disinfected (iodine tablets). To prevent diarrhea, be wary of dairy products that might contain unpasteurized milk; and be highly selective when eating food from street vendors. If you develop diarrhea, be sure to drink plenty of fluids, preferably with an oral rehydration solution containing lots of salt and sugar. If diarrhea is bloody or persists for more than 72 hours, or is accompanied by fever, shaking chills or severe abdominal pain, seek medical attention.

» **Typhoid** Caused by ingestion of food or water contaminated by a species of salmonella known as Salmonella typhi. Fever occurs in virtually all cases. Other symptoms may include headache, malaise, muscle aches, dizziness, loss of appetite, nausea and abdominal pain. Possible complications include intestinal perforation, intestinal bleeding, confusion, delirium or (rarely) coma. A pretrip vaccination is recommended.

ENVIRONMENTAL HAZARDS

» **Animal Bites** Do not attempt to pet, handle or feed any animal. Any bite or scratch by a mammal, including bats, should be promptly and thoroughly cleansed with large amounts of soap and water, followed by application of an antiseptic such as iodine or alcohol and contact a local health authority.

» **Insect Bites** No matter how much you safeguard, getting bitten by mosquitoes is part of every traveler's experience in the country. The best prevention is to stay covered up – wear long pants, long sleeves, a hat and shoes, not sandals. Invest in a good insect repellent, preferably one with DEET. Apply to exposed skin and clothing (but not to eyes, mouth, cuts, wounds or irritated skin). Compounds containing DEET shouldn't be used on children under the age of two, and should be used sparingly on children under 12. Invest in a bug net to hang over beds (along with a few thumbtacks or nails with which to hang it). Many hotels in Costa Rica don't have windows (or screens), and a cheap little net will save you plenty of nighttime aggravation. The mesh size should be less than 1.5mm. Dusk is the worst time for mosquitoes, so take extra precautions.

» **Sun** Stay out of the midday sun, wear sunglasses and a wide-brimmed hat, and apply sunblock with SPF 15 or higher, with both UVA and UVB protection. Drink plenty of fluids and avoid strenuous exercise when the temperature is high.

Internet Access

» Costa Rica has plenty of internet cafes and many businesses have wi-fi.

» Expect to pay US$1 to US$2 per hour in San José and tourist towns.

» Wi-fi is common in all mid- and top-end hotels.

Language Courses

» Spanish-language schools operate all over Costa Rica and charge by the hour for instruction.

» Many courses can be found in central San José and the suburb of San Pedro, and the Central Valley.

» It is best to arrange classes in advance. A good clearing house is the **Institute for Spanish Language Studies** (ISLS; ☎2258-5111, in USA 800-765-0025; www.isls.com), which has eight schools in Costa Rica.

Legal Matters

» If you are arrested your embassy can offer limited assistance. Embassy officials will not bail you out and you are subject to Costa Rican laws, not the laws of your own country.

» In Costa Rica the legal age for driving, voting and having heterosexual sex is 18 years.

» Keep in mind that travelers may be subject to the laws of their own country in regard to sexual relations.

Drivers & Driving Accidents

» Drivers should carry their passport and driver's license at all times.

» If you have an accident, call the police immediately to make a report (required for insurance purposes).

» Leave vehicles in place until the report has been made and do not make any statements except to members of law-enforcement agencies.

Maps

Detailed maps are unfortunately hard to come by in Costa Rica. An excellent option is the 1:330,000 Costa Rica sheet produced by International Travel Map, which is waterproof and includes a San José inset.

WHAT'S THAT ADDRESS?

Though some larger cities have streets that have been dutifully named, signage is rare in Costa Rica and finding a Tico who knows what street they are standing on is even rarer. Everybody uses landmarks when providing directions; an address may be given as 200m south and 150m east of a church. A city block is *cien metros* – literally 100m – so 250 *metros al sur* means '2½ blocks south,' regardless of the distance. Churches, parks, office buildings, fast-food joints and car dealerships are the most common landmarks used – but these are often meaningless to the foreign traveler who will have no idea where the Subaru dealership is to begin with. Better yet, Ticos frequently refer to landmarks that no longer exist. In San Pedro, outside San José, locals still use the sight of an old fig tree *(el antiguo higuerón)* to provide directions.

Confused? Get used to it...

» The **Fundación Neotrópica** (www.neotropica.org) publishes a 1:500,000 map showing national parks and other protected areas. These are available in San José bookstores and over the internet.

» The Instituto Costarricense de Turismo (ICT) publishes a 1:700,000 Costa Rica map with a 1:12,500 Central San José map on the reverse. These are free at ICT offices in San José.

» Online, **Maptak** (www.maptak.com) has maps of Costa Rica's seven provinces and their capitals.

» Few national park offices or ranger stations have maps for hikers. Topographical maps are available for purchase from **Instituto Geográfico Nacional** (IGN; ☑2257-7798; Calle 9 btwn Avs 20 & 22; ◷7:30am-noon & 1-3pm Mon-Fri).

» The Mapa-Guía de la Naturaleza Costa Rica is an atlas no longer published by Incafo that included 1:200,000 topographical sheets, as well as English and Spanish descriptions of Costa Rica's natural areas. Out-of-print used copies can be purchased on the internet.

Money
ATMs

» ATMs, or *cajeros automáticos*, are ubiquitous in all but Costa Rica's smallest towns.

» Most ATMs also dispense US dollars or Costa Rican colones.

Cash & Currency

» The Costa Rican currency is the colón (plural colones), named after Cristóbal Colón (Christopher Columbus).

» Bills come in 500, 1000, 5000, 10,000, 20,000 and 50,000 notes, while coins come in denominations of 5, 10, 20, 25, 50 and 100.

» Note that older coins are larger and silver, while newer ones are smaller and gold-colored.

» Paying for things in US dollars is common, and at times is encouraged, since the currency is viewed as being more stable than colones.

» Newer US dollars (ie big heads) are preferred throughout Costa Rica.

» When paying in US dollars at a local restaurant, bar or shop the exchange rate can be unfavorable.

Credit Cards

» Expect a transaction fee on all international credit-card purchases.

» Holders of credit and debit cards can buy colones in some banks, though you can expect to pay a high transaction fee.

» Cards are widely accepted at midrange and top-end hotels, as well as top-end restaurants and some travel agencies.

» All car-rental agencies require drivers to have a credit card.

Exchanging Money

All banks will exchange US dollars, and some will exchange euros and British pounds; other currencies are more difficult. Most banks have excruciatingly long lines, especially at the state-run institutions (Banco Nacional, Banco de Costa Rica, Banco Popular), though they don't charge commission on cash exchanges. Private banks (Banex, Banco Interfin, Scotiabank) tend to be faster. Ensure the bills you want to exchange are in good condition or they might be refused.

BARGAINING

» A high standard of living along with a steady stream of international tourist traffic means that the Latin American tradition of haggling is unpopular in Costa Rica.

» Do not try to bargain for hotel room rates as it is very uncommon.

» Negotiating prices at outdoor markets is acceptable, and bargaining is accepted when hiring long-distance taxis.

DOLLARS VS COLONES

While colones are the official currency of Costa Rica, US dollars are virtually legal tender. Case in point: most ATMs in large towns and cities will dispense both currencies. However, it pays to know where and when you should be paying with each currency.

In Costa Rica you can use US dollars to pay for hotel rooms, midrange to top-end meals, admission fees for sights, tours, domestic flights, international buses, car hire, private shuttle buses and large-ticket purchase items. Local meals and drinks, domestic bus fares, taxis and small-ticket purchase items should be paid for in colones.

All of our listings have prices in US dollars. With regard to transportation, our use of either dollars or colones reflects the preferred currency for a given mode.

Taxes

» Travelers will notice a 13.39% sales tax at midrange and top-end hotels and restaurants, while hotels also charge an additional 3% tourist surcharge.

» Everybody must pay a US$26 airport tax upon leaving the country.

Tipping

It is customary to tip the bellhop/porter (US$1 to US$5 per service) and the housekeeper (US$1 to US$2 per day) in top-end hotels, less in budget places. On guided tours, tip the guide US$5 to US$15 per person per day. Tip the tour driver about half of what you tip the guide. Naturally, tips depend upon quality of service. Taxi drivers are not normally tipped, unless some special service is provided. Top-end restaurants may add a 10% service charge onto the bill. If not, you might leave a small tip to show your appreciation, but it is not required.

Traveler's Checks

With the popularity of ATMs and credit cards, traveler's checks are increasingly uncommon in Costa Rica. They can be exchanged at banks, typically only for US dollars or Costa Rican colones.

Photography

» Always ask permission to take someone's photo.

» With the prominence of digital cameras, it is increasingly difficult to purchase high-quality film in Costa Rica.

» Most internet cafes can burn your digital pictures on CD, and cheap media is available for purchase in most large towns and cities.

Post

» Air-mail letters cost about $0.35 for the first 20g.

» Parcels can be shipped at the rate of $7 per kilogram.

» You can receive mail at the main post office of major towns.

» Mail to San José's central post office should be addressed: (Name), c/o Lista de Correos, Correo Central, San José, Costa Rica.

» Letters usually arrive within a week from North America, longer from more distant places.

» The post office will hold mail for 30 days from the date it's received.

» Photo identification is required to retrieve mail and you will only be given correspondence with your name on it.

» Note that in addresses, apartado (abbreviated 'Apdo') means 'PO Box'; it is not a street or apartment address.

» You can ship parcels inexpensively within the country using the public bus system. Packages travel onboard buses and are dropped off at any terminal along their routes. Clients receive a receipt number after paying for the service; the number is relayed to the recipient, who retrieves the package at the destination bus terminal.

Public Holidays

Días feriados (national holidays) are taken seriously in Costa Rica. Banks, public offices and many stores close. Public transport is tight and hotels are heavily booked. Many festivals coincide with public holidays.

» **New Year's Day** January 1

» **Semana Santa** (Holy Week; March/April) The Thursday and Friday before Easter Sunday is the official holiday, but most businesses shut for the whole week. From Thursday to Sunday bars are closed and alcohol sales are prohibited; on Thursday and Friday buses stop running.

» **Día de Juan Santamaría** (April 11) Honors the national hero who died fighting William Walker in 1856; major events are held in Alajuela, his hometown.

» **Labor Day** May 1

» **Día de la Madre** (Mother's Day; August 15) Coincides with the annual Catholic Feast of the Assumption.

» **Independence Day** September 15

» **Día de la Raza** (Columbus Day) (Columbus' Day) October 12

» **Christmas Day** (December 25) Christmas Eve is also an unofficial holiday.

» **Last week in December** The week between Christmas and New Year is an unofficial holiday; businesses close and beach hotels are crowded.

Safe Travel

For the latest official reports on travel to Costa Rica see the websites of the **US State Department** (www.travel.state.gov/travel) or the **UK Foreign & Commonwealth Office** (www.fco.gov.uk).

Earthquakes & Volcanic Eruptions

Costa Rica lies on the edge of active tectonic plates, so it is decidedly earthquake-prone. Recent major quakes were in 1990 (7.1 on the Richter scale) and 1991 (7.4). Smaller quakes and tremors happen quite often – particularly on the Península de Nicoya – cracking roads and knocking down phone lines. The volcanoes in Costa Rica aren't really dangerous as long as you stay on designated trails and don't try to peer into an active volcano's crater. As a precaution, always check with park rangers before setting out in the vicinity of active volcanoes.

Hiking Hazards

Hikers setting out into the wilderness should be adequately prepared for their trips.

» Know your limits and don't set out to do a hike you can't reasonably complete.

» Carry plenty of water, even on very short trips.

» Carry maps, extra food and a compass.

» Let someone know where you are going, so they can narrow the search area in the event of an emergency.

» Be aware that Costa Rica's wildlife can pose a threat to hikers, particularly in **Corcovado National Park**.

Ocean Hazards

Approximately 200 drownings a year occur in Costa Rica, 90% of which are caused by riptides: strong currents that pull the swimmer out to sea. Many deaths in riptides are caused by panicked swimmers struggling to the point of exhaustion. If you are caught in a riptide, do not struggle.

Simply float and let the tide carry you out beyond the breakers, after which the riptide will dissipate, then swim parallel to the beach and allow the surf to carry you back in.

River-Rafting Hazards

River-rafting expeditions may be particularly risky during periods of heavy rain – flash floods have been known to capsize rafts. Reputable tour operators will ensure conditions are safe before setting out.

Thefts & Muggings

The biggest danger that most travelers face is theft, primarily from pickpockets. There is a lot of petty crime in Costa Rica so keep your wits about you at all times and don't let your guard down.

Shopping

Avoid purchasing animal products, including turtle shells, animal skulls and anything made with feathers, coral or shells. Wood products are also highly suspicious: make sure you know where the wood came from.

Coffee & Alcohol

» Coffee is the most popular souvenir, available at the Mercado Central in San José and at any supermarket throughout the country.

» The most popular alcohol purchases are Ron Centenario, Café Rica (coffee liqueur) and guaro (local firewater). All are available at duty-free shops inside the airport, or in supermarkets and liquor stores in every town and city.

Handicrafts & Ceramics

» Tropical-hardwood items include salad bowls, plates, carving boards, jewelry boxes and a variety of carvings and ornaments. The most exquisite woodwork is available at **Biesanz Woodworks** (2289-4337; www.biesanz.

com; ☺8am-5pm Mon-Fri, 9am-3pm Sat) in Escazú. All of the wood here is grown on farms expressly for this purpose.

» Uniquely Costa Rican souvenirs are the colorfully painted replicas of carretas (traditional oxcarts) produced in Sarchí.

Solo Travelers

Costa Rica is a fine country for solo travelers, especially if you get in with the backpacking community. Inexpensive hostels with communal kitchens encourage social exchange, while a large number of language schools, tours and volunteer organizations will provide every traveler with an opportunity to meet others. However, it isn't recommended to undertake long treks in the wilderness by yourself.

Most female travelers experience little more than a 'mi amor' ('my love') or an appreciative hiss from local men. But in general, Costa Rican men consider foreign women to have looser morals and to be easier conquests than Ticas (female Costa Ricans). Men will often make flirtatious comments to single women, particularly blondes. Women traveling together aren't exempt from this. The best way to deal with this is to do what the Ticas do – ignore it completely. Women who firmly resist unwanted verbal advances from men are normally treated with respect.

In small highland towns, dress is usually conservative. Women rarely wear shorts, but belly-baring tops are all the rage. On the beach, skimpy bathing suits are OK – topless or nude bathing aren't.

Solo women travelers should avoid hitchhiking.

Do not take unlicensed 'pirate' taxis (licensed taxis are red and have medallions) as there have been reports of assaults against women by unlicensed drivers.

Birth-control pills are available at most pharmacies without a prescription.

Telephone

» Cellular service now covers most of the country and nearly all of the country that is accessible to tourists.

» Public phones are found all over Costa Rica and Chip or Colibrí phone cards are available in 1000, 2000 and 3000 colón denominations.

» Chip cards are inserted into the phone and scanned. Colibrí cards (more common) require you to dial a toll-free number (199) and enter an access code. Instructions are provided in English or Spanish.

» The cheapest international calls from Costa Rica are direct-dialed using a phone card. To make international calls, dial '00' followed by the country code and number.

» Pay phones cannot receive international calls.

» To call Costa Rica from abroad, use the country code (506) before the eight-digit number.

» Due to the increasing popularity of voice-over IP services such as Skype, and more reliable ethernet connections, traveling with a laptop and headset can be the cheapest way to call internationally.

Time

Costa Rica is six hours behind GMT, so Costa Rican time is equivalent to Central Time in North America. There is no daylight-saving time.

Toilets

» Public restrooms are rare, but most restaurants and cafes will let you use their facilities, sometimes for a small charge – never more than 500 colones.

» Bus terminals and other major public buildings usually have toilets, also at a charge.

» Don't flush your toilet paper. Costa Rican plumbing is often poor and often has very low pressure.

» Dispose of toilet paper in the rubbish bin inside the bathroom.

Tourist Information

» The government-run tourism board, the **ICT** (☑in USA 800-343-6332; www.visitcosta rica.com), has two offices in the capital.

» The ICT can provide you with free maps, a master bus schedule and information on road conditions in the hinterlands. English is spoken.

» Consult the ICT's flashy English-language website for information.

» From the USA call the ICT's toll-free number for brochures and information.

Travelers with Disabilities

Independent travel in Costa Rica is difficult for anyone with mobility constraints. Although Costa Rica has an equal-opportunity law, the law applies only to new or newly remodeled businesses and is loosely enforced. Therefore, very few hotels and restaurants have features specifically suited to wheelchair use. Many don't have ramps, and room or bathroom doors are rarely wide enough to accommodate a wheelchair.

Outside the buildings, streets and sidewalks are potholed and poorly paved, making wheelchair use frustrating at best. Public buses don't have provisions to carry wheelchairs and most national parks and outdoor tourist attractions don't have trails suited to wheelchair use. Notable exceptions include **Volcán Poás** (☑2482-2165; admission US$10; ⊙8am-3:30pm), **INBio** (☑2507-8107; www.inbioparque.com/en;

4km south of Heredia, Santo Domingo; adult/student/child US$23/17/13, parking US$3; ⊙8am-3pm Fri, 9am-4pm Sat-Sun; 🖈) and the **Rainforest Aerial Tram** (☑2257-5961; www.rainforestrams.com; adult/ student & child US$55/28, full-day tour with lunch & guided hike US$99/56; 🖈).

Visas

Passport-carrying nationals of the following countries are allowed 90 days stay with no visa: Argentina, Canada, Israel, Japan, Panama, the USA and most Western European countries. Citizens of Australia, Iceland, Ireland, Mexico, New Zealand, Russia, South Africa and Venezuela are allowed to stay for 30 days with no visa. Others require a visa from a Costa Rican embassy or consulate.

For the latest info on visas, check the websites of the **ICT** (☑in USA 800-343-6332; www.visitcostarica.com) or the **Costa Rican embassy** (www.costarica-embassy.org) in Washington, DC.

Extensions

» Extending your stay beyond the authorized 30 or 90 days is time-consuming, making it easier to leave the country for 72 hours and then re-enter.

» Extensions can be handled by the office of **Migración** (Immigration; ☑2220-0355; ⊙8am-4pm) in San José, opposite Channel 6, about 4km north of Parque La Sabana.

» Requirements for extensions change, so allow several working days.

Onward Tickets

Travelers officially need onward tickets before they are allowed to enter Costa Rica. This requirement is not often checked at the airport, but travelers arriving by land should anticipate the need to show an onward ticket.

If you're heading to Panama, Nicaragua or another Central or South American country from Costa Rica, you may need an onward or round-trip ticket before you will be allowed entry into that country or even allowed to board the plane, if you're flying. A quick check with the appropriate embassy – easy to do via the internet – will tell you whether the country you're heading to has an onward-ticket requirement.

Volunteering

Costa Rica offers a huge number of volunteer opportunities, by both local and expat organizations. Word of mouth is a powerful influence on future volunteers, so a majority of programs in Costa Rica are very conscientious about pleasing their volunteers. Almost all placements require a commitment of two weeks or more.

English Teaching

Many travelers in Costa Rica are extremely keen to learn and/or perfect their Spanish, but there are English teaching opportunities for people of all backgrounds.

Amerispan Study Abroad (www.amerispan.com) Offers a variety of educational travel programs in specialized areas.

Sustainable Horizon (www.sustainablehorizon. com) Arranges volunteering trips such as guest-teaching spots.

Forestry Management

Despite its relatively small size, Costa Rica is home to an impressive number of national parks, a good number of which protect some of the most pristine rainforest on the planet. If you're interesting in helping to save this

---

GRAPPLING WITH THE SEX TRADE

Exit the baggage claim at the international airport in San José and you'll be welcomed by a sign that reads 'In Costa Rica sex with children under 18 is a serious crime. Should you engage in it we will drive you to jail.' For decades, travelers have arrived in Costa Rica in search of sandy beaches and lush mountainscapes. Unfortunately, an unknown percentage of them also come in search of sex – not all of it legal.

Prostitution by men and women over the age of 18 is perfectly legal. But the tourist juggernaut of the last few decades has fueled illicit activities at its fringes – namely child prostitution and, to a lesser degree, human trafficking. To be clear: having sex with a minor in Costa Rica is illegal, carrying a penalty of up to 10 years in jail. But child prostitution has nonetheless flourished. In fact, a number of aid groups, along with the country's national child-welfare agency (Patronato Nacional de la Infancia; PANI), estimate that there may be as many as 3000 child prostitutes in San José alone. In turn, this has led to women and children being trafficked for the purpose of sexual exploitation, as documented in a 2008 report issued by the US State Department.

Alarm over the problem has crescendoed steadily since 1999, when the UN Committee on Human Rights issued a statement saying that it was 'deeply concerned' about child-sex tourism in Costa Rica. Since then, the government has taken a number of measures to crack down. They've established national task forces to combat the problem, trained the police force in how to deal with issues of child exploitation and formed a coalition against human trafficking. But enforcement remains weak – largely due to lack of personnel and funding. On its end, the USA – the principal source of sex tourists to Costa Rica – has made it a prosecutable crime for Americans to have sex with minors anywhere in the world.

There are also countless challenges in fighting the problem. Tourism remains one of the country's primary sources of revenue – and, unfortunately, that includes the countless travelers who arrive specifically to seek sex. Along with Thailand and Cambodia, Costa Rica is one of the most popular sex-tourism destinations in the world, according to Ecpat International, a nonprofit dedicated to ending child prostitution. The phenomenon has been magnified by the internet: there are entire sex-tourism websites that chronicle – in grotesque detail – where and how to find sex or, in the words of one, how to find '18-year-old girls for less than the price of a good steak.' In all of these, Costa Rica figures prominently. While these sites are not necessarily illegal, they do promote a permissive image of the country – one that can lead some travelers to think that child sex is acceptable.

Various organizations fight the sexual exploitation of children in Costa Rica, which you can contact to learn more about the problem or to report any incidents you encounter. See the websites of Ecpat International (www.ecpat.org) and Cybertipline (www.cyber tipline.com).

threatened ecosystem, and perhaps gaining a valuable skill set in the process, consider a placement in a forest-management program.

Cloudbridge Nature Preserve (www.cloudbridge.org) Trail building, construction, tree planting and projects monitoring the recovery of the cloud forest are offered to volunteers, who pay for their own housing with a local family. Preference is given to biology students, but all enthusiastic volunteers can apply.

Tropical Science Center (www.cct.or.cr) This long-standing NGO offers volunteer placement at Monteverde Cloud Forest Reserve. Projects can include trail maintenance and conservation work. Volunteers are expected to work from 7am to 4pm Monday to Friday and to 11:30am Saturday. The cost for housing and food is $20 per day. Placements have a two-week minimum.

Fundación Corcovado (www.corcovadofoundation.org) An impressive network of people and organizations committed to preserving Parque Nacional Corcovado.

Monteverde Institute (www.mvinstitute.org) A non-profit educational institute offering training in tropical biology, conservation and sustainable development.

Organic Farming

Costa Rica is certainly at the forefront of the sustainable food movement. Home to virtual living laboratories of self-sufficient farms and plantations, Costa Rica is perfectly suited for volunteers interested in greening their thumbs.

Reserva Biológica Dúrika (www.durika.org) A sustainable community that is centered upon a 75-sq-km biological reserve.

WWOOF Costa Rica (www.wwoofcostarica.org) This loose network of farms is part of the large international network of Willing Workers On Organic Farms (WWOOF). Placements are incredibly varied. WWOOF Mexico, Costa Rica, Guatemala and Belize have a joint $33 membership, which gives potential volunteers access to all placement listings.

Finca La Flor de Paraíso (www.la-flor.org) Offers programs in a variety of disciplines from animal husbandry to medicinal-herb cultivation.

Punta Mona (www.puntamona.org) An organic farm and retreat center that is based on organic permaculture and sustainable living.

Rancho Margot (www.ranchomargot.org) This self-proclaimed life-skills university offers a natural education emphasizing organic farming and animal husbandry.

Wildlife Conservation

If you're interested in sea turtles or rehabilitating rescued animals, Costa Rica is one of the best places in the world to get hands-on experience with wild animals. Whether you're an aspiring veterinarian or just concerned with the plight of endangered species, there are some programs that can help you get a little closer to some of Mother Nature's charismatic creatures. See also **Fundación Corcovado** (www.corcovadofoundation.org).

Earthwatch A broadly recognized international volunteer organization, Earthwatch efforts in Costa Rica work with the sea turtle population. Activities include night patrolling and documenting nesting turtles.

Sea Turtle Conservancy (www.conserveturtles.org) From March to October, this Puerto Limón organization hosts 'eco-volunteer adventures' working with sea turtles and birds. They have projects as short as one week.

CCC (www.cccturtle.org) Assist scientists with turtle-tagging and research on green and leatherback turtles.

Profelis (www.grafischer.com/profelis) A feline conservation program that takes care of confiscated wild cats, both big and small.

Work

It is difficult for foreigners to find work in Costa Rica. Labor laws favor Costa Ricans. The only foreigners legally employed in Costa Rica are those who work for their own businesses, possess skills not found in the country, or work for companies that have special agreements with the government.

Getting a bona fide job necessitates obtaining a work permit, which can be a time-consuming and difficult process. The most likely source of paid employment is as an English teacher at one of the language institutes, or working in the hospitality industry in a hotel or resort. Naturalists or river guides may also be able to find work with either private lodges or adventure-travel operators, though you shouldn't expect to make more than survival wages.

Transportation

GETTING THERE & AWAY

Entering the Country

» Entering Costa Rica is mostly free of hassle, with the exception of some long queues at the airport.

» The vast majority of travelers enter the country by plane, and most international flights arrive at Aeropuerto Internacional Juan Santamaría, outside San José.

» Liberia is a growing destination for international flights; it is in the Guanacaste province and serves travelers heading to the Península de Nicoya.

» Overland border crossings are straightforward and travelers can move freely between Panama to the south and Nicaragua to the north.

» Some foreign nationals will require a visa. Be aware that you cannot get a visa at the border. For more information on visas see the Directory (p528).

Passport

» Citizens of all nations are required to have a passport that is valid for at least six months beyond the dates of your trip.

» When you arrive your passport will be stamped.

» Though seldomly enforced, the law requires that you carry your passport at all times.

Onward Ticket

» Officially, travelers are required to have a ticket out of Costa Rica before they are allowed to enter. This is rarely and erratically enforced.

» Those arriving on land with no onward ticket can purchase one from international bus companies in Managua, Nicaragua and Panama City.

Air

Airports & Airlines

» Costa Rica is well connected by air to other Central and South American countries, as well as the USA.

» International flights arrive at **Aeropuerto Internacional Juan Santamaría** (☎2437-2400; www.aeris.cr), 17km northwest of San José, in the town of Alajuela.

» Aeropuerto Internacional Daniel Oduber Quirós in Liberia also receives international flights from the USA, the Americas and Canada. It serves a number of American and Canadian airlines and some charters from London. Flights into Liberia have increased since the 2012 opening of a new terminal.

» The national airline, Lacsa (part of the Central American Airline consortium Grupo TACA), flies to the USA and Latin America, including Cuba.

» The US Federal Aviation Administration has assessed Costa Rica's aviation authorities to be in compliance with international safety standards.

CLIMATE CHANGE & TRAVEL

Every form of transport that relies on carbon-based fuel generates CO_2, the main cause of human-induced climate change. Modern travel is dependent on airplanes, which might use less fuel per kilometer per person than most cars but travel much greater distances. The altitude at which aircraft emit gases (including CO_2) and particles also contributes to their climate change impact. Many websites offer 'carbon calculators' that allow people to estimate the carbon emissions generated by their journey and, for those who wish to do so, to offset the impact of the greenhouse gases emitted with contributions to portfolios of climate-friendly initiatives throughout the world. Lonely Planet offsets the carbon footprint of all staff and author travel.

Tickets

» Airline fares are usually more expensive during the Costa Rican high season (from December through April).

» December and January are the most expensive months to travel.

Central & Latin America

» **American Airlines** (www.aa.com), **Delta** (www.delta.com), **United** (www.united.com) and **US Airways** (www.usairways.com) have connections to Costa Rica from many Central and Latin American countries. Grupo TACA usually offers the most flights on these routes.

» **Nature Air** (www.natureair.com) now flies from Liberia to Granada, Nicaragua. Note that rates vary considerably on season and availability.

» Grupo TACA offers daily direct flights to Caracas, Guatemala City and San Salvador. TACA and Mexicana have daily flights to Mexico City, while both TACA and COPA have several flights a day to Panama City. Rates vary considerably on season and availability.

Other Countries

» More than one-third of all travelers to Costa Rica come from the USA.

» Flights from Houston, Miami or New York are most common.

» From Canada, most travelers to Costa Rica connect through US gateway cities,

though Air Canada has direct flights from Toronto.

» From the UK, Costa Rica is served by British Airways and Virgin, typically with at least one stop.

» Most flights from the UK and Europe connect either in the USA or in Mexico City. High-season fares may still apply during the northern summer, even though this is the beginning of the Costa Rican rainy season.

» From Australia and New Zealand, travel routes usually go through the USA or Mexico. Fares are highest in June and July even though this is the beginning of the rainy season in Costa Rica.

Land
Border Crossings

» Costa Rica shares land borders with Nicaragua and Panama. There is no fee for travelers to enter Costa Rica, however, there have been several reports of towns having recently added their own entry/exit fees, usually US$1.

NICARAGUA
Sapoá–Peñas Blancas

Situated on the Interamericana, this is the most heavily trafficked border station between Nicaragua and Costa Rica.

» The border station is open from 6am to 8pm daily on both the Costa Rican and Nicaraguan sides – though local bus traffic stops in the afternoon. This is the only

official border between Nicaragua and Costa Rica that you can drive across.

» Travelers must fill out an exit form and submit it with their passport.

» Waiting times at this border can be several hours. Plan on at least one hour to cross the border.

» **Tica Bus** (in Managua 222-6094, in Panama City 262-2084), **Nica Bus** (in Managua 228-1374) and **TransNica** (in Managua 278-2090) all have daily buses that serve points north and south. Regular buses depart Peñas Blancas, on the Costa Rican side, for La Cruz, Liberia and San José.

» The Costa Rican and Nicaraguan immigration offices are almost 1km apart; most people travel through by bus or private car. Travelers without a through bus will find golf carts (a small tip is requested) running between the borders, but many walk.

» Costa Rica does not charge visitors to cross the border.

» Nicaragua charges visitors to cross the border. People leaving Nicaragua pay US$2. Entering Nicaragua costs US$7 until noon; after noon it costs US$9. All fees must be paid in US dollars.

» Note that Peñas Blancas is only a border post, not a town, so there is nowhere to stay.

San Carlos–Los Chiles

Very rarely used by travelers, this crossing must be done by boat.

» Boats ferry across the Río San Juan and connect via a 14km bus ride to San Carlos. Alternatively, boats can be hired for the entire trip, though this is more expensive.

» The Costa Rica border control office is open from 8am to 5pm daily.

» Regular boats (US$10 to US$15, 45 minutes) leave San Carlos and travel the Río Frío to Los Chiles at 10:30am and 4pm. Extra boats are scheduled as needed.

» At other times, boat workers can usually be found by the ENAP dock in San Carlos.

» The road that travels from the southern banks of the Río San Juan in Nicaragua to Los Chiles is reserved for federal employees. You will not be able to enter Costa Rica this way.

» Those entering Costa Rica have to purchase a US$2 exit stamp at the San Carlos *migración* (immigration) office, 50m west of the dock. Once you enter Costa Rica you'll have to stop at the Costa Rica *migración* for your entry stamp.

» Traveling from Costa Rica to Nicaragua you will need to pay a US$7 fee when you enter before noon, US$9 after noon.

PANAMA

Note that Panama is GMT -5, one hour ahead of Costa Rica.

Paso Canoas

The Carretera Interamericana (Pan-American Hwy) is by far the most frequently used entry and exit point with Panama, and is open 24 hours a day.

» The border crossing in either direction is generally straightforward.

» Get an exit stamp from Panama at the *migración* office before entering Costa Rica.

» There is no charge for entering Costa Rica.

» Northbound buses usually stop running at about 6pm. Travelers without a private vehicle should arrive during the day.

» Those with a private vehicle are likely to encounter long lines.

» Tica Bus travels from Panama City to San José (US$25 to US$35, 15 hours) daily and crosses this border post. In David, Tracopa has one bus daily from the main terminal to San José (nine hours). In David you'll also find frequent buses to the border at Paso Canoas

(US$2.50, 1½ hours) that take off every 10 minutes from 4am to 8pm.

» If traveling to Panama, you will have to pay US$5 for a tourist card, which is valid for 30 days.

Guabito–Sixaola

Situated on the Caribbean coast, this is a fairly tranquil and hassle-free border crossing.

» Immigration guards regularly take off for lunch and you may have to wait a while to be processed. The border town on the Panamanian side is Guabito.

» The border is open from 8am to 6pm in Panama and from 7am to 5pm in Costa Rica. Both sides close for an hour-long lunch at around 1pm, which means that there are potentially two hours each day when you'll be unable to make it across the border quickly. Get to Sixaola as early as possible; while there are a couple of sleeping options, it won't be the highlight of your trip if you have to spend the night. Before crossing the bridge, stop at the Costa Rica *migración* to process your paperwork. Walking across the bridge is kind of fun, in a vertigo-inducing sort of way.

» If you are coming from Bocas del Toro, it's faster and cheaper to take the ferry to Changuinola (US$5 to US$7, 45 minutes), from where you can take a quick taxi to the border or to the bus station (US$5). One daily bus travels between Changuinola and San José at 10am (US$15, eight hours). Otherwise, you can walk over the border and catch one of the hourly buses that go up the coast from Sixaola.

Río Sereno–San Vito

This is a rarely used crossing in the Cordillera de Talamanca. The border is open from 8am to 6pm in Panama and from 7am to 5pm in Costa Rica. The small village of Río Sereno on the Panamanian

side has a hotel and a place to eat; there are no facilities on the Costa Rican side.

» Regular buses depart Concepción and David in Panama for Río Sereno. Local buses (four daily) and taxis go from the border to San Vito.

Bus

A lot of travelers enter the country by bus. Furthermore, an extensive bus system links the Central American capitals and it's vastly cheaper than flying.

» If crossing the border by bus, note that international buses may cost slightly more than taking a local bus to the border, then another onward from the border, but they're worth it. These companies are familiar with border procedures and will tell you what's needed to cross efficiently.

» There will be no problems crossing borders, provided your papers are in order. If you are on an international bus, you'll have to exit the bus and proceed through both border stations. Bus drivers will wait for everyone to be processed before heading on.

» If you choose to take local buses, it's advisable to get to border stations early in the day to allow time for waiting in line and processing. Note that onward buses tend to wind down by the afternoon.

» International buses go from San José to Changuinola (Bocas del Toro), David and Panama City in Panama; Guatemala City in Guatemala; Managua in Nicaragua; San Salvador in El Salvador; and Tegucigalpa in Honduras.

Car & Motorcycle

The cost of insurance, fuel and border permits makes a car journey significantly more expensive than buying an airline ticket. To enter Costa Rica by car, you'll need the following items:

» valid registration and proof of ownership

» valid driver's license or International Driving Permit

» valid license plates

» recent inspection certificate

» passport

» multiple photocopies of all these documents in case the originals get lost.
Before departing, check that the following elements are present and in working order:

» blinkers, head- and taillights

» spare tire

» jerry can for extra gas (petrol)

» well-stocked toolbox including parts, such as belts, that are harder to find in Central America

» emergency flares and roadside triangles.
Insurance from foreign countries isn't recognized in Costa Rica, so you'll have to buy a policy locally. At the border it will cost about US$15 a month. In addition, you'll probably have to pay a US$22 road tax to drive in.

You are not allowed to sell the car in Costa Rica. If you need to leave the country without the car, it must be left in a customs warehouse in San José.

Sea

» Cruise ships stop in Costa Rican ports and enable passengers to make a quick foray into the country. Typically, ships dock at either the Pacific port of Caldera or the Caribbean port of Puerto Limón.

» It is also possible to arrive in Costa Rica by private yacht.

GETTING AROUND

Air

Scheduled Flights

» Costa Rica's domestic airlines are **Nature Air** (☏2220-3054; www.natureair.com) and **Sansa** (☏2290-4100; www.flysansa.com). Sansa is linked with Grupo TACA.

» Both airlines fly small passenger planes, and you're allocated a baggage allowance of no more than 12kg.

» Space is limited and demand is high in the dry season, so reserve and pay for tickets in advance.

» In Costa Rica schedules change constantly and delays are frequent because

Domestic Air Routes

of inclement weather. You should not arrange a domestic flight that makes a tight connection with an international flight back home.

» All domestic flights originate and terminate at San José. Destinations reached from San José include Bahía Drake, Barra del Colorado, Golfito, Liberia, Neily, Palmar Sur, Playa Nosara, Playa Sámara/Carrillo, Playa Tamarindo, Puerto Jiménez, Quepos, Tambor and Tortuguero.

Charters

» Travelers on a larger budget or in a larger party should consider chartering a private plane, which is by far the quickest way to travel around the country.

» It takes under 90 minutes to fly to most destinations, though weather conditions can significantly speed up or delay travel time.

» The two most reputable charters in the country are **Nature Air** (☑2220-3054; www.natureair.com) and **Alfa Romeo Aero Taxi** (www. alfaromeoair.com). Both can be booked directly through the company, a tour agency or some high-end accommodations.

» Luggage space on charters is extremely limited.

Bicycle

» With an increasingly large network of paved secondary roads and increased awareness of cyclists, Costa Rica is emerging as one of Central America's most comfortable cycle touring destinations.

» Mountain bikes and beach cruisers can be rented in towns with a significant tourist presence, for US$10 to US$15 per day. A few companies organize bike tours around Costa Rica.

Boat

» Ferries cross the Golfo de Nicoya, connecting the central Pacific coast with the southern tip of Península de Nicoya.

» The **Countermark ferry** (☑2661-1069) links the port of Puntarenas with Playa Naranjo four times daily. The **Ferry Peninsular** (☑2641-0118) travels between Puntarenas and Paquera every two hours, for a bus connection to Montezuma.

» On the Golfo Dulce a daily passenger ferry links Golfito with Puerto Jiménez on the Península de Osa, and a weekday water taxi travels to and from Playa Zancudo. On the other side of the Península de Osa, water taxis connect Bahía Drake with Sierpe.

» On the Caribbean coast there is a bus and boat service that runs several times a day, linking Cariari and Tortuguero, while another links Parismina and Siquirres.

» Boats ply the canals that run along the coast from Moín to Tortuguero, although no regular service exists. A daily water taxi connects Puerto Viejo de Sarapiquí with Trinidad on the Río San Juan. The San Juan is Nicaraguan territory, so take your passport. You can try to arrange boat transportation for Barra del Colorado in any of these towns.

Bus
Local Buses

» Local buses are a cheap and reliable way of getting around Costa Rica. The longest domestic journey out of San José costs less than US$20.

» San José is the transportation center for the country, though there is no central terminal. Bus offices are scattered around the city: some large bus companies have big terminals that sell tickets in advance, while others have little more than a stop – sometimes unmarked.

» Buses can be very crowded, but don't usually pass up passengers on account of being too full. Note that there are no buses from Thursday to Saturday before Easter Sunday.

» There are two types of bus: *directo* and *colectivo*. The *directo* buses should go from one destination to the next with few stops; the *colectivos* make more stops and are very slow going.

» Trips longer than four hours usually include a rest stop as buses do not have toilets.

» Space is limited on board, so if you have to check luggage, be watchful. Theft from overhead racks is rampant, though much less common than in other Central American countries.

» Bus schedules fluctuate wildly, so always confirm the time when you buy your ticket. If you are catching a bus that picks you up somewhere along a road, get to the roadside early.

» For information on departures from San José, pay a visit to the **Instituto Costarricense de Turismo** (ICT; ☑2222-1090, in USA & Canada 866-267-8274; www. visitcostarica.com; Plaza de la Cultura, Calle 5 btwn Avs Central & 2) office to pick up the reasonably up-to-date copy of the master schedule, which is also available online at www.visitcostarica.com.

Shuttle Buses

The tourist-van shuttle services (aka gringo buses) are an alternative to the standard intercity buses. Shuttles are provided by **Grayline's Fantasy Bus** (☑2220-2126; www.graylinecostarica.com) and **Interbus** (☑2283-5573; www. interbusonline.com). Both companies run overland transportation from San José to the most popular destinations, as well as directly between other destinations (see their websites for the comprehensive list). These services will pick you up at your hotel, and reservations can be made online or through local travel agencies and hotel owners.

Car & Motorcycle

» Drivers in Costa Rica are required to have a valid driving license from their home country. Many places will also accept an International Driving Permit (IDP), issued by the automobile association in your country of origin. After 90 days, however, you will need to get a Costa Rican driver's license.

» Gasoline (petrol) and diesel are widely available, and 24-hour service stations are along the Interamericana. At the time of research, fuel prices averaged US$1.25 per liter.

» In more-remote areas, fuel will be more expensive and might be sold at the neighborhood *pulpería* (corner store).

» Spare parts may be hard to find, especially for vehicles with sophisticated electronics and emissions-control systems.

Hire & Insurance

» There are car-rental agencies in San José and in popular tourist destinations on the Pacific coast.

» All of the major international car-rental agencies have outlets in Costa Rica, though you can sometimes get better deals from local companies.

» Due to road conditions, it is necessary to invest in a 4WD unless travel is limited only to the Interamericana.

» Many agencies will insist on 4WD in the rainy season, when driving through rivers is a matter of course.

» To rent a car you need a valid driver's license, a major credit card and a passport. The minimum age for car rental is 21 years.

» Carefully inspect rented cars for minor damage and make sure that any damage is noted on the rental agreement. If your car breaks down, call the rental company. Don't attempt to get the car fixed yourself – most companies won't reimburse expenses without prior authorization.

» Prices vary considerably, but on average you can expect to pay over US$200 as the standard rate for an SUV, including *kilometraje libre* (unlimited mileage). Economy cars are much cheaper, as

little as US$80 a week. The price of mandatory insurance makes this more expensive, often doubling the rate.

» Costa Rican insurance is mandatory, even if you have insurance at home. Expect to pay about US$15 to US$25 per day. Many rental companies won't rent you a car without it. The basic insurance that all drivers must buy is from a government monopoly, the Instituto Nacional de Seguros. This insurance does not cover your rental car at all, only damages to other people, their cars, or property. It is legal to drive only with this insurance, but it can be difficult to negotiate with a rental agency to allow you to drive away with only this minimum standard. Full insurance through the rental agency can be up to US$50 a day.

» The roads in Costa Rica are rough and rugged, meaning that minor accidents or car damage are common.

» Note that if you pay basic insurance with a gold or platinum credit card, the company will usually take responsibility for damages to the car, in which case you can forego the cost of the full insurance. Make sure you verify this with your credit card company ahead of time.

» Most insurance policies do not cover damages caused by flooding or driving through a river, so be aware of the extent of your policy.

» Rental rates fluctuate wildly, so shop around. Some agencies offer discounts for extended rentals. Note that rental offices at the airport charge a 12% fee in addition to regular rates.

» Thieves can easily recognize rental cars. Never leave anything in sight in a parked car – nothing! – and remove all luggage from the trunk overnight. If possible, park the car in a guarded parking lot rather than on the street.

» Motorcycles (including Harleys) can be rented in San José and Escazú.

FLAT-TIRE SCAM

For years Aeropuerto Internacional Juan Santamaría has suffered from a scam involving sudden flat tires on rental cars. Many readers have reported similar incidents and it is commonly reported, but it continues to happen.

It happens like this: after picking up a rental car and driving out of the city, the car gets a flat; as the driver pulls over to fix it, the disabled vehicle is approached by a group of locals, ostensibly to help. There is inevitably some confusion with the changing of the tire, and in the commotion the driver gets relieved of their wallet, luggage or other valuables.

This incident has happened enough times to suggest that somebody may be tampering with rental cars to 'facilitate' these flat tires. It certainly suggests that travelers should be very wary – and aware – if somebody pulls over to help after getting a flat on a recently rented car. Keep your wallet and your passport on your person and lock your doors whenever you get out of your car.

Road Conditions & Hazards

» The quality of roads varies from the quite smoothly paved Interamericana to the barely passable rural back roads. Any can suffer from landslides, sudden flooding and fog.

» Most roads are single-lane and winding, lacking hard shoulders; others are dirt-and-mud affairs that climb mountains and traverse rivers.

» Drive defensively and expect a variety of obstructions in the roadway – from cyclists and pedestrians to broken-down cars and cattle. Unsigned speed bumps are placed on some stretches of road without warning.

» Roads around major tourist areas are adequately marked; all others are not.

» Always ask about road conditions before setting out, especially in the rainy season; a number of roads become impassable in the rainy season.

Road Rules

» There are speed limits of 100km/h or less on all primary roads and 60km/h or less on secondary roads.

» Traffic police use radar, and speed limits are enforced with speeding tickets.

» Tickets are issued to drivers operating vehicles without a seat belt.

» It's illegal to stop in an intersection or make a right turn on a red.

» At unmarked intersections, yield to the car on your right.

» Drive on the right. Passing is allowed only on the left.

» If you are issued with a ticket, you have to pay the fine at a bank; instructions are given on the ticket. If you are driving a rental car, the rental company may be able to arrange your payment for you – the amount of the fine should be on the ticket.

DRIVING THROUGH RIVERS

Driving in Costa Rica will likely necessitate a river crossing at some point. Unfortunately, too many travelers have picked up their off-road skills from watching TV, and every season Ticos (residents of Costa Rica) get a good chuckle out of the number of dead vehicles they help wayward travelers fish out of waterways.

If you're driving through water, follow the rules below:

» **Only do this in a 4WD** Don't drive through a river in a car. (It may seem ridiculous to have to say this, but it's done all the time.) Getting out of a steep, gravel riverbed requires a 4WD. Besides, car engines flood very easily.

» **Check the depth of the water before driving through** To accommodate an average rental 4WD, the water should be no deeper than above the knee. In a sturdier vehicle (Toyota 4-Runner or equivalent), water can be waist-deep.

» **The water should be calm** If the river is gushing so that there are white crests on the water, do not try to cross. Not only will the force of the water flood the engine, it could sweep the car away.

» **Drive very, very slowly** The pressure of driving through a river too quickly will send the water right into the engine and will impair the electrical system. Keep steady pressure on the accelerator so that the tailpipe doesn't fill with water, but go slowly.

» **Err on the side of caution** Car-rental agencies in Costa Rica do not insure for water damage, so ruining a car in a river can come at an extremely high cost.

A portion of the money from these fines goes to a children's charity.

» Police have no right to ask for money, and shouldn't confiscate a car, unless: the driver cannot produce a license and ownership papers; the car lacks license plates; the driver is drunk; or the driver has been involved in an accident causing serious injury.

» If you are driving and see oncoming cars with headlights flashing, it often means that there is a road problem or a radar speed trap ahead. Slow down immediately.

Hitchhiking

Hitchhiking is never entirely safe in any country and Lonely Planet doesn't recommend it. Travelers who hitchhike should understand that they are taking a small but potentially serious risk. People who do hitchhike will be safer if they travel in pairs and let someone know where they are planning to go. Single women travelers should use even greater discretion.

Hitchhiking in Costa Rica is uncommon on main roads that have frequent buses. On minor rural roads, hitchhiking is more commonly practiced. To get picked up, most locals wave down passing cars. If you get a ride, offer to pay the driver when you arrive by saying *¿Cuánto le debo?'* (How much do I owe you?). Your offer may be waved aside, or you may be asked to help with money for gas.

USING TAXIS IN REMOTE AREAS

Taxis are considered a form of public transportation in remote areas that lack good public-transportation networks. They can be hired by the hour, the half-day or full day, or you can arrange a flat fee for a trip. Meters are not used on long trips, so arrange the fare ahead of time. Fares can fluctuate due to worse-than-expected road conditions and bad weather in tough-to-reach places.

The condition of taxis varies from basic sedans held together by rust to fully equipped 4WDs with air-con. In some cases, taxis are pick-up trucks with seats built into the back. Most towns will have at least one licensed taxi, but in some remote villages you may have to get rides from whomever is offering – ask at *pulperías* (corner stores).

Local Transportation

Bus

Local buses operate chiefly in San José, Puntarenas, San Isidro de El General, Golfito and Puerto Limón, connecting urban and suburban areas. Most local buses pick up passengers on the street and on main roads. For years, these buses were converted school buses imported from the USA, but they have slowly been upgraded and now many include coach buses.

Taxi

In San José taxis have meters, called *marías*. Note that it is illegal for a driver not to use the meter. Outside of San José, however, most taxis don't have meters and fares tend to be agreed upon in advance. Bargaining is quite acceptable.

In some towns there are *colectivos* (taxis that several passengers are able to share). Although *colectivos* are becoming increasingly difficult to find, the basic principle is that the driver charges a flat fee (usually about US$0.50) to take passengers from one end of town to the other.

In rural areas, 4WD are often used as taxis and are a popular means for surfers (and their boards) to travel from their accommodations to the break. Prices vary wildly depending on how touristy the area is, though generally speaking a 10-minute ride costs between US$5 and US$15.

Taxi drivers are not normally tipped unless they assist with your luggage or have provided an above-average service.

WANT MORE?

For in-depth language information and handy phrases, check out Lonely Planet's *Costa Rican Spanish Phrasebook*. You'll find it at **shop.lonelyplanet.com**, or you can buy Lonely Planet's iPhone phrasebooks at the Apple App Store.

Language

Spanish pronunciation is easy, as most sounds have equivalents in English. Also, Spanish spelling is phonetically consistent, meaning that there's a clear and consistent relationship between what you see in writing and how it's pronounced. If you read our colored pronunciation guides as if they were English, you'll be understood. Note that kh is a throaty sound (like the 'ch' in the Scottish *loch*), v and b are like a soft English 'v' (between a 'v' and a 'b'), and r is strongly rolled. The stressed syllables are in italics in our pronunciation guides.

The polite form is used in this chapter; where both polite and informal options are given, they are indicated by the abbreviations 'pol' and 'inf'. Where necessary, both masculine and feminine forms of words are included, separated by a slash and with the masculine form first, eg *perdido/a* (m/f).

BASICS

Hello.	Hola.	o·la
Goodbye.	Adiós.	a·*dyos*
How are you?	¿Cómo va? (pol)	ko·mo va
	¿Cómo vas? (inf)	ko·mo vas
Fine, thanks.	Bien, gracias.	byen gra·syas
Excuse me.	Con permiso.	kon per·*mee*·so
Sorry.	Perdón.	per·*don*
Please.	Por favor.	por fa·*vor*
Thank you.	Gracias.	gra·syas
You're welcome.	Con mucho gusto.	kon *moo*·cho *goo*·sto
Yes./No.	Sí./No.	see/no

My name is ...

Me llamo ...	me ya·mo ...

What's your name?

¿Cómo se llama Usted?	ko·mo se ya·ma oo·ste (pol)
¿Cómo te llamas?	ko·mo te ya·mas (inf)

Do you speak English?

¿Habla inglés?	a·bla een·gles (pol)
¿Hablas inglés?	a·blas een·gles (inf)

I don't understand.

Yo no entiendo.	yo no en·tyen·do

ACCOMMODATIONS

Do you have a ... room?	Tiene una habitación ...?	tye·ne oo·na a·bee·ta·syon ...
single	sencilla	sen·see·ya
double	doble	do·ble

How much is it per night/person?

¿Cuánto es por noche/persona?	kwan·to es por no·che/per·so·na

Is breakfast included?

¿Incluye el desayuno?	een·kloo·ye el de·sa·yoo·no

campsite	área para acampar	a·re·a pa·ra a·kam·par
hotel	hotel	o·tel
hostel	hospedaje	os·pe·da·khe
guesthouse	casa de huéspedes	ka·sa de wes·pe·des
youth hostel	albergue juvenil	al·ber·ge khoo·ve·neel

TIQUISMOS

These colloquialisms and slang terms (*tiquismos*) are frequently heard, and are for the most part used only in Costa Rica.

¡Adiós! – Hi! (used when passing a friend in the street, or anyone in remote rural areas; also means 'Farewell!' but only when leaving for a long time)

bomba – gas station

buena nota – OK/excellent (literally 'good note')

chapulines – a gang, usually of young thieves

chunche – thing (can refer to almost anything)

cien metros – one city block

¿Hay campo? – Is there space? (on a bus)

machita – blonde woman (slang)

mae – buddy (pronounced 'ma' as in 'mat' followed with a quick 'eh'; it's mainly used by boys and young men)

mi amor – my love (used as a familiar form of address by both men and women)

pulpería – corner grocery store

¡Pura vida! – Super! (literally 'pure life,' also an expression of approval or even a greeting)

sabanero – cowboy, especially one who hails from Guanacaste Province

salado – too bad; tough luck

soda – cafe or lunch counter

¡Tuanis! – Cool!

¡Upe! – Is anybody home? (used mainly in rural areas at people's homes, instead of knocking)

vos – you (singular and informal, same as *tú*)

air-con	aire acondi-cionado	ai·re a·kon·dee·syo·na·do
bathroom	baño	ba·nyo
bed	cama	ka·ma
window	ventana	ven·ta·na

DIRECTIONS

Where's ...?
¿Adónde está ...?   a·don·de es·ta ...

What's the address?
¿Cuál es la dirección?   kwal es la dee·rek·syon

Could you please write it down?
¿Podría escribirlo?   po·dree·a es·kree·beer·lo

Can you show me (on the map)?
¿Me puede enseñar (en el mapa)?   me pwe·de en·se·nyar (en el ma·pa)

at the corner	en la esquina	en la es·kee·na
at the traffic lights	en el semáforo	en el se·ma·fo·ro
behind ...	detrás de ...	de·tras de ...
far	lejos	le·khos
in front of ...	en frente de ...	en fren·te de ...
left	a la izquierda	a la ees·kyer·da
near	cerca	ser·ka
next to ...	a la par de ...	a la par de ...
opposite ...	opuesto a ...	o·pwes·to a ...
right	a la derecha	a la de·re·cha
straight ahead	aquí directo	a·kee dee·rek·to

EATING & DRINKING

Can I see the menu, please?
¿Puedo ver el menú, por favor?   pwe·do ver el me·noo por fa·vor

What would you recommend?
¿Qué me recomienda?   ke me re·ko·myen·da

Do you have vegetarian food?
¿Tienen comida vegetariana?   tye·nen ko·mee·da ve·khe·ta·rya·na

I don't eat (red meat).
No como (carne roja).   no ko·mo (kar·ne ro·kha)

That was delicious!
¡Estuvo delicioso!   es·too·vo de·lee·syo·so

Cheers!
¡Salud!   sa·lood

The bill, please.
La cuenta, por favor.   la kwen·ta por fa·vor

I'd like a table for ...	Quisiera una mesa para ...	kee·sye·ra oo·na me·sa pa·ra ...
(eight) o'clock	las (ocho)	las (o·cho)
(two) people	(dos) personas	(dos) per·so·nas

Key Words

appetisers	aperitivos	a·pe·ree·tee·vos
bar	bar	bar
bottle	botella	bo·te·ya
bowl	plato hondo	pla·to on·do
breakfast	desayuno	de·sa·yoo·no
cafe	café	ka·fe
(too) cold	(muy) frío	(mooy) free·o
dinner	cena	se·na

food	comida	ko·mee·da
fork	tenedor	te·ne·dor
glass	vaso	va·so
hot (warm)	caliente	kal·yen·te
knife	cuchillo	koo·chee·yo
lunch	almuerzo	al·mwer·so
main course	plato fuerte	pla·to fwer·te
market	mercado	mer·ka·do
menu	menú	me·noo
plate	plato	pla·to
restaurant	restaurante	res·tow·ran·te
spoon	cuchara	koo·cha·ra
supermarket	supermercado	soo·per·mer·ka·do
with/without	con/sin	kon/seen

Meat & Fish

beef	carne de vaca	kar·ne de va·ka
chicken	pollo	po·yo
duck	pato	pa·to
fish	pescado	pes·ka·do
lamb	cordero	kor·de·ro
pork	cerdo	ser·do
turkey	pavo	pa·vo
veal	ternera	ter·ne·ra

Fruit & Vegetables

apple	manzana	man·sa·na
apricot	albaricoque	al·ba·ree·ko·ke
asparagus	espárragos	es·pa·ra·gos
banana	banano	ba·na·no
bean	frijol	free·khol
cabbage	repollo	re·po·yo
carrot	zanahoria	sa·na·o·rya
cherry	cereza	se·re·sa
corn	maíz	ma·ees
cucumber	pepino	pe·pee·no
fruit	fruta	froo·ta
grapes	uvas	oo·vas
lemon	limón	lee·mon
lentils	lentejas	len·te·khas
lettuce	lechuga	le·choo·ga
mushroom	hongo	on·go
nuts	nueces	nwe·ses
onion	cebolla	se·bo·ya
orange	naranja	na·ran·kha
peach	melocotón	me·lo·ko·ton
pea	petipoa	pe·tee·po·a

pepper (bell)	pimentón	pee·men·ton
pineapple	piña	pee·nya
plum	ciruela	seer·we·la
potato	papa	pa·pa
pumpkin	calabaza	ka·la·ba·sa
spinach	espinaca	es·pee·na·ka
strawberry	fresa	fre·sa
tomato	tomate	to·ma·te
vegetable	vegetal	ve·khe·tal
watermelon	sandía	san·dee·a

Other

bread	pan	pan
butter	mantequilla	man·te·kee·ya
cheese	queso	ke·so
egg	huevo	we·vo
honey	miel	myel
jam	jalea	kha·le·a
oil	aceite	a·sey·te
pastry	pastel	pas·tel
pepper	pimienta	pee·myen·ta
rice	arroz	a·ros
salt	sal	sal
sugar	azúcar	a·soo·kar
vinegar	vinagre	vee·na·gre

Drinks

beer	cerveza	ser·ve·sa
coffee	café	ka·fe
(orange) juice	jugo (de naranja)	khoo·go (de na·ran·kha)
milk	leche	le·che
tea	té	te
(mineral) water	agua (mineral)	a·gwa (mee·ne·ral)
(red/white) wine	vino (tinto/ blanco)	vee·no (teen·to/ blan·ko)

Signs	
Abierto	Open
Cerrado	Closed
Entrada	Entrance
Hombres/Varones	Men
Mujeres/Damas	Women
Prohibido	Prohibited
Salida	Exit
Servicios/Baños	Toilets

EMERGENCIES

Help!	*¡Socorro!*	so·ko·ro
Go away!	*¡Váyase!*	va·ya·se

Call ...!	*¡Llame a ...!*	ya·me a ...
a doctor	*un doctor*	oon dok·tor
the police	*la policía*	la po·lee·see·a

I'm lost.
Estoy perdido/a. es·toy per·dee·do/a (m/f)

I'm ill.
Estoy enfermo/a. es·toy en·fer·mo/a (m/f)

It hurts here.
Me duele aquí. me dwe·le a·kee

I'm allergic to (antibiotics).
Soy alérgico/a a soy a·ler·khee·ko/a a
(los antibióticos). (los an·tee·byo·tee·kos) (m/f)

Where are the toilets?
¿Dónde está el baño? don·de es·ta el ba·nyo

SHOPPING & SERVICES

I'd like to buy ...
Quiero comprar ... kye·ro kom·prar ...

I'm just looking.
Sólo estoy viendo. so·lo es·toy vyen·do

Can I look at it?
¿Lo puedo ver? lo pwe·do ver

I don't like it.
No me gusta. no me goos·ta

How much is it?
¿Cuánto cuesta? kwan·to kwes·ta

That's too expensive.
Está muy caro. es·ta mooy ka·ro

Can you lower the price?
¿Podría bajarle po·dree·a ba·khar·le
el precio? el pre·syo

There's a mistake in the bill.
Hay un error ai oon e·ror
en la cuenta. en la kwen·ta

ATM	*cajero*	ka·khe·ro
	automático	ow·to·ma·tee·ko
credit card	*tarjeta de*	tar·khe·ta de
	crédito	kre·dee·to

Question Words		
How?	*¿Cómo?*	ko·mo
What?	*¿Qué?*	ke
When?	*¿Cuándo?*	kwan·do
Where?	*¿Dónde?*	don·de
Who?	*¿Quién?*	kyen
Why?	*¿Por qué?*	por ke

market	*mercado*	mer·ka·do
post office	*correo*	ko·re·o
tourist office	*oficina*	o·fee·see·na
	de turismo	de too·rees·mo

TIME & DATES

What time is it?	*¿Qué hora es?*	ke o·ra es
It's (10) o'clock.	*Son (las diez).*	son (las dyes)
It's half past (one).	*Es (la una) y media.*	es (la oo·na) ee me·dya

morning	*mañana*	ma·nya·na
afternoon	*tarde*	tar·de
evening	*noche*	no·che

yesterday	*ayer*	a·yer
today	*hoy*	oy
tomorrow	*mañana*	ma·nya·na

Monday	*lunes*	loo·nes
Tuesday	*martes*	mar·tes
Wednesday	*miércoles*	myer·ko·les
Thursday	*jueves*	khwe·ves
Friday	*viernes*	vyer·nes
Saturday	*sábado*	sa·ba·do
Sunday	*domingo*	do·meen·go

January	*enero*	e·ne·ro
February	*febrero*	fe·bre·ro
March	*marzo*	mar·so
April	*abril*	a·breel
May	*mayo*	ma·yo
June	*junio*	khoon·yo
July	*julio*	khool·yo
August	*agosto*	a·gos·to
September	*septiembre*	sep·tyem·bre
October	*octubre*	ok·too·bre
November	*noviembre*	no·vyem·bre
December	*diciembre*	dee·syem·bre

TRANSPORTATION

boat	*barco*	bar·ko
bus	*bús*	boos
plane	*avión*	a·vyon
train	*tren*	tren

first	*primero*	pree·me·ro
last	*último*	ool·tee·mo
next	*próximo*	prok·see·mo

Numbers		
1	uno	oo·no
2	dos	dos
3	tres	tres
4	cuatro	kwa·tro
5	cinco	seen·ko
6	seis	seys
7	siete	sye·te
8	ocho	o·cho
9	nueve	nwe·ve
10	diez	dyes
20	veinte	veyn·te
30	treinta	treyn·ta
40	cuarenta	kwa·ren·ta
50	cincuenta	seen·kwen·ta
60	sesenta	se·sen·ta
70	setenta	se·ten·ta
80	ochenta	o·chen·ta
90	noventa	no·ven·ta
100	cien	syen
1000	mil	meel

airport	aeropuerto	a·e·ro·pwer·to
aisle seat	asiento de pasillo	a·syen·to de pa·see·yo
bus stop	parada de autobuses	pa·ra·da de ow·to·boo·ses
cancelled	cancelado	kan·se·la·do
delayed	atrasado	a·tra·sa·do
platform	plataforma	pla·ta·for·ma
ticket office	taquilla	ta·kee·ya
timetable	horario	o·ra·ryo
train station	estación de trenes	es·ta·syon de tre·nes
window seat	asiento junto a la ventana	a·syen·to khoon·to a la ven·ta·na

A ... ticket, please.	Un pasaje de ..., por favor.	oon pa·sa·khe de ... por fa·vor
1st-class	primera clase	pree·me·ra kla·se
2nd-class	segunda clase	se·goon·da kla·se
one-way	ida	ee·da
return	ida y vuelta	ee·da ee vwel·ta

I'd like to hire a ...	Quiero alquilar ...	kye·ro al·kee·lar ...
4WD	un cuatro por cuatro	oon kwa·tro por kwa·tro
bicycle	una bicicleta	oo·na bee·see·kle·ta
car	un carro	oon ka·ro
motorcycle	una motocicleta	oo·na mo·to·see·kle·ta

child seat	asiento de seguridad para niños	a·syen·to de se·goo·ree·da pa·ra nee·nyos
diesel	diesel	dee·sel
helmet	casco	kas·ko
mechanic	mecánico	me·ka·nee·ko
petrol/gas	gasolina	ga·so·lee·na
service station	bomba	bom·ba
truck	camión	ka·myon

I want to go to ...
Quisiera ir a ...   kee·sye·ra eer a ...

Does it stop at ...?
¿Hace parada en ...?   a·se pa·ra·da en ...

What stop is this?
¿Cuál es esta parada?   kwal es es·ta pa·ra·da

What time does it arrive/leave?
¿A qué hora llega/   a ke o·ra ye·ga/
sale?   sa·le

Please tell me when we get to ...
Por favor, avíseme   por fa·vor a·vee·se·me
cuando lleguemos   kwan·do ye·ge·mos
a ...   a ...

I want to get off here.
Quiero bajarme aquí.   kye·ro ba·khar·me a·kee

Is this the road to ...?
¿Por aquí se va a ...?   por a·kee se va a ...

(How long) Can I park here?
¿(Cuánto tiempo)   (kwan·to tyem·po)
Puedo parquear aquí?   pwe·do par·ke·ar a·kee

The car has broken down (at ...).
El carro se varó en ...   el ka·ro se va·ro en ...

I've had an accident.
Tuve un accidente.   too·ve oon ak·see·den·te

I've run out of petrol.
Me quedé sin   me ke·de seen
gasolina.   ga·so·lee·na

I have a flat tyre.
Se me estalló una   se me es·ta·yo oo·na
llanta.   yan·ta

GLOSSARY

adiós – means 'goodbye' universally, but used as a greeting in rural Costa Rica

almuerzo ejecutivo – literally 'executive lunch'; a more expensive version of a set meal or *casado*

alquiler de automóviles – car rental

apartado – post-office box (abbreviated 'Apdo')

artesanía – handicrafts

ATH – *a toda hora* (open all hours); used to denote ATMs

automóvil – car

avenida – avenue

avión – airplane

bahía – bay

barrio – district or neighborhood

batido – fresh fruit drink, similar to smoothie

biblioteca – library

bocas – small savory dishes served in bars

bomba – short, funny verse; also means 'gas station' and 'bomb'

bosque – forest

bosque nuboso – cloud forest

buena nota – excellent, OK; literally 'good note'

caballo – horse

cabaña – cabin; see also *cabina*

cabina – cabin; see also *cabaña*

cajero automático – ATM

calle – street

cama, cama matrimonial – bed, double bed

campesino – peasant, farmer or person who works in agriculture

carreta – colorfully painted wooden oxcart, now a form of folk art

carretera – road

casado – inexpensive set meal; also means 'married'

casita – cottage or apartment

catedral – cathedral

caverna – cave; see also *cueva*

cerro – mountain or hill

cerveza – beer

ceviche – local dish of raw, marinated seafood

Chepe – affectionate nickname for José; also used when referring to San José

cine – cinema

ciudad – city

cocina – kitchen or cooking

colectivo – bus, minivan or car operating as shared taxi

colibrí – hummingbird

colina – hill

colón – Costa Rican unit of currency; plural *colones*

comida típica – typical local food

cordillera – mountain range

correo – mail service

Costarricense – Costa Rican; see also Tico/a

cruce – crossing

cruda – often used to describe a hangover; literally 'raw'

cueva – cave; see also *caverna*

culebra – snake; see also *serpiente*

Dios – God

directo – direct; refers to long-distance bus with few stops

edificio – building

estación – station, eg ranger station or bus station; also means 'season'

farmacia – pharmacy

fauna silvestre – wildlife

fiesta – party or festival

finca – farm or plantation

floresta – forest

frontera – border

fútbol – soccer (football)

gallo pinto – stir-fry of rice and beans

garza – cattle egret

gasolina – gas (petrol)

gracias – thanks

gringo/a (m/f) – US or European visitor; can be affectionate or insulting, depending on the tone used

guaro – local firewater made from sugarcane

hacienda – rural estate

hielo – ice

ICT – Instituto Costarricense de Turismo; Costa Rica Tourism Board, which provides tourist information

iglesia – church

indígena – indigenous

Interamericana – Pan-American Hwy; the nearly continuous highway running from Alaska to Chile (it breaks at the Darién Gap between Panama and Colombia)

invierno – winter; the rainy season in Costa Rica

isla – island

jardín – garden

josefino/a (m/f) – resident of San José

lago – lake

lavandería – laundry facility, usually offering dry-cleaning services

librería – bookstore

llanura – tropical plain

machismo – an exaggerated sense of masculine pride

macho – literally 'male'; figuratively also 'masculine,' 'tough.' In Costa Rica *macho/a* (m/f) also means 'blonde.'

macrobiótica – health-food store

maría – local name for taxi meter

mercado – market

mercado central – central town market

Meseta Central – Central Valley or central plateau

mestizo/a (m/f) – person of mixed descent, usually Spanish and indigenous

metate – flat stone platform, used by Costa Rica's pre-Columbian populations to grind corn

migración – immigration

Minae – Ministerio de Ambiente y Energía; Ministry of Environment and Energy, in charge of the national park system

mirador – lookout point

mole – rich chocolate sauce

mono – monkey

mono tití – squirrel monkey

motocicleta – motorcycle

muelle – dock

museo – museum

niño – child

normal – refers to long-distance bus with many stops

obeah – sorcery rituals of African origin

ola(s) – wave(s)

OTS – Organization for Tropical Studies

pájaro – bird

palapa – shelter with a thatched, palm-leaf roof and open sides

palenque – indigenous settlement

panadería – bakery

páramo – habitat characterized by highland shrub and tussock grass

parque – park

parque central – central town square or plaza

parque nacional – national park

pastelería – pastry shop

perezoso – sloth

perico – mealy parrot

playa – beach

posada – country-style inn or guesthouse

puente – bridge

puerto – port

pulpería – corner grocery store

punta – point

pura vida – super; literally 'pure life'

quebrada – stream

queso – cheese

rana – frog or toad

rancho – small house or houselike building

refugio nacional de vida silvestre – national wildlife refuge

río – river

sabanero – cowboy from Guanacaste

selva – jungle

Semana Santa – the Christian Holy Week that precedes Easter

sendero – trail or path

serpiente – snake; see also *culebra*

Sinac – Sistema Nacional de Areas de Conservación; National System of Conservation Areas

soda – informal lunch counter or inexpensive eatery

supermercado – supermarket

telenovela – Spanish-language soap opera

Tico/a (m/f) – Costa Rican; see also *Costarricense*

tienda – store

tiquismos – typical Costa Rican expressions or slang

tortuga – turtle

valle – valley

verano – summer; the dry season in Costa Rica

vino – wine

volcán – volcano

zoológico – zoo

behind the scenes

SEND US YOUR FEEDBACK

We love to hear from travelers – your comments keep us on our toes and help make our books better. Our well-traveled team reads every word on what you loved or loathed about this book. Although we cannot reply individually to postal submissions, we always guarantee that your feedback goes straight to the appropriate authors, in time for the next edition. Each person who sends us information is thanked in the next edition – the most useful submissions are rewarded with a selection of digital PDF chapters.

Visit **lonelyplanet.com/contact** to submit your updates and suggestions or to ask for help. Our award-winning website also features inspirational travel stories, news and discussions.

Note: We may edit, reproduce and incorporate your comments in Lonely Planet products such as guidebooks, websites and digital products, so let us know if you don't want your comments reproduced or your name acknowledged. For a copy of our privacy policy visit lonelyplanet.com/privacy.

OUR READERS

Many thanks to the travelers who used the last edition and wrote to us with helpful hints, useful advice and interesting anecdotes:

Lina Andersson, Deborah Bakker, Jolande Bakker, Julie Bergeron, Laura Berli, Fanny Bernadet, Helen Bonser, Jim Brady, Carla Caamaño, Sandra Chatelain, Robert Chmura, Lauren Cleaver, Nick Dillen, Luke Duggan, Sophie Durandet, Maria Eugenia, Chani Fajka, J-f Gregoire, Peter Grossnickle, Rina Hakimian, Kaya Hansen, Sandy Hunter, Karyn Kaplan, Tsipi & Raanan Kessel, Christina Kolmert, Eline Kooijman, Wojtek Kosarzecki, Lauri Koseff, Branton Kunz, Edo Lamoree, Corina Landert, Alison Lee, Jean-Claude Lefebvre, Tomas Ludvik, Jorge Marin, Matt Muir, Steven Neumeier, Barry O'Hara, Elia Petrou, Tom Phillips, Berni Picado, Gail Pike, Rosa Prado, Sarah Riches, Chris Ridderbeks, Chris Ross, Mateo Saavedra, Jonathan Saborío M, Perrine Sandrea, Bryan Scholes, Alex Serrano, Henrik Stabell, Carl Stein, Bianca Tate, Ingrid Thuet, Eelco Timmerman, Marcel Unkelbach, Silke Van Deelen, Jan Van Der Holst, Arie Van Oosterwijk, Frans Van Woerkom, Robert Vogt, Kari Volkmann-Carlsen, Magdalena Wodyńska, Maria Wright, Kristina Ziccardi

AUTHOR THANKS

Nate Cavalieri

Thanks most to Felipe Pardo, a Manuel Antonio guide and godsend, who found and returned a book of notes for this guide after I dropped them on a trail. For the information and the company, thanks also to Jorge Picado, Matt Sulkis, Carlos Meneo and Jenny Shrum. Thanks to Cat, Adam, Wendy and the Christo team who made working on this title a pleasure.

Adam Skolnick

Many thanks to Mariana Estrada; the entire Pension Santa Elena family; Le Tois Dora; Joel at Celeste Mountain Lodge; Miranda and Phoenix; Prue, Josie and Margaret in Santa Teresa; and Aidan and Vicky in Mal País. Thanks especially to Emilio and Pablo for an incredible afternoon of spearfishing and lobster diving. Thanks also to co-conspirators Nate, Wendy, Cat Craddock and Christo. And to sweet and lovely Georgiana Johnson.

Wendy Yanagihara

Thanks to everyone who knowingly and unknowingly gave me intel in Costa Rica or otherwise helped me along on the road. Special thanks to Marise and Pierre, Natalie, Andrés, Castor, Cristian, Sebastian, Alex and Amelia, Vicky Taylor and the South African pirates who kidnapped me in Bocas del Toro. *Fuerte abrazos* to Victoria for hanging with Jasper, and to Austin for post-research adventures in Nicaragua.

Cover photograph: Frog, Parque Nacional Tortuguero, Paolo Giocoso/4Corners Many of the images in this guide are available for licensing from Lonely Planet Images: www.lonelyplanetimages.com.

ACKNOWLEDGMENTS

Climate map data adapted from Peel MC, Finlayson BL & McMahon TA (2007) 'Updated World Map of the Köppen-Geiger Climate Classification', *Hydrology and Earth System Sciences*, 11, 163344.

This Book

This 10th edition of Lonely Planet's *Costa Rica* guidebook was researched and written by Nate Cavalieri, Adam Skolnick and Wendy Yanagihara. The previous edition was researched and written by Matthew D Firestone, Carolina A Miranda and César G Soriano. The 8th edition was researched and written by Matthew D Firestone, Guyan Mitra and Wendy Yanagihara.

This guidebook was commissioned in Lonely Planet's Oakland office, and produced by the following:

Commissioning Editor Catherine Craddock-Carrillo

Coordinating Editor Nigel Chin

Coordinating Cartographer Marc Milinkovic

Coordinating Layout Designer Frank Deim

Managing Editors Barbara Delissen, Bruce Evans, Dianne Schallmeiner

Managing Cartographers Shahara Ahmed, Alison Lyall

Managing Layout Designer Chris Girdler

Assisting Editors Janice Bird, Cathryn Game, Lauren Hunt, Kim Hutchins, Joanne Newell, Kristin Odijk, Charlotte Orr

Assisting Cartographer Mick Garrett

Assisting Layout Designer Nicholas Colicchia

Cover Research Naomi Parker

Internal Image Research Aude Vauconsant

Language Content Branislava Vladisavljevic

Thanks to Dan Austin, Anita Banh, Laura Crawford, Ryan Evans, Larissa Frost, Tobias Gattineau, Asha Ioculari, Carol Jackson, Jouve India, Pat Kinsella, Kellie Langdon, Alex Leung, Bella Li, Trent Paton, Averil Robertson, Fiona Siseman, Gerard Walker, Jeanette Wall, Amanda Williamson

index

N

000 Map pages
000 Photo pages

how to use this book

These symbols will help you find the listings you want:

👁	Sights	👉	Tours	🍷	Drinking
🏄	Beaches	🎉	Festivals & Events	☆	Entertainment
🏃	Activities	🛏	Sleeping	🛍	Shopping
🍃	Courses	🍴	Eating	ℹ	Information/Transport

These symbols give you the vital information for each listing:

📞	Telephone Numbers	📶	Wi-Fi Access	🚌	Bus
🕐	Opening Hours	🏊	Swimming Pool	⛴	Ferry
P	Parking	🥗	Vegetarian Selection	Ⓜ	Metro
🚭	Nonsmoking	📖	English-Language Menu	Ⓢ	Subway
❄	Air-Conditioning	👪	Family-Friendly	Ⓣ	London Tube
@	Internet Access	🐾	Pet-Friendly	🚋	Tram
				🚆	Train

Reviews are organised by author preference.

Look out for these icons:

TOP CHOICE	Our author's recommendation
FREE	No payment required
🌿	A green or sustainable option

Our authors have nominated these places as demonstrating a strong commitment to sustainability – for example by supporting local communities and producers, operating in an environmentally friendly way, or supporting conservation projects.

Map Legend

Sights
- Beach
- Buddhist
- Castle
- Christian
- Hindu
- Islamic
- Jewish
- Monument
- Museum/Gallery
- Ruin
- Winery/Vineyard
- Zoo
- Other Sight

Activities, Courses & Tours
- Diving/Snorkelling
- Canoeing/Kayaking
- Skiing
- Surfing
- Swimming/Pool
- Walking
- Windsurfing
- Other Activity/Course/Tour

Sleeping
- Sleeping
- Camping

Eating
- Eating

Drinking
- Drinking
- Cafe

Entertainment
- Entertainment

Shopping
- Shopping

Information
- Post Office
- Tourist Information

Transport
- Airport
- Border Crossing
- Bus
- Cable Car/Funicular
- Cycling
- Ferry
- Metro
- Monorail
- Parking
- S-Bahn
- Taxi
- Train/Railway
- Tram
- Tube Station
- U-Bahn
- Other Transport

Routes
- Tollway
- Freeway
- Primary
- Secondary
- Tertiary
- Lane
- Unsealed Road
- Plaza/Mall
- Steps
- Tunnel
- Pedestrian Overpass
- Walking Tour
- Walking Tour Detour
- Path

Boundaries
- International
- State/Province
- Disputed
- Regional/Suburb
- Marine Park
- Cliff
- Wall

Population
- Capital (National)
- Capital (State/Province)
- City/Large Town
- Town/Village

Geographic
- Hut/Shelter
- Lighthouse
- Lookout
- Mountain/Volcano
- Oasis
- Park
- Pass
- Picnic Area
- Waterfall

Hydrography
- River/Creek
- Intermittent River
- Swamp/Mangrove
- Reef
- Canal
- Water
- Dry/Salt/Intermittent Lake
- Glacier

Areas
- Beach/Desert
- Cemetery (Christian)
- Cemetery (Other)
- Park/Forest
- Sportsground
- Sight (Building)
- Top Sight (Building)

OUR STORY

A beat-up old car, a few dollars in the pocket and a sense of adventure. In 1972 that's all Tony and Maureen Wheeler needed for the trip of a lifetime – across Europe and Asia overland to Australia. It took several months, and at the end – broke but inspired – they sat at their kitchen table writing and stapling together their first travel guide, *Across Asia on the Cheap*. Within a week they'd sold 1500 copies. Lonely Planet was born.

Today, Lonely Planet has offices in Melbourne, London and Oakland, with more than 600 staff and writers. We share Tony's belief that 'a great guidebook should do three things: inform, educate and amuse'.

OUR WRITERS

Nate Cavalieri

Coordinating Author, Central Pacific Coast, Southern Costa Rica, Península de Osa & Golfo Duce Nate Cavalieri traveled extensively in Latin America on a 2009 trip around the world, but quickly realized that Costa Rica required a lengthy return visit for his undivided attention. Nate lives in Oakland, California, where he writes about life's most colorful diversions: travel, music and professional cycling. His dozen titles for Lonely Planet include guides to the Caribbean, Mexico, Northern California and Colorado. For this edition he took up surfing, got really into the mythology of the Quetzal and nearly destroyed an economy-class rental car. You can check in on him via Twitter (@natecavalieri) or visit www.natecavalieri.com.

Adam Skolnick

Northwestern Costa Rica, Península de Nicoya, Northern Lowlands Adam Skolnick writes about travel, culture, health, sports and the environment for Lonely Planet, *Men's Health*, *Outside* and *Travel + Leisure* among others. He has authored and co-authored 16 previous Lonely Planet books, and has travelled and reported throughout Central America. You can read more of his work at www.adamskolnick.com.

Wendy Yanagihara

San José, Central Valley & Highlands, Carribean Coast On her first trip to Costa Rica in 1996, Wendy wandered out to Zarcero to check out the loopy topiaries of the public plaza, and met Evangelisto Blanco himself (the man behind the landscaping). Fifteen years later, she was pleased to discover that both Zarcero and Señor Blanco have changed only slightly. She has covered the Nicoya Peninsula and northern zone before for Lonely Planet, but on this trip she discovered the surprising delights of San José and a taste for Caribbean *rondón*. When not on the road for Lonely Planet, she lives in southern California.

Published by Lonely Planet Publications Pty Ltd
ABN 36 005 607 983
10th edition – October 2012
ISBN 978 1 74220 018 7
© Lonely Planet 2012   Photographs © as indicated 2012
10 9 8 7 6 5 4
Printed in China